KU-149-346

Contents

Contents

THE CAMBRIDGE HISTORY OF POLITICAL THOUGHT
1450–1700

EDITED BY

J.H. BURNS

Professor Emeritus of the
History of Political Thought,
University of London

WITH THE ASSISTANCE OF

MARK GOLDIE

Lecturer in History
and Fellow of
Churchill College, Cambridge

CAMBRIDGE
UNIVERSITY PRESS

HAMPSHIRE COUNTY LIBRARY

320.
01

0521477727

C003021643

Published by the Press Syndicate of the University of Cambridge
The Pitt Building, Trumpington Street, Cambridge CB2 1RP
40 West 20th Street, New York, NY 10011–4211, USA
10 Stamford Road, Oakleigh, Melbourne 3166, Australia

© Cambridge University Press 1991

First published 1991
First paperback edition 1994

Printed in Great Britain at the University Press, Cambridge

British Library cataloguing in publication data
Burns, J.H. (James Henderson), *1921–*
The Cambridge history of political thought, 1450–1700.
1. Europe. Politics. Theories, history
I. Title   II. Goldie, Mark
320'.094

Library of Congress cataloguing in publication data
The Cambridge history of political thought, 1450–1700 /
edited by J.H. Burns with the assistance of Mark Goldie.
p.   cm.
Includes bibliographical references.
ISBN 0 521 24716 0
i. Political science – History.   I. Burns, J.H. (James Henderson)   II. Goldie, Mark.
JA81.C283   1990
320'.09-dc20   89–22282   CIP

ISBN 0 521 24716 0 hardback
ISBN 0 521 47772 7 paperback

Contents

Contents

Contents

Contributors

BRENDAN BRADSHAW
Lecturer in History and Fellow of Queens' College, Cambridge

PETER BURKE
Reader in Cultural History and Fellow of Emmanuel College, Cambridge

J.H.BURNS
Professor Emeritus of the History of Political Thought, University of London

J.C. DAVIS
Professor of English History, School of English and American Studies, Univerity of East Anglia

ALFRED DUFOUR
Professor of Legal History, Department of Legal History, Faculty of Law, University of Geneva

JULIAN H. FRANKLIN
Professor of Political Science, Columbia University, New York

MARK GOLDIE
Lecturer in History and Fellow of Churchill College, Cambridge

ANTHONY GRAFTON
Professor of History, Princeton University

DONALD R. KELLEY
Professor of History, University of Rochester

ROBERT M. KINGDON
Professor of History, University of Wisconsin, Madison

HOWELL A. LLOYD
Professor of History, University of Hull

Contributors

NOEL MALCOLM
Former Fellow in History and English, Gonville and Caius College, Cambridge

FRANCIS OAKLEY
President Emeritus and Edward Dorr Griffin Professor of the History of Ideas, Williams College, Massachusetts

NICOLAI RUBINSTEIN
Professor Emeritus of History, Westfield College, London

J.H.M. SALMON
Professor Emeritus of History, Brun Mawr College, Pennsylvania

J.P. SOMMERVILLE
Associate Professor of History, University of Wisconsin, Madison

RICHARD TUCK
Lecturer in History and Fellow of Jesus College, Cambridge

JAMES TULLY
Associate Professor of Political Science and Philosophy, McGill University, Montreal

CORINNE C. WESTON
Professor Emeritus of History, Herbert H. Lehman College, The City University of New York

DAVID WOOTTON
Professor of Politics, Department of Government, Brunel University, London

BLAIR WORDEN
Lecturer in History and Fellow of St Edmund Hall, Oxford

Acknowledgements

My greatest debt as general editor of this volume is to Mark Goldie for the invaluable contribution he has made since January 1987 to every aspect of the editorial work. I must also thank Quentin Skinner and Richard Tuck for placing their expert knowledge and their time at my disposal when the book was first being planned.

Mark Goldie and I wish to thank Richard Fisher for his unfailing help and support at the Cambridge University Press and Linda Randall for her patient and painstaking copy-editing. Our thanks are due also to Jane Palmer for prodigious typing and manifold secretarial support.

Since this volume marks the end of my editorial contribution to what has grown into a continuing series, I take the opportunity of belatedly expressing my gratitude to those who helped me in many ways in the editing of *The Cambridge History of Medieval Political Thought*. I owe a very special debt to Patricia Williams, then of the Press, for her enthusiastic furthering of the original one-volume project; to Jeremy Mynott for continuing support; once again to Richard Fisher, and to his predecessors Stephen Barr and Jonathan Sinclair-Wilson; to Linda Randall for bearing a particularly burdensome load of copy-editing; and to two contributors whom it is not invidious to single out here – David Luscombe, who sustained me with his advice and reassurance in so many ways; and Joe Canning who came promptly and generously to the rescue at a moment of crisis.

J.H.B.

Introduction

The political ideas examined in this volume were generated in a period that requires its historians, in an especially marked degree, to 'look before and after'. A watershed between 'medieval' and 'modern' European history has conventionally been located in the late fifteenth century and the beginning of the sixteenth – the period which saw the final eclipse of the Byzantine Empire, the flowering of the humanist Renaissance, and the first stages of the Protestant Reformation. Yet the society of the three centuries following that period has increasingly been represented as a 'world we have lost' – a world essentially pre-modern because pre-industrial (at least in terms of what Marx called 'machinofacture') and pre-capitalist (if by 'capitalist' we mean to refer to a society having an urban proletariat as a major characteristic). Demographically, the population explosion accompanying the social transformations of the eighteenth and nineteenth centuries brought into being mass societies of an unprecedented kind. In political terms, it is true, there may seem to be less reason to question the modernity of the period here under scrutiny. There is a genuine sense in which the 'sovereign state' – even if its lineaments are more clearly discernible in medieval Europe than has sometimes been supposed – took firmer shape in and after the sixteenth century. Yet even here the need to distinguish an 'early modern' from a later phase is evident. The European nation-state of the nineteenth and twentieth centuries is a very different entity from the typically dynastic states (or the surviving republics) of that Ancien Régime which was shaped in the period with which we are here concerned. The modern democratic state, the welfare state, the *dirigiste* or corporatist state, the bureaucratic state, the state organised around political parties (or around a single party) – all these, in forms we could readily recognise, are developments of the past 200 years. The monarchies which dominated the political scene for three centuries or so before the French

Revolution – whether they were absolute or limited monarchies – belonged to a quite different world. The republics of the sixteenth and seventeenth centuries, even if they might ascribe sovereignty to the *populus*, were hardly 'people's republics' or 'democracies' as we understand those terms.

This is not, of course, to imply that the world of early modern Europe was merely a world of medieval survivals, of a continuity with the middle ages not to be broken significantly within our period. Decisive changes had taken place: there are features in early modern society and institutions that can and must be differentiated from what had gone before as well as from what was to follow. Yet it seems equally clear that, as the differentiation between 'early modern' and 'later modern' has sharpened, that between 'early modern' and 'medieval' has softened. This is manifestly a point to be considered in depth in the book as a whole; but it is one worth exemplifying and exploring briefly even in this introductory essay. An illustrative area of particular importance is that of ecclesiastical polity. In the traditional view, this was perhaps the clearest exemplification of 'the end of the middle ages'. The collapse of the universal authority of the papacy marked the demise of 'medieval christendom'. The *respublica christiana*, insofar as it took visible shape, did so, from the sixteenth century onwards, in the form of 'national churches'. Here above all, it seemed, the sovereignty of the new, modern state was asserted and vindicted. Even in Catholic Europe – in Spain, in France, in the Habsburg Empire – this pattern prevailed. Now it cannot be doubted that this view, so far as it goes, is substantially correct; but how far does it in fact take us towards an understanding of the ecclesiastical polity of early modern Europe?

If we think of the modern state as 'secular', as accepting (or even insisting upon) a separation of church and state, then we are again bound to question the modernity of early modern political society and of much of its political thinking. The states of Europe in the sixteenth and seventeenth centuries, whatever else they may have been were not secular states. They were, or at least they strove strenuously to be, confessional states, in which membership of the political community was inseparable from membership of a coextenive ecclesial community. The *respublica christiana* survived vigorously, however much the doctrinal ground of its being might be disputed. Again, the notion of a *christianitas* of which the universality, even the unity, was compatible with political diversity and with the exercise of substantial control of the church by the state was not simply a development of post-Reformation times. Already in the later middle ages means had

2

been found of reconciling papal authority with the 'free empire' of temporal (but by no means secular) rulers. Here as elsewhere the period from the late fifteenth century to the end of the seventeenth saw neither innovation nor even the unfolding of what had been implicit or latent, but rather the fuller and faster development of tendencies already explicitly present and manifest in late medieval society. These and other related themes are here illuminated not only in those chapters (6–8 especially) dealing directly with ecclesiological issues, but also in those which explore the impact of law and legal concepts on political ideas (e.g. chapters 3 and 10).

Complexity and ambiguity are likewise to be found in intellectual and cultural history. The great movements of the Renaissance and the Reformation did indeed mark significant new departures. That is why those movements dominate the early chapters of the book. Yet neither humanism nor Protestantism – to say nothing of the continuing vitality of other intellectual and spiritual traditions – retains in recent historiography quite the appearance it formerly had. This is in part a result of lengthening the chronological perspectives, of recognising the significance of what might be called proto-humanism and of earlier instances of the genus 'renaissance'; or of acknowledging that the Reformation and the Counter-Reformation of the sixteenth century are themselves part of a much longer 'age of reform' in western Christendom (Ozment 1980; Oakley 1979). It is also a matter of perceiving greater complexity in the relationships between what might otherwise be seen as antithetical groups or movements. Intellectual activity did not, could not, take place in rigidly separated channels. One man in his time could play different parts as circumstances required: Giovanni Francesco Poggio, son of the great Poggio Bracciolini, could write both a humanist's discourse on princely government (Poggio 1504) and a scholastic jurist's treatise on papal and conciliar authority (Poggio 1512?). Again, as we ourselves move further away from the educational dominance of the classical tradition and from the influence of religious concepts derived from both Catholicism and Protestantism in their sixteenth-century forms, it becomes harder to accept the modernity of the principles and values embodied in those modes of thought and teaching.

When, almost at the end of the volume we find (in chapters 18–20) the stubborn persistence of theological issues that had preoccupied late medieval scholastics, it may yet again seem that distinctive modernity has been submerged. Yet there are after all intellectual criteria of that

3

modernity which do come to us from the early modern period, and perhaps especially from the seventeenth century. The philosophy and what we would call the science of that seminal era, whatever indebtedness there may have been to the insights of late scholasticism, do convey the sense of novelty expressed in Bacon's *Great Instauration*. Neither the rationalism nor the empiricism of the age of Descartes and Hobbes, of Locke and Leibniz, has proved definitive; but both may be seen as characteristic of a recognisably modern way of thinking. Nonetheless such a theme or thesis – classically expounded in Alfred North Whitehead's *Science and the Modern World* (1926) – requires cautious scrutiny: we need, for instance, to remind ourselves that the thought-world of an Isaac Newton is remote in many ways from our concerns and our assumptions. As ever, there is no evading the historian's responsibility for reading the evidence as far as possible in its own terms. Such a reading may lead us to adopt and transplant Galileo's *eppur si muove*: the world of ideas, like the world of institutions and social relationships, moved decisively in the period with which we are concerned. Nor is the historical importance of that movement in any way lessened by the recognition that the process has continued, perhaps even more decisively, in the transformation of the world we have lost into the world in which we find ourselves.

The history of political thought in early modern Europe could obviously be written in different ways. Mere chronicling is perhaps the only historiographical mode ruled out by the nature of the subject. Some chronological ordering there must indeed be; and the division of this volume into five parts reflects that need. Such dividing-lines cannot, however, be rigid. Plainly the concerns of Renaissance thinkers continued into the period of Reformation and Counter-Reformation when the ideas analysed in Part II were generated. And a theme like the constitutionalism discussed in chapter 9, besides projecting long shadows beyond the notional terminal date of the chapter in the early seventeenth century, demands that the source of the light casting those shadows be sought in the period mainly examined in Part I. Late scholastic thinkers such as John Mair and Jacques Almain, writing in the early decades of the sixteenth century, were to be significant for some ways of thinking throughout the seventeenth. Recurrences and overlaps, then, are both unavoidable and deliberate. Chronological sequence can provide no more than a broad flexible framework for the investigation.

Within that framework, again, different schemes of subdivision suggest themselves. The thematic scheme adopted below need not be defended here: it must be judged by its fruits in historical elucidation of an intricate and complex mass of material. At the same time there are at least two other options calling for preliminary comment, both because of their own claims and because each has in fact had a certain modifying effect on the structure the book has aquired between planning and completion.

There is, first, the possibility of treating the history of political ideas as the history of modern Europe in general is often treated; as a series of inter-related but discrete national histories. J.W. Allen's *History of Political Thought in the Sixteenth Century* largely exemplified this approach; and it is noteworthy that when Allen carried his investigation into the next century he did not undertake to look further afield than English political thought (Allen 1928, 1938). Now it is indeed quite clear that, in comparison with the middle ages, there is much greater national diversity in political discourse from the mid-fifteenth century onwards. To ignore this, or even to reduce it (as, in general, has been done here) to a secondary role in determining the arrangement of the material, carries the risk that important aspects of the subject will be left in shadow. It may be the case here, for instance, that – despite the recurrence of a thinker like Suárez in several chapters – Spanish political thought, in a period when Spain was a dominant European power, has received less than due attention. Yet a case can be made for accepting this kind of possible lack of proportion as the necessary price for sustaining a more illuminating approach to the subject as a whole.

The transformation as well as the survival of the *respublica christiana* in this period has already been noted. We now need to consider the emergence of the notion of a 'republic of letters'. This was surely not the least important contribution made by humanism to European intellectual life; and for all the diversity in experience and in the articulation of that experience in political reflection and analysis, the sense of a 'common market' in ideas persists. George Buchanan's *De jure regni apud Scotos* was at one and the same time a response to a crisis in one small realm and part of a European debate on monarchy engaging general concern across national frontiers. Its author's correspondence with other humanists graphically illustrates the kind of intellectual community within which that debate took place. It is with European political thought in this sense that the chapters below seek to deal.

Do chapters 13, 14, and 15 stand out as exceptions to this norm? Is there even some reflection here of an 'anglocentricity' only too likely to be found in a history published in English and written almost wholly by British and

North American scholars? Not necessarily so. For one thing, these chapters are grouped in a part of the book which opens with a chapter bringing out very clearly the affinities between English and French conceptions of absolute monarchy and exemplifying the tendency in recent historiography to soften the sharp contrast conventionally made between England and continental Europe in such contexts. And, to the extent that there is then a considerable concentration on the importance of English experience, this is by no means a mere manifestation of intellectual chauvinism. There was, it is true, conflict and debate elsewhere in Europe in the early and middle years of the seventeenth century – perhaps even a 'general crisis' of authority across the entire continent. Yet the British and particularly the English aspect of that crisis threw issues into uniquely sharp relief and generated an unrivalled wealth of ideological dialectic. Specifically English the ideas – or at least their expression – may be in many instances; their historical significance nonetheless transcends such limitations.

As it happens, two English thinkers who do *not* receive attention mainly in the chapters just referred to illustrate the second possible approach to the subject which, while not predominant has had its influence here. Hobbes and Locke would be universally recognised as major intellectual figures; and here, like Pufendorf, Spinoza, Grotius, Bodin, Machiavelli, these thinkers have chapters or substantial parts of chapters devoted to their ideas. There is neither space nor need here to rehearse the now well-worn theme that the history of political thought is at best imperfetly written in terms of a succession of 'great thinkers'. And yet, however one conceives the nature of that history, the fact remains that figures emerge every now and then – and they were perhaps especially numerous in our period – who demand sustained analysis and who cannot, without distortion, simply be 'reduced to the ranks'. A balance must be struck between recognising this and responding to the demand of other, lesser voices to be heard. If there is dissonance as well as counterpoint (and sometimes harmony) in the composition, it must be hoped that such a result is inseparable from the nature of the subject.

I
Renaissance
and Counter-Renaissance

I

Humanism and political theory

ANTHONY GRAFTON

i Scholarship and power: a problematic partnership

In 1599 the Habsburg archduke and his Infanta came to the university of
Louvain to hear a humanist teach. The outstanding local scholar Justus
Lipsius proved more than equal to this challenging task, as he explained to a
friend in a characteristically immodest letter:

> I had to perform in the School of Theology, after what they call a theological
> 'Actus'. So I stood up and began to speak . . . after an extemporaneous introduction
> I explained a short text from Seneca's *De clementia*, beginning: 'The prince's
> greatness is firmly founded if all know that he is at once above them and on their
> side etc.' I explained the text from Seneca, I say, and in it the task of princes, and
> finally I added a reflection on the happy result that would stem from this, that is
> that we Belgians would feel towards them the benevolence and loyalty we had
> always felt for our rulers. That's it. They heard me with such sympathy that the
> prince never took his eyes off me; he inclined towards me not just mentally but
> bodily. So did the other nobles present, and they in turn received the favour of the
> ambassador of the king of Spain, a scholar, and one who favours me, as you should
> know. The Infanta was there too. I leave you to imagine what – or if – she
> understood. Now you know what went on here – the unusual, or possibly unique,
> event of a female prince coming to these exercises. I, and other prudent men, may
> begin to cherish better hopes for the republic, since the princes are openly
> beginning to show themselves favourably disposed to their Belgians and their
> ways.   (Lipsius 1637, II.454)

The lesson could hardly have gone better.

Lipsius' lecture to his Habsburg patrons encapsulates in one exemplary
case the humanist enterprise in political thought. We encounter a scholar
firmly committed to the belief that practical instruction for the most urgent
tasks in political and social life can best be found in Greek and Roman texts.
We see him extract from one of these a message not particularly Roman
but directly germane to the Habsburgs, whose refusal to learn or even

9

accommodate themselves to the customs of their Burgundian subjects had helped to provoke the Dutch Revolt. We see his audience nod eagerly in agreement even when they do not understand what he is saying. In short, we see the ancients made to live again as political counsellors. And yet, in this as in other instances, the more closely we scrutinise the exercise, the more it puzzles us. Is this the limited free speech allowed to a famous and valued counsellor, an independent intellectual challenging the authorities? Or is it a prearranged public ritual of conciliation between Habsburgs and Spanish officials on the one hand and Belgian dignitaries on the other? Did Lipsius mean – or expect – his advice to carry weight? Did Lipsius – until 1591 the leading scholar in the Protestant provinces of the Netherlands, an intellectual architect of their successful military resistance to Spain, a designer of the new model army led with such brilliance by his pupil Maurice of Nassau – really think that a Habsburg would come to hear about Seneca, attain enlightenment, and put an end to the revolt? The letter seems rich and vivid, yet the images it calls up are soon dispelled, and we are left, much like Alice, able to see the humanist's smile of satisfaction but not to grasp his meaning in a way that satisfies us.

The same interplay of fascination and frustration recurs when we trace the brand of scholarship Lipsius represents back to its Italian roots. To be sure, not every humanist and every fact proves difficult to place or assess. We know where the movement started. We can trace its spread and watch it take on institutional form. But we must remember the element of the mysterious in the humanists' enterprise as we try to grasp their distinctive forms of political discourse and teaching.

ii   *Dictatores* and philologists

We begin in the thirteenth century, with the growth of two parallel and related intellectual traditions in the Italian city-states. On the one hand, *dictatores* sprang up in every city and in many universities. These men, neither lawyers nor orators in the modern sense, performed a variety of necessary public functions, commercial, administrative, and legal. They developed an elaborate and stylised method for writing, in epistolary form, about matters of private and public interest. They kept formulary books of model letters and contracts, boiler-plate which could be copied or adapted to serve the needs of a businessman writing to a partner or a government clerk keeping records. And they soon came to play an active role in the small permanent governments that the Italian city-states developed to collect taxes and administer justice (Witt 1982).

On the other hand, intellectuals simultaneously began to form small cohesive groups and create new forms of literature and scholarship in the same cities. These men came from a variety of social orders and practised a variety of professions. Some, like the Paduan lawyer Lovato Lovati, were laymen; others, like the *Mansionarius* of the Verona cathedral, Giovanni de Matociis, were priests. But all shared a dedication to seeking out unknown or little-known classical texts. All tried to sort out the historical and philological problems the new texts posed (like the relation between the Pliny of the *Natural History* and the Pliny of the *Letters*, the nephew of the former, which Giovanni de Matociis explained). All tried to decode and master the most difficult and novel formal features that the texts presented (like the metres of Senecan tragedy, which Lovati became the first man in centuries to try seriously to scan). And many wrote substantial works of their own, ranging from derivative and traditional compendia to innovative histories and poems, in which they put their classical discoveries to work (Weiss 1947; Holmes 1986).

The two groups were not cut off from one another. Some early humanists worked with or as *dictatores* in public life. Some of the *dictatores* found the direct study of the Roman law and other classics to be to their professional advantage. Albertino Mussato, the best known of these early humanists, even tried to use the most advanced scholarship of his world to practical political effect. He not only mastered Seneca's metres but used them to write a Senecan tragedy on the tyranny of Ezzelino da Romano. He hoped that this powerful composition might dissuade his fellow citizens from giving in to the tyrannical della Scala. Cola di Rienzo similarly used the *lex regia* to persuade his fellow Romans to restore their republic to greatness.

When the *dictatores* and early humanists addressed themselves to political issues, they drew on Cicero and Seneca to dramatise the need for concord and pursuit of a common good; and to that extent a pre-humanist political discourse came into being, which adumbrated many features of later humanist political writing. It did not, however, annex the advanced philology of its time; the scholarship of the humanists remained a private preoccupation of scholars and writers, throughout the fourteenth century. The most original and learned scholar of the time, Petrarch, studied Roman inscriptions and Livy's history with great intensity. He loved the brilliant early centuries of Roman history, which he saw as the culmination of human accomplishment, far more than the more recent but more obscure Christian centuries. He chose his favourite books – which he carefully listed at an early date – almost exclusively from Roman literature. And he modelled his literary career on those of Virgil and Ovid as he knew them from their works and the ancient commentaries. But he did not make any effort to recreate in his own world the Roman ethos of active life in the service of the state – the ethos that Virgil celebrated and Cicero practised. He often adverted to the superiority of solitary contemplation to impure political action. He showed no special affection for the republic of Florence from which his family came. And when he learned from the *Letters to Atticus* that his beloved Cicero, his favourite philosopher, had also been an engagé politician, he reacted not with admiration but with horror. Cicero's involvement in earthly politics seemed to him a terrible error – one that compromised Cicero's standing as a moral philosopher and revealed undreamt-of corruption in the classic heart of pagan culture: 'How much better it would have been for a philosopher to grow old in the quiet countryside . . . Farewell, my Cicero, from the land of the living . . . in the year 1345 from the birth of the God you did not know' (*Familiares* 24.3). The most advanced classical scholarship of the fourteenth century, in other words, served literary and philosophical rather than practical and political ends (Mommsen 1959; Baron 1988).

iii   Humanism in the service of the city-state

Between 1390 and 1420, to be sure, the situation changed. Coluccio Salutati, a provincial notary who became the chancellor of Florence, finally fused humanistic scholarship and political action. As a humanist he avidly collected classical manuscripts, corrected texts, and supported young scholars like Poggio Bracciolini and Leonardo Bruni who also sought out, copied, and made available new classical texts. As a statesman he employed his new information and ideas on behalf of Florence. Defending her against the aggressive and effective ruler of Milan, Giangaleazzo Visconti, he articulated a new ideology of republicanism to counter Milanese propaganda and rally other cities to Florence. He presented Florence as the true heir of Roman liberty, founded by Roman citizens and therefore directly descended fom the republic (Garin 1952, pp. 20, 32 Witt 1983).

Bruni, later to become chancellor of the republic in his own right, went much further along the same road. His commitment to republicanism led him to reassess all values, including his own strict early classicism. He defended Dante, for example, as an exemplary active citizen (where Petrarch had remained aloof and uninvolved); more remarkably still, he defended Dante's use of the vernacular, arguing passionately that 'each language has its own perfection and its own sound, and its polished and learned diction', so that Italian as well as Latin poetry could make the basis of a valid claim to eternal fame (Griffiths *et al.* 1987, p. 93). He developed an acute and robust theory of history, one both coherent in its explanation of events and original in its refusal to follow traditional ways of ordering the past. Bruni held that talent, in politics and literature alike, could produce great achievements only in a society that rewarded virtue. This, Rome had ceased to do by the time it became an empire. The emperors, in their violence and suspicion, decimated the Roman people whom they should have protected. Rome itself, like the great trees that 'overshadow small plants that arise in their vicinity and keep them stunted', had crushed the old cities of Etruria (Watkins 1978, p. 33). History written by Bruni did not apply the old strait-jacket of the four Monarchies to the chaos of local events; it did not even magnify Rome's greatness. Rather, it celebrated what had always seemed the most tragic of all events, the fall of Rome, as the precondition of the rise of Italy's medieval free cities – above all the greatest of them, Florence. And Bruni did not hesitate to argue, in terms and forms borrowed from Thucydides and other ancient celebrators of the greatness of republican Athens, that the liberty and free access to office that Florentines enjoyed were a sufficient explanation of their unique institutions and achievements (Baron 1988, I, pp. 24–93). No wonder that the creator of this 'Copernican Revolution in historiography', as Baron has called it, became the best-paid official and one of the best-known citizens of Florence, as his splendid tomb still shows.

From the 1420s, then, humanism had shown that it could forge a civic ideology that crystallised the aspirations of leading citizens and evoked the loyalty of ordinary men and allies. It could produce effective propaganda in the modest form of broadsides and letters or the far larger and more intellectually ambitious one of Bruni's *History*. It naturally won the interest and support of established members of the social and political elites throughout Italy. In Florence and Venice, for example, members of the ruling order began in the first decades of the fifteenth century to have their sons educated classically. In Florence those present at the committee meetings of influential citizens that took place at every time of crisis began to cite classical examples as sources of valid political precept and example (Brucker 1977; King 1986). And they began to see themselves as the humanists portrayed them: as the heirs of Rome and the defenders of republican liberty, stability, and law. At the same time, however, the Visconti rulers of Milan, the Aragonese rulers of Naples and the popes in Rome also began to hire humanists to legitimate their very different political goals and achievements. Despots and popes won credit above all for support of the arts, but they also often appeared in the texts written about them as the ideal defenders of a classically defined common good (Bentley 1987). Humanism, in short, had established itself as vital to the public justification of political power: it could legitimate or attack a regime, defend a war, instil patriotism, and offer advice in time of crisis.

As humanist skills became fashionable in government offices and princely courts, the humanists themselves began to demand – and to achieve – the creation of a new network of institutions. They founded schools where their new literary skills could be learned through direct encounters with the classical texts. They revived the classical notion, forged in Athens and re-forged in republican Rome, of the *vir bonus dicendi peritus* – 'the good man skilled in public speaking' – as the ideal product of education (Kristeller 1979; Gray 1963). They forcefully pointed out that the normal educational systems of their time – the innovative, popular, and intellectually aggressive Italian university faculties of medicine and law, with their emphasis on technical skills and their determined modernisation of classical texts to serve current needs – could not produce morally reliable generalists able to speak effectively in public, in assembly, court, or diplomatic delegation, on any subject. And they urged that close study of rhetoric would provide the skills, and close study of history and moral philosophy would develop the moral strength, that would enable active members of the elite to govern themselves, their families, and their states 'far more effectively than the pettifoggers and shysters of our day' – as Lodovico Carbone put it in the 1450s, when setting out to teach Roman history from Lucan and Valerius Maximus (Müllner 1899, pp. 88–9).

The humanists never convinced all members of the elite to accept the most ambitious planks in their programme. Teachers of rhetoric and history never enjoyed salaries a third as large as those normally paid to lawyers, and a degree in law continued to seem desirable and attractive to thousands of young members of the patriciate (Grafton and Jardine 1986). Moreover, the rise of new schools of formal theology in Italy, which reached real prominence at the same period as the humanist schools, also offered a non-humanist path to power and activity in the one world-wide political organisation, the church. Bernardino of Siena and Antonino of

Florence were by no means the only influential Italians of the mid-fifteenth century to follow this path to power and authority (Kristeller 1979; Seigel 1968). Yet in many respects the humanists did triumph. They transformed the tastes and sensibilities of the elite. Classical texts written – after the 1470s printed – in the clear round script that the humanists revived from Carolingian manuscripts became the proper load for a patrician's shelves to bear. Young lords and merchant princes found themselves forced to study Latin texts, word by word, and to weave the fruits of their reading into their own compositions. Ambrogio Traversari spoke with pleasure of the sight of the young Gonzaga prince and princess that he met in Mantua in 1435. The boy recited 200 verses of his own composition as well as Virgil had recited *Aeneid* 6 to Augustus, while the girl, though only ten years old, wrote a finer Greek hand than many professional scholars (Traversari 1759, Bk 15, ep. 38) Ludovico Sforza of Milan, trying to produce a gift worthy of his formidable mother Bianca Maria, wrote out for her a neat fair copy of his tutor's lectures on a treatise on rhetoric, the *Ad Herennium*, then thought to be by Cicero (Filelfo 1967). The humanists, in other words, did impart a new set of skills and tastes to many members of the political elite. Chanceries and courts across Italy participated in a common discourse and possessed a common set of standards of civility and elegance (Grafton and Jardine 1986).

iv 'Civic humanism' and its rivals

But did this revolution in the canons of taste and the form of public discourse also lead to revolutionary change in political thought? Here opinions differ sharply. Hans Baron, perhaps the most influential of all Renaissance scholars in the last two generations, has argued that the Florentine humanists with whom we have become acquainted were the founders of secular political thought and the modern republican tradition. Challenged by the Visconti, virtually bereft of allies, Florence maintained itself against high odds as the champion of liberty in Italy. When Giangaleazzo died in 1402 and the Milanese state lost cohesion – as the Italian despotates so often did when a ruler died – Florence triumphed, or at least survived. And this victory transformed the lives and ideas of its citizens and intellectuals (Baron 1966).

True, the great old chancellor Salutati never fully abandoned his loathing, founded on medieval beliefs, for the murderers of Caesar. For all his interest in new texts and critical techniques, he retained his loyalty to a

Trecento intellectual style, practising allegorical forms of classical scholarship that his younger contemporaries would abandon. Bruni by contrast changed radically. Before the crisis, so Baron argued, Bruni had written a clever dialogue in which his friend Niccolò Niccoli tore apart the unclassical styles and defective scholarship of Florence's three great fourteenth-century writers, Petrarch, Dante, and Boccaccio. Bruni and Niccoli shared a classicism so rigorous that it led them to condemn all products of modern culture as inferior – indeed, to assert, against Salutati, that modern men could write nothing of value. After the crisis Bruni wrote a phosphorescent work *In Praise of Florence*, modelled on Aelius Aristides' ancient work in praise of Athens. He lavishly praised the unique qualities of Florence's republican government, mercantile wealth, physical beauty. He wrote a second dialogue to correct and complete the first, a palinode in which Niccoli refuted his own criticisms of the fourteenth-century writers and praised modern Florence heartily – if less powerfully than he had attacked it. And throughout his life, much of it to be spent a chancellor, Bruni took every opportunity to praise Florentine civic virtues and values. He used powerful ancient models like Thucydides' funeral oration of Pericles and Livy's history of Rome to brilliant effect (Baron 1966).

Others went as far and further. Poggio produced a dialogue *On Avarice* in which one speaker explored the possibility that acquisitiveness of the kind normal and necessary in the mercantile elite was not a sin but a vital civic virtue: 'For money is vital, like a set of sinews that sustain the republic, and since the avaricious have so much of it, they must be esteemed a foundation of the state . . . Moreover they often add great adornments to the cities' (Garin, 1952, pp. 270, 272). Palmieri wrote powerfully on the duties of the good citizen as he had learnt them from the Florentines who came to political maturity in the Milanese crisis (Baron 1988, I, pp. 155–7, 234–5). Even Machiavelli owed his insights into the nature of republicanism very largely to his predecessors of a century before in the Florentine chancery. For Baron, then, the Florentines were the first intellectuals to adopt an implicitly secular and civic view of politics, and to use the tools of classical rhetoric to give that view powerful expression in works on philosophy, literature, and history.

More recent scholarship has modified Baron's theses in a variety of ways. The crisis of 1402 now seems less prominent than Baron thought it, and other ones, like the slightly later war with Ladislas of Naples, seem more so. More important, the humanists seem less radical than Baron thought them. Closer examination of the central texts Baron relied on – few of which in fact explicitly concentrate on political questions – has revealed that none of them yields the unequivocal messages Baron found in them except at the price of over-interpretation and deliberate indifference to their genres. Bruni's two dialogues, for example, are clearly modelled on the dialogues of Cicero, in which different positions were deliberately presented with comparable eloquence by one author, speaking through the mouths of different characters (an exercise known as argument *in utramque partem*). The attack on and the defence of Florence form part of a single conception and were meant to be read together, whether they were written simultaneously or not (Quint 1985; Mortensen 1986). Poggio's dialogue *On Avarice* – to which we will return – offers its defence of sin as a paradox, and winds up with a blistering attack on avarice by a powerful speaker (Oppelt 1977). Moreover, the timing of events is less precise than Baron held, the connection between external circumstances and political ideas far less tight. It now seems likely, for example, that Bruni's dialogues were not only written to stand together but also at the same time the political crisis came before either was drafted, and presumably affected the attitudes of the second no more than those of the first.

Above all, it has become clear that the complex of ideas and values Baron labelled as 'civic humanism' did not even win the full assent of the Florentine elite. Niccoli, for example, came from a Florentine family of wealth and power and served the state in important public offices. Yet he never adopted the favourable view of republican culture that Bruni espoused. Attacks on him circulated, ridiculing him for his obsession with collecting manuscripts and correcting their spelling and punctuation. Surely, the attackers suggested, to spend one's life worrying about whether a Latin word should be spelt *nihil* or *nichil* is to create much ado about nothing (Gombrich 1976). Thus one could belong to the Florentine elite and serve the Florentine state in the years of crisis without ever necessarily fusing civic service with scholarly tastes. A commitment to civic service, moreover, did not necessarily imply a commitment to republican ideals. Bruni perhaps compromised his own adherence to republican government by committees chosen by lot when he stayed on as chancellor under Cosimo de' Medici, who took over and subverted the Florentine republic after 1433; more likely, as James Hankins has argued, he saw himself as committed not to republicanism as an ideology but to public service as a calling – to deploying his considerable skills loyally in the service of the Florentine government (Hankins forthcoming; cf. Baron 1988, I, p. 9). And Poggio, who succeeded Bruni as chancellor, seems to have been less a civic humanist than an old, loyal servant intent on getting through state meetings as soon as possible so he could return home for his dinner.

If the civic humanists of Florence had an ideology less clear and cohesive than Baron thought, moreover, they also had more rivals than he admitted through the fifteenth century. First, their friends and colleagues in princely states often held a diametrically opposed view of the needs and nature of society, arguing that a prince could uphold justice and maintain peace far more effectively than a republican government, with its liability to faction and corruption. If Poggio thought that Scipio had been Rome's greatest hero, Guarino of Verona thought Caesar deserved that honour – and the two of them fought out their rival conceptions in an elaborately staged debate (Oppelt 1974). Guarino could not have agreed more fully with the Florentines that the study of the ancient world should produce moral, active citizens now. He too found inspiration in Cicero for these views. 'What better goal can there be for our thoughts and efforts [he asked at the start of a course on Cicero *De officiis*] than the ability, precepts, and studies by which we may come to guide, order, and govern ourselves, our households and our political affairs?' (Sabbadini 1896, p. 182) Guarino too saw classical texts as the best available source of advice for public life. But the rules he extracted from his texts were hardly civic in their implications. 'Whatever the ruler may decree', he explained to his son, 'must be approved of with a calm mind and the appearance of pleasure. For men who can do this are dear to rulers, make themselves and their relatives prosperous, and win high promotion' (Guarino 1915–19, III, p. 439). Similarly, but less cynically, the influential teacher Pier Paolo Vergerio combined a belief that 'that man excels all others in character and way of life who devotes himself to the government of the state' with the further belief that princes normally preserved the rule of law most effectively, and that the best civic life would normally be attained in their service (Robey 1973).

Second, the secular and civic values that Bruni sometimes expounded had intellectual competition of a serious kind from ideas that seem far less familiar to modern readers. We have seen that history provided men like Bruni with a genre in which they could both assert the primacy of the values they believed in and present an implicitly secular and highly politicised characterisation of human life. Yet their history was not the only literary form of the public memory to thrive in fifteenth-century intellectual circles. Another popular one – one that the Latin west had inherited from Islam in the twelfth century – rested on the belief that the conjunctions of Jupiter and Saturn that take place roughly every twenty years have a powerful shaping effect on earth, and aligned the great turning points in ancient and modern history with the stately, regular dance of the stars. This belief clearly implies a vision of politics different from either that of the Florentines or that of their debate partners in Milan and Ferrara – a vision in which providence still controls man directly and human decisions, accordingly, play a limited and secondary role. Historical astrology of this kind, prominent in fourteenth-century Florentine chronicles, was banned from historiography by Bruni and Poggio (Baron 1988, I, pp. 68–71). But it was hardly banned from Renaissance society. Great buildings – notably churches and palaces – continued to be built at astrologically propitious times. Horoscopes – including the horoscope of the founding of Florence – continued to fascinate intellectuals and eventually received treatment in the great official pictorial versions of Florence's founding in the sixteenth century (Cox-Rearick 1984). And in the time of Savonarola, late in the fifteenth century, it became clear that this and other providential interpretations of history had a stronger claim on many than the secular and civic ones for which Bruni is now celebrated.

Finally, recent research on medieval political and legal thought has shown that the jurists and philosophers of the Italian universities had at least as much to say about the practical needs and goals of the Italian communes as the humanists did. Jurists, not humanists, established and invoked the secular principle that in a crisis of the state *necessitas legem non habet* ('necessity knows no law'). Scholastics, not humanists, first revived the Aristotelian writings that offered a set of secular categories for analysing states as monarchical, aristocratic, or popular. A scholastic trained in Paris, Marsilius of Padua, drew out the implications of Aristotle's view for the autonomy of the human city far more thoroughly than any humanist ever would (Rubinstein 1982). And his application of the Aristotelian principle of the *bonum commune* to the popular government of Italian communes was no individual aberration; he drew on the patriotic enthusiasm of humanists like Mussato, and, even more directly, on the political thought of earlier Italian scholastics and pre-humanists who had already shown that Latin morality and Greek categories could fit and help to explicate Italian realities (Skinner 1986). Mendicants, not humanists, first admitted in their theological writing that merchant cities needed merchants to carry out their political and economic functions. 'The rich', wrote Bernardino of Siena, 'are necessary to the state' (Oppelt 1977, p. 574). And mendicants elaborated the rich store of casuistic doctrine that permitted merchants and bankers to charge interest without committing usury, by redefining interest as compensation for potential and actual loss of income. They also drew up the first, impressive sketches of doctrine about fair wages and prices (Bec 1967).

v   The topics of humanist political discourse

What remains when all subtrahends are removed is still important. The humanists created a new language for talking about citizenship and the state. As specialists in discourse they made their way to prominence and power, offering in a language far more attractive and accessible than that of scholasticism a description of society as it is and prescriptions for what society should be that often fitted the needs of their time with supple elegance. This language, flexible, rich, and largely classical, was shared by civic humanists and monarchists, Florentines and Ferrarese. For the remainder of this essay we shall explore it, dividing its lexicon of concepts into three categories that the humanists themselves would have seen as legitimate. Humanist social and political language explicates the duties of the patrician towards household, city, and state. To deal with the household may seem to the twentieth-century reader a conflation of the personal and the political. Yet in fifteenth-century cities it seemed evident that the two forms of economic and administrative order were analogous and intimately related. Teachers of ethics like Ioannes Argyropoulos argued that they had to show from their texts that 'man is born not for himself but for others as well, but not just any others, only those for whose care and rule he is responsible. These fall into two categories; some belong to the household, some to the state' (Müllner 1899, pp. 12–13). Teachers of history like Ludovico Carbone promised to show their pupils how 'to organise the family and administer the state' (Müllner 1899, pp. 88–9). And all tended to assume in humble practice – whatever they might proclaim in lofty theory – that on these matters the classical philosophers had basically 'the same doctrines as our writers do' (Bruni 1928, p. 71).

First, then, the family. Here the humanists had much to say. They began by making classical materials available in a new way. Francesco Barbaro wrote an elaborate treatise *De re uxoria* in which he vulgarised the ideas and anecdotes of Plutarch about how to marry, raise children, and preserve a peaceful home (Garin 1952, pp. 104–37; Kohl and Witt 1978, pp. 189–228). Leonardo Bruni retranslated the pseudo-Aristotelian treatise *Oeconomica*,

'On Household Management', and used his knowledge of Greek history and customs to provide it with a commentary that made clear much that the scholastics had misunderstood – and even some points that the author himself (whom Bruni thought to be Aristotle) might have left obscure. Bruni was at pains to show that the text did not treat women, as it seemed at first to do, as domestic equipment on a par with cattle. He argued at length, in fact, that a wife had a status and rights guaranteed by laws which no husband could licitly violate (Griffiths *et al.* 1987, pp. 300–17). This work became a humanist bestseller; more than 200 manuscript copies of it survive, still bearing the marks left by owners who included clerics and laymen, scholars and merchants – a cross-section of the Italian elite (Griffiths *et al.* 1987). Others elaborated in treatises on education the doctrines on marriage and management of children that they had found in the witty, anecdotal essays of Plutarch and the systematic treatise of Quintilian (Woodward 1899).

So far as relations between husbands and wives, fathers and children were concerned, the humanists essentially fitted their classical sources to Italian realities. The major classical text on marriage, Plutarch's *Coniugalia Praecepta*, calls for husbands to remain on top, but does so in a moderate and qualified way. Plutarch insists that husbands accommodate themselves to their wives and not expect them to be constantly obsequious and complaisant in the style of courtesans. Barbaro, adapting Plutarch to an Italian world where husbands married young wives late in their own careers, speaks only to husbands and advises wives simply to be silent and obey. He twists Plutarch's anecdotes to support total subordination of women. In the same style, later treatises like Leon Battista Alberti's Italian dialogues *On the Family* offer a splendid male fantasy of docile young wives being ruled and instructed by powerful, mature husbands in everything from storage of food to sexual relations. If sometimes fanciful, though, these texts are far from insignificant. In a society that often seemed obsessed with the need to preserve the family against the aggression of rival families, the suspicions of state officials, and the high rate of infant mortality, they offered attractive and apparently effective advice that actually ratified the demographic realities of the time. But they did so at the double price of distorting classical sources and of ignoring many difficult modern situations, such as arose when a young and vigorous widow like Alessandra Scala came to control a family or a princess became the ruler of a state (Grafton and Jardine 1986, ch. 2).

More ambitious – and probably far more influential – were the humanists' efforts to provide a moral rationale for the existence and power of the rich merchants and princes of their time to earn and spend their money without shame. They found in Aristotle above all justification for conspicuous expenditure: 'But great expenditure is becoming to those who have suitable means to start with, secured by their own efforts or from ancestors or connections, and to people of high birth and reputation . . . For all these things being with them greatness and prestige' (*Nicomachean Ethics* 1122b30ff). They thus came to argue that wealth was not simply something 'indifferent' – something that could be used for good or for ill – but that its possession could be the foundation of a virtue in its own right. 'Magnificence', the proper expenditure of large sums, was a virtue peculiar to the rich; and the rich, in Florence and elsewhere, and their panegyrists rapidly appealed to these views as they dropped the traditional medieval habit of concealing wealth from tax officials and rivals and went in for display (Fraser Jenkins 1970). Great families, in Florence above all, built themselves palaces that cut them off from the street-corner life of the city and loggias that offered in its place a private sociability for family and close friends (Goldthwaite 1981; Kent 1977). They became – most notoriously in the case of Cosimo de' Medici – patrons of architecture on the vast scale previously reserved for the church and secular rulers, and patrons of visual artists and dealers in fine clothing and antiquities as well (Gombrich 1985). And they and those who designed for them, like Alberti, continually insisted that this new world of display was the conscious and virtuous exercise of magnificence in action. 'Men of public spirit', Alberti wrote in the preface to his work on architecture, 'approve and rejoice' at the sight of such activity (Fraser Jenkins 1970).

As personal display came to seem desirable and virtuous, acquisitiveness too took on a newly laudable character. True, the humanists did not actually advance new economic doctrines to supplant those of the medicants. But they did defend the activities of the merchant in a newly aggressive way, as vital to the exercise of virtue.

When the venerable Giannozzo in Alberti's *On the Family* insisted that his young relatives should examine their consciences nightly to determine if they had missed an appointment or an opportunity, failed to meet a commitment, or to act in good time, he spoke a language of innerworldly asceticism that the mendicants could not use – and that would have lacked any justification without the alternate ideologies of magnificence and civic service that Alberti espoused through other *personae* (Baron 1988, 1, ch. 10). In later bourgeois society 'money is very ashamed of itself', as Lionel

Trilling rightly pointed out. In fifteenth-century Italy the humanists devised a language in which money could speak without shame, if only as the sign and basis of a new idea of virtuous conduct. Humanist doctrines on the government of the household, in other words, were modern and attractive; and they helped to reshape the social and physical space in which the Italian elite lived.

Humanist doctrines about the nature and government of cities, like those on households, began from classical sources but were not confined to them. The humanists knew from Aristotle and his followers how to divide an urban population into ordinary people and patricians. They learned from Livy how the circumstances of a city's founding shape the character and virtues of its people. But they also learned from medieval intellectuals how to compile a powerful dossier in praise of the city to which they belonged, enumerating its saints and spectacles in overwhelming detail. And even their most classical descriptions of a city's virtues tend to enfold or reflect late medieval discussions of urban history and power.

Humanist texts on cities may at first seem somewhat bland to the uninitiated reader. Examples of epideictic rhetoric, oratory in praise (or blame) of a person or thing, they pile up the virtues and attributes of the cities they describe with little obvious regard for details or qualifications. Salutati defending Florence against Antonio Loschi and Bruni praising Florence both extol the city's climate, health, agriculture, trade, commerce, walls, and buildings – referring neither to the lowered scale of manufacturing and banking after the crash of the fourteenth century nor to the insalubrious conditions caused in Florence by some of her characteristic industries, like the tanning works and fullers' shops. Bruni explicates Florentine institutions as built around a central check, a *cautela* – the system of choosing members of the governing committees by lot from a large body of citizens that supposedly prevented the great families from controlling urban policies. Yet he wrote this at a time when one small group of families was in fact manipulating the city's policies towards war and expansion to serve their own economic interests, as well as opening up positions in the government to more citizens than before. Such rhetoric blurs the outlines of real cityscapes and institutions.

The classical and clerical sources of the humanists' language, moreover, did not offer them terms and tools for dealing with certain crucial features of Renaissance urban life. Florence, we know from several recent books, was less a single coherent city-state in the classical sense than a congeries of districts and guilds to which most citizens felt their primary loyalties – and

23

from which they received such governmental interference as they met (Kent and Kent 1982). But the classical language of social analysis of cities has little terminology for these intermediate bodies, and the works in praise of cities accordingly paid little attention to them. True, the Venetian humanists devised a more elaborate and novel language to deal with their city's unique constitution, its powerful doge, closed governing body, and remarkable social harmony (King 1986). And reality slips through the rhetoric in Florence as well – as when Bruni, writing for his Greek friends at the Council of Ferrara–Florence, admitted that his city was now dominated by men of wealth and connected that fact with the replacement of the old civic militia by mercenary armies, who fought for money rather than sentiment (Griffiths *et al.* 1987, p. 174). On the whole, however, it remained a language of praise (Goldbrunner 1983).

Yet the humanists' civic discourse was novel in at least two vital ways. In the first place, they based cities' claims to antiquity and high origins on direct study of the ancient sources. Salutati's argument for Florence's Roman heritage, for example, rested on a passage in Sallust's history of Catiline in which he described discontented veterans of Sulla's army sent out to resist the inhabitants of Fiesole, turning rebellious after losing their property. Such arguments became more and more elaborate over time, as Bruni and others traced their cities back to Rome, to the Etruscans, and even – in the notorious case of Viterbo – to Isis and Osiris. And they often led to the bold invention of acts and documents where these were lacking, since, as Salutati had already admitted, the passage of time made urban origins tantalisingly obscure. Yet they had a powerful impact on political propaganda throughout Europe, and the invention of traditions about Trojan, Roman, or Greek origins that became a staple of Renaissance pageantry and propaganda had its origins in the Italy of the humanists (Baron 1988, I, ch. 3; Cipriani 1980).

In the second place, the humanists dwelt on the physical appearance of their cities with a new artistry and interest. They treated Florence under the Medici, Rome under Nicholas V, and Milan under the Sforza as cities rationally planned both to give aesthetic pleasure and to further economic activity and political power. Bruni, for example, emphasises in his *Praise of Florence* the city's ideal situation, splendid public buildings, clean and wide streets. The humanists in the papal curia did the same, ceasing to lament the decay of Roman inscriptions and buildings – and their misidentifications by past scholars – as papal architects rebuilt and population returned to the acres of sheep meadow within the old walls. These descriptions often misrepresented reality. They treated confused and over-built cities, with narrow streets and polluted rivers, as ideal and rational creations like the cities imagined in Antonio Filarete's treatise *Sforzinda* and Alberti's *On Architecture*. Yet in doing so they challenged rulers to build systematically and further the creation of rationally planned colonies – and a few such cities, like the fortress of Alessandria, were actually built. More importantly, perhaps, they helped to create the tradition of including detailed physical descriptions of public buildings, churches, hospitals, and open spaces in political writing – and of insisting on the effects of the built environment on its human inhabitants. These motifs became standard ones in the utopian writing of the sixteenth century, from Thomas More's *Utopia* to Tommaso Campanella's *City of the Sun*. To that extent the apparently unrealist epideictic orations of the humanists had a real impact – if not on most cities, at least on some of the most powerful and persistent western visions of what a good city should be. The image of the city as a rational, planned space, its buildings and quarters differentiated not by tradition and accretion but by logic and science, received its most powerful crystallisation in Leonardo's drawings. It is salutary to remember that these high Renaissance creations of one who called himself a 'man without letters' have their roots in the political writing of the humanists (Garin 1969).

The state, finally, *respublica* as opposed to *civitas*, called forth a great deal of discussion from the humanists. Writers about kingship, on the one hand, naturally directed their attention to relations between a court and all its subjects rather than the more limited political space of the city where a court was normally located. This they did partly because their rulers genuinely formed the heads of a wider political community, and – especially in Naples and Milan – found both special problems and special opportunities in the existence of lesser nobles and formerly independent cities in their domains. But they also did so because the tradition of writing on kingship that they inherited, stemming from Isocrates in classical Greece and brilliantly continued by John of Salisbury and many others in the middle ages, dictated this approach. An almost unvarying series of topics – including the proper relations between a king and his counsellors, the question of whether a king is above or below the law, and the king's moral duty to devote himself to the good of his subjects, avoiding excess taxes and unnecessary war – formed the staple of this genre in its Renaissance incarnation from Petrarch on. Modern readers know these topoi best from Machiavelli's inversions of them in *The Prince*, with its obsessive insistence on the role of fear and the vital importance of warfare. And for all the mordant injustice of his work, it must be admitted that the humanists of the fifteenth century added little of substance to the traditions that they drew upon (Born 1928).

Republican writers often addressed – but did not always have much of substance to say about – the increasingly large territorial states that surrounded Florence and Venice. In defending Florence against Antonio Loschi, Salutati tried to articulate an ideology that justified Florence's presence outside her own walls. Florence stood, he claimed, as the defender of *libertas*, not just at home but in the rest of north Italy; her territorial state was the necessary consequence of the need to defend republicanism against the aggression of the Visconti tyrant. This argument sounds pleasing now, but as Nicolai Rubinstein has shown, it would have evoked remarkably varied reactions around 1400 (and in fact did so from Salutati's literary opponent, Loschi). In Florentine political discourse *libertas* had a variety of meanings, including the republican constitution at home and freedom from interference from other powers. But it did not mean that formerly autonomous states that now came under Florentine rule would be granted autonomy in their own affairs. Pisa, captured in 1406 and made to serve as the base of the Florentine galley fleet, was occupied by a garrison and ruled by Florentine governors and tax collectors. Loschi did not fail to point out that *libertas* was more a cloak for self-interest than a programme for the political development of north Italy (Rubinstein 1982). In short, humanist political discourse did not offer an incisive analysis of the larger and larger political entities, centred on Milan, Florence, Venice, Rome, and Naples, that divided up the Italian political scene in the course of the fifteenth century, like monstrous paramecia seen on a microscope slide devouring smaller organisms.

What the humanists did offer, as usual, was a flexible and persuasive language of praise and justification for the states and rulers that they served. In this realm of epideictic discourse the humanist mastery of the ancient texts, with their rich resources of argument, anecdote, and metaphor, and the humanist command of rhetoric itself proved a decisive advantage. Any ruler and any subject could be provided with a terminology appropriate to the social and intellectual standing of both. Thus, as Alison Brown has shown, classical topoi could be deployed in praise of Cosimo de' Medici in at least three ways. A Greek humanist like Argyropoulos, appointed to a formal position in the Florentine *studio*, could draw on Plato's *Republic* to describe his master as the embodiment of the philosopher-king that Plato had thought could not exist except as an ideal. Members of established Florentine families like Donato Acciaiuoli could remain more reserved – and reveal less awareness of the political realities – by treating Cosimo as simply *primus inter pares*, a noble and beneficent citizen who had saved the state from chaos, held only a few offices, and devoted himself to the public good. And the admirers and beneficiaries of Cosimo's lavish patronage of the arts, drawing on the rich resources of Horace and Virgil, could compare Cosimo to Augustus and Maecenas, the great benefactors of the Augustan age whose most lasting material was the classic literary works they had supported (Brown 1961).

Humanist epideictic proved remarkably supple and inventive. Some orators employed premises that seemed unexceptionally Roman and republican to praise absolute – and absolutely non-Roman – rulers. Thus Pier Paolo Vergerio, theorist of education and student of Cicero, insisted firmly on the preeminence of the active life in public service: 'That man excels all others in character and way of life who devoted himself to the government of the state and to sharing in the labor for the common good.' At one point he went even further, arguing like a good Florentine that 'the best philosophy . . . dwells in cities and shuns solitude, strives both for its own advantage and for that of all', and denouncing Augustus as a tyrant. On the whole, however, the one string that he plucked in every context was the need for justice and the rule of law rather than violence. It comes as a surprise to learn from David Robey that he used these principles to build an edifice of praise for the Carrara of Padua, a family not known for their rigorous adherence to legal codes (Robey 1973). And while one could argue – as Castiglione later would – that such idealised statements were a way of confronting the actions of a ruler with the values they violated, of teaching by indirection, the lasting impression one receives is of men deliberately setting out to conceal and divert attention from inconvenient realities. When Bartolomeo Fonzio set about praising Lorenzo de' Medici, a far less active patron than Cosimo (though a fine poet in his own right) and a more overt manipulator of Florentine government, he did so in the exalted term of Virgil's Fourth Eclogue; 'You have at last restored the rule of Saturn [the Golden Age] . . . The arts are restored, poets are prospering' (Gombrich 1985). Angelo Poliziano, similarly, finely conflated Virgil, Ovid, and others in a mock epic in which Lorenzo himself was made to learn not how to found a new race but how to love (Poliziano 1979). These praises of Lorenzo had a clear political purpose despite their exalted sound. They distracted attention from the recent rise of the Medici

27

and Lorenzo's personal lack of the military prowess which had distinguished princes in most traditional panegyrics (he himself confessed that he
was not 'a hard hitter' and won tournaments only because the judges
wanted him to). And they did create a powerful image of Lorenzo as a
patron of the arts – an image which persisted in histories of the Renaissance,
despite his lack of means and low scale of real expenditure, into the twentieth
century. Sometimes, indeed, the curtain-drawing seems painfully visible –
as when Poliziano, writing the history of the conspiracy of the Pazzi against
the Medici, modelled his work on Sallust's *Catiline* but completely omitted
any counterpart to Sallust's social and political exposition of why
conspiracy had taken place. To include such an explication was to call
attention to the recency and illegitimacy of Medicean rule. Poliziano
accordingly ignored social and political preconditions of revolt and instead
included a stunningly vivid account of the rituals of inversion by which the
Florentine crowd had humiliated the Pazzi alive and even dead (Poliziano
1958).

   In one area – and perhaps only in one city – humanist political discourse
did transcend propaganda. In Venice, as Margaret King has recently
shown, the fifteenth century saw the patriciate which dominated the
Venetian economy and monopolised political life take a strong interest in
humanistic scholarship. The Venetian elite, with its tradition of service to
the state in a wide variety of positions at home and in the Venetian outposts
(and eventually its growing empire in Italy) forged from partly classical
ingredients and partly modern ones a new set of ideas. Ermolao Barbaro,
for example, a great scholar and also a great state servant, wrote in classical
Latin an account of the duties of the resident ambassadors of Venice, those
officials of a new kind who made it possible for states to survive in the
turmoil and continual rapid reversals of Italian politics. Here he articulated
an ideal of absolute subservience, not to a single ruler but to the state as a
whole, that had no counterpart in previous political discourse. Barbaro
argued that the ambassador must place himself absolutely at the disposal of
the home government, obeying its commands without hesitation or
scruple, as a deliberate and dutiful sacrifice of that independence of action
which a patrician normally cherished in other spheres (Barbaro 1969). This
call for absolute obedience to the political needs of the state, brief, cogent,
and simple, resounds with reality and modernity just as powerfully as
Bruni's admission of the role of money in Florentine affairs (King 1986;
Branca 1973).

   Specialists in discourse, the humanists did not articulate a new and

28

compelling full-scale analysis of the new and dangerous political world that they inhabited. They praised, they blamed, they concealed; the classical themes and ideas they revived more often proved a template to be imposed on obdurate facts than a lens through which to inspect them more closely. And even when they obtained, translated, and discussed such powerful ancient works of political philosophy as Plato's *Republic* or of political reflection a Thucydides' history, they used them more as grab-bags of anecdote and edifying platitude than as models for comparably ambitious intellectual projects. These they left to the later writers of the age of the New Monarchies and after. Yet epideictic, though usually stereotyped and sometimes cloying, is far from insignificant. The humanists' idealisations of institutions and individuals took on a powerful life of their own, inspiring later thinkers and deceiving later historians. For that alone they deserve close scrutiny.

2

Italian political thought, 1450–1530

NICOLAI RUBINSTEIN

The middle of the fifteenth century was a turning point in the relations between the Italian states, and the relative stability which Italy enjoyed until the Neapolitan expedition of Charles VIII in 1494 forms part of the background to the history of its political thought during that period. The peace of Lodi had put an end, in 1454, to a succession of wars which had begun in the 1420s. It had been followed by the conclusion of an Italian league, aimed at safeguarding the integrity of the Italian states as well as peace among them; in fact, wars were chiefly prevented or contained by triple and dual alliances between the five greater powers which were its members, Milan, Venice, Florence, the papacy, and Naples.

To the relative stability and equilibrium in inter-state relations, threatened primarily by the expansionist policies of Venice and the papacy, there corresponded a similar stability in the internal conditions of the Italian states, although it too could be temporarily threatened. Domestic crises occurred in Milan in 1476 with the assassination of Duke Galeazzo Maria Sforza; in Florence in 1478 with the Pazzi conspiracy, but these were of short duration; far more serious and lasting was the revolt of the Neapolitan barons against Ferrante of Aragon in 1485. The lesser princes, such as the Malatesta at Rimini and the Este at Ferrara, were more vulnerable; a judicious policy of placing themselves under the protection of one or more of the greater powers, as well as serving them as *condottieri*, could help them to achieve security and dynastic survival.

i   Monarchies and republics, 1450–1500

The Italian states of the fifteenth century could be divided into monarchies and republics; but within these categories, there was a great variety of constitutional structures. Of the former, only the kingdom of Naples conformed to the type of western European monarchies; the others, with the exception of the Papal States, had communal or feudal origins; and even the most powerful and the longest established among them, such as that of the Visconti at Milan and those of the Este at Ferrara and Modena, were not entirely independent of superior – imperial or papal – authority and of popular support, and could consequently not rely on the same measure of sovereignty as a 'natural lord' like the king of Naples. Of the republics, the two leading ones, Venice and Florence, differed substantially in their political institutions; in Venice, the aristocratic constitution, established at the turn of the thirteenth century and perfected in the course of the fourteenth, remained the solid foundation of government and administration; in Florence, the republican institutions, which went back to the end of the thirteenth and the early fourteenth centuries, were at crucial points gradually eroded by the Medici and adapted to secure an ascendancy which was consolidated in 1458 and greatly increased under Lorenzo de' Medici. Other republics experienced, in their turn, the rise of single families to supreme political power, or even to signorial position, as did Bologna under the Bentivoglio and Siena under the Petrucci while, like the despots of that region, Bologna and other communes of the Papal States were liable to have their independence substantially curtailed by the reassertion of papal authority and the consequent extension of the central administration.

The history of Italian political thought during this period reflects, in several respects, these developments and problems. Treatises on princely government composed by humanists continued the medieval tradition of Mirrors of Princes,[1] but there were significant differences between those addressed to lesser rulers whose security could be enhanced by good government, and eulogistic works addressed to the king of Naples which emphasised the majesty of a 'natural' monarch.

Bartolomeo Platina's *De principe*, written in 1470 for Federico Gonzaga, heir of the marquess of Mantua (Platina 1979), while broadly modelled on Giles of Rome's *De regimine principum*, is a typical product of humanist didactic literature; making ample use of the works of moral philosophers such as Cicero, he illustrates his teachings by a wealth of examples drawn from ancient history. Platina takes for granted the superiority of monarchy as the best form of government (pp. 53–6), as well as the absolute authority of the prince; but this authority, which in fact corresponded to that of Italian despots, was to be tempered by his duty, spelled out under the

---

1. See Gilbert 1939, pp. 46off (repr. 1977, pp. 98ff).

headings of the cardinal and other political virtues, to govern his subjects justly and liberally and see to it that his officials did so likewise. The *optimus princeps* is, briefly, a benevolent despot, and as such the opposite to a tyrant who, deprived of friendship and loyalty, is liable to be toppled from power (pp. 70–1). His is also a military leader, as the Gonzaga were; the third book of the treatise deals with warfare and military science.

Some of Platina's practical advice for the security of the ruler appears, undiluted by humanist rhetoric and learning, in Diomede Carafa's *I doveri del principe*, composed before 1476 for the duchess of Ferrara, Eleonora of Aragon (Carafa 1899). States are ruled by love or by fear, he says, and it is preferable for the ruler to be loved (p. 266), yet at the same time he is advised to keep armed forces, for then his subjects will 'see to it to be obedient and will not indulge in wicked thoughts' (p. 270). Legitimate rulers have so often lost their power that it is essential to guard oneself against such an eventuality by making military and financial provisions, but above all by having soldiers at one's disposal to deal with emergencies (p. 272). For all this, the lord should treat his subjects as if they were his children, dispense justice equitably through his officials, and whenever possible avoid wars, which may harm them as much as him (pp. 276ff, 289). Compared with this pragmatic and paternalistic view on how to preserve power in a north Italian principality, whose ruler had only recently acquired the ducal title, the Neapolitan humanists have a more exalted vision of monarchy.

Giovanni Pontano, in his *De principe* (*c.* 1468; Pontano 1952), states, after a passing reference to the importance for the prince of justice and religion, that among the traditional princely virtues he should above all observe *humanitas* and liberality; for inhumanity is the mother of hatred, and it should be the prince's aim to be loved by his subjects (pp. 1040, 1042). But what determines most the opinion they have of him is what some call his majesty, which is the special property of the prince, 'principum propria' (p. 1046). It has its origin in his nature, but must be cultivated by art and diligence; it differs from Cicero's *decorum*, which belongs to private persons, not to kings; and it is borne out by the prince's behaviour (p. 1060). Pontano ends his advice to the young Alfonso, duke of Calabria, to whom the work is dedicated, by urging him to sustain the majesty of the prince by correct deportment, gestures, and dress – 'a subject neglected by the ancient philosophers' with which he could fill many books.

It was to majesty that in 1492 Iuniano Maio devoted an entire book, which he dedicated to King Ferrante, the duke of Calabria's father. He begins his *De maiestate* (Maio 1956) by displaying his humanist learning in a long discourse, studded with quotations from classical authors, on the meaning of the term, follows this up by enumerating the princely virtues, and devotes, after describing the burdens of majesty, the penultimate chapter to the magnificence of the prince. His examples are drawn, in the customary humanist fashion, from antiquity, but are supplemented, in appendices to the various chapters on the prince's virtues, by others derived from the life of Ferrante, who thus appears as an exemplary prince.

These manuals for princes ignore, in contrast to Aquinas' *De regimine principum*, the existence of other forms of government: apart from a glancing observation in Platina's *De principe*,[2] the humanists keep strictly to their purpose of exhorting and celebrating monarchs. As rhetoricians schooled to defend 'the other side' (*alteram partem*), they were also perfectly capable of performing the same service for republics. Platina adapted, in 1474, his advice book for princes to fit the virtual ruler of the Florentine republic, and his image of Lorenzo de' Medici as *optimus civis* of the republic probably came closer to political realities and to Lorenzo's own views of his position than the eulogies of friends and clients (Platina 1944; see Rubinstein 1986, pp. 141ff). The Sienese Francesco Patrizi wrote two successive treatises praising first republics and then monarchies as the best constitutions; he admits in his *De regno et regis institutione* (Patrizi 1594b), which he dedicated to Alfonso, duke of Calabria, probably in the early eighties (Battaglia 1936, p. 102), that 'there will be those who will say that these things are self-contradictory' and that the same person cannot consistently argue both in favour of monarchies and republics. To this he replies somewhat feebly that 'men are free to praise alternatively whomever they wish' (I, 1), and launches into a celebration of monarchy. In his *De institutione reipublicae*[3] he had pointed out that while monarchy was theoretically the best form of government, it was liable to degenerate (I, 1). 'Born and educated in a free city', he considers 'the life of a well-ordered republic safer.' Even though a prince possessed all the virtues, in a republic, which was 'nearly immortal', they may be spread over many citizens. As for its constitution, he counts himself among those who preferred one that was 'mixed of all classes of men' (I, 4), in which not arbitrary power, but 'only law rules' (I, 5). Yet happy are those republics

2. Platina 1979, p. 56: 'Laudare optimatum rem publicam popularemve, quarum altera ad tyrannidem vel paucorum potentiam facile descendit, altera ad principem vergit, instituti nostri nequaquam est'.
3. Patrizi 1594a. See Battaglia 1936, p. 101: completed between 1465 and 1471.

which, 'as Plato says, are governed by the wise and learned' (I, 8). In the *De regno*, on the other hand, he concedes that a well-governed republic 'may be praised' (I, 3), but it is prone to turn into a tyranny or mob rule. He quotes a large number of classical authors to support his arguments in favour of monarchy; it is of divine origin, and the king resembles God on earth (I, proem, IX, 2). In describing the ideal prince, Patrizi says, he is going to imagine one 'who may never have existed', thus following the example of Plato who 'conceived a new, imaginary, perfect city' (II, 4). He provides an extensive and detailed advice book for princes, with a long catalogue of their virtues. Foremost among these is justice (II, 1); magnificence 'is fitting only for kings and princes', and differs from liberality, the former concerning 'the great and the public', the latter 'the small and the private' (VII, 11). Under a just king, there reigns what Plato calls 'civil or social friendship' among the citizens, which 'is more appropriate to the king than any other' (VIII, 10) – a form of consensus which should form the foundation of a well-ordered state (Battaglia 1936, p. 124). In many ways, Patrizi follows the tradition of the medieval *specula principis*; but he does so by amply drawing on classical authorities and exemplars, as he had done in his *De institutione reipublicae*, which may help to explain why these two rather unwieldy humanist works enjoyed an impressive degree of popularity during the sixteenth century (pp. 102ff).

While the humanist authors of advice books for princes were concerned with their moral virtues, Giovanni Simonetta's history of Francesco Sforza, the *Commentarii*, written in the seventies as a semi-official work which could serve the dukes of Milan as propaganda, offers a different and more realistic picture of a new prince (Simonetta 1932–59; see Ianziti 1988, pp. 151ff). Simonetta portrays the *condottiere* founder of the Sforza dynasty as a military leader endowed with qualities, among them foresight and speed of decision, that were conducive to the success of his actions, even though these could at times be considered to be immoral, the end, that is victory, thus justifying cruel means such as the sacking of towns (Ianziti 1988, pp. 184ff). Similar lessons could be drawn from Flavio Biondo's innovatory history of contemporary Italy, which as early as 1437 had elicited the comment that it provided precepts for political action at home and abroad.[4] Historiography could serve as a corrective to eulogistic works on princely conduct in showing a new sense of the power politics of fifteenth-century Italy, in which both princes and republics were involved.

4. Ianziti 1988, pp. 51–3, on Lapo da Castiglionchio's letter to Biondo praising his third *Decade*.

Only one humanist attempted a systematic comparison between the monarchical and the republican forms of government, and it may not be a coincidence that Aurelio Brandolini, although once a resident of Naples, was a native of Florence, where the enduring tension between republican and Medicean views on government had kept alive the issue, so important in the political literature of the early Quattrocento, of the relative value of republic and monarchy. Brandolini, who began his dialogue *De comparatione rei publicae et regni* at Buda, originally planned to dedicate it to King Matthias Corvinus of Hungary, who figures in it as the principal interlocutor; after the king's death in 1490 he completed it, with a dedication to Lorenzo de' Medici, in Florence (Brandolini 1890, pp. 79–80, 81–4). In the dialogue, Domenico Giugni, a Florentine resident in Hungary, defends the republican form of government; Matthias defeats his arguments that it secures liberty, equality, and justice more effectively than a monarchy. While he does so in a general fashion, the republic which Giugni defends is Florence. As a result, the debate turns on the superiority of that city's republican institutions, which Giugni describes in considerable detail and which are subjected to a scathing critique by the king. His task is facilitated by the fact that Giugni is concerned less with the actual working of those institutions than with their original purpose, and thus conforms to the idealisation of the Florentine republic by civic humanists such as Bruni. He does not take into account the changes brought about by the Medici and the ascendancy of Lorenzo de' Medici, which Matthias sees, precisely, as the saving grace of the Florentine republic. In the end, Brandolini may have agreed with this view, if his dedication of the dialogue to Lorenzo is an indication; Matthias' critique of Florentine republican institutions and his praise of monarchy should, he says, be acceptable to a man who was 'in ea re publica princeps' (p. 84). Brandolini tried to compare the Florentine republic with a feudal monarchy; comparisons between different types of monarchical and republican regimes, so obvious to modern historians, are notably absent from the political literature of the period. However, the admiration of the Venetian republic which we find among Florentine patricians during the fifteenth century implies a comparison between its aristocratic constitution and the government of Florence under the Medici (see Gilbert 1968).

Another comparison which continued to be discussed by the humanists, that between *condottieri* warfare and native militia, could have political implications. Platina advised the prince on practical grounds to choose his troops from his own territory (Platina 1979, p. 162). Patrizi, who considered *condottieri* unreliable, in his turn proposed, in the *De institutione reipublicae*, to raise a militia from the *contado* (Patrizi 1594a, p. 42; III, 5; IV, 4; see Bayley 1961, pp. 231–3). The admiration for the heroes of antiquity, perpetuated in innumerable examples by classical authors such as Valerius Maximus, and represented, in the fifteenth century, in public palaces in paintings of famous men, made the connection between civic patriotism and military valour a favourite humanist topos. In contrast to warfare, scant attention is paid in the political literature to the relations between states. Platina's sole reference to them in the *De principe* occurs in the chapter 'de fide'; like earlier authors of *specula principis*, he conceives the question in ethical terms; following Cicero, he demands that 'servanda [est] fides' (Platina 1979, pp. 116–19; cf. *De officiis*, III.29.104). For new and wide-ranging insights into the realities of foreign policy and diplomatic practice, we have to turn to despatches of ambassadors and letters of statesmen such as Lorenzo de' Medici, whose correspondence shows, among reflections on the relations between states in war and peace and on the techniques of power politics, the emergence of the concept of balance of power as a prerequisite of Florentine independence and influence and as a foundation of the peace of Italy.

Among the Italian republics, the political thought of Venice in the fifteenth century was, like its constitution, marked by stability and continuity. There is no evidence of debates on political principles, of discussions of problems affecting the government, as in Florence. The Venetian republic is seen as a uniquely successful realisation of the notion of the mixed constitution. Since the turn of the century, humanists had supplemented the Venetian tradition, according to which during the barbarian invasions the city was founded in the lagoon by emigrants from the mainland as the home of liberty and justice;[5] her constitution, they argued, conformed to classical models. The translation, at the middle of the century, of Plato's *Laws* was taken by its translator to provide triumphant support for this thesis: George of Trebizond asserts, in his preface to Francesco Barbaro and the Venetian republic, that its founders followed Plato's teaching by creating a constitution that was a mixture of monarchy, aristocracy, and democracy (George of Trebizond 1970, pp. 498–501, 1984, pp. 198–203). He thus reinforced the argument, stated as early as *c.* 1300 by Henry of Rimini, that Venice possessed a mixed constitution (Robey and Law 1975, p. 54), an argument which remained a fundamental theme of

5. On the 'myth of Venice' see Gaeta 1961; Fasoli 1958; Robey and Law 1975; King 1986, p. 174 n. 231 (bibliography).

Venetian political thought[6] and which was authoritatively reaffirmed in the 1520s by Gasparo Contarini in his widely read *De magistratibus et republica Venetorum* as the principal reason for the incomparable excellence of the Venetian constitution.[7]

The principal classical authority for Venetian political thought was, however, Aristotle, whose *Politics* could also be interpreted to favour aristocracy.[8] Lauro Quirini made a digest of that work, which he dedicated in about 1450 to the Doge Francesco Foscari under the title *De republica* (Quirini 1977b, pp. 123–5; on the date, p. 109). Quirini considers that political regime the best which preserves liberty through being governed, with the consent of the people, by 'nobiles et generosi' (p. 142). Quirini's hierarchical vision of Venetian society under the government of 'the few but elected'[9] also underlies his *De nobilitate*, in which he affirms that no republic remained so long 'in unanimous concord' as Venice (Quirini 1977a, p. 89). Unanimity was a central political theme of Venetian humanism, and the nobility was uniquely fitted to secure it (King 1986, pp. 92, 172ff).

There could be differences of opinion on the precise structure of that nobility. In his *De bene instituta re publica*. Domenico Morosini, at the beginning of the sixteenth century, follows Aristotle more faithfully than Quirini had done. He advocates a society ruled, to the exclusion of the excessively powerful and of the plebs, by 'middling' citizens whom he identifies with the true Venetian nobility; a view which may have been prompted by a reaction against those nobles who had led the republic into a dangerous expansionist policy.[10] Venetian expansionism on the mainland had been a major issue in determining Italian attitudes to Venice throughout the fifteenth century. Among Florentine patricians, criticism of that policy went uneasily hand in hand with admiration for Venice's aristocratic constitution. During the second half of the century, the Turkish advance, from which Venice suffered more than any other Italian state with

---

6. Cf. the *De Republica Veneta* by Pier Paolo Vergerio, of about 1400, ed. Robey and Law 1975, pp. 38–9 (on the date, p. 29); see Gilbert 1968, pp. 468ff.
7. Contarini 1589, fos. 4r, 8v: 'Eam vero in hac repub. moderationem ac temperamentum adhibuere, eamqu. mistionem omnium statuum qui recti sunt, ut haec una Respub. et regium principatum et optimatium gubernationem et civile item regimen referat . . .'. On Contarini's constitutional theory see Gilbert 1969, pp.110ff (repr. 1977, pp.262ff).
8. As it was, for instance, by Vergerio; see above, n. 6. Aristotle considered aristocracy the best form of the mixed constitution: *Politics* IV, 1293b.
9. Quirini 1977b, p. 136: 'paucorum sed electorum', pp. 142–3.
10. Morosini 1969, p. 76. See Cozzi 1970, pp. 418ff, 429; King 1986, pp. 140–50. The work was written between 1497 and Morosini's death in 1509.

the exception of Genoa, added further recriminations for her lukewarmness in supporting crusades, and Paolo Morosini defended, in a letter to the Milanese chancellor Cicco Simonetta, the republic on both counts as being 'avid for peace and content with her own boundaries' (King 1986, p. 139).

That the evolution of political thought was far richer and more varied in Florence than in Venice was due, in large part, to the political vicissitudes of the Florentine republic from the end of the fourteenth century onwards. The shift, after 1434, from the aristocratic regime of the early fifteenth century to Medicean ascendancy gave rise to new political ideas; but owing to its gradual development and oblique nature, and to the survival of republican values and institutions (Rubinstein 1966, pp. 7ff), it did not bring about a clear break with the ideology of civic humanism. Matteo Palmieri's dialogue *Vita civile*, which was written about five years later,[11] at a time when Cosimo de' Medici and his supporters were well on the way to establishing their control of government and legislation by manipulating elections to the Signoria and having legislation passed by specially constituted councils, contains no reference whatsoever to these developments. We are still in the civic world of the early fifteenth century, which had been celebrated by Bruni. The central figure of the dialogue is a patrician of the old elite, Agnolo Pandolfini, and the work is designed 'to show the proven life of the virtuous citizens' of Florence rather than of imaginary citizens, such as those described by Plato (Palmieri 1982, p. 7). Modelling his moral teachings largely on Cicero's *De officiis*, his educational ones on Quintilian, Palmieri follows Bruni in using classical sources, including Aristotle's *Politics*, to formulate a republican theory that conformed to the political conditions and problems of his city. The central principles of that theory are, as for Bruni, the supremacy of the common good, justice, equality, civic unity, and liberty. Office-holding, which is meant to serve the common good, is seen as representing 'the universal persona of the entire city',[12] justice involves equitable distribution of offices and taxes without regard to ancestry; his ideal is a meritocracy rather than an aristocracy, although he shares the views of the patricians who wanted the plebs to be excluded from government (pp. 136, 137–8, 187, 191). He insists, as Florentines had done since the days of Dante, on the destructive consequences of civil discord – a disease of the body politic which, as history shows, could be mortal (p. 133). Florence had only recently been

11. On the date (between 1437 and 1440) see Belloni 1978.
12. Palmieri 1982, pp. 131–2: 'rapresentare l'universale persona di tutta la città, et essere facta animata republica'.

torn by party struggles, which in the end had brought Cosimo and his faction to power, and Palmieri's warning to those 'who own sweet liberty' that there is no greater cause of 'civil dissensions and seditions' than unjust government,[13] may well have been addressed to the new ruling group.

Palmieri could still believe that the Medici regime, in its formative period, would not seriously alter the political traditions of the Florentine republic. The restoration and extension, in 1458, after a brief period of abolition, of the Medicean controls taught Florentine republicans a different lesson; but the vigour and militancy with which republican values were reasserted during a spell of anti-Medicean reaction in 1465/6 bear witness to their survival in Medicean Florence.[14] So, with a sense of fatalistic resignation, does Alamanno Rinuccini's dialogue *De libertate*, which he wrote, during the war of the Pazzi conspiracy, in 1479 (Rinuccini 1957). Rinuccini condemns Lorenzo de' Medici (who had succeeded Cosimo's son Piero in 1469), as a tyrant, under whom the ancient laws of the city were being violated and equality, 'the chief foundation of the citizen's liberty', and freedom of speech and elections by lot abolished, while only few citizens were allowed to participate in government (pp. 283ff). Since resistance was impossible, it was preferable, rather than serve under such a regime, to retire into the private sphere of contemplative life (p. 302). That Rinuccini joined, in the following year, the special council set up to consolidate the Medici regime, reflected an ambivalence characteristic of patrician attitudes to it (Rubinstein 1966, p. 312). Rinuccini's political ideals were still those of the civic humanists of the early Quattrocento, his principal classical sources, like Bruni's, Aristotle and Cicero; and it was the *Politics* which provided him with the view, fundamental for his political theory, that a free republic resembled 'one body with many heads, hands, and feet' (Rinuccini 1957, p. 284; cf. *Politics*, III, 1281b).

Rinuccini, like Palmieri before him, also quotes Plato; but Plato had by then become, in Florence, the favourite classical source for those who, by way of eulogy or prescriptive teaching, pointed to the union in the same person of political power and philosophy as the key to Lorenzo's position in Florence (Brown 1986, pp. 388ff). At the same time, the image of his grandfather was transformed from that of the republican statesman, who by public decree had been posthumously named 'pater patriae', to that of

13. Palmieri 1982, pp. 135–6: 'Piglino exemplo coloro che posseggono la dolce libertà'.
14. Pampaloni 1961, 1962; see also Rubinstein 1966, pp. 136ff, 1968, pp. 456–60; Phillips 1987, pp. 169ff.

the philosopher-ruler (Brown 1961). In the version of the *De principe* which he dedicated to Lorenzo under the title *De optimo cive*, Platina held him up as an example of 'the father and leader' of the republic. In this dialogue, Cosimo himself quotes Plato's 'divine words' that 'republics will only then be happy when the learned and the wise begin to rule them, or those who rule them place all their endeavour in learning and wisdom' (Platina 1944, pp. 185, 212). Cristoforo Landino, in his *Disputationes Camaldulenses*, written about the same time, quotes the same passage, while Marsilio Ficino, in his dedication to Lorenzo of the *Theologia Platonica*, asks him to combine philosophy with the 'supreme authority in public affairs'.[15] But Ficino did not always give that authority his wholehearted support (Fubini 1984, pp. 24ff), and Platina subjected it to the observance of republican liberty, of which the 'optimus civis' should be the guardian (Platina 1944, pp. 192–3). However much eulogists may have praised Lorenzo in Platonic terms, Platina came closer to the real nature of a regime in which the position of its leader as the virtual head of the state had gradually evolved within the framework of the republican constitution.

The enemies of Lorenzo described him as a tyrant, a description which was as far removed from reality as that of a philosopher-ruler; and the fall of the Medici in 1494, two and half years after his death, was hailed as a liberation from tyranny. That such 'tyranny' was contrary to the nature and customs of the Florentine people was one of the chief arguments of Girolamo Savonarola's *Trattato circa el reggimento e governo della città di Firenze* (Savonarola 1965, II, 3, pp. 469–71). Republican restoration had been followed, under his inspiration and guidance, by a fundamental reform of the Florentine constitution with the creation of a great council of over 3,000 citizens which, like that of Venice which served him as a model, was both the sole legislative and the electoral body of the republic's magistracies. Savonarola's treatise, which he wrote at the beginning of 1498 at the request of the Signoria, was designed to show that the great council, the guardian of the city's liberty and representative of its people, was divinely established, 'sent by God', and that a republican constitution was in accordance with its nature (III, 2). To prove this, he drew on the scholastic Aristotelianism of St Thomas Aquinas' and Tolomeo of Lucca's *De regimine principum* (Weinstein 1970, pp. 290ff). In about 1430, Leonardo Bruni had used the *Politics* to describe the Florentine constitution as mixed of aristocracy and democracy (Rubinstein 1968, pp. 447–8); Savonarola, in

15. Landino 1980, p. 11; see Rubinstein 1986, pp. 143–4. Ficino 1576, p. 78; see Brown 1986, p. 395.

the wake of sixty years of Medicean ascendancy and, in the end, virtual rule, used Aristotle's argument that different constitutions were suitable to different peoples (*Politics*, III, 1288a), to prove that, while monarchy was theoretically the best form of government, republican government was natural to the Florentines, 'the most intelligent (*ingegnosissimo*) of all the peoples of Italy', 'whose nature it is not to support the rule even of a good and perfect prince' (I, 3). The same Aristotelian argument had been related by Toloméo to republican Italy in general (Aquinas 1948, IV.8, p. 76): Savonarola applied it, two centuries later, in an Italy in which only few of the old republics had survived the spread of despotism, to Florence in particular. At the same time, he blends the teachings of the *De regimine principum*, which went in its entirety under the name of Aquinas, with traditional Florentine notions of republican liberty (Weinstein 1970, pp. 305ff) – just as, in his chapters on tyranny, he combines Aquinas' description of the tyrant's devices with allusions to the tyrannical rule of the Medici (II, 2, 3). That rule had been discussed, in very different terms and with a different purpose, by the humanist Platina in his *De optimo cive*; a quarter of a century later, the Dominican friar from Ferrara provided the new Florentine republic with an authoritative declaration of its guiding principles. But Savonarola's theologically inspired political theory was ill-adapted to the problems which that republic had to face during the years following on its establishment, at a time when the balance of power in the peninsula had been upset as a result of the French invasion of 1494. To some of these problems, Machiavelli reacted in his first political writings in a spirit that had little in common with Savonarola's religious and moral stance; but they both shared a whole-hearted commitment to the republican cause.

ii   A new epoch: Machiavelli

Although only briefly successful, Charles VIII's expedition to conquer Naples, the Anjou claims to the kingdom having recently devolved to the French crown, proved a turning point in the history of the Italian states. It not only put an end to the relative stability which had prevailed during the preceding forty years; large parts of the country soon passed under foreign domination: in the first years of the sixteenth century the duchy of Milan under the rule of France, the kingdom of Naples under that of Spain; and in 1509, the league of Cambrai came close to destroying the *terraferma* empire of Venice. The destabilisation of inter-state relations offered Cesare Borgia the opportunity of creating a new territorial state in central Italy at the expense of local rulers. At the same time, conquests were liable to be short-lived: Cesare Borgia's dominion collapsed after the death in 1503 of his father, Pope Alexander VI; the French lost Milan in 1512, by which year the Venetians had recovered many of their mainland territories. In Florence, Piero de' Medici's opposition to the French expedition against the king of Naples, an ally of Florence, had led to his expulsion in November 1494 and to the establishment of a new republican regime. Eighteen years later, the withdrawal of the French, Florence's only ally, from northern Italy after the battle of Ravenna resulted in the fall of that regime and the return of the Medici; and the restored Medici supremacy was greatly enhanced, in 1513, by the election of Lorenzo's son Giovanni to the papal throne as Leo X.

These events form the background to a new epoch in the history of Italian political thought, whose dominant figure was Niccolò Machiavelli. His two great political works, *Il Principe* and the *Discorsi sopra la prima deca di Tito Livio* grew out of his humanist knowledge of ancient history, blended with his experiences of Florentine and Italian politics during a period when the Florentines were desperately trying to safeguard their dominions and, above all, to recover Pisa. Elected in 1498, after the execution of Savonarola, as second chancellor of Florence and then as secretary of the Ten, the magistracy responsible for the conduct of foreign and military affairs, he was employed in many diplomatic missions in Italy as well as in missions to the French king and the king of the Romans. Machiavelli thus acquired an extensive and diverse knowledge of diplomacy and war and of the problems of territorial administration in the rapidly changing world of Italian politics at the beginning of the sixteenth century. A passionate critic of mercenary warfare, he strenuously agitated for the creation, and was intimately involved with the organisation, of a Florentine militia recruited from the *contado* (Bayley 1961, pp. 247ff; Ridolfi 1972, pp. 126ff, 137ff, 154ff). His earliest political writings mirror these concerns. Their predominant themes relate to the security and to the recovery of the city's territories at a time when, in the midst of a war against Pisa which had rebelled against her rule in 1494, Florence was being confronted with other such rebellions in the wake of the advance of Cesare Borgia. They also raise questions and present answers which foreshadow his major works (Marchand 1975, pp. 371ff). Foremost among these is the question of the role of force in politics: it is central for his advice, written in the year after the loss and recovery of Arezzo, on how to deal with rebellious subjects of the Valdichiana, where he recommends the solution adopted by the Romans 'that rebellious populations must be either benefited or squashed (*o beneficare o spegnere*), and that any other method is highly dangerous':[16] the 'middle path' (*via di mezzo*) has to be avoided at all costs;[17] it was another matter of whether the use of force or of love, *o la forza o l'amore*, were preferable.[18] The question of the proper use of force also underlies his writings on the Florentine militia, and involves that of civic education: introduced in the *contado* only, the militia would, he was hoping, be extended to the city itself and thus help to generate civic virtue.[19] These are themes which reappear, in a much more systematic and penetrating form, in *Il Principe* and in the *Discorsi*, together with others which are first formulated or adumbrated in his earliest writings – such as the role of fortune in man's actions, the lessons which history can offer them ('I have heard it said that history is the teacher of our actions').[20] Closely related to this question is his advice, although 'it is not customary to refer' to them,[21] 'to imitate those who had been the rulers of the world'.[22] There are also passages which almost literally anticipate *The Prince*, as when he states, in 1506, that in certain circumstances 'to a new ruler, cruelty, perfidy, and irreligion are useful in order to achieve reputation' (Machiavelli 1961a, p. 231: 'Ghiribizzi')'.

It was in keeping with the nature of Machiavelli's employment by the republic that, in contrast to his concern with territorial and military policies, the discussion of domestic affairs is all but missing from his earliest writings; only after the fall of the republic in 1512 does the political and social structure of the state become a dominant theme of his political thought. In December 1513 Machiavelli, who had lost his post in the chancery in the preceding year in the wake of the restoration of the Medici (he had even been imprisoned under suspicion of having participated in a conspiracy against them), completed a short work which he first called *De principatibus* and which he sent to his friend Francesco Vettori in Rome, in the hope of finding employment with the Medici.[23] In one of its opening sentences, he states that, having written on republics, he will now deal with

16. *Del modo di trattare i popoli di Valdichiana ribellati*, in Machiavelli 1961b, pp. 73–4. On the date (1503) see Ridolfi 1972, p. 450; Marchand 1975, pp. 102–4.
17. Machiavelli 1961b, p. 72; see Whitfield 1969, pp. 37ff.
18. *Discorso fatto al magistrato dei dieci sopra le cose di Pisa*, in Machiavelli 1961b, p. 13.
19. *Discorso dell' ordinare lo stato di Firenze alle armi*, in Machiavelli 1961b, p. 100.
20. *Del modo di trattare*, in Machiavelli 1961b, p. 73.
21. Letter to Giovan Battista Soderini ('Ghiribizzi'), in Machiavelli 1961a, pp. 229–30. On the date (1506) of this letter, which had previously been dated 1512, see Ridolfi and Ghiglieri 1970; Martelli 1969.
22. *Del modo di trattare*, in Machiavelli 1961b, p. 73.
23. Letter to Vettori of 10 December 1513, in Machiavelli 1961a, pp. 301–6.

principalities (II). It seems probable that by that time he had written part of what was to become the first book, which deals primarily with republican institutions, of the *Discorsi sopra la prima deca di Tito Livio*, and that he interrupted his work on republics to write *Il Principe*.[24]

The central figure of *Il Principe* is the new prince: Machiavelli asks by what means he can establish and maintain his power, and what role *virtù* and fortune play in this process. Machiavelli starts from the premise that to want to acquire power is entirely natural to man (III), and the lesson he is teaching the new prince is how to do so first at home and then abroad. In this context, his belief in the superiority of native over mercenary armies acquires fresh importance; arguments in favour of the former are now marshalled for the prince instead of the republic (XII–XIV). Similarly, the chapter on 'mixed principalities' (III), which discusses the problems of holding newly acquired territories, recalls his experiences with the problems Florence had to face in her dominions. Loosely following the model of Mirrors of Princes (Gilbert 1938, pp. 9, 231ff), he firmly rejects the method of the many authors – one of them was Patrizi – 'who have imagined republics and principalities which have never been seen or are known to exist'. His purpose was to write something useful to those who understand, and so he preferred to examine matters as they are in reality, the 'verità effettuale della cosa', rather than in imagination (XV). Accordingly, the famous chapters (XV–XVII) on the qualities required for a ruler who wants to preserve his power invert the moral teachings of the medieval and humanist advice books for rulers by proposing an alternative code of political conduct. This prescribes, wherever necessary, the use of cruelty and deceit as inevitable means, owing to the innate wickedness of men, to achieve the desired end. 'It is necessary for a prince who wants to maintain himself to learn how not to be good, and to use or not to use this knowledge according to necessity'; for 'one who wants to make a profession of goodness in all things will be ruined among so many who are not good' (XV). While avoiding hatred and contempt (XVII, XIX), he 'must not mind the infamous reputation of cruelty, to keep his subjects united and loyal' (XVII), as long as his cruelties are committed 'all at once for the

---

24. Unless, as has been argued by Baron, according to whom no part of the *Discorsi* was written in 1513, the sentence in *Il Principe*, II, is a later interpolation (see below). The chronology of the composition of the *Discorsi*, and in particular the question whether part of Book I was composed or drafted before *Il Principe*, is controversial: see Gilbert 1953; Hexter 1956; Sasso 1957, 1958; Bertelli, in Machiavelli 1960, pp. 109ff; Baron 1961; Bausi 1985. On the composition of *Il Principe*, see Chabod 1927. All references to the two works are to the edition in Machiavelli 1960.

necessity of security, and afterwards not persisted in' (VIII). He 'ought not to keep faith, when by doing so he acts against his own interest' (XVIII). Briefly, 'a prince, and particularly a new prince, cannot observe all those things on whose grounds men are considered good', and 'must often, in order to maintain his power, act against faith, against charity, against humanity, against religion', while at the same time feigning to have all these qualities. 'Let the prince aim at conquering and maintaining power (*lo stato*); the means will always be judged honourable and praised by everyone, for the crowd (*il vulgo*) is always taken in by appearances' (XVIII). At the same time, these teachings are qualified by the role fortune plays in the prince's actions, and the interaction of fortune and *virtù*, an ambivalent term which, derived from the Latin *virtus*, may broadly be defined as that quality of energy, vitality, and courage which enables man to achieve greatness and power in the face of the impersonal force of fortune (see Price 1973; Diesner 1985). The interaction of fortune and *virtù*, which had preoccupied him since the years he spent in the Florentine chancery, is one of the key questions of *The Prince*, and central to his account of the rise and fall of Cesare Borgia, whom he had set up as a model for the new prince (VII). His answer is not free of ambiguities: he adopts classical and humanist notions in stressing the capacity of *virtù* to curb or defeat fortune, but concedes, in chapter XXV, that fortune controls one half of our actions. What ultimately matters is whether men's nature is in agreement with fortune or not; yet even so he insists, in the concluding sentences of that chapter, that 'it is better to be impetuous than cautious', for fortune, 'as a woman, is a friend of the young, for they are less cautious, fiercer, and command her with greater audacity'. It is a theme which Machiavelli takes up in the *Discorsi* in the context of reflections on the role of the individual in the process of historical change (II, 29).

Il Principe ends with a passionate appeal to the Medici to take the lead in liberating Italy from foreign domination (XXVI). A Medici was pope, and there were unequalled opportunities 'for a new prince' to take up arms against the 'barbarians'. There were, in fact, plans, in 1513, to create a territorial state for Leo X's brother Giuliano, to whom, in December of that year, Machiavelli intended to dedicate the *De principatibus*, and it has been argued that he had these plans in mind when composing it.[25] He dedicated the work, in 1515 or 1516 (Ridolfi 1972, pp. 257, 525–7), to Leo's nephew Lorenzo, who then acted as the pope's lieutenant in Florence,

25. Machiavelli 1961a, p. 267; Clough 1967, pp. 61ff. But see Sasso 1967, pp. 84ff.

and there were those in the city who believed Machiavelli was teaching Lorenzo how to become her absolute ruler: 'to the rich it seemed that his *Prince* had been a lesson to teach the Duke to deprive them of all their properties, to the poor, of all their liberty' (Busini 1860, p. 84: letter of 23 January 1549). But if *Il Principe* contained a specific message to the Florentines, it has rather to be sought in chapter IX on the 'civil principality' ('principato civile'), where Machiavelli advises the 'private citizen' who 'with the support of the other citizens becomes prince of his fatherland', his *patria*, to found his power on the people rather than on the nobility, the *grandi*, because such a power base would give him greater security (cf. XX; see Sasso 1967, pp. 96ff, 1980, pp. 346ff). To gain popular favour, he could use a variety of methods, *molti modi*, which Machiavelli refrains, no doubt prudently, from spelling out; but the traditional use, derived from Aristotle, of the term *politicus* or *civile* to describe constitutional government based on popular consent can hardly have been absent from Machiavelli's mind when he was writing that chapter (see Rubinstein 1987, pp. 44ff). 'These principalities decline', he says at its end, 'when they change from the *ordine civile* to the absolute one' (cf. *Discorsi* I, 25, 26); and in the *Discorsi* he writes (I, 16; cf. I, 58, III, 1) that the king of France, whose rule conformed to the requirements of the *vivere politico* or *civile*, had 'pledged themselves to obey an infinite number of laws, which encompass the security of all their peoples' (see below, p. 54).

The *Discorsi* are also designed to demonstrate that, although the government of monarchies as well as of republics can conform to the *vivere civile*, it is in the republics that it finds its fullest expression. Republicans took it for granted that the *vita civile* was characteristic of republics; Savonarola had described it as natural to the Florentines (see above, pp. 40–1); Machiavelli saw it realised to perfection in ancient Rome. In order to discover the reasons for Rome's success in creating 'a perfect republic' (I, 2), he takes as his text the first ten books, or decade, of Livy's *History of Rome*, which cover the history of the city from the origins to 293 BC, but he also draws on later books of that work. In the opening sentence of the proem of the first book of the *Discorsi*, he proudly affirms that he has chosen to 'enter a new path . . . not yet trodden by anyone'. Considering, he says, that antiquity is so greatly revered that, to cite only one of innumerable examples, sculptors are made to imitate fragments of ancient statues acquired at great cost, it is a matter of surprise and sadness that the examples of virtuous actions provided by ancient history are 'admired rather than imitated'. 'Infinite numbers of those who read it enjoy hearing of the

46

various incidents contained in it, without any thought of imitating it, since they believe this to be not only difficult but impossible'. To remedy this 'error', he proposes to write a commentary on Livy's *History* (in fact, he says, on all its extant books), so as to learn from that work the kind of lessons 'which one should seek to acquire through the knowledge of history'. The premise for this enterprise is the fundamental identity of human nature from antiquity to the present time, 'the world' having 'always been the same' ('sempre essere stato ad uno medesimo modo'), only what is good or bad in it shifting from region to region (II, proem).

By taking as the text for his political theory an historical rather than, like his scholastic and humanist predecessors, a philosophical work, Livy' *Ab urbe condita* rather than Aristotle's *Politics*, Machiavelli endowed his enquiry from the start with an historical dimension. His generalisations and his rules for political action (see Machiavelli 1950, I, pp. 93ff; Butterfield 1940, pp. 37ff, 71ff) are, as a result, derived from his study of Roman history as well as from his own experience. At the same time, by writing the *Discorsi* in the form of a commentary, he renders a systematic analysis of that theory often singularly difficult, at times artificially contrived. Yet, despite occasional inconsistencies and even contradictions, a coherent scheme of political ideas does emerge from a reading of the *Discorsi*; and this is helped by the fact that the first eighteen chapters disregard the chronological sequence of Livy's *History* and discuss, in a fairly systematic fashion, fundamental concepts and problems which are subsequently presupposed and partly treated at greater length.[26]

Machiavelli's historical and empirical method of political enquiry underlines, and largely explains, his apparent lack of interest in some of the basic questions of classical and scholastic political philosophy – such as the role of justice in the state, the nature of law, the limits of political obligation, and the relationship between the temporal and the spiritual power (Plamenatz 1963, I, p. 16). In the proem of the *Discorsi*, he enumerates, in his turn, the questions to which a correct reading of ancient history can provide answers: they concern the institutions (*ordini*) of republics and of kingdoms, the preservation of political regimes, military organisation and judicial administration, and territorial aggrandisement. In the *Discorsi*, these questions are encompassed in the basic theme presented to Machiavelli by Livy's *History*: why and in what ways Rome became a

---

26. Gilbert 1953, p. 150 (repr. 1977, p. 127) suggests that these chapters constituted the draft of a separate treatise on republics on which Machiavelli was working in 1513 and which he later used in the final version of the *Discorsi*.

'perfect republic'. The point of departure for Machiavelli's attempt to answer this question is Polybius' cyclic theory of constitutional change (I, 2), although he does not mention him by name. Polybius saw the mixture of constitutional forms as the only way by which the inexorable process of corruption, to which all simple constitutions are subject, and hence the cycle through which they pass, could be for a time arrested; the Roman republic owed its duration to its mixed constitution. By taking the sixth book of Polybius' *Histories* as his guide for his interpretation of the history of Rome, Machiavelli also follows Polybius' view that even Rome, despite the exemplary character of her constitution, was not exempt from the process of corruption.[27] In sharp contrast to the condemnation, traditional in Italian political thought since the thirteenth century, of civic division as destructive of republican regimes, including that of ancient Rome, he considers class conflicts the chief cause of the evolution of her constitution, and thus of her stability and greatness. Two legislators, Romulus and Numa, had laid the foundations of that constitution, just as Lycurgus had laid those of Sparta; but the laws and institutions they had established had been designed for a monarchy. Yet, though defective, they could, after the expulsion of Tarquinius, serve as the foundations for a *vivere civile e libero* (I, 2), that is, a republic. The role of the lawgiver is central to Machiavelli's political thought; in Rome, however, he provides, in contrast to Sparta, only the foundations on which later generations were to build, in the course of struggles between social classes, 'a perfect republic' (I, 2).[28]

That all states are divided into two classes, the nobles and the people, the *grandi* and the *popolo*, whose 'humours', or desires, conflict with one another (I, 4), is one of the major premises of Machiavelli's political theory.[29] The *umori* form part of Machiavelli's notion of the state as a body politic in which, as in the human organism, contrasting humours can be contained or reconciled. In *Il Principe*, the new ruler is advised to make use of this division in his own interest by choosing the people as his chief supporter: 'who becomes a prince through the favour of the people, should preserve its friendship'; who does so 'against the people through the favour of the nobles, should above everything else seek to acquire that of the people' (IX). According to the *Discorsi*, the mixed constitution created in Rome a balance between these contrasting 'humours' by dividing power

27. See Sasso 1967, pp. 161–280 (revised Sasso 1987–8, I, pp. 3–118); Walbank 1972, pp. 131ff. On the eventual decline of the mixed constitution, Walbank 1972, pp. 145–6.
28. The basic concept is again Polybian: see *The Histories*, VI.10.12–14; the Romans achieved the same result as Lycurgus not 'by any process of reasoning, but by the discipline of many struggles and troubles' (trans. W.R. Paton, Loeb edn, III, p. 293).
29. '. . . e' sono in ogni republica due umori diversi, quello del popolo e quello de' grandi'.

between those two classes. Machiavelli insists that, contrary to received opinion, in Rome class conflicts had a constructive effect by creating a constitution which made possible centuries of domestic stability (I, 4). He also maintains that, through the active share in political life assigned by it to the people, that constitution provided the foundation of Rome's military power and hence of its empire (I, 5); while the Venetian constitution, mixed in its turn, had, by making the nobility the ruling class of the state at the expense of the people, deprived the republic of the strength needed to preserve its conquests (I, 6). It was only when in Rome selfish economic interests came to prevail, in the class conflicts, over political ambitions (see Price 1982), that these conflicts took, at the end of the second century BC, a disastrous turn, leading first to the victory of the nobility over the people and finally to the overthrow of the republic itself by Caesar. The event which set this process in motion was the Gracchi's attempt to enforce the agrarian laws at the expense of the patricians, because it resulted in such 'hatred between the plebs and the senate, that it led to armed struggle and to bloodshed' (I, 37; see Cadoni 1978a), and thus to the breakdown of the political balance of the *vivere civile* which the same class conflicts had helped to bring about at the time of the early republic through perfecting its *ordini*.

Machiavelli distinguishes between *ordini* and *leggi* (see Whitfield 1955; repr. 1969); in Rome, the former were the political institutions created by the founders of the monarchy and then of the republic, the latter were laws that were introduced subsequently; they could supplement or enforce, but only rarely change, the *ordini*. He explains this distinction in *Discorsi*, I, 18: the constitutional arrangement of the Roman republic, with the division of power between consuls, senate, and tribunes, and with their methods of elections to office and of legislation 'changed little or not at all'; what changed were the laws that were designed to restrain, among other corrupt practices, the anti-social ambitions of the citizens. In view of the fact that Machiavelli often uses *ordini* and *leggi* as interchangeable terms, it is important to bear this distinction in mind. Legislators have to assume, he says at the beginning of the *Discorsi* (I, 3) 'that all men are evil' and that they 'never do good unless induced by necessity'. His concept of law, like that of Marsilius of Padua, is unreservedly positivist: the validity of human law depends in no way upon its conformity to a higher law. This son of a lawyer omits entirely, from his discussion of law, the term 'law of nature', crucial for medieval juristic theory;[30] perhaps it is not without an ironic

---

30. Canning 1988, pp. 454ff. Geerken 1987 argues that Machiavelli's use of the term *ordini* relates to Cicero's concept of natural law (pp. 40–1). For the generally accepted view on this question see *ibid.*, pp. 37–8.

twist that in Bartolomeo Scala's dialogue *De legibus et iudiciis*, Bernardo Machiavelli figures as representing, in Platonic terms, this tradition (Brown 1979, pp. 292–4). Good laws produce *buona educazione*, and 'good education' generates, in its turn, 'good examples' (I, 4), that is, of civic virtue. For Machiavelli, good laws are not concerned with individual rights, but with civic duties, with checking ambition and restraining or reconciling conflicting bids for power. They benefit the citizens insofar as they secure domestic peace, concern for the common interest, and security of life and property, with which the vast majority of citizens is anyway satisfied: only 'a small part of thcm want to be free in order to command'; in no republic does the ruling group exceed forty or fifty members (I, 16). Good laws also serve the citizens by providing the foundations of empire. Religion and military service make it possible for the laws to fulfil their creative functions, the former by instilling unquestioned loyalty to the state, the latter by complementing civic virtue with military prowess. Numa was the second founder of Rome, for the religious institutions which he introduced were 'among the prime reasons for the happiness of that city'; they 'caused good *ordini*, and good *ordini* produce good fortune', which in its turn was the cause of Rome's successful military exploits (I, 11). 'Where military service (*milizia*) is good, the *ordine* must needs be good', and it is rare that this is not accompanied by good fortune (I, 4). Indeed, Machiavelli goes so far as to maintain that 'the foundation of all states is the good *milizia*'; and where it does not exist, 'there cannot be either good laws or anything good' (III, 31). This reformulates his statement in *Il Principe* (XII) that 'the principal foundations of all states . . . are good laws and good arms', and that 'there cannot be good laws where there are not good arms, and where there are good arms there must be good laws'.[31] The *milizia* is also essential for republics whose aim is territorial aggrandisement, and which should follow Rome's example in arming the people (I, 6). But good arms cannot be easily introduced, and when introduced preserved, without religion (I, 11).[32] While reinforcing the case for the essential role religion plays in the state by generating civic virtue, Machiavelli's argument has also a bearing on his critique of Christian religion as being less capable than the pagan religion of ancient Rome of producing fortitude and love of liberty among the citizens: 'the ancient religion . . . beatified only men who were replete with worldly glory . . . Our religion has glorified humble and

---

31. See *Arte della guerra*, proem, in Machiavelli 1961b, pp. 325–7.
32. ' . . . dove è religione facilmente si possono introdurre l' armi; e dove sono l'armi e non religione, con difficultà si può introdurre quella'.

contemplative men rather than men of action'; although he adds that this is caused by a false interpretation of our religion, which 'allows us to exalt and defend the fatherland' (II, 2).

While institutions and laws promote civic virtue, they require, for being observed, in their turn 'good customs' ('buoni costumi'): 'just as good customs need good laws for being maintained, so laws need good customs for being observed' (I, 18) – an apparently circular argument, which reflects a fundamental premise of Machiavelli's political thought: the dependence of institutions for their proper functioning on social conditions. These are, in their turn, subject to change. As a result, good laws and institutions that were introduced at a time when social conditions were healthy cease to be so, indeed may be harmful, when they have become corrupt (I, 17, 18). Machiavelli's theory of the role of institutions and laws in political life is sociological as well as historical.

Polybius' theory of cyclic change relates, in Machiavelli's formulation, to 'variations of government' ('variazioni de' governi'), which follow 'the cycle passing through which all commonwealths have been and are governed' (I, 2).[33] According to Polybius, all simple constitutions had a built-in tendency to change into corrupt forms; even the mixed constitution was destined to decay and fall. In the first chapters of the *Discorsi*, Machiavelli had analysed the origins and progress of the 'perfect' mixed constitution of Rome. Three subsequent chapters (I, 16–18) are concerned with the decline of that constitution, and with corruption in general. The result is a general theory of political degeneration which is firmly based on social foundations.

'Since all human affairs are in a state of movement (*in moto*), and since they cannot stand still, they must either rise or decline' (I, 6); and Machiavelli recapitulates, at the beginning of book III: 'it is abundantly true that the life of all things in this world has its end'. The goodness, *bontà*, which republics and monarchies had at the time of their creation, 'degenerates in the course of time' unless they are renewed (III, 1; see below p. 52). This degeneration affects not only *ordini* but society at large. *Ozio*, idleness, is singled out as one of its immediate causes, since it threatens civic virtue (I, 1); it is a hallmark of the feudal society which Machiavelli considers to have been, in Italy, a primary cause of corruption (I, 55; see Waley 1970, p. 95). Another such cause is inequality, in contrast to the basic equality among citizens which should reign in republics, and which has

---

33. On the extent of the influence on Machiavelli of Polybius' cyclic theory, see Sasso 1967, pp. 166ff, 232ff, 1987–8, I, pp. 7ff, 75ff.

made it possible for the German towns to maintain an uncorrupted *vivere politico* (I, 55); yet another, the seizure by the government of absolute power, 'for absolute power (*una autorità absoluta*) corrupts the material (*la materia*), in the shortest of time' (I, 35).

What did Machiavelli mean by *materia*? 'Other *ordini* and regimes (*modi di vivere*) are required according to whether their subject is bad or good, nor can the same form exist where the *materia* is entirely contrary' to it, he states in I, 18. In other words, the *ordini* are the form, the *materia* the society to which they are applied; and the society can be virtuous like that of republican Rome, whose history bears witness to the 'goodness of its *materia*' (I, 18, III, 8), or it can be corrupt. Where the *materia* is good, as in Rome, class war and civil unrest, *i tumulti ed altri scandoli*, do not damage it; where it is corrupt, 'the well-ordered laws are of no avail', unless applied with extreme force (I, 17). This process of social degeneration is inevitable, it can only be arrested or reversed by one man using such 'extreme force' in imposing laws capable of restoring society to its pristine health: 'and I do not know whether this has ever occurred and whether it is possible that it should occur' (I, 17). As far as republics are concerned, to renew one in this way 'presupposes a good man, and to become through violence the ruler of a republic an evil one', and consequently it happens extremely rarely that a good man seizes power by evil means, though the end is good, or that an evil man, once he has become a prince, should use the authority he has thus acquired to a good end: it is therefore practically impossible 'to maintain or newly create a republic in corrupt cities' (I, 18). Elsewhere, Machiavelli is less pessimistic: states, like religious bodies (*sètte*), which are equally subject to degeneration, can be renewed by taking them back to their origins (*principii*), and 'those are better ordered and have longer life, whose institutions (*ordini*) makes their frequent renewal possible' (III, 1). Reformers occupy, in his political theory, a place second only to that of founders. 'Truly, should a prince seek worldly glory, he should covet to possess a corrupt city, not in order to spoil it entirely as Caesar, but to re-order it as Romulus did' (I, 10): 'one ought to take it as a general rule, that it never or rarely happens that a republic or a kingdom is either well ordered at the beginning, or completely reformed apart from its ancient institutions, unless this is done by one person' (I, 9). Yet, such a reform was liable to be only temporary: once its architect was dead, the city would return to its former state (I, 17). The problem is compounded by the fact that, while absolute power is essential to effect the reform of a corrupt society, it is itself, as we have seen, a source of corruption.

Machiavelli's sociological analysis of corruption forms part of a general theory of the suitability of political institutions to different societies at different points of their evolution. Institutions differ also according to whether a state is organised with a view to territorial aggrandisement or to security within its own borders. The former was the case of ancient Rome, the latter is that of modern Venice. A state which wants to expand should therefore follow, in fashioning its institutions, the example of Rome; to seek aggrandisement where the institutions, and in particular those concerning warfare, are not devised accordingly, means to court disaster, as the recent example of Venice's – in fact only temporary – loss of her mainland possessions shows (I, 6). As for the notion of the suitability of institutions to different societies, it derives ultimately from Aristotle;[34] Tolomeo of Lucca had applied it to Italy, Savonarola, following him, to Florence (see above, pp. 40–1); Machiavelli refines Savonarola' formulation by arguing that some nations require monarchies, others republics because of their different social structures; 'a republic should therefore be set up where there is . . . a great equality, and vice versa a principality where there is great inequality'; to ignore this political fact of life will nearly always lead to failure (I, 55). At the same time, Machiavelli considered republics to be superior to monarchies. 'As for prudence and stability, I say that a people is more prudent, more stable, and has better judgement than a prince' (I, 58); 'a republic has a longer life . . . than a principality' (III, 9); the 'common good is only observed in republics' (II, 2); they 'observe treaties far better than princes' (I, 59); they show more gratitude to their citizens than princes to their subjects (I, 29); Rome's rise to world power began after the expulsion of the kings and the establishment of the republic. In fact, 'cities have never increased their empire or wealth unless they were free', for is it 'the common good which makes cities great' (II, 2).

Machiavelli rejects the 'common opinion', according to which 'the people, when in power, is variable, fickle, and ungrateful, and distinguishes between the 'disorganised' ('sciolta') multitude and the one which is 'regulated by the laws'. It is the 'well-ordered people' 'which would be at least as stable, prudent, and grateful . . . as even a prince who is considered wise, while a prince who is unrestrained by the laws' would in these respects be worse than a people. At the same time, if one compared a prince and a people both bound by the laws, 'one would see more *virtù* in the latter than in the former; if unrestrained by them, 'one would see less errors in the people than in the prince' (I, 58).

Despite the superiority of the republic, good government can also be

---

34. *Politics* III, 1288a, IV, 1296b, V, 1327b. See Butters 1986, p.413.

provided by a monarchy, and not only at the foundation of states, or at their reform, where the untrammelled action by one man is essential. In a corrupt society, an absolute ruler can provide the only solution; for 'where the *materia* is so corrupt that the laws do not suffice to restrain it', what is needed to reform it is a monarchy 'which with absolute and excessive power restrains the excessive ambition and corruption of the powerful', as would be the case of most of Italy (I, 55). But also in societies in which corruption has not reached a stage where only an absolute ruler stands any chance at all of reforming them, monarchy can be a suitable form of government. The prime example of a good monarchy is, for Machiavelli, contemporary France. One of the reasons why he considered that country 'among the well-ordered and well-governed kingdoms' of his age was precisely because its king had succeeded, through the establishment of the *parlement*, in placing 'a bit in the mouth' of the great nobles and had thus checked their ambition and insolence (*Il Principe*, XIX); another, and more cogent reason, was that he had 'pledged himself to observe an infinite number of laws which encompass the security of all his peoples' (I, 16); with the result that the kingdom of France is 'more regulated by laws than any other of our time of which we have knowledge' (I, 58).

A monarchy bound by law was, like a republic, a *vivere politico*, and as such the opposite to tyranny. Since the early fourteenth century, Italian republicans had identified the *politeia* of Aristotle's *Politics*, as *vivere politico* or *civile*, with republican government; Machiavelli departs from this tradition by extending the term *politicus*, as Fortescue had done in England and Seyssel, recently, in France, to constitutional monarchies (Rubinstein 1987, pp. 44ff, 49ff). Machiavelli's eulogy of the kingdom of France, which is 'regulated by laws', serves to underline its distinction from a tyranny (see Matteucci 1972, pp. 215ff). His unreserved condemnation of tyranny relates to the classical and medieval notion of it as a corrupt form of monarchy, but also to Italian republican traditions: after the rise of despotic regimes in the Italian cities in the thirteenth century, tyranny was seen not only as a corruption of monarchy but above all as the antithesis to republican liberty. It is this republican tradition which prevails in the *Discorsi* where, after dealing with the heroic age of the Roman republic, he comments on the succession of crises which led to its destruction by Caesar was, for Machiavelli, a tyrant, like other citizens 'who had become tyrants of their fatherland' (I, 16). The new prince of *Il Principe* who comes to power as a private citizen, 'di privato . . . diventa principe' (VIII), is, by this definition, a tyrant as soon as he seizes absolute power (IX; cf. *Discorsi* I, 25,

26), although Machiavelli never uses the term in this work, even where he condemns princes for their criminal and cruel actions (VIII).

It is one of those points where *Il Principe* and the *Discorsi*, though dealing with the same subject, approach it from different viewpoints – a difference which was due to the different purposes of the two works, rather than to changes in Machiavelli's political thinking. This forms part of the wider question of the relationship between the republican theory of the *Discorsi* and the advice offered in *The Prince* to the new ruler. The apparent conflict between the political teachings in these two works has been interpreted as due to the former belonging to an earlier phase in the development of Machiavelli's thinking about politics,[35] but it can also be explained by the different situations in which they were written and by their different purposes. The two works have major themes in common. Thus the problem of *virtù* and fortune is again taken up in the *Discorsi*, but given a less voluntarist and more historically defined slant than in *The Prince*: the emphasis is now placed on men's character conforming to the point in history at which their action takes place: 'the cause of the bad or the good fortune of men depends on their behaviour happening to be in conformity with the times' (III, 9). This is, incidentally, yet another reason why a republic is superior to a monarchy; for owing to the 'diversity' existing among its citizens, it is better equipped than a prince to 'adapt itself to the diversity of the times' and consequently enjoys life and good fortune over longer periods (III, 9).

Another theme, central for the teachings of *Il Principe*, is the rejection of Christian morality as the guide of political action. In *The Prince*, while considered objectionable in theory, this is justified in practice on the grounds of the innate wickedness of man; 'for how one lives is so far removed from how one ought to live, that he who leaves what is done for what ought to be done will experience his ruin rather than his preservation' (xv). Here the use of immoral methods is defended as essential for the success and the security of the prince, whereas in the *Discorsi* the end is also postulated as justifying the means as long as it serves the common good. Writing of Romulus' murder of Remus, Machiavelli comments that it is to be accepted that, 'although the fact accuses him, the effect excuses him', it being a 'general rule' that a state can only be well ordered, or reformed, by one person, and that he who intends to do so not for his own sake or for that of his successors, but for the common good and the fatherland, 'should seek

---

35. See Baron 1961, pp. 247ff, repr. 1988, pp. 193ff, and above, n. 24.

to be alone in authority' (I, 9). It is for the sake of preserving the republic that he justifies the execution by Brutus, the first consul, of his own sons for having plotted against it. However, much the same also applies to the founder of a tyranny: 'he who establishes a tyranny and does not kill Brutus, and who creates a republic (*uno stato libero*) and does not kill the sons of Brutus, lasts only a short time'; in both cases 'it is necessary to take exemplary (*memorabile*) action against the enemies' of the new regime (III, 3). The necessity to use extraordinary methods at their foundation applies to republics as well as to principalities: 'he who sets out to govern a multitude either in the form of a republic or of a principate, and does not secure himself against those who are hostile to the new order, creates a regime which will be short-lived' (I, 16). The chapter on fraud (III, 40), with its distinction between private and public morality, reads as if it were taken straight from *The Prince*: 'although to use fraud is detestable in any action, in the conduct of war it is nevertheless praiseworthy and glorious'. For the aim is the good of the community, in this case of the fatherland in its relation to other states; and, as he says in the following chapter (III, 41) – one of the last of the work: 'when one decides wholly on the safety of the fatherland (*patria*), there should be no consideration of what is just or unjust, kind or cruel, praiseworthy or ignominious; rather, setting aside any other regard, one should entirely adopt that decision which saves its life and preserves its liberty'.

The term *patria* recurs, about ten years after he had completed the *Discorsi*, in a letter Machiavelli wrote, at a moment of supreme crisis, when the imperial army was advancing on Florence: 'I love my fatherland more than my soul' ('amo la patria mia più dell'anima').[36] What is the relevance of his *patria* to an understanding of that work? There are no explicit references to the internal politics of Florence in *Il Principe*, except to support his argument about the importance of arms for a prophet: Savonarola, a *profeta disarmato*, 'was ruined . . . when the multitude ceased to believe in him' (VI). Yet, if our interpretation is correct, there is a veiled lesson on Medicean rule in the chapter on the 'civil principality' (IX; see above, p. 46). The *Discorsi* were perhaps read by Machiavelli around 1516 to a select literary circle at Florence which met in the Rucellai garden.[37] To what extent has this political commentary on the history of the 'perfect' Roman republic to be understood in the context of Florentine politics, and

---

36. To Francesco Vettori, 16 April 1527, in Machiavelli 1961a, pp. 504–5.
37. Ridolfi 1972, pp. 265–6. According to Nerli 1859, II, p. 12, 'a loro istanza compose il Machiavello quel suo libro de' discorsi sopra Tito Livio'.

as providing, apart from 'general rules', special lessons for his compatriots? His observations on the city and on individual citizens, scattered through that work, are mostly critical; yet when he discusses the chances of reform in corrupt Italy, he distinguishes regions such as Lombardy, in which the *materia* had degenerated to an extent where only absolute power could restrain the excesses of the nobility, from the three Tuscan republics Florence, Siena, and Lucca, 'where there exists so much equality that a prudent man who was familiar with the civic institutions (*civilità*) of antiquity could easily introduce a constitutional government (*uno vivere civile*)' (I, 55).

Central to the problem of the role of Florence in the *Discorsi* is the question to what extent Machiavelli's innovative view of the effects of internal division on the evolution of the Roman republic was relevant to his interpretation of Florentine history. It was only later, in his *Istorie fiorentine* (Machiavelli 1962), which he wrote between 1520 and 1525, that he tried to explain why civil conflict was beneficial in Rome but harmful in Florence; but it is probable that when he discussed the political and institutional equilibrium which the struggles between the nobility and plebs had brought about in ancient Rome, he was also thinking of the antagonism between *ottimati* and *popolani*, between aristocratic and democratic tendencies, which had reemerged in Florence after the creation of the great council in 1494 and which played a major role in the political life of the republic during Machiavelli's years in its chancery. The preface to the third book of the *Istorie fiorentine* contrasts the political balance which class struggle had produced in Rome with the oppression of the nobility by the people after its victory in Florence; and in the preface to the seventh book he insists that factions, *sètte*, are, unlike class division, always detrimental to the common good, and have always been harmful to Florence. In the *Discorsi*, most of the explicit references to his city are to her recent past (see Rubinstein 1972, pp. 23ff); but towards the end of the first book, Machiavelli attempts a comprehensive interpretation of her history. During the last two centuries, he writes, which are reliably documented – of which 'si ha di vera memoria' – she has never succeeded in establishing a regime 'which allowed her to be truly called a republic' (I, 49).

About two years after the completion of the *Discorsi*, he made this conclusion the starting point for an analysis of the constitutional development of Florence designed to provide the basis for a proposal to reform the ruling Medicean regime. The *Discursus florentinarum rerum*, written after the death in 1519 of the virtual ruler of Florence, the younger Lorenzo de'

Medici (Machiavelli 1961b, pp. 261–77), forms part of a group of political pamphlets advising the Medici how to secure their power through reforms. Machiavelli's is the most radically republican of these writings: he advocates the restoration, with some substantial changes, by Leo X and Cardinal Giulio, the only surviving legitimate members of the main branch of the family, of the republican constitution the Medici had overthrown in 1512. He repeats, and expands, his critical interpretation, in the *Discorsi*, of his city's constitutional history: it had never been a true republic or a true principate. Her social structure, characterised by a 'very great equality', requires a republican constitution (pp. 261, 267). The Medici were, by reestablishing and reforming such a constitution, to act as the reformers Machiavelli had praised, in the *Discorsi*, as the saviours of their country: 'no one is as much extolled in any of his actions as those who through laws and institutions have reformed republics and kingdoms' (p. 275; cf. *Discorsi*, I, 10). This appeal, which joins that to the Medici, at the end of *Il Principe*, to liberate Italy from the barbarians, proved, in its turn, to be a complete failure. It contrasts with his observations, in the *Discorsi*, on the obstacles facing reform in an age of corruption (I, 17, 18), and thus reflects on the problem, fundamental for Machiavelli's theory of the lessons of history, of the validity of 'general rules'.

iii Florence and Venice: Guicciardini

Machiavelli's *Discursus florentinarium rerum* was, like other Florentine political writings such as those by Niccolò Guicciardini, Lodovico Alamanni, and Alessandro de' Pazzi (Albertini 1955, pp. 41ff, 85ff), concerned with practical questions regarding the reform or the consolidation of the restored Medici regime. The hopes of Machiavelli and of other republicans that the Medici would initiate a constitutional reform leading to a restoration of the republican constitution were dashed by the discovery, in 1522, of a conspiracy against them. Francesco Guicciardini's *Dialogo del reggimento di Firenze* (Guicciardini 1932, pp. 3–172), which he began before that event, during the pontificate of Leo X, and completed about four years later during that of the second Medici pope, Clement VII (pp. 296–7), proposes such a reform within the context of a wide-ranging analysis of Florentine government and politics under the early Medicean regime and under the republican regime established in 1494. Unlike Machiavelli, Guicciardini was a member of an old patrician family which had played a prominent role under Lorenzo de' Medici and had later supported the new republic; as the heir to a family tradition of active participation in government, he was, again in contrast to Machiavelli, drawn to an aristocratic rather than to a democratic view of Florentine politics. At the same time, although holding high office in the administration of the States of the church under two Medici popes, he considered, when writing the *Dialogo*, a republican constitution more suitable to his city than Medicean rule. The purpose of the *Dialogo* explains why its republican theory is, unlike that of the *Discorsi*, strictly related to Florence; but just as the *Discorsi* have Florentine implications and undertones, so the political ideas expounded in the *Dialogo* often transcend their Florentine dimension and assume a general character, which comes fully into its own in the *Ricordi*, or maxims, which Guicciardini penned in the course of the manifold activities of his political life.

The central question of the *Dialogo* is whether the Medici regime or a republican constitution was more congenial to Florence. The work belongs, like the *Discorsi*, to the Italian debate on the respective merits of monarchies and republics. It is also, like Machiavelli's political writings, strictly related to empirical facts. Guicciardini resolutely rejects any evaluations of forms of government based on normative classifications of constitutions (p. 15). Similarly, he subjects traditional concepts of liberty and equality, basic for Florentine political thought and authoritatively formulated by Bruni, to a devastating critique: in most cases these terms serve, he believes, to conceal bids for power on the part of the underprivileged (p. 38). The only criterion he accepts for a comparative evaluation of constitutions concerns, pragmatically, their 'effects' ('effetti'). Those constitutions are the best, 'where the laws are most observed and justice is best administered, and where there is most consideration of the good of all, while at the same time social distinctions are respected' (p. 16). His rejection of classical constitutional theory as his guide does not prevent him from proposing the mixed constitution as the ideal form of government for the Florentine republic; but he does so with reference not to a classical author, as Machiavelli had done, but to contemporary Venice. It is Venice, not ancient Rome, which he holds up as a model republic, a view which goes hand in hand with a critique of Machiavelli's interpretation of Roman history[38] and altogether with a rejection of his axiomatic belief in the lessons of history (p. 68).[39]

38. Guicciardini 1932, pp. 148ff. Cf. his *Considerazioni intorno ai Discorsi del Machiavelli sopra la prima deca di Tito Livio*, Guicciardini 1933, pp. 10ff, 43.
39. Cf. Guicciardini 1951, p. 121 (c110): 'Quanto si ingannano coloro che a ogni parola allegano e Romani! Bisognerebbe avere una città condizionata come era loro, e poi governarsi secondo quello essemplo . . .'

At the same time, Guicciardini insists, like Machiavelli, on the importance of the suitability of constitutions to the societies for which they are devised; and like Savonarola, and like Machiavelli in the *Discorsi*, he accordingly considers republican liberty to be 'natural' for Florence (pp. 98–9). Again like Savonarola, he contrasts that liberty with the government of Florence under Lorenzo de' Medici; but he does so within the context of a detailed comparison of the Medicean regime before 1494 with that of the new republic. Savonarola had condemned the former as a tyranny, Guicciardini argues that it had respected republican institutions and traditions, and had preserved at least the image of liberty.[40] While preferring republican liberty as natural to Florence, he nevertheless rates the early Medicean regime higher than the republican one that had replaced it in 1494 on the grounds of its better 'effects' for the government of the city, because its errors were due to rational calculation, those of the people to ignorance; and ignorance, 'which has neither measure nor rules' (p. 51), is more damaging than errors due to malice (pp. 46, 50–1, 55).

As early as 1512, Guicciardini had, in a short discourse on the reform of the republican regime of 1494,[41] singled out the guiding principle of the ideal republican constitution, which he expounds in the second book of the *Dialogo*, after having completed the comparison between the two regimes under which Florence had been governed in the recent past. That principle is a balance between the conflicting claims to power of the upper and lower classes, to be secured by a constitution in which an elite of wise and experienced citizens plays a decisive and moderating role and holds in check 'the ignorance of the multitude' (p. 227). This does not only apply to Florence: 'at all times, experience has always shown that it is the virtue of few citizens which has governed and which governs the republics' (p. 238). In the *Dialogo*, the senate, composed of 'the most virtuous and best qualified citizens', holds the balance between the potentially excessive authority of the head of the republic, the Gonfalonier of Justice, and the people assembled in the great council, by providing 'a moderating element between tyranny and popular licence' ('uno temperamento tra la tirannide e licenzia populare') (p. 118). His model, as for other institutions of his ideal

40. ' . . . non era venuto su come uno stato di uno principe assoluto, ma accompagnato co' modi della libertà e della civilità, perché ogni cosa si governava sotto nome di republica . . . la imagine era che el governo fussi libero' (p. 77). In his *Storie fiorentine*, composed in 1508–9, he had described Lorenzo as a benevolent despot (Guicciardini 1931, p. 80): ' . . . bisogna conchiudere che sotto lui la città non fussi in libertà, nondimeno che sarebbe impossible avessi avuto un tiranno migliore e più piacevole'.
41. *Del modo di ordinare il governo popolare* ('Discorso di Logrogno'), in Guicciardini 1932, pp. 218–59.

Florentine republic, is the Venetian senate. Venice, which, he says, 'for so many centuries has preserved the same form of government without ever experiencing seditions or civil discord' (p. 139), has 'the best government not only of our own times, but perhaps the best that any city had ever possessed in ancient times, for it has a share of all forms of government, of one, of the few, and of the many, and has moderated them all in such a way as to derive from each of them most of its advantages and avoid most of its disadvantages' (pp. 138–9). In a veiled critique of Machiavelli's idealisation of ancient Rome as the 'perfect republic', Guicciardini, apparently oblivious of his earlier rejection of the standard classifications of constitutions, shares, in a far more subtle and comprehensive form, the admiration with which some Florentine patricians of the fifteenth century had regarded the mixed constitution of Venice – an admiration which re-emerged after the creation in 1494 of the great council, conceived by Savonarola in imitation of Venice, and which contributed to attempts by the aristocrats, the *ottimati*, first in 1502 and then during the last days of the republic in 1512, to reform the republican constitution by creating a senate (Gilbert 1968, pp. 475–6, 484, repr. 1977, pp. 190–1, 198). Yet Guicciardini, with all his insistence on the divisive role of a political elite – 'in reality, the entire weight of government (*tutto 'l pondo del governo*) lies, in the end, on the shoulders of very few men, and this was always so in all republics in ancient as in modern times' (Guicciardini 1932, p. 242) – does not want this elite to be exclusively formed of aristocrats. He condemns oligarchy as leading to oppression and discord (pp. 139–40): what he has in mind is a meritocracy of the wisest and the best citizens who, while not identical with the patricians, would be more likely be found in their ranks than in those of the people (pp. 118–19).

The detailed account of the constitutional arrangements that were to establish and to secure ·Guicciardini's 'well-ordered' republic (p. 101) reflects a deep-rooted Florentine belief in the political efficacy of institutional reforms and manipulations. Guicciardini shared Machiavelli's views on the creative force of *ordini*, but they were meant to create, rather than civic virtue and imperial power, good government and internal stability. He too believed that their suitability was historically conditioned: Florence, he writes, was by now an old city, 'and rather declining than growing' ('piú presto in declinazione che in augumento'), and hence less capable of being reformed (pp. 81–2, 145). When he began composing the *Dialogo*, at a time when constitutional reforms were being discussed in the city, he had not been without hope that his project of an ideal Florentine constitution could contribute to republican reform before he reached old age.[42] By the time he completed this work he seems to have abandoned that hope,[43] and a few years later, after the fall in 1530 of the last Florentine republic, under which he had suffered from political persecution, he gave his full and unreserved support to the nascent principate of the Medici.

The *Dialogo* is not only a blueprint for a republican reform of Florence. In his pragmatic insistence on political 'effects' rather than norms, Guicciardini breaks with the traditions of classical political philosophy even more incisively than Machiavelli. His critical analysis of the concepts of liberty and equality, while related to Florence, are meant to have general validity, and the same applies to his observations on the connection between power and violence: 'if one carefully considers their origins', he says of states, 'they are [all] violent, and with the exception of republics, and this only within their boundaries (*nella loro patria*), there is no power whatever which is legitimate' (p. 163). Like Machiavelli, he considers conquest a natural desire 'it is pleasant to make acquisitions' ('lo acquistare è cosa dolce': p. 160), in whose pursuit Christian virtures may not have any place. 'Who nowadays wants to keep dominions and states should, whenever possible, use compassion and goodness, and where this is not possible, it is necessary that he use cruelty and pay scant regard to his conscience.' For 'if one wants' to govern and rule 'in the way it is done today', it is impossible to do so 'according to the precepts of Christian law' (p. 162).[44]

Guicciardini included the observation that power is nearly always founded on violence almost literally in his *Ricordi*. The *Ricordi*, which he collected between 1512 and 1530,[45] were designed by him to spell out, in the form of general maxims, the quintessence of his public and private experiences in Florence and abroad. Many of them recall the views expressed in the *Dialogo*, others range over a wider area. In a republic, 'only those should govern who are able to do so and deserve it' (C 109), for 'who speaks of a people really speaks of a mad animal which is crammed with a

---

42. 'E però potrebbe questa fatica mia non riuscire al tutto inutile e venire eziandio, innanzi che io invecchiassi, el tempo suo da publicarsi' (Guicciardini 1932, p. 299; first version of the proem of the *Dialogo*).

43. In the final version of the proem he writes that he had composed the *Dialogo* 'massime . . . per mio piacere e recreazione né con intenzione di publicarlo' (Guicciardini 1932, p. 5).

44. Cf. also *Del modo di ordinare*, in Guicciardini 1932, p. 222: 'Non è altro lo stato e lo imperio che una violenzia sopra e' sudditi.'

45. Guicciardini 1951, pp. ixff. The following references to the *Ricordi* are to this edition. Q refers to the collection of 1512, A to *Ricordi* written between 1512 and 1525, B to that of 1528 and C to the final one of 1530. See also Scarano 1980, pp. 89–178 ('Le redazioni dei "Ricordi"').

thousand errors and confusions, without taste, discernment, and stability' (c 140). 'Do not believe those who preach liberty so effectively, because . . . perhaps none of them has anything but his private interests in mind' (c 66). In fact, 'those men conduct their affairs well in this world, who always keep before their eyes their own interests' (c 218). What the 'liberty of republics' (*la libertà delle republiche*), according to a maxim written before 1525 (A 119), really means is that it is the 'servant of justice, for it has not been founded for any other purpose than to prevent anyone being oppressed by another'. If one could be certain that justice was observed under the rule of one or a few, 'there would be no reason to desire' that liberty. Indeed, together with republican liberty, princely rule is a major theme of the *Ricordi*, reflecting his experience of Italian politics. Princes do not always conform to the classical norm of being 'established not for their own interest but for the common good' (c 172); in the *Ricordi*, in fact, he calls them often tyrants – unlike Machiavelli in *Il Principe*, he does not avoid the term to describe absolute rulers. There are 'prudent' tyrants, as well as 'bestial and cruel' ones (c 98, 99, 101). Guicciardini is here concerned less with tyranny as such, which he condemns, in one of the earliest *Ricordi* (Q² 23), as being held together 'by the blood of the citizens', than with rules of behaviour to be adopted towards a tyrant. 'To save oneself from a bestial and cruel tyrant', the only effective rule is 'to flee from him as far and as quickly as possible' (c 101). Otherwise it is best to take as one's guide Tacitus, who tells one 'what are the thoughts of tyrants' (c 13) and who 'teaches very well . . . those who live under a tyrant how to live and conduct themselves prudently, just as he teaches tyrants the means of founding a tyranny' (c 18; see Schellhase 1976, pp. 94ff).

The years around 1530 formed a turning point in the history of Florentine political thought. Machiavelli died in 1527, shortly after the last restoration of the republican regime; after its fall in 1530, Guicciardini became a counsellor of Duke Alessandro de' Medici and, after his assassination in 1537, helped Cosimo I to succeed him as duke; he spent his last years writing his greatest work, the *Storia d'Italia*. But Guicciardini's hope of a republican reform, which he had expressed in his *Dialogo del reggimento di Firenze*, was not extinct among Florentine republicans. Shortly after the fall of the last republic, Donato Giannotti combined, in his *Della repubblica fiorentina* (1531–4), a painstaking survey of the evolution of the Florentine constitution with a critical analysis of the shortcomings of the last two republican regimes and with a detailed project of constitutional reform which would create one such regime that would be both stable and lasting (see Albertini 1955, pp. 146ff). Giannotti began this work while he was confined to his villa near Florence because of his association with the last republic: he had held Machiavelli's former post in the chancery, to which he had been appointed in 1527. The year before, he had written, in Padua, a dialogue *Della repubblica de' Viniziani*, which has been described as representing 'the climax of Florentine political thinking on Venice in the Renaissance period'.[46] Giannotti may have been motivated by the publication, in 1526, of the *Della republica* by Antonio Brucioli, a member of the Orti Oricellari group who had fled from the city after the conspiracy of 1522.[47] Brucioli draws, in his dialogue, the picture of an ideal republic which is largely modelled on Plato and Aristotle, but intends to deal with those republics only 'which have existed or which could exist', refusing, as Machiavelli and Guicciardini had done, to discuss imaginary ones; some aspects of his scheme evidently refer to Florence, as for example the importance he ascribes to the militia (Brucioli 1982, pp. 101, 120ff; see Cantimori 1937, pp. 95ff). Giannotti, in analysing the Venetian constitution and describing its evolution, claims to be following the example of Aristotle who 'composed special books on all states existing in his time and known to him' (Giannotti 1850, pp. 3–4). Despite all his admiration for the laws and institutions of the Venetian republic and for the 'wise mixture' ('prudentissimo temperamento') of its constitution (p. 17),[48] he did not set up a model for Florence a city in which the members of the great council were descended from the nobles who, at the city's foundation, 'formed' its 'body' (p. 33). Like Guicciardini, he considers the mixed constitution the most suitable form of government for Florence (Giannotti 1990, I, 5);[49] but in a city in which there were few nobles (*grandi*) and a large middle class (pp. 98–9), the mixture of constitutional elements should be weighed in favour of the people, and should 'inclinare nel popolo' (III, 3). At the same time, the great council, 'the city's ruler' ('il signore della città') (p. 166), was to be composed of the '*grandi*, the *mediocri*, and the *popolari*', to the exclusion of the plebs (p. 166). Giannotti believed that his mixed constitution, his 'governo ottimamente temperato' (p. 102), was superior to that of Rome as described by Polybius (and, he might have added, by Machiavelli): had the government of Rome been weighted in favour of the

---

46. Gilbert 1968, p. 490 (repr. 1977, p. 204). On the date of composition see Ridolfi 1942, p. 77.
47. Brucioli 1982, dialogue VI; see Cantimori 1937, pp. 88ff; Albertini 1955, pp. 79–83.
48. For Giannotti's use of the word *temperare* see Giannotti 1990a, III, 2 ('Come si debbe temperare lo stato misto').
49. 'Che Firenze è subietto capacissimo del governo misto'. Cf. III, 4.

people or the senate, she would have avoided civic struggles (III, 2). He
visualises his ideal Florentine constitution in the form of a pyramid, whose
apex is formed by the Gonfalonier of Justice, its base by the great council,
with the senate on the intermediate level (III, 4).[50] Following Machiavelli's
views on military service, and drawing on his own experience during the
siege of the city, he considers the civic militia an essential part of the
reformed republic (IV, 1). Like Guicciardini, he intends, in his work, 'to
deal exclusively with the government' of Florence, and with the 'kind of
republic that is suitable' to her (I, 2); but, unlike Guicciardini, who
composed his *Dialogo* before the short-lived republican restoration of 1527,
he has the advantage, of which he makes ample and detailed use, to subject
to critical analysis not only the republican regime of 1494, but also that of
1527, and to single out their defects and shortcomings – an analysis which
then serves him as the foundation of his own programme of a well-ordered
and stable republican constitution. That he could still hope that such a
constitutional reform could be introduced at a time when Alessandro de'
Medici was consolidating his absolute authority in Florence under the
protection of the emperor contrasts with Guicciardini's diffident attitude
towards the realisation of his own reform programme (Guicciardini 1932,
pp. 5, 299–300; see above, pp. 61–2). Giannotti's treatise became, in its
idealistic optimism, the major intellectual document of the republican
exiles, whose hopes of a restoration of the city's ancient liberties and more
recent reforms were definitively dashed in 1537 by Cosimo I's victory over
them in the battle of Montemurlo.

50. He had used the same metaphor in his description of the Venetian constitution: Giannotti 1850,
   pp. 37–8.

3

Law

DONALD R. KELLEY

'Civil science is the true philosophy', declared the fifteenth-century jurist Claude de Seyssel in his commentary on the Digest, 'and is to be preferred to all other fields because of its purpose' (Seyssel 1508, fo. 1). Down at least to the eighteenth century this conviction was maintained by professional lawyers of various political persuasions, and indeed expanded because of the increasing interaction between jurisprudence and modern political thought and institutions. The original Roman formula, enshrined in the first lines of that great anthology of classical jurisprudence, the Digest of Justinian, was joined to a deep reverence for judicial expertise and for the holy office of the 'priests of the laws'; but in its Byzantine context legal science was subordinated to, and conscripted by, the absolutist and imperialist designs of the emperor; and this strategy was resumed by early modern European jurists, especially those serving monarchs – kings of France, Spain, and England – who claimed to be 'emperors' in their own kingdoms. Civil law continued to be concerned predominantly with private matters (personal status, family, succession, property, obligations, and the like), though increasingly it came to be subordinated to and shaped by legislation. 'True philosophy' was in many ways bound to modern ideas of rulership. This is why political thought in its widest sense cannot be understood apart from law and jurisprudence.

i The old legal heritage

In the fifteenth century the European legal tradition was vastly complex but displays, from a modern perspective, three fairly distinctive aspects, corresponding to civil, canon, and customary law.[1] By then each of these

---

1. Classical surveys are headed by Koschaker 1958, Calasso 1954, Wieacker 1967, Cavanna 1983–7, Coing 1985–9, and Stintzing and Landsberg 1880–1910; but see also Fassò 1968 and Carlyle 1903–36, VI; and for bibliography Coing 1973–7.

had been formulated in modern written terms, rationalised and in various ways modernised, and subjected to several generations of adaptive 'interpretation'. Civil law, revived in the twelfth century and expanded into 'civil science' through academic and practical jurisprudence, has at all points been central to the legal tradition, since it provided both the model and the quarry for 'canonist science', and since it provided the conceptual basis and the terminology for European customary law, whether through 'scientific' incorporation (the *jus feudale* being regarded as part of 'Roman law' in Italy and the empire) or simply as a standard of comparison (as in England and, more systematically and officially, in France). All three sub-traditions were, of course, transformed: civil law from Romano-Byzantine books of authority to an eclectically construed and adapted common law, its sibling rival canon law from hierocratic ecclesiological doctrine into a subordinate system of private rules, and customary law from a mélange of barbarian, feudal, and communal usages into distinctive, though still localised, national systems. All of these were given a certain common basis through interpretation in terms of natural and divine law and subjection to legislative authority.

Of the modern European legal tradition in general Rome was ever, according to the ancient formula (Digest I, 12, 1, 13; Code I, 33), the 'common fatherland' (*Roma communis patria*). Centuries after the fall of Rome the structure and spirit, the language and the methods, of its law preserved their sway not only through derivative legal systems, Romanist or Romanoid if not Roman, but also through attitudes, assumptions, and what Justice Holmes once called 'inarticulate major premises'. In a famous passage Holmes' friend Alfred North Whitehead advised historians to attend not merely to positions consciously argued by writers in bygone ages, but also to 'fundamental assumptions presupposed by all disputants' (Whitehead 1948, p. 50). In jurisprudence and to a considerable extent in political philosophy such presuppositions have been reflected most comprehensively in certain titles, especially the early titles, of the Corpus Juris Justiniani published in the 530s. The Institutes and the Digest in particular represented a significant part of general 'liberal' as well as specifically legal education in many European universities. In order to suggest the significance of the legal tradition for political thought suffice it here to set down some of the major rubrics, formulas, concepts, and topoi of Roman jurisprudence as they were transmitted to modern thought (Schulz 1936; Kelley 1990).

I   Toga and sword. 'The imperial majesty should be armed with laws as well as glorified with arms, that there may be good government in times both of war and of peace' (Institutes, proemium, further elaborated in the prefaces of the Digest). From Justinian (and before) to Napoleon (and beyond) this formula was invoked to express the two aspects of rulership, and usually the turning from conquest to social control and political organisation.

2   The divine origin of law. 'We have wished God to become the author and head of the whole work', declared Justinian of his Digest, adding moreover that his collection 'shall prevail for all time hereafter' (constitution *Tanta*). Such has been the claim of virtually every official legal collection, or 'codification', of medieval and modern times, reflecting the need to claim perfection or infallibility on transcendent grounds, and establishing a legal and ideological canon binding legal interpreters.

3   The reverence for antiquity. The authority of civil law derived in no small measure from its age and pedigree, going back some 1,400 years to the 'founding of the city', according to Justinian (constitution *Tanta*); and for lawyers this entailed also going back to origins, or sources, for full understanding (Digest I, I, 2, *de origine juris*). Celebration of and reliance upon antiquity, and especially upon founding fathers, has likewise been characteristic of European jurisprudence and political thought down to modern times.

4   Absolutism. Despite respect for the 'fathers of jurisprudence', Justinian insisted that henceforth the only source of law was the imperial will – 'for how can antiquity abrogate our laws?' (constitution *Tanta*) – and so he forbade all judicial discretion, all 'interpretation', in the hope of preventing the 'vain discord of posterity'. This heaven-storming ambition, expressed in a variety of famous formulas, especially that 'What pleases the prince has the force of law' (*Quod principi placuit legis habet vigorem*) and that the prince is above the law (*legibus solutus*) (Digest I, 4, I, and I, 3, 31, and Institutes II, 17, 8), was revived by later monarchs; and the concept of sovereignty itself (related to the *imperium* as well as to *majestas*) was further developed by medieval and early modern legists, most famously by Jean Bodin in the sixteenth century. Yet in this case, too, there was a counter-thesis, namely:

5   Popular sovereignty. The aforementioned idea that the prince's will was law was justified (though in effect undermined) by the second clause of the formula, referring to the famous *lex regia*, according to which the prince received his authority from the people, that *populus* which alone, originally, possessed 'majesty'; and this principle was reinforced by another formula, the equally famous *Lex Digna Vox*, declaring that 'It is a word worthy of majesty of the ruler that the prince professes himself bound to

the law' (Code I, 14, 4). The conflict between this proto- 'constitutionalist' argument and the preceding 'absolutist' formulas has informed much of western political thought.

6   Distinction between public and private law (Digest I, I, I, 2). This distinction, which corresponds to those between individual and society, or government, between domestic and political economy, and between ethics and politics, has become even more deeply and perhaps incorrigibly embedded in western thought (Müllejans 1961; Longo 1972).

7   Natural law (Digest I, I, I, 3, and Institutes I, I). The *jus naturale*, associated with the 'natural reason' underlying custom and the 'law of nations' (Gaius, Institutes I, I, I), came to be identified with the loftier 'reason' of Stoic philosophy and distinguished in Greek fashion from convention or culture, later 'positive law'; and it was in this form that 'natural law', whether distinguished from or identified with 'divine law', was elaborated by medieval and modern jurists (Gierke 1950; Tuck 1979).

8   The law of nations (Digest I, I, I, 4, and Institutes I, I). The *jus gentium*, assembled originally by Roman jurists from the customs of foreign nations taken into the Empire, was expanded by medieval and modern lawyers to include other, non-western cultures, resulting in a massive expansion of the field of comparative legal and institutional studies (Lombardi 1947).

9   The structure of law. 'All the law which we make use of relates either to persons, things, or actions' (Digest I, 5, I, and Institutes I, 2, 12, from Gaius, Institutes I, 2, 8). Prehistorical in origin, this formal principle of private law has come to inform western social and political thinking over many centuries, serving among other things to establish the boundaries of public law (Kelley 1979b; Goudy 1910; Affölter 1897).

10   The status of persons, or condition of man (Digest I, 5 *et seq.*, and Institutes I, 3 *et seq.*). This famous rubric has furnished the juristic locus for celebrations of the dignity of man (rarely including women), arising from natural and civil 'liberty', defined according to various familial, economic, and social qualifications (Duff 1938; Zatti 1975).

11   The idea of property. The second member of the Roman trinity (No. 9 above), the category of 'things', represents above all the materials of the natural world which, when prehended or occupied by persons, become the basis of possession or property in a general, legal, or 'civil' sense; and the social problems created by this institution have been perhaps the major concern of Romanist legal systems from Justinian to Napoleon, as well as a central theme of political thought (Maiorca 1937).

12   The idea of action. This third category, while originally limited to

legal initiatives aimed at redress of injuries (*legis actiones*), introduces more generally fundamental assumptions of legal and political voluntarism, which is to say the central role of human will in private (as in public) law, and the importance of values, including public as well as private interest, in legal and political decisions (Bekker 1871; Orestano 1978).

13   Customary law (Digest I, 1, 1, 6, and I, 3, 32–40. Defined originally as 'unwritten' as distinguished from 'written law', *consuetudo* evolved into a complex tradition and conceptual system by which Germanic and other European (and non-European) customs could be incorporated into Roman law and later discussed in more general philosophic and later anthropological terms (Schmiedel 1966).

14   The idea of interpretation (Digest I, 3, *passim*, and L, 16 and 17, including the essential titles *de regulis juris* and *de verborum significatione*). Here is the source of many of the conventions, 'commonplaces', and 'maxims' of legal (and implicitly political) thought, including perhaps obvious notions of 'equity' and the value of 'liberal' as distinguished from 'strict' interpretation, which is to say emphasis on the judicial and customary rather than the legislative source of law (Stein 1966).

15   The criticism of law. Going back to the ancient distinction between practitioners (*pragmatici*) and philosophical jurists (*jurisconsulti*), lawyers have been regarded with ambivalence, but never before the object of such extremes of adulation and vituperation – ranging from identification with 'nobility' and virtue to denunciations, satirical, moral, religious, and political.

ii   Civil science in the Renaissance

These are some of the major assumptions, attitudes, and principles inherited and developed by the legal tradition, especially in its 'modern' form, as Seyssel characterised his fellow Bartolists (Seyssel 1566, p. 3). Adaptation of these themes, of course, differed among the various national branches of the Roman legal tradition. The classic modern formulation came in 'jurisprudence Italian style', and from the fifteenth century this modernised law was 'received' into the imperial courts of Germany. At the other extreme was England, which maintained a vernacular tradition of customary and '"common" law' touched only marginally by Roman influence, civilian or canonist. Indeed, in his *De Laudibus Legum Anglie*, Sir John Fortescue defined (or rather idealised) English law as the very obverse of civil law, whose arbitrary and illiberal spirit was epitomised by the formula that the prince's will was law (Fortescue 1949, ch. XIX *et seq.*). In France and Spain, as in England, neither Roman law nor its feudal supplements had specific 'authority', but of course it was taught in the universities and had profound ideological as well as methodological impact, certainly in terms of the themes summarised above (Coing 1973–7, II, pt I, ch. I).

One of the conditions of the massive expansion of jurisprudence in early modern Europe was what one historian has called 'the triumph of the professionals', a phenomenon itself arising from the shift from customary to 'written law', and specifically to Romano-canonical procedures.[2] From the thirteenth century jurists trained 'in both kinds of law' (*utriusque juris*) created a large Romanist, or at least Romanoid, jurisprudence; in France and Spain the same process was carried out by the *légistes* and *letrados* and by the royal courts which overwhelmed popular and eventually feudal forms of justice. The *parlement* of Paris in particular, branching off from the royal council from the early fourteenth century, stood at the apex both of the French system and of the legal profession, and (especially from the time of the Great Schism) acquired political and even legislative as well as judicial authority, which continued into the eighteenth century, especially through remonstrances and 'interpretation' of ordinances. In Germany the formal *Rezeption* gave official status to the incursions of learned law made over the previous century or so, and consequently the older popular courts and finders or 'sayers' of law (*Weistümer, Oberhöfe* and to some extent the *Schöffen*) were in large part supplanted by the imperial and territorial courts. There were the closest ties with the schools of law, which from the sixteenth century were called upon to submit expert judgements in response to 'records dispatched' from the courts (*Aktenversendung*). Magistrates and lawyers were themselves trained and in effect licensed by these schools, whether law faculties or technical schools like the English Inns of Court, and so were part of the academic as well as administering establishment.

The connections between legal and political thought are evident above all in this academic context. In the universities civil, canon, and feudal law were all taught according to a conventional scholastic method, which (though introduced by thirteenth-century French jurists) came to be named after its eponymous hero Bartolus and later was referred to as the 'Italian method' (*mos italicus*) (Engelmann 1939; Canning 1987). Of the founding fathers (especially Bartolus, his mentor Cino da Pistoia, and his

2. Dawson 1960, p. 69, 1968; also Strauss 1986, Dahm 1972, and Piano Mortari 1962.

disciple Baldus) the most important epigones in the later period were Filippo Decio (d. 1535), Giason del Maino (d. 1519), and Claude de Seyssel (d. 1519), who taught at Turin in the 1480s; but there were also distinguished representatives of 'Bartolism' in Germany, France, Spain, and even England who took the Italian master as their model (*nemo jurista nisi Bartolista* was a common proverb even in France) (Pasquier 1621, p. 706). The Bartolists were masters of political thought as well as of legal science and set about literally to 'civil-ise' the world by bringing the activism of the *civis*, the urbanity of the *civitas*, and the regularity of the *jus civile* to the social groupings and political forces that agitated the cities and countryside of Renaissance Europe.

'Civic humanism' has been the subject of much debate and no little exaggeration in recent years, in part because of the tendency to allow humanist rhetoric to drown out, and in some ways to discredit, the more pedestrian work of professional lawyers. Political posturing and propagandising as well as more conspicuous engagement in contemporary issues have overshadowed the contribution of jurists to political and social thought, as indeed Aristotelian political philosophy has tended to overshadow the texts of civil law. Yet as historians used to notice, civilians of the Bartolist persuasion possessed not only technical legal expertise but also the values and aspirations of a new *civilità*, a commitment to the ideals of citizenship, and often a favourable attitude toward republican liberty and even resistance to 'tyranny' – though like humanists, of course, they could as easily be conscripted into the service of despotism. These attitudes were expressed independently of the political 'causes' and the 'Machiavellian moment' often associated with 'civic humanism', and so it seems plausible to distinguish a cast of mind of rather longer intellectual *durée*, which might be called 'civil humanism'.

Between Italian and northern European civil science, however, as between Italian and northern humanism, there were significant differences and even rivalries. Politically, this had to do above all with the authority of 'Roman law', consequently with the position of the emperor; and it was expressed generally as an opposition between 'Citramontanes' and northern 'Ultramontanes', a division which was intensified through the Habsburg–Valois conflict of the sixteenth century. French, Spanish, and German jurists challenged the formula that the emperor was literally 'lord of the world' (*dominus mundi*), as the glosses on the title *Cunctos populos* had it, and took the position that the authority of civil law arose entirely from its rationality or 'rationability' – that, according to a modern formula, it was accepted 'not by reason of empire but by the empire of reason' (*non ratione imperii sed rationis imperio*) (Aubépin 1855, p. 139).

Yet these European *doctores legum* had a common professional commitment, spoke the same technical language, believed in the same exalted goals, and applied the same methods; they constituted, according to one of their eighteenth-century members, a veritable 'republic of jurisconsults' (Gennaro 1733). This 'republic' was at once a licensed profession, an international academic guild, and a secular intelligentsia with overweening intellectual and political ambitions. Its members were the products of, and often taught in, the various university law faculties of Europe (numbering some seventy-five by the sixteenth century). Like their academic rivals in the faculties of theology, philosophy, and medicine, jurists agreed generally on the authoritative texts in which 'doctors of law may not allege error', according to Baldus (Baldus 1535, fo. 4); namely, Justinian's Digest, Institutes, Code, and Novels for 'legists'; Gratian's *Decretum* and the thirteenth- and fourteenth-century decretals for 'canonists'; and both, of course, for those who took their degrees *utriusque*. There was disagreement about the status, or 'authenticity', of feudal law (that is, the *Consuetudines Feudorum*, which Italian 'feudists' accepted as the 'tenth collation' of imperial law following Justinian's Novels because of the presence of certain constitutions by medieval emperors), while Protestant and Anglican jurists rejected canonist tradition as a whole (at least on principle) from the second quarter of the sixteenth century (Laspeyres 1830). But explicitly or implicitly, the form and much of the content of Roman law remained in force, effective in education and legal mentality if not always in law courts, down to the end of the old regime, and indeed long after. In various transformations since the thirteenth century Roman legal science has been a permanent part of the environment of political thought; and in some respects – social and economic dimensions and various ideological and institutional applications – it has had a deeper impact than its chief rival, Aristotelian political science, which has for so long dominated the history of political thinking.

The methodology of 'jurisprudence Italian style' changed little between the time of Bartolus and that of Bodin, although issues multiplied and opinions proliferated through a variety of conventional genres derived from pedagogical as well as practical concerns: elementary summaries, extracted 'questions', legal briefs (*consilia*), and endless monographs based usually on particular titles of the Romano-Byzantine canon, or its canonist or customary counterparts (Kelley 1979a). Essential to teaching and inevitable in legal practice was the accumulation of opinions, pro and contra, whether or not a professional consensus (*communis opinio*) could be attained; and indeed a fundamental dialectic (*duplex interpretatio*) was so inherent in jurisprudence that it seems impossible to tie Roman legal doctrines to any particular political or ideological position – absolutist, constitutional, or revolutionary. Nor did European legists acknowledge any impingement from other disciplines, including theology, which on the contrary, declared Barthélemy de Chasseneuz was actually contained in the law (Chasseneuz 1586, fo. 207). Legal science was even exempt from the rules of grammar and historical truth, as certain defenders of the Donation of Constantine insisted (Maffei 1964, ch. III); and it was not ignorance but professionalism which led jurists to accept certain etymologies which obviously contradicted linguistic possibility (perhaps most famously in the derivation of the fief from faith (*feudum a fide seu fidelitate*) in the *Consuetudines Feudorum* I, 3) (Lehmann 1896). For, as Seyssel put it, the purpose of etymology was to get at the essence (*quidditas*) of a term; and in general the aim of jurisprudence was justice, or equity, before logic or historical truth (Seyssel 1566, p. 11). Much the same can be said about the vast accumulation of conventional legal 'maxims' which grew out of centuries of legal experience.

Civil science purported to be a whole world, then, a complete encyclopaedia of learning which could claim superiority to other fields, including philosophy, medicine, and theology, because of its unique combination of natural and social philosophy. On the one hand it was a true 'science', as generations of jurists proclaimed, because of its universality and its rationality and above all because it offered understanding in terms of cause and effect – referring to 'cause' in a richly moral and legal as well as technical Aristotelian sense (Cortese 1962–4, II, as index). 'To know is to understand through causes', Chasseneuz explained (*scire est per causas cognoscere*); and 'legists and canonists understand through causes' (*legistae et canonistae cognoscunt per causas*) (Chasseneuz 1586, fo. 209). On the other hand jurisprudence displayed characteristics of a liberal art (*studium liberale*, Chasseneuz called it) (fo. 207), and more especially it had to take into account factors of human will and social and cultural circumstances. Jurists were obliged to determine facts as well as to apply principles. As Seyssel summed it up, 'Civil science consists in action, not in speculation' (Seyssel 1566, p. 11). This further illustrates the point that there has been a current of 'civil' as well as 'civic humanism'.

iii Humanism and jurisprudence

The humanist movement in Italy had a profound effect on the study of Roman law, and Justinian's Digest in particular became a major target of philological and historical criticism. To Lorenzo Valla and other 'legal humanists' Roman law was best understood not as the basis of professional jurisprudence but rather as a great monument of classical learning, unfortunately mangled and distorted by its Byzantine editors. 'Wherever the Latin tongue holds sway', Valla wrote in his *Elegantiae Latinae linguae* (II, preface), 'there is the Roman Empire.'[3] Even more than the Greekisms of Tribonian and his colleagues, Valla deplored the barbarisms of medieval jurists such as Bartolus, whose pseudo-philosophical interpretations and impossible etymologies had, he thought, corrupted the 'golden science' of the ancients almost beyond recognition. Valla's aim, and that of such followers as Angelo Poliziano, Ludovico Bolognini, Guillaume Budé, Lelio Torelli, and Antonio Agustín, was to reconstruct the historical meaning of classical texts and so to achieve a closer understanding of the culture of 'antiquity'. From the pristine Roman tradition, Valla banned not only feudal but also canon law, 'of which the greatest part is Gothic', he remarked (1962, p. 80), and of which some is fabricated, as he showed in his devastating exposure of the Donation of Constantine. In these ways Valla hoped to humanise and to liberalise the 'true philosophy' which he, too, took civil law to be.

The impact of humanist philology was apparent not only in the fields of textual exegesis and juridical lexicography but also in an area more obviously significant to political thought, namely, the practice and theory of 'interpretation'.[4] Modernly as well as classically, the dispute was between those (humanists as well as the old glossators) who demanded strict construction of legislative will and those who (with the Bartolists and especially canonists) inclined toward what jurists called 'extension' (*interpretatio extensiva* or *extensio interpretativa*) and which came to be identified with the underlying meaning or reason of law (*mens* or *ratio legum*). 'For reason', as Andrea Alciato wrote in his great commentary *De Verborum significatione*, 'is the soul and life of a particular law' (Alciato 1565, p. 20). At stake in this controversy was not only a concept of hermeneutics – the letter versus the spirit of a law – but also control over the political and

3. Valla 1962, p. 196; Duker 1711; and see Kelley 1970a.
4. Maffei 1956 and Troje 1971; see also Kisch 1972 and 1969, and Kelley 1987.

social meaning and application of laws. What was reflected in the great stream of *extensio* literature generated especially from the late fifteenth century was an early phase of the interminable struggle between legislative and judicial authority. In this debate the inclination of humanism was in general toward the authoritarian position.

More specifically in Valla's polemic we can see the making of an even more publicised controversy in early modern European jurisprudence, that between the 'Italian' and 'French' methods (*mores italicus* and *gallicus*) as they were later called, in fact a particular skirmish within the larger war between scholasticism and humanism, which was also reflected in the work of Valla. The popular view of this controversy is illustrated by a little dialogue by Claudio Tolomei, *De Corruptis verbis iuris civilis dialogus* (1517), which introduced Poliziano as spokesman for the innovating 'grammarians' and Giason del Maino for the professional Bartolists, who actually endorsed such neologisms as *guerra* (for *bellum*) and so, more generally, modern departures from ancient ideas and institutions (Tolomei 1517, sig. Aiii). The case for legal humanism was elaborated by a long series of manifestos in the sixteenth century, especially by the French disciples of Alciato, and attacked by a smaller number of tracts defending old-fashioned Bartolism, perhaps most notably by Alberico Gentili's *De Iuris interpretibus dialogi sex* (1582), which denounced the pedantry and the amateurism of the philologists and historians poaching on the territories of the legal profession.[5] Like Seyssel, Gentili was convinced that law was a practical civil science not a scholarly pastime, a systematic discipline to be placed in the service of particular 'causes' not a form of literature.

This was the position taken by most jurists, even Alciato, though he boasted of having been the first in a thousand years to teach law 'in the Latin manner'. Alciato denounced the ignorance of the glossators (*Accursiani*), but he had little more use for the irrelevant 'folly' (consciously using the term of his friend Erasmus) of grammarians, especially of their 'emperor' Valla; and he celebrated the work of Bartolus and such later professional interpreters as his own teacher Giason, 'without whom . . . we should have no science'.[6] Neither grammar nor rhetoric nor even philosophy had authority over this science since justice always had priority over the aims of these other disciplines. In general the search for the true 'method for studying law' could be satisfied by neither the Italian nor the French extremes; rather it had to combine the best of both and to pursue in a

5. Gentili 1582; and see Astuti 1937 and Panizza 1981.
6. Alciato 1617, col. 1, and cf. cols. 188, 377; and see Viard 1926.

systematic way the ultimate goal of making civil science into 'true philosophy'.

In the early sixteenth century this enterprise was taken up in a most innovative fashion by a great 'triumvirate' of legal scholars, including Budé, Ulrich Zasius, and Alciato. All three deplored Accursianism (*Accursianitas*), devoted themselves to textual emendation of the text of the Digest, supported the idea that civil law was a member of the humanities (*studia humanitatis*), and at the same time tried to reveal the philosophical riches of civil law, termed 'civil wisdom' (*civilis sapientia*) by Budé.[7] In particular they associated Ulpian's famous definition of jurisprudence (as *ars boni et aequi*) with the 'equity' (*epieikeia*) of Aristotelian philosophy, which 'emended' the legalistic rigour implied by the formula, 'the most general law is the most injurious' (*summum ius, summa iniuria*). On the whole and in their own ways these men also accepted the notion of princely absolutism established by Justinian, though they, of course, had a historical interest in earlier institutions and sources of law; and they were intensely aware of the differences between antiquity and the vastly changed traditions of 'today' (*hodie*, in the conventional formula). Yet these traditions, if divergent, were nonetheless derivative of ancient customs; and so, for example, all three scholars seemed to agree, for similar ideological purposes, that feudal customs had a basically Roman provenance (Kelley 1964).

Inevitably, there were political differences between Budé, Zasius, and Alciato, arising especially from the old conflict between Ultramontanes and Citramontanes. Alciato and Zasius perforce supported the imperialist party and the Romano-Germanic idea of 'translation of empire', which was to say the theoretically universal hegemony of Charles V, while Budé reached back to Gallican doctrines. 'The point', as Alciato stated the fundamental issue, 'is to determine whether the king of France recognises the emperor as superior', and his answer was taken from the most authoritative of all jurists. 'Bartolus says yes (*quod sic*) . . .', he continued, 'for the emperor is lord of the whole world' (*dominus totius orbis*, according to the famous gloss on *Cunctos Populos*).[8] Zasius took much the same position and declared also in favour of the emperor's absolute power (*legibus solutus*), though he added that the emperor could neither break

---

7. Budé 1535, fo. 3, on Digest I, 1, 1: critical edition in Kisch 1960, studying the legal concept of equity (*epieikeia*). Cf. Baron 1562, II, (letter to Marguerite of Navarre, 154): 'divina illa iuris sapientia'.
8. Alciato 1617, I col. 9, on Digest I, 1, 1. See also Mochi Onory 1951, pp. 96ff; Post 1964, pp. 413ff; Gilmore 1941; Goez 1958.

contracts nor override judicial decisions on this ground, especially not since the 'reception' of Roman law in 1495. Zasius had no quarrel with the complementary authority of canon law, but he would hardly go as far in his opinions as Alciato, who defended the Donation of Constantine on grounds of prescriptive legitimation (Zasius 1550, pp. 241, 347). Yet both worked within the conventions of Roman universalism and Roman imperialism which were increasingly offensive to the new forces of what has been called 'juridical nationalism'.

iv The French school

No French jurist could agree with these Romanist formulations, especially during the Habsburg–Valois conflicts of the sixteenth century. Budé's strategy generally was to appropriate for the French ruler those political and institutional principles most useful for national monarchy. The result was to lead him to a series of essays in comparative law, which offered critical analogies between *roy* and *princeps, regalia* and *imperium, parlement* and senate, chancellor and praetor and other offices, customs, and archival records. Other French jurists, who took a more professional and less historical line, appealed to contrary formulas, derived characteristically from canon law, that in fact the emperor had never been 'lord of the world' (*imperator nunquam dominus mundi*) and that the French king was himself 'emperor in his kingdom' (*rex imperator in regno suo*), and, according to the canonist companion text, 'recognised no superior in temporal things' (*non recognoscat superiorem in temporalibus*) (Schramm 1960; Kantorowicz 1957, ch. vii). One classic formulation was that of Chasseneuz, whose *Catalogus gloriae mundi* (1529) invoked Giovanni Pico della Mirandola's *Oration on the Dignity of Man* to establish proper rankings, political as well as natural, including the preeminence of Francis I and his predecessors over all the rulers of Europe (Chasseneuz 1586, fos. 138ff).

French royalism was celebrated more insistently by practising lawyers with official commissions, such as Jean Ferrault and Charles de Grassaille, though they likewise exploited Roman as well as indigenous sources. With Chasseneuz and others they carried on the task of collecting, proving, and giving political shape to the 'regalian rights' (*regalia*) of the French crown (Ferrault 1542; Grassaille 1545). Among these 'marks of sovereignty', as they were in the course of becoming, were principles of exclusive legislation (*solus rex facit constitutiones seu leges in regno Franciae*), independence from foreign law (feudal as well as civil and canon), expressed especially in the formula that the French king 'recognises no one in temporal things' and is 'above all other kings' (*super omnes reges*), the title 'most Christian',, the power to work miracles, the exclusion of women from royal succession (the so-called *Lex Salica*), and a variety of particular secular and ecclesiastical privileges. Of these royal prerogatives Ferrault listed twenty, Grassaille forty, Chasseneuz fifty-six, and through legal investigation and argumentation they continued to multiply (Franklin 1973; Fell 1983–7). In a sense they represent the particulars of that principle of sovereignty (*majestas*) which Bodin would provide with philosophic form. In their way, legal history and antiquarianism accumulated juridical and ideological arsenals for the defence of government and other institutions and interested parties, including the legal profession itself.

The great centre of the 'French method' (*mos gallicus*, as distinguished from the old-fashioned *mos italicus*) was the University of Bourges, where the intellectual progeny of Alciato (*Alciatei* is the term applied in later legend) emerged in the 1540s to establish their law faculty as perhaps the most distinguished in Europe (Kelley 1981b; Piano Mortari 1978). The two leading figures were Eguinaire Baron and François Le Douaren, whose respective followings in the second half of the sixteenth century developed into academic factions and then confessional 'parties' (the latter inclining toward evangelical religion). Among the disciples of Baron were François Baudouin and, indirectly, Jacques Cujas; on the side of Le Douaren the most prominent were François Hotman and Hugues Doneau. With François Connan and Jean de Coras, these were the leading figures in the French school, whose first aim was the restoration of Roman law in terms of form as well as substance. Their work, together with that of such like-minded scholars as Agustín and Torelli, formed the basis of the 'new jurisprudence' of that 'golden age', in which law itself became the basis of an encyclopaedic cultural ideal. 'The civilised man is the jurisconsult' (*Homo politicus, id est jurisconsultus*), as Baudouin put it (Baudouin 1559, p. 20).

In the massive work of this school several parallel or intersecting trends may be seen, beginning with one area of enquiry inherent in 'civil science' from the start, namely, comparative law and politics. This was inevitable because of the necessity of adapting ancient law to modern conditions, the need to reconcile civil with canon law, and the acceptance of feudal law into the Roman canon; but it was given special urgency in France because of the status of Roman law as 'common law', and because of the political threat posed by any official 'reception' of what was regarded as the 'emperor's law'. Like Budé French jurists in general proceeded to reject or to plunder Roman law sources as it suited royal or national needs, but in any case it was essential to include them in legal education even if they might be treated invidiously. A good example is the work of Baron, whose teaching from the mid-1520s led him to publish a series of 'bipartite commentaries' on the Institutes and Digest of Justinian, taking up various French counterparts to the standard categories of Roman law, including questions of sovereignty, legislation, justice, and indeed the whole range of institutions making up what Seyssel had celebrated as the 'grand monarchy of France'.[9] 'To the Roman *princeps* we oppose the French *rex*', Baron wrote sententiously, 'for in establishing and promulgating law he follows reason more closely than the emperor' – recalling the formula that civil law was accepted 'not by reason of empire but by the empire of reason' (Baron 1550, p. 5). In the spirit of what has been called 'juridical nationalism' Baron went on to glorify the liberal and constitutional traditions of French government and society.

The 'French method', too, was carried over into vernacular jurisprudence – not only in the editing of medieval texts but also in the Romanising, or at least 'civilising', of native legal traditions. A striking case is the work of Louis Le Caron (Charondas), graduate of Bourges and pioneer of 'vernacular humanism' in France. In his *Pandectes ou Digestes du droit françois* (1587) Le Caron set out to fulfil the ideal of the profession of law to embody 'true philosophy', which he also called 'la Philosophie chrestienne' and linked to the political philosophy of Plato.[10] Le Caron rehearsed the old formulas that the French king was 'emperor in his kingdom' and even 'the image of God'. Yet in opposition to royalists like Bodin, Le Caron identified the true 'mark of sovereignty' not with the legislative power but, following Plato, with justice itself – which in practice meant the judiciary. During the civil wars Le Caron even endorsed the inflammatory notion of 'mixed monarchy' (equivalent to lèse-majesté some argued), pointing out the corrective force of custom (*usus legum corrector*) and recalling the originally elective character of the French monarchy. Legal judgement rather than political power represented for Le Caron the cornerstone of that magisterial discipline which he did not hesitate to call 'la Science politique'.

---

9. Baron 1562, I, p. 38. on Digest I, I, I; and see Moreau-Reibel 1933. Cf. Seyssel 1961; 1981.
10. Le Caron 1587, p. 3; 1637, p. 34; and see Kelley 1976a.

v Rivals to Romanism

Civil science was a fundamentally comparatist discipline. The study of law was European-wide and tied not only to modern civil science but also to emergent native traditions and their attendant problems, such as those of 'territoriality' and the 'conflict of laws'. Feudists of all countries made Latin commentaries on vernacular texts, customs as well as statutes, and so did studies of comparative law at least implicitly, whether invidiously or approvingly. The Spanish 'national school' tried to establish a 'concordance' of Hispanic and Roman law, largely to the advantage of the former. In Germany several authors assembled a treatise designed to show 'the difference between civil and Saxon law', and others carried on antiquarian research into the Germanic past in order to deepen such studies. English civilians preserved a tenuous tradition through the 'Doctors' Commons' and tried to preserve the respectability of Roman law.[11] In the early seventeenth century William Fulbeke drew a 'parallel or conference of the civil law, the canon law, and the common law of this realm of England', for example, while John Cowell compiled an *Institutes of the Lawes of England* in the effort to join English substance with Roman forms.[12] One of their colleagues went so far as to call civil law the 'mother' of common law, although the most judicious conclusion was probably that of Sir Henry Spelman, who thought 'the Foundations of our Law to be laid by our German ancestors, but built upon and polished by materials taken from the Canon Law and the Civil Law, (Spelman 1733, p. 100).

In France vernacular jurists like Etienne Pasquier and his colleague Antoine Loisel followed much the same moderate line as Baron and Spelman. Pasquier composed an *Interpretation de Institutes de Justinian*, which began as a translation but which ended up as an extensive discussion of French counterparts to conventional Roman institutions, commending French law for its rejection of absolutism in public law and of rigidity in private law. The authoritarian formula *Quod principi placuit* 'need not be taken cruelly', he wrote, and the notorious 'paternal power' (*patria potestas*) 'has no place among us' (Pasquier 1847, p. 26). More ingenious and original was Loisel's *Institutes coutumiers*, which sought the spirit of French law in proverbs and popular literature as well as in provincial customs. The

11. See Kagan 1981; Garcia Gallo 1956; Van Kleffens 1968; Wieacker 1967; Levack 1973.
12. Fulbeke 1618; Cowell 1651, opposing Coke's more famous work of the same title. See Kelley 1974 and Thorne 1976.

message was much the same: Loisel did not deny royal authority – 'Qui veut le Roy', he quoted, 'si veut la loy' – but stressed its popular roots and limitations and repeated that 'Droit de puissance paternelle n'a lieu'.[13] Though a seeker and celebrator of custom, Loisel was no populist, and it might be better to see him as a professional chauvinist. He also published a sort of hagiography of French legists, which he named in honour of his old friend (*Pasquier, ou Dialogue des avocats*) and in general agreed with him in emphasising, contrary to Roman convention, the value of judicial authority as a necessary supplement to princely power.

The comparative approach was reinforced among French jurists both by the movement for a 'reformation of customs', led by the first president of the *parlement*, Christofle de Thou, and by the growing debates over the cultural and political provenance of the French nation – Roman, Germanic, or even (as Connan suggested) Celtic (Filhol 1937)? The 'Germanist' persuasion was represented most effectively by that 'prince of legists' Charles Du Moulin, who began by rejecting the consensus view about the Roman origins of feudalism. His own programme included the defence of the 'ancient liberties' of the Gallican church and especially the unification of French customs under a national monarchy purged of Romanism, both papal and imperial (Thireau 1980). His protégé Hotman pushed Germanist arguments to a further extreme. In his *Antitribonian* (1567, published 1603) he offered a systematic critique of the evils of Romanism introduced by the universities in terms of persons, things, and actions; and for purposes of a 'reformation' concluded that 'the laws of a country should be accommodated to the state and not the state to the laws' (Hotman 1603, p. 6). In the wake of this 'anti-Tribonianist' manifesto Hotman offered, in his famous *Francogallia* (1573) a historical survey of the Celto-Germanic traditions of the French monarchy, emphasising its liberal, consensual, and even elective character, in contrast to the 'tyranny' of Romanism. This sort of anti-Romanism was reflected also in the work of English common lawyers, from Sir John Fortescue to Sir Edward Coke (both chief justices of the king's bench), and for much the same reasons. From the time of Henry VIII, as an eighteenth-century historian, John Ayliffe, wrote, 'the books of Civil and Canon law were set a-side to be devoured of Worms, as savouring too much of Popery', while in the next century civil law was inevitably associated with the 'prerogative' and growing despotism of the Stuart kings (Ayliffe 1714, p. 188).

---

13. Loisel 1935, pp. 19, 23; and see Reulos 1935.

Perhaps the major source of criticism of written 'law' in general was the Protestant Reformation as understood by Martin Luther, who set out to evaluate the whole tradition of the church formulated by the canonists. What he ended up doing, was, in the spirit of Pauline doctrine, to reject the Romanist (and in effect crypto-Judaic) law entirely; and indeed his symbolic burning of the Corpus Juris Canonici (provoked in part by his discovery of Valla's declamation against the Donation of Constantine) was one of the emblematic gestures of the age, and well publicised in his subsequent pamphlet, *Why the Books of the Pope and his Disciples were Burned* (1520).[14] Much of the ecclesiastical polemic of the next two generations continued the canonist debate started by Luther and taken up by Calvin and other evangelical reformers. Problems of church and state, of divine and human law, and of various political doctrines such as conciliarism and Gallicanism, were discussed in the context of canon law. (It is curious that this field, so productively cultivated by medievalists, has been relatively neglected by students of modern history and political thought. For many ordinary folk as well as jurists the virtues and vices of Romanism were manifested more directly in the canonist tradition than in the more academic doctrines of the laws of Justinian.)

In this connection it should be noted, too, that Protestant ideas of resistance owed much to the secularising of notions of Christian 'liberty of conscience' preached by Luther and by the associated insistence of being freed from the 'law' (Skinner 1978; Kelley 1981a, ch. 5). This is another case of creative, or at least transformative, interpretation. It was in any case Protestant lawyers, beginning with the defenders of the Schmalkaldic League and defiant towns like Strasburg and Magdeburg and including Huguenot publicists like Hotman and Doneau, who took over from theologians the leadership of protest, shifting the arguments for resistance from biblical to constitutional and political grounds, with the help of various concepts of feudal and civic 'liberties' and the private notion of 'resisting force with force' (*vim vi repellere licet*). It was an often inarticulate commonplace of the legal tradition that the private sphere in general – the sphere of popular custom – was excluded from interference by public authority, to the extent indeed that the 'reformation of customs' could be effected only through consent of all three estates.

---

14. Luther 1957. For Melanchthon's much more favourable view of 'law' see Kisch 1967.

vi   Custom and the law of nations

In the broadest view and religious questions aside, the poles of early modern jurisprudence were 'written law' (that is, the Justinianian canon) and unwritten 'custom'. Historically the two were linked, as recognised in the old juridical formula deriving law from fact (*lex ex facto oritur*), but there was always a fundamental rivalry between the two (Zasius 1550, III, col. 16). Since the twelfth century *consuetudo* could have written form, but in any case it was always a major source of 'interpretation' – being indeed, according to the Digest (I, 3, 37), 'the best interpreter of written law.'[15] Such was in particular the view of many continental feudists and virtually all English common lawyers. The force of custom was always popular rather than princely, or at least feudal rather than royal, social rather than political; and despite its irrational or prerational implications (being dependent on social or judicial memory) it commanded respect even at the height of enthusiasm for rationalist methods. Of the Parisian *coutume* Claude de Ferrière wrote in his seventeenth-century commentary, 'It unites the law, interprets it, and sometimes corrects it' (a vernacularist paraphrase of the old civilian gloss) (Ferrière 1679, p. 1). English common law, of course, was interpreted entirely as a species of custom – and finally, in the age of constitutional conflict, as 'immemorial custom'. Often overlooked, the rich tradition of late medieval and early modern customary jurisprudence was an important source of political and social thinking and especially, in its peculiarly empirical way, for the search for the 'spirit of the laws'.

Custom represented the most basic aspect of positive jurisprudence, which came to include a variety of legal opinions expressed in law reports, legal briefs (*consilia*), and monographic publications, as well as commentary on and interpretation of legislation. Like custom, judicial opinion in particular continued in some ways to be conceptualised according to Roman convention, which is to say the old civilian (and canonist) rubric of 'matters judged' (*de rebus judicatis*). One of the best examples is the treatise on this topic published by Pasquier's friend Pierre Ayrault, for whom the true source of law was not the will of the legislator but the concrete wisdom of the magistrate (Ayrault 1677, 1576). Whence his interest in legal procedure and the history of procedure, and especially the relativity and mutability of the circumstances which judges had to take into account. Like

---

15. See Puchta 1828–37, Brie 1898, and Lebrun 1932, as well as Calasso 1954.

his colleague Montaigne, Ayrault was both impressed and depressed by the variability of customs and the instability of laws; but his remedy was not withdrawal into self-preoccupation – a sceptical stance adopted by Montaigne but rejected by more activist colleagues, such as Le Caron (Le Caron 1555) – but rather it was to develop a more sophisticated and socially useful science of law. It was above all the task of the judge, especially in the midst of political chaos (Ayrault was writing at the height of the civil wars), to keep in mind that the ultimate goal was not private fulfilment or even abstract justice but always 'public utility', another time-honoured Roman concept.

Through positive as well as abstract jurisprudence, then, Roman law had come to permeate European social and political thought, whether officially 'received' or not. Civil law in its modern forms (the *usus modernus Pandectarum* in the phrase of Samuel Stryk) was practised internationally and produced another intellectual polarity, which was a specifically juridical version of the famous 'quarrel of ancients and moderns'.[16] This battle of books, with the humanists representing the 'ancients' and conventional professionals the 'moderns', had its champions in all countries: in Italy the ancients were defended by Alciato and the moderns by Gentili (for example); in Germany there were Gregor Haloander and Benedikt Carpzov; in Spain Agustín and Diego de Covarruvias; in England Sir Thomas Smith and (again) Gentili; and above all in France the two heroic figures, Cujas and Du Moulin (Schulz 1953, ch. 4). 'What has this to do with the Pretorian edict?' was the question Cujas was supposed to have asked about legal matters; 'What has the Pretorian edict to do with us?' is the question Du Moulin and his colleagues might have put. The war has never really ended, though in general the 'moderns' succeeded in occupying, or at least leaving their mark on, large parts of the European legal tradition.

The general framework for the interpretation of positive law in its various national forms was, once again, of ancient Roman devising, though vastly expanded since antiquity. The 'laws of nations' (*jus gentium*), produced by military and then commercial contacts between Rome and 'barbarian' peoples, consisted both of a law common to all *gentes* and, as Baron repeated from medieval jurists, a particular law (*jus proprium*) for each nation.[17] It is too often forgotten that much political and legal argumentation in the Renaissance was carried out within the confines not

16. Wieacker 1967, p. 204; Stintzing and Landsberg 1880–1910; and Sollner 1975.
17. Baron 1562, I, p. 29; and see Cortese 1962–4, I, pp. 55ff, and Wagner 1978.

of the *jus civile* but of the *jus gentium*. Not only 'actions' but also 'peoples' and 'tyrants' belonged to the law of nations according to often repeated formulas (*actiones, populi, tyranni sunt de jure gentium*). This was the true basis of the right to self-government enjoyed by every state. Aside from its relationship to modern 'international law', in other words, the *jus gentium* (or *jus novissimum gentium*) represented the expanding and extra-European horizons of modern political and social thought. Most portentously, the *jus gentium* represented the legal face of that 'universal history' in which Bodin found the basis both for his juridico-historical 'method' (*Methodus ad facilem historiarum cognitionem*, 1566) and for his massive treatise on comparative public law (*Les Six Livres de la République*, 1576). 'In universal history', Bodin declared, 'one finds the better part of law' (*In historia iuris universi pars optima latet*) (Bodin 1951, p. 108). In this way he opened further that 'world of nations' (in Giambattista Vico's famous phrase) which would be explored by historians and social and political philosophers. For Vico, indeed, drawing here especially upon Grotius, the 'natural law of nations' (*diretto naturale delle genti*), derived from the right to self-defence, was one facet of his 'new science'.[18]

vii   Rational jurisprudence

One of the major preoccupations of the later sixteenth century was the massive, interdisciplinary search for a proper 'method' of learning, whether pedagogical or scientific. This quest was carried on in philosophy, theology, and history, but nowhere more intensively or more controversially than in continental jurisprudence of the sixteenth and seventeenth centuries.[19] As in other fields, some jurists inclined toward the old Aristotelian dialectic and others toward the new rhetorical approach usually associated with Peter Ramus. The first is illustrated by Matteo Gribaldi's treatise of 1541 on the 'method and reason' of legal study, which utilised Aristotle's transcendentals and predicaments and especially his system of four causes; the second by discussions of legal dialectic and rhetoric by humanists like Claude de Chansonnette (Cantiuncula) and Christoph Hegendorf, who preferred the innovative approach to logic of Agricola, later to be developed by Ramus and Johann Frey, whose conception of the 'perfect jurist' was based directly on bifurcation in the

18. Vico 1911–41, II.1, pp. 126–7 (*Diritto universale*, ch. 136), IV.1, p. 26 (*Scienze nuova*, no. 31); and see Fassò 1971.
19. Gilbert 1960; Ebrard 1948; Carpintero 1977; and Vasoli 1977.

style of Ramus.[20] But despite this formalism most jurists tended to arrange the material of law according to its own structure and 'topics', its own conventional modes of arguing from reason and authority, yet with attention to facts as well as principle and sometimes the flexible concept of 'equity' as well. This was the sort of theoretical literature that 'extended' the idea of legal interpretation from its original suspect status (Justinian's ban) to its position as a fundamental 'part of law', as Pietro Gammaro argued in his *De Extensionibus* of 1520.[21] This enhanced 'interpretation' implied a wider view of judicial discretion, hence a more intense rivalry with legislative authority, and it also contributed to the mainstream of modern philosophical hermeneutics.

One of the most comprehensive discussions of legal 'method' came in the work of Coras, who also had visions of legal system and who emphasised the centrality of the notion of causation to the 'science' of law (Coras 1560, 1568). In Aristotelian terms this meant that the 'people' (*populus*) itself was the efficient cause, the particular business or social actions the material cause, the general law relevant to the case the formal cause, and the common good the final cause: *Salus populi suprema lex*, he quoted, though of course placing the whole process under the purview and control of the legislative sovereign. For Coras legal coherence and monarchical authority were two sides of the social coin of the realm. This conviction also appears in his defence of paternal power (*la puissance paternelle*), which seemed to him perhaps more fundamental than royal or even divine authority to the extent that it is in the family that a sense of order is first instilled and obedience learned, if ever (Coras 1572). With a more practical and perhaps solider learning in the law Coras supplemented the 'absolutist' views given currency by the better known work of his colleague Bodin.

Perhaps the central impulse of modern professional jurisprudence, at least on the continent, was the search for a general system, which was often a way of subordinating law to politics. The pioneers of what Savigny would call 'systematic' jurisprudence were Le Douaren, Connan, and especially Doneau, who carried the message into Germany; and of course it later came to include such self-conscious 'jusnaturalists' as Jean Domat and Samuel Pufendorf (Voeltzel 1936; Todescan 1980). The discussions of these jurists began with the conventional rubrics of civil law but departed from

---

20. Gribaldi 1541; Cantiuncula 1545; Hegendorf 1537; Hotman 1560; and Fregius 1581, among many others: the best collection is Reusner 1588. See also Kisch 1970; Kalinowski 1982; Troje 1969; and Coing 1973–7, II, pp. 724–54.
21. Gammaro 1584, fo. 248; and see Piano Mortari 1956, and Conring 1666, pp. 149ff.

them in the name of 'interpretation' and 'extension' and reordered them in the cause of the 'reason' or 'spirit' of the laws (*ratio, mens legum*), which had to be extracted from texts formerly depending on 'authority' even more than 'reason'. Their concern was with the definition of law in general, its divisions, distinctions, and 'distribution', and with such concepts as equity, custom, justice, sovereignty, and 'public utility' as well as with the ancient hope of 'reducing law to an art' (*de jure in artem redigendo*, in the Ciceronian phrase). In fact Roman law had often been referred to rhetorically as 'written reason' (*ratio scripta*); and what these systematists were doing was to attempt to realise the ancient claims of jurisprudence to be 'true philosophy' (*vera philosophia*), though their success had to wait for two centuries and a revolution before the Romanoid legislative creation of Napoleon (Arnaud 1969). It should be added that feudal custom, too, was the object of such attempts at rationalisation, as in Antoine Le Conte's *Methodus de feudis* of 1599 and in Paul Challine's *Méthode générale pour l'intelligence des coutumes de France* of 1666, representative of a vast (and vastly neglected) literature.[22]

Other products of the impulse to philosophical or legislative system included the 'republics' envisioned by Bodin, Pierre Grégoire de Toulouse, and Henning Arnisaeus, for whom public law assumes a dominant position over the legal and social concerns of jurisprudence.[23] Bodin's work far transcended the limits of jurisprudence, of course; that of Grégoire likewise has high philosophic aspirations but kept closer to legal forms. To Grégoire the 'republic' suggested not only an ideal society but a total cultural cosmos, and as an organising principle he preserved Justinian's (and Gaius') tripartite division of persons, things, and actions as the basis for a syncretistic effort to arrange and to explain all human, natural, and divine law. The 'republic', he declared, 'is a community of one society of things and life, which makes up a single civil body composed of many different parts, so that its members, under a single supreme power and under one head and spirit intended for the benefits and comforts of this mortal life, may more easily achieve eternal life'.[24] In this connection Grégoire explicitly attacked the counsels of that 'most pernicious man Machiavelli,' whose rejection of conventional religion and morality – and more especially of law! – made him a devil figure for French jurists, not only Protestants like Innocent Gentillet but orthodox Catholics like Grégoire

22. Le Conte 1599; and see Theuerkauf 1968, on the medieval background.
23. Arnisaeus 1615; and see also Hoke 1976, and Gross 1973. On Bodin, Denzer 1973.
24. Grégoire 1609, also 1580 and 1591; and see Collot 1965 and Gambino 1975.

(Kelley 1970b). On the other hand, Grégoire, in his eclectic and anthropocentric synthesis, was pleased to make use of the 'Francogallic' interpretations of Hotman as well as the absolutist theorising of Bodin, whose political and religious positions had been poles apart.

All of these topics of discussion – legal humanism, comparative law, the conflict of methods, the law of nations, and the search for system – converge on the main theme of early modern legal and political thought. Natural law (*jus naturale*) had been variously identified with divine law, 'right reason', the law of nations, and even custom, which was at least a 'second nature' (*altera natura*). From Bartolus to Grotius it was also conventional to distinguish a 'primary' from a 'secondary law of nature', the first being in accord with natural reason, as Baron wrote, and the second reflected in the collective behaviour of peoples (Baron 1562, I, p. 29). Among the early founders of modern (Gierke calls it 'antique-modern') natural law were Johann Oldendorp, Bodin, and the Spanish theologian-jurists, including Francisco de Vitoria and Francisco Suárez, creators of the so-called 'second scholasticism'; but of course the major figures were Hugo Grotius, Johannes Althusius, Pufendorf, and other seventeenth-century theorists who appealed increasingly to pure reason and made analogies with the 'new' natural philosophy which 'cast all in doubt' but which also promised a straighter path to certainty.[25] From the rhetorically inspired Ramus' 'method' of sixteenth-century jurists, the success of pure reason seems complete with Leibniz' *Nova methodus discendae docendaequae jurisprudentiae* of 1667; and of course such rationalism also came to inform political thinking.[26] 'In opposition to positive jurisprudence . . .', as Gierke put it, 'the natural-law theory of the state was Radical to the very core of its being'; and it figured centrally in the great intellectual war of the age of Descartes, Hobbes, and Leibniz, which Ernst Troeltsch described as the first struggle between 'naturalism' and 'historicism'.[27]

This dichotomy is certainly reflected in much of the legal theory of that age of naturalist system-building. Ultimately, it derives from the ancient distinction between nature and custom – which in legal terms is to say, according to Aristotle, between law that was natural (*physikon*) and law that was arbitrary (*nomikon*). The contrast is drawn perhaps most sharply by Hobbes' *Dialogue between a Philosopher and a Student of the Common Laws of England* (1661), which raised the humble men of reason (*mathematici*)

25. See Macke 1966, Wolf 1963; also Grossi 1972, I; and in general Scupin *et al.* 1973.
26. Leibniz 1667; and see Sturm 1968, Schneider 1967, Dickerhof 1941; also Kelley 1988.
27. Gierke 1950, pp. 35–6; cf. Troeltsch 1922.

above the arbitrary and authoritarian men who invoked custom or even consent (*dogmatici*) and who, like Descartes, preferred a Euclidean to a Justinianian model of learning (Hobbes 1971, p. 53). It is a striking and unusually neglected fact that many of the most distinguished jusnaturalists – including Domat and Leibniz as well as Grotius and Pufendorf (if not Hobbes) – followed the spirit and often the letter of Roman forms, substance, and terminology (including the Gaian tradition of persons, things, and action), and that they depended profoundly on the scholarship of 'recent' jurisprudence (*hodierna* is Leibniz' term), including most of the names discussed here. Yet it remains true that the central thrust was to shift attention from the authoritarian source of law to its fundamental but metahistorical rationale – in this way to transform the meaning of the old civilian formula, 'spirit of the law' (*mens legum; esprit den lois*), from original intention to philosophical justification. 'Whether natural or arbitrary', as Domat declared in *Les Loix civiles dans leur ordre naturel* (1702), 'all rules base their usage on the universal justification which is in their spirit' (Domat 1702, I, p. 6). In the next century this quest for 'the spirit of the laws' would be carried on even more profoundly by Montesquieu and Vico.

viii   The new legal heritage

The impact of Romanist, Romanoid, or rational jurisprudence on public law was overwhelming. In the areas of private law it was hardly less extensive but much harder to trace and to assess, since it was conventionally resorted to as a standard of custom or, as Hermann Conring wrote, 'measure of positive law'.[28] In many ways it reshaped the materials gathered under the three conventional rubrics of civil law. The law of persons was extended increasingly by notions of citizenship, civil 'liberty', and resistance; and it was expanded as well by commercial forces – the legal aspect of that 'individualism' which is usually described in other material or cultural contexts. The law of things was extended through Roman concepts of prescription, giving definition to vague 'custom'; possession, which came to supplement 'seizin'; and especially property, which helped to transform feudal lordship (*dominium*) into 'private' ownership (*dominium directum* as distinguished from *dominium utile*) and which was reinforced through criminal law (Meynial 1908; Choppin 1662). Legal 'actions' were elaborated in connection with commercial law in particular, which shifted

---

28. On Conring see Wolf 1963, pp. 220–52.

emphasis from quasi-moral questions of usury to technical questions of economic exchange and 'interest', and which helped to raise the idea of 'contract' to a more general, a social and political, level of discussion. But these problems go far beyond, or below, the history of political thought as commonly understood and in any case still await adequate historical investigation. By way of conclusion suffice it to suggest a few of the major themes and transformations in the tradition of European law between the Renaissance and the threshold of the Enlightenment.

1   The expansion of the legal profession. Established as a lay intelligentsia from the thirteenth century, jurists (*legistae, canonistae, feudistae*, and other professional specialities) not only formed national guilds and a university monopoly but also became an integral part of government and a new office-holding nobility. The education of this professional elite thus became an important part and extension of higher learning in general and in many ways an important substratum of social and political thought, furnishing terms, materials, and forms of conceptualisation for the understanding of modern European society.

2   The debates over 'method'. From Baron and Le Douaren to Leibniz, and beyond, jurists (paralleling philosophical methodologists from Ramus to Descartes, and beyond) enquired first into the pedagogical organisation of legal study and then into the practical application and theoretical formulation of human law. Because of the overlapping of questions of fact, value, reason, and public interest, these debates touched also on the methodology of emergent political and social as well as legal 'science', especially with the attempt to accommodate geographical, cultural, and historical factors both in judgements and in the theory of law.

3   Legal hermeneutics. From being a questionable and indeed illegal practice, legal 'interpretation' became a major genre in which questions of sources, authenticity, authorial 'intention', and rational and contextual 'meaning' were discussed with great sensitivity and ingenuity – thus marking the convergence of the legal theory of interpretation with the older philological, philosophical, and theological varieties. It marked, too, a new phase in the endless conflict between (interpretive) judicial and (declarative) legislative interests (Kelley 1983).

4   Legal antiquities. From the fifteenth century serious enquiries were undertaken in legal and institutional history, medieval as well as ancient; and before the advent of anti-historical natural law theories such historical materials and interpretations were fundamental in the treatment of legal and especially political issues. Arguments from history – authority,

precedent, the 'ancient constitution', and even 'immemorial custom' – drew strength from legal antiquarianism (Pocock 1957, 1987).

5   Divergent national traditions. However closely or remotely connected with civil and canon law, all of the indigenous national traditions drew upon and compared themselves with the Roman model and, what is more, frequently returned to it, whether through the judgements and interpretations of learned men or through a more official 'reception', a modern adaptation of Roman law (the *usus modernus Pandectarum*), or even construction of a Romanoid code.

6   The law of nations. Vastly expanded as a Romanist law common to the *gentes* and peoples undreamt of by the ancients, the *jus gentium* became also, in the work of jurists like Vitoria and Grotius, the basis for a *jus inter gentes*, which produced the first stage of modern 'international law', as well as the basis for Vico's system of 'universal law', the first form of his 'new science' (cf. n. 18 above).

7   Legal systematics. The impulse to system, evident already in Gaius and the editors of Justinian, was implied in the dialectical method employed by Bartolists and, in somewhat different ways, by Ramist and Ramoid methodisers of the sixteenth and seventeenth century; but it was most fully realised by the French system-builders from Doneau and Connan to Domat. Originally pedagogical or philosophical in inspiration (in order to reform or to improve upon the Institutes of Justinian), this impulse was also significant for the great efforts of codification beginning in the eighteenth century.[29]

8   Natural law. The attempt to define the *jus naturale* (or *jus naturale gentium*) was a rationalist offshoot of legal systematics, but the seventeenth-century aim was deliberately to depart from Roman convention, as exemplified by Domat's classic treatise devoted to arranging 'civil laws according to their natural order', analogous to seventeenth-century mathematical and metaphysical systems but also in keeping with earlier juridical invocations of 'geometrical' forms by Le Douaren, Coras, and others.

9   The idea of sovereignty. Based literally on ancient Roman 'majesty' (according to Bodin), this dominating conception drew also on the attributes of 'empire' and on a vast accumulation of modern regalian rights, privileges, and precedents – 'marks of sovereignty' – which were largely the creation, and in the curatorship, of the professional lawyers, especially those in the employ of the national monarchies.

29. Tarello 1971; Gagner 1960; Vanderlinden 1967; Gaudemet 1977; Ebel 1958.

10   The idea of custom. Again of ancient lineage, 'custom' (*consuetudo*, produced by *mos*) acquired a social and cultural as well as a legal significance, suggesting the prehistorical origin and corrective 'spirit' of written law. It marks a crucial point of intersection between jurisprudence and history, anthropology and sociology, at least in retrospect.

11   The idea of liberty. Associated traditionally with the civil law rubric on 'the condition of men', this fundamental human attribute was conceptually enhanced by Germanic and Protestant views of freedom. Detached from this legalistic context this theme was taken over in often derivative political affirmations about the general, 'natural' as well as civil, 'rights of man'.

12   The idea of resistance. Tied in many ways to the idea of liberty, this distinctively modern theory joined also religious and constitutional protest and private law notions of self-defence into what was potentially – and, in the context of natural law, actually – a defence of revolution in a modern sense.

13   The idea of private property. Regarded in effect as an extension of 'personality', this is the most important of a number of concepts of political economy developed by jurists in the economic conditions of a commercial age, and associated increasingly with values derived from labour, production, exchange, and 'interest'.

14   The idea of contract. Elaborated from Roman precedents, this juridical device was expanded mightily not only in the economic but also in the political domain, where philosophical arguments transformed the notion into a 'social contract' interpreted in a variety of ways, libertarian and authoritarian.

15   The idea of the 'perfect jurist' (*jurisconsultus perfectus*). First as a sixteenth-century topos and then as a legal genre, this Renaissance idealisation, formed by the convergence of traditional civil science and legal humanism, portrayed the learned yet activist lawyer as the master of legal, social, and political science – the fulfilment in modern terms of the ancient ideal of 'true philosophy'.

16   As ever, but more ingeniously and more indignantly, critics of law and of lawyers carried on the protests against the pretensions, dishonesty, and duplicity apparently inseparable from the methods of the legal profession. To the idealised 'perfect jurist' celebrated in sixteenth- and seventeenth-century literature, Luther opposed the old proverb, 'The lawyer is a bad Christian.' From either point of view the law has remained a central force in modern history and political thought.

In general, under the intimidating influence of the new natural philosophy, old-fashioned civil science seemed to be eclipsed by the rising star of natural law and to be estranged from political philosophy. Some defenders of positive jurisprudence protested against the extreme and empty rationalism represented by fashionable social contract theories. Samuel Rachel lodged such a complaint against Pufendorf, for example; and J.W. Textor argued that the 'law of nations' was the product not only of reason but of positive law and historical precedent (Rachel 1676; Textor 1916, ch. 1). Later Vico drew upon the old tradition of civil law to lay the foundations of a 'new science' constructed wholly on human, anti-naturalistic principles. For Vico 'certainty' was the product first not of reason but rather of 'authority' understood in a cultural and historical sense. Law too had to be understood as an accumulation of national experience, not a quasi-geometrical construct; and only through historical and comparative investigation could one achieve that 'system of universal law' underlying Vico's *New Science*.[30] On the whole, however, these objections were lost in the wave of enthusiasm for an abstract and universal reason which raised the 'philosophical school of law' into a position of dominance which – among critics as well as defenders of the old regime – prevailed until the historical school of the nineteenth century. Civil law was overshadowed by natural law – and 'civil science' by natural science. Nor has the balance ever been restored.

30. Vico 1911–41, II.1, pp. 83, 126, 254, etc.; and see Kelley 1976c.

4

Transalpine humanism

BRENDAN BRADSHAW

i Renaissance eloquence: rhetoric and philosophy

Skirting the problematical subject of the reception of Renaissance humanism outside Italy (Skinner 1978, I, ch. 7) this chapter addresses itself directly to humanism as an established phenomenon north of the Alps. Chronologically it spans what may be described as northern humanism's epic phase: the period from roughly the last decade of the fifteenth century when, with the writing of such scholars as Robert Gaguin in France, Conrad Celtis in Germany, and John Colet in England, humanist discourse in the north acquired a native voice, down to the late 1530s when, with the death of the generation of Erasmus and Budé, and the burgeoning of the Reformation and the Counter-Reformation, northern humanism lost its discrete character as a cultural force – succumbing to the role of handmaiden in the service of a variety of other cultural forces. The specific concern of the chapter is to explore the intellectual and ideological content of the political literature generated by northern humanism in this epic phase. Thus, having skirted a historigraphical Scylla, it will be necessary to engage with a Charybdis.

Charybdis looms in the form of a well-established orthodoxy which denies Renaissance humanism any specific philosophical content. It does so by defining humanism in exclusively literary and educational terms, as a movement devoted to the cultivation of *bonae literae* and the *studia humanitatis*. Accordingly, it is argued, the involvement of humanists with the larger questions of religion, morality, and politics must be distinguished from their proper role as humanists, In such instances, the argument goes, the humanist is to be viewed as bringing an array of technical literary and rhetorical skills to bear on issues extrinsic to the discipline itself. And, it is urged, the variety of ideological standpoints which humanists can be seen

95

to assume in these areas testifies to the lack of any specific philosophical content to humanism as such.[1] Approached in this way, therefore, the political literature of northern humanism presents, strictly as a humanist corpus, a mode of discourse, no more – a form, so to speak, without substantial content.

Such a thesis might seem amply justifed in the case of the political literature of northern humanism. For here a cursory survey conveys the impression of an ideological hotchpotch. By way of illustration one might point to the ideological gulf that yawns between the *Utopia* (1516) of Sir Thomas More and the exactly contemporaneous *La Monarchie de France* (1515) of the Swiss, Claude de Seyssel: the one provides a scathing indictment of the political elites of northern Europe: the other is written in a spirit of piety towards a royal patron, Francis I, and an adopted *patria*, and extols the French monarchy accordingly as the ideal form of common-wealth. Equally, the reductionist definition would serve to explain the marked contrast in ideological viewpoint observable in the political writings of those rival princes of northern humanism, Erasmus and Budé: as between the moral idealism of Erasmus and his excoriation of militarism and of institutional violence, and the staid conservatism of the legist Budé (Tracy 1978, *passim*). Or again, the orthodoxy seems to find support in the writings of a younger generation of humanists, in the contrast provided, for instance, by Thomas Starkey's *Dialogue between Pole and Lupset* (1529–32), with its startlingly frank avowal of populist and republican sentiments, and the best-selling *Boke Named the Governour* (1531) of his fellow Englishman, Sir Thomas Elyot, which anxiously defends the old order and the virtues of lineage and degree.

A cursory survey of the political commentary of the northern humanists, therefore, seems to substantiate the orthodox thesis by which humanism is reduced to a mode of discourse and an array of rhetorical techniques lacking a profounder philosophical perspective. What the corpus seems to reflect, indeed, is the readiness of humanists to put their literary expertise to work as polemicists and propagandists on behalf of a variety of mutually antipathetic ideologies – often, allegedly, for no better reason than considerations of professional advancement. Superficially attractive though this thesis might seem, it is not borne out by a closer scrutiny of the literature. And the import of the analysis offered here is to give it the lie. As will be seen, the political commentary of northern humanism is informed

---

1. This interpretation originated with Paul Otto Kristeller. For one among many statements of his position, see Kristeller 1961, ch. 1, esp. pp. 8–13, 17–19. Kristeller's interpretation has been extensively applied in recent times, e.g. Fox and Guy 1986, ch. 1, esp. pp. 31–3.

by a common perception of the human condition, a world view, a philosophy of life, on which the literary and educational enterprise of the humanists is also found to be grounded. No doubt the world view to which the humanists subscribed turns out on inspection to be a capacious construct. No doubt also it was variously apprehended and interpreted, and proved capable of accommodating a variety of ideological standpoints. Nevertheless, the crucial consideration is that beyond the ambiguities and the variables a common nucleus of values and assumptions is found which constitutes the matrix of a distinctively humanist ideology. The latter provides the agenda for the exposition which follows. The task is twofold: to identify those seminal concepts which comprised the matrix of the humanist ideology and to trace their impact in each case upon the political thought of northern humanism.[2]

Before proceeding to that agenda, however, some preliminary consideration must be given to the formal composition of the texts which constitute the basis of the analysis. That is especially necessary because the humanist mode of discourse often conveys an impression of intellectual superficiality which has played no small part in lending credence to the historiographical orthodoxy just discussed. The nub of the problem lies in the humanist notion of Eloquence. This is commonly taken to refer to a merely rhetorical attainment: stylistic competence, a facility of expression in accordance with the standards of *bonae literae*, i.e. the best practice of classical antiquity, in contrast to the barbarouly functional latinity of the scholastics. Such a notion of humanist Eloquence is valid enough in so far as it goes. It is, indeed, the case that a discursive, literary presentation is of the essence of humanist Eloquence by contrast with the dialectical-analytical mode of the scholastics. However, misconceptions result when humanist Eloquence is reduced on this basis to a mere matter of stylistic elegance, and when the humanists' enthusiasm for *bonae literae* is taken to entail an antipathy towards systematic analytical procedures in reaction to the perceived sterility of dialectical analysis. In fact humanist Eloquence aspired to combine the functions of philosophy and rhetoric, allying the intellectual rigour of the former to the persuasive power of the latter: the challenge was to construct a discourse that would be both attractively literary in its form and seriously philosophical in its substance.[3] So far as the corpus under consideration is concerned two basic strategies can be

---

2. For a different approach by means of a close thematic analysis of the texts, see the magisterial treatment of Skinner 1978, I. 7, 8, 9.
3. Seigel 1968, pt I; Kennedy 1980, chs. 5, 10. For a contemporary corroboration from a northern humanist, see Elyot, *The Governour* (1531), Bk I, ch. 12.

discerned by means of which commentators in the north sought to develop a mode of political discourse which would satisfy the demand of humanist Eloquence for both literary appeal and philosophical rigour. One was by resort to a literary-fictional approach in which a literary form – dialogue, fictitious narrative, allegory, satire – was exploited as the vehicle for a sustained philosophical discourse. More's *Utopia* stands as the enduringly brilliant example: in contrast, the somewhat earlier *Tree of Commonwealth* (1510) of Sir Edmund Dudley provides an example – one among regrettably many – of the lugubriousness to which the medium lent itself at the hands of less-gifted rhetoricians. The alternative procedure – also, perhaps, the more common – was to construct a straightforward prose discourse, designed to achieve literary appeal by means of stylistic embellishment and the deployment of a range of apt *exempla* culled from literature, history, and, not least, scripture. The genre at its best is exemplified in the *Adages* of Erasmus, in which an original series of expositions of classical proverbs are developed through succeeding editions into a collection of brilliantly contrived propagandist essays on religious, moral, and political issues. By way of a counter example, Elyot's *Boke Named the Governour* might be cited as all too characteristic of the earnest pedantry which permeated commentary in this vein. Ultimately, however, the literary merit of the corpus of northern humanist political commentary is not the relevant issue for the discussion which follows. What matters is its philosophical content which historians too often tend to miss, bemused by the rhetorical packaging and by an inadequate grasp of what was entailed in the practice of humanist Eloquence.

ii   The renaissance of politics

Proceeding, then, to the agenda proper, an obvious starting point is provided by a consideration of the influence on the political thought of the northern humanists of the seminal concept which has been taken to characterise the era in which they flourished and to which nineteenth-century historians have given the name, the Renaissance (Skinner 1978, I, *passim*). The claim of the aspiration towards rebirth or renewal – the notion which the term Renaissance was coined to describe – to constitute a seminal concept of the era in which humanism enjoyed its vogue need not, presumably, be pressed (Ferguson 1948, *passim*). Perhaps it needs to be emphasised, however, that the aspiration provides as characteristic a feature of the intellectual environment of politics in the period as it does of literature and the arts with which it is more commonly associated. Indeed, the case has been made that the emergence of the aspiration was conditioned in the first instance by the exigencies of Italian politics rather than by autochthonous pressure within the cultural domain (Ullmann 1977, *passim*). Be that as it may, the impact of the notion upon the political thought of the northern humanists is manifest in their writings. Indeed, it can be seen to provide the fundamental inspiration of the genre of northern humanist political commentary as a whole. In that connection, a significant parallel is to be observed between the perspective on politics adopted in humanist writings and that adopted towards literature and the arts. In each case a critical stance is assumed towards the conventions and forms of the received culture and an alternative model is promoted based on the practice of classical antiquity conceived in idealised terms. In this regard, *Utopia* presents the classic paradigm with its scathing critique of the chivalric culture of late medieval Europe in Book I set over against the ideal political order of Utopia depicted in Book II. True, for the purposes of the fiction, the ideal is located at a geographical distance from late medieval Europe rather than in the classical past. However, the provenance of the ideal is not in doubt: Hythlodaeus, the protagonist both of the critique of contemporary barbarism and of Utopian civility is presented as a Platonic philosopher. Similarly, the political commentary of Erasmus pivots on the contrast between the wisdom of the political values enshrined in the classical heritage and the folly of contemporary practice. His well-known colloquy, *Convivium Religiosum* (1521), daringly apostrophising 'St Socrates', elegantly exemplifies the approach. More to the point for present purposes, the same thought-pattern is found to inform the political commentary of the conservative stream of humanist writers in the period. In the writings of these, it is characteristically expressed in the form of the paradoxical axiom of radical conservatism – given utterance here perhaps for the first time in the literature of western political thought: the necessity to change in order to remain the same. Thus Seyssel's *La Monarchie* begins by extolling the perfections of the French constitution, embodying, as he claims, the Aristotelian ideal of mixed government, i.e. the attributes of monarchical, aristocratical, and popular rule, but then proceeds to urge a scheme of administrative reform of quite radical constitutional implications in order to bring the reality into line with the ideal. The same cast of thought, altered in the focus of its concern, is reflected in Elyot's *The Boke Named the Governour*. There, drawing especially upon the Neoplatonic tradition, he gives classic expression to a message which conservatively minded humanists had begun to preach several decades earlier – Celtis in Germany (*Inaugural Oration*, 1492), Dudley in England (*Tree of Commonwealth*), and Budé in France (*De Asse*, 1515) – the need for a profound transformation of the chivalric culture and lifestyle of the English nobility, from a warrior to a civil ethos, in order to maintain their traditional role of political leadership intact. Thus, as this cross-section of the literature exemplifies, humanist political commentary at this period revolves upon the notion of renewal under the inspiration of an idealised perception of classical antiquity. Whatever the differences otherwise, the ideological thrust of the commentary is invariably progressive, urging advance from an imperfect present towards an ideal inspired by classical antiquity. That progressive orientation provides the first example of the way in which humanist political thought in the north took a distinctive ideological impress from the matrix of seminal ideas which moulded the intellectual environment in which humanist culture flourished.

The task now is to give specific content to the aspiration towards renaissance or renewal as it took form in the political thought of northern humanism. This can be done by means of a closer analysis of the literary corpus. In that connection, attention is to be directed in the first instance to the sub-categories into which the literature breaks down. Here a twofold classification emerges in accordance with the themes around which the treatises are organised. These are conveniently illustrated in the classic contributions of Erasmus and More to the genre, the titles of which conveniently summarise the burden of the discourse: *Of the Formation of a Christian Prince* (1516) and *Of the Best State of a Commonwealth and of the Island of Utopia*. Humanist political discourse, therefore, was preoccupied with the practical problem of the reform of government in its personnel and its processes. However, as reference to the treatment of these issues in the commentary shows, the two converge, as lines of approach, on a single all-absorbing consideration: how the means of government – human and instrumental – were to be brought to fulfil its end. And ultimately, by reference to the end of government as envisaged in the commentary, it can be seen that the concern of the humanists was not strictly political at all. For the reform of government, as presented in the literature, is directed to the reform of the social order as a whole. In that connection, a consideration of the rhetoric through which the aspiration of the humanists was articulated proves highly illuminating. Interest here focuses on a term which enjoyed a special vogue in humanist political discourse before entering upon a long and eventful career in the rhetorical currency of early modern Europe, namely the term *respublica* – together with a variety of vernacular equivalents. What needs to be emphasised in that connection is the unique resonance which the term acquired in humanist usage precisely through association with the notion of a renaissance. And the key to its uniqueness lies in its fidelity to the original Platonic usage from which it derived, namely to convey an abstract and teleological concept: the notion of a political community flourishing under a just and beneficent political order (see below, pp. 116–17). That ideal of the *respublica* – usually put into English as 'the commonwealth' – constitutes the criterion on which the humanist critique of late medieval political culture was based and the inspiration of the humanists' aspiration towards the renewal of the political order.

iii *Humanitas* and the *imago Dei*

Against that background the discussion may proceed to consider the place of a second seminal idea in moulding the distinctive content of humanist political commentary in the north. This is the Renaissance concept of Man. Although the subject is historiographically fraught, as will soon appear, the historicity of the concept, as such, hardly calls for comment, manifest as it is in the artistic and literary artefacts of the period: in art, in the distinctive Renaissance preoccupation with the human form as embodying the ideal of perfect beauty (Gombrich 1950, chs. 1, 15); in literature in a corresponding genre most famously represented by Giovanni Pico della Mirandola's *Oration on the Dignity of Man* (1486).[4] The motif, therefore, is as characteristic of the Renaissance as the aspiration towards renewal itself: indeed, they are corollaries. However, the impact of the concept on humanist political thought provides a more problematical subject. The problem revolves upon the significance which is to be attached to the concept of *humanitas* as deployed in humanist discourse. Here two traditions of interpretation have tended to dominate, each of which serves valuably to emphasise a particular aspect of the term's contemporary usage, though neither, as will be suggested, comprehends the full referential range intended by the humanists.

One approach, mentioned earlier, seeks to confine Renaissance humanism within a scholarly, academic ambience and may, therefore, be described, at the risk of some confusion, as scholasticist. It stresses the humanists' concern for the revival of rhetoric and literature as academic

---

4. The theme has generated a considerable historical literature. For a sampling, see Kristeller 1972; Trinkaus 1982; Skinner 1978, I, pp. 94–101.

disciplines, and their resistance to the overweening influence of scholastic philosophy (e.g. Kristeller 1961, ch. 1). Set within that framework, *humanitas* acquires a strictly academic range of reference. It relates simply to the *studia humanitatis*, the cluster of arts subjects, colloquially referred to in academic parlance as the humanities. Thus, as noted earlier, Renaissance humanism is deprived of any distinctive philosophical content and, *ipso facto*, of any distinctive political ideology. Humanists, it is argued, espoused a variety of political standpoints which they vindicated by recourse to their humanistic skills and learning but not strictly in their capacity *as* humanists. The difficulty with this interpretation is that it ignores the basis on which the *studia humanitatis* were promoted and vindicated. The humanists did not take a stand on the principle of *ars gratia artis*. Rather, they regarded their subject as supremely well adapted to that larger purpose to which they believed their educational enterprise to be directed, namely, moral formation (Garin 1965). In this respect, it may be remarked in parenthesis, their cast of thought reflects a distinctively Platonic, or, more strictly, Socratic influence.

It is precisely in this moral orientation that the second tradition of interpretation finds the key to the meaning of *humanitas*. Here appeal is made to the term's classical provenance. Set in that context it refers to a moral quality extolled by the philosophers and poets of classical antiquity, a way of acting in accordance with those unique faculties which set the human species above the animal kingdom: reason, speech, and moral freedom (Trinkaus 1970, *passim*; Ullman 1977, ch. 4). Such an explication advances understanding of the term as deployed by the humanists in two related respects. It draws attention to the common moral stance which the humanists brought to bear in their writings, corresponding to the common set of cultural and aesthetic values which they espoused. And, as a corollary, it reveals the objective to which the promotion of the *studia humanitatis* was directed: the restoration of *bonae literae* not as an end in itself but as a means towards the restoration of *humanitas* as embodied in the ideal of the *vir humanus* (Garin 1965, pp. 78–113; Ullmann 1977, ch. 4). In that light, it is possible to see that the notion of *humanitas* as deployed by the humanists did, indeed, extend to comprehend, if not a full-blown philosophy, at least a world view, an ideology, a common outlook on life and art, grounded upon an exalted anthropology (Trinkaus 1970, *passim*).

Nevertheless, this account does not seem entirely satisfactory as applied to the political thought of the humanists. The difficulty arises in relation to the polemical function which is assigned to the term *humanitas* in humanist political commentary. According to the tradition of interpretation under discussion this, in a word, may be described as secularist. The suggestion is that the *vir humanus* was invoked as a means of affirming the autonomy of the secular order against a medieval Christian ideology which sought to sacralise it, and, thereby, to give the church ultimate control of it.[5] The objection to such an explanation is that the thrust of humanist political thought in the north is, in fact, holistic. As perusal of the political treatises of the humanists abundantly indicates, the controlling conception is of a renewed *Christian* society – a truly Christian commonwealth – not of a restored secular political order on the classical model.[6] It seems, therefore, that the humanists' understanding of *humanitas* somehow comprehended such a holistic vision. In that regard, an illuminating insight is provided by those artistic and literary artefacts referred to earlier, in which the Renaissance concept of Man is celebrated. As the iconography of the art and the literary tropes abundantly testify, the human ideal which is here affirmed expresses not a polemical tension between a classical and a Christian conception but a harmonious fusion of the two. And the inspirational source of the synthesis is no less clear. It is the account of Man in his original state of perfection contained in the opening two chapters of the Book of Genesis. In effect, the humanists baptised the classical ideal of the *vir humanus* by subsuming it under the biblical ideal of Man as the *imago Dei* (Trinkaus 1970, *passim*). This, then, was the end to which the humanists' promotion of the *studia humanitatis* was directed: not the revival of *bonae literae* as a good in itself; nor yet the revival of the classical ideal of the *vir humanus*, secular man, as such. What the humanist aspired to was the revival of the classical ideal subsumed under the biblical ideal of Man as the image of God.

The way is now clear to proceed to a consideration of the impact of the Renaissance concept of Man on the political thought of the northern humanists. The first point which should be made in that connection is that the topos of the *imago Dei* is found to pervade the body of humanist literature in the north in the same way as in Italy. True, the genre of formally elaborated treatises *De dignitate hominis* may be less well represented – though Juan Luis Vives' *Fabula de homine* (1518) provides a charming exception in which the Genesis account is decked out in the trappings of classical allegory. More to the point, the motif of 'the excellent dignity of man' is encountered as a recurring trope within the political

---

5. This tradition of interpretation may be traced back to Burckhardt. However, I have especially in mind the thesis argued in Ullmann 1977.   6. See below pp. 104–5.

commentary itself and in a form, moreover, which comprehends both the classical and biblical concepts: for instance, as a philosophical gloss on the Genesis account, as in Elyot's *Governour* (Bk III, ch. 2); or, as a Neoplatonic allegory – thus Celtis' lyrical eulogy on Man as 'the earthly star' (*Oration*, ch. 11) and Starkey's 'sparkle of divinity' (*Dialogue*: 1989, p. 9); or in the form of a literary trope as in Erasmus' 'St Socrates' (*Convivium Religiosum*).

How, then, did this exalted conception function in the political thought of the northern humanists? The answer, as will now be clear, comes to hinge on the ideological implications of subsuming the classical ideal of human perfection under the biblical one. In that connection a crucial insight is provided by the humanists' deployment of the classical notion of *respublica* as the ideal of government and as the moral criterion by which to assess the political practice of the governing elites of contemporary Europe. To return to a point made earlier: the thrust of this pivotal ideological conception, as deployed in the political commentary of the humanists, was towards the affirmation of a Christian not a secular political order. The classical ideal was held up not as the criterion of absolute perfection but as pointing towards an even loftier ideal, enjoined on Christian rulers, *a fortiori*, by reason of the greater excellence of the Christian dispensation. This rhetorical structure is readily apparent in the mainstream tradition of humanist commentary where the mode is straightforwardly exhortatory. Here the lesson is explicitly drawn in the manner of a moral *exemplum* – as, for instance, when Antonio de Guevara appeals from the 'pagan' ideal of a heroic death in battle to the 'Christian' ideal of the holy life of the peace-maker.[7] More tellingly, however, the same thought process is reflected in humanist polemic in the satirical mode, despite its iconoclastic force and studied ironies, as practised to such devastating effect by Erasmus, More, and, indeed, Rabelais. Here, as so often, *Utopia* holds a special interest, not so much for the light it throws on the mind of More himself but for the way it serves to illuminate the mind-set of the humanists of his generation. In *Utopia*, then, the notion of *respublica* is applied as a rhetorical ploy on which the polemical structure of the work as a whole pivots. Thus, the injustices of the nominally Christian commonwealth depicted in Book I are high-lighted by appeal to the justice of the non-Christian commonwealth of Utopia depicted in Book II. Nevertheless, as More signals at several points throughout the text, the Utopian polity remains less than perfect, limited as it is by the dictates of reason, unguided by the higher light of revelation.[8]

---

7. Guevara 1919, p. 130.   8. These are pinpointed in Skinner 1987, pp. 147–52.

Accordingly, that consummation, the conversion of the island to Christianity, provides the conclusion to Hythloday's narrative (Bradshaw 1981,
pp. 6–14). Despite the savage indictment of the contemporary establishment, therefore, and the appeal to the classical ideal of a justly ordered
respublica, *Utopia* reflects a deeply Christian consciousness. Undoubtedly,
the polemic is calculated to undermine the political culture of late medieval
Christendom but it is conducted on behalf of a Christian, not a secular,
alternative. More precisely, the message which the Utopian polemic seeks
to convey is that the construction of a truly Christian political order must
rest upon the foundation of a just secular one (Bradshaw 1981, pp. 6–14).
Here lies the key to the significance of the Renaissance concept of Man as it
functioned in the political thought of the humanists. By virtue of this
anthropological perception, the humanists sought to bring to bear the
values and insights of classical political thought, grounded on the notion of
the *vir humanus*, in pursuit of their aspiration to construct a truly Christian
commonwealth.

In considering the consequences of this approach for the political
thought of the humanists the first step is to grasp its ideological
implications. These may best be observed, following the interpretative line
of the secularists discussed earlier, in the light of the polemic which the
humanists conducted against the political culture of late medieval Christendom. Accordingly, the discussion returns to the starting point provided by
the secularists. That is the contrast between the anthropological perception
which moulded humanist political thought and the perception which
dominated the cultural ethos of late medieval Europe: the view of Man as
fallen from grace, corrupt in nature, and in need of redemption, derived,
ironically, from the same source as the humanist one, the opening chapters
of the Book of Genesis. As the secularists rightly insist, that deflating
anthropological perception, in the radically pessimistic formulations of St
Augustine conveyed to the late middle ages in Pope Innocent III's bleak
account of the human condition, *De miseria humanae conditionis*, provides
the polemical referent of the Renaissance concept of Man as deployed in
the reform treatises of the humanists.[9] Nevertheless, as pointed out earlier,
the secularists' account of the ideological implications of the contrast is
unacceptable. It is not satisfactorily explained in terms of a conflict between
a sacralising medieval ideology and a secularising Renaissance one. The

9. Ullmann 1977, ch. 4. On the humanist polemic against the anthropology of the Christian middle
   ages, see Skinner 1978, I, pp. 88–101.

ideal which the humanists sought to promote was not the *vir humanus* as such, but that classical concept subsumed under the biblical concept of the *imago Dei*. And the purpose of the humanists in doing so was profoundly Christian, not to desacralise the political culture of late medieval Christendom but, as they believed, to reChristianise it. While, therefore, the hoary jurisdictional debate between church and state survived into the early modern period with fateful consequences, it does not provide the frame of reference within which the polemic of the humanists was conducted. As perusal of the relevant literature abundantly shows, the humanists' critique of the political culture of late medieval Christendom was informed by a more fundamental, functional preoccupation. It concerned the central question to which political thought in the classical tradition addressed itself: the means by which the polity is to be directed to the end of a justly ordered *respublica*.

This, therefore, is the frame of reference within which the ideological significance of the contrast between the anthropological perception of the humanists and that which dominated late medieval Christendom must be explicated. Situated in that context the contrast is seen to reflect a conflict between two approaches to the practice of government: the one voluntarist, characterised by strategies of coercion, and reflecting a perception of human nature as fallible and predisposed towards evil; the other rationalist, characterised by strategies of persuasion, and reflecting a perception of human nature as perfectible and disposed to virtue. In ideological terms, therefore, the contrasting anthropological perceptions under consideration reflect, on the one hand, the humanists' repudiation of conventional Augustinian assumptions about government as a necessarily coercive and punitive process – a consequence of the fall of Adam – and, on the other hand, their commitment to a more benign approach, designed to assimilate the classical tradition of political thought, grounded on the ideal of the *vir humanus*, within a Christian frame of reference.

iv   Political Wisdom

In turning to explore the consequences of the humanists' commitment to a reason-centred approach to government, a third seminal idea of the Renaissance presents itself for consideration. That is the Renaissance idea of Wisdom. Some explication of that notion must, therefore, be offered before proceeding. First, its centrality to the intellectual ethos of the Renaissance must be emphasised. Its status is indicated, for instance, by a flourishing genre of Wisdom literature, stemming from Petrarch's *De sapientia*, and represented most famously – though by no means uniquely – in the north by Erasmus' *Praise of Folly* (1507).[10] To the testimony of the literature may be added the corresponding development in art of a genre centred upon the theme of *homo sapiens*, familiar examples of which include Raphael's *School of Athens* and the *Allegory of Philosophy* of Albrecht Dürer. The concept of Wisdom claims a place, therefore, alongside the aspiration towards renewal itself, and the exalted anthropological notion just now considered, within that matrix of ideas which moulded the culture of the Renaissance. Of more specific relevance to the subject in hand is the matter of intellectual provenance. In this regard two points require to be emphasised. One concerns the classical inspiration of the concept. What is of significance here is the syncretism of the humanists' approach to the Wisdom literature of classical antiquity and the consequent fusion, in the notion of Eloquence, of two ideologically congenial but methodologically disparate schools of thought: the Socratic philosophical tradition, mediated through Plato, and the rhetorical, literary stream, represented for the humanists above all by Cicero and the Stoics.[11] In this combination, therefore, lies the intellectual source of the humanists' commitment to *philosophia de caelo revocata* – i.e. a mode of philosophical reflection that was existential, moral, and practical – and their aversion, by the same token, from the essentialist quiddities to which Aristotelian philosophy tended, most especially as represented by scholastic dialectic (Guthrie 1969, III, pp. 417–25). The second point which a consideration of the intellectual provenance of the Wisdom idea serves to highlight is the Christian orientation of the concept. In view of the earlier discussion of humanist anthropology this point need scarcely be laboured. All that needs to be said is that the same intellectual strategy can be seen to operate here as applied in the christening of the *vir humanus*. The classical concept was subsumed under a Christian one: in this case mainly by reference to the Wisdom tradition of the Old Testament and to the treatment of the theme in the Pauline epistles – St Paul is made to play Plato to Jesus' Socrates, as in the remarkable conclusion to Erasmus' *Praise of Folly* (Bradshaw 1982, esp. pp. 429–40). The relevance of these considerations emerges in connection with the explication of the motif's precise intellectual content.

Here, once more, Erasmus offers an illuminating insight in a phrase

10. Two major studies of Renaissance Wisdom are Rice 1958 and Kahn 1985. On the classical Wisdom tradition, see Guthrie 1969, III, ch. 14, and 1975, IV, ch. 4.
11. Kahn 1985, ch. 2; Seigel 1968, chs. 1, 3; Rice 1958.

which has been claimed to convey 'the one ideal of wisdom peculiarly characteristic of the Renaissance'. It is *virtus cum eruditione liberali coniuncta* (Rice 1958, p. 204). What commends that phrase is its encapsulation of the Socratic–Ciceronian perception just discussed, of learning as a moral process – directed to the fulfilment of the human potential – and, as a corollary, the repudiation of knowledge pursued for its own sake, and the disparagement of metaphysics and the science of nature for their lack of moral relevance. The insight thus provided into the mind-set of the humanists has to do with the nexus which is here highlighted between *sapientia* and *humanitas*. For, as has been rightly observed, the Erasmian phrase might equally well be taken to characterise that latter notion (Rice 1958, p. 214) – as the *potentia*, so to speak, which issues in Wisdom. In elucidating the significance of this association it is necessary to correct once again a confusion arising from the secularist tradition of interpretation. In that tradition the nexus is taken to reflect the secular thrust of the humanist concept, inspired, supposedly, by the classical ideal of Wisdom as the rationally acquired virtue of the *vir humanus*, over against a medieval conception of it as supernaturally infused knowledge.[12] In the light of the background provided here that view calls for little comment. Suffice it, therefore, to illustrate the Christian orientation of the humanist concept by reference to another phrase as quintessentially Erasmian as it is characteristic of the mind-set of Renaissance humanism. That is the phrase in which Erasmus extols the gospel as the *philosophia Christi*, the Christian Wisdom in which classical Wisdom finds its consummation (Bradshaw 1982, pp. 422–9).

Clearly, then the significance of the nexus between *humanitas* and *sapientia* in the minds of the humanists requires to be reformulated. In fact, its meaning becomes abundantly evident by references to treatments of the theme in the humanist genre of Wisdom literature: as, for instance, in the systematic exposition by Erasmus himself in the *Antibarbari* (Bradshaw 1982, *passim*) or, in more didactic form, in a host of manuals of the *ars vivendi* variety, represented in the north, for instance, by the *Introductio ad sapientiam* (1524) of Vives – translated into English by Richard Morison (1540) – or Elyot's *Of the Knowledge which Maketh a Wise Man* (1533) (Fox and Guy 1986, pp. 65–73), or, indeed, by Erasmus' own best-selling *Enchiridion Militis Christiani* (1504). The concept which emerges from these constitutes the epistemological corollary, as it might be said, of the

---

12. Thus Rice 1958, see esp. ch. 8. Cf. Ullmann 1977, esp. pp. 198–202.

anthropological conception which the humanists purveyed by recourse to the biblical ideal of the *imago Dei*. It is the notion of Wisdom as an attribute acquired through the combined resources of Reason and Revelation, each contributing uniquely yet reciprocally towards that consummation (Bradshaw 1982, pp. 422–9). Situated in the context of the cultural ethos of late medieval Christianity the ideological thrust of that conception – and the force of the Erasmian rhetoric – is readily apparent. Over against a deeply entrenched patristic current of thought, whereby Revelation was set apart, as transcending and superseding mere human reason, the humanists sought to affirm a view of the two as complementary and interdependent (Bradshaw 1982, pp. 414–16). Thus, in this view, the knowledge acquired by rational means points towards Revelation as to its perfection, while the knowledge to which Revelation gives access requires to be appropriated by means of rational endeavour. Viewed in conjunction, therefore, the two seminal Renaissance ideas here discussed – of Man and of Wisdom – can now be seen to reflect an even more fundamental conception on which, indeed, the ideology of Renaissance humanism was ultimately grounded. That is the notion of an ontological symbiosis as between the natural and the supernatural orders and, by way of corollary, of nature and grace as the divinely appointed means by which Man is enabled to attain his perfection as the *imago Dei*. Here in that harmonious ontological conception lies the key to the function of Wisdom, as perceived by the humanists, in the practice of politics and government.

Proceeding then to consider that question, what first requires to be noted is the way in which Wisdom is singled out among the virtues in humanist political discourse. Its status is well reflected in the revival of the Platonic ideal of the philosopher-prince, a figure who provides an ubiquitous trope in the writings of humanists, both those in the Erasmian mould, such as More, Vives, and Starkey, and those of a more conservative cast, such as Erasmus' German contemporary, Celtis, or, in the next generation, Elyot. Whatever their differences otherwise – with one another or, indeed with Plato, as we shall see – all agree in singling out Wisdom as the preeminent political virtue. The second feature of note points up the relevance of the earlier epistemological discussion. It concerns the rationale which the humanists provided for their sapiential option. The point of fundamental significance in that regard is the humanists' perception, in line with Socratic–Platonic epistemology, of intellect rather than will as the dynamic source of action (Guthrie 1969, III, pp. 450–61). Thus, by way of example, Erasmus' classic *Institutio Principis Christiani* (1516) which opens with a paean to Wisdom and goes on to impress upon the young Charles V that whereas 'good will may suffice in the ordinary citizen, since he is directed by the laws, it [good will] is of little avail in a prince unless accompanied by wisdom which shows him how to attain what he desires' (*Institutio*: 1936, p. 187). The precise implication of this perception is pinpointed by Elyot when he declares – in another classic advice book of a later vintage and at a significant distance ideologically in other respects from that of Erasmus – that 'sapience in the governaunce of a commonwealth is of more efficacy than strength and puissance' (*Governour*, Bk III, ch. 23). In short, the effect of the humanist attempt to assimilate the insights of classical political thought within a Christian frame of reference was, in the first instance, a commitment to an ideology of Wisdom as against one of Power as the instrument of politics.

The third significant feature of the Wisdom motif as treated in the political commentary of the humanists concerns the ambiguity, nevertheless, as hinted earlier, of the response evinced by the Platonic tradition of political reflection. The attitude is highlighted in a topos significantly as ubiquitous in humanist political commentary as the trope of the philosopher-prince. Its effect is to disavow the Platonic tradition of political thought – or, by euphemism, 'ancient philosophy' – as impractically idealistic, in fact, as *philosophia in caelis*, and to affirm an alternative approach on the basis of its practical utility. Thus, the Swiss humanist, Seyssel, in an entirely characteristic proem to his *La Monarchie de France* emphasises the novelty of his treatise insofar as it addresses the state of the historic French commonwealth and not that abstraction of 'ancient philosophy', the ideally best commonwealth. However, the most illuminating example of the humanists' attitude – in part because the most paradoxical – is provided once again by More's *Utopia* – as it happens a work exactly contemporaneous with Seyssel's *La Monarchie*. This must be discussed at some length since it directs attention to what was most distinctive about the concept of Wisdom as it functioned in the political thought of the humanists.

In *Utopia* the disavowal of Platonic political thought takes two forms. One consists in a prefatory poem and an epistle, obligingly supplied by More's collaborator, Peter Giles, which acclaim the merits of *Utopia* to the disadvantage of Plato's *Republic* (More 1965, pp. 21–5). The second takes the form of a debate which develops within the text between Morus and the Platonic philosopher Hythlodaeus. The polemic is mutually reinforcing despite the inevitable irony. The point of Giles' coy banter is to draw attention to the realism with which More constructs his 'best state of a commonwealth' as a credible entity existing in the world of human experience, by contrast with Plato's idealised abstraction. And, indeed, as can be seen by reference to the account of the island commonwealth provided by Hythlodaeus in book II, Utopia is no idyllic arcadia. It enjoys no special environmental advantages. It is peopled not by paragons but by mortals of ordinary intellectual and moral calibre – descended, as elsewhere, from ignorant and uncivilised forebears. And the Utopians maintain their justly ordered commonwealth in the midst of a world of *Realpolitik* in which their moral idealism is everywhere discarded in the pursuit of power, wealth, and self-advantage.

The irony of the polemic appears on turning to the debate between Hythlodaeus and Morus.[13] For here Hythlodaeus is found defending the Platonic proposition of which the *Republic* constitutes the *locus classicus*, that the philosopher must stand aloof from politics. In doing so he shows that he has not grasped the meaning of the Utopian commonwealth of which he himself is the advocate. It is left to Morus to point up the message. The basis of the Platonic argument is that the philosopher's approach to government is incompatible with that of the politician. The philosopher is concerned to show how government is to be conducted by reason and virtue in the interests of the commonwealth. The politician perceives government as a function of power and wealth directed towards self-interest. In consequence, the philosopher must steer clear of politics for two reasons. First, because involvement would not serve the interests of the commonwealth: in politics the philosopher's advice would be spurned as irrelevant to the concerns of government. Secondly, because involvement would place the philosopher's moral integrity in jeopardy: politics is conducted by means of dissimulation and compromise which are incompatible with the philosopher's adherence to reason and virtue.[14] This, then, is the Platonic argument, placed in the mouth of Hythlodaeus, which Morus rebuts in a profoundly illuminating interjection. His first ploy is to direct the Platonic argument against academic philosophy, thereby turning the tables on Plato. Thus, the imperviousness of politicans to philosophical advice is attributed to the form in which it is offered, i.e. academically, as abstract prescriptions endowed with universal validity, remote, therefore, from the politicians' pragmatic way of thinking – 'scholastica, quae quiduis

13. For a different interpretation of this debate to which, however, I am indebted, see Skinner 1987, pp. 123–35.
14. On the Socratic–Platonic argument, see Guthrie 1975. IV, pp. 91–3, 498–502.

putet ubiuis convenire' (More 1965, p. 98 line 11). Morus then proceeds to resist Plato's categorical stricture against the philosopher's involvement in politics by expounding an alternative mode of philosophical discourse, a 'more political philosophy' which undermines the twin pillars of Plato's objection. He explains what he has in mind by recourse to a metaphor which reflects More's own boyhood experience, that of the actor who improvises a part in a pantomine:[15] 'she (*philosophia civilior*) gets to know the scene, accommodates herself to the matter in hand, and plays her part accordingly with decorum' (More 1965, p. 98 lines 11–14) – not coming on stage, as he says, in a philosopher's gown or intruding a tragic oration into a comedy. Thus, by accommodating itself to the constraints of the political forum philosophy can, contrary to Plato's contention, aspire to an effective voice in politics. Furthermore, as the histrionic metaphor serves to indicate, the accommodation required pertains to form and not to substance. It is a strategy which enables the philosopher to represent the claims of reason and virtue in credible form to those pragmatically minded politicians responsible for the conduct of government. Plato's moral objection is overthrown, therefore, since the philosopher uses his involvement in politics in the interests of the commonwealth and not for private advantage. Thus More proceeds to clinch his case as he began by turning Plato's argument back upon academic philosophy. His contention is that the academic's self-righteous repudiation of the constraints of politics – the necessity to engage in dissimulation and compromise – constitutes the real moral abdication. To do so, he vehemently protests – invoking another much favoured humanist metaphor – is to abandon the ship to the storm because you have no control over the winds. The polemical point of the so-called 'Dialogue of Counsel', therefore, concurs with the message which More sought to convey through the realism of his account of the Utopian commonwealth. The point is, *pace* Plato, that the philosopher can and, therefore, must pursue the ideal of the commonwealth in the world of *Realpolitik*.

The implications for the concept of Wisdom as it functioned in the political thought of the humanists remain to be considered. These may be elucidated by reference to the notion of *philosophia civilior* which Morus opposed to the *philosophia scholastica* represented by the Platonic philosopher Hythlodaeus. In that connection two features of the *philosophia civilior* as it emerges in the course of the debate assume fundamental significance.

15. This is recounted in the biographical memoir of his son-in-law, William Roper, ed. E.E. Reynolds 1963, p. 3.

One pertains to its correspondence – the quarrel notwithstanding – with the *philosophia scholastica* of Hythlodaeus. This arises at the fundamental level of ideological orientation. Both are concerned to show how government may be directed by reason and virtue in the interests of the commonwealth. In that respect, therefore, both stand in a tradition of political thought characterised by adherence to Wisdom rather than to Power as the means of pursuing the goals of the commonwealth – a tradition deriving ultimately from the rational idealism of Socrates–Plato. The second feature of note, by contrast, pertains to the precise issue in the quarrel between Morus and Hythladaeus. This, it is clear, revolves upon the question of intellectual method. Where, as Morus observes, academic philosophy proceeds by abstraction, seeking prescriptions of universal application – *quiduis putet ubiuis convenire* – *philosophia civilior* proceeds by accommodation, seeking, like an actor, to address itself to a specific context, to the exigencies of time, place, and circumstance. The significance of these different procedures appears by reference to an earlier discussion of the intellectual provenance of the humanist concept of Wisdom. For what the quarrel between Morus and Hythlodaeus brings to light is the consequence for the political thought of the humanists of the fusion which they effected as between the rational idealism of Socrates–Plato and the rhetorical tradition of Wisdom represented by Cicero. In that connection More's histrionic metaphor is especially illuminating. Both the metaphor itself and the terms on which More draws in developing it – accommodation, harmony, propriety, decorum – reveal behind the figure of Morus, the advocate of the *philosophia civilior*, the figure of the Ciceronian orator.[16] Confronted, therefore, with the gulf opened up by Plato between the rational idealism of Socratic Wisdom and the contingent world of practical politics, More looked to rhetoric, in the manner of Cicero, to provide a bridge.

It is precisely this conception of rhetoric as the means of pursuing the morally ideal in the real world of politics which led the humanists to extol their 'political Wisdom' over the abstract prescriptions of 'ancient philosophy'. Against that background, in turn, the full significance of the humanists' commitment to *humanitas* at last emerges. It is *humanitas* which provides access to the political wisdom to which the humanists looked to fulfil their aspiration for a truly Christian commonwealth.

16. The point is persuasively demonstrated in Skinner 1987, pp. 128–31. On Cicero's fusion of rhetoric and philosophy and the Renaissance revival of the Ciceronian notion, see Seigel 1968 *passim*; Kahn 1985, chs. 1–4.

v   *Humanitas* and the Christian commonwealth

It will be sufficiently clear by now that, as argued from the outset, the humanists' commitment to *humanitas* served to generate a body of political commentary in the north which was distinctive, not only in form but also in substance. Formally what resulted was a distinctive mode of political discourse, a way of conducting political thought in accordance with the norms of Renaissance Eloquence (see above, pp. 97–8). Of more fundamental historical significance, however, the effect was also to produce a genre of political literature distinctive in its substantial content by reason of the characteristically Renaissance intellectual matrix within which it was moulded. In that respect, the distinctiveness of humanist political commentary in the north derives in the first instance from the exalted anthropological conception which provides its ideological pivot – and on which, indeed, the entire enterprise of the Renaissance may be said to pivot – that of the classical *vir humanus* subsumed under the biblical ideal of the *imago Dei* (see above, pp. 102–3). Inspired by that lofty ideal, the humanists sought to renew the political culture of northern Europe by assimilating the values and insights of the classical Wisdom tradition of political thought within a Christian frame of reference (see above, pp. 106–9). The precise implications of that approach for the practice of politics and government remain to be considered. These may best be observed, following the procedure adopted hitherto, by relating the political commentary of northern humanism to its contemporary context.

Proceeding, therefore, to that exercise, what presents itself first for consideration is the moral challenge which the humanists offered to the assumptions and values on which the practice of government in the late medieval period was grounded. The issue here is highlighted in the contrast between the rational idealism of the classical Wisdom tradition and the Augustinian world view which served to condition the political culture of late medieval northern Europe.[17] More specifically, the issue revolves upon the contrast, noted earlier, between the rationalist approach to the conduct of government and the strongly voluntarist approach to which the Augustinian world view lent itself (see above, pp. 108–9). In brief, from the Augustinian standpoint, government was seen as the secular corollary of supernatural grace, in that it provided an antidote in the secular domain to the evil propensities of fallen human nature (Markus 1970, ch. 4). As such,

17. On Augustinianism in the late middle ages, see Wright 1982, ch. 1; Oberman 1977, ch. 6.

however, it fulfilled its function in an altogether different manner, appropriate to the domain of fallen nature to which it pertained. Thus, whereas grace operates inwardly, moving the individual soul to spiritual regeneration by supernatural power – divine charity – government operates externally by human power – the secular sword – moving society to outward conformity to the norms of social justice and public order. In the Augustinian secular cosmology, therefore, government was perceived as an instrument of coercion and punishment necessary for the maintenance of justice and order in the domain of corrupt human nature. The effect was a political morality which served to endorse violence as the necessary sanction of government by appeal to the shibboleths of the 'just war' and 'severe justice'.[18] Against that background the nature of the moral challenge which the humanists offered to the political culture of the late medieval period clearly emerges. Its source is found in the assimilation of the values and insights of the classical Wisdom tradition within a Christian frame of reference. The effect of christening the Wisdom tradition was virtually to invert the Augustinian categories. First, it led the humanists to take as their anthropological starting point, not the Fall of Man, but his creation, in which he was dignified by the unique status of the *imago Dei*. Secondly, it led them to construct a secular cosmology, not on the basis of the evil propensities of human nature, vitiated by the corruption of the will, but rather on the basis of human nature's capacity for self-perfection, having been endowed with a rational faculty and thereby with the attributes of *humanitas* – intellect, speech, and moral freedom (see above, pp. 102–3). Thirdly, in contrast to the dourly negative conception of the political order which the Augustinian world view entailed, the humanists were led to conceive the function of government in benignly teleological terms. This was the context in which their aspiration towards a truly Christian commonwealth emerged. In the light of Man's unique dignity as the *imago Dei* and the capacity for self-perfection which his *humanitas* conferred, the humanists were led to adopt the moral ideal by which the classical Wisdom tradition of political thought had been inspired, the conception of government as directed by reason and virtue to the goal of *respublica*, the commonwealth (Guthrie 1975, IV, pp. 434–544). Inspired by that ideal, in turn, the humanists sought to regenerate the political culture

18. The classical historical evocation of this ethos is Huizinga 1924, ch. 1. Huizinga's account is generally corroborated by a more recent study of the mental environment of late medieval English politics – the environment which conditioned the perception of the author of *Utopia*: James 1978, pp. 2–22; cf. Hexter 1965, pp. l–liv. For the underlying moral tradition see Keen 1966, chs. 5, 6.

of late medieval Christendom and, in doing so, to challenge the Augustinian values which it embodied.

In that light, the commonwealth ideal now emerges as the fourth and culminating component of that matrix of Renaissance ideas from which the political thought of the humanists derived ideological coherence. Its precise impact, as such, therefore, calls for explication. Conveniently that question may be pursued in the context of the present discussion for, as has been seen, *respublica* constitutes the moral criterion against which the humanists measured the contemporary practice of politics and government, and found it wanting. In elucidating the implications of the notion as deployed in humanist political commentary, an instructive case-study presents itself, yet again, in Thomas More's *Utopia*, considered now, at last, precisely as a treatise on the reform of the commonwealth. Here, as will be seen, the concept reveals its full potential as the pivot of a devastating critique of the political *status quo* and of a reforming manifesto. Attention for these purposes centres upon the three-pronged ideological thrust with which More endowed the notion and upon its corresponding threefold intellectual provenance.

First to be considered is its application to the process of government, strictly as such, as a criterion of justice by means of which More sought to expose the moral bankruptcy of contemporary governmental practice and to promote an alternative. The key to the content of *respublica* in that respect lies in its original Platonic formulation. In the *Republic*, the *res* which Plato posits as the end of government is defined not in terms of tangible material values but as moral betterment – the good proper to man in virtue of his rational nature – while *publica* is taken to comprehend the entire body politic, not just its ruling or political element (Guthrie 1975, IV, pp. 434–9, 411–18). Conceived in those terms, as Hythlodaeus relentlessly demonstrates in Book I of *Utopia*, the commonwealth was flagrantly disregarded in contemporary governmental practice. This was directed neither towards human betterment nor towards the general welfare. Rather, it was directed towards the material benefit of the ruling elites in the form of wealth, power, and public reputation, to the detriment, moreover, of the general welfare since, as Hythlodaeus shows, the pursuit of these goals produced socially harmful consequences – war, extortionate taxation, repressive legislation, idleness, crime, and poverty (More 1965, pp. 86–97; cf. Hexter, *ibid.*, pp. l–liv). Highlighting the message, More has Hythlodaeus present in Book II the example of Utopian government, directed in accordance with the Platonic criterion. Here, indeed, government is ordered to human betterment and to the general welfare; civil administration is its concern, not war and foreign aggrandisement; service of the public interest is its aim and not private profit; virtue is its criterion of merit and not privilege of birth or riches; need is the criterion on which distributive justice is based, not mere possession; reform is the end to which the criminal code is directed, not vindictive punishment. The effect of the Utopian contrast, therefore, is to affirm a cluster of values, based on the Platonic concept of *respublica* as just government, by appeal to which More was enabled to expose the moral bankruptcy of the contemporary practice of government and to provide a moral basis for its reformation. This Platonic conception, with its attendant cluster of values, presented as the criterion of just government, constitutes the first aspect of the ideology of the commonwealth as it emerges in the pages of *Utopia*.

The second aspect shifts attention from the specifically governmental range of reference with which Plato's formulation originally endowed *respublica* to its wider political register. That conception may be approached by means of the paradox of the Utopian perspective on politics. In its preoccupation with human corruptibility this might seem to reflect a truly Augustinian anthropological pessimism, for all the commitment to *humanitas* of the treatise otherwise. In fact, as closer scrutiny reveals, what the Utopian preoccupation reflects is an aspect of the inversion of the Augustinian world view, produced, as noted earlier, by the humanists' perception of Man as the *imago Dei*. The crucial indicator in this regard is the ideological orientation of the pessimism in each case. Augustinian pessimism – to repeat – served to condition a voluntarist approach to government, which stressed its coercive and punitive function, and to provide a corroboratory political morality centred upon social obedience, public authority, and the sanction of force. The Augustinian preoccupation with human corruptibility, it might be said, reflects a perception of the political order haunted by the spectre of 'anarchy from below'. Considered in that light, the ideological orientation of Utopian pessimism presents a significant contrast. To adapt the metaphor, the spectre which haunts the Utopian perception of politics is that of 'tyranny from above' (Fenlon 1981). In more explicit terms, from the Utopian perspective the threat posed to the political order by human corruptibility is perceived to emanate from those who exercise power rather than from those upon whom it is exercised. The significance of the contrast is that it serves to highlight in turn the intellectual source of More's anthropological pessimism. As will be clear, this is not satisfactorily explained by reference

to a medieval Augustinian world view. Rather, its ideological thrust points
to a source that is classical and humanist, namely, Cicero's characteristic
preoccupation with the threat which the abuse of power poses to the
respublica. In line with the syncretism of the humanists' response to the
classical Wisdom tradition, therefore, the Utopian concept of *respublica* is
found to reflect a Ciceronian as well as a Platonic intellectual provenance.

Proceeding to elucidate the Utopian conception within the intellectual
framework thus provided, attention comes to focus on the two features
which are basic to Cicero's conception of a just *respublica*. One is the 'rule of
the wise', by which, in line with the Platonic conception, government
devolves upon the intellectual and moral elite – as idealised in Cicero's
Orator. The second, departing from the Platonic conception, is the notion
of constitutional government – as it would now be called – a system of
political organisation devised so as to comprehend the general will by the
processes of election, consultation, representation, and consent.[19] Turning
to *Utopia* with these principles in mind, their implications for the Utopian
polemic emerge once more by means of the contrast which conventional
European practice presents to Utopian arrangements. Thus, the effect of
Hythlodaeus' political critique in Book I is to undermine the credibility of
the monarchical regimes of northern Europe as representing 'the rule of the
wise'. Invoking their public record, his own encounters with the
establishment mentality, and the deliberations, as he persuasively re-
constructs them, of European monarchical councils, he provides a
sweeping indictment of the ruling elites which comes to rest on two
gravamina. One is moral corruption: evidenced in the war-mongering and
dishonesty which marks the practice of international relations; in the
extortion, repression, and manipulation of the law in which governments
engage in the conduct of civil administration; and in the self-interested
flattery and moral cowardice which passes for counsel-giving. The second
charge is intellectual decadence, as manifested by the inability of the ruling
elites to respond to new ideas or to the notion of progress – More satirises,
with characteristic brilliance, the combination of incomprehension, negative traditionalism, and self-complacency with which reforming proposals
are greeted (e.g. More 1965, pp. 56–9, 70–1, 80–7). Utopia, of course, as
Hythlodaeus shows in Book II, presents an altogether different picture.
There the 'rule of the wise' does, indeed, obtain. Government devolves
upon those of proven moral and intellectual calibre. And the practice of

19. Hunt 1954, esp. pp. 197–205. Watson 1986 edn. Kennedy 1980, pp. 90–100.

politics, consequently, is marked by rationality and moral probity: international relations are conducted on the basis of natural justice, not cynical opportunism; civil government is marked by intellectual openness and a desire for progress;[20] and the political ethos is characterised by a common commitment to the service of the commonwealth not by competition for personal advancement. Here, once again, Utopian practice is found to embody a cluster of values derived from the classical ideal of *respublica* which serve both to undermine the moral credibility of European practice and to provide a moral basis for its reformation. However, the full subversive potential of the Ciceronian concept only emerges when this aspect of the Utopian polemic is set in the context of the contrast which Utopia presents with regard to constitutional arrangements. Here, replacing the hereditary monarchies and royally appointed governments of the European system, Utopia flourishes under a carefully elaborated constitution in which the features of election, consultation, representation, and consent mark all aspects of the political system, including the selection of the ruler himself and his executive council (More 1965, pp. 122–5). Thus, in the process of undermining the moral credibility of the monarchical regimes of northern Europe, *Utopia* is found to endorse a full-blooded Ciceronian republicanism: in Europe the choice of the ruling elite devolves upon the arbitrary processes of heredity and political patronage, with the consequences of corruption and stagnation, as Hythlodaeus' critique demonstrates; in Utopia the political system encompasses the general will by means of election, consultation, representation, and consent, thus ensuring the rule of the wise and the service of the commonwealth.

By way of addendum here, attention must be drawn to the manner in which the Utopian contrast serves to emphasise an important corollary to the principle of the 'rule of the wise', derived from the Ciceronian ideology. This relates to the question of the political responsibilities of the intellectual – the subject which, as will be remembered, provided the issue in debate between Hythlodaeus and Morus in the so-called 'Dialogue of Counsel' (see above, pp. 111–12). The contrast which emerges in this instance is between, on the one hand, the representative of the European intelligentsia, Hythlodaeus, the philosopher, who holds aloof from politics, through disdain for its pragmatism and compromises, and, on the other hand, the Utopian intellectual elite who engage in politics in a spirit of

20. On the conduct of foreign affairs, see More 1965, pp. 196–203. On the Utopians' intellectual openness, see *ibid.*, pp. 106–9, 180–5.

service to the commonwealth (More 1965, pp. 130–3). It is left to Morus to point up the message that the claims of the commonwealth over the private interest – even the lofty interests of the intellectual – are not diminished in transition from the ideal world to the real world of politics.

The third ideological thrust of the commonwealth ideal as elaborated in *Utopia* presents its most problematic and also, perhaps, its most enduringly attractive aspect. Here the concept acquires a distinctively populist range of reference. The focus shifts from the abstract ideal conceived by Plato and Cicero – *respublica* as such – to a social group, the *populus*, envisaged, moreover, as comprising not only the 'poor commons', but also the marginalised and criminalised elements of late medieval European society – the destitute, the incapacitated, the vagrants, the beggars. Proceeding to explore this dimension of the Utopian ideal in the light, as hitherto, of its intellectual provenance, a novel feature presents itself. That is its failure to strike a resonant chord within the classical Wisdom tradition. Thus, by default, attention comes to focus on the significance of the baptism of the classical concept by reason of its assimilation within a Christian frame of reference. The effect, as exemplified by *Utopia*, in any case, was the fusion of two radical moral traditions: the classical Wisdom tradition of political thought, pivoting on the ideal of *respublica*, and a Judaeo-Christian tradition of social morality, inspired by the ideal of Messianic justice, i.e. the emancipation of the poor, the weak, and the socially ostracised. Originally developed within the prophetic literature of the Old Testament, reiterated in the Messianic preaching of Jesus in the gospels, and finally embodied in the eschatological ideal of the Acts of the Apostles, of a Christian community 'holding all things in common', this radical tradition provides the inspirational source of the populist dimension of the Utopian commonwealth.[21]

Explication of the Utopian ideal within that frame of reference returns the discussion, in the first instance, to Hythlodaeus' searing critique of the political *status quo*, considered now in its specifically social content – as an indictment which leads him to denounce 'the commonwealths [which] nowadays anywhere do flourish' as but 'a conspiracy of rich men procuring their own commodites under the name and title of the commonwealth' (More 1965, pp. 240–1; 1974, p. 132). As an exposé of social injustice, two features of Hythlodaeus' critique hold a special interest. One is the way in which *republica* is pressed into service on behalf of an ideology of

---

21. Vawter 1961; Gelin 1965. The moral tradition lying behind the perception of social justice in *Utopia* is treated in Bradshaw 1981, pp. 14–21.

biblical populism. That abstract political concept now, in effect, comes to be identified with the welfare of the commons and, in doing so, to affirm a series of 'preferential options' which precisely reflect the social stance of biblical populism: solidarity with the poor, the weak, and the 'downcast' over against the rich and the powerful perceived as the exploiters and oppressors of their social inferiors. Thus, Hythlodaeus' analysis of the 'ills of the commonwealth' takes the form of an indictment in which the oppression and exploitation perpetrated by the ruling elites of Europe upon the 'poor commons' are precisely delineated: dynastic war-mongering with its associated extortionate taxation; aristocratic power-politics with its socially disruptive factionalism and violence; various forms of profiteering – land-clearance, rack-renting, price-rigging; all of this aided and abetted by a Draconian system of justice directed to social control and to the protection of private property (More 1965, pp. 58–97). The second notable feature of the analysis as an exposé of social injustice is the way in which the religious sanction to which biblical populism traditionally appealed is now powerfully reinforced by reference to the sanction invoked by the classical Wisdom tradition, human rationality. What gives the critique of Hythlodaeus its sharp satirical edge is his indictment of the conduct of the ruling elites, not merely as oppressive and exploitative of the 'poor commons' but, *ipso facto*, as irrational insofar as it leads directly to those 'ills of the commonwealth' with which they seek vainly to grapple in their capacity as governors: destitution, dearth, idleness, vagrancy, mendicancy, crime, and social violence. Turning, then, to Book II to highlight the message of the polemic, attention comes to focus on the social order of the Utopian polity. The significance of the contrast there provided is nicely pinpointed in the criticism commonly voiced in the historiography that the social order of Utopia consigns its inhabitants to an existence of drab uniformity – in dress, in housing, and in lifestyle generally.[22] So, indeed, it might seem from the perspective of the socially advantaged – whether of the twentieth or of the sixteenth century. However, the prospect of life in Utopia seems altogether more inviting from the perspective of the socially disadvantaged. First, the struggle for survival on the threshold of destitution has been eliminated: the problems of poverty and dearth have been resolved; the exigencies of sickness and old age are provided against; full employment is available for the able-bodied while, at the same time, a six-hour working day ameliorates the drudgery of manual labour. Second,

22. A recent example is Marius 1984, pp. 152–70. See also Dorsch 1966–7, pp. 345–53.

social privilege has been abolished: advancement in the public domain is based on merit; education is universally available; avocation is determined by talent and aptitude. Third, power is benign and exercised in the interests of the common people: justice is equitable and compassionate; war is avoided unless necessitated in the interests of the *publica* and is then so conducted as not to cause general hardship. In short, the 'ills' which governments inflict on the lower orders elsewhere are resolved by government as conducted in Utopia. The 'poor commons' have been emancipated. Thus the significance of the Utopian contrast viewed from the social perspective is that it affirms a conception of social justice in accordance with the criterion of biblical populism and, in doing so, provides a cluster of values which serve both to undermine the credibility of the social order of contemporary Europe and to provide a moral basis for its reformation.

The question of how this justly ordered commonwealth is to be attained finally takes the discussion to a consideration of the Utopian political strategy. In that context, the much-debated issue of Utopian communism at last arises. What significance is to be attached to Hythlodaeus' insistence, in line with Utopian practice, that the abolition of private property and the institution of a communist system of socio-economic organisation constitute the necessary conditions for the attainment of a commonwealth? Without aspiring to resolve the apparently irresolvable, some light may be thrown on that question by adhering to the interpretative procedure hitherto adopted, namely by viewing Utopian practice, not as a blueprint for precise replication, but as a rhetorical device designed to affirm a set of values which serve both to undermine the credibility of conventional European practice and to provide a moral basis for its reformation. Examined from that perspective, communism does not seem to function within the framework of the Utopian polemic as an unambiguously affirmed value. It constitutes the one feature of the Utopian political order regarding which the reiterated affirmations of Hythlodaeus encounter sustained objections from Morus. And, significantly, the latter's argument comes to rest on the same ground which he occupies in his stand in the 'Dialogue on Counsel': the need to accommodate philosophical ideals to the exigencies of practical politics. Seen in these terms, the import of the debate on Utopian communism seems to be to vindicate the pragmatic realism of the Ciceronian political activist over the uncompromising and, therefore, ineffectual idealism of the Platonic philosopher – thus both affirming the ideal and removing it from the domain of practical politics at the same time.[23] The effect of the debate, secondly, however, as in the case of the 'Dialogue on Counsel', is to reveal beyond the issue in controversy a broader area of consensus by virtue of the common commitment of Hythlodaeus and Morus to the ideology of classical Wisdom. And the effect of the consensus, in turn, is to highlight by way of contrast the divergence between the Utopian political strategy, grounded on the values and insights of the classical Wisdom tradition, and the approach adapted by the ruling elites of contemporary Europe. In this way, the issue of political strategy comes to be subsumed under the issue on which the entire Utopian polemic hinges: on the one hand, the injustice of the political order of late medieval Christendom, grounded upon Augustinian voluntarism, with its pessimistic assumptions about human nature and its approbation of the sanctions of coercion and violence; on the other hand, the justice of the Utopian political order, grounded on the values and insights of the classical Wisdom tradition, and thus directed by reason and virtue to the attainment of *respublica*. Here the clinching argument of the polemic emerges – and the discussion of the Utopian concept of the commonwealth returns to its starting point. For the message conveyed by means of the contrast in this respect, as in others, is unambiguous if paradoxical. It is that *humanitas* provides the means, through the resources of reason, rhetoric, and moral virtue, to direct government to the end of a truly Christian commonwealth.

The specific implications of this conception, as embodied in Utopian practice, provide the final cluster of values which More sought to bring to bear in order to undermine the moral credibility of the contemporary political order and to provide a moral basis for its reformation. These may be summarised under three broad categories. The first is rational planning. In accordance with the Platonic conception, Utopia represents a triumph of social and institutional engineering through which the community as a whole is enabled to achieve human fulfilment, freed from material want and directed to intellectual and moral betterment.[24] In contrast, the hidebound traditionalism of contemporary Europe, with its uncritical veneration of custom and tradition, serves to perpetuate a political order which, as Hythlodaeus' critique has shown, is designed to serve the interests of the ruling elites alone and, *ipso facto*, to generate poverty and moral

---

23. Bradshaw 1981, pp. 18–21, 24–7. The case presented there seems compatible with the revised interpretation presented in Skinner 1987, pp. 146–57.
24. On Utopian rational planning see More 1965, pp. 78–9, 146–7, 158–9, 208–10. Cf. Hexter 1952, pp. 56–62.

corruption. The second category relates to the corollary of rational planning in the Platonic conception – as transformed, however, under the inspiration of Ciceronian rhetoric. It concerns value-formation based on reason as the means of securing social and political harmony in the polity, as against reliance on the exercise of coercive authority. In Utopia, the resources of rhetoric are deployed on behalf of an imaginatively orchestrated programme of formal education, civic ritual, and popular propaganda designed to inculcate public virtue and to secure personal commitment to the Utopian ideology. The contrast is with the ruthlessly authoritarian approach of contemporary European governments to the problems of social and political order. There, reliance is placed on Draconian penal legislation and violent repression deployed in vain pursuit of mere external obedience. The third category relates to perhaps the most remarkable and, certainly, the least remarked on, aspect of the Utopian strategy. It concerns the means whereby the polity accommodates itself to the world of *Realpolitik*, a world in which moral values are thrust aside in the self-interested pursuit of power, wealth, and reputation. Here the term statecraft may be applied to the Utopian strategy in full awareness of the word's Machiavellian resonances. Reason and rhetoric, deployed as the means to counter political subversion, emerge in Utopian practice in the form of a series of prudential expedients which disconcertingly mirror Machiavelli's contemporaneous reformulation of the meaning of political virtue (Skinner 1978, I, pp. 128–38; Butterfield 1940). These run the gamut from the irreproachable – foresight and circumspection – to the morally reprehensible – dissimulation, bribery, assassination, ultimately warfare. Nevertheless, a fundamental difference is to be discerned between Utopian statecraft and the Machiavellian version. And this serves as the basis, in turn, of a contrast between Utopian practice and *Realpolitik* as practised by the political entrepreneurs of contemporary Europe – a major inspirational source, according to the author himself, of Machiavellian *virtú*. The distinction lies in the criterion which governs practice in each case. For the latter, the interests of the ruler – what maintains his state – constitute the criterion of political conduct. They constitute the 'necessity' which for Machiavelli supersedes the claims of orthodox morality. In contrast, Utopian statecraft is practised within the constraints of moral orthodoxy. Its criterion is the interests of the commonwealth. These constitute the moral absolute by appeal to which deviations from the morally ideal may be justified on the grounds of 'the lesser evil';[25] thus the deployment of

25. The classical origins of this conception may be traced to Cicero, *De Officiis*, on which see Hunt 1954, ch. 6.

mercenaries as 'war-fodder' in preference to peace-loving natives, or the resort to espionage and assassination as a means of averting full-scale warfare (More 1965, pp. 202–9). In that light the final implication of the contrast between Utopian statecraft and contemporary European power politics emerges. The message is that the goal of the commonwealth may be pursued even in the amoral world of *Realpolitik*. In that regard, Morus' sober insistence, articulated in the course of the 'Dialogue on Counsel', on the political function of the humanist is most apt. 'You must with a crafty wile and a subtle, train, study and endeavour yourself, as much as in you lieth, to handle the matter wittily and handsomely for the purpose; and that which you cannot turn to good, so to order it that it be not very bad' (More 1965, pp. 98–101; 1974, p. 48). Not the least of the ironies of *Utopia*, as the 'Dialogue on Counsel' shows, is that Morus, better than Hythlodaeus, grasped the meaning of the Utopian message: in the resources of reason, rhetoric, and moral virtue, the humanist possesses the means and, therefore, incurs the duty, to pursue the interest of the commonwealth even in the world of *Realpolitik*.

Analysed in the light of its intellectual provenance, therefore, the Utopian ideal of the commonwealth is seen to represent a fusion of classical and of Christian values. As such, it comprehends three distinctive ideological elements. First, harking back to the conception of *respublica* in its original Platonic formulation, it affirms a philosophical ideal of government as directed by rational means to the attainment of public virtue. Secondly, reflecting the more political range of reference which the notion acquired in the Ciceronian rhetorical tradition, it affirms the ideal of a republican constitution as the guarantee of good government directed in accordance with the Platonic conception. Thirdly, it comprehends a notion of social justice, derived from the Judaeo-Christian tradition. In this dimension it affirms the populist values of biblical social morality, encapsulated in the Messianic aspiration for the emancipation of the *populus* from poverty and social oppression. Here the controlling conception of the Utopian ideology presents itself. It is the vision of *humanitas*, the means to which classical Wisdom looked for the realisation of *respublica*, brought to bear in order to realise the Messianic aspiration for an emancipated *populus*.

It remains to assess the representative character of the Utopian ideal by relating it to the corpus of humanist political writing. In short, the question which arises is whether, as a treatise for the reform of the commonwealth, *Utopia* can claim the status of a humanist manifesto. In proceeding to consider that question, an instructive comparison is offered at the outset in the form of an analogous political discourse produced by the acknowledged leader of the humanist circle with which More was associated. The text is the *Institutio Principis Christiani*, written by Erasmus for the young Habsburg monarch, Charles V, partly as a treastise on the education of a prince and partly as a manual of instruction for use in such circumstances. This context is relevant to the comparison in that it explains Erasmus' rhetorical strategy. In contrast to the satirical and calculatedly shocking mode of *Utopia*, the mode of the *Institutio* is sober and discursive, befitting the dignity, as well as the personal gravity, of the young prince to whom the work is dedicated. Nevertheless, as shall be seen, for all the constraining circumstances, the ideological stance which Erasmus' treatise adopts is unmistakably Utopian.

The ideological affinities of the *Institutio* are already suggested in the paean to Wisdom which occupies its 'Dedicatory Epistle'. They emerge in specific terms as the discourse itself gets under way by means of the usual preliminary consideration of the best form of government. Here, the conventionality of the format is belied by the unconventionality of Erasmus' conclusion. Remarkably, in the context of the political culture of post-feudal northern Europe, and all the more so in a treatise addressed to a monarch in the process of accumulating a vast empire by inheritance, Erasmus proceeds to undermine the credibility of hereditary monarchy.[26] His ploy is to present it, in effect, as a historical anachronism, a survival, as he claims, of barbaric custom, over against which he sets out elective monarchy as the system rationally designed to secure a monarch 'apt to rule' in the interests of the commonwealth (*Institutio*: 1936, pp. 139–40). The Ciceronian register, thus struck, resonates throughout the treatise, as the characteristic republican values are affirmed in some of Erasmus' most intensely expressed pages: government by consent and under the law; political liberty based on a common humanity; the heinousness of political corruption and tyranny (e.g. *Institutio*: 1936, pp. 163–4, 174–9, 199). Meanwhile, consideration of the qualities necessary in a prince 'apt to rule' serves to introduce a second aspect of the Utopian ideology and, by the same token, a second dimension of the *Institutio's* tacit polemic against the cherished values of the contemporary political culture. Predictably, no doubt, the prince 'apt to rule' in Erasmus' treatment, turns out to be the ubiquitous philosopher-king of humanist political treatises. More signifi-

---

26. For a study of the political ideas of Erasmus which differs in emphasis and in which the radical edge is considerably blunted, see Tracy 1978.

cantly, however, as closer inspection reveals, he also provides an embodiment of the values of Utopian *respublica*, as conceived in accordance with the Platonic conception of political justice: he governs in the public interest, not for dynastic or personal profit; his concern is civil affairs, not foreign wars of aggrandisement; he relies on reason and not on power as the sanction of political authority; he observes merit and not privilege of birth or wealth as the criterion of public status; he administers justice with a view to reform and not to vindictive punishment. The casualty of the polemic here is the heroic warrior-king much-celebrated in medieval chivalry who now, in the pages of the *Institutio*, merges into the spectre of the classical tyrant – arbitrary, aggressive, vainglorious, deluded by flatterers, avaricious, cruel, a war-monger, and a perverter of justice.[27] Finally, as the discussion proceeds from a consideration of the qualities of the Christian prince to a consideration of the practice of government in the Christian polity, the *Institutio's* populist stance is highlighted in two features. One relates to the exercise of political authority. The radical position adopted here is sufficiently indicated in the novel biblical exegesis on which the discussion pivots. Erasmus disposes of the standard text, Romans 13:1–6, with its authoritarian connotations – 'Be obedient to the powers that be' – by expounding it, in humanist fashion, in relation to its context, as an admonition to Christians living under pagan government. On the other hand, he directs attention in a lengthy excursus to the text which he urges as normative for the exercise of all Christian authority, religious or political, Matthew, 20:25–6. Thus Christ, the humble servant, set over against the lords of the world who 'make their authority felt', becomes the model for the Christian magistrate (*Institutio*: 1936, pp. 162–80). The second feature relates directly to the issue of social justice as the *Institutio* proceeds to provide guidelines for the Christian prince on those aspects of government which, in the early sixteenth century, especially impinged on the well-being of the *populus*: taxation, social privilege, criminal justice, warfare. Here the Utopian preferential option for the poor against the rich is clearly affirmed and, in the process, the Utopian indictment is echoed that the existing political order amounts to a conspiracy of the rich against the poor 'in the name of the commonwealth'. Thus attention is directed to the ways in which the political system operates to reinforce social inequality by, for instance, enabling the 'wealth of the multitude' to be appropriated by the few, by taxing necessary, not luxurious, goods, by repressing crime and

---

27. A contrast between the virtuous prince and the tyrant is presented in *Institutio*: 1936, pp. 162–5.

social discontent instead of addressing the underlying problems of dearth and unemployment, above all, by embroiling the community in the devastation of warfare – the 'sea of all calamities' to the denunciation of which Erasmus devotes a final impassioned chapter. The effect of affirming the Utopian ideology here, as elsewhere, therefore, is to undermine, at the same time, some of the most cherished shibboleths of the contemporary political culture: in this case, the inviolable rights of property and heredity, the divinely ordained wisdom of lineage and social hierarchy, the axiomatic morality of severe justice and dynastic warfare.

A comparison of *Utopia* and the contemporary *Institutio* reveals, therefore, a common ideological standpoint. Both are concerned to affirm the threefold Utopian ideal of a rationally governed, constitutionally organised, and socially just commonwealth. That is the first significance of the comparison. Nevertheless, it is also important to note that the polemical thrust of the *Institutio* is reformist rather than revolutionary. Thus, the moral which Erasmus draws from his demystification of hereditary monarchy is not that the system must be supplanted but that its deficiencies must be remedied – in the first instance by equipping the heir to fulfil his task by means of an appropriate educational formation. Here a second aspect of the ideological correspondence of *Utopia* and the *Institutio* emerges: the conviction that the existing ills of the commonwealth can be reformed by a strategy of rational planning, value-formation, and statecraft. Thus the *Institutio*, it might be said, provides the spectacle of Morus, in the guise of Erasmus, accommodating the Utopian ideal to the political environment of early sixteenth-century northern Europe.

In assessing the claims of *Utopia* to the status of a humanist manifesto, a second contemporaneous treatise, produced in very similar circumstances to the *Institutio*, offers a valuably contrasting perspective. That is *La Monarchie de France*, written by the Swiss humanist, Seyssel, as a guide for the young Francis I in governing the patrimony which he had just inherited. The effect of the comparison here is to reveal, in the first place, a significantly different ideological thrust to Seyssel's treatise. In contrast to Erasmus' manifestly Ciceronian predilections, the Swiss humanist does not hesitate to assure the young Francis I that monarchy in general, and the French monarchy in particular, constitute the best form of government; moreover, that heredity constitutes the best form of monarchical succession (*La Monarchie*: 1981, Bk I, chs. 4–8). Again, in contrast to Erasmus' Platonic emphasis on the claims of merit, (i.e. rational virtue) as the criterion for public office and status, Seyssel presents lineage and degree as part of a divinely ordained cosmic order which, as such, require to be buttressed by political status and social privilege (*La Monarchie*: 1981, Bk I, chs. 13–16, Bk II, ch. 18). Such a view of the cosmic order is scarcely compatible with a populist social perspective and, unsurprisingly, Seyssel's analysis of the 'ills of the commonwealth' contains no trace of the social exploitation detected by More and Erasmus. Here, then, is a humanist political standpoint markedly more in tune with the *status quo* than the stance reflected in the Utopian ideology. Nevertheless, the significance of the comparison lies also in the fact that, Seyssel's social conservatism notwithstanding, closer examination reveals a basic ideological affinity with his more radical fellow humanists. In the first place, as already noted at an earlier stage of the discussion, the treatise of Seyssel shares with those of More and Erasmus a common reformist aspiration – a critical perspective on the present state of the commonwealth and a commitment to remedying the situation. Secondly, in more specific terms, the reforms which Seyssel proceeds to adumbrate reflect a conception of the 'best state of a commonwealth' in generic agreement with the Utopian model. Thus, while acknowledging the absolute status of the French monarchy, he nevertheless emphasises the existence of 'bridles' in the form of religion, law, and 'policy' (i.e. its governmental institutions) which effectively preclude the possibility of arbitrary government. And a major concern of Seyssel's programme of reform is to reinforce the constitutional restraints upon the monarchy by means of a conciliar system (*La Monarchie*: 1981, Bk I, chs. 9–12, Bk II, chs. 4–7). Similarly, Seyssel's responsiveness to Plato's notion of political justice is reflected in two features of his reforming programme. One is an aversion to coercive sanctions as a normal mode of government: the monarch must manifest his *humanitas* in the form of the princely virtues – liberality, clemency, honour – and must strive to overcome force by reason (*La Monarchie*: 1981, Bk IV, chs. 2–4, Bk V, ch. 13). The second is his insistence that the claims of ancient lineage to social privilege and public honour must be supported by moral attainment – *noblesse oblige* – hence the value of humanist education (*La Monarchie*: 1981, ch. 18). Finally, despite the absence in Seyssel of the radical conception of social justice which informs the populist critique of More and Erasmus, his programme, nevertheless, reflects a concern to relieve the social plight of the *populus* by alleviating the burdens of taxation and repressive legislation and by providing moderate opportunity for upward social mobility (*La Monarchie*: 1981, Bk II, chs. 22–5). Examination of Seyssel's treatise in the light of the Utopian ideology serves to draw attention of one further point of identity on which a comment may be made in conclusion. That is the strategy which both espouse as a means of reforming the ills of the commonwealth. In the same tradition as *Utopia* and the *Institutio*, *La Monarchie* sets out to show the way in which the ills of the commonwealth can be reformed by the threefold formula of rational planning, value-formation, and statecraft – and, in doing so, of course, it affirms what it seeks to exemplify.

Unity, as well as diversity, therefore, is found to mark the comparison between *Utopia* and Seyssel's treatise. Both features are significant for the purpose of relating the Utopian ideal to the corpus of humanist political commentary. Examination of the corpus in detail would serve to reveal a bifurcation of the humanist approach to the problem of the reform of the commonwealth. On the one side are ranged the Erasmians who espouse the radical conception of *Utopia*, seeking to accommodate it to the contemporary political environment without repudiating its controlling vision of an emancipated *populus*. That tradition is well represented in the writings of Vives in the 1520s[28] and in the striking contribution of Starkey in the 1530s.[29] On the other side, the conservatism of Seyssel is abundantly evident in the political reflections of his more distinguished colleague, Budé, or in the next generation, in the classic *Boke Named the Governour* of the Englishman, Elyot.[30] The source of the fundamental solidarity in humanist political commentary has been explained and, it is hoped, now satisfactorily demonstrated. It can be traced to the common intellectual matrix provided by a series of seminal Renaissance ideas within which their reflection was conducted. Inspired by an ideal of the dignity of Man and of the human capacity for self-perfection, the humanists were at one in their dissatisfaction with the political culture of their time and in their commitment to its reformation. To explore the intellectual sources of the

28. The key texts of Vives for these purposes are *De pace inter Caesarum et Franciscum* (1525). *De disciplinis* (1531), *De subventione pauperum* (1526), *De concordia* (1526), *De pacificatione* (1526). Vives – like More – rejected the Anabaptists' assertion of communism as an absolute prescription of Christian morality in *De communione rerum* (1535). Cf. Noreña 1970.
29. Starkey's major tracts on politics are *A Dialogue between Pole and Lupset* (1529–32), ed. Mayer 1989, and *The Exhortation to the People* (1537), ed. Heritage 1878. A recent study which fails to take account of the Utopian affinities of Starkey's *Dialogue* and, accordingly, presents it as an affirmation of aristocratic oligarchy is Mayer 1989. See also Bradshaw 1979, pp. 467–9.
30. For a comparison of the political ideas of Budé and Erasmus see Tracy 1978, *passim*. A recent study of Elyot sees a 'basic inconsistency' between his ascription of absolute political authority to the Prince in Book I and the severe limitations placed upon princely power by the constraints of virtue in Book III, Fox and Guy 1986, p. 57. Elyot's 'inconsistency' is entirely characteristic of the constitutional conservatism displayed by the humanist tradition represented here by Seyssel. Cf. Lehmberg 1960; Major 1964.

difference between the two traditions does not come within the scope of the present study. Briefly, the key is to be found in the temporising possibilities offered by the conservatives' espousal of Neoplatonism and the Aristotelian *via media*.

This tension notwithstanding, the significance of the humanist achievement must be emphasised before concluding. The discussion returns, therefore, to the Utopian ideal of *respublica*. It was the concept and the rhetoric of *respublica* which gave the notion of renaissance or renewal as embodied in the political thought of northern humanism its specific content. The socially benign orientation of that ideal assumes special significance in the light of the historical juncture at which it emerges. This was precisely the moment when, as announced in the works of Machiavelli, a novel notion of political morality began to establish itself. Meanwhile, as the phenomenon of Martin Luther signified, the old Augustinian perception underwent dramatic rehabilitation. Fatefully for the course of intellectual development in the west thereafter – and, specifically, for the course of the development of political thought – these two highly influential thinkers shared a common anthropological starting point: a profoundly pessimistic assessment of the human capacity for self-perfection.[31] In consequence, under the auspices of this unlikely alliance, political thinkers in the early modern period found themselves increasingly fascinated by the spectre of Leviathan. At this crucial turning point in the history of western political thought, therefore, the humanists' recovery of the ideal of *respublica* and of the Messianic aspiration for an emancipated *populus* can be claimed to have preserved for the west the line of continuity between its moral tradition and the political morality not only of classical antiquity but of the Judaeo-Christian scripture.

---

31. On Machiavelli's anthropological pessimism see *The Prince*, ch. 17. For one example among many of Luther's radical appraisal of the consequences for human nature of Adam's Fall see his exegesis of Genesis, ch. 2, in Trinkaus 1979.

5

Scholasticism: survival and revival

J.H. BURNS

Endings, in the history of ideas, are no easier to identify with certainty than beginnings. Scholasticism, that product of the mature intellectual culture of medieval Europe, was to experience, even within the period surveyed in this volume, more than one revival. Revitalisation might indeed be a better term; for that which has not died need not in the strict sense be revived, and there is ample evidence to indicate that the scholastic tradition, however exhausted it might seem at times to be, clung stubbornly to life. The advent of the printing press ensured the preservation, the transmission, and the wider dissemination of many scholastic texts. Nor was this characteristic only of the late fifteenth and early sixteenth centuries – when it was only to be expected that what were still the standard works in theology and philosophy would be committed to print. Well into the seventeenth century we find, most notably, the twelve-volume edition of the work of Duns Scotus published in 1639. A year later – an instance of particular relevance here – Jean Buridan's commentary on Aristotle's *Politics* was printed at Oxford. The place is as significant as the date – as a reminder that academic conservatism played its part in keeping the scholastic mode alive. Hobbes' attack on the schoolmen – from whose works, nonetheless, he no doubt took more of his ideas than he cared to acknowledge – indicates, again, that the doctrine he had received at the turn of the century was still to the fore some fifty years later.

By that time, indeed, a new scholasticism had developed vigorously alongside the old. This chapter, however, is not concerned with what has

The following abbreviations are used in this chapter:
CHLMP   The Cambridge History of Later Medieval Philosophy, ed. N. Kretzmann, Anthony Kenny, and Jan Pinborg (Cambridge: Cambridge University Press, 1982)

DBI   Dizionario Biografico degli italiani, ed. A.M. Ghisalberti *et al.* (Rome: Istituto della Enciclopedia Italiana, 1960–)

been termed the *Barockscholastik* of Robert Bellarmine and Suárez.[1] The focus here is on the hundred years or so from the mid-fifteenth to the mid-sixteenth centuries. There can of course be no sharp lines of division in such a matter; but it is at least arguable that late medieval scholasticism can claim – especially perhaps in political thought – its own distinctive historical importance, setting aside its relationship to the scholastic theology and philosophy which developed in the late sixteenth century and beyond in response to the challenges of the Reformation and Counter-Reformation.

It is true that late medieval scholasticism has been seen as a spent force even before the period here in question. Of almost 150 authors deemed worthy of a biographical note in *The Cambridge History of Later Medieval Philosophy* no more than ten or a dozen can be regarded as having flourished within the hundred years referred to above. The philosophical work of those years is certainly no longer dismissed as trifling and insignificant. Thus the notion of an 'eclipse of the insights of medieval logic' by 'a humanistic, rhetorically-orientated logic' is now seen to stand in need of substantial modification (*CHLMP*, p. 787). The grounds for modification are located particularly in developments down to about 1530 to which major contributions were made by thinkers who, as we shall see, were important also in the political thinking of the period. Yet all this is still advanced in a chapter headed 'The eclipse of medieval logic' in a section entitled 'The defeat, neglect and revival of scholasticism'; and the 'revival' in this context belongs essentially to the second half of the sixteenth century or later. Historians of philosophy, it seems, would still find little plausibility in any suggestion that scholastic writers of the period 1450–1550 produced original work of importance to them.

With theology – and political ideas were at least as firmly embedded in theological as in philosophical thinking – things are rather different. Here revaluation by recent scholarship has increasingly rated the late fifteenth century as a period of major importance. A figure like Gabriel Biel, who will receive at most a passing reference in a history of philosophy, emerges in the theological perspective as a thinker of stature and extensive influence (Oberman 1967a, 1967b; Oakley 1979). Nor are historians of theology now concerned merely to identify, whether for praise or for blame, 'forerunners of the Reformation'. There is, indeed, obvious interest and importance in locating the roots of those doctrines which made Protestantism the force it was to be in early modern Europe. That, however, is not the only significance of the ideas in question; and it is in any case essential to

---

1. See pp.237–40, 292–7 below.

understand those ideas in their genesis within medieval thinking and in the society from which that thinking emerged.

Such issues commonly arise on the frontier between theology and the theory of society and politics. A good illustration is afforded by the question of 'individualism', with particular reference to the concept of rights in medieval thinking. Whether we are to look here to a 'Gersonian' theory of active individual rights (Tuck 1979) or rather to the developing doctrine of conscience from the twelfth century onwards (Tierney 1983), we must at all events come to terms with a revised understanding of the place of the individual in medieval thought and experience (Black, in Burns 1988, pp. 588–606). It may be the case that a figure such as John Wessel Gansfort expressed an 'emphatic insistence on the individual-subjective conscience' over against 'the objective, collectivist, corporational standpoint'. Yet this is not necessarily to say that such an insistence 'can be seen as the decisive turning-point from the wholeness point of view to the individualistic standpoint' (Ullman 1975, p. 305). Other considerations apart, it is plain that a good deal of further work is needed on late medieval sources in order to unravel the strands in a complex pattern.

In any case, theologies and perceptions of man in relationship to society can properly be regarded as contexts in which the late fifteenth and early sixteenth centuries have more to offer than the comparative aridity of scholastic philosophy in the period might lead one to expect. A similar claim can also be made in respect of more narrowly 'political' ideas – ideas about authority, government, and law. Here, indeed, historical recognition is of somewhat longer standing. Half a century ago and more, the importance of a writer like Jacques Almain, or of his teacher John Mair (Major) was duly acknowledged (Carlyle 1903–36, VI, pp. 241–8; Allen 1928, pp. 336–7). Acton and Figgis for that matter had seen the importance of a tradition of thought stemming from the conciliar movement generated by the Great Schism of 1378–1418 (Acton 1910, p. 17; Figgis 1916, pp. 41–70). Yet here too more recent scholarship may claim to have made an essential contribution: the almost explosive growth, in the third quarter of the twentieth century, in the exploration of 'conciliarist' ideas has lengthened and deepened the perspectives in which those ideas are to be properly understood.[2] Not the least important aspect of this is the recognition that before we consider conciliarism as a 'political theory', we

---

2. The publication since 1969 of the *Annuarium historiae Conciliorum* is one indication of the historical aspect of this interest.

need to understand it as an ecclesiology – or rather a group of ecclesiologies. Theology, and especially the theology of the church, can never be very far below the horizon as we survey this intellectual landscape.

The terrain is extensive, variegated, and uneven: for its exploration some kind of provisional sketch map is essential. Different 'projections' (to continue the cartographical metaphor) are available, though each of them will no doubt – as such projections must – tend to misrepresent and distort in some respects even if it illuminates in others. Such mapping as is possible here must leave out many details while emphasising some features at the expense of others. What follows will concentrate mainly on some half-dozen authors, whose arguments will be examined in relation to three major themes or patterns in the thinking of the period. The first of these is the dialectic between different schools in philosophy and theology generally; the second is the theory of *dominium*; and the third, the issue between papalist and conciliarist views of the polity of the church, together with their consequences for civil or temporal government.

i   Schoolmen and schools of thought

Of an earlier phase in the history of medieval thought it has been said that 'The label of nominalism . . . lies like a pall . . . across the philosophy and theology of the fourteenth century' (Leff 1976, pp. 12–13); and no doubt the tendency of such labelling is, for the fifteenth century, too, to obscure 'heterogeneity' and 'eclecticism'. That there was a full measure of eclecticism will be evident enough in what follows. Yet there can at least be no doubt as to the importance attached to identifications and affiliations of this kind by fifteenth-century thinkers themselves. The point is well illustrated in the case of Gansfort. The issue between one school of thought and another seemed to him of such moment that his primary object in moving from Heidelberg, where he had taught the realism learnt as a student at Cologne, to Paris was 'to confute the opinions of those two most famous masters, Henry Zomeren and Nicolaus of Utrecht, and win them from the opinions of the Formalists to those of the Realists, to which I subscribed' (Gansfort 1917, I, p. 285). Gansfort's reference here to 'the Formalists' is a valuable reminder that the issue was not a simple confrontation between 'nominalism' and 'realism'; Scotist doctrine was still important and indeed experienced a notable revival in this period. Within three months, however, it was Gansfort himself who changed his position: and by the end of a year he had moved from the 'formalism' he found in Scotus and others to the nominalism he was to uphold during and after his stay of some sixteen years in Paris. This involved taking sides in a dispute then sharply dividing the university; and if, as seems likely, Gansfort left Paris in 1474 or 1475, this may well have been connected with the imposition of the royal ban on nominalist teaching which prevailed for seven years, till 1481.[3]

Jacobus Hoeck, with whom Gansfort was later to argue at length on the subject of indulgences, was, as *prior Sorbonicus*, a leading opponent of the nominalists; and Gansfort made a particular point, in the later controversy, of the philosophical position upon which he based his doctrinal stance. It was no mere matter of scoring points against an adversary's 'wavering words' by insisting that 'our Nominalist school will not permit such inconsistency and incoherence' (1917, I, p. 302, 1966, p. 890). Nor was Gansfort's concern simply to argue that theological mastery depended upon philosophical rigour: 'who could ever attain to that apex of theology, to which Peter d'Ailly climbed, without definitions, divisions, argumentations, distinctions, and logical instances?' (1917, I, p. 308, 1966, p. 895). The relationship between philosophy and theology reached beyond this into the heart of Gansfort's teaching. When discussing the love of God he invokes the nominalist analysis of 'intension' and claims that 'By adopting the view of the nominalists it becomes easy to understand what should be taught, viz., that we ought to grow in love' (1917, I, p. 323, 1966, p. 907).

These may appear to be, and in some degree are, matters remote from 'political thought'. Yet there are connections. The problem of indulgences was in part a problem of authority, and Gansfort's position depends upon his convictions as to where authority ultimately lies. Nothing in Hoeck's argument, perhaps, disturbed him more than the claims made for papal authority in doctrinal matters: 'I am not a little horrified at your admonition that the pope's authority ought to have more weight with me than reason . . . you admonish me in matters of this sort to regard the authority of the pope, not merely as a substitute for reason, but as superior to it!' The reference here to reason is, for Gansfort, inseparable from the test of scriptural warranty:

What, I ask, am I to regard as reason in these matters? Is it not the Holy Scriptures? Do you wish to put the authority of the pope above the Holy Scriptures? The will of the pope and the authority of Scripture have not been placed on an equal footing so that, just as the will of the pope should be regulated by the truth of Scripture, so that truth should be regulated by the will of the pope.

(1917, I, pp. 304–5, 1966, p. 892)

3. On the effects of the ban see, e.g., Renaudet 1953, pp. 90–4; Ritter 1963, pp. 31ff.

And when he finds even 'the venerable Gerson' apparently departing from this position, Gansfort feels constrained to suppose that this was only the result of anxiety to avoid the scandal and schism that might result from pressing the claims of strict theological truth with too much vehemence (cf. 1917, I, p. 308).

What is certainly striking is Gansfort's readiness to appeal, more or less directly, from papal authority to the individual's reason and conscience. There is scarcely a pause at the 'conciliarist' position which retained so strong a hold for many thinkers – and not least among those of nominalist inclination. Yet, as always, caution is needed before identifying the connection between nominalism and individualism. Not only does Gansfort, of course, attribute essential authority to the church, while denying that this authority can be identified with that of either pope or council. It is also important to take account of the special place he accords to 'the wise man'. And, perhaps most important of all, he insists that 'Every man in his individual capacity (*quisque privatus*) ought to assume that no assembly of distinguished men will err in its definitions' (1917, II, p. 204, 1966, p. 781). Gansfort's individualism allows both for the validity of collective judgements and for the superiority of some individual judgements to others.

Parisian nominalism rapidly recovered after 1481 from what had been a reverse rather than a defeat. By the turn of the century, in the academic generation of John Mair and his first pupils, 'terminism' had indeed achieved substantial preponderance in philosophical teaching. It was against that preponderance that Peter Crockaert, at first a follower of Mair's teaching, led a Thomist revival which, as we shall see, was to be important for political thinking in the first half of the sixteenth century. Paris itself was not, it is true, to be a major centre of Thomist thinking in those directions; and for that matter the most important Thomist of the first quarter of the century, Tommaso de Vio, later Cardinal Cajetan, owed nothing to Parisian teaching. It is also the case that other, earlier manifestations of Thomist vitality in thinking about society and government demand some consideration. These matters, however, can be most appropriately discussed in later sections of this chapter: the focus for the moment may remain on the fortunes of nominalist thinking, especially in centres other than Paris.

There had always been, of course, major nominalist centres in Germany and more widely in central Europe. In the fifteenth century Erfurt seems to have had special importance, and it was certainly there that Gabriel Biel absorbed the 'Ockhamism' that was to pervade his later teaching (Picascia

1979, p. 138). That teaching phase in Biel's career came late in life, for he was already in his sixties when he came to the University of Tübingen, founded in 1476. In its earliest years the Tübingen theology faculty was presided over by Johann Heynlin (Johannes a Lapide: *c.* 1428/31–96). Heynlin came to Tübingen from Basle, but the formative part of his career – spanning a period of over twenty years from 1453 to 1475 – had been spent in Paris. There, as a prominent member of the arts faculty and latterly in theology, his position had been firmly on the realist side, and this seems to have been the initial tendency in theological teaching at Tübingen. Heynlin's 'reign', it is true, was brief: he left Tübingen in 1479. Five years passed, however, before Biel began to teach there; and, influential though he clearly was, there is no reason to suppose that other than 'Ockhamist' influences vanished at once – or perhaps at all – from the university. Conrad Summenhart (d. 1502) outlived Biel and had preceded him at Tübingen. Like Heynlin he had gone there from Paris, where his studies were pursued during the ban on nominalist teaching; and his earlier formation, at Heidelberg, had been in the realist *via antiqua*.[4]

Biel's own position is doubtless essentially nominalist (Oberman 1967a; Picascia 1979). Yet it can also be argued – at least in those aspects of the matter that are most relevant here – that he exemplifies the more eclectic, less school-dominated features of fifteenth-century thought. He had himself studied not only at Erfurt but also at Heidelberg (where teaching was offered in both *via antiqua* and *via moderna*), and at Cologne (a major centre of Albertist and Thomist realism). The middle decades of his career had been spent in largely non-academic activities – he was provost of several collegiate churches and a notable preacher. It is thus in no way surprising to be told that when he came to Tübingen to teach theology according to the *via moderna* his doctrine 'had a markedly pastoral orientation' (Oakley 1979, p. 237). Biel was sufficiently concerned with vindicating a substantial role for human reason in the process of salvation to have incurred Luther's censure as a 'pelagianiser' if not a Pelagian (Ozment 1980, pp. 233–5).[5] In discussing the crucial question of free will, Biel draws extensively on older medieval thinkers such as Anselm and Bernard of Clairvaux; but on some of the critically important philosophical issues, the influence of the nominalist tradition, represented by Ockham and Gregory

---

4. For Haynlin, *Auctarium Chartularii Universitatis Parisiensis*, 6: 250 n. 7; for Summenhart, 539 n. 5. For the early history of the Tübingen theological faculty, see Hermelink 1906; Oberman 1977, chs. 3–6; and cf. Picascia 1979, p. 33. Summenhart's early teaching, however, would have been in the arts faculty.
5. Opinions on this question have varied: cf. Oakley 1979, p. 147 and n. 26.

of Rimini, is strongly marked (Biel 1973–84, II, pp. 480–96).[6] On the other hand, when examining the problem of 'original justice' and the 'natural rectitude' of the will, it is to Scotus rather than to the nominalists that Biel turns for support: Ockham is mentioned it is true, but only as having in this matter 'imitated' Scotus (II, pp. 555–61).[7]

Biel's eclecticism is also apparent in matters with a more directly political bearing, though here, indeed, his indebtedness to Parisian nominalism is both clear and fully acknowledged. In the important discussion of law in his commentary on Book III of the *Sentences*, he proceeds wholly on the basis of positions laid down by Jean Gerson. An obligatory law is a true (or valid) sign informing a rational creature of the right reason of him who prescribes it, enjoining or prohibiting some act. The 'sign' may be mental, vocal, or written; and while the reference to 'right reason' is crucial, so too is the element of will, implied at some points but for the most part explicit and emphatic. All this is applied to human law – for which Biel adopts Gerson's characterisation, *positiva praeceptiva* – in both its canon and its civil form. The whole analysis comes almost verbatim from Gerson.[8] Scotus too is invoked, however, both in regard to natural law and in discussing the dispensing power. With Aquinas also among the authorities cited, the impression of a composite rather than anything like a monolithic theory is heightened (III, pp. 627–33).

The preponderance of Gerson's authority in this key passage remains striking; and it reflects a pervasive Gersonian influence on the thought of the period. Gerson's works, substantial in scale and varied in genre, often had political implications even when their primary concern was not political. The *De vita spirituali animae* is a notable instance. Its analysis of law, utilised by Biel, was used in the same way by, among others, John Mair (Mair 1519, fo. 15vA). Nor was the penetration of Gerson's ideas restricted to narrowly academic contexts. It has been shown that the vernacular *Meroure of Wyssdome*, written for James IV of Scotland by John Ireland in 1490, incorporates extensive unacknowledged borrowings from Gerson.[9] If it is arguable that, in terms of nominalist philosophy and

6. These nominalist references occur, for instance, in the discussion of such questions as proving free will or establishing whether the will is a sufficient cause of actions.
7. 'Hanc quaestionem tractat *Doctor subtilis* [Scotus] II dist. 29, quem in hac materia imitatur Occam.' There are no other references to Ockham under this heading.
8. Biel refers directly both to the *De vita spirituali animae* and to the *De potestate ecclesiastica*.
9. This was first established by Mr David Brown of the University of Glasgow and will be fully documented in Dr Craig McDonald's forthcoming edition for the Scottish Text Society of Books VI and VII of the *Meroure*. See also Mason 1987, esp. pp. 129–31, 139–41. For Ireland see Burns 1955 (an account now, however, needing substantial revision).

theology in general, Pierre d'Ailly is the most influential fifteenth-century thinker,[10] there is certainly a case for according priority to Gerson's influence on the political ideas of the latter part of the century and beyond. Once again, however, caution is needed in categorising a thinker and characterising his influence. Gerson is not properly to be seen as exemplifying anything like a direct antithesis to the teaching of Aquinas (see Tierney 1983; Burns 1983b). And the most substantial study of Biel's theory of law suggests that 'Biel's concept of law . . . approximates very closely to the Thomist concept' (Ott 1952, p. 264). The tendency for a diversity of approaches to converge is something to be borne in mind in examining the theory of *dominium* in this period.

ii   Lordship, rights, and society

The case of Wessel Gansfort has already illustrated a possible connection between nominalism and some kind of individualism, and there will be occasion to look later at another aspect of Gansfort's thought. His writings did not, however, lend themselves to sustained theoretical analysis. For the concepts of *dominium* and rights as these were deployed in late fifteenth-century thinking it is necessary to look elsewhere; and it may indeed be best to begin by turning away from the nominalist tradition to a thinker whose ideas were cast in a different mould. Antoninus of Florence belongs, indeed, to the very margins of the period covered here; his *Summa Theologica* was written, or at least begun, in the late 1440s. Its influence, however, was exerted – and widely diffused – in the second half of the century and later.[11] As a Dominican, Antoninus was in some sense *ex professo* a Thomist; but his concern was not to expound Aquinas' system as a whole, but rather, taking that system as his foundation, to develop its implications in the context of human action and relationships. The importance of his *Summa* is epitomised in the claim that it was 'the first work to have embraced the study of moral theology on such a scale' (Mandonnet, cit. *DBI*, III, p. 529a). Antoninus' moral concerns, moreover, mirrored the problems of his own society – of the bustling mercantile economy of Florence, where he was already archbishop when the *Summa* was written. Antoninus, indeed,

---

10. Of the few thinkers of the period to receive much attention in *CHLMP*, d'Ailly is given the most extensive treatment.
11. The frequency of early printings of the *Summa* indicates its 'immense diffusion and success' (*DBI*, III, p. 530b, where seven editions in the period down to 1550 are mentioned; but this is by no means a complete list).

might well command more attention in a history of economic thought than in the context of political ideas. Yet *dominium* is so central in late medieval political thinking that such a substantial and widely known discussion of the theme must be relevant here.

What Antoninus has to say on this topic is no doubt sufficiently Thomist in approach. Nutural law of itself prescribes community of goods: it is by *jus gentium* – more precisely it is by positive law in accordance with *jus gentium* (and therefore not contrary to natural law) – that the distribution of private property necessary since the Fall has been made (Antoninus 1959, III, pp. 180–1). As to the relationship between rights so established and *dominium*, Antoninus' view is not clear-cut. He reports the existence of different opinions, including the 'Gersonian' position: 'According to some doctors *dominium* and *jus* mean the same thing . . . so that if a man has a right to anything he has lordship in it as well (III, p. 186). Antoninus himself seems to prefer a view in which, while all *dominium* entails *jus*, the converse does not hold: there can be rights, such as those of children against their parents, the possessor of which does not have lordship. Antoninus defines *dominium* as 'the right of having, possessing, and enjoying something either simply as one chooses or according to some determinate mode, based on a certain superiority or authority' (III, p. 186). Now the *dominium* of a property-owner is, it seems, one level in a hierarchy or pyramid of *dominia*, at the apex of which we find God – 'in the beginning things and possessions belonged to no one but God' (III, p. 176). The human authority by which individual *dominium* is established exists by divine delegation, and such authority is the instrumentality whereby God has chosen to act in a matter provided for neither by natural law nor, directly, by divine law.

Antoninus' theory of *dominium* in respect of property and rights thus forms part of a more general theory of temporal lordship: and this wider theory is emphatically papalist. Under God, universal dominion lies with the pope exercising 'authority and regal power'. The emperor is indeed 'lord of the world and *princeps*', but he is at the same time absolutely subject to the authority of the pope, who may judge, confirm, or depose him (III, p. 165). Within this structure – resonant, if in rather hollow tones, with the renewed self-confidence of the post-conciliar papacy – we find a fairly conventional account of political power ordinarily exercised either by a king or by a city-state. This is based on the characteristically Thomist view that 'rule and government' are necessary for the well-being of those who cannot govern themselves. Common consent is invoked as the basis for an essentially voluntary subjection, though it seems fair to say that the emphasis on consent is less marked than it was to be in 'nominalist' thinkers such as Biel, Mair, and Almain (cf. III, p. 181). It is at the same time clear that Antoninus, drawing heavily on juristic as well as on theological sources, transmitted to later generations a substantial common stock of ideas to be used by other writers without such use implying a strong commitment to a firmly held doctrinal position derived from one school or another.[12]

To return from this excursion into mid-century Thomist thinking to the work of Biel is indeed to be struck as much by similarities as by divergences. Biel too, when discussing *dominium* in Book IV of his *Collectorium* on the *Sentences*, is concerned to establish the basis of private property rights, given that these are not the work of either natural or divine law. His primary (and largely acknowledged) debt for the arguments he uses is to Duns Scotus. From Scotus he takes the view that 'just positive laws' are necessarily the basis of private possessions and that such laws may be made either by paternal or by political authority. That authority, furthermore – especially in its political form – retains its control even after it has established and distributed property rights. When discussing the transfer of property, Biel insists that this can be effected, not only by private transactions, but also by acts of public authority (Biel 1973–84, IV. 2, pp. 5–9).

Once again, therefore, we have a theory of property predicated upon a theory of political authority – and indeed, in this instance, upon a more general theory of society. The legitimacy of public acts transferring property, according to Biel, stems from the consideration that 'in the fact of community there is supposed to be included the consent of every member of that community' (IV.2, p. 8) – a point, once again, derived directly from Scotus.[13] Consent is here the ground of law, and law is treated as equivalent to, or interchangeable with, decisions by the ruler. The theory of *dominium* has again brought us to questions of a political and governmental nature; but for further light on Biel's answers to such questions it is necessary to consider a rather different part of his discussion. The context is still, as before, that of restitution (the entire analysis forming part of an account of the sacrament of penance). Now, however, Biel's concern is with the use of violence and its justification. The 'just war' is a relevant instance; and one factor in its justness is the legitimacy of the authority by which it is waged.

12. For instance, a key passage in the *Summa summarum* of Silvestro Mazzolini da Prierio (1539, fo. 159v, cited in Tuck 1979, p. 5) is taken almost word for word from Antoninus.
13. '. . . quia in facto communitatis supponitur includi consensus cuiuslibet de communitate'. The Scotus reference is to his discussion of the same passage in Book IV of the *Sentences* (dist. 15, q.2.).

Relying on the authority of the canonists and – notably – of Aquinas, Biel accepts the view that this authority belongs to *principes* and that it belongs most fully to that *princeps* – be he king or emperor – who has no superior. Even subordinate authorities, it is true – including 'counts' and 'communities' as well as 'princes' – have the right to make war on *those within their own jurisdiction* who cannot otherwise be reduced to order. Throughout *principes* are seen as guardians of the common weal, entrusted with an authority to be used for the common good (IV.2, pp. 66–70).[14]

Biel is well aware, however, that the poor, and subjects in general, are often oppressed and unjustly exploited by rulers, and this consideration leads to another dimension of his theory. The question is again one of restitution; but it is now a matter of the duty of those holding temporal *dominium* to restore what they have unjustly taken from their subjects. This obligation derives, Biel argues, from the nature and basis of temporal authority itself. Like private property, it is the product, not of natural law or right, but of *jus humanum*. To be legitimate (*iusta dominandi auctoritas*) it must be grounded in the people's choice and consent. For Biel this is so regardless of the way in which authority may in one case or another have been acquired – by direct election, by 'just war against infidels or rebels', by legitimate succession, or through appointment by some superior jurisdictionally entitled to make it: 'all these legitimate modes are reducible in their origins to the choice and consent of the people' (IV.2, p. 85). This is what distinguishes *principatus politicus* from paternal authority (the origin of which lies in natural right). The ruler's authority extends to the making as well as the execution of law; but it is throughout an authority to be used *ad utilitatem et commodum rei publicae*. Used for contrary, selfish purposes, it becomes tyrannical (IV.2, pp. 85–6).[15] Thus the ruler has the right to levy taxes, but a just ruler will restore to his subjects anything he has taken illegitimately. If the ruler's authority has itself been acquired illegitimately, by usurpation, he is morally bound to surrender it – provided that this will not have consequences for the community worse than those of his usurpation (IV.2, pp. 85–90). The echo here of a familiar element in Aquinas' doctrine is no accident; throughout this part of his exposition Biel invokes the authority of St Thomas, either directly or through the medium of Antoninus.[16] As to the direct question of whether subjects are bound to

---

14. The Aquinas reference is to IIa IIae, 40, I. Biel's other references here are mostly to canonists, notably Hostiensis and Raymond of Penyafort.
15. In this connection Biel cites Aquinas, *De regimine Iudaeorum*, as quoted by Antoninus.
16. There are also direct references to Antoninus' *Summa*: see esp. Biel 1973–84, IV.2, pp. 93ff.

obey a usurping tyrant, Biel bases his cautiously negative answer directly on Aquinas' *Summa*. His caution is indeed even greater than St Thomas'; for his concept of legitimate disobedience seems to extend only to the case of authority illegitimately held, not to that of legitimate authority unjustly used (IV.2, pp. 104–5).[17]

There is nothing 'radical' in all this, nor is it in any way contradictory that Biel's earliest work should have been a *Defence of Apostolic Obedience* (Biel 1968). His views on papal and conciliar authority will call for brief notice later. Here it is more relevant to emphasise the absence from his social and political thinking of any marked 'individualism'. His views are essentially 'communitarian', and he does not seem to have concerned himself with the problems of the origins and basis of communities as such. He does, it is true, refer at one point to a people as 'united' or 'made one' (*populus adunatus*), but there is no account of any process of *adunatio* (Biel 1973–84, IV.2, p. 86).

It has been said of Biel's nominalist contemporary Gansfort that his 'political philosophy was permeated with voluntarism' and that in it 'the right of resistance was given firm shape and sharply drawn contours' (Ullmann 1975, p. 306). Certainly Gansfort is emphatic that 'unworthy' rulers are to be removed from office. The place of consent and election in his thinking is, again, something more politically effective than a mere theoretical postulate: for Gansfort a properly constituted state is one in which supreme authority is either conferred for no more than a year at a time or is at least subject to checking by those who confer it (Gansfort 1966, p. 765, 1917, II, p. 176). This is the basis for a decidedly active theory of resistance, in which kings who do wrong are not simply to be passively disobeyed but must be driven from the throne (*deberent regno deturbari*: 1966, p. 766, 1917, II, pp. 176–7). At the same time there is no simple contrast between rulers, who may become tyrannical, and communities, who will collectively rectify matters. Communities too may err; and Gansfort insists that laws contravening the law of God, even if they have been made by the consent of the people (*communi consensu multitudinis*), must in no circumstances be obeyed (1966, p. 754, 1917, II, p. 160). The need to obey God rather than man is paramount, but in the case of misgovernment there is the usual cautionary note – resistance is permitted,

---

17. The Aquinas reference is to IIa IIae, 104, 6. The key phrase (*ad 3.*) is 'si [principes] non habeant justum principatum sed usurpatum, vel si injusta praecipiant . . .'. The second clause does not figure in Biel's formulation.

even enjoined, but only if its consequences will not prove to be the greater evil.

Returning to Tübingen and to Biel's colleague, Summenhart, we find views which like those of Gansfort, though in a different context, may be regarded as individualistic. Summenhart's account of *jus* and *dominium* at the outset of his massive *Septipertitum* on contracts has been seen as an elaboration of a 'Gersonian' theory of rights (Tuck 1979, pp. 27–8). Caution is required here, however. We have seen already, in the case of Antoninus, that the issues are by no means clearly defined. If we look briefly at a prominent exponent in Paris and later in Germany of Scotist thinking in the late fifteenth-century, Etienne Brûlefer, the same point emerges. Brûlefer, like Antoninus, rehearses different views of the relationship between *jus* and *dominium* and of both to *proprietas* – only to set all these niceties aside and proceed on the basis of treating the three concepts as, for practical purposes, the same (Brûlefer 1500, fo. 169v). In Summenhart's case the debt to Gerson in respect of the theory of *dominium* is clear enough; but it would be a mistake to regard him as simply an exponent of 'Gerson's kind of nominalism' (Tuck 1979, p. 27). It has been noted already that Summenhart's early formation had been in the *via antiqua*, not the nominalist *via moderna*; and though he was no doubt influenced by his association with Biel, that influence again had its eclectic aspects. In Summenhart's account of law, as in Biel's more elaborate analysis, the Scotist element is strong. Law derives its efficacy from the authority of the lawgiver (though for it to be a truly just law that authority must be guided by wisdom); and legislative authority belongs (once men have advanced from a state of life in which paternal power is sufficient) to political rulers, constituted as such by the consent of their subjects. Summenhart distinguishes two basic forms of political power – regal and (as we would say) republican, the latter exemplified in the city-states of Italy. (There are verbal echoes in this passage of Antoninus' formulation of the point.) The essential importance of consent is illustrated by Summenhart from the situation of David before the death of Saul: though chosen by God and anointed by Samuel, his right was only *ad regnum*, not yet *in regno* – a right to *exercise* royal power could come only from his acceptance by the people (Summenhart 1513, I.vii, sig. b2rA).

So far as private property is concerned, Summenhart fully accepts the view that it is a right grounded in human law. If, however, his analysis is compared with Biel's (strongly Scotist) account, a point of some interest emerges. The necessary 'positive law', Summenhart argues, might emanate neither from paternal authority nor from political power in its ordinary sense, but from 'a dictate of common consent'. This consent is apparently envisaged as something other than the collective authority of a politically constituted *communitas* or republic. The justice of such a law would rest on the principle *volenti non fit injuria* (1.ix, sig. c5rB). There is in this both a flexible concept of law and, arguably, a distinctly individualistic concept of consent – though neither, it must be said, is fully developed.

Despite individual differences and tendencies determined by commitment to one school of thought or another, the theory of *dominium*, government, and society in the late fifteenth century may on the whole be seen as reflecting a convergence and conflation, if not quite a synthesis, of elements that might initially have appeared to be dialectically opposed. A sharper dialectic may be expected in controversies more directly concerned with the organisation and exercise of political authority.

iii Conciliarists and papalists

The issue between conciliarist and papalist views of authority in the church had not, of course, sunk totally out of sight in the half-century following the final liquidation of the conciliar movement as such with the dissolution of the Council of Basle–Lausanne in 1449. Despite the effective papal victory at that point, the conciliar theory remained alive, its arguments available for deployment in limited but sometimes sharp controversies. Biel's 1462 *Defensorium Obedientiae Apostolicae* was the product of one such controversy, in which Gregor Heimburg had vehemently asserted the anti-papal position (Thomson 1980. pp. 15–17).[18] Biel's brief, then, was to defend papal authority; and he did so vigorously, arguing, for instance, that no positive law could bind the pope and that a papal definition, command, or other act contrary to positive law must be reverently obeyed (Biel 1968, pp. 142–3). Yet when, twenty-five or thirty years later, he wrote his exposition of the canon of the mass, he regarded the council, representing the whole community of believers, as the supreme tribunal in the church, having authority over all its members, even the pope; and he explicitly cited in this context the decree *Frequens* of the Council of Constance (Biel 1963–71, II, p. 199). A moderate and carefully hedged conciliarism, again, had been expressed in the late 1450s by Denis

18. The controversy, arising from a disputed election in the archdiocese of Mainz, is further examined by the editors of Biel 1968. See also Becker 1988, pp. 346–52.

Rijkel (commonly known as Denis the Carthusian). Arguably no more than a 'quasi-conciliarist' (Black 1979, p. 24), Denis at least gave, in his *De auctoritate summi pontificis et generalis concilii* (Rijkel 1908, pp. 531–676), an elaborate restatement of the arguments; and in his *Epistola ad principes catholicos* (pp. 505–34) he is emphatic as to the culpable failure of popes to summon a council subsequent to that of Basle–Lausanne to deal with the problems – not least the Ottoman threat – facing Christendom.[19]

Denis Rijkel's work is significant in the wider context of fifteenth-century intellectual history, though that significance can only be touched on here. On the one hand, committed as he is to the hierarchical vision of his namesake the (pseudo-) Areopagite, he exemplifies the importance of Christian Neoplatonism for the thinking – including the political thinking – of his age (see Black 1970, pp. 57ff). At the same time, his heavy reliance on the authority of Aquinas is a reminder of the vitality of Thomist realism in the mid-fifteenth century. Looking, from that point of view, at the work of the great Parisian conciliarists of the early decades of the century, d'Ailly and Gerson (representing as they did a different philosophical tradition), Denis is concerned to argue that their conciliarism was in fact consonant with his own moderate position. A more radical interpretation of Parisian conciliarism was to emerge – or reappear – forty years after his death.

To say that is not to deny an affinity between the moderate, eclectic positions adopted by Biel and Rijkel and the thinking of the Parisian nominalists and conciliarists of the early sixteenth century. There is, indeed, a real continuity of thought. When Almain's commentary on Book III of the *Sentences* was first published, posthumously, in 1516 (with a dedication to Mair), it embodied lectures delivered in 1512 which had avowedly followed Biel's lead.[20] At the same time, the direct influence of Ockham is especially clear in Almain's work. Not only did he write a specific exposition of Ockham's *Octo quaestiones* on papal power: there is constant reference – not always uncritical, but always respectful – to Ockham throughout the works Almain wrote between his *Moralia*, first published in 1510, and his premature death in 1515. Yet Almain also reflects the characteristic eclecticism of the period in frequent references not only to

---

19. It is noteworthy that these and other writings by Rijkel were printed in the early 1530s.
20. The editor was Nicholas Maillard (for whom see Farge 1980, pp. 295–301); his dedicatory epistle to Mair is reprinted in Burns 1954, pp. 97–8. A passage in that letter may have given rise to the suggestion that Almain had edited Biel's commentary on the *Sentences* (cf. Oberman 1967a, p. 20). It is clear, however, from the editorial note at the end of the text (Almain 1518, fo. 107) that Almain followed Biel in his 1512 lectures: 'in tertium sententiarum profitendo Gabrielem [Biel]'.

Scotus[21] but also to Aquinas; and references to Aquinas are particularly
significant in his 'political' writings.

The fact that Mair and, especially, Almain produced works that may
properly be termed political was, naturally, the result of political
circumstances. The conciliarism they absorbed from the Parisian academic
tradition and especially from Gerson could have remained inert: it hardly
stirs, indeed, in Mair's writings before 1518.[22] The precipitating factor was
Louis XII's essentially political manoeuvre in bringing together at Pisa (and
later Milan) a council of the church intended to undermine the authority of
the pope, Julius II. Denounced as a schismatic *conciliabulum*, the council
nevertheless asserted in practice – to the point of declaring Julius deposed –
the full rigour of conciliar theory. That theory was to be emphatically
restated during the council by Almain and after the event by Mair.[23]
Almain's *Libellus de auctoritate ecclesiae* had been prompted by a sharp attack
on conciliarist principles by Tommaso de Vio, later – as Cardinal Cajetan –
to be one of Luther's principal adversaries; and Cajetan himself restated his
case in reply to its critics. In this polemical confrontation political
arguments of considerable importance were advanced.

Almain's position – with which an analysis of the argument may
conveniently begin – was based on the concept of *dominium naturale*. This,
its nature, and its relationship to 'civil dominion' are the subject-matter of
his *Quaestio in vesperiis habita*, written perhaps before – though only just
before – the resurgence of the conciliar controversy: its main elements are
in any case redeployed in the 1512 *Libellus*, written in response to Cajetan's
De comparatione auctoritatis Papae et concilii of 1511.[24] Individual human
beings, Almain argues, are naturally – that is, divinely – endowed with a
right to whatever is necessary to sustain and preserve life and promote well-
being. This right extends to the legitimate use of force to repel force – even
to the killing, if need be, of an attacker. So far as the proprietary aspect of
dominium naturale is concerned, Almain seems to have envisaged the
possibility of a form of natural appropriation going beyond the simple
right to take and use whatever was needed to support life. At one point,

21. Almain's *De penitentia* was based explicitly on Scotus' commentary on dist. 15 of Book IV of the
Sentences. The importance of Scotist doctrine at this period is also reflected in the fact that John Mair
superintended, in 1517–18, the first printed edition of Scotus' *Reportata parisiensia* (cf. Mair 1892,
p. 410).
22. For some 'stirrings' in 1510 and 1512, see Burns 1981, p. 48 and nn. 77, 78.
23. On Mair's position and circumstances in this connection, see Burns 1981, p. 50 nn. 89, 90.
24. Almain undertook the response at the instance of the Paris faculty of theology. For a full account
see La Brosse 1965.

certainly, he endorses the view we have already seen in Summenhart – that 'common consent' without the intervention of any other common authority could authorise such appropriation (Almain 1518, *In Quartum*, fo. 30rA). Even at the natural level, indeed, there is for Almain a collective or corporate as well as an individual dimension: some of the 'natural rights' he has in mind have to do with the interests of the human race as a whole – such, for instance, are the rights husbands have over their wives' bodies (fo. 26vA). In general, however, Almain's views on the social dimension in human life are expressed in the context, not of the natural order, but of what has been 'superadded' to that order since, and in consequence of, the Fall.

Dominium civile has two elements, *dominium proprietatis* and *dominium jurisdictionis*; and Almain follows John of Paris closely in his strong emphasis on the distinction between them (Almain 1518, *Expositio*, 1.vi, fo. 7rB). It is the jurisdictional aspect that needs analysis if we are to establish the more strictly political implications of Almain's theory. Jurisdiction is ultimately a coercive power – it involves the *jus gladii*, the right when necessary to put offenders to death. There is an evident analogy here with the individual's *dominium naturale*; but Almain makes it clear enough that jurisdictional authority is not something delegated by individuals. Nor, on the other hand, does it inhere as of right in a ruler or ruling group. It is indeed a delegated power, but its source lies in the community for whose corporate benefit it is to be used (see Burns 1983a). Three questions arise from this. First, what is the source of the right the community transfers or entrusts to its rulers? Second, what is the nature of the community itself and of its relationship to its individual members? Third, how should political power be organised in order to ensure its proper use?

As to the first point, Almain once again is clear that the authority of the community does not derive from its individual members, since it is an authority they do not, as individuals, possess. Nor can he see any other answer to the question than to say that the power in question comes from God (Almain 1518, *Quaestio*, fo. 62v, *Libellus*, fo. 46r). There *is* a close analogy between individual and corporate right – an analogy extending further when we note that neither the individual nor the community can 'abdicate' this right or be legitimately deprived of it. But it is an analogy between two parallel entities, each of which is natural or divine in origin.

In answering the second question, Almain makes one of his most important references to Aquinas, citing him (both in the *Quaestio* and in the

Libellus) for the argument that the community's right to punish capitally is analogous to the surgeon's cutting off 'a gangrenous member'. The 'organic' view here is strongly developed. Almain invokes the Pauline notion of society as a body comprising different members and insists on the consequence that each individual is 'ordered' to the body politic, serving its common purposes as limbs and organs are subordinated to the needs of the natural body to which they belong (Almain 1518, *Expositio*, III.1, fo. 35r).[25] Any kind of individualism here takes second place to a strongly 'communitarian' view.

As for the third question, one of the community's basic rights is to provide by its own collective decision for its own government. It may choose to do this by vesting jurisdictional power in the hands of one man or of a body of men; and, if the latter, either in a small group or in the many. Of this classic Aristotelian trio of possibilities Almain – and Mair – are quite clear that monarchy or kingship is the best, and that, as such, it was surely the form of government established by Christ in the church. The analogy between papal and royal power is elaborately developed by Mair (see Burns 1981, esp. pp. 50–6). It is, however, crucial for the conciliarist case to show that the virtues of monarchy are compatible with – are, indeed, inseparable from – the essential powers of the community. In the end, no doubt, the most essential of those powers is the power to call to account and if need be depose an erring king or pope. This follows in particular from Almain's insistence on the inalienability of the community's natural right to safeguard its own well-being (Almain 1518, *Quaestio*, fo. 62v). The general principle is that 'the whole community has power to depose the king if he rules not to the advantage but the destruction of the polity' (Almain 1512, sig. Aiv). When this is applied to the church it means that 'if such power were conferred on the pope that he could not be punished by the whole church even if he exercised it destructively and not beneficially, then the ecclesiastical polity would be less well ordered than civil society' (sig. Civ). And this is inconceivable in a polity constituted by the *legislator optimus*, Christ himself (cf. Mair 1518, fo. 69vA). Mair again, writing in less immediately polemical circumstances than Almain, analyses more fully some of the theoretical implications of the argument. It means, he says, that there are, strictly speaking, two sorts or levels of political power in a properly ordered community. There is, *regulariter*, the ordinary authority of the ruler, supreme as he is over every individual or corporate member of

25. The Aquinas reference is to IIa IIae, 65, 1; and cf. Burns 1983a, p. 372 n. 14.

the 'mystical body'. That power, however, is in the end essentially instrumental or 'ministerial' in character: it is, *casualiter* – in certain eventualities – subordinate to the collective authority of the community. The community necessarily acts through representatives – the council in the case of the church, the estates in the temporal realm and it has always available in its *proceres*, its leading men, those whose right and responsibility it is to act for the common good (see Burns 1981, pp. 38–40).

Both Mair and Almain thus emphasise the close parallelism they see between the ecclesiastical and the civil polity. They face problems here, to be considered later. First, it is important to note how Mair, writing more discursively than Almain, and as the author of a work – his *Historia Majoris Britanniae* (1521) – devoted to temporal concerns, exhibits more fully the political consequences of the theory they both embrace. In this context it becomes clear that the community, through its representatives, has powers at its disposal other than the reserve power of deposition. The estates, in Mair's understanding of the matter, have, for instance, the judicial or quasi-judicial function of determining disputes over the royal succession; their consent is needed for the imposition of taxes; and, though legislation in general may best be left to the ruler in his role as wise legislator, guided by counsel but in the end 'laying down the laws authoritatively' (Mair 1528, fo. 85rB, 1530, fo. 98v, 1510, fo. 100rB), there are, nonetheless, matters on which the estates – and the council in the case of the church – have the right and the duty to 'impose binding laws' on the ruler. These laws are in effect 'constitutional laws' prescribing specific limits to the ruler's authority.[26] The community's power to impose such laws is an element in what may reasonably be called its contituent power. That term is all the more appropriate in view of the fact that the power extends to the right of a free people to choose and to change the form of government.[27] And it is just here that the theory encounters a major difficulty, duly seized on by Almain's antagonist in 1511–12.

Had Cajetan confined himself to a firm restatement (which he does, of course, provide) of the papalist view of the church as a pure monarchy under the authority of the pope, his work would be a good deal less interesting than it is for the history of political ideas. In fact he does more. Particularly in his 1512 rejoinder to his critics, he carries the fight directly to

---

26. See Burns 1981, pp. 41–3; and for 'constitutional laws', Mair 1510, fo. 101vA: 'rex non debet imponere aliquid in humeris populi ultra leges regni . . . Rex deuincitur tenere leges consuetudinales regni.'
27. Mair 1518, fo. 70vB: 'Populus autem liber pro rationabili causa potest policiam mutare.'

his adversaries. In doing so he directly questions their fundamental claim
that the very nature of monarchy – at least in its legitimate form – not only
allowed but required the limits discussed above. Almain, for instance,
argued that there was no contradiciton between monarchy in its best form
and the existence of a juridical power independent of the ruler (Almain,
1518, *Expositio*, III.vi, fos. 41–2). To this kind of argument Cajetan's
response is that such arrangements *do* impair the monarchical principle. To
claim for the community the powers claimed by the conciliarists is in effect
to say that such a community is governed, not monarchically, but by a
regimen populare. Now this cannot be true of the church, nor is the church in
any sense a *libera communitas*. Almain and Mair had acknowledged that the
church could not claim a free community's right to change the constitutional order, and recognised that the papal authority could not be said to
derive, like that of temporal rulers, from the consent of the people: 'a king
has authority from the men over whom he rules . . . but the pope is
ordained by God' (Mair 1518, fo. 70rA). For Cajetan this is the difference
that makes all the difference. He is ready, even eager to accept that in
temporal realms the community does enjoy the powers claimed for it by his
opponents – eager because he is concerned to assert as strongly as possible
the uniquely divine character of ecclesiastical authority. In developing his
argument he puts forward political ideas of some importance.

Cajetan insists that to determine the location of the 'casual' power in a
political system is in effect to define its constitutional character. If that
power rests with the people, the system is fundamentally a *regimen populare*.
Certainly there can be, under such a system, a form of kingship or
monarchical rule; but however powerful that rule may be, it lacks the final
determining authority, and the governmental authority it wields is only
what Cajetan calls *regimen medium* (Cajetan 1582, p. 52). Elsewhere Cajetan
makes a similar point, using the now more familiar term 'executive power'
to describe the authority in question, and distinguishing it from *potestas
praeceptiva*. The latter, he says, is what Aquinas calls *auctoritas regiminis*
(Hennig 1966, p. 24). It was, the argument runs, this 'preceptive' power
that was committed to Peter, and therefore to the pope as Peter's successor;
the other apostles – and therefore *their* successors, the bishops – received
only 'executive' power. This sustains Cajetan's papalist ecclesiology. In its
temporal application, the argument about *regimen medium* both supports
the notion of a prior, 'constituent' power and, arguably, foreshadows
Bodin's crucial distinction between sovereignty and government.

Cajetan's analysis goes further. He acknowledges that there are some realms in which the king is, like the pope, ordained or appointed by God, whereas in other cases royal authority is conferred by the community. This, however, makes no difference, in his eyes, to the royal power enjoyed by the king: in both cases, and always, political power in the temporal order belongs in some ultimate sense to the people. The importance of this argument, both in itself and in relation to later developments, is evident. Cajetan is concerned to make as absolute a distinction as he can between civil and ecclesiastical authority, so as to undermine the conciliarist exploitation of their supposed similarity. That assimilation was under attack elsewhere. Giovanni Franceso Poggio (1442–1522), for instance, in his *De potestate papae et concilii*[28] (probably published in 1512), insists that the ecclesiastical order is not a *regimen politicum* but a monarchy established by Christ (Poggio 1512?, sigs. [H iv]v–[I 3]r). Cajetan, however, is prepared, it seems, to push his argument to the point of saying in effect that all political authority in the temporal order is, in Sir John Fortescue's terminology, *politicum*, even if it is also in many cases *regale* (cf., e.g., Cajetan 1582, p. 54).

There is thus a curious convergence, so far as temporal society is concerned, between the two opposing sides in the ecclesiological debate. Neither Cajetan nor his conciliarist opponents, for one thing, saw any place for an absolute, independent, sovereign power in the state. And if, in the church, Cajetan (like another Thomist two generations earlier, Juan de Torquemada) envisaged a more purely monarchical regime than Mair or Almain could have accepted, he would doubtless have agreed with them that a fully absolute power – *suprema potestas regularis et casualis independens* (Mair 1518, fo. 71r) – belonged, in the church, to Christ alone. Whether such a power subsisted, or could subsist, in the state, and if so where it was lodged, were questions as yet unresolved in the political thought of the early sixteenth century.

Cajetan's role as the leading Thomist of his generation has already been mentioned; but the importance of that role in the Thomist revival which coincided with the early stages of the Protestant Reformation needs further emphasis. His commentaries on St Thomas' *Summa*, first published between 1514 and 1519, soon established the position as standard authorities they were to retain for the best part of 400 years after his death in 1534. In the third quarter of the sixteenth century, however, the most

---

28. This is mistakenly attributed by Black (1970, pp. 54n, 54–6, etc., as index) to Poggio Bracciolini. The author was in fact one of the great humanist's five legitimate sons.

important and creative Thomist thinking was done neither in Italy nor in
France but in Spain. There is, it is true, a significant connection with the
Paris of Mair and Almain. Mair – who incidentally owned a copy of Part III
of Aquinas' *Summa* with Cajetan's commentaries[29] – had a substantial
number of Spanish pupils, several of whom also came under the influence
of Peter Crockaert and contributed to the revived study of St Thomas in
the 1520s.[30] It was in this milieu that Francisco de Vitoria and Domingo de
Soto pursued their Parisian studies before returning to exert their seminal
influence in the universities of Spain. A brief note on their teaching –
Thomist in its essential character, yet revealing consciousness of the insights
of nominalism and (especially, if debatably, in Vitoria's case) of humanism
– may serve as a conclusion to this chapter.

Within the framework of a firm, though not entirely unproblematic,
restatement of the Thomist theory of law, and in particular of natural law
(Hamilton 1963, pp. 14–18; Skinner 1978, II, pp. 149–54), Vitoria and Soto
expound a view of political society strikingly similar in some respects to
what we have seen in Almain. Thus the community is regarded as naturally
endowed with an inalienable right to safeguard its own interests – a right
analogous to that which is enjoyed by individuals (Vitoria, cit. Hamilton
1963, pp. 34–5). This right, however, can be effectively exercised only by a
governing authority to which the community has transferred its God-
given but collectively inoperative power. At this point a divergence from
positions like those of Mair and Almain manifests itself. It had been a
conciliarist commonplace that the ruler, while supreme over every
individual subject, was subordinate to his subjects as a collective body – the
principle *maior singulia minor universis*. Vitoria rejects that principle,
holding that in a 'true monarchy' the king 'is not only above all individual
citizens, but also above the community as a whole' (Hamilton 1963, p. 39).
The distinction between 'true monarchy' and forms of monarchical
government in states that are essentially 'popular' is reminiscent of the view
taken by Cajetan; but it is not wholly clear whether the term 'true' implies
the absolutism of what James VI and I was to call 'free monarchy'. The idea
that political power as such always in some sense inheres in the community
is deeply ingrained in the Thomist thinking of the early sixteenth century.
This becomes especially clear when Vitoria discusses the crucial problem of
'church and state'. Like Cajetan he insists on the distinction between an

29. Durkan and Ross 1961, p. 128.
30. See, in addition to Renaudet 1953, Villoslada 1938 and Farge 1980, pp. 424–31 (on Vitoria).

ecclesiastical power conferred directly by Christ and a civil power transferred to the ruler by the community to which it belongs. Yet his position is hardly one of extreme papalism. Certainly he rejects the conciliarist view, arguing that the authority of councils is derived, not from their status as representing the whole body of the faithful, but rather from the decision of the bishops to set up such an authority. On the issue between conciliar authority, so undertood, and papal power he remains deliberately neutral (Hamilton 1963, pp. 71–4).

The Spanish Dominicans of this period raised issues that were to be further discussed and elaborated by their Jesuit successors, Luis de Molina and Suárez, and, in the Italy of the Counter-Reformation, by Bellarmine. That post-medieval scholasticism lies beyond the scope of this chapter (cf. below, pp. 237–40, 292–7). Vitoria and Soto are transitional figures; it is significant that both lived on into the period of the Council of Trent (Soto participated in it), but neither survived to see its conclusion. The unresolved problems in their thought are perhaps symptomatic of a more general tension in late medieval scholastic political theory. If we return, finally, to Mair, we may see that tension exhibited in a number of ways. In his theory of *dominium* there is the contrast between a wide-ranging individual right and a circumscribed political authority: 'the king does not have such unrestricted power (*ita liberum dominium*) over his realm as I have over my bible' (Mair 1516, fo. 76rB). At the same time the corporate, 'communitarian' authority from which limits to political power are derived still leaves the ruler free to wield a wide-ranging competence: 'it is better to have one supreme monarch in the realm, by whose will all matters are governed, provided that he takes counsel of wise men and then, whether they agree or dissent, decides as he pleases' (Mair 1509, fo. 87rB). In an age of expanding royal power, scholasticism yielded no clear resolution of the developing issue between 'absolutism' and 'constitutionalism'.

II
Religion, civil government, and the debate on constitutions

6

Christian obedience and authority, 1520–1550

FRANCIS OAKLEY

Continuities with the medieval past are no less evident in the political ideas to which the Protestant Reformation gave rise than in the religious and theological commitments that characterised it. In both respects, however, it constituted also a striking break with the centuries preceding, and scholars have devoted an enormous amount of attention to wrestling with the problem of continuities and discontinuities. By a long-established route, the characteristic approach to Martin Luther's startling departures in word and deed from the norms of medieval orthodoxy and the dominant patterns of late medieval political thinking sets out from the decline of the later medieval papacy into legalism, fiscalism, confusion, and corruption. Encompassing the onset of the Great Schism in 1378, the emergence in the conciliar movement of a constitutionalist opposition to the jurisdictional claims of Rome and in the policies of European rulers of a set of comparable claims that overlapped and rivalled them, that approach moves on to the more radical challenges posed to the whole hierarchical order of the church by such heretics as the Waldensians, Wycliffites, and Hussites. It takes special note of the rise of the nominalist theology and of the retreat from the externals of religion reflected in the mysticism of Germany, the Netherlands, and England, as well as in the later flowering of the *devotio moderna* and the humanist *philosophia Christi*. And it terminates on the eve of Luther's great challenge with an emphasis on the deepening tension between the intense piety – 'churchliness' even – of the populace and the increasing calcification of the ecclesiastical establishment, and a concomitant emphasis on the growth of anti-clericalism (Moeller 1965, pp. 3–31, 1966, pp. 32–44).

The following abbreviations are used in this chapter:
LW *Luther's Works*, ed. J. Pelikan *et al.*, 54 vols, (St Louis: Concordia Publishing House, 1955–76)
WA *Martin Luthers Werke*, 92 vols. in 105 (Wei-
marer Ausgabe) (Weimar: H. Bohlau, 1883–1983)
WA, DB *Martin Luthers Werke. Die deutsche Bibel* (Weimar: Böhlau, 1906–61)

This traditional approach should be neither ignored nor privileged. It can tell us much about the ease with which the secular rulers of Europe were able to assert a sovereign jurisdiction over their national or territorial churches, and also about the warmth and enthusiasm with which Luther's views were initially received – especially by the lower orders in the cities of northern Germany and by those of humanist sympathies. Many of the latter, indeed, by a 'constructive misunderstanding' they later had reason to regret (Moeller 1972, p. 29) took Luther to be one of themselves, merely a more passionate and providentially effective exponent of their own Erasmian ideals. At the same time, this approach sheds little light upon the religious formation of Luther himself, or upon the nature of those profound and novel views which he propagated with such conviction, passion, and force. In common with those of his followers who best understood him, Luther was a good deal more than a mere critic of the late medieval ecclesiastical order. The wellsprings of his religiosity lay less, that is, in any reaction to the medieval Catholic system at its weakest and most decadent, than in the profound inadequacies he attributed to it even at its strongest and most pure. To convey that point adequately it will be necessary to construct a different type of interpretative context, one that reaches out to embrace theological developments matured long before the troubles that overtook the Latin church during the fourteenth and fifteenth centuries.

i   Theological and canonistic fundamentals

Despite the fact that the historical account in which it is embedded is open to criticism at more than one point, a good case can be made for choosing as one's point of departure the distinction between church and sect that formed part of the sociological typology elaborated long ago by Ernst Troeltsch, sociologist, historian and theologian (Troeltsch 1960, I, pp. 334, 340–1, II, p. 994). By the 'church' Troeltsch meant the type of socio-religious organisation that reaches out to comprehend and to Christianise society as a whole, and that contrives to do so by manifesting a willingness to compromise with the mores it finds embedded already in society. As a corollary, it foregoes any rigid insistence upon the subjective holiness of its individual members, stressing instead its holiness as an institution, locus as it is of the regenerative working of the Holy Spirit through the preaching of the Word and the administration of the sacraments.

While the church thus strives to include the masses, the 'sect' resigns itself to excluding them. Setting up as its goal the achievement of the exacting moral ideal proclaimed by Jesus in the Sermon on the Mount, it becomes of necessity a voluntary society. Deemphasising its sacramental powers, it eschews, accordingly, all talk of institutional sanctity, stressing instead the subjective holiness of its individual members. Driven to seek the purer maintenance of its ideals in separated communities subsisting at the margins of society, it awaits the future dawning of the millennium, and, sometimes, when the end of the world seems imminent and the establishment of the kingdom of God on earth within its grasp, it feels justified in resorting to revolutionary violence in order to hasten that happy culmination.

For Troeltsch, of course, the terms 'church' and 'sect' refer, not to concrete historical entities existing in the real world, but rather to persistent tendencies in Christianity, inextricably interwoven in the course of historical events. And if 'the main stream of Christian development', Protestant as well as Catholic, flowed 'along the channel prepared by the Church-type', never was it confined more fully within that channel than it was in medieval Europe, where the sectarian element, so strongly represented in the early church, was effectively marginalised, and where, in the hierarchical Latin church presided over by its papal theocrats, the church-type was most purely realised and most coherently developed.

The very coherence of that development presupposed the working of two fundamental factors. The first was the progressive transformation of Christianity in the years following Constantine's grant of toleration from the proscribed cult of a suspect minority into the empire's official religion, and of the church from a voluntary private organisation into a public, all-inclusive society, increasingly indistinguishable in its totality from what we would call the state, and possessed of an authority both political and coercive. The second factor was the crucial doctrinal departures of the fourth, fifth, and sixth centuries that did so much to enhance in the world of Latin Catholicism the dignity and importance of the priestly hierarchy. Reflecting the more juridical approach to the church that distinguished the thinking of the Latin theologians from their Greek counterparts, and reflecting also an assessment of man's moral capacities far gloomier than that current among the theologians of the eastern church, these distinctively western theological tendencies came together in the thinking of St Augustine of Hippo (354–430) in such a way as to set the agenda for much of subsequent western theologising, Protestant as well as Catholic.

Thus, in the wake of his great controversies with the Donatists and Pelagians, the norm of orthodoxy came to embrace his anti-Donatist teaching on the church, with its non-sectarian emphasis on the objective and the sacramental, and its insistence that the authenticity and holiness of the sacramental channels of divine grace depended upon the personal moral worthiness neither of minister nor of recipient. His harsh views on nature and grace, however, were admitted only with modifications that served to bring them into line with his anti-Donatist doctrine of the church.

Endorsed in the authoritative position adopted in 529 by the Council of Orange was Augustine's emphasis on the devastating impact of Adam's original sin on the religious and moral capacities of all his descendants. Also endorsed was the assertion that without some prior gift of divine grace man can do nothing to please God, since even the desire to believe presupposes the prevenient workings of the Holy Spirit. But there was no mention of his doctrine of irresistible grace, and the idea that God had predestined some men to damnation was roundly condemned. It clearly lay within man's power, therefore, to spurn the divine advances, and it was suggested only a little less clearly that man retained some power freely to cooperate with God's grace, and, by an assiduous exploitation of the sacramental ministrations of the visible church, to do something, at least, to further his own salvation. It was this version of Augustinianism, packaged and popularised in the Latin west by the influential writings of Pope Gregory the Great (590–604) and underpinning the authority and prestige of the sacerdotal hierarchy (for most of the sacraments, to be efficacious, had to be administered by the priesthood), that was to form the bedrock of medieval orthodoxy.

Recognising the public character of the church's authority and attaching great importance to the sacerdotal and sacramental, medieval thinkers devoted considerable effort to the analysis of ecclesiastical power. From the twelfth and thirteenth centuries onward, canon lawyers began to employ in that effort (though sometimes in the teeth of theological opposition) categories and concepts drawn from secular legal and political thinking. By the eve of the Reformation – and the formulations of the prominent Parisian theologian, Jacques Almain, may be taken as representative – it had become customary to distinguish ecclesiastical power into a power of order (*potestas ordinis*) and a power of jurisdiction (*potestas jurisdictionis*).[1] Whereas the former is the truly sacerdotal, sacramental power at whose heart lies the mysterious power to make present in the eucharist the 'true body of

---

1. See Almain, *Espositio* (1706), 1019D–25D, 1068A–C; *Tract. de auct. eccl.* (1706), 979D–89A. For useful discussions of the distinction, see *Dictionnaire de droit canonique* 1935–65, VI, pp. 1148–50, *s.v.* 'Ordre en droit canonique', VII, pp. 77–108, *s.v.* 'Pouvoirs de l'église'.

Christ', the latter is the administrative, judicial, legislative (and, therefore, magisterial) power over the church, the 'mystical body of Christ'.[2] The latter power, moreover, was said to be twofold in that it was exercised over both the internal and the external forum. The former (which Almain calls the *potestas jurisdictionis in foro interiori* or, sometimes, *in foro poenitentiali*) is the power of administering the sacraments to the faithful, and it is devoted to the private good of the individual. It is a power exercised above all by means of sacramental penance and can be exercised only over those who voluntarily submit themselves to its sway. That is not the case, however, with the power of jurisdiction in the exterior or public forum (*potestas jurisdictionis in foro exteriori et publice*), which is a coercive power exercised even over the unwilling, instituted by Christ 'with the purpose of compelling the faithful to live in accord with the evangelical laws', and to which it pertains 'to punish sins, confer benefices, promulgate laws (*constitutiones*), excommunicate, degrade, confer indulgences', and so on.[3] Late medieval papalists and conciliarists alike had this latter power in mind when they spoke of the fullness of power (*plenitudo potestatis*) in the church. It is, in effect, a truly governmental power, one closely akin to that wielded by temporal rulers. Because of that, Almain notes, some papalists were tempted to overextend it to such a degree as to engross every prerogative pertaining to the secular prince, while Marsilius of Padua denied it to be a power rightfully possessed at all by the church.[4] But, in so doing, Almain insists, Marsilius 'deviated from the faith' (*Exposition*, 1706, 1037D, 1041A, *On Ecclesiastical Authority*, 1706, 980D).

ii Luther and early German Lutheranism

Among the overextensions of the power of jurisdiction that Almain dismissed as improper was the claim that it could be used to ameliorate by indulgence the condition of souls presently in purgatory – except, he conceded, merely 'by way of suffrage' (*On Ecclesiastical Authority*, 1706,

---

2. Note that by the mid-twelfth century theologians had begun to designate the eucharist, not as the *corpus Christi mysticum*, but as the *verum corpus Christi*. The former term was transferred now to the Church. By Almain's day it had acquired corporational and political associations and was being used almost as a synonym for *corpus morale et politicum*. See Lubac 1944, pp. 117–37; Kantorowicz 1957, pp. 193–206.
3. '...[Q]uantum ad Ecclesiasticam Potestatem juridicam et publicam, quae respicit Forum exterius, ad quam spectat peccata punire, conferre Beneficia, Constitutiones edere, excommunicare, degredare, Indulgentias conferre...'. *Espositio* (1706), 1024A.
4. For an analysis of Almain's views on the subject, see Oakley 1977, pp. 111–32; for those of the high papalist, Johannes de Turrecremata, see Izbicki 1981, pp. 48–51.

98 1B–3A). In October 1517, only two years after Almain's death, it was at that same contested claim that Martin Luther levelled some of the harshest of his Ninety-Five Theses, the articles for academic disputations that came to be seen in retrospect as the opening salvo in his bold attack upon the pretensions of Rome. But the nature of Luther's challenge to the medieval Catholic order proved to be a much more radical one than that opening salvo might suggest. Moved by a heartfelt desire to strip away the all-too-human accretions of centuries, to return to the unsullied gospel of Christ as it speaks through the scriptures, and emboldened by a reading of those scriptures determined in marked degree by the travail of his own spiritual crisis, Luther was led to call into question the church's jurisdictional power in the internal no less than the external forum, the power of order no less than the power of jurisdiction, reaching beyond those issues, indeed, to subvert those fundamental theological equations hammered out a thousand years earlier concerning the respective roles in the salvific process of human effort and divine grace.

That such was the case became increasingly clear to Luther himself during the critical half-dozen years subsequent to the posting of his theses: years marked by the furore that broke out when those theses were translated into the vernacular and widely publicised, by the disputations and interrogations that culminated in papal condemnation and imperial ban, and by the sustained burst of literary activity that reached its peak in 1520 when he produced the four historic works: *The Freedom of the Christian, The Babylonian Captivity of the Church, Address to the Christian Nobility, On the Papacy at Rome.* So clear was it, indeed, that when replying later on to Erasmus' tract, *On Free Choice of the Will* (1524), he concluded by praising the latter because, 'unlike all the rest, you alone have attacked the real issue, the essence of the matter in dispute, and have not wearied me with irrelevancies about the Papacy, purgatory, indulgences and such like trifles' (*Bondage of the Will: LW*, XXXIII p. 294; *WA*, XVIII, p. 786).

That reply was framed in the book that Luther himself considered to be his best theological work. It constituted a fierce and uncompromisingly Augustinian rejection of the moderate and characteristically humanistic case Erasmus had made for according, in the process of salvation and in response to the prompting of divine grace, some modest role to the free will of man, for attributing at least 'something to human choice which has not withdrawn itself from the grace of God' (*On Free Choice*, 1969, p. 90).

Such craven qualifications were perfectly traditional, and they signal the line Erasmus was finally committed to drawing between himself and

Luther. But the latter was unable to conceal his impatience with them. Instead, he evoked Augustine's harsh doctrine of original sin and his great eschatological vision of mankind as divided until the Day of Judgement into two opposed communities, invisible here and now because their memberships are ineradicably intertwined, but known nonetheless to God. He spoke of a kingdom of God (*regnum Dei*) to which true Christians belong, and of a kingdom of Satan (*regnum Satanae/diaboli*) into which are gathered the rest of mankind. Between those kingdoms, he insisted, 'there is no middle kingdom'. They are mutually and perpetually in conflict with each other (*Bondage of the Will: LW*, XXXIII, p. 227; *WA*, XVIII, p. 743). Only with the Day of Judgement will Satan finally be routed and Christ come to reign in glory. Until then, the human will is like a beast over which two riders contend. We are 'captive, subject, and slave either of the will of God or the will of Satan' (*LW*, XXXIII, p. 70; *WA*, XVIII, p. 638). If we are fortunate enough to be 'delivered from the dominion of darkness' it is not by our own strength but by the grace of God, through which alone citizenship in the *regnum Dei* is granted. For once 'the foreknowledge and omnipotence of God are accepted' it is necessary to conclude that 'we are under necessity'. Indeed, we must go to extremes, deny free will altogether, and ascribe everything to God (*LW*, XXXIII, pp. 227, 190; *WA*, XVIII, pp. 782, 719).

Despite such extreme formulations, however, and notwithstanding the commitment to the doctrine of double predestination that they undoubtedly entail, it would be wrong to conclude that the desire to safeguard the divine omnipotence was the motivating force in Luther's thinking or that he subscribed to any sort of philosophical determinism. With regard to 'what is beneath him', the mundane activities of day-to-day life, he was perfectly willing to concede free will to man. It was only in 'matters pertaining to salvation or damnation' that he utterly denied it (*LW*, XXXIII, p. 70; *WA*, XVIII, p. 638). Nor would it be correct to view the grim equations of divine election as the pivot upon which his theology turned. For him, the doctrine of election evoked God's forgiveness rather than his wrath, it was a source of hope rather than of fear, a conclusion rather than a premise. That premise lay elsewhere, in the doctrine of justification by faith, the principle that shaped his entire theology and informed his social and political thinking. To that transformative insight he had attained only after years of bitter experience as a devout monk who had faithfully followed the medieval prescriptions for seeking righteousness by works, exhausting the ascetic exercises and sacramental remedies available to him in an anxious but ultimately unsuccessful quest for an abiding assurance of God's forgiveness. To such a degree did the quest fail, indeed, as he himself tells us, that he had more than once been 'brought to the very depth and abyss of despair, so that I wished I had never been born a man' (*LW*, XXXIII, p. 190; *WA*, XVIII, p. 719; cf. *LW*, XXXIII, pp. 288–9; *WA*, XVIII, p. 783). We have it on Luther's own later (and not always reliable) testimony that the critical breakthrough occurred around 1518–19, and that it involved the startled but ecstatic recognition that the 'justice' or 'righteousness of God' (*justitia Dei*) could mean something other than that active punishing justice associated with the grim fact that we are bound to the prescriptions of the Old Testament law even while, as slaves to sin, we inevitably fall short of those prescriptions. He had been driven to the edge of final despair when his reading of Paul's Epistle to the Romans (1:16–17) had led him to doubt that the righteousness of God revealed by the gospel could be anything other than that punishing justice. But then it had dawned on him that the justice of God revealed in the gospel must be interpreted otherwise, as the salvific gift that God bestows upon his chosen ones, as the 'passive righteousness' by which the merciful God justifies us through faith. And with that critical insight, Luther says, 'I felt as if I was altogether born again and had entered into Paradise itself through open gates' (preface to the Latin writings, 1565: *LW*, XXXIV, p. 337; *WA*, LIV, p. 186).

Scholars continue to wrangle about the dating of that moment and the importance to be attributed to it. Some have pushed it back as far as 1513–14. Others have shied away from the whole idea of linking Luther's mature doctrine of justification by faith with any sudden epiphany, and have argued instead for seeing it as the outcome of a gradual evolution in his thinking across the years 1513–19. All would concede, however, that his terminology shifted somewhat across those (and later) years, posing for his commentators vexing problems of interpretation. All would agree, further, that his theology underwent considerable development during that period. But, whatever the case, all would also agree that his autobiographical remarks accurately register the seismic nature of the spiritual shock in the life of the believer generated by the breakthrough to the doctrine of justification by faith.

Although some of his more systematic formulations emerged only in subsequent writings, what Luther did as his theology matured during the critical years from 1518 to 1522 was to relate the dialectic nature of his own religious experience (induced by the antinomies of sin and grace, despair and faith, divine wrath and divine mercy) to a comparable dialectic

between Old Testament law and New Testament gospel. The commandments of the Old Testament 'are intended to teach man to know himself,
that through them he may recognise his inability to do good and despair of
his own ability', may learn the bitter lesson, indeed, that left to his own
moral striving there is 'in himself nothing whereby he may be justified and
saved' (*Freedom of the Christian: LW*, xxxi, p. 348; *WA*, vii, p. 52).
Salvation comes instead from above, bestowed as a gratuitous gift upon
those true Christians whom God, of his incomprehensible mercy, has
chosen to deliver from bondage to Satan. And it is in the New Testament,
in virtue of Christ's great sacrifice on the cross, that God reveals himself as a
forgiving and merciful father who promises man that the justification
which has eluded him while he struggled 'to fulfil all the works of the law'
will now be accomplished 'quickly and easily through faith' (*LW*, xxxi, p.
349; *WA*, vii, p. 53). It must always be remembered, of course, that true
faith reflects neither human choice nor human achievement. It is, instead, a
gift of God, 'a divine work in us, which changes us and makes us to be born
anew of God..., makes us altogether different men in heart and spirit and
mind and in all our powers, and it brings with it the Holy Spirit' (*Preface to
Romans: LW*, xxxv, p. 370; *WA*, DB, 7, 7).

The formula 'salvation by grace alone through faith' has often been
suggested as a helpful substitute for the expression 'justification by faith'.
What the idea entailed was the abandonment of Luther's own earlier
patristic and medieval view of justification as a gradual and lifelong process
of effortful spiritual regeneration to be completed only in the next world.
Instead, justification by the forgiving love of God in Christ was now
viewed as a present reality, and the Christian life of true sanctification
understood, not as a laborious *sine qua non* for salvation, but rather as its
effect, 'Good works do not make a good man, but a good man does good
works.' And 'as faith makes man a believer and righteous, so faith does
good works' (*Freedom of the Christian: LW*, xxxi, p. 361; *WA*, vii, p. 613).
Possessed now of Christian liberty, freed from the bondage of the law and
the corrupting imperative to work out his own salvation, the believer was
liberated likewise from the claims the church had traditionally made to
mediate between him and his creator. Indeed, with justification wholly a
divine gift and an instant reality conditioned only by faith, the church in its
innermost essence could be nothing other than the communion of the
saints, the spiritual body of the elect. And, in its manifestation here on earth,
that church could be nothing other than the community of believers,
distinguishable by the fact that in it one can find the Word truly preached

and the sacraments rightly administered. Those sacraments, moreover, were now on scriptural grounds reduced in number to two and interpreted, not as indispensable channels of grace but simply as visible testimonies to the Word. As a result, their centrality in the process of salvation was denied, and, with it, the age-old hierarchical ordering of the church. The dismissal as unscriptural of the sacrament of orders, the assertion that all true Christians share equally by faith in Christ's kingship and priesthood, the erasure, therefore, of the notion that the clergy constituted a spiritual estate distinct from the laity and superior to them, the redundancy of the monastic vocation for a belief-system in terms of which not even the most strenuous of moral strivings could affect one's eternal destiny – all of these represented crucial departures from the norms of medieval orthodoxy. They served to obliterate the traditional distinction between clergy and laity, to reduce the ministry to the functional status of one divinely ordered calling among many, and to lay the foundations for a body of political thinking markedly different from that dominant in the centuries immediately preceding.

The key to that difference is to be found in the complex way in which, at least from 1522–3 onwards, Luther conceived of the setting in which man lives his life. Had that setting been framed totally by his vision of the great eschatological struggle between the two warring kingdoms, with the true Christians arrayed as citizens of the *regnum Dei* and the rest of mankind subjected, as bondsmen of Satan, to the *regnum diaboli*, things would doubtless have been otherwise. Then, his political thinking might have focused almost exclusively upon the necessary ordering in this world of the affairs of those who were not true Christians and who would destroy one another were they not coerced into some semblance of order. This was all the more likely, indeed, in that Luther, just as Augustine before him, saw an intimate connection between the powers and principalities of this world and the sovereign sway of the *regnum diaboli* over the hearts and minds of the bulk of mankind, including some who make an outward profession of Christianity but who are not destined to be numbered in the body of the elect. This again was all the more to be expected in that from time to time he appeared to be suggesting that the coercive power of the temporal government exists only to cabin and confine the citizens of the *regnum diaboli* and that true Christians are not subject to its sway, or, at least, are so subject only by virtue of the Christian love that impels them to avoid giving (by their own rejection of its authority) a bad example to the neighbour who needs the discipline of coercive government.

Had this been the controlling element in his thinking, his political teaching would have been something akin to that of those Anabaptists who insisted that true Christians were not to be subject to the rule of the temporal sword but to that of the Word above. But it was not the controlling element. That role is played, instead, by his crucial discrimination in Christian man of two distinct natures, the concomitant distinction he draws from 1522–3 onwards between the two orders or realms (*Reiche*) God has established for man's existence in this world, and the related (indeed, overlapping) distinction he draws between the two divinely instituted orders of government (*Regimente*) pertaining to those realms (Cargill Thompson 1980, pp. 42–59; Cranz 1959, pp. 113–73).

The Christian, Luther insists, is at the same time both righteous and a sinner (*simul justus et peccator; semper peccator, semper justus – Lectures on Romans: Scholia: LW*, xxv, p. 332 and 434; *WA*, LVI, pp. 343 and 442). In saying that, he means that through faith the Christian stands before God (*coram Deo*) as wholly righteous here and now, because God of his gratuitous mercy no longer imputes his sins to him. In relation to God, he is made a new man, a spiritual person, through Christ wholly righteous. As such, he belongs to that spiritual order or realm (*das geistliche Reich*) which pertains solely to the direct relationship between man and God. And, as such, he is subject of God's spiritual governance (*das geistliche Regiment*), an inward governance over the heart which God exercises in this world, not by the deployment of coercive force, but rather via the Word and its proclamation through preaching and the sacraments.

Even in this world, as a consequence of his complete justification, the Christian is gradually being sanctified. But as a Christian in this world, no man can be solely a spiritual person. As a natural creature, with all the needs and proclivities pertaining to that status, he is subject to the laws that govern the world of nature. Further than that, as a natural creature who is also a human being, he is a *Weltperson*, a person who exists in relation to others as well as to God, and one who still reels under the impact of original sin. If he has been forgiven, it is by no means because he is sinless, but in spite of the sins he still, willy-nilly, commits. As such a person, and no less than his unredeemed fellow men, he belongs not only to the spiritual but also to the temporal realm (*das weltliche Reich*), and is subject to the divinely instituted temporal governance (*das weltliche Regiment*) that embraces the world of human society as well as of nature, working, as a result, to bring about a type of justice. But this is not, Luther insists, that salvific justice which is taught by the gospel and makes men righteous before God, for that comes only through faith. Instead, it is a civil, or 'external' justice, which concerns only the outward actions of men. It is 'to be sought in offices and works' (*Whether Soldiers, too, Can be Saved*: *LW*, XLVI, p. 95; *WA*, XIX, p. 625), and is taught by reason and the natural law that is imprinted in the hearts of all men, pagan no less than Christian, unredeemed as well as redeemed.

This is the source of the most striking emphases of Luther's political theology, emphases that served to wrench thinking about political life out of the orbit in which it had revolved during the late middle ages. Four in all, these emphases inserted a marked discontinuity into the history of political thought and set the agenda in terms of which political thinkers, for a century and more, were to go about their business.

First among these emphases was the very fact that his thinking about political life was, indeed, a political *theology*, one continuous with his great theology of salvation, and, in common with that body of thought, grounded in a heartfelt wish to return to the pure Christian vision conveyed by the scriptures and especially by the Pauline epistles. That he should so often evoke a scriptural warrant (Romans 2:14–15) for the notion that there is a natural law underpinning the external justice of the temporal order is consistent with that emphasis. So, too, is the fundamental and highly influential importance he attached to the authority of the New Testament in the determination of questions pertaining to the political life.

The second emphasis was his denial to the church of any power that could properly be called jurisdictional. That church, it will be recalled, was for him embodied here on earth, not in the form of any hierarchically ordered sacerdotal structure, but rather of a community of faithful Christians in which the Word is truly preached and the sacraments rightly administered – preached and administered, moreover, by ministers neither more nor less priests than other baptised Christians. Hence, as early as 1520, in his *Address to the Christian Nobility*, Luther dismissed the canon law as an all-too-human tool of papal exploitation (*LW*, XLVI, p. 131; *WA*, VI, p. 409). Hence, also, he insisted that the function of ministers in the church was as instruments of God's spiritual governance to proclaim the gospel, to rebuke sin – even when it occurs in high places – and to admonish the faithful to live in accordance with Christ's teaching. Of coercive power they had none. Their role was one of service; their power, no more than the power of persuasion; their authority, the authority of the Word that addresses itself to the inner hearts of men.

Third among these emphases was the concomitant importance he attached to temporal rulers, whose standing in society he greatly enhanced. This was not only because he now saw them as possessing a monopoly on the use of coercive force, but also because, as the masks (*larvae*) behind which God conceals the exercise of his temporal governance, they are to be obeyed as much for conscience sake as for fear. 'Civil law and the sword', he tells us – citing the two biblical texts on which he placed so enormous and influential an emphasis – are 'in the world by God's will and ordinance' (Romans 13:1–7; 1 Peter 2:13–14; *Temporal Authority: To What Extent it Should be Obeyed*: *LW*, XLV, pp. 85–6; *WA*, XI, p. 247). Temporal government is a 'remedy for sin' a divinely instituted means to maintain at least an external peace, to stave off the anarchy that threatens in a fallen world to engulf society. And, precisely because of its divine ordination, it is neither to be abused by an immoral ruler commanding his subjects to do wrong, nor actively resisted by subjects even when they groan under the heel of a tyrant. Even tyrants are ministers of God, and they may (as Paul points out) be instruments of his wrath. Should a ruler order what is immoral, we should remember that 'it is no one's duty to do wrong; we must obey God (who desires the right) rather than men' (*LW*, XL, p. 125; *WA*, XI, p. 277). Should he be a tyrant, while it is our religious duty to disobey him if he commands us to do what is evil, it is also our religious duty passively to bear the consequences of that disobedience: Though 'we should not sanction it, or lift a little finger to conform, or obey', even 'outrage is not to be resisted but endured' (*LW*, XLV, p. 125; *WA*, XI, p. 267). And that admonition applies no less to true Christians than to pagans or to the mass of the unregenerate. All are equally subject to God's temporal governance in matters external – ministers as well as their flocks, Christians as well as pagans (*Address to the Christian Nobility*: *LW*, XLIV, pp. 130–1; *WA*, VI, pp. 409–10). Christians, moreover, are so subject not simply for charity's sake, to set an example of obedience for their unregenerate brethren to follow, or by way of service in the divinely ordained calling of magistrate or soldier. The reason for their subjection lies, rather, in the fact that they, too, as Christians in the world (*simul justus ergo et peccator*) *need* the burden of the law to curb, in their dealings with others, the evil promptings of their own sinful nature.

Finally, the fourth of these emphases was the firmness of the distinction he strove to maintain between the spiritual and temporal realms and between their respective modes of governance, as well as the force of his insistence that they not be confused. It had been characteristic of medieval thinkers after the reception of Aristotle in the twelfth and thirteenth centuries to see the temporal and spiritual as hierarchically related, the temporal being ordained to the spiritual as the lower to the higher end. But Luther saw them as distinct and, in a sense, parallel – concerned with different aspects of man's existence, exerting different modalities of authority, resorting to different instrumentalities of persuasion (*Temporal Authority: LW*, xlv, pp. 88–91; *WA*, xi, pp. 249–51). And the confusion of the two (*confusio regnorum*) he saw very much as the work of the devil, who prowls like a roaring lion seeking whom he may devour, prompting subjects to rebel, priests and potentates alike to abuse their legitimate powers, striving, in effect, to subvert the whole divinely ordained order of things.

This accounts for the bitterness of his attacks in *The Babylonian Captivity* and elsewhere on the papal church (indeed, the papal 'Antichrist' – *LW*, xxxvi, p. 72; *WA*, vi, p. 537), not only for intruding itself improperly in the domain of temporal governance and claiming to be the immediate source of the power that temporal rulers wield, but also for introducing into the church of God a regime of laws, jurisdiction, and coercion. Such a regime properly belongs to the temporal realm alone; it has no place in spiritual governance. The same factors explain his insistence on the limits of temporal power, his criticism of rulers, however Christian in aspiration, who went beyond their legitimate duty to protect the external order and peace of the church, legislating upon matters essentially religious, attempting vainly to impose beliefs upon their subjects, intruding upon the interior disposition of the soul, and introducing into spiritual matters (where it is for the Word alone to persuade) the alien coercion of the law (Cargill Thompson 1984, pp. 131–3).

In this context can best be understood the harshness, during the Peasants' Revolt in Germany, of his final tirade *Against the Robbing and Murdering Hordes of Peasants* (May 1525). In his earlier *Admonition to Peace* (published in 1524 and before the outbreak of extensive hostilities), while he had warned the peasants that 'tumult and rebellion' could not be justified by 'the fact that the rulers are wicked and unjust', he had also rebuked the princes for their 'stubborn perversity' and the oppression of their rule (*LW*, xlvi, pp. 19 and 25; *WA*, xviii, pp. 309 and 295). That position was entirely consistent with the political theology he had earlier delineated in his *Temporal Authority: To What Extent it Should be Obeyed* (1523). The unbalanced stridency with which he finally condemned the peasants as 'faithless, perjured, disobedient, rebellious murderers, robbers, and blasphemers', and the brutal vigour with which he urged the princes to 'stab, smite, slay' them, was not only rooted in his horror of rebellion against the powers that be as a direct repudiation of Paul's teaching in Romans 13. It also sprang from the fact that he now saw the peasants as honouring and serving the devil by promoting the *confusio regnorum*, 'making Christian freedom a completely physical matter' cloaking this 'terrible and horrible sin [of rebellion] with the gospel', and becoming thereby 'the worst blasphemers of God' (*LW*, xxxix, pp. 49–55; *WA*, xviii, pp. 357–61).

Such were the characteristic emphases, the controlling tendencies in Luther's political thinking. The later history of the Lutheran and territorial churches notwithstanding, they help explain why a Sebastian Castellio, for example, could later on seek support in Luther's writings for his own argument that no one can be coerced into belief. They also help explain why Erastianism never came fully to dominate the Protestant world. But their main impact lies elsewhere. Forcible resistance to the princes and potentates of this world had rarely been an occasion for moral anguish among late medieval Catholics. But Luther's rejection of it as sinful transformed it for the remainder of the sixteenth century and a goodly part of the seventeenth as well into the central and critical question confronting European political thinkers. As the next chapter makes clear (see below, pp. 200–3), this was a question on which Luther himself changed his mind in the 1530s, though only with great difficulty and in the face of changed political and religious circumstances in Germany. During those later years, with comparable difficulty and behind a screen of cautious qualifications, he also changed his mind somewhat on other issues, permitting now a certain degree of coercion even in religious matters, and, more broadly, enlarging the role of the prince in the governance of the church. But if changed circumstances played their role in inducing him to modify his fundamental positions, so too did the sheer difficulty he and other early reformers encountered in trying to hold to the firm line of distinction he had drawn between the spiritual and temporal *Regimente*.

Among those early reformers some, it is true – Johannes Brenz at Schwäbisch-Hall, for example, or Huldreich Zwingli at Zurich, or Martin Bucer at Strasburg, or, indeed, the more radical Thomas Müntzer at Zwickau – showed less interest in maintaining the type of separation between the two realms and the two systems of governance for which Luther had argued. But others did, and Luther's own change of viewpoint was in some measure worked out in dialogue with theirs. And of those early German Lutherans who addressed themselves in anything more than a fragmentary fashion to theoretical political questions, notably Eberlin

von Günzburg, Andreas Osiander, and Philip Melanchthon, it was the last
– colleague, neighbour, beloved friend – who was closest to Luther, serving
sometimes, it may be, even as teacher rather than disciple.

In the final edition of the *Loci communes*, which reflected the shifts in his
thinking made across the years in response to changing religio-political
circumstances, Melanchthon rejected as 'a Judaic dream and an odious error'
any notion of 'a worldly kingdom of Christ' in which 'only the saints will
rule and wield the sword, blotting out the godless and capturing all
kingdoms'.[5] That had been the error of Thomas Müntzer, and it is always
'very harmful to portray the Church of God as a worldly kingdom'
possessed of coercive powers of a legal type. 'Only the worldly power', he
says, 'should punish with fist and sword'. To that worldly power,
moreover, Melanchthon now assigns a role in ecclesiastical and religious
matters that goes well beyond anything he or Luther had originally
envisaged. Worldly power, he says, 'does not merely exist to serve to satisfy
the stomachs of men', or to maintain peace, or even to punish immoral acts
that do not disturb the peace. It is also 'obliged for the good of the Church
to supply necessary offices, pastors, schools, churches, courts, and hospitals'.
Beyond that, indeed, rulers are 'obliged to accept the holy gospel, to
believe, confess, and direct others to true divine service'. They must also
'prohibit, abolish, and punish' such offences as 'external idolatry, blasphemy, false oaths, untrue doctrine, and heresy'. And this means,
Melanchthon insists, citing the example of some of the Old Testament
kings and of such Christian rulers as Constantine, Theodosius, and
Charlemagne, that rulers 'are obliged to have knowledge of the Christian
doctrine and to pass judgement on false doctrines' (*Loci communes, On
Christian Doctrine*, esp. 36: Melanchthon 1965, pp. 335–7).

Such claims reveal the distance Melanchthon himself had travelled since
those early days when his thinking had been more closely aligned with
Luther's insistence on the separation of the spiritual and temporal
Regimente, and especially since the mid-1530s, when he had begun to
ascribe a 'right of reformation' to temporal rulers and to develop his notion
of the prince as the *praecipuum membrum ecclesiae*. Luther never went so far,
and even in his last years expressed misgivings about the intrusion of

---

5. I cite the English translation of Manschreck 1965, pp. 260, 273. The original *Loci communes* had been
   published in 1521 and the greatest changes to the tract were made between the late 1530s and 1555,
   when Melanchthon altered it quite markedly and enlarged it fourfold. Manschreck's translation is
   based on two German editions of the 1551 version, the German translation having been made by
   Melanchthon himself. The 1559 Latin version of the work is printed in Melanchthon 1951–75, II.1,
   pp. 164–352, II.2.

princely power into the affairs of the church. By the mid-1530s, nonetheless, having had to confront the Anabaptist threat and the urgencies of church organisation in Saxony and elsewhere, he had come to abandon 'his belief that the Gospel must never be defended by force and was beginning to replace it by the Melanchthonian doctrine that secular rulers had a duty to do all in their power to promote and defend true religion, by force if need be' (Cargill Thompson 1984, p. 117). By so doing, he was led to marginalise the originally sectarian elements in his thinking and to move in the direction of a church answering in its sociological dimensions to Troeltsch's 'church-type' Christianity. By so doing, whether wittingly or unwittingly, he also lent credence to the very large claims that his followers and their fellow travellers in the world of the Lutheran diaspora made for the religious dimension of the royal office.

iii The Lutheran diaspora and the emergence of the royal supremacy

During the early 1520s, long-established affiliations, both commercial and academic, helped foster the spread of Lutheran ideas eastward to the Baltic states, westward to England, northward to Denmark and Sweden, and thence, respectively, to Norway and Iceland, on the one hand, and Finland on the other. In all of these countries it was, above all, the needs and sympathies of the secular authorities that were finally to determine the fate of those new ideas. But only in England, surprisingly, and, to a much lesser degree, in Sweden, did reformers of Lutheran sympathies produce any significant body of writing on matters of political theology.

The Swedish contribution, indeed, was slight enough, its central moment being the *Krönungspredikan* of Olaus Petri, the great reformer who had studied at Luther's Wittenberg from 1516 to 1518, whose religious commitments from about 1523 onwards were clearly Lutheran, and who, with his brother Laurentius, did more than anyone else to shape the liturgy and piety of the Swedish Reformed church. The *Krönungspredikan* was a sermon preached at the coronation of Gustavus Vasa in 1528 – some years before that king finally committed himself unambiguously to a form of Lutheranism – and it understandably proffers no systematic statement. Its message, indeed, is a rather simple one. Emphasising that kingship is 'a Christian office' (*Christelegit embete*) divinely ordained for the public well-being, Olaus Petri warns the king of the dangers and temptations of his position, urging him to rule not for his own sake but for that of his subjects, and reminding him that his duties extend beyond the securing of temporal peace and tranquillity to the watchful oversight of the clergy of the realm that they not slight their responsibility to preach the Word of God (*Coronation Sermon*: 1914–17, I, p. 316). Again, brandishing such well-worn texts as Peter 2:13–14, or Matthew 17:24–27, or (above all) Romans 13:1–7, he lays an even greater stress on the duty of all subjects, clergy as well as laity, and in all matters that do not infringe God's commandments, to be loyal and obedient to the king, not simply for fear of punishment but for conscience sake. And striking the familiar Pauline theme to which he was to return later on in his great *Svenska Kronik*, even tyrants and wicked rulers are ministers of God, instruments of his wrath to punish those that do evil (*Swedish Chronicle*: 1914–17, IV, pp. 78, 114).

Similar themes were emphasised by the earliest English sympathisers with Lutheran ideas – men such as William Roy and William Tyndale who, like Olaus Petri, had spent time at Wittenberg, or Simon Fish and Robert Barnes who had not, but who were in close touch with the new theological currents flowing in north Germany and the Rhineland. Thus Roy's *A Brefe Dialoge bitwene a Christen Father and his stobborn Sonne* (1527), translated from a German original, stressed the divinely ordained nature of the temporal ruler's authority and the gravity, therefore, of the subject's obligation to obey them. Similarly, Fish's *The summe of the holye Scripture* (1529), another translation from a continental original, reproduced almost word for word the section of Luther's *Temporal Authority* that sets forth his teaching on the two *Regimente*.[6]

That teaching found a fairly faithful echo in the first version (1531) of Barnes' *A supplication ... unto the most gracyous prynce Henrye the eyght*, with its clear emphasis on the separation of the temporal and spiritual realms and their respective systems of governance, its insistence that kings are the ministers of God in the temporal realm and must never, therefore, be resisted by force, its conviction, nonetheless, that they must be humbly disobeyed if they exceed their bounds and interfere in spiritual matters. For 'Christen men are bounde to obey in suffering the kynges tyranny, but not in consenting to his unlawfull commaundement' (*Supplication*: 1573, p. 295). A comparable note is struck even more insistently by Tyndale in *The Obedience of a Christen man and how Christen rulers ought to governe* (1528), a work which denounces the intrusion of pope and prelates into the temporal

---

6. For these two works see Clebsch 1964, pp. 232–9, 245–51, and esp. 249 n. 18 for Fish's borrowings from Luther. Cf. *WA*, XI, pp. 247–55.

realm and their engrossing of lands, liberties, and jurisdictions as nothing other than a 'wily tyranny which increaseth more and more daily'. That tyranny kings should not hesitate to overthrow as a damnable derogation from their own divinely ordained authority. Was it not St Paul's teaching that every soul should for conscience sake be subject to the powers that be? From that injunction neither pope nor bishops can claim any exemption, 'for here is no man except; but all souls must obey' (*Obedience*: 1848, pp. 206, 178). Unless, of course, we are commanded to do evil. And then the Christian, while necessarily disobeying, is called to offer no further resistance but 'to suffer even the bitter death for his hope's sakes, and because he will do no evil' (p. 332).

When the book was drawn to his attention in 1529, Henry VIII is reported as having found *The Obedience of a Christen man* 'a book for me and all kings to read' (Mozley 1937, p. 143). But it is worthy of note that all of these early Protestant writings predated the failure of his attempts to secure his much-needed divorce, the consequent decision to break with Rome, and the great propaganda campaign that ensued. By the years 1534–5 Barnes, and in some measure Tyndale too, had come to envisage the king's authority as minister of God as extending now beyond the temporal to encompass the spiritual. That is to say, they had moved from their own earlier Lutheran emphasis on the strict separation of the temporal and spiritual realms and in a direction more congenial to the propagandists of the royal supremacy. But if that move reflected at least in part a more fundamental shift in their theologies away from a strictly Lutheran position and in a direction parallel to that taken by Johannes Oecolampadius, Bucer, and other Rhinelanders,[7] no theological concerns of comparable profundity can be said to have perturbed the thinking of those royal propagandists whose works, with the vigorous encouragement of Thomas Cromwell, began now to dominate the arena of public debate.

The political theories of the early English Protestants had been, after all, political *theologies*. They had been grounded in the novel Lutheran soteriology. They had stressed the primacy of faith and its rejection of the efficacy of good works, its preoccupation with the preaching of the Word, its reinterpretation of the notion of 'church', its refusal to the church thus interpreted of any power to mediate via sacramental channels the divine graciousness, and its concomitant denial of anything other than a functional

7. This is the thesis persuasively argued by Clebsch 1964, esp. pp. 54–65. For the shift in Barnes' political thinking see also Cargill Thompson 1960, pp. 133–42.

distinction between clergy and laity. In contrast, the ideologists of the royal supremacy, whatever their novelties, laid down no challenge to the fundaments of Catholic belief. In his responses to Henry VIII's comments on the *Bishops' Book* (1537) Thomas Cranmer, it is true, already proto-Protestant in his doctrinal commitments, came very close to according to the king the *potestas ordinis*, at least insofar as it involved the ordination of priests. But Edward Foxe, bishop of Hereford, despite claims periodically made to the contrary, did not.[8] In this he was at one with the other propagandists for the royal supremacy, who left in the hands of the priestly hierarchy the sacramental powers traditionally ascribed to it. Instead, from Richard Sampson, Foxe, and Stephen Gardiner at the outset, to Thomas Starkey, Christopher St German, Richard Taverner, and Johannes Beckinsau later on, they focused their attention with varying degrees of explicitness, on the *potestas jurisdictionis*, and, within it, on the *potestas jurisdictionis in foro exteriori* – the truly governmental power over the church possessed in its fullness, or so the high papalists claimed, by the pope alone.

That they should define the church simply as the 'congregation of the faithful' and deny to the pope the ultimate possession of the *plenitudo potestatis* within it was not in itself revolutionary at all. The fourteenth- and fifteenth-century advocates of the strict conciliar theory had done likewise, basing their case on the more fundamental claim to the fullness of jurisdictional power possessed by the *congregatio fidelium* – the universal church itself and the general council representing it. And that traditionally conciliarist position was clearly stated in the Henrician pamphlet *A declaracion of a general concile* which Sawada views as the work of one of Cromwell's propagandists – probably of Henry Cole, friend of Starkey and Sir Richard Morison (Sawada 1961, pp. 197–214). But if such early propagandists as the anonymous authors of *A Glasse of the Truthe* (1533) and the *Articles devised by the holle consent of the Kynges moste honourable counsayle* (1533) could safely evoke the decrees of the Councils of Constance and Basle on the superiority of council to pope (Pocock 1870, II, pp. 407, 526–7), or, like Foxe in his *De vera differentia* (1534), could bolster their attacks on papal jurisdiction by a less specific nod in the direction of conciliar authority (Foxe 1534, fos. 9ʳ–9ᵛ, 17ʳ–17ᵛ), those writing after 1536 could not. In that year Pope Paul III had convoked a general council to

---

8. The text of Cranmer's responses is printed in Burnet 1830, IV, pp.128–30. They are discussed in Scarisbrick 1968, pp.403–4, 415–17. For Foxe's alleged attribution of a *potestas ordinis* to the king, see Baumer 1940, p.82; Morris 1953, p.54; and (more cautiously) Skinner 1978, II, p.96 n. 1. But see to the contrary Oakley 1987, pp.347–53.

assemble in 1537 at Mantua. The possibility of a council's actually responding to the pressing question of church reform now became a live option. As a result, therefore, the defenders of the royal supremacy were forced to address the delicate issue of the relationship of the royal authority to that of a general council. This they did in boldly unflurried fashion, insisting, as did Starkey in his *Exhortation to . . . Unitie and Obedience* (1540?) and the anonymous author of *A Treatise concernynge generall councilles, The Byshoppes of Rome and the Clergy* (1538), that general councils fall into the realm of 'thinges ... indifferent' and that their decrees are 'of none authoritie among the people in any countrey, tyl they be confirmed by princely power and common counsell' or that they could not lawfully be executed without the royal assent (Starkey 1540, fos. 8^v–9^v; Sawada 1961, p. 205).

By this insistence, and by their treatment of the relationship of king to general council in the context of the more fundamental relationship between royal and priestly power, these men revealed just how far beyond the old conciliarist position the publicists of the Henrician Reformation had been led to go in their attempts to defend and define the royal supremacy. While the conciliarists had denied to the pope the fullness of jurisdictional power, they had not questioned the divine foundation of the papal office itself. That Marsilius of Padua had certainly done, but then he was something more (or other) than a conciliarist,[9] and it is understandable that in the wake of the crucial *Act in Restraint of Appeals* of 1533 Cromwell should have commissioned the humanist, William Marshall, to produce the first English translation (1535) of Marsilius' *Defensor Pacis*.

By then, however, the attacks on papal jurisdiction as unscriptural and usurped that had formed the backbone of Sampson's *Oratio* (1534) had been extended further in Foxe's *De vera differentia*. And they were subsumed in Gardiner's *De vera obedientia* (1535) under the rubric of a more sweeping onslaught on the distinction between the church's spiritual and the prince's temporal government that had formed the very foundation of the traditional ecclesiologies and political theories. 'Forsothe', Gardiner said, 'a blynde distinccion and [one] full of darkenesse' (Gardiner 1930, sig. Dvi^v). If God 'hathe committed the office of teaching and the ministerie of the sacraments' to some, that office would appear to involve little more than a *potestas ordinis*, clearly not any true *potestas jurisdictionis* and certainly not any sort of exemption from the rule of the prince, who is 'Prince of all the

---

9. See Oakley 1977, pp. 131–2, arguing against Bäumer 1971, pp. 12–15, 265.

people and not of parte' (sig. Dvi and Eiii*). If God did indeed commit some authority over the church to the apostles and their successors, by that commission 'that which beforehand is committed of God to princes is in no wise taken awaye' (sig. Dvi). To say, therefore, that the king is 'the supreme headde of the church of England' involves no novelty. How could it? The church of England being 'nothing else but the congregatione of men and women of the clergie and of the laytie united in Christian profession', and the realm of England being a Christian realm, it is really no different than to say that he is 'headde of the realme of Englande' (sig. Di*–i*, Dii*–ii*). And such by God's will he is. For, as the scriptures tell us, he is 'God's lieftenaunt', 'as it were the ymage of God upon earthe', upon our obedience to whom the scriptures impose no limits and add not 'one sillable of excepicion' save only 'the obedience due to God' himself (sig. Diii*–iii*, Div*–iv*).

In all of this, Gardiner's views are clearly in accord with the famous words in which the *Act in Restraint of Appeals* (1533) had asserted the king's jurisdictional omnicompetence within the territorial boundaries of his 'realm of England' (Tanner 1951, pp. 41–6). What was involved was not simply the rejection of any lingering papal claim to power of a temporal nature, or the denial to the pope of a plenitude of jurisdictional power within the church, but rather the arrogation to the crown of the entire fullness of jurisdictional power *in foro exteriori* previously wielded by the church, and the redefinition of the spiritual authority possessed by the priestly hierarchy in such a way as to limit it to the *potestas ordinis* and the *potestas jurisdictionis in foro interiori*.

The power of jurisdiction *in foro exteriori* had traditionally included the magisterial power of rendering binding judgements on matters doctrinal, and Gardiner, evoking the example of the Old Testament kings and early Christian emperors, notes that Solomon by David's appointment took care 'of holy as spirituall maters', asserts that Justinian 'made lawes concerning the glorious Trinitie and the catholike faith of Bishoppes', and concludes that 'a Kynge ordayned of God ... should take charge of spirituall and eternal affaires before and rather than corporal maters' (Gardiner 1930, sig. Dviii, Eiiii). Similarly St German, who emphasised that the church is constituted of laity as well as clergy. While denying in *An Answer to a Letter* (*c.* 1535 – the final and most radical of his pamphlets) that parliament had the authority to grant to the king such powers in things 'mere spirituall' as those of consecration, absolution, administration of the sacraments, he nonetheless asked: 'why should not the parlyament then which representeth the whole catholyke churche of Englande expounde scrypture rather than the convocacyon which representeth onely the state of clergy' (St German 1535?, sig. Aiii^v–Avi, Biii^v–Biii^v, Gvi^v; cf. Baumer 1936–7, pp. 649–51)?

In so arguing, of course, and in this he stood with Starkey and Morison, he was ascribing the headship of the church and the fullness of jurisdictional power to the king-in-parliament, rather than thinking in terms of a simply personal headship, as had Sampson, Foxe, and Gardiner. On that issue the propagandists of the royal supremacy did not speak with a single voice. They were at one among themselves, however, and with Barnes and Tyndale before them, in their Pauline insistence on the sinfulness of resistance to the powers that be. That insistence became more strident in the wake of the northern uprising of 1536 and after the publication in Rome of Reginald Cardinal Pole's *Pro ecclesiasticae unitatis defensione* (1538?). For that work, replying to Sampson's *Oratio*, pressed the papal claim to headship of the universal church, denied the royal supremacy, and appealed to the Emperor Charles V to come to the aid of the oppressed people of England (Pole 1538?, ch. III, fo. lxxxii–cxiii). Thus, in *An Exhortation to styrre all Englyshe men to the defence of theyr countreye* (1539) Morison dismissed the 'pestyferous Poole' as 'trayterous Cardinall', and emphasised that the king was 'our Kynge, our ruler, by the wyll and ordinance of god, he is goddis mynister, unto whose charge god hath commytted this realme' (Morison 1539, sig. Avii^v, Ci^v, Cii^v). Thus Taverner in his *Garden of wysdome* (1539) noted that kings 'represent unto us the parson even of god himself', so that God 'adourneth them wyth the honourable title of hys own name callying them Goddes' (Taverner 1539, fo. 14). And thus, following the route from royal theocracy to royal christology, another author was apparently moved even to refer to King Henry as 'the Son of Man' (Anon., cited in Baumer 1940, p. 86).

Notwithstanding the strong Protestant emphasis on obedience, this growing cult of kingship was not necessarily welcomed in truly Protestant circles. Bucer, who had earlier praised the *De vera obedientia*, became after 1539 increasingly critical of the role in ecclesiastical matters that Gardiner was intent on claiming for the king. He denounced him, indeed, as 'the corrupter of the English Church' and accused him of scheming to establish a regime of Caesaropapism in France as well as England (Gardiner 1930, p. xii). That fact is at once both noteworthy and ironic, since Bucer himself did not hesitate to ascribe to the Christian magistrate an important role in the establishment and maintenance of the true religion. And when with the accession of Edward VI in 1547 the gates were opened to the influx of Protestant ideas into England, Bucer moved there and wrote for the guidance of the young king his *De regno Christi* (1550). For the Protestant ideas that now began to exert a dominant influence over English religious life stemmed, not from the 'evangelical' religion of the older Lutheran sources, but from the 'reformed' Protestantism of the Swiss and south-west German cities.

iv   Zwingli, Bucer, the young Calvin, and the
Reformed tradition

The proponents of the Reformed tradition looked to Luther for inspiration and shared in marked degree his most fundamental theological and political commitments. These commitments entailed a political theology of formidable complexity, and the current level of scholarly disagreement on the subject is really quite high. No attempt, therefore, to differentiate the political thinking of such reformers as Zwingli or Bucer from that of Luther himself is likely to command universal assent. Differences, nonetheless, there undoubtedly were – of nuance, certainly, and something more. Temperament, theology, timing, social and political context – all of these, and especially the two last, contributed to the emergence of those differences. While Zwingli, Bucer, and Calvin all adhered to Luther's doctrine of justification by faith, it did not occupy the central, controlling position in their theologies that it had in his. For him, after all, it had been grounded in a transfiguring personal encounter with God's forgiving love in Christ and had entailed a conception of the Christian life as, above all, a free and joyful outpouring of gratitude to a supremely merciful heavenly father. For them, however, that controlling position was occupied by something at once less experiential and more theoretical, the doctrine of God's unconditioned and controlling will. They saw the heart of the Christian life, accordingly, as a humble and painstaking obedience to the divine will as it is revealed in the scriptures. And that obedience they saw as extending, not only to the norms of faith and of moral living, but also, and in great detail, to matters of ecclesiastical life, practice, and discipline.

In Zwingli's thinking, as a result, the sharpness of the contrast that Luther drew between the law and the gospel was blunted.[10] Both are a form

---

10. See esp. *On Divine and Human Justice* (1905–59, II, pp. 484–93). I follow here the careful analysis of Walton 1967, pp. 158–67.

of law, the one no less a declaration of God's will than the other, and the difference between them is a matter of degree, not of kind (*On Divine and Human Justice*: 1905–59, II, esp. pp. 487–93). Without denying them, Zwingli softened the harshness of Luther's other dualisms between the spiritual and temporal realms and spiritual and temporal governance. His emphasis on the law and his preoccupation with the fulfilling of God's will necessitated immediately for him a related preoccupation with the human instrumentalities whereby, in a world in which the elect and reprobate are inextricably intertwined, that will was to be interpreted and that law enforced. And he was moved by that preoccupation with a degree of urgency that the *young* Luther, at least, does not appear to have felt.

Considered as the body of the elect, its membership known only to God, the church is invisible. But considered as the body of all those 'who make profession of faith in Christ the whole world over', it is visible. And because that visible body is a mixed one, numbering in its ranks some who lack the gift of faith and 'are called Christians falsely', it is 'in need of government for the punishment of flagrant sinners'. Among the 'shepherds in the church', then, Zwingli adds, 'we may number princes'. Their authority 'is necessary to the completeness of the body of the church' and 'without civil government a church is maimed and impotent' (*Exposition of the Faith*: 1953, pp. 265–6). Against Hugh, bishop of Constance, it is true, and rejecting the notion that force could compel belief, he argued in 1522 that Christ's kingdom was not of this world (Walton 1967, p. 122). In its loftiest aspect it is an inward and spiritual kingdom that dawns in the hearts of the individual believer, a kingdom to which no worldly and external jurisdiction can extend, for 'man is not God, since God alone knows the hearts of men and we know them only by their fruit' (*Exposition of the 67 Articles*: 1905–59, II, p. 329). In its subordinate reaches, however, Zwingli clearly regarded that kingdom as also in some measure external, and in 1528, commenting on those at Constance who had objected to the magistrate's regulation of religious practices, and explicitly brushing aside Luther's insistence that Christ's kingdom is not external, he argued that Christ himself and his apostles and disciples had concerned themselves with external religious observances, and that so, too, therefore, might the magistrates of a city (*To Ambrosius Blarer*: 1905–59, IX, pp. 452–4).

It is true, again, that in his critically important sermon of 1523 *On Divine and Human Justice* and in a way that paralleled Luther's distinction between the spiritual and temporal *Reiche*, Zwingli contrasted the two forms of justice that govern our conduct in this world: the divine and the human.

The former 'concerns only the inner man: how one should love God and one's neighbours' (*On Divine and Human Justice*: 1905–59, II, p. 484). It constitutes an inner spiritual standard the attainment of which only divine grace can make possible and the observance of which only God can judge. In relation to this divine justice and its correlative law all that even the clergy can do is, by proclaiming the Gospel, to delineate its norms for the guidance of their fellow believers, rulers as well as the populace at large, and to alert them to the shortcomings of human justice. For this latter form of justice, and the human law that is grounded in it, concerns only 'the outer man'. Epitomised by the ten commandments and concerned with no more than exterior conformity to the divine will, it relates to the realm of civil government (for the clergy wield no separate authority), and the realm in which the sanction of coercive force holds sway. For 'the judges and rulers are servants of God', because through the law they compel men to follow the dictates of human justice; 'he who is not obedient to their justice acts also against God' (II, pp. 484, 488).

So far, so good. The gulf between the two forms of justice might well seem complete. But Zwingli then goes on to evoke the impact on the Christian magistrate of the hearing of the Gospel, which will bring him and his subjects 'to inward piety and greater perfection than [mere] human justice requires'. It being his office 'to carry out all things according to the divine will', it now becomes his duty to shepherd his subjects towards that greater perfection, to proscribe 'all that is contrary to the divine Word', to nudge the external religious practices of their communities (e.g. the divine worship, the administration of the sacraments) into greater conformity with the higher norms of divine justice (II, pp. 504, 522, 525). And by so arguing, Zwingli betrayed his characteristic tendency – manifest also in the almost contemporaneous *Exposition of the 67 Articles* (1523) – to detect reverberations of harmony where Luther had heard only discord, to move towards reuniting what Luther had put asunder, and, having discriminated so sharply the invisible church from the visible, to identify the latter with the assembled civic community itself. As he said elsewhere, when the gospel is preached and all, including the magistrate, heed it, 'the Christian is nothing else than the faithful and good citizen, and the Christian city is nothing other than the Christian Church'.[11]

---

11. 'Sic principes vestri non turgent fastu, sic prophetae commode, fideliter ac erudite docent, sic plebs tranquilla et doctrinam et imperium capit, ut jam dixisse olim non poeniteat Christianum hominem nihil aliud esse quam fidelem, ac bonum civem, urbem Christianam nihil quam ecclesiam Christianam esse.' Zwingli, *Jeremiah-Erklärungen* (1905–59, XIV, p.424).

Robert Walton has emphasised that by these positions, staked out in *On Divine and Human Justice* and some related sections of the *Exposition of the 67 Articles*, Zwingli simply 'made explicit' what had been implicit in his cooperation with the magistracy from the beginning (in 1518) of his ministry at Zurich (Walton 1967, p. 224). Further, Walton argues, his stance was very much in harmony with the late medieval communalist tradition at Zurich in accordance with which its civic government had come to wield a far-reaching power of jurisdiction over the affairs of the church. His argument parallels that of Bernd Moeller, who, in a classic statement, claimed that for Zwingli at Zurich, as for Bucer at Strasburg, the urban context in which they lived and worked helped mould their theology and accounts in part for the difference between their political and ecclesiological thinking and that of Luther. 'To understand and appreciate the characteristics of this theology', he said, 'one must see it as the result of the Reformation message filtered through the actuality of the free city' (Moeller 1972, p. 89).

Of course, had Zwingli met in the process of the reform at Zurich the type of foot-dragging on the part of the civic authorities that Bucer had periodically to cope with at Strasburg or that Calvin encountered during the first phase of his pastorate at Geneva, he might not have endorsed the intrusion of the magistrate into matters religious and ecclesiastical with quite so much ardour. In the *De regno Christi*, certainly, Bucer grumbled that a number of princes or magistrates had 'accepted some preaching of the gospel only in order that they might confiscate the rich properties of the church', and commented sadly that although 'in a great many places the entire doctrine of the Kingdom of Christ' had been 'faithfully announced to the people, ... I for one cannot say in what churches it has yet been firmly accepted and Christian discipline publicly constituted' (*On the Kingdom of Christ*, I, 4: 1959, p. 213). Nonetheless, even in that work, the ripe fruit of reflection on a lifetime of reforming endeavour, Bucer viewed both state and church as instrumentalities of the dawning kingdom of God, and still affirmed his guiding commitment to their harmonious integration in the common task of religious reform: that of transforming their people into 'devout and righteous' citizens 'who rightly acknowledge and worship their God and who are truly helpful toward their neighbours' (*On the Kingdom of Christ*, I, 2: 1959, p. 180). Among the theological initiators of Reformed Protestantism, indeed, it was left to Calvin to sound a clear note of reserve about the role of the temporal authority in matters religious, to emphasise in such matters the independence and superiority of the clerical authority, and to do so in so forceful a manner as to make that emphasis henceforth a distinguishing feature of the Reformed tradition, evoking from hostile contemporaries and modern commentators alike sweeping comparisons between his Genevan ideal and the triumphal papalism of the high middle ages.

At Geneva the facts of the matter were a good deal more complex than such dramatic comparisons might suggest. But it is true that from the moment of his arrival there in 1536 Calvin placed a very heavy emphasis on the independence of the ministers in the task of imposing a godly discipline on the inhabitants. Indeed, he proposed an ecclesiastical ordinance that would have left in clerical hands the crucial power of excommunication, and he pressed his demands so vigorously as to bring about in 1538 his own dismissal and exile. Even when he returned to Geneva in 1541, after the chastening experience of exile and the opportunity to learn at Strasburg from Bucer's more supple tactics, while he was careful to signal his respect for the political supremacy of the city's governing councils, he still pressed them to permit the restoration of 'pure discipline'. His persistence paid off. In 1555 he succeeded at last in gaining for the consistory of pastors and elders – the essentially ecclesiastical organ of religious and moral oversight – the full power of excommunication that the magistrates had previously manoeuvred by careful qualifications to deny.

His struggle for clerical independence in Geneva notwithstanding, there is little reason in general, and with reference to the young Calvin none, to follow in the footsteps of his sixteenth- and seventeenth-century critics and accuse him of having compromised Luther's controlling emphasis on obedience to the temporal powers that be. It is true that he did introduce a few ambivalent sentences into the final (1559) edition of his *Institutes of the Christian Religion*. It is also true that in the dedicatory letter to Francis I of France which prefaced the very first version of the *Institutes* (published in March, 1536, prior to the start of his first ministry in Geneva), Calvin was bold enough to insist that the 'King who in ruling over his realm does not serve God's glory exercises not Kingly rule but brigandage' (*Institutes of the Christian Religion*, pref.: 1960, p. 12). In that same edition, moreover, as in all subsequent editions of the *Institutes*, he followed in the footsteps of Zwingli and Melanchthon, and, for that matter, of Cicero before them, and in a classic passage evoked the example of the *ephors* at Sparta, who, he said, 'were set against the Spartan kings'. 'If there are now', he added, 'any [comparable] magistrates of the people, appointed to restrain the wilfulness of kings, ... [with] such power as the three estates exercise in every realm when they hold their chief assemblies', then it is clearly their duty, as divinely ordained protectors of the people, to oppose 'the fierce licentiousness of kings' (IV, XX, 31: 1960, p. 1519).

But such quasi-constitutionalist statements are framed by a firm denial to private persons of any right of forcible resistance even to tyrannical oppression. Tyrants, after all, may be the instruments of God's wrath. And even if we have the duty to disobey if commanded to do wrong, we are equally bound to accept without recourse to violence the consequences of that disobedience. Such statements are framed also by a persistent emphasis on the veneration due to temporal rulers as God's 'vicegerents', wielders of an authority grounded not in human perversity but in 'the divine providence and holy ordinance', members of a calling that is 'not only holy and lawful before God', but also the most sacred and by far the most honourable 'in the whole life of mortal men' (IV, XX, 4 and 31: 1960, pp. 1489–90, 1518). Such statements are framed, again, by an unremitting insistence that the new gospel was not 'the opportunity for sedition', that Christian liberty was 'in all its parts a spiritual thing', something 'to keep within its own limits' and not to be misinterpreted and placed in the service of anarchy and licentiousness (pref., III, xix, 9, IX, XX, 1: 1960, pp. 30, 460, 1486). As early as August 1535, he set out to assure Francis I that Protestants were not 'contriving the overthrow of Kingdoms'. And with good reason. He was writing, after all, in the immediate aftermath of the Anabaptist attempt to establish by violent revolution a new Jerusalem in the imperial city of Münster – the dramatic incident which even more than the Peasants' Revolt of 1525 suggested a compromising link between Protestantism and sedition and succeeded in alarming more than the conservatives of the day. And it seems clear that it is the Anabaptists and related radical reformers that he has in mind when he subsequently excoriates the 'outrageous barbarity' of those 'fanatics' and tumultuous spirits, those 'insane and barbarous men' who 'furiously strive to overthrow' the civil government which God has himself ordained for our well-being (IV, XX, 1–3: 1960, pp. 1485–8).

v   The radicals of the Reformation

Calvin was at one with both Luther and Zwingli before him when he saw the Anabaptists as blasphemous purveyors of sedition and viewed the career of Müntzer and the later outburst at Münster as accurately revelatory of their true intentions. Their negative view of the radicals

of the Reformation proved determinative for subsequent historical interpretations. It is by way of reaction to a well-established derogatory
stereotype that the scholarship of the first half of the present century, much
of it Mennonite, strove to depict as 'normative' the 'evangelical Anabaptism' typified by Conrad Grebel and his Swiss Brethren, who broke in 1523
with Zwingli's budding state-church at Zurich and in 1525 formally
adopted the practice of adult baptism. Such earlier north German radicals as
Andreas Bodenstein von Karlstadt at Wittenberg or Müntzer at Zwickau
were disavowed as progenitors, and it was emphasised that Grebel had
rebuked Müntzer in 1524 for his advocacy of violence. Similarly, the
apocalyptic revolutionaries at Münster were bracketed as aberrations from
the norm. They were merely fanatics of the fringe who had properly to be
dissociated from the mainstream of Reformation radicalism, which was
committed quintessentially to the practices of toleration and adult baptism,
to the ideals of pacifist non-resistance to the powers that be, and quietist
separation from the evils of society at large.

But if this more positive appraisal succeeded in imposing a certain unity
on the teeming complexities of what has sometimes been referred to as the
'left wing' of the Reformation, over the past twenty years that achievement has itself been called into question. After all, even Heinrich Bullinger,
Zwingli's successor at Zurich, and the man whose hostile account of
Anabaptism did much to establish the negative stereotype, perceived the
diversity within the movement he labelled as Anabaptist. The current
disposition of many scholars, therefore, is simply to admit that diversity, to
concede that among the Anabaptists themselves there was a plurality of
traditions, to abandon as misleading the practice of labelling all radicals as
'Anabaptists' and as futile the attempt to trace them all back to a single
source – whether it be north German or Swiss. Hence the tendency is to
assume that 'the proper focus in the history of Anabaptism is on interacting
groups and sects rather than on a unified movement' (Stayer 1973, p. 20).

Among these interacting groups and sects three principal 'families' have
been identified. The first can be traced back to Grebel and his followers in
Switzerland, the second to Hans Hut and Hans Denck in south Germany
and Austria, the third to Melchior Hoffman and Jan Matthijs in north
Germany and the Netherlands. Between and among these families there
were complex cross-currents, disagreements, and affiliations, but in origin
– and in some measure in their particular inspiration – they appear to have
been distinct. While it was the religious and political upheaval engineered
by the magisterial reformers that liberated their own spiritual energies,

those energies were fuelled in some cases, not so much by the religious concerns characteristic of the great reformers, but by motifs of late medieval provenance – whether apocalyptic, mystical, or anti-clerical, or, alternatively, by a heartfelt desire, grounded in a simple biblical literalism, to recover the type of moral purity seen to be characteristic of the apostolic church but unattainable in the new but already hopelessly compromised established churches of the Reformation. Widespread among them all, though variously grounded theologically, was a very un-Protestant emphasis on the role of free will in the process of salvation. Similarly, there was a widespread view of the visible church on earth as itself a voluntary community composed only of the truly regenerate, of men and women the very quality of whose lives attested to the possession of a conscious and transformative faith and who, by accepting Christian baptism, publicly attested to their regeneration. Along with that went also a concomitant tendency to separate not only from the established ecclesiastical bodies of the day, Protestant as well as Catholic, but also from involvement in the coercive instrumentalities of political society.

This last tendency was at first no more than that. Even apart from those apocalyptic spirits who were willing to resort to revolutionary violence in order to inaugurate the rule of the saints, there were other radical leaders, and in the Netherlands and Switzerland as well as south Germany, who were willing to urge their followers to participate in the political process in order to elect magistrates with compatible religious ideals, or, as in the case of Balthasar Hübmaier, to endorse a vision of the relationship of church and state close to that of Zwingli himself. Only in February, 1523, in the historic formulations of the *Schleitheim Confession*, did the Swiss Brethren themselves accept Michael Sattler's teaching of non-resistant, separatist apoliticism. Only in the late 1530s did the followers of Hut in south Germany rally to the same standard. Only after the death of Menno Simons in 1561 did the Mennonites, who traced their origins back to the Melchiorites of north Germany and the Netherlands, fall finally into line.

It was at the term of their development rather than in their origins that most of the radicals of the Reformation acknowledged the *Schleitheim Confession* as a normative statement of their beliefs and coalesced into those apolitical Anabaptist congregations that manifested so clearly the features characteristic of Troeltsch's 'sect-type' Christianity. Hewing closely in their public no less than their private lives to the New Testament ethic at its most exacting, and rejecting any attempt to draw from the Old Testament any norms governing their relationship to civil society, they affirmed their adhesion to the voluntary church of the regenerate. Entry into that church was to be by adult baptism given only to 'those who have learned repentance and amendment of life and who believe truly that their sins are taken away by Christ' (*Schleitheim Confession*: Wenger 1945, p. 248). The purity of the commitment involved was to be sustained by a stern discipline guaranteed in the last resort by the imposition of the ban but nourished on a day-to-day basis by a policy of withdrawal 'from Babylon and the earthly Egypt', and from 'fellowship with . . . the wicked' (Wenger, 1945, p. 249). Separation, that is, not only from 'all popish and anti-popish works and church services, meetings and church attendance', but also from all bearing of arms, taking of oaths, recourse to courts of law, service as magistrate, involvement in civil affairs (Wenger 1945, p. 249). The sword of temporal authority is certainly divinely ordained, not for the regenerate, however, who have no need of it, but for the curbing and punishment of the wicked, who do. It is ordained, in effect, 'outside the perfection of Christ' (Wenger 1945, p. 250). Unlike Luther and Zwingli, therefore, true Christians will not accept the protection of the sword, much less, like Müntzer and his followers, resort to it in the name of the gospel.

Sattler's endorsement of this type of non-resistant separatism, and the later rallying of other Anabaptists to the same apolitical standard, reflect the bitter experience of persecution and their repeated failure to gain for their reforms the sustained support of the political authorities. But it bears witness also to the revulsion they themselves sooner or later came to feel for the revolutionary violence resorted to by Müntzer in 1525 and by the followers of Matthijs at Münster in 1534–5. And though there was certainly no identity of viewpoint between Müntzer and the radicalised Melchiorites of Münster, the crusading apocalypticism they both shared, and their belief that the kingdom of God was finally dawning on earth, can plausibly be illustrated from the *Sermon before the Princes* that Müntzer preached at Allstedt on 13 July 1524, in the presence of the duke of Saxony and his son.

In common with one of the pamphlets Bernhard Rothmann was to write later on in 1534–5 in defence of the New Jerusalem at Münster and with which it shared many a point in common, Müntzer's *Sermon* focused on a much-favoured apocalyptic text, on Nebuchadnezzar's dream, and Daniel's interpretation of the four great kingdoms of history and the final kingdom which 'the God of heaven will set up . . . which shall never be destroyed' (Daniel 2:44). Announcing that 'the spirit of God is revealing to many elect, pious persons a decisive, inevitable, imminent reformation [accompanied] by great anguish', and insisting that 'it must be carried out to completion', he urged the princes not to let themselves be deceived by 'the false clerics and the vicious reprobates' of the day (*Sermon before the Princes*: 1957, pp. 62, 64–5). Among those false clerics, he struck out particularly at the Lutherans for teaching that 'the princes are in respect to their office a pagan people ... able to maintain nothing other than a civil unity' (p. 65). That teaching ran counter to the very words of Paul himself (Romans 13:1–4), who tells us that the ruler does not bear the sword in vain, that he is the instrument God uses to visit his anger upon the wrongdoer. If 'Christ's government', therefore, is not to be ruined and if the true reform is to be achieved, rulers must not hesitate to use the sword to drive God's 'enemies from the elect' (pp. 65–6), to 'wipe out the godless', to pluck the weeds 'out of the vineyard of God' (p. 68), to 'eliminate ... the wicked who hinder the Gospel' (p. 65). Should they so hesitate, he warned, the sword would be 'taken from them' (p. 68), for 'the poor [laity of the towns] and the peasants' see the advent of the kingdom far better than do they (p. 63). And, as if to underline this last point, Müntzer welcomed the Peasants' Revolt as an apocalyptic sign and himself joined forces with the peasants at Mulhausen.

Such views, it is now clear, did not die with Müntzer. They survived even the New Jerusalem at Münster and Menno Simons' successful efforts to lead the bulk of the Melchiorites away from revolutionary activism and back to their originally peaceful commitments. In the late 1530s, quasi-terrorists of unrepentantly Müntzerite convictions were to be found in central Germany; years later, the followers of Jan van Batenburg, who was said to have taught that robbery and murder of the obdurately unconverted was no sin, kept alive a form of violent Melchiorite apocalypticism in north Germany and the Netherlands.

In the course of less than two decades the impact of the Protestant Reformation upon the political thought of the age had been a dramatic one indeed. It had succeeded in diverting the mainstream of political thinking from its established medieval course into a complex of essentially scriptural channels leading, at one extreme, to the apocalyptic justification of revolutionary violence, at the other, to an enhancement in status of the temporal authority and an enormous emphasis on its claims to loyalty and obedience. If the former development was the less characteristic, it was powerfully influential by virtue of the reactions it inspired. It ended by nudging the Anabaptists in the direction of non-resistant separatism – an essentially apolitical stance that made its mark on the history of political thought only indirectly, and then a full century later in England. There the Separatists, having first adopted from their more radical forebears the idea of the church as a free and voluntary association of believers bound together by promise and consent, were led amid the turmoil of religious unrest and civil war to apply to the civil polity that same individualistic, consensual and implicitly contractarian model. At the same time, and during the era of Reformation itself, the turbulence of their radical brethren made it even harder for Lutherans and Calvinists alike, when confronted in mid-century with increasingly menacing political conditions, to modify the absolute nature of their original teaching on the sinfulness of forcible resistance to the powers that be. That teaching, rather than anything else, was the fundamental doctrinal contribution made by the magisterial reformers to the development of European political thinking. It was the failure of those reformers to command for their views a universal allegiance, rather than any more faithful deduction from their doctrinal premises, that led their followers to modify that original teaching. And when finally they did so, they opened up the way, ironically enough, not to any great theoretical novelties, but rather to the revival of medieval constitutionalist ideas.

7

Calvinism and resistance theory, 1550–1580

ROBERT M. KINGDON

The second generation of the Reformation was dominated by the followers of John Calvin. Calvin, to be sure, was but one of a number of theologians who provided intellectual leadership to the new type of Protestantism that emerged in these years. And he built upon a base that had already been constructed by Huldreich Zwingli in Zurich, Martin Bucer in Strasburg, and others. But he achieved such prominence within the movement, both among its advocates and its opponents, that it can fairly be called Calvinist. This new type of Protestantism was created in a number of free cities in what is now southern Germany and Switzerland, and continued to bear traces of its civic origins. It developed institutions that were able to penetrate into hostile parts of Europe outside of the Holy Roman Empire, and thus came to be the form of Protestantism most common in areas outside the German heartland of the movement. And it also tended to become particularly militant, not hesitating to mobilise political and military forces in order to win its way. This militant posture made it necessary for Calvinists to develop theories in justification of political resistance: they did develop such theories, some being both subtle and influential.

In the development of Calvinist resistance theory, Calvin himself played a role which was seminal but not major. For the greatest political challenges to his movement developed after his death. Calvin first won intellectual prominence in 1536, with the publication of the first edition of his *Institutes of the Christian Religion*, but he did not win institutional prominence until 1555, the year his supporters won control of the city of Geneva, and he did not gain an international role until the 1560s, when his followers took the leadership in promoting militant movements in his native France, in the Netherlands, in Britain, and in parts of Germany. It was especially at the times those followers faced annihilation in the ensuing religious wars, most particularly after the St Bartholomew's massacres of 1572 in France, that a highly articulated resistance theory was developed. But this was long after Calvin's death in 1564, and thus had to be the work of his successors.

i Knox and the anti-Marian resistance

Well before Calvin's death, however, one group of his followers developed a body of resistance theory. These were the English and Scottish Marian exiles, refugees from the England of Mary Tudor and the Scotland of Mary of Guise, resident in a number of Reformed cities on the continent, including Calvin's own Geneva. Like many ideological refugees before and since, these Marian exiles spent much of their time in conspiring against the government which had driven them out, in looking for ways to create a more congenial government that might make possible their return home. The Marian exile was short, as exiles go, for Mary Tudor sat upon the throne of England for only five years, from 1553 to 1558, and few of the refugees were gone from Britain for that entire period. But her rule was precarious, many of her subjects uncertain and upset, and this could only encourage their compatriots in foreign exile to call most stridently for resistance. A number of these exiles wrote political pamphlets and had them printed in major Protestant publishing centres on the continent, for circulation among fellow exiles to keep strong their commitment to the cause and for smuggling into England to encourage subversion of the government. Among these exiles, three wrote particularly interesting statements of resistance theory. They were John Ponet, the former bishop of Winchester, in exile in Strasburg; Christopher Goodman, a former professor at Oxford, in exile in Geneva; and John Knox, the future leader of the Reformation in Scotland, with Goodman in Geneva. It can be argued that none of these three was a true Calvinist, that their theologies had been formed under the influence of Swiss and Rhenish theologians well before they came to know Calvin. Still they fell under his spell while on the continent, most obviously Knox, and their followers helped plant Calvin's thought as the reigning form of theology back in Britain after the exile. For these reasons it is fair to call their resistance ideas an early form of Calvinist theory.

The first of these three to publish a political tract was Ponet. His *A Shorte Treatise of Politike Power, and of the true obedience which subjectes owe to kynges and other civile governours . . .*, was printed anonymously in 1556 in

Strasburg.[1] It was not only one of the earliest statements of a Calvinist theory, it was also one of the most radical – for it called for popular revolution and tyrannicide. In form this treatise is divided into eight sections, the first seven in turn exploring separate political questions, the last issuing a general warning to the lords and commons of England. Of these sections, the most important for an understanding of Ponet's resistance theory is number 6, devoted to the question: 'Whether it be lawful to depose an evil governor and kill a tyrant.' Ponet's answer is a resounding yes, documented by many examples of depositions and assassinations drawn from the Old Testament, ecclesiastical history, and English history. They include general uprisings, depositions by legal process, and assassinations by individuals. Ponet gives the impression that anyone who can get away with an act of violent resistance to a tyrant should. He does not limit the duty of resistance to any particular kind of agent. Some of his examples, however, do suggest a limitation of a sort that was to be important in later Calvinist theory. He points out, for example, that the popes who were deposed at the Council of Constance were deposed by the cardinals who created them (pp. 103–5), thus intimating that the granting of power in an election is conditional and can be revoked if that power is misused. And in an earlier section, number 1, on the origins of government, a classic Christian argument that all governing power is derived from God fleshed out with an Aristotelian analysis of the types of government, he points to institutions within many governments designed to hold rulers to their duties, to prevent tyranny. These include the ephors of Sparta, the tribunes of Rome, the members of the imperial 'council or diet' in Germany, the members of the parliaments in England and France, all representatives of the people charged with keeping a check on executive power (pp. 11–12). Ponet does not return to these institutions in his analysis of resistance, however, so they do not play a very important role in his theory.

Ponet's target, furthermore, is not so much the government of England as it is her church. The individuals he singles out for his most violent attacks are her Catholic bishops, most notably Stephen Gardiner – his Catholic rival for Winchester – and Edmund Bonner – who supervised in London the greatest number of burnings of Protestants. He also attacks in vaguer terms the Spanish advisers to the queen, as foreigners seeking to force

---

1. Hudson 1942 includes as an appendix a facsimile reprint of the *Shorte Treatise of Politike Power*.

Englishmen out of their rightful positions. But he never mentions Mary Tudor at all. And he makes it clear that he did not approve of the attempt engineered by John Dudley, duke of Northumberland, to substitute Lady Jane Grey for Mary at the beginning of her reign. The government which Ponet wants to see deposed is an ecclesiastical government; the tyrants he wants to see assassinated are its bishops. His theory, therefore, is still very much a part of the general Protestant struggle against Catholics that marked the early stages of the Reformation. It is religious; it is sectarian; it does not have the more political and secular significance of later theories.

There is an important shift in target in the pamphlets of Goodman and Knox which appeared two years later, in 1558, from the press of Jean Crespin in Geneva. They still lambast the Catholic bishops and Spanish advisers, but their primary target is Mary Tudor, and there is an almost hysterical misogyny to their argument. Goodman is the more comprehensive and the more interesting of the two for students of theory. His *How Superior Powers Oght to be Obeyd of their Subjects* began as a sermon on Acts 4, but was extended into a full treatise on resistance, developing one general lesson: we must obey God rather than man.[2] It has some of the shape of a scholastic treatise, with two chapters, 8 and 9, raising objections to his own argument from first the New Testament and then the Old Testament, followed by formal refutations to each. Goodman was also radical, as radical as Ponet, calling for popular revolution and tyrannicide. The unusual feature of his argument is its misogyny. Applying his general precept, that we must obey God rather than man, he proceeds to argue that we must obey God in the principles by which we choose rulers rather than follow our own fantasies. But those principles preclude the choice of a woman for that 'is against nature and God's ordinance' (p. 52). Just as a woman is incapable of ruling a family or holding an inferior office within a government, so is she totally unfit for supreme rule. Mary is unfit not only because she is a woman, furthermore, but because she is a 'bastard by birth' (p. 97) and thus barred by the laws of inheritance from rule, and is also an 'open idolatress' (p. 99) who deserves death. Furthermore, this sentence can be executed by anyone who can manage it. Goodman explicitly refuses to limit the right of resistance to magistrates and inferior officers, arguing that 'common people also' (p. 142) must make their princes obey God's laws. The vengeance of God upon an idolatrous community will fall upon the

---

2. Goodman's *How Superior Powers Oght to be Obeyd* (1558) is available in a facsimile reprint with a brief introduction by C.H. McIlwain.

entire community, not just its leaders. It is therefore the responsibility of all to avert the calamity which the pollution of idolatry will otherwise bring upon the community. A good example, says Goodman, is Matathias in the books of the Maccabees who 'was no public person' (p. 76) yet led the revolt against Antiochus that ended in the killing of the tyrant. Goodman's treatise, like Ponet's, is religious and sectarian, and indeed has an even nastier polemical edge. But it does have a more openly political content, since its prime target is the head of state, the queen.

There is an even more sharply developed misogyny in Knox, for Knox spent much of his life organising resistance to the rule of women – first Mary Tudor, then Mary of Guise as regent of Scotland, finally her daughter Mary Stuart. Knox was also much more prominent as an actual leader of resistance than either Ponet or Goodman. Ponet, indeed, died before he could return to England. But Knox became the chief ideological leader of the Protestant movement in Scotland, with some influence south of the border into England. Knox's political writings, in consequence, have some of the practical quality of an active leader, closely adapted to the circumstances for which they were written.

The first and best known of these writings is his *First Blast of the Trumpet Against the Monstrous Regiment of Women* (Knox 1846–64, IV, pp. 363–420). It is a real classic of misogyny, elegantly organised and developed with a relentless scholastic logic. His purpose, he tells us in the preface, is to demonstrate 'how abominable before God is the Empire or Rule of a wicked woman, yea, of a traiteresse and bastard' (p. 365). He then develops three separate proofs of this proposition: the first is from nature, quoting Aristotle and the Corpus Juris Civilis to the effect that women are inherently unstable and should thus not possess political or judicial authority; the second is from Scripture, quoting Genesis and St Paul to suggest that God himself prefers that women be subject not only to their husbands but to men in general; the third is from order and equity, and advances an organic analogy, comparing society to a body and man to its head, backed by analogies from the animal kingdom. In proper scholastic fashion he then states and refutes objections drawn from the Old Testament, the New Testament, and the history of certain other governments. He concludes that it is a duty of the nobility and estates that had elected women as rulers to correct their mistake by deposing those women. Only at this point does the argument enter the domain of resistance theory, and the conclusion is not elaborated very much. Knox's primary target throughout this treatise is Mary Tudor of England, but he acknowledges in passing that the argument also applies to Scotland, then ruled by Mary of Guise, as regent for Mary Stuart.

Knox then turns to his native Scotland and writes a number of pamphlets attacking its government. They are *The Copy of a Letter Delivered to the Lady Marie, Regent of Scotland* (first printed in 1556), *The Appellation ... to the nobilitie, estates, and communaltie* (of Scotland), and *A Letter Addressed to the Commonalty of Scotland*, all published in Geneva in 1558 (Knox 1846–64, IV, pp. 429–60, 465–520, 521–40). These three treatises take the form of appeals against a sentence issued by the convocation of the Catholic church of Scotland back in 1556, convicting Knox of heresy and ordering his execution. In form, therefore, they are primarily diatribes against the Catholic clergy and pleas for intervention by the secular authorities in this as in other matters of church business. The tyrants Knox attacks are Catholic bishops and abbots, the resistance he encourages is by laymen against clerical rule. In this they are reminiscent of Ponet, or for that matter of Protestant polemic in general. The most temperate of the three is the letter to the queen regent, Mary of Guise. It is polite and respectful, almost courtly in tone. There is almost none of the misogyny of the *First Blast*, save for one rather condescending passage in which he expresses regret that the instability that goes with her sex will make it impossible for her rule to last very long (p. 452). Above all it is a plea that she intervene to lift the condemnation of Knox and other Protestants, even though she remains Catholic, and inaugurate a policy of toleration for the two faiths. His emphasis on the power of a ruler to control religious matters led one king, James VI of Scotland and I of England, to claim in this pamphlet support for his own Erastian views on the rights of a monarch to control a national church, although James exaggerates the point somewhat (Knox 1846–64, IV, pp. 425–8).

Knox's argument is expanded and made somewhat more concrete in the *Appellation*. Here he develops the contention that his condemnation by the Catholic clergy violated due process of law, as codified by the civil lawyers, and that in any event the matter should be settled in a secular court. He goes on to argue that it is the primary purpose of all secular government to see to the 'reformation of religion ... and punishment of false teachers' (p. 485), and thus calls upon their assistance in his campaign to rid Scotland of its Catholic clergy. He insists that this is an obligation laid by God not only upon kings but also upon all magistrates and other officers of government, particularly in times when a king fails to undertake this duty. In fact he argues that each and every member of a community is responsible for the suppression of idolatry, his code word for Catholicism, and that God will punish the entire community if this is not done. He follows the scholastic format of the *First Blast* in raising and then refuting a number of objections to this thesis. Most of his examples of proper suppression of idolatry are drawn from the Old Testament, which he insists must continue to serve as a guide to Christians in matters of this sort. In an aside, he says that it is 'the duty of the Nobility, Judges, Rulers and People of England' to resist and put to death Mary Tudor, for permitting the return of 'idolatry' to that country (p. 507). This is the only open appeal to resistance in the pamphlet. His target is primarily the Catholic clergy of Scotland, he rarely mentions its royal government, his goal is to persuade the lay nobility of the realm to join his campaign against Catholicism.

Finally in his *Letter to the Commonalty* Knox again appeals that his condemnation be lifted so that he might have freedom to preach, and calls upon the general population to join in this campaign. He does not advise them to join in any form of armed resistance, however, contenting himself with asking them to disobey the Catholic clergy and refuse to pay tithes and other financial dues owed to them.

At the very end of this piece, Knox adds an outline of a proposed *Second Blast of the Trumpet*. In this outline he promises to develop the following propositions: (1) lawful kings do not receive their power by inheritance but rather by election; (2) it is never legitimate to elect an idolater as king or to any public office; (3) even a promise to an elected idolater is not binding; (4) if an idolater has been mistakenly elected to public office, those who elected him can and should depose him. Here at last is a real resistance theory, insisting upon the conditional nature of all political power, designed to justify Protestant attempts to overthrow Catholic rulers. But it is only an outline, without any development. Knox never did get around to writing this treatise.

Taken together, these pamphlets of Knox's hardly provide a resistance theory of any generality. They argue for resistance to women and Catholic clergymen, not to governments in general. They also did not have much influence. The *First Blast*, in particular, proved to be a considerable embarrassment to the general Calvinist community. Its arguments quite obviously applied not only to the Mary but also to Queen Elizabeth I. She was fully aware of them and never forgave Knox or his Genevan hosts for issuing this pamphlet. In vain Calvin wrote to Elizabeth's chief minister, William Cecil, to protest that he had not read and certainly had not approved of the misogynous writings published by the English in his city.[3]

---

3. Calvinus Cicellio, n.d. (probably March 1559), in Calvin 1863–1900, XVII, pp. 490–2.

In vain Calvin's chief lieutenant, Theodore Beza, added a clause on this matter to the next version of the *Confession* he prepared as an authoritative summary of the Calvinist faith, a summary printed in many editions and translations throughout the rest of the century. That clause supported the occasional rule of women, specifically denying that the biblical texts used by Knox on the subjection of women to men were applicable when it came to deciding who should rule a kingdom.[4]

It is possible that Knox's appeals to the Scots had more effect. Soon after they were issued, Knox returned to Scotland and helped the covenanted Lords of the Congregation overthrow the government of the queen regent and establish a Reformed church of Scotland. In this case, however, action really went beyond theory. In any case Scotland was peripheral to most of Europe and its policies were not followed closely elsewhere.

In general, then, these English Calvinist arguments for resistance, radical though they were in part, had little general impact, even within the Calvinist community. Most Calvinist resistance theory followed a very different line of development and built upon a somewhat different set of sources. An important ingredient in those sources was Lutheran.

ii   The development of Lutheran resistance theory

It may come as a surprise to some to hear of a Lutheran theory of resistance, since modern Lutheranism has often been politically passive, docilely accepting the form of government under which it lives, whatever that may be. In the early sixteenth century, however, there was a vigorous Lutheran resistance movement. Indeed it can be argued that this resistance made possible the very survival of Protestantism. That movement first took shape in 1530, after the imperial diet in Augsburg had once again failed to resolve the religious split provoked by Luther's attack on indulgences back in 1517, and the emperor resolved to suppress Lutheranism by military force. In response to that threat, a group of Lutheran principalities and cities had organised the Schmalkaldic League, committed to defending their faith by armed force.

To justify this resort to force, lawyers on the staffs of the two leaders of this league, Hesse and Saxony, developed resistance theories. These two powers still remembered all too well the Peasants' Revolt of the preceding

---

4. The relevant passage of Beza's *Confession de la foi chrestienne* (1560) is reprinted as an annexe II to Beza 1971, pp. 70–5.

decade, which had threatened their power along with imperial power. So they wanted to be very careful to develop a resistance theory that would not justify revolt by anyone in the general population but would permit the revolt they planned to lead. They wanted, in other words, to limit the right to revolt to lawfully constituted if inferior agencies in the imperial government, to 'inferior magistrates' in the terminology of the period. The Hessian argument was based upon an interpretation of the imperial constitution. It began with the fact that the emperor is indeed elected, by the seven great prince-electors, supported by the lesser princes and cities of the empire. It then insisted that this election is conditional, granting power that is provisional and partial, not absolute. The lesser princes retain the responsibility for the proper exercise of religion within their realms. Thus any emperor who seeks to force them to change religious policy is overstepping the bounds of his authority and forfeiting his claim to general power. In these circumstances he may and should be resisted, with armed force if necessary. The Saxon argument for resistance was based on an appeal to the Roman civil law, specifically as recorded in that great compilation, the Corpus Juris Civilis, then being received by governments all over Europe as a useful guide to the structure and ultimate principles undergirding local systems of law. It was based specifically on the principle that it is always permissible to use force to repel force, and it pointed further to clauses permitting citizens to resist the orders of a manifestly unjust judge, who was not applying the law as he should in his decisions. The emperor, the Saxons argued, was behaving like an unjust judge in condemning their religious policies. His orders, thus, could not be accepted and must be resisted (Skinner 1978, II, pp. 195–9).

Luther and the other theologians who provided intellectual leadership to this movement were persuaded to accept these arguments, at first in a memorandum drafted by Luther in Torgau in 1530, which simply acknowledged that the lawyers were probably right if their understanding of the nature of the imperial government was correct,[5] later in a number of publications, most notably Luther's *Warnung an seine lieben Deutschen* of 1531.[6] Nothing came of these resistance arguments at the time, since the emperor became distracted by problems in other parts of his immense holdings and did not proceed to mobilise an army to suppress Lutheran Protestantism. In 1546, however, after Luther's death, the imperial threat did materialise and resulted in the first Schmalkaldic war. That war ended

5. Luther 1883–1983, Briefwechsel V, p. 662.　　6. *Ibid.*, 30, III, pp. 276–320.

in 1548, with a smashing imperial victory and was followed by imperial decrees imposing a religious compromise on all of Germany, the Interims of Augsburg and Leipzig. Many Lutherans accepted these compromises, often after some haggling and modification, most notably Philip Melanchthon, Luther's most prominent successor. But a few of Luther's most devoted followers, the so-called Gnesio-Lutherans, refused to accept any compromise, and insisted on continuing resistance to the imperial armies. The most important centre of these Gnesio-Lutherans was the city of Magdeburg in northern Germany. This comparatively small and powerless city flatly refused to enforce the new imperial legislation or to permit the entry of imperial commissioners. And it called upon all good Lutherans to join in continued resistance. This position was explained and justified in several manifestos issued by the magistrates and pastors of Magdeburg in 1550, most notably a Confession of the pastors drafted on 13 April.[7] These manifestos developed the argument that inferior magistrates such as the elected officials governing Magdeburg had an obligation to resist imperial law. They adapted and applied the arguments earlier advanced in the chanceries of Hesse and Saxony. They argued that all governments, both superior and inferior, are bound to enforce certain natural laws inherent in all human society, as, for example, the laws governing marriage. If the superior level of government seeks to legislate positive laws in violation of these natural laws, it must be resisted. The imperial government in 1550 was violating natural laws in seeking to impose upon Magdeburg a false and idolatrous form of religion. The magistrates of Magdeburg, thus, had to resist this imperial initiative.

Magdeburg's call to revolt succeeded. The Schmalkaldic armies were re-grouped and re-vivified. The imperial government was not able to defeat them as before and finally, in 1555, abandoned the effort. In the Religious Peace of Augsburg of that year it was decided to end all attempts to impose religious unity throughout the empire. Each subordinate element within the imperial government, each 'inferior magistrate', whether a principality ruled by one man or a city ruled by a council, was permitted to choose whether it would adopt the Catholic or the Lutheran form of worship. This compromise settlement has often been described as embodying the principle of 'cuius regio eius religio'. It effectively ended the need for Lutheran resistance. The Gnesio-Lutheran initiative had won for the entire

7. *Bekenntnis Unter-/richt und vermanung der Pfarr-/hern und Prediger der Christlichen/Kirchen zu Margdeburgk./Anno 1550. Den 13. Aprilis.*

t the end! Check out the books about
en's Library at '595.7'

Brown, M
6/12

Lutheran movement a secure place within the structure of imperial government. Lutherans in consequence turned to a posture of political passivity for much of the rest of the century.

The Schmalkaldic revolt and the theory used to justify it, however, gained wide attention in other parts of Europe. Chroniclers and historians told and retold the story. Probably the most prominent of them was Johannes Sleidan, a diplomat who followed closely the political developments of this period, and then became a historian. His *De statu religionis et reipublicae Carolo Quinto Caesare*, printed in several editions and translations from 1555 on, spread word of the Lutheran struggle throughout Europe. It recounted the story of the 1530 Diet of Augsburg, of the organisation of the Schmalkaldic League, of Luther's Torgau memorandum of 1530, of the defeat of the League, and of the heroic role of Magdeburg in its revival. It summarises the argument of the Confession of the pastors of Magdeburg adopted in April of 1550, for example, in these words: 'It is lawful for an inferior magistrate to resist a superior that would constrain their subject to forsake the truth' (Sleidan 1689, p. 496).

iii   The Calvinist inheritance from the Schmalkaldic war: Peter Martyr Vermigli

Theologians in the Calvinist camp, furthermore, began to weave Lutheran arguments for resistance into their biblical commentaries. Thus Peter Martyr Vermigli, the erudite Reformed theologian who helped introduce a Calvinist version of the faith into England in the Edwardian period, and developed it further both in Strasburg, before and after his visit to England, and in Zurich, in the later years of his life, adopted a version of the Hessian constitutional argument for the resistance of inferior magistrates. It can be found in both his published commentaries on Romans, first printed in Basle in 1558, and on Judges, first printed in Zurich in 1561. It is then repeated in further editions of these commentaries, and a critical part of the Judges commentary is included in the posthumous collection of his *Common Places*, a basic resource for Calvinist clergymen throughout the rest of the century.[8] In the Romans commentary, Vermigli names the Roman senate and the German College of Electors as examples of bodies that can resist princes 'if they transgress the ends and limits of the power which they have received' (1980, p. 11). In the Judges commentary, in a

8. Vermigli 1980 contains the cited texts in Latin and in Tudor English.

locus aimed directly at the problem of 'whether it be lawful for subjects to rise against their prince', he again refers to the Electors of the empire, saying that for them 'undoubtedly if the prince perform not his covenants and promises, it is lawful to constrain and bring him into order, and by force to compel him to perform the conditions and covenants which he had promised, and that by war when it cannot otherwise be done' (pp. 99–100). Vermigli, observe, was close to the Marian exiles in both Strasburg and Zurich. Indeed, a number of them had been his students back in England. But he did not buy their radical arguments for popular resistance. He rather preferred the more limited arguments of his Lutheran neighbours and hosts in Strasburg, arguments of which he may well have gained knowledge from his friend and colleague Sleidan.

References to the Magdeburg defiance of imperial authority also begin to creep into Calvinist activity in this period. Thus Beza includes an allusion to the Magdeburg resistance in a polemic against Sebastian Castellio's plea for religious liberty, first published in 1554, in Latin, then again in 1560, in French. The main thrust of this pamphlet is to argue for the necessity of repressing heretics as flagrant as Michael Servetus, but it not only insists that a government must suppress heresy within its jurisdiction, it also insists that a government must prevent the imposition of false doctrine from outside its jurisdiction and it points to Magdeburg as a notable example of a government which had recently acted thus to maintain pure religion.[9] Knox also used the Magdeburg example in 1564, when he presented a copy of the 'Apology of Magdeburg' to Secretary Lethington at a meeting of a General Assembly of the church of Scotland, as a way of encouraging continued resistance to the government of Mary Stuart (Knox 1949, II, pp. 129–30).

The Lutheran theory of resistance, as it developed from 1530 to 1550, just like the Marian exiles' theory of resistance, as it was stated from 1556 to 1558, remains primarily religious in nature. Each assumes its form of Protestantism is true and must be protected against Catholic repression. Each argues that its adherents have a religious obligation to fight for the true faith. Neither tries to make an appeal across religious boundaries for support in resistance to supreme political authority. Neither tries to develop a truly political theory of resistance. That final step was taken only later, by French Calvinists, following the St Bartholomew's massacres.

Before we move to the mature French Calvinist theory of resistance,

---

9. The relevant passage of Beza's *De haereticis a civili magistratu puniendis*, in French translation (1560), is reprinted as annexe 1 to Beza 1971, pp. 69–70.

however, we should note that elements of it were anticipated well before the massacres of 1572. Calvin himself, although he usually insisted upon a general obligation of Christians to obey their rulers, briefly conceded a few times a possible right of resistance. The most celebrated of these concessions is to be found in a short passage near the very end of his *Institutes of the Christian Religion*, arguably the most influential single synthesis of Protestant theology produced in the sixteenth century, first published in 1536, then translated, expanded and refined by its author in a number of editions down to 1560. That passage reiterates his general teaching that private individuals must never resist their rulers, no matter how tyrannical. But it then notes that in certain governments there are institutions established to limit the powers of kings 'as in ancient times the ephors were set against the Spartan kings, or the tribunes of the people against the Roman consuls, or the demarchs against the senate of the Athenians; and perhaps ... such power as the three estates exercise in every realm when they hold their chief assemblies' (IV. 20. 31: Calvin 1961, II, p. 1519). Calvin grants that these institutions which represent the people and which have a constitutional responsibility to limit royal power must fulfil that responsibility. Similar passages calling for a limit to the exercise of royal power can be found in several of Calvin's biblical commentaries. All these passages, however, are brief and casual. They do only a little to shade Calvin's general insistence on the duty of Christians to obey their governments.

Similarly Pierre Viret, a close associate to Calvin in the building of Protestant churches in French-speaking Switzerland and France itself, and perhaps an even more popular preacher and publicist, observed in a pamphlet entitled *Remonstrances aux fideles qui conversent entre les Papistes*, published in 1547, that resistance led by inferior magistrates is sometimes legitimate:

if there comes some tyrant who instead of guarding those whom he has promised and sworn to guard and in the place of performing the duties which his office requires of him, he deliberately tyrannizes those whom he owes preservation ... [then] if such a people have an honest means of resisting the tyranny of such a tyrant by means of their legitimate magistrates and are able by this means to avoid slavery, then they ought to follow the counsel of St Paul: ... 'if you can gain your freedom and enjoy liberty, then avail yourself of the opportunity' [I Cor. 5:21].[10]

We have already noted that Beza, Calvin's closest associate and principal successor, included in his 1554 polemic against Castellio an approving allusion to the example of the magistrates of Magdeburg in defying the

---

10. See Linder 1966, p. 133, for English translation of and commentary on this passage.

imperial threat to impose upon their city a corrupted form of religion. Both these passages, however, like Calvin's remarks, are casual asides in writings devoted primarily to other purposes.

iv   The Huguenots and the French wars of religion

More extended analysis of political matters followed these asides, particularly following the outbreak of the French wars of religion in 1562. That outbreak was made possible by a serious decline in royal authority following the premature death of King Henri II in 1559, as three of his sons succeeded him, the first two of whom were so young on accession that they could not rule effectively, thus exposing the kingdom to the instability the rule of a minor king almost always entailed. Francis II ruled for a year, but real power was held by members of the Guise family, relatives of his young wife, Mary Stuart. He was succeeded by the even younger Charles IX, with real power now vested in a regency council dominated by the queen-mother, Catherine de Médicis. Tensions between powerful factions of aristocrats jockeying for power were reinforced by religious differences which finally exploded into open warfare, which was to plague France for most of the rest of the century, leaving much of the country a smoking ruin and inducing psychic scars, traces of which persist to this day. The political tracts provoked by the beginning of these wars, however, are not of great interest to students of political theory. Most of them are by Protestant apologists in the suite of the prince of Condé, seeking to justify his recourse to arms. They insist on continued Protestant loyalty to the crown and claim that Condé and his followers, now called Huguenots by the opposition, had gone to war only to protect the kingdom from wicked advisers to the king. On occasion they even accuse these advisers of attempting to kidnap the king and his relatives, and insist that the main Protestant goal was to rescue the royal family. Chief among the targets of their attack were members of the Guise family, above all the cardinal of Lorraine. These advisers are blasted with a singular ferocity, as in François Hotman's polemic, *Le Tigre* (1560).[11] But these early tracts explicitly deny any disloyalty to the crown of France and thus find no need to justify resistance to it. In these early years of the wars of religion, the leaders of the Protestant party were optimistic, hoping to win the royal family to their side, hoping

---

11. Hotman's *Epistre envoiée au tigre de la France* appears in a facsimile reprint with commentary by Charles Read in Hotman 1970.

to convert all of France to their cause. Calvinism was still spreading fast within the kingdom, winning control of entire cities and certain rural areas. The first years of war dampened that optimism somewhat, but did not dash it entirely.

All this changes in 1572, following the St Bartholomew's massacres. In the few weeks following the assassination in Paris of the Admiral Coligny, then principal leader of the Protestant party, dozens of additional political and military leaders were killed, and thousands of humbler Protestants were murdered. Altogether perhaps as many as 10,000 people were put to death in about a dozen cities.[12] These massacres had a shattering effect upon French Protestants and their allies in other countries. They ended for good their hopes of winning all of France to their cause. They could not be dismissed as the work of a few wicked advisers, because they had been openly ordered by the king himself, supported by his mother and the older of his two remaining brothers. They could not be dismissed as the work of a malevolent minority, because mobs of Catholic fanatics had taken to the streets and chopped Protestants to pieces by the thousands. It was obvious to all that Protestantism in France was an endangered minority without the resources to win for itself security within the kingdom.

These circumstances forced the Protestants of France to develop a new political theory of resistance. To survive they had to resist the royal government, for it had committed itself to a policy of exterminating Protestants. But they had to develop a resistance theory that was in no way democratic, for the general population, especially in the larger cities, had shown itself quite willing to help implement a policy of extermination. And they had to develop a theory that would win the assistance of opponents to the government who were not themselves Protestant, for Protestantism was now too weak a movement militarily to save itself. These were the circumstances that led to the extraordinary flowering of Calvinist resistance theory that followed the St Bartholomew's massacres.

Many of the pamphlets following the massacres, to be sure, continued the tradition of straightforward diatribe, now attacking not only the Guises but also members of the royal family. And, indeed, the most widely circulated pamphlets, such as the *Reveille-matin* which appeared in several editions in just a few years,[13] possess this character. The queen-mother, Catherine de Médicis, was a particularly favoured target, in part because

---

12. See Estèbe 1968, p. 19, on the widely varying estimates of numbers of victims (2,000 to 100,000); pp. 143–55 on the geography of the massacres.
13. For detailed analysis of this work, see Kingdon 1988, ch. 4, Kelley 1981, pp. 301–6.

she was a foreigner, an Italian, with a number of Italian advisers in her entourage. A number of these pamphlets accused the Italians of introducing the wicked and amoral political tactics of Machiavelli into France. The most developed version of that argument is to be found in Innocent Gentillet's *Anti-Machiavel*.[14] Several of these pamphlets, however, contained more reasoned and considered political argument. Foremost among them were Hotman's *Francogallia*, first published in 1573; Beza's *Du droit des magistrats*, first published in anonymous French translation in 1574; the *Vindiciae contra tyrannos*, first published under the pseudonym of Stephanus Junius Brutus in 1579.

Hotman's *Francogallia* was in form not a political tract at all. It was rather a constitutional history of France, with particular attention to the period in which the cultures of the Germanic Franks and the Romanised Gauls were fused to form an entity distinctively French. It had clearly been in preparation for some time and was part of a publishing programme upon which the great French Calvinist jurisconsult had been working for years. In fact it is quite likely that much of the text of the *Francogallia* was written before the massacres of 1572.[15]

As a work of history, Hotman's book has its strengths. It firmly rejects some of the more extravagant notions of early French historians – that the country was first settled by Trojans, that its earliest inhabitants spoke Greek. It uses many of the same early chronicles describing the barbarian invasions following the collapse of Roman imperial power that modern historians of the subject would use. But it is far from an objective work of history. For Hotman clearly had a thesis to develop, and he did not hesitate to force the facts to fit it. He made much of the elective nature of the early Frankish monarchy and claimed to find traces of it surviving to his day, although he granted a growing role to inheritance. Above all he insisted upon the integral role within French government of a Public Council representing all elements of the kingdom's population. He found traces of such a Council from the very beginning and he found it persisting almost to his day, taking the form of the Estates General in the most recent centuries. This Council, Hotman argued, rightfully held ultimate power within the state. It created and could depose kings, for it was the custodian of the immutable fundamental laws by which all kings of France were required to govern. It had to share with the crown in making the most important

14. Mastellone 1972 provides an expert survey of this current of thought. Gentillet 1968 is a good critical edition of the 1576 printing of the most influential text.
15. Hotman 1972 is a fine variorum edition of the Latin originals with an English translation. See pp. 38–52 for information on the genesis of this work.

decisions in government policy, including decisions to tax, and most explicitly the right to regulate religion. Hotman conceded that the power of this Council had been attenuated in recent centuries, and blamed some of this weakening upon the pernicious influence of the Roman Catholic church. Lawyers from Rome had introduced new forms of law and a general spirit of litigiousness. Clergymen supported by Rome had usurped for themselves an entire estate within the Public Council. New courts, most notably the *parlements*, had sprung up, arrogating to themselves powers rightfully belonging to representative institutions.

Hotman made no overt attempt to apply the lessons of his history to his own day. But they were obvious to many of his contemporaries. They justified resistance to royal authority and to judicial authority, providing such resistance was led by an institution that represented the general population. Soon a number of such institutions developed, particularly in the south and west of France, generally called *assemblées politiques*. They were made up of noblemen, both Protestant and Malcontent Catholic, backed by representatives from cities that had remained under the control of local governments independent of the crown. And these bodies mobilised armed forces to begin again the fight against the royal government of France. We even have record that at one of these *assemblées politiques*, held in 1573, copies of the *Francogallia* were passed around and helped to convince the participants of the need to return to war.[16]

Another pamphlet passed around at the same *assemblée* for the same purpose was the anonymous *Du droit des magistrats* which we know was written by Beza, then still in unpublished form, although soon to appear in print.[17] It reached a similar conclusion using some of the same historical evidence as Hotman. In fact it is clear the two treatises were finished in Geneva at the same time, and that Beza either read Hotman's draft or discussed the subject with him at length. But Beza's pamphlet was much less a work of erudition and scholarship, and much more a tract for its times, although it, too, seldom mentions recent events. Close analysis of it, however, reveals that it was quite cleverly designed to encourage the very policy of resistance French Protestants and their Malcontent Catholic allies were then contemplating.

Beza's starting point is his claim that God must be obeyed above all

16. Reported by de Thou in his *Histoire universelle* in many editions in both Latin and French from 1620 on: e.g. 1734, VII, pp. 18–19.
17. De Thou 1734, VII, p. 19, identified, here only as 'un livre qui avoit paru en Allegmagne du tems du siege de Magdebourg', in reference to the claim on the title page of this work to be an expanded reprint of a 1550 Magdeburg pamphlet, in evident allusion to the *Bekenntnis*.

human authorities. This means that there are times when human law must be disobeyed, even if those who disobey must endure punishment, even martyrdom. He insists that individuals must never go beyond passive disobedience, if they are faced by a legitimate ruler turned tyrant, and includes a nasty aside against the Anabaptists for ignoring this rule. He then proceeds to analyse types of tyranny and makes use of a classic distinction between tyrants who are usurpers and tyrants who are legitimate rulers. The tyrant who is a usurper, either by illegally seizing power within the government under which he lives or by invading a territory over which he has no legitimate claim, poses no theoretical problem. He can be resisted by anyone who can manage the job and by any means, including assassination. But the other type of tyrant, the legitimate ruler who turns sour and wicked, does pose a problem for Beza. He proceeds to divide the population living under such a ruler into three categories: (1) private individuals; (2) inferior magistrates, such as provincial governors and city mayors, who share power under a king's direction over restricted local areas; (3) magistrates whose constitutional duty it is to serve as a check or bridle on royal power. It is this sharp division into two types of subordinate magistrates that is one of the most striking and useful parts of Beza's theory. The private individuals, of course, are not allowed to resist with force, but must limit themselves to passive disobedience, prayers, and repentance. The inferior magistrates hold power by what amounts to a reciprocal contract with the king, a contract embodied in their oaths of office. If any king abrogates his side of this agreement by encroaching on the local responsibilities of these magistrates, then they are free to abandon their side of the contract requiring loyalty to the crown and may join in armed resistance. The magistrates who advise the king, primarily through the Estates General, have a constitutional duty to hold him to his responsibilities. If he fails, they may organise armed resistance against him, even depose him if that prove necessary.

This part of Beza's argument is developed in some detail, with proofs derived from scripture, from history, and from law. He provides some thirteen 'examples' of magistrates of this type, ranging from the ephors of Sparta and the tribal chiefs of ancient Israel to the parliament of England and the Estates General of France, including representative institutions from Poland, Spain, the Holy Roman Empire, and several other countries. Most of these institutions, Beza insists, play an essential role in creating kings and in advising kings, retain the right to depose kings, and certainly are entitled to lead armed resistance to kings if that seems necessary and expedient. This argument is then further supported with allegations from the Roman Corpus Juris Civilis, which Beza seems to equate with natural law, including references to the laws of contract, the laws on inheritance, the laws of marriage, and the laws regulating and limiting the powers of parents over children, husbands over wives, and masters over slaves.

To this point, Beza's argument would seem to be a call for a meeting of the French Estates General to organise opposition to the crown, and in this it parallels Hotman. But Beza then faces squarely the probability that a hostile king is not likely to call an estates that would favour his opponents. So Beza then insists that in this situation it is the duty of the inferior magistrates who oppose the power of the tyrant to take the initiative and call an equivalent of the estates, a representative body prepared to take on the constitutional duty of organising resistance to the crown laid upon certain advisers to the king. What Beza was calling for was much like the *assemblées politiques* summoned by the Huguenot aristocrats of Languedoc, soon allied with the Malcontent Catholic governor of that province, Henri de Montmorency-Damville. Beza's theory, therefore, precisely fitted the needs of the Calvinist party in France at that time. It admirably justified the very programme of resistance they were contemplating.

Beza's theory, however, was not limited in utility to that time and place. It was cast in such general terms that it would continue to prove useful for decades to come. It was cast, indeed, in terms so general that it could even be used by partisans of other religious causes. The fact that Beza had had to conceal his identity as the book's author, had had even to conceal the place of its publication, helped make this broader use possible. Between 1574 and 1581, the *Du droit des magistrats* appeared in ten French editions, four of them within Simon Goulart's general collection of documents provoked by the religious warfare of that time, the *Mémoires de l'estat de France sous Charles neufiesme*.[18] And between 1576 and 1649, it appeared in about seventeen Latin translations, often bound with such other political classics of the period as the *Vindiciae contra tyrannos* and Machiavelli's *Prince*.[19] Few expressions of Calvinist resistance theory of this period were so influential for such a long period of time.

The one Calvinist work which clearly rivalled Beza's treatise in influence was the one so often published with it, the *Vindiciae contra tyrannos*. Its preface was dated 1577 and it was planned as early as 1575, but it was not

---

18. Beza 1971, pp. xliv–xlv, contains a list of French editions.
19. Beza 1965 is a good critical edition of the Latin version; pp. 21–3 contain a list of Latin editions.

actually published until 1579, when a first Latin edition appeared in Basle. That was followed by eleven more Latin printings, often in combination with other works, one French translation in 1581, a partial English translation in 1588, and full English translation in 1648 and 1689.[20] Its content makes it clear that the *Vindiciae* was prepared in the same French Calvinist circle as the *Francogallia* and the *Du droit des magistrats*. Indeed, it borrows from them at points: all three, for example, tell the story of a fictitious oath sworn by the subjects of the king of Aragon at his coronation to make clear the provisional nature of their award of power to him (Giesey 1968). The identity of the *Vindiciae*'s author remains a mystery. There is some evidence that the author was Hubert Languet, a French Protestant who spent much of his career in Germany as a diplomat in the service of the Elector of Saxony. There is also some evidence that the author was Philippe Duplessis Mornay, a younger French nobleman who became an important lay leader of the French Reformed party. There are theories about other possible authors and even about collective authorship. To me the most probable hypothesis is that Languet prepared a first draft and gave it to his younger friend Mornay, who then arranged for its publication, perhaps after extensively revising it.[21]

In the years between the writing of the *Du droit des magistrats* and the *Vindiciae*, the situation had changed somewhat for the French Calvinist party. The alliance they had sought with the Malcontent Catholics had been struck and they had even won support within the French royal family, from the duc d'Alençon, younger brother to the new king, Henri III. Their joint armies had gone to war against the royal government. Fellow Calvinists in the Netherlands, furthermore, had helped spark a revolt against the king of Spain, rallying behind the standard of the prince of Orange. Militant Catholics in both Spain and France had reacted by organising their own forces more tightly, most notably in the first French Catholic League. That League had dominated a meeting of the Estates General in 1576, making clear that this was not an institution likely to be of much use in organising resistance for a Calvinist party. More and more Calvinists found themselves relying on an international coalition of prominent aristocrats and leaders of governments, both Protestant and Catholic, drawn from France, the Netherlands, Britain, and Germany, facing a similarly international coalition of prominent aristocrats and

20. Mornay 1979 is a facsimile edition of the 1581 French translation, with a fine critical apparatus. For a list of editions, see pp. 397–9.
21. See Mornay 1979, pp. i–v, for a review of theories of authorship ending with this conclusion.

leaders of governments, single-mindedly Catholic, drawn from France, the Netherlands, Italy, and Spain. The *Vindiciae* incorporates an attempt to adjust to this new situation.

In form the *Vindiciae* is a scholastic treatise, organised around four basic questions, including a number of formal objections with responses, presenting an argument so carefully constructed that it does indeed resemble, as the author of its preface claims, a geometric proof. It is longer and more fully documented than the *Du droit des magistrats*, thus making more clear the sources upon which both drew. These are the questions around which the *Vindiciae* is built: (1) Must subjects obey a prince who commands something against God's law? (2) Is it lawful to resist a prince who wishes to break God's law and ruin the church? (3) Is it lawful to resist a prince who oppresses the state? (4) May neighbouring princes rescue the subjects of a tyrant? The answers to these questions are (1) No, (2) Yes, (3) Yes, and (4) Yes. In explaining these answers, the author develops at the beginning a distinctive theory of two contracts: a first between God and the general population, both ruler and ruled; a second between a ruler and his subjects. Like all contracts, these bear mutual obligations, and if one party fails to fulfil his obligations, the other party is released from his. Thus a king who flouts the laws of God loses divine support as mediated through the leaders of the religious community, and a king who breaks his promises to his subjects loses the obedience they had promised to him.

The longest and most interesting part of the *Vindiciae* is the answer to question three, for it develops a theory of government and a theory of resistance which is really secular, cut loose from the religious foundations of much of the rest of the treatise and most of earlier Calvinist resistance theory. It first presents an extensive analysis of the nature of royal power, arguing from several different angles that such power always depends upon popular consent, a consent that is conditional and can be revoked. Then it turns to an analysis of tyranny, developing in some detail the classic distinction, now derived explicitly from Bartolus, between the tyrant by usurpation and the tyrant by exercise. The tyrant by usurpation poses no problem for the author of the *Vindiciae*, any more than he does for Beza. Any and all members of the community, even the 'least of the people' (Mornay 1979, p. 210), are permitted and even obliged to resist such a tyrant. If assassination is necessary to dispose of a usurper, no one should shrink from attempting it. The tyrant by exercise does pose a severe problem, however, for his misbehaviour does not release private individuals from their obligation to obey him. But the officers of the kingdom can resist this type of tyrant. In fact they have an obligation to resist, which the author illustrates at some length by comparing it to the obligations laid upon a co-tutor by Roman civil law. Just as the co-tutors of a minor are obliged to restrain or replace a principal tutor who is betraying his trust by misusing the property of their joint charge, so the inferior officials of a royal government must restrain or replace a king who is betraying his trust by oppressing his people.[22] In his effective use of this and other legal analogies, as in his earlier use of contract theory, the author of the *Vindiciae* uses law most effectively to build resistance theory. He builds upon but goes beyond his Lutheran and British and French Calvinist predecessors in this respect.

The *Vindiciae*, like the *Du droit des magistrats*, distinguishes two types of royal officials who may lead resistance, but the distinction is not quite the same. One type is again made up of inferior magistrates, local officials with local or regional responsibility, like provincial governors and city mayors. The other type is made up of crown officials with national responsibility, like peers of the realm, constables, and marshalls. Little is now said of the Estates General or the vaguer Public Council. Calvinists were now clearly pinning their hopes on a somewhat different coalition of support. Indeed, in some ways they had returned to the earlier Lutheran formula of resistance by inferior magistrates, only this time permitting such resistance not only in the name of a religious cause but also in the name of the urge for freedom from tyranny.

Finally, in its fourth question the *Vindiciae contra tyrannos* gives an international dimension to the Calvinist struggle for survival. Foreign princes of the true religion are urged to intervene in order to rescue the oppressed subjects of their neighbours. Such intervention is justified if necessary to protect members of the one true church, but it is also justified if necessary to protect victims of a more secular tyranny.

v   The deposition of Mary Stuart

Meanwhile, events in Scotland provoked yet another version of Calvinist resistance theory. In 1561 Mary Stuart, on the death of her first husband, Francis II, king of France, had returned from the continent to claim personally her inherited right to rule Scotland. She remained loyal, however, to the Catholic faith in which she had been raised and to which

---

22. Giesey 1970, pp. 48–53, contains an extended commentary on the significance of this legal allegation.

her French relatives of the Guise family were so committed. This brought her into immediate conflict with the Protestant regime that had been established in her absence by the covenanted Lords of the Congregation, assisted by Knox. That conflict was softened in 1565, when the queen married and made king Lord Darnley, but it worsened seriously in 1567, when Darnley was murdered and Mary then married one of those responsible for the killing, the earl of Bothwell. A revolt of nobles led by Mary's natural brother, the earl of Moray, led to her expulsion from the kingdom, the proclamation that her infant son was now King James VI, and the granting of actual power to Moray as regent. Mary took refuge in the England of Elizabeth I where she passed the rest of her life under house arrest.

This violent expulsion of a legitimate ruler shocked Catholic Europe, most obviously Catholic France. It embarrassed royalist England, in spite of its Protestant commitments. Catholic and royalist sympathisers in Scotland, England, and other countries, began working for the restoration of Mary as the rightful ruler of Scotland. Moray and his associates in the regency government of Scotland needed a defender of their policy. They found one in George Buchanan, a brilliant humanist intellectual who had spent much of his career on the continent, primarily in France, with a brief interlude in Portugal, and who had recently returned to his native Scotland. Buchanan had earned an international reputation for a translation of Linacre's Latin grammar and for his elegant Latin poems and plays. He had become a Protestant, using his talents for that cause in Latin paraphrases of the psalms and plays on biblical themes.[23]

Buchanan possessed exactly the skills in communication needed by the government of the regent Moray to defend both at home and abroad its deposition of Mary Stuart. He was pressed into service as a negotiator and a propagandist for that government. This led him to write three politically significant books. The first to be published was his *A Detection of the Doings of Mary, Queen of Scots* (Buchanan 1571). It is a biography designed to blacken as thoroughly as possible the reputation of the deposed queen, by making her personally responsible for the murder of her husband and consort, Darnley, and thus to justify her deposition by the Scots. It was supported by an appendix containing love letters allegedly written from Mary to the murderer Bothwell and discovered in a casket of her personal

---

23. McFarlane 1981 supplies a full biography and, in its appendix A, a full list of all the editions of Buchanan's works.

valuables. This exposé was published in Latin, English, Scots, and French, with most of the editions appearing in London, beginning in 1571. It was designed initially to persuade the government of England to stand firm in its decision to keep Mary under house arrest rather than permitting her either to return to Scotland or to retire to France. It was used also to justify throughout Britain and at the court of France the policy of the regent.[24]

Another of Buchanan's contributions to resistance theory was a detailed history of Scotland, the *Rerum Scoticarum Historia*, upon which he worked much of his life although it was first published in 1582. It was designed in part to find as many precedents as possible for the deposition, imprisonment, and even execution of rulers who had turned tyrannical.[25]

The most sophisticated of Buchanan's contributions, however, was his *De jure regni apud Scotos*.[26] It is the one that deserves the most attention from students of political theory. This tract was apparently written shortly after the deposition of Mary Stuart but circulated only in manuscript until its first publication in 1579. It was reissued several times between 1579 and 1581 by presses both in Scotland and on the continent. It was published even more frequently in editions combined with the *Rerum Scoticarum Historia*, beginning in 1583 and continuing into the seventeenth and eighteenth centuries.[27] The *De jure regni apud Scotos* was dedicated to the boy king, James VI, and was ostensibly designed to assist in his education. Its release in 1579, however, suggests continuing nervousness within the government of the regency about its legitimacy, a nervousness no doubt kept alive by the continuing plots to assassinate Elizabeth I of England and to crown Mary in her place, plots hatched among English Catholics and encouraged from the continent.

In form the *De jure regni apud Scotos* is very much the work of a humanist. Not only is it written in elegant Latin but it is cast in the shape of a Platonic dialogue, with the Scottish diplomat Thomas Maitland, who had recently returned from France, acting as the straight man, and Buchanan himself

---

24. For its use in France, see Kingdon 1988, pp. 131–3.
25. Gatherer, in Buchanan 1958, supplies an analysis of Buchanan as an historian and excerpts from both the *Rerum Scoticarum Historia* and his other works about Mary. For an important, though debatable, account of Buchanan's historical work in relation to his political ideas, see Trevor-Roper 1966.
26. There is no modern edition of the *De jure regni apud Scotos*: Buchanan 1969 is a facsimile of the first edition (Edinburgh, 1579). Translations into English can be found in Buchanan 1949, by Arrowood, and Buchanan 1964, by MacNeill, but neither includes a full critical apparatus and both contain problems in translation. See the reviews of them by J.H. Burns in the *Scottish Historical Review*, 30 (1951): 60–8, 48 (1969): 190–1.
27. See McFarlane 1981, pp. 512–14, for a full list of these editions.

presenting the heart of the argument. It does not use the more traditional scholastic shape of many of the other Calvinist resistance tracts we have examined, most notably the *Vindiciae contra tyrannos*. The dialogue form had been used, to be sure, by French Calvinist political theorists, for example in the *Reveille-matin*, but never to sustain an argument as comprehensive and coherent as that developed by Buchanan. The documentation of the *De jure regni apud Scotos*, furthermore, is heavily classical. It appeals to examples drawn from Greek and Roman history and to sentiments expressed by classical authors, almost exclusively in its first half, still heavily in its second half.

In content the *De jure regni apud Scotos* concentrates on two definitions. One is of kings, the other is of tyrants. It defines a king as one who gains power by popular consent, who rules by law, and who is subject to law. But law is not static. It is to be made and changed by the estates of the realm (Mason 1982, pp. 19–20); and for its interpretation and application a king must have a council of wise men and must permit himself to be guided by them. A tyrant, on the other hand, seizes power unilaterally and claims that he can create laws and that he need not be bound by them. He also does not accept advice. Kings rule for the benefit of their subjects. Tyrants rule only for their own personal gain.

The classic exhortations to obedience, Buchanan argues, apply only to true kings, not to tyrants. He examines at some length the biblical injunctions to obedience, especially in the Pauline epistles, in reaching this conclusion (chs. lxii–lxx). He also examines the *lex regia*, the principle of Roman civil law embedded in the Corpus Juris Civilis which undergirds imperial and royal claims to power (chs. xlix–l). Neither are absolute, he insists. Both apply only to rulers who are legitimate.

Since the rule of tyrants is not legitimate, they can be deposed. It is not always necessary to depose a tyrant, Buchanan concedes, since a usurping tyrant can become a ruler sensitive to his subjects' needs. But precedent and principle both prove that a tyrant can be deposed if necessary. A tyrant can be removed by legal action, leading to imprisonment or exile. A tyrant can be resisted by military force. A tyrant can even be assassinated, if that is the only way to dispose of him or her. And the specific tyrant Buchanan has in mind, he makes clear at the beginning, is Mary Stuart.

There is much of Buchanan's theory that was to prove useful to later generations of theorists. Its starting point is a quick analysis of the state of nature before the creation of society and government. It includes an embryonic version of social contract, drawn explicitly from the Roman law of contract. But it lacks much of the specificity of continental Calvinist theory, failing to identify with any precision institutions that are entitled to lead resistance to a tyrant and implement a deposition. It implies that a king's privy council can restrain and depose him, and thus would justify regents like Moray. This implication is not developed, however. Buchanan's theory is also more radical than that of continental Calvinists in its encouragement of general revolt and in its endorsement of tyrannicide. In this it reverts to the position of Ponet.

Unlike his British predecessors and more like his French contemporaries, however, Buchanan presents a theory that is really secular. There is little within the *De jure regni apud Scotos* that is explicitly Protestant, much less Calvinist. There are, to be sure, a number of passages attacking the tyrannical abuse of papal power by specified recent popes and supporting conciliarism as a better form of church government. But these passages could as easily come from an anti-clerical Gallican as from a Protestant.

Buchanan's theory provoked a storm of protest, both in Britain and on the continent. Indeed it was in good part in retort to Buchanan that the Gallican polemicist William Barclay early in the seventeenth century coined the term 'monarchomach', or king-killer, to apply to this entire body of resistance theory. As Barclay himself was aware, however, this theory by 1580 had in fact developed into a form so general that it could be and was used by many who were not Calvinists. The next use of theory of this type in France was by Catholic members of the League, first against the mediating *politique* position to which Henri III had moved, then against the Protestant and *politique* Catholic position of his successor, Henri IV. Calvinist resistance theory survived to be of use to other Calvinists, however, most immediately in the Netherlands where the revolt against Spain raged on, well into the seventeenth century; next in the German Empire, most conspicuously in the Palatinate, where Calvinist theorists took a lead in organising the resistance to imperial authority that exploded into the Thirty Years War, 1618–48; finally in the revolt of Calvinist Puritans against royal power in England, 1640–60. But those are stories for later chapters.

8

Catholic resistance theory, Ultramontanism, and the royalist response, 1580–1620

J.H.M. SALMON

i Patterns of controversy

The preceding chapter has outlined the development of Huguenot doctrines of resistance during the first half of the French religious wars. It was one of the ironies of the time that, in the second half, some French Protestant writers turned to support royal authority while their most bitter enemies among Catholic enthusiasts occupied the vacant ground with Catholic theories of resistance. The Holy League, in which these doctrines were evolved, relied not only upon secular justification of armed opposition but also upon the power of the papacy to depose temporal sovereigns and authorise armed opposition for religious reasons. In response, royalist theory was associated with the tradition of independence within the Gallican church. In England at the same time the Anglican settlement was defended against Puritan pressure for further reform and a Catholic campaign for reconversion that in one aspect was peaceful and non-political and in another welcomed papal deposition and foreign invasion. Not surprisingly, English and French royalism had much in common, however different the institutions and traditions of the two countries. In the early seventeenth century a European debate took place over the respective powers of kings and popes which invoked and redefined ideas generated by the French Holy League.

The three principal strands in secular Huguenot resistance theory were also contained in the ideas of the League. There were: loyal resistance to malevolent and Machiavellian advisers who had usurped royal authority; constitutional opposition to a king who had overstepped limitations defined by law and history; and communal defiance of a tyrant in the name of the ultimate power, or 'popular sovereignty', of the commonwealth over the ruler. While the three strands were often interwoven, and the second served to particularise the more general and contractarian terms in which the third was framed, they also help to distinguish three phases through which Leaguer, no less than Huguenot, theory unfolded.

For the Huguenots the 'evil counsellors' mode had fitted the opposition of the 1560s, constitutionalism had been appropriate to the wars of 1567–70, and popular sovereignty had been part of the Protestant response to the massacre of 1572. The League began as a movement opposing the favourable treaty granted the Huguenots in 1576. In 1584 the death of Alençon-Anjou, heir and younger brother to Henri III, the last Valois king, made the Protestant Bourbon leader, Henri de Navarre, heir presumptive to the throne. While the Huguenots joined Catholic *politiques* in support of royal dynasticism, the League reformed to oppose the succession of a heretic by reinterpreting law and history and proposing a fundamental constitutional law of the catholicity of the crown. At a meeting of the representative Estates General dominated by the League in 1588, Henri III had the League's leaders, Henri de Guise and his brother the cardinal de Guise, murdered, and prominent deputies arrested. Popular sovereignty, papal deposition, and tyrannicide then became the motifs of Leaguer thought. Navarre's Catholic uncle, the cardinal de Bourbon, was declared king and the last Valois assassinated. When the cardinal de Bourbon died in 1590, the League promoted the idea of a genuinely elective monarchy, only to find its endeavours to choose a Catholic ruler frustrated by the rivalries of its own aristocratic leaders. As he fought to secure his title as Henri IV, Navarre relied increasingly upon absolutist doctrines of divine right and royal sovereignty. He converted to Catholicism during a meeting of the Leaguer Estates General in 1593, but the war continued because the papacy withheld absolution for two years and Spain provided military support for the remnants of the League.

Although a similar pattern, dictated by contingent twists in political circumstance, marked the development of both Protestant and Catholic ideas of resistance, there were some signal differences in secular as well as in religious doctrines. While the Huguenots became resigned to the role of a minority fighting for toleration, the League spoke more authoritatively for the control of the ruler by a united Catholic people, and carried the implications of the concept to more radical conclusions. While both factions adhered to the Renaissance mode of curing present corruption by restoring ancient institutions to their supposed pristine virtue, the League became more conscious of the utilitarian need to bend tradition to serve the present, to create, rather than to restore, fundamental law. While the two parties found allies in foreign powers, it was the League that seemed linked to anti-national forces in Habsburg imperialism and Roman universalism, and hence provoked a patriotic response that weakened its own unity. While Huguenots and Leaguers both found partial justification for revolt in Christian belief, the theocratic element in the League created a greater tension between religious and secular priorities. Finally, while the two opposition movements both experienced inner social tensions, such tensions were far more pronounced within the League. A small but vocal section of the Leaguer group in Paris known as the Sixteen suggested the possibility of social revolution.

ii The Catholic League

The manifesto of the 1576 Catholic League had the preservation of Catholicism as its ostensible objective, but it was essentially an aristocratic document, expressing in the third of its twelve articles a certain ambivalence between past and present with the demand to restore 'rights, pre-eminences, franchises and ancient liberties such as they were in the time of Clovis, the first Christian king, and to find, if possible, even better and more profitable ones under protection of the aforesaid League'.[1] The role of the estates and their supposed origin in Merovingian Gaul became a theme within the League as it had been in François Hotman's *Francogallia*. In 1577, when the estates were meeting at Blois a circular entitled *Instruction des gens des troys estats* was passed among Leaguer deputies, calling for the estates to be recognised as a part of the regular machinery of government (Baumgartner 1975, p. 59). An analysis of the estates that was more objective than either the Huguenot or the Leaguer version of the institution was published at this time by Matteo Zampini, an Italian jurist at the court of Henri III (*Degli stati di Francia*, 1578). Zampini agreed that the estates had extensive powers, but he also pointed out that they were only convened at the king's discretion, and that they had no voice in the appointment of the ruler except when the succession was disputed.

The succession was the centre of debate when the new League, bound by treaty to Philip II of Spain and dominated once again by the house of Guise, formed in 1585. The manifesto, issued in the name of the cardinal de Bourbon, insisted, like its counterpart of 1576, upon the banning of heresy,

---

1. 'Droits, prééminences, franchises et libertés anciennes telles qu'elles estoient du temps du roy Clovis, premier roy chrestien, et encores meilleures plus profitables si elles se peuvent enventer, sous la protection susdite.' Palma-Cayet 1823, p. 255.

the rights of the aristocracy, the reduction of taxes, and the active participation of the estates in government. It went further, however, in its open criticism of the king, its provisions for the third estate, and its readiness to employ force: 'We have all solemnly sworn and promised to use *main forte* and take up arms to the end that the holy church of God may be restored to its dignity as the true and holy Catholic religion' (Salmon 1975, p. 238). The League did indeed use armed force to occupy a number of towns, and, when Henri III capitulated to most of its demands, its forces were associated with the royal armies in the renewed war against the Huguenots. Meanwhile a pamphlet war was directed against the defenders of Navarre, who in 1585 had been excommunicated by Pope Sixtus V.

While Zampini and Antoine Hotman, the brother of the Huguenot polemicist, defended the claims of the cardinal de Bourbon to the succession in juristic treatises, more general arguments were advanced by Louis Dorléans, a barrister and member of the Sixteen who was later to disown his more radical colleagues. In 1586 Dorléans published at least four works, in the best known of which, *Advertissement des catholiques anglois aux françois catholiques*, he pretended to be a Catholic Englishman warning French Catholics of the tyranny they would have to endure under a heretic. Like Antoine Hotman, Dorléans had the conservative instincts of a defender of judicial tradition, especially the rights of the high court of *parlement*, where he was later to become the League's advocate-general. Yet his religious enthusiasm led him to adopt contrary positions, which he expressed with the rhetorical skill of one trained by the humanist Jean Dorat. The so-called Salic law of the succession had been invented in the early fourteenth century, but most French jurists, François Hotman being exceptional in this respect, regarded it as coeval with the original Frankish monarchy (Hotman 1972, pp. 97–9). This was the fundamental law to which the supporters of Navarre appealed, whereas the propagandists of the League relied upon Roman law arguments about the relative proximity of Navarre and his uncle to Henri III. More important to the Leaguer case, Dorléans stressed catholicity as more fundamental than antiquity. His *Apologie ou défence des catholiques unis* (1586) declared that the Salic law was pagan and must yield to later Christian principles.

The law of succession became less important when the League began openly to espouse the doctrine of election through the Estates General. The Sixteen adopted this view as early as 1587 when their clandestine organisation prepared a circular for like-minded groups in other cities. They and their policies emerged into the open in the following year, when they installed their own government in Paris after expelling the king from his capital in the day of barricades. In a surrender more abject than that of 1585 Henri III declared the catholicity of the crown and the exclusion of a heretic as fundamental law in his Edict of Union. This did not entirely satisfy the League, since it regarded the establishment or confirmation of fundamental law to be the prerogative of the estates the king had agreed to convoke. The edict was the subject of Dorléans' *Responce des vrays catholiques françois* (1588). Here he referred to the crimes of the monarchy under the first two dynasties, and stressed the priestly function of the *rex-sacerdos*, a concept that became widespread in 1589, when the cardinal de Bourbon as 'Charles X' was frequently likened to Melchizedek. Dorléans wrote of the paramount role of the estates and treated the *parlement* as their permanent *abrégé*, with power to disallow royal legislation. He made use of the Huguenot concept of inferior magistrates, whom he called *regnicoles*.[2] As the estates assembled at Blois the Sixteen issued a tract entitled *Articles pour proposer aux estats et faire passer une loy fondamentale du royaume*. While these constitutional arguments held the field, attacks upon the king's favourites proliferated. The most notable was a satire comparing Epernon, the so-called 'archimignon' of Henri III, with Piers Gaveston, who had been executed by the barons under Edward II (*Histoire tragique et memorable de Gaverston ... iadis mignon d'Edouard II*, 1588). The author was Jean Boucher, the leading preacher of the Sixteen. When Henri III murdered Henri de Guise and his brother at Blois Boucher began to prepare the best known Leaguer exposition of popular sovereignty.

After the coup at Blois Boucher persuaded the theological faculty of the University of Paris to anticipate papal action by declaring Henri III deposed, a decision ratified by the *parlement* after that body had been purged by the Sixteen. The revolutionaries set up other *ad hoc* institutions, soon to be counterbalanced by the conservative custodian of the Leaguer version of the monarchy, and brother to the martyred Henri de Guise, Charles de Mayenne. In these acts appeared the two sources of tension within the political thought of the League: the relationship between secular and clerical jurisdiction, and the social differences between the aristocratic leadership on the one hand and the bourgeois and clerical revolutionaries on the other.

Boucher's *De justa Henrici Tertii abdictione* (1589) was in press at the time of the regicide of Henri III, and was adjusted to meet the new

---

2. Dorléans 1588, pp. 158–9.

situation. The argument was divided into three parts: whether church and people may depose a king for just cause; whether Henri de Valois should be deposed; whether, pending his actual removal, he might be resisted in arms. Boucher explicitly denied that the pope possessed 'the full and direct jurisdiction' over the secular power he exercised over the ecclesiastical order. He asserted that by giving the church authority to depose kings he did not suggest that the pope had the power to act arbitrarily or to change the laws of the kingdom. As the vicar of Christ, the pope was obliged to take note of any occasion in a Christian state when the ruler harmed the church or endangered the salvation of the people by fostering 'schism, perjury, and apostasy'. When admonition and censure proved ineffective, the pope should 'release the people from the bond of obedience and arrange for the flock redeemed by Christ to be committed to more appropriate care'.[3] This was a cautious restatement of the indirect power of Rome based on the claim that the spiritual end was superior to the temporal.

Nor was Boucher, despite his activist fervour, any kind of social radical. Before explaining the right of the people to depose kings, he insisted that by 'the people' he did not mean 'the undisciplined and turbulent mob known as the many-headed monster', but, rather, nobles, senators, and men of virtue and integrity, 'a prudent multitude assembled by law'.[4] Their authority as the representatives of the people arose from the original purpose of government. The form of government was the product of human artifice, although the choice of monarchy followed the model of God as ruler of the universe. Men, who were free by nature, had recognised the inconvenience of allowing everyone to do as they wished, and desired a means of enforcing conformity to law. Hence they had 'consented to transfer to some one person the political power they possessed immediately in themselves, and this for the sake of the public utility'.[5] Boucher did not elaborate on this tantalisingly brief account of the creation of government or on the state of society before it was established. He intended to demonstrate the superiority of the commonwealth over the king, and to argue that it was inconceivable that a ruler created for such a purpose

---

3. '... tum populos obedientiae vinculo eximat, denique operam ut alteri commodiori grex a Christo redemptus commitatur'. Boucher 1591, I, v, p. 13.

4. 'Quod antequam exponimus, intelligendum populi nomine isto loco non inconditam ac confusam turbam, quae bellua multorum capitum est ... sed procerum, senatorum, ac praecipua virtutis, probitatis, iudiciique ac dignitatis authoritate hominum prudentem ac iure coactam multitudinem sumi.' *Ibid.*, I, ix, p. 19.

5. 'Multi in id consenserunt, ut quae penes eos immediate politica potestas erat, ad unum aliquem publici commodi causa transferretur.' *Ibid.*, I, xii, p. 23.

would be allowed to betray it. Later he declared that, while the king was invested with highest authority (*summum imperium*), a perpetual sovereignty (*majestas*) was exercised on behalf of the commonwealth by the *comitia* or estates.[6]

Apart from his emphasis on the role of the church and his suggestion of a free state of nature, Boucher's most obvious difference from the Calvinist resistance writers was his long and vituperative attack upon the character and crimes of the king. The theoretical sections of this treatise offered a comprehensive synthesis of the ideas of his heretical precursors. He used the same biblical, classical, and medieval authorities as they, but his allusions, especially to classical writers, were more profuse and ingenious. He cited Cicero's adage that the safety of the people should be the supreme law (*salus populi suprema lex esto*). He repeated the commonplace that the king, though greater than the people considered individually, was less than they as a whole (*rex maior singulis, universis minor*). He used Roman law principles of tutorship and corporation theory. He depicted Louis XI as the subverter of the ancient constitution, stressed the supposed role of the peers as arbitrators, recalled Claude de Seyssel's three bridles upon royal power, and reminded his readers of the chancellor's duty to refuse an unjust royal edict. At times he came very close to François Hotman's vision of the Frankish past. 'It was the custom of the ancient Franks', he wrote, 'to salute the king they elected by raising him on a shield and carrying him round the camp.'[7] Like Hotman, Boucher explained that the Franks preferred to choose the best candidate from a particular dynasty. He repeated the passage in *Francogallia* citing Plutarch on the way a dog or horse was chosen for personal qualities as well as its breeding, and avoided any reproach of plagiarism by replacing Hotman's words with synonyms.[8]

Boucher's *De justa Henrici Tertii abdicatione* put less stress upon contract than *De jure magitratuum* and *Vindiciae contra tyrannos*, and there was nothing in the two Calvinist works to parallel his hint about a state of nature. Boucher did not follow up this remark with anything on a precise contract between ruler and ruled until much later in the work, when he accused Henri III of violating public faith, and went on to say: 'Moreover public faith is necessarily conjoined with the king. For it depends upon

6. 'Populus summus ei imperium defert.' *Ibid.*, III, iii, p. 230. 'Maiestatem reipublicae penes ordines ac comitia praecipue esse.' *Ibid.*, III, vii, p. 242.
7. 'Et veterum Francorum mos fuit, ut regem a se electum super clypeum elevatum ac per castra circunductum, salutarent.' *Ibid.*, I, xvi, p. 29. Cf. Hotman 1972, vi p. 232.
8. Boucher 1591, I, xvii, p. 29. Cf. Hotman 1972, vi, p. 220.

that mutual contract by which the king pledged his faith to the people, and in turn the people pledged theirs to him.'[9] This, like accounts of the coronation ceremony, was simply an elaboration of the principle of trust, and was inserted to show that a king who violated it became a private citizen and might be put to death. A more interesting use of contract theory was the invocation of scriptural authority to prove both the supremacy of the church and the continuance of the power of the people over the king after he had been constituted. Boucher claimed that 'the priest takes precedence over the people, and the king over the individual, and the people or kingdom over the king'. To support this he quoted II Chronicles 23:16 (Paralipomenon in the Vulgate): 'Jehoiada made a covenant between himself and all the people and the king, that they should be the Lord's people.' This, according to Boucher, 'means that the king is included in the people, not the people in the king, nor are the king and the people to be seen as separate entities, but the pact is made with God by both together'.[10] The tripartite contract between God, king, and people in *Vindiciae contra tyrannos* was intended to show that the people might act against a king who failed to keep his part of the agreement. In *De justa Henrici Tertii abdicatione*, however, the point was not simply the superiority of the people to the king, but the superiority of the priest to both. The church was the direct creation of God, the state of human will. Although church and people had their separate roles in depriving a king, the general argument cast the shadow of theocracy.

The second significant Leaguer treatise published at this time of crisis was *De justa reipublicae Christianae in reges impios et haereticos authoritate* (1590), composed after the assassination of Henri III and directed aganst Navarre. The author, who used the pseudonym Gulielmus Rossaeus in a later edition, was probably the Catholic Englishman William Reynolds. He covered the same themes as Boucher, but with greater depth and originality and without the extensive personal abuse of *De justa Henrici Tertii abdicatione*. He treated the origin of government in more detail, discussed the collaboration of church and people more convincingly, and differed from Boucher in his refusal to associate popular sovereignty with the estates alone.

---

9. '[Publica fides] pendet enim id ex mutuo contractu illo, quo rex populo fidem suam, huic vicissim suam populus obligavit.' Boucher 1591, III, iii, p. 239.
10. 'Eiusmodi est illud quod "pepigit Ioida foedus inter se universumque populum ac regem ut esset populus Domini." ... ut ex eo intelligas in populo regem non in rege ac populum esse, nec separatim a rege ac populo, sed simul ab utroque factum foedus cum Deo esse.' *Ibid.*, I, xviii, p. 32.

Both Boucher and Reynolds cited George Buchanan's *De jure regni apud Scotos* (1579) on tyrannicide. Buchanan's work differed substantially from Huguenot resistance theory. He derived government from a state of nature and placed an active sovereignty inalienably in the people. This had much in common with the early sixteenth-century conciliarist Jacques Almain, and, to less extent, with Almain's teacher John Mair, under whom Buchanan had studied. Reynolds was more ready than Dorléans and Boucher to admit that a Calvinist, however mistaken in religion, might profess acceptable ideas about secular government. Buchanan argued that mankind had escaped from a pre-social condition by an impulse to communal living, a light divinely infused in human minds. A sense of mutual obligation developed in formed society, but there were also those in whom self-interest dominated, and for this reason government had been instituted. Unfortunately, the same self-interest infected the rulers chosen by the people, so that laws had to be devised to restrain them. Popular authority was not delegated to the higher orders but reposed in those citizens who put the public welfare foremost. 'And so', Buchanan wrote, 'if the citizens are counted not in terms of their number but in terms of their worthiness, not only the better, but also the greater part will stand for liberty, morality, and security' (Salmon 1987, pp. 138–54). Buchanan did not define precisely how the people dealt with tyrants. History revealed a variety of ways in which the popular will had become effective. A ruler should be a free man ruling over free men: a tyrant treated his subjects as slaves. A king who subverted the society he was appointed to preserve and broke the *pactio mutua* between himself and his people became a public enemy whom even private citizens could put to death. This was the only occasion when Buchanan mentioned a contract in *De jure regni*.

Reynolds described an original state of nature very like Buchanan's. Each in his way was attempting to reconcile the Aristotelian tradition (in which, man being by nature a social animal, it was impossible to conceive a pre-social human existence) with passages in Cicero suggesting that man had once lived as a bestial, solitary, wandering being. To Reynolds a natural force within men living in this barbarous way had impelled them to form a society, and, once they had done so, they became conscious both of its advantages and the need to create a frame of government to restrain a minority driven by lust and greed. St Augustine, as well as Aquinas, was among Reynolds' authorities. If God had endowed men with the drive to live communally, it was depravity that obliged them to devise laws. Governmental forms and measures to discipline rulers 'emanated from the will and approbation of peoples' (Salmon 1987, p. 149). Reynolds illustrated these assertions with an array of examples drawn not only from Europe and classical and biblical times but also from Calicut, Cochin China, the Moluccas, and the Indians of the New World. Like Buchanan and Boucher, he briefly referred to a contract of government and stressed the coronation as a formal acknowledgment of the ruler's obligations and the people's consent. Like Buchanan, but unlike Boucher, he refused to endow the estates with the ultimate sovereignty, which resided inalienably in the people. All legitimate monarchy was limited. Signs of tyranny were taxation without consent, infringement of constitutional laws, and threats to the established religion. In Christian countries, and particularly in France, where the catholicity of the crown was fundamental law, rulers must obey the church. The episcopacy must approve popular choice in the appointment of a king, and a synod, as well as the pope, might declare a ruler a tyrant meriting deposition.

In 1591 a number of Leaguer pamphlets described the crown as elective and denied the hereditary claims of Navarre. Pressure mounted to call the estates to elect a Catholic king and remain a directive force in government. A list of articles presented by the Sixteen to the Paris municipal government proposed that the estates should nominate the royal council, control taxation and the creation of offices, and meet without the king, who should possess no legislative veto (Baumgartner 1975, pp. 179–82). The Sixteen, deserted by their members within the municipal elite and no longer in control of the city government, reverted to terrorism and had to be temporarily suppressed by Mayenne. However, the Leaguer lieutenant-general needed the radicals to offset the growing peace movement in his party. Despite his desire to avoid convoking the estates, which might threaten his own authority, Mayenne had finally to issue instructions for their assembly. The Leaguer estates of 1593 met with the express intention of electing a king. They failed because of the rivalries of the various aristocratic candidates, the patriotic reaction against a Spanish attempt to promote the claims of the Infanta, and the timely announcement of Navarre's conversion. Two tensions within Leaguer thought emerged in 1593 and in the ensuing year, when Paris surrendered to Navarre, now clearly established as Henri IV. Both were the products of extremism, the one social and the other religious.

The theme of social conflict was apparent within royalist satire of the League as well as within Leaguer propaganda. The proceedings of the estates were mocked by a group of *politique* sympathisers and men of letters in a manuscript secretly circulated at the time and subsequently expanded and published as the *Satyre Ménippée* (1594). The social anarchy provoked by the exploitation of the lower classes in the wars of the League was a serious point made by this Rabelaisian burlesque. The fictitious speech put into the mouth of the spokesman for the second estate confessed the profits derived by the nobility in continuing the conflict at the expense of the unprivileged. Another section of the satire described a series of tapestries displayed for the assembly which portrayed as their motif the contemporary peasant risings and the activities of urban radicals such as the Sixteen. *Politique* satire may have exaggerated the lowly social status of the Sixteen, but it was not mistaken in detecting an anti-noble bias among the revolutionaries. The articles submitted to the Paris *hôtel de ville* deplored the proliferation of petty nobles and called for a reduction in their numbers. Oudart Rainsart, one of the principals in the Sixteen's murder of the first president of the Leaguer *parlement* and two other magistrates in November 1591, had published at that time a tract in which he denounced the nobility in general and suggested that their titles had been based upon the brigandage of their ancestors (*La Représentation de la noblesse hérétique sur le théâtre de France*, 1591). Even Dorléans, who had broken with the terrorists in the Sixteen but remained a violent critic of Navarre, reproached the vices of the nobles on both sides in the satire he composed in the summer of 1593 (*Le Banquet et apresdinée du conte [sic] d' Arète*, 1594).

The most remarkable Leaguer document attacking the elite was *Le Dialogue d'entre le maheustre et le manant* (1594), attributed to the organiser of the 1591 murders, François Morin de Cromé. So radical were its opinions that the royalists published a doctored version in which the speeches of the labourer or *manant* were allowed to stand as testimony of the extremism of the Sixteen (Salmon 1987, pp. 264–6). The nobility of the sword, the magistracy, and the episcopacy, whether they supported Navarre or Mayenne, were all the subject of bitter accusation for their treatment of the unprivileged. Behind the lament of the *manant* at the suffering of the people lay the implication of popular rights and the belief that common folk alone constituted true believers and served as the agents of divine will. Cromé suggested that the hereditary nobility be replaced with an aristocracy of virtue (Cromé 1977, p. 189).

The Sixteen had appealed directly to the pope, as they had to the king of Spain. The *manant* represented a combination of social radicalism and Catholic fervour which had earlier appeared in the tracts of Jean de Caumont. 'Jesus Christ will conquer', Caumont had written. 'Jesus Christ will reign. Jesus Christ will be king of France' (*Advertissement des advertissements*, 1587, p. 30). Caumont's *La Vertu de la noblesse* (1585) had been as severe an indictment of noble depravity and atheism as Cromé's *Dialogue*. The preachers of the League – not only those associated with the Sixteen – often voiced a kind of theocracy, and this was particularly apparent in clerical reaction to the supposed hypocrisy of Henri IV's conversion. Jean Porthaise of Poitiers published *Cinq sermons . . . de la simulée conversion* (1594), granting the pope direct power over secular government and allowing the clergy to depose a ruler for secular tyranny as well as heresy. There was a theocratic tinge to Boucher's own sermons against the conversion, even though he accorded the pope merely indirect power (*Sermons de la simulée conversion et nullité de la prétendue absolution de Henry de Bourbon*, 1594). It was not until he had fled to the Spanish Netherlands after the king's recovery of Paris that Boucher solved the problem of the dual sovereignty of pope and people. In justifying the attempted regicide by Jean Chastel in December 1594 (*Apologie pour Jean Chastel*, 1595), he wrote that the pope should excommunicate an unjust or heretical ruler, but the people should effect his deposition and punishment. Should it prove impossible to assemble the estates for this purpose, or should the nobility prove too corrupt to act, the people must appeal to the pope, whose judgement might be executed by private citizens. Boucher went on to defend the Jesuits who had been expelled by the *parlement* of Paris from the area of its jurisdiction. He singled out for criticism the published speech against the society by Antoine Arnauld that had led to their condemnation.

The combination of Ultramontanism with popular religious enthusiasm caused problems for the Leaguer magistracy, among whom Gallican sentiment still existed. When the papal nuncio to the League, Cardinal Cajetan, arrived in Paris in 1590 with the Jesuit Robert Bellarmine in his train, the judges of the Leaguer *parlement* would not register his bull without the reservation of the Gallican liberties. Two years later another legate, the cardinal of Piacenza, brought a bull confirming the excommunication of Navarre and requiring the election of a Catholic sovereign. On this occasion the judges registered the document without qualification, and it was their advocate-general, Dorléans, who justified their action with his *Plaidoyé des gens du Roy* (not published until 1594). Dorléans supported the indirect power of the pope to depose a secular ruler when the latter threatened the spiritual welfare of his subjects, but he went beyond this in support of Ultramontanism and denied that the procedure by which the *parlement* employed its supervisory powers in matters of clerical administration, the *appel comme d'abus*, could be invoked against a papal bull. Three months after delivering these opinions Dorléans completely reversed himself and spoke in the estates opposing the clergy's request to receive the decrees of the Council of Trent. He was in fact a member of a commission of the *parlement* to examine the Tridentine articles which produced a thoroughly Gallican finding. This did not prevent the Leaguer estates of 1593 from approving the decrees. However, the *parlement* had the last word, for its subsequent declaration against the election of a foreign prince as contrary to the Salic law effectively prevented the deputies of the estates from choosing a candidate. The twists and turns in the positions of Dorléans demonstrate the League's dilemma between patriotic sentiment and extra-national loyalties.

iii   Gallicanism

Gallican sentiment, though far from unanimous in its support of Navarre, was an important element in the development of royalist theory in response to the League. Ecclesiastical Gallicanism, affirming the independence of the French church from both pope and king, had its roots in the Pragmatic Sanction of Bourges in 1438. Political Gallicanism, presenting an alliance of church and crown to limit papal authority, had been strengthened during Henri II's dispute with Rome in the early 1550s. At the Council of Trent in 1562 the French contingent had supported the Spanish demand that the institution of bishops by apostolic succession should be declared *iure divino*. The speech by the Jesuit general Diego Lainez helped to defeat this proposal in favour of the overriding authority of the successors of St Peter. It was from this point that the Jesuits were seen as the enemies of Gallican liberties and the prime defenders of Ultramontanism. Nothing in the Tridentine decrees dealt directly with the respective powers of pope and king, but the decrees were generally viewed as a threat to the Gallican independence defended by the *parlement* and, on occasion, by the Sorbonne. Henri III, whose erratic piety at times induced him to forget Gallican traditions, personally favoured the unqualified reception of the decrees but the opposition of the *parlement* frustrated his intentions. In 1579 the king approved the reforming ordinance of Blois, only to find the pope resentful of royal enaction of ecclesiastical legislation promulgated under his own direct authority. The extreme to which *parlementaire* reaction could extend was demonstrated in *Advertissement sur la réception et publication du concile de*

Trente (1583) by Jacques Faye d'Espesses, *président-à-mortier*. Faye not only suggested a papal plot to undermine regal power, but indulged in personal criticism of Gregory XIII (Martin 1919, pp. 203–6).

The excommunication of Navarre and his cousin Condé by Sixtus V in 1585 could not but be regarded by defenders of political Gallicanism as another expression of papal interference in temporal affairs. Huguenot writers, who turned at this time from resistance theory to defence of Navarre's dynastic rights, cleverly catered to this Gallican reaction. Philippe Duplessis Mornay superintended the personal response of the princes, while François Hotman went a little too far to catch Gallican support in the insults he flung at Sixtus in his pamphlet *Brutum Fulmen*. Both these works were translated into English, since they had a ready appeal to Anglicans who had experienced Pius V's similar excommunication of Elizabeth in 1570 (*An Answer to the Excommunication by Sixtus V*, 1585; *The Brutish Thunderbolt or, rather, feeble fire-flash*, 1586). So also was the *politique* and Gallican rebuttal of the bull by Michel Hurault (*Anti-Sixtus*, 1590). After the assassination of Henri III the *politique* followers of Navarre realised the importance of attracting Gallican support by emphasising the Ultramontane element in the League. Thus the *politique* jurist Louis Servin published his *Vindiciae secundum libertatem ecclesiae Gallicanae* in 1591 in answer to Bellarmine's defence of the indirect power of the pope (*De Summo Pontifice*, 1586). Servin provided an extreme statement of political Gallicanism in which the pope was described as merely the chief among bishops, and the king was so much in control of the French church that he could release himself and others from excommunication, Protestant though he was. The theory of divine right was clothed in dynastic mystique by Servin, who stressed the king's descent from remote Germanic ancestors, and reminded his readers of the original rights of the church of 'Gallo-Francia', now threatened by papal usurpation and Spanish aggression. Similar themes were pursued in *Philippiques contre les bulles et autres pratiques de la faction d'Espagne* by François de Clary. They were repeated too, by Charles Faye, brother of Faye d'Espesses, in the speech denouncing Gregory XIV's bulls in favour of the League which he delivered to a sparsely attended royalist clerical assembly at Tours in 1591 (Salmon 1987, pp. 169–70). Heightened rhetoric, and a history designed to show royal control of the church in early times and the gradual expansion of papal ambition, marked Gallican writing in the embarrassing circumstance of rule by a heretic king. The Gallican myths about Clovis and the early councils were treated more realistically in the *Traicté des libertez de l'église gallicane*, composed in 1591 by the antiquarian Claude Fauchet, but even in this erudite work the author was clearly pleading a cause.

After Henri IV's conversion, his recovery of Paris, and the defection to him of nearly all the Leaguer bishops and *parlementaire* judges, a triumphant Gallicanism expressed itself through the works of Jacques de la Guesle, Jacques Leschassier, Etienne Pasquier, and the brothers Pierre and François Pithou. Of these Pierre Pithou's short treatise on the liberties of the Gallican church, licensed by the reunited *parlement* after the king's entry to his capital, became the best known statement of the principles of political Gallicanism (Salmon 1987, p. 172). The *parlement* proceeded to decree the expulsion of the Jesuits, who were denounced before the court by Arnauld as the accomplices of the would-be regicidal assassin, Pierre Barrière. Arnauld's speech, and an earlier indictment of the Jesuit order by Etienne Pasquier received wide circulation in France and England (*The Arrainement of the Whole Societie of the Jesuites in France*, 1594; *The Jesuite displayed, containing the original and proceedings of the Jesuits together with the fruits of their doctrine*, 1594). Clement VIII made the return of the Jesuits and the reception of the Tridentine decrees conditions for his absolution of Henri IV in 1595. The king honoured the first in 1603, but the *parlement* blocked fulfilment of the accord. Yet, while Gallicanism was in the ascendant, it was not unambiguous. Some former members of the League had more sympathy with the ecclesiastical variant than they had with the political. In his *Traicté des libertez de l'église gallicane* (1594), Antoine Hotman, the former Leaguer, cited the conciliarists Jean Gerson, Pierre d'Ailly, and Almain, and criticised the belief that kings were justiciable by God alone.

iv   *Politique* royalism

Gallicanism became associated with the theory of the divine right of kings. This doctrine and the absolutist version of sovereignty were the hallmarks of *politique* royalism. The Toulousain jurist Pierre de Belloy sought to answer both the secular and the Ultramontane arguments of the League. His *Apologie catholique* (1585) was yet another response to Navarre's excommunication, while *De l'authorité du Roy* (1587) refuted the constitutional theories of Dorléans and others. Kings, according to Belloy, held their power directly from God, and, since they were responsible to God alone, the pope had no power to depose them. He might excommunicate, but even a heretic king held divinely approved authority. Belloy denied that power was originally in the people and government a human artefact, for the first kings were created after the Fall as patriarchs. Using Bodin's terms, Belloy described royal authority as *puissance souveraine*, which consisted in 'giving law to all in general and each in particular without the consent or will of anyone else whatsoever' (Allen 1941, p. 384). To rebel against the image and lieutenant of God was to rebel against God Himself.

Before Belloy, the Gallicised Scot Adam Blackwood had provided an original defence of absolute monarchy. The first two parts of his *De conjunctione religionis et imperii* (1575) were written before the League and directed at Calvinism, which Blackwood held to be inherently subversive of monarchy. The third part did not appear until 1611 and denounced the doctrines of the League as a kind of Calvinism in disguise. *Pro regibus apologia* (1581) was aimed at his fellow-countryman, Buchanan. It was replete with Roman law citations to show that kingship by nature was unlimited and unmixed. Blackwood wrote realistically of the origin of monarchy in force and made little attempt to justify it in moral terms. It partook of the attributes both of a father and of a master of slaves. At the same time Blackwood, unlike Belloy, showed great respect for the papacy, and outlined a doctrine of non-resistance in which religious and secular authority complemented each other. Such views were an inappropriate defence for royalism in the heyday of the League.

The absolutist views of Bodin, described elsewhere in this volume, were, of course, of great importance in this period. One of his disciples, who chose not to put as much stress upon divine right as Belloy, was Pierre Grégoire, a civilian and canon lawyer at Pont-à-Mousson in Lorraine. Grégoire kept out of the public debate with the theorists of the League and published a detailed and exhaustive analysis of political forms and theories at the conclusion of the religious wars (*De republica*, 1596). Kings, in his view, derived their authority from the people by an irrevocable transfer of power, in terms of the Roman *lex regia*. Although he declared mixed government to be impossible under the logic of Bodinian sovereignty, he was aware of Bodin's distinction between the form of government and the method of its administration, which could admit aristocratic and democratic elements. Since ordinary positive laws were simply the command of the sovereign, the ruler could not be limited by them, but he was restrained by divine and natural law. The estates could be convoked only by royal authority. They existed to submit grievances, to constitute regencies in royal minorities, to consent to new taxes, and to aid in reforming the frame of government when called upon to do so (Carlyle 1936, p. 444). Grégoire was thus a moderate absolutist who took constitutional practice into account. No Gallican, he supported publication of the Tridentine decrees in France. He admitted that a pope might depose the Holy Roman emperor but he could not deprive a king of his right in a hereditary monarchy.

A stronger anti-papalist stance was taken by Grégoire's successor at Pont-à-Mousson, the Catholic Scotsman William Barclay. His views developed in the course of a controversy at the university there between the law faculty and the Jesuits. His absolutist *De regno et regali potestate* (1600) was a kind of *summa* of the ideas of divine right, sovereignty, and Gallicanism developed by *politique* royalists during the later religious wars. His treatise took the form of a detailed refutation of Huguenot and Leaguer resistance theorists, for whom he coined the term *monarchomachi*. Unlike Grégoire, he did not concede original authority to the community, but believed with Belloy that kings were appointed directly by God and were responsible only to Him. Even when electors chose a king in a non-hereditary monarchy, they were simply expressing God's will and held no constitutive power (*De regno*, III, 3). Monarchy began with Adam, the first patriarch, and it was the only form of government approved by God. A sovereign king was *supra ius, contra ius, extra ius*. Laws were his commands and, insofar as they existed otherwise, served merely to take the place of his express will when he was absent. A limitation on kingship was a contradiction in terms and an invitation to anarchy. François Hotman's historical version of the estates was a myth, for they depended upon royal authority, as, indeed, did any kind of privilege (*De regno*, IV, 14–18). Barclay followed the monarchomachs through all the standard biblical and classical texts and found answers to their arguments. Yet, despite his indefatigable perseverance in defending royal absolutism, he made vital concessions to resistance theory which were to be cited by his critics throughout the seventeenth century, including Locke himself. Not only did he allow resistance to a usurper but he also admitted that a king who handed over his realm to a foreigner, or who flagrantly undertook its destruction, could be resisted in arms (*De regno*, III, 8 and 16).

Barclay's loyalty to king and church served as a model for those royalist English Catholics who opposed Jesuit influence at the end of Elizabeth's reign. James I, who invited such Protestant scholars as Isaac Casaubon and Joseph-Juste Scaliger to write in his anti- papal cause, also asked Barclay to serve as his propagandist, but the Scot was too good a Catholic to pay the price of his pension with conversion to Anglicanism. This was also the attitude of his son, John Barclay, who saw through the press his father's posthumous attack against Ultramontanism in general and Bellarmine in particular, *De potestate Papae* (1609, English version 1611). This work followed Belloy in making an absolute distinction between the spiritual and temporal spheres. The pope might excommunicate a ruler, but he had no power to absolve subjects from their secular allegiance. While the state served no spiritual end, the clergy who resided within it were subject to the civil power. The Jesuit opponents of monarchy by divine right also distinguished between church and state, but they did so in order to claim the indirect power of the pope in temporal affairs and to deny secular control of ecclesiastical administration.

v Jesuits and Ultramontanes

The Jesuits were seen as the most fervent defenders of Ultramontanism and also as supporters of secular resistance theory. In practice the society did not display the monolithic unity its critics claimed, especially in the context of the French religious wars (Martin 1973). Most of their political writings achieved a level of detachment and abstraction seldom equalled by their opponents, but they were also capable of casuistry and dissimulation, as the English Jesuit Robert Parsons demonstrated. In terms of their theory of natural law, they assumed the neo-Thomist mantle worn earlier in the sixteenth century by the Spanish Dominicans, with whose theology of grace the Jesuit Luis de Molina had decisively broken. Nor were Jesuit political doctrines necessarily accepted by the papacy. Sixtus V preferred to excommunicate Navarre and Condé *in plenitudine potestatis* and he so disapproved of the indirect theory advanced by Bellarmine in *De Summo Pontifice* that he planned to place the volume of disputations in which it was published upon the Roman Index. The theory of the direct power of popes over kings was advanced by Alexander Carrerius in *De Potestate Romani Pontificis adversus impios politicos* (1599) and, as has been noted, it sometimes appeared in the propaganda of the League.

Bellarmine's early works were directed against the Lutherans, the humanists, and the conciliarists. In the latter respect he followed Lainez in maintaining the pope's monopoly of the keys of St Peter, the pope's legislative authority within the church, and the unalterable nature of the ecclesiastical hierarchy (Skinner 1978, II, pp. 138–41). *De Summo Pontifice* insisted that a Christian king had a duty to defend the true faith under pain of deprivation. Subjects need not obey a heretical ruler, and it was for the pope to judge whether he was a heretic and whether or not he should be deposed. Under the pseudonym of Franciscus Romulus, Bellarmine published an answer to Belloy's *Apologie* (*Responsio ad praecipua capita*

Apologiae quae falso catholica inscribitur, 1587). He also acted as a polemicist against James I's oath of allegiance, assuming the name of Matthaeus Tortus in his *responsio* of 1608 and using his own name in reply to Barclay's *De potestate Papae* (*De potestate summi pontificis in rebus temporalibus*, 1610).

Bellarmine, and more particularly the two Spanish Jesuits, Molina and Francisco Suárez, expounded a Thomist view of natural law in their discussion of secular government. Natural law was understood by men through the rational apprehension of it imprinted upon the mind by the Creator, and it served as the measure of justice in human positive law. Molina's *De justitia et jure* (1592) was based upon lectures he had given in Portugal sixteen years earlier, while Suárez' *De legibus ac Deo legislatore* (1612) was the product of his teaching at Coimbra in the mid-1590s, and perhaps even of an earlier time when he was Bellarmine's colleague at the Jesuit college in Rome. Both these works viewed the ruler as effectively limited in his acts and ordinances by their consonance with natural law.

The interpretation of *ius naturale* was the key element in the account of the origin of political society provided by Molina and Suárez. As has been seen, Reynolds attempted to reconcile Aristotelian and Ciceronian traditions in *De justa authoritate*. It was difficult for a theorist to conceive a pre-social state of nature, unless man was to be in some way de-natured and reduced to a bestial condition. If natural man were to be so described, then it was hard to explain how he had escaped into civilised society. Humanists who followed Stoic and Ciceronian accounts of natural depravity did not, with the exception of Mario Salamonio and Buchanan, derive theories of political obligation from the transition to organised communal living. Nor did Protestant theorists of resistance, Buchanan again excepted, argue from a state of nature, preferring to stress pacts between a ruler and pre-existent community. For conciliarists, following the fifteenth-century tradition of Gerson, property and hence natural rights existed in the pre-social condition, and consequently the state of nature could not be entirely barbarous (Tuck 1979, p. 27). The paradox of conciliarism, however, was that these individualistic premises were lost to sight with the organicist language used to describe a corporate people, among whom individual good was subordinate to the common good. The Jesuits were enemies of conciliarism, and as theorists they were aware of Aquinas' observation that the king was greater than the people as a whole – a remark denied in the conciliarist and monarchomach adage *rex singulis maior, universis minor*. This was the problem to which Molina and Suárez achieved a compromise solution.

The two Jesuits wanted to demonstrate that political society was the immediate creation of men and served purely temporal ends, whereas the church was the immediate creation of God for higher spiritual ends. Molina used the actual term *status naturae* (Skinner 1978, II, p. 155) and asserted the absence of political organisation after the Fall. Suárez argued in *De legibus* that men abandoned their natural freedom to 'come together by individual will and common consent in one political body, under the single bond of society to aid each other through mutual organisation for a single political end, and by that means to bring into being one mystical body, which in moral terms can be called an entity for its own sake and consequently needs a single political head'.[11] The power thus created to enact positive law was vested in a government, sometimes established in a mixed form but more often transferred to a ruler ('the single head'). Both Molina and Suárez saw this transfer not as a delegation but as an alienation, and it was in this sense that they could agree with Aquinas that the king was superior to the community, whether viewed integrally or as a discrete mass of individuals. However, the scholastic practice of presenting other interpretations and pursuing qualifications and corollaries left some issues in doubt. In the succeeding chapter Suárez made the case that God alone could bestow power immediately, citing St Paul, Romans 13:1 ('There is no power but of God: the powers that be are ordained of God'). He even went on to point out that, according to some, only God could make law, for no one but the giver of life could take it away, law had a divine purpose to promote virtue and fulfil conscience, and God had reserved to Himself the punishment of wrongdoers ('Vengeance is mine: I will repay saith the Lord': Romans 12:19). Then in his next book (*De legibus*, IV, 2, p. 123), Suárez resumed his original theme, declaring that, while power might be found in the prince, it had to be bestowed by the people to be just. He went on to develop the less ambiguous attitudes to tyranny and resistance to be found in his *Defensio fidei Catholicae* (1613), directed against James I's *Apologie for the Oath of Allegiance*.

Some modern commentators have depicted the thrust of Suárez' theories as favouring royal absolutism.[12] No one who reads attentively his

---

11. 'Alio ergo modo consideranda est hominum multitudo, quatenus speciali voluntate seu communi consensu in unum corpus politicum congregantur uno societatis vinculo, et ut mutuo se iuvent in ordine ad unum finem politicum, quomodo efficiunt unum corpus mysticum, quod moraliter dici potest per se unum, illudque consequenter indiget uno capite.' Suárez 1613a, III, 2.4, p. 121.

12. On this question see Skinner 1978, II, pp. 177–84. A more emphatic statement that Suárez meant total alienation is provided by Tuck 1979, p. 56. Sommerville 1982, pp. 531–3, criticises both Skinner and Tuck. For a balanced view, albeit with some confusion, see Carlyle 1936, pp. 334–8, and Hamilton 1963, pp. 32–43.

answer to James I's *Apologie* can maintain this interpretation, and certainly those who read the *Defensio* at the time of its publication had the contrary impression. Suárez asserted the right of self-defence under natural law for both the individual and the commonwealth, and he conflated the latter with contractarian doctrines of resistance. In this respect he endorsed and elaborated the statements of the most prestigious adversary of King James:

Bellarmine actually said that the people never transfers its power to the prince without retaining it in a particular sense for use in certain circumstances. This is not a contradiction, and it does not invite the people to claim liberty as the fancy takes them ... These circumstances are to be understood as associated either with the conditions of the prior contract or with the requirement of natural justice, for pacts and just conventions are there for a purpose. That is why, if the people transferred power to the king while reserving it to themselves in some grave causes and affairs, it is lawful for them so to make use of it and to preserve their right.[13]

Suárez made it clear that a legitimate king could not be attacked for occasional acts of tyranny, but only when he threatened to destroy the commonwealth and massacred its citizens. Then alone could a king be resisted and deposed by public authority. No one could anticipate the decision of the appointed judges, nor could anyone act to avenge a personal wrong. A king once dethroned, or formally declared a heretic, could be killed by a private man, who became thereby the instrument of public authority. Like medieval theorists of tyrannicide, Suárez allowed private individuals to kill a tyrant usurper (*Defensio*, 1614, VI.6–22, col. 815–22).

Much of the *Defensio* was devoted to the superior jurisdiction of the pope, which was occasionally defended as a direct as well as an indirect power over temporal rulers.

Indeed this power is vested in the Supreme Pontiff who by right of his superior role has jurisdiction to reprove even the greatest kings as if they were his subjects, as shown earlier. Hence if the crimes lie in the spiritual sphere, as is the case with heresy, he can punish them directly, even to the point of deposition from a kingdom should a king's stubbornness and the preservation of the church's common good require it. What is more, if vices in the temporal sphere amount to sins he can also reprove by direct power insofar as they may be harmful to a

---

13. 'Quod vero Bellarminus ex Navarro dixit populum nunquam ita suam potestatem in Principem transferre, quin etiam in habitu retineat, ut ea in certis casibus uti possit, neque contrarium est, neque fundamentum populis praebet ad se pro libito in libertatem vindicandum ... Qui casus intelligendi sunt, vel iuxta conditiones prioris contractus, vel iuxta exigentiam naturalis iustitiae, nam pacta et conventa iusta servanda sunt. Et ideo si populus transtulit potestatem in regem reservando eam sibi pro aliquibus gravioribus causis aut negotiis, in eis licite poterit illa uti, et ius suum conservare.' Suárez 1614, III.3.3, col. 253.

Christian commonwealth in temporal terms, and in any event he can punish them indirectly, insofar as the tyrannical rule of a temporal prince always presents the gravest danger to the salvation of souls.[14]

In the following section of the *Defensio* Suárez went on to claim that the pope might call upon a Christian commonwealth to revolt against an oppressive ruler, just as he might order subjects who had prematurely rebelled against a tyrant to return to their obedience if the moral dangers of civil war seemed too great. The pope might also authorise a foreign prince to invade the realm of a king who had been declared a heretic. Despite Suárez' reservations about the occasions when popular revolt and the exercise of the pope's coercive powers were inappropriate, it is not surprising that Gallican and Anglican royalists saw his *Defensio* as a singularly aggressive example of papalist theory. He had made the pope the arbiter of natural law morality as well as of heresy, and had linked indirect to direct papal authority.

The ideas of Juan de Mariana provide another variant of Jesuit political thought. In *De rege et regis institutione* (1599) Mariana said little about papal authority over kings and a great deal about popular authority over the ruler. Perhaps it was his humanist education at the University of Alcalá that led him to question Aquinas on the king's superiority to the community. He wrote in national rather than universalist terms and, like Buchanan, composed a history of his country in which he exemplified his constitutionalist principles. When he sought general premises, he postulated an explicit state of nature, and, unlike Molina and Suárez, stressed not natural right but the bestiality that prevailed there. In a passage resembling one in Reynolds' *De iusta authoritate* he described the weakness of these subhumans in contrast with the protective and offensive weapons the rest of the animal creation possessed (*De rege*, I, i). The defencelessness of mankind had led to the formation of social groups, which imposed rules that merely exacerbated the predatory habits of their members. Since the rules proved as vexatious as the vices they were supposed to remedy, individuals agreed with one another to form a better organised society and appoint an

14. 'At vero in Summo Pontifice est haec potestas tanquam in superiori habente iurisdictionem ad corripiendum reges etiam supremos tanquam sibi subditos, ut supra ostensum est. Unde si crimina sint in materia spirituali, ut est crimen haeresis, potest directe illa punire in rege etiam usque ad depositionem a regno, si pertinacia regis et providentia communis boni Ecclesiae ita postulent. Si vero vitia sint in materia temporali, quatenus peccata sunt, etiam potest illa corripere per directam potestatem, quatenus vero fuerint temporaliter nociva reipublicae Christianae, indirecte saltem poterit ea punire, quatenus tyrannicum regimen temporalis principis semper etiam est salutati animarum perniciosum.' *Ibid.*, VI.4.16, col. 819.

administrator. In his sixth chapter Mariana said clearly what royalists read into all Jesuit writers, namely that no people would establish a governor under terms that would permit him to oppress them. Curiously, Mariana gave less emphasis to the deposition of a king by the representatives of the community than he did to the right of private men to kill a tyrant who prevented the assembly of the estates or *cortes* (*De rege*, I, vi, pp. 75–7). It was this assertion that earned Mariana his notoriety as the prophet of tyrannicide, and his enunciation of the principle was assumed by the enemies of the Jesuits to be the general tenet of the order.

vi   English Catholicism

Parsons also professed at times ideas differing from those of Bellarmine, Molina, and Suárez. A subtle and prolific polemicist, he displayed an opportunism in tune with the vicissitudes of Elizabethan Catholicism, and his ideas must be seen in this context. The political thought of Catholics after the Anglican settlement displayed a wide variety of opinion, sometimes anticipating, and sometimes following in the wake of Leaguer and Gallican writers. In the 1560s, when little pressure was placed upon recusants, a few Catholic intellectuals in exile offered radical criticism of the Anglican settlement. In answer to Bishop John Jewel's defence of the new regime, Thomas Harding's *Confutation of a Book* (1565) and other works maintained the papal power of deposition. He asserted that all temporal authority was subordinate to the vicar of Christ, and that, whereas priests held jurisdiction directly from God, the office of the ruler was derived from the people. John Rastell, also responding to Jewel in a number of tracts, defended the direct authority of popes over kings and cited Boniface VIII's bull *Unam Sanctam* with approval (*Confutation of a Sermon*, 1564). In 1570 Pius V excommunicated Elizabeth in the bull *Regnans in Excelsis*, which began in terms not very different from those of Boniface:

He that reigneth on high, to whom is given all power in heaven and earth, has committed one holy, Catholic, and apostolic church, outside of which there is no salvation, to one alone upon earth, namely to Peter, the first of the apostles, and to Peter's successor, the pope of Rome, to be by him governed in fullness of power. Him alone He has made ruler over all peoples and kingdoms.

(Pritchard 1978, p. 11)

An echo of these extreme claims was heard in a work by Nicholas Sanders (*De visibili monarchia*, 1571), in which resistance was justified by an original schema of three historic stages: patriarchal authority; kings ruling through the consent of their subjects; and, following the incarnation, kings whose prime duty was to promote the true faith under direction of the priesthood (Holmes 1982, pp. 28–9).

In the decade that followed William Allen launched the mission for the reconversion of England with the priests trained in his seminary at Douai. From 1580 Parsons and a number of English Jesuits trained in Rome also took part in the mission. Despite their complicity in Catholic plots against the queen, Allen and Parsons issued pamphlets claiming that the priests and fathers preached loyalty and non-resistance, and had received papal approval not to execute the bull. Faced with the persecution and martyrdom of their followers, and aware of Spanish plans for the Armada, the leaders of the mission abandoned the theory of non-resistance after 1583. In response to William Cecil's *Execution of Justice in England* (1583), which asserted that prosecutions were for treason and not for religious reasons, Allen wrote his *True, Sincere, and Modest Defence of the English Catholics* (1584). He defended the pope's powers of deposition and even justified the papal invasion of Ireland in 1579, although he continued to insist that the priests had not encouraged sedition. Allen depicted Catholic political doctrine as the product of 'men of order and obedience', whereas Protestant resistance theory aimed at leading 'opinionative and restless brains to raise rebellion at their pleasure under pretense of religion' (Allen 1965, p. 142). In words later to be echoed by Suárez, the sixth chapter of his *Defence* expatiated on the theme

that it is much to the benefit and stability of commonwealths, and specially of kings' scepters, that the differences between them and their peoples, for religion or any other cause for which they may seem to deserve deprivation, may rather be decided by the supreme pastor of the church, as Catholics would have it, than by popular mutiny and fantasy of private men, as heretics desire and practice.

(Allen 1965, p. 173)

In subsequent works (*The Copie of a Letter Concerning ... Daventrie*, 1587; *An Admonition to the Nobility and People*, 1588) Allen issued an open invitation to revolt against a heretic queen who had violated 'the universal moral law of Christendom'.

After 1584 Parsons was even more active in justifying resistance than Allen. His best known work in this vein was *A Conference about the Next Succession to the Crowne of England*, published under the pseudonym of N. Doleman in 1594. In the first part of the book the fictitious civilian who expounds the general principles of monarchical succession sounds very like Reynolds. He describes the need for law, after the establishment of communal life, 'to repress the insolent and assist the impotent, else living together be more hurtful than apart' (*Conference*, p. 7). Hereditary monarchy was probably the best kind of government, despite the wilful passions of kings. This did not mean divine right monarchy, however, for it was 'left unto every nation and country to choose that form of government which they shall like best and think most fit for the nature and conditions of their people' (*Conference*, p. 9). Parsons said explicitly that kings were appointed with '*potestas vicaria* or *delegata*' (*Conference*, p. 73). They were partners with their people in a contract confirmed in the coronation oath, and they were controlled by laws and national assemblies. If a ruler set out to destroy the commonwealth instead of advancing the public good, his authority might be revoked, for it was 'not likely . . . that any people would ever yield to put their lives, goods and liberties in the hands of another without some promise and assurance of justice and equity' (*Conference*, p. 82, cited by Pritchard 1978, p. 20). Mariana, as noted, was to say exactly the same thing.

Like Mariana, Parsons had little to say about relations between church and state, apart from insisting that the preservation of religion was the highest priority in a commonwealth. He adapted his opinions to the occasion and the audience. When he prepared a Latin version for the eyes of the pope he added a new chapter on papal authority of which Suárez would have entirely approved. 'Where the public good, and especially the well-being of religion, requires it,' Parsons wrote, 'the pope, with a pre-eminent right, can direct, restrain, check or even correct and punish any civil magistrate whatsoever if he stubbornly strays from the true path of eternal salvation, on account of which all magistracy was founded, or turns others from that path by his government' (Holmes 1982, p. 154).

After the death of Cardinal Allen in the year *A Conference* was published, deep resentments against the Jesuits became manifest in the internment centre for Catholics in Wisbech on the part of the secular priests, and in the Jesuit-directed English seminary in Rome on the part of the seminarians. In 1598 George Blackwell, reputedly a puppet of the Jesuits, was appointed archpriest in charge of English seculars. The priests twice appealed to Rome, and on the second occasion, with the help of the French ambassador, received some satisfaction in a brief forbidding Jesuit influence in their administration. However, Blackwell remained in office and the seculars were ordered in the brief not to continue their contacts in Anglican circles, notably with Bishop Bancroft in London. The covert liaisons of the appellants with French and English governments revealed the common policy of the two monarchies towards papal claims in temporal matters.

The eighteen tracts published by the appellants in their cause between 1601 and 1603 strengthened the black legend of Jesuit plotting and sedition, and popularised royalist doctrines. The appellants, who could not totally renounce papal rights, were particularly indebted to French royalist theory. Some of them had attended Pont-à-Mousson, and several draw their arguments from Grégoire and Barclay. Their particular target was Parsons' *Conference*. Parsons responded to some of their works by retreating to a moderate position where he ceased to defend secular grounds for resistance but continued to uphold the indirect power of the pope. William Watson was the most outspoken of the appellant controversialists – so much so that Christopher Bagshaw, a leading appellant and personal enemy of Parsons, asked him to moderate his invective. Watson played up the patriotism of the seculars as against Parsons' Spanish sympathies, which he recognised as similar to the earlier attitudes of the radical Leaguers in France. In *Important Considerations* (1601), a tract by the seminary priest Thomas Bluet to which Watson added a preface, Leaguer resistance theory was attributed to the Jesuits and compared with 'the hufmuf Puritan popularity' of Calvinist resistance doctrine (Salmon 1959, p. 35; Milward 1977, p. 119). It was Watson who arranged an English version of new denunciations of the Jesuits by Pasquier and Arnauld similar to those that had appeared in translation in 1594 (*The Jesuites Catechisme*, 1602; *A Discourse Presented of Late to the French King*, 1602). This aspect of the archpriest controversy may serve as a reminder of the inter-relationship of *politique* and Anglican royalist theory.

vii The defence of Anglicanism

Under the Anglican settlement the role of the queen as supreme governor of the church was thought to be jurisdictional rather than sacerdotal, and no one expected her to pronounce on doctrine. Such was the assumption of Bishop Jewel in his *Apologie ... in Defence of the Church of England* (1562) and in his subsequent response to his Catholic critics. Jewel found nothing new in ecclesiastical control by the temporal ruler, arguing that 'good princes ever took the administration of ecclesiastical matters to pertain to their duty' (Cross 1969, p. 139). Constantine and his successors had summoned councils of the church, a function now usurped by the bishop of Rome. In response to Allen, Thomas Bilson offered the same opinion in

The True Difference between Christian Subjection and Unchristian Rebellion (1585). However, Puritan pressure for further reform provided doctrinal change with political overtones, and from time to time Elizabeth took a stand on matters that were more than jurisdictional. In this she encountered such opposition from Archbishop Grindal that she was obliged to suspend him. Even his successor, John Whitgift, who had refuted the publications of the Presbyterian lobby before directing the repression of Puritan forms of worship, suffered some humiliation at her hands (Porter 1958, pp. 364–75).

Underlying the problem of distinguishing between jurisdiction and doctrine was the question of the respective legislative powers of parliament and convocation in religious matters. It was the general assumption of the queen and her archbishops that the supreme governor would rule the church through the bishops and convocation, but parliament was allowed to confirm the thirty-nine articles of faith defined by the assembly of the church. Richard Hooker's *Lawes of Ecclesiasticall Politie* (Books I–IV, completed in 1593) was an attempt to plaster over the gap between theory and practice and to justify the whole settlement in terms of parliamentary action. His basic position was that, since the members of the church of England were the same persons who composed the commonwealth of England, there were not two societies but one, ministered to in respect of their religious and secular needs by two sets of officials under one supreme governor.

In his posthumous eighth book Hooker provided a general definition of the ecclesiastical authority of kings:

When, therefore, Christian kings are said to have spiritual dominion or supreme power in ecclesiastical affairs and causes, the meaning is that within their own precincts and territories they have an authority and power to command even in matters of Christian religion, and that there is no higher nor greater that can in those cases overcommand them, where they are placed to command as kings.

(*Lawes*, VIII, 2.3, p. 332)

Those mistaken enough to challenge the power of the supreme governor were of two kinds, one believing 'that the supreme power in causes ecclesiastical throughout the world appertaineth of divine right to the bishop of Rome', and the other declaring 'that the said power belongeth in every national church unto the clergy thereof assembled' (*Lawes*, VIII, 2.4, pp. 333–4). Those in the latter category claimed that king and parliament had 'no more lawful means to give order to the church and clergy in those things than they have to make laws for the hierarchies of angels in heaven' (*Lawes*, VIII, 6.10, p. 401). Their error lay in their neglect of the principle that it was the consent of all which alone gave laws their binding force. Admonitions and instructions might be issued by the clergy for articles of faith, forms of prayer, and religious ceremonies, but these, to Hooker, were not laws. 'We are to hold it a thing most consonant with equity and reason that no ecclesiastical laws are made in a Christian commonwealth without consent as well of the laity as of the clergy, but least of all without consent of the highest power' (*Lawes*, VIII, 6.7, p. 393). Such was Hooker's defence of the parliamentary basis of the church of England and of the authority of the supreme governor.

The status of episcopacy was another key issue. In the early years of the settlement the bishops were content to derive their authority from the crown, and, while they insisted upon the hierarchical organisation of the church, they did not see a bishop as a different kind of priest from an ordinary clergyman. In 1589 Richard Bancroft responded to continuing anti-episcopal sentiment with a sermon stressing apostolic succession. There followed a series of tracts asserting the divine right of episcopacy (Hadrian Saravia, *De diversis ministrorum Evangelii gradibus*, 1590; Matthew Sutcliffe, *A Treatise of Ecclesiasticall Discipline*, 1591; Thomas Bilson, *The Perpetual Government of Christes Church*, 1593). Within ecclesiastical Gallicanism the doctrine of apostolic succession had defended clerical independence against king as well as pope. In England it could be seen as a challenge to Erastian control, and the radical pamphleteer Martin Marprelate pointed out that the divine right of bishops might be inconsistent with the authority of the supreme governor. Bancroft in his *Survey of the Pretended Holy Discipline* (1593) was careful to remark that bishops, although *iure divino*, received their jurisdictional rights from the temporal ruler. Potential tension between crown and episcopacy was minimised by their common front against Presbyterianism (Collinson 1982, pp. 1–38). Calvinist doctrines of grace appealed to many of the bishops but Calvinist church discipline was anathema.

It was also at this time that the idea of the divine right of kings began to be encouraged within Elizabethan court circles (Sommerville 1983, pp. 229–45). Saravia, the author of one of the works on *iure divino* episcopacy, also published a book defending royal divine right (*De imperandi authoritate et Christiana obedientia*, 1593). Saravia was a Fleming naturalised in England who served for a time as professor of theology at Leiden before returning to become a canon of Canterbury cathedral. He was a severe opponent of resistance theory, *De imperandi authoritate* being directed particularly at Buchanan and Reynolds. The doctrine of the divine right of kings was developed in England at the same time as a change occurred in English royalist attitudes towards the conflict in France. Bilson's *True Difference*, anxious to reverse Allen's contrast in resistance theory between Catholic legalism and Protestant anarchy, defended the Huguenots by asserting that they had not opposed the king, but had merely supported the constitutional rights of Navarre and Condé, and defended themselves against unjust persecution orchestrated by the house of Guise. After 1584 and the change of front in Huguenot doctrine, there was less need to discriminate between one kind of resistance and another. In his *Survey of the Pretended Holy Discipline*, Bancroft, like Saravia, condemned both the Calvinist and the Leaguer versions of resistance. This was also the trend in *politique* propaganda, in which the divine right of kings responded to both religious and secular justifications of rebellion.

Much of the *politique* and Gallican literature, including the works of Belloy, were appearing in English translations in the later years of Elizabeth (Salmon 1959, pp. 174–80). Their frequent citation in the writing of English royalists suggests that it was not James I who introduced the theory of divine right monarchy to England but that both he and those English writers who anticipated him in this regard were jointly indebted to French ideas. The connection, rather than the antagonism, between *iure divino* episcopacy and *iure divino* monarchy is also more comprehensible in the light of this circumstance. In both France and England during the time of the League and after, bishops were the defenders of monarchy against popes and presbyteries. James I was the supporter of divine right episcopacy, and the aphorism 'no bishop, no king,' which he delighted in so much that he used it twice in one day at the Hampton Court conference to discredit Presbyterian influence, was less contradictory than it might seem (Fincham and Lake 1985, pp. 174, 187).

viii James I, the oath of allegiance, the Venetian Interdict, and the reappearance of French Ultramontanism

James I's political views had been plain for all to see in *The Trew Law of Free Monarchies* (1598) five years before he succeeded Elizabeth. J.N. Figgis described his theory of the divine right of kings as consisting of four propositions: monarchy was divinely ordained; hereditary right was indefeasible; kings were accountable to God alone; and non-resistance and passive obedience were enjoined by God (Figgis 1965, pp. 5–6). James regarded the right of Scottish kings to have been established by conquest, and the dependency of existing institutions followed from this:

The kings therefore in Scotland were before any estates or ranks of men within the same, before any parliaments were holden, or laws made: by them the land distributed (which at first was wholly theirs), states erected and decerned, and forms of government devised and established: And so it follows of necessity that the kings were the authors and makers of the laws, and not the laws of the kings ... And according to these fundamental laws already alleged, we daily see that in the parliament (which is nothing else but the head court of the king and his vassals) the laws are but craved of his subjects, and only made by him at their rogation and with their advice. (James I 1918, p. 62)

When he faced the need to manipulate the English parliament, James modified these opinions, even if the concessions were offered as royal lectures which at first sight seemed to reassert his overriding authority. The most significant of such occasions was a speech to parliament in 1610 when the king began: 'The state of monarchy is the supremest thing upon earth, for kings are not only God's lieutenants upon earth, and sit upon God's throne, and even by God Himself they are called Gods' (James I 1918, p. 307). Such declarations have been regarded as airy rhetoric, but there is good reason to take them seriously. James was comparing himself with God as the guarantor of the hierarchical order of things, and he went on to imply that natural law was a real limitation upon himself, just as God bound Himself to His own ordained law. More than this, just as there was a distinction between God's absolute and ordained law, so there was a difference between the king's absolute and ordinary prerogative (Greenleaf 1964, pp. 58–67; and Oakley 1984, pp. 93–118). It was in the latter area that he permitted the subject's rights to be heard, even if regal power was the source of the positive law that defined such rights. James elaborated this later in the speech when he discussed the origins of authority and constitutional law:

So in the first original of kings, whereof some had their beginnings by conquest, and some by election of the people, their wills at that time had served for law. Yet how soon kingdoms began to be settled in civility and polity [policie], then did kings set down their minds by laws, which are properly made by the king only; but at the rogation of the people, the king's grant being obtained thereunto. And so the king became to be *lex loquens* after a sort, binding himself by a double oath to the observation of the fundamental laws of his kingdom ... So as every just king in a settled kingdom is bound to observe that paction made to his people by his laws, in framing his government agreeable thereunto, according to that paction which

God made Noah after the deluge ... And therefore a king governing a settled
kingdom leaves off to be a king and degenerates into a tyrant, as soon as he leaves
off to rule according to his laws.   (James I 1918, pp. 301–10)

These pronouncements were compatible with *Trew Law* but they extended
and modified the theory by placing it in the context of English practice.
Echoes of the vocabulary of the opposing camp, including words and
phrases to be found in the writings of his former tutor, Buchanan, and of his
contemporary Jesuit critics, sounded in the royal utterance. But through his
subtle reasoning James had bent their meaning to his own purpose, and
offered an absolutism consistent with the observance of natural and
constitutional law.

Some royalist statements at the time of James' accession suggested
variations on the themes preferred by the king. Most of these were
responses to Parsons' *Conference*, which had proposed the Infanta as
Elizabeth's successor, although Parsons himself, hoping that James would
authorise toleration for Catholics, now supported the Scottish claimant and
was preaching non-resistance. The trend of these responses was to rely
upon Roman law concepts and authorities. Sutcliffe (*A Briefe Replie*, 1600;
A Full and Round Answer, 1604) cited the French civilians and treated
Parsons as the purveyor of the treasonable doctrines of the League. Sir John
Hayward, who was associated with Sutcliffe in the foundation of Chelsea
College (an institution to counter Roman propaganda), produced *An
Answer to the First Part of a Certaine Conference* in 1603. He attacked Parsons
as a Leaguer and relied upon Belloy, adding a theory of the irrevocable
transfer of power from the people to the king. The Scot Sir Thomas Craig,
who had been a pupil of the celebrated defender of political Gallicanism,
Charles Du Moulin, composed his *Right of Succession* in Latin in 1603, and
quoted Bodin and Belloy, to whom his translator was to add Blackwood
and Barclay when the book appeared in English a century later. Roman
law was becoming an increasingly important ingredient in English royalist
thinking at this time, and the regius professors of civil law at Oxford and
Cambridge, Alberico Gentili and John Cowell, were distinguished
representatives of the trend. It was Cowell's *Interpreter* (1607), with its
absolutist interpretation of royal prerogative, that was to be a prime source
of friction between James I and parliament at the time of the king's 1610
speech.

The paranoia stimulated by the Gunpowder Plot of 1605 led to an act
imposing a stringent oath of allegiance upon Catholics in the following

year, and this in turn began an international debate in which the king was one of the principal controversialists. Thomas Morton's *Exact Discoverie of Romish Doctrine* (1605) appeared immediately after the plot and blamed it upon Catholic doctrines justifying rebellion and papal deposition. This was elaborated in *A Full Satisfaction concerning a Double Romish Iniquitie* (1606) which, like Hayward, interpreted the *lex regia* to mean that authority had at first resided in the community and had been alienated to the ruler and his descendants. The indefatigable Parsons reacted to the oath with *A Treatise tending to Mitigation towardes Catholicke Subjectes in England* (1607), and Morton, now chaplain to the king, answered it with *A Preamble unto an Incounter with P.R.* (1608). Before Parsons returned to the debate with Morton in *A Quiet and Sober Reckoning with M.T.*(1609), he had entered the lists against the king's first contribution and published *The Judgment of a Catholicke English-man* (1608). This in turn involved him in exchanges with another of the king's champions, Bishop Barlow. In his duel with Morton and Barlow, Parsons revealed that his advocacy of non-resistance did not imply his renunciation of the indirect power of papal deposition. His desire to score debating points led him into the absurdity of portraying Rossaeus as a supporter of royal authority. Identifying Rossaeus as William Reynolds, Morton made the most of this piece of equivocation (Salmon 1959, p. 71).

The exchanges with Parsons are but one example of the way in which the controversy ramified. Its expansion to unprecedented European dimensions followed the appearance of James I's *Apologie for the Oath of Allegiance* (also entitled *Triplici Nodo, Triplex Cuneus*, 1607), to which the king added his *Premonition to all Most Mighty Monarchs* (1609) and his *Remonstrance for the Right of Kings* (1616). The papacy issued two briefs forbidding English Catholics to take the oath, and, when Blackwell himself disobeyed, it was Bellarmine who published a letter of remonstrance addressed to him. The king's *Apologie* answered the briefs and the letter, moving Bellarmine to further refutation. His opinions, as well as the contributions of Barclay and Suárez, have already been described, and there is little more to be said about the positions adopted on both sides. Casaubon and Lancelot Andrewes, and many other scholars and clerics, enlarged upon the king's arguments, while the Jesuit Martin Becan of Mainz was the most prolific of a regiment of papal champions.

The beginnings of the controversy about the oath of allegiance coincided with an interdict imposed by Pope Paul V on the republic of Venice. This extreme act was a response to Venetian subordination of Catholic clergy to civil jurisdiction and to the republic's limitation of the right of the church to acquire property. The coordinator of Venetian propaganda against the interdict was Fra Paolo Sarpi, an outspoken critic of Roman corruption who developed a circle of anti-papal correspondents among Gallicans and Protestants and who is best remembered for his later *History of the Council of Trent* (1619). Sarpi rapidly put into print an Italian version of Gerson's criticism of the improper use of papal excommunication. To this Bellarmine, aware of the dangers of a revived conciliarism, responded with *Riposta ad un libretto di Gio. Gerone* (in Bellarmine 1606), and Sarpi looked to his French friends to continue the debate.

Gallican sentiment had strongly opposed the return of the Jesuits to France in 1603 but the pleas of Arnauld and Pasquier in the previous year had been ineffective. It received a further check when the Sorbonne censured Servin's publication of some of his more extreme pleadings in the cause of political Gallicanism. But the Sorbonne had less of a quarrel with the ecclesiastical variant of Gallicanism that regained support in the aftermath of the League. Ecclesiastical Gallicanism made much of the argument that papal jurisdiction had been unjustifiably expanded since the early centuries, when the provinces of the church and the bishop of Rome himself had followed the teaching of the councils. This viewpoint was readily adaptable to the Venetian crisis, and it was in this vein that Edmond Richer, soon to be elected syndic of the Sorbonne, answered Bellarmine and produced a new edition of the works of Gerson, together with excerpts from d'Ailly, Almain, and Mair (*Ioannis Gersonii doctoris et cancellarii Parisiensis opera*, 1606; Salmon 1987, pp. 181–3).

It was also in this period that the antiquarian justifications of Gallicanism by Jean du Tillet and Claude Fauchet were published, and the revised versions of Pasquier's *Recherches de la France* were set in print with the inclusion of his diatribes against the Jesuits. These represented the *parlementaire* interpretation of the Gallican liberties, which was not in sympathy with growing Ultramontane opinion within the French clergy and the renewed clerical pressure to receive the Tridentine decrees. Works by officials of the *parlement*, supporting Sarpi's Venetian campaign and equating the Gallican position with that of the church of Venice, continued to appear. Notable among them were Leschassier's *Consultatio* (*Consultatio Parisii cuiusdam de controversia inter sanctitatem Pauli Quinti et serenissimam rempublicam Venetam*, 1607) and Servin's *Pro libertate* (*Pro libertate status et reipublicae Venetorum Gallo franci ad Philenetum epistola*, 1606).

In this way the Venetian crisis fuelled the oath of allegiance controversy and strengthened the alliance of Catholic and Anglican theorists against the papalist camp. Events in France further extended the debate. The assassination of Henri IV in 1610 seemed to confirm the worst fears which the allegedly Jesuit doctrine of tyrannicide had inspired. Nothing that the king's Jesuit confessor, Père Coton, could say to expose the falsity of the sinister reputation the society had acquired altered the popular impression. Despite the crescendo of Gallican condemnation for the Jesuits and the papalist doctrines to which they were thought to subscribe, the regency of the king's widow, Marie de Médicis, tried to find a middle way between continued clerical support for Ultramontanism, which was manifest in many spiritual reforms throughout the French church, and the kind of anti-Jesuit mania expressed by the *parlement* of Paris and a group within the Sorbonne. The *parlement* had ordered the burning of Mariana's *De rege* after the murder of Henri IV. In 1611 it took up the cause of Richer, the syndic of the Sorbonne, who had moved to block a dissertation proclaiming the pope infallible and superior to church councils. In the course of these proceedings Richer published his *De ecclesiastica et politica potestate* maintaining that the pope could excommunicate but not depose a temporal sovereign, that the collective body of the church represented in a council alone possessed infallibility, and that the clergy were subject to the civil power in temporal matters. Richer's conciliarist position and his affirmation of individual clerical rights of spiritual jurisdiction proved too extreme for moderate Gallican opinion. He received clerical censure and was deposed from the office of syndic of the Sorbonne. Even the *parlement* would not entertain his appeal, but Servin, the advocate-general, persuaded the court to have the Jesuits declare their adherence to the first two of the propositions extracted from Richer's tract. In 1613 the Sorbonne censured Becan's *Controversia Anglicana de potestate pontificis et regis*, written in defence of Bellarmine, and in the following year the *parlement* burnt Suárez' *Defensio fidei Catholicae*, an act anticipated in England.

Cardinal Du Perron acted as the spokesman for the regency against Gallican excess. He readily condemned the doctrine of tyrannicide, and accepted royal authority as directly empowered by God in temporal affairs. He felt obliged, however, to defend the papal right of deposition, and resisted an attempt in the Estates General of 1614–15 to propose a fundamental law protecting the crown against this right. James I's *Remonstrance* was a direct reply to the cardinal's speech. In this way events in France prolonged the oath of allegiance controversy. Although Du Perron chose not to publish the comments he composed on the *Remon-*

strance, he wrote a long answer to a piece printed in 1612, in which Casaubon, with royal guidance, had defended King James' religion against the cardinal's suggestion that he was no Protestant. This *Réplique à la Réponse* was published posthumously in 1620 as one of the last shots to be fired in this ideological war, which had lasted fourteen years and produced a vast quantity of polemical literature (McIlwain 1918, pp. xlix–lxxviii; Milward 1978, pp. 128–31; Hayden 1974, p. 144).

The papal camp had continued to defend the theory of indirect power, while the supporters of divine right monarchy had continued to accuse their opponents of advocating secular revolt as well as papal deposition. The arguments, in short, were basically those expressed earlier in the context of the League, the Elizabethan defence of Anglicanism, and the archpriest controversy. Although this was a period of intense religious belief, its association with political conflicts pointed to increasing secularisation. That the same patterns and motifs could be repeated by states and factions of differing religious alignment suggested that the real priorities in political ideals were all too human.

9

Constitutionalism

HOWELL A. LLOYD

i The idea of constitutionalism

The term 'constitutionalism' had no currency in the political thought of the late fifteenth and sixteenth centuries. A nineteenth-century augmentative of 'constitution', itself derived from the Latin *constitutio*, the term signifies advocacy of a system of checks upon the exercise of political power. Such a system is commonly taken to involve the rule of law, a separation of legislative from executive and from judicial power, and representative institutions to safeguard the individual and collective rights of a people who, while governed, are nonetheless sovereign. As we shall see, ideas which would contribute to later conceptions of that kind were present in the thought of the period. But for those thinkers the term 'constitution', which certainly formed part of their technical vocabulary, conveyed a very different meaning. They used it first and foremost in a sense consistent with the definition to be found in Justinian's lawbooks, a definition which drew no distinction between the legislative and judicial spheres: 'whatever the emperor has determined (*constituit*) by rescript or decided as a judge or directed by edict is established to be law: it is these that are called constitutions' (Institutes, 1.2.6). A constitution was an explicit declaration of law by the prime political authority. Hence, in England, Chief Justice Fortescue's view that 'when customs and the rules of the law of nature have been reduced to writing and published by the sufficient authority of the prince and ordered to be kept, they are changed into a constitution or something of the nature of statutes'.[1]

But 'constitution' had a wider meaning and broader implications. So

---

1. Fortescue 1949, p. 36; cf. the title of Pierre Rebuffi's compilation of royal acts and his glosses upon them: *Commentaries on Constitutions or Royal Ordinances*.

much was evident from the writings of classical philosophers, not least the later Stoics whose influence upon Renaissance humanism was profound. Both Cicero and Seneca had written of the 'constitution of nature', and with it of the nature of man, constituted of body and soul.[2] Both had also used the term to describe the formal condition of an entire body politic. Moreover, according to Cicero, in the case of the Roman *respublica* the 'wisest and best-regulated condition (*res cum sapientissime moderatissimeque*) has been laid down (*constituta esset*) by our ancestors' (*De legibus*, III.v.12). Beyond particular decrees, constitutions were sets of historically established, even fundamental, laws: they were, as the *Indice de la Bible* put it in 1564, 'the whole of the laws and institutions handed down by tradition'.[3] And Cicero had gone further, affirming that the optimum condition which he had in mind was 'the mixed form of polity (*temperationem reipublicae*)' (*De legibus*, III.v.12). Once more such sentiments found sixteenth-century echoes. Thus the historian Bernard du Haillan held that in principle France's form of rule imposed 'bridles' upon the king, at least in respect of the apparatus of government. The 'administration of the public weal' was 'divided and distributed' among 'all the Estates proportionately according to their condition', an arrangement that ensured 'harmony and consonance'. Regrettably, however, the 'beautiful order instituted in our monarchy is corrupted', and 'we retain only the shadow of those first fine constitutions' (Du Haillan 1609, fos. 174v–5r).

Given these and similar usages, it entails no anachronism to describe as 'constitutionalist' contemporary ideas to the effect that power ought to be exercised within institutionally determined limits. Such ideas may be expected to have flourished in the age of Renaissance and Reformation, of humanist learning, of critical and historical reappraisal of the Roman texts. The very section of Justinian's lawbooks where 'constitutions' were defined by reference to the ruler's law-declaratory power could be construed in terms of popular sovereignty. There, as medieval publicists had remarked and diligently pondered, the definition stood juxtaposed with a statement of the *lex regia*: the source of the emperor's authority lay in an act arguably of delegation on the part of the Roman people (Institutes, 1.2.6). Roman precedents apart, the age in question saw in the sphere of practical politics developments surely conducive to fresh building upon constitutionalist foundations which medieval thinkers had already laid. In the western

---

2. Cicero, *De finibus*, iv.6, 7; Seneca, *Epistulae morales*, xcv.52, and *De clementia*, 1.iii.5.
3. Cited in *Trésor de la langue française* (1978), VI, p. 10.

European realms a major feature of such developments was a vigorous assertion of the secular authority *vis-à-vis* the church. In England the assertion proceeded through the representative assembly of a self-sufficient 'empire' whose laws were the work of king and people acting together 'at their free liberty by their own consent'.[4] In France it occurred within a context of 'Gallicanism' which, as expounded by its leading late scholastic theoreticians, would reserve ultimate authority in the secular as in the ecclesiastical community to assemblies of either body's *valentior pars*.[5] The phrase recalled the views of Marsilius of Padua for whom legislative power should rest with the 'whole body of the citizens or the weightier part thereof' (Marsilius 1956, II, p. 45). While his views had an influence upon the moving spirits of England's Henrician Reformation (Elton 1974, II, pp. 228–9), a greater influence upon Gallican positions was that of Jean Gerson, advocate of a moderate conciliarism and so of the merits of a mixed form of rule at least as the means of checking possible monarchical excesses.[6] In Spain royal powers to nominate bishops, tax clerics, and wield the formidable weapon of the Inquisition sprang from papal concessions which owed nothing to specifically Marsilian or Gersonian promptings. Yet Spanish thinkers continued to credit the pope with 'indirect' power in the temporal sphere – a concept traceable to John of Paris, precursor of Marsilius, participant in early Gallican controversy, and exponent of the thesis that the pope had a power *per accidens* to be used against incorrigible kings through the medium of the people from whom the secular ruler derived his authority.[7]

And yet, propositions about how to deal with an heretical or a tyrannical ruler belong to the sphere of resistance theory rather than of constitutionalism properly conceived. The former has to do with exceptional circumstances, the latter with the nature, scope, and distribution of power in normal times. Amid the upheavals and sectarian conflicts of sixteenth-century Europe proponents of resistance arrived, it has been claimed, at 'a recognisably modern, secularised thesis about the natural rights and original sovereignty of the people' (Skinner 1978, II, p. 338). Whatever its modernity, that thesis stood opposed in the era of Renaissance courts and princes to the theory of regal power, reinforced in the course of the period

---

4. 24 Hen. VIII. c. 12; 25 Hen. VIII, c. 21.   5. For instance, Burns 1981, esp. pp. 58–9.
6. On the ambiguities of Gerson's position, see Tierney 1982, pp. 95–6.
7. John of Paris 1969, pp. 138, 97, 113, and 1971, pp. 14–15, 156, 103, 124. See also Melía 1977, pp. 54, 196ff.

by a new concept of the state as the locus of legislative sovereignty.[8] It is in these rival theses, both coherently enough expressed, that the prime achievements of sixteenth-century political thought are most obviously to be found. By comparison, the products of specifically constitutionalist thinking seem sterile and diffuse. Du Haillan's regret for the erosion of France's 'constitutions' reflects the relative decadence of their theoretical concomitants. Deductive minds of constitutionalist inclination continued eclectically to revolve positions already stated by civilians and canonists, by Bartolus, Aquinas, Isidore of Seville, with lavish infusions of Aristotelian principles and occasional appeals to feudal norms. Their chief accomplishment was to apply to the kingdoms of the west ideas long since adumbrated in relation to empire, church, and city-state. In any case, few men devoted their minds systematically and consistently to the task of formulating political theory along constitutionalist lines. The elements of constitutionalism lie scattered among works, whether academic treatises or *thèses de circonstance*, whose authors for the most part were preoccupied with other issues and in many instances altered their political opinions in the course of their writing careers.

Even so, those elements remained vital ingredients in the thought of the time. For the period at issue here belongs, it has recently been argued, to a continuous tradition of western thought traceable perhaps to the fourteenth, perhaps to the twelfth, century or even beyond (esp. Tierney 1982 and Skinner 1978). In the forging of that tradition debates over 'the proper limits of lawfully constituted authority' were formative upon the conceptual vocabulary of political discourse (Tierney 1982, p. 7). Thus all contemporary discussions which impinged upon the relation between power and society necessarily deployed at least some of the elements in question, albeit with varying degrees of emphasis and from differing perspectives. A preserve of no particular disciplinary, methodological or theoretical school, they figured in the writings of jurisprudents and moral

8. Lloyd 1983, pp. 146–68. Statements of typical regalist positions occur in the following French or English works: on the king as directly appointed by God, Grassaille 1538, p. 133; on the king as *imago Dei*, Budé 1557, p. 69; on monarchy as the norm throughout the natural order, Elyot 1531, fo. 7v; on the monarchical as the earliest form of rule, Smith 1982, p. 60; on the prince as *causa causarum*, Rebuffi 1589, p. 36; on the head (i.e. king) as the seat of 'intellect' and source of all power in the body politic, Chasseneuz 1546, fos. 132r, 284v; for an application of the Neoplatonist concept of *processio*, to the same effect, Bodin 1945, p. 287; on the *merum imperium* as belonging in a monarchy solely to the prince, Barclay 1604, cited by Gilmore 1941, pp. 89, 90; for denial of all lesser jurisdictions except those received through royal *concessio*, Du Moulin 1681, I, p. 128; on the subject's duty of obedience, Gardiner 1930, p. 98.

philosophers, scholastics and humanists, proponents of resistance and of absolutism alike. This chapter's first main section aims to extract those elements from a selection of French, English, and other western European writings of the period *c.* 1470 to *c.* 1600. It will present them in consecutive fashion, and regardless at this stage of context and chronological variations, within a framework of three principal themes: the origins and end of political society; custom and the rule of law; and the distribution of power among the organs of mixed government. A brief indication of the context of political thought in four western European countries is given in sections (v) to (viii), as a preliminary in each case to a fuller statement of the position of one major thinker who, at the end of the sixteenth century or at the opening of the seventeenth, exhibited some claim to be reckoned a constitutionalist.

ii   The origins and end of political society

Kings were divinely appointed. The proof lay in scripture. Yet it did not follow that God appointed them directly, nor that the institution of kingship was coeval with human society. The 'minister' whom St Paul described as 'ordained of God' was 'a revenger to execute wrath upon him that doeth evil' (Romans 13:1,4). Without the presence of evil, therefore, there would have been no need of kings – a point implicit in Augustine's writings as in those of Luther long after him, for all the latter's stress upon the providential source of princely power. And although sin was inescapably a part of the condition of fallen man, what had sprung initially from it was not necessarily kingship as the means of chastising the wicked, but political society itself. This, after all, was what Augustine had in fact suggested, in terms echoed in sixteenth-century Flanders by his Spanish commentator Juan Luis Vives and in France by the Scotsman John Mair.[9] The urge that prompted men to form a society of any kind might itself be the product of 'divine inspiration', as Mair's fellow Scot and pupil George Buchanan affirmed (Buchanan 1579, p. 10). The powers of political society as such might in turn be 'what God placed in men', as Jacques Almain, another of Mair's pupils, maintained.[10] Yet it remained the case that the people were prior to their monarchical ruler and possessed the capability of participating in his appointment. As Mair himself indicated, kings were

9. Vives 1782–90, v, pp. 229, 276–7, 388–9; Mair 1519, fo. c^r, col. 2.
10. Almain, *De auctoritate*, in Gerson 1706, ɪɪ, col. 978.

'introduced' by a 'people', already formed into a 'polity', and had powers 'conceded by them'. There was scriptural evidence for this; and although Mair chose to except the Israelites from his analysis, others found that the same applied to God's chosen people.[11]

A people, once politically formed, existed as a 'community'. The community could be interpreted as a corporate entity: in Almain's view it existed 'as one body of which all are members one of the other'. This was the entity that 'gives authority to the prince', an authority which 'is first in the community'.[12] The thesis drew upon corporation theory rooted in Roman law. A people and its power as a corporate whole were distinguishable from and greater than a mere assemblage of individuals. God remained the ultimate source of that power. Were this not so, the Spanish Jesuit Luis de Molina explained, and were the community's existence dependent upon the concurrence of 'the parts from which it is formed into one', it would have had from the time of its formation 'no authority' over those of 'its cohabitants who might not have wished to offer agreement to it', nor subsequently over any new arrivals (Molina 1602–3, I, col. 115). Of course, the community had many of the attributes of a natural association too. 'Most harmonious with nature', it was, wrote the Spanish Dominican Francisco de Vitoria, 'self-sufficing' and 'of all societies that in which men most easily may obtain necessities'. Man could not exist 'in solitude'; and obedience to the 'public power' was consistent with 'natural law'. But it was an error to argue from the assumption that man was 'created free'. Political society as such did not consist simply of 'each individual'; it did not exist for the sake of 'private utility'; and it had not originated as an 'invention of man'. Possessing its power 'by divine ordinance', it 'embraced its citizens with that power, as if they were the members of one body, in order to preserve the whole unimpaired' (Vitoria 1933–6, II, pp. 178–83).

But other thinkers did not shrink from adducing the agreement of its members as a condition of the community's formation. Some suggested that the agreement amounted to a contractual undertaking. It sprang, according to the Spanish Jesuit Juan de Mariana, from men's recognition of a need 'to bind themselves with others in a compact of society (*societatis foedere*)' (Mariana 1605, p. 16). Hence the origins of 'royal and princely power' which began, as the Roman patrician Mario Salamonio declared,

11. Mair 1519, fos. ciii^r, col. 1 – ciii^v, col. 1; cf. for instance, Goodman 1558, p. 48.
12. Almain, *Quaestio resumptiva*, in Gerson 1706, II, cols. 963–4.

'by the compacts of men' whom 'God created equal' (Salamonio 1544, fo. 11r). Compacts rested upon voluntary and rational consent. Well-worn foundation myths indicated the relevance of these conditions to the making of political society and, taken in conjunction with assumptions about human nature, served also to show how it was that legitimate government took various forms. Supplementing Aristotle with Plato, the English civilian Sir Thomas Smith recounted how different forms of 'commonwealth' had emerged from the initial rule of the 'great grandfather' over an expanding domestic society. Commonwealths, whether aristocratic or democratic, could be accounted 'natural' insofar as they conformed with 'the nature of the people'; yet every commonwealth was 'the common doing of a multitude of free men collected together and united by common accord and covenants among themselves' (Smith 1982, pp. 57–64). In Jean Bodin's view, while man was naturally gregarious he formed associations 'by his own volition'. Kingship arose when 'the full liberty of everyone' was 'handed over by the separate citizens to one' (Bodin 1945, pp. 213–14, cf. p. 29). At the very least, the process involved some exercise of that 'deliberate choice' which Aristotle reckoned a prime requisite of political justice.[13] But nowhere was that requisite accommodated more persuasively to humanist minds than in Cicero's foundation myth. Far from exhibiting an ineluctable sociability, men in the state of nature had wandered severally abroad 'in the manner of beasts', until at last some eloquent speaker persuaded them to recognise the benefits of having ordered institutions. Thus political society owed its origins neither to divine intervention nor to natural expansion from a domestic base so much as to the triumph through rhetoric of reason over appetite.[14]

Even so, it remained the case that reason had led a good many people to opt for monarchical rule. The act was surely decisive: a deliberate transfer of collective power and a commitment thereafter absolutely to obey. In the imagery of proponents of regal power, the king was identified with 'intellect' to which 'appetite' as exemplified elsewhere in the body politic had always to defer.[15] Yet, given that the community was the immediate source of the ruler's authority, it could be held on a number of grounds that by the act in question only a limited power was transferred to him. First, a

---

13. Aristotle, *Nicomachean Ethics*, 1111b4–1112a18, 1134a16–1134b18.
14. Cicero, *De inventione*, i.ii. See, for instance, Starkey 1871, p. 53; Alciato, *Opera* (1546), cited by Tuck 1979, p. 36.
15. For instance. Chasseneuz 1546, fos. 132r, 284v. For a constitutionalist variation on this theme, with the 'reasonable appetite' identified as a mean contributing actively to the conduct of 'politic and regal' rule, see Le Roy 1598, p. 26.

people could scarcely transfer to its king a power greater than it itself possessed. As Salamonio concluded from examining the case of the Roman people and the *lex regia*, the authority of the prince 'cannot be more and stronger than what the people itself can do' (Salamonio 1544, fo. 16r). Secondly, the people might not have transferred all of its power to its ruler. By Molina's assessment, while princes exercising power 'conceded to them by the commonwealth' must be obeyed, there might still be matters which continued to 'depend upon the approval of the people'; and although 'the king remains superior not only to each part of the commonwealth, but also to the commonwealth as a whole so far as the power conceded to him extends', if he 'should wish to assume power not conceded to him the commonwealth would certainly be able to resist him'.[16] Thirdly, and most importantly for constitutionalist positions, even in the exercise of the power that was in fact 'conceded' the king remained, in Salamonio's phrase, 'not the lord (*dominus*)', but 'the minister of those who commit themselves to his charge' (Salamonio 1544, fos. 13r, 17v).

The significance of those grounds became especially apparent when account was taken of why men had been persuaded to submit themselves to rulership at all. It was evident to Smith that the descendants of the original ruler had done so precisely in order to 'defend themselves', and 'to save the politic body too' (Smith 1982, pp. 60, 62). The 'especial defence and safety of the whole body' were the paramount concerns of 'all just and lawful forms of empires', according to the French Aristotelian Louis Le Roy.[17] Self-preservation was not only a rational concern for a collectivity of people. It could also be seen as every individual's private right under natural law. As Vitoria put it, 'every man has by natural law the power and the right (*ius*) to defend himself', there being 'nothing more natural than to repel force with force' (Vitoria 1933–6, II, p. 182). A correspondence could accordingly be urged between the position of the individual and the position of the community as a whole. Like Vitoria a student at Paris – though more closely attuned to the ideas of Gerson, their precursor there – Almain expressed the concept of a natural *ius* in terms of *dominium*, a term which in the usage of such Parisian legists as Charles Du Moulin related rather to legally verifiable property rights. To Almain every man had a 'natural *dominium*', defined as a '*facultas* or power' rooted in 'natural law'

16. Molina 1602–3, I, col. 118; further discussion of the relative superiority of king and commonwealth as a whole occurs below, p. 272.
17. Le Roy 1598, p. 26, contrasting such forms of rule with 'lordly' government where the people were treated as slaves.

whereby 'everyone is bound to keep himself in being'. This *dominium* included 'the power to strike down an assailant' and was 'inalienable'. An equivalent *facultas* appertained to the community as a whole. In Almain's view that entity derived its power from God and not from its individual members. Nevertheless, it was as an entity equally bound to preserve itself. When it 'constituted' a king it 'conceded' to him its 'right of the sword'. But the concession could not be absolute: no more alienable by a people than by an individual, the right continued to inhere in the community itself. Should the king's behaviour redound to the 'destruction' of the community, he forfeited his power and might be removed. And in any case, the *dominium* which he enjoyed in relation to that power was 'merely that of an administrator (*solum ministeriale*)'.[18]

The situation of such a king compared poorly with that of the potentate whom regalists described as self-moving, himself conceding to lesser magistrates jurisdictional power which flowed only from him and of which, as Du Moulin maintained, none of them might have *dominium*. And even in its narrower proprietary sense that same term had constitutionalist implications. From Du Moulin's account of it the king, though divinely appointed, emerged as no outright proprietor of public power in his realm. What he could and did concede to others was *dominium* of a kind, in the sense of a right of use (*utile dominium concedere possit*). What he himself retained was *dominium directum* which included the power to intervene should a jurisdiction be neglected or abused. But he could not 'altogether alienate or abdicate or, as they say, make expropriation of territories, honours or jurisdictions'. These remained indissociably the 'members' of the realm itself. The king, as its 'head', could not 'subsist' without them; and should he attempt to alienate them even on the strength of his 'certain understanding and proper motion', he would be 'murderer of his own official dignity' (Du Moulin 1681, I, pp. 78–9). The position bore upon the question of the realm's fundamental laws. It also tallied with Almain's insistence upon the community's inalienable rights, though Du Moulin conceived of the 'goods and rights (*iura*) of the kingdom and the commonwealth' in specifically different legal terms. And he too concluded that the king, who stood in relation to those rights 'like a husband in respect of his wife's dowry', was 'not accounted *dominus* or proprietor of his kingdom, but *administrator* [*sic*]'.[19]

18. Almain, *Quaestio resumptiva*, in Gerson 1706, II, cols. 961–4; cf. *De auctoritate*, in Gerson 1706, II, col. 978. See also Burns 1983; and, for Vitoria's refusal to equate *jus* with *dominium*, Tuck 1979, p. 47. On the Gersonian theory of natural rights, see Tuck 1979, pp. 25–7.
19. Du Moulin 1681, I, p. 135. Cf. on the marriage analogy Kantorowicz 1957, pp. 221–3, and Hanley 1983, pp. 83–5.

Of course, there were kings who had gained simply by force of arms power over the people whom they ruled. A conquered people doubtless submitted to 'lordly' government as Le Roy described it – though even they, according to Fortescue, accepted subjugation in order to be 'protected' from other possible assailants. To that extent they shared a common aim with any people who 'incorporated themselves into a kingdom in no other way (*non alio pacto*)' than 'by their own choice'. And even an unconquered people 'wishing to erect itself' into 'a body politic' had always 'to place in authority one man for the government of all that body' which otherwise would resemble 'not a body but a trunk'. In the case of such a people, however, the kingly head 'was set up for the guardianship (*ad tutelam*) of the laws of the subjects and of their bodies and goods, and to this end he has power flowing forth from the people itself, so that it is not permitted to him to have dominion (*dominari*) over his people by any other power' (Fortescue 1949, pp. 28, 34, 30, 32). Here were pregnant terms – some more fructiferous than others, in Fortescue's usage. *Dominium* for his purposes meant governmental authority, *pace* its ethical and proprietary connotations. Nor did his use of *pactum* necessarily denote that specifically contractual relationship between king and people[20] with which scholastic thinkers were sufficiently familiar and of which radicals such as Buchanan would make vigorous play.[21] But the significance of the term *tutela* was unmistakable. The concept of the ruler as guardian of the realm and of his people's well-being had for centuries been a commonplace of juristic thought (instances in Ullmann 1981, p. 500). On Cicero's authority Salamonio would define the term in relation to princes as 'the administration (*procuratio*) of the commonwealth, for the benefit of those who are entrusted and not of the ones by whom the trust is held' (Salamonio 1544, fo. 26v). As in the marriage analogy, the king as *tutor* was once more, and literally, administrator of his charge.

Cast, then, as administrator and as *minister* not directly of God but of the realm or of the people who 'transferred'[22] power to him, the king was subject to legal constraints. Furthermore, the community's interests – rather than his own – in which he was bound to use his power were identifiable with the end of political society itself. For scholastics and humanists alike, Aristotle had persuasively formulated that final cause

20. Burns 1985, pp. 797, 788 n. 43.
21. Buchanan 1579, p. 96: 'mutua igitur regi cum civibus est pactio'.
22. 'Transmittit', in Fortescue 1949, p. 30, holding that power thereafter resided 'in the head and all the members together'; 'transtulit' in Salamonio 1544, fo. 55v, arguing that it remained ultimately with the *universus populus*. Strictly, the idea of transference married ill with the tutorial principle: it was not from the ward that a guardian received his authority (Lloyd 1981a, p. 67).

which involved far more than mere preservation: 'the end of the state is the good life' (*Politics*, 1280b39). Even Bodin, critical enough of Aristotle, endorsed that position: commonwealths were established 'for the sake of living well' (Bodin 1945, p. 276). 'Living well' signified concern for the common good as distinct from individual well-being. Men should not live, as the Englishman Thomas Starkey put it, 'to their own pleasure and profit, without regard to the weal of their country'. And although the common good had its material side, what it meant above all to Starkey as to generations of scholastic and humanist thinkers was maintenance of 'peace', avoidance of 'discord', promotion of 'concord and unity' within the commonwealth as a whole. For the sake of this true end men should cultivate 'virtue' and apply it 'to the common profit and utility'.[23] 'Virtue', indeed, might be cultivated to best purpose without benefit or otherwise of kings at all: in a regime of 'liberty', of republican self-government, and so of fulfilment of the individual in 'political life' through action as opposed to contemplation.[24] But to the English humanist, whatever the desirability of such activity, 'the mother of all virtue' was that men should be 'obedient to reason' – the efficient cause of how political society first came to be (Starkey 1540?, fo. 5r). And this line of discussion led, as in the case of the monarchical adminstrator, to the conclusion that political life and government with it must be conducted under the law. For 'the laws, which be sincere and pure reason', Starkey affirmed, 'must rule and govern the state, and not the prince after his own liberty and will' (Starkey 1871, p. 181).

iii   Custom and the rule of law

The proposition that the common good was the end of political society was applicable also to law. 'The end of law is the common good, upon which our happiness depends': thus the Spanish Dominican Domingo de Soto, in terms faithful to the traditions of Thomist Aristotelianism.[25] But law was no mere instrument for political use in pursuit of a common good which at

23. Starkey 1871, pp. 2, 46–50, 5–6; Starkey 1540?, sig. a.ijv, etc. On the idea of *pax et concordia* in pre-humanist thought, Skinner 1986; I am grateful to Professor Burns for drawing this item to my attention.
24. 'Affection' for 'liberty' or 'self-government (*del vivere libero*)' was the key to the 'greatness which Rome attained after freeing itself from its kings' (Machiavelli, *Discorsi*, II.2: 1950, I, pp. 361–2). The *locus classicus* for the ambiguities of Stoic doctrine on the action/contemplation antithesis is Cicero, *De officiis*, I.xliii–xliv. See also Pocock 1975, p. 114 and *passim*; and, for comparative comment on the positions of Leonardo Bruni, Almanno Rinuccini and others, Rubinstein 1968.
25. Soto 1569, fo. 5v, employing for 'happiness' the characteristic Thomist term *beatitudo*. Cf. Aristotle, *Nicomachean Ethics*, 1129b; Aquinas, *Summa*, Ia IIae, 90.2.

any time might be ill-advisedly conceived. By that same tradition, law was a measure of human acts in relation to justice – a property which, to Aristotle as to Plato, was essential to the very existence of the political community.[26] And although Augustine had appeared to deny the latter proposition, he too had pronounced justice to be a necessary constituent of law, so that – as Soto once more repeated – an unjust law would be a contradiction in terms.[27] It followed that law, properly conceived, afforded a people its surest means of attaining a condition at once of common good and of justice. So Fortescue, Du Moulin and others more enamoured than they of Romanist precepts could cheerfully adopt the time-honoured formula of the *Digest* for their summary definitions of law: 'the art of the good and the just'.[28] Again, Justinian's lawbooks yielded grounds for urging the exercise of political authority in accordance with law and not simply by its means, so that, as Du Moulin commented with approval, 'imperial edicts or mandates against justice or the laws are not valid' (Du Moulin 1681, III, p. 589). No writer drew the constitutionalist implications of such positions more plainly than Claude de Seyssel, himself a commentator upon the Roman texts and a self-confessed admirer of his Bartolist predecessors in the field (Seyssel 1981, p. 9). Stressing, like Starkey, the desiderata of 'concord' and 'unity' among the citizens, Seyssel found that these depended upon 'obedience to the king' (Seyssel 1961a, pp. 127, 167). But royal power was regulated by three 'bridles' – 'religion', 'justice', and '*police*'. Each of these in turn was tied to the maintenance of law.[29] And so, in sum, the 'public good' in the case of that 'most civil and best-constituted (*mieux policié*)' monarchy of France rested four-square upon laws 'established in such a way that they can scarcely be broken and annulled' (Seyssel 1961a, pp. 120, 99–100, 115).

But simply to insist upon the maintenance of law was to obscure important issues. There were varieties of law, as Aquinas had shown (*Summa*, Ia IIae, 91). It was true that all of them derived in some degree from God's eternal law, 'prime right reason', and, in the English common lawyer

---

26. Aquinas, *Summa*, Ia IIae, 90.1, 2, 95.2, 97.1. Aristotle, *Nicomachean Ethics*, 1135a1, *Politics*, 1253a36–8. Plato, *Republic*, s.427. Cf. Cicero, *De legibus*, I.vi.19 (*iuris atque iniuriae regula*).

27. Augustine, *De civitate dei*, ii.21, and xix.24, *De libero arbitrio*, i.33. Soto 1569, fo. 15r (*lex iniusta non est lex*).

28. *Digest*, I.i.1; Fortescue 1949, p. 8; Du Moulin 1681, I, p. 835.

29. The king must live 'in accordance with law and the Christian religion'; he was appointed 'primarily to maintain and do justice', and so he must govern through 'good laws, customs and ordinances'; and *police*, a concept which embraced matters as various as the preservation of the social hierarchy, the taking of counsel and the practice of trade, again was indissociable from 'laws, ordinances and praiseworthy customs' (Seyssel 1961a, pp. 116, 150–1, 154).

Christopher St German's phrase, 'synonymous' with justice. The eternal law was by definition immutable. Again, the first principles of the law of nature were 'written in the heart and so impossible to blot out nor even to alter in relation to place or time' (St German 1974, pp. 8, 14). But below such strata in the hierarchy of laws came others where change and diversity were indeed admissible. Aquinas had admitted that 'secondary precepts' of the law of nature, though deduced from its first principles, might 'nevertheless be changed on some particular occasions' (*Summa*, Ia IIae, 94.5). Human laws must be more changeable still. More specific than natural laws, they nonetheless consisted in statements of general rules; and, as Aristotle had noted, particular cases were bound to occur where rigorously to apply those rules would be to perpetrate injustice (*Nicomachean Ethics*, 1137a31–1138a3). One way of tempering 'the rigour of the law' lay in supplementing its rules with 'equity' which St German explained in terms of the principle of *epikeia*: 'an exception by divine or natural law from the general rules of human law ... which exception is tacitly understood in all general rules of positive law' (St German 1974, p. 96). To resort to 'equity' was not to alter the law itself: rather, it wss to ensure that the just intention of the law be fulfilled despite the frailty of its letter. Nevertheless, the very principle of the hierarchical relationship between natural and human law testified to the latter's mutability. For 'human law', in Soto's words, 'is derived from natural law by human reason, deriving the species from the genus'. And human reason was inherently imperfect, while human affairs were perpetually in flux. Therefore, Soto concluded, 'because human reason does not sufficiently foresee all future things, to this extent law itself is mutable'.[30]

Who, then, might do the altering? Here the Thomist dicta, especially when coupled with civilian maxims, seemed to point to a regalist answer. An act of law involved command: however beneficent and just its end, law, to be efficacious, must be imperative (*Summa*, Ia IIae, 92.2). Smith could equate it with 'the ordinance of that part which doth command' (Smith 1982, p. 50). 'In truth', declared Molina, himself a commentator upon Aquinas' ethical writings, 'the binding force of positive law springs from the command and will of the one commanding' (Molina 1602–3, I, col. 10). Surely the 'one commanding' must be the monarchical ruler. The 'force of law', as the *Digest* statement of the *lex regia* had it, lay in 'what has satisfied the prince' (*Digest*, 1.4.1.1). Of course, power of command was not

---

30. Soto 1569, fos. 17v, 26v; cf. Aquinas, *Summa*, Ia IIae, 97.1 (*responsio 2*).

confined to the king alone. Among others who exercised it were noblemen holding fiefs and able, as even the regalist Barthélemy de Chasseneuz recognised, 'to make edicts and statutes within the limits' of their jurisdictions (Chasseneuz 1528, fo. 377r). But although in a sense such noblemen were tantamount to 'princes', it was by virtue of the king's concession that they enjoyed both the fiefs and the powers in question. Moreover, their 'edicts' had only a limited application, could not prevail against the king's own legislative acts, and, strictly, were not to be accounted 'laws' at all. So Bodin argued, with a degree of emphasis which led him in due course to formulate a definition of law purely in terms of 'the commandment of the sovereign' (Bodin 1583, p. 216; cf. 1945, p. 177).

But few contemporary thinkers would follow the theorist of legislative sovereignty quite so far. While command was a necessary property of law, it was not sufficient for law to exist. Civilian maxims, for all their voluntarist and absolutist implications, had long since been interpreted to demonstrate a distinction between law as such and the ruler's will. That the prince was *lex animata* signified to dialecticians the presence at least of inanimate law, separate from his command.[31] That he held all rights (*iura*) 'in the casket of his breast'[32] meant his possessing knowledge – *certaine science*, in the terminology of the enabling clause in French royal acts – of rights which need not have originated with him and of which he must take full account in positing or activating laws of his own. Whether or not such rights were 'natural' to men, they could certainly be categorised with a range of qualities which should appertain to laws. Isidore of Seville had provided a seminal list of those qualities; and early modern jurists continued with Aquinas to construct their analyses around it.[33] While justice and 'common utility' were conspicuous in Isidore's formula, it specified as well that positive laws should be 'in accordance with the custom of the country'. And this last drew attention to a 'ground of law' quite other than the ruler's will and of central constitutionalist importance. It indicated how the people, for all that they had transferred power to the ruler, nevertheless retained extensive means of regulating their own affairs in at least quasi-legislative fashion. For custom was made by the people. It differed radically from positive laws, which derived their force from

---

31. Maxim in *Novellae*, 105.2.4; cf. Kantorowicz 1957, pp. 134–5.
32. Maxim derivsed from Code, VI.23.19.2 (*toto iure quod nostris est scrinis constitutum*); cf. Post 1953, p. 311.
33. Isidore, *Etymologiarum*, v.xxi (*Patrologia Latina*, LXXXII, p. 203). St German 1974, p. 27; Rebuffi 1613, p. 16; Suárez 1612, pp. 31ff.

instantaneous acts whereas custom, remarked Bodin, 'gains its force little by little, and over long years by a common consent of all' (Bodin 1583, p. 222). The element of consent was vital, as Bartolus had stressed and as the Toulouse jurist Jean de Coras accepted: custom was 'that which the established practices of men have brought in by the tacit consent of the citizens' (Coras 1603, qu. Fell 1983, I, p. 117 n. 15). Indeed, owing to that element custom was tantamount to a contractual agreement. Echoing Bartolus more appreciatively, Salamonio could define it as 'a kind of compact (*pactio*), if it is concluded by the citizens' common consent'.[34] Likewise, Du Moulin could refer to it as the *pactum commune civium*; and, as he observed elsewhere, 'the substance and basis of all contracts begins from and consists in the concurrence and consent of the co-contracting parties' (Du Moulin 1681, II, p. 680, IV, p. 402).

Long debated, the proposition remained contentious that imperative law should be compatible with consensual custom despite the divergence of their sources. The difference between them might in a measure be reduced by detecting, with Vitoria, a contractual element even in law that emanated from the ruler's will. According to the Dominican, 'although the establishing of law is a matter for the will of the king, it is not a matter for his will whether he is bound or not bound thereby: just as in the case of pacts, for whoever enters freely into pacts is still bound by them' (Vitoria 1933–6, II, p. 206). But it was one thing to contend that a ruler was bound by his own laws, quite another to hold that his law-making power was limited by custom, and yet another to demonstrate whether and how the Isidorean requirement should be satisfied. The simplest solution was to dismiss that requirement altogether. Thus the Parisian legist Etienne Pasquier, asserting that custom must always give way to law: 'law being made by the prince and custom by the people, a custom which runs directly counter to law is never admissible' (Pasquier 1723, I, col. 1092). Other thinkers were not so sanguine. Soto analysed the problem by taking up Isidore's own differentiation between written and unwritten custom, and linking it with different forms of rule. Unwritten custom 'has the force of law'. In a republic, custom promulgated as law 'by the consent of the commonwealth' would coincide with 'the usage of the people'. Under princely rule, however, 'custom is not law of itself', but depended for its 'interpretation' upon 'the will of the prince'. Therefore, 'law is not moved according to custom' – and yet 'it should not conflict with the custom of the

---

34. Salamonio 1544, fo. 19v, in effect applying Bartolus' own adaptation of the Digest phrase (1.3.35: *conventio civium*) to show that custom was equivalent to law. On Bartolus' contribution and the significance of 'consent' in his interpretation, Ullmann 1962, p. 714 and *passim*.

country' (Soto 1569, fos. 14v–15v, 27r–v). While the position was ambivalent, it implied a potentially useful analytical distinction between the substance of a measure and its motive force, comparable with the difference between inanimate and animate law. But given, as the Spanish fiscal Castillo de Bobadilla argued, that the king might be assumed 'to confirm all reasonable customs', then 'the custom of the country overcomes the statute and has more force than law' (Castillo de Bobadilla 1597, I, p. 568). In any case, the converse of Pasquier's bald assertion was equally tenable, even in Paris. There Pierre Rebuffi, devoting to Isidore's formula an extensive gloss, could propound that 'a royal edict made against custom has no force'. It was true that the ruler could dispense with custom in particular cases. But such enactments were in effect ones rather of equity than of law, for law was by definition general. And, in general, laws that ran counter to custom endangered the community's well-being – the end of political society, and of law itself. For, as Rebuffi argued, 'a man cannot be bound by law in such a way that he alone in the society of others would have contrary rules of behaviour and live according to them. Therefore, a law against the custom of the inhabitants is cancelled by the contrary custom' (Rebuffi 1613, pp. 9, 33–4).

One means of avoiding confrontation between law and custom lay in assigning each to a distinct sphere. According to the Digest, the public was distinguishable from the private sphere of affairs, *ius publicum* from *ius privatum* (Digest, 1.1.1.2). Hailed by Du Moulin a 'the prime and supreme division of jurisprudence', it tallied with his own association of custom with contractual agreements between particular parties. To the private sphere belonged 'contracts, wills, dues and obligations for landholding, inheritance practices' – all matters concerning individual or family affairs and therefore subject to 'what the usage of men allows'; and a good king would be 'neither capable nor desirous nor mindful of derogating from it' (Du Moulin 1681, I, pp. 738, 22, II, p. 731). The public sphere involved, as the legist Louis Charondas Le Caron explained, matters 'which concern the condition of the commonwealth (*l'estat de la république*) and not of each one in particular'. It included the 'authority' and 'jurisdiction' of 'magistrates', the management of 'war, peace', and military recruitment – all things 'without which the public estate cannot subsist and endure' (Le Caron 1607, pt i, col. 60). These matters, moreover were subject to the ruler's prerogative power and therefore to his edicts.[35] But although attempts at

---

35. Thireau 1980, pp. 237–9. Cf. Smith 1982, pp. 85–8, the terminology alluding to the traditional distinction between the ruler's 'absolute' and his 'ordinary' power.

specific differentiation between the public and the private sphere had a bearing upon the question of mixed government, they did not suffice to resolve the difficulty of the relation between custom and the ruler's law. As Du Moulin himself acknowledged, custom embraced 'all things which concern the necessities of civil and human life' – a point implicit in Rebuffi's observation on 'rules of behaviour' which governed how men lived 'in the society of others'.[36] Coras summarised the problem succinctly: 'that which is of public utility bears upon the convenience of individuals', while 'that which principally concerns the utility of private persons is linked by consequence to the utility of the commonwealth'. In his opinion it followed that the ruler's law must be preferred to custom, for public should always take precedence over private concerns.[37] Yet it could be argued to the contrary that custom not only had a justifiable relevance to the conduct of public affairs, but even had shaped the prime elements of public law.

Those elements were the 'fundamental laws'.[38] In France they related to properties which Du Moulin had ascribed to the realm in terms of *dominium* (see above, p. 262). The ruler could not alienate any part of the territories and rights of the royal domain; nor could he devise the realm at will, for the crown must descend by primogeniture in the male line, and females were barred from the royal succession. Arguing from the writings of 'all the old historians of our Francogallia', the radical François Hotman maintained that each of these 'definite laws' sprang from 'established and ancient custom'.[39] Even the more absolutist but no less historically minded Bodin of the *République* cited with approval evidence that the kingdom's laws of succession were rooted in the 'ancient custom' of the Franks (Bodin 1583, p. 983). To these elements other historians would add further 'beautiful laws' by which the kingdom was 'established' and which together constituted its '*police*' (Du Haillan 1609, fo. 10v). Paradoxically, the more numerous those elements, the greater the possibility of ascribing at least some of them to kings 'acting of their own volition' (Du Haillan 1609, fos. 172v, 170v; cf. Pocock 1957, p. 17). Yet all such laws imposed limits upon royal power; and the dominant tradition of thought in sixteenth-century France

36. Du Moulin 1681, I, p. 22. For Rebuffi, see above, p. 269; and, for 'mixed government', below, pp. 273ff.
37. Coras 1603, qu. in Fell 1983, I, p. 198 n. 22, also p. 197.
38. A concept certainly present in the sixteenth century, though the term itself may perhaps be later in the case of France. See Hanley 1983, p. 50 n. 4; but cf. Lemaire 1907, dating the term's introduction to Leaguer propaganda of the 1570s. For England, Gough 1955, p. 12.
39. Hotman 1972, pp. 458–78 (a new chapter in the 1586 edition).

accounted at least for those prime 'fundamental laws' on the basis of customary usage (Church 1941, pp. 83–93). In England, which boasted no comparable array of 'definite laws', the concept of fundamental law was nonetheless familiar, and even more far-reaching. In his lengthy discourse upon the 'grounds of English law (*fundamenta legis anglie*)', St German gave greatest prominence to 'general customs of old time used throughout the realm' which 'in the proper sense are called the common law'. These were what underpinned the exercise of public authority as well as the conduct of private affairs. Thus, while continental jurists might locate the jurisdiction of courts in the public sphere and derive them from acts of institution or concession by the ruler, in England 'the custom of the realm is the source and foundation (*fundamentum*) of the various courts in that realm' (St German 1974, pp. 72, 44, 46, and 30–77 *passim*). And it was in the light of the 'reason' of the common law that judges in those same courts interpreted even the public enactments of king-in-parliament (Gough 1955, pp. 18–21). In the case of England it seemed evident that over the public and private spheres alike the rule of custom prevailed, at least in the sense of the rational principles of the common law.

Custom, then, rested upon the concurrence of the people concerned, had a bearing upon the common good, and was itself a foundation of law. It followed that the altering of law from time to time must call for some reference to the people. From Fortescue onwards English thinkers endorsed this conclusion to the full. What Starkey chose to call 'the civil law' consisted of 'custom and law' taken together; and this law, unlike the given law of nature, 'taketh effect of the opinion of man' and 'resteth wholly in his consent' (Starkey 1871, pp. 15, 121, cf. 1540?, fos. 71r, 73r–4r). On the continent, more orthodox civilians could also arrive at an advocacy of consent, though by a different route. The maxim *quod omnes similiter tangit ab omnibus comprobetur*,[40] originally specific to the conduct of joint guardianship in Roman law, had passed through the hands of medieval canonists and conciliarists to graduate from a private-law rule of procedure into a 'principle of public law' (Congar 1958, pp. 211–12, 258). Radicals such as Hotman in France or John Junius de Jonghe in the Netherlands vouched it to warrant the view that matters concerning the well-being of the people as a whole should be 'decided upon' by their 'counsel and

40. Code, VI.59.5.2. As has often been remarked, the canon law adaptation of the formula in the thirteenth-century *Liber Sextus* came closer to stipulating consent: *quod omnes tangit debet ab omnibus approbari* (*Corpus iuris canonici*, II, col. 1122, *regula iuris*, xxix).

authority'.[41] In early modern constitutional thought, however, the *quod omnes tangit* formula figured less frequently than another which fifteenth-century conciliarists had again revived in the wake of earlier civilians: *rex major singulis minor universis*.[42] This maxim gained added significance by association with the doctrine that the ruler was an administrator who obtained his authority from the people as a whole. Matters that touched the very form and survival of the entity entrusted to him ought certainly to be referred afresh to its consent. Thus Mariana, rejecting the opinion of his fellow Jesuit Molina,[43] repeatedly invoked the maxim in question to prove the king's inability without 'the consent and definite decision of the whole people' to alter laws governing the royal succession and the 'form of religion' too (Mariana 1605, pp. 68, 70, 71–3, 81). Taxation also, though in a sense separable from the fundamental laws as such, was nonetheless linked with the issue of the community's preservation. As Soto observed, while the 'commonwealth has transferred its power to the prince' its members had not transferred to him 'their own material resources (*proprias facultates*)'; and yet it might be 'necessary' for him 'to make use of' these 'for the protection of the commonwealth' (Soto 1569, fo. 107v). He had, therefore, in the view of the French chancellor Michel de L'Hôpital, to ask his 'subjects' that they 'should consent' to extraordinary subventions, his prime justification for doing so being the 'necessity' of the defence of the realm.[44]

Thus, although human law was mutable and doubtless – in a monarchy – derived its force from the king, he could act of his own volition only to a limited degree. So much followed from the doctrine of the rule of law: the doctrine that power should be exercised in accordance with a normative system which had as its end the good of the community. Within the system positive human law formed a stratum bounded and conditioned by the

---

41. Hotman 1972, p. 296; Junius de Jonghe, *Discours* (1574), in Kossmann and Mellink 1974, p. 124. For the significance of Hotman's use of the maxim, Giesey 1972. On the importance of the king's taking 'counsel', see Pasquier 1723, I, col. 81; Seyssel 1961a, p. 133. Continental thinkers distinguished more circumspectly than their English counterparts between 'consultation' and 'consent'.
42. Tierney 1975, p. 246, for the medieval development of the maxim.
43. Above, p. 261 – though according to Molina the king could not alter the succession laws for these concerned 'the whole commonwealth'; and even 'the commonwealth itself cannot do it' after the realm's first institution: 1602–3, II, col. 277.
44. L'Hôpital 1824–6, I, p. 392, II, pp. 163–5. Others matters of policy where consent might be due included monetary mutation. Cf. Smith 1982, p. 86, assigning this to the king's 'absolute power', with Du Moulin 1681, VI, p. 119, holding that it should be done 'not by the prince alone in a monarchy ... but also according to the consent and usage of the people, and the custom of commerce'.

imperatives of divinely instituted and natural law on the one hand and the customs of the community on the other. The limitations upon royal power were consistent with a concept of a mixed constitution or even of divided sovereignty: that king and people should act jointly in certain areas of rule or, *mutatis mutandis*, that each respectively was now supreme and now subordinate. Such ideas, as Bodin and others recognised, were beset both with logical and with practical difficulties.[45] Logic at least was better satisfied by the thesis that kings were administrators and not proprietors of power for their use of which they stood always answerable under the law to whoever had appointed them. Alternatively, it could be argued that the king himself was head and therefore part of the community which as a whole stood supreme. Insofar as his use of power was limited by that whole or by the legitimate roles of its other members, this meant not a division of sovereignty so much as a mixture or distribution of governmental functions. But to present any argument purely in such terms as these was to rely upon mere analogy and abstraction. If a people had a collective constitutional role, by means of what organic institution might they perform it? If governmental functions were to be distributed, what were the organs that should exercise them, and the constitutional significance of the relations of those organs to one another and to the king? While some of these questions might be easily answered, together they too confronted would-be constitutionalists with considerable difficulties.

iv   Mixed constitution or mixed government

In the kingdoms of western Europe it was obvious that not all of the people could participate directly in constitutional or in collective governmental affairs. Almain summarised the difficulty: 'the community is not able easily to come together regularly'. The solution, however, was equally plain: 'it should delegate [its authority] to another or to others who can easily assemble'.[46] Holders of delegated authority were tantamount to proctorial representatives. Given that their principals had assigned them full power (*plena potestas*), a principle which again had crept under canonist influence from private law into the conduct of public affairs, they could perform whatever those principals or constituents were competent to do as if the latter had been present (Post 1943, pp. 363–4; cf. Brown 1972, and below,

---

45. See below, pp. 281–2, for Hooker's opinion.
46. Almain, *Quaestio resumptiva*, in Gerson 1706, II, col. 965.

p. 293). Hence the civilian Smith's elucidation of the position of the English parliament. Its 'consent' was 'taken to be every man's consent' because 'every Englishman is intended to be there present, either in person or by procuration and attorneys'. While Almain had thought in corporationist terms of the community and its powers of delegation, Smith by his phrasing adumbrated an individualistic conception of the basis of parliamentary authority. But with those phrases he coupled the view that parliament 'representeth and hath the power of the whole realm, both the head and the body' (Smith 1982, p. 79). Hackneyed enough, the metaphor nonetheless invoked an alternative idea of representation, less legal than metaphysical though rooted once more in medieval ecclesiology (Kantorowicz 1957, pp. 206–7). Properly constituted representatives together 'epitomised' or embodied the *corpus mysticum reipublicae*.[47] Meeting as an assembly of estates in the presence of the king, they made actual what must otherwise remain an abstraction. They gave substance to the qualities and collective will which appertained to the people not severally, but as a corporate whole.

The people, then, had institutional means of performing whatever role or function that should belong to them. Yet regalists might reply that the essence of the realm was sufficiently represented by the king in person. Was he not the head of the corporate entity in question? Was not the head the seat of reason – the very medium of a people's attaining to its political form, and of that form's retention (see above, n. 8 and p. 260)? But the person of the king was a complex phenomenon. Du Moulin explained that while 'the majesty and dignity contained in the commonwealth' were indeed 'represented' by the prince, they appertained to his 'intellectual person' as distinct from his 'private person'. And while that 'private person' was 'the organ and instrument of the said intellectual person', other organs also 'form part of the mystic person of the prince' (Du Moulin 1681, VI, pp. 513–14, 408). Indeed, that plurality of 'representatives' could be seen to function with the king himself as the realm's joint guardians, ensuring that 'what touches all' should be 'approved by all' in the maxim's root civilian sense. Among those other organs was the royal council, which the regalists Chasseneuz and Charles de Grassaille described in concert as 'part of the prince's person'. If he was *lex animata*, his councillors 'are the soul of the prince (*anima principis*) and make the king reign' (Chasseneuz 1546, fo.

---

47. *Vindiciae contra tyrannos*: Mornay 1979, pp. 62, 228. For Du Moulin's and Hotman's citations of the idea as expressed by Jean de Terre Rouge in 1418/19, Giesey 1960, p. 158.

148r, col. 2; Grassaille 1538, p. 166). Among them, too, were members of the judiciary: those of the Paris *parlement* saw themselves as a 'mystical body ... representing the person of the king', and their court as 'the king's true seat, authority, magnificence and majesty' (qu. Maugis 1913–16, I, p. 375). A comparable status could be claimed for the Estates General itself. In respect of that assembly Du Moulin repeatedly grounded his opinion upon a declaration of Charlemagne's successor 'Louis the Pious, first French emperor of that name'. On that evidence it was 'certain that the majesty, splendour and virtue of the empire resides rather in the assembly of the members of the estates of the empire than in the sole head taken separately, or in the organic person of the emperor' (Du Moulin 1681, IV, p. 514, cf. p. 418).

However, merely to identify such candidates for association with the ruler's person was not enough to clarify their respective constitutional roles. In view of the doctrine of the rule of law, the position of the judiciary and of the people's representative assembly lay especially open to discussion. In England the discussion was muted. Fortescue might insist upon the independence of the judges who would apply the law without fear or favour 'even if the king should command the contrary by his letters or by word of mouth' (Fortescue 1949, p. 126). Later judges might incautiously pronounce that the common law as interpreted in the courts 'doth control acts of parliament and sometimes shall adjudge them to be void'.[48] But Smith's contribution carried greater conviction: that in England 'the most high and absolute power' resided in parliament which coupled legislative with judicial authority, abrogating 'old laws', making 'new', and 'giving judgement' between 'private man and private man' (Smith 1982, pp. 78, 89). In France these issues excited keener debate. On the question of the judiciary's independence Seyssel outbid Fortescue: judges of the *parlements* were 'perpetual and it is not in the power of kings to depose them'. Furthermore, their courts 'were instituted principally for this end and purpose of bridling the absolute power that kings would use'. But all this fell within the category of 'distributive justice'.[49] As to collective matters concerning the community as a whole, both Le Roy and Du Haillan seemed to postulate a separation of powers between the *parlements* and the estates, the one dealing with 'particular causes', the other with 'great affairs' and 'general complaints' (Le Roy 1598, p. 230; Du

48. Coke's notorious words on Dr Bonham's case, 1606 (8 Coke Reports (1658), p. 118).
49. Seyssel 1961a, pp. 117–18. Cf, Seyssel 1961b, p. 81 where he credited 'the sovereign courts' with 'inappellable and final cognizance' of 'all ordinances concerning the interests of parties'.

Haillan 1609, fos. 184v–5r). The view approximated to the alleged distinction between the private and the public sphere of law. At least in respect of the *parlements* it could commend itself to L'Hôpital who held that the 'function (*estat*)' of those 'sovereign courts' was strictly 'to adjudicate differences between subjects and to administer justice' (L'Hôpital 1824–6, II, pp. 12–13, 60–6). But, as Du Haillan himself noted, the Paris *parlement* claimed also a legislative function (Du Haillan 1609, fo. 182v). Its leading members asserted as much, in direct response to the chancellor (L'Hôpital 1824–6, II, pp. 17–18; Hanley 1983, p. 151). The authority of Pasquier was on the magistrates' side: the court 'was always intended for public affairs and verification of edicts' – a procedure whereby kings submitted to 'the civility of the law', and the people at large 'observe without complaint' any act so verified (Pasquier 1723, I, cols. 64, 66).

And yet those who urged the significance of such institutions themselves shrank from the ultimate constitutionalist implications of their own arguments. In the last resort the role of the king himself was overriding. 'To rule', announced Smith in his work's opening sentences, was 'to have the supreme and highest authority of commandment'. And even in parliament 'the last and highest commandment' appertained to 'the prince' who 'is the life, the head and the authority of all things that be done in the realm of England'.[50] Seyssel was no less emphatic: notwithstanding the *parlement*'s functions, the king must always preserve 'his sovereignty and pre-eminence over all his subjects, of whatsoever dignity, estate, or condition they may be, without allowing his power to be lost or usurped in any manner whatsoever' (Seyssel 1961a, p. 157). Du Haillan dismissed objections that his statements adduced traditional Aristotelian recommendations of a mixed constitution with supreme authority either shared or divided among monarchical, aristocratic, and democratic elements. For 'we do not say at all that France is a state (*estat*) composed of three modes of government, nor divided in three, each having its own absolute and equal power'. The king 'is absolutely royal, monarchical, and sovereign, bearing all the marks of absolute power and sovereignty'(Du Haillan 1609, fo. 171r). As for separation of powers, L'Hôpital described how the king himself gave 'justice to each and every one' and was 'legislator' too. Furthermore, he could do these things in assemblies of estates as well as in

50. Smith 1982, pp. 49, 78, 88; cf. Bodin 1583, p. 141, maintaining that, for all the activities of the English parliament and the consent that it expressed, 'the entire sovereignty belongs without division to the kings', and that parliamentary 'consent' in no way derogated from the royal power of 'command'.

royal *séances* of the *parlements* (L'Hôpital 1824–6, I, p. 380). The latter's legislative pretensions might in some measure be accommodated when the monarch held his *lit de justice* assembly to deal with matters of public or constitutional law. On those solemn – and infrequent – ritualistic occasions, magistrates in the setting of their court deliberated with the king, peers, and other dignitaries of the realm upon affairs touching what Francis I termed 'the entire universal monarchy of the kingdom'. But L'Hôpital did not hesitate to use such an occasion to stress that the king was as much overseer of justice as maker of ordinances for the public weal.[51]

Even so, a unitary form of constitution with supreme authority vested comprehensively in the monarch was no bar to a mixed form of government with orderly distribution of functions among the members of political society. In the case of England, according to Smith, lords and commoners from the yeomanry upwards participated in governing the country at large: each 'hath his part and administration in judgements, corrections of defaults, in election of offices'. And yet, 'I cannot understand that our nation hath used any other and general authority in this realm neither aristocratical nor democratical, but only the royal and kingly majesty' (Smith 1982, pp. 77, 56). In the case of France, Du Moulin found enlightenment in the remainder of Louis the Pious' declaration to the estates. The 'ministry' of the realm – as distinct from its 'majesty' – was 'divided in parts, so that each one of you in his place and order may be recognised to have a part of our ministry'. But even 'in this ministry the highest place may be seen to consist in our person'.[52] Considerations of order dictated that 'public commodities, honours, and charges' be 'divided according to the condition of every estate', wrote Le Roy; for every political society 'is composed of degrees or estates, as it were parts, which estates must be held in concord by a due proportion of each to other, even as the harmony in music' (Le Roy 1598, pp. 263–4). The musical analogy correlated in turn with that elaborate number mysticism so beloved of Renaissance Neoplatonist metaphysicians. 'Harmonical proportion' mixed the 'arithmetical' and 'geometrical' proportions which were appropriate respectively to democratic and aristocratic 'forms of government' (Bodin 1583, p. 1017; cf. Le Roy 1598, p. 241). But, as Bodin

---

51. Hanley 1983, pp. 75, 167–9; cf. the author's claim that the emergence of the *lit de justice* assembly in the sixteenth century marked 'a new theory of the ancient constitution, separating constitutional-legislative and judicial authority' (p. 172).

52. Du Moulin 1681, II, p. 537: although the syntax is convoluted it does not seem intended to apply 'division' to the 'highest place'. Hotman quoted the same extract, but not the earlier part of the declaration (above, p. 275): see Hotman 1972, pp. 294–6, 346.

insistently explained, 'the constitution of a commonwealth '*l'estat d'une république*) is different from its government ànd administration' (Bodin 1583, pp. 273, 1050, etc.). 'Harmonical' distribution of governmental functions was fully compatible with a 'pure' and 'well-ordered monarchy'. In such a monarchy the 'sovereign prince', who was 'as the intellect', also represented the 'unity' from which 'depends the union of all numbers', so that from his power 'all others [orderly] depend'. And while those dependent 'estates' rightly 'have a part in offices, benefices, judicatures, and honourable charges' and so formed 'a pleasant harmony', the prince's 'majesty' suffered 'no more division than unity itself'.[53]

So the regalist position comfortably accommodated the desiderata of mixed government with their attendant reciprocity of governmental with social order. Against that position one thinker at least summoned up enough conviction to prescribe a form of rule calculated 'to restrain from the prince such high authority' and equipped with institutions grounded upon all the main constitutional elements: that the king was appointed by the people and remained their minister, subject to law, subordinate to the community as a whole, and dependent at all times upon its counsel and consent. Not content merely to argue for the popular origins of kingship, Starkey urged the merits of elective monarchy. Every king in turn should be 'chosen by free election of the citizens in the country', able to 'make him a prince and him that is a tyrant so to depose' (Starkey 1871, pp. 102, 107, 167). Once appointed, his use of power should be regulated by a system of checks and balances. The system consisted in a series of councils: one to attend upon the king himself so that without its 'authority' he 'should do nothing pertaining to the state of his realm'; another to act as watchdog over the former, to choose its members and to 'represent the whole state'; and a parliament to elect and authorise the latter council in turn whilst not itself meeting except upon some great occasion (*ibid.*, pp. 169–70, 182). The scheme postulated some division of functions. In addition to distributing offices, the king's council should act as an administrative tribunal; and for its part the council of 'state' should deal with foreign affairs. But the distinguishing feature of Starkey's prescription for a 'mixed state' was his explicit intention to ensure that in it no 'one part hath full authority' and so

---

53. Bodin 1583, pp. 264, 1056–7, preferring Plato's to Aristotle's view of 'unity' which 'is not a number at all, nor to be ranked among the numbers'. The word 'orderly' was inserted by Richard Knolles in his 1606 translation of the *République* (Bodin 1962, p. 791), a version based upon both the French and Latin texts and rigorously faithful to neither.

that each principal 'part' should act continually as a check upon the doings of the rest (*ibid.*, pp. 170, 181).

A community with faulty institutions, Starkey believed, must lack material well-being. His strictures upon England's social and economic needs reverberated in the writings of other 'commonwealthmen' (see Jones 1970). But his specific proposals for constitutional emendation – the proposals of an enthusiast for positive reform by means of strong and effective rule – remained a dead letter, unpublished in his lifetime and for centuries afterwards. While the elements of constitutionalism were grist to the mill of outright resistance theorists, more moderate thinkers who also entertained them fought shy of seeming to emasculate the king in normal times – of advocating a genuine distribution of power among institutional structures in a manner that would reduce him to the status of a mere executive. Even Mariana, momentarily inclined to ascribe just such a status to kings and no moderate in his advice for removing tyrants, 'freely' allowed 'supreme regnal power in the kingdom to exist in all things which by the practice of the people, by established custom and by settled law are permitted to the will of the prince'. In these respects, 'whether military affairs or declaring law to the subjects or creating commanders and magistrates', the king was greater 'not only than individuals, but also than the whole'. It was true that matters such as taxation and the fundamental laws were 'reserved' to the whole people 'or those who administer its parts, men of the first rank chosen from all the orders', when they 'assemble in one place'. But for the rest, and manifest tyranny apart, 'there is no one who should resist [the ruler] nor examine the reason for his conduct' (Mariana 1605, pp. 70, 72–3; cf. Skinner 1978, II, pp. 346–7). Such ideas were better attuned than Starkey's to the prevailing mood as western Europe approached the age of absolutism.

v   England: Hooker

In England successful royal government rested heavily upon the cooperation of noble and landed elites in the communities of the realm: men who in the course of the sixteenth century, were acquiring an intensified involvement in royal administration at the local level and at least the rudiments of a legal education as well. Taught at the Inns of Court as distinct from the universities where continental lawyers got their schooling, England's remarkably unified common law differed in vital respects from European traditions so permeated with civilian influences. A fundamental difference lay in the extent to which common law procedures revolved around the role of the lay jury. As with legislative procedure, the outcome of legal process hinged upon the prior approbation of representatives of the communities concerned. It was here, in the mode of establishing proof through jury trial together with the mode of establishing statute through parliamentary assent, that Fortescue discerned the distinguishing characteristic and surest guarantee of the English form of rule as *dominium politicum et regale*. In his view, a principal mark of the excellence of that form of rule lay in its continuity and lack of change: since its foundation 'the realm has been ruled continuously by the same customs as it is now' (Fortescue 1949, p. 38). Yet the Tudor regime in due course carried through changes so significant in their effects upon the secular and ecclesiastical institutions of the realm as to amount, it has been argued, to a revolution (Elton 1953). At least on the religious front, the changes in question were successively and directly shaped by the monarch's own predilections – a determining factor implicitly acknowledged in the assumptions of Stephen Gardiner and Edward Foxe that what must replace the authority of Rome was a personal royal supremacy over the *ecclesia anglicana*.[54] Even so, English political thinkers remained steadfast with Fortescue in canvassing the themes of consultation, consent, and the rule of law. In the years of the Marian reaction those themes reinforced the version of resistance theory presented by the Calvinist John Ponet: that kingship was 'an office upon trust', that kings ought 'to be obedient and subject to the positive laws of their country', that the making of laws required 'the consent of the people' which had historically to be sought in 'parliaments', and that 'men may revoke their proxies and letters of attorney when it pleaseth them: much more when they see their proctors and attorneys abuse' those delegated powers (Ponet 1556, sig. C.vij.b, B.vj.b, G.vj).

From the Calvinist standpoint the Elizabethan religious settlement removed the need for extremes of resistance, though not for pressure to remodel yet again a church 'but halfly reformed'. In order to vindicate that settlement with its endorsement of the royal supremacy and to disarm its Puritan critics, Richard Hooker began in 1593 to publish his eight books *Of the Lawes of Ecclesiasticall Politie*.[55] While much of the work dealt in

---

54. Gardiner 1930, pp. 114–16, 156, etc; Foxe 1548, fos. lxiiii[r], lxxi[r], etc. On the Elizabethan settlement of religion as the product of the queen's intentions, Jones 1982.
55. All references are by Keble's divisions of Hooker's chapters, as given in the Belknap Press edition (1977–82, ed. Speed Hill).

theological controversy, it examined afresh the familiar themes of Tudor political literature. Hooker's treatment of those themes was philosophically more ambitious and more systematic than those of any of his English contemporaries. He claimed 'coherence' for his treatment, with the 'more general meditations' of the earlier portions illuminating and reciprocally illuminated by the 'specialities' of the later (Preface, 7.6–7, 1.1.2). Authority came ultimately from God. In some cases He appointed kings directly. In others – as, evidently, the English case – He left men 'free' to 'make choice of their own governor' (VIII.2.5; cf.1.10.4). Nevertheless, 'all government was instituted' for the 'common good', goodness being the 'perfection' to which all things 'incline' (VIII.3.4; 1.5.1–2). The 'most certain token of evident goodness' was 'the universal consent of men' (1.8.3). But the freedom and consent in question were scarcely matters of men's un-trammelled volition. They were driven to make their choice of governor by consequence of 'natural inclination, whereby all men desire sociable life and fellowship' (1.10.1). For social life was a theatre of 'mutual grievances, injuries and wrongs'; and from this condition men had no escape, 'but only by growing unto composition and agreement amongst themselves, by ordaining some kind of government public, and by yielding themselves subject thereunto' (1.10.4). Even so, it was from 'the whole entire body politic' and by its consent that such a king as England's received his 'power of dominion' (VIII.3.2). The same principle of consent applied to the church, viewed as a 'natural society' (1.15.2). Resorting, as in his teleological account of 'goodness', to Aristotelian metaphysics, Hooker argued that 'church' and 'commonwealth' were 'names betokening accidents unabstracted'; and such names 'betoken not only those accidents but also, together with them, the subjects whereunto they cleave' (VIII.1.5; cf. Gardiner 1930, pp. 92ff). The 'subjects' in question were the members of the society of England: 'with us one society is both the church and commonwealth' (VIII.1.7). And just as the entire 'commonwealth' might bestow 'dominion over itself' upon a king, so too 'by human right' might a Christian king receive 'supreme power in ecclesiastical affairs' (VIII.3.1).

The question arose, in what sense did 'dominion' or 'supreme power' appertain to the monarch? While it was true that 'the king through his supreme power may do sundry great things himself', there were other things, such as altering 'the nature of pleas' or of courts, which he 'alone hath no power to do'. Yet it did not follow that the power in question was divided. Hooker was at pains to stress how 'inconveniences may grow where states are subject unto sundry supreme authorities'. Rather, the power of the king was limited by law: 'unto all his proceedings', Hooker insisted, 'the law itself is a rule' (VIII.3.1–4). But laws in turn were mutable. Elaborating upon the Thomist account of the hierarchy of laws, Hooker argued that every level of human law and even divine law too 'containeth sundry both natural and positive laws'. The latter were 'changeable according as the matter itself is concerning which they were first made'. The making and altering of divine law was the province of 'God Himself' (I.15.1, 3). As for human laws, the principle of universal consent in respect of that 'goodness' which was the 'end' of society and government applied equally to them: for laws were the means of rendering social and governmental actions 'suitable, fit and correspondent unto their end' (I.2.1). Men should 'make their own laws' (VIII.6.5). Whatever the 'power of dominion' which a community first possessed and then might transfer to its king, the 'principal use' of 'public power' was 'to give laws unto all that are under it';[56] and 'diligent care' should be taken that 'the commonwealth do not clean resign up herself and make over this power wholly into the hands of any one'. That power of making laws 'should belong to the whole, not to any certain part of a political body' (VIII.6.1, 5). And in England 'the body of the whole realm' was 'the parliament' where, 'although we be not personally ourselves present, notwithstanding our assent is, by reason of others agents there in our behalf' (I.10.8).

The royal supremacy thus emerged as a supremacy of king-in-parliament. While the functions of government were divided, it was there, in parliament, that a unified supremacy of power seemed to lie. But, at considerable cost to the coherence of his treatment, Hooker was not content to leave the matter there. Even though the king's position could be described as one of 'dependency' upon 'the whole entire body politic',[57] the degree of his dependency remained tenuous. It sprang from that initial 'composition and agreement' which men had made 'amongst themselves', and their 'ordering some kind of government public' to escape the consequences of their natural sociability (I.10.4). Hence, at least in the English case, kings 'were first instituted by agreement and composition made with them over whom they reign, how far their power may lawfully extend' (VIII.3.3). Here was the language of contract, and with it a possibility of distinguishing a social from a governmental compact, and the latter in turn from an agreement with a king. Yet Hooker did not pursue such distinctions, either in anticipation of his seventeenth-century suc-

56. I.16.5; cf. Bodin 1583, p. 221, on the 'first mark of sovereignty'.
57. VIII.3.2, citing the 'maior singulis universis minor' formula.

cessors into the sphere of social contract and individual natural rights,[58] or even with his own contemporaries into the realms of resistance theory. Considerations of compact might serve to elucidate the origins of royal government. They amounted to very little by way of offering practical restraints upon a king. Agreements or compositions of whatever kind could scarcely have the status of contract unless they were legally enforceable. No means of enforcement figured in Hooker's account of the king's position. On the contrary: after the monarch's first institution, the initiative lay plainly with him.

For kings succeeded one another not 'by the voluntary deed of the people', but by hereditary right. And with the passage of time those first 'articles of compact' were mostly 'either clean worn out of knowledge, or else known unto very few' (VIII.3.2–3). It was true that subsequently they were supplemented by 'positive laws' which, like all laws, were acts of 'public obligation'. Even so, and for all the emphasis upon parliamentary consent, in the making of laws the king had 'chiefest sway' (VIII.6.7). That sway might appear to involve no more than a power of veto, 'the right of excluding any kind of law whatsoever it be before establishment. This doth belong unto kings as kings.' But the establishment of laws was itself an act of predominantly royal power: 'that which establisheth and maketh them is power, even power of dominion, the chiefty whereof amongst us resteth in the person of the king' (VIII.6.11–12). And that legislative supremacy was coupled with judicial supremacy, such that law itself afforded no justification for resisting the king and no redress against him if he should abuse his power in defiance of all the principles which Hooker had laid down. However disturbing the conclusion, it could not be denied. It rested upon the very laws of nature as expounded in Aristotelian physics. For 'as there could be in natural bodies no motion of any thing unless there were some which moveth all things and continueth unmovable, even so in politic societies there must be some unpunishable or else no man shall suffer punishment'. The king was that unmoved mover: and him 'therefore no man can have lawfully power and authority to judge' (VIII.9.2).

vi   France: Coquille

In contrast to his English cousins, the king of France had an ever-growing multitude of quasi-bureaucratic officials to exercise authority in his name. In no sector of royal government was bureaucracy better developed than in

---

58. Cf. D'Entrèves 1939, pp. 128–31; Cargill Thompson 1972, pp. 40–3.

the administration of justice with its hierarchy of courts and its host of magistrates and *praticiens*, so many of them university-trained *in utroque jure*. The size and influence of the magistracy sprang from the procedures of the law itself, geared in royal courts to inquisitorial modes of proof as distinct from the jury-centred methods of the English common law. Critics of the regime denounced the magistracy as 'hangers-on and flatterers of royalty', upon whom kings could rely 'to be accommodating to their schemes', *pace* the sovereign courts' much-vaunted function of judicial review of royal acts (Hotman 1972, pp. 520, 504). The *parlements*' response to royal edicts of pacification during the civil wars of the sixteenth century scarcely warranted such denunciations. Even so, Parisian juristic opinion was indeed shifting decisively away from the conciliarist views which attended early sixteenth-century royal expeditions into Italy, and towards that endorsement of regal power in the public sphere at which such thinkers as Charles Loyseau would arrive in the reign of Henri IV (Renaudet 1953, pp. 547, 549; Lloyd 1981b). And yet, notwithstanding this appearance of concentration in official hands and ultimately in the hands of the king, power in late Valois France remained diffused among the multiple components of an essentially pluralist system. Royal office-selling served to perpetuate and to institutionalise patrimonial attitudes towards government and its tasks. Such attitudes were rooted in feudal values which in turn persisted, associating judicial and political authority with possession of land in the form of fiefs and status in the form of lineage. Moreover, provincial and local assemblies of estates flourished in various quarters of the realm, offsetting the relative failure of their national counterparts and testifying, in conjunction with the presence of provincial *parlements* and the active survival of seigneurial courts, to the decentralised character of the French polity. Nowhere was that character more plainly evident than in the sphere of private law. Efforts at redaction of the kingdom's multifarious customs stopped far short of realising Parisian jurists' hopes for a unified *droit commun coutumier*. And the customs provided, to the mind of the *procureur-général* of the duchy of Nevers, a clinching proof of the people's constitutional standing *vis-à-vis* their king.

Writing mainly in the last two decades of the sixteenth century, Guy Coquille produced no rounded statement of his political thought, but scattered his ideas about his numerous works.[59] Rich in historical and legal

---

59. All references are to Coquille's collected *Œuvres* (1703). In vol. I pages, printed in two columns, are numbered consecutively throughout. Vol. II, printed likewise, falls into two parts, the numbering of each part beginning afresh at p. 1. References to vol. I thus give page followed by column numbers; and to vol. II, part, page, and column numbers.

materials, they were relatively innocent of philosophical content, heavily conservative in tone, and not infrequently self-contradictory.[60] But Coquille's central ideas rested firmly enough upon two bases. The first was his conviction that maintenance of the rights of the feudal nobility was vital to a stable polity and necessary to the 'prosperity' of kingship itself. The peers of the realm were the vehicle whereby at the coronation the people concluded with their king 'a mutual obligation', made 'as if by stipulation';[61] and it was they who convened provincial estates from which deputies were sent to the Estates General (1.282.1). Apart from these high constitutional functions, it was to the nobility at large, 'born and raised in greatness' and 'stimulated by the example of their ancestors', that the kings of France had 'communicated hereditarily part of their [own] greatness and authority' (II.ii.130.1). And although the king was 'true sovereign', there were, nonetheless, degrees of 'sovereignty' – a term which in this connection, and despite Bodin's efforts, Coquille continued to interpret in a specifically feudal sense. Deriving it 'from the Latin *supremus*', he applied it to positions of superiority in the feudal hierarchy, such that 'the seigneur suzerain or sovereign' had 'many others seigneurs subject to him, and these subject seigneurs have other seigneurs subject to them' and so might be accounted 'sovereign' in their turn (II.ii.154.2). These relationships, with the distribution of sovereignty which they entailed, were geared to tenure of land (II.i.41.2). Half a century after Du Moulin had attacked the position that jurisdictional rights appertained inherently to feudal patrimonies, Coquille persisted in holding that 'the right to exercise justice' belonged 'inseparably to the seigneurie and fief', so that 'it is said in France that judicial rights are patrimonial to the seigneurs'.[62] By virtue of those rights, seigneurs could not only adjudicate between private litigants, but also 'command' and 'make by-laws' in respect of public concerns (II.i.38.2). Royal courts and their agents strove persistently to encroach upon the rights in question (II.i.307.2, 309.2). In doing so they abraded 'the ancient constitution (*établissement*) of this kingdom' which had placed 'the power of justice in the hands of the second estate' (1.282.1). To leave that power in seigneurial hands was a surer guarantee of the well-being of local

60. For instance: 'the government of this kingdom is a true monarchy which has none of the characteristics of democracy nor of aristocracy' (1.276.1); 'the ancient constitution of the French *république*, mixing democracy with aristocracy and monarchy' (II.ii.125.2). Again: consultation with the Estates General was 'of the essence of the crown' (II.ii.125.1) and 'in certain cases the estates have power and authority of greater power and effectiveness than of counselling the king' (1.277.1); '[the estates have] no part nor connection whatsoever with anything to do with government' (1.276, 1–2).
61. 1.230.2, alluding to the verbal contract *stipulatio* in Roman law which Coquille had studied at Orleans.   62. Du Moulin 1681, I, pp. 127–9; Coquille, 1.340.2, II.i.7.1.

communities than to assign it to some 'hired creature (*personnage emprunté*) who is mercenary and who has no purpose nor aim of special friendship towards those to whom he renders law' (1.279.1).

Coquille's theory of law furnished the second basis of his thought. Its bedrock was the customs. Emphasis upon these led him to accentuate the popular origins of royal government and the role of the provincial estates. It also led him to distinguish between three categories of law in a manner which again implied a distribution of sovereignty, though this time in a legislative sense. At the realm's 'first constitution (*établissement*)' it was 'the people' who had 'established kings'. They had done so 'by way of joint agreement (*compromis*), in order to avoid the confusion which would arise if in any affair of importance it should be necessary to seek the opinion of all'. But the people 'did not transfer all power indiscriminately and absolutely (*incommutablement*) to the kings'. Rather, they retained 'the right to establish law over themselves: which are the customs and unwritten law' whereby the people's 'intercourse, transactions, and other affairs are regulated' (II.ii.125.1, 1.280.2). Although Parisian legists regarded the customs as 'entirely local', they were in fact 'our true civil and common law in every province'.[63] The 'prime movement' of this 'civil law was in the will of the people of the three orders and estates of the provinces by tacit consent' (1.280.2). It did not follow that in the making of the customs the king had no part to play. The provincial estates are 'assembled by the authority of the king'. This was a mark of his 'supreme sovereignty' (II.ii.125.2). Once that assembly had declared the customs, 'the authorisation of them belongs to the king' once more, for it was he who 'breathes life into the law' (1.280.2, cf. 1.445, II.i.1.1). Nevertheless, 'it is indeed the people who make the law' and 'the making of law is a right of sovereignty' (II.ii.125.2). Secondly, there were 'general laws and ordinances for the universal *police* of the realm'. The making of these was 'one of the principal rights of the majesty and authority of the king'. Laws of this kind were 'published and verified in the *parlement*' – a necessary part of the process of promulgation, for 'otherwise the people are not bound by them' (II.ii.2.1). But the *parlement* was no 'partner (*compagne*)' in the royal power, and its function remained simply to 'exercise justice in particular cases, and not to make laws' (1.281.2). There existed a third category, of 'perpetual laws, important for the state of the realm'. These were a matter for the Estates General. For the purpose of its assembly, 'the power of all the people is

---

63. II.i.239.1, 238.2; cf. II.ii.1.1 and 1.286.1, etc.

transferred' to the 'deputies' who met in the presence of the king, the princes of the blood, and other dignitaries (II.ii.2.1, 1.281.2). It was an assembly where the king's 'sovereignty' and that of the people evidently stood combined in a single gathering.

Coquille's three forms of law corresponded in some degree to a differentiation between the private and the public sphere, with fundamental laws providing the third category. But such a distinction was incidental to his main intention, and in any case was not sustained. Although the king's 'rights of majesty' in respect of the kingdom's 'universal *police*' extended also to powers in respect of war and other affairs, the customs could equally be described as 'loix politiques' (1.280.2). What mattered most in Coquille's system was the 'reciprocal' relationship between king and people, seen rather as interdependent and interacting parts of the realm's 'political and mystical body' than as discretely sovereign in antithetical spheres (1.230.2, 277.1, 281.2, etc). Thus, the people were the source of their king's legislative authority and must have knowledge of his acts, while he in turn was necessary to the actualisation of the law-making potential which they themselves retained. The difficulty for France, and the cause of 'many inconveniences and disadvantages', had been the inclination of kings for a century or more to 'command more absolutely', neglecting to summon the estates, licensing intrusions upon seigneurial jurisdictions, generally setting constitutionalist principles at naught (1.280.1). For this Coquille had no remedy to offer beyond regret for the non-observance of those principles and reminders from his provincial perspective that they retained a greater relevance to France's government than his Parisian counterparts seemed any longer disposed to acknowledge.

vii   The Netherlands: Althusius

In 1604, the year after the publication of his *Politica methodice digesta*,[64] the Calvinist Johannes Althusius settled in east Friesland as syndic of Emden. East Friesland formed part of the empire; yet town and province had close ties with the Dutch. The *Politica*'s enlarged second edition was dedicated to one of the republic's component parts, the States of Friesland, which Althusius extolled for the 'praiseworthy example of your own and of the

---

64. All references are by chapter and section numbers as given in the Harvard Political Classics edition (1932, ed. Friedrich), reprinted from the third edition of 1614.

other provinces confederated with you' in 'war against the most powerful king of Spain' (Preface, p. 8). In that war the rebels had taken their principal stand upon a contractual view of rulership, historically based.[65] Charters and treaties had been concluded from time to time between the several provinces and their respective dukes and counts. Prominent among such agreements were Brabant's *Blijde Inkomst* of 1356 and the *Groot-Privilege* of 1477, both of which affirmed that obedience to the ruler was conditional upon his and his agents' observing provincial and local 'privileges, rights, customs, and usages'.[66] For the rebels, the contents of these and related documents were tantamount to a written constitution; indeed, what was recorded there approximated to sovereignty itself (cf. Kossmann 1981, p. 12). Even so, its defence resided in the people not as a multitude of individuals, but as a corporate body actualised through the representatives of their communities.[67] The obvious candidates for that representational role were the members of the States General. Yet as Francis Vranck, pensionary of Gouda, explained in 1587, it was in fact the 'boards of town magistrates and councillors, together with the corporation of nobles, [who] undoubtedly represent the whole state and the whole body of the inhabitants'.[68] The constitution of the Dutch republic as it emerged from the struggle with Spain abundantly warranted that view. Its affairs were effectively in the hands of those very boards, assemblies of patricians, who controlled not only their own towns, but also the membership of provincial states and, beyond them, the States General as well. And although Althusius composed his treatise in the light of the constitution rather of the empire than of those provinces, the ideas which it presented had an obvious appeal to the latter.

Althusius grounded his system upon the principle of *consociatio* (i.2). Men as individuals were not 'adequately equipped by nature' to be 'self-sufficient'. They were therefore 'led and as it were impelled' to adopt 'the symbiotic life'; and this involved 'the bond of a uniting and associating compact (*pactum*)' (i.3–4, 6). In such a life there had to be a differentiation of

65. Ample documentation in Kossmann and Mellink 1974.
66. *Blijde Inkomst* (*Joyeuse Entrée*) (both Brabantine and Latin texts) printed in Van Bragt 1956, pp. 95–121; *Groot-Privilege* (Brabantine text) in De Blécourt and Japiske 1919, pp. 3–7. I am grateful to my colleague Professor P.D. King for much help with translating the latter document; and to Professor E.H. Kossmann of Groningen for bibliographical advice on political thought in the Netherlands prior to the revolt. The constitutional foundations of the Netherlands system are usefully discussed in Van Uytven and Blockmans 1969 and in Blockmans 1983.
67. The rendering of the *quod omnes tangit* formula in articles drafted for agreement with the Archduke Matthias in 1577 is indicative, *omnes* becoming 'communities (*Gemeynte*)': see Griffiths 1968, pp. 311–12.   68. *Corte verthoninge* (1587), in Kossmann and Mellink 1974, p. 278.

political roles. The 'common and perpetual law' of all associations was that some should be 'rulers' or 'superiors' and others 'subjects' or 'inferiors'. This again was consistent with 'the law and arrangement of nature': if 'all were equal and each should wish to rule others by his own will', the consequence would be 'discord' and the 'dissolution of society' (i.11–12, 37). Thus, although Aristotelian analytical methodology indicated 'the efficient cause of political *consociatio* to be the consent and compact (*pactum*) of the communicating citizens', such a formation had its roots rather in 'necessity' than in those citizens' free and voluntary acts as individuals (i.29, 33). However, from classical jurisprudence it transpired that 'by natural law all men are equal'.[69] It followed that men could lawfully be subject to no one 'except by their own consent and voluntary deed'. Accordingly, they must 'transfer to another their rights' to which no one else could have legal claim 'without just title received from their owner (*domino*)' (xviii.18). Thus to that initial compact was added a 'reciprocal contract', but this time between the political 'body' already constituted and whatever party it proceeded to adopt as its ruler, the rights in question being those of the people as a whole (xix.7, ix.3, 5, 12, etc., xviii.10). In such a contract the 'obligation' of the 'promisor' or ruler 'comes first (as customarily happens with mandatory contracts)' (xix.7). For the people was 'prior' and 'superior to its governors', just as 'every constituting body is prior and superior to what it constitutes' (xviii.8, 92, xxxiii.20, etc.). Even so, ruler and people alike were subject to the rule of law: 'law presides over all and singular, it is above and superior to all' (xviii.94). 'Common law (*lex communis*)' as set out in the Decalogue 'explains the common law of nature to all peoples'. By 'proper law' it was 'adapted to some particular polity', and within every polity there were 'special laws' for particular regions and for groups within those regions: such laws were formulated by 'common agreement' (xxi.29, 30, ix.7, iv.17, vi.43, 17). Furthermore, a commonwealth as a whole might have its 'fundamental law' which 'is nothing other than certain covenants (*pacta*)' to which its members subscribed (xix.49). 'Common consent' accordingly informed the legal structure of every political society within a framework of divine and natural law; and without law 'neither household nor city nor commonwealth nor the world itself can stand' (x.8).

Taking these considerations as axiomatic, Althusius proceeded to describe political society as an ascending series of corporate groups. All were 'political', though two were 'simple and private': the 'domestic

---

69. xviii.18. Cf. Digest, L.17.32; also Cicero, *De legibus*, I.x.30.

society' of household or kinship group, 'seedbed of all symbiotic associations' (iii.42, ii.1.14,); and the '*collegium*', formed by participants in the same occupation 'solely through their pleasure and will' (iv.1). Public association consisted of the city, the province, and the realm or commonwealth (*respublica*). Each formed one 'body', the 'members' of which were groups occurring below it in Althusius' schema (v.10, vii.29, ix.3, 5, 12, etc.). Thus, the members of the province were 'its so-called orders and estates, or major *collegia*', while the members of the realm were 'cities, provinces, and regions' and 'not individual men nor families nor *collegia*'.[70] Each public association had its head who administered its affairs and 'represents' it (v.25, viii.53, xix.98). Each had also its assembly – city *senatus*, provincial *conventus*, general *concilium* for the realm at large (v.50, viii.64, xviii.56) – which 'represents' its membership and so, in effect, the entire people of its zone of influence (v.55, viii.5, xvii.57). The head had coercive power over individuals and the several members within his jurisdiction (v.49, viii.61, xxiv.32, xxvii.27). But, *major singulis*, he was *minor universis* (v.49, viii.67, xviii.71). And, further, the principle *quod omnes tangit* dictated that his legislative proposals be subject to review by the relevant body of representatives (xvii.60, v.59, viii.64ff, xviii.68). At the level of the realm matters were complicated by the role ascribed to 'ephors'. Distinct from the *concilium*, they were 'in the likeness of a guardian bearing and representing the person of the whole people' who 'resemble a ward or minor' in their charge (xviii.11, 12). Ultimately the ephors' role was tantamount to that of the inferior magistrates of Calvinist resistance theory which, Althusius thought, was exemplified in the Dutch Revolt (xviii.83, cf.75; xxxviii.28–45, 55). But as guardians the ephors were entrusted with powers of administration. Although the authority of the united members of the realm exceeded theirs, theirs collectively was greater than its head's or supreme magistrate's (xviii.25–9, 73). They controlled him by law; and it was they who reviewed his administrative decrees, while the *concilium* dealt with such 'grave affairs' as taxation, fundamental laws, and the rights of 'sovereignty (*maiestas*)' (xviii.51, 68, xvii.56).

Sovereignty, for Althusius as for Bodin, was 'indivisible' and consisted chiefly in legislative power. But, unlike Bodin. 'I can in no wise ascribe this supreme power to a king or optimates.' These had only its 'administration

---

70. viii.2, ix.5. In the first edition, prior to Althusius' move to Emden, the 'province' did not rank as a fully-fledged 'public association'. In respect of the 'realm'. Althusius used the terms *regnum* and *respublica* more or less interchangeably, declaring that he could find no reason for distinguishing between them (ii.3).

and exercise by concession from the associated body' to which the power in question must always belong (ix.19, 16, 22, 23, 18). Even so, the constitution of every realm was in some sense 'mixed'. It exemplified monarchy, not simply in the shape of the supreme magistrate, but when the *concilium* was 'deemed to be as one voice and will'. It exemplified democracy through the 'many voices' contained in that same assembly, and aristocracy by virtue of the 'intermediate magistrates' (xxxix.14). The system was one of checks and balances: 'what is monarchical in the commonwealth keeps within bounds of duty and conserves what is aristocratic and democratic' which, in turn, 'checks what is monarchical' (xxxix.15). It also involved a separation of functions between its administrative institutions: 'a king has charge and rules in those things for which he has received the power of ruling and governing, not in those which have been reserved to the power and judgement of the ephors' (xviii.99). The separation emerged most noticeably in respect of ecclesiastical administration. The church had its own structure and its distinct responsibility for 'those things' which 'concern eternal life and salvation' (viii.16, xxviii.5). But the secular magistrates, provincial and supreme, had also their responsibility for the 'inspection, defence, management, and direction of ecclesiastical affairs' (xxxviii.5). These exhibited 'therefore a dual administration', one for the magistracy and one for 'church ministers', whereby 'each directs and submits to the other, and whereby each assists the other in the separate administration entrusted to its charge' (xxviii.5). But these Genevan arrangements had still to do with administration: the church as such, by the will of God and 'by the religious covenant' concluded between Him and 'the members of the realm', was 'committed to the whole people whom its ministers, ephors, and supreme magistrate represent' (xxviii.15, 18).

And yet, while sovereign power was a property of the people, those to whom they 'transferred' it (*transtulit*: xviii.10, 56, etc.) had also its reality. Mere administrator though he might formally be, the supreme magistrate had the authority to identify just causes of war, to coin money and assess its value, and generally to exercise all those rights which thinkers had traditionally linked with *majestas* (xxxv.5, xxxii.31). It was by his 'sole will that the law of a city is constituted', from him that the 'administration and power' of provincial heads 'is conceded' and with it their capacity 'to give force of law' to the decisions of provincial assemblies (v.42, viii.53, 65). Even the general *concilium*, although 'all public affairs of the realm are laid before it', had no automatic right of assembly, but depended for its summons upon the supreme magistrate once more (xvii.57, xxxiii.5). While it fell to the ephors to constitute him in office, the supreme magistrate might succeed to that office by 'hereditary or successive' right, a procedure which had much to commend it (xviii.64, xix.25, 74–91). As for the ephors themselves, Althusius' elaborate description of how they were 'elected by the consent of the whole people' carried the significant rider that 'sometimes' the 'supreme magistrate or optimates have the power' to elect them. What mattered was that ephors be persons 'who have great political power (*potentia*) and wealth' so that 'the *maior et sanior pars* of the people prevails' (xviii.59, 60, 62). Likewise at the level of the city, the *senatus* was a *collegium* 'of the soundest select men' who might 'be elected by the *senatus*' itself (v.54, 60). The remaining citizens were 'inferior' and 'the subjects of the whole or of those who represent it' – just as 'the individual people of the realm by themselves are the subjects and servants of their administrators' (v.26; xviii.15). All this tallied at least with the letter of that Aristotelian principle which Althusius had adduced at the outset: in every political association, by natural law, some must command and other obey (*Politics*, 1254a1–3). With ceaseless reiteration of constitutionalist maxims, he explored his corporatist vision of political society, intent upon reconciling as intimately as possible forms of association with forms of rule. But for practical purposes, and doubtless to the satisfaction of the Dutch, the system which emerged from that exploration was distinctly oligarchic; and it left open the door for a powerful monarch removable only if he should transgress too outrageously the requirements of the rule of law.

viii   Spain: Suárez

The power of Spain's rulers rested first and foremost upon the kingdom of Castile, the driving force in the unification of the Iberian peninsula. There the king seemed equipped to rule in authoritarian fashion, through a council reduced in membership to consist mainly of *letrados* and by means of a proliferation of officials combining administrative with judicial responsibilities at every level. Most authoritarian of all was the Castilian crown's practice of empire in its colonies of the New World, where native people were treated as subjugate inhabitants of the king's private domain and granted to *encomenderos* with utter disregard of their indigenous institutions (Parry 1940, p. 71). In Aragon and the provinces of Catalonia and Valencia federated with it, however, traditions of contractual monarchy continued to inform political attitudes. Those traditions, encapsulated in the famous Aragonese oath of allegiance (see Giesey 1968), found institutional expression through assemblies of the *cortes* and through other distinctive organs established to safeguard regional and local franchises. Even in Castile, resentment towards the alleged misgovernment of Habsburg-imported officials flared into rebellion in 1520, the rebel leaders taking their stand upon defence of the customs which earlier rulers had ratified (*fueros*) and calling for regular meetings of representative assemblies with deputies (*procuradores*) firmly answerable to their constituents (Perez 1970, p. 546). Despite the defeat of the *comuneros*, the principle that *procuradores* were strictly mandatories and not plenipotentiaries on the English model survived to facilitate a revival of the Castilian *cortes* later in the century (Thompson 1982, pp. 39–40). And even the Amerindians found their defenders, principally in the shape of the Dominican Bartolomé de Las Casas with his insistence that the system of *encomienda* breached both fundamental and natural law and exposed the king to the charge that 'he who uses authority badly is not worthy to rule' (Las Casas 1957–8, v, pp. 97–8; cf. Maravall 1972, I, pp. 338–9). Such ideas could continue to strike chords in a Spain where, although the intellectual climate was growing less favourable to critical political thought,[71] the universities were expanding apace, their theology faculties increasingly penetrated by Thomist influences, their law faculties attracting in mounting numbers the sons of noblemen and prospective royal officials, to follow a curriculum modelled upon the Bartolist school of Bologna (Kagan 1981, pp. 140–4). Where teachers of the calibre of Vitoria and Soto held sway, pupils could scarcely remain indifferent to the central questions of ethics and jurisprudence.

No teacher surpassed the Jesuit Francisco Suárez in exploring those questions on the basis of the Thomist tradition and the methods of scholastic disputation. Suárez' political ideas, expounded most fully in his lectures *On Laws and God the Lawgiver*,[72] were rooted in his philosophy of law. Law as such was 'a certain measure of moral acts' (1.i.5). It was thus a measure of right (*ius*), defined as 'a certain moral power (*facultas*) which every individual has, either over his property or over what is owed to him' (1.ii.4–5). Right, however, was reciprocally a measure of law, in turn definable as 'a common, rightful (*iustum*) and stable precept which has been

---

71. Following the early sixteenth-century impact of Erasmian humanism, on which Bataillon 1950 remains the classic study.
72. All references are to the Coimbra edition of 1612, cited hereafter by book, chapter, and section numbers.

sufficiently promulgated' (II.xvii.2, I.xii.5). Neither term contained the other's full meaning; yet law implied right, and right implied the possibility of law (II.iii.12, I.ii.*passim*). Law was divisible, Thomist fashion, into several categories.[73] Human law, though indirectly an 'effect' of the eternal law, was 'something created and temporal' and 'gets its force and efficacy immediately from the will of the human legislator' (II.iv.8). Like all law, human law proceeded from a superior to an inferior: it was 'established by the free will of someone having power to command' (I.v.[24], II.ii.9, 6). But the human legislator's power of command was not arbitrary. His freedom in this regard was limited by the 'ground and essence of law that it should prescribe what is just'. Here justice signified the good of the community: for, by the same token, it was 'of the ground and substance of law that it be made for the common good' (I.ix.2, I.vii.1). Furthermore, the element of command was not dissociable from an element of consent: 'the consent of the people is needed in some way for all law' (VII.xii.1). All this, however, was bound up with the question of how the human community was formed and how the human legislator obtained his power.

Here Suárez began from the Aristotelian commonplace that man 'naturally and rightly craves to live in a community' (III.i.3, cf.12). Even so, a community's formation remained 'dependent upon human volition', for men were 'naturally free' (II.xvii.9, III.iii.6). Not until they were 'bound together by some compact (*aliquo foedere*)' did they form a community as distinct from a mere multitude (I.vi.19). As with Hooker and Althusius, the opportunity arose to investigate that 'moral bond (*morale vinculum*)' in terms of an initial social contract. No more disposed than they to pursue the matter, Suárez hurried on to the question of political authority. While the community once formed might be 'imperfect, or domestic', a 'perfect' community had the 'capability of political government' which meant that it exhibited 'political power' (III.i.3, I.vi.19, III.ii.3). That power, quite distinct from the 'power of dominion' held by the head of a domestic community, consisted chiefly in the authority to legislate (I.viii.5, III.i *passim*). The power resided in the community itself and not in its individual members.[74] Nor did it spring from several members: 'this power does not react in human nature until men are gathered together into one perfect

---

73. I.iii.5–21. The eternal law was 'not promulgated' except through 'some divine or human law' (II.iv.10); and, while both divine and natural law indicated the 'divine will' (II.vi.13), natural law resided 'in the reason', in 'the actual judgement of the mind' (II.v.12, 14).
74. III.iii.1, dismissing a syllogism which purported to prove the contrary.

community and are politically united' (III.iii.6). Yet the proof was analogical. Just as man 'has power over himself and over his faculties and members for their use,' so too, 'directly by natural law, the 'single mystical body' of the community as a whole 'has power and government over itself and consequently has power over its members also' (III.iii.6, III.ii.4, cf. Suárez 1613b, III.v.11). What the community did with its power by way of establishing a form of rule was a matter of 'human counsel and decision' (III.iv.1). It might itself retain 'supreme legislative authority', but this would lead to 'infinite confusion and bickering' (VII.xii.1, III.iv.1, cf. 8). It might consign only some of its power to a prince, with the result that 'the monarchy would not be perfect, but mixed and democratic'; this, however, 'is not ordinarily the case' (VII.xiii.5, cf. III.iv.1). Through accidents of title 'several kingdoms' might find themselves to be 'under the same king', each requiring that 'provision be made for it by its own laws' (I.vii.14) – circumstances strongly reminiscent of the condition of the Spanish realms. All in all, Suárez was of the opinion that 'monarchy' or rule 'by one head' afforded 'the best' form of 'political government'. Nevertheless, the source of the monarch's power was an act of transfer on the part of the community as a whole, expressive of its 'own consent' (III.iv.1, III.iii.7).

In transferring its power to a king, a community did not deliver itself into 'despotic servitude'. The transfer was made 'under obligation, the conditions under which the first king received the kingdom from the community'. Those conditions could be described in terms of a 'pact or agreement (*pactum vel conventio*)' (III.i.7, III.iv.3, 5). They consisted, however, not so much in specific articles of contract as in broad agreement as to the ensuing mode of rule. The king should 'rule politically (*politice*)'.[75] He who ruled otherwise ruled tyrannically. In extreme circumstances such a ruler might lawfully be deposed – though only when threatened with its own destruction should a community resort to deposition. In such a case 'the commonwealth as a whole, and by the public and common deliberation of the citizens and nobles', might call the tyrant to account before a 'public council'. Even then, deposition required papal endorsement. 'To punish' was 'an act of jurisdiction' and so 'of a superior'; and to that extent the pope, who had direct power to punish the spiritual offences of men of all degrees, had indirect power also over tyrannical princes (Suárez 1613b, VI.iv.15, 12, 17). In normal circumstances the position of the church itself constituted a limitation upon the ruler's power. The church

---

75. Suárez 1621: *de charitate*, Disp. XIII, sect. viii.2.

was autonomous and independent: 'a lay prince cannot bind clerics by his express will' (Suárez 1612, VII.xvi.11). As for his lay subjects, despite their transference to him of the power to make law, they continued collectively to possess a residual capacity to nullify his acts. Custom was established through repeated performance of 'voluntary acts' on the part 'of the community as a whole' or 'of the greater part' of its members, over a period of time sufficient to manifest 'the consent of the people' (VII.i.8, 12). And a reasonable custom which was also prescriptive, 'if it should be contrary to a law, abrogates that law' (VII.i.12, VII.xviii.14). Indeed, in order to abrogate a law the ruler's tacit connivance at 'the resistance of the people' was enough. Thus law in effect could be made by 'the people joined with its head' in a manner where the king's role was scarcely more than passive (VII.xviii.20, xiv.4).

So Suárez' position accommodated significant elements of the constitutionalist tradition. But the balance of his arguments leaned decisively the other way. The king was not to be seen as administrator or *tutor* of the realm; nor was his relation to public authority one of delegation. The community's act of transfer endowed him with full legal title to political power and cast him as its 'proper owner (*proprius dominus*)' (III.iv.9). The *minor universis* principle was dismissed: 'the power having been transferred to the king, he is thereby made superior even to the kingdom that gave it'.[76] Whatever the people's residual law-making capability, there was no question of limiting the king's own legislative power on the strength of custom. His express injunction sufficed for 'forbidding a custom contrary to it', whether retrospectively or prospectively; and sometimes he might 'dispense' even from 'precepts of the natural law' (VII.vii.5, II.xiv.11). Manifest tyranny aside, there existed no legal machinery to enforce constraints upon him: kings were not bound by the coactive force even of their own laws, although they ought to 'call to mind the directive constraint of the laws' (III.xxxv.28, cf, 15). As for his subjects as individuals, the king by virtue of his power might, 'to the extent necessary for obligatory government', override their rights 'even if such a right (*ius*) has been positively given by nature' (II.xiv.18). *Pace* the language of rights, what must take precedence was the interest of the community as a whole: 'the common good is preferred to private good whenever they cannot exist at the same time' (I.vii.14). And the former was identifiable with the king

---

76. III.iv.6. Cf., however, Suárez 1621: *de charitate*, Disp. XIII, sect. viii.2: in circumstances of manifest tyranny 'the whole commonwealth is superior to the king'.

himself. 'The good of the prince *qua* prince', observed Suárez portentously, 'is reckoned the common good, since he himself is the common and public person' (I.vii.11). In sum, the thrust of Suárez' arguments as the seventeenth century opened was towards the supremacy and licensed encroachment of the public over and upon the private sphere at the behest of the monarch's will – and so towards absolutism.[77]

77. A sense of the distinctiveness and relative immunity of the private from the public sphere nonetheless remained: for instance, it was 'most absurd' of 'certain jurists' to argue that 'temporal kings can, by their own absolute power and arbitrary volition, alter rights of ownership over property or usurp those rights for themselves" (II.xiv.15).

10

Sovereignty and the mixed constitution: Bodin and his critics

JULIAN H. FRANKLIN

The account of sovereignty in the work of Jean Bodin was a major event in the development of European political thought. Bodin's precise definition of supreme authority, his determination of its scope, and his analysis of the functions that it logically entailed, helped turn public law into a scientific discipline. And the vast system of comparative public law and politics provided in his *Les Six Livres de la République* (1576) became the prototype for a whole new literary genre, which in the seventeenth century was cultivated most in Germany.

But Bodin's account of sovereignty was also the source of much confusion, since he was primarily responsible for introducing the seductive but erroneous notion that sovereignty is indivisible. It is true, of course, that every legal system, by its very definition as an authoritative method of resolving conflicts, must rest upon an ultimate legal norm or rule of recognition, which is the guarantee of unity. But when Bodin spoke about the unity of sovereignty, the power that he had in mind was not the constituent authority of the general community or the ultimate coordinating rule that the community had come to recognise, but the power, rather, of the ordinary agencies of government. He advanced, in other words, a theory of ruler sovereignty. His celebrated principle that sovereignty is indivisible thus meant that the high powers of government could not be shared by separate agents or distributed among them, but that all of them had to be entirely concentrated in a single individual or group.

This thesis was controversial even as applied to the more consolidated kingships of France, Spain, and England, and it was hopelessly at odds with the constitution of the German Empire and other monarchies of eastern Europe and Scandinavia. Yet so seductive was the idea of indivisibility that it remained a celebrated issue among academic jurists for at least a half-century after Bodin wrote. And even after the error was exposed, around the end of the first quarter of the seventeenth century, it lingered on in one form or another. In this chapter I shall deal only with the earlier and main phase of the controversy. I shall try to explain how Bodin's theory of sovereignty came about and how his confusion as to indivisibility was cleared up in the course of the debate on the locus of sovereignty in the German Empire.

i Bodin's doctrine and its limitations

The idea that concentration of power in the ruler is an essential condition of the state as such might seem at first sight to have been absolutist in its inspiration, and Bodin, when he published the final version of his political doctrine in 1576, indeed argued that the king of France had all the power that a government could legitimately exercise and that apparent restraints on royal power were not constitutional requirements, but mere re-commendations of prudence and good government (Franklin 1973, pp. 54ff). Yet the earlier history of Bodin's thought suggests a somewhat different genesis. In his *Methodus ad facilem historiarum cognitionem* (1566), Bodin was not an absolutist, or was at least evasive on that subject, and his interest in the theory of sovereignty was clearly technical and quasi-academic (Franklin 1973, pp. 35ff).

In the earliest phase of his career as an aspiring teacher at the law school of Toulouse, Bodin had apparently undertaken to identify those powers of a sovereign that could not also be held as a right of office by ordinary magistrates (Franklin 1973, pp. 23–5). To say that a magistrate 'held' or 'had' a power by his right of office had been taken, by most medieval jurists, to mean that he could exercise that power according to his own discretion and without direct reliance on the king so long as he remained within whatever legal limits might apply. Not all powers were or needed to be held this way, of course. The public officer might be acting solely on delegated power subject to immediate control. But by medieval notions, that sort of officer was little better than a servant. High officers of state, who exercised some degree of *merum*, or pure, *imperium*, held their *imperium* by right. And since the *merum imperium* could include very high powers of the state, this conception of the right of office was naturally associated with a decentralised administration.[1]

With the growing consolidation of power in the French and other

---

1. For an historical survey of the issue of *merum imperium* in medieval and post-medieval legal theory going back to the thirteenth century, see Gilmore 1941.

Renaissance monarchies, this view of office was increasingly attacked, and most strenuously of all by Andrea Alciato, the great Italian legal humanist of the early sixteenth century, who held that the possession of *merum imperium* by right of office was a corruption of Roman civil law, that every power in the state, other than (abusive) feudal grants, was merely a right of exercise derived by delegation from the prince (Alciato 1582, cols 29ff). This opinion was obviously favourable to royal power. And given Bodin's constant preference for strong monarchical authority, one might have expected him to welcome Alciato's view.

But Bodin was also an erudite and cautious legal craftsman and throughout his career he constantly attempted to reconcile the new idea of royal dominance with the French juridical tradition of which he was a great admirer and connoisseur. Against Alciato, accordingly, and the whole tradition of juridical interpretation in which he stood, Bodin held that by the customary rule of public law in France, high magistrates could hold the *merum imperium* by right of office at least to the extent of imposing capital punishment. But against the medieval exponents of this view, he did not include those prerogatives that could make the magistrate a partner or rival of his prince. These could not be 'held', but could be exercised by delegation only (Bodin 1951b, pp. 174–6, 1961, pp. 432ff).

Unlike Alciato and his followers, accordingly, Bodin divided the *merum imperium* into a (minor) part that could be held by magistrates and a (major) part held only by the prince. And by this conservative route he was led, ironically, to a new and theoretically momentous question as to the character of sovereignty. He now sought to determine those powers that could not be held by magistrates, but only exercised, if the prince was to be accounted sovereign. Although this topic had sometimes been touched upon by other jurists of the time, Bodin was to treat the question in a more fundamental and systematic way than anyone before him. He now proceeded to derive the necessary rights, or 'marks', of sovereignty from the concept of supremacy itself. The question that he asked, in other words, was what prerogatives a political authority must hold exclusively if it is not to acknowledge a superior or equal in its territory.

Bodin's first reflections on this question almost surely go back to his early career as an academic jurist at the University of Toulouse (which he left in 1559 after failing to secure a permanent appointment). But the scope and depth of his investigation was decisively shaped by a far-reaching methodological commitment that carried him well beyond the conventional approach to legal studies. At some point of his Toulousan period, Bodin concluded that issues of legal theory could not be settled in the traditional fashion of the medieval civil lawyers by appeal to Roman norms alone. The use of high philological technique in the study of the Roman law by the great French school of legal humanism had prepared the way for a methodological revolution in which Bodin became a leading figure. The humanists, rejecting the medieval style of scholastic exegesis, had attempted to get back to the original meaning of the Roman texts, and to recover the underlying system of the Corpus Juris. But the further they went, the more critical they became of Roman law itself. The Corpus Juris, to list their main complaints, seemed incomplete in many areas, and most especially in public law; Justinian had often been cryptic and inaccurate in representing the best of Roman legal thought; many rules, some of which seemed basic to the system, were peculiar to the Roman state and obsolete for France; the Corpus Juris had not been arranged as a logically coherent system, and could not be reduced to a system because of its defects and omissions. The intellectual authority of Roman law was thereby shaken, and this had a number of important repercussions (Franklin 1963, pp. 36ff).

One of these was a new appreciation of domestic legal custom (Franklin 1973, pp. 37ff; cf. Kelley, 1970). But an additional motif, especially strong in Bodin, was the idea of remedying deficiences in the system of Roman law by consulting the materials of universal history (Franklin 1963, pp. 59ff). This in large part was the theme of his *Methodus ad facilem historiarum cognitionem*. The only way, says Bodin in the preface, to construct a truly universal legal science is to compare 'all the laws of all, or the most famous, states and to select the best variety'. A few years earlier, perhaps while he was still at Toulouse, he had produced a grandiose design for this comparison with his *Juris universi distributio* or *System of Law in its Entirety*; and the *Methodus* presents a preliminary statement of his findings for the area of public law in its very lengthy chapter vi.

In this fashion an enterprise that very likely started as an enquiry into the specific prerogatives of the ancient Roman emperors and the kings of France was transformed into a study of sovereignty in every kind of state. In Bodin's design, the basis for comparing states, and explaining their schemes of public law, was to determine and describe the locus of sovereignty in each. He was thus required to work out common principles of sovereignty that would apply to democracies and aristocracies as well as monarchies, and to variants of each of these in different times and places.

One consequence of this was a comprehensive and general definition of the rights of sovereignty. The Corpus Juris offered virtually nothing on the theory of public powers since it was primarily a scheme of private law. And the lists of regalian powers used in feudal law were mainly catalogues of particular privileges. In Bodin's *Methodus*, however, the essential rights are distinguished and reduced to five main heads:

And so having compared the arguments of Aristotle, Polybius, Dionysius [of Halicarnassus], and the jurists – with each other and with the universal history of commonwealths – I find that supremacy in a commonwealth consists of five parts. The first and most important is appointing magistrates and assigning each one's duties; another is ordaining and repealing laws; a third is declaring and terminating war; a fourth is the right of hearing appeals from all magistrates in last resort; and the last is the power of life and death where the law itself has made no provision for flexibility or clemency. (Bodin 1951b, pp. 174–5)

This classification is not quite as modern as it seems. It becomes clear in the *République* that Bodin thinks of the legislative power (which he now puts first among the rights of sovereignty) as a very general power to command, so that it implicitly includes all others. Hence the modern distinction between legislation, as the making of a rule, and execution, as the application of a rule, is not yet fully grasped, and that confusion we shall see is costly. And yet Bodin makes a very important, and even decisive, step towards an adequate account of public powers.

A second consequence of Bodin's comparative enterprise was his celebrated claim that sovereignty is indivisible, which he seems to have come to only at this point. In seeking to determine the form of state for ancient Rome and certain other classical republics traditionally reputed mixed, Bodin was finally led to ask, in strictly juridical terms, for the locus of sovereignty in a mixed constitution – in a constitution, that is, wherein the sovereign was said to be compounded of monarchy, aristocracy, and democracy, or any two of these.

Thus put, the question was completely new, since Polybius, and other exponents of the mixed constitution, thought of it more as a balance of effective influence than as a legal formula for partnership in sovereignty. And Bodin's answer was that, beyond the three simple forms of state, 'no fourth had existed, or could even be imagined' (Bodin 1951b, p. 177). The difficulty with a mixed constitution, in other words, was not merely prudential or political. As Bodin saw it, the unity of a legal system seemed

302

logically to require the unification of power in a single ruler or single ruling group (Franklin 1973, pp. 23ff).

This opinion is, of course, mistaken. Apart from federal decentralisation, which I leave aside for the purpose of this chapter, a constitution can be mixed either by sharing or by distribution. Where sovereignty is shared, the outcome is a compound polyarchy, the members of which, each retaining its identity within the whole, are the king, the senate, and the people, or any two of these, who may participate with different weights in different governmental functions. The idea of such a compound is not always easy to imagine. The President of the United States, for example, is, by virtue of his veto, a member of the legislature along with the two houses of Congress. Yet it is hard to imagine an act of legislation as the 'will' of such a complex entity, and more normal to think of it as an act of Congress subject, within certain limits, to approval by the President.

Where the constitutional principles of mixture are well understood, this way of speaking does not lead to theoretical confusion. But in the sixteenth century the mixed constitution had not yet been explored juridically, and where it occurred it was the legacy of traditional restraints and *ad hoc* adaptations that were not reflected in the legal terminology. In the limited monarchies of Europe, the king was still addressed as sovereign even though he might require the consent of the estates or other body for the conduct of some of his affairs, and commentators on the ancient Roman republic often passed over the traditional claims of the senate to a legislative veto.

Hence jurists of the sixteenth century were readily misled. The mixed systems of their own time or of the past were hard to grasp as authentic partnerships in sovereignty, while the mixtures they imagined and triumphantly proved to be impossible were irrelevant. Bodin, for example, assumes that the only sense in which a constitution might be mixed by sharing would be to give each of the partners the entirety of power simultaneously, which is of course juridically absurd:

But to institute the dominion of one, together with that of the few, and also with that of the many, simultaneously, is not only impossible but cannot even be imagined. For if sovereignty is by its nature indivisible, as we have shown above, how can it be allotted to one and to all at the same time? The first mark of sovereignty is to give law to all in general and to each in particular, and to command them. But will the citizens yield to being bound against their will when they, in turn, are empowered to coerce the person who commands them? If they willingly obey their majesty collapses; and yet if both parties refuse to be commanded, and there is no one obeying or commanding, it will be anarchy rather than a commonwealth, which is worse than the cruelest tyranny.[2]

A second way of mixing constitutions (as distinct from sharing) is by distributing the rights of sovereignty to different partners separately. This entails express or implied coordinating rules by which the powers thus separated, and above all the legislative power, are adjusted to each other's functions. It supposes, more specifically, that the legislature, although supreme in making rules, cannot apply them and cannot control directly that authority which is constitutionally charged with execution. But this possibility was also difficult to recognise at the time that Bodin wrote. In the best known example of 'mixture', which was the classical Roman republic, the highest forms of executive and judicial power were joined with the legislative in the people, so that it was technically not mixed in this respect. In European monarchies executive and legislative power were linked in the person of the king. Indeed, even Locke, much later on, who recommended the separation of executive and legislative power and had an example of it in the English constitution, still thought that the former was naturally subject to the latter, and that the executive independence of the English king hinged on his legislative veto. Without that veto, Locke believed, the two houses of parliament would be entitled to make and unmake executives at will (Locke 1960, pp. 414–15).

Bodin's attempt to show that distribution must be futile as a scheme of mixture thus seems to start by holding that all other powers would be in conflict with the power to make law. And as though to complicate the issue, he adds, alongside the legislative, another all-inclusive power (as Bodin interprets it), which is the right of taking oaths of fealty. The

---

2. Bodin 1586, II.1, p. 176. The phrase 'as we have shown above (*ut antea demonstravimus*)' in this quotation probably refers to 1.10, especially pp. 149–50, where Bodin, following Baldus and Cyno da Pistoia, observes portentously that a sovereign cannot share his power with a subject and still remain a sovereign. The implication seems to be that sharing somehow cancels sovereignty as such, as opposed to altering only the persons who hold it. This interpretation is confirmed by the passage just quoted.

In the French version, the original of which goes back to 1576, the result of this attempt to mix by sharing is described as democracy. 'And what individual can give the law, if he is himself constrained to take it from those to whom he gives it? The conclusion follows necessarily that, if no one in particular has the power to make law, and the power belongs to all together, the commonwealth is democratic.' *République*, II.1 (1961, p.254). One possible interpretation of this cryptic passage is suggested by Arnisaeus' comments on sharing, below p.321. The key clause in Bodin's passage would then be '... [if] the power belongs to all ...' and the error would then consist in not seeing that 'all' do not participate equally or even directly, that the people and the aristocracy vote as corporations.

breakdown of the attempted distribution follows from the conflict between these two powers, without excluding resistance also arising from the independent claims of all the rest. But no matter how the picture is construed, it is evident enough that Bodin is innocent of any notion of constitutional coordination of co-equal parts.

Let us produce, if that is possible, or at least let us imagine, a commonwealth in which the people would have the power to create magistrates, dispose of the public treasury, and to decide on life and death; while the nobility would be assigned the right of making laws, deciding war and peace, and levying taxes; and the citizens, collectively as well as individually, would be obliged to render an oath of fealty or homage to the king without exception of any other person, and the king, who is above all the other magistrates, would hear appeals in the last instance. By this method the rights of sovereignty will seem to be divided three ways: – the aristocrats and nobles will claim a part, the democrats and commoners a part, and the king will also claim a part – as a result of which a blend of royal power, aristocracy and democracy will seem to exist. But I deny that this ever was or can be done. For the aristocrats and nobility, who have the supreme power of making law – the power, that is, of laying commands and prohibitions on everyone – will use it to control the commoners and the prince, and will forbid homage to be rendered to the prince, while the prince will have bound everyone to swear to him and will permit obedience to no one but himself. And as each will vigorously wish to defend his own rights and not give up those he would assume, this arrangement will be incompatible with the nature of government in that the same actor that has the highest right of command would be forced to obey another who is yet his subject. This makes it clear that where the rights of sovereignty are divided between the prince and his subjects, a state of confusion must result in which the issue of supreme authority will always be decided by the force of arms until the highest power is in one man, in a few, or in the entire body of citizens.[3]

Bodin was thus confused about indivisibility, his greatest problems coming in trying to show that sovereignty could not be shared. His attempts to show that it was undivided in the Roman and other constitutions commonly regarded as mixed depended on a certain misunderstanding of their institutions. He failed to recognise the independent legislative function of the senate which thus shared power with the people in the earlier phase of the Roman constitution, and overlooked the powers of analogous councils in other ancient and modern city-states. On

---

3. Bodin 1586, II.1, p. 184. See also the sentence which follows directly after the passage on the sharing of sovereignty previously quoted: 'But if the people are given the power of making the laws and creating the magistrates, while all of the remaining powers are allowed to the senate or the magistrates, it will have to be acknowledged that the state is popular. For the power given to the senate and the magistrates is entrusted to them on loan and can be taken back at the people's command' (1586, II.1, p. 176).

the other hand, in treating contemporary European kingships, the thesis of undivided sovereignty was sustained by avoiding any clear definitions of the scope of public power. Only thus could Bodin account for the constitutional realities of the French kingship without acknowledging that sovereignty was shared.

For despite the centralisation and growth of royal power in the Renaissance, medieval notions of limited government still lingered on in French constitutional opinion. Commentators in the main tradition going back to Claude de Seyssel, held that the king of France, although sovereign and the source of all authority, was expected to act according to the law and not to change it without the advice of some semi-independent council like the high court, or *parlement* of Paris (Seyssel 1981, pt I, chs. viii–xii, pp. 49–58). Bodin not only accepted these restraints on royal power, but gave them even greater scope and weight. He held that a king of France could not change well-established law without the consent of the provincial or general estates, and that decrees in conflict with that law could be refused enforcement by the *parlements* (Franklin 1973, pp. 34ff).

The admission of these limitations seems at first sight to be in glaring conflict with Bodin's claim that sovereignty undivided was vested in the king. But when he wrote the *Methodus*, Bodin was implicitly working with a concept of limited supremacy. A king's authority, accordingly, could be sovereign yet less than absolute. He could be bound by fundamental law in the broader sense of well-established custom, which he could not change without consent. But if his regular powers were normally sufficient for the conduct of affairs and if nothing could be done apart from his initiative, he seemed nonetheless to be supreme. By such criteria a proper monarch like the king of France could be distinguished from the doge of Venice or the emperor of Germany, who were little more than figureheads, and might even be deposed for cause.

There is a certain common sense to this relaxed conception of supremacy, and it might be roughly workable.[4] But as the use of it in later writers shows, it is ultimately too flexible. The distinction between fundamental and ordinary law (which parallels the distinction between constituent and ordinary sovereignty) is legitimate, and indispensable, in constitutional theory. But where the scope of 'fundamental' becomes too indefinite and broad, the utility of sovereignty as a juridical concept is undermined. Bodin would have done better, therefore, to have defined the ruler's sovereignty as absolute (except with respect to the law of nature and

---

4. Which was once my own opinion: Franklin 1973, pp.38–40. But see Gierke 1966, p.161.

fundamental law more narrowly defined), and have conceded that its functions were divided among the king, the *parlements*, and the estates.

But the incoherence in Bodin's theory of sovereignty was to be eliminated in a different way. By 1576, when his *République* appeared, he had come to the conclusion that sovereignty was absolute, by which he meant that a truly sovereign authority must have all the power that a state could legitimately exercise. To this extent the clarification of his doctrine was reasonable enough. But since Bodin continued to insist that sovereignty was indivisible, he concluded, necessarily but wrongly, that there had to exist in every commonwealth a single individual or group in which the entire power of the state was concentrated. Furthermore, since he had never doubted that the king of France was truly sovereign, it now seemed utterly clear that the king of France was absolute. And this applied to kings of England and of Spain as well.

Bodin was probably led to this revised idea of sovereignty by two considerations. One, almost surely, was further reflection on the logic of indivisibility, a thesis which had earlier been more or less intuitive. He must now have recognised that if there were legitimate acts of governance which a king could not perform without the consent of the estates or *parlement* then these consenting agents must have a share in his authority. Hence, consistent with the principle of indivisibility, he had to conclude that sovereignty was absolute, that the exercise of supreme authority could not be restrained within its territory by any independent agent. But Bodin would have been confirmed in this conclusion by another, more political, concern with the issue of resistance to a tyrant-king. At the time of the *Methodus* he had managed to avoid this question. Ten years later, however, in the midst of recurrent civil wars, the right of resistance was publicly asserted by the opponents of the crown, and Bodin, alarmed, construed it as a recipe for anarchy.[5] But the very key to resistance doctrine was the set of restraints on royal power that Bodin had earlier been inclined to admit. He must now have seen, at least intuitively, that binding restraints upon the ruler implied some sense in which the community was higher than the king and would have power to act against a tyrant. It would have been seen to follow, therefore, that the absolute power of the king of France and of every other proper sovereign was not only an analytic truth but the very foundation of political stability (Bodin 1961, Preface).

The outcome, accordingly, of Bodin's revised idea of sovereignty was

5. On French resistance theory see Franklin (ed.) 1969; and see Skinner 1978, II, ch. 7–9, on the more general doctrinal and political setting for assertions of a right of resistance and revolution in the period.

systematic elimination, in the *République*, of all enforceable limitations on the king's authority. This is not to say that there were no restrictions morally. Bodin strenuously insisted that absolute kings were subject to the law of nature – that they were bound to respect the liberty and property of free subjects, and that they were obligated by contracts entered into with private citizens. Bodin even managed to hold that, except in emergencies, new taxation required the consent of the estates if it was not to be a mere taking of the subject's property. But for violations of the law of nature the king was answerable to God alone, and was not required, in construing it, to have approval from the courts or the estates. Bodin believed that a prudent king would heed the remonstrations of the *parlement* and he recommended that the estates be frequently consulted. But these were in no way binding obligations. They were mere recommendations of humanity and prudence (Franklin 1973, pp. 79ff; Bodin 1961, pp. 149ff).

Bodin continued to believe that a king was also 'bound' by customary fundamental law. But this domain of law, which had been left vaguely broad in the *Methodus*, was now narrowed down to two arrangements – one prescribing the rule of succession to the throne, the other forbidding alienation of the royal domain without consent. Both rules were designed to keep the state intact, rather than to limit the royal right of governance. Their guarantee, moreover, was simply that attempted alterations or alienations by a sitting king would be disallowed upon his death. Hence neither the law of nature nor fundamental law could justify a challenge to absolute authority or resistance to a sitting king (Franklin 1973, pp. 70–9).

This systematic elimination of binding institutional restraints was a distortion of constitutional practice. But given the elements of ambiguity in the French tradition, the break was not easy to detect. The obligation of the king to keep existing law had always been presented tactfully. In the 1560s the obtaining of consent before changing well-established law was considered to be the normal and unvarying practice, but the invocation of absolute authority had not been totally excluded. The right of the estates had not been specified precisely in the older commentators; and there was even some uncertainty attaching to the status of the *parlements* (see Church 1941, ch. 3). They did not quite assert a veto on royal legislation, so much as a right of continued remonstration until such time as their complaints were heeded. Hence Bodin's change in 1576 would not have been obvious to many of his readers, and Bodin himself must have regarded his position in the *République* as a mere clarification of a doctrine he had always held.

As Bodin presented it, however, the idea of absolute kingship would not have seemed threatening to moderate contemporaries, and might have even been attractive. In one way or another he had managed to account for almost all the limitations that had been traditionally considered indispensable. And although he had undermined the legal force of checks upon the king, he still expected them to operate as in the past. He confidently believed that the complaints and administrative pressures of the magistrates would restrain impulsive rulers and he optimistically expected that the political value of the estates was sufficient to assure their consultation. Bodin's account of sovereignty would thus have appeared to be compatible with civilised and law-abiding government. Yet it seemed to provide an ironclad defence against any justification of resistance from below, which was to recommend it strongly in the troubled circumstances of the later sixteenth century (Bodin 1961, II.5, pp. 297ff).

ii   The question of sovereignty in the constitution
of the German Empire

Hence, despite its basic error, Bodin's theory of sovereignty was received not only in France but in Spain and England also, where it was even less consistent with constitutional realities. In the epoch of resurgent royalism that followed the religious war, it was neither safe nor patriotic to question the logic of sovereignty. Jurists who continued to insist on the binding force of limitations generally abstained from challenge. They simply documented limits on the king while maintaining an attitude of reverence, and catalogued the legal precedents without speculation on the locus and character of sovereignty. It was only in the German Empire, where the monarch was universally and even officially acknowledged to be limited, that Bodin's central thesis posed an inescapable challenge to academic jurisprudence. And even here the issue was not clearly joined until the first decade of the seventeenth century.

Before this time the only knowledgeable answer to Bodin seems to have come from the French jurist, Vincent Cabot, who briefly yet lucidly set forth four formulas by which a mixed constitution could be instituted.

I shall not pursue these points further, since it is enough to have shown that there can be a mixed state and that it can come about in four ways, as is evident from what I have said. First, if one partner has one kind of supreme power, and another another; as when the king may constitute magistrates at his discretion, the aristocrats decide as to war and peace, and the people make the laws. Next, if they [all] have the same power but not with respect to the same persons, as in the

309

Roman republic where, as I said, the punishment of crimes committed in Italy was in the senate if they were done by provincials and in the people if by citizens. Further, if they [all] have the same power over the same persons, but one cannot act without the other; as if the prince could not establish magistrates, make law or complete any other act of supreme power without the senate and the people. Last, if one can do some things alone, and cannot do other things without consent, while the others alone cannot do anything. (Cabot 1752, p. 623)

Yet this first, very promising attempt was destined to have little influence. Apart from a passing reference to Poland, there is no comment on any European monarchy that might have sparked a controversy. Almost all of the illustrations are drawn from ancient Rome. Cabot, furthermore, does not diagnose the basis of Bodin's confusions, or offer an alternative theory of sovereignty, which alone was calculated to dispel the belief in indivisibility. Cabot, in short, was not yet part of a continuing debate; his ideas were not developed further by himself or noted, except occasionally, by later writers.

Among German writers, on the other hand, the issue raised by Bodin was more immediate and urgent. The emperor was more drastically restricted in his power than any of the kings of western Europe. Political power was decentralised among the individual 'estates'[6] of the empire – most epecially the Electors and the territorial princes, but also the cities which held directly of the emperor. And largely to guarantee these local privileges, limitations on the emperor by institutions representing the estates were extensive and jealously enforced. Not only was the emperor bound to make no law without the consent of the estates assembled in a diet, but some of his highest executive and judicial functions were jointly exercised with representatives of the estates in general or with the Seven Electors which, as the most preeminent estates, often acted on behalf of all. Appointment to vacant fiefs of the empire thus required consent of the estates, and cases in which an estate was a party under imperial law were heard not in the prince's court but in the high court of the empire in which the estates shared jurisdiction with the emperor. Most of these arrangements, along with others, were recorded in capitulations which had been undertaken by emperors at the time of their election and which thus afforded authoritative texts of fundamental law. The recesses, or ordinances, which embodied the legislation agreed to in a diet were often enacted in the name of estates together with the emperor.

---

6. The term 'estates' in German usage often refers to the individuals having independent powers in the empire, although sometimes also to groups of individuals having a common status (as in 'three estates'). In what follows the primary meaning will usually be clear from the context.

In the sixteenth century, furthermore, these limitations were generally accepted by the legal commentators. It is sometimes suggested in the secondary literature that opinions on the status of the emperor, who was regularly a Catholic Habsburg, were divided along confessional lines – that Catholics tended to magnify the office with the Calvinists tending to be more militant on the rights of the estates and the Lutherans hewing to a conciliatory middle course. Such differences no doubt existed on the level of attitudes and programmes. But as to the basic facts of the German constitution there seems to have been little disagreement, at least among the more eminent and influential legal commentators. Since all of them were either professors at territorial universities or councillors to territorial princes and imperial cities, or both of these at once, they were hardly inclined to question the rights of the estates. In the first two decades of the seventeenth century, their accounts of constitutional restraints, not only in outline but also in detail, were pretty much the same. All agreed, moreover, that an emperor who defied restraints could be formally deposed for tyranny. The removal of Wenceslas in 1400 was generally taken without question as a precedent.

Yet these same commentators were by no means willing to embrace Bodin's conclusion that, strictly speaking, the German Empire was no longer a monarchy in any sense at all. Beginning with the Golden Bull and then with various electoral capitulations of the fifteenth century, the emperor, according to Bodin, had become utterly subject to the assembled estates, which, having acquired all the legislative power, could command the law as they saw fit and depose the emperor if he proved unwilling to comply. The emperor still retained the titles and honours of a king. But the German Empire, like the kingdoms of Denmark, Sweden, and Poland, was neither a monarchy, nor yet a mixed constitution, but a principate. The prince in these systems was but the first citizen and chief magistrate of an aristocratic state, who was properly compared with the doge of Venice, not a sovereign ruler like the king of France (Bodin 1961, II.6, pp. 321ff, II.1, pp. 262, 270).

German jurists and humanists writing around 1600, however, were not yet ready to make a cipher of the emperor. The territorial estates still looked to the empire for their common defence and for the settlement of disputes among them, for which purpose the emperor's initiative was needful, since the diet was primarily an instrument of limitation rather than of governance. Some independence of power in the emperor thus seemed residually useful; and in an age of resurgent royalism monarchical status for the emperor seemed also to be requisite for German dignity. Hence,

Bodin's equation of the emperor and the doge of Venice was offensive to patriotic and feudal sensibilities. Not all the commentators of all the different regions were equally sensitive in this respect, but none had reason to defend Bodin, while most had reason to oppose him. Indeed, with the one exception of Henning Arnisaeus, and that only partial, all the leading writers of the early 1600s insisted that the German emperor was a true monarch in some sense or another.

By thus asserting both monarchy and the right of the estates, the Germans were drawn into conflict with Bodin's theses on the indivisibility of sovereignty. The constitutional circumstances favouring such a confrontation were also present in other monarchies of central and northern Europe, which Bodin had also characterised as principates. But it was only in Germany that an intellectual culture existed which favoured theoretical elaboration of the issues. The first two decades of the seventeenth century marked the introduction of schools of public law in various sections of the empire. Beginning about 1600 a mass of brochures, dissertations, and treatises began to appear on politics and public law in general and German public law particularly, in which the analysis of sovereignty was inevitably a central topic.[7] By the middle 1620s, as we shall see, a satisfactory theory of mixed constitutions was finally presented (see below pp. 323ff). But this was only after much confusion and a number of false starts, a review of which will help to indicate the difficulties of the problem and the importance of its resolution.

Thus Johannes Althusius, although known as a critic of Bodin, endorsed his view on indivisibility. Bodin's real error, for Althusius, was his attribution of absolute power to the ruler, which the latter rejected as both immoral and inaccurate. An absolute power, he agreed, could indeed be found in every commonwealth. But for Althusius, here as so often transmitting the monarchomach position, that power was inalienably vested in the people and was held by the ruler only as a delegated power subject to conditions. This distinction between the constituent power of the people and the ordinary power of the ruler, or, as it would soon be called, between real and personal majesty, was an advance in the theory of sovereignty. But it did not dispose of the issue of indivisibility. For where,

---

7. On the development of schools of public law in this period, the classical account is Stintzing 1880–4, I.15.4ff. A brief but excellent recent account is Hoke 1968, pp. 17–39. For the history of doctrine the classical account is Stintzing 1880–4, II.17; Gierke 1966 *passim*; and Gierke 1957. For a concise modern survey see Hoke 1968, pp. 54–93, 152–64. A full treatment of the history of doctrines of sovereignty in German thought is Gross 1973, chs. 1–5.

as in Germany, the prince was limited by law, he required the consent of the estates not only for changes in the constitution, but for ordinary acts of legislation, from which it followed, on Althusius' own account, that the form of state, or personal majesty, was mixed. And indeed when Althusius came to consider 'the forms of supreme magistrate' in the very last chapter of his treatise, he was bound to admit that the German Empire, like the French monarchy, contained an element of aristocracy. Yet he was still unwilling, or perhaps unable, to understand such a kingship as prevailed in Germany as a mixed constitution, and felt justified in calling it a monarchy since that was the component which he took to be predominant.

> Therefore, the kingdom of Germany or of France is a monarchy, even though the power of the emperor or king is limited by the high court (*parlamento*) and the councils of the realm. I have not denied this [monarchical status] in ch. 14 as Arnisaeus thinks, in his *Doctrina Politica*, ch. 8. For even though there is something of aristocracy in this French and German monarchy, or kingdom, that does not mean that it ceases to be a monarchy. For the forms of commonwealth are to be judged from the preeminent, prevailing, and predominant part.
>
> (Althusius 1932, ch. 39, p. 404)

Institutional restraints upon the king are thus treated as moderations of the royal principle rather than as alterations of the form. In practice no systems ever is, or can be, pure, and all three components of monarchy, aristocracy, and democracy will always be present, even though one of them predominates and gives the state its name. This admixture of components, furthermore, is desirable as well as unavoidable, since it works against abuse of power, and the best arrangement, indeed, is a 'tempered' monarchy more or less as in the German Empire (ch. 39, p. 405). But in admitting this tempering of forms, Althusius does not acknowledge mixture in the strict sense of the sharing or distribution of the rights of (personal) sovereignty. Indeed, he comes close to rejecting it explicitly in a critical comment on Cabot's four suggestions. 'I do not approve these mixtures', says Althusius, 'nor do use and practice admit them, except insofar as the people in the election of a king or supreme magistrate has reserved certain powers to itself. That sort of mixture is the best, as I have said. And such is thought to have existed in the Spartan commonwealth' (ch. 39, p. 405).

The problem in Althusius is not that his account is wrong, but that the concepts of predominance and tempering are non-technical and imprecise. Political predominance does not exclude legal division of the rights of sovereignty, since the powers may be shared unequally and in such a way that one of the parties is situated more strategically for the advancement of its policies. Conversely, even where sovereignty is legally concentrated in a single individual or group, the pattern of effective influence need not correspond. And where, as in Germany, the tempering of monarchy depended on binding rules, as Althusius clearly thought, the limitation is not merely political but also constitutional, and the system is a mixture in one or more of the ways discriminated by Cabot.

It thus appears that Althusius' distinction between a tempered kingship and a mixed constitution simply cannot be technically maintained. In any event it could hardly be stretched to cover the German emperor. The 'certain powers' that the people had reserved, in Germany as well as Sparta, were so far-reaching as to threaten the very notion of the emperor's 'predominance' no matter how construed. The point is made against Althusius by Arnisaeus, who was Bodin's shrewdest and most independent follower among the German commentators. Arnisaeus, too, felt constrained to admit the existence of impurities and deviations in simple forms of states, but only insofar as they did not compromise the very form. Althusius, he thought, was one of those who had been too permissive in describing the monarchy of France. Along with the Huguenot resistance theorists, he had acknowledged reservations of power to the people that removed France from the ranks of monarchy:

A similar error is to be found in Junius Brutus, *Vindiciae contra tyrannos*, in Hotman's *De antiq. jur. Gallo*,[8] and in Althusius' *Politica*, c. 14, all of which exclude the French kingdom from the class of monarchies in that the first law of the kingdom as Hotman reports it in ch. 23 of his *De antiq. jur.* is that nothing bearing on the general condition of the kingdom can be decided by the king without authorisation of the public council.[9]

Unlike Althusius, Bartholomaeus Keckermann was willing to admit not only tempered forms of state but fully mixed constitutions in which each of the partners had an equal role. Yet he too was never led to break with Bodin on the indivisibility of sovereignty. Keckermann seems to have thought of mixture as a tempering of a simple form, which had been carried as far as it could go. But tempering or moderation, no matter whether the dose thereof was large or small, did not suggest to him, any

---

8. This refers to *De antiquo jure regni Galliae*, a posthumous edition of Hotman's *Francogallia*.
9. Arnisaeus 1606, VIII, pp. 159–60. For Althusius' embarrassed denial of this charge in the third edition of his *Politica* see p. 313 above. Arnisaeus, it may be noted, achieved consistency in his own criterion of monarchy only by interpreting all of Hotman's limitations on the king of France as royal courtesies.

more than to Althusius, a genuine sharing of the rights of majesty. Searching for a looser, more 'Bodinian' solution, Keckermann believed that he had found it in a distinction between state and government introduced for this purpose by none other than Bodin himself. Bodin, he claimed, had ultimately backed away from his strict rejection of the mixed constitution. He 'does not deny', says Keckermann, 'that one form may be tempered by another in its mode of government, as when a monarchy is aristocratic in its mode of government, or even democratic. But this is the very thing we want, namely that the simple forms of commonwealth can be moderated by each other' (Keckermann 1608, II.iv, p. 560).

This, however, is a serious misrepresentation of Bodin for whom the form of governance is not a modification of the form of state. The form of government, as distinguished from the state, is rather the pattern by which the sovereign distributes offices among the various classes of his subjects. Since the powers of these offices and the right to hold them are at the discretion of the sovereign, at least in strictest law, the form of government, no matter how desirable, is not a constitutional requirement. Although Bodin does not put it exactly in such words, his meaning is abundantly clear:

We will thus hold it for settled that the state of a commonwealth is always simple even if the [form of] government is contrary to the [form of] state. Thus monarchy is altogether opposite to a popular state, and yet sovereignty can be vested in a single prince who governs democratically, as I have said. This will not, however, introduce mixing (*confusion*) of a popular state with monarchy, which are indeed incompatible, but rather of monarchy with popular government, which is the most stable monarchy of all.[10]

With Keckermann, on the other hand, there is no distinction between the distribution of offices as an ordinary rule and as a constitutional requirement. His model of a monarchy governed aristocratically is the French system as it is described by François Hotman, the *Vindiciae contra tyrannos*, and Althusius; and this is also his model for the German Empire on which his comments are tactfully oblique (Keckermann 1608, II.iv, p. 563). Hence Keckermann, like many other writers after him, could eat his cake and have it too. He speaks of a mixed constitution. He describes a mixed constitution. But by misapplying Bodin's terminology, he is able to avoid speaking of divided sovereignty, and somehow manages to think of the state as monarchy. He merely fails to notice that the terms 'state' and

10. Bodin 1961, II.7, p.339, and compare 1586, II.7, p.234, for a slightly modified version in the Latin. See also 1961, pp.1013–14.

'government', in Bodin's usage, refer to different levels of authority, the first to the ownership of power and the second to the exercise thereof in accordance with the owner's will. Keckermann, therefore, admitted mixture but failed to see the implications for the theory of sovereignty.

A solution similar to Keckermann's was also proposed by Hermann Kirchner, the humanist and historian, who was among the most creative theorists of sovereignty in the first quarter of the seventeenth century. Kirchner's *Respublica* (1608) is the *locus classicus* for the principle of double majesty or the distinction between constituent power and the ordinary power of the state. That distinction is virtually present in Bodin, who speaks, in his *République*, of fundamental laws on the succession to the throne and on the inalienability of domain that an incumbent ruler cannot alter even though he is absolute for all ordinary purposes. Althusius, citing this as an implicit recognition of the people as the source of all authority, already spoke in passing of *duplex majestas*, or double majesty.[11] But he regularly preferred to reserve the term sovereignty or majesty for the constituent power of the people and to describe the power conceded to the government as *potestas administrationis*. With Kirchner the distinction is more clearly drawn and generalised in what was to become the standard terminology. There was in every commonwealth, he held, a *majestas realis*, or constituent supremacy, which always remains in the people as the source of all authority, and *majestas personalis*, or ordinary supremacy, which is delegated to the prince, or government, on whatever terms the people may prescribe.

Given the sharpness of this and other formulations in Kirchner, we might expect him to have read Bodin correctly as to state and government, and to describe the latter merely as administrative arrangements enacted by the holder of (personal) majesty. Yet when he offers an account of the mixed constitution, Kirchner makes the same mistake as Keckermann. 'But you will easily settle the issue', he informs his reader, 'if you hold that the state of a commonwealth differs from the principle of government and mode of administration, as did Bodin, indeed, when he saw that he had trapped himself. For he avowed it to be possible that the state could be royal and yet be governed democratically' (Kirchner 1614, p. 53).

Kirchner then goes on to describe the modern German Empire as a

---

11. Commenting on Bodin's unwitting admission of an ultimate layer of sovereignty on which the king's is based, he comments '... even according to Bodin there is a double majesty of the kingdom and of the king ...' (1932, ch. 9, p. 93). But the term *duplex majestas* could have been borrowed from Kirchner.

monarchy tempered by an aristocratic plan of government. 'And yet', he says,

the advice and consent of the aristocratic element, which serves the empire as rowers do a ship, takes nothing from its royal keel ... and does not diminish the authority of the royal power in promulgating laws but only graces and augments it ... And this is evidenced by the opinion of Bodin himself, who contends that the French kingdom is absolutely monarchical, ... although they never granted their kings absolute authority uncontrolled by law but rather tempered the course of royal governance with the advice and consent of assemblies and convocations, of the *parlements* and of the peers of France.   (p. 54)

That Kirchner here is thinking of consent as a binding requirement is indicated not only by his choice of words but by his citation of Hotman as his prime authority on French procedures (pp. 54, 94). And later on, the rule for Germany – as for England, Spain, and France – is said to be 'that the king may decide nothing pertaining to the state of the kingdom as a whole without the authority of the public council' (p. 94). Yet Kirchner somehow managed to persuade himself that Bodin too could be listed among those who ratified this formula. In Book III, ch. I of the *République*, Bodin held that a weighty senate is indispensable to a well-ordered monarchy. Kirchner cites this chapter without considering Bodin's express insistence that the proper role of a senate is advice and nothing more (p. 54).

By loose and careless use of Bodin's distinction between state and government, Kirchner felt able to account for mixture while still ignoring the divisibility of sovereignty, and to speak of the empire as an aristocratically governed monarchy by glossing over the question of a partnership in sovereign authority. Was personal majesty vested solely in the emperor? If so, how does one account for binding limitations in his mode of governance? Or if personal majesty was shared between the emperor and the estates, why, then, should the empire be called a monarchy? Given the looseness of the terminology, Kirchner's distinction between state and government allowed such questions to be bypassed.

So loose was it, indeed, that the distinction could be used to draw the very opposite conclusion! Kirchner had intended to account for mixture and was so understood by other writers of the time. But with just the slightest twist, his distinction between state and government could be made to show that the German monarchy was pure and even absolute, yet still without denying the facts of the imperial constitution! This, indeed, was the purpose for which Kirchner's argument on moderated monarchy was most often used. And one of the main architects of that adaptation was

Daniel Otto who was among the most prolific and ingenious commentators on the theory of sovereignty and the constitution of the empire in the first quarter of the seventeenth century.

In an article of 1620, 'An mixtus detur reipublicae status?' ('Is There such a Thing as a Mixed State?'), Otto denies that Kirchner, any more than the others who defended mixture, have found a rationale, and he then proceeds to turn the distinction between state and government against them. The form of state, he observes, denotes the essence and substance of a commonwealth; the form of administration merely indicates its quality. But a change of qualities, or accidents, does not affect the essence of a thing, so that Bodin was perfectly consistent in conceding the possibility of mixture in administration while denying it in the state itself. It thus follows that Kirchner, Keckermann, and others who defended mixture in this way have begged the question. And Otto felt able to conclude, triumphantly, that the empire was a simple monarchy!

Since all of this is so, we confidently conclude that the modern empire is a monarchical state, and a simple one at that, because not even a particle of the imperial majesty is shared with the princes of the empire ... And although in some areas the state is tempered by aristocratic principles, it cannot on that account be called aristocratic or mixed ... It is clear enough from what has been said that the mode of administration does not change the form of state. (Otto 1620, p. 652)

But Otto's dissent from Keckermann and Kirchner is simply a different conclusion from the same mistake as to the distinction between state and government. With Bodin, the function of those who assist the sovereignty in governance is merely to advise or to carry out his orders. The consent of the estates in Germany, however, which extended to almost all the great affairs of state, was a constitutional requirement – a fact which Otto himself does not deny, but rather openly admits!

For although there are many rights of majesty that the emperor cannot exercise without the approval and consent of the imperial estates – as is evident from imperial capitulations and from that clause so constantly used in imperial recesses, *darüber wir uns mit ihnen und sie hindwiderumb mit uns verglichen* – yet nevertheless monarchical power is not removed.

For what really counts, is whether the rights of supreme majesty are constrained, or detracted from. The first of these surely diminishes absolute power, but does not always cancel the existence of a supreme magistrate. The second leaves no [supreme] magistrate at all, because there can be no [supreme] magistrate who is lacking in the rights of sovereignty. (p. 653)

The sovereignty of the emperor is thus held to be constrained but not defective, diminished in its absoluteness but still supreme. Yet sovereignty constrained in matters of ordinary law is sovereignty shared, especially when it is limited as thoroughly and pervasively as it was in the German Empire. It thus turns out that Otto's talk about essence and qualities, substances and accidents, as applied to state and government, uses distinctions without a difference since the 'qualities' were prescribed and the 'accidents' constitutionally required.

There are two other assertions connected with Otto's view of the emperor's sovereignty that should perhaps be mentioned briefly. One is the argument that the feudal tenure of the German princes and the oath of fealty attached thereto imply subjection to the emperor and are inconsistent with their possession of a share of sovereignty. Yet Otto does not deny, and does not wish to deny, the hereditary status of the princes or the collective right of the estates. The language of subjection in the oaths that he cites is thus at odds with well-established constitutional norms, and should have been regarded as mostly ceremonial (p. 651). The second contention, more curious for modern readers, is that the emperor 'enjoyed' or somehow 'made use of' absolute authority. By this language Otto does not intend to deny constitutional limitations on the emperor. Like other champions of a German monarchy before him, he means merely that there are still certain areas of government in which the emperor can act alone without consent and at his own discretion. Otto suggestively notes that such power is the residual expression of an authority that was plenary in ancient Roman times. But he has no intention of denying that this 'absolute' authority has been narrowed in its scope and strictly delimited by law. 'We turn now', he says, in another of his essays,

> to our Romano-German Emperor, and we ask whether he can still be considered absolute (*an etiamnum solutus dici possit*). The basis of doubt is that the emperor cannot exercise the rights of majesty without consent of the Electors and the estates . . . The basis of decision is that the absolute power conceded (*legibus soluta potestas concessa*) to the emperor has never been taken back *in toto*, either tactily or expressly . . . Hence he still enjoys that power. . .[12]

---

12. 'An princeps legibus sit solutus?' (1616, p. 519). This use of 'absolute' is also to be found in Gottfried Antonius and Theodor Reinking. In the course of a complex polemic with Hermann Vulteius and his followers, Antonius assumed the position of a champion of mixture in the German constitution, the very point of which was to show that the emperor had 'absolute' power in some respects. 'Whatever was conceded to the emperors by Roman law, and has not subsequently been taken back tacitly or expressly, they still enjoy and use . . . In Roman law, however, the power conceded to the emperors was absolute . . . nor can it be shown that it was ever tacitly or expressly taken back completely. Therefore, they still enjoy and use that power' (*De potestate Imperatoris*, in Antonius 1614, p. 625). For the position of Vulteius, who as early as 1599 attempted, almost allusively, to explain the German constitution by the state-government distinction, see *Ad titulos Codicis qui sunt de iurisdictione et foro competenti*, p. 511 (on III.xxiv.1.i of Code). For brief summations of the debate, which is often too confused for easy summary, see Stintzing 1880–4, I, pp. 462–3, II, p. 39; Hoke 1968, p. 23; Gross 1973, pp. 138–41. Reinkingk (1631, I, *classis* iii.xiii, no. 25–9) uses arguments similar to those of Antonius and Otto to glorify the emperor.

Otto's case for the sovereignty of the German emperor thus depends not so much on a misrepresentation of the constitutional relationships as on ambiguity of terms. But it must not be thought that this cluster of equivocations was peculiar to him. It was an attractive device for patriotic commentators who hoped to strengthen allegiance to the empire by enhancing the symbol of the emperor. Thus all the arguments we have noted in Otto are also to be found in Theodor Reinking whose loyalist treatise on the empire continued to be republished well into the eighteenth century.[13]

But the confusion of this period on the mixed constitution was not only the result of sentimental or patriotic attachment to the principle of monarchy in the German constitution. For there were at least two very highly sophisticated legal commentators who fully recognised the sharing of sovereignty in the German constitution yet could only think of it as a polyarchy rather than a mixture. The problem here was not that they failed to understand the legal relations among the partners of a mixed constitution. It was rather their inability to see that a mixed sovereign was a compound corporation in which at least one of the members was itself a corporate body. They thus assumed, mistakenly, that constitutions like the classical Roman or the contemporary German were properly described as (simple) polyarchies.

Thus Arnisaeus clearly recognised that in the early period of the classical Roman republic the legislative power was shared between the senate and the people. In Bodin, as we have noted, the formula by which the senate authorised and the people decided was denied or misinterpreted. But Arnisaeus treats this as a mode of mixture, or rather of attempted mixture, in which 'the same right of majesty is given separately to two or more estates, but to each one in a different way', so that neither has the whole of it (Arnisaeus 1606, viii, p. 163, cf. 1615, II.vii, p. 875). And although he believed that such a system is likely to be unstable for political reasons, he does not find sharing or conjoint ownership of sovereignty to be formally inconsistent with the coordination of political authority.

But for this very reason, ironically, he refuses to admit that sovereignty held conjointly is a form of mixed constitution. In a mixed constitution, he assumes, the rights of sovereignty may well be separated and the separated rights distributed to different partners – which, indeed, is to construct a

---

13. Stintzing 1880–4, II, p. 40. For parallels to Otto's evasions in Reinking see, among other places, especially: 1631, I, *classis*, ii.1, nos. 56, 89, 137, 196.

compound sovereign. But he believes that if a constitution is to be mixed by means of sharing, this can only be if the entirety of any power or set of powers is granted to each of the partners in the same way at the same time! This, of course, is a juridical absurdity which is, however, absent from the Roman scheme of legislation since power there was shared conjointly by the senate and the people. But how, then, is that arrangement to be classified? For Arnisaeus it is simply a version of polity in Aristotle's sense because it seeks to balance the interests of the nobles and the commoners by giving equal weight to each.

Yet in this [Roman] arrangement there is no mixture of commonwealths since neither the senate nor the commoners control the rights of majesty, but these are handed to each of them conjointly. Since, then, patricians and plebeians rule in equal measure, how else portray this state than as a polity (*Rempublicam in specie*)? For it is not the mode of administration (*modus dispensationis*) but the degree of domination (*gradus dominationis*) that constitutes the form of a commonwealth, and so long as the commoners and the nobles participate on an equal basis, they join together into a true and legitimate commonwealth. An example may be taken from the Roman republic, the gradual degeneration of which into a democracy after the introduction of the tribunes is beyond all doubt . . . and yet the distinction between the power (*potestatem*) of the commoners and the authority (*authoritatem*) of the senate did not cease to exist up to the change of regime, or up to the age of Livy, Florus, and Dio. (1615, p. 876).

But this expansion of the concept of a polity leads to confusing ambiguities. In a constitution mixed by sharing, like the Roman, the constituent elements are separate corporations, each of which casts its vote independently of the other. In the idea of polity as it is found in Aristotle, on the other hand, sovereignty is located in a single assembly wherein all participate as individuals although certain voting procedures are adopted to promote a balanced outcome. It is thus a kind of moderate democracy which, at least in its juridical principle, is very different from a mixed constitution. Arnisaeus, indeed, is not unaware of the difference between vote by order and vote by head. Speaking of polity (*respublica in specie*), he notes the difficulty of maintaining the equality of nobles and people (which is the very meaning of polity) where voting is individual, and then continues:

Since it might not be possible in this manner to keep the patricians and the commoners within the confines of a shared commonwealth because the commoners would be preponderant, Aristotle points out another way in *Politics* IV, chs. 8–9, which he calls *mixin* [mixing], or blending of oligarchy and democracy, and in which he locates the nature of the polity (*reipublicae in specie*). If all the citizens are admitted to the suffrage on a man by man basis, the majority may crush the minority, as has been said. But if the entire order of patricians is accorded a right equal to that of the entire order of commoners, without regard to the weight of numbers, then a form of shared commonwealth comes about in which the commoners can do no more than the nobility by virtue of their great numbers. There is, moreover, a distinction between this commonwealth and a mixed system, as we will show more fully in c.vi, sec. 1, since in a mixed commonwealth the rights of sovereignty are distributed among all the parts of the commonwealth, whereas in this they remain in all of them undivided, so that the first is a compound and this one mixed in such a way that it does not deviate from simplicity in its essence, given that to admit all the citizens into the government of the commonwealth on an equal footing (*aequo jure*) is the sign of a simple not a compound commonwealth. In a compound the king, the aristocrats, and the people each have different rights, but in this form all citizens of either order are regarded as having one and the same right. Aristotle, *Politics* IV ch. 9, has proposed both techniques since in either case all the citizens are admitted to partnership in the commonwealth, except in one way conjointly, in the other by separate rights (*divisim*). We will speak of both ways in our chapter on the mixed commonwealth. But here we will briefly note some things than can help to understand the polity. In this commonwealth, therefore, the order of the nobility – whether it has obtained this prerogative by virtue, by wealth, or by excellence of birth – ought to be distinguished from the order of the commoners so that in deliberations the opinion of a whole order may be heard, not that of individuals. (1615, II.v, pp. 825–6).

Arnisaeus here treats voting by order as but one more device of political moderation, rather than as a separate juridical form. His concept of polity, by thus embracing both a simple and a compound polyarchy, can refer to two quite different things, and becomes imprecise and ambiguous in its meaning. On the other hand, when he is dealing with the distribution of powers, Arnisaeus can be accurate. He describes the German constitution as a mixture of aristocracy and monarchy (with the monarchical element held preponderant in his account of 1606, and the aristocratic in his account of 1615) (1606, p. 183, 1615, II.vi.5, p. 1084). But the element of mixture here admitted is merely the reservation to the emperor of certain residual executive powers, which produces a separation, or distribution, of powers between the emperor and the diet. This Arnisaeus regards as an authentic and even desirable division of the rights of sovereignty. But insofar as there are powers that are shared, or held conjointly, he calls the outcome aristocracy since, for the reasons we have given, he can have no other term for it. Just as the partnership of nobles and people is 'polity', so that of king and nobles is 'aristocracy'.[14]

---

14. This is evident from the context as in 1615, II.vi.5, p. 1073. And in the same place there is a critical comment on Paurmeister which seems to agree that the term aristocracy is properly applied to the element of sharing in the German constitution.

No less surprising, and similarly misleading, is the account by Tobias Paurmeister, whose *De jurisdictione Imperii Romani* is one of the most acute and influential treatises of this period on German public law. Paurmeister had no difficulty in recognising the shared jurisdiction of independent partners as an arrangement in which each of the partners had a veto. Speaking of the empire, he says,

> The supreme power of the empire . . . is distributed in two halves, one of which is held by Caesar, the other by the estates collectively. A division of this sort once existed between Caesar and the people, for Suetonius, writing about Caesar, notes that the power of the popular assemblies was divided [between them] – although in this case through separated areas of jurisdiction (*sed pro partibus divisis*). But now the entire power of the empire, except for the power of bestowing special rights and privileges, is shared, without divided jurisdiction (*pro partibus indivisis*), between the emperor and the estates. The half that belongs to the estates is distributed as three-sixths, of which the Electors have one, the Princes another . . . and the senate of the imperial cities the third.   (Paurmeister 1608, ii.ii, no. 20, pp. 342–3)

But although this idea of fifty-fifty sharing is later repeated in refuting Bodin's claim that sovereignty in the German constitution was entirely vested in the princes and the delegates of the cities, Paurmeister does not go on to a criticism of Bodin on the mixed constitution (ii.ii. no. 34, pp. 356–7). On the contrary, in Book ii, chapter i, he classifies the imperial system as an aristocracy or kind of oligarchy in accordance with a classification which holds that all regimes may be divided dichotomously into the rule of a few (oligarchy) and the rule of many (democracy) (ii.i, nos. 7–9, 11–12, pp. 322, 324). This classification, much like Arnisaeus', is not exactly wrong, but it does not express, or even hint at, the fact of mixture in the German constitution, and might be readily taken to deny it. The terms oligarchy or aristocracy, then as well as now, would ordinarily convey the idea of a polyarchy in which those entitled to participate would vote not by corporation but by head, and it would therefore fail to indicate that the emperor in the German constitution had an independent share.

iii Besold and the mixed constitution

A clear understanding of the sharing of sovereignty and an adequate formula for the German constitution appear only with the work of Christoph Besold, who was the first to formulate the concept of a compound polyarchy. Besold seems to have put forward this conception in the first decade of the seventeenth century and then to have worked out the implications in the course of a running debate with Otto. His earlier statements are virtually inaccessible. But we are fortunate in having what seems to be a complete as well as final version of his views in the form of an article, 'De reipublicae statu mixto', in a collection of his writings (1626).

Besold begins by observing that truly pure forms of state are almost never encountered in reality. But in contrast with Althusius, this does not lead him to propose that all systems be considered as virtually simple, but rather to insist that the mixed constitution is the most common form of state, and particularly so in modern Europe, in the monarchies of which the king is usually the prince of a mixed constitution (Besold 1626, p. 211).

The mixture of a constitution, furthermore, cannot be comprehended by the distinction between state and government, since the form of government exists *de facto* at the ruler's discretion, not as a *de jure* constitutional requirement. 'And surely if a commonwealth is defined not by law but by the mode of governance, then a master who embraces his servant in filial love would be his father not only in affection but in law, which no one will readily assert' (p. 211). Besold here refers approvingly to Otto's criticism of Kirchner and others who held similar views. But unlike Otto he is completely clear on the difference between arrangements of administrative convenience and requirements of fundamental law:

And if a king most often follows the advice of the estates of his realm and of the leading men among his people, the mode of ruling is no doubt aristocratic. But this is not to say that the form of the commonwealth is mixed unless it appears that sovereign power is shared with them in some degree. That happens only if the estates have the faculty not only of advising but also and at the same time of preventing and prohibiting; and the prince is bound to abide by their counsel or dissent.

(p. 213)

By ignoring this difference, Otto has managed to conclude that a king could be constrained in his authority and the state remain a simple monarchy. But if a prince requires the consent of others for the ordinary conduct of affairs, it makes no sense to speak as if he ruled alone. 'He [Otto] thinks it to be a point of great importance', Besold comments, 'whether the rights of a supreme authority are constrained or taken away, etc., which I do not deny. For if they are constrained it is a mixture, and if taken away a pure aristocracy' (pp. 212–13).

Thus the rights of sovereignty had to be capable of being shared, Bodinian objections notwithstanding. The core of these objections, as they had been elaborated and refined by Otto in an attack upon Besold and others, was that the logical consequence of sharing sovereignty was to annihilate it altogether. And Besold's main contribution was to formulate the consequence of sharing as the institution of a compound polyarchy:

It is never possible he [Otto] says, either in nature or even in imagination for supreme authority or majesty to be shared with an inferior and still remain supreme. It remains supreme, I answer, but not in one individual. It is rather in the whole body, or corporation, of those who rule (*archonton*) but in such a way that it is not distributed equally among the parts. The prince will be conceded some large degree of eminence (which will be larger, of course, than what the doge has in the Venetian commonwealth) or else it will be an aristocracy.   (p. 212)

The polyarchic outcome, furthermore, does not require that the king and the estates be equal partners. It can also exist where the king enjoys preeminence and is the focus of political allegiance. In a mixed constitution 'sovereignty is in the corporation (*collegium*) even though the head of that corporation, as often happens, may be above the other members in a variety of ways', and although the oath of allegiance may be rendered to the prince, it need not entail obedience to him outside his particular jurisdiction (p. 212). Even the emergency power of the prince, if such indeed exists, applies only to occasions that are foreseen by law and custom (p. 220). The components of the polyarchy, finally, are not individuals but orders, on which account it may be distinguished from democracy. Arnisaeus, Besold notes, refused to acknowledge the sharing of sovereignty as mixture:

And there seems to be some room for doubt here since a state of this kind, where all three forms of commonwealth are commingled without separation of the rights of sovereignty, may seem rather to be democracy. But in a democracy the majority decides; here the king, the nobles, and the commoners constitute three orders, and cast three votes, so that the majority of the people cannot preempt the others.
                                                                    (p. 227)

In replying to Otto on the mixed constitution Besold is thinking of sovereignty shared between two or more partners in a compound polyarchy. But when he goes on to the German constitution, he notes that a state is also mixed when different rights of sovereignty are assigned to different agents. His purpose here is to account for the *reservata* of the German emperor, such as the right of hearing certain fiscal and feudal cases in his own tribunal as well as certain rights in foreign affairs and the conduct of warfare, which he could still exercise without the consent of the Electors or estates. Otto does not reach this issue because he managed to believe that all the rights of sovereignty belonged to the emperor alone. With Besold, on the other hand, the rights of sovereignty shared by the emperor and the estates belonged to a compound body that was juridically distinct from the emperor alone so that the issue of separated powers was readily confronted.

If Besold is brief on separation, it is largely because the issue had already been resolved by Arnisaeus, who at least in this respect had broken cleanly with Bodin. The parts of sovereignty are in some sense indivisible, Arnisaeus had observed, since no one of them can be exercised without the cooperation of the others. But this is not to say that these parts, although functionally inseparable, cannot be vested in separated agents so long as they are harmonised and coordinated by fundamental law.

> For there are a number of powers and rights the union of which produces complete sovereignty. And although it is impossible for sovereignty as a whole and in its entirety to be shared among several agents, there is nothing to prevent its parts from being separated and distributed to several agents such that there is a fragment of sovereignty in each of them, and yet in the body as a whole complete and supreme sovereignty results from the union of the fragments of sovereignty coming together into one. (Arnisaeus 1606, viii, pp. 164–5)

Bodin's mistake was that he not only failed to see this need for harmonisation but gave such scope to certain parts of sovereignty that they swallowed all the rest:

> He [Bodin] concedes rights to the particular components such as carry with them the entirety of majesty, and this may not be done as we said a little while ago. Thus the power to make law on all topics cannot be given to some one component because power over everything goes with it. Nor can subjects be obligated to the king in all respects in this mixed commonwealth, because to do this is to lay the supreme power in the king's lap. (p. 166).

Properly delimited and coordinated, therefore, the rights of sovereignty can be distributed among separate agents. And this is also the conclusion in Besold, who praises mixture of this sort as conducive to political stability:

> The mixed state admits of many variations. Sometimes the rights of majesty are divided, as when the king has some of them and the senate some, or the optimates some and the commoners some. Sometimes they are shared, as when the king does not have them without the senate or the senate without the king, or when the commoners and the nobles enjoy them simultaneously. Sometimes the supreme power is tempered in other ways [outside of mixture]. In the first kind of mixed state, the rights of majesty are separated and different ones are assigned to different estates. This mixture seems to be the most finely balanced harmony, for some powers are best exercised by one person, such as the power of judging and imposing punishments, while there are others in which the participation of the orders or estates could hardly be denied without inequity. The right of undertaking a war is one of these perhaps, as well as others of a similar order.[15] (Besold 1626, p. 213)

15. Besold, it may be noted, deals with the German constitution mainly as an example of distribution. He is not quite willing openly to list it under 'ephoristic' monarchies in which sovereignty is shared but does not rule that out (p.216). Poland is his first example of shared sovereignty, a form much

Besold's refutation of Bodin and his followers was thus complete on all the main themes of indivisibility. And although he is perhaps indebted to Arnisaeus for his account of separation, his formulation of the more controversial principle of sharing seems to be original as well as luminous, and so decisive for a modern reader.[16] But in order to understand the difficulty of this question for contemporaries and their reluctance to acknowledge sharing as a form of mixture, it is worth showing how Otto, at least, attempted to maintain his view in the teeth of Besold's argument.

There had been, as we have said, a number of exchanges between Otto and Besold, and to a modern reader the first version of Besold's *De statu reipublicae mixto*, which must have appeared about 1620, should have left the question settled. But Otto in a last reply to Besold complained that the question had been begged. In his *De maiestate imperii et imperantis* of 1623, Otto contends that the concept of a compound polyarchy is not a mixture since power is in the whole and not the parts, and that it precludes the distribution of power to the parts which, Otto seems to think, is Besold's own criterion for mixture:

In response to my [earlier] argument Besold replies that supreme authority continues [after sharing] but in a corporate body or college of rulers (*archonton*) rather than in one person. To which I reply that there is no mixture here and that this state in no way differs from a polyarchy, in which sovereignty is attributed to all collectively rather than to all as individuals. But let us go on. Even though (you say) the rights of majesty are entirely in the corporation, they can nonetheless be so divided that the king has some of them, and the senate some, or the aristocrats some and the commoners some; and the senate does not have them without the king, or the commoners and the nobles assert them simultaneously. But I reject this. If the rights of majesty are assigned to the corporation as such in a polyarchic state, I simply do not see how the same can be assigned to the individual parts.

(Otto 1623, p. 31)

Otto's confusion here is twofold. In the first place, he blurs the difference between a simple and a compound polyarchy. This appears to be the same sort of error that we saw in Arnisaeus. But it is now more surprising, since it comes after Besold's clarification. In the second place, Otto utterly confuses *distribution* of the rights of sovereignty – in which some rights go to one partner and others to another – with *sharing* of the rights of sovereignty – in which the partners act together. But these two modes of mixture are clearly

recommended, he says, by Althusius, the *Vindiciae contra tyrannos*, Buchanan, and Hotman. The *reservata*, one should also note, are singled out by Antonius to show that the emperor is truly a monarch. See above p.319 n.12. And they are cited by Keckermann a one indication that the monarchical element predominates in the German mixture: 1608, ii.iv, pp.570ff.

16. For another contemporary account see Frantzke 1621, which is a competent analysis of the sharing and distribution of the rights of majesty, and seems to be dependent on Besold and Arnisaeus.

and expressly distinguished in the passage from Besold Otto paraphrases (see p. 326). Besold never suggests that the same rights of sovereignty could be shared and divided among the same partners at the same time that would of course be logically absurd.

With the appearance, in Besold, of a theoretically decisive account of the divisibility of sovereignty in a mixed constitution, we bring this chapter to a close. This is not to suggest that all of Besold's conclusions were immediately or universally taken up. Almost to the end of the eighteenth century, there were theorists who continued to treat the obligation of a king to obtain consent to legislation as sovereignty limited rather than sovereignty shared (Gierke 1957, p. 154). And there were some who followed Pufendorf in holding that the several rights of sovereignty could not be separated, so that the German and even the English constitution were to be regarded not as proper states in which some individual or body ruled, but as irregular systems which were held together merely by comity among independent parts.[17] Yet such resistance notwithstanding, a change of perspective occurs around the end of the first quarter of the seventeenth century on which Besold's influence, although often indirect and difficult to measure, was no doubt considerable (Gierke 1957, p. 118). Around that time the German empire is deliberately expounded as a mixed constitution, in something close to Besold's usage of that term, by authoritative commentators on German public law (see esp. Hoke 1968, pt II). And among theorists of sovereignty, there is an unbroken succession, starting with Besold, in whom the sharing of sovereignty as well as the distribution of its parts are correctly identified as modes of mixture that are ultimately consistent with the coordination of governmental functions (Gierke 1957, pp. 155–6, 1966, p. 170ff).

17. Pufendorf 1934, pp. 1016ff, 1038–9, 1769, II.vii.9, pp. 693–5, II.viii.12, pp. 706–8; Gierke 1957, pp. 154–5.

11

Utopianism

J.C. DAVIS

i   Christian social morality and the best state

In the fifty years after its first publication in 1516, Thomas More's *Utopia* appeared in ten further Latin editions and in French, Dutch, English, German, and Italian translations. Widespread and profound as its influence was, its ambivalence generated both utopian and anti-utopian imitators. In other words, the spread of More's fictional device – the 'discovery' of an ideal society – was not always utopian in its political thought and the utopian impulse proper was not necessarily derived in the profoundest sense from the imitation of a model.

The fifteenth-century rediscovery of Plato and Plutarch stimulated the early modern 'best state' exercise and encouraged a debate on constitutions which replicated the seed-bed out of which the classical utopia had sprung (Logan 1983; Ferguson 1975, p. 28; Manuel and Manuel 1979, pp. 95–100). But some aspects of civic humanism and of Reformation thought endorsed and broadened the idea of social redemption through individual moral performance, typified for the late middle ages by the Mirror of Princes tradition (Skinner 1978, I, pp. 126–35). Still others gradually excited a vast outpouring of millennial expectation, especially on the Protestant side of the Reformation divide. These two traditions of discourse about social idealisation – by individual moral effort or by a millennial and literal *coup de grace* – were quantitatively much more important in early modern Europe than the reemergent utopian mode which existed in dialogue with them. It is helpful, therefore, to distingish utopianism as a form of social idealisation.[1]

If we define utopia as the envisaging of a best commonwealth, or ideal

---

1. Davis 1981a, ch. 1, 1984a; cf. Sargent 1979, Introduction; Pissavino 1985.

society, of sinful human beings in a fallen world without benefit of divine agency, then More may be said to have reinaugurated the exercise. He did so in a multi-faceted work designed not only to reconcile scholasticism with humanism, expedience or prudence with virtue, Stoic and Epicurean with Christian values, but also to counsel his fellow Christian humanists against the self-indulgence of criticism without praxis, satire without responsibility. Implicitly, the *Utopia* said that the task of translating an agreed and correct set of values into political practice involved much more than moral exhortation. Did others attempt the utopian exercise in the same vein; in simple and admiring imitation of Hythlodaeus rather than More; under the influence – as More was – of the monastic model's attempt to subdue sin in a social context; or for other reasons? The answers are, of course, various.

The frame which holds that variety together is not utopianism itself but the strenuous search for ways of pursuing the best state/good life exercise of the ancients so as to make predominantly Christian social morality effective. It would be wrong to see this as purely Neoplatonic in inspiration (Goldie 1983; cf. White 1982). It was far too eclectic for that and in its utopian form owed much to the scholastics' emphasis on law and institutions (Logan 1983, pp. 75–7). A considerable body of literature throughout the period continued to see the best state/good life exercise as a moral one, a matter of will, and hence tended in the direction of the perfect moral commonwealth, however that morality was defined. At one end of the spectrum was Machiavelli's analysis of the problem of *buono ordini* in an age of corruption with his resultant stress on human will. Closer association with Christian aspiration, however, produced such works as Joannes Ferrarius Montanus' *A Work touching the Good Ordering of a Commonweal* (1559), with its attempt to reconcile Stoic, Platonic and Christian concerns. The message remained simple: as ungodliness caused corruption so godliness was the essential path to social perfection. Injunctions from scripture, perhaps additionally from the classics, were the basis for social harmonisation *via* individual moral renewal (e.g. Filippe 1584; Caraffa 1688). In the mid-sixteenth century Gaspar Stiblin, disgusted with corrupt monasteries and decayed societies, called for moral renewal and a social discipline of austerity, asceticism, and rigorous ethics (Stiblin 1555; cf. Firpo 1963). From the early seventeenth century Lipsian neo-Stoicism powerfully reinforced this tradition and extended its moral exhortation from princes to bureaucrats and standing armies (Oestrich 1982, Part I, esp. p. 50). By the later seventeenth century, writers in this mode were beginning to attenuate the Christian moral basis of social renewal by depicting perfect moral commonwealths based on natural or rational principles, buttressed if necessary by rational rather than revealed religion (e.g. Gilbert 1700). Understandably, in a hierarchical and almost universally monarchical society, the most prolific form of writing was that which focused on the moral responsibilities and performance of princes and their advisers. Antonio de Guevara's *Relox de les principes* (1529) may typify this perfect prince literature.[2] The education of the prince and his advisers was frequently seen as a prerequisite of their perfect rule but it was moral, rather than prudential, education which was stressed. In this sense, Erasmus' *The Education of a Christian Prince* (1516) fits into this tradition and we should remember that More's utopian fiction of the same year may in part be read as a critique of attitudes behind that work. In a republican, rather than imperial or monarchical, setting the focus shifted from the model emperor or prince to the virtuous aristocracy. So the ideality of Traiano Boccalini's ideal Venice was sustained by an aristocracy which invariably gave preference to public good over private interest and did so, not because of any peculiar institutional constraints, but because of their exemplary moral character (Boccalini 1706, Advices v, xxv). Nevertheless, in a century, the seventeenth, when hierarchy was challenged from both above and below and the aspirations of monarchy came under attack, there was a tendency to shift from reciting the moral precepts fit for princes to analysing the legal and institutional framework necessary to sustain princely perfection. It was necessary to mould the people's manners 'by Wholsome Laws' and to model royal government 'by good Policy'.[3]

As we move from the Mirror of Princes to regulated monarchy idealised, we may observe that the greater the doubts about human moral performance, the harsher the sanctions invoked. Eberlein's *Wolfaria* (1521) verged on the hysterical with its demands for the drowning of drunkards, public execution of adulterers, and decapitation of those who taught 'any prayer but the Lord's prayer' (Eberlein 1521). The 'profound Peace' of George Psalmanazar's idealised Formosa was based on violent and harsh punishments severely executed (Psalmanazar 1704, pp. 163–6, 214). In a Machiavellian sense, it was recognised that severity was necessary if corrupt customs were to be overcome in creating a virtuous society, but custom could appear stronger than force. For Paolo Paruta the true form of

2. Guevara 1529; Furio Ceriol 1570?; Torres 1596; Bellarmine 1619; Santa Maria 1650; Saavedra Fajardo 1700; Salici 1627; Mendo 1662. For Fajardo's neo-Stoicism, see Oestrich 1982, p. 103.
3. Barnes 1675; see also Fénelon 1701; Vairasse D'Allais 1702; *Antiquity Reviv'd* 1693; R.H. 1660.

government was that 'by which people living in peace and union, may work righteously, and obtain civil Felicity'. But 'immoderate Authority' and violent sanctions would only unbalance the commonwealth if the problem of custom were not addressed.

in a well-ordered City, the Laws ought to be confirmed by the Manners and Education of the Citizens, the which is of more force to make men honest, than is the fear of punishment; nay, from hence Actions arise according to true Honesty and Vertue; for they proceed from a vertuous Habit, which is only acquired by Exercise.

For this 'good institutions of life' were necessary and Paruta's work became a search for institutionally well-balanced commonwealths in the Polybian sense (Paruta 1657, esp. pp. 1, 3, 11). The search for the best commonwealth would result then in compendia of comparative constitutionalism or, more or less fictive, political gazetteers.[4] The knowledge associated with such encyclopaedic enterprises could be imagined as incorporated in the miracle lawmaker – Solon, Lycurgus, Utopus – whose skills in constitutional architecture were such as to engender new forms of behaviour as if they had been ancient custom (see Paruta 1657, p. 11, on Lycurgus). The point, however, was to establish good customs by appropriate institutions and this approach linked utopianism with constitutionalism in an ambivalent relationship. If we take constitutionalism to be concerned with the setting up of institutional contrivances to enable government to proceed without personal dependence in a world of deficient actors, then utopianism has, with constitutionalism, a common purpose. That is the prevention of corruption associated with anti-social viciousness, of the pursuit of self-interest against the collective interest, and of the effects of sheer laxity and ignorance. However, whereas constitutionalism seeks to limit the anti-social effects of these things in order that politics may continue, policies be chosen, adapted or abandoned in pursuit of the common good, utopianism stops that pursuit of policy. Its constitutional engineering is deemed so complete that there is no longer any need for policy.

The perceived obstacles to the achievement of an ideal society were sin and pride, *fortuna*, and the ironies of moral inefficiency. In the ideal of heroic moral performance and efficiency – the perfect moral commonwealth – these were overcome by exemplary moral performance. In the millennium they were overcome by the sword of justice and judgement in the hands of a returned redeemer and his saints. In Arcadia or Cockaigne social problems dissolved in individual satisfaction or satiation. In all four

4. E.g. Sansovino 1578; Cavalcanti 1805; Botero 1659; *Treasurie* 1613–19.

cases the obstacles were overcome or brushed aside. In utopia they persisted and must be contained rather than abolished. Human beings remained recalcitrant in their pride, sinfulness, and egotism. Deviance was not only a necessary feature of utopia, it was essential if the efficacy of utopian controls were to be realised (Fox 1969). Isolation was one recourse against *fortuna* but watchfulness, discipline, and control were also necessary. Tight discipline and severely circumscribed choice reduced the gap between moral intention and moral consequences but never entirely eliminated it. In utopia social problems were contained, not dissolved or overcome, and the utopian approach to containment was therefore holistic, systemic, and continuous. Every aspect of life must be regulated in a coordinated way. Institutions, educational programmes, legal sanctions, and custom must converge to the desired end, and all of these processes must operate impersonally and continuously. One obvious model for such an operation was the medieval monastic ideal and this is reflected in the utopias of More, Campanella, Franceso Doni, Eberlein, and Johann Valentin Andreae (Seibt 1980; Lapouge 1973; Coleman 1982; Seguy 1971). What is distinctive about the utopian writers of the early modern period is that they project this totalism of discipline and control on to society at large. Their cue is Solonic: 'I have made laws, for the good man and the bad alike, and shaped a rule to suit each case, and set it down' (Ferguson 1975, p. 44). Their inspiration is frequently classical but, we must ask, what is the contemporary intellectual background to this way of solving the problem of social idealisation?

One dimension of the recurrent Renaissance exercise of fusing the scholastic and the humanist was the search for an institutional context for virtue. In his utopian variant, More, in implied criticism of the effective limits of the moral exhortation and satire typical of the work of his humanist friends, envisaged an institutional grid within which virtue was embodied and to a large degree predetermined. Central to the final configuration, however, was the question: what is virtue? There was a hiatus between the Christian humanist answer that virtue was the realisation of the *philosophia Christi*, observing a preset, fixed, moral code through acting in charity to God and man, and the civic humanists' answer derived from Aristotle and Boethius that virtue was something realised and defined in action by the operation of human will in a civic setting (Pocock 1975, Part I). In the former case, if all acted according to the code as interpreted for their social role, the ideal society of the perfect moral commonwealth would be realised; but this did mean suspending belief in the irremediable sinfulness of humanity. In the latter, or civic humanist, case the prospect of a polarisation between good citizen and good man, in the Christian sense, began to open up; a polarisation which became identified with the writings of Machiavelli. More attempted in the *Utopia* to resolve the good man/good citizen, morality/expediency issue by showing that the pursuit of a rational self-interest, including that of a carefully defined pleasure (Surtz 1957; More 1965, Introduction, Part I, by J.H. Hexter), and the pursuit of virtue could be reconciled in a world of less than perfect and less than morally heroic individuals. But virtue was predetermined and More did not leave sinful humans living in a deficient natural order to struggle unaided for moral achievement and social harmony. Rather a grid of institutional regulation, bureaucratic sur- veillance, and educational socialisation locked virtue on to the people, rulers and ruled alike, and dealt with them when they threatened to elude its grasp. The moral philosophy of More's Utopians was central to his whole design, and social morality has remained the issue central to utopianism.

The moment at which this sort of choice again became relevant was, however, a moment in the broader intellectual history of the late Renaissance. For utopia reemerges as a means of solving or restating an intellectual problem; its initial function is in the realm of ideas not of praxis. The desire to give coherence, if not synthesis, to the currents of neo-Stoic, scholastic, and humanist thought, with the reawakening of Christian social aspiration as catalyst, is the background out of which the idea of utopia sprang. It has repeatedly been argued that other elements contributed to that moment: the transition from feudalism to capitalism (e.g. Marin 1984, pp. 153, 198–9); the discovering of the New World (Levin 1970, p. 68); state building, gross instability, and the perceived inadequacies of curial politics. All of these appear a more tangible seed-bed but in fact turn out to be both difficult to grasp and hard to relate to the concerns of specific utopias. What is clear is the radical nature of utopia's emergence in the realm of political thought. It ran athwart the political languages of the sixteenth and seventeenth centuries; rejecting immemorialism, cutting across constitutionalism, abandoning patriarchalism, classical republican- ism and order theory, and turning its back on ideas of sovereignty. As what Goethe called a 'pedagogic province', it wags its finger at other modes of thought. As 'a figure in discourse', it is 'written and imagined within the discourse which criticises it' and which it, in turn, criticises.[5]

5. For Goethe see Stern 1980–1, p. 99; Marin 1984, p. xxi.

ii Holy experiments in a fallen world

There were, of course, a number of alternative discourses in this period to which utopian constructs might relate and we may distinguish types of utopia accordingly.[6] More's *Utopia* identified itself, in the text as well as in the prefatory and appended letters and verses, as a product of a humanist concern with literature, language, and moral philosophy. But the axis of the work is the suggestion that there is a conceivable social ideal in which fallible humans live in a society of moral dignity and worth without the aid of revelation and that, moreover, such an ideal cannot be arrived at by moral effort in a curial context or even by the legislative effort (More 1965, p. 103) of good men struggling in a corrupt world. However imaginative, fictional, or satiric the device, therefore, More has to suggest ways in which political and social arrangements could be made which would conduce to that end. He had to think through some of the fundamental issues of politics, but not all of them. For, while he had to work *with* fallible human material, he did not have to work *through* it. The first stage in the solution of the problem was a work of supreme artifice: the creation of an artificial island by manual excavation. The second was to construct a constraining social and institutional order which would oblige fallible human beings to behave in ways compatible with social harmony and morality. Human beings always acted reasonably in pursuing their interests as defined by circumstance. The point was, therefore, to reconstruct social circumstance so as to reconcile private and communal interest. Accordingly, since private property inspired only private interest, communal property must be substituted for it (More 1965, pp. 237–9). The institutional, legal, and educational apparatus of *Utopia* was carefully designed, in extension of this, to guide flawed individuals into better social performance. Organisation and a bureaucratic order were perfected to this end and this was the essential perfection of utopia. Individual citizens could fail to meet the required standards, and punishments, including slavery and death, must be sustained to control and condition behaviour. Beyond this the system of control and conditioning was seen as total in its sweep. All acts and relationships were subject to control. All were public; none private (Davis 1981a, pp. 52–4).

Almost a century later, Campanella's *City of the Sun* pursued the same themes. Private property was the source of self-love. 'When self-love is

6. For alternative approaches to categorisation see Manuel and Manuel 1979; Thomas 1985; Shklar 1969; Hansot 1974; Holstun 1987.

destroyed, only concern for the community remains' (Campanella 1981, p. 39). But the attack extended beyond the privacy of property to sexuality and to personal characteristics such as generosity, fortitude, diligence, and so on (*ibid.*, pp. 22, 28–33). In these respects, the differences between More and Campanella were ones of degree and detail rather than substance. The most significant contrast between the two related to science and scientific knowledge. Campanella's ideal city was in form a huge memory system with all scientific knowledge depicted on its concentric walls. Scientific knowledge was already complete and could be kept in 'only one book'. There was no mention of scientific research. Moreover, science, associated by Campanella with astrology, was the knowledge of natural law and regularity. Like rigidly enforced civil law it countered the appearance that the world was ruled by chance, a realm of contingency.[7] More's Utopians allowed for miracles 'which occurred without the assistance of nature' (More 1965, p. 137). Campanella's made no such allowance.

Francis Bacon affords yet another contrast with Campanella, for, while the latter assumed the existence of a finite and complete body of scientific knowledge at the service of the utopian state, Bacon attempted to portray an ideal society in which scientific activity remained a continuing activity. But this, as Bacon recognised, was to embrace the freedom, fortuity, and power of scientific discovery within a framework of total control made necessary by the aberrance of individuals. Bacon's scientists were thus ambiguously depicted as moral paragons charged with adjudicating on the apparently miraculous but also liable to cheat and lie, and therefore subject to the same controls as other citizens (Bacon 1627, p. 43). In the *New Atlantis* these contradictions come home to roost and they have dogged the scientific utopia ever since; either utopia controls science or science subverts utopia (Davis 1984b; Thomas 1985, p. 167). Nevertheless, given the early modern commonplace that science, as knowledge, was power, it is remarkable that so little political theorising, other than the utopian, attempted to come to terms with science in the period (Manuel and Manuel 1979, p. 213).

Bacon's followers could escape the tensions generated in his unfinished utopian exercise by transferring his scientific aspirations to a millennial context (Webster 1975; Tuveson 1964). There was an element of this, too, in the pansophist aspiration of a chain of scientific and religious figures running from Giordano Bruno through Christopher Besold, Johann

7. Campanella 1981, pp. 18–20, 60. On this theme see Davis 1984a.

Heinrich Alsted, and Andreae to Leibniz (Hall 1972; Manuel and Manuel 1979, Part III). It would be mistaken to overemphasise the utopian form of this, as it would the hermetic content (Vickers 1979). The millennial element, more evident in so much of this post-Reformation excitement and despair, could readily lead to a perfect moral commonwealth or an Arcadian harmony. In this context, it was a Protestant emphasis on godly discipline which was more likely to lead to utopia. At its loudest and most punitive, this can be seen in Eberlein's *Wolfaria* (1521), in more sophisticated form in Andreae's *Christianopolis* (1619). Both of these Lutheran utopias confronted the problem of how the godly society could be established in a sinful and chaotic world. Not surprisingly, the answer came to look remarkably monastic, or in Andreae's case, and despite the religious differences, was modelled on what he saw as 'the guidance of social life' in Geneva (Montgomery 1973, I, pp. 43–4; Andreae 1916, pp. 13, 27–8). Accepting the long haul facing Lutheran reform in his day, Andreae placed elaborate stress on education. Under Comenian influences, this theme flourished again in mid-seventeenth-century England. Samuel Gott's *Nova Solyma* (1648) attempted to reconcile millenarian and utopian impulses by setting an ideal society of converted Jews in the Holy Land, itself a symbol of the Last Days. But his work, and his education theory, was riven by tensions between the self-rule appropriate to the saints and the godly discipline necessary to the natural man. Despite strenuous efforts to develop an educational theory and practice which could free the one and constrain the other, the tensions remained (Davis 1981a, ch. 6).

One approach to resolving those tensions was the withdrawal of the saints into a holy experiment. In an ambience of sectarian proliferation and experiment, mid-seventeenth-century England saw a scattering of sect-type, small community experiments and writings. From the first it was recognised that economic viability was a critical problem for such experiments. So Peter Cornelius Plockhoy's *A Way Propounded* (1659?), proposing equality, had to elaborate detailed economic arrangements for the production and distribution of goods within his society and in commerce with a wider world. This was also a feature of John Bellers' *Proposals for Raising a College of Industry* (1695). Bellers saw his proposed community as being financed on a joint-stock basis and in many ways anticipated the idealised organisation of the proto-factory as set forth, for example, in the *Law Book* of the Crowley ironworks in north-east England (Plockhoy 1659?; Bellers 1695, 1987; Flinn 1957; Davis 1981a, ch. 11).

A variant on this resolution of the tensions between the Christian liberty of the saved and the godly discipline of all could be observed in the writings of Gerrard Winstanley. In his writings of 1648–9 Winstanley envisaged universal redemption and the dissipation of forms of social control. Between 1649 and 1652 he moved from small community experiments – the Diggers – of whose actual organisation we know very little but which were conceived in a spirit of millenarian expectation, to a very detailed set of proposals for a much broader scheme to be sponsored, as he hoped, by Cromwell. *The Law of Freedom* (1652) proposed a communistic society for all those willing to settle on waste and common land plus the confiscated estates of the king, church, and royalists. Commonwealth's government would be set up without commerce, under continuous supervision and subject to 'Laws for every occasion and almost for every action that men do.' Sin, 'unreasonable ignorance', and covetousness made law necessary. True freedom was not to be confused with commercial freedom, liberty of preaching, sexual freedom, or inequality. '*True Commonwealth's Freedom lies in the free Enjoyment of the Earth*' (Winstanley 1941, pp. 515, 519, 528–9). All these things were to be subject to control and supervision. Winstanley moved, therefore, from the redemption of all and their consequent liberty, to a vision of society locked in battle with covetousness and waywardness, comprehensive in its pursuit of godly discipline.[8] Peter Chamberlen's *The Poore Mans Advocate* (1649), with its proposal to settle the poor, on what Winstanley called commonwealths land, to become self-supporting and relieve the propertied of tax burdens, may be read as an ironic counterpoint to the more comprehensive proposals of *The Law of Freedom* (Chamberlen, 1649).

An attempt to reconcile Protestant aspirations and classical republicanism of a Polybian/Machiavellian kind was made in the French utopia of 1616, *Histoire du Grand et Admirable Royaume d'Antangil* (Lachèvre 1933). Set south of Java, the island of Antangil was divided into 120 provinces and, in decadic fashion, into groups of households, parishes, and towns. A Council of State of three wise, prudent, and experienced men from each province advised the king and a senate of 100 great and wise men. The wickedness of men made a monarch necessary but kings themselves were subject to corruption and viciousness.[9] Balance was therefore necessary; a king as a check on oligarchy, a senate as a check on tyranny. The system was described in the immense detail typical of the early modern utopia,

---

8. For the dispute over whether Winstanley saw the need for repression as permanent see Davis 1976; Hill 1986.
9. Lachèvre 1933, chs. III, IV, V. 'il ne s'est ven aucun bon Roy en quatre ou cinq cents ans' p. 43.

with special emphasis on military and judicial organisation and on education.

The idealisation of a mixed constitution could focus on an existent state, usually a city-state, as in Ludovico Zuccolo's myth of San Marino or Gasparo Contarini's of Venice (Manuel and Manuel 1979, pp. 151–3). The most elaborate attempt to recast the classical republican ideal for a large rural society was James Harrington's *Oceana* (1656). But Harrington's emphasis was ultimately not so much on the freedom with which participating citizens should be encouraged to exercise their civic responsibilities as on making the republic inviolable to sin and corruption; 'it is the duty of the legislator to presume all men wicked' (Harrington 1977, p. 290). To reconcile power and authority; the one, the few, and the many; the bearing of arms and the exercise of citizenship, Harrington developed a constitutional apparatus of such complexity that the machinery was all. Participation was reduced to privatised ritual rather than social interaction (Davis 1981a, ch. 8, 1981b). While J.G.A. Pocock has identified as neo-Harringtonian those who sought to free Harrington's thought from the machinery and reestablish a participatory ideal, others, in utopian vein, continued the elaboration of constitutional contrivances (Davis 1981a, ch. 9; Pocock 1975, chs. 12–14). In part, Harrington's problem and his response to it were integral to the problem of a Polybian balance in a society where a king had been executed for attempting to subvert the laws, where the threat of a militarily based oligarchy was real, and where the spectre of popular anarchy or antinomian excess appeared equally real.

In the context of the Italian city-states a more aristocratic, if equally utopian, version of the classical republic could be pursued. In Francesco Patrizi's *La Città felice*, citizenship was limited to the leisured – military commanders, magistrates, and priests. Slaves and the common people were to be carefully controlled. Leon Battista Alberti, in a sense, provided the architectural setting for this two-class society with different designs for the rural household and the city. Ludovico Agostini, in his *La Repubblica Imaginaria*, insisted on the obligation of all, including nobles and scholars, to work, but political participation was restricted to the nobility who were expected to respond in terms of the highest paternalistic moral standards (Manuel and Manuel 1979, pp. 170–2, 174–5). At this point, utopia, concentrating on the moral standards of an ideal aristocracy, begins to merge with a perfect moral commonwealth, and may be seen as an extension of the municipal courtesy book, weaning the aristocrats from a community of honour to a community of civility (Curtin 1985).

Growing knowledge of the New World stimulated not only the 'discovery' of ideal societies but the sense of a *tabula rasa* on which new forms of ideal society could be depicted. Almost always the initial formulation was Arcadian. From Christopher Columbus through Peter Martyr Vermigli to Bartolomé de Las Casas the expected encounter was with noble savages inhabiting a golden age, the simplicity and innocence of which were to be contrasted with European civilisation and sophistry (Levin 1970, p. 68). In 1516, the year of the *Utopia*, Las Casas planned to complete the model of Cuba, Hispaniola, San Juan, and Jamaica by adding Christianity. In the 1530s Vasco de Quiroga, seeing that contemporary European customs were not appropriate for the Golden Age, recommended the implementation of More's utopian design. In the first half of the seventeenth century the Jesuits in Brazil, Uruguay, Argentina, and Paraguay sought in their *reductions* to maintain the innocence of the natives through a paternalistic and morally controlled communism. Spain's first fictional utopia, *Sinapia* (*c.* 1682), still reflected faith in a paternalistic, primitive communism, with a purified Christianity providing strong moral guidance. But, in the same work, mixed forms of government were appearing with an elected prince and magistracy as well as careful separation of judicial, military, and religious offices (Cro 1979; Caravaglia 1981).

Running through the multifarious depictions of social ideality in a New World setting are contrasting themes of Arcadian primitivism and utopian constraint. By the later seventeenth century, mixed government forms came to predominate in the latter. As early as 1594, Richard Beacon, addressing the problems of England's 'first colony', Ireland, could settle that theme in a Machiavellian meditation on the reform of the Irish which is in many ways a striking anticipation of Harrington (Beacon 1594). But, closer to the *tabula rasa* of the New World, greater extremes could, at least at first, be contemplated. Nowhere is the transition in terms of ideality better expressed than in the early history of Virginia. Described in 1606 as 'Earth's only Paradise' (Drayton 1606), Virginia's Arcadian status soon slipped into damnation through the wilfulness and sinfulness of men. By 1609, quarrelling, faction, disorder, disease, famine, and retaliation by the natives had reduced the colony to chaos. Of 900 who had emigrated to Virginia only 60 survived. Between 1609 and 1611 Sir Thomas Gates, Thomas West and Sir Thomas Dale elaborated a series of rules for the colony which were codified and edited by William Strachey in 1612 as *Lawes Divine, Morall and Martiall*. Godly discipline pursued the devil in

Virginia with a vengeance. Impiety, blasphemy, and insubordination became capital offences. Sabbatarianism and a regime of daily worship were strictly enforced. Trade, the disposition of property, prices, and hygiene were closely controlled. Discipline in the wilderness paid close attention to work, tools, trade with the natives, and moral order generally (Strachey 1612). A similar pattern may be observed in Plockhoy's proposals for the Dutch colony of the New Netherlands in the 1660s (Harder and Harder 1952, ch. 4 and pp. 174–204). In post-Restoration England a more aristocratically detached attitude to the possibilities of colonial self-government could be taken. This is reflected in the constitutions devised for New Jersey in the 1660s and 1670s, all combinations of Leveller and Harringtonian ideals (Boyd 1964). The Carolina constitution of 1669, which appears to have been written by John Locke, was more directly classical-republican and Harringtonian in inspiration, but the most elaborate exercise of this type was the 1683 scheme for the government of Pennsylvania.[10]

Always there was a tendency for utopia to blur into other ideal society forms. The conventions of the utopian genre might be maintained but there could be a subversive softening of focus with regard to substance. One sees this, for example, in Joshua Barnes' *Gerania* (1675), in form utopian, in fact Arcadian; or by the early eighteenth century in Simon Berington's *Memoirs of Sigr. Gaudentio di Lucca* (1737) depicting a society untouched by the Fall and ruled, in familial bliss, by natural law (Barnes 1675; Berington 1737).

As we have seen, and as Fénelon's *Telemachus* would remind us, utopia, especially in its monarchist forms, could spill over into perfect moral commonwealth or something approaching the Mirror of Princes tradition. The mere existence of the perfect utopian lawgiver – Utopus, Solamona, Olphaeus Megaletor – would appear to confirm this. Was this the utopian concession to the final dependence of things social on good nature and good will: the chink in the utopian armour? Or, was the utopian lawgiver God? If this were so, the laws of utopia would be divine or natural law. Utopia would be a realm of grace, transcending sin, not a world of contrivance locked in battle with sin. In Arcadia and Cockaigne the lawgiver was unnecessary because everyone gave laws to themselves. In the perfect moral commonwealth, the law was not given but taken as given and everyone

10. *The Two Charters granted by King Charles IId to the Proprietors of Carolina* (n.d.), British Library 1061 g 10; Franklin 1740. For John Eliot's earlier experiments with Indian self-rule in his 'praying towns' of New England see Holstun 1987.

obeyed it. There was no sovereign legislator above the law because he created it. In the millennium, God was the lawgiver, hence its fulfilment was universal. In utopia, the lawgiver was necessary because law could not come from God or nature. It must have a source in human will, but, since all humans were deficient in will, it had to come from a fictionalised human who escaped the normal limitations ascribed to the utopian individual. It is not, however, the matter of lawgiving which distinguishes utopia but the designing of *ordini*, mechanisms of an institutional kind, bureaucratic procedures and sanctions which check the propensity to disregard, breach, or subvert laws. Christianity provided a moral code and the utopian said that was not enough. To be efficient in the elimination of wickedness, it was necessary to do more than pronounce rules and leave it to the exercise of human free will. Utopus was a system designer, not primarily a lawgiver or a pronouncer of moral maxims. In this sense, owing little to God, nature, or tradition, utopia was a kind of sacrilege (Lapouge 1973) and a pre-Christian fictional setting could be deployed to offset this. In our period, although these strands have a more continuous existence, the early struggle of utopianism was with the efficacy of simple moral renewal, in the middle period with a Christian millennialism, and in the later with a growing Arcadianism resting its faith in natural law.

Utopian thought only takes on historical meaning if placed in the context of ideal society alternatives, for it represents a choice between competing modes of social idealisation. The choice may seldom be completely or unambivalently made but many ideal society theorists of the early modern period saw themselves as actively confronting such a decision. Robert Burton, for example, in his approach to his own utopian exercise, rejected Arcadianism, millennial transformation, and the perfect moral common-wealth.[11] Beyond this, utopia can be seen as a kind of limiting case in respect of all the cardinal issues of early modern political thought. If constitutional-ism, for instance, was the attempt to find institutional contrivances and procedures which would legitimate and mitigate the risks of rule by imperfect human agents, then utopianism is close to the constitutional enterprise. What distinguishes it is its radical view of that undertaking. However antique its fictive constitution, utopia has always been created whole at one particular point in time. It is not immemorial or confirmatory of custom. Rather, as utopians frequently insisted, laws were not to be moulded to men but men were to be moulded by and to the laws. In utopia

11. Burton 1932, I, pp. 96–7, 102, 106, 130–6, II, pp. 189, 202; Davis 1981a, ch. 4.

fortuna was conquered by the establishment of predictability, moral meaning, and efficiency. Citizens lost their capacity for *virtú* but the republic no longer ran the risk of corruption. Equally, utopia jeopardised the bases of monarchy. Kings were no more than bureaucrats – once the great lawgiver had done his work. Utopia reversed the problem of politics in a providential order by ending the play of particular providence in its changeless perfection and also by ending politics. To the issue of whether there could be a language of politics separable from that of private morality, utopia provided a brusque answer by its simultaneous termination of politics and elimination of the private. Utopia could take the classical aspirations of humanism and the monastic/sect-type aspirations, on both sides of the Reformation divide, reconcile them, and set them within limits. Later, as in *Antangil* or *Oceana*, it absorbed military aspirations too. When change became a natural law, utopia, because of its fixity of purpose and structure, ceased to be a limiting case in political thought. The more recently modern vision has been of the millennium or time perfected, with or without its precedent cataclysm, or of Arcadia, space, and nature perfected. We continue to talk about utopia only because we fail to distinguish it.

It is not appropriate to reduce the history of early modern utopianism to transitions in economic or social structure, to the revival of Platonism or to a single set of linguistic conventions, since the social backgrounds out of which it sprang were so diverse and the intellectual affinities of its progenitors were so eclectic and diverse. The importance of early modern utopian thought is not in what it can tell us about the contexts and paradigms within the confines of which much early modern political thought is held to have taken place. Rather, its usefulness is in opening up for us the potentialities of early modern political thought given the adoption of certain liberating and constraining conventions. In this period, utopia flourished alongside perfect moral commonwealth, millennium, Arcadia, and Cockaigne. It did so as a profound criticism not only of existing society but also of the other ideal society alternatives. Its emergence reflected a new sense of the history of collective Christian moral effort and a disillusionment with the apparent naivety of the Christian humanists' faith in moral renewal based on pure scriptures. By the seventeenth century its disillusionment was directed more at the future prospects and present dangers of millennialism. Later in that century utopia's confrontational focus shifted to a renewed Arcadianism and an embryonic faith in progress. It is easy to overestimate the extent to which the aspirations of the classical utopia were displaced in the early modern period (Shklar 1969; Hansot 1974; cf. Davis 1984a) and to underestimate the continuity of form flowing through into the period of modern utopianism. Only in the fugal context of its counterpoint with other ideal society forms does utopia's history take on a dynamic.

III

Absolutism and revolution in the seventeenth century

12

Absolutism and royalism

J.P. SOMMERVILLE

i The meaning of absolutism

The purpose of this chapter is to describe the main tenets of absolutist and royalist thinking in the seventeenth century. That century, we are often told, saw the making of absolutism, especially in France. There, the Estates General fell into disuse after 1615, and its demise brought death to the principle that taxation requires the consent of the taxed. In the 1620s Louis XIII subdued the Huguenots in a crusade which harnessed militant Catholicism to the service of the monarchy. In the 1630s war with Spain led to a massive increase in the crown's military capacity – and troops could be used to suppress insurrection at home as well as to defeat enemies abroad. The introduction of *intendants* brought local government under central control, and this development was given added impetus when the *intendants* assumed military powers. After the temporary setback of the Fronde, royal power resumed its progress, and in the latter decades of the century French absolutism entered its golden age. Louis XIV completed the work of Richelieu and Mazarin. In 1673 the *parlement* of Paris was formally deprived of the right to remonstrate against royal edicts before registering them. In 1682 the Declaration of the clergy of France unambiguously asserted the independence of kings from papal control in temporal matters.

Elsewhere events often ran a similar course. In 1660 the Danish Estates met for the last time. In 1680 the Swedish Riksdag engineered a constitutional revolution which effectively introduced absolutism. In Prussia the Great Elector taxed without consent and used troops to enforce his will. By the end of the century, we might argue, absolutism was made or in the making in most European states. Even in England its triumph sometimes looked likely, and was averted only by the execution of one king and the deposition of another. Even in republics – Holland, Venice – there were those who expressed absolutist ideas.

Plainly, royal power increased in many European countries. Nevertheless, the enforcement of the king's will required the cooperation of local elites. The need to secure the support of provincial notables placed stringent limitations upon the king's effective freedom of action. Growing awareness of this truth has led some historians to call for radical refinement of current conceptions of absolutism. Andrew Lossky, for example, has argued that 'one must invent a concept of "limited absolutism" to describe the rule of Louis XIV' (Lossky 1984, p. 15). Perhaps 'absolutism' is a term of little value for analysing seventeenth-century political practice. Worse still, its use may foster the mistaken beliefs that kings ruled in an arbitrary and despotic fashion (or at least that they could have done so if they had pleased), and also that the political structures of European states conformed to a single model.

Arguably, there are also problems in using the term 'absolutist' to describe seventeenth-century theory (as distinct from practice). James Daly has demonstrated that in England there was no single, settled idea of absolute monarchy (Daly 1978). Contemporaries used the term in a variety of ways. It might be thought that a point of substance underlies this perception about usage: there was no agreement on the nature of absolute monarchy because there were no absolutists. In fact, as we shall see, there were absolutists in England as on the continent. Whatever may be true about practice, 'absolutist' *does* usefully describe a distinctive set of ideas, current in much of Europe. An understanding of these ideas illuminates the intentions and therefore the practice of kings and statesmen in the seventeenth century.

Let us begin with some definitions. Absolutists were thinkers who held that the prince is accountable to God alone for his actions within his realm, that his commands ought to be obeyed by his subjects provided that they do not conflict with divine poitive or natural law, and that he (and those acting on his command) ought never to be resisted actively by his subjects. A prince could be any specific person or persons, for though absolutists generally preferred monarchy to aristocracy and democracy, they seldom claimed that it was the only valid form of government. There are, indeed, difficulties with this – and any – definition of absolutism. The reason is that there was no *single* absolutist theory. Rather, there were several different traditions of thought which, in the seventeenth century, were used to free rulers from accountability to their subjects. One such tradition was the idea of the divine right of kings which proposed that all rulers (whether kings or not) derived political power *directly* from God. Certainly, many absolutists adopted this theory. But others derived the ruler's power from an irreversible grant by the people. Moreover, some thinkers who drew the king's power immediately from God believed that the king alone could not validly change human laws; they cannot therefore be classed as absolutists (e.g. Coke, *Reports*, VII, fos. 12b–13b; IV, preface, p. xix). Another point on which absolutists disagreed was the nature of the relationship between royal power and the spiritual power of the church. For example, William Barclay and Paolo Sarpi adopted conflicting views on this question, though their general political positions were so close that it seems sensible to call them both absolutists (see Wootton 1983, pp. 58–9 for their views on church–state relations).

Though absolutists differed on important questions they did all look to the prince as the supreme maker and interpreter of human laws (at least in temporal matters), and they held that the prince could not be deposed by the church or by his subjects. Royalists, by contrast, cannot easily be defined in terms of any coherent doctrines. The term royalist was used in England in the 1620s sometimes to mean royal absolutist (Sibthorp 1627, pp. 13, 16), and sometimes (seemingly) to mean someone who supported the king's financial policies (Russell 1979, p. 152). It was not, however, until the 1640s that the word came into wide usage, and then it usually denoted an adherent of the king in the Civil War. A number of the king's most famous propagandists in the 1640s were absolutists, though they generally toned down their claims for popular consumption. But a good many of Charles' supporters (including Falkland and Edward Bagshaw) rejected absolutist thinking. It would be unwise to impose any great intellectual consistency on English royalists of the Civil War period. Perhaps royalism is best defined merely as a tendency to support the king in the political controversies of the day. Not all royalists were absolutists. Nor were all absolutists royalists. In the Civil War many parliamentarians claimed that there was, or at least ought to be, an absolute sovereign in every state, though they denied that sovereignty was vested in the king in England. In this chapter, however, it is with advocates of royal absolutism that we shall be primarily concerned.

Armed with these definitions, we are now in a position to investigate the nature and development of absolutist thinking in the seventeenth century. We shall concentrate particularly on France and England. There are differences of detail in the arguments put forward by absolutists in these two countries. But a great many of the fundamental absolutist contentions were voiced equally by thinkers throughout Europe and on both sides of the confessional divide between Protestants and Catholics. The first major episode in the history of seventeenth-century absolutist thought was the controversy over church–state relations that resulted from the Interdict of Venice and from the almost simultaneous enactment of James I's oath of allegiance in 1606. In this controversy a number of French and Venetian Catholics sided with English (and French and German) Protestants. Similar international and cross-confessional alliances recurred later in the century. In 1644 the Huguenot Synod of Charenton condemned the actions of their English co-religionists in taking up arms against the king (Galland 1928, p. 110), and in 1690 both Pierre Bayle (in his *Avis important*; cf. Yardeni 1985, pp. 332–3) and Jacques-Bénigne Bossuet (*Cinquième avertissement*; extracts in Bossuet 1966, pp. 83–5) denounced Pierre Jurieu's notions of popular sovereignty. Bossuet's arguments illustrate a further point about absolutist thinking in the seventeenth century, namely its essential lack of development. Changes of emphasis did indeed occur. But the underlying arguments remained, for the most part, static. Let us begin by examining these arguments.

ii Sovereignty and monarchy

The two main objectives of absolutist writers were to defend the independence of the prince from foreign (and especially papal) jurisdiction in temporal matters, and to end constraints upon his rule at home. Both objectives were commonly achieved by the assertion of the Bodinian doctrine of sovereignty. Sovereignty was sometimes treated as a logically necessary feature of every state, but more frequently it was portrayed as the only practical alternative to anarchy, and (given the nature of man) mayhem. The prince alone should possess coercive power within the state, said Bossuet, 'otherwise all is confusion and the state returns to anarchy' (*Politique tirée des propres paroles de l'Ecriture sainte*, 4, 1, 3, in Bossuet 1966, p. 111). To divide sovereign power would be to undermine the peace of the commonwealth and to infringe the biblical precept that no one should serve two masters (*Politique tirée*, 4, 1, 3, in Bossuet 1966, pp. 112–13). 'It is impossible', declared the Oratorian Jean Senault in 1661, 'to divide authority and keep the peace' (Senault 1661, p. 24). 'Without kings', pronounced H. Du Boys in 1604, 'human life would be nothing but confusion and disorder' (Du Boys 1604, p. 23). 'Take Soveraignty from the face of the earth', said the Englishman Robert Bolton in 1621, 'and you turne it into a Cockpit. Men would become cut-throats and Canibals one unto another . . . We should have a very hell upon earth, and the face of it covered with blood, as it was once with water' (Bolton 1635, p. 10). Agreement between people was possible only if they submitted to a single government which united them all, said Bossuet, for even Abraham and Lot could not agree, though they were godly men (*Politique tirée*, 1, 3, in Bossuet 1966, pp. 71–2).

The necessity of sovereignty, then, was deduced from contentions about human nature and mankind's objectives, and not merely from the abstract concept of the state. This is a point of some importance, for it explains why the advent of Bodinian sovereignty did not lead absolutists to abandon theorising in terms of God's laws and man's purposes. The concept of sovereignty was itself underpinned by attitudes towards human nature and needs: in order to fulfil God's purposes and his own goals, man required the protection of an absolute sovereign. This applied even in the state of innocence, and there people were naturally ready to obey. After the Fall, however, pride led to disobedience, and coercion became necessary (Baricave 1614, p. 453; Donne 1610, p. 83).

Unlimited and indivisible sovereignty was necessary to the security of the state. It mattered little whether a community in which sovereignty was divided could strictly be classified as a state. The important point about such a community was that it could not long survive. According to Hadrian Saravia (a native of Flanders who spent his later years in England defending the Protestant establishment against the criticisms of the monarchomachs), mixed government spelled doom for any community (Saravia 1611, pp. 163–4). In the opinion of Moïse Amyraut, a Huguenot divine, the English Civil War resulted from the fact that sovereignty had been divided between the king and parliament; in France, by contrast, the king alone was sovereign and the state secure (Amyraut 1650, p. 143). 'No prudent man doubts', said Isaac Casaubon (a Huguenot who defended Venice at the time of the Interdict, and who later went to England where he served James I in his political controversies with Catholics), 'that the well-being of the commonwealth cannot be provided for unless there exists in it a single sovereign; whether it be ruled by one man, as in a monarchy; or by more, as in an aristocracy or democracy. For even in these latter forms sovereignty is undivided'[1] (Casaubon 1607, pp. 89–90).

---

1. 'Pro certo et confesso ponimus . . . & de quo nemo prudens dubitat: saluti Reip. consuli aliter non posse, quam si unus numero in illa sit Principatus: sive ille ab unico sustineatur, ut in statu monarchico: sive a pluribus, ut in optimatu, vel populari statu, nam & in istis, unus est numero Principatus.'

Stable states, it could be presumed, had pure forms of government – monarchy, aristocracy, or democracy. The form was defined by the locus of sovereignty. So a king whose power was limited was no true monarch. Where the people could call their rulers to account, said Marc'Antonio De Dominis (a Venetian who likewise served James I in his anti-papal polemics), the state was a democracy (De Dominis 1620, p. 531; the reference to mixed government at p. 921 should be interpreted in the light of this passage). Again, a king who held his power from the pope was no true sovereign. The kings of England, said Cardin Le Bret, had always derived their power from the church of Rome. They had, in consequence, never possessed sovereignty (Le Bret 1632, p. 10).

Of the three pure forms of government monarchy was generally deemed the best. This thesis was defended on both empirical and metaphysical grounds. Monarchy upon earth corresponded most closely to God's rule over the universe, to the eagle's dominion over birds (Poisson de la Bodinière 1597, p. 7; Verstegan 1622, pp. 142–3), and to the government of that puzzlingly feminine monarch the queen bee[2] over the hive – a model commonwealth. Such analogies, underpinned by a Neoplatonic conception of the universe as a hierarchy, in which each part was related to all the others by similitude or correspondence, featured in absolutist writings throughout the century (the use of similitudes in early-seventeenth-century English thought is emphasised in Greenleaf 1964, pp. 1–94, and in Daly 1974, p. 19). Neoplatonic preconceptions were by no means incompatible with arguments from history and experience, for history was interpreted in the light of ethical and metaphysical presuppositions. Bodin has sometimes been seen as a political scientist, but it is clear that his methodology, even if it was overtly inductive, relied in practice upon deductions from first principles provided by his world view: theory determined what Bodin found in history (Parker 1981, pp. 257–63). Bossuet's *Discours sur l'histoire universelle* was likewise saturated with preconceived notions about the past, and not least with providentialist ideas (e.g. Bossuet 1966, pp. 55–8).

It is likely that the use of analogies and of scriptural citations by absolutist writers decreased in the course of the seventeenth century, while appeals to reason became commoner. The extent of these changes should not, however, be exaggerated. In 1661 Senault still accepted the hackneyed idea

---

2. The ruling bee was shown to be a queen in Butler 1609, but was generally treated as male until much later. Mandeville still talked of the king of the bees in the early eighteenth century (Mandeville 1924, I, p. 17 and elsewhere).

that man is a microcosm of the universe, and used analogies with other parts of creation to mount arguments about human society (Senault 1661, pp. 2–4). At the end of the century Bossuet completed his major political work – the *Politique tirée des propres paroles de l'Ecriture sainte* – in which he overtly drew political conclusions from the Bible. On the other hand, reason features strongly in the absolutist arguments of early seventeenth-century writers. In 1649 Claude de Saumaise did indeed claim that by appealing not to examples but to 'reason' he had developed a 'new kind of argument'[3] (Saumaise 1650, p. 314). In fact, neither Saumaise's methodology nor his specific arguments were in the least original. Scriptural examples had long been regarded as compatible with reason – the law of nature. Scripture and natural law, said John Milton in reply to Saumaise, did 'exactly agree', and he declared that this had always been his opinion (Milton 1931–40, VII, p. 267). Both the Bible and reason served as guides to God's law.

God ruled the universe through laws. Some of these were positive, applying only at a particular time and place. Examples were the judicial and ceremonial laws of Moses – which God had given to the Jews of the Old Testament – and the laws of grace, which had been revealed to Christians, and which spelled out the nature and powers of the Christian church. Other divine laws were natural, applying eternally and deducible from manifest truths about human nature. By obeying the laws of nature men could promote their own temporal welfare and thereby acquire the leisure to pursue the higher goal of spiritual felicity. Obedience to natural law did not, however, lead people to salvation, for fallen man could be saved only by God's grace. Protestants were divided from Catholics on the theology of grace, but this did not prevent them from agreeing on the contents of the law of nature. It was in the law of nature – reason – that political principles were grounded. That is why religious opponents were so often able to unite in their political theorising.

The purpose of the law of nature was to lead mankind to temporal welfare. The promotion of the public good was a major moral duty. 'The goal of a lawful king', said Senault, 'is public utility' (Senault 1661, p. 18), and Casaubon likewise placed the utmost weight upon the obligation 'to

---

3. English absolutist ideas on natural law are discussed in Sommerville 1986b, pp. 12–17, 20–1, 29–30. Keohane, 1980. p. 304, argues that theories of natural law were 'almost absent from French political discourse in the first half of the seventeenth century'. This is difficult to sustain, for the law of nature was often used quite unselfconsciously by French writers, e.g. Martelière in 1610 (Martelière 1612, pp. 45, 48); Balzac in his *Prince* of 1631 (Balzac 1665, II, p. 85). On other occasions it was treated more elaborately, e.g. by Richer in *c.* 1617 (Richer 1692, pp. 68–70).

consult the public weal' (Casaubon 1607, p. 89; cf. Réfuge 1633, p. 399). At the same time natural law was held to impose certain specific and absolute duties, summarised in the ten commandments. What should be done if adherence to one of these duties led to public disaster? The answer was that it could not. Obedience to God's commandments was always beneficial, while divine providence would invariably visit calamity upon those who disobeyed, even if the intention of such disobedience was to promote the public good. 'Impiety is the cause of all the misfortunes of states', said Senault, while piety gave security to monarchs and felicity to their kingdoms (Senault 1661, pp. 175, 162; cf. Lever 1608, p. 1).

By obeying God's commandments, kings could promote the welfare of their subjects. The king was accountable to God for his actions. Bossuet reminded kings that it was horrible sacrilege to misuse the powers that God had granted them (*Politique tirée*, 3, 2, in Bossuet 1966, p. 150). Jean de la Bruyère stressed the onerousness of the king's task: he was responsible to God in all his actions for the welfare of his subjects, and ignorance could never excuse him (La Bruyère 1966, p. 249). Le Bret underlined the 'rigour of the penalties' with which God would punish rulers who failed to do their duty (Le Bret 1632, p. 698). It was true that a king who was accountable to his people was no true king (Saumaise 1650, p. 315; Hayward 1603, p. 36) and that sovereigns were responsible to God alone (Le Bret 1632, p. 9; Charles I 1628, p. 9). But the fact that rulers were not subject to any temporal authority by no means implied that their misdeeds would go unpunished: they *were* subject to the awful majesty of God.

The idea that sovereigns are subject only to God was central to absolutist thought. It was often but not always accompanied by the notion that sovereigns derive their power immediately from Him. There was wide agreement on the contention that God has constructed human nature in such a way that government is necessary for mankind. 'Government', said Bolton (in a passage which he cribbed from the Frenchman Pierre Charron), 'is the prop and pillar of all States and Kingdoms, the cement and soule of humane affairs, the life of society and order, the very vitall spirit whereby so many millions of men doe breathe the life of comfort and peace; and the whole nature of things subsists' (Bolton 1635, p. 10; Charron 1604, p. 266). Government, considered abstractly, was the divinely appointed instrument by which people could achieve the temporal goals of their nature. So government was, in some sense, the work of God. It did not follow, however, that the powers of particular governors were derived directly from God. For it was arguable that God had at first granted political authority to every independent multitude, and that kings (or aristocracies) had arisen only when the sovereign people transferred authority to one (or a few) men. Arguably, too, the transference had taken place on conditions stipulated by the people. If the prince infringed these conditions, power would revert to the people.

The notions that kings were subject to contractual limitations which had been imposed upon them by an originally sovereign people, and that they might be resisted or even deposed if they ignored these limitations, were rejected by absolutists. Some argued that the king's power was not in fact derived from an act of transference by the people. The original multitude might, perhaps, have appointed the person(s) of its ruler(s), but those rulers drew their authority from God alone. A husband's power over his wife and children was natural, for God had, as it were, imprinted husbandly and fatherly power in human nature. The wife's consent made a particular man her husband, but it was God alone who gave power to husbands and fathers (De Dominis 1620, pp. 527–8; Digges 1643, p. 113). In the same way, royal and papal power were often held to stem directly from God, though kings might at first have been elected by the people, and popes still were elected by cardinals. In both cases, election nominated the person of the ruler but did not transfer power to him (Barret 1612, p. 28; Buckeridge 1614, p. 291; Marsilius 1606, p. 205). The king's power was derived from God alone, and it was, therefore, to God alone that he was accountable for its exercise.

This theory of the origins of government was common throughout the seventeenth century. According to one version of it, royal and paternal power were not just similar (in that both were derived from God alone), but identical. In other words, the power of any independent father over his offspring *was* royal power. Conversely, the authority of a king over his subjects *was* patriarchal. By identifying royal with patriarchal power, writers were able to harness conventional social theory – which emphasised the divinely appointed duty of children to obey their fathers – to the king's cause. They were also able to demolish the claim that the first states had been independent, self-governing communities. For, if patriarchal power was kingly, it followed that the first fathers – and in particular Adam – had been kings. Monarchy, then, was the original form of government.

While many writers, both on the continent and in England, claimed that royal power was derived immediately from God, others accepted the notion that the community had at first been sovereign, and yet deduced absolutist conclusions from this premise. They argued either that the community's transference of power to a ruler had been unconditional, or that the king's power had arisen by conquest (which was morally equivalent to an absolute transference), or, finally, that the consequences of any attempt to enforce contractual limitations upon a ruler were likely to be so unpleasant that it ought always to be avoided. The idea that royal power arose from a grant by the people had been widely voiced in France during the wars of religion, and both Huguenots and Leaguers had drawn radical implications from it. In the seventeenth century the same idea continued to flourish but was increasingly used to absolutist ends. One of the main developments in Catholic ideology during the seventeenth century lay precisely in the increasing conservatism with which the idea of an original transference of power was interpreted. In France this development was connected to the highly successful equation of anti-absolutist ideas with Protestantism by royal propagandists.

In 1614 Jean Baricave, a French cleric, published a word-by-word refutation of the Huguenot *Vindiciae contra tyrannos*. According to Baricave it was Wyclif, Luther, and Calvin who had first introduced the idea that subjects may legitimately take up arms against their prince. He admitted that some Catholics had adopted similar views, but insisted that they derived their ideas from Protestants (Baricave 1614, pp. 15, 91). The intention of Calvinists in France, he claimed, was to introduce republicanism, on the model of Geneva and the United Provinces (Baricave 1614, p. 153; other French examples are discussed in Parker 1980, pp. 155–6; the emperor Ferdinand II likewise equated Protestantism with disloyalty: Evans 1979, p. 68). It was by Huguenot ideas that Henri IV's Catholic assassin François Ravaillac had been influenced. The Jesuit Juan de Mariana's doctrines on resistance had been justly condemned in France, and yet they were less noxious than the teachings of the *Vindiciae* (Baricave 1614, pp. 91, 241). Baricave's arguments were paralleled by those of English Protestants, who likewise condemned the resistance theories of both papist and Puritan monarchomachs, but who gave priority to the papists (Owen 1610; Maxwell 1644, pp. 12–15; Nalson 1677, p. 201; Brady, quoted in Clancy 1964, p. 196). In both countries the equation of religious heterodoxy with anti-absolutist political ideas was a regular part of royalist polemics. In England, however, the identification of popery with rebellion never proved fully convincing for, from the 1620s onwards, the opponents of absolutism persuasively argued that popery was in fact linked to arbitrary government – and the French experience confirmed their thesis.

Baricave decried the ignorance of people who did not know that God grants popes and kings their authority, using those who elect them merely 'to designate and name the person' (Baricave 1614, p. 343). Princes received their power immediately from God: there was no intermediary between God and the king. Despite Baricave's suspicions, many Protestant thinkers maintained precisely the same position, which was voiced by the Huguenot national synod in 1617 (Hespérien 1617, pp. 5–6). Theories of legitimate resistance were rarely articulated by French Protestants in the seventeenth century (Parker 1981, pp. 156–9, 1983, pp. 111–12; the period after 1685 and the resistance theorist Jurieu are discussed in Dodge 1947). The idea of the divine right of kings was not confined to any single religious or professional group. According to the jurist Jean Domat 'it is immediately from God that princes hold their power' (Domat 1705, II, p. 142). The Gallican bishop Pierre de Marca declared that the notion of an original transference of power from the people to the king was not only anarchic but also contrary to scripture, which made it plain that 'royal power is immediately conferred by God upon each king'. Kings might at first have been elected – though even here God inspired the electors – but their authority stemmed directly from God as the author of the law of nature (Marca 1641, p. 147).

In Venice Sarpi similarly affirmed that 'in temporal matters absolute princes are subject to none but God, from whom their power is immediately derived' (Sarpi 1606, p. 633). The Venetian De Dominis wrote at length in favour of the same thesis, taking issue with the Jesuit Suárez' arguments for original transference. In De Dominis' opinion, it was blasphemous to suggest that God had at first set up democracy, the worst form of government (De Dominis 1620, pp. 919–20). When De Dominis came to England in 1616, such ideas had already been circulating there for some time. James I held that kings derive their power from God alone, though the person of the king had on occasion been determined by popular election (Tanner 1930, pp. 15–16). Thomas Morton (who defended James I's oath of allegiance against Catholics) followed the Venetian Johannes Marsilius in distinguishing sharply between the origins of a king's title and the source of his authority: 'the title unto an authority is not without the meanes of man, but the authority it selfe is immediately from God' (Morton 1610, I, p. 246; Marsilius 1606, p. 205). According to Lancelot Andrewes, kings draw their power from God alone, and in some cases at least (Saul, David) their persons had also been appointed by Him (Andrewes 1610, pp. 18, 21). Sir Robert Filmer, whose father-in-law was Andrewes' predecessor as bishop of Ely, held that God first gave Adam kingly power, but he acknowledged that not all later kings were Adam's direct descendants. Providence could change the ruling dynasty and even the form of government. Yet, by whatever means the ruler acquired his title, his power was still from God alone (Filmer 1949, p. 62).

iii   Patriarchalism

Filmer confirmed his thesis about the divine origins of royal authority by *equating* kingly and paternal power. Many writers argued that royal and fatherly power were analogous, and that the fifth commandment enjoined obedience to magistrates as well as to parents. Filmer went further, claiming that the power of any sovereign ruler was *identical* with the power of an autonomous father – and virtually everyone agreed that fathers derive their power from God alone (Filmer 1949, p. 62). The first father was, of course, Adam, who had ruled over the whole world by right of fatherhood (Filmer 1949, p. 58). Later kings held power which was, like Adam's, fatherly, whether their title to it arose 'by election, donation, succession or by any other means' (Filmer 1949, p. 106). Since Adam had been a king the notion of original popular sovereignty stood refuted, and no place was left 'for such imaginary pactions between Kings and their people as many dream of' (Filmer 1949, p. 57).

Filmer's *Patriarcha* was first published in 1680, twenty-seven years after its author's death. The date of composition of the book remains uncertain, though the notion that it was written after the outbreak of the English Civil War is difficult to sustain (Daly 1983; Tuck 1986). Fortunately, the precise date is of relatively minor historical interest, since the political doctrines expressed in it were mostly unoriginal. Many of its most famous contentions were voiced by theorists of the Jacobean period and, indeed, by the Elizabethan Saravia.

Saravia was born in Flanders, but became naturalised as an Englishman in 1568, and was a translator of King James' Authorised Version of the Bible. His *De imperandi authoritate* was published by the royal printer in 1593 as an antidote to the writings of Catholic and especially Protestant monarchomachs. In it Saravia struck at the doctrine of original freedom, declaring that 'by nature men are not born free, since 'by the law of nature the son is in the power of his father' (Saravia 1611, p. 125). He inveighed against those who praised liberty 'as if the highest happiness of human life were to be found in it'; in reality, desire for freedom arose from self-love, the root of all evil and the cause of Adam's downfall (Saravia 1611, p. 119; a very similar passage is in Filmer 1949, p. 53).

4. 'Homines natura non nascuntur liberi.' 'Naturae lege filius familias in patris est potestate'.

Scriptural history, said Saravia, made it clear that mankind's original condition had not been one of freedom: 'the true origin of political authority is taught by sacred history, which shows that government was not the invention of man but the constitution of God and nature, and that the first governments were paternal[5] (Saravia 1611, p. 167). The Book of Genesis demonstrated that political power existed from the very beginning of mankind's history. Saravia concluded that 'fatherly power was kingly, that is to say supreme, amongst the first authors of the human race, whether we look at those centuries of the first age before the Flood, or at those which followed under Noah and his sons and grandsons; and by the law of nature fathers were princes over their descendants'[6] (Saravia 1611, p. 167). The power of a father (and king) included the right to nominate his successor, but if he failed to do so succession proceeded by primogeniture (Saravia 1611, p. 167). God could, however, alter these arrangements. Providence could change the form of government or the person(s) of the governor(s). In every state, however, the power of the ruler was the same, and came from God alone (Saravia 1611, p. 160).

The ideas that royal power is essentially patriarchal, and that the first fathers were kings over their subjects (and children) were relatively common in early seventeenth-century England. Patriarchal and regal rule, said Andrewes, were 'both one in effect' (Andrewes 1610, p. 13). Bishop John Buckeridge, Dean Thomas Jackson, and Bolton each said much that was later to be regarded as characteristic of Filmer (Sommerville 1986b, p. 31). The only innovatory aspect of Filmer's patriarchal theory is the thoroughness with which he expressed it. Nor was his treatment of other questions original. He did indeed derive royal power from God alone, and parted company with Sir John Hayward, Barclay and Adam Blackwood on this matter (Daly 1979, pp. 20–1). Yet, in doing this, he found himself in agreement with a vast number of other thinkers. Again, Filmer held that royal power was not limited by any human authority or law. In this he agreed with such theorists as his friend Peter Heylin, and the civil lawyer John Cowell, both of whom wrote before 1640 (Heylin 1637, p. 156; Cowell 1607, sig. 2Q1a).

Later, when Civil War came, a number of royalists argued that His

---

5. 'Ex sacra historia docetur vera imperii origo, & quod non hominum fuerit inventio, sed Dei & naturae constitutio, & prima imperia fuisse paterna.'
6. 'patriam potestatem regiam, hoc est, summam fuisse apud primo humani generis authores, sive secula prioris aevi ante aquarum inundationem spectemus, sive quae post secuta sunt sub Noaho, & ipsius natis ac nepotibus: & Patres illos iure naturae principes fuisse eorum quos procrearunt'.

Majesty was, in fact, limited by human laws. This was the position of Bagshaw, a common lawyer whose views on the origins of government resembled Filmer's, but who nevertheless subordinated the royal will to the customary law of the land (Daly 1979, pp. 178–9; Bagshaw 1660, pp. 101–6). Some of the king's propagandists also claimed that Charles was limited by English law, and at times implied that this was an arrangement which the monarch alone could neither justly nor validly alter (Ferne 1642, p. 15, 1643, p. 6; Digges 1642, p. 12, 1643, pp. 10, 64, 128). It is not surprising that such publicists emphasised the moderation of the king's cause, for their task was to persuade the uncommitted to side with King Charles. Yet they were often very imprecise on just how royal power was limited, and it is arguable that if pressed most of them would have agreed with Filmer's views.

It has been said that the 'bizarre' system of Filmer's *Patriarcha* left 'no echo in the French literature of the time' (Lacour-Gayet 1898, p. 463). Filmer's system was not bizarre, but it is, seemingly, true that no fully developed patriarchalist theory of government was voiced in seventeenth-century France. Nevertheless, elements of such a theory are to be found in a number of French writers. Elie Merlat, for example, held that fathers and masters originally possessed the power to inflict the death penalty upon their children and servants (Merlat 1685, p. 55). Baricave attempted to refute contractualist accounts of the origins of government by showing that Adam and Noah had been kings and that kingship therefore existed from the beginning of time (Baricave 1614, pp. 354, 451). Bossuet declared that 'all men are born subject', since their fathers have power over them, and he held that states developed from families (*Politique tirée*, 2,1, in Bossuet 1966, p. 104). Senault asserted that 'the first fathers were kings of their children, just as the first kings were fathers of their subjects'. 'Monarchy', he said, 'is almost as old as the world itself', for Adam had been king in Eden (Senault 1661, p. 22). None of these authors, however, placed any great weight upon these patriarchalist propositions, and some contradicted patriarchalism by distinguishing between royal and paternal power (e.g. Baricave 1614, p. 561). Systematic patriarchalism flourished in England but not France. The reasons for this are obscure. Filmer's own influence probably had little to do with the popularity of the theory in England. Patriarchalism was arguably more popular before than after Filmer, and few writers quoted him (specific examples of Filmer's influence are discussed in Schochet 1975, pp. 163, 165, 175, 185, 202–3, but even here the evidence is not always conclusive). Of course, patriarchalism was a variant of the divine right of kings. In other words, patriarchalists held that kings derive their power from God alone. In France many absolutists did not subscribe to this view. A high proportion of legal thinkers, and of theologians, continued to maintain that royal power arose from an act of transference by the people.

iv Contract, conquest, and usurpation

When De Dominis attacked the political theories of Robert Bellarmine and Suárez, he argued that every ruler derived his power from God alone, and concluded that kings are exempt from papal control. Edmond Richer agreed with the conclusion but rejected the premise. Richer, who had been syndic of the Sorbonne until his ultra-Gallican views led to his dismissal, broadly followed the teachings of Jean Gerson and Jacques Almain on the origins of government. Royal power, he said, was derived from the people and not from God alone, so De Dominis' theory was mistaken (Richer 1692, pp. 154–5). Yet, he maintained, the Venetian was correct to condemn the views of such men as Suárez. The fact that the people had once possessed power did not imply that they could ever recover it. Public tranquillity would be undermined if princes could be resisted by their subjects. Kings were, in consequence, irresistible, and accountable to God alone. One private individual could use force to defend himself against attack by another, but no individual could ever use force against the king. For the death of the king would doubtless cause public harm, while God's law of nature required that we promote the public good (Richer 1692, pp. 159, 133).

Cardinal Du Perron strongly disagreed with Richer's views on church–state relations. When the third estate attacked the pope's claims to power in temporals in the Estates General of 1614–15, Du Perron spoke in favour of the papal position. His political theory was Ultramontane, and its principles were not far removed from those of Leaguer resistance theorists. Du Perron, however, was careful to tone down the practical implications of his thinking, and the same holds good of most Ultramontane theorists in the years after the assassination of Henri IV. The *parlement* of Paris condemned Mariana's *De rege*, which had allowed resistance by private individuals in special circumstances. After 1610, the Jesuits and their allies tried to distance themselves from the ideas of Mariana. Suárez heavily qualified popular rights of resistance but nevertheless incurred the wrath of the *parlement* of Paris, which condemned his *Defensio fidei* in 1614. Other

Ultramontanes were still more circumspect than Suárez, and many disguised the anti-absolutist implications of their contractualism. The English author of *The Image of Bothe Churches* (possibly James Pateson) was so cautious on the subject of resistance that he can be read as an absolutist. He spent much space on showing that Calvinists were seditious, and quoted Bodin on sovereignty (Pateson 1623, p. 218). Yet there is little in his book which formally contradicts the ideas of the Catholic monarchomachs. The Protestant contractualist Hugo Grotius published his *De Jure Belli ac Pacis* at Paris in 1625. This work is sometimes regarded as an unoriginal re-hash of neo-scholastic (and especially Suárezian) ideas (Edwards 1981, pp. 148–55). Since Rousseau, it has also commonly been seen as a major text of early modern absolutist thinking (Rousseau, *Du contrat social*, ch. 2). In a sense, it is both, for neo-scholastic authors became increasingly absolutist in the seventeenth century.

Grotius was not the only contemporary jurist to toy with absolutist notions. Absolutist ideas became increasingly influential amongst French jurists in the late sixteenth and early seventeenth centuries, though a number of these writers continued to trace the origins of royal power to a grant by the people. Le Bret's *De la souveraineté du Roy* of 1632 set out what was virtually the official ideology of the government of Richelieu and Mazarin (Bonney 1978, pp. 26, 115). Le Bret insisted that the king had a monopoly of legislative power (Le Bret 1632, pp. 64–75). Popular acclamation of the sovereign at the time of the coronation did not imply that royal power was in any sense dependent on the people, for kings were accountable to God alone. The coronation ceremony was useful in giving the people an opportunity to pay homage to a king whom God had set over them; it did not indicate that kingship was elective (Le Bret 1632, p. 27). Yet the people had originally been sovereign. To prevent the rich and powerful from abusing their positions 'the first men . . . established kings, and gave them sovereign authority over them' (Le Bret 1632, pp. 3–4). Once kings had been instituted, however, they became sovereign legislators (Le Bret 1632, p. 64). Le Bret used the Bodinian concept of sovereignty to show that even if kings had at first derived their powers from the people, they were now accountable to God alone. Bodinian sovereignty allowed absolutist conclusions to be drawn from contractualist premises. The people had at first been sovereign, said the Jansenist Pierre Nicole, and the prince's power arose from a popular grant, but now kings 'hold their power from God alone' (Nicole 1670, p. 186).

Saumaise condemned the English Independents for executing Charles I, and for setting up the 'new monster of military government' (Saumaise 1650, p. 328). He held that the idea of perpetual popular sovereignty, which underlay the Independents' actions, was a recipe for anarchy (Saumaise 1650, p. 320). A king who could be judged by his subjects was unworthy of the name of king, for kings are by definition accountable to God alone (Saumaise 1650, pp. 314–15). The English claimed that *salus populi* had justified Charles' execution, but their reasoning was faulty. The safety and welfare of the people was, indeed, the purpose of government. It did not follow, however, that kings could ever be resisted or deposed. Indeed, what followed was the precise reverse: since *salus populi* was so important a goal, kings were irresistible. For we could never expect a single moment of peace in the state if royal power were revocable (Saumaise 1650, pp. 333–4). 'The same reason which demands that the people should not be without a ruler, also demands that the ruler should not be changed' (Saumaise 1650, p. 335). So the original transference of power from the people to the prince was irreversible (Saumaise 1650, pp. 333, 335).

Saumaise vested original sovereignty in the people as a whole, and not in individuals. Most theorists likewise denied that individuals had ever held political power, and displayed little interest in the pre-political condition of mankind. An exception was Bossuet, whose account of the origins of government was heavily indebted to Hobbes. Bossuet denied that the people had been sovereign before the institution of kings. Rather, anarchy had prevailed in that state, which was, indeed, a condition of perpetual war of all against all. To escape from a situation in which 'everyone is master and no one is' individuals therefore renounced their noxious natural liberty, which led only to fear and confusion. This renunciation of liberty was not, however, a renunciation of sovereignty: to suggest otherwise was 'to confuse the independence which every man has in a state of anarchy, with sovereignty'. Manifestly, where everyone was independent, no one was sovereign (*Cinquième avertissement*, in Bossuet 1966, pp. 83–5).

Bossuet's use of Hobbes illustrates the point that with very minor alterations the doctrines of *Leviathan* could be made to look quite traditional. In effect, Bossuet's theory was little different from conventional divine right thinking. The people *nominated* their sovereign by renouncing their natural liberty, while he alone kept his. They did not transfer sovereignty to him for they had never possessed it. In 1643 the English royalist pamphleteer Dudley Digges likewise posited an original state of complete liberty in which we all had 'an unlimited power to use our abilities, according as will did prompt' (Digges 1643, p. 2). The misery of this condition, he held, would soon persuade people that it was rational to renounce their native liberty by agreeing 'not to resist publique authority' (Digges 1643, pp. 5–6). Yet whoever held this public authority derived the right of executing criminals not from the people but from God alone.

In Digges' theory the original people are constrained by natural law to institute government. They do this by giving up their right to defend themselves against attack by some specific person(s) whom they thus effectively designate as their ruler(s). The ruler's coercive power, however, stems from God alone. The idea that princes may not be actively resisted by their subjects was, of course, utterly conventional amongst royalists and absolutists. The only novel feature of Digges' approach was that he posited a state of original liberty. This served two functions, neither of which contributed much of substance to his theory. First, it underlined just how unpleasant life without government would be. Secondly, it allowed him to score an important polemical point against his parliamentarian adversaries. They claimed to be fighting for their native liberty; Digges showed that native liberty was anarchy (Digges 1643, pp. 1–2).

Digges' intentions were polemical. The same goes for other royalist pamphleteers such a Henry Ferne, Henry Hammond, and Sir John Spelman. There were, of course, differences between them, but these propagandists had a great deal in common. All used a wide variety of arguments in order to win the debate with parliament. Digges, for instance, appealed to patriarchalism (Digges 1642, p. 5, 1643, pp. 61–2), the concept of sovereignty (Digges 1643, pp. 31–2, 59), the notion of an irreversible original transference of power (Digges 1642, pp. 1–2, 68–9), and conquest (Digges 1643, pp. 81, 116). These elements recur in varying proportions in royalist writings throughout and after the 1640s.

The Norman conquest provided Robert Brady with a basis for absolutist claims in 1681 (Brady 1681; discussed in Pocock 1957, pp. 195–9). In the 1640s conquest featured in the work not only of Digges but also of Ferne (Ferne 1643, p. 32; Sharp 1983, pp. 97–102). Like Digges, he held that William of Normandy had conquered England, and that the conquest had given him a valid title to the crown. The idea that conquest, at least in a just war, gives the victor absolute sovereignty over the vanquished was widely accepted on both sides of the Channel. Since the conqueror could put the defeated population to death, the argument ran, it was only reasonable that he acquire absolute rights over it if he chose to spare it (Bossuet, *Cinquième avertissement*, in Bossuet 1966, pp. 270–1). Saumaise claimed that unless conquest conferred title, no contemporary prince could call his kingdom his own. England, he said, had been conquered by Saxons, Danes, and Normans (Saumaise 1650, pp. 366, 367). For Saumaise, of course, the fact that a king was a conqueror implied little about his authority. All kings held sovereign power. So conquerors held no more power over their subjects than other princes. They might have fewer moral obligations, but that was a different matter.

In England, some absolutists asserted that the country had been conquered by William but, like Saumaise, placed little weight upon this contention. Such men include James I, Saravia, and, indeed, Digges and Ferne (James I 1616, p. 202; Saravia 1611, p. 288). Others – Hayward, William Fulbeke, Cowell – argued a rather stronger case, claiming that the current monarch was an absolute ruler *because* the royal line began with a conqueror (Sommerville 1986b, pp. 68–9). These three were civil lawyers, and civil law texts recorded that political power at first belonged to the people, who later decided to transfer it to a prince. This left open the possibility that in England they had transferred it on certain conditions, limiting the king's power. Arguably it was to close off this possibility that Hayward and the rest stressed conquest. For conquest, civil lawyers agreed, left the king absolute. Most absolutists, however, relied on arguments other than that from conquest. Most anti-absolutists were aware of this. The question of whether William of Normandy had acquired the throne of England by lawful succession or by conquest never lay at the centre of political debate in the seventeenth century (contrasting views on this question are to be found in Pocock 1957, pp. 42–5, 53–5; Skinner 1965; Wallace 1968, pp. 22–6; Dzelzainis 1983, pp. 43, 61).

Victory in battle was a sign of God's favour. Providence could change the royal line by transferring it to a successful invader or rebel. God made kingdoms, said Bossuet, and could give them to whomever He chose (Bossuet 1966, p. 58). The implication of this thesis was that hereditary right is not indefeasible, and most absolutists admitted this. It was easy to accept that an omnipotent deity might depose one monarch and set another in his place. It proved less easy to reach agreement on how subjects were to recognise that God had in fact changed their sovereign. Some authors argued that a usurping line acquired legitimacy after it had been in power for a century, or for three generations (Daly 1979, p. 121n; Barret 1612, pp. 417–18). In the ecclesiastical canons of 1606, however, the representatives of the English clergy affirmed that a usurping regime became legitimate as soon as it was 'throughly settled'. James I took exception to this clause which would have sanctioned any successful rebellion (Overall

1844, p. 51, preface pp. 6–9). Yet the idea that a usurper's government becomes valid once it has been effectively established continued to be influential in England, particularly in the controversy over the Engagement of 1649, and again after the Glorious Revolution. In 1690 Archbishop Sancroft published the canons of 1606, and soon afterwards William Sherlock drew on them to justify the rule of William and Mary (Goldie 1980, p. 514).

Two main arguments were used to justify the claim that a usurper became a legitimate king if he established his rule. The first was that success testified to divine approval, and this providentialist doctrine was regularly expressed both at the time of the Engagement Controversy and again after 1688. The second argument linked protection with obedience. A prince who failed to protect his subjects, so the reasoning went, forfeited his claims to their allegiance. Conversely, a usurper who did protect a people acquired a right to their obedience. In 1645 William Ball declared that 'it is an Axiom Politicall, where there is no protection there is no subjection' (Ball 1645, p. 14). He claimed that if king or parliament failed to protect the people's rights, they might defend them by force. The maxim that 'as protection draws subjection, so subjection draws protection along with it' was also used by Robert Austine in 1644 to justify parliament's use of force (Austine 1644, p. 2), but it was not until the Engagement Controversy began in 1649 that the idea really came into its own. In 1651 Hobbes gave forceful expression to the theory, employing it to defend obedience to the commonwealth (Skinner 1972).

Absolutist thinking in the early seventeenth century was divided and often imprecise on exactly what constituted a valid title to the crown. In England after 1649 some erstwhile royalists were thus able to accommodate themselves to the new regime without sacrificing their old principles. Providentialists could construe the commonwealth as providentially ordained. Consistent supporters of Stuart rule, on the other hand, might find themselves forced to alter their doctrines. Filmer is an example. In *Patriarcha* he claimed that Providence could change the line of succession, and even the form of government (Filmer 1949, p. 62). Later, he changed his mind on both points. In the *Directions for obedience to government in dangerous or doubtful times* (1652), Filmer argued that 'a usurper can never gain a right from the true superior', but that amongst usurpers the earliest had the best title (Filmer 1949, p. 234). One obvious implication of these principles is that if genealogists discovered the heir of Adam (the first legitimate ruler), or of some ancient usurper, the claim of the Stuarts to the throne of England would be undermined. In challenging the title of the commonwealth, Filmer constructed arguments which not only contradicted his earlier theory but also cast doubt on the claims of the Stuarts, and, indeed, of every ruling house in Europe. The *Directions* was appended to *Observations upon Aristotles politics touching forms of government*, in which Filmer claimed that there was only one form of government, namely monarchy. Once monarchy had been abolished in England, Filmer decided that non-monarchical forms of government were invalid.

v   The limits of absolutism

The case of Filmer illustrates that civil war led to ideological shifts amongst Englishmen. It is sometimes difficult to tell how far such shifts were cosmetic rather than substantial. Property provides an example. Before the Civil War, lawyers and clerics in the king's service often vindicated His Majesty's right to take his subjects' goods without their consent in what he deemed to be a case of necessity. From 1640 onwards, however, Charles' propagandists emphasised royal respect for rights of property, and the necessity of consent. It was not the king, they said, but the so-called parliament which threatened the subject's property (Digges 1642, p. 97). After the Restoration, too, many royalists wrote circumspectly on the question of property. Clarendon, for examrle, dissented from Hobbes' notion that sovereigns might take a subject's goods at will, and reminded him of 'the ill consequence which must attend the very imagination that the Nation had lost its Propriety' (Hyde 1676, p. 109). The Civil War demonstrated that Englishmen were fond of their property, and could grow violent if it were subverted. Many post-Restoration royalists bore this lesson in mind, though some continued to assert that the monarch had absolute power over the property of subjects (Leslie 1709, p. 42).

In later seventeenth-century England royalists grew increasingly reluctant to assert the king's right to tax without consent. In France, by contrast, the notion that taxation ordinarily requires consent was swiftly eroded. Bodin famously insisted that kings had a duty to obtain the consent of their subjects before they levied taxes, though he admitted that this rule lost its force in emergencies (Bodin 1962, pp. 663–5). He looked to the Estates General as the appropriate institution to vote taxes in France. After 1615 this institution fell into disuse. Even before then many theorists had abandoned the idea that consent is normally needed to validate royal levies. Neither Charles Loyseau nor Pierre de L'Hommeau deemed consent necessary (Church 1941, p. 328; on Loyseau see Gilmore 1950).

Baricave claimed that the king could commandeer the resources of his subjects in order to preserve the state. Only necessity and the public good could justify sovereigns in seizing goods. Yet even if they had no such justification, the subject could never resist. Later, Le Bret vigorously rejected the idea that princes may take their subjects' goods arbitrarily. He insisted that a king ought not to pursue his own personal advantage at the expense of his people. The public good, however, took precedence over private interests. So the king could levy taxes without consent whenever the public good required such a course (Baricave 1614, pp. 573, 576; Le Bret 1632, pp. 632, 634, 637).

Louis XIV himself held that kings have 'the full and free disposition of all the goods possessed by ecclesiastics as well as laymen', to use according to the needs of their state (Louis XIV 1860, I, p. 209). He did not bother to mention the old idea that taxation requires consent. Nor did Senault, though he was careful to stress that monarchs hold no property in their subjects' goods, and that they are bound to rule in the public interest. Only necessity could justify taxation, he said, and a prudent king would explain to his subjects why taxes were necessary – or risk rebellion. Senault criticised French taxation not because the king ignored consent but because his levies fell disproportionately upon the poor, causing hardship (Senault 1661, pp. 350–1, 354–6). Fénelon likewise attacked the disastrous effects of royal policies rather than the king's right to finance them without consent (Fénelon 1920, pp. 143–57).

French theorists claimed that the subject held property in his lands and goods. In an arbitrary or seigneurial monarchy, they argued, the king alone possessed property. In France, however, royal rule was absolute and not arbitrary. That is to say, the king could not justly take his subjects' possessions at will. Seigneurial monarchy was regarded as contrary to Christian principles (Bossuet, *Politique tirée*, 8,2, in Bossuet 1966, p. 115; La Bruyère 1966, p. 247). Just occasionally, authors affirmed that the people of France held only usufruct and not full property (Church 1941, pp. 259–60; Lacour-Gayet 1898, p. 428). Mostly, however, thinkers insisted that the sovereign could tax only when public necessity demanded. Since the king was irresistible this stipulation was evidently unenforceable.

The doctrine that necessity justifies taxation was more easily swallowed when the necessity was obvious – as it was in France in the 1630s. Amongst theorists, however, the thesis had won wide favour well before the war with Spain, and its vogue continued even after victory began to look likely. In 1640 a *conseiller* of the *parlement* of Paris argued that there was no necessity, since Louis XIII's troops were victorious everywhere. He was arrested and exiled (Bonney 1978, p. 116). At the time of the Fronde, the idea that taxation requires consent was indeed revived, but thereafter it faded rapidly. In England, on the other hand, the same idea flourished – partly, at least, because there was no obvious emergency in the 1630s when Charles I levied Ship Money.

Before 1640, English clerics frequently vindicated the king's right to tax without consent, and specific levies were validated in famous legal test-cases. The legal decisions were sometimes based on narrow technical grounds, and occasionally royal rights over property were justified by reference to the Norman conquest. Saravia, for example, stated that after William the Conqueror had obtained the lands of England by right of war he graciously restored possession of them to their former owners, but 'reserved to himself direct dominion'[7] over them (Saravia 1611, p. 288). Digges likewise argued that the Conqueror had granted his subjects only the *utile dominium* of the land, himself retaining direct dominion (Digges 1643, pp. 91, 116). The main argument in favour of extra-parliamentary taxation, however, was not based on any particular reading of medieval history. As in France, absolutists claimed that the prince's power to rule in the public interest included a power to take his subjects' goods when necessity demanded. The sovereign alone was the judge of necessity (Sommerville 1986b, pp. 160–3).

Theft was prohibited by the eighth commandment. In the public interest, absolutists allowed the prince to take goods without consent. Were they condoning a breach of divine law for the sake of promoting the common good? Under Charles I, the claim was sometimes advanced that for 'reason of state' the king could perform actions which would otherwise be unjustified, and similar assertions were commonly made in Richelieu's France. Those who expressed such opinions occasionally drew their ideas from Machiavelli. An example is Louis Machon, who prepared a defence of Machiavelli at Richelieu's request (Church 1972, pp. 416–30; Machon and Gabriel Naudé are discussed in Thuau 1966, pp. 318–50). Even Machon, however, was anxious to reinterpret Machiavelli's views in order to make them conform to traditional Christian morality. Machon's work remained unpublished, and most theorists were more cautious about praising the Florentine's ideas. Arguably, some nevertheless fell under his spell. However, it is far from clear that the growth of talk about 'reason of state' amongst absolutists in the early seventeenth century bears witness to an

---

7. 'directo sibi dominio reservato'.

increase in Machiavelli's influence or, indeed, to any significant change in moral thinking. Two points are important here. First, so-called traditional morality itself placed great weight upon the public good. Secondly, most theorists who wrote in favour of 'reason of state' were careful to stress that the sovereign's power was limited by his Christian duties.

In 1625 two Jesuit pamphleteers attacked French foreign policy, claiming that it irreligiously placed narrow national interests before the Catholic cause (Church 1972, pp. 121–3). In the later 1620s and 1630s a number of French Catholics likewise looked askance at Richelieu's alliances with heretics against Spain, the champion of Catholicism, and accused the Cardinal of Machiavellian practices: like Machiavelli, Richelieu subordinated Christian morality to the public safety. Such accusations should not be taken too seriously. Devout, Hispanophile Catholics themselves gave a very high priority to the maintenance of the public good. Of course, they denied that 'the least sin against God may be committed for the welfare of the commonwealth'[8] (Coquaeus 1610, p. 493). Some held, however, that actions could cease to be sinful if they were performed in a good cause. 'Such is the force of the public good', said the English priest Edward Weston, 'that at its bidding many things are rendered good and lawful which would otherwise, of their own natures, be found contrary to right reason'[9] (Weston 1613, p. 240). Jesuits (and other Catholic moralists) were capable of evading the more rigid of God's commandments by reclassifying their contents. Mental reservation was distinguished from lying, for example, and permitted if the cause were just. The effect of this development was to allow acts which had previously been classified as lying, provided that they led to public or at least private benefit. In 1625 the English Benedictine John Barnes convincingly argued that some of the casuists placed such great emphasis upon the public good that their teaching was indistinguishable from Machiavelli's (Barnes 1625, p. 106). Many of such casuists were Jesuit opponents of Richelieu's foreign policy.

Richelieu and his propagandists in fact insisted that statesmen should scrupulously abide by the demands of Christian morality (Church 1972, esp. p. 501). 'True reasons of state do not clash with the maxims of religion', said Jean de Silhon, and in 1661 Senault argued that piety and prudence

---

8. 'pro salute Reipublicae non licet ne minimum quidem peccatum in Deum committere'.
9. 'Imo tanta vis tantumque est imperium boni publici, et alti dominii, eius causa, in cives, ut ad illius mandatum multa reddantur bona ac legitima, quae alioquin naturis suis a recta ratione aliena invenirentur.'

were fully compatible (Silhon quoted in Church 1972, p. 164; Senault 1661, pp. 123–5). Few authors denied that there were unchangeable moral rules by which the prince was bound to abide. His duty to govern in the public interest did, indeed, force him to ignore human positive laws when they came into competition with the common good. Some precepts, however, were eternally binding. The king's will did not define what was just except in cases where superior laws were silent (Baricave 1614, p. 505). The laws of God were to be obeyed in preference to the prince's decrees. If a subject *knew* that the sovereign's edict was contrary to a divine injunction, he was bound to obey God and not the king. Where he merely suspected that the prince's command was unjust, however, he had an obligation to give the king the benefit of the doubt, and a further obligation to overcome his conscientious scruples, and so avoid obeying half-heartedly (Le Bret 1632, p. 193).

Kings sinned if their orders contravened the laws of God and nature. Since God's law required that they keep their promises, they also sinned if they broke human law (which they promised to uphold at the time of their coronation) – unless, of course, the public good necessitated such action. Two other varieties of law which imposed limitations upon monarchs were fundamental law and the canons of the church. French absolutists gave especial emphasis to fundamental law, which bound the king not to alienate the royal domain, and which (as Salic law) governed succession to the throne.

Perhaps introduced into France in the 1570s, the term fundamental law soon acquired a European vogue. It long remained imprecise, however, and was interpreted according to each writer's theoretical predilections. Absolutists sometimes assimilated it to the law of nature. Jérôme Bignon, for example, held that Salic law was drawn 'from nature itself' and Bodin also declared that government by women was contrary to the law of nature (Bignon 1610, p. 254; Bodin 1962, p. 746). Others gave it scriptural warrant, for Christ had said that the lilies (meaning the crown of France) did not toil or spin, and this evidently meant that labourers and women were excluded from the succession (Bacon 1671, II, p. 227; Senault 1661, p. 44). A third possibility was that Salic law had been instituted by an originally sovereign people before it transferred authority to a monarch (Nicole 1670, p. 186; Le Bret 1632, pp. 32–3).

Perhaps the only consistent element in absolutist interpretations of fundamental laws is that they were construed as strengthening the crown. Like Bodin, Jean Savaron affirmed that the king held only the usufruct of the royal lands in France, and insisted that an inalienable domain was essential to strong monarchical power (Savaron 1620, pp. 10–11; on Bodin see Burns 1959). Savaron was attacked for these views, which suggested that the king was subject to laws imposed upon him (Savaron 1620, p. 12), and others preferred to construe this limitation on the royal will as moral, not legal, in nature. Baricave, for instance, argued only that the king *ought* not to alienate the domain without just cause, and stressed that he was its true proprietor (Baricave 1614, pp. 590, 610). Again, Bossuet held that fundamental law in general had only directive force over the prince. The king could validly abrogate any law – fundamental or otherwise – though he could do so sinlessly only when the public good dictated. In the case of fundamental laws it was unlikely to be wise to abrogate them, for they were precisely those laws upon which the stability of society depended (*Politique tirée*, 4,1,3–4, in Bossuet 1966, pp. 111–14; 1,4,8, in Bossuet 1967, pp. 28–9).

Fundamental law placed only minor restrictions on royal power. Arguably, more serious limitations were imposed upon the king's freedom of action by the ecclesiastical authority of the church. In England, only the most extreme of Erastian theorists denied that the clergy possessed spiritual authority independently of the prince. Most writers held, indeed, that clerics could not exercise such power without royal licence; but spiritual power itself, they said, was given immediately to churchmen by God and not by the king. In France, many thinkers granted the clergy still wider powers. Ecclesiastical Gallicans questioned the rights over the church which the king had gained in the Concordat of Bologna. Ultramontane Catholics were reluctant to condemn the indirect deposing power of the pope, and in 1614–15 it was the clergy who torpedoed the third estate's article on this matter in the Estates General.

By tolerating high clericalist thinking among churchmen the French crown ensured that zealous Catholicism was equated with loyalism (see Parker 1983, p. 50, and for a central European parallel Evans 1979, pp. 65–6). Again, the survival of Ultramontane ideas amongst the clergy benefited the crown by fusing anti-clericalism with absolutism. In 1639 Pierre Dupuy published a collection of treatises which emphasised royal power in ecclesiasticals. The book was condemned by the Assembly of the Clergy, and a Doctor of the Sorbonne wrote a reply to it. In 1640 the *parlement* of Paris in turn condemned the Doctor's work (Martimort 1953, p. 99; Lacour-Gayet 1898, p. 360). That same year members of the English parliament attacked the clergy's canons largely because of the absolutist doctrines which they propounded. In England, absolutism came to be equated with the narrow sectional interests of the clergy. In France, by contrast, it was anti-absolutist ideas which were identified with private interests. As the century progressed the French clergy themselves shifted ground until by 1682 they unambiguously rejected the papal deposing power and other Ultramontane ideas (Martimort 1953, pp. 461–74).

Clerics also aided absolutism's cause by presiding over the ritual in which monarchs touched (and hopefully cured) scrofulous patients. This royal power was supernatural and served to mark kings out from ordinary mortals. James I was notoriously sceptical about his ability to cure the King's Evil, but other thinkers took the ritual much more seriously. James' chaplain William Tooker claimed that it was from English monarchs that the kings of France had derived their talents in this area – a thesis staunchly rejected by the sieur de Lancre in 1623 (Thuau 1966, p. 24). Senault spoke of the king's miraculous power to cure scrofula, claiming that it was acquired when His Majesty was anointed (Senault 1661, pp. 86, 100–1). 'There is', he said, 'something supernatural about monarchy' (Senault 1661, p. 24), and others agreed, but it seems likely that the magical qualities of kingship bulked larger in popular sentiment than in the considered reflections of theorists.

In England, the royal touch was in high demand in the second half of the seventeenth century. During two decades Charles II laid a hand upon an average of more than twelve sufferers per day (Thomas 1973, p. 228). Popular belief in the magical powers of monarchs does not seem to have declined in the late seventeenth century. Amongst English theorists, absolutist ideas did grow less popular towards the end of the century. This was not, however, because of the growth of scepticism. The main alternatives to absolutist thinking were just as vulnerable to sceptical attack. Nor did absolutism fade because its opponents won the polemical debate, whatever Whig publicists might claim. Any explanation of the failure of absolutism in England must take full account of the ineptitude of James II and his father, and arguably it was royal incompetence which later led Frenchmen to follow the English example. The king's actions helped to convince his subjects of the truth of one of the ideologies which rivalled absolutism. In England during the early seventeenth century the most important of these ideologies centred on the ancient constitution and the common law.

13

England: ancient constitution and common law

CORINNE C. WESTON

A new history centring on law and government, pervasive respect for common law, and an increasingly confident and aggressive House of Commons – this congruence of elements nourished in Stuart England the doctrine of an ancient constitution. The authors of the new history were usually common lawyers with scholarly interests, often referred to as legal antiquaries, who interpreted the historical past from the standpoint of their own day. Assuming the antiquity of Englishmen's rights and liberties and their constant assertion through the centuries, they ransacked historical records for the requisite evidence and interpreted their findings in light of common law. Their list of rights and liberties, composing *in toto* the ancient constitution, proved surprisingly protean, ranging from freedom of speech in parliament to its regular meetings and, after civil war directed political thought into new channels, even legal rights concerned with parliamentary representation and the role of the House of Commons in law making – subjects little scrutinised in the pre-1642 political world.

Whether the human source of these rights and liberties was the king or community became a leading question in Stuart political thought. According to the Jacobean House of Commons, reasoning from common law, the rights and liberties of the commons of England, enjoyed from time immemorial, were an inheritance from their ancestors, a statement making the community their human source. James I's rejoinder expressed impa-

The research was supported (in part) by a grant from PSC-CUNY Research Award Program of The City University of New York. A version of a portion of this chapter was presented on 3 April 1986 at the Folger Institute Center for History of British Political Thought, which is supported by grants from the Research Programs Division of the National Endowment for the Humanities (an independent federal agency), the John Ben Snow Memorial Trust, the George Washington University, and the Exxon Education Foundation. I wish also to thank Dr J.H. Baker, St Catharine's College, Cambridge, for his kindness in reading this chapter and giving valuable suggestions. For the views here expressed I alone am responsible.

tience with 'anti-monarchical' words about ancient liberties unless it were added that he and his ancestors had granted them; but the king pledged, of his own will, to respect privileges enjoyed by long custom and lawful precedent. This language bespoke the political theory of order dominant in early Stuart England by which the king, as God's vicegerent, was the human source of political power and authority and hence of ancient rights and liberties. In this exchange of opinions, reflective of divergent ideologies, were seeds of a dispute that endured to the Glorious Revolution.

i   The common law mind and the ancient constitution

That the doctrine of the ancient constitution is recognised as a distinctive component of Stuart political thought is due largely to J.G.A. Pocock's *Ancient Constitution and the Feudal Law* (1957), which highlighted the role of a common law outlook in shaping that doctrine and ensuring its wide reception. 'Belief in the antiquity of the common law', he writes, 'encouraged belief in the existence of an ancient constitution, reference to which was constantly made, precedents, maxims and principles from which were constantly alleged, and which was constantly asserted to be in some way immune from the king's prerogative action.'[1] The source of that doctrine was Sir Edward Coke, whose *Reports*, published in eleven parts in 1600–15, and *Institutes of the Laws of England* (1628–44) contain the legal and historical ideas linking ancient constitution and common law. The *Reports* supplied law cases for generations of students, and the *Institutes* was a great legal text-book. Their popularity could only have been enhanced by the great prestige of an author who was at one time speaker of the Elizabethan House of Commons, successively chief justice of the common pleas and king's bench, and prominent parliamentary leader. To William Prynne, and countless others, Coke was 'that eminent patron and pillar of the common law . . . whose quotations . . . are generally received, and relied on by a mere implicit faith, as infallible oracles, not only by most young students and professors, but most ancient sages of the law in their

---

1. Pocock 1987, p. 46. This work, which first appeared in 1957, was reissued in 1987 with additional chapters in which Pocock has expanded and in some instances refined his earlier position. Other works on the ancient constitution include Butterfield 1944; Gough 1961; Hill 1958, pp. 50–122; Nenner 1977; Smith 1987. On progress in writing history, see Kenyon 1984, pp. 5–17. The terms 'antiquaries' and 'historians' were used interchangeably in the seventeenth century.

arguments and resolutions; yea by many members of parliament in their debates and conferences' (Prynne 1669, 'To all Ingenuous Readers', p. 3).

Coke was the oracle of the law, that law of two kinds: common law and statutory law, the first sometimes described as unwritten law, the second as written law. The latter is the product of a legislating parliament consisting of the king and two houses, which could make new laws or alter, repeal, or enforce the old, whereas common law is usually defined in terms of ancient customs and described as a customary or traditional law with deep medieval roots, not willed by a legislator but declared by royal judges in common law courts, and already ancient when declared. Both influenced political thought; but it was common law that gave ancient constitutionalism its distinctive flavour. Two main conclusions pertinent to this discussion flowed from this law: not all ancient customs formed part of common law, which was an earned and demonstrable status; and the adjective 'immemorial' was confined to ancient customs with that status. By itself antiquity was not enough.

The authoritative statement is in the *First Part of the Institutes* (1628), often referred to as 'Coke on Littleton', where it is explained that customs attain force of law by title of prescription. This common law principle became conspicuous in Stuart discourse when it was applied to ancient customs embodying rights and liberties. If these customs were to be allowed by the common law, they must be in accord with reason and God's will expressed in the scriptures. But other criteria were more prominent in political argument. Before customs could be deemed prescriptive, they had to have existed before (or beyond) time of memory without written record to the contrary. Stuart polemicists used the date of Richard I's coronation, 3 September 1189, to divide time before memory from time of memory. They considered that in a legal sense whatever was before 1189, so far as customs were concerned, was before time of memory; whatever was since that time was said to be within time of memory. Sir Thomas Littleton, writing in the fifteenth century, reported that some found a title of prescription at common law 'where a custom, or usage, or other thing, hath been used for time whereof mind of man runneth not to the contrary (*a tempore cujus contraria memoria hominum non existit*)', that is, before time of memory. To be deemed prescriptive, customs must also have been exercised regularly and constantly before and after 1189; usage must have been long, continued, and peaceable without the interruption, for example, of a Norman conquest (1 *Institutes*, lib. 2 cap. 10, section 170). If these conditions were met, a customary usage was established that demonstrated tacit consent; and the rights and liberties involved were allowed by the common law.

The influence of these rules of law governing prescription in the much-studied and often-cited 'Coke on Littleton' became even stronger, if this is possible, when Chief Justice Henry Rolle – member of a circle that included John Selden and Chief Justice Matthew Hale – included them in his *Abridgment* (1668). Like Coke, Rolle was active in early Stuart parliaments, sitting in all of them from 1614 to 1629. This work, thought to have been completed before 1640, has a lengthy section on prescription, which is peppered with allusions to 'Coke on Littleton'. Hale, who edited Rolle's *Abridgment*, took the same view of prescription, as did Whig polemicists of the late seventeenth century.[2]

Two related declarations of the Jacobean House of Commons, the *Form of Apology and Satisfaction* (1604) and the *Protestation* (1621) reveal the role of prescription in early Stuart political thought. The first dealt with the source of parliamentary privileges, the second, specifically, with the issue of freedom of speech in parliament; both reflected the view that parliamentary privileges were the ancient and undoubted birthright and inheritance of English subjects and implied that these were held by an ancient right independent of the King, contrary to James' emphatic claim that he and his ancestors were the source of privilege. The matter was important since a derived authority was considered inferior to an original one. In making the point Prynne quoted with approval from Mario Salamonio that 'every creator is of greater power and authority than its creature and every cause than its effect' (Prynne 1643, pp. 35–6).

Although the *Apology* is important in its own right, it is viewed here in the context of the 1621 proceedings. At that time the respected antiquary, William Hakewill, read from it to the House of Commons and numerous speakers found in it the model to be adopted. Harking back to the earlier episode hints in itself at customary usage, and this common law principle determined the course of action to be followed. Christopher Brooke, recorder of York and substantial member of the house, went to the heart of the matter: 'We hold our privileges by prescription and prescription is inheritance.' Another report had him asserting: 'We have our privileges

---

2. Wharam 1972, pp. 262–5; Hale 1971, pp. 3–4; Rolle 1668, pp. 264–72. The same view of 1189 is in Brooke 1573, fo. 149v. The date is from Stat. West. 1.c.39 (Hale 1971, p. 4; Pollock and Maitland 1968, 1, p. 168). For the opinion that only a 'godly and rational' custom could become part of common law, see Sommerville 1986a, pp. 254–5, 1986b, pp. 92–4. William Petyt supplies a prime example of a representative Whig common lawyer and antiquary who relied on Rolle (Weston and Greenberg 1981, p. 342 n. 16). See also Tyrrell 1694, pp. 585–6, 591.

and liberties by prescription time out of mind.' William Noy was practical: 'Let us use whatsoever liberties we have hitherto used . . . To use our liberties is the best maintenance of our liberties.' And Serjeant Ashley, chairman of the grand committee that prepared the *Protestation*, offered in summary: 'A legal use breedeth a right; and [is] as good, as a legal grant.' Acting like a court, the House of Commons on 18 December approved the *Protestation* and ordered its inclusion in its journal, there to remain as of record. The king's studied response revealed full awareness of the threat to the theoretical basis of monarchy when in the presence of his privy council he tore out the offending pages and in a proclamation dissolving parliament took the exceptional step of justifying publicly his conduct. Members had entered a protestation for their liberties in language that might serve in the future to invade most of his rights and prerogatives. He then went beyond words, punishing such ring-leaders as Coke, Hakewill, Sir Robert Phelips, and John Pym.[3]

Like it or not, members of parliament felt compelled to assert their rights and privileges in this situation. The governing rule was that the law aids the vigilant, not those who slumber on their rights; and negligence in asserting a right, in conjunction with lapse of time, could mean its loss or abandonment. No such risk attended the king's prerogative because of the principle *nullum tempus occurrit regi*. Since time did not run against him, a right which he failed as sovereign to exercise was not lost through inaction or omission. He could not be viewed as failing to act because cares of government took up his time, and he ought not to suffer from his officers' negligence. The lines were drawn in the famous words of the *Apology*, quoted in 1621 by Hakewill, Phelips, and Pym, that 'the prerogative of princes may easily and do daily grow; the privileges of the subject are for

---

3. Hexter 1978, pp. 24–43; Tanner 1930, pp. 274–95; *Commons Debates 1621*, 1935, VI, p. 238 (Brooke), p. 240 (Noy); *Journals of the House of Commons*, I, p. 664 (Ashley), p. 666 (Noy), p. 667 (Hakewill). See also Nicholas 1766, II, pp. 332–3. Modern scholars usually focus on precedent rather than on a sequence or pattern of precedents. Consult Gardiner 1965, I, p. 182, for the distinction in the *Apology* between Queen Elizabeth and James I; and *ibid.*, IV, pp. 255–7, for the queen's attempts to restrict freedom of speech in parliament and Gardiner's conclusion that customary usage was on the side of the Commons. As for the practice by which the speaker at the beginning of parliament petitioned the king to enjoy the privileges of the house during that parliament, the authors of the *Apology* stated: 'Our making of request in the entrance of parliament to enjoy our privilege is an act only of manners, and doth weaken our right no more than suing to the king for our lands by petition'. See also Hakewill, *CJ* I, p. 667; Glanville 1775; Nicholas 1766, II, p. 338; Atkyns 1689, pp. 21–2, 33; Judson 1964, pp. 258–9. How customary usage was determined can be seen in Hakewill 1641, pp. 34–93; Thomas Hedley in *Parliamentary Debates, 1610*, 1862, p. 73; Glanville 1775, *passim*; Sir Robert Holbourne in the Ship Money case, Howell 1809–28, III, cols. 1007–10. Holbourne considered that danegeld must be accepted without protest if the levy were to become a practice: *ibid.*, cols. 1000–1. Hakewill's speech against impositions in 1610, printed in 1641, ran on the same lines. See also Weston and Greenberg 1981, pp. 142–5.

the most part at an everlasting stand. They may be by good providence and care preserved; but, being once lost, are not recovered but with much disquiet'.[4]

By 1628, with the Petition of Right at centre stage, the main concern was national liberties; and parliamentary leaders relied on Magna Carta, with six supporting statutes, to justify their position. This very complicated episode is not easily fitted into an account of a prescriptive ancient constitution, or so it first appears. For the events at Runnymede were comfortably within time of memory; and despite Coke's assertion that Magna Carta had been confirmed thirty-two times, this mattered less because the confirmations had ceased in the early fifteenth century. Yet spokesmen for the House of Commons were uninterested in Charles I's offer to confirm Magna Carta once more, preferring instead to include in the Petition their own definition of ancient liberties. This display of confidence could have been rooted in the belief that Magna Carta was a statute and as such required no further confirmations. By the late thirteenth century it held primacy of place in lawyers' private collections of statutes, and in the middle of the sixteenth century it circulated as the 'first statute' in the predecessors of the *Statutes at Large*.

But the single fact that Magna Carta was not seen in the seventeenth century as a statute in the modern sense renders it more likely that the authors of the Petition of Right were thinking in terms of prescription. For that document was usually described not as making law but as declaring and confirming common law. Witness the remark of John Glanville, spokesman for the House of Commons in a conference with the Lords. They were relying, he stated, 'upon the good old statute called Magna Carta, which declares and confirms the ancient common laws of the liberties of England'.[5] Pressed to identify these laws, he would have turned to the laws of Edward the Confessor (1042–66) – printed in William

---

4. Russell 1979, p. 56; Hexter 1978, pp. 37–8, 41; *Commons Debates 1621*, II, p. 501. Phelips declared on 12 December: 'We are put upon rocks, either to discontent his majesty, or lose our liberties' (*ibid.*, p. 514). Chitty 1820, p. 379. Sommerville 1986b, pp. 173–4. Conrad Russell dismisses the *Protestation* as 'a powerless piece of paper, a last vain protest by a dying parliament' (Russell 1979, p. 142). More likely, parliamentary leaders considered that they had succeeded in their main objective of placing their affirmation of parliamentary privilege on record; and James' response suggests that this was his estimate, too. But Russell also notes that Coke in 1628 – in the tense situation preceding Charles I's second answer to the Petition of Right – called for a reading of the *Protestation* (Russell 1979, p. 379). For a view of early Stuart England different from Russell's, see Hexter 1978; Rabb and Hirst 1981.

5. *Commons Debates 1628*, III, p. 565. See also Hedley in 1610, quoted in Sommerville 1986b, p. 98. That Glanville differentiated between a statute declaring law (Magna Carta) and one making new law appears in *Commons Debates 1628*, III, pp. 565–6. Unlike the latter, Magna Carta, because it declared common law, was not subject to the king's dispensing power.

Lambarde's *Archaionomia, sive De Priscis Anglorum Legibus* (1568) (cited hereafter as *De Priscis Anglorum Legibus*) – and to the coronation charter and laws of Henry I (1100–35), which added to the reputation of Edward's laws. In compiling Saxon laws Lambarde used *Leges Edwardi Confessoris*, a medieval lawbook that F.W. Maitland considered bad and untrustworthy, with characteristics suggestive of a political pamphlet. Be that as it may, this version of the Confessor's laws became the standard authority in the long period between the first publication of *De Priscis Anglorum Legibus* and the 1680s, when it came under fire in circumstances to be related.

Were these laws statutes in the modern sense or 'ancient common laws', as Glanville had posited? Coke, commenting on one of them, wrote as if the Confessor's laws were the product of a legislating parliament; but a formidable obstacle hindered this conclusion. The parliament rolls, where the laws should have been recorded, were nowhere to be found. Yet it was widely assumed that the records had in fact existed, so firm was the conviction that parliaments were immemorial. Scholars as assiduous as Prynne and as learned as Selden wrote of the 'missing' parliament rolls. Prynne, keeper of the Tower records after the Restoration, reported the absence of legal records from William I to the first year of King John. They were 'utterly lost'. And Selden placed the matter in perspective, writing 'The proper place of the laws as well of those times (as of ours) was in their rolls of parliaments, all which are lost.'[6] Also attesting the high value placed on the parliament rolls was the abundance of theories about their fate. Their loss was due to negligent keepers or to high officials failing to return them after borrowing them for special occasions, or even to the iniquity of the times when King John and Henry III warred with their barons or Lancastrians with Yorkists. The prevailing parties could have suppressed records injurious to their respective parties. And then there was the reprehensible Richard II, said to have 'defaced and razed' the parliament rolls.[7]

This was the situation confronting the antiquaries, who influenced speakers in parliament or were among them; and out of their solution emerged the line of reasoning that Glanville followed in 1628. Lacking the essential legal records to establish that the Confessor's laws were actually

---

6. 4 *Institutes*, p. 36 (commenting on the law of tithes in the Confessor's laws); Selden 1672, pt II, p. 590; Prynne 1657a, preface; Stowe MSS (British Library) 543, fos. 70–5. See also Pollock and Maitland 1968, I, pp. 97–106, esp. p. 103; and Sir Francis Ashley's Middle Temple autumn reading, 1616, on the 'statute' of Magna Carta, ch. 29 (Thompson 1948, pp. 285, 287–8).

7. Johnson 1693, pp. 51–4; Atwood 1690, p. 34; Prynne 1657a, preface, n.p.; Lambarde 1957, p. 136.

statutes, Stuart scholars concerned about rights and liberties had no alternative except to work from historical materials such as medieval chronicles and annals and to apply common law reasoning to whatever evidence of such rights and liberties existed in the historical record. Nowhere was the influence of common law reasoning more apparent than in their accounts of the Norman conquest. Minimising the elements of force and compulsion in 1066 or else stressing a post-conquest political accommodation between the Conqueror and his new subjects, reaffirmed by Henry I's coronation charter, they denied an interruption at the conquest in the customary usage of Saxon rights and liberties.

The salient point was that these had crossed the great divide in the laws of holy King Edward, or St Edward, as Coke termed him. Not so much their giver as their preserver in the wake of the Danes, he was described as repairing, embellishing, and confirming them. But more than this. Picking and choosing from the great heap of his predecessors' laws, he was praised as the creator of common law, indeed, as its father. Stuart Englishmen, unaware that Edward's laws were apocryphal, perceived in Magna Carta their reincarnation; and associating the great charter of English liberties with the most sanctified of Saxon kings – he was canonised in 1161 – they brought forth the astonishing common law cult of holy Edward's laws. How great an influence the cult exerted appears from the bishop of Lincoln's speech in the House of Lords in 1628. Recording its import, a listener wrote: 'He conceives that by *lex terrae* [the law of the land] is meant the laws of Edward the confessor.'[8] The bishop's comment would have been perfectly intelligible to an audience convinced that in 1215 the ancient customs in the Confessor's laws – and hence English rights and liberties – were still allowed by the common law, their security assured by the events at Runnymede.

How could this be demonstrated? Contemporary explanation drew on the repeated confirmations of Edward's laws in the great charters of Norman and early Angevin kings. It is urged here that this historical process, amply documented in the medieval record, meant to the men of 1628 that the liberties in those laws had continued to be exercised in post-conquest England. And, further, that the habit of associating the common law principle of prescription with the confirmations provides the prime explanation for their omnipresence and pride of place in Stuart political

<hr/>

8. *Commons Debates 1628*, II, p. 333; V, pp. 172, 321 Coke 1777, IV, pp. x–xi; Johnson 1693, p. 54; Prynne 1657a, preface, n.p.. Raphael Holinshed's *Chronicles*, first published in 1577, nourished the assumption that the Confessor was father of common law.

literature. That is, this historical process was widely perceived as the legal mechanism by which rights and liberties embodied in ancient customs had retained the legitimacy and force of common law in the dangerous years after the Norman conquest. The standard account of the confirmations to which everyone turned is in the preface to Coke's *Eighth Reports*, where he dwells on the manner in which William the Conqueror consolidated his hold on the kingdom. He had earlier called upon twelve of the most discreet and wise men of each shire to declare the Confessor's laws; and from their declarations, which he amended with baronial advice, William had composed his own Magna Carta, 'the groundwork of all those that after followed'. Calling attention to similar confirmations by Henry I, King Stephen, Henry II, and King John, Coke wrote of the ancient laws and liberties confirmed at Runnymede that these were 'partly in . . . the charter of King Henry, and partly taken out of the ancient laws of King Edward'.[9] Adding these confirmations to those of Magna Carta and treating that document as a declaratory statute, the common law mind confidently linked the Confessor's laws with the Petition of Right, holy Edward with Charles I, Saxon with Stuart liberties.

Where, after all, was there to be found a more solid and convincing body of evidence for customary usage than that displayed by the repeated confirmations of the Confessor's laws, with Magna Carta magnificent in support? And how better to prove that Saxon and Stuart liberties in a legal sense were one and the same? Witness this recital of confirmations, in which Magna Carta was pivotal, the drumbeat of the confirmations as consequential as the rights and liberties being confirmed. That document, writes a modern scholar,

9. Coke 1777, IV, fos. iv–x. See also Twysden 1849, pp. 40–4, 57–8; *Commons Debates 1628*, II, pp. 333–4; Fox 1956, pp. 53, 61; Pocock 1987, pp. 42–5. For the persistence of these views throughout the century, see Petyt 1680a, 'Preface', pp. 34–5, and *A Collection of State Tracts* 1705, pp. 520, 575–97. The lengths to which Coke's statement could be taken can be seen in Cooke 1682, reprinted under a different title in 1689. That the Confessor's laws commanded what looks like an inordinate amount of attention in Stuart England had much to do with their use in the generation before Magna Carta. J.C. Holt tells how the barons at Runnymede pressed their reform programme on King John in the name of the Confessor's laws and Henry I's coronation charter; and he finds a parallel between this earlier movement, extensively discussed by medieval annalists and chroniclers, and that in the early seventeenth century before the Civil War. Both in 1215 and in 1642 rebellion was 'prefaced by an antiquarian movement which sought restraint of the crown'. Holt 1965, pp. 96–8, 133–7, 1985, pp. 13–17. Indeed, medieval political literature was so abundant in Stuart England, its message so germane, that its presence alone is almost enough to explain why the common law cult of the Confessor's laws became the core of the Stuart doctrine of the ancient constitution.

played a key role as the most celebrated link in the chain whereby the liberties of immemorial antiquity were confirmed and passed on to future generations. For Magna Carta did nothing new. It simply did what William I had allegedly done when he confirmed the laws of the Confessor; what Henry I had done in his coronation charter; what Edward I was to do when he confirmed the charters in 1297; and what parliament was to ask Charles I to do in 1628 when it presented him with the Petition of Right.[10]

The coronation oath, beginning with Edward II (1307–27), likewise confirmed the Confessor's laws; and it performed, accordingly, much the same function as the confirmations of the charters. As late as 1690, William Atwood wrote of 'the confessor's laws, received by William I and continued downwards by the coronation oath required to this very day'.[11]

That the authors of the Petition of Right thought in these terms appears from Pym's famous speech of 4 June 1628. After noting that durable commonwealths often reformed and recomposed themselves according to their first ordinance, he discerned the 'plain footsteps' of the ancient constitution in Saxon England. Its principles, outliving the Norman conquest, imposed limitations upon William the Conqueror; if his successors defied them, still the Norman kings restored the ancient constitution by issuing charters and statutes reaffirming its principles. To Pym, 'the petitions of the subjects upon which those charters and acts were founded were ever petitions of right, demanding their ancient and due liberties, not suing for any new'.[12] Such remarks reflect a juridical not an historical cast of mind, and in this respect as in the argument itself he was representative of the House of Commons in the 1620s.

The same theme, more specifically stated, runs through Hale's comment later in the century. In his view Magna Carta, the Charter of the Forest, and most of the king's grants to his people were 'not so much new grants of new liberties but restitutions of those very liberties which by the primitive and

---

10. Ashton 1979, pp. 18–19, 360 n. 9; Sir Dudley Digges' speech, *Commons Debates 1628*, II, pp. 333–4, V, p. 172. See also *A Collection of State Tracts* 1705, pp. 591–2.

11. Atwood 1690, p. 103. In another passage he writes of 'the Confessor's law received by William I and continued downwards as the noblest transcript of the common law'. *Ibid.*, p. 73.

12. Kenyon 1966, p. 17. The speech was given three days before Charles I accepted the Petition. Pym's views are further described in Sommerville 1986a, pp. 253–4, 258. Prynne evoked the same theme in his reading on the Petition at Lincoln's Inn, 17 February 1662, and, in addition, called upon one of the Confessor's laws known as the 'office of a king' (Stowe MSS 302, fos. 47ff, but esp. 57v–58). In 1623 and 1624 Pym was member of the committee of privileges and elections. Its chairman was Glanville, and the membership also included Coke, Digges, Noy, Phelips, and Selden. The reports of the committee point to a preoccupation with prescription as the basis for settling the representation of boroughs and determining their electoral qualifications (Glanville 1775, *passim*; *CJ* I, p. 717).

radical constitution of the English government were of right belonging to them'. He came to the point. 'Such were the grants of King William of the laws of Edward the confessor, the grant of the great charters by King John, Henry 3, Edward the 1st, the Statutes de Tallagio non concedendo & divers others which were the original rights and liberties of the subject.' These rights and liberties, which had grown out of a reciprocal contract between king and subjects, were embodied for the most part in acts of parliament and parliamentary concessions wherein the subjects granted such things to the king as aids and supplies and he in turn granted them laws and liberties. But these acts of parliament before time of memory were not like statutes after 1189: they were part of the common law, drawing their strength from 'mere immemorial usage or custom'. There was 'as great reason to conclude them to be parts of the original and primitive institution of the English government *by their long usage & frequent concessions & confirmations of princes in so long and continued series of time, as if an authentic instrument of the first articles of the English government were extant* [italics added]' (Hale 1966, p. 511, 1971, pp. 4, 17).

The ancient constitution was, then, a Saxon constitution, for which Tacitus stood warrant, its ideas and institutions as old as the name of England even if some proponents, notably Coke, pushed them further back in time. Either way, law and government had begun before time of memory, and there had been customary usage of rights and liberties. Little wonder that parliamentary leaders, historians and polemicists, with this historical record in mind, placed the subject's rights and liberties on the same foundation as the royal prerogative: both were allowed by the common law. This point of view was nourished by the growing interest in Saxon studies and old English law displayed in the publication of another historical record shedding light on the Confessor's laws. This was Selden's edition of Eadmer's annals, which contained what were described as the laws and rights that William assured the people of England after the conquest. They were said to be much the same as the Confessor had observed. Selden published these so-called laws of William I in 1623 with supportive extracts from the anonymous Lichfield chronicle and the writings of Ingulphus of Croyland. Moreover, two new editon of *De Priscis Anglorum Legibus* were published in 1644. One of them, to which Sir Roger Twysden contributed, contained the laws of the Confessor, William I, and Henry I – an arrangement suggesting continuity at the conquest. Contemporaries also gleaned historical data about the Confessor's laws from such medieval historians and annalists as Matthew

Paris, Roger of Wendover, Roger de Hoveden, and Henry de Knighton. Interpreting these materials had its own difficulties; too often interpretation suffered from defective linguistic skills and ignorance of political feudalism, though remarkable progress was made in both areas during the century.[13]

The laws themselves dealt with protection of the church, payment of tithes, fines for criminal offences, the definition of danegeld, and the like – a farrago of items from which Stuart Englishmen fashioned legal and constitutional principles of wide application. Thus the makers of the Petition of Right, relying on these laws, asked the king to refrain from the practice of forced loans and other financial exactions without parliamentary consent, arbitrary imprisonment, compulsory quartering of troops on the civilian population, and martial law in peacetime. After civil war introduced new complexities into political thought and new issues surged to the front, the antiquity of the House of Commons became, for reasons to be seen, the object of enquiry. Supporters of that house, insisting on its immemorial character, appealed to the law of tithes (*De Apibus*) in *De Priscis Anglorum Legibus*, often cited as c. 8, fo. 139. It ran a prosperous course. Termed that 'mighty law' by the Whig Edward Cooke, it had been enacted 'à rege, baronibus, & populo', translated as 'by the king, his barons, and his people'. On this peg were hung two highly important prescriptive rights: the right in the commons of England to parliamentary representation and that of the House of Commons to an equal share in lawmaking with the king and the House of Lords. The popularity of this enacting clause owed much to Coke, who cited it in his influential *Fourth Part of the Institutes* (1644). It was invoked in many quarters – in the writings of Nathaniel Bacon at the end of the 1640s, Bulstrode Whitelocke in the late 1650s, the Whigs William Petyt and Sir Robert Atkyns in the 1680s. Even the High Tory historian, Sir William Dugdale, the most eminent medievalist of his generation, concluded from it that parliamentary representation had surely existed in some form before 1189.[14]

13. Kliger 1952, *passim*; Kenyon 1984, pp. 13–17. See also Prynne 1657b, pp. 313–21, for an account of the Confessor's laws and supporting bibliography. Digges traced parliaments to the Saxons and cited Tacitus (*Commons Debates 1628*, II, p. 334). So did Lambarde 1957, pp. 126–7; Hakewill 1641, p. 128. Nathaniel Bacon's *An Historical Discourse of the Uniformity of the Government of England* (1647–51) made Saxon England the major source of Stuart political institutions (Weston and Greenberg 1981, pp. 66–7). The Saxons are said to have laid the foundations of common law in Dugdale 1666, p. 4. And see Twysden 1849, pp. 13, 119–27, 134; Tyrrell 1694, p. 584; *Collection of State Tracts* 1705, p. 321. Selden's views are discussed in Christianson 1984, pp. 276–308, esp. pp. 278–80, 306–8, 311 n. 34. Also see Sommerville 1986b, pp. 90, 100–4, and n. 9 above.

14. *4 Institutes*, p. 36. See also *Institutes* (1642), p. 442 (marginal note). And see Cooke 1682, p. ci; Bacon 1647–51, I, p. 59; Whitelocke 1766, II, p. 140; Petyt 1680a, 'Preface', p. 11; Atkyns 1689, p. 25; Dugdale 1666, p. 15. That Cooke was insisting on customary usage appears in pp. xlv–xlvi.

As high in favour, though for a different reason, was the Confessor's law known as the 'office of a king', cited as c. 17 in *De Priscis Anglorum Legibus*. Its wide audience was due to its provenance, to be sure, but also to its inclusion in John Foxe's *Acts and Monuments*, known as the 'Book of Martyrs', with a circulation second only to the Bible. First published in English in 1563, it was frequently reprinted and early placed in churches and other public places. At the end of the seventeenth century an estimated 10,000 copies were available to eager readers, and this says nothing of the numbers reached by way of the pulpit. Cited in conjunction with the radical quotation known as 'Bracton and Fleta', the coronation oath, and two highly influential medieval treatises, the *Mirror of Justices* and the *Modus tenendi Parliamentum*, the 'office of a king' began:

> The king, because he is the vicar of the highest king, is appointed for this purpose, to rule the earthly kingdom, and the Lord's people, and, above all things, to reverence his holy church, to govern it, and to defend it from injuries; to pluck away wicked doers, and utterly to destroy them: which, unless he do, the name of a king agreeth not unto him, but he loseth the name of a king.

Further, he was to preserve the lands, rights, and liberties of the crown, establish good laws and customs, do justice with the counsel of his *proceres* – a word long translated to denote both lords and commons – and act in all things with good advice and premeditation.[15]

This law, exceedingly useful in a century rife with suspicion of popish plots, was attractive generally to theorists with a community-centred view of government. Prynne put it to good use, as did the pamphleteers of the Exclusion Crisis (1679–81) and the Glorious Revolution. They perceived in the 'office of a king' one of the very few pieces of historical evidence for an original contract, which their political enemies challenged them to produce. According to a radical Whig, 'Englishmen never believed that the king of England could violate the laws and overturn the state at his pleasure, without making himself thereby liable to punishment. [This] clearly appears from the laws of St Edward' (*A Collection of State Tracts*, 1705, p. 506). Another wrote with James II's policies in mind: 'That noble

---

15. The 'office of a king' is in all editions of *De Priscis Anglorum Legibus*. See, too, Foxe 1843–9, II, pp. 89–91; Prynne 1643, pp. 36–7, 43–4, 47, 51–6; Prynne 1657b, p. 320; Atwood 1690, pp. 28–9; Sheringham 1660, pp. 41–2, 53–4; Tyrrell 1694, pp. 697, 704–10, 760; n. 12 above. Sir Henry Spelman also knew it (Pocock 1987, p. 184). It had a medieval background (Holt 1965, pp. 48, 79, 1985, p. 13). The Bracton and Fleta quotation is discussed in Weston and Greenberg 1981, pp. 62, 78–9, *passim*. See also Weston 1984, pp. 85–104; *Collection of State Tracts* 1705, pp. 303, 419, 506; *State tracts* 1692–3, Part II, pp. 270, 493. For the word 'proceres' see Twysden 1849, p. 122; Brady 1684, 'Glossary', p. 57; Tyrrell 1694, p. 376.

transcript of the original contract, the confessor's law, . . . shows, that if a king does not answer the true end for which he was chosen, he loses the name, or ceases to be king.'[16]

But if the ancient constitution was in truth a Saxon constitution, how to explain references in political literature to perpetual rights and liberties? Here, again, resort must be had to the principle of prescription. These rights and liberties pertained to the House of Commons, explained Atkyns, common law judge and Whig historian, if that house has 'been ever from the beginning of the government a part and member of the parliament'. The word 'ever' simply meant that the house had met regularly since time before memory, that is, before 1189; and despite the reference to the 'beginning of the government', it technically had no beginning. As Hale stated, whatever was before time of memory was supposed 'without a beginning, or at least such a beginning as the law takes notice of'; and Twysden, discussing parliamentary representation, reported that a custom was no custom if it had a beginning; that is, if it began within time of memory. Atkyns also assigned the House of Commons 'a perpetual being, to speak in the language of the law'. Consequently its rights and liberties, easily extrapolated to mean English liberties, were independent of the king: they were derived from the original constitution of the government. The situation must be very different if the House of Commons began within time of memory; its powers and privileges were at risk if they were 'by the mere [pure] grace and indulgence of princes'.[17] Happily, no problem existed on this score. It was usual to consider that a right or liberty had existed before 1189 if it were present in the medieval records with the expressions 'time out of mind', 'in all times past', 'of old times', 'from time whereof the memory of men runs not to the contrary', and the like; and deeming the right perpetual in a legal sense, the new historians and Stuart publicists wrote of it as having 'ever' existed, 'always', and 'for all time'.

This legal parlance may have shaped Pocock's version of the ancient constitution in cardinal respects. Despite the alteration in his view expressed in 1987, when his *Ancient Constitution* (1957) was reprinted with a 'Retrospect', his remarks in the 1950s – in an influential article on Dr Robert Brady as well as in his *Ancient Constitution* – ought to be briefly

---

16. Atwood 1690, p. iv. There is material on the original contract, in *ibid.*, pp. 28–39; *Collection of State Tracts* 1705, pp. 136–8, 303, 325, 419, 576–91, esp. 577, 591. The most extreme use of this argument is in chapter viii of John Milton's regicide tract, 'A Defence of the People of England' (1651). The matter is discussed at some length in Greenberg 1989.

17. Atkyns 1689, p. 17; Hale 1971, p. 4; Tyrrell 1694, pp. 584–9; Herle 1643, p. 17; Atwood 1681, p. 10; Twysden 1849, p. 126.

recapitulated because of their powerful impact. Ascribing to Coke and his disciples 'a theory of the law's unchanging continuity', he indicates that their interest in common law as fundamental law was greater than in parliament as a modern legislature actively making new law. And he writes of common lawyers carrying the doctrine of an immemorial law or parliament to the point of denying that these had originated by human action or at a fixed time lest they be subject to a human sovereign, that is, the king.[18]

Yet Stuart historians were more aware of change in their laws than the Pocock of the 1950s allows. Even Coke, though less historically minded than a Selden or Twysden, recognised that common law was not immutable when he brought it within the purview of courts and parliament. He also displayed modernity in outlook when he differentiated between making and declaring law and asserted the high power of statutes *vis-à-vis* common law. This is not the place to discuss his view of parliament except to indicate that he and contemporaries, too, had a strong interest in early parliaments, the latter, at least, by no means reluctant to date their beginnings. The chronicles of early Stuart England cited as the first parliament Henry I's great council at Salisbury in 1116, the phrase 'first parliament, 1116' typically appearing in the margin. In short, the attributes assigned by Pocock to Stuart historians are explicable in terms of their legal understandings but are not apposite with regard to their historical scholarship. When Coke's disciples wrote as if customs or laws or institutions had 'ever' existed – which they certainly did – they were in all likelihood making use of legal language. By the end of the century they would have been happy, indeed, to establish that the modern parliament had existed before 1189. No more was thought necessary or even desirable.[19]

In Pocock's hands the emphasis in Stuart England on the great antiquity

18. Pocock 1951, pp. 189–90, 1987, pp. 36, 37, 153, 189–90, 234–5. For a sense of how Pocock's work is construed, see Kenyon 1984, p. 23; Pallister 1971, p. 35. Evidence is mounting, however, that the minds of the antiquaries were more richly stocked than he allows and that they were better historians: Sharpe 1979, pp. 224–5; Pallister 1971, p. 32; Pawlisch 1985, pp. 161–75; Thompson 1948, pp. 360–1; Christianson 1984. See also Kelley 1974, pp. 24–51, 1976, pp. 143–6; Brooks and Sharpe 1976, pp. 133–42.
19. See nn. 18 above and 21 below; Pallister 1971, p. 47; Thompson 1948, p. 260; Evans 1938, pp. 206–21; Sommerville 1986b, pp. 91, 96; Weston 1972, p. 417 n. 17; Hakewill 1641, pp. 126–8; Tyrrell 1694, p. 584. Sommerville 1986a, pp. 251–5, questions Pocock's version of an immemorial common law but does not associate customary usage with Stuart interpretations of the Norman conquest. However, he rightly objects to Pocock's proposition that in the age of Coke 'to admit to a conquest was to admit an indelible stain of sovereignty upon the English constitution'. That strain, of course, could be erased.

of common law flows into a widespread acceptance of a fundamental law restrictive of king and parliament alike. Charles II's Restoration and the Revolution of 1689 were 'efforts to restore the fundamental law, rather than to establish the sovereignty of king-in-parliament'; and when parliament claimed sovereignty, it did so as guardian of a fundamental law, which it had not made. The transition from this claim to the assertion that parliament was sovereign was 'both incomplete and largely unrealized' (Pocock 1987, pp. 49–50, 234). A similar outlook pervades C.H. McIlwain's *High Court of Parliament* (1910), where it is contended that the medieval view of lawmaking as declarative of fundamental law persisted in the seventeenth century. If this means that those who reasoned in this way had no sense of making new law, parliament becomes a high court rather than a modern legislature and fundamental law a barrier to legal sovereignty. As earlier noted, Coke distinguished between declaring old law and making new; but the ideas derived from McIlwain are nonetheless often sanctioned by reference to Coke's judgement in Bonham's case (1606) that when a statute was 'against common right or reason, or repugnant, or impossible to be performed', common law could 'control it and adjudge such acts to be void'. The more usual opinion today is that he was advancing a principle of strict statutory interpretation compatible with the high authority of parliament.[20]

Moreover, generalisation about fundamental law in Stuart England is tricky because the term is so elusive. As used by Pocock, it was less influential than he suggests, even before 1642. For one thing, there was familiarity with Jean Bodin's doctrine of legal sovereignty in his *République* (1576), a work known to Tudor scholars that was studied at Cambridge and available in numerous French and Latin editions prior to its publication in English in 1606. Bodin made authority the central feature of his system of politics. Defining sovereignty as the most high, absolute, and perpetual power over the citizens and subjects of a commonwealth, he emphasised as the chief mark of sovereignty the power to give laws and command to all in general and to everyone in particular. Whoever made law possessed the further powers of abrogating, declaring, and correcting it. Was, then, the

---

20. Gough 1961, pp. 30–47: Gough's conclusion is based on Samuel Thorne's 1938 article on Bonham's case. For more recent scholarship, see, for example, Gray 1972. Gray believes that Coke's opinion, delivered orally as judge, did not advocate a doctrine of judicial review though he came closer to this view when he reported the decision in the preface to his *Eighth Reports*. He also adduces fresh evidence to demonstrate that contemporaries understood Coke to be advancing a doctrine of judicial review, but recognises that 'Coke had no specific quarrel with the supremacy of parliament, and that on balance his writings strongly upheld it' (*ibid.*, pp. 36, 49, and *passim*).

English king, who could not repeal a law without the two houses, a Bodinian lawgiver? The answer was affirmative: despite this limitation he was an absolute sovereign with no companions in lawmaking. Though the two houses seemed to have great liberty, their role was limited even in lawmaking; they proceeded by way of supplication and request to the king, and he had a complete power of veto. Nor was his law-making power diminished by exercising it in parliament. The king was much greater in such assemblages where his people acknowledged him as their sovereign even though he conceded more at these times than usual (Weston 1972, pp. 413–14).

Bodin's influence expanded during the Civil War, but even earlier there were elements conducive to this line of thought. Witness the high regard for statutes in 1628 when parliamentary leaders preferred this mode of binding Charles I to a petition of right. That they thought in terms of a modern legislating parliament was equally apparent when their political allies among the antiquaries scoured the medieval record for evidence of early parliaments. 'None of them', remarks a modern scholar, 'seems to be aware of any difficulty in the idea of enacted law in their own time or the time of Ine.'[21] Conversant with the laws that Saxon kings had made with their witenagemots, they were at least as interested in lawmaking as in common law viewed as fundamental law; and they may well have wondered what the promised restitution of the Confessor's laws amounted to if the witenagemot, the sacred anchor and sanctuary of English liberties, as one writer put it, had not survived the conquest (Petyt 1680a, 'Preface', p. 40). And there was their obvious interest in the *Mirror of Justices* and the *Modus tenendi Parliamentum*, prime sources for Saxon law and government that encouraged the self-confidence of the Stuart House of Commons.

Only a word about the *Mirror* is possible here despite its importance in polemical literature. Long attributed to Andrew Horn, though the attribution is now considered very doubtful, it circulated in manuscript after 1550 but went unpublished until 1642, appearing in English for the first time in 1646. Its doctrine that the king had 'companions' in parliament, who were to hear and determine complaints about 'wrongs done by the kings . . . and their special ministers' appealed greatly to parliamentarians,

---

21. Evans 1938, p. 217. Coke's recognition that statutes overruled common law is in 1 *Institutes*, lib. 2, cap. 10, sect. 170, 2 *Institutes* proem, n.p., and pp. 20–1, 4 *Institutes*, p. 36. Other contemporary views are Hakewill 1641, p. 98; Holbourne in Howell 1809–28, III, cols. 978, 979, 982, 1000–1. See also Thompson 1948, p. 360; Judson 1964, pp. 85–6.

who also welcomed the statement that King Alfred had provided as 'perpetual usage' that parliaments meet at least twice a year.[22] Yet the *Mirror* was a lesser authority for parliamentary history than the *Modus*, written about the same time but much earlier on the political scene, fitting easily and naturally into the confirmations of the charters and becoming their mainstay. The only surviving medieval treatise on parliament, it was published in English by John Hooker in 1572, in a work entitled *The Order and Usage of the Keeping of a Parlement in England*, which was inserted into the 1587 edition of Raphael Holinshed's *Chronicles*. It appeared in another English edition in 1641, this one attributed to Hakewill and said to have been completed by 1610. The *Modus* was well known to the Elizabethan society of antiquaries, whose members after devoting a meeting to the antiquity of parliaments were apparently planning another on parliamentary privileges when the society came to an abrupt end under James I, not in the circumstances an altogether surprising development. By this time the treatise was expanding into the world of politics. Members cited it in the 1621 House of Commons, and no less a personage than Sir John Eliot read from it to the house in 1628.

There were actually two 'Moduses', an English and an Irish one, each with a distinctive proem relevant to the common law cult of the Confessor's laws. Dealing with a period of the highest importance to the common law mind, they seemed to provide conclusive evidence of a parliament with a House of Commons, its composition the same as its Stuart counterpart, that had continually existed from the Confessor to Henry II (1154–89). The author of the *Modus*, impressively knowledgeable in the ways of parliament, furnished a detailed account of that institution, telling about summonses to parliament, its composition, procedure, powers, business, etc. The treatise was surprisingly favourable to parliament, especially the House of Commons. If the king was at first sight the principal figure in parliament as its head, beginning, and end – *caput, principium, & finis Parliamenti* ran the quotable tag – still his role was in cardinal respects subordinate to the two houses. He could not dissolve parliament until he had answered his subjects' petitions – a point made by Coke, Pym in the Short Parliament of 1640, Prynne during the Civil War, and radical pamphleteers in the 1680s. The House of Commons was the

---

22. Horn 1895, pp. 7–8. The popularity of the *Mirror* in Stuart England is noted by Kliger 1952, p. 121. It was used in conjunction with the notorious Bracton and Fleta quotation: Prynne 1643, pp. 36–7; Petyt 1680a, 'Preface', pp. 40–1; Atwood 1690, pp. 34–5; Tyrrell 1694, p. 697.

superior house; with the king it even constituted a legal parliament in the absence of the Lords.[23]

The *Modus* was as important to Coke's account of parliament as Magna Carta to his comments on common law. As early as 1593, as speaker of the House of Commons, he called its members' attention to the treatise; and its reputation grew apace when he included the proem to the English *Modus*, written in Latin, in the famous preface to his *Ninth Reports* (1613). Its message, translated into English, was breathtakingly germane:

> Here is described the manner in which the parliament of the king of England and of his Englishmen was held in the time of King Edward, the son of King Ethelred, which manner was related by the more distinguished men of the kingdom in the presence of William, duke of Normandy, conqueror and king of England: by the conqueror's own command, and through his approval it was used in his times and in the times of his successors, the kings of England.
>
> (Pronay and Taylor 1980, p. 80; see also *ibid.*, p. 56)

Customary usage had been observed since William and his successors had held parliament in the manner of the Confessor; and to cap it all, the composition of their parliaments was that of Coke's own day. He possessed the *Modus* 'in a fair and very ancient written hand' and in it 'the assembly of the kings, the lords, and commons, according to the manner continued to this day, is set down'. The phrase *conventus nobilium & sapientum, etc.* in early medieval records encompassed both houses of parliament (*Reports*, 1777, V, fos. *iv–*iv verso). Coke returned to the *Modus* in the *Fourth Part of the Institutes*, which, along with the prefaces to the *Eighth* and the *Ninth Reports*, supplied contemporaries with the history of their political system.[24] Much of his earlier statement was replicated in the *Fourth Part*, but he also explained that Henry II had exported the *Modus* to Ireland as a model for the Irish parliament, and Coke noted its effects on the makers of

---

23. *Reports* 1777, V, fos. *iv–*v; 4 *Institutes*, p. 11. Elizabeth Read Foster notes that whatever the view of modern historians, the *Modus* 'had long been considered an authoritative guide to the past when Stuart Englishmen took it up' (cited in Pronay and Taylor 1980, pp. 54–5). Hooker is discussed in Snow 1977. Others who owned or had access to the *Modus* include Glanville, Selden (who questioned its authority for the Confessor's reign), Petyt, and the Elizabethan society of antiquaries who met from 1572 to 1604 and in 1614, and whose papers were published in Dodderidge 1658 and reprinted in 1679 and 1685. The *Modus* was discussed under 'parliament' in John Cowell's *Interpreter* (1607) and John Minsheu's *Guide into Tongues* (1617). Both appeared in new editions before the Civil War. See also Prynne 1643, p. 31; *Proceedings of the Short Parliament* 1977, p. 149; *Commons Debates 1628*, II pp. 306–7; *State Tracts* 1692–3, Part I, p. 165 and Part II, pp. 222–3.

24. For the influence of the preface to the *Ninth Reports*, see the *Priviledges and Practice of Parliaments* (n.p. 1640), pp. 1–2. Written as early as 1620–1, it was printed in 1628, 1640, 1641, and 1680. See also Baxter 1659, pp. 458, 479–80. Although he recommended in addition Bacon 1647–51 and Prynne 1643, still he thought it not really necessary for the cause in hand to prove 'the antiquity of their [parliament's] being, or their power'.

Magna Carta. Their familiarity with its contents was evident when ancient reliefs of entire earldoms, baronies, and knights' fees were reduced in accordance with amounts in the treatise. He also pointed to provisions early made for regular meetings of parliament, listing as the appropriate statutes Edgar c. 5, 4 Edw. 3 c. 14, and 36 Edw. 3 c. 10, the last-named providing for annual parliaments.[25]

Lambarde's *Archeion* (1635), completed as early as 1591, added to the reputation of the *Modus* when he named it *Modus tenendi Parliamentum tempore Regis Edward filii Ethelredi* and reported that it could be seen 'in many hands'. Less committed to it than Coke, though their comments ran on the same lines, Lambarde gave a much more polished and coherent account of the relationship between title of prescription and the concept of an immemorial House of Commons. These aspects of *Archeion* made it the tract *par excellence* on the ancient constitution before the Civil War and help to explain the great popularity of Lambarde's comments later in the century, as does the continued circulation of *De Priscis Anglorum Legibus*. By 1601 he was keeper of the records in the Tower of London, and he has been described as the prince of legal antiquaries. Like Coke he employed an argument for an immemorial House of Commons that relied on the decayed condition of certain boroughs in Tudor England. Assuming their greater prosperity when first created, Lambarde turned to Saxon England as a place of suitable circumstances. As he put it, the 'interest' that boroughs had in parliament grew 'by an ancient usage before the conquest, whereof they cannot show any beginning'. He also discussed 'a contrary usage in the self-same thing', illustrated by boroughs of 'ancient demesne' – a method of proof known to Coke. Since they were exempted from sending burgesses to parliament and contributing to the wages of knights representing counties, there must have been a parliament. Where otherwise would less privileged boroughs send their burgesses?[26]

And what about the Norman conquest? Had the Saxon parliament, with its House of Commons, survived that cataclysmic event? After all, customary usage was essential for title of prescription, and it would be of little avail to find a House of Commons in Saxon England if it was brought

25. 4 *Institutes*, pp. 9, 12 Coke referred readers to 2 *Institutes*, pp. 7–8 for the relationship between the *Modus* and Henry I's coronation charter. The Long Parliament ordered the publication of the *Fourth Part*. See Husband 1643, p. 709, for the statement in the declaration of 26 May: 'It is well known that the laws for holding a parliament once a year lay asleep for a long time (yet the practice was no argument against the right).'
26. Lambarde 1957, pp. 132–3; Atkyns 1689, p. 18. Selden, too, wrote of seeing numerous copies of the *Modus* (Selden 1631, pp. 739, 743).

to an end in 1066. Like many contemporaries Lambarde explained away the conquest. Evidence of a full parliament could be found in Henry I's coronation charter with his promise to restore the law of Edward the Confessor and acknowledgement that he had been crowned by the common council of the realm. It was awkward that the members of that common council were referred to as *barones*, a choice of language that seemed to preclude a House of Commons; but Lambarde explained that the Germans had translated *barones* as freemen and Matthew Paris had applied the word to London's citizens. This meant that 'barons of the realm' included both lords and commons, and Lambarde considered the matter settled conclusively when Henry I coupled this language with the words 'common council', signifying parliament.

At this juncture Lambarde made a contribution to the doctrine of the ancient constitution on lines much like those developed after 1642 by parliamentarian writers. Not only did he find a prescriptive right of representation by which the commons of England (that is, the counties and boroughs) returned members to the House of Commons (a right independent of the king), he also wrote of the king and the two houses as 'three estates' and ascribed the voice of the two houses in parliament to prescription. That this voice meant that the two houses shared the law-making power with the king could be seen from the enacting clauses of statutes, where it was stated 'that the king, his nobility and commons, did ordain and enact the same'.[27] Lambarde was asserting that the shares of the lords and commons in law-making had a source independent of the king – these were 'radically' from the community, as contemporaries would have said – and he was implying, moreover, that the two houses were equal partners in lawmaking with the king. The growth in specificity and this particular pattern of political ideas made Lambarde's *Archeion* of great interest during the remainder of the century, especially after large-scale debate erupted over the antiquity of the House of Commons and its role in law-making; and on such occasions his name was linked with Coke's.

Yet, when all is said and done, the doctrine of the ancient constitution was less influential in pre-Civil War England than the political theory of order espoused by James I.[28] Although it appeared at times as if the two sets of ideas coexisted harmoniously even within the mind of a Coke or a Pym,

---

27. Lambarde 1957, pp. 134–5, 138–40. *Archeion* may have been written in part as a response to the episode in which Arthur Hall described the House of Commons as a newcomer to parliament but was obliged to recant (Mendle 1985, pp. 58–9, 103–4).
28. Weston and Greenberg 1981, *passim*. See also Greenleaf 1964; Russell 1965.

these were nonetheless incompatible; and the period of personal rule, which ancient constitutionalists deemed illegal, hardly lessened the sense of grievance so evident in the 1620s. It is not coincidental that the Short Parliament, uncommonly preoccupied with parliamentary privileges, insisted on redress of grievances before supply, nor that the first statute enacted by the Long Parliament was the triennial act. Also passed at this time was the act for abolishing Ship Money, which condemned the judgement against John Hampden as contrary to the Petition of Right and provided that all points of that document be in force. Then there was the act abolishing star chamber, which quoted Magna Carta and four of the six supporting statutes (Thompson 1948, pp. 369–70). At this time, too, Hakewill's English edition of the *Modus* appeared. Moreover, the Long Parliament very early provided for the recovery of Coke's papers, confiscated at his death by Charles I, and on the day of the earl of Strafford's execution (12 May 1641) ordered their publication. In this way the last three volumes of the *Institutes* reached the public. Coke's commentary on Magna Carta is in the *Second Part* (1642), while parliament occupies the first and longest chapter of the *Fourth Part*.

Whatever harmony existed between the order theory and ancient constitutionalism disappeared with the advent of the Answer to the Nineteen Propositions (June 1642). In this singularly influential declaration, the king, at least publicly, turned his back on his father's position when he described 'the ancient, equal, happy, well-poised and never enough commended constitution of the government of this kingdom'. The human source of this ancient constitution was not the king, as James had averred, but the earlier experience of Englishmen – an admission that what contemporaries termed the 'original' of government and law was the community and the very point put forward by the authors of the *Apology* and *Protestation*. Of equal interest were Charles' observation that there was a mixture of monarchy, aristocracy, and democracy in the government, which could be seen when the 'three estates' of king, lords, and commons made law jointly, and his repeated references to his 'share' in that important power, fast being seen as the sovereign power. Rejecting the Nineteen Propositions as unacceptable on the ground that they threatened social and political harmony, the king repeated the famous dictum: 'Nolumus leges Angliae mutari' ('We do not wish that the laws of England be changed').[29]

---

29. Sharp 1983, p. 40; Weston 1965; Weston and Greenberg 1981, *passim*. Key portions of the Answer are in Weston 1965, pp. 259–65; Kenyon 1966, pp. 21–33, 1986, pp. 18–20. The king's remarks ought not to be confused with the earlier views of John Ponet, John Aylmer, Thomas Cartwright,

ii 'Coordination' and the royalist response

Whatever Charles I's intentions, the Answer opened the door to a host of radical political ideas injurious to the kingship that flourished in the atmosphere of civil war. Foremost among them was a coordination principle in lawmaking that became almost at once the hallmark of a remodelled ancient constitution. Its author was the relatively obscure Puritan clergyman, Charles Herle; the pertinent tract his *Fuller Answer to a Treatise Written by Doctor Ferne* (December 1642). Inspired by the king, Herle wrote of the monarchy or highest power in the kingdom as compounded of three coordinate estates – king, lords, and commons – whom no subordinate authority could resist. This mixture, which Charles I had applauded, meant that the two houses were coordinate with the king and in no important way subordinate to him: they were 'a co-ordinative part in the monarchy or highest principle of power' because they shared in lawmaking. It was not enough to insist on a coordination in lawmaking: there was also the need to explain the original frame of the coordinate government of the three estates in parliament. That government had been consented to and contrived by the people in its first constitution and had been confirmed by 'constant custom time . . . out of mind, which . . . amounts to a law, wherein the rule is *Quod non disprobatur presumetur*, it cannot be disproved from taking place upon all occasions, therefore it is to be presumed to have continued from the beginning' (Weston and Greenberg 1981, pp. 52–8; Herle 1642, revised edn, p. 4). Anyone urging otherwise bore the burden of proof; unless he could demonstrate that confirmation had not taken place on all occasions, the ancient constitution, the coordination principle at its core, was prescriptive.

The sweep of a pen had placed the king beside the two houses on the same political plane. As Hale noted, the great mistake was in making him but one of three estates. If he were one of three estates, and not their head, 'it were to make a co-ordination and a kind of parity between him and them'. Hale's own view was very different: the three estates were the lords

Sir Thomas Smith, and Robert Parsons. They too described the government as a mixture of monarchy, aristocracy, and democracy, but they did not single out lawmaking as the exemplar of the mixture and allot equal shares in that power to king, lords, and commons. Nor were they enunciating a modern theory of legal sovereignty, though perhaps Smith's *De Republica Anglorum* should be excepted from this generalisation. Mendle 1985 is an account of the background to the Answer differing in critical respects from that in Weston 1965 and Weston and Greenberg 1981. Cf. Sommerville 1986b, pp. 174–5, 187 n. 71, and Weston and Greenberg 1981, pp. 282–4 n. 14, 304–5 n. 13.

spiritual, lords temporal, and commons, the king their sovereign head (Hale 1976, p. 13). Those who reasoned this way treated the king in parliament as the sovereign lawmaker, a role that permitted his retention of the royal prerogatives acknowledged to be his before the Civil War. This became the royalist position by the late 1640s: but others such as Philip Hunton, following Herle on such vital points, placed sovereignty in king, lords, and commons in parliament (Weston and Greenberg 1981, pp. 58–61). As the principle of parity became the foremost consideration, some writers, noting that two estates were more than one, subordinated the king to the two houses, a line of argument that Prynne developed ingeniously in his highly successful *Soveraigne Power of Parliaments* (1643). It was second only to Herle's *Fuller Answer* in the history of the coordination principle. Prynne worked from the Answer, certainly, but in particular from the declaration of the Long Parliament of 2 November 1642 and from the *Mirror*, the *Modus*, the preface to Coke's *Ninth Reports*, and 'office of a king' in the Confessor's laws, the confirmations of the charters, the coronation oath, and the like (Weston and Greenberg 1981, pp. 61–6; see Prynne 1643, pp. 32, 36–7, 41–3, 51–3, 56, etc.).

This assimilation of the king's constitution with the common-law cult of the Confessor's laws accelerated with the publication of the *Fourth Part of the Institutes*. Registered with the company of stationers on 6 August 1644, it provided the Answer with the appropriate historical background by reinforcing and supplementing Coke's earlier discussion of parliament. The confluence of these important political ideas produced a profound and lasting change in political thought. If ever a marriage was made in heaven between two sets of political ideas, it was this union between the coordination principle, sprung from the Answer to the Nineteen Propositions and carrying the sanction of a king soon to be a royal martyr, and an immemorial House of Commons, supported by the authority of the greatest lawyer of the age. Few doubted the immemorial character of the kingship and House of Lords, but the House of Commons was vulnerable on this score. For a golden moment this was no source of apprehension. The redoubtable Coke, relying on the *Modus* and evoking the law of tithes, and Lambarde in *De Priscis Anglorum Legibus* and *Archeion* had seen to that.

In contemporary parlance, then, the three estates of king, lords, and commons, given their equal shares in lawmaking, their immemorial character, and the human source of their powers, were coordinate, coeval, and coessential; and in their united voices was the sovereign power of the kingdom. At this juncture common law became clearly subservient to the modern theory of parliamentary sovereignty, its primary role thenceforth one of demonstrating that a sovereign parliament, in which king, lords, and commons made law as three coordinate estates, had existed on a constant basis time out of mind. Despite the seeming paradox ancient constitutionalists would now combine common-law language and reasoning with the advocacy of the modern theory of parliamentary sovereignty. As political debate centred on the citadel of power, discussion entered new territory; and much was said about the prescriptive right of the commons to representation in parliament and the nature of the law-making process. To Atwood, the right of coming to parliament was an established liberty in 1215, and Twysden wrote similarly.[30] But there were those in the royalist ranks who found this proposition unacceptable; and one of the most respected among them harked back to the implications of the Norman conquest. Conquerors, he pointed out, did not allow such coordinations or admit so many sharers in the rights of sovereignty as was being fantasised. Nor was there among the Confessor's laws anything that could 'give the least colour or pretence for such a co-ordination as is conceited'.[31]

The spearhead of the royalist response was the anonymous *Freeholders Grand Inquest* (1648), the most formidable anti-coordination tract of the century. The practice until recently has been to assign the *Freeholders* to Sir Robert Filmer on the strength of a modern edition of his writings edited by Peter Laslett in 1949. This theory of authorship has seemed reasonable because the *Freeholders* circulated in the late seventeenth century in Filmerian collections. Even then there was a dissident voice. No less an authority than Anthony Wood assigned the tract without reservation to Sir Robert Holbourne, a royalist who moved in circles close to the crown in Civil War Oxford. In the early twentiety century G.K. Fortescue, editor of the Thomason tracts, agreed with Wood; and J.W. Allen, an authority on early Stuart tracts, denied Filmer's authorship. Yet though Laslett's attribution seemed to settle the matter, the controversy was renewed in the

---

30. Atwood is quoted in Pallister 1971, p. 36; Twysden 1849, pp. 126–7, 134–5 (for the confluence of ideas see *ibid.*, pp. 13, 33, 40–4, 57–9, 82–6, 119–25, 126–8, 134, etc.); Baxter 1659, pp. 456–90; Weston 1965, pp. 73–4, 107–9, 112; Whitelocke 1766, I, pp. 179–98, 366–80, 423–32 and II, pp. 43–57, 111–39, 140, 168, 251, 255, 308–11, 331–8. Both Twysden and Whitelocke are thought to have written in the 1650s. See also *A Collection of State Tracts* 1705, pp. 506–7, and Acherley 1759. Pocock sees a union of ancient constitutionalism with James Harrington's *Oceana* (1656): resulting neo-Harringtonianism is said to be a vital element in the 'country' ideology in Charles II's reign and afterwards (Pocock 1975, pp. 406–22; Pocock, in Harrington 1977; Pocock 1985).
31. Sheringham 1660, pp. 53, 54–5. This was written within the context of the 'office of a king'. See also *ibid.*, pp. 41–2. The tract was first published in Paris under the title *A Remonstrance of the Unlawfulnesse of the War* (1652).

1980s. For reasons given elsewhere, it is assumed here that Holbourne was author of the *Freeholders*.[32]

The tract is remarkable for the strategy employed to counter Herle and Prynne. Holbourne would demonstrate two main propositions: (1) no coordination marked the law-making process and (2) there was no prescriptive right in the commons of England to representation in parliament. To do so, he turned to royal writs of summons to parliament and enacting clauses of statutes for evidence of an inequality among king, lords, and commons that must make impossible any claim of parity or coordination in lawmaking. They could also be utilised to prove that the House of Commons had reached Westminster within time of memory. The two ideas reinforced each other: if there was no prescriptive right to representation, no coordination marked lawmaking. After all, how could a House of Commons, arrived at Westminster within time of memory, associate on equal terms in the important area of lawmaking with the king and House of Lords, both accepted as immemorial? The contemporary value system permitted only the denial that the House of Commons was in these circumstances a genuinely independent estate of parliament, coordinate with the king and the House of Lords. If it was not a coordinate estate, there was no coordination in lawmaking; and sovereignty, undivided and unshared, resided in the king alone.

But what of the pervasive and hitherto unchallenged assumption that the House of Commons had always formed part of the common council of the kingdom? Holbourne now took deliberate aim at the doctrine of the ancient constitution, writing that even though early writs made no mention of calling knights, citizens, and burgesses to parliament, some might think their coming so customary as to make this unnecessary. To clarify the writ and satisfy those who thought the commons 'always' part of the common council he would insist

1. That anciently the barons of England were the common council of the kingdom.
2. That until the time of Hen. 1 the commons were not called to parliament.
3. Though the commons were called by Hen. 1 yet they were not constantly called, nor yet regularly elected by writ until Hen. 3 time.

For the first point Holbourne found parliaments among the Saxons but not with a House of Commons; and he was explicit that parliaments after the conquest contained no such house. Quoting from Henry I's coronation

32. The authorship of the *Freeholders* is discussed in Weston 1980, 1987; Daly 1983.

charter, he found that William I had amended the Confessor's laws with the consent of his barons; but unlike Lambarde, he translated *barones* to denote earls and bishops without the commons. And in another passage he resisted the temptation to include the commons under the term *proceres*.[33]

The other two points are treatable as one. Holbourne would grant the presence of commons in parliament before time of memory but not in a form recognisable to Stuart England. All the people of the kingdom were called in Henry I's reign, and multitudes came, but the king had legislated only with barons in the common council. Moreover, Holbourne lays special emphasis on the point that, even when the commons were called, this was neither constant nor based on regular election until Henry III's reign. Not until 1265 (49 Hen. 3), the year of the earliest extant writ of summons to knights of the shire, was the representative body of the kingdom established. Only then was there customary usage of representation; that which Henry III 'began a little before his death, Edward I and his successours constantly observed and continued'.[34]

These conclusions were replete with implications. A House of Commons founded within time of memory was obviously not immemorial; and the coordination principle would have to discarded. The king whose writs had summoned representative elements to parliament was the founder and master of such a house. Inferior to the king and House of Lords, whose longevity was not in question, it was at best a junior partner in an arrangement that required three equal partners if the coordination principle was to have viability. In the new circumstances controversy about the human source of political power and authority in the state must be settled in the king's favour. Not only the rights and privileges of the House of Commons were at risk; so was the position of parliament itself.

Six months after the publication of the *Freeholders*, royalist defeat at Preston set in motion events that led to Charles I's execution and the proclamation of a republic without king and House of Lords. In these disjointed times the tract might well have slipped from sight without the support forthcoming from Prynne. Appalled at the king's fate and adamantly opposed to the Levellers and commonwealthmen, who in his

33. Holbourne 1648, pp. 6–10. The account in this chapter revises that in Weston and Greenberg 1981, pp. 128, 145–7; 319 n. 9, where Prynne receives credit that belongs to Holbourne. The latter was working from Selden's edition of Eadmer's annals, in which the Confessor's laws, as approved and amended by William I, are printed. Holbourne did not disclose whose ideas he was attacking, but see the appraisal in Prynne 1662, p. 230.
34. Holbourne 1648, p. 14. The *Freeholders* has a surprisingly lengthy section on parliamentary privilege sympathetic to James I (*ibid.*, pp. 50–64).

view had undermined the monarchy and destroyed it, he set out to restore king, lords, and commons as three coordinate estates but with special safeguards to restrain the House of Commons. The result was a series of major political tracts that for twenty years, in season and out, kept alive the ideas in the *Freeholders*. It was an altogether extraordinary performance. But Prynne's contribution was more extensive than this when, clinging tenaciously to the coordination principle, he nevertheless dealt it a severe blow by producing massive evidence that there was no House of Commons before 1189. One of his methods was to adopt a definition of time of memory which imparted a very different time sense to phrases in medieval records such as 'time out of mind', 'in all times past', etc. (Weston and Greenberg 1981, p. 141). So great were his services to the crown that he was appointed keeper of the Tower records at the Restoration, and in the grand controversy over legal sovereignty that raged during the remainder of the century his name was grouped with 'modern writers' on government whose writings affrighted supporters of the ancient constitution.

As early as February 1648 Prynne's retreat from radicalism was manifested in an attack on Coke's sponsorship of the *Modus* so savage, prolonged, and ultimately successful that pro-court writers such as Brady and his fellow High Tory historians felt no need to deal with the subject.[35] If the *Modus* were to go, the best surviving evidence from the middle ages for an immemorial House of Commons would vanish with consequences devastating for the doctrine of the ancient constitution. Prynne also demonstrated at length an inconsistency in representation after 49 Hen. 3 that wrought havoc with the accepted idea of an ancient right in the commons of England to representation in parliament. This argument has received extended consideration elsewhere (Weston and Greenberg 1981, ch. 5), but not his critique of the *Modus*. What Prynne did was mount a successful attack on the credibility of the proem to the English *Modus* by denying that the treatise was an authority for the Confessor's reign and that the Conqueror and Henry II had accepted it. Nor, despite Coke, had it influenced the makers of Magna Carta.

For one thing, the historical record revealed that for hundreds of years there were no knights and burgesses in parliament; only the king and his nobles. This was so despite 'the spurious pretended ancient (though in truth late ridiculous) treatise, styled *Modus tenendi Parliamentum* on which Sir

35. For Brady's reaction see n. 36 below. An obvious exception to this generalisation is the aged Fabian Philipps, whose last major tract is understandable only in these terms. Philipps 1687, pp. 673, 688–95, 698–70, and *passim*.

Edward Coke and others most rely' (Prynne 1658, p. 20, 1664, pp. 552, 553–4). The *Modus* was replete with anachronisms if associated with the Confessor's reign. Thus the word 'parliamentum', which appeared 148 times and was present in almost every line besides the title, was new in Henry III's reign, and it was strange to find it unaccompanied with such contemporary terms for parliament as *concilium, concilium magnum, commune concilium*, etc. Noting that the first clause in the treatise appeared to have been transcribed from Magna Carta, where *commune concilium* was the term for parliament, he concluded that the *Modus*, rather than inspiring Magna Carta, as Coke believed, had been written at a later date. There was also the troublesome matter of parliamentary writs. According to the *Modus*, the king had issued them to the wardens of the Cinque Ports to summon two barons from every port and to sheriffs and others to summon two knights from each county and two citizens and burgesses from every city and borough, but Prynne was unable to find an historical record of such writs before 49 Hen. 3. Nor were the sums paid to such representatives, as recorded in the *Modus*, consonant with known facts. Despite statements about sums allotted for this purpose, for example, to the barons of the Cinque Ports, no such writs were issued until Edward I's reign. His argument concluded on a triumphant note: 'I suppose no antiquary or lawyer can produce one precedent of any parliament or great council held in England or Ireland according to this *Modus*, either before, at, or since the conquest, in any of our histories, parliaments, close rolls, records, or journals.'[36]

But if there were no representatives in parliament before 1189, how to explain their absence? The stage was set for the necessary historical explanation when Dugdale made available to Tory scholarship a complete printing of Sir Henry Spelman's *Glossarium Archaeologus*, known as the *Glossary*. The first volume, published in 1626, reached the letter 'L' but the second, published in 1664 for the first time, included under 'P' an article on parliament entitled 'Parlamentum' that proved of high value to the court. Since Dugdale had financial assistance from two extremely powerful political figures, Lord Chancellor Clarendon and Bishop Gilbert Sheldon

36. Prynne 1664, pp. 567–8. See the general discussion, pp. 553–608, esp. 559–60. The repercussions are in Tyrrell 1694, pp. 378, 380, 1696–1704, III, Part II, pp. 71–2. See n. 35 above. Brady's reaction is in Stowe MSS 366, fo. 2v. Although he was influenced as well by Selden, it was Prynne's discussion, in particular, in the fourth volume of his *Parliamentary Writs*, that led Brady to write admiringly that Prynne was 'very full and hath clearly confuted this *Modus* and proved it an imposture in this piece, and also in his animadversions upon the 4th Institutes'.

(soon archbishop of Canterbury), probably more than scholarly patronage
was at work. Spelman's reputation for disinterested scholarship and his
discovery of political feudalism would make it possible to exploit the
Norman conquest on behalf of a Bodinian kingship. What he did was set
forth the main lines of a feudal kingship after 1066 that was thoroughly
incompatible with the historical vision of the ancient constitutionalists. At
its centre were the lord–vassal relationships by which the king granted
landed estates (fiefs) to his vassals (Norman military men), who owed him
in return military service and court duty. As his tenants *in capite*, they
attended his *curia regis*, the nearest equivalent in the feudal world to an early
parliament. Nor was there a substantial class of freeholders to serve as
electors or members of a House of Commons, and he reported in a much-
quoted sentence that there was no sign of commons in parliament 'ab
ingressu Gulielmi I. ad excessum Henrici 3'. Yet Spelman left the ancient
constitution otherwise intact by accepting the idea that William had
confirmed the Confessor's laws, and he sought to reconcile his findings
generally with the confirmations of the charters (Pocock 1987, pp. 111–16).

Profiting from the *Glossary*, Dugdale published two major works
associating political feudalism with parliamentary history: *Origines Juridiciales* (1666), which passed through three editions by 1680, and his
Baronage of England (1675). His main contribution in the political sense was
in *Origines Juridiciales* where he advanced a new version of parliamentary
representation before 1189. In much of what he wrote he followed the lines
marked out by Coke and Lambarde. From Coke he took the standard
account of the confirmations of the charters, which ensured customary
usage of the ancient rights and liberties in the Confessor's laws for the
period from William I to Magna Carta and thence to Edward I; from
Lambarde, the conclusion that there had indeed been parliamentary
representation before 1189. Working from *Archeion* and *De Priscis
Anglorum Legibus*, he found the law of tithes decisive. It had been made 'à
rege, baronibus, & populo'. At this point, however, he departed from the
Whigs, who equated 'populo' with the House of Commons. Not so.
According to Dugdale tenants *in capite* represented their sub-vassals in the
common council and modern representation was born almost overnight in
49 Hen. 3. This was to concede a parliamentary representation before 1189,
but not in a form acceptable to Coke's and Lambarde's disciples. Haunted
by the vision of an early House of Commons fully capable of serving as a
coordinate estate in lawmaking, they were less than grateful; as one of them

said: they were being asked to accept 'a fancied way of being represented by such as they never chose, tenants *in capite*, by military service'.[37]

iii   History and sovereignty in the Exclusion Crisis

Like a modern jackhammer breaking up a pavement, these repeated blows at the doctrine of an ancient constitution were too much to endure in silence. By the time of the Exclusion Crisis its supporters were likely to be Shaftesbury Whigs though the doctrine was by no means confined to that party. The leading Whig polemicist was Petyt, the common lawyer and legal antiquary who would figure prominently in the well-known Brady controversy. An exponent of a shared parliamentary sovereignty, he considered that the new view of the Norman conquest endangered the idea of an immemorial House of Commons. With Spelman and Dugdale in mind he wrote that though the Conqueror had got the imperial crown of England and introduced several arbitrary laws, such as new tenures, yet he had not made such an absolute conquest, nor had the kingdom received so universal a change as 'modern authors' had published to the world, as if by a general confederacy and without examination of the truth. They had fathered upon this 'revolution' all the alterations they could imagine (Petyt 1680a, 'Preface', pp. 17–18). In this atmosphere Petyt collected materials for a broad defence of coordination. Yet his extremely influential *Antient Right of the Commons of England Asserted* did not appear until 1680, directly after the republication of the *Freeholders Grand Inquest*.

To establish an immemorial House of Commons Petyt relied, not on the *Modus*, but on the early fourteenth-century case of the burgesses of St Albans. It was said to provide ample proof that cities and boroughs at this time were sending members to parliament by a general custom or law that had originated time out of mind. The burgesses had petitioned Edward II to send two representatives to parliament on the ground that this was customary practice 'in all former times'; and making use of this phrase and other language in the petition as a point of departure, Petyt established to

---

37. Dugdale 1666, pp. 4–18; Atwood 1681, p. 4; see also the 'Preface'. According to Dugdale, the modern parliament began in 49 Hen. 3 when Simon de Montfort in the king's name summoned knights and burgesses to parliament for the first time. This explanation for the 'revolution of 1265', as Whigs derisively termed it, had been initially popularised by Prynne, who assumed, however, that Henry III issued the necessary writs. To explain the change in historical terms was to strengthen the court case; to attribute it to a rebellious baron, with memories of civil war and interregnum still fresh, was to minimise parliament: Dugdale 1666, p. 18, 1675, pp. 756–7 (de Montfort). Prynne worked from James Howell's *Cottoni Posthuma* (Howell 1651, pp. 345, 346).

his own satisfaction a continuity of representation between Richard I and Edward II. Still short of his goal of going 'higher' than Richard I, as the 1189 rule required, he turned to 'Bracton'. Since the latter's reputation as a great judge was at its height in Henry III's reign, presumably his lifetime spanned Richard's and John's reigns. Fortunately he had left a record of the rule by which parliament made law in his lifetime and in 'ages before': it revealed that there had been representation in the process. A measure had the force of law if it were 'justly declared and approved by the council and consent of the great men [the House of Lords] and by the general consent of the commonwealth [expressed in the House of Commons], the authority of the king preceding'. The decisive statement had come from the admired 'Bracton', and Petyt was deeply chagrined by Brady's failure to deal squarely with it.[38]

Petyt was chary of the word 'coordination', which was being linked in political literature with the death of Charles I, preferring language that stressed the 'shared' quality of lawmaking. In Petyt's view the people had had a share in their public councils since the beginning of their history. Thus the Britons had called their parliament 'kyfr-y-then' because their laws were ordained there. Much more was known about the Saxons, who had brought their laws and government from Germany. Tacitus was authority for the fact that the commons formed part of their witenagemots. After the country was reunited under a Christian monarchy, Englishmen had kept their ancient witenagemots or parliaments, where Saxons made laws and managed the great affairs of the king and kingdom. And relying on *De Priscis Anglorum Legibus*, Petyt reported that the Confessor had reformed and confirmed ancient Saxon laws and also made new ones. Nor could there be any doubt about the role of the House of Commons in legislation. Petyt would supply authorities from which it was 'apparent and past all contradiction that the commons in those ages were an essential part of the legislative power, in making and ordaining laws, by which themselves and their posterity were to be governed'.

The witenagemot had survived the Norman conquest, and notwithstanding William's high power and severe policies, the customary usage of parliaments persisted. This could be seen from the confirmations of the charters and the evidence in *De Priscis Anglorum Legibus*. Working from the edition of 1644, to which Twysden had contributed, Petyt reported

---

38. Petyt 1680a, 'Discourse', pp. 1–44, 123–6, 'Appendix', pp. 147–8; 1681, p. 14, 1739, pp. xiii–xiv. See also Tyrrell 1694, pp. 309–12, 344, esp. 312.

that William had early issued a Magna Carta granting and confirming the Confessor's laws. One of them was said to reveal that the king could legislate only with the consent of the common council of the kingdom. He also found that William's Magna Carta had much in common with King John's and other great charters. They provided for the 'restitution and declaration of the ancient common law and right of the kingdom', words that to Petyt ensured the continuance of parliament. As he said, 'What could the promised restitution of the laws of Edward the confessor signify, if their witenagemot, or parliament . . . was destroyed and broken?' Since the Saxon parliament contained a House of Commons, Petyt considered that all his authorities and reasons proved conclusively that the commons had votes and a share in lawmaking in the governments of the British, the Saxons, and the Normans. They were an essential part of the government before and after the Norman conquest, and the same generalisation applied to the House of Lords. Petyt also placed an unlimited law-making power in parliament; on this point he left no doubt of his modern outlook, writing: 'When any doubts and differences of opinions arose amongst lawyers, concerning what the common law was in points of great and weighty importance, such doubts and differences were by the ancient course and practice declared and settled, not by the judges of Westminster Hall, but by the law-making power of the kingdom.'[39]

A formidable adversary now intervened on the side of the court. This was Dr Brady, master of Caius College, Cambridge, and royal physician to Charles II and James II, whose historical writings were much indebted to the historical scholarship of Holbourne, Prynne, Spelman, and Dugdale though he clearly excelled them in the use to which he now put a hard-earned understanding of political feudalism and its distinctive vocabulary. If his erudition has to be acknowledged, still his examination of early English history was always subservient to the larger cause of placing a legal sovereignty in the Stuart kingship. What he did was set out to establish that the commons of England did not constitute an estate in parliament before 49 Hen. 3 and that earlier freemen, as the term was understood in his day, had no share in lawmaking unless they were represented by tenants in chief. But he went further than this by promulgating a full-blown conquest theory with implications for the seventeenth century: the Norman

---

39. Petyt 1739, pp. 10–12, 45, 66–7, 1680a, 'Preface', pp. 3–12, 32–40, 54, 73–4, 'Discourse', pp. 123–4, 'Appendix', pp. 146–7; Tyrrell 1694, pp. 326–7. Clearly parliamentary privilege was a subject dear to Petyt, who printed the *Apology* and *Protestation* in his *Jus Parliamentarium* and long extracts from the debates of 1621. On another occasion he reprinted the Petition of Right: 1680b, pp. 126–37.

conquest meant that the Stuart king was sovereign on the lines that Bodin had made familiar. Brady was insistent that there had been a genuine conquest, followed by the introduction of a feudal kingdom that precluded a shared law-making power before time of memory. The combination of military conquest with an arbitrary power in the king as sole lawmaker rendered Brady's historical writings horrendous to the advocates of an ancient constitution. So fierce was his assault on that doctrine that he seemed to an early eighteenth-century Whig 'the very learned advocate of slavery'; and 100 years after his death even conservative polemicists shunned him as a Stuart apologist of illiberal and absolutist sympathies. They preferred the researches of a pre-Civil War Spelman or Selden.[40]

That Brady had an ideological interest in the Norman conquest appears from his account of William after Hastings. Whoever noted his actions in drawing his army about Westminster at the time of his coronation, his construction of fortresses and castles in London, and his 'dictating laws' must believe that his intention was to rule by the sword from the first. The phrase 'dictating laws' stands out. After winning England by the sword, the Conqueror had imposed Norman feudal law on his subjects to establish his mastery over the defeated kingdom and provide unmistakable proof of its subjugation; and Brady discussed the laws that William deliberately imposed at this time. The thrust of the argument was plain: the Conqueror was, as the contemporary phrase went, the 'original' or human source of the law. There was no law independent of William and his successors in this period of time so critical to title of prescription. To take up this position was to depart sharply from Coke, who, Brady stated, had ignored the entrance of a new and foreign law at the conquest that became the English law. He had written as if common law had grown up with the first trees and grass, 'abstracting it from any dependence upon, or creation by the government'.[41]

But was Coke wholly mistaken? What of the repeated confirmations of the Confessor's laws, so well attested in historical accounts? Had these not ensured the continuity of Saxon law and government after 1066, and did this not mean that Saxon law and government, in a legal sense, had a life independent of the crown, exactly what Coke had claimed? Brady would

40. Weston 1972, pp. 425–7; Weston and Greenberg 1981, pp. 187–92; Brady 1684, 'The Introduction' and also 'An Answer to Mr Petit's Book', pp. 11 (margin), 16, 'An Answer to . . . *Argumentum Antinormanicum*', pp. 251–2; St Armand 1725, p. 89; Lee 1982, p. 175 n. 54.
41. Brady 1684, 'An Answer to Mr Petit's Book', pp. 13–14, 'An Answer to . . . *Argumentum Antinormanicum*', p. 237; Brady 1685, 'General Preface', p. xlvii, 'Preface to the Norman History', pp. 155–6, 157.

admit that William had indeed confirmed the Confessor's laws but no more than this. Dwelling at length on the common-law cult of the Confessor's laws he broke new ground by undermining the credibility of Lambarde's collection of those laws; the account of William's Magna Carta as detailed by Coke and supported by Selden's edition of Eadmer's annals, Ingulphus of Croyland, and the Lichfield chronicle; and the customary interpretation of Henry I's coronation charter and Magna Carta itself. Nor did he overlook the enacting clause in the law of tithes. Far from being a mighty law, it was an uncouth expression used on one occasion only and but slender proof of a House of Commons in Saxon parliaments that shared the law-making power. By itself 'populus' signified neither great nor little people but only laity, and it ought to be interpreted according to the usage and practice of the time. The Confessor's laws were no more than penal laws, which William I had selected, approved, and published by command, doing so for the benefit of his Norman but not his Saxon subjects. Moreover, he had added to the Confessor's laws, not simply corrected them. The message was stark: the bulk of English law after 1066 had come from Normandy with the Conqueror; and post-conquest common law was substantially feudal law. Contrary to Coke, ancient English kings had planted early English law, and in another passage Brady wrote of this action as taken with the assistance and advice of their great councils in all ages as they found it expedient. They had acted in response to the petition and request of their people.[42]

Brady would also establish that there were no elements in these great councils corresponding to the two houses of parliament. There was not even an independent nobility, much less a counterpart to the freeholders of Stuart England that would make possible a House of Commons of the kind envisaged by Petyt and his friends. The social and political conditions illuminated by Domesday Book would not permit the people (the two houses) to be lawmakers, as troublesome men proclaimed. After 1066 a Norman military class held land of the king, to whom its members owed military and court duty; and the *curia regis* was no more than a tenurial council of tenants in chief. After first accepting Dugdale's version of early representation, Brady decided it was 'probable the commons were not at all represented before 49 H. 3'. Subjugated Englishmen, mired in serfdom,

---

42. Brady 1685, 'General Preface', pp. xlvii–xlviii, 1684, 'An Answer to Mr Petit's Book', pp. 14, 16–17, 20, 29, 31, 'An Answer to . . . *Argumentum Antinormanicum*', pp. 256–69, esp. 262 (see also pp. 296–8); 1684, 'Glossary', pp. 24–6. His discussion of Magna Carta is described below.

were outside this political world: they were not the ones who attended the *curia regis* or contended for the 'liberties' in royal charters; no indeed. The *liberi homines* named there were Norman military men or their descendants and their sub-vassals, and the liberties in contention were for the most part relaxations of rigorous exactions and usages of feudal law relating to fiefs held of the Conqueror and his successors. If that law was too harsh for tenants in military service, only the king, as its source, could adjust or correct it.[43] As for St Albans, it too was part of feudal arrangements. The burgesses had not prescribed to come to parliament 'merely as from a borough, but as from a town that held in chief of the king, and this service was incident to their tenure'.[44] So much for the idea of a right at common law to representation in medieval parliaments and the concept of an immemorial House of Commons.

The final blow was the Tory historian's use of the great charters to demonstrate the Bodinian character of the early English kingship. These were statutes, the king their only maker – a generalisation applicable even to Magna Carta, so long the exemplar of the Confessor's laws, its role so pivotal in the confirmations of the charters. At Brady's hands a whole new frame of reference was taking shape. The authority of Magna Carta was now said to be due to the king's grace, the point being that King John was the sole lawmaker when he granted the demands of the Norman military men and their ecclesiastical allies. As Spelman had written, 'what was determined by the king and council in that age, and confirmed by his seal had without doubt the force of law'. But did not this suggest that lawmaking was a shared power? Not at all. The role of the great council was limited to making charters at the stage when these were only petitions and requests. To be sure, the barons had offered King John a schedule of terms that he was in no position to reject; yet the fact remained that the authority of Magna Carta was due to its being a royal grant, confirmed by royal seal. The only legal sanction required by the rebellious barons was the king's assent: the tenor of all royal charters was 'we grant, we confirm, we give for us and our heirs, to them and their heirs, etc.'. It was the king's

---

43. Brady 1685, 'General Preface', pp. xxv–xxviii, lxvii–lxviii, 1684, 'The Epistle to the Candid Reader', n.p., 'An Answer to Mr Petit's Book', pp. 17–18, 'Animadversions upon . . . *Jani Anglorum facies Nova*', p. 169, 'An Answer to . . . *Argumentum Antinormanicum*', pp. 252, 255, 256, 265–6. And see 'Glossary', pp. 50–4. For the shift in his view of representation before 49 Hen. 3, see Brady 1684, 'The Introduction', n.p., 'An Answer to Mr Petit's Book', p. 112 (margin).
44. Brady 1684, p. 38. In this connection see, too, the comment on Brady's *Historical Treatise of Cities and Burghs or Boroughs* (1690) in Weston and Greenberg 1981, pp. 185–6; Smith 1987, pp. 25–6.

power and authority alone that gave life to the charters: they contained no such phrase as 'by authority of parliament', words arousing Brady's indignation (Brady 1685, pp. xxxiv, xli–xlii, xlviii; Tyrrell 1694, p. 719).

The outcome of the Glorious Revolution determined the form of legal sovereignty that would prevail, and in this context it is irrelevant that Brady's historical scholarship was superior to that of supporters of the doctrine of an ancient constitution. Together, Charles I and Coke had provided that constitution with sanctions of the most august kind; and while the reputation of the *Modus* had been injured, it was not out of the political wars and it would be generations before Spelman's *Glossary* replaced the political understandings generated by that treatise. In 1689 time still ran on the side of the ancient constitution. At the Revolution, Brady gave up his position as keeper of the Tower records to Petyt, who held it for the rest of his days. Pocock writes graphically that 'it is possible to regard the fall of James II as a triumph on the plane of historical thought for the concept of the ancient constitution; . . . in the microcosm of the tower records office the Revolution meant the fall of Brady and the substitution of Petyt' (Pocock 1987, p. 229; Dickinson 1977, pp. 77–83). On the political plane it signalled the fall of a theory of Bodinian sovereignty and the final recognition that legislative sovereignty resided in king, lords, and commons.

The shift in political power meant that Brady's scholarship would make its way only gradually, but that it was far advanced by the mid-eighteenth century appears from David Hume's *History of England* (1762). When he wrote, the Revolution was secure, and the modern idea of progress was replacing the doctrine of an ancient constitution. Drawing on Spelman, Dugdale, and Brady, as he turned to a consideration of the antiquity of the House of Commons, Hume explained that no one doubted but that the king and his great barons composed early parliaments.

The only question seems to be with regard to the commons, or the representatives of counties and boroughs; whether they were also, in more early times, constituent parts of parliament? This question was once disputed in England with great acrimony; but such is the force of time and evidence, that they can sometimes prevail even over faction, and the question seems, by general consent, and even by their own, to be at last determined against the ruling party. It is agreed that the commons were no part of the great council, till some ages after the conquest; and that the military tenants alone of the crown composed that supreme and legislative assembly. (Hume 1762, I, p. 407; Dickinson 1977, pp. 140–2.)

The epitaph was premature only if one reads into it that the doctrine of the ancient constitution was completely dead. Several generations would have to pass for that result to be achieved.[45] But as Hume's commentary indicates, by the time that he was writing, it was really all over. A turning point had indeed been reached.

45. The appeal of the Saxon constitution persisted for another two centuries, but the common law argument seems to have lost ground steadily during the eighteenth century (Burrow 1981, pp. 18–35, 100–2). For the theme of the Saxon constitution consult Smith 1987 *passim*, but esp. pp. 28–41, 50–4, 57–63, 80–102, 113–22, 137–40; Lee 1982, pp. 167–79. Smith accepts Pocock's sharp distinction between 'Cokean immemorialism' and a Saxon or Gothic constitution, as described in Kliger 1952; Pocock 1987, pp. 56–8. Signs of the common law argument are in Squire 1745; Acherley 1759; Brewer 1976, pp. 260–1; Peters 1971; Colbourn 1965 *passim*, but esp. pp. 7, 21–39, and Appendix II. Petyt's reasoning was perpetuated in the essay on parliament in Giles Jacob, *A New Law Dictionary* (1729). In an eleventh edition by 1797, it contained still another discussion of the case of the burgesses of St Albans.

14

Leveller democracy and the Puritan Revolution

DAVID WOOTTON

i The Leveller movement

The Levellers were a political movement united around the programme of the first Agreement of the People (3 November 1647; Wolfe 1944, pp. 223–34).[1] That Agreement is the first proposal in history for a written constitution based on inalienable natural rights. It embodied three essential principles. The first, though ambiguously expressed, was taken by contemporaries to be that any property qualification for the franchise should be abolished: even the poor should have the right to vote. The second was that the representative assembly should have supreme authority in making law, appointing magistrates, and conducting foreign policy: the king, if any, was to be accountable to his subjects. The third principle was that the powers of government be limited by the principles of natural justice. This meant, first, that all laws must apply equally to all subjects: there must be no privileged estate or corporation. This also implied the illegality of all monopolies. Second, all subjects had the right to freedom of conscience, entitling them to dissent from any established state religion. This also implied a right to freedom of expression. Third, conscription was banned: subjects could not be compelled to serve in an army if they disapproved of the cause for which it was to fight, although they could be compelled to pay taxes. Finally, all laws 'must be good, and not evidently destructive to the safety and well-being of the people'. This implied both the right of juries to refuse to enforce bad law, and an ultimate right of revolution: if the people's representatives betrayed their trust, the nation as a whole could assert its ultimate sovereignty.

---

1. For a fuller discussion of the Leveller movement, see Aylmer 1975; and, on Civil War radicalism in general, Dow 1985.

It is hard for us, at this distance in time, to grasp how revolutionary this document was. All European societies of the time had privileged estates and corporations, all placed limits (often very narrow ones) upon religious worship and expression, all excluded the poor from political life, and all but a few were ruled by hereditary monarchs who claimed an absolute authority over the lives and estates of their subjects. The Levellers were not merely seeking to establish in England freedoms that existed elsewhere, in Holland or in Venice, but to establish for the first time freedoms which (outside a mythical historical past, that of Anglo-Saxon England) never had existed, and were not to come into existence for over three centuries. The Agreement thus poses in an acute form a common historical problem: read in what appears to us to be its natural sense it seems a remarkably modern document. This modernity must either be explained, or be shown to be illusory.

There is, at first sight, nothing about the origins or education of the Leveller leaders themselves which helps to explain the novelty of the Agreement (Aylmer 1970). Their backgrounds are precisely what one might expect for the political leaders of a movement which claimed to speak for people who had previously had no voice in politics: men whom John Lilburne described in 1653 as 'the hobnails, clouted shoes, the private soldiers, the leather and woollen aprons, and the laborious and industrious people in England' (E708(22), p. 15).[2] The Leveller leaders were on the lower fringes of the social and educational elite, with enough in common with the poorer classes and small businessmen to act as their spokesmen, but at the same time with the social and educational confidence which would make them potential leaders. These were men who had both worn leather or woollen aprons and sat at school desks. Perhaps half of them could read Latin and half could not, half were the sons (usually younger sons) of gentlemen and half were not. In this respect they straddled the major social and educational divides of the nation. But probably all were in some sense Londoners and had had some experience of trade or waged labour.

London was of growing importance in the economic and political affairs of the nation. The street demonstrations of London apprentices and small merchants had ensured both the execution of Strafford in 1641 and the

---

2. I cite Civil War pamphlets which are in the Thomason collection and have not been recently reprinted by the catalogue numbers of G.K. Fortescue, *Catalogue of the Pamphlets, Books, Newspapers and Manuscripts Relating to the Civil War, the Commonwealth and Restoration, collected by George Thomason, 1640–61* (London: British Museum, 1908). These works do not appear in the bibliography, which does, however, list modern collections.

failure of Charles' attempts to regain control of London thereafter. Their political support had provided a basis for the strategy of appealing downwards to the people embodied in parliament's Grand Remonstrance of November 1641 and had made it possible for the supporters of parliament to gain control of the common council in December 1641. The military support of their trained bands had turned back the king's forces at Turnham Green in November of 1642. The financial support they continued to provide through taxation was the precondition for parliament's survival. This was the world, on the fringes of the political life of the gentry elite, in which the Leveller leaders acquired their political skills: Lilburne, for example, had been active in the demonstrations of 1641 (Pearl 1961; Manning 1976; Lindley 1986).

In 1641 support from outside parliament made possible the success of the radicals in the Commons. In the late 1640s the Levellers must have hoped a new alliance with members of the gentry elite would strengthen their hand. They did receive some support from the republican MP Henry Marten, the future regicide MP John Hutchinson, and Col. Thomas Rainsborough, son of a vice-admiral and MP. However, the crucial novelty of the Levellers' strategy, from the moment they appeared as a political movement in 1646 until their final destruction as a unified force by Cromwell in 1649, was that they sought to mobilise support around a programme which had little to offer the political establishment, and to negotiate with established authorities on a basis of equality in an attempt to have that programme accepted. The precondition for success was the creation of an autonomous and informed political culture amongst their supporters, a culture which would stabilise and orientate a mass movement deprived of establishment leadership. Hence the urgency with which the Leveller leaders published pamphlet after pamphlet, writing in the crisp language of everyday speech and seeking to tie indissolubly together general principles and specific grievances.

Only in a society where Puritanism and commerce had encouraged the spread of literacy amongst the common people could such a political campaign have offered any prospect of success. Only where censorship of the press, generally so effective in early modern Europe, had broken down could political leaders seek to express the values and interests of the politically dispossessed. Only where the anonymity of market relations had made possible independence of expression without fear of economic sanction could merchants and artisans afford to lay claim to their rights. Only where petitions, street demonstrations, and voluntary military service showed some prospect of changing the course of political events – only under conditions of civil war – could such a strategy seem worth undertaking.

Yet from the beginning the Leveller movement was flawed by three fatal weaknesses. First, much of its support derived from two aggrieved groups: the religious sects, who wanted toleration; and the rank and file of the New Model Army, who wanted fair treatment (in particular they wanted their back-pay and protection against prosecution for offences, such as horse-stealing, committed in time of war). Throughout the period of Leveller strength the Presbyterian majority in the Commons was hostile to both toleration and the army; but in 1649 Cromwell was able to break the back of support for the Levellers by offering limited toleration to the sects and regular pay to the soldiers.

Second, the basis of the Leveller programme was always a call for elections. But the practical situation after both the first and second Civil Wars was that popular hostility – even in London, where support for the Levellers was most extensive – to war taxation and centralised government would have led to the electoral defeat of the radicals and the cause they stood for. Cromwell, Henry Ireton, and the officers of the New Model Army were eventually willing to accept the Leveller arguments for the use of force against parliament and for the prosecution of the king; but the Levellers had no effective strategy for consolidating power and preparing the ground for elections. They were willing to see the temporary exclusion of known royalists from the electorate, but not the postponement of elections themselves and the establishment of military dictatorship. They thus had no strategy for handling the transition from revolutionary war to peaceful settlement.

Third, the Levellers knew from the beginning that no matter what support they could muster among the rank and file of the army, the officers distrusted the egalitarianism of their constitutional proposals. Yet they never prepared effectively for a trial of strength with the officers. At Ware, in November 1647, a Leveller-inspired mutiny by two regiments was easily overawed by Fairfax and Cromwell and one mutineer was executed. At Burford, in May 1649, a second mutiny was overwhelmed, and three mutineers were executed. Neither uprising was adequately prepared; the timing of both was more convenient for Cromwell than for the Leveller movement. The Leveller movement never acquired any independent military strength.

These three weaknesses reflect, as we shall see, the distaste of Lilburne and

William Walwyn for the arts of political compromise and the techniques of military force. In order better to understand the failure of the Leveller movement we need to look more closely at their conception of political activity.

ii Puritans and revolutionaries

H.N. Brailsford (1873–1958) wrote, in his posthumous work, *The Levellers and the English Revolution*, 'to our generation fell the good fortune of re-discovering the Levellers' (1961, p. xi). This remark points up a number of problems that bedevil the study of the Levellers. In the first place they had in their own day and for subsequent generations no standing as serious political thinkers. They did not write in Latin, quote authorities, or define their own relationship to established traditions of political theory. Second, to claim for them an important role in the events of the Civil War is to adopt a view of those events which is open to dispute, for earlier historians found it easy to overlook them. Lastly, if the Levellers were important to Brailsford's generation, that is surely because they seemed to speak in peculiarly modern accents to the preoccupations of the day: their message was one of political and social equality, and it is no accident that they were rediscovered by the first generation of historians to see universal suffrage and the coming to power of socialist and communist parties. When Brailsford was born, there was not a single self-styled democracy in the world, or a single socialist government. When he died, throughout Europe and the English-speaking world a great part of the reforms that Eduard Bernstein, whom Brailsford singled out as 'the forerunner of us all' (p. xiii) in Leveller scholarship, and fellow social democrats had campaigned for had come, in the years after the Second World War, to be approved by politicians of both left and right. The rediscovery of the Levellers coincided with the triumph of democracy, and the welfare state.

The last decade has seen a decline in the historiographical fortune of the Levellers. A view of the Civil War as the first – if least thoroughgoing – of the revolutions of the modern world has been rejected as anachronistic, and the Civil War, it is now argued, is better understood as a conservative rebellion of the provinces against the innovations of central government, or as the last of Europe's religious wars (Morrill 1976, 1984). In such a context the Levellers appear once more as marginal figures: based in London, but resolutely opposed to political centralisation; sectarian in their origins, but outspoken advocates of toleration in a world of confessional strife. Do they deserve a central place in the history of political theory? This question, which no one would have paused to ask before Brailsford's birth, and which he and his contemporaries felt confident they could answer, has become inescapable within a few decades of his death.

In answering it, it is important to remember that anachronism, which is often treated as being merely the danger of making the past seem modern, is in fact both the Scylla and the Charybdis of the historian's voyage. On the one hand there is prochronism, which invents changes before they really happened; on the other there is parachronism, which blindly insists that current events have yet to occur. If Brailsford's generation struck the rock of prochronism, the most recent generation has tended to overstress our distance from the past and underestimate the rapidity of change, for fear of reading the present into the past. In order to steer a course between these two dangers we must begin by looking at the Levellers through the eyes of contemporaries.

Thomas Edwards was a leading Presbyterian minister who may conveniently personify the values that generations other than Brailsford's have taken to be at the heart of the parliamentarianism of the English Civil War. During 1646 he published, under the running title of *Gangraena*, three attacks on 'the errors, heresies, blasphemies, and pernicious practices of the sectaries of this time' (1977, title-page, pt 1). His purpose was to uphold Calvinist theological orthodoxy and social and constitutional conservatism against the radicals who were seeking to take advantage of the political and religious divisions within the gentry establishment.

When the first part of *Gangraena* appeared the New Model Army was already assured of military victory over the king. By mid-year the king had surrendered and, at the end of the year, when the final part appeared, peace with the king, on the terms of the Newcastle Propositions, seemed near. A conservative, Presbyterian majority in parliament appeared to be on the verge of bringing the war to a conclusion fairly close to that which Pym had envisaged when war began in 1642: the national church reformed, the powers of the monarch permanently restricted. Three years later, however, the king was to be executed and a republic declared, while the church remained divided, so divided that religious toleration was one of the few long-term consequences of the Interregnum.

The winter of 1646 and the spring of 1647 saw the Great Rebellion, the attempt to defend the constitutional reforms of 1641 while grafting on to them religious reforms unacceptable to the king, slide into revolution. Even as the fighting was taking place the parliamentary side had fallen into disagreement over the nature of the church reform it wanted, and over the extent to which toleration should be allowed to those unable to accept a national church settlement. Military victory brought home the unpleasant truth that the outcome of the religious conflict depended on the terms of the constitutional settlement. Constitutional conservatism meant Presbyterian victory; only constitutional radicalism could save the Independents and the sects. As a result the gangrene that Edwards had set out to attack not only took hold, but for the first time directly threatened the survival of the traditional body politic. If the Long Parliament had at first stood united against the king over constitutional questions, and had then divided over questions of religion, constitutional questions were now once more to the fore; but this time the threat to parliament's survival came not from the king, but from the populace and the army, and parliament found itself not united but divided.

Gangraena mirrors this transition from constitutional consensus to political revolution. The gangrene of the first two parts is the gangrene of heresy, which Edwards wishes to see rooted out. The sectaries, who plead for toleration and who go so far as to attack the very notion of a state church, are his enemies, amongst their number men such as Lilburne, Walwyn and Richard Overton. But by the time the third part appeared in December Edwards was aware of a new enemy: religious divisions amongst the parliamentarians were now beginning (for the first time) to seem less important than fundamental disagreements over the constitution of the kingdom. He announced his new preoccupations as follows:

The reader shall find in this book the sectaries' design and practise not to be only corrupting religion . . . but to be against magistracy and civil government . . . opposing settled government, and bringing an anarchy and confusion into church and state . . . they have *in terminis*, in divers pamphlets and some sermons, declared against monachy and aristocracy, and for democracy: they have expressed themselves in such a manner concerning that that they make it no other than an anarchy, making all alike, confounding of all ranks and orders, reducing all to Adam's time and condition and devolving all power upon the state universal and promiscuous multitude, whom they make the creator and destroyer of kings, parliaments and all magistrates at their mere pleasure, without tying them to any rule, or bounding them by any laws.   (Preface, pt III)

Edwards might justly claim, on the strength of these words, to have been the first discoverer of the Levellers. The prime targets in part III of *Gangraena* were the men who were later to be recognised as the leaders of the Leveller party; his main complaint against them was that in the past six months they had adopted a radical political egalitarianism which showed no respect for the constitution. Where his earlier attacks had met with no less than five indignant rebuttals and satirical denials from Walwyn, the future Leveller, alone, part III was met almost with silence. Even Lilburne, who could never resist an argument, was bound to admit that Edwards' account of his views was largely correct: his defence was merely that such radicalism was a reasonable deduction from the parliament's principles (E373(1); cf. Sharp 1988). The Agreement of the People, of 3 November 1647, must have seemed the clearest possible confirmation of Edwards' charges, and it was during that month that the term 'Leveller' came into use to identify the position he had described (Brailsford 1961, p. 309).

Political theories are inseparable from the vocabulary with which they are expressed. For Edwards the views of the Levellers implied a rejection of all established law, and a return to a lawless equality which could have existed only before sin entered Eden. He claimed their views were in conflict with the constitution (the need to preserve which they denied) and with biblical revelation (the very necessity for which they seemed to question by invoking a prelapsarian innocence and equality). But he had no positive language with which to describe them. Significantly, he could not call them 'revolutionaries' or (without periphrasis) 'democrats': he could not begin to think of them in the terms that came naturally to Brailsford's generation. Nor, for that matter, could they think of themselves in those terms.

Here lies a central problem for the study of the Levellers. 'Revolutionary' and 'democrat' are terms which imply a measure of self-consciousness: you cannot be one, any more than you can be a ballet dancer or a darts player, if you do not know that that is what you are. And yet Edwards' description reads transparently to us as a description of revolutionaries and democrats. Much of the history of ideas consists in rendering clear what is at first obscure. In cases such as this, however – and this is where our assessment of the Levellers has to differ from that of Brailsford's generation – it is necessary first to render what seems simple, complex; what seems transparent, opaque.

Let us take first the term 'revolutionary', which I have already applied to the Levellers several times. Most men in the seventeenth century believed that legitimacy was a product of precedent, of tradition, of history, and took it for granted that the decisions of their ancestors must properly determine their own actions. In all the European rebellions of the mid-seventeenth century the rebels claimed to be defending traditional liberties against innovating monarchies. How was it possible to shake oneself free of this incubus of tradition and conceive of a revolution, especially since the very concept of revolution was unavailable?

The term 'revolution' only came to have its modern meaning of a seizure of power by the people as a consequence of the French Revolution (for a range of views: Snow 1962; Elliott 1969; Zagorin 1969, pp. 1–18; Straka 1971; Stone 1972, pp. 50–54; Hill 1986). Seventeenth-century authors use the term 'revolution' as a metaphor derived from astronomy (Copernicus had written *De Revolutionibus*) to mean a major shift in the location of power, a turn in the wheel of fortune, and hence as often a restoration as a 'revolution' in our sense of the word. Locke wrote of 'the many revolutions which have been seen in this kingdom, in this and former ages' (Locke 1967, p. 432). The modern conception of revolution, since 1789, has, however, often been highly specific: revolution has been taken to involve a transfer of power from an oppressive minority to an oppressed majority, and a consequent change in the policies, the personnel, and the structure of government. There was no single seventeenth-century word for an event of this sort. Of course one can find in authors such as James Harrington and Locke descriptions of political revolutions even in the modern sense. But it could be argued that this is only because they had the events of the Civil War to look back to. When they looked back to the revolution of 1649 they were looking back, however, to a revolution that had been carried out by a House of Commons seeking to restore the ancient constitution and defend what it took to be its ancient rights and privileges, a revolution in which the execution of the king was only an unintended consequence, and which was, therefore, properly speaking, no revolution at all.

In fact there is evidence that in the early stages of the Civil War some people were willing to put aside the language of a conservative defence of historical rights and adopt a language that amounted to a call for revolution: in this respect the English Civil War differed in its inception from other seventeenth-century rebellions (Allen 1938; Sirluck, in Milton 1953–82, II; Manning 1978; Wootton 1990). And, indeed, it was partly because of pressure from such people (for whom revolution was an intended rather than an unintended consequence of revolt), and from the Levellers in particular, that the same king whose person parliament had declared to be sacrosanct and whose authority it had sworn to uphold in the Solemn League and Covenant was put on trial and condemned as a tyrant. The condemnation of the king was accompanied by the condemnation of monarchy, the abolition of the House of Lords, and the declaration of a Commonwealth.

'Revolution', properly so called, needs an ideology of innovation and not merely restoration. The House of Commons had one to hand in republicanism. Admiral Blake spoke on behalf of his government when, in Spain in 1651, he said that 'monarchy is a kind of government the world is weary of' and predicted that within ten years it would diasppear from France and Spain (Merriman 1938, p. 95; cf. also Hugh Peters, quoted in Brailsford 1961, p. 672). What was in prospect was a new epoch in world history. There appears to be nothing hopelessly anachronistic, then, about the identification of revolutionary political theories in mid-seventeenth-century England.

It would be wrong, however, to put too much stress upon republicanism as a revolutionary ideology in the 1640s. Existing republics, such as Venice, were generally intensely conservative and highly oligarchic political systems. This made them attractive models for politicians seeking an alternative to monarchy, but meant that republicanism was largely irrelevant to the preoccupations of the Levellers. Indeed, when they realised that Cromwell was not going to adopt the Agreement of the People they were prepared to enter into negotiations with the Stuart court in exile with a view to a restoration of the monarchy on acceptable terms. Both republicans and Levellers, however, were prepared to advocate constitutional revolution, despite the fact that the ties that bound men to the notion of an 'ancient constitution' had been strong: it was only because something had acted to dissolve those ties that revolution could legitimise itself. Religion was a much more important issue than the question of whether England should have a king, more important perhaps even than the idea that no ruler should be absolute, and it was religion which played the crucial role in undermining men's faith in the ancient constitution.

The similarities between Laud's beauty of holiness and Catholic ceremonial, combined with the suspicion that the Irish rebels had acted with royal connivance, convinced many in 1641 that the monarchy was acting in the Catholic interest (Lamont 1979, pp. 76–123). From 1639 Lilburne had been amongst those few sectarians arguing that the church of England was part of the Beast, one of the limbs of Antichrist. It was a small step from this view to the conclusion that the king was an agent of Antichrist, and that the struggle against royal absolutism formed part of an eschatological drama. In the early months of the Civil War the traditional view that the end of the world was not far off was supplemented by a view that had previously had only limited support: that the struggle between the forces of Christ and Antichrist during these last days would be decisively won by the Christian forces, a victory which would inaugurate the rule for a thousand years upon the earth of either Christ himself, or his saints.

Parliament was thus able, while seeking to insist on the supposedly conservative character of its constitutional proposals, to find in millenarianism a revolutionary doctrine tailor-made for its purposes. Millenarianism not only implied a decisive conflict which must lead to the ultimate victory of one side or the other, it also dispensed with the need to appeal to past precedents, replacing them by biblical prophecies. The prototype of a parliamentary sermon in support of war with the king was provided by Stephen Marshall's *Meroz Cursed* of 23 February 1642 (Trevor-Roper 1967, pp. 294–344). Here the attack upon those who do the work of the Lord negligently, those who withhold their hands from shedding of blood, is justified by appeal to the apocalyptic context within which the coming war is to be seen: the work is to 'revenge God's church against Babylon', while supporters of the monarchy had 'entered their names into the dragon's muster book' (Christianson 1978, pp. 227–8).

The approach of the last days meant that politics need no longer be conceived in terms of cyclical repetition but could be thought of in terms of innovation. In 1644 George Gillespie explained to the Commons that 'If we . . . consider the great revolution and turning of things upside down in these our days, certainly the work is upon the wheel: the Lord has . . . prepared the instruments of death against Antichrist' (Hill 1971, pp. 86–7). Thus eschatology could facilitate the transition from the idea of a turning wheel of fortune to the idea of an irreversible historical change, and could be used to justify belief in the inauguration of a new era of unparalleled prosperity, a utopia whose practicality was guaranteed by the prophecies of Daniel and the Book of Revelation (Webster 1975).

It might be thought that this vision of the Civil War as one of the final acts in the great conflict between Christ and Antichrist can have been shared only by a few eccentrics and bigots. But it may in fact help us to unpick the tangled skein of 'the Puritan revolution': a term invented by Samuel Rawson Gardiner a century ago. Recently it has been claimed that not only is the word 'revolution' anachronistic, but the word 'Puritan' has no clearly defined meaning when used either by contemporaries or by historians (Finlayson 1983). Nevertheless, contemporaries did employ religious terms – terms which might more properly be described as chiliastic than Puritan – to justify supporting radical parliamentarianism rather than conservative royalism.

The main impetus to revolution thus came not from any secular theory of revolutionary change but from a radical development of Protestant eschatology. It was religion which made the Civil War possible and was the primary factor leading to the deposition of the king. For some, religion came to be supplemented by a genuine constitutional radicalism; whilst many others, who had espoused millenarian language in 1642, came – as did Edwards – to see the sectaries as a greater threat than the king to the establishment of a godly society. Thus millenarian language ceased to serve as a guarantor of unity once the king had been defeated. If a few, like Hugh Peter, who began his sermon at the opening of the king's trial by recalling Simeon, whose expectation that he would live to see the coming of Christ had been fulfilled, and who preached after the king was condemned from Isaiah's denunciation of the king of Babylon, continued to use it, others, like Lilburne himself, had abandoned it entirely.

How far did the Levellers succeed in putting forward arguments for revolutionary change which could replace the millenarianism of the early stages of the Civil War? This question helps to expose the relative disadvantage of the Levellers in comparison with both millenarians and modern revolutionaries. Millenarians and revolutionaries think in party terms: the godly and the ungodly, the Plain and the Mountain, the reactionary and the progressive. The Levellers, however, systematically opposed any division of the political world between godly and ungodly: they opposed, partly for religious reasons, the very frame of mind which had made Civil War possible. They were willing to identify 'malignants' – those who had supported the king – and deny them full civil rights for a limited period, and they were willing to propose concrete policies that a government should adopt. But they presumed that, once the justice of their constitutional proposals was recognised, there would be no need for continuing party-political activity. For them 'party' was a term of abuse. In *The Second Part of England's New Chains Discovered* (1649) they attacked 'mere politicians . . . governed altogether by occasion, and as they saw a possibility of making progress to their designs' (Haller and Davies 1944, pp. 175–6). They could easily (as they came to lament) be charmed by those who called upon them 'to lay by all discontents, to forget and forgive, and to unite all against the common enemy', promising not to 'discountenance honest men . . . nor endeavour to set up a party' (pp. 180–1). They saw themselves as representing the antithesis of a party: 'an unanimous and universal resolution in all well-minded people' (p. 182). One of the central planks of their programme was a strict separation between the legislative, the executive (including the army), and the law courts, 'to the end all officers of state may be certainly accountable, and no factions made to maintain corrupt interests' (Wolfe 1944, pp. 299, 403). They never envisaged presenting themselves as a faction for election, or claimed to be the appropriate officers in a new government. They never saw themselves as seeking to concentrate power in their own hands.

Underlying the Leveller attitude to political activity was the belief that government existed to further an identifiable common interest, and that honest men should have no difficulty in agreeing on the nature of that interest or the best means to attain it. It should therefore be possible to take decisions by consensus. In this respect their assumptions were those of their day: parliament sought to proceed by consensus and avoid divisions determined by votes, just as the Levellers and officers did at Putney (Kishlansky 1981). Cromwell himself, it has been argued, was unable to establish a stable form of government simply because he failed to establish within parliament a loyal party of supporters, committed to united action (Trevor-Roper 1967, pp. 345–91). Their failure to break with these assumptions, however, greatly handicapped them in their efforts to bring about a revolution.

Nor were they ever willing to sacrifice what they saw as fundamental principles in the pursuit of power: they even opposed the execution of the king on the grounds that he had been tried, not by a jury according to a known law, but by a prerogative court. Millenarians were better placed to maintain that there were no common interests or common standards applicable to all citizens, and those who practised 'a waiting upon providence' were, as the Levellers protested, able to change their policies and principles with the times (Haller and Davies 1944, p. 176). In short, millenarians or revolutionaries would have been better than the Levellers at thinking about the seizure and exercise of power.

It would be wrong to conclude that because the Levellers did not see themselves as a political party they did not exist as a political movement (Brailsford 1961, pp. 309–18; Carlin 1984): they had a common programme, and raised funds by subscription from their supporters. But they constituted what might be termed a 'petitioner party' rather than a prospective party of government. The whole history of the movement was written in the court cases of its leader, Lilburne, as he begged for justice in the face of his accusers: first Laud and the star chamber, then the king at Oxford when he was captured during the Civil War, then the Lords and the Commons, and finally the Commonwealth and the Protectorate. And the organisation of the movement centred around the drafting and circulation of petitions: an effective method of mobilisation, but one which seemed to acknowledge that power properly lay in others' hands.

The Levellers relied upon persuasion to overcome 'error of breeding, long custom and sway of times' and 'erroneous zeal' (Haller and Davies 1944, p. 187). When persuasion failed and they sought – at Ware and at Burford – to organise army mutinies, they proved predictably unorganised and ill-prepared. To see the Agreement of the People as embodying revolutionary proposals is perfectly correct; and it is scarcely anachronistic to see the Levellers as trying to carry out a revolution. In doing so, however, they failed to act as a revolutionary party: the concept may be an anachronistic one, but there is nothing anachronistic about the idea of ruthlessly pursuing ideological ends through strict discipline and unprincipled opportunism. The Jesuits, after all, were constantly portrayed in such terms, as was Cromwell. The Levellers knew what they were doing when, rightly or wrongly, they preferred failure to certain sorts of success.

Their defeat, however, was bound to lead to a reassessment of a strategy which invited failure. The interest in classical republicanism shown by Sir John Wildman and Edward Sexby in later years implies not a blind willingness to attach themselves to the radical movement of the moment, whatever it might be, so much as an implicit criticism of the helpless inactivity of the Leveller movement when Cromwell and Ireton deprived them of the initiative in the autumn of 1647, and again a year later. Republicanism might be socially less radical, but it stressed the notion of effective political and military action. Between Walwyn's *The Power of Love* of 1641 (Haller 1934, II, pp. 271–304) and Sexby's *Killing No Murder* of 1657 (Wootton 1986, pp. 360–88) lay the failure of the Leveller movement and the belated development of a preoccupation with political realism. Levellers like Wildman and Sexby turned in the end to a Machiavellian politics of conspiracy and violence. Even Lilburne in exile read Machiavelli in order to understand what had gone wrong.

There was, however, an alternative to this new preoccupation with power. Between the spring of 1649 and the spring of 1650, the self-proclaimed True Levellers, under the leadership of Gerrard Winstanley, sought by cultivating waste land on communist principles to found a new society in the interstices of the old (Hill 1972; Aylmer 1984). Their strategy was pacific and principled: by gathering support they hoped slowly to deprive the propertied economy of its labour force. Far from claiming with the Levellers that political liberty was consistent with respect for private property, and that all that was required to eliminate injurious social inequality was to abolish monopolies and institute responsible government, the Diggers, or True Levellers, sought indeed to confound all ranks and orders and to reduce all to Adam's time and condition. They were Edwards' vision of disorder made flesh.

It was not only their rejection of private property which separated the True Levellers from their defeated predecessors. Winstanley had come to the view that God was nothing but the principle of reason, Christ nothing but the principle of universal love, that there was no life after death, and that heaven and hell were to be found only in this world. He saw men as the agents of their own redemption. But, far from abandoning conventional Christian language along with conventional Christian beliefs, he set out to make systematic use of millenarian imagery to express the nature of the revolutionary change he aspired to bring about. Setting aside the largely secular language of the Levellers, he sought to reshape religious images of irreversible change for his own purposes, maintaining that Babylon was soon to be brought down, and Eden to be restored.

iii   The Levellers and the constitution

The Leveller conception of political activity was based upon their confidence in the independent judgement of the common man. Yet the Levellers never called themselves democrats. What was straightforwardly obvious to Edwards was that they were opposed to monarchy and aristocracy. The question of opposition to monarchy may be divided into two subsidiary questions. In the first place there was the question of the attitude to be adopted to Charles I. Parliament in 1642 had insisted that the king's person was inviolable. Evil councillors could be brought to account, but the king's own evil actions were to be attributed to such councillors for 'the king could do no wrong'. The future Levellers were in the forefront of those contesting this view. In works such as the *Arguments proving we ought not to part with the militia* (669 f 10(60)) and Lilburne's *The Just Man's Justification* (both of June 1646) they called for the king to be subjected to exemplary punishment: a view which stood in direct opposition to the official policy of negotiation with the king and was only to win more general support with the outbreak of the second Civil War, responsibility for which the Levellers insisted must be laid at his door.

But to punish – inevitably to execute – the king was not necessarily to abolish monarchy. Republicanism was advocated as early as March of 1646 in *The Last Warning to all the Inhabitants of London* (E328(24)), followed by *The Remonstrance of Many Thousand Citizens* (Wolfe 1944, pp. 109–30) of July, and *Regall Tyrannie Discovered* (E370(12)) of January 1647, all probably the work of Overton, who held that one of the chief lessons to be drawn from history was that 'none but a king could do so great intolerable mischiefs' (Wolfe 1944, p. 115) as Charles and his predecessors had sought to do, and that the mystique of kingship had played a dangerous role in persuading men all too often to fight against their own liberties.

Opposition to monarchy had been accompanied by attacks on the members of the House of Lords as the mere creatures of royal favour, in contrast to the Commons, the representatives of the people. In June of 1646 Lilburne was imprisoned by the Lords for refusing to recognise their jurisdiction over a commoner (he had been attacking the earl of Manchester, former commander of a parliamentary army). In July Overton too was imprisoned for publishing *An alarum to the house of lords against their insolent usurpation of the Common Liberties* (E346(8)). Lilburne had insisted that Magna Carta's guarantee of trial by one's peers meant that commoners must be tried by commoners. But at the same time he attacked the very authority to which he appealed. The key statute laws which laid out the powers of king and parliament, such as Magna Carta and the Petition of Right, did not, Lilburne complained in *The Just Man's Justification*, go far enough to 'preserve the splendor and glory of that undivided Majesty and Kingship that inherently resides in the people, or the state universal, the representation or derivation of which is formally and legally in the state elective or representative and none else' (E340(12), p. 14). The attack upon king and Lords thus led to a direct statement of the ultimate supremacy of the people and the legal sovereignty of the Commons. Overton too insisted that in the eyes of God all men were equal, and true Christians should treat each other as equals. Amongst the first Christians there would have been no scope for titles such as 'gracious lords' or 'favourable lords', for they recognised 'no ruler, nor government, but by common election and consent', in other words government by the equivalent of the House of Commons (E346(8), p. 1).

Alongside their attack on the king, the lords, and statute law, Lilburne and Overton mounted an attack on the whole English legal system as the creation of William the Conqueror, who had swept away the laws of the Saxons and created the common law (Hill 1958; for a differing view: Seaberg 1981). Where once men had been tried promptly in English in the hundred courts, now they often had to attend distant courts, to await the passage of the law terms, to struggle with Latin and Law French, and to deal with an unwritten law, a judge-made law based supposedly on precedent. With such a law it was impossible to know exactly what the law was, and the resulting confusion benefited only lawyers, a profession unknown before the conquest, and the king. 'The mainstream of our Common Law, with the practice thereof, flowed out of Normandy, notwithstanding all objections can be made to the contrary, and therefore I say it came from the will of a tyrant' (E340(12), p. 13). The law must be reformed to embody central principles of equity and divine law, such as the right not to be required to incriminate oneself by being obliged to answer questions under oath, for self-incrimination was no better than self-execution, a legal suicide.

Despite appeals to Anglo-Saxon practices it was impossible to reconcile this view of the constitution with historical precedent, and easy to show that the position adopted by Lilburne and Overton was seditious. Overton's reply was to deny that the existing constitution deserved to be respected, 'for whatever our forefathers were, or whatever they did or suffered, or were enforced to yield unto, we are the men of the present age, and ought to be absolutely free from all kinds of exorbitancies, molestations, or arbitrary power' (Wolfe 1944, p. 114).

Edwards was thus correct in seeing in the writings of Lilburne and Overton an attack on monarchy, aristocracy, and the existing law and constitution. But did this make them democrats? The first step to answering this question is to realise that in one sense all supporters of parliament were democrats: after the publication of *His Majesty's Answer to the Nineteen Propositions* (Wootton 1986, pp. 171–4) in 1642, parliament claimed to be defending the 'mixed constitution' of England, in which the king represented monarchy, the House of Lords aristocracy, and the House of Commons, the representative of the people, democracy. The novelty of the Leveller position in the second half of 1646 was their insistence that the democratic element in the consitution was the only legitimate element: in attacking king and lords they were necessarily advocating an unmixed democracy, despite the fact that democracy on its own was, on the authority of Plato and Aristotle, widely believed to be the worst of all possible forms of government.

Edwards' complaint though was that the Levellers had gone beyond merely advocating supremacy for the House of Commons: they had advocated an egalitarian democracy, in which there would be no recognition of rank or status. In fact when part III of *Gangraena* was published it was no more than a few days since the Levellers had committed themselves unambiguously to this position. In *London's Liberties in Chains* (E359(17)) of October 1646 Lilburne had argued that every free man of the city should have a vote in city elections, and that in parliamentary elections rotten boroughs should be abolished and representation made proportionate to the amounts contributed in taxes by the different boroughs and counties: a policy which would have given London an overwhelming influence in parliament. But it was not until December, in *The Charters of London*, that he committed himself to a definition of the franchise which explicitly excluded a property criterion and implied that representation should be on the basis of population, not wealth, claiming that 'the poorest that lives has as true a right to give a vote as well as the richest and greatest' (E366(12), p. 4).

A year later, in October 1647, the Levellers had abandoned their strategy of the second half of 1646, which had been one of appealing to the Commons to transform the constitution and to represent the interests of the people. The Presbyterian majority in the Commons was committed to settlement with the king and the disbanding of the army. The Levellers in London, calling for religious toleration and constitutional change, shared a common interest (and common principles) with the representatives of the rank and file in the army, called agitators, who were opposed to disbandment without settlement of arrears of pay or legal indemnity for actions taken during the war. Both groups agreed to advocate the sweeping away of parliament and its replacement by a new representative, a policy outlined in the Agreement of the People. At Putney, from 28 October to 11 November, they met with the army commanders to debate the merits of this programme (Woolrych 1986). Rainsborough, an MP and an officer who nevertheless supported the rank and file and the Levellers, echoed Lilburne as he explained the Leveller programme:

For really I think that the poorest he that is in England has a life to live, as the greatest he; and therefore, truly sir, I think it's clear, that every man that is to live under a government ought first by his own consent to put himself under that government; and I do think that the poorest man in England is not at all bound in a strict sense to that government that he has not had a voice to put himself under.
(Woodhouse 1938, p. 53)

It would thus seem straightforward to conclude that the Levellers were in 1647 advocates of manhood suffrage: and one might well feel a certain sympathy with Edwards, who had complained that if all men were to have the vote, why not women (and children) too (1977, pt III, p. 154)? But this conclusion would be premature. The outcome of the discussions at Putney was a resolution of the general council of the army: 'That all soldiers and others, if they be not servants or beggars, ought to have voices in electing those which shall represent them in Parliament, although they have not forty shillings per annum in freehold land' (Woodhouse 1938, p. 452).

Was the abandonment of the traditional property qualification for county elections a victory for the Levellers, or was the exclusion of servants and beggars a defeat for the first democratic party in European political history? Scholars are sharply divided on this, as they are on the question of who exactly was meant by the terms 'servants' and 'beggars'. In May 1649 four of the Leveller leaders, imprisoned in the Tower by Cromwell, their short-lived movement dissolving around them, issued a final, uncompromising declaration of principles: the vote was to be given to 'all men of the age of one and twenty years and upwards (not being servants, or receiving alms, or having served the late king in arms or voluntary contributions) . . . those who served the king being disabled for ten years only' (Wolfe 1944, pp. 402–3). This very much suggests that the Levellers had been satisfied with the general council's resolution in November of 1647 and had accepted the outcome of the Putney debates as representing their own views. If so, they not only did not call themselves democrats, but were not democrats in our terms.

But what did the exclusion of servants and beggars imply? In December 1648, the army, victorious in the second Civil War, purged from parliament supporters of Presbyterianism and opponents of the execution of the king. The defeat for Edwards' allies looked like a victory for Lilburne's: as the army acted a committee of Levellers and Independents met to hammer out a constitution they believed the army would require the purged parliament to adopt. According to this second Agreement the electors were to be (excluding for the time being those who had supported the king) 'natives or denizens of England, such as have subscribed this agreement; not persons receiving alms, but such as are assessed ordinarily towards the relief of the poor; not servants to, or receiving wages from any particular person. And in all elections (except for the universities) they shall be men of one and twenty years old, or upwards, and housekeepers.' (Wolfe 1944, p. 297). If this second Agreement was intended to express the same position as the first and third, the Levellers intended to exclude from the vote all those who received poor relief, as opposed to those who contributed towards it; all employees in what would now be termed the private sector; and all who were not heads of households. On this basis well over half the adult male population would have been excluded from the vote (Macpherson 1962).

It is possible to argue, on the other hand, that the second Agreement is not really a Leveller document, but a compromise reached between Levellers and Independents with a view to ensuring the support of the army officers. It has been argued that the exclusion of servants and beggars after

Putney and in the third Agreement was much more limited in scope than the exclusion proposed in the second Agreement: servants, it is said, would normally have been taken to mean only living-in servants; beggars, 'sturdy beggars' who begged from door to door and had no fixed abode. Such an exclusion would have affected only a small minority of the population. Moreover, living-in servanthood was a temporary condition which mainly affected adolescents. Apprentices, for example, were living-in servants, but nobody continued to be a living-in servant after marriage, and, as nearly all men married, nearly every male would – on this reading of the Agreement – have had the vote for the greater part of his adult life.

We thus have three alternative accounts of the Leveller position: one which would see them as democrats, forced into a series of reluctant compromises from October 1647 on (Davis 1968; Morton 1970; Hampsher-Monk 1976; Thompson 1980); one which would see them as intending, at least for the most part, to give the vote to all heads of households, excluding living-in servants and vagabonds only (Thomas 1972); and one which would take them to be excluding (as the second Agreement does) all wage-workers and recipients of poor relief, in other words the greater part of the nation (Macpherson 1973). The crucial difficulty in choosing between these interpretations is the ambiguity of the word 'servants', which could mean in normal usage *either* living-in servants as contrasted to wage-workers in general, *or* all employees (Kussmaul 1981).

The best solution to this problem is to start from the fact that the Levellers were unambiguously committed in 1647 to the proposition that even the poor should vote. This clear rejection of a property test is effectively meaningless if the intention was to exclude all but the self-employed from the franchise, and we should therefore conclude that the second Agreement represents an unhappy compromise, not the Levellers' considered position, and that the third Agreement, which returns to the wording which resulted from the Putney debates, represents a minimum statement of their true convictions, which permitted the exclusion of living-in servants, but not the poor. Perhaps the Levellers, before they reached Putney, had even aspired to the establishment of manhood suffrage: if so, it is important to note that they show no sign of having felt that they had abandoned an issue of principle in giving up the idea of one man one vote. For them the principle lay elsewhere, in the rejection of the property test.

We have difficulty in believing that the householder franchise could have been anything but an unprincipled compromise because we are used to thinking in terms of the inalienable rights of individuals. We need to find our way back into the world of Thomas Cartwright, who had written, when discussing voting in the Presbyterian system of church government, 'all men understand that where the election is most freest and most general, yet only they have to do which are heads of families' (Thomas 1972, p. 72). The Levellers should be seen as advocating 'the most freest and most general' franchise, but as seeing no necessary contradiction between this and giving the vote only to heads of households. In fact they were seeking to extend to the country as a whole the franchise which already existed in those urban constituencies where the electorate was most broadly defined.

Nor did the exclusion of servants from the vote involve the Levellers in any inconsistency. Children were to be denied the vote because they were subject to a natural, pre-political authority, their parents. Wives had chosen to subject themselves to the authority of their husbands; servants to the authority of their masters. They were already, in Rainsborough's phrase, 'under government'. But heads of households were free and independent individuals who could properly be subject to no authority they had not themselves chosen. In the seventeenth century the household, gathered together under the authority of the father, seemed the natural unit of economic, political, and religious activity. Wage-labour cut across this natural system of independent households by subjecting men and women to the economic control of their neighbours. This provided a reason for arguing that the poor could not in practice vote independently. A contrasting argument, much used at Putney, was that the poor, far from being subservient to the rich, would vote to dispossess them. But the Levellers show no sign of having been persuaded by either argument: they insisted that the poor were rational individuals, capable of making sound judgements. The householder franchise embodied this principle, without giving the vote to people – wives and servants – who had directly subordinated their own judgements, in the affairs of this world at least, to someone else's. If the Levellers were guilty of an inconsistency it was merely in not asking themselves whether women (widows, for example) could ever be heads of households (see Gentles 1978, pp. 292–4): but this was an ambiguity that they were not alone in failing to face squarely.

We can summarise the Leveller position by saying the Levellers planned to give the vote to those who were entitled to wear their hats at home. The head of the household wore his hat at home while his sons and servants doffed theirs. Members of parliament wore their hats while in the parliament chamber to symbolise the fact that they alone were masters there. Radicals like Henry Marten argued that juries should wear their hats in court to symbolise the fact that they – not the judges – were the ultimate authority. And the Quakers, of course, were soon to refuse to take their. hats off to any man, insisting that sons living at home should not even take their hats off to their fathers. There is no reason to suppose that the Levellers had ever intended to commit themselves to a view on the franchise which flew as directly in the face of existing social conventions as did the Quaker refusal to do hat honour.

To call the Levellers democrats, without periphrasis, is to think in terms of the inalienable rights of individuals, not the proto-political authority of fathers, and to forget the extent to which seventeenth-century wives and servants were presumed to be able to alienate their rights, in the one case permanently, in the other temporarily. The Leveller case was not that political rights could not be alienated, that monarchy, for example, could never be legitimate: it was, first, that the present generation could not be governed by the decisions of its ancestors, any more than the status of wife or servant could be inherited; second, that certain rights (such as freedom of conscience) were inalienable, and could be claimed even by wives and servants, just as they could be by subjects against their rulers; third, that the contract between ruler and subject was a conditional one, like that between master and servant, not an unconditional one, like that (in the view of everyone but Milton) between husband and wife, and that in the event of tyranny the people could reclaim their alienated rights; and, fourth, that the best form of government was one which gave the poor not only an initial say in the form of government but also a continuing say in policy-making. The Levellers were not democrats: rather they believed that all authority must be originally founded on genuine consent, which, in the event of tyranny, the people had a right to withdraw, or, as Edwards protested, that the 'promiscuous multitude' have a right to be 'the creator and destroyer of kings, parliaments and all magistrates at their mere pleasure'.

This principle of popular sovereignty was far more fundamental to their thinking than the franchise or any constitutional question, for they believed that it provided the only secure protection for those inalienable rights which the sects wished to claim against Presbyterianism. The Levellers were willing to give the benefit of the doubt to constitutional proposals that fell short of the householder franchise, for they did not see the right to vote as inalienable: hence their willingness to approve the second Agreement of the People. But they were not willing to agree to proposals which embodied what seemed to them oppressive principles contrary to the inalienable rights of both men and women: hence their refusal during the Whitehall Debates which followed hard on Pride's Purge (December 1648) to retreat from the principle of freedom of conscience. This, much more than the franchise, was an issue of principle in the eyes of the Levellers.

The difference between the Levellers and their opponents was not generally couched in terms of constitutional forms, despite passing references by men like Richard Baxter (1696, p. 53) and Edwards to democracy, because the Levellers were primarily seen as appealing to pre-constitutional rights of nature, rights which many felt to be incompatible with constitutional government, and because the term democracy itself was so uncertain in its meaning. But the demise of the Leveller movement did not mean the demise of the householder franchise they had advocated. Harrington consistently defended such a franchise, while seeking to combine it with bicameral government and a property test for election to the upper house. A few years later, Sir William Petty, the founder of political economy, was to express his approval of 'democracy', meaning by it the franchise advocated in the third Agreement of the People (Amati and Aspromourgos 1985). To call the Levellers 'democrats' is misleading and anachronistic. But if one means by the term what Petty meant by it, the prochronism is one of decades, not centuries. When we feel the need to use the word 'democracy' in describing Leveller proposals, we are responding as contemporaries and near-contemporaries did to the revolution in political thought that they had inaugurated.

iv   Free grace and toleration

We have seen that the Levellers were not, strictly speaking, revolutionaries or democrats, although it is hard to avoid these terms in describing their convictions. This leaves us with a final problem, that of where their convictions came from. The simplest solution was provided by Marchamont Nedham in 1647:

> A Scot and a Jesuit, joined in hand
> First taught the world to say
> That subjects ought to have command
> And Princes to obey.
>
> (E411(8), p. 33)

Neither the Jesuits nor the Scots, however, had clearly envisaged a situation where power would revert from the estates of the realm, who normally were expected to sit in judgement on a tyrant, to the individual subjects. They foresaw circumstances in which the estates might be prevented from acting and individuals might temporarily have to act on their behalf, assassinating, for example, a tyrant who was preventing the estates from meeting; or circumstances in which constituencies might have to recall their representatives for dereliction of duty. But they did not conceive of a situation where the absence of a constitutional check on tyranny would lead to the dissolution of government, a return to the state of nature, and the establishment of a new constitution. Although there was some discussion of this as a theoretical possibility in the early stages of the Civil War, the first author to regard this, not as a dreadful prospect or a counsel of despair, but as a practical proposal was the author of *England's Miserie and Remedie* (1645; Wootton 1986, pp. 38–58), a work which appeals to the authority of George Buchanan. As we have seen, the broad franchise that existed in some borough constituencies in early seventeenth-century England may have facilitated the construction of this radical theory of popular sovereignty.

At first sight this would seem a full and complete picture of the origins of Leveller views on popular sovereignty. It is not, however, the one that historians have generally favoured. And, indeed, some further element appears necessary to complete this account. For why was the idea of starting a state *de novo*, which had simply never been considered by previous thinkers, who had assumed that legitimacy derived from past undertakings, rapidly embraced by the Levellers? Why were they prepared to go so far as to insist that no individual could be subjected to an authority that was not of his own choosing? Why were they prepared to consider something close to democracy a viable form of government?

The simplest answer to these questions consists in the claim that the Levellers were applying to politics the religious practices of the sects (Robertson 1951, pp. 28–9; Morton 1970, pp. 14–16). For decades sectarians had separated themselves from the established church, established new churches based on covenants, which were nothing other than contracts or agreements, and had governed these new churches on democratic principles (Tolmie 1977). Lilburne was a separatist by 1638. Overton may have been a member of a Dutch Baptist congregation in 1615–16, and was once more a Baptist in 1646. Much of the Levellers' strongest support came from the leaders of separatist congregations, such as Samuel Chidley (Gentles 1978). The Levellers never claimed that their political philosophy derived from separatist religious principles: to do so would have been immediately to restrict its potential support to those who were separatist in religion. Nevertheless, the connection between politics and religion is apparent in, for example, Overton's claim that the first Christians governed themselves 'by common election and consent'. The daily practice of the sects thus made thinkable what was previously scarcely conceivable: constitutional revolution and democratic accountability. The political philosophy of Robert Bellarmine and Buchanan, as expounded by Samuel Rutherford or John Maxwell, provided opportunities for anyone who wanted to extend these practices from church to state.

Unfortunately, the argument cannot rest here. Our second simple answer is no more complete than the first. Central to the classical theology of the sects was the stress on the difference between the small number of the elect, the saints gathered into churches, and the mass of the reprobate. How could practices appropriate for a godly minority be equally suitable for an ungodly majority (Woodhouse 1938, pp. [1]–[100])? The gathered churches depended on their ability to expel backsliders from their communion, but the Commonwealth was necessarily an inclusive, not an exclusive, community. It was therefore natural for Puritans to argue that only the godly should rule. Milton and Baxter maintained that the wicked should be denied civil rights, while the Fifth Monarchists expected Christ himself to come and separate the godly from the ungodly, establishing the saints in unshakeable control.

How then could sectarian theology lead to democratic philosophy? One answer to this question has been to see key Levellers as adopting a rationalist position which denied the significance of the Fall, and thus of the Puritan distinction between the godly and the ungodly. Overton has often been presented as a rationalist because in *Mans Mortalitie* (1644; 1968) he argued that reason showed the soul to be mortal: but this is no evidence that he did not believe in the promise of resurrection to be found in the gospel (Burns 1972). Walwyn claimed to learn true Christianity from the sceptical Montaigne. He attacked all existing churches and clergy without exception. He was accused of denying that the Bible could be shown to be the word of God and of believing that there was no hell. When he defended himself by affirming his belief in the Bible he scarcely mended matters by comparing reading it to searching for a pearl lost in a field, while his defenders admitted that he had in the past believed that all would be saved.

Walwyn himself thought that the proper test of a doctrine was its utility. For him Christianity was above all a religion of the Golden Rule. Christian love had led the apostles to communism, and must lead present-day Christians to political and perhaps social revolution. He did not seek to defend this view by quoting texts, but merely redefined Christianity in the light of it: 'The politicians of this world would have religious men to be fools, not to resist, no by no means, lest you receive damnation: urging God's Holy Word whilst they proceed in their damnable courses; but (beloved) they will find that true Christians are of all men the most valiant defenders of the just liberties of their country' (Haller and Davies 1944, p. 299).

Walwyn himself was scarcely likely to confess to religious scepticism – the claim that he no longer believed in universal salvation was surely made in knowledge of the fact that the Blasphemy Ordinance of 1648 provided the death penalty for denying there was a day of judgement after death – but, whatever his private convictions, they can scarcely be adduced to explain the approval his views met with from a Lilburne or a Chidley. If sceptical arguments made a contribution to Leveller thinking – and we will see that Walwyn was not alone in insisting on the limits of natural reason – there must also have been a way of defending Leveller political philosophy as compatible with good theology.

Some historians have argued that Leveller political thinking was dependent upon a particular theological doctrine, that of 'free grace', termed by its opponents antinomianism (e.g. Davis 1973). Free grace, they argue, meant that Christ had died for all, and that all would (as Walwyn at one time believed), or at least in principle could (as those who believed in free will would claim), be saved. By denying that any were predestined to damnation, and by insisting that even sinners could be saved, it opened the way to a new sense of the equality of all men in God's eyes, and thus made a democratic political theory plausible. Walwyn, who proudly claimed to have been converted to what others termed antinomian principles, is seen by these commentators, not as a sceptic, but as a Christian radical who drew political conclusions from the theology of free grace (Mulligan 1982). Lilburne, an orthodox Calvinist at the beginning of the Civil War, is said to have been converted to it, a conversion which made the Leveller movement possible. Thus the author of *Vox Plebis* (1646) could appeal to free grace against feudal bondage, and treat the law of nature and the law of grace as identical, as if the Fall had been without consequence:

For as God created every man free in Adam, so by nature are all alike freemen born; and are since made free in grace by Christ; no guilt of the parent being of sufficiency to deprive the child of this freedom. And although there was that wicked and unchristian-like custom of villeiny introduced by the Norman Conqueror; yet was it but a violent usurpation upon the law of our creation, nature . . . and is now, since the clear light of the Gospel hath shined forth . . ., quite abolished as a thing odious both to God and man . . .   (E362(20), p. 4)

This argument is an elegant one. Leaving aside minor objections – such as the difficulty of tracing Lilburne's evolution from orthodox Calvinism to Quakerism – it unfortunately suffers from a central defect: the doctrine of free grace in no way implied a belief in universal salvation (Solt 1959; Wallace 1982), which is why Walwyn was able to continue appealing to free grace even when his friends had denied that he still believed that there would be no hell. It did not even imply a belief in free will. Roger Williams, who certainly believed that only a chosen minority would be saved, advocated free grace, and John Saltmarsh's *Free Grace* (1645; E1152(1)), was not, as has been claimed, an attack upon the Calvinist doctrine of election (Morton 1970, pp. 45–69), but a defence of a strict interpretation of it against those who would make salvation dependent on repentance, a holy life, and good works. Saltmarsh took it as axiomatic that some were elected to salvation before all time: but he also maintained that all those who had true faith would be saved through Christ's free grace, whether they were sinners or not. So much was promised in the gospel, and it was unprofitable to try to determine whether one's own faith was of the sort peculiar to the elect, the sort which guaranteed salvation.

The late 1640s certainly saw widespread uncertainty about the meaning and truth of the Calvinist doctrine of predestination, and this may well, as A.S.P. Woodhouse maintained, have helped to undermine Puritan inegalitarianism. But the central theological issue which was crucial to the religious defence of Leveller principles was one which was largely irrelevant to the debate over predestination and free will, and quite separate from the question of universal salvation. It was, however, central to the doctrine of free grace, whether in the form in which it was presented by Saltmarsh, or the more radical form in which it was adopted by Walwyn, and it lay at the heart of the debate over antinomianism. The issue was that of the relationship between the Old and New Testaments (Woodhouse 1938, pp. [53]–[7], [87]–[90]), and it was in fact the central issue between the separatists and those who advocated religious uniformity.

All Christians agreed that in part God's revelation of his covenant in the Old Testament merely prefigured his promise of salvation in the New.

Thus baptism replaced circumcision, and the new dispensation of grace in part abrogated the Mosaic law, which was a mere 'shadow' of it. The crucial debate between the exponents of free grace or 'antinomians' and the orthodox Presbyterians was over how far this principle that the old law was merely a 'type' of which the gospel was the 'antitype', merely a prefiguration which must now be dispensed with, should be extended. For Williams, whose *Bloudy Tenent* of 1644 (1963) was one of the first and most influential defences of a nearly universal toleration, the principle was a radical one which undermined the whole idea of a holy commonwealth (Miller 1953; Bercovich 1967). The state of Israel in the Old Testament had been a holy commonwealth sustained by legal compulsion, but it merely prefigured the church, which was to be a purely voluntary assembly sustained by faith. The New Testament provided no portrait of Christian magistracy: if God's commands to the Old Testament kings could not be adduced as of continuing validity, then Christians could have no claim to impose their beliefs on others. There was therefore no need for Christians to seek to enforce through the civil law the Old Testament injunctions requiring religious uniformity. The spheres of competence of church and state must be sharply separated, and the state must concern itself only with this-worldly affairs according to the principles of natural reason.

This decisive distinction between the political dispensation of the Old Testament and the spiritual dispensation of the New was rejected by Presbyterians. They maintained that the ten commandments were of continuing force and covered idolatry, heresy, and blasphemy. The magistrate was as much under an obligation to repress heresy as to punish murder. The Independents took the view that even if the magistrate could not compel people to adopt the true religion he was certainly under an obligation to prevent them from openly practising and advocating false religions. For both Presbyterians and Independents the nation of Israel provided the ideal exemplar for a national church. Only the sects and the Levellers, who were opposed to the whole idea of a national church, were prepared to maintain that the magistrate had neither compulsive nor restrictive power in matters of religion.

In December 1648 at Whitehall, Independents, Levellers, representatives of gathered churches and army officers debated the terms of a new constitution – the officers' Agreement – which they expected to see imposed upon parliament, and much of the debate centred on the question of toleration (Polizzotto 1975). Ireton, who at Putney had been the leading opponent of Leveller views on the franchise, was here the leading opponent of their views on toleration. Ireton's claim was that the first four of the ten commandments were known to be true from natural reason and from divine revelation, that they had not been abrogated by the gospel, and should therefore be enforced by the magistrate. To these claims the radical Independent John Goodwin, who was at this time ministering to a gathered church and working in uneasy collaboration with the Levellers, replied that while certain moral principles were self-evident by the light of nature, monotheism was not, and therefore should not be required of people by the magistrate on the grounds that it was a precept of natural law. As for Ireton's claim that Old Testament magistrates must be a model for Christian magistrates, he appealed to the theology of type and antitype to deny that the state of Israel was anything other than a prefiguration of the church.

Goodwin's arguments, both those from theology and those from natural reason, but particularly those from natural reason, were supported by Wildman: 'It is not easy by the light of nature to determine [that] there is a God. The sun may be that God. The moon may be that God. To frame a right conception or notion of the First Being, wherein all other things had their being, is not [possible] by the light of nature' (Woodhouse 1938, p. 161). In view of this, even if the magistrate believes he knows the truth, he must recognise that he is at least as likely to err as anyone else, and admit that by imposing uniformity he is more likely to do harm than good.

The Levellers thus saw the state as a purely secular institution, required to conform only to the principles of natural reason, and obliged to leave to the individual questions of private conscience which depended on belief, not certain knowledge. Not only could people not be compelled to believe against their will; they could not alienate the right to worship as they thought best, for in matters of religion and worship 'we cannot remit or exceed a tittle of what our consciences dictate to be the mind of God, without wilful sin' (Wolfe 1944, p. 227).

This approach to the question, in terms of the rights of the individual, not the duties of the magistrate, was one that Ireton could not accept: even if natural reason might provide no decisive court of appeal, revelation clearly outlawed idolatry and required its punishment. In the end the dispute between the Levellers and their opponents on the question of toleration therefore turned on a central question of theology, that of the relationship between Old Testament and New. For Ireton, the appeal to the Old Testament was a valid one; for those who defended 'free grace' such an appeal could not be employed to alter or extend in any substantial way the teaching of the New.

When Walwyn insisted that free grace was the *unum necessarium*, it was not because it implied universal salvation, but because the doctrine of free grace required this sharp dichotomy between Old Testament and New, between the Mosaic law, which demanded obedience, and the Christian gospel, which offered salvation. If sinners could be saved, it was impossible in this world to know who were the saints who should rule and who the reprobate who should obey: free grace had democratic implications. If the Old Testament dispensation had been abrogated, government must be seen as man-made according to the principles of natural reason, not divinely ordained, and what man had made he could change so that it more adequately served his purposes. If grace was free, then the magistrate was not obliged to punish the wicked for their own moral good and as an example to others, but only insofar as was necessary for the protection of society. He no longer had any role to play in the salvation of men's souls, or any obligation to prevent the ungodly from sharing power with the godly.

In April 1649 Overton summed up the central issue in the toleration debate as follows:

As I am in myself in respect to my own personal sins and transgressions, so I am to myself and to God, and so I must give an account; the just must stand by his own faith. But as I am in relation to the Commonwealth, that all men have cognizance of, because it concerns their own particular lives, livelihoods and beings, as well as my own; and my failings and evils in that respect I yield up to the cognizance of all men, to be righteously used against me. So that the business is, not how great a sinner I am, but how faithful and real to the Commonwealth; that's the matter concerneth my neighbour . . . And till persons professing religion be brought to this sound temper, they fall far short of Christianity; the spirit of love, brotherly charity, doing to all men as they would be done by, is not in them.

(Haller and Davies 1944, p. 231)

This appeal to brotherly love sounds straightforward, but it could persuade only those who had abandoned the idea of a holy commonwealth modelled on the Old Testament state of Israel, and who no longer expected God to punish idolatry with plague and fire, to hold whole communities responsible for the sins of a few in their midst. It could thus persuade only those who were sceptics and rationalists, or, more importantly, those who accepted the radical type/antitype theology expounded by Williams.

Leveller arguments were thus founded on a theological presumption: that men, created free in Adam, born free by nature, had indeed, as *Vox Plebis* put it, been once again 'made free in grace by Christ' after the servitude of the Mosaic law. This presumption did not require a belief in free will or general redemption; but it did require a belief that the Old

Testament was now of allegorical rather than literal significance, and that politics was now a matter for natural reason, not revelation. This presumption guaranteed that there could be no Presbyterian Levellers, and only cautious collaboration between Independents and Levellers. As Goodwin protested during the Whitehall Debates, to write the Leveller view on toleration (a view he agreed with in principle) into a constitution would be to adopt a theological position. Far from implying a mere practical toleration for all religious views, it implied that the government condemned the religion of the majority, which was based upon a different conception of grace.

Once again, anachronism beckons. The Levellers were not revolutionaries, but advocates of revolution; not democrats, but nearly so; not secular thinkers, but (for the most part at least) Christians who welcomed for theological reasons the idea of a secular society; not original philosophers, and yet the first to give practical political expression to arguments which had previously seemed no more than hypothetical possibilities. Certainly, they are not our contemporaries; but equally certainly their capacity to think and argue was not restricted by any conventional commitment to hierarchy, tradition, or outward godliness. There was never any prospect of their views gaining general acceptance in their own day; but Hobbes may have paid attention to them (Wootton 1986, pp. 56–8), and Locke was almost certainly influenced by them (Ashcraft 1986), as Tom Paine was by Locke. Eventually whole societies were to acknowledge the principles of the Agreement of the People, principles born out of second-hand scholastic philosophy (see Tierney 1982) combined with the practice and, equally importantly, the theology of the sects. Out of the disjointed and discarded arguments of Bellarmine and Buchanan, coupled with those of Saltmarsh and Williams, the Levellers built a coherent political philosophy. In large part that philosophy is still ours today, although, since few of us now believe the arguments out of which it was first constructed, or share the experiences which first gave it meaning, a study of its origins can serve only to emphasise the continuing difficulty of defending it against the claims of precedent and privilege.

15

English republicanism

BLAIR WORDEN

i Sources and resources

The contribution of seventeenth-century republicanism to the development of western political thought was made principally in England. In Italy the vitality of Renaissance republicanism had been largely extinguished by 1600; in Holland the emergence of the independent United Provinces produced little systematic exploration of republican principles;[1] in France, Spain, and the empire the domestic opposition to the advances of absolutism was particularist rather than republican. In England, the breakdown of political institutions between 1640 and 1660 stimulated a more profound reexamination of political belief and practice. The ideas of the English republicans are not easy to classify. Writing in order to shape events, they adapted their arguments and their emphases to immediate circumstances. Usually writing in opposition to the prevailing power, they drew heavily on ideas of contract and resistance and of natural rights which were not peculiarly republican. Their constitutional proposals were flexible, and the form of government often mattered less to them than its spirit. The term republican was not, on the whole, one which they sought, and was more commonly one of abuse. Nevertheless, a republican tradition can be identified which was to enter the mainstream of eighteenth-century political ideas in Britain, on the continent, and in America.[2]

In the emergence of that tradition there were three main stages. The first, and most fruitful, belongs to the Interregnum of 1649–60. It was a response to the execution of Charles I in 1649, to the abolition of monarchy and of the House of Lords in the same year, and to the ensuing failure of a series of

---

1. For introductions to what there was of it, see Kossmann 1960; Rowen 1978; Haitsma Mulier 1980.
2. The most recent literature on seventeenth-century republicanism is summarised by Pocock 1985, pp. 215–34. See also Nuzzo 1984.

improvised Puritan regimes to provide a durable alternative to kingship –
an alternative which the republican writers of the Interregnum sought to
provide. The first into the field was Marchamont Nedham; the most
eloquent was John Milton; and the most penetrating and influential was
James Harrington, even though in some respects his ideas were eccentric to
the prevailing character of the movement. The second stage was a response
to the political crisis of 1675–83, when the menaces of absolute monarchy
and of a Catholic succession brought the prospect of renewed civil war; it
was now that the republicans Henry Nevile and Algernon Sidney made
their main contribution to political thought. The third stage was produced
by the fresh constitutional anxieties of the 1690s. Although the Revolution
of 1688–9 had dispelled the immediate threat of tyranny, liberty seemed
newly endangered by the expansion of the executive, by corruption, by the
emasculation of parliamentary independence, and, from 1697, by the
maintenance of a standing army in peacetime. The principal republican
writings of this period were by Robert Molesworth, Walter Moyle, John
Trenchard, John Toland, and the Scot Andrew Fletcher (for whom see
Robertson 1985).

Despite the developments and adjustments of republican thought
between 1650 and 1700, there are enough consistent elements in republicanism to enable us to study it as a body of ideas. At its centre was a
desire to learn from and to emulate the achievements of the commonwealths of classical antiquity – principally Sparta and, above all, Rome. It
was in England that the classical vision of Italian Renaissance humanists was
preserved (and adapted) in the seventeenth century, and it was from there
that it subsequently reentered political thought elsewhere. Humanist
political thought in England rested on a base of educated interest in classical
politics that broadened significantly from around 1570. By 1640 Thomas
Hobbes had developed his belief, which he was often to express, that the
English monarchy owed its difficulties to the study by its subjects of 'the
books of policy, and histories, of the ancient Greeks and Romans' – not
least Aristotle's *Politics*.[3] His claim has made little impression on historians,
who have been struck rather by the constitutional conservatism of Charles
I's parliamentary opponents, by their reluctance to move beyond the
insular and customary terms of conventional debate, and by the improvised
and limited content of the political theory used to justify regicide in 1649. It

---

3. Hobbes 1839–45, II, pp. 153, 171–2, III, pp. 202–3, IV, pp. 219, 314–15, VI, pp. 192–3, 233. Cf.
 Harrington 1977, p. 178.

is indeed doubtful whether anyone in pre-Civil War England believed that the fundamental principles of the ancient constitution could be changed. Even in the later seventeenth century republicanism seemed to most people a bookish, utopian ideal, beyond the reach of humans whose natural weaknesses made the 'outward pomp and gilding' of monarchy indispensable (Foxcroft 1898, II, pp. 287–8, 460–1). In any case the lessons to be drawn from classical politics were not necessarily republican ones. There were probably as many critics of the instability of republican Rome as admirers of its virtues, and more admirers of Augustus Caesar than of Marcus Brutus.

Yet within Hobbes' overstatement lay a substantial point. Republican ideas might be missing from the political treatises of the generations before the Civil War, but they were often explored in imaginative literature: in Sir Philip Sidney's *Arcadia* and the verse of his friend Fulke Greville (Worden 1986); and in plays by Shakespeare, Jonson, and their contemporaries which indicate not merely the public interest in the evils of courts and tyranny but the alertness to Roman political thought and history which playwrights could expect from their audiences. The same concerns are evident in the private written reflections of noblemen and gentlemen dismayed by the growing powers and the growing ostentation of the Renaissance monarchies of England and the continent and by the corresponding decline of representative institutions – a process to which the decay of the Roman republic and the rise of the empire appeared to offer pressing parallels (Worden 1981, pp. 185–90). A similar dismay can be found after the Restoration of 1660, when it was 'country party' or 'country Whig' politicians and landowners to whom republican works came to be principally addressed and among whom republicanism – albeit in a diluted form – exerted its political influence.

The fountainhead of the classical political inheritance was Aristotle. His was the vocabulary with which seventeenth-century men studied the forms of government and conceived of politics as the pursuit of the good life. His account of constitutions was supplemented by Book VI of Polybius' *Histories* – although this was an exclusive taste, not yet available in English. Plutarch's *Lives*, which taught morality rather than theory, was a less demanding and more widely read work, the *Life* of Lycurgus having a special interest for republicans. Cicero, who equipped them with a conception of political justice and of its relationship to good government, probably did more than anyone to shape their reading of Aristotle. Livy provided the essential map of Roman history, and struck a responsive chord with his lament for the lost virtues of an earlier age. Tacitus supplied vivid images of tyranny which the evils of Stuart rule were often held to reflect. The histories of Sallust and Quintilian were likewise keenly studied. History to republicans was the beginning of political wisdom. Believing that 'the same causes will produce like effects in all ages',[4] they saw the past as a storehouse of examples, where constant, universal principles underlay the fluctuations of events – although sometimes, as in the works of Algernon Sidney and of Fletcher, there is a competing awareness of history as an organic process, and a greater interest in the relationship of event to context.

Republicans found their principal guide to antiquity in Machiavelli (Raab 1964; Pocock 1975). Despite the obloquy that still attached to his name, Machiavelli's influence was widespread, especially after the appearance in English of *The Discourses* (1636) and *The Prince* (1640). Although the study of Machiavelli was never thought of as a substitute for a knowledge of the broad classical inheritance on which he had provided an angled commentary, we shall find ways in which the outlook of English republicans was essentially Machiavellian. But republican ideas were not stimulated only by books. They were nourished, too, by travel. On the continent, Englishmen were able to compare the sway of popery, poverty, and tyranny in France and Spain with the heroic exploits of the small republics: of the prosperous United Provinces, which had cast off the Spanish yoke; of Switzerland, the capital of the reformed religion; and of Venice, which had thwarted the Counter-Reformation papacy. Admiration for the United Provinces was curbed by a suspicion that its constitution, a bizarre and improvised solution to the needs of war, could not last; Switzerland was admired more for its military than for its constitutional organisation; but Venice, which seemed uniquely to have learned how to combine liberty with stability, aroused acute interest among Englishmen, who loved to visit it, who by 1600 were already suspected of imbibing republican principles there (Norbrook 1984, p. 130), and who studied its elaborate constitution mainly in the accounts by Donato Giannotti (not available in English) and Gasparo Contarini (translated in 1599).

English republicanism was 'a language, not a programme' (Pocock, in Harrington 1977, p. 15). Only rarely were its exponents uncompromisingly opposed to kingship (cf. Fink 1945; Weston 1984). They did point

4. *Argument* 1697, p. 5. Cf. Harrington 1977, pp. 311, 687, 770; Sidney 1772, pp. 134, 220.

repeatedly to the inherent disadvantages of monarchy: hereditary kings were often incapable and usually behaved as if they were owners rather than servants of their countries; elective monarchies, preferable in other respects, produced wars of succession; and even virtuous rulers, bound by constitutional restraints, were liable to be corrupted by power and to extend it at the subject's expense. Yet republicans knew from Aristotle and Polybius that a healthy and durable state is one in which there are mixed or balanced the three principles of government – the rule of the one, of the few, and of the many – and their corresponding forms – monarchy, aristocracy, and democracy. Even in the 1650s, when it was much easier to argue publicly against monarchy than it became after 1660, Harrington and his followers were prepared to concede a role for a 'single person' in government, albeit usually a temporary one. Republicans after the Restoration, sometimes more concerned to emphasise the people's right to set up whatever form of government they chose than to assert the merits of a particular form, were normally willing to concede the validity of 'mixed', 'regular', 'regulated', 'limited', 'legal monarchy', which they contrasted with the evil of 'absolute monarchy'[5] (or occasionally of hereditary monarchy, although in general they conceded the people's right to establish hereditary rule[6]). After 1688, anxious not to jeopardise the admittedly restricted gains which the Revolution had brought, the heirs of Harrington became even readier to distance themselves from the 're-publican pretences' of outright opponents of monarchy, even though the language of 'mixed monarchy' became less attractive to republicans now that the court had adopted it for its own (Toland 1702, p. 4; Harrington 1700, p. vii).

Republicans never claimed that the existence of the English monarchy was constitutionally invalid. Even Nedham, celebrating in 1650 the overthrow of the ancient constitution the previous year, thought 'no sober man' capable of affirming that Englishmen had lived 'in times past under an unlawful magistracy' (Nedham 1971, I, p. 322). The republican complaint was rather that the true character of the monarchy had been perverted. In the middle ages it had been an elective rather than an hereditary institution, even if for convenience the people had usually elected the eldest son.[7] Although for varying reasons all republicans believed medieval kingship to

5. Sidney 1666?, pp. 22, 67, 195–211, 1772, pp. 111, 160, 164, 248, 266–7, 333, 339–40, 437; *Argument* 1697, p. 2; Moyle 1969, p. 243; Fletcher 1732, pp. 8–9, 39, 383, 390. Cf. Harrington 1977, p. 401.
6. Sidney 1666?, pp. 17, 31; Sidney 1772, pp. 80, 139; Moyle 1969, p. 226.
7. Milton 1953–82, III, p. 203; Sidney 1666?, p. 12; Sidney 1772, pp. 45–6, 91, 95, 203, 321, 377.

have been unsatisfactory, they agreed that only in more recent times had the institution become intolerable. Admittedly the role which they envisaged for a 'single person' in their own time is hard to locate. That perhaps is because, true to their country party perspective, they showed so little interest in the working of the executive. Once the constitution had been remodelled on classical principles, they seemed to imply, there would be little for an executive to do.

Less important in the minds of republicans than the presence or absence of a king was the distinction, which they inherited from the Protestant resistance theorists of the later sixteenth century, between government imposed from above and that derived from consent. The former was rule in the interest of one or a few men, of a 'separate and distinct interest' from the people. The latter was government in the interest of the whole: a 'commonwealth' governing for the 'common weal'. Equally important in republican minds – although no more original – was the distinction between the rule of law and the rule of men.[8] Law was the embodiment of reason: men who ruled other than in the service of law became the slaves of will, lust, and passion, while those who served or supported them were guilty of idolatry, of the enslavement and debasement of the will. A commonwealth where law prevailed, whether or not it had a king, was a 'free state': its antithesis was tyranny. With one half of their minds republicans condemned the tyrannical evils wrought by kingship in the world around them; with the other they clung to the Aristotelian and Ciceronian equation of true kingship with law and justice and reason, and to 'that excellent maxim of the ancients (almost exploded in this age) that the interest of kings and of their people is the same' (Nevile 1675, 'Letter', p. 4). They offered first and foremost a criticism of tyrants rather than of kings. 'If I attack tyrants,' asked Milton, 'what is this to kings . . .? As a good man differs from a bad, so much, I hold, does a king differ from a tyrant' (Milton 1953–82, IV (i), p. 561). 'Nothing is farther from my intention', echoed Sidney, 'than to speak irreverently of kings' (Sidney 1772, p. 160). Even so, in the seventeenth century the reign of a true Aristotelian king was, observed Sidney, merely 'a distant imaginary possibility' (p. 387). The republicans' criticisms of existing monarchies were too penetrating to be met within the ancient constitution, whose grip on the seventeenth-century political imagination they helped to loosen.

8. Milton 1953–82, III, pp. 199–200; Harrington 1977, pp. 170, 205, 401; Sidney 1666?, p. 200; Sidney 1772, p. 1; *Argument* 1697, p. 2.

ii Writers and writings

Although the Civil War prompted a fresh interest in Venice and in classical constitutions (Smith 1971, pp. 38–9), it was only after the execution of the king that the aim of emulating them was extensively canvassed. The erection of the Commonwealth in 1649 introduced the one period in the seventeenth century when kingship was outlawed and when the term 'free state' unambiguously meant a kingless commonwealth. To show 'that a free state is much more excellent than any other form' was the aim of Nedham (Nedham 1971, IV, p. 101). Although the liveliest writer among the English republicans, his adoption of republicanism was opportunist. A royalist caught plotting against the new regime, he earned his pardon by becoming editor in 1650 of the government's newspaper *Mercurius Politicus* and by writing, over the next two years, editorials to justify the abolition of monarchy and to win support for the republic. Some of them were taken from his *The Case of the Commonwealth of England Stated* (1650); others would reappear in his *The Excellency of a Free State* (1656). As editor, Nedham found himself in the role, unusual for an English republican, of advocate rather than critic of government policies, to the development of which his editorials were finely attuned. Classical, continental and English history were looted for illustrations of the superiority of republics, illustrations which have a distinctively Machiavellian ring. It was at the same time (1651–2) that Nedham's friend Milton was exploring Machiavelli's writings (Milton 1953–82, I, p. 512). Milton wished the new republic to become 'another Rome in the West' (VII, p. 357); and the background to Nedham's editorials is the military and naval exploits which earned the infant Commonwealth heady comparisons with republican Greece and Rome. Nedham's newspaper gave a mouthpiece to a republican group in parliament which included Algernon Sidney and Harrington's friend Nevile (Worden 1981, pp. 195–9). But Nedham was close too to army radicals who were impatient of the Commonwealth's tardiness in introducing social reform. Nedham is perhaps socially the most radical of the republicans, for his attacks on kings are assaults also on that 'lordly interest' (Nedham 1971, IV, pp. 213ff, 245ff) to which peers and the rich were likewise thought to belong, and against which much of the army's social criticism was directed. While other republicans admired Venice, Nedham dismissed it as an oligarchy or 'multiplied monarchy';[9]

9. Nedham 1971, III, pp. 310–11, IV, pp. 165ff, 245ff, 293ff, 389ff, V, pp. 5ff, 37ff.

and unlike other republicans he was drawn more to democratic Athens than to aristocratic Sparta. His aim was to win support for the Commonwealth from independent freeholders, the class which republicans saw as the equivalent, in the predominantly agricultural society of England, to the citizenry of republican Rome and of Machiavelli's Florence.

With the appearance in 1656 of Harrington's *Oceana*, we encounter a major thinker. Harrington belonged to a family of ancient gentry in the Midlands. Having travelled on the continent in the 1630s, he kept out of the Civil Wars, but in 1647 entered the service of the imprisoned king, for whom he developed a warm fondness, and whose execution was a great blow to him. At one level *Oceana* – like the Horatian Ode of Harrington's intimate friend Andrew Marvell – can be understood as an attempt to come to terms with the brutal abolition of the old order and with the new facts of power. The work was also a response to Oliver Cromwell's seizure of power in 1653. It is likely that Harrington was in touch with the 'commonwealthmen' – a group of parliamentary and army leaders who wished to restore the republic Cromwell had destroyed. Even so, *Oceana* was ostensibly loyal to the Protector, whom it invited to fill the role of republican lawgiver. Harrington's hostility to him became evident only in 1659, after Cromwell's death, when Harrington published *The Art of Lawgiving* and some shorter works. His purpose now was to persuade his countrymen to grasp the opportunity created by the collapse of the Protectorate to design the constitution afresh. By the autumn his hopes were probably failing. It was now that the Rota Club, a brilliant constitutional talking-shop, was founded under his chairmanship. The club disintegrated as the return of monarchy approached in 1660. In 1661 Harrington wrote a pithy manuscript work 'A System of Politics', but thereafter his days as a creative political thinker were past. Harrington is not an easy writer. Thrilling aphoristic perceptions leap from passages of uncertain syntax and meaning. But persistence is rewarded.

Oceana is a plea for the political philosophy of Machiavelli, 'whose books are neglected' (Harrington 1977, p. 161), against that of Hobbes, whose *Leviathan* had appeared in 1651. Many features of Hobbes' thought dismayed Harrington: his scorn for the lessons of history and experience, for classical political thought, for the principle of mixed government, and for civic participation; his pessimistic account of human nature; his reduction of politics to mechanical and abstract hypotheses. With Machiavelli, Harrington began by reflecting on the past. Like Machiavelli, too, he believed that political stability and health could be attained only by a radical departure from the practice of the present and by a return to the wisdom of antiquity: to what Harrington called 'ancient prudence'. Europe, he believed, had turned fatally to 'modern prudence' when the barbarian invasion broke the Roman Empire and 'deformed the whole face of the world with those ill features of government which at this time are become far worse in these western parts, except Venice' (p. 161). His repudiation of medieval politics presented a fundamental challenge to the conventional terms of discussion. To Charles I's parliamentary opponents – and to Harrington's republican successors – the 'Gothic' polities of Europe and the 'ancient constitution' of medieval England, whatever their defects, had sustained a liberty which early modern monarchy had undermined. Harrington swept such notions aside. The Gothic constitution had been 'no other than a wrestling match' between crown and nobility (p. 196); and now it was in ruins. Salvation lay not in its resurrection but in its abandonment, and in the adaptation of classical political principles to English circumstances. To those principles he added, as he believed, a discovery of his own which, if the nation would only grasp it, would transform political understanding and make possible, amidst an instability even more chronic in England than elsewhere in mid-seventeenth-century Europe, the creation of a perfect and permanent commonwealth.

That discovery was 'the doctrine of the balance' (p. 580). Its premise was that political power always follows economic power; and to Harrington, as to most of his republican successors of the century, economic power was landed power. As his admirer David Hume was to say, Harrington 'made property the foundation of all government' (Smith 1971, p. 147). The secret of political stability, in Harrington's eyes, was to ensure that the balance of political power in a nation reflected the balance of economic power. That principle, he believed, had often been dimly perceived: by Machiavelli, 'who hath missed it very narrowly' (Harrington 1977, p. 166), but also by Aristotle, by Plutarch, by Walter Ralegh and Francis Bacon (two authors from whom he derived much of his understanding of English history), and by Harrington's contemporary John Selden (whose studies of land tenure, together with those of Sir Henry Spelman, made the formulation of Harrington's thesis possible). Harrington turned the principle of the balance into the starting point of constitutional design. In classical terms, the predominant form of government – monarchy, aristocracy, or democracy – must be chosen according to the distribution of landed wealth. But Harrington also believed that the only government capable of answering to the 'interest' of the whole community, and so of achieving 'a full perfection' (p. 180), was a predominantly democratic one (although not a purely democratic one, for Harrington's classical instincts rebelled against all pure forms of government). It so happened that economic developments had made the 'popular government' or 'equal commonwealth' which he wished to see in England not only possible but inevitable. The disintegration of the Gothic polity in the Civil Wars had given England an opportunity to establish a commonwealth which would not merely emulate the glory of the Roman republic but, by building the principle of the balance into its constitution, achieve the immortality which republican Rome had been denied.

The Gothic polities, in Harrington's eyes, had been predominantly aristocratic. To his republican successors of the Restoration period, that characteristic was a virtue; but not to him. He believed that the English monarchy, having given the nobility its feudal lands, had become dependent upon it for order and for warfare, while the commons were bound to the nobility by feudal tenure. The nobles determined the occupancy of the throne, and their quarrels on that score involved the tenured commonalty in wars which could profit it nothing. Eventually the monarchy, anxious to free itself from noble control, had destroyed the feudal system – and so destroyed itself. First it created, alongside the old nobility, a new nobility which owed its position to royal favour alone – and which, lacking economic power, 'had no shoulders' to support the crown (p. 196). But the fatal blows were delivered between 1485 and 1547: by Henry VII's legislation against noble wealth and retinues, and then by Henry VIII's dissolution of the monasteries. Those policies had produced a massive redistribution of land in favour of the commons, who naturally demanded a political power proportionate to their prosperity. By the time of James I parliaments were 'running unto popularity of government like a bowl down the hill' (p. 680); and Charles I, whose policies in the 1630s put the strength of the monarchy 'unto unseasonable trial' (p. 609), was left to discover that the crown had lost its base of power. The outcome of the Civil War showed that 'Wherever the balance of a government be, there naturally is the militia of the same' (p. 605). Military power, like parliamentary power, had passed to the commons. The simultaneous collapse of kingship and of the House of Lords in 1649, and the rise of the House of Commons to supremacy at their expense, gave plausibility to Harrington's thesis (as, no doubt, they had been largely instrumental in producing it), and won it a considerable measure of acceptance.

Harrington's claims about recent English history were not based on

452

research. His statements about both the pace and the extent of the transfer of land were vague when they were not guessed; and in the hands of his supporters and successors both the chronology and the arithmetic were subjected to arbitrary variation. Friends and critics alike complained of Harrington's refusal to acknowledge the influence of motives other than economic ones, and of his inability to understand how hard to bridge would be the gap between men's true interests and their own perceptions of them. Nevertheless, Harrington offered his contemporaries a new and compelling approach to the problem of understanding the experience of civil war through which they had lived. His claim that 'the dissolution of this government caused the war, and not the war the dissolution of the government' (p. 198) challenged men to overcome the divisions and bitterness of the conflict, and to examine impersonal forces which neither king nor parliament had understood. Charles I's intentions had not been sinful. He had seemed a tyrant only because the commons had lacked power commensurate with their property. Harrington had his own political sympathies in the 1650s, as we shall see, but he was justified in claiming that 'I never was nor am of any party' (p. 390). His relative detachment distinguishes him from the general movement of seventeenth-century republicanism – as does his consequent lack of interest in theories designed to justify resistance.

The author of *Oceana* offered not only a diagnosis of England's problems but a cure. The transfer of power to the commons would be secured and immortalised by two 'superstructures': an 'agrarian law' and 'rotation' (p. 180). Although he knew that agrarian laws had often been blamed for the decline of republics, he believed that the problem had always lain not in the legislation but in the failure to adhere to it. Harrington's 'agrarian' would outlaw extremes of wealth and poverty. No one, he proposed, should be allowed to inherit land worth more than £2,000 p.a. The principle of 'rotation' would find expression in the regular election and replacement of office-holders and of the people's representatives. In common with Nedham (Nedham 1971, IV, pp. 37ff), and indeed with the wide body of radical opinion which had pleaded for 'successive representatives' to replace the Long Parliament, Harrington thought of 'motion' in office-holding as a counter to both stagnation and corruption (Harrington 1977, p. 248). It would enforce that accountability which all republicans were anxious to see; and it would meet the Aristotelian precept, stressed too by Nedham (Worden 1977, p. 362) and endorsed by later republicans as well, that men must learn how to obey as well as to command. It would also provide an antidote to faction, for the elimination of which Harrington proposed an intricate system of ballot voting modelled on the practices of Venice.

In Harrington's commonwealth there would be two elected assemblies, the first with the power of debate, the second with the power of resolution: the first would formulate proposals which the second, without discussion, must either accept or reject. This division of power would forestall that tendency to corruption which, he believed, the Levellers' scheme for a single sovereign assembly would produce (Harrington 1977, pp. 656–7). It would also ensure that the commonwealth profited not only from the experience of the many (who would have the power of resolution) but from the wisdom of the few (who would have the power of debate). There was, Harrington thought, a God-given 'natural aristocracy' of wisdom (p. 173). In any community of citizens – as in any herd of cattle – about a third of the members will emerge as natural leaders of the rest. Only if the constitution took account of their superiority, and confined the power of debate to them, would the principle of reason flourish in the common-wealth. In England the natural leaders were the gentry, whose command of the processes of debate would be secured by electoral property qualifica-tions. For 'there is something first in the making of a commonwealth, then in the governing of her . . . which . . . seems to be peculiar unto the genius of a gentleman' (p. 183). At the same time, lacking the power of resolution, the gentry would be prevented from governing in their own sectional interest; for 'the wisdom of the few may be the light of mankind, but the interest of the few is not the profit of mankind, nor of a commonwealth' (p. 173). It was 'popular government' that came 'the nearest unto the interest of mankind' and so 'unto right reason' (p. 172). To Harrington 'reason' and 'interest' were natural allies, a point he illustrated by his example of two girls sharing a cake: '"divide", says one unto the other, "and I will choose; or let me divide, and you shall choose"' (p. 172). In Harrington's commonwealth, a rational division of power would find acceptance on the same principle. Yet while 'interest' plays a key part in Harrington's system, he believed that political activity should transcend it. He wanted Englishmen to 'raise ourselves out of the mire of private interest unto the contemplation of virtue' (p. 169). The straightforward antithesis between private interest and virtue was subjected to increasing scepticism in the seventeenth century (Gunn 1969), but not, on the whole, by republicans. Only at the end of the period was an anonymous republican – probably Moyle, who often brought clarity to points where his hero

Harrington had left confusion or contradiction – prepared to portray the harmonising of private with public interest as a matter of artificial manipulation, in which man's natural selfishness would be harnessed to, rather than extinguished by, the common good (*Short History*, 1698, p. iii)

Oceana is written – as Harrington's later, more succinct works are not – in a fictional form, and its elements of playfulness and fantasy can give an impression of remoteness from reality. Yet he was convinced that his country's happiness depended upon the implementation of his ideas; and in 1659, his despair mounting as the nation's republican opportunity seemed to slip away, he modified his proposals in the hope of securing their acceptance (Harrington 1977, pp. 662, 664–5). Despite the alien names he gave to the constitutional devices or 'orders' of Oceana (the equivalent to the *ordini* of Venice), they bore close resemblance to existing English practices of local government and electoral regulation. His proposals bore resemblances, too, in language and content, to much of the 'common-wealthmen' programme of the 1650s. There is his dislike of the 'negative voice' of the peers (p. 261); of 'covetousness' and 'pomp and expense' (pp. 240, 353); of the 'grandees' (pp. 265, 286) and of the oligarchical Rump Parliament (pp. 205–6, 243, 295, 737, 744–5); of the usurping and perfidious 'tyrant' Cromwell (pp. 729, 737, 750, 859) – a word he would never have used of Charles I; of Cromwell's major-generals and the decimation tax that financed them (pp. 196, 228, 316). There is his enthusiasm for electoral and legal reform (pp. 237, 472–3); his eagerness to improve the lot of younger sons (pp. 237, 472–3) and of the oppressed commons of Scotland (pp. 159, 240, 331); his adoption of the language of the 'good old cause' (pp. 660, 730), of an 'equal commonwealth' and an 'equal representative' (p. 227); and his Miltonic admiration for the 'ancient heroes' among the army commonwealthmen (p. 744). Even so, Harrington had serious disagreements with the radicals of 1659. Believing as he did in good laws rather than good men, he mistrusted those self-appointed guardians of the good old cause like Sir Henry Vane who wished, either through a 'standing senate' or through the rule of the saints, to entrench their own authority, and whom Harrington believed to be as susceptible to corruption as everyone else (pp. 204, 731, 736, 744–5). He was also sure that so long as the commonwealthmen excluded former royalists from politics, their government would be the rule of a 'party', not a 'commonwealth' (p. 204).

One of Harrington's critics was John Milton. Milton's republican values can be found not only in his prose but in his greatest poetry. For him perhaps more than for any other republican, politics are a public projection of the war waged between reason and passion within every soul. There can be no true political reformation which is not also a reformation of manners and morals, of the household, of education (Milton 1953–82, e.g. II, pp. 229–30, 476, III, p. 190, IV(i), p. 680). John Aubrey's statement that Milton's 'being so conversant in Livy and the Roman authors, and the greatness done by the Roman commonwealth' had led him to write against monarchy is a simplification, but has the merit of directing us to the formidable reading which seems to have led Milton towards republicanism even before the Civil War. It was apparently in 1637–8 that he noted the opinion of Sulpicius Severus 'that the name of kings has ever been hateful to free peoples', and between 1640 and 1642 that he recorded the view of Machiavelli that 'a commonwealth is preferable to a monarchy' (I, pp. 421, 440). Like Harrington, Milton learned from the Civil War to renounce insular and backward-looking solutions to England's problems: his countrymen would 'miscarry still' unless they turned for guidance to 'foreign writings and examples of best ages' – and in particular to Mediterranean thought and history (v(i), p. 451).

The development of Milton's republicanism is not easy to chart. His pamphlets of the earlier 1640s, of 1649–50, and of 1654 were written at times when the regimes for which he wrote them were reluctant to encourage candid republican speculation. Even when republican enthusiasm comes to the surface of his writings it is qualified by his doubts whether his countrymen are 'fit' for republican rule (I, p. 420, II, pp. 226–7, III, p. 581, v(i), pp. 402–3, 449, VII, pp. 356–7, 363). In the Interregnum he consistently supported the prevailing power. That disposition led him first to hail the 'glorious and heroic deed' of regicide (III, p. 212), an event seen by other republicans as the victory not of their principles but of brute force; and then, unlike all the republicans except his friend the trimmer Nedham, to support the Protectorate of Oliver Cromwell. Only in early 1660, in *The Ready and Easy Way to Establish a Free Commonwealth*, did his republicanism become uninhibited. He was hostile now even to the element of monarchy proposed by advocates of what he called 'the fond conceit of something like a Duke of Venice' (VII, p. 374). 'And now is the opportunity', he proclaimed, 'now the very season wherein we may obtain a free commonwealth, and establish it for ever in the land, without difficulty or much delay' (VII, p. 367). But while Milton resembled Harrington in viewing the political crisis of 1659–60 as a republican *occasione*, he at this time rejected Harrington's 'new or obsolete forms, or foreign models' (VII,

ideas, which he was less willing than other republicans to adjust to changed circumstances, makes him seem at times an almost anachronistic figure within the movement. For Harrington was a prophet whom the Restoration appeared to have proved wrong. In the 1650s, Harrington had explained the collapse of the Stuart monarchy: in the 1670s the same monarchy seemed to most of its critics – but not to Nevile – to be moving towards an invincible tyranny. Republicanism changed its role accordingly. It became a defence of constitutional liberty against the threats of popery and of a standing army. The ancient, 'Gothic' constitution was found to have had virtues that Harrington had missed. Whereas Harrington had seen the ownership of property as a qualification for political participation by citizens, his successors thought of it as a guarantor of independence and a handmaid of constitutional freedom.

Not only had monarchy been restored in 1660: so had the House of Lords; and it was from the Lords that the Whig leader the earl of Shaftesbury conducted from 1675 a campaign distinguished by what has been called 'neo-Harringtonianism' (Pocock 1971, 1972, pp. 104–47), in which the medieval nobility was restored to the glory of which Harrington's diagnosis had deprived it. Milton had praised 'those faithful and courageous barons' of the middle ages, 'who lost their lives in the field, making glorious war against tyrants for the common liberty' (Milton 1953–82, III, p. 343). After the Restoration that theme was developed by a republican writer whose rhetoric was often close to Milton's, Algernon Sidney, himself descended from the proud baronial family of the Percies, and a son of the earl of Leicester. Sidney fondly recalled the 'ancient', 'warlike', 'powerful, gallant nobility' whose members had 'spirits suitable to their births' and had been able, by protecting the weak and curbing the insolent, 'to restrain the exorbitances that either the king, or the commons, might run into' (cf. Molesworth 1694, p. 70). His ideal nobility was not the Norman but the Saxon one. It had been a large class, too large for the crown to corrupt it (cf. Milton 1953–82, IV(i), p. 484) and it had supplied the natural leaders of the freeholder class – of 'the people'. Its modern counterparts were to be found in numerous knights and gentry whose claim to noble status had been usurped by an 'effeminate', 'unarmed', 'titular nobility'. The usurpers were 'court-parasites' who lacked 'the interest and estates' to fulfil the true role of a nobility and owed their position to royal favour alone. Unfortunately, Sidney did not dwell on the economic processes which had produced the gap between the true and the false nobility. Harrington's language of the balance is present in Sidney's writing, but so fleetingly that we cannot tell whether Sidney has subtly adapted Harrington's diagnosis or merely imperfectly remembered it (Worden 1985, pp. 17, 23).

Like Nevile, of whose family the Sidneys had long been political allies, Sidney was an influential member of the Commonwealth government in 1652–3. Like Nevile he visited Italy both during and after the Puritan Revolution. In exile following the Restoration, he returned to England from France in 1677, and was executed for treason in 1683 for plotting against Charles II. In the eighteenth century Sidney was to acquire a legendary status as a Whig hero and martyr. Since the collapse of the Whig mythology in the nineteenth century his work has been unduly neglected. He published nothing of substance in his lifetime, when his works were incomplete and unrevised. His two principal writings were 'Court Maxims Refuted and Refelled', a manuscript written in the mid-1660s and only recently discovered, and the long treatise posthumously published in 1698 as *Discourses concerning Government*. 'Court Maxims' was written in Holland in the hope of inciting a rising in England during the second Anglo-Dutch war and of securing the aid of Dutch republicans in the party of John de Witt. The *Discourses*, too, was written with an insurrectionary purpose, and the manuscript of it was cited by the prosecution at Sidney's trial as evidence of treason.

Although – or because – the *Discourses* lacks the analytical rigour of Harrington's thought, it was to exercise an influence wider than his and probably wider than that of any other republican work of the seventeenth century. It is a book of great clarity, elegance, and learning. It is also repetitive, and so long that the reader is easily lulled into inattention and so into missing the energy and life of the work. It was written in 1681–3, the time when, it has lately been argued (Ashcroft 1980), Locke was writing his *Second Treatise of Government*, which the *Discourses* often resembles. Those were the years when, after the failure of parliamentary opposition in 1679–81, Whigs turned in desperation to radical actions and arguments. Offering a page by page refutation of Sir Robert Filmer's *Patriarcha*, the posthumous appearance of which in 1680 seemed to Whigs to represent a new and menacing development in Tory political thought, the *Discourses* was, like 'Court Maxims', a plea for resistance and tyrannicide. In neither of those works, both of which have a destructive rather than a constructive purpose, does Sidney outline the government he would like to see. His clear preference is for a mixed government in which aristocracy is the predominant form,[10] but beyond that the theoretical content of his republicanism has largely to be guessed from tantalising asides. Even so his writings give plausibility to the claim of Bishop Burnet, who knew him well, that Sidney had 'studied the history of government in all its branches beyond any man I ever knew', and that he had possessed a knowledge of 'the Greek and Roman commonwealths' unsurpassed in Burnet's experience. They also illustrate the depth of Sidney's conviction that 'all that was ever desirable, or worthy of praise and imitation in Rome, proceeded from its liberty' (Sidney 1772, p. 119).

The third stage of seventeenth-century republicanism was launched by the publication in 1694 of *An Account of Denmark* by Robert Molesworth. After a long preface which declared his republican principles, Molesworth described the dire consequences of the monarchical coup in Denmark in 1660 – the year also, of course, of the monarchical coup in England. In 1711 Molesworth explained his principles further in his preface to a translation of François Hotman's *Francogallia*. Despite the undoubted impact of *An Account of Denmark*, the republican campaign of the 1690s took wing only in 1697–9, when the government's determination to maintain its land forces after the Peace of Ryswick, which had ended the war with France, provoked the political and intellectual debate known as the standing army controversy. The literary strategy adopted by republicans in that period, resourcefully coordinated by radical publishers and editors, took two forms. First there were pamphlets against standing armies, written by Moyle, Trenchard, the Irishman Toland, and Fletcher of Saltoun in Scotland, whose *Discourse concerning Militias*, published in 1697, reappeared in expanded form the following year. The other principal pamphlets were Toland's *The Militia Reformed* (1698) and two anonymous works on which Toland, Moyle, and Trenchard probably collaborated, although Moyle's is likely to have been the guiding pen: the helpfully entitled *An Argument Showing that a Standing Army is inconsistent with a Free Government, and absolutely destructive to the Constitution of the English Monarchy* (1697); and *A Short History of Standing Armies* (1698). The second aspect of the republican campaign was the publication of a series of works which were to become the standard texts of country party ideals in the eighteenth century: the *Memoirs* of the Civil War regicide Edmund Ludlow (1698–9); Milton's *Historical and Political Works* (1698); Sidney's *Discourses* (1698); Nevile's

---

10. Sidney 1772, pp. 22, 100, 103, 146, 161–2, 186, 258–9, 390, 463, 493.

Plato Redivivus (republished in 1698); and the works of Harrington (1700). Some of these writings now became available in print for the first time: the others became significantly better known as a result of their republication. Toland, the editor of Harrington, seems also to have edited the works of Ludlow and Sidney (Ludlow 1978, pp. 17–39).

Of Toland's colleagues in the campaign against standing armies, Trenchard was to achieve a greater fame in the reign of George I as the author, with Thomas Gordon, of *The Independent Whig* and *Cato's Letters*. Moyle was a Cornish MP and antiquary whose principal republican works were not published in his lifetime. They were *An Essay of the Lacedaemonian Government* and the more important (although evidently unfinished) *An Essay upon the Constitution of the Roman Government*, a study in which he applied the principle of 'the great Harrington' that 'the balance of dominion changes with the balance of property' (Moyle 1969, p. 232). The republicanism of Fletcher of Saltoun, a figure less close to the other principal republicans of the 1690s than they were to each other, was fuelled by his resentment not only against the English exploitation of his country but against Scotland's acquiescence in it. He was to be a central figure in the development of civic humanism in Scotland and in the study of the relationships between national identity, political stability, and economic progress.

Criticism of standing armies drew on the widespread anxiety among the gentry (Tory as well as Whig) about the growth of the executive and about the corruption of parliament by court patronage – an anxiety sharpened by the high taxation by which the army was financed. The wills of Englishmen were being enslaved by 'mercenary soldiers'. Republicans insisted with Machiavelli that defence should be entrusted to armed and independent citizens, whose manhood would be incomplete without a term of military service and without experience of the 'military discipline' which was essential to moral and social discipline.[11] Whereas Hobbes and the Levellers thought every man was entitled to pay or persuade another to fight in his place, republicans found the idea of 'substitution' an affront to citizenship (e.g. Fletcher 1732, pp. 50–1). Citizen armies would be not only more virtuous than mercenary ones but more effective, for as Sidney put it 'we see everywhere the difference between the courage of men fighting for themselves and their posterity, and those that serve a master' (Sidney 1772, p. 182). Despite their agreement on the interdependence of civic and

11. Harrington 1977, p. 228; Sidney 1666?, pp. 66, 180; Sidney 1772, p. 232; Fletcher 1732, p. 64.

military fulfilment, republicans were not at one about the nature of the ideal citizen army. Harrington (1977, p. 197) praised the 'excellent infantry' which had been achieved by English freeholder-commoners after their emancipation from feudal tenure. His successors, here as elsewhere, had more aristocratic preferences. They idealised the feudal array, and argued that now as in the middle ages the landed rulers of England should lead its people out to battle. Only if the nobility and gentry controlled the nation's arms, the later republicans believed, could property give its due protection to liberty.

In the hope of persuading the audience of 1697–9 that national military security could be safely entrusted to local militias – a proposition which recent advances in the art of war had made implausible – Toland and Fletcher put forward elaborate schemes for militia reform. In the vision which informs their proposals – a vision part civic, part feudal; part classical, part insular – some of the tensions within English republicanism can be seen. They are the tensions of a movement consistently critical of conventional political assumptions yet consistently dependent for its influence on its ability to play on them. Sometimes republicanism of the later seventeenth century seems merely to reflect the reestablishment of aristocratic political values in that period. Sometimes republicans seem to have deserved the mockery to which they were subjected by Daniel Defoe, who questioned their favourable image of the middle ages, doubted whether the medieval nobility had had a protective rather than an oppressive role, and suggested that if, as republicans complained, noble power was broken, then patronage, which they so hated, was necessary as a binding and stabilising force in its place (Pocock 1975, pp. 432–5). Yet despite the prevailing aristocratic tone, something of the social radicalism of the 1650s, of Nedham and Harrington, survived. So did Harrington's language of 'an equal commonwealth'. Moyle located Rome's greatness in its period as an 'equal commonwealth', and showed how kingship and nobility had been obstacles to her greatness. Molesworth warned against 'insolent' treatment of the commons by the nobles (Molesworth 1694, p. 76; cf. Sidney 1772, p. 464).

'Equality' had never been an absolute aim. Even Nedham had pleaded not for 'an equality (that were irrational and odious) but an equability of condition among the members, so that no particular man or men shall grow over-great' (Nedham 1971, IV, pp. 325ff, 344) – the principle which Harrington's 'equal commonwealth' was designed to implement. 'Equal' could mean 'more equal' or, on the Aristotelian principle of distributive justice, equality 'proportionate' to merit; or an 'equal' commonwealth might be one where the principle of rotation ensured a fair distribution of office-holding.[12] Two principles of political prudence were embodied in the idea of 'equality'. The first was a dislike of the extremes of wealth and poverty, which were enemies to both virtue and stability (e.g. Moyle 1727, p. 51; Fletcher 1732, pp. 27, 438). The second was the Aristotelian location of virtue in the mean, in 'mediocrity' or 'the middle sort'. Sometimes the middle sort was the gentry (Molesworth 1694, sig. A3v); sometimes it was the nobility, the middle of the three estates (*Argument* 1697, p. 2; Holles 1693, p. 459); but often, too, the middle sort consisted of the freeholder-citizens – a class distinguished from 'servants', whom republicans, defining liberty as 'independency upon the will of another' (Sidney 1772, p. 10), wished to exclude from political participation. Republicans subscribed to the conventional praise of the English yeoman and to the belief that England's superiority over other countries lay in the existence of a free yeoman class.[13] The tension between the equalitarian and the aristocratic strains of late seventeenth-century republicanism can be glimpsed in the writings of Toland, the editor both of Harrington, who wanted 'an equal commonwealth', and of Sidney, the spokesman for the ancient nobility. Toland tried to have it both ways, by declaring that the 'eternal fame' which 'some' of the ancient nobility had 'worthily acquired, is wholly owing to those glorious actions they performed' for their country in war, 'and not in the least to that immoderate power they might then exercise over the people' (Toland 1698 p. 604).

iii   The Machiavellian tradition

Among the modifications of republican thought over the second half of the seventeenth century lay elements of continuity which are best described as Machiavellian. With few exceptions the republicans shared Machiavelli's respect for, and his belief in the autonomy of, political activity; his conception of civic activity and participation; his concern for national glory (though not without reservations); his approach to history; his understanding of the proper relationship between politics and religion.

Toland emphasised a common republican view when he emphasised

12. Nedham 1971, IV, pp. 325ff, 344; Milton 1953–82, IV(i), pp. 366–7, VII, pp. 359, 383; Moyle 1969, pp. 242–3, 247.
13. Harrington 1977, p. 197; Molesworth 1694, sig. B1r, p. 86; Bethel 1671, p. 7. Cf. Nevile 1969, pp. 114, 119–20.

that 'the politics, no less than arms, are the proper study of a gentleman' (Harrington 1700, p. ix). There was no wisdom without political wisdom. Virtue and vice, happiness and misery, were determined by political institutions and constitutions. Manners were corrupted, said Harrington, only when the 'balance' was corrupted (Harrington 1977, p. 202). 'Nothing is more certain', averred Nevile, 'than that politic defects breed moral ones' (Nevile 1969, p. 87; cf. Sidney 1772, pp. 183, 236). Republicans mistrusted thinkers who preferred climatic to political explanations of national character; the climate of Rome, observed Toland, had been the same under the republic as it was under the papacy.[14] The republicans' respect for politics did not make them advocates of Machiavellian 'reason of state', to which on the whole they expressed conventional country party hostility.[15] To them the most admirable political skill lay in the designing, not the running of a state. For Harrington the initial construction was all: 'as no man shall show me a commonwealth born straight that ever became crooked, so no man shall show me a commonwealth born crooked that ever became straight (Harrington 1977, p. 276). The working of a constitution, he thought, should resemble an eternal and rapturous motion of spheres (p. 342). One of his successors compared the ideal constitution to 'a piece of clockwork; and having such springs and wheels, must act after such a manner'.[16] Hence the republican reverence for the lawgiver, and for the 'abstruse science' of 'political architecture' which could insulate institutions from social and economic change.[17] Only Algernon Sidney viewed politics as a necessarily dynamic or evolutionary process. Whereas other republicans believed that the proper response to political problems was to follow Machiavelli's principle of 'renewal' (e.g. Milton 1953–82, I, p. 477; Moyle 1969, p. 253) – of returning to the original purity of the constitutional design – Sidney thought it necessary to go further: to 'add' constitutional provisions, which must be 'variable according to accidents and circumstances'. Constitutions drawn up in times of 'virtuous simplicity' were bound to contain initial flaws which must be rectified as communities gained experience (Worden 1985, p. 19).

Harrington eliminated not only historical movement from his ideal commonwealth, but tension. Other republicans, by contrast, subscribed to Machiavelli's view that conflicts, even 'tumults', could be evidence of

14. Toland 1706, p. 596. Cf. Molesworth 1694, pp. 41, 75; Fletcher 1732, p. 68.
15. E.g. Harrington 1977, p. 171; Sidney 1666?, pp. 70–1.
16. *Short History* 1698, p. iii. Cf. Moyle 1727, pp. 59–60.
17. Harrington 1977, p. 609; Sidney 1666?, p. 20; Sidney 1772, pp. 64, 98; Nevile 1969, pp. 68, 111; Fletcher 1732, pp. 3–5, 380.

political life. Sidney, remarking on the capacity of tyrannies to extinguish political expression, waxed eloquent in his Tacitean scorn for writers who 'give the name of peace to desolation' (Sidney 1772, pp. 118, 132–4, 198, 223–5, 254–5). Nedham argued that by the contests between nobles and people in Rome 'the spirits of the people were kept warm with high thoughts of themselves and their liberty (which tended much to the enlargement of their empire)' (Nedham 1971, IV, pp. 309ff); Moyle argued that the same events, 'though for the present creating some little disorders in the state, introduced excellent orders into the government, and were succeeded by lasting quiet and tranquillity'.[18] Moyle's acknowledgement that 'tranquillity' was the desirable norm indicates the difficulty, experienced by other republicans, too, of appearing to recommend instability to a seventeenth-century audience. Even so, some republicans were prepared to claim that the conflicts between king and people, or between lords and commons, in the history of England had been 'the contending billows that kept it afloat' (Molesworth 1694, sign. A5r–v).

Machiavelli, putting vitality before stability, also preferred a 'commonwealth for expansion' to one merely for 'preservation'. The transient glory of Rome's conquests was more desirable than the humble permanence of Venice. Not all seventeenth-century republicans thought England equipped for 'expansion'. There was a feeling that she should respect the natural boundaries which 'providence' had given her, and that conquest was not in her 'interest'.[19] The humanist mistrust of war and glory for their own sakes surfaced in the awareness that, in Sidney's phrase, 'rules of morality' should be consulted before an aggressive foreign policy was launched;[20] and republicans were conscious that Rome's expansion had produced luxury and tyranny and decline. There was also a belief that conquests should be undertaken only if – again in Sidney's phrase – they were 'suitable to the constitution' of the conquering state (Sidney 1666?, p. 14). They were not suitable to monarchy or aristocracy, because men would not fight vigorously for possessions which would benefit only the rulers and not the ruled, and because no government ruling in the interest of a few could risk arming the people. To be a 'commonwealth for expansion', noted Harrington, was a talent 'peculiar unto popular government' (Harrington 1977, p. 329). In support of that thesis re-

18. Moyle 1969, p. 246. Cf. Milton 1953–82, I, p. 505, III, p. 388; Hall 1700, p. 15; Nevile 1969, p. 194; Sidney 1772, pp. 111, 124, 188, 214–15, 479.
19. Milton 1953–82, I, pp. 499, 597; Sidney 1666?, pp. 151–2; Sidney 1772, p. 119; Nevile 1969, p. 143; Fletcher 1732, pp. 21, 66; Bethel 1671, p. 1; Holles 1693, pp. 458–9.
20. Sidney 1666?, p. 14. Cf. Milton 1953–82, I, pp. 499, 597, and *Paradise Regained*, III, 43–107.

publicans strove to demonstrate that Rome's greatness had been achieved in periods of republican or popular rule.[21] In the same way a contrast was repeatedly drawn between the shameful pacifism and humiliating betrayals of Stuart foreign policy and the glorious exploits, equal at least to those of Greece and Rome, which had been achieved by the Long Parliament.[22] That parliament's annexation of Ireland and Scotland, and its proposed union with the Dutch, excited an interest in the question how new territorial acquisitions could be best governed: as colonies, or through the formation of equal or unequal leagues, or through the naturalisation of the conquered peoples.[23] The same subject was explored by Moyle at the end of the century (Moyle 1969, pp. 228–9, 249–53).

Harrington departed from Machiavelli in believing it possible to combine expansion with stability – although here he seems to have carried few republicans with him. He dissented from the traditional belief that Rome had collapsed beneath the weight of her empire. She had fallen because, neglecting her 'equal agrarian', she had allowed the profits of conquest to be appropriated by nobles. English expansion was both a necessity and a moral obligation. It was a necessity because – as Sidney was likewise to insist – international relations were a race for recovery among the fallen Gothic nations. The country which first recovered its vigour would dominate the continent; and if England missed her chance France would take hers.[24] The moral obligation to expand was announced by Harrington in apocalyptic language characteristic of the Puritan Revolution. England, liberated from Gothic rule, must relieve the oppressed peoples of Europe, for 'if thy brother cry unto thee in affliction, wilt thou not hear him?'. England had a 'duty' to emulate the imperial role of Rome. With Cicero, Harrington believed that Rome had 'rather undertaken the patronage than the empire of the world'; and 'if we have given over running up and down naked and with dappled hides, learned to write and read, to be instructed with good arts, for all these we are beholden to the Romans' (Harrington 1977, pp. 192, 322–3, 332). Imperialist dreams lived on after 1660, when Sidney thought that England 'might conquer a great part of the world' if her constitution were reformed (Sidney 1772, p. 178). Yet doubts and scruples remained. Fletcher rebelled against his predecessors' willingness to think of international affairs as an inevitable jungle.

21. Nedham 1971, III, p. 279, IV, pp. 149ff; Sidney 1772, pp. 119, 128–38; Moyle 1969, pp. 228–9, 248.
22. Worden 1981, pp. 195–9; Milton 1953–82, VII, p. 356.
23. Harrington 1977, pp. 323–5, 329; Worden 1981, pp. 198–9.
24. Harrington 1977, pp. 332, 456; Sidney 1772, pp. 174–5, 179.

Since the rise of one nation must mean the suffering of another, it was time to outlaw the foolish pursuit of international glory and to seek means to international security. Molesworth lamented the arms race of his time and the fear which made all monarchs reluctant to 'disarm'. Like Fletcher, Molesworth wanted an international order where men would be 'citizens of the world'.[25]

Despite his aversion to political tension and disorder, Harrington subscribed to the idea of civic virtue and participation, and evidently believed that his procedures for debate and resolution would promote it. He was at one with his fellow republicans in seeing the choice between a tyranny and a free state as the choice which Machiavelli had offered between two sets of values. In republican eyes, 'courts' inevitably generated 'luxury' and its 'inseparable companion, idleness', while commonwealths were distinguished by the 'frugality', 'industry', 'sobriety', and 'honest poverty' of their citizens.[26] Republican freedom was not a mere absence of restraint. Milton's distinction between 'liberty' and 'licence' was drawn, too, by Nedham and by Sidney:[27] and all republicans would have applauded Milton's contempt, in *Samson Agonistes*, for 'nations grown corrupt', which preferred 'bondage with ease' to 'strenuous liberty'. In 1659–60, a time of grave hardship, Milton was ready to ban the 'luxurious expenses of a nation upon trifles or superfluities', and to insist on the enforcement of civic virtue at whatever economic cost (Milton 1953–82, VII, p. 386; cf. *ibid.*, III, pp. 437–8). Other republicans shared his dislike of 'money'.[28] Their Puritanism on that score must not be exaggerated: many republicans were concerned to generate wealth, not least in order to solve the problem of poor relief;[29] and the country party hostility to the 'moneyed interest' made only a limited impact on republican thought before 1700 (Sullivan 1982, p. 164). Even so, civic self-fulfilment, like military self-fulfilment, would be a Spartan process. The sanctions of civic loyalty would be severe. The state would be bound together by strict oaths of association, by stiff treason laws, and by severe punishments, even the death penalty, for breaches of civic responsibility.[30] Education, always a chief instrument in republican plans or reform, would rigorously instil

25. Fletcher 1732, pp. 437–31; Molesworth 1694, p. 126; Molesworth 1721, p. xiv.
26. Nedham 1971, III, p. 294, IV, pp. 133ff; Harrington 1977, pp. 188, 202, 684–5, 687; Milton 1953–82, I, p. 475; Sidney 1666?, pp. 68, 74; Worden 1985, p. 18; Molesworth 1694, sig. A4v.
27. Milton, Sonnet XII; Milton 1953–82, II, p. 225, III, p. 190, v(i), p. 131; Nedham 1971, III, p. 295, V, p. 69; Sidney 1772, p. 3.
28. Sidney 1772, pp. 134, 425; Moyle 1727, p. 52, 1969, p. 239; Fletcher 1732, p. 429.
29. Bethel 1671, p. 7; Fletcher 1732, p. 375; Moyle 1727, pp. 28–30; *Argument* 1697, p. 2; *Short History* 1698, p. 3.
30. Nedham 1971, III, pp. 309–10, V, p. 6; Harrington 1977, pp. 623–4, 684–5; Moyle 1969, p. 232; Molesworth 1721, p. vi; Fletcher 1732, pp. 57–8.

civic values. Pupils, thought Molesworth, should be exposed not merely to 'the study of words and languages' but to 'the weightier matters of true learning . . . such as good principles, morals, the improvement of reason, the love of justice, the value of liberty, the duty one owes to one's country and the laws, . . . the right notion of a generous and legal freedom'.[31] The formidably austere training camps which Fletcher planned for his reformed militia would require youths to study ancient history between military exercises and exhort each other to the promotion of 'public liberty'. They would be 'as great a school of virtue as of military discipline': pupils 'would learn greater and better things than the military art, and more necessary too' (Fletcher 1732, p. 64; cf. pp. 3–5).

An essential aspect of civic fulfilment was what Harrington called 'participation of magistracy' (Harrington 1977, p. 277). Admittedly republican enthusiasm for that idea was sometimes ill at ease with the country party's suspicion of power and with its posture of stoical indifference to it; but country party sentiments often belonged to men who felt themselves unjustly excluded from office by 'court-parasites' – and who found solace in the republican belief that the occupancy of government posts should be determined by virtue and merit instead of favour. Milton and Sidney were especially anxious to respect the Aristotelian principle that virtue – wherein, rather than in high birth, true nobility lay – must be rewarded by office: if one man stood out from his countrymen he should be king (a suggestion they tended to invert as soon as they had made it, so that it served to demonstrate the injustice of subordinating outstanding citizens to the worthless kings of the seventeenth century);[32] if a few were prominent they should rule as a nobility; where men were equal they should rule equally. So the predominant form of government should be determined by the distribution of merit rather than – as Harrington proposed – of property. As Sidney put it, '*detur digniori* is the voice of nature' (Sidney 1772, pp. 39, 61). The reward of merit was not only a matter of fairness or of ensuring the political acquiescence of the virtuous. If commonwealths existed for the good life, then they were to be judged by the moral qualities of their citizens and by the number of 'heroes' or 'patterns' (of which Rome had boasted so many) among them.[33]

Like Machiavelli, English republicans believed themselves to be living

---

31. Molesworth 1694, sig. B4r. Cf. Nedham 1971, III, pp. 293–4, V, pp. 6, 53–7; Harrington 1977, pp. 227, 228, 300, 304; Milton 1953–82, II, pp. 362–415, VII, pp. 383–4; Sidney 1772, p. 379; Moyle 1727, p. 61; Harrington 1700, p. x; Toland 1698, pp. 596, 605–6.
32. Milton 1953–82, III, pp. 204, 460–2, 486, IV(i), pp. 366–7, 438; Worden 1985, p. 24.
33. Milton 1953–82, I, p. 421; Sidney 1772, pp. 60, 117, 134, 185, 214, 218–21, 233, 236, 238–9, 381; Nevile 1969, pp. 90–1.

through a critical period – although Harrington's view of his time was more optimistic than that of his successors. The later republicans believed the Gothic constitutions and the free city-states to have been undermined by the rise of the Renaissance monarchies in the fifteenth century – in France, in Burgundy, in Spain, in Italy, in Scotland, in England.[34] The 'subtle arts' of kings, complained Sidney, had 'subverted the Laws' and thus 'broken this golden chain' of Gothic polities (Sidney 1772, p. 252). It was left to Fletcher and Moyle, late in the century, to revert from Sidney's censoriousness to Harrington's insistence on impersonal rather than moral explanations. Fletcher thought that the decay of Gothic monarchies, although fatal to liberty, had not been 'introduced by the contrivance of ill-designed men' but caused rather by the economic and social consequences of the invention of the compass, of gunpowder, and of printing. Those discoveries were 'in themselves excellent' (Fletcher 1732, pp. 6, 10), but they had bred in the nobility a taste for luxury which had destroyed their independence and which had led to the revolution in landownership described by Harrington. Moyle argued that the causes of constitutional change must be sought not in 'moral reasons' but in 'the only true ground and foundation of power, property' (Moyle 1969, p. 231).

However they explained Gothic decline, Harrington's successors were agreed that in their own century history had taken a grimmer turn. Absolutism had been achieved in France and the Habsburg lands, and in England the early Stuarts had succeeded, in Sidney's words, in 'turning a legitimate monarchy into tyranny' (Sidney 1666?, p. 122). The skies had darkened further with the coups of 1660 in England and Denmark. To Sidney, the reign of Charles II was a black tyranny; to republicans of the next generation, the 1690s were a period of black corruption. Admittedly the Revolution of 1688–9 did produce a tendency to think of England less as a victim of a general European trend than as a country which, through providence or geography or mere luck, had retained a liberty that the rest of Europe had lost.[35] But England might succumb at any moment; and the republicans of the 1690s were as anxious as Sidney and Nevile had been that – in phrases which echo down the republican literature of the century – the constitution be reformed 'in time', before decay had made renovation 'too late'.[36]

34. Nedham 1971, III, p. 231, IV, pp. 112ff, 149ff, 165ff, 213ff, 261ff, 357ff, V, pp. 22–4, 136–8; Worden 1985, p. 17; Nevile 1969, p. 137; Moyle 1969, p. 231.
35. Molesworth 1694, sig. A6v; Fletcher 1732, p. 26; *Short History* 1698, pp. 2–4, 16; Moyle 1727, p. 62.
36. Harrington 1977, p. 188; *Copy of a Letter* 1656, p. 7; Worden 1985, pp. 17–18; Nevile 1969, pp. 81, 99; Moyle 1969, p. 256.

In their approach to history, both classical and European, republicans liked to show how 'example' and 'experience' illustrated timeless principles of 'reason' – reason being the root of the tree whereof example and experience were branches (Harrington 1977, p. 454; Sidney 1772, p. 182). Their arguments had an element of circularity. When its evidence supported them they invoked the sanction of antiquity, and argued that the medieval history of parliament, of the succession or of the coronation oath gave the verdict of custom and precedent to the Whig rather than the Tory case. But when history failed to support their beliefs they abandoned it, and rebuked history for failing to follow the principles of reason. Sidney asserted, in terms close to Locke's, the authority of 'not so much that which is most ancient, as that which is the best' (Sidney 1772, p. 404). The landmarks of medieval liberty, like Magna Carta, were important less because of their antiquity than because they gave expression to principles of reason written in the hearts of men (Nevile 1969, p. 124; Sidney 1772, p. 433). In any case the origins of government, lost in 'fable' or 'oral tradition' (Nevile 1969, p. 84; Sidney 1772, p. 402), could be discovered only by reason, not by research. Time and again republicans declared it 'impossible', 'not to be imagined', that any people would in time past have surrendered the rights which monarchs now claimed over them,[37] and which, being inherently in the people, were in any event inalienable by them.[38]

The republicans' confidence in 'reason' seems to contrast markedly with the Calvinist pessimism of the Puritans and nonconformists with whom they often found themselves in alliance. Equally, republican enthusiasm for classical and pagan civilisation looks barely compatible with Puritan fundamentalism. The republicans also differed from the Puritans (as well as from Hobbes) in their stress on the positive aspects of man's sociability. No Calvinist could have warmed to Molesworth's premise that, even in a fallen world, 'liberty' was 'natural' and its absence a 'disease' that arose from 'nature debauched, depraved or enforced' (Molesworth 1694, sig. A1v). It may seem curious to us that the republicans of 1659 secured the cooperation of the Puritan Ludlow, who was indignant at the belief – which many republicans would have privately acknowledged for their own – 'that we are to take the history of the Holy Scriptures as those of Titus Livius or Polybius' (Ludlow 1978, sig. A1v). How can Ludlow have become a friend of Nevile, who in parliament in 1659 was charged with atheism after reportedly saying that he preferred reading Cicero to the Bible?

---

37. Sidney 1772, pp. 13, 25, 55, 337, 424, 464; Nevile 1969, pp. 85, 127; Moyle 1969, p. 233.
38. Milton 1953–82, IV(i), p. 467; Molesworth 1694, sigs. B8v–C1r.

The problem is a genuine one. Yet the religious commitment of the republicans is easily underestimated or misunderstood. Certainly they were sharply anti-clerical. They resented the clergy's interference in politics, blamed Europe's wars of religion on it,[39] and thought the clergy responsible for the development of Tory and authoritarian political theory in the seventeenth century.[40] Yet their charge against the clergy was not that they had promoted religion but that they had perverted it. For republicans, politics was a supremely religious activity. The commonwealth was 'a minister of God upon Earth' (Harrington 1977, p. 323; Sidney 1772, p. 329). The achievement of a perfect state would fulfil a divine instinct among citizens; for, as Harrington wrote, 'the contemplation of form is astonishing to man, and has a kind of trouble or impulse accompanying it, that exalts his soul to God'. Harrington – unlike his successors – did not believe that human frailty need impair his immortal commonwealth, 'for as man is sinful, but yet the world is perfect, so may the citizens be sinful and yet the commonwealth be perfect' (Harrington 1977, pp. 320, 837). That aspiration was not an irreligious one. There are hints, indeed, that Harrington saw in politics the road not only to the secular self-fulfilment of citizen-freeholders but to that recovery from the Fall which it was the religious purpose of Bacon and Milton and Samuel Hartlib to accomplish (Webster 1975). The apocalyptic strain in Harrington's imperialism was close to Puritanism. So were the republicans' insistence on 'frugality' and 'industry' and their belief, which enabled Nevile and Sidney to make common cause with Restoration nonconformists, that the English were 'a very debauched people' (Nevile 1969, p. 196; Worden 1985, pp. 26–7). Like the Puritans, too – albeit in a somewhat different spirit – republicans regarded the Old Testament as a fundamental source of political wisdom. From Deuteronomy 17 and from 1 Samuel 8 they knew that God had not wanted monarchy, either for the Israelites or as a pattern for other nations. God's preference had clearly been for a free state, although he had allowed his people liberty to make their own choice.[41]

In the Hebrew polity, as it stood before the Israelites inflicted kings upon themselves, Harrington and Sidney saw a mixed constitution which embodied the principle of 'balance' likewise to be found in the commonwealths of Greece and Rome. In that respect Harrington thought Israel

39. Nedham 1971, IV, pp. 373ff; Harrington 1977, pp. 186, 216; Moyle 1969, p. 216.
40. Worden 1985, p. 21; Sidney 1666?, pp. 8, 40; Nevile 1969, p. 150; Moyle 1727, p. 62; Molesworth 1694, sigs. B6v–7r.
41. Nedham 1971, IV, pp. 357ff; Milton 1953–82, III, pp. 206–7; Sidney 1772, pp. 12, 67–8.

'that original whereof all the rest of the commonwealths seem to be copies'.[42] Thus the Old Testament provided the essential introduction to political 'prudence'. 'They', wrote Harrington, 'that under colour of religion, in matter of government, slight prudence are mistaken or do not mean honestly. Neither God nor Christ ever instituted any policy whatsoever upon any other principles than those of human prudence.' The clergy – in whose enmity to himself Harrington saw a parallel to the clerical conspiracy that had damaged the reputation of Machiavelli – were at fault in calling it 'irreverent or atheistical' to derive political instruction from the classical lawgivers as well as from Moses. Harrington saw no conflict between his own Christian values and his pagan ones. Had it not been 'by the help of the arts' which Rome had cultivated that Christianity had spread? God gave guidance to men through the light of nature, which was visible to pagans as well as Christians. Thus 'ancient prudence' had been 'first discovered unto mankind by God himself in the fabric of the commonwealth of Israel, and afterward picked out of his footsteps in nature and unanimously followed by the Greeks and Romans' (Harrington 1977, pp. 161, 192, 547, 629).

The clergy were held responsible by republicans for the erosion of civic virtue. Milton blamed them for that 'low dejection and debasement of mind in the people' that had produced the 'idolising' of kings (Milton 1953–82, III,p. 343). Nevile thought that 'priestcraft' had 'deformed the face of government in Europe, destroying all the good principles and morality left us by heathens': he aimed 'to restore the good policy (I had almost said with . . . Livy the sanctity too) of the heathens, with all their valour and glorious endowments'. The clergy's political influence was, he maintained, 'a solecism in government' which the Reformation had disastrously failed to eliminate (Nevile 1675, 'Letter', pp. 7–8). In opposition to the clergy, republicans argued for liberty of conscience, which, they proclaimed, was the natural companion of a free state.[43] Yet while republicans sometimes pressed for a complete separation of church from state, there was a powerful strand within republicanism which emphasised the need for a 'national religion'. For, as Harrington had it, 'religion is nothing else but the national conscience'; and the national conscience, the religious dimension of civic virtue, required national institutional expression.[44]

Whatever resemblances of moral tone republicanism may have borne to

42. Harrington 1977, p. 205; cf. Sidney 1666?, p. 117.
43. Harrington 1977, p. 742; Moyle 1969, pp. 212–15. Cf. Milton 1953–82, III, pp. 509, 570.
44. Harrington 1977, pp. 185, 217–18, 307, 678; Nevile 1969, p. 153; Moyle 1969, p. 213.

Puritanism, there were not many similarities of theology. There is, indeed, little theological substance to the writings of Harrington and his successors. Enemies to idolatry in religion as in politics, they strove to expose, through reason, the hollow mysteries of dogma. Republicanism always had affinities with the Arminian and Socinian criticisms of Calvinist theological rigour (Worden 1981, p. 195); and by the late seventeenth century, when Toland and Moyle were warring against 'creeds and catechisms', republicanism seemed the natural friend of deism. Moyle thought that 'the common principles of religion all mankind agree in' (Moyle 1969, p. 210). Molesworth would have extended toleration to pagans, Jews, and Turks (Molesworth 1721, pp. xii–xiv). Religion had become not merely an ally of civic virtue but scarcely distinguishable from it. Republicans agreed with Machiavelli that the Christian religion, in the corrupted state to which the clergy had reduced it, was subversive of those qualities – manliness, courage, appetite for glory – on which civic and military health depended. Fletcher proposed to ban the clergy from his militia training camps, where laymen would teach each other 'Christian and moral duties' (Fletcher 1732, p. 57). Moyle praised Numa, the father of the Roman religion, who 'interwove his moral precepts with his religious doctrine'. Rome, indeed, provided Moyle's model of a 'national religion', for Numa had supplied 'the wisest and most politic system of religion that ever any lawgiver founded'. Moyle and Molesworth endorsed the 'pious cheats' with which the Romans had fostered civic bonds: the use of oracles and augurs, the doctrine of the immortality of the soul ('an opinion of great use and service to the state'), the myth of the Elysian Fields where men who died for their country found eternal happiness. In the propagation of those 'cheats', it seems, the clergy might find a place after all. Molesworth wanted 'generous notions of liberty' to be 'inculcated from the pulpit, and enforced by the learned arguments of able divines' (Moyle 1969, pp. 207–12; Molesworth 1694, sigs. B4v, C3v).

In exploring the deficiencies of monarchy the republican writers of seventeenth-century England addressed a fundamental problem – perhaps the fundamental problem – of contemporary politics, and gave men an alternative perspective and an alternative language to those of the more insular tradition of law and precedent. Yet in their writings thought is often an inch away from prejudice. Harrington alone – whose arguments were more often repeated by his successors than modified by them – was an indisputably creative and innovative thinker. In the eighteenth century, in the prose of Trenchard and Gordon and Bolingbroke, republican prejudice declined almost into republican cliché. The significant legacy of the ideas we have inspected lay in a broader field, where Harringtonian ideas were adapted to political purposes of which Harrington might scarcely have approved. Classical political language, and the doctrine of the balance, became commonplace in eighteenth-century political discussion – and in eighteenth-century vindications of oligarchy (Smith 1971, pp. 145–8). The ideal of the independent citizen likewise entered the mainstream of English political culture. Those outlooks cannot necessarily be attributed to the republican tradition alone, but they are probably inconceivable without it. The tradition left its mark on high thought and low; for, as Pocock has written, 'the myth of the standing army, the Gothic society of free landed proprietors, and the rise of luxury and bureaucracy, was both the worn language of tediously insincere parliamentary debate and one of the seminal ideas of eighteenth-century historiography' (Pocock 1971, 1972, p. 146). Adam Ferguson and David Hume wrote history to illustrate a civic humanist thesis which seventeenth-century republicanism had done much to shape. So did Edward Gibbon – in whose library the seventeenth-century republicans were well represented.[45] To recall Gibbon on Christianity is to suspect the existence of another durable legacy of republicanism, in the alliance it had formed with deism. And the posthumous impact of the seventeenth-century movement was not to be felt in Britain alone. In France the principal texts of the tradition were to guide Montesquieu into the tradition of Renaissance political humanism (Shackleton 1964, pp. 8–10); and across the Atlantic they were to play a major part in 'the ideological origins of the American Revolution' (Bailyn 1967; Pocock 1985, p. 216n).

45. Keynes 1980, pp. 144, 184, 198, 203, 251, 268. Cf. Ludlow 1978, p. 40n.

IV
The end of Aristotelianism

16

Tacitism, scepticism, and reason of state

PETER BURKE

i Reason of state

The historian Friedrich Meinecke, a bold climber of what he liked to call the 'mountain-peaks' in the history of ideas, once wrote despairingly of the literature on reason of state that 'There are real catacombs here of forgotten literature by mediocrities' (Meinecke 1957, p. 67n). All the same, these catacombs are well worth the effort of exploration to any historian concerned with the history of arguments, attitudes, and mentalities as well as with the achievements of outstanding individuals. Shifts in political attitudes are generally marked, sooner or later, by the coinage of new terms, as the traditional vocabulary comes to appear increasingly inadequate to express the new insights. In the later sixteenth century, an important new 'keyword' was 'reason of state'.

To be exact, the Italian phrase *ragione degli stati* had been employed, around the year 1547, by Giovanni della Casa – the archbishop best known for his courtesy book – in an oration to the emperor Charles V, but it was only in 1580s or thereabouts that the new coinage passed into general currency. By the time Giovanni Botero published his *Ragione di Stato* (1589), the first of a whole shelf of books bearing that sort of title, it was, as he noted in the dedication, a 'constant subject of discussion' in some courts. The claim is plausible enough, since Botero's book went through at least five more Italian editions by 1606, while the phrase *ragion di stato* appears in the titles of at least eight more Italian treatises on politics by the year 1635.[1]

Botero was quickly translated into German, French, Spanish, and Latin, and so contributed to the international circulation of the new term; *razón de*

---

1. Frachetta 1592; Palazzo 1606; Canonhiero 1614; Zuccolo 1621; Buonaventura 1623 (written *c.* 1601); Zinano 1626; Settala 1627; Chiaramonti 1635.

estado, ratio status, raison d'état. (The Germans tended to use the Latin phrase, the English, until the 1620s at least, to use the Italian, or to replace it by 'policy'.) The concept was central to political thought for about a century, and appeared not only in theoretical treatises but also in practical memoranda, including the *Testament politique* of Cardinal Richelieu and the *Mémoires* of Louis XIV. In an age when abstractions were frequently personified, reason of state made an appearance in woodcuts and engravings in female form, and once, on stage, as the quack doctor 'Meister Ratio Status' offering his patient 'pills of hypocrisy' (Rist 1647).

What exactly was this reason of state? The political writers of the period who use the phrase – and there are certainly enough of them – do not employ it in quite the same way. Its ambiguity may well have been the secret of its success. The term 'reason' was, of course, quite slippery enough by itself. The Latin *ratio* sometimes has the force of 'method', or 'plan', as in the case of the Jesuit Plan of Studies (*Ratio Studiorum*). In sixteenth-century French, a *livre de raison* was an account book. In Italian, *ragione* was associated not only with 'reason' but also with 'discourse', 'accounts', and 'law'; the thirteenth-century Palazzo della Ragione in Padua, which still stands, is not the 'Palace of Reason' but the Town Hall.

When Della Casa used the phrase *ragione degli stati*, it was in deliberate contrast to *ragione civile*, 'civil law', implying that the rulers of states were above the law (*quod principi placuit*, and so forth). The law was also in Botero's mind when he came to propose a definition of reason of state in the first chapter of his treatise. Actually he proposed not one definition but two, which overlap but do not coincide. 'State is a stable rule over people', he began, 'and reason of state is the knowledge of the means by which such a dominion may be founded, preserved, and extended.' A moment later he added that the term has a more specific connotation and refers to 'such actions as cannot be considered in the light of *ragione ordinaria*', which the translators of his treatise have rendered 'ordinary reason' but makes better sense, I think, if it is taken to mean 'ordinary law'.

In a book published only three years after Botero's, Girolamo Frachetta made his dichotomy both sharper and more explicit. There are two kinds of reason of state, he explained, the true and the false. True reason of state is simply political prudence, he continued, while false reason of state is the pursuit of self-interest. Many evil deeds have been committed in the name of reason of state by such tyrants as the Roman emperor Tiberius (Frachetta 1592, fos. 38a, 43b). Two years later, it was the turn of Scipione Ammirato to offer a definition of the phrase, which was, he declared, 'on our lips all day', yet remained ill-understood. 'A prince should not be described as acting from reason of state if it can be shown that this was done through ordinary legal channels (*per ragione d'ordinaria giustizia*).' The phrase refers to cases when the law is broken, or more exactly overridden, by the ruler for the public good. Great princes, he declares, such as the emperor Tiberius and King Henri III of France, have on occasion been obliged to have dangerous individuals, such as Sejanus and Henri duc de Guise, put to death without trial (Ammirato 1594, Book 12, ch. 1; the examples will recur).

A generation later, Ammirato was criticised by the lawyer Lodovico Zuccolo for suggesting that reason of state necessarily involved breaches of the law. Zuccolo, who pointed out with some disdain that in his time 'even the barbers and other base craftsmen discuss reason of state in their shops and other haunts and ask questions about it', himself argued that an action may be described as having been performed for reasons of state whenever it helps in the conservation of the particular form of government then in force. Thus, it is from reason of state that the Grand Turk kills his brothers when he becomes sultan, because the Turkish despotism requires the elimination of possible competitors for supreme power. Like his predecessors in the genre, Zuccolo thought in dichotomies, but his basic distinction was the one between theory and practice, rather than those between legal and illegal, or true and false reason of state.

By the 1620s, most of the main points about reason of state had been made, and these points would simply be repeated in later treatises, whether their authors were Italians, Germans, Spaniards, or Frenchmen. For this reason it will probably be more useful to outline an 'identikit' picture of the typical contents of these treatises than to discuss any one of them in detail.

A number of political writers of the time condemned reason of state altogether, like the poet Francisco Quevedo, who claimed that the greatest master of this art was Pontius Pilate, who had condemned Christ for precisely this reason. It was more common, however, to draw a distinction between two kinds of reason of state, 'true' or 'good' on one side and 'false' or 'devilish' on the other. The distinction might be made in terms of ends; good reason of state is what serves the common good, bad reason of state is what serves the individual ruler. Alternatively, it would be drawn with reference to the means employed. True reason of state is limited by justice, piety, the law of God, and so on, while false reason of state condones the breach of treaties and even political assassination. There was general agreement that a line should be drawn between the two kinds of reason of state. Where exactly to draw it was, of course, another matter and a more controversial one.

The central concept was quickly associated with a cluster of other terms. 'Interest', for example, occurs more and more frequently in political and also in historical writing in Italy, France, and elsewhere from the end of the sixteenth century. It forms the organising concept of Henri duc de Rohan's treatise, *De l'interest des Princes et Estats de la Chrestienté* (1638). 'Reason of state', declared another French writer of the time, 'is nothing but reason of interest *(raison d'intérêt)*' (Béthune 1633).

'Prudence' is another term which regularly recurs in the reason–of–state literature from Botero onwards. Botero himself devotes the second book of his treatise to the subject, which he reduces to the form of maxims. Prudence was often associated with 'state secrets' *(arcana imperii)*, and also with simulation and dissimulation, the opposite but complementary arts of appearing to be what you are not and of not appearing to be what you really are. Although some writers in the genre denounced simulation as hypocrisy, it was more common to allow it to form part of true reason of state.

As for false reason of state, it was agreed that this was something the ruler needed to know about, just as the physician needs to know about poisons. Variations on this medical metaphor recur frequently in this literature. (It may not have been only a metaphor: some of the works on reason of state were actually written by physicians.) The state, or 'body politic' is described as being subject to 'illness', so that the ruler or minister has to be able to interpret pathological symptoms, just like a good physician. He also needs to know when to prescribe a little blood-letting; here the metaphor provides a justification for warfare. The physician of the state needs to be able to guide his patient through its various 'crises'; 'crisis' was still an essentially medical term at this period, and referred to the turning point in an illness, when the fate of the patient was decided. This extended metaphor of political sickness and health could, or course, be treated in a more or less original way. It has been noted that Montaigne employs the notion of political illness, but chooses to say nothing about cures or physicians (Clark 1970). When, at the end of the Thirty Years War, Johann Rist put 'Master Reason of State' on to the German stage in the garb of a quack doctor, he was simply giving a new twist to an idea which had been fashionable for two generations (Rist 1647).

An associated idea is that politics, like medicine, is a professional skill, whether it is to be described as an art (for some writers, the 'art of arts'), or as a 'science'. Political behaviour was generally considered to follow rules or principles, so that it could be reduced to maxims or 'aphorisms' (a term associated with the ancient Greek physician Hippocrates and so an extension of the medical metaphor). This specialised skill in matters political is to be acquired, according to many of these writers, not only by experience but also by the study of history and of different forms of government, from China to Peru. Botero did in fact draw examples from both of these empires (not to mention Iran and Burma), and went on to compile the *Relazioni Universali*, a survey of the whole world which paid considerable attention to variations in the form of government. Like the rise of the reason-of-state genre itself, this work suggests that a serious attempt was being made to put the study of politics on a sound empirical basis by collecting detailed observations in a systematic manner, as was being done in medicine, botany, astronomy, and other disciplines.

How new was all this? Botero's lucid and well-informed but rather pedestrian study of reason of state may have launched a new literary and political genre, but it did not really break new intellectual ground. The author had the wit to provide his book with an intriguingly up-to-date title, but its contents were rather more traditional. They are, as he was well aware, reminiscent of Machiavelli, although he is quick to point out that Machiavelli 'bases his reason of state on lack of conscience' (Botero 1589, dedication).

The problem for Botero, as for later writers in the genre, was that, much as they might dislike Machiavelli's recommendations, they could not do without his ideas. Where the political thinkers of the preceding centuries had concentrated on such questions as the best form of government or the duties of the ruler, Machiavelli produced how-to-do-it books, 'political science' (in the twentieth-century sense of the term), rather than 'political philosophy'. The reason-of-state writers had similar aims, as we have just seen, and so, whether they attacked him or tried to ignore him, they could not escape their debt to Machiavelli. Generally they attacked him. He was denounced as the master of the devil's reason of state. 'Machiavellism' (the term was occasionally used by contemporaries) was associated with 'atheism' (in other words, the denial of providence); with the worship of the state ('Politiolatry', it was sometimes called); and with the *politique* party in the religious wars. However, some of the very writers who denounced Machiavelli so vigorously will be found recommending simulation, dissimulation, and even the breaking of treaties, just as he did. What they produced may be described, according to taste, as a more Christian or simply a more hypocritical version of Machiavelli.

It would, of course, be mistaken to treat Machiavelli as the first writer to make recommendations of this kind. Confidential memoranda of the early sixteenth century – and this was, after all, what *The Prince* had been intended to be – analyse political situations in a similar way; the reports of Venetian ambassadors, for example, or the analyses of the state of affairs in Florence after the restoration of the Medici. There is a sense in which the idea of reason of state goes back to the twelfth and thirteenth centuries, to John of Salisbury, for example, who discussed the 'argument of common benefit' (*ratio communis utilitatis*), and to Thomas Aquinas, who was prepared to argue that 'necessity knows no law' (*necessitas legem non habet*). This was, of course, a time when Roman law was being revived, and the Romans, too, had a concept not unlike that of reason of state; Cicero's *ratio reipublicae*, for example (Post 1961). It is possible to go back still further, to the Greeks. As Ammirato remarked, Thucydides and Polybius may be regarded as writers on reason of state. So, of course, can Aristotle, who was concerned with the creation of a science of politics based, like botany, on a collection of empirical data. In the fifth book of his *Politics*, as European intellectuals of the sixteenth and seventeenth centuries knew very well, he described two methods by which tyrannies may be made to endure. Some of the reason-of-state authors cite Aristotle constantly, as Frachetta does, for example, or frame their definitions in his terms, writing, for example, of 'a *habitus* of the practical intellect, called prudence'. However, the ancient writer whose work could most easily be assimilated into the reason-of-state tradition was, of course, Tacitus.

ii Tacitism

The political opinions of Cornelius Tacitus are not easy to discern. As the greatest modern authority has remarked, 'Tacitus gives little away' (Syme 1958, p. 520). His ironic manner reveals a contempt for flattery and other forms of servility and also a certain impatience with theory, but leaves ambiguous his attitude to the Roman monarchy. Although he obviously disliked what went with it, Tacitus may well have regarded the institution as the lesser evil. As a result of his ambiguity he could be claimed as an ally by both the opponents and the supporters of monarchy in early modern Europe, the 'red' and the 'black' Tacitists, as they were called in an essay published in Italy not long after the First World War (Toffanin 1921).

There were certainly enough of these 'Tacitists'. Interest in Tacitus as a political writer spread rapidly in the later sixteenth century. Between 1580 and 1700, more than 100 authors wrote commentaries on Tacitus, and the majority of these commentaries were political ones. A few of them were critical (just as a few contributions to the reason-of-state genre were attacks on the idea and its implications), but in practice the distinction between critical admirers and admiring critics was not very sharp. Meanwhile, the *Annals* and the *Histories* of Tacitus went through edition after edition (at least sixty-seven editions in the half-century 1600–49), in response to the growing demand (Burke 1969).

At this time, Tacitus was viewed as a master of reason of state and the commentaries on him were in effect a parallel genre to the reason-of-state literature, and flourished at much the same time, *c.*1580–*c.*1680. It does not look like coincidence that the author of the first political commentary on Tacitus (published in 1581), Carlo Pasquale (or Paschalius), was, like the author of the first treatise on reason of state, Botero, a Piedmontese (Momigliano 1977). Indeed, the two men almost certainly met in 1585, in France. It was doubtless at the court of France, as well as Rome and Turin, that Botero heard reason of state discussed, and Tacitus quoted, and in his own book he refers to Tacitus no less than forty-four times.

An important contribution to the rise of Tacitism was made by one of the greatest classical scholars of the later sixteenth century, the Fleming Justus Lipsius. The dedication of his 1574 edition of Tacitus to the emperor Maximilian II pointed out the political parallels between 'our times' and those of the Roman historian, a point which Lipsius amplified in later editions. In his *Politicorum libri sex* (1589), 'this learned and laborious tissue' as Montaigne called it, not so much a treatise as an anthology of quotations from classical writers, selected to convey a message, Lipsius gave Tacitus pride of place, with 547 citations (Cicero, the runner-up, received only 227). This book went through fifteen editions in the next decade, and by 1604 it had been translated into seven modern languages (Oestreich 1982, p. 57).

Although he did not use the phrase *ratio status*, preferring to discuss different kinds of *prudentia* (a term which Lipsius helped to popularise in this context), the *Six Books of Politics* made both an important and an early contribution to the reason-of-state genre, a contribution which was virtually ignored by Meinecke. Lipsius' fourth book in particular is concerned with this topic, discussing as it does what maintains a kingdom and what overthrows one, and distinguishing various kinds of dissimulation or deceit, 'small', 'medium', and 'large' – advocating the first, tolerating the second, and condemning only the third. This book demonstrates – if demonstration be needed – the link between the rise of the idea of reason of state and the revival of Tacitus.

So do the *Discorsi sopra Cornelio Tacito* (1594), by Ammirato, whose definition of reason of state has been discussed already. Ammirato's success in the bookshops was considerably more modest than that of Lipsius, but all the same his book was translated into Latin and French and had gone through at least eight editions by 1619. Three years after Ammirato came another important commentary, the *Discorsi sopra i primi cinque libri di Cornelio Tacito* (1597), by Filippo Cavriana. Cavriana is one of the authors whose work suggests that modern historians should not be too quick to dismiss the idea of the body politic as mere metaphor. A physician by profession, Cavriana had a particular admiration for two ancient writers, Tacitus and Hippocrates, and he considered that they had much in common. Like some writers already quoted, he believed that 'illnesses affect states as they do human bodies, but they can be cured by wise statesmen in the same way that skilled physicians cure bodily ills' (Cavriana 1597, p. 12). As Hippocrates taught medicine by means of aphorisms, so Cavriana taught politics, or rather, allowed Tacitus to do the teaching, by extracting aphorisms from his narrative, amplifying them, and elucidating them. The parallel with Hippocrates was to become a standard one.

By the beginning of the seventeenth century, the trickle of commentaries on Tacitus was becoming a flood. To discuss individual commentators one by one is impossible, because they are so numerous, but it is also unnecessary, because they repeat one another. As in the case of the abundant literature on reason of state, the most useful procedure would seem to be to summarise the typical contents of a contribution to the genre.

The commentators read Tacitus with their eyes firmly fixed on political techniques (not to say tricks), techniques which they generally studied from the prince's point of view, sometimes from that of the courtier. As Milton once complained, they 'cut Tacitus into slivers and steaks', taking his maxims out of context and adding to their store of predigested political prudence by turning specific cases into generalisations in a manner which modern readers will find highly implausible (it would be good to know whether many contemporaries would have agreed with them or not). The preface (signed 'A.B.') to an English translation of Tacitus' *Histories* published in 1640 was making typical points more concisely than usual when it told the reader that 'In Galba thou mayest learne, that a good prince governed by evil ministers is as dangerous as if he were evill himselfe . . . By Vitellius, that he that hath no vertue can never be happy . . . By Vespasian, that in civil tumults an advised patience, and opportunity well taken are the only weapons of advantage.'

The commentators tended to concentrate on Books 1–6 of Tacitus'

Annals, in which the emperor Tiberius is the protagonist. In the index to Ammirato's *Discorsi*, for example, references to Tiberius take up a whole column; in Cavriana's *Discorsi*, three columns; and in Pasquale's *Observations*, five columns; while some monographs were exclusively devoted to the emperor's doings. One writer compared these books to Xenophon's *Education of Cyrus* as a representation of the idea of a perfect prince. The example of Tiberius is cited again and again in discussions of the art of political dissimulation; or of the need, on occasion, for rulers to have subjects executed without trial; or of the value of listening in silence to the advice of subordinates. A brief phrase will often stimulate pages of comment. Four words of Tacitus, *Tiberium Neronem maturum annis* ('Tiberius was mature in years'), was enough to launch Cavriana into a discussion of the dangers of royal minorities.

The parallels between the Rome of Tiberius and the courts of early modern Europe were constantly made explicit, whether the commentators believed that human nature never changes, or, with Lipsius and Montaigne, that Tacitus was of particular relevance to their own troubled times. 'You would often think it is us whom he is describing and criticising' (*vous diriez souvent qu'il nous peint et qu'il nous pinse*) (Montaigne 1580–8, Book 3, ch. 8). When they read Tacitus on Tiberius, some contemporaries could not help thinking of rulers of the last century or so. The cold, cruel, cunning emperor so skilled in the art of dissimulation reminded some readers of Louis XI of France, who was frequently quoted as saying that 'who can't feign, can't reign' (*qui nescit dissimulare, nescit regnare*). For other readers the true parallel was still closer to hand. Tiberius reminded Lipsius – at least in his Protestant days – of the duke of Alba, and other commentators thought of Alba's master, Philip of Spain. In the early seventeenth century, Richelieu was a parallel which sprang easily to the minds of both supporters and opponents of the cardinal.

Again, when they considered the career of Sejanus, the commander of the guard who became the favourite of Tiberius – 'a blend of arrogance and servility', as Tacitus described him, who 'concealed behind a carefully modest exterior an unbounded lust for power' – some early modern readers could not help thinking of the favourites of their own day. Some identified Sejanus with the earl of Essex, others with the duke of Buckingham. It was to draw a parallel with Buckingham, then at the height of his power, that Sir John Eliot quoted Tacitus on Sejanus – in the Latin – in a speech in the House of Commons in 1626. Charles I's reaction was that 'he must intend me for Tiberius', and Eliot was sent to the Tower.

487

It was this sense of the political relevance of Tacitus to an age of powerful favourites, absolute monarchs and civil wars which accounts for the growing interest in his writings in the late sixteenth and early seventeenth centuries. The statistics of editions, translations, and commentaries provide a mere outline of his influence. For the colouring we have to turn elsewhere, to the arts, and especially to the drama. Tacitean plays were no more purely aesthetic than commentaries on the *Annals* were purely antiquarian. Both genres carried political messages and were expressions of political thought. The appeal of Tacitus to seventeenth-century playwrights was all the greater because subjects from ancient history were considered more dignified than modern ones. They also had a better chance of getting past the censors, while audiences could be relied on to draw political parallels with their own time; indeed, they would do this whether the dramatist liked it or not.

Although Corneille wrote a fine play about *Otho* (1664), and his seizure of power from his weak predecessor Galba, Tacitean dramas cluster around the figures of two emperors, Tiberius and Nero. The first group includes Ben Jonson's *Sejanus* (1603), and Cyrano de Bergerac's *Mort d'Agrippine* (1653), which deals with the unsuccessful attempt at revenge by the widow of Germanicus, the adoptive son of Tiberius who had been poisoned at his orders. The second group includes two plays about another Agrippina, Nero's mother (his rival for power and ultimately his victim). One was written by the English poet Tom May (1628), the other by the German dramatist Daniel Casper von Lohenstein (1665).

These plays and others in the genre are Tacitean not only in the sense of taking their plots from Tacitus (whose *Annals* sometimes seem closer to melodrama than to normal history), but also in that of drawing on his maxims in a manner not far removed from that of the political commentators. Both Jonson and Lohenstein acknowledged their debts in their notes, Lohenstein citing Tacitus more than 200 times altogether, while Jonson referred to him 59 times in the notes to the first act of *Sejanus*. It is scarcely an exaggeration to claim that the true subject of these plays is reason of state, a phrase which Jonson was one of the first Englishmen to use and one which makes its appearance in Tom May (line 489), Cyrano de Bergerac (act I, scene 5), and Pierre Corneille (act I, scene I). The plays also refer again and again to dissimulation, flattery, 'policy', tyranny, 'absolute' power, and 'the times necessity'. No wonder that Louis XIV's minister Louvois is said to have remarked that to judge Corneille's *Otho*, 'it would have been necessary to fill the pit with ministers of state'.

Tacitus also provided subjects for operas, from Monteverdi's *L'incoronazione di Poppaea* (1643) to Handel's *Agrippina* (1709); and for such paintings as Poussin's *Death of Germanicus* and Rembrandt's *Conspiracy of Civilis*. Monteverdi and his librettist may not have wished to convey any message other than 'Love conquers all', but the Rembrandt, at least, has a clear political significance. Painted for the Town Hall of Amsterdam at the time when the success of the Dutch Revolt against Spain was at last a matter for public celebration, in 1648, Rembrandt's work showed the Batavians, the ancestors of the Dutch, in the process of organising an insurrection against Roman domination.

Tacitus was clearly fashionable in the seventeenth century – which is not to say that the appeal of his work was mere fashion, without good reasons behind it. However, he did not appeal to everyone. Indeed, there was something like an anti-Tacitist movement in this period, although it was rather small in scale. From Botero onwards, there was a tendency to associate Tacitus with Machiavelli and to condemn them both as immoral. More precisely, Botero's association was between Machiavelli and Tiberius: 'I was amazed that so impious an author and so wicked a tyrant should be held in such esteem that they are thought to provide ideal examples of the methods by which states should be governed' (Botero 1589, dedication). Again, in the *Satyre Ménippée*, the French wars of religion were blamed on the cult of Tacitus. In the early seventeenth century, the rival statesmen Richelieu and Olivares were both suspected of an admiration for Tacitus which was supposed to have encouraged them in harsh measures.

Treatises were written against Tacitus, or more exactly against the uncritical acceptance of Tacitus. There were demands that he be 'scoured' or 'sieved', the good advice separated from the evil like wheat from chaff. In his *Tacito abburattato (Tacitus Sieved)* (1643), the Genoese patrician Anton Giulio Brignole Sale concentrated on the danger of taking maxims out of context and using them to analyse situations to which they did not apply, while a host of objections to Tacitus were marshalled by another Genoese, Raffaelle dalla Torre, in his *Astrolabio di stato* or 'political astrolabe' of 1647. One of the most vigorous criticisms, a work called 'The Skowrers' (which unfortunately remains both anonymous and unpublished), is the work of a British writer.[2] The author complains that the writings of Tacitus are taken

---

2. 'Averrunci or The Skowrers: Ponderous and New Considerations upon the first six books of the Annals of C. Tacitus'. MS in the Durazzo Giustinian library, Genoa, uncatalogued when I saw it in 1982.

as 'canonical scripture' by some people, 'speciallie among popular or democratical statesmen' (p. 87). His own aim is, on the contrary, to destroy their authority or, as he puts it, to 'apocryphate' them. Tacitus, he declares, is 'a most slipperie and perilous' writer. 'The indiscreet or unwarie reading the description of Tiberius . . . where the reader is subject to a king . . . will train up and teach such a person to prie into, examin, judge and forejudge the deeds and words of his sovereign to the worse, not onlie his deeds and words but also his gestures looks and postures' (p. 71). Falling into the trap himself a few pages later, he describes the reign of the late Queen Elizabeth as 'a true copie of the times of Tiberius' (p. 76). The moral is that there is no point in prohibiting Machiavelli as long as Tacitus is permitted to circulate freely.

A similar ambivalence runs through what is surely the most brilliant of the many political commentaries written on Tacitus, the *Osservationi* or *Observations* of Traiano Boccalini, first published in 1678 but written around the year 1600. The author spent much of his life as a judge in a Roman tribunal and as an administrator in the Papal States. However, his sympathies, in the political and ideological conflicts of the early seventeenth century, were not with Rome but with the republic of Venice, 'the honour and the strength of Italy', a 'miraculous city' which has 'the divine benefit of liberty' and a model government, including, so he claimed, an aristocracy uncorrupted by luxury.

Boccalini disliked monarchies in general and hated Spain in particular as a cruel and despotic regime which reminded him of Rome under Tiberius. Giving a typically ironic twist to the common comparison of princes to physicians, he described Philip II as dealing with the revolt of the Netherlands by sending 'the medicine of the Duke of Alba' (1678, p. 221). Bitter medicine indeed. Boccalini had much in common with Tacitus, but he could not approve of a writer whose works taught tyrants how to hold on to power. Others might praise Tacitus for producing a manual of statecraft like the *Cyropaedia* of Xenophon; Boccalini called it an anti-manual, a cruel 'Tiberipaedia'. Yet he could not but admire the skill with which Tacitus penetrated the secret designs of princes, pulling away the 'cloak' or 'mask' of idealism to reveal the workings of naked 'interest' underneath. In his *Ragguagli da Parnasso* (*News from Parnassus*, a topical satire of which the more innocuous parts were published in his lifetime), Boccalini described Tacitus as getting into trouble for inventing a new kind of spectacles, which would enable ordinary people to see princes' most secret thoughts (Book 2, ch. 71).

iii   Stoics and sceptics

The preceding two sections have drawn attention to a group of men who could neither accept reason of state nor do without it. They hated the cruelty and deceit of politics, but they wished to be free from political illusions. For some of these men, the most attractive political ideal was that of the ancient Stoics.

Unlike Plato and Aristotle, the Stoics formulated their political theories after the decline of the city-state. Some of them believed in republican liberty, like Cato of Utica, who killed himself when he saw that the Roman republic was doomed. Others were prepared to accommodate themselves to monarchy, like Seneca, who became an adviser to his former pupil the emperor Nero. The Stoics had a good deal to say about liberty, but the freedom on which they placed most emphasis was an interior freedom, defended in the last resort by suicide. It was based on a self-discipline the purpose of which was to achieve a serenity or 'constancy', impervious to the slings and arrows of outrageous fortune. The favourite Stoic images of the wise man were those of an oak tree standing firm against the buffeting of the winds, and of a rock resisting the waves. Such a political philosophy was obviously appropriate to what Seneca once called a 'stormy age of the state', and this was precisely the appeal of Stoicism in the sixteenth and seventeenth centuries. It was not so much a political theory in the strict sense of the term as an attitude or set of attitudes.

The values of Stoic republicanism appealed to some, including the banker Filippo Strozzi, who killed himself in 1538, in imitation of Cato, on the failure of his attempt to restore Florentine liberty, and the author of the *Vindiciae contra tyrannos*, who used the name of Cato's nephew – and Caesar's assassin – Marcus Junius Brutus. There was also the *Discours de la servitude volontaire* (written about 1550, and published posthumously in 1576), by the French magistrate, Montaigne's friend Etienne de La Boétie. La Boétie praised Cato and condemned tyranny, which he stripped bare in the manner of the Stoic emperor Marcus Aurelius. Marcus Aurelius had recommended, in good Senecan fashion, that 'Where there are things which appear most worthy of our approbation, we ought to lay them bare and look at their worthlessness and strip them of all the words with which they are exalted. For outward show is a wonderful perverter of the reason' (*Meditations*, 6.13). La Boétie followed this method (not far removed from the *V-Effekt* or deliberate alienation recommended by Bertolt Brecht), but with more radical intentions than the emperor's. He pointed out that the festivals, rituals, plays, and medals of ancient and modern monarchs were so many *drogueries*, 'drugs', in other words, the opium of the people, intended to tranquillise them, to make them submissive.

The new Stoics of the sixteenth and seventeenth centuries were not necessarily republicans. Far from it. One of the most famous of them in his own day was the Spaniard Antonio de Guevara, Charles V's court preacher and the author of an imaginative biography of Marcus Aurelius, the *Libro áureo* (1528), which held him up to Charles as a model. The most influential version of political Stocism, however, was the resigned monarchism of Lipsius. His dialogue *On Constancy* (1584), set in a garden at Liège, a 'wholsome withdrawing place from the cares and troubles of the world', was often reprinted and translated and did much to make Stoic attitudes fashionable. *On Constancy* was written for private citizens, while Lipsius' even better-known *Politicorum libri sex* was supposedly written for the ruler. It drew heavily on Seneca as well (as we have seen already) as on Tacitus, whose moral and political views seem in any case to have been fairly compatible with those of the Stoics.

Lipsius was also concerned to fit his political philosophy into a Christian framework. His task was not too difficult, although Stoicism had originated in pagan times. Stoic constancy had much in common with the Christian virtue of patience and in any case, as Lipsius was careful to point out, the Stoic philosophy had appealed to some of the fathers of the church.

There was even a sense in which Stoicism was in harmony with reason of state. Like *yin* and *yang*, the two doctrines were complementary opposites, reason of state teaching the activities suitable for a ruler, Stoicism the passivity or resignation suitable for his subjects, who were recommended to exercise absolute power over their passions rather than resist the absolute power of the monarch. Since the 'stormy age of the state' to which Seneca referred had come round again, and Europe was racked by the 'Eighty Years War' (1568–1648), it is no wonder that the Stoic views reformulated by Lipsius on the basis of his experience of civil war in the Netherlands should have attracted widespread interest and gained considerable acceptance.

It has even been suggested, by the late Gerhard Oestreich, that Lipsius and Stoicism both played an important part in the military reforms of the period, and more especially the creation, by Maurice prince of Orange and other rulers, of a standing army as part of the apparatus of the early modern state. 'Lipsius . . . sets up the Roman Stoic ethic as the morality and ideology of the new army' (Oestreich 1982, p. 50). A stress on military discipline can indeed be found in both the writings of Lipsius and the reorganised armies of the seventeenth century. However, it should be pointed out that the discipline with which the ancient Stoic philosophers were concerned was self-discipline, the self-control of heroic individuals, very different from the new military discipline which was not voluntary but imposed, and on masses not individuals. If the military reformers did indeed derive their ideals from philosophy, as well as from practical needs (or from the example of the Roman army, from which Seneca had derived his metaphor of discipline), then their transformation of that philosophy was a profound one.

Whatever its relevance to the so-called 'military revolution', there can be little doubt of the success of the neo-Stoic movement or of the political importance of the literature it engendered. Towards the end of the civil wars in France, the magistrate Guillaume Du Vair transposed Lipsius into French terms in his dialogue *De la Constance* (1594). Even the garden is there; a Parisian one this time, in which the dialogue's protagonists discuss the ruin of the state and reach the resigned conclusion that 'The afflictions that are borne constantly . . . lift us up to heaven' (Du Vair 1622, p. 111). Library inventories reveal the interest taken in Lipsius by Cardinal Richelieu and other French intellectuals of the early seventeenth century. In Spain, too, Lipsius and Stoicism were taken seriously. Richelieu's great adversary the count-duke of Olivares owned the works of Lipsius and the writer Quevedo presented Olivares as a Stoic hero, as Richelieu was by Jean de Silhon. In England, Stoic values were expressed in Sir Philip Sidney's *Arcadia* (1590), in which Pamela is portrayed as constant in adversity 'like a rock amidst the sea, beaten both with the winds and with the waves, yet itself immovable'. Lipsius and Du Vair were translated, and in 1629 Richard James sent Sir John Eliot a copy of Lipsius' *On Constancy* to console him during his imprisonment in the Tower of London.

For dramatic presentations of Stoic values – and their relevance to politics – we may of course turn to the stage. George Buchanan's *Baptistes* (written *c.* 1540) presents St John the Baptist as a Stoic hero constant in his resistance to tyranny (a passive resistance, as recommended by Calvin). The Roman plays of Robert Garnier, written during the French civil wars of the 1560s and 1570s, celebrated similar values, and so did those of Corneille, written shortly before the renewal of civil war in the 1640s. The 'Tacitean' drama discussed above might equally well have been called 'Senecan', partly because Seneca himself wrote tragedies on which many early modern plays were modelled, and partly because he made frequent

493

appearances on the seventeenth-century stage, for example, in Monteverdi's *Poppaea* (1643), Lohenstein's *Epicharis* (1665), and Racine's *Britannicus* (1669), not to mention the *Death of Seneca* (1645) by Tristan L'Hermite.

One of the best-known adherents of the neo-Stoic movement has not yet been discussed: Michel de Montaigne. A great friend of La Boétie, whose constancy in dying he recorded, Montaigne drew heavily on Seneca in his early essays, as he was the first to admit. Like La Boétie, he imagined the powerful stripped of the accessories which made them respected. 'The Emperor, whose pomp dazzles you in public . . . look at him behind the curtain and you see nothing but an ordinary man' (1580–8, Book 1, ch. 42). However, Montaigne did not use this image as an argument against monarchy. His position was one of scepticism. On the beams of his study were painted the sentences 'All that is certain is that nothing is certain', and 'I suspend judgement.'

It may seem odd to attribute a political theory – or indeed any kind of theory – to sceptics, but their suspension of judgement was not without political consequences. Even the decision to be apolitical is in a sense a political decision; and in any case the sceptics (ancient and early modern) were not apolitical. They were not apathetic in this sense, despite the ideal of *apatheia* ('constancy'), which they shared with the Stoics. Their point was essentially what we would call a 'relativist' one: that political arrangements, like other customs, vary from place to place and from time to time, and that there is no reason to argue that one such arrangement is in itself better than another. Where the Stoics believed in natural law, Carneades, the leader of the academic sceptics, argued that what was law was not natural and that what was natural was not law. The wise man, according to the sceptics, will live his life in conformity with the customs of his country, although he will not accept the arguments put forward for the superiority of those customs.

This was the attitude of Montaigne. His belief was that disputes about the best form of government (disputes which were common in his day) were of no practical value. They were (as we might say) purely utopian or indeed 'academic'. He took pleasure in pointing out that people brought up to self-government regard monarchies as unnatural, while those who are accustomed to monarchy do exactly the reverse. He defended the political system under which he lived, the French monarchy, for purely pragmatic reasons. 'In public affairs', he wrote with brutal candour, 'there is no course so bad, provided that it is stable and traditional, that is not better than change and alteration' (1580–8, Book 2, ch. 17). The price of political revolution (*mutation d'estat*) was, he thought, always too high. On the other hand, he had nothing but contempt for traditional modes of justifying particular regimes. 'The laws are maintained in credit', he wrote, 'not because they are just but because they are laws. That is the mystical foundation of their authority; they have no other' (1580–8, Book 3, ch. 13). A remarkable (not to say shocking) statement to make in the sixteenth century, and one not unlike the notorious definition of law as 'the command of the sovereign' put forward some sixty years later by Thomas Hobbes. Both men were, of course, writing after years of civil war, to which any kind of stability was coming to seem preferable.

Their reaction was not so different from that of Stoics such as Lipsius and Du Vair who expressed their desire for a quiet life in a more heroic language, although for his part Montaigne came to regard the Stoic ideal of constancy as unnatural or even inhuman. Still closer to Montaigne was the pragmatic attitude expressed by the engineer Simon Stevin: 'Everyone must always consider as his rightful authority those who at the present are actually governing the place where he chooses his dwelling, without concerning himself about the question of whether they or their predecessors have reached their position justly or unjustly' (*On Civil Life* (1590), ch. 2: Stevin 1611). The main difference was that Stevin was a Netherlander, writing in a more mobile and decentralised society than France. In the Civil War in the Netherlands, it was not unrealistic to suggest to those who disliked a particular urban regime that they should simply go elsewhere.

Another political thinker who was close to Montaigne was his acquaintance Pierre Charron, whose treatise *De la Sagesse* (1601), includes a discussion of prudence (*prud'hommie*). Whether or not he was a true sceptic in the strict epistemological sense, Charron was impressed by 'the diversitie and strangenes' of alien customs, from suttee to male prostitution. His political reflections, like Montaigne's, were inspired by his experience of the French religious wars, as his chapters on treason, faction, sedition, and popular revolt (let alone civil war) make obvious enough. Charron drew Montaigne's conclusion that 'Lawes and customs are maintained in credit, not because they are just and good, but because they are lawes and customes'; that all alteration 'is very dangerous, and yeeldeth alwaies more evill than good'; and that the best thing for everyone is to follow 'the lawes and customes which he findeth established in the countrie where he is' (Book 2, ch. 8). He has no time for utopias, and dismisses the political ideas of Plato and Thomas More as mere 'painting in the air' (Book 3, ch. 51).

Passages such as these make it easy to see why Charron has often been regarded as a mere plagiary of Montaigne. However, there is more to his treatise. Although he criticises the life of retirement as a form of cowardice, Charron has considerable sympathy for Stoic values, praises constancy and tranquillity of mind, quotes Seneca again and again, and acknowledges a considerable debt to Lipsius, notably in his discussion of the various types of prudence. Charron might also be described as a Tacitist; at any rate he laces his recommendations with frequent quotations from Tacitus, and holds a similar view of the contrast between appearance and reality in politics. 'That which is done in publike is but a fable, a fiction, the truth is secret and in privat' (Book 1, ch. 53). Charron also deserves to be regarded as a writer on reason of state, although he does not use the phrase. He was very much concerned with the *état* (still a new concept in France), and especially with its conservation. He was prepared to advise the prince 'among foxes to counterfet the foxe', and to save the commonwealth 'by the self-same meanes that others would undermine and overthrow it', means which include not only dissimulation but also the execution without trial of dangerous individuals (Book 3, ch. 4). He was even prepared to cite Machiavelli without the usual words of condemnation.

In short, Charron's *De la Sagesse* brought within the covers of one treatise all the political attitudes discussed in this chapter. His eclecticism seems to have had considerable appeal; at all events, his book was reprinted, translated, and generally taken more seriously in the seventeenth century than the essays of Montaigne. Cardinal Richelieu, for example, owned his books and was accused by Olivares of wishing to introduce Charron's irreligious 'wisdom' into France.

Another of Charron's admirers was Richelieu's librarian Gabriel Naudé. Naudé's own treatise, *Considérations politiques sur les coups d'état* (1639), is written in a tone of sceptical (or Stoic) detachment, recommends ministers to keep calm, and draws on Seneca, Lipsius, and Montaigne as well as Charron. However, Naudé was also well aware of Tacitus and Machiavelli, and his book is essentially concerned with reason of state; indeed, it is the most trenchant of the many contributions to the genre. He takes up the term 'coup' (*colpo*), which had been used in a casual way in the earlier Italian literature, and makes of it a technical term to describe bold actions in extraordinary circumstances, where the ordinary rules or maxims do not apply. Henri III's assassination of Henri duc de Guise, for example, is treated as a violent remedy for the sickness of the state ('kill or cure'), and so is the Massacre of St Bartholomew's Day, of which Naudé remarks coolly that it was 'very just', but could be criticised for having been merely 'done by halves' (1711, p. 101; cf. Freund 1975). Like La Boétie and Montaigne, Naudé was well aware of the political utility of ritual and mystery, and remarks on the conversion of Clovis that 'the sacred Oil and the Auriflamb . . . were so many Contrivances of State to give Authority to the change of his Religion, which he would make use of as a powerful Machine to ruine all his little neighbouring Princes' (1711, p. 87). It should · not be thought that the ideas of legitimation and of social function were altogether strange to the seventeenth century.

With Naudé we have reached the last major work in any of the genres discussed in this chapter. As Meinecke pointed out long ago, the Italian reason-of-state literature 'completely dwindled away in the second half of the century' (Meinecke 1957, p. 126). So did the commentaries on Tacitus. Amelot de la Houssaye's *Morale de Tacite* (1683) is an interestingly late example, but it is concerned, as the title suggests, more with morals than with politics. There was also a reaction against Stoicism, or at least against the Stoic hero, in the middle of the seventeenth century, a reaction expressed in his usual lapidary form by La Rochefoucauld when he wrote that 'the constancy of the wise is no more then the art of hiding their agitation' (La Rochefoucauld 1665, no. 20). Queen Christina of Sweden, no bad indicator of intellectual fashions, shifted enthusiasms in later life from Stoicism to mysticism (Stolpe 1959).

As for the sceptical approach to politics characteristic of Montaigne and Charron, it was attacked head-on by Grotius, whose *De Jure Belli ac Pacis* (1625), included a critique of Carneades, and by implication of those modern sceptics who had denied the existence of the law of nature (Battista 1966, p. 213), while Pascal transformed Montaigne's political theory into something very different by combining it with the Augustinian view of government as the unfortunate consequence of original sin (Auerbach 1959). Later in the century, John Dryden could still profess his attachment to 'Montaigne's principles, that an honest man ought to be contented with that form of government and with those fundamental constitutions of it which he received from his ancestors and under which himself was born' (q. Bredvold 1934, p. 131), but in Dryden's day this kind of political relativism was being driven out – at least for a time – by the geometrical method.

Dryden formed his political views in the Exclusion Crisis, as Montaigne had formed his in the French civil wars. None of the movements discussed in this chapter can be understood unless we remember that their political context was the age of international and civil wars (seen by many as religious wars), which racked Europe in the sixteenth and seventeenth centuries, more especially in the eighty years between the Revolt of the Netherlands and the Peace of Westphalia. If the Italians, French, and Netherlanders were the principal innovators in this area of political thought, while the Spaniards, Germans, English, and others seem to have followed in their tracks, this may well be because the involvement of the Italians, French, and Netherlanders in political upheavals took place earlier than it did elsewhere. Reason of state and Tacitism offered rulers and their counsellors advice on dealing with the extraordinary problems of the times; Stoicism taught private citizens how to endure their extraordinary calamities; while scepticism was in large measure a reaction against conflicting claims to political legitimacy. The divergences between Stoicism, scepticism, and reason of state should not of course be forgotten. Stoics, for example, believed in natural law; sceptics undermined it; reason of state overrode it. Yet the intellectual movements which have been discussed here are at least connected in the sense of offering solutions to the same pressing problems of their day.

17

Grotius and Selden

RICHARD TUCK

i The context of Grotius' career

When the history of recent moral philosophy was written at the end of the seventeenth and the beginning of the eighteenth century, a consistent account was given of the role of Hugo Grotius. In the eyes of men like Samuel Pufendorf, Christian Thomasius, Jean Barbeyrac, and their successors, he was the one who 'broke the ice' after the long winter of Aristotelianism; who provided a new theory of natural law which could supplant both the discredited theories of the scholastics and the anti-scientific and sceptical writings of Renaisance authors such as Montaigne and Pierre Charron. He was the inventor of a new 'science of morality', which was taken up in various ways by all the major figures of the seventeenth century, including Hobbes, Locke, and Pufendorf himself. His first important follower, they also all agreed, was John Selden, though the relationship between the two men was by no means a straightforward one (see Tuck 1979, pp. 174–5).

As we shall see, there is a sense in which these historians were absolutely correct; Grotius *did* see something for the first time which was to be crucially important in the succeeding century, namely that there could be a systematic moral and political philosophy which met the objections levelled against such an enterprise in the late sixteenth century. But this insight was hard-won, and embodied in a series of works which were to some extent *pièces d'occasion*; to understand the generation of his political philosophy, it is necessary to look first at his public career.

On 18 March 1598, shortly before his fifteenth birthday, Hugo Grotius left his native Holland on an embassy to the king of France. Despite his youth, he had been chosen by Johan van Oldenbarnevelt, advocate of the States of the province of Holland since 1586 and in effect the chief minister of the United Provinces, as an appropriate companion on one of the major diplomatic missions during the war between the Netherlands and Spain, and their joint enterprise marked the beginning of a political partnership which was to endure until Oldenbarnevelt's fall and execution in 1619. They both came from the same kind of social background; Grotius' father Jan de Groot was one of the regents of Delft – that is, one of the small group of magistrates who governed the city and who chose from among themselves delegates to sit in the States of Holland, the medieval parliamentary assembly which governed the province in the absence of the king. They were not elected, but coopted by the existing regents, and increasingly became a closed and hereditary group. Oldenbarnevelt, though not by birth a Hollander, came from a similar regent family in Amersfoort in the province of Gelderland. Both turned to the law for their career, though in Grotius' case this decision followed a brilliant and precocious career at the University of Leiden (which he entered at the age of eleven) and the appearance of a number of editions of classical texts. His decision to enter the legal profession was marked during the mission to France by the conferment on him of the degree of *doctor utriusque juris* by the University of Orleans in May. But the difference in age and position between Oldenbarnevelt and Grotius meant that the younger man was very much the protégé of the older, and his fortunes rose or fell with those of his patron.[1]

By virtue of his political position, Oldenbarnevelt had the resources at his disposal to reward his friends, and Grotius benefited accordingly. In 1601 he was made historiographer of Holland, a post which was not purely honorary – a monetary subsidy was also granted to him (at first he was on trial, but in 1604 he was secured in the post). In 1607 he became *advocaat-fiscaal*, one of the treasury officials of the States of Holland, and in 1612 received his greatest office when he was appointed pensionary of Rotterdam, becoming at the same time one of that city's representatives in the States of Holland. The pensionary was a kind of chief executive of the city, and Oldenbarnevelt had himself held this post immediately before becoming the States' advocate. In 1613 Grotius led an important delegation to King James in England.

Throughout this period he was producing a multitude of papers and speeches for Oldenbarnevelt, acting as a kind of political adviser and,

---

1. For the association of Grotius and Oldenbarnevelt, and the latter's career, see den Tex 1973, *passim*. The best account in English of Grotius' life is Knight 1925.

sometimes anonymously and sometimes openly, as a propagandist for his patron's ideas; he even lived next door to Oldenbarnevelt in The Hague.[2] But throughout the second decade of the century, Oldenvarnevelt's adminstration ran into more and more opposition over its policy of a degree of religious toleration. Eventually an open breach developed between his supporters in the States General of the United Provinces (primarily the representatives of the cities, though by no means all of them) and his opponents, a coalition of clergymen and some municipal leaders (notably those of Amsterdam) headed by the stadtholder Maurice. Since under the United Provinces' constitution Maurice controlled the military power of the provinces (rather like the governor of an American state), the only way in which Oldenbarnevelt could secure himself when the crisis point was reached was by attempting to raise a rival military force; he failed, and was arrested for high treason. After a lengthy trial he was executed at The Hague on 13 May 1619. Grotius was naturally implicated in his fall, and faced trial also; he was almost sentenced to death, but in the end was reprieved and sentenced to life imprisonment in the fortress of Loevestein in the south of Holland, and his estate confiscated. His reprieve was partly the result of his betrayal at the trial of his old friend and patron. He escaped in dramatic and romantic circumstances (in a basket of books, appropriately enough) two years later, and fled to France – his escape was probably winked at by the stadtholder, embarrassed by the presence on Dutch soil of such an eminent captive. Grotius was not to return to Holland for twenty-three years, except for a brief visit in 1631 when he was threatened with arrest and had to flee to Hamburg; he lived the remainder of his life after his escape from Loevestein as a pensioner of royal courts, first of France and then from 1634 onwards of Sweden, where he was one of Queen Christina's gallery of European intellectuals and was employed by her as resident ambassador in Paris. Paris was thus his usual base from 1621 to 1645. In that year he visited Sweden *via* Holland and was received with honour in Amsterdam. Intrigues at the Swedish court seem to have determined him to resign his ambassadorship, which the queen eventually allowed him to do; he may have planned to return to Holland, but the ship on which he was travelling to Lübeck was blown ashore on the coast of Pomerania, and Grotius fell ill. He died in Rostock on 28 August 1645, and it was only his body which finally returned to Holland, where it was buried in the church of Delft.

---

2. See the address on the letter from De Vigier, March 1608, Grotius 1928, p. 106 and n.

Oldenbarnevelt's rise and fall had something of a classically tragic character, and was indeed the subject of a tragedy by John Fletcher. But it was also in one sense one of the formative dramas of the modern world: the issues at stake included the question of religious toleration, the emancipation of ethics from theology, and the location of sovereignty within the Dutch state. On all of these issues, Grotius had something important to say.

He began, like his master, by accepting many of the ideas to which rulers in the 1590s all over Europe were attracted – the impossibility of reaching a universal consensus on ethical and religious matters, and the importance of maintaining a powerful state which could prevent this lack of consensus from tipping over into civil war. This is the set of ideas associated most famously with Justus Lipsius (who was a friend and teacher of Grotius' father), and they found a ready audience in both the northern and southern Netherlands – the two halves of a nation which had after all been destroyed by just such a civil war.[3] Inscribed above the front door of Oldenbarnevelt's house was the motto, 'Nil Scire Tutissima Fides ('To Know Nothing is the Surest Faith') (den Tex 1973, I, p. 7); but at the same time he worked hard to sustain the political unity of the United Provinces and their military strength – based on a disciplined army modelled on the Roman legions described by Lipsius.

But the group of writers round Oldenbarnevelt at the turn of the century, including Grotius himself and his old friend Jan de Meurs, saw that Lipsius' particular brand of political theory was not really appropriate to the problems of a nation without a *prince*, and they produced a number of remarkable essays in which they argued for the recognition of the United Provinces as a true aristocratic republic, comparable to Venice or (in their own interpretation of these constitutions) Athens and Rome. Grotius in a very early piece revealed his sympathy with the oligarchic Venetian constitution and his belief that it resembled that of the United Provinces (Stevin 1599, sig. *2ff.), and in a longer work he composed in 1601–2, entitled *Parallelon rerumpublicarum* (the bulk of which is now lost), he produced a systematic comparison of the Netherlands with both Athens and Rome. Attacking both the traditional notion of the mixed constitution and the Bodinian view that Rome was a democracy, he argued that the 'ordinary and day-to-day authority' at Rome was possessed by the nobility.[4] Hostility to the idea of a mixed constitution ran throughout his

---

3. For Lipsius, see Oestreich 1982. His sympathy with scepticism is discussed briefly in Tuck 1983, p.48. See also pp.92–3 above.   4. Grotius 1928, p.29; 1801, *passim*.

work, despite the traditional view that Venice exemplified it; in the view of these early seventeenth-century Dutch republicans, Venice was in fact a true oligarchy or aristocracy.

ii Dutch republicanism and the transition to natural law

In his major constitutional work of this period which actually appeared in print, his *De Antiquitate Reipublicae Batavicae* of 1610, Grotius began by quoting Tacitus – 'all nations are ruled either by the people, the leading inhabitants (*primores*), or an individual'.[5] The 'Batavians' or Netherlanders had always, he claimed, been ruled by *primores*, with whom a kind of prince had often been associated; but this did not make their constitution any more mixed, or less purely aristocratic, for the prince acted like a president or chairman of the oligarchs. Like Selden at the same time in England, Grotius read Tacitus and the other classical writers on the customs of the Germanic and Gaullish tribes as giving an account not of balanced or limited kingship (which had, for example, been François Hotman's reading) but of true aristocracy without a monarchical element.[6] In a piece written for Oldenbarnevelt but never published until 1967, Grotius even argued that the States General of the United Provinces should be reconstructed on avowedly aristocratic, non-representative lines (De Michelis 1967, pp. 171–89). It actually consisted of mandated delegates from the provincial States, but Grotius claimed that to prevent civil strife and further the war, it should consist of self-appointing senators like the regents of his native city. In a number of other papers and letters he wrote before the Truce of 1609, Grotius expressed his whole-hearted support for the war, and his fear that constitutional change of this kind would be threatened by peace (e.g. Grotius 1928, p. 85; Van Eysinga 1955).

Unlike the Venetian writers on republicanism, however, Grotius and the other Dutch republicans linked their aristocratic theories with a defence of imperialism more like that of the populist Florentine republicans. Grotius' *Annales et Historiae* (note the Tacitist echo), the product of his years as historiographer to the States of Holland, chronicle the rise of the Dutch overseas empire and analyse its economic base; while in 1604 he started

---

5. Grotius, *De Antiquitate*, ch. I (1630, p. 17). The (unacknowledged) quotation from Tacitus is from the *Annals*, IV.33.
6. Grotius, *De Antiquitate*, ch. II (1630, pp. 33ff): Selden, *Analecton Anglo-Britannicon*, ch. III (1726, II, cols. 877–9).

work on a comprehensive defence of Dutch naval activity against Spain and Portugal in the East Indies. The form this took represented something new in his work: it went beyond the humanist reflections of the *Parallela* (which, he remarked in March 1605, 'now begins to displease its author' (Grotius 1928, p. 53), and involved Grotius in thinking about what moral rules could underpin the confrontation of two societies anywhere in the world. This is the work which lay in manuscript until it was discovered in 1864 (except for part of it which was published in 1609 as the *Mare Liberum*), and which was misleadingly entitled by its first editors *De Iure Praedae*. In fact, Grotius always referred to it in his correspondence as his work *De Indis*. The object of the work was two-fold. One was to persuade Dutch public opinion that the seizure of prize ships in the East Indies by ships of the Dutch East India Company was legitimate (for some members of the Company, particularly the Mennonites, seem to have been unsure about this), but the other was the wider object of demonstrating to an international audience (and particularly one familiar with the Spanish neo-scholastic literature) that the Dutch activity was legitimate. What the Dutch were trying to do in the Indies was to persuade native rulers (often by a show of military force) to trade with them rather than the Spaniards, and in many cases to help native guerrilla forces in their wars with Spanish-backed rulers – a classic example of informal imperial activity. In 1608 the Zeeland Chamber of the East India Company asked Grotius to publish part of the work as the *Mare Liberum*, though by the time it appeared the relevant agreements with Spain had already been made. Grotius himself had considered publishing the more general and theoretical parts in November 1606; he admitted that the issues they covered had been dealt with by 'many both ancient and modern writers', but claimed that he believed it to be possible to 'throw new light on them by employing a secure method and by combining divine and human law with the principles of philosophy' (Grotius 1928, p. 72).

This is indeed exactly what the *De Iure Praedae* (as I shall continue to call it) attempts. Its first chapter contains a critique of the customary humanist way of talking about such matters, and a remarkable manifesto for a wholly new method. He rejected both the use of positive civil law as a guide and the attempt to employ scriptural exegesis, as well as the idea that a simple comparative history was all that was needed. Instead, he proclaimed the need to do as the ancient jurists had done, and to 'refer the art of civil government back to the very fount of nature'.[7] This call for a return to a

---

7. Grotius, *De Iure Praedae*, MS, p. 5 (1950, I, p. 7).

naturalistic style of argument was accompanied by an even more remarkable breach with the general Renaissance Aristotelian methodology in the human sciences. Aristotle divided sciences into the categories of practical and theoretical – ethics and politics belonged to the practical, and mathematics and similar studies to the theoretical. And yet Grotius now outlined his own methodology as follows:

First, let us see what is true universally as a general proposition; then, let us gradually narrow this generalisation, adapting it to the special nature of the case under consideration. Just as the mathematicians customarily prefix to any concrete demonstration a preliminary statement of certain broad axioms on which all persons are easily agreed, in order that there may be some fixed point from which to trace the proof of what follows, so shall we point out certain rules and laws of the most general nature, presenting them as preliminary assumptions which need to be recalled rather than learned for the first time, with the purpose of laying a foundation upon which our other conclusions may safely rest.

(*ibid.*, MS, p. 5: 1950, I, p. 7)

And, indeed, the whole work is tightly organised as a series of discussions round nine fundamental 'rules' and thirteen associated 'laws'. In the writings of the scholastics, their concentration on the law of nature as a foundation for their arguments had led them also to blur the distinction between the practical and theoretical sciences – according to Aquinas, the distinction was merely that in the practical sciences deductions from the fundamental and *a priori* axioms were more difficult and contentious than in the theoretical sciences. Grotius' return to the law of nature as the basis for his discussion led him to make the same move, and to instate mathematics as the methodological model for the human sciences – a development which was to determine more than anything else the character of seventeenth-century European political thought.

The idea that there could be a universal and deductive science of ethics akin to mathematics, however, rested in the *De Iure Praedae* not simply on a reiteration of the beliefs of the scholastics. Grotius argued first that the form of any moral rule was the pronouncement by an agent or agents of what their will was to be (a claim compatible, of course, with the most extreme relativism). This was true both of God and of man, and he based his whole discussion on a set of fundamental and formal rules.

   I What God has shown to be his will, that is law.
  II What the common consent of mankind has shown to be the will of all, that is law.
 III What each individual has indicated to be his will, that is law with respect to him.

IV What the commonwealth had indicated to be its will, that is law for the whole body of citizens.

V What the commonwealth had indicated to be its will, that is law for the individual citizens in their mutual relations.

VI What the magistrate had indicated to be his will, that is law in regard to the whole body of citizens.

VII What the magistrate had indicated to be his will, that is law in regard to the citizens as individuals.

VIII Whatever all states have indicated to be their will, that is law in regard to all of them.   (*ibid.*, 1950, I, pp. 369–70)

But such a formal system did not help his argument unless the contents of these acts of will, and particularly of God's, could be uncontentiously determined. This was the occasion for Grotius' striking and original idea, an idea of great simplicity whose consequences occupied him for the rest of his life. He went back to the principles of the Stoics upon which men like Lipsius had based their pessimistic and relativist view of the world, and in particular the Stoic claim that the primary force governing human affairs is the desire for self-preservation. But he interpreted this desire in *moral* terms, as the one and only *universal right*: no one could ever be blamed for protecting themselves, but they could never be justified in doing anything harmful which did not have the end in view. This was the content of God's will for mankind, which could be deduced simply by looking at the natural world.

From this fact the old poets and philosophers have rightly deduced that love, whose primary force and action are directed to self-interest, is the first principle of the whole natural order. Consequently, Horace should not be censured for saying, in imitation of the academics [i.e. the sceptics], that expediency might perhaps be called the mother of justice and equity.[8]

Upon this basic principle of self-interest, he argued, were grounded the two principles of the law of nature (and hence the first two 'Laws' which he set out as corollaries to his 'Rules'): 'It shall be permissible to defend one's own life and to shun that which threatens to prove injurious' and 'It shall be permissible to acquire for oneself, and to retain, those things which are useful for life.' But because men feel a certain sense of common kinship with one another, there are two other laws of nature: 'Let no one inflict injury upon his fellow' and 'Let no one seize possession of that which has been taken into the possession of another' (*ibid.*, MS, pp. 6, 7: 1950, I, pp. 10,

8. Grotius, *De Iure Praedae*, MS, pp. 5, 5a (1950, I, p. 9).

13). Grotius was quite clear that self-interest is the primary and overriding principle, and that altruism must in some way be explicable in terms of self-interest.

The order of presentation of the first set of laws and of those following immediately thereafter has indicated that one's own good takes precedence over the good of another person – or, let us say, it indicates that by nature's ordinance each individual should be desirous of his own good fortune in preference to that of another. (*ibid.*, MS, p. 11: 1950, I, p. 21)

It is important also to stress that according to Grotius this natural sense of society with all other men does not entail any obligation to *help* them: it merely entails an obligation to *refrain from harming* them. It is only in organised states that something more emerges:

there are laws peculiar to the civil convenant, . . . which extend beyond the laws already set forth, as follows: first, *Individual citizens should not only refrain from injuring other citizens, but should furthermore protect them, both as a whole and as individuals;* secondly, *Citizens should not only refrain from seizing one another's possessions, . . . but should furthermore contribute individually both that which is necessary to other individuals and that which is necessary to the whole* [my italics].
(*ibid.*, MS, pp. 11a 11: 1950, I, p. 21)

The natural society of men is one in which individuals pursue their own interests up to the point at which such a pursuit actually deprives another of something which they possess; it is not one of benevolence as we would customarily understand the term, and it is very far removed from the Aristotelian picture of the *zoon politikon*.

A theory about how we acquire possessions in a state of nature is obviously essential to an argument of this kind, and Grotius provided such a theory in that part of the work which was later printed as the *Mare Liberum*. His central argument was that men can have *a kind of* property in nature – the second law of nature, as he had outlined it, after all precisely endorsed the acquisition of the things necessary for life by an individual. This was only a kind of property, or *dominium quoddam* as he put it, because the salient feature of the developed system of private property was absent: no one could claim a persistent and unique right over a part of the material world that they were not at the time putting to some direct use (*ibid.*, MS, p. 101: 1950, I, p. 228). However, such a developed system would grow naturally out of the primitive condition of mankind as culture and technology developed: the growth of agriculture meant fields had to be cultivated on a systematic basis to produce consumables, and the man who cultivated the field could claim a property right in it. A system of conventions could then arise to allocate particular pieces of property, like taking seats in a theatre.

Not only private individuals, but also groups of people and states acquired their possessions in this manner. This further claim is linked to one of the most important themes of the work, that the rights enjoyed by a state and its government cannot be different in kind from the rights enjoyed by an individual in the state of nature. 'Just as every right of the magistrate comes to him from the state, so has the same right come to the state from private individuals (*ibid.*, MS, p. 40: 1950, I, p. 929). Civil society developed out of a state of nature in which men were already bound by the fundamental laws of nature, and it was brought about largely because of the increasing numbers of people.

[Relatively small] social units began to gather individuals together into one locality, not with the intention of abolishing the society which links all men as a whole, but rather in order to fortify that universal society by a more dependable means of protection, and at the same time, with the purpose of bringing together under a more convenient arrangement the numerous different products of many persons' labour which are required for the uses of human life.

(*ibid.*, MS, p. 10: 1950, I, p. 19)

One of the main arguments against such an account of civil society in earlier literature had been that only a prince or a supreme magistrate could possess the power to punish offenders, since that appeared to be a special right which no individual could possess and which therefore no individual could transfer either to the state or to the magistrate; but Grotius was quite clear that this was not so. The first four laws of nature together entailed a right to exact restitution for wrongs committed against one, and since, as he said, 'an injury inflicted even upon one individual is the concern of all . . . primarily because of the example set', each person in a state of nature had an interest in restraining or punishing anyone who infringed another's rights and deprived them of their possessions. He supported this claim with the identical argument that Locke was later to use in the same context, that modern states claim the right to punish foreigners for their transgressions, and that such a right must arise from the law of nature and not from civil law (*ibid.*, MS, p. 40: 1950, I, p. 92).

Although his purpose in the *De Iure Praedae* was not to defend the oligarchic Dutch constitution, Grotius nevertheless revealed that he did not believe that Dutch opposition to Spain was grounded on any obvious principle of *popular* resistance. As he said, 'not every regime devoid of a prince is a popular government'. Liberty was important, but defined in the following way:

if the principate has already been abolished, and a republican form of government set up, the course properly to be followed by citizens in doubtful cases will be indicated by the laws that favour the claims of liberty . . . This principle holds good, above all, with reference to that form of liberty which is neither immoderate not unbridled (for liberty attended by these attributes is more accurately called 'licence'), or in other words, with reference to that free status which is confirmed by the princely power of the governing officials, by the authority of the country's most important men, and by the goodwill of the citizens.

(ibid., MS, pp. 135, 136: 1950, I, p. 301)

His vision was still that of an aristocratic republic, 'free' in the sense of being without a monarch, fighting to establish its right to engage in an aggressive imperialism.

As can be seen from this account of its main arguments, the *De Iure Praedae* is an astonishing book. In it we find laid out most of the themes (and the dilemmas) which were to occur in all his successors until the end of the eighteenth century. Sceptical moral relativism is answered by being absorbed into a new 'scientific' ethics: the 'necessities' of Lipsius and his followers become 'rights' which can be used to generate a complex system of rights and duties. What Grotius built on this foundation was the common habitation for his successors. The idea that civil society is a construct by individuals wielding rights or bundles of property, and that governments possess no rights that those individuals did not possess, is the main assumption of all the great theorists of the seventeenth and eighteenth centuries.

iii   The Arminians and the problem of religious toleration

While Grotius was able to develop these ideas in the years before the Truce in relative isolation from urgent polemics, almost all his work in the decade between 1609 and his trial in 1619 was devoted to the single end of defending Oldenbarnevelt's position in the religious controversies which tore Dutch society apart. In the process, he had to modify and sharpen some of his ideas, but his basic vision of the world remained very stable, and he was able to apply it to what was to be a central issue for all the writers of this century, the relationship between church and state. The controversies had initially developed during the first years of the century over the teaching of Jacob Arminius, professor of theology at Leiden from 1603 until his death in October 1609.[9] Arminius had long been worried about the notoriously

---

9. For the details of Arminianism and the controversies over it, see Harrison 1926 and den Tex 1973, esp. chs. 10 and 12.

harsh Calvinist theory of salvation, that God determined to whom he would extend his grace and therefore who would be saved – human effort counted for nothing, except as a necessary (but not sufficient) condition for observers to say that someone counted as one of God's elect. Arminius proposed instead that God did not determine *in particular* who was to be saved, but rather *in general*: he offered grace, but it might be refused. Despite the allegations of his orthodox opponents, this did not make Arminius like the kind of late medieval Catholic whose repudiation had been the foundation of Protestantism, for he did not say that man might *claim a right* to salvation; a good analogy (though not one which Arminius actually used) would be with a parent who offers to buy something for his child. The child can refuse the offer, but he cannot buy the article for himself. But it was a sufficiently different vision from the other Calvinists to make them very alarmed.

The dispute over Arminius, though in origin a technically theological one, inevitably spilled over into a political conflict. Arminius himself never abandoned the traditional Calvinist view that doctrinal matters had to be settled by a synod, and that the role of the magistrate was to summon such an assembly, preside over it, and accept its conclusions. But his supporters realised that they could not win the day in such a synod, and in 1609/10 one of them, Johannes Uyttenbogaert, resolved on a decisive break with the political traditions of Calvinism as well as its theological ones, arguing that the States of each province and not the synod should control worship, preaching, the administration of sacraments, the care of the poor, and the final appointment of preachers, elders, and deacons.

This meant that the Arminians had created a coalition between themselves and anyone who (like Grotius himself), whilst not an Arminian, was nevertheless sceptical about ecclesiastical authority. The Arminians succeeded in manipulating this coalition very quickly: in January a group of ministers under Uyttenbogaert's chairmanship drew up a statement of their theological position, the famous 'Remonstrance', and on 22 August the States passed the resolution that 'Preachers of the opinions expressed in this remonstrance should be free from the censure of other preachers.' The States had thus unequivocally committed themselves to a piece of ecclesiastical regulation, and the issue of ecclesiastical authority was henceforward inextricably bound up with the theological battle between Remonstrants and 'Counter-Remonstrants' (as the Arminians' opponents came to be called).

Grotius' public involvement in this struggle began in 1613, when he published his first polemical work concerned with ecclesiastical power, the *Pietas Ordinum Hollandiae et West-Frisiae*. The occasion of the work was twofold: one object was to defend the resolution of 22 August 1610, while the other was to defend the appointment of Conrad Vorstius to a chair at Leiden in May 1611. Vorstius had been accused of heresy (including Socinianism) by the orthodox at Leiden, yet in face of this opposition the States of Holland had ratified his appointment: precisely the same issues were thus involved in his case as in the Remonstrance. The central argument of the *Pietas Ordinum* was that the secular authorities could force the church to tolerate a particular theological position; the will of the state could govern its members in all matters except those which involved their destruction. The work occasioned a considerable pamphlet battle, to which Grotius himself contributed. For the next six years he worked away at these issues, much of his labour being centred on a new toleration resolution (passed in January 1614) which would restate in a possibly more acceptable form the principles of the 1610 resolution (den Tex 1973, II, pp. 550–2).

Although this passed by a bare majority, many of the most important towns, and particularly Amsterdam, refused to accept it: both Grotius' belief in the need for a strong and sovereign States, and his belief in the nullity of ecclesiastical power, came together at this point. The next years were spent trying to persuade the recalcitrant towns to come into line – on 23 April 1616 Grotius went to Amsterdam and delivered a public address (later printed) to its council urging them to accept the resolution, but without success.[10] The Counter-Remonstrants continued to urge the calling of a synod, and Oldnebarnevelt's refusal to do so put him under ever increasing pressure. In the end the stadtholder intervened, and added his voice to the demand; Oldenbarnevelt clearly feared that he would be forced by military pressure to give way, and on 23 July 1617 the States of Holland passed the so-called 'Stern Resolution' in effect seeking to wrest military authority away from the stadtholder. This was the climacteric of Oldenbarnevelt's career: his opponents organised behind the stadtholder and succeeded in bringing the advocate down, together with his associate the pensionary of Rotterdam. Despite the urgent character of the political demands put upon him during these years Grotius had managed by the time he went to prison in addition to his more polemical writings and speeches to finish two longer works: one, a defence of the orthodox theory of Christ's role as mediator for our sins, against the views of the Socinians,

---

10. Grotius 1679, III, pp. 177–94; den Tex 1973, pp. 563–4.

was published in 1617, but the other, his general work on ecclesiastical authority the *De imperio summarum potestatum circa sacra*, remained unpublished until 1647. Both seem to have been written at least in draft form at about the same time, in the late summer of 1614 (Grotius 1928, p. 349 (*De imperio*), p. 367 (*Defensio*)).

It is important to stress that in none of his writings during these years did Grotius actually endorse the Arminians' theology. His position was consciously that of a conciliator: in 1613, in a correspondence with the English theologian John Overall, he argued that a compromise between Arminius and Calvin was the desirable position to adopt.[11] Moreover, his *Defensio fidei Catholicae de Satisfactione Christi* against the Socinians was intended to be a similar contribution to an eirenic enterprise – he circulated it to a number of leading Calvinist theologians as evidence of his recruitment into the 'great war' against the heresy (it was received distinctly coolly, it should be said) (Grotius 1928, p. 397). The issue at stake in the conflict was not so much one of theological truth: it was whether the state had the right to make a judgement about what the church should allow to be taught. Part of Grotius' case was that to allow such a right in Holland would occasion no great risk: the judgement which the secular rulers such as himself were capable of making was wholly orthodox; but part involved a matter of higher theory, that the state had a perfect right to legislate on any 'sacred' matter.

This was the heart of his case, and he established it in both the *De imperio summarum potestatum* and the *Defensio Fidei Catholicae* by showing the invalidity of any distinction between sacred and profane matters. To do so, he had to set out once again the fundamentals of his political theory, and show how they implied the nullity of ecclesiastical power. He drew on his original insight in the *De Iure Praedae*, that the laws of nature had to be principles which all people, sceptics and non-sceptics alike, would concede to be true, and that they were therefore an extremely minimal set of rules. The laws of nature, as he now put it, were 'moral impossibilities', and this very strong definition enabled him to make a distinction between what was customarily taken to be part of the law of nature (such as God's commands to men in the Decalogue) and what was *truly* part of it, following as a *logical* necessity from some non-controversial assumption about the world (*De imperio*, c. III.2: 1679, III, p. 211).

---

11. He sent Overall an essay entitled *Conciliatio Dissidentium de Re Praedestinaria et Gratia Opinionum*: Grotius 1679, III, pp. 351–60. See Grotius 1928, pp. 240ff.

In the *Defensio Fidei Catholicae* he made this distinction clear, as part of an argument against the Socinian claim that a just God could not waive punishment due to an offender without the breach of a fundamental moral law (and that the conventional account of the Atonement was therefore morally repulsive).

As in physics, so in moral matters, something is called 'natural' either properly or less properly. 'Natural' in physics is properly used about the necessary essence of anything – as when we say that a living creature must have sensations. It is used less properly about something which is convenient and suitable, as when we say that it is natural for a man to use his right hand. Similarly in morality, those things are properly natural which necessarily follow from the relationship of the things themselves to a rational nature – such as the immorality of lying. Other uses, as when we say that a son should succeed his father, are less proper.

(Defensio, c. III: 1679, III, p. 311)

Rather similar things about the necessity of the laws of nature were said by many scholastics, but Grotius' originality lay in his very narrow-minded approach to what actually constituted logical necessity. As he said in the *De imperio summarum potestatum*, 'given that it is certain that God the Father, the Son and the Holy Ghost is the one true God, it is part of the law of nature that we worship Him. God's commands either to individuals, or to nations, or to the whole human race, belong to another category and may be called the divine positive law' (*De imperio*, c. III.3: 1679, III, p. 212). God's commands even to the whole of humanity were not *certain*, or logically necessary, in the same way as the proposition that because he is the true God he must be worshipped. The latter proposition must be true at any time or place, whereas the content of God's commands can alter, and frequently has done so in human history.

This minimalist approach to the laws of nature implied among other things that the Decalogue, which had been used very generally as a compact statement of the laws of nature, was in fact merely a statement of positive law which could be altered (and which Grotius later observed had not been given to the Gentiles anyway). At this stage he did not draw this radical conclusion explicitly but the implications of his discussion were already clear; when his friend the Remonstrant J.A. Corvinus described the Decalogue as divine positive law and not the law of nature, in a tract of 1622 defending the Remonstrants' theology, the orthodox Antonius Walaeus (who had been the minister at Oldenbarnevelt's execution) exploded that this was doctrine 'hitherto unheard of among Christians' and he was probably right (Corvinus 1622, p. 160; Walaeus 1643, p. 168).

The conclusion which Grotius did draw explicitly at this time, and which the minimalist account of the law of nature was particularly good at underpinning, was that there was no natural and universal basis for a distinction between religious and secular authority. Civil society had as a matter of natural necessity to be governed by a sovereign with coercive power, and that sovereign was circumscribed in his activities by both the laws of nature and the divine positive laws applying to his people. But there was no area of special religious or sacred matters into which he could not intrude, for 'sacred' things could not be distinguished from 'profane'. It is true that in modern states there is a division of expertise, and some men spend their lives studying 'religious' matters; but this no more establishes a fundamental division between civil and religious responsibilities than does the similarly specialised study of medicine.[12]

iv   Grotius' *Of the Law of War and Peace*

Ironically, given their detestation of him, and of what they took to be the 'atheist' implications of his views on church government, it was men like Walaeus who gave Grotius the chance to produce work pulling together all the themes which he had considered since writing the *De Iure Praedae*. They did so, of course, by jailing him for two years in Loevestein, and thus giving him a period of enforced rest and study. He seems to have begun his time in prison by studying classical poetry once again (among other things editing the poetic fragments contained in the Byzantine compilation of Johannes Stobaeus), and by reading the New Testament with a critical eye. The great product of this period was a poetic treatise in Dutch on the truth of the Christian religion, the *Bewijs van den waren Godsdienst*, which was published in 1622 and which was in effect translated into Latin as the famous *De Veritate Religionis Christianae* (1627). Towards the end of his stay, however, his mind turned once again to jurisprudence and political theory; in the early part of 1620 he wrote an introduction to Dutch law, the *Inleiding tot de Hollandsche rechts-geleertheyd* (published in 1631), and in the course of the year following his escape he obviously decided to write a major treatise on natural law. He first mentioned his project in a letter to his brother William in November 1622 (Grotius 1936, p. 254). It was finished and rushed by the printers to the Frankfurt book fair in March 1625 under the title *De Jure Belli ac Pacis libri tres*. The king of France received a dedicatory copy in

---

12. See, e.g., his remarks in *De imperio*, ch. IX,7 (1679, III, p. 248).

May. While the title (and the subsequent fate) of the work might suggest that it was merely concerned with the laws of war, Grotius made clear in the first sentence of Book I that his subject-matter was 'all the differences of those who do not acknowledge one common Civil Right' – in other words, his aim was to delineate the natural, pre-civil state of man in great detail, though since that state could be studied most easily in international relations he concentrated on them. There is not in fact much stress on the *desirability* of peace – one of his objects was still (as it had been in the *De Iure Praedae*) to legitimate war.

The works of this period are those which made Grotius' reputation in Europe, and which led to his being hailed later as one of the founders of the Enlightenment. But in fact they largely recapitulated and systematised ideas which he had first had up to twenty years earlier. Thus *De Jure Belli* builds on the same distinction between the law of nature and the divine positive law (or as he now called it, the divine 'voluntary' law) which we saw adumbrated in the *De imperio summarum Potestatum* and the *Defensio Fidei Catholicae*. Natural law

is the Rule and Dictate of Right Reason, showing the Moral Deformity or Moral Necessity there is in any Act, according to its Suitableness or Unsuitableness to a reasonable Nature, and consequently that such an Act is either forbid or commanded by God, the Author of Nature. The Actions upon which such a Dictate is given, are in themselves either Obligatory or Unlawful, and must, consequently, be understood to be either commanded or forbid by God himself; and this makes the Law of Nature differ not only from Human Right, but from a Voluntary Divine Right; for that does not command or forbid things as they are in themselves, or in their own Nature, Obligatory and Unlawful; but by forbidding, it renders the one Unlawful, and by commanding, the other Obligatory.

(*De Jure Belli*, I.i.10: 1738, pp. 9–10)

Elsewhere, he said in a notorious phrase that the laws of nature would be valid 'though we should even grant, what without the greatest Wickedness cannot be granted, that there is no God, or that he takes no Care of human Affairs' (*ibid.*, Prolegomena 11: 1738, p. xix). This did not, of course, mean that God could not still be seen as in *some* sense the author of the laws of nature: he had after all made man in such a way that his essence was that of a rational, social being, and the world in such a way that society could not be preserved if men behaved towards one another in certain ways.

But what was really important and striking about Grotius' argument in the *De Jure Belli ac Pacis* as much as in the *De Iure Praedae* was the account he gave of the functional necessities for any social existence. Once again, his argument eschewed the rich and complex Aristotelian account of social life, with its stress on friendship and on the development of the virtues. Instead, it began as before with a statement of what the sceptic believes (this time in the person of Carneades, the famous head of the sceptical Academy) (*ibid.*, Prolegomena 5: 1738, p. xiv), and then proceeded to find principles which could be common ground between the relativist and the anti-relativist; principles, that is, which even the relativist would have to concede underlay any possible social life. The sceptical relativists whom Grotius had in mind, such as Montaigne or Charron, had not questioned the possibility or even the desirability of social life *as such*; what they had questioned was the universality of any particular moral principle.

In particular, Grotius still argued that the right of self-preservation and the law against *wanton* injury were the crucial foundations for any social life, including the minimal sociability of international relations.

Right Reason, and the Nature of Society, . . . does not prohibit all Manner of Violence, but only that which is repugnant to Society, that is, which invades another's Right: For the Design of Society is, that every one should quietly enjoy his own, with the Help, and by the united Force of the whole Community. It may be easily conceived, that the Necessity of having Recourse to violent Means for Self-Defence, might have taken Place, even tho' what we call *Property* had never been introduced. For our Lives, Limbs, and Liberties had still been properly our own, and could not have been, (without manifest Injustice) invaded. So also, to have made use of Things that were then in common, and to have consumed them, as far as Nature required, had been the Right of the first Possessor: And if any one had attempted to hinder him from so doing, he had been guilty of a real Injury.
(*ibid.*, 1.2.1: 1738, pp. 25–6)

This initial natural right of consuming material objects was the basis for Grotius' account of the acquisition of property, just as in the *De Iure Praedae*, and his theories of both property and punishment in the *De Jure Belli ac Pacis* follow the *De Iure Praedae* almost exactly (with one significant alteration, which we shall examine presently). But he was not much clearer than he had been before about a number of the implications of his general theory. First of all, he now argued explicitly that traditional theology was of very little use to moral philosophy, for the 'divine voluntary law' which actually applied to Christians was extremely slight. He dismissed the whole of the law given to the Jews as obviously given only to them. 'A Law obliges, only those, to whom it is given. And to whom that Law is given, itself declares, *Hear O Israel*' (*ibid.*, 1.1.16: 1738, pp. 17–18). Even the law given to believers through Christ, he argued, was of a rather tenuous character; the new Testament shows what is lawful for Christians to do; which Thing itself, I have notwithstanding, contrary to what most do, distinguished from the Law of Nature; as being fully assured, that in that most holy Law a greater Sanctity is enjoined us, than the mere Law of Nature in itself requires. Nor have I for all that omitted observing, what Things in it are rather recommended to us than commanded, to the Intent we may know, that as to transgress the commands is a Crime that renders us liable to be punished; so to aim at the highest Perfection, in what is but barely recommended, is the Part of a generous Mind.   (*ibid.*, Prolegomena 51: 1738, p. xxxiii)

Christians, Grotius argued, must always be careful to distinguish between Christ's *commands* and his *advice*: the primitive Christians in their enthusiasm tended to confuse the two, but much of what Christ said did not carry any obligation, viewed properly.

On the whole, then, men (other than Jews) had to manage their lives with the assistance only of the laws of nature; and in religious affairs, those laws specified a minimal set of beliefs which must be enforced on all men. Everything else should be left to the individual, all things being equal. The minimal set were 'that there is a Deity, (one or more I shall not now consider) and that this Deity has the Care of human Affairs'; 'Those who first attempt to destroy these Notions ought, on the Account of human Society in general, which they thus, without any just Grounds, injure, to be restrained.' The laws of nature did not similarly prescribe any other religious beliefs – 'other general Notions, as that *There is but one God*, that *No Object of our Sight is God*, not the World, not the Heavens, not the sun, nor the Air; that *The World is not eternal, nor its compound Matter, but that it was created by God*, have not the same Degrees of Evidence as the former' (*ibid.*, II.20.46,47: 1738, pp. 444–5). The *De Veritate Religionis Christianae* confirms this: there, Grotius argued that there are natural and rational grounds for religious feeling in general, but that Christianity is to be preferred only because it is (so to speak) an 'ideal type' religion, capturing with great clarity all that other religions also contain.[13] It followed that there were no good grounds for enforcing Christianity upon non-Christians, much less enforcing a particular interpretation of Christianity.

As for those who use professed Christians with Rigour, because they are doubtful, or erroneous as to some Points either not delivered in Sacred Writ, or not so clearly but to be capable of various Acceptations, . . . they are undoubtedly very unjust . . . But suppose the Error to be more palpable, and such as one may be easily convicted of before equitable Judges, from the holy Scriptures, and from the

---

13. See particularly Grotius, *De Veritate*, I.2–7, II.8–16 (1679, III, pp. 4–7, 36–44).

concurrent Opinions of the primitive Fathers; even in this Case it is requisite to consider how prevalent the Force of a long standing Opinion is . . . Besides, to determine how criminal this is, it is requisite to be acquainted with the Degrees of Men's Understanding, and other inward Dispositions of Mind, which it is impossible for Men to find out.   (*De Jure Belli*, II.20.50: 1738, p. 449)

His experiences since 1619 had made him clearer about the wide limits of toleration than he had been when engaged in the struggle with the Counter-Remonstrants.

The second implication of his general theory which Grotius now made explicit was its anti-Aristotelian character. We saw that in effect he had abandoned an Aristotelian methodology in the *De Iure Praedae* but there is no open critique of Aristotle in that work. In the *De Jure Belli ac Pacis* it is very different: Grotius in this work remarked that 'I could only wish that the Authority of this great Man had not for some Ages past degenerated into Tyranny, so that Truth, for the discovery of which Aristotle took so great Pains, is now oppressed by nothing more than the very Name of Aristotle' (*ibid.*, Prolegomena 43: 1738, p. xxviii). In particular, he attacked the Aristotelian theories of the virtues and of justice: the virtues could not reasonably all be taken to consist in a mean, and the essential feature of justice was respect for one another's rights, not any distributive principle (*ibid.*, Prolegomena 45: 1738, p. 30). Both these points were straightforwardly related to his general theory. As in the *De Iure Praedae*, mathematics is the model for the moral sciences in the *De Jure Belli* – 'as Mathematicians consider Figures abstracted from Bodies, so I, in treating of Rights have withdrawn my Mind from all particular Facts' – and there is no distinction between a theoretical and a practical science (*ibid.*, Prolegomena 59: 1738, p. xxxv). But this means that, at least in principle, a definite and *a priori* science of ethics is possible, in which there will be little room for individual judgement or the exercise of *phronesis*. The idea that virtue is a mean is intimately bound up with the idea that ethics is practical (in the Aristotelian sense), for the selection of the mean point is essentially a matter of skill and judgement, and cannot be reduced to the application of a clear-cut rule. Furthermore, the basic provisions of the law of nature according to Grotius relate to the recognition of one another's rights and property: justice is thus primarily the maintenance of that natural moral order, and only secondarily something to do with the distribution of goods. After the *De Jure Belli*, it was impossible for anyone who wished to think about politics in a modern way – that is, in terms of natural rights and the laws of nature – to pretend that they were still Aristotelians, and much of the criticism levelled at

Grotius' work came from people who were unwilling to abandon the Aristotelian inheritance (e.g. Felden 1653).

In addition to these general implications of his theory, Grotius perceived that it had one consequence for his account of both property and government which he had overlooked in the earlier work. Given that the preservation of the self was an overriding principle and that it was to preserve themselves that men entered society, no society could expect its members not to continue to preserve themselves from wanton attack. Necessity must be a legitimate plea, even within civil society; and this entailed a modification in his account of private property. Grotius explained the origins and development of property in the same way as in *De Iure Praedae*, but he now concluded that if the point of dividing a common world into private estates was to advance the interests of the individuals concerned, then it was absurd to think that such a division would rule out the use of another's possessions *in extremis* (*De Jure Belli*, II.2.6: 1738, p. 149).

For the same reasons he was now much clearer about the continued existence of a right of resistance within civil society. Given that the point of entering civil society is self-protection, there can be no reason for not resisting where one's physical existence is at stake, unless one is being attacked by men aggrieved by one's own wanton injury of one of their number (*ibid.*, II.1.3–5: 1738, pp. 131–3). This proviso is what keeps his theory at this point from sliding into Hobbes', but the gap is not great, and Hobbes himself managed to bridge it fairly easily. Certainly, traditional arguments for non-resistance to an aggressive and unjust sovereign had no appeal for Grotius, though he conceded that one of the things which Christians (as distinct from natural men) are obliged to do is suffer death rather than resist.[14]

In all other respects than one's personal survival, one can be completely subordinated to the demands of civil society, and Grotius now argued that a people could be similarly subordinated to their prince, remarking in a notorious passage that

we must first reject their Opinion, who will have the Supreme Power to be always, and without Exception in the People; so that they may restrain or punish their Kings, as often as they abuse their Power. What Mischiefs this Opinion has occasioned, and may yet occasion, if once the Minds of People are fully possessed with it, every wise Man sees. I shall refute it with these Arguments. It is lawful for

14. This is the implication of his contrast between the actions of David or the Maccabei and those of the primitive Christians: Grotius, *De Jure Belli*, I.4.7 (1738, pp. 113, 115–17).

any Man to engage himself as a Slave to whom he pleases; as appears both by the *Hebrew* and *Roman* Laws. Why should it not therefore be as lawful for a People that are at their own Disposal, to deliver up themselves to any one or more Persons, and transfer the Right of governing them upon him or them, without reserving any Share of that Right to themselves? neither should you say this is not to be presumed: for the Question here is not, what may be presumed in a Doubt, but what may be lawfully done? In vain do some alledge the Inconveniences which arise from hence, or may arise; for you can frame no Form of Government in your Mind, which will be without Inconveniences and Dangers . . . but as there are several Ways of Living, some better than others, and every one may chuse what he pleases of all those Sorts; so a People may chuse what Form of Government they please: Neither is the Right which the sovereign has over his Subjects to be measured by this or that Form, of which divers Men have divers Opinions but by the Extent of the Will of those who conferred it upon him.

(ibid., 1.3.8: 1738, p. 64)

Characteristically, having given support to absolutism in this passage, he withdrew many of its familiar supports elsewhere. The critical question in his eyes was, indeed, 'the will of those who conferred' the sovereign power upon a person or institution. The superficial character of the form of government was uninstructive: men could be misled by it into thinking that (for example) a prince was superior to his States when in fact historically and legally the reverse was the case. A great deal of care was needed actually to distinguish the focus of sovereignty in a state, and Grotius made a number of (to contemporaries) surprising claims – such as that sovereignty is not necessarily perpetual (and thus the Roman dictator was a sovereign) and that it may be divided, though not in the way that mixed constitution theorists held – the example he gave was the later Roman Empire, with its two emperors (*ibid.*, 1.3.17: 1738, p. 86). Kings would have a hard time in practice proving that they were Grotian sovereigns: what mattered to Grotius by 1625 was that there should be a definite sovereign in every state, not that it should be a monarch or any other similar institution.

The *De Jure Belli ac Pacis* represents Grotius' final and public break with both Aristotelianism and scepticism. In it he in effect promulgated a manifesto for a new science of morality, in which the radical disagreements of the previous generation could be subsumed into a consensus on a minimalist morality and theology. Beyond this consensus, the way of life or set of beliefs which a man chose were a matter only for him, and a great variety was possible: 'there are several Ways of Living, some better than others, and every one may chuse what he pleases of all those Sorts' (*ibid.*,

1.3.8: 1738, p. 64). To anyone who believed strongly in the truth of propositions beyond the minimal core – as all Grotius' old Calvinist opponents in the Netherlands did – his views were likely to be anathema, and his criticisms of Calvinist doctrines in both theology and politics seemed to many of them to mean that he had simply deserted Protestantism for Rome. This was, of course, far from being the case; he remained throughout his life a deviant Protestant (like all his major successors in this genre of political theory) and not a Catholic. But his activities in the last twenty years of his life were not calculated to win back any Calvinist support. He wrote very little straightforward political thought from 1625 until his death; largely a second and extended edition of *De Jure Belli ac Pacis*, and some notes on the Corpus Juris Civilis, on his own *Introduction to the Jurisprudence of Holland*, and on Campanella's *Political Aphorisms*. All simply restate the fundamental arguments of the *De Jure Belli*.

What really engaged his attention was working out the full theological implications of his ideas, and he did so in a series of works published between 1638 and 1645. Their common theme, already adumbrated in his earlier work, was that Christians are actually *required* to believe very few dogmas, and that the statements of faith of the major churches (and in particular the Tridentine decrees and the Confession of Augsburg) can be interpreted in a minimalist manner, such that a rational Christian can see himself as part of a universal Christian church with a continuous history from the time of Christ to the present day. Grotius was now absolutely clear about the irrelevance to Christianity of the Decalogue. Catholics cannot be condemned by other Christians for idolatry, since the prohibition on graven images in the ten commandments referred exclusively to the Jews – there can be no natural prohibition on the kinds of images which Catholics construct. 'Certainly images are forbidden by a precept of the Decalogue; but since it is a positive precept, and one given to the Hebrews because of particular circumstances, it no more obliges the new people of Christ, than the law of the Sabbath. Images are aids to memory.'[15] In 1640 he published an extensive commentary on the Decalogue to make this point even clearer.

In his old age, Grotius (contrary to a common expectation) became progressively more radical in his thinking, particularly on theology. Reading these later works, one has a strong sense of a man excited by his

---

15. Grotius, *Commentatio ad loca quaedam Novi Testamenti quae de Antichristo agunt*, Appendix (1679, III, p. 485).

own ideas, and conscious of their novelty and importance. That excitement was infectious; Grotius' achievement in both theology and moral philosophy caught hold of the imagination of many of his readers in the late 1620s and 1630s. But it did so in part, like most major ideas, because the ground was prepared: elsewhere in Europe other people had begun to think along lines broadly similar to his, conscious like him of the problems posed by the irreconcilable religious and political conflicts of the previous generation. In some ways Hobbes was the true heir of Grotius, but his first heir was taken by contemporaries to be another Englishman, Selden.

v   Selden

Although England had not itself suffered a civil war in the late sixteenth century, its survival as a nation had been caught up in one of them – the Netherlands civil war and the Spanish attempt to defeat the rebels through an invasion of England. The problems of the European wars were as starkly visible west of the North Sea as east of it, and the men who ruled England in the late sixteenth century were cast to a great extent in the same mould as Oldenbarnevelt (the circle of the earl of Essex, for example, fostered the same kind of Tacitism as the Lipsians in the Netherlands, France, and Spain). James I disliked this intellectual style, preferring theological verities, but even under him and completely under his son, Englishmen were aware of its attractions and limitations.

Selden grew up in very much the same intellectual world as Grotius, though his social background was quite different.[16] He was the son not of an urban aristocrat but of a yeoman farmer in Sussex, and he did not move by birthright in the world of international scholarship, but by his own efforts in a relatively open educational system. Born in 1584, he was spotted as exceptionally bright at the local grammar school, and was sent to an inexpensive Hall at Oxford. Encouraged by his tutor and friends there to make the law his career, on some recommendations from Oxford he became the legal agent of the earls of Kent, as well as developing a practice as an advocate. His financial and political fortunes continued to be dependent on the good will of the Kents and their friends in a group of politically active and independent-minded noblemen. He resided for much of his life in the Kents' household, in his later years as the generally acknowledged lover of the widowed countess of Kent. In the 1620s and

16. For Selden's life, see the DNB article by Edward Fry, Christianson 1984 and Tuck 1982.

again in the 1640s he was a member of parliament, in the former decade one of the leaders of the opposition to Buckingham and in the latter a central figure among the moderate parliamentarians (his decision to stick by parliament in the Civil War being seen as highly significant by contemporaries).

As a young man his interests and attitudes were very similar to those of the young Grotius. Like the Dutchman, the Englishman wrote both poetry and history, and mixed with poets and dramatists. His historical writings, also, were concerned with the antiquity of his country's constitution and its legal order; and in a remarkable piece of synchrony with Grotius, he argued in a work written before the *De Antiquitate Reipublicae Batavicae* was published that the ancient constitution of pre-Roman Britain, like that of other pre-Roman peoples, was a pure aristocracy with no trace of kingship.[17]

In a series of works written between 1607 and 1617 he outlined a *political* history of the English law – a history in which the themes of the Tacitist (necessity and reason of state) were deployed to explain the changes in the English legal system. The history of England as he saw it was one of conflict between interest-groups – kings, barons, and commons – which periodically reached agreement about the terms on which they could coexist. Fundamental documents like Magna Carta were testimony to this process; he described it as 'an instrument of public liberties, through mediation of what is above all law, necessity'.[18]

But the similarity with Grotius goes even further. Like the United Provinces, England faced in the first two decades of the century a conflict between different kinds of Protestantism (though unlike the United Provinces, the government in England never supported the Arminians in their calls for help from the state: James firmly backed the Counter-Remonstrants at the Synod of Dort). There is no doubt that Selden immediately sympathised with the campaign against independent ecclesiastical authority, and in 1617, the year of the 'Stern Resolution', he published his famous *History of Tithes*, with a preface containing a denunciation of the malicious, lazy, and ignorant clergy who over the centuries had blocked intellectual progress.[19] The principal argument of the work is very close to Grotius' much more general theme in the *De imperio summarum potestatum*, namely that there is no conceptual difference

17. Selden, *Analecton Anglo-Britannicon*, ch. III (1726, II, cols. 877–9).
18. Selden, *England's Epinomis*, ch. X (1726, III, col. 41).
19. Selden, *The History of Tithes*, Preface (1726, III, p. 1073).

between 'religious' and 'secular' matters, and that both come under the civil law. Selden chose as his example of this the history of tithes, believing that it showed particularly well that 'sacred' things were simply things which the civil sovereign had decided to allocate to ecclesiastical purposes. The work occasioned a great deal of opposition, both from clergymen in the church of England and from the government. Selden was summoned before the privy council to explain his views, but an adroit use of internal court politics enabled him to escape any further action – Selden knew quite well how to live in an Ancien Régime.

Those court politics in fact led in the following year to Selden being commissioned to write a reply to Grotius' *Mare Liberum*. The English claimed exclusive fishing rights in the North Sea, and Grotius in an aside in the *Mare Liberum* had criticised this as unreasonable. James now wanted a reply to the Dutch insistence on continued fishing in English waters. Selden had already considered writing a treatise on maritime jurisdiction, for the similarity between his ideas and Grotius' could not have been overlooked by him (Grotius visited England in 1613, and they had several friends in common, but there is no evidence that they ever met). His *Mare Clausum* as we actually have it, however, is a product of another seventeen years' reflection on Grotius, including a careful reading of the *De Jure Belli ac Pacis*, for changing international politics in 1618 determined that the book should not be published as it stood.

It finally appeared during another fishing crisis in 1635, and was greeted with enthusiasm by readers such as Hobbes and – though, of course, with reservations – by Grotius himself.[20] It was followed five years later by a work whose composition had been eagerly followed by the leaders of European intellectual life, particularly the group associated with Marin Mersenne in Paris – the *De Iure Naturali et Gentium juxta Disciplinam Ebraeorum.*[21] Both the *De Iure Naturali et Gentium* and the *Mare Clausum* deploy similar arguments, though the underlying theoretical assumptions of Selden in the late 1630s are much clearer in the later (and far longer) work.

As its full title suggest, the *De Iure Naturali et Gentium* had on the face of it a highly idiosyncratic purpose – to examine the classical Jewish account of the laws of nature. Selden drew on a wide range of Hebrew literature, but his principal source was the Talmud. He was aware that his project might

---

20. See Hobbes 1839–45a, VII, p. 454; Historical Manuscripts Commission 1893, p. 128; Grotius 1967, p. 461; Grotius 1969, p. 133.
21. Mersenne 1963, pp. 318, 357, 1967, p. 294.

seem peculiar, and he devoted the first book of the work to an explanation of why he chose to work from Hebrew sources.

Like Grotius in the *De Jure Belli ac Pacis*, Selden took the moral scepticism of Carneades very seriously. One chapter of the *De Iure Naturali et Gentium*, like the Prolegomena to *De Jure Belli ac Pacis*, centres on Carneades' claim that there can be no universal law of nature because of the widespread and fundamental moral disagreement between societies (*De Iure Naturali*, 1.6,7: 1725, I, cols. 131, 138). Selden entirely accepted the force of Carneades' point against traditional moral philosophy, and he added some of the familiar arguments of other sceptics (including the famous story in Herodotus about the confrontation between a horrified Greek and an equally horrified Indian over their different funeral practices). But, like Grotius, Selden took his task to be the discovery of general moral principles which even a sceptic of the Carneades type would have to accept. According to Selden, scepticism was entirely justified if directed against the idea that we can naturally and veridically perceive a moral reality – the idea which he associated with Aristotle and with medieval Aristotelianism. But it was not justified if it denied the existence of any moral obligation whatsoever, for he argued that to be under an obligation is to be in the power of some superior whose punishments we fear. 'The idea of a law carrying obligation irrespective of any punishment annexed to the violation of it . . . is no more comprehensible to the human mind than the idea of a father without a child' (*ibid.*, 1.4: 1726, I, col. 106). Without such a superior to lay an obligation upon them, he several times emphasised, men would be in a state of total moral freedom; there was nothing in man's *nature* which implied the existence of any *laws* of nature. But this state of moral freedom was limited and ordered once men recognised that pain and destruction could be avoided only if they obeyed the commands of some being in whose power they lay.

A sceptic might accept that there was such a being, namely God, but still raise questions about how confident we could be about the content of what God has commanded. Here, Selden used two interlinked arguments. On the one hand, we possess (he claimed) a reasonably good historical record of God's pronouncements to the whole of mankind, in the form of the seven *praecepta Noachidarum*, the laws given to Noah's sons after the Flood. These do not appear in the Bible, but were the subject of much Talmudic speculation, and were presented by Selden as the following. Men must abstain from (1) idolatry, (2) cursing the divine name, (3) murder, (4) adultery, (5) theft. They must (6) institute judges to ensure these precepts are followed, and (7) abstain from eating the flesh of living animals. This last prohibition was regarded by Selden as a minor and subsidiary matter; the first six gave the minimal content of the law of nature, and indeed of any social life (*ibid.*, 1.10: 1726, I, col. 158).

On the other hand, even before the Flood and even among men sundered from knowledge of it, human beings (Selden argued) can apprehend what God requires of them. They do so through the 'active intellect'; but it is important to stress that Selden took great care not to let his use of this notion put him back in the scholastic tradition which he despised. What he did was to resurrect and entirely endorse in a very extreme manner the Averroistic tradition (found also in Jacopo Zabarella and Bodin), according to which there is an active intellect *exterior* to individual men which provides them with direct knowledge of reality, including moral reality.[22] The analogy he and the others in this tradition used was with a light illuminating an object and thereby allowing the eye to see: the human mind is like the eye, and can malfunction in various ways, but it can in principle determine the nature of objects once they are illuminated by the active intellect, which is in some sense outside the mind. He condemned the late medieval theory according to which the active intellect was a natural part of the mind, upholding Roger Bacon (a hero also of the preface to the *History of the Tithes*) as someone who had seen the truth but whose views had been swamped and stigmatised as heretical by Aristotelians.

It is not clear that he had understood the Averroist position; but what is clear is that the active intellect on Selden's account is an external power, literally identifiable with God (or perhaps, he added, with the angels), which can give human beings a direct revelation of what God requires of them, comparable to the more concrete revelation the sons of Noah received. This is compatible with his view that the best means of determining God's requirements is through the text of the *praecepta*, for just as the best means in practice of understanding geometry is not to work it out for oneself from first principles (though one might be able to do so), but to read Euclid, so the best way of establishing securely the contents of the law of nature is to look at the historical record of God's pronouncements to men.

Selden's general theory, for all its idiosyncracies, thus lay squarely in the

---

22. Selden, *De Iure Naturali*, 1.9 (1726, I, cols. 152–7). For Bodin and Zabarella, see col. 156 note t; Sommerville 1984.

Grotian, anti-Aristotelian tradition. Scholasticism as he understood it in its post-Aquinas form was fundamentally flawed by its naive ethical natural-ism and its reliance on Aristotle, and the sceptical critique of this kind of law of nature was entirely justified. But a post-sceptical moral science was possible, and he shared Grotius' general sense that self-preservation (in the form of his account of fear of divine punishment) would be a key to its creation. He gave two hints about its character which were to be of great importance to his successors. One was that we can conceive of men being totally free prior to the imposition of a law of nature; as Selden said, he hypothesised this just as a geometer hypothesises an infinite line, but it was a conceptual possibility (*De Iure Naturali*, 1.4: 1726, I, col. 105). It was not part of the *nature* or *essence* of men that they were under moral obligations. The other was that our clear and distinct idea of what God requires of us could be the basis for an account of natural law which would escape the sceptical criticisms of traditional naturalism. In the writings of both Hobbes and Locke we can find these hints taken up and their implications explored without Selden's unwieldy scholarship and amateur metaphysics.

Upon this foundation, Selden was able to erect his critique of Grotius. First, the strong distinction between natural law and divine voluntary law, upon which Grotius set such store, was, of course, utterly obliterated and divine voluntary law reinstated as the source of natural law, though with the important proviso that only when God spoke *universally* to men did he lay down laws of nature. The Decalogue was as uninteresting to Selden as it had become to Grotius. (This was a point made already in the *Mare Clausum*.)[23]

Second, the fifth *praeceptum* was a ban on theft, which Selden interpreted widely as legitimating private property and enforcing the principle that contracts must be kept. Since this command was enforced by divine penalties, no human calamity could be pleaded against it: the claim of necessity had no place in human society if contracts were to be kept. As so often, Selden put the matter most pungently in *Table Talk*, a collection of his remarks edited after his death by one of his friends. 'If I sell my lands, and when I have done, one comes and tells me I have nothing else to keep me. I and my wife and children must starve, if I part with my land. May I therefore not let them have my land that have bought it, and paid for it?'[24] Furthermore, contracts even about such things as the sea, which could not

---

23. Selden, *De Iure Naturali*, 1.3 (1726, I, cols. 100–5); Selden, *Mare Clausum*, 1.4 (1726, II, col. 1193); Selden, *Table Talk*, 'Sabbath' (1726, III, col. 2069).
24. Selden, *Table Talk*, 'Law' (1726, III, col. 2041).

be justified in terms of their necessity for the satisfaction of material needs, could still be binding. This was the heart of Selden's case against Grotius in the *Mare Clausum*, though he also argued that mere abundance did not rule out ownership – the whole earth was as abundant as the sea, yet it was quite conceivable for someone to own it all (as the Roman emperors had claimed to).[25]

However, Selden's critique stopped at this point. He fully endorsed most of the other features of Grotius' theory, such as his anti-clericalism and his account of sovereignty; he argued himself that voluntary slavery both of individuals and of whole nations was perfectly possible – contracts must be kept whatever the consequence.

If our fathers had lost their liberty, why may not we labour to regain it? *Answer.* We must look to the contract, if that be rightly made, we must stand to it. If we once grant we may recede from contracts, upon any inconveniency that may afterwards happen, we shall have no bargain kept. If I sell you a horse, and you do not like my bargain, I will have my horse again.[26]

But also like Grotius, he was not sure what in any instance represented the sovereign in a society. This came out clearly when the English Civil War began: in 1642 he wrote strongly against the king's attempts to raise an army using commissions of array, arguing that without any specific right the king could do nothing. His chief scorn was directed at the claim by the king's ministers that the king had a right to raise an army by virtue of public necessity: given that the plea of necessity, in Selden's view, could never be used *within* the legal order, the king's use of it was equivalent to an admission that civil order had completely broken down, and with it his own special position within the society. Selden said the same about parliament's similar use of necessity as a justification for its Militia Ordinance:

whereas necessity is pretended to be a ground of this ordinance, that can be no true ground of it, for in that case where there is a true and an apparent necessity every man hath as great a liberty to provide for his own safety as the two Houses of Parliament; neither can any civil court pretend to do anything out of necessity which they cannot do by the ordinary rules of law and justice, so when such a real necessity come there must be a stop of the courts of justice.

(Tuck 1982, p. 149)

In the end, however, he stuck by parliament: in time of war, it was better that the people of England should win than that their king should do so.

---

25. Selden, *Mare Clausum*, 1.22 (1726, II, col. 1260).
26. Selden, *Table Talk*, 'Contracts' (1726, III, col. 2024).

His last years, before his death in 1654, were spent on an extension of the *De Iure Naturali et Gentium* into the realm of more specifically political thought, with an account of the power of the Hebrew Sanhedrim. The centre of the work is an attack on ecclesiastical power, and a demonstration that the Sanhedrim had possessed all religious rights including the right to excommunicate; it was bitterly resented by contemporary Anglicans, though enthusiastically welcomed by the leaders of the Independent party who were now in power in England (Anon. 1849, p. 148). Selden was by now a close friend of Hobbes (who had sent him a complimentary copy of *Leviathan*), and the *De Synedriis* reflects many of the same concerns as Books 3 and 4 of *Leviathan*. The book also contains a discussion of the Sanhedrim's power to try the kings of Israel, in which Selden judiciously refrained from denouncing it as a usurpation of sovereignty (a denunciation usually made in earlier commentaries on the Hebrew constitution). The respect in which he was held by the rulers of the new republic is well illustrated by the fact that Cromwell in 1653 considered approaching him and Oliver St John to draft a new constitution for England. It was also rumoured in 1650 that he was to be approached to answer Claudius Salmasius' *Defensio Regia*, a task which eventually fell to one of Selden's great admirers, John Milton.[27]

Selden deserved his place in the seventeenth- and eighteenth-century 'histories of morality', and has not deserved his subsequent oblivion. As we have seen, he was neither a simple *epigone* of Grotius nor a mean-minded critic: he provided an extension and modification of the theory of natural law which Grotius had developed. Each of them built on their youthful enthusiasm for the new politics of Lipsius and his followers; Grotius to a great extent incorporated it into a new theory of the moral life, while Selden made a much crisper distinction between the arena of law and that of necessity. But together they presented their readers with the possibility of a new science of morality, an account of natural law in openly anti-Aristotelian and post-sceptical terms, and it was the modification and extension of this science which was to preoccupy their successors in the seventeenth century.

27. Anon. 1849, p. 147; Patin 1846, I, p. 17; Tuck 1982, p. 137.

18

Hobbes and Spinoza

NOEL MALCOLM

i Hobbes

When the Parliament sat, that began in April 1640, and was dissolved in May following, and in which many points of the regal power, which were necessary for the peace of the kingdom, and the safety of his Majesty's person, were disputed and denied, Mr Hobbes wrote a little treatise in English, wherein he did set forth and demonstrate, that the said power and rights were inseparably annexed to the sovereignty; which sovereignty they did not then deny to be in the King; but it seems understood not, or would not understand that inseparability. Of this treatise, though not printed, many gentlemen had copies, which occasioned much talk of the author and had not his Majesty dissolved the Parliament, it had brought him into danger of his life.   (Hobbes 1839–45a, IV, p. 414)

Such was Hobbes' own account, written twenty-one years later, of the origins of his first work of political theory, *The Elements of Law*. Hobbes had himself been an unsuccessful candidate for election to the Short Parliament (Beats 1978, pp. 74–6), so no doubt he followed its proceedings closely. The disputed 'points of the regal power' emerged most pointedly in John Pym's famous speech of 17 April, which asserted fundamental constitutional rights of parliament against the crown ('Parliament is as the soule of the common wealth', 'the intellectual parte which Governes all the rest') and attacked 'the Doctrine that what property the subject hath in any thinge may be lawfully taken away when the King requires it'. The latter point was taken up by Sir John Strangways on the following day: 'for if the Kinge be judge of the necessitye, we have nothing and are but Tennants at will' (Cope and Coates 1977, pp. 149, 155, 159).

The king dissolved this parliament on 5 May. Four days later Hobbes signed the dedicatory epistle of his treatise, which was addressed to his patron, the staunchly royalist earl of Newcastle; he explained that the principles he was expounding were 'those which I have heretofore acquainted your Lordship withal in private discourse, and which by your command I have here put into method' (Hobbes 1928, p. xvii). The polemical purpose of the work is evident, and is reflected in its circulation in numerous manuscript copies, at least nine of which survive. (Three of them were written by scribes and signed by Hobbes: this suggests a form of clandestine publication by a production-line of copyists.)[1] Hobbes' argument was designed to show first of all that government by a civil sovereign was necessary, and secondly that the reasons which made it necessary also made the sovereignty absolute. He attacked those who 'have imagined that a commonwealth may be constituted in such a manner, as the sovereign power may be so limited, and moderated, as they should think fit themselves'; he sought to overturn the claim that the sovereign power can be 'divided' or shared between king and people, and (in a transparent reference to the recent proceedings in parliament) he denounced those who 'when they are commanded to contribute their persons or money to the public service . . . think they have a propriety in the same distinct from the dominion of the sovereign power' (II.i.13, II.viii.4, 1928, pp. 68, 135). It was Hobbes' argument on this last point above all which made him fear for his life when the next parliament assembled in November and began its impeachment of Strafford (Aubrey 1898, I, p. 334; Zagorin 1978). Within a few days Hobbes fled to Paris, where he was to remain for eleven years; and it was there that he wrote his two other major works of political theory (*De Cive*, printed in 1642, and *Leviathan*, printed in 1651), each of which in turn developed and added to the arguments of *The Elements of Law*.

That Hobbes' career as a political writer should have begun with a polemically royalist work in 1640 is, in biographical terms, not very surprising. His entire adult life, since his graduation from Oxford in 1608, had been spent in the service of aristocratic families as a tutor, secretary, and companion. Employed at first by the Cavendish family at Hardwick and Chatsworth, he had gained some experience of quasi-public affairs cooperating with the second earl of Devonshire as an active member of the Virginia Company (Malcolm 1981). In 1629 (prompted, it has been suggested, by the Petition of Right of the previous year: Reik 1977, p. 37) he had published a translation of Thucydides, who appealed to him for his

---

1. These three MSS are: BL Harl. MS 4235; Chatsworth, Hobbes MSS A2B and A2A (which now lacks the dedication, but cf. the description in Todd 1973).

dispassionate analysis of the ways in which democratic governments could be corrupted and manipulated. For most of the 1630s Hobbes was a tutor to the young third earl of Devonshire; wardship over the young earl was exercised by his cousin, the earl of Newcastle, who helped to awaken Hobbes' philosophical interests and no doubt his royalist sympathies.

The Elements of Law is not, however, simply a piece of royalist propaganda. Its importance lies in the way that it derives its political conclusions from a set of philosophical assumptions. Hobbes' philosophical awakening had taken place, it seems, during the 1630s when he had become preoccupied with an area of overlapping fundamental problems in physics, metaphysics, and epistemology. He had adopted enthusiastically the Galilean principle of the subjectivity of secondary qualities; this meant that a secondary quality such as heat did not inhere in a 'hot' object, but was a feature of the experience of someone perceiving that object, and could be causally explained in terms of the primary qualities which belonged to the object itself (such as the shape and motion of its particles). For Hobbes, this principle was a lever which could be used to overturn scholastic physics and metaphysics. He attacked the notion that the ultimate reality of physical things consisted in their intelligible 'forms' or 'essences'; scholastic philosophy had used this explanation to account for the way in which our process of sense-perception begins with the action of physical causes (light acting on the eye, for example) but ends with an immaterial mental object in the intellect. Most medieval philosophers, drawing on a mixture of Aristotelian and Neoplatonist thought, had distinguished between physical existence and non-physical intelligibility ('esse existentiae' and 'esse essentiae'), and had subordinated the former to the latter in the order of real being. A tree physically existed by virtue of being an expression of the essence of a tree, and so the mind could abstract this essence from its perceptions of a tree's physical properties.

This view of the world as constituted by intelligible essences had usually also assumed that these essences were systematically related to each other in an economy of perfection: they all participated in absolute Being, which was unitary and was derived from (or was perhaps identical with) God. The rational order of the whole system could be described in terms of the laws of reason or laws of nature which governed all its parts. This way of describing things gave rise to a way of valuing them: a thing became better the more it fulfilled its essential nature, and thereby fulfilled its place in the whole system of essences. The more arboreal a tree was, the more it expressed its essential nature. Human beings also had an innate teleology to fulfil, but as rational beings they were conscious of their own ends and were able to direct their actions towards them. In Richard Hooker's words, 'A law therefore generally taken, is a directive rule unto goodness of operation . . . The rule of natural agents that work by simple necessity, is the determination of the wisdom of God . . . The rule of voluntary agents on earth is the sentence that Reason giveth concerning the goodness of those things which they are to do' (*Laws of Ecclesiastical Polity*, I.viii.4, 1888, I, p. 228).

Hobbes rejected this notion of reason intuiting natural teleological values, because he rejected the metaphysics and theology from which those values were derived. His most thorough attack on the old metaphysics came in a monumental refutation of a work by a Catholic Aristotelian, Thomas White; this refutation, which remained unpublished till 1973, was written in 1642–3. The fundamental principle from which Hobbes argued in this work was that of God's freedom to create the world if, how, and when he pleased (1973, chs. 30–4), a principle which severed any intrinsic connection between the natures of created things and the nature of God, and reduced 'essences' to mere descriptions of existing things (p. 381). These metaphysical assumptions can already be seen at work in an earlier manuscript, probably written between 1637 and 1640, in which Hobbes had asserted that 'the original and summ of Knowledge stands thus: there is nothing that truly exists in the world but single and individuall Bodyes producing single and individuall acts or effects' (Rossi 1942, p. 102). And in another early manuscript, probably also written in the 1630s, he had begun to apply these principles to the construction of a system of psychology in which all change was to be accounted for in terms of mechanical causation (the 'Short Tract', printed in Hobbes 1928, pp. 152–67).

Scholastic psychology had explained the operation of desire, for example, in terms of the mind's apprehension of the 'form' or essence of the desired thing; Hobbes explained it in terms of a strictly causal process leading from sense-perception to the setting in motion of the body's 'animal spirits' (conceived of as a fine fluid in the nervous system), causing the body's motion towards the desired thing. The 'thought' of the desired object was simply that part of the sequence of motion which took place in the brain, where it might also interact with memory's store of residual motions from previous sense-impressions. Hobbes denied that the *feeling* of desire was a special kind of thought, and analysed it as a combination of having the mental image of the desired object and beginning to move towards it (1839–45b, V, p. 261). This idea of the 'beginnings of motion' became a key feature of Hobbes' psychology and physics; later described by him as 'conatus' or 'endeavour', it enabled him to reduce intentions to infinitesimal actions.

For Hobbes, reason neither participated in the nature of desire nor supplied any substantive knowledge of values. 'For the Thoughts, are to the Desires, as Scouts, and Spies, to range abroad, and find the way to the things Desired' (1651, p. 35).[2] Reason could only calculate means to ends, applying the merely formal principles of ratiocination to the brute facts of sense-experience and desire. The ends themselves were supplied by the causal mechanism of desire and aversion. Such a view of human nature might suggest that even if one tried to move from 'is' to 'ought' by assigning value to the fulfilment of desire, one would still not be able to form any universal value system: values would be individual rather than general, refracted and fragmented into a number of conflicting egoisms. There is, as we shall see, a deep sense in which Hobbes' values *are* individual rather than universal, but it is not simply a matter of having an 'egoistic' moral psychology. Motivation in Hobbes' account is necessarily egoistic only in a nugatory, definitional sense: each person strives to fulfil his own desires. This does not mean that the contents of those desires cannot be concerned with the good of others. The definitions of the passions which Hobbes supplies in chapter 16 of *Leviathan* include '*Desire* of good to another, BENEVOLENCE, GOOD WILL, CHARITY. If to men generally, GOOD NATURE' (p. 26; cf. Gert 1965 and 1967). It is true that Hobbes did tend to explain the passions in terms of self-interest, as when he wrote that '*Griefe*, for the Calamity of another, is PITTY; and ariseth from the imagination that the like calamity may befall himselfe' (p. 27); but is is often unclear in such cases whether 'ariseth from' explains the feeling in the sense of analysing its true content or in the sense of pointing to its causal predecessor. The origin of many of these definitions is found in Hobbes' early summary of Aristotle's *Rhetoric*; Aristotle is often as ambiguous as Hobbes and almost as reductive. And when Hobbes translated *Rhetoric* 1369b18 as 'In summe, every *Voluntary* Action tends either to *Profit*, or *Pleasure*' (1986, p. 55), we can see that draining away Aristotle's teleology from his psychology can leave us with a very Hobbesian residue.

Hobbes' contemporary critics denounced him for arguing that men were naturally selfish and hostile towards one another. His reply was

---

2. References to *Leviathan* are given in the form of page numbers in the first edition: these can be located in the text of the 1968 Penguin edition (ed. C.B. Macpherson) and in the margin of the 1909 Clarendon Press edition (ed. W.G. Pogson Smith).

commonsensical: first, that although men were sometimes benevolent, a state could not be founded on benevolence alone, and secondly, that 'though the wicked were fewer than the righteous, yet because we cannot distinguish them, there is a necessity of suspecting, heeding, anticipating' (1983, p. 33). A third reason, more important but less commonsensical and less directly stated, also emerges: the primary state of conflict between individuals posited by Hobbes is not a contingent, factual conflict which might not exist if people ceased to be irascible or competitive, but rather a necessary jural conflict between people whose *rights* overlap or conflict in some sense with one another until they have been renounced.

In order to show that men can all agree on the need to pass from a state of conflict to a state of peace, Hobbes argues that it is possible to abstract a set of universal rules of human action from the contingent facts of conflicting individual desires. Individual desires are various and are constantly in motion, so they can be neither consummated in the achievement of a final, systematic goal (Hobbes rejects the notion of a 'summum bonum' in this life), nor dispensed with by means of Stoic withdrawal. (When Hobbes characterises life as a 'restlesse desire of Power after power' (1651, p. 47), he is not making the empirical observation that men are power-hungry, but merely conjoining his view of life as motion with his definition of power as the 'present means, to obtain some future apparent good' (p. 66).) Only one desire can have any sort of priority over all other desires, namely the desire to avoid death; being alive is a necessary condition, the present means to all future apparent goods. Having established this one general truth over and above the mass of individual desires, Hobbes proceeds to draw from it a system of means towards the avoidance of death, providing a set of rules of action which all men must find valid if they reason correctly. The most important means towards self-preservation is peace, the establishment of stable and trustable social relations. And the optimum means towards peace can be formulated as 'Laws of Nature' or moral principles which will be immutably and eternally true. In this way Hobbes has performed the transition from the subjective and relative vocabulary of 'good' and 'evil' ('good' meaning 'object of desire') to an objective system of virtues and vices which can apply universally.

And therefore so long a man is in the condition of meer Nature, (which is a condition of War,) as private Appetite is the measure of Good, and Evill: And consequently all men agree on this, that Peace is Good, and therefore also the way, or means of Peace, which (as I have shewed before) are *Justice, Gratitude, Modesty, Equity, Mercy*, & the rest of the Laws of Nature, are good; that is to say, *Morall Vertues*. (p. 80)

Hobbes has thus cleverly passed from 'is' to 'ought' almost without appearing to take upon himself the responsibility for using normative language: given that men use such language in an unreliable way to express their own desires, Hobbes offers a reliable, systematic use of it in the form of 'Laws of Nature' with which they must all agree. The laws are 'Conclusions, or Theoremes concerning what conduceth to the conservation and defence of themselves' (pp. 122–3); although usually framed conveniently as imperatives, they would be more correctly spelt out as theorems of the form: 'given that you desire to do x y and z, if you reason correctly you will also desire to do the following'. The laws of nature specify an optimum set of actions designed to bring about peace, the optimum condition for self-preservation. But there will also be occasions when obeying those laws will endanger an individual's life rather than preserving it (e.g. when faced with a man of violence); in such circumstances the need for self-preservation will dictate breaking the laws of nature and responding with violence in self-defence. This entitlement to go against the laws of nature in order to fulfil the purpose which they serve is called the 'right' of nature. In chapter 14 of *Leviathan* Hobbes shows that both laws and right flow from the same source, which he calls the 'rule' of nature: 'That every man, ought to endeavour peace, as farre as he has hope of obtaining it; and when he cannot obtain it, that he may seek, and use, all helps, and advantages of Warre' (p. 64). Whilst the laws put forward a determinate set of actions, the right covers an indeterminate range of possible actions contrary to natural law; hence Hobbes' statement in the same chapter that 'RIGHT, consisteth in liberty to do, or to forbeare; Whereas LAW, determineth and bindeth to one of them' (p. 64). But in any particular set of circumstances when the right needs to be used, using it will be no less necessary than obedience to the laws normally is when they can safely be obeyed. Calling the right a 'liberty' does not mean that at critical moments of self-defence it is a matter of indifference whether the right be used or not; it connotes rather the right's nature as an 'entitlement' to act against the usual requirements of natural law.[3]

This account has so far been concerned with what might be called an internal valuation of men's actions: each man has to consider his own need

3. Hence it is not necessary to accept the argument (Warrender 1957) that the laws of nature cannot be based on self-preservation because self-preservation is a right, and rights involve 'liberty to do, or to forbeare'. It must also be stressed that Hobbes' argument in Leviathan is not that men have a right to preserve themselves but that they have a right to attempt to preserve themselves. On this important distinction see Viola 1979, pp. 88–9.

for preservation, and this need generates a particular set of laws and a general right. In the state of nature, when conditions are always potentially hostile and the scope for acting in accordance with the laws of nature is reduced almost to vanishing point, all sorts of actions may be justified by the right of nature. But some actions will still not be justified by it, if they do not meet the internal standard of conduciveness to self-preservation. In an important note added to the second edition of *De Cive*, Hobbes explained that wanton cruelty or drunkenness in the state of nature would not be covered by the right of nature (1983, p. 73). Yet elsewhere Hobbes clearly stated that in the state of nature 'Every man by nature hath right to all things, that is to say, to do whatsoever he listeth to whom he listeth, to possess, use, and enjoy all things he will and can' (1928, II.xiv.10, p. 55; cf. 1651, p. 64, 'this naturall Right of every man to every thing'). This suggests a different use of the term 'right'; we might call it Hobbes' account of men's external rights, that is, their rights *vis-à-vis* other men, as opposed to his internal account of rights overruling laws in the system of actions for self-preservation.

The old undifferentiated notion of a right or 'ius' as 'that which is right' was still in the process of being broken up during this period (see Tuck 1979); although Hobbes was one of its main attackers, his own arguments are sometimes ambiguous because he uses the term in more than one way. His internal account of the right of nature made a procedural and categorial distinction between it and the laws of nature, but still conceived of it as an 'objective' right of the traditional kind, a way of justifying actions because in their particular circumstances they were *right* to do. Externally, however (in the field of inter-personal relations), Hobbes put forward a strong version of the modern 'subjective' notion of a right, a freedom or liberty of action which, far from being generated by any normative requirements, consisted of an absence of obligations. Hobbes was presupposing a sort of moral vacuum so far as inter-personal moral duties were concerned. This was a condition of his argument that the only standard by which an action could be judged to be wrong in the state of nature was the internal standard of conduciveness to self-preservation: in the state of nature there is no requirement to 'respect' the rights of others, no duty towards other people. To illustrate: if in the state of nature A snatches B's food, this action can never be judged to be wrong on the grounds that A has some duties towards B which he is thereby breaking. A has no duties towards him or anyone else, and therefore his (external) rights of action are total and all-encompassing. So the only standard by which the action can be judged to be wrong is the (internal) standard of conduciveness to self-preservation: by this standard A will have the right to snatch the food if his preservation requires it, but he will not have that right if he does not need the food and is merely increasing his chances of suffering retaliatory hostility.

Separating external and internal rights in this way helps us to see that although the natural laws and natural rights concerned with preservation are in some ways similar to a traditional corpus of 'objective' rights and duties, they are still fundamentally different from any normal set of universalisable moral rules. These laws and rights are universal only in the sense that they are duplicated in every individual. Their derivation is essentially egoistic: each person may assign a value to modesty, humility, generosity, etc., but his reason must ultimately be that each quality has an instrumental value *to him*. The altruism which flows from obedience to natural law is, for Hobbes, a form of enlightened self-interest, and it can only be expected of individuals once they have joined together in the common security of the state.

There is a danger, in following Hobbes' account of the state of nature and the formation of political society, that the reader begins to treat it as a literal, historical narrative. Hobbes presented it in this way for the sake of exposition, but willingly admitted of the state of nature that 'I believe it was never generally so, over all the world' (1651, p. 63). He concluded that families in the state of nature were to a limited extent miniature political societies, because children could be deemed to have consented to obey their parents (pp. 102–6). His own favourite example of a state of nature was that of the relations between sovereign states (p. 63); in a letter to a friend he also suggested, rather unsatisfactorily, that soldiers or travelling masons, who passed through various states but owed settled allegiance to none of them, might also be thought of in this way.[4] But in essence the state of nature is the product of a thought-experiment in which Hobbes considers what rights of action and reasons for action men would have if there were no common authority to which they could turn to settle their disputes, or on which they could rely to give stability to their expectations of how other men would act towards them.

Conversely, when Hobbes describes the formation of political authority

---

4. This letter does not survive, but the reply of its recipient does, objecting that these two instances are not proper examples of the state of nature 'because this is only a war of each against each successively and at different times': Peleau to Hobbes, Bordeaux, 4 January 1657. (Chatsworth, Hobbes papers, letters from foreign correspondents, letter 34. I am grateful to the trustees of the Chatsworth Settlement for permission to cite this letter.)

through a covenant he is not tying his argument to a putative historical event, but trying to characterise the kind of commitment which members of society must have towards the political arrangement which they accept. Contract theories of the state have often taken a quasi-historical form because of the element of contingency which is one possible reason for appealing to the notion of a contract. Instead of marshalling general principles to prove that the political arrangement in question is the only just and proper arrangement that could have been made, contract theorists can argue that it is one of a number of possible arrangements, and that men are bound to this one simply by the fact that they have agreed to it. In some cases, notably that of John Selden, the contract theory of the state did have a genuine, though complex, historical character; on the question of when resistance to the government becomes justified, his maxim was that 'we must look to the contract', and this required the services of legal and constitutional historians (such as himself). More frequently, however, contract theory became an excuse for ahistorical arguments about what people 'must have' rationally contracted to do; in other words, a way of presenting *conditions* which ought to be deemed to be incorporated in any grant of power from people to government. Hobbes followed this ahistorical tendency, but with a radical difference: he used the notion of necessary consent as a lever to overturn all claims about implicit conditions or limitations of the rights of government.

Hobbes was able to do this because of the unitary nature of his foundation for natural law: self-preservation. The main Ciceronian and Thomist traditions of natural law saw self-preservation as the ground floor, so to speak, of a whole structure of human needs and values, and it was out of those higher-order values that rational contractarians could construct the implicit conditions which they thought were involved in the grant of power from people to government. In Hobbes' argument, self-preservation is a sheer need which takes precedence over other needs; that a subject should be preserved by his government is the only essential condition of his allegiance to it. Since, in Hobbes' theory, self-preservation could *in extremis* justify doing anything, the subjects must have granted their government the power to do anything for the sake of their preservation. Their consent to this eliminated all scope for further 'conditions' or constraints.

It may still be wondered, however, whether Hobbes' account needed to use a concept of contract at all: in any argument which hinges on the phrase 'must have contracted', it is surely the reasons for saying 'must have' which are doing the real work. Hobbes' reasons are laid down in his laws of nature, which enjoin people to enter society, submit to arbitration, and so on. Indeed, the third law of nature is 'that men performe their Covenants made' (1651, p. 71). If the reasons for obeying covenants are to be found in a system of prudential rules, why has Hobbes not drawn up his whole theory of obedience in terms of long-term benefits and dispensed with the notion of contract altogether? The answer must be that contract was only a formal device in Hobbes' theory, but a device which served some important subsidiary purposes. First, it enabled him to insulate the language of justice from the rest of the moral vocabulary: a sovereign government might be iniquitous, that is, it might break the laws of nature, but it could not be unjust, because injustice consisted of breach of contract. (In Hobbes' theory, the sovereign is not a party to the contract: the contract is between the subjects, who agree to hand over their rights and power to the sovereign: p. 89). In a classic example of his reductive technique of argument, Hobbes dispensed with the traditional claims of distributive and commutative justice, reducing the former to equity and the latter to contractual justice (p. 75). The claim that rulers cannot be convicted of injustice had not been without polemical point in the England of 1640.

Secondly, Hobbes' theory requires people to renounce not only rights of action but also rights of judgement. Only the sovereign can judge what will be necessary for the preservation of peace in the state: if subjects claimed the right to judge this, they would be undermining the sovereign's role as final arbiter and frustrating the purpose for which a sovereign was instituted. (This too had had a topical relevance in the late 1630s, following the Ship Money case.) The notion of a covenant is a kind of shorthand for the type of commitment to obedience this requires, in advance of any knowledge of the contingencies of particular decisions by the sovereign.

The state forces its subjects to keep their covenant by annexing punishments to its laws. 'Covenants, without the Sword, are but Words, and of no strength to secure a man at all' (p. 85). But Hobbes is not arguing here that the desire to avoid punishment is the only motivation for obeying the laws. The prospect of punishment is a short-term consideration, necessary to concentrate the minds of passionate men, and thereby to create secure surroundings for those who do wish to keep their covenant. And there is always an adequate long-term consideration prompting this wish, namely the conduciveness to self-preservation of peace and stable government. Hobbes is sometimes associated with modern 'positivist' or 'realist' theories of law which explain the obligation to obey laws in terms of the motivation to avoid the punishments which those laws predict; but in Hobbes' theory there is thus always a further motive to obedience. This point comes out strongly in his criticism of the doctrine of 'passive obedience' in *Behemoth*, his history of the Civil War. 'Every law is a command *to do*, or *to forbear*: neither of these is fulfilled by suffering' (1889, p. 50). Laws do not propose value-free alternatives of action leading to punishment and action leading to non-punishment; there is always a value attached to obedience to laws, because there is always a duty towards the legislator, whose continuing authority ensures peace.

Hobbes does, however, raise an apparent exception to this principle when he writes about 'the Obligation a man may sometimes have, upon the Command of the Soveraign to execute any dangerous or dishonourable Office'. Here he concludes: 'When therefore our refusall to obey frustrates the End for which the Soveraignty was ordained, then there is no Liberty to refuse: otherwise there is' (1651, p. 112). This seems to transgress Hobbes' rule that only the sovereign can decide whether an action is necessary for the safety of the state. But, leaving aside the mention of dishonour (which is not fully supported by the rest of Hobbes' theory), it is clear that Hobbes is concerned here with the uncertain, probabilistic borderline at which the need to obey gives way to the need for self-preservation; the 'danger' referred to here is danger to the subject's life, and it was an immovable sticking point in Hobbes' theory that no one could ever covenant to kill himself (p. 69). It cases of capital punishment, Hobbes argued, the convict had a right to resist his gaolers and executioners. But it was also an important feature of his argument that at the same time the sovereign (who could commit no injustice) had a right to execute the man. The sovereign acted with the rights of the people, on their behalf.

The most striking formulation of this point comes in *De Cive*, where Hobbes writes that 'The *People* rules in all Governments, for even in *Monarchies* the *People* Commands' (1983, p. 151). He contrasted the 'people', which was the corporate entity created by the political agreement of its members, with the 'multitude', which was any mere aggregate of individuals. His intention was to undermine those who claimed to speak on behalf of 'the people' against their ruler, by showing that individuals gained a corporate identity only by virtue of being united under a sovereign. But since the 'people' was also the term which Hobbes used for the sovereign itself in the case of a democratic constitution, this argument had the probably unintended consequence that the foundation of any type of state had required a primary phase of democracy. In the quasi-historical accounts of *The Elements of Law* and *De Cive* this is what happened, and the democracy then dissolved itself if it handed over sovereignty to a monarchy or an aristocracy (1928, p. 94, 1983 pp. 109–11): even if the hand-over occurred at the first gathering of the people, the fact that it did so by majority vote would imply the momentary existence of a democratic constitution. Hobbes was obviously troubled both by the quasi-populist appearance of his argument in these works (as if democracy were somehow more natural), and by the theoretical awkwardness of identifying the corporate will of the state with an entity, the 'people', which apparently continued to exist after it had disappeared, like the grin of the Cheshire Cat. In *Leviathan* he streamlined his account by treating the original majority principle as a necessary procedural assumption (rather than as a mini-constitution), and worked out a new way of describing the continuing corporate entity as the 'person' of the state. Together with this concept of a 'person', which was drawn from the legal fiction that corporations could act as persons at law, he employed the related legal vocabulary of 'authorising' and 'representing': the sovereign (whether an individual or an assembly) represents its subjects because it is authorised to act as the bearer of their 'person', and they have a unitary 'person' only by virtue of being represented by a unitary sovereign (1651, pp. 80–3; see also Polin 1953, pp. 229–40, and Forsyth 1981). Throughout his account, Hobbes allows that the sovereign may be an aristocratic council or a democratic assembly; although he gives reasons for preferring a monarchy (pp. 95–8), the nature of the sovereignty is the same in each case.

The notion of authorising is taken up again when Hobbes considers the sovereign's legislative action and permissive inaction. 'All Lawes, written, and unwritten, have their Authority, and force, from the Will of the Common-wealth; that is to say, from the Will of the Representative' (p. 139). Customary law thus has its validity not from any intrinsic force of its own but from being 'authorised' by the sovereign, who could cancel it if he wished. (This was the starting point for Hobbes' attack on the claims of common law jurists in his *Dialogue . . . of the Common Laws of England.*) In a wider sense, all activities within the state are authorised by the sovereign so long as they are not forbidden. The state authorises geometry professors to teach geometry just as it authorises people to walk through public parks; this does not mean that everyone is acting on instructions from the state, and it does not mean that the sovereign authority is making the professors' geometry true, or obliging people to believe it. Of course the range of things which *might* be forbidden by the state is almost unlimited; but

Hobbes' theory supplies no reason for the state to use this power except for the preservation of peace and prosperity. It is in the sovereign's interest to allow individuals to pursue their own interests, because this produces a more contented and prosperous population: 'where the publique and private interest are most closely united, there is the publique most advanced . . . The riches, power, and honour of a Monarch arise onely from the riches, power, and honour of his Subjects' (p. 96; cf. Gunn 1969, pp. 65–81). Hobbes summarised his argument at one point in the *Elements of Law* by saying that it was the sovereign's duty by the law of nature 'to leave man as much liberty as may be, without hurt of the public' (1928, p. 141).

Hobbes' apparently unobjectionable claims about the authorisation of geometry teachers shadowed forth his argument on a much more contentious subject: the status of the church within the state. He regarded the church as a society of men engaged in teaching the doctrine of the Bible. The sovereign might authorise this teaching in the strong sense of endorsing as laws the injunctions to action which the teaching contained; or the sovereign could authorise it in the looser sense of permitting the activity of teaching. The distinction between belief and action was an important one: 'For internall Faith is in its own nature invisible, and consequently exempted from all humane [i.e. 'human'] jurisdiction' (1651, p. 285). If the church claimed an independent authority to direct the actions of men within the state, this was contrary to the unitary and absolute nature of civil sovereignty. The church's own actions must be subject to the civil power, and those actions must include not only acts of worship but also writing and speaking. But Hobbes distinguished carefully between forbidding teaching and forbidding men to believe what they were taught: 'such Forbidding is of no effect; because Beleef, and Unbeleef never follow mens Commands' (p. 271). Provided that the church did not claim independent rights of action, and provided that the doctrine it taught was not subversive to the peace of the state, Hobbes' theory allowed for a great degree of religious toleration. Ideally the sovereign should have no more reason to interfere with the church than with geometry lessons. Hobbes is only loosely to be described as an Erastian; he did not think that any strong connection between state and church was necessary, and his theory permitted Roman Catholicism in England, for example, provided that it were understood that the pope appointed teachers of doctrine in England only on sufferance from the English sovereign (p. 296). After the Restoration, Church of England bishops such as Edward Stillingfleet and Samuel Parker used Hobbesian arguments to justify government action against the Dissenters, on the grounds that they were a threat to civil peace; but in some ways it was the Dissenters who were wielding the most centrally Hobbesian arguments when they said that religious beliefs should not be subject to civil compulsion.

The difficulty, of course, was that some versions of religious belief would not fit into Hobbes' scheme, because they did involve belief in rights of action or jurisdiction independent of the sovereign. Most varieties of institutional Christianity taught beliefs of this sort, and Hobbes' arguments on this point are thus fiercely anti-clerical and above all anti-Catholic. But even within the Roman Catholic church there were traditions of Marsilian and Gallican argument on which Hobbes could draw in his attack on papal power (Malcolm 1984, pp. 82–3). Within the Anglican church Hobbes was in some ways following in the tradition of rationalist religion, of writers such as William Chillingworth and Falkland at Great Tew. Hobbes agreed with them that the essential doctrinal truths contained in the Bible were few and easily knowable (1651, pp. 325–6). And in the third part of *Leviathan* he subjected the Bible to a more thorough course of rational textual criticism than had been attempted by any previous English writer. His aim was to show that scripture, far from demanding beliefs or actions contrary to those of his own theory, actually matched and confirmed his account of men's duties at every point. It may be tempting to describe this as a rather cynical *arrière-pensée* on Hobbes' part; but, equally, it can be described as a necessary consequence of his own theological position. His theology, as we have seen, severed all essential links between the nature of God and the nature of the world. Natural theology might arrive at the knowledge that God existed, but it could supply no further knowledge of his nature. Evidence of God's will could exist in the form of something historically contingent, such as the text of scripture; but in order to interpret this evidence, principles of interpretation had to be applied, and they could not be derived from the evidence itself. It was inevitable, then, that in interpreting the Bible men would use their natural reason and interpret away any aspect of it which appeared to conflict with the dictates of natural reason – dictates already arrived at in the first two parts of *Leviathan*. Hobbes' similarity to rational theologians such as Falkland was therefore only skin-deep. They read rational beliefs into the Bible because they felt they had substantive knowledge of the rational nature of God; Hobbes did the same because of his *lack* of knowledge of God's nature, which forced him to interpret the Bible by the light of human nature and human reason. Denounced and dismissed as an 'atheist', Hobbes countered with a reply which it is hard to gainsay: 'Do you think I can be an atheist and not know it? Or, knowing it, durst have offered my atheism to the press?' (1839–45a, VII, p. 350).

ii Spinoza

Outside England, the Dutch republic was the country where Hobbes' writings exerted their greatest influence. The conditions of intellectual life there were favourable to 'free-thinking', with a flourishing book trade on which regulation and censorship were comparatively lightly enforced. The second edition of *De Cive* was printed there in 1647; a Dutch translation of *Leviathan* appeared in 1667; and an important collection of Hobbes' Latin writings, including his new Latin version of *Leviathan*, was published in Amsterdam in 1668.

Given its recent birth and the continuing uncertainty of some of its constitutional arrangements, the Dutch republic was a country in which basic questions of political theory were often of pressingly topical concern. Hobbes' pupil, the second earl of Devonshire, had written about 'such as professe to reade Theorie of Statisme; fellows that swarm in most places abroad, especially in *Germany*, or those places where the *Dutch* most usually frequent, that nation being easie and apt to be gulled by these Imposters' (Cavendish 1620, p. 40). The word 'Statisme' has overtones of 'étatisme' and 'raison d'état'. Where the internal workings of the state were concerned, this meant a value-free, comparative study of constitutions as power structures; where their external actions were concerned, it meant a study of all the tricks and devices of diplomacy and warfare – a study which could be amply justified by the dependence of Dutch foreign policy, throughout the seventeenth century, on kaleidoscopically shifting patterns of uncertain alliances. The leading academic exponent of this sort of power-analysis was M.Z. Boxhorn, who taught at Leiden University from 1633 to 1653; he published an edition of Tacitus in 1643, and in his own political writings he used examples from Tacitus to show that rulers would always be impelled by self-interest to encroach on the liberties of their subjects (e.g. Boxhorn 1663, pp. 18–22; Kossmann 1960, p. 20; Wansink 1981, pp. 93–100, 149–53).

The history of the Dutch republic had also fostered public interest in another area of political controversy: the relation between religion and the state. The main patterns of argument had been laid down in the second decade of the century, when the Remonstrants (liberal theologians who followed Jacobus Arminius) had appealed to the civil powers to protect them against the hard-line Calvinist Counter-Remonstrants. Pro-Remonstrant writers, such as Grotius in his *De imperio summarum potestatum circa sacra* (written *c.* 1614 and printed posthumously in 1647), had developed a theory of jurisdiction in which all power over human actions – including teaching, preaching, and acts of worship – had to be vested ultimately in the civil authority. Churches, in this theory, were regarded as voluntary associations within the state. The Remonstrants defended a policy of religious toleration by arguing that the Calvinist church had no jurisdictional power to persecute, and by claiming that religion was essentially a matter of beliefs, not actions, thus implying that a variety of religious beliefs should pose no threat to the state's activities. There was a natural congruence between this attitude and the Tacitean view of religion, which regarded public religious observances as part of the trappings, the psychological theatre, of the state, and therefore as something which must be controlled by the civil power. In the abstract, of course, these arguments did not dictate whether the civil power should be monarchical or republican. The contingencies of political history ensured that the Remonstrants and tolerationists sided with republicanism, while the supporters of the princes of Orange upheld the powers of the Calvinist church. But these alignments were not quite accidental. For it was the republican theorists who, in their attempt to work out from first principles what the nature and powers of the state should be, came closest to developing a rationalist-utilitarian type of political theory from which the traditional categories of sacerdotal and ecclesiastical power were most likely to be absent.

By the mid-century, the influence of Descartes' philosophy in the Dutch academic world was giving a powerful impetus to the desire to replace traditional bodies of theory with new systems of deductive science. Cartesianism flourished at the Universities of Utrecht and Leiden, where its influence was strongest in the areas of medicine and physics. The anti-scholastic nature of Descartes' views on human psychology was taken further by Dutch Cartesians such as Henricus Regius and Gerard Wassenaar at Utrecht, who developed a more mechanistic, materialist philosophy of mind which denied the existence of innate ideas and described the mind as a 'mode' of the body. This was a version of Cartesianism which was ideally suited to the reception of Hobbesian theories too. And Hobbes' work, for Cartesians, could usefully remedy the lack of any political theory in Descartes' own writings. Lambert van Velthuysen for example, who had studied at Utrecht in the 1640s, published defences of Descartes, Copernicus, and Hobbes, and in the preface to his 'apologia' for *De Cive* he defended Hobbes' work as if it were a straightforwardly Cartesian enterprise: all previous attempts at political philosophy were flawed, he wrote, because they had not used 'this device of doubting everything', and had failed to deduce their various principles from one single starting point (1651, sig. ★5r).

All these strands of argument – reason of state, Tacitism, religious toleration, the defence of unitary civil power, republicanism, Cartesianism and Hobbesianism – came together in the work of the most influential Dutch political writers of the 1650s and 1660s, the brothers Johan and Pieter de la Court. After the death of William II in 1650, and during the childhood of William III (who was born a few days after his father's death), most of the Dutch provinces found themselves operating a truly republican constitution for the first time, holding in abeyance the office of 'stadtholder' which had previouly been filled by the princes of Orange. Under John de Witt, the quasi-presidential 'grand pensionary' of Holland, a vigorous campaign of republican propaganda was waged to persuade Holland and the other provinces to abolish the office of stadtholder altogether. The brothers de la Court and Spinoza were among the most prominent writers to support him.

Both brothers had studied at Leiden in the early 1640s, where they had become Tacitists and Cartesians, and Pieter had gone on in 1645 to study medicine under Regius at Utrecht (Van Thijn 1956, pp. 309–15). Johan may have been responsible for the unauthorised printing of some lectures by Boxhorn, the *Commentariolus*, in 1649: the work bears a suspicious resemblance to Johan's own notes on the lectures, which he heard in 1643 (Wansink 1981, pp. 150–1). And a more spectacular example of literary piracy was Pieter's publication, over his own initials ('V.D.H.': 'van den Hove', the Dutch equivalent of 'de la Court') of a book, *Naeuwkeurige consideratie van staet (A Close Examination of the State)*, which was in fact written by that other pupil of Regius, Wassenaar (Haitsma Mulier 1984). Wassenaar's book seems to have given the de la Courts the idea of combining Tacitus and Machiavelli with a Cartesian theory of the passions, so that the task of political philosophy was seen as that of constructing the state as a mechanism to regulate the passions of individuals and force both rulers and ruled to identify their individual interests with the common good. And it was with this task in mind that the brothers de la Court turned eagerly to the writings of Hobbes.

The writings of the de la Courts form a homogeneous group of works, in which the same arguments keep reappearing.[5] 'Self-love is the origin of all human actions', begins the *Consideratien* (1660, p. 1). 'Self-preservation is the supreme law of all individuals' (*Discoursen*, 1662a, p. 91). Men are governed by their passions, and most men are therefore evil by nature; without a political power to keep them in check they will lead a diffident and violent existence in a 'state of nature', each judging partially in his own cause (*Consideratien*, 1660, pp. 1–8). People are equal by nature, and only the state, an artificial human construct, has introduced inequalities (p. 346, mispaginated '246'). Once the state is established, the subjects owe it a debt of gratitude for their protection; and they are justified in rebelling only when their individual lives are threatened (p. 347, mispaginated '247', *Discoursen*, 1662a, p. 27).

Thus far, the Hobbesian overtones are obvious. The 1660 *Consideratien* shows a close familiarity with *De Cive*, and the later editions suggest a reading of *Leviathan* as well. But this is a version of Hobbes from which all the jural categories – rights, covenants, authorisation – have been stripped away. For Hobbes, the essential conflict in the state of nature is a conflict of *rights*. For the de la Courts, it is a conflict of passions; there is thus no qualitative distinction between men's relations in the state of nature and their relations in civil society. 'All obedience is caused by compulsion' (*Discoursen*, 1662a, p. 29). Each individual wishes to live according to his own will (*'t Welvaren*, 1911, p. 10): this principle means that force is required to get any individual to live according to the will of another, and it also means that rulers will constantly be trying to extend their wills more fully over their subjects.

---

5. The corpus of their works, however, poses many problems of individual attribution. Most of the major works appeared over the initials 'V.H.', 'V.D.H.', or 'D.C.', but other works which have been attributed to them appeared anonymously. Johan died in 1660; he is thought to have been largely responsible for the *Consideratien* of that year, which was expanded in subsequent editions by Pieter, and Pieter may well have quarried material from Johan's papers in putting together the other works of the 1660s. The major works are:
't Welvaren der stad Leiden (*The Prosperity of the City of Leiden*), MS dated 1659, ed. F. Driessen (Leiden: Nijhoff, 1911).
Consideratien en exempelen van staat (*Observations and Lessons on the State*) (Amsterdam, 1660); 2nd (expanded) edn published 1661 under the title *Consideratien van Staat ofte Polityke Weeg-Schaal* (*Observations on the State; or, the Political Balance*); 3rd edn (also expanded) and 4th and 5th edns published under this title, 1662.
Politieke Discoursen (*Political Discourses*) (Amsterdam, 1662)
Interest van Holland (*The Interest of Holland*) (Amsterdam, 1662); 2nd edn, expanded with two additional chapters possibly by de Witt, published 1669 as *Aanwysing der heilsame politike Gronden en Maximen van de Republike van Holland en West-Vriesland* (*An Indication of the Salutary Political Principles and Maxims of the Republic of Holland and West Friesland*).
On other works by the de la Courts see Geyl 1947.

As a result of this line of argument, the problems of constitution-building assumed a central place in the work of the de la Courts. For Hobbes, the nature of an individual's covenantal commitment to obey the sovereign power would be the same, regardless of the constitutional form which that sovereign power assumed. The arguments in favour of monarchy in *De Cive* and *Leviathan* thus have a purely secondary status in Hobbes' overall theory. But for the de la Courts the primary problem was to design a constitution which could keep the encroaching wills of both rulers and ruled in check. Monarchy was the least attractive solution, because any individual entrusted with power was likely to use it for his private benefit (*Consideratien*, 1660, pp. 13–74). Government by a large assembly was better, because in such a gathering the divergent private passions would tend to cancel each other out (p. 203, mispaginated '103'); and since the basic urge of each individual was to live according to his own will, any more or less democratic system would enable individuals to obey the will of the government and at the same time obey their own will, which was a component of the government's will (p. 353, mispaginated '253'). If this sounds like a version of consent theory, then it is a version quite unlike Hobbes': this version does not explain the nature of sovereignty, but is confined to one type of constitution. It merely gives a democratic government a psychological advantage which may, in effect, increase the amount of power which the government can wield.

These considerations may prompt the conclusion that the de la Courts owed little to Hobbes beyond their starting point in mechanistic psychology. But there was one important area of their argument which did draw directly on Hobbes' political theories: their views on the unitary nature of sovereign power and the relation which this implied between church and state. The state, they argued, must have power over all external acts, and therefore over all acts of religious worship. To further the interests of both rulers and ruled, it must exercise this power for purely secular ends, namely peace and prosperity. Hence the need to tolerate all religions which are not themselves subversive of the state (*Discoursen*, 1662a, pp. 19–24). And for the subject, mere outward conformity is sufficient (pp. 69–74). The peculiarly Hobbesian twist to this argument is the insistence that 'the public determination of what is good and what is evil belongs only to the sovereign: otherwise the political state will change, through the conflict of many private judgements, into a state of nature' (p. 24). This argument struck at the moral jurisdiction of the Calvinist church, and was accompanied by some thoroughly Hobbesian jibes against the deleterious effects of clerical power on intellectual life (pp. 36–41).

The late 1650s and early 1660s saw numerous attempts by the Calvinists to reassert their moral and intellectual jurisdiction. Pressure was brought to bear on the university authorities at Leiden to curb the teaching of Cartesianism and 'the application of philosophy to the prejudice of theology' (Molhuysen, 1913–24, III, pp. 109–12); the anti-clericalism of the de la Courts' writings provoked a storm of sermons and pamphlets (Van Gelder 1972, p. 253); and in Utrecht, where the Hobbesian philosopher van Velthuysen had penned similar attacks on clerical power in 1660 (*Ondersoeck* and *Het predick-ampt*), the leading anti-Cartesian, Gisbertus Voetius, wrote a major defence of the jurisdictional powers of the Calvinist church (*Politica ecclesiastica*, 1663). In 1665 a brief but important treatise attacking the Calvinist arguments, *De jure ecclesiasticorum* (*The Right of the Clergy*) was published over the pseudonym 'Lucius Antistius Constans'. This work, which was once attributed to Spinoza himself, draws so heavily on the arguments of the de la Courts that it can quite plausibly be attributed to Pieter de la Court (e.g. by Van der Linde 1961, p. 16); but it goes beyond the de la Courts' other published works in its attempt to assimilate the jural concepts of contract and 'jus' ('right'). It distinguishes between right and power, but observes that the former without the latter is worthless (pp. 54–5). Differences of right within the state are created by the power of the state; and the state's power arises either through the conquest of the weak by the strong, or through a social contract, whereby people transfer their 'right and power' to the ruler (pp. 9–12). Just as the notion of 'right' is weakened, in the course of this argument, by its constant association with 'power', so too the notion of contractual obligation is absorbed into the pattern of factual power relations: the 'conventio' ('agreement') can be entirely implicit, something to be identified 'not in words but in deeds' (p. 35).

This is the background against which we must situate Spinoza's own writings on the nature of the state. It was in 1665 that Spinoza started work on what was to become his major political treatise, the *Tractatus theologico-politicus* (henceforth cited *TTP*), aiming, as he explained to one correspondent, to defend 'the freedom of philosophizing . . . for here it is always suppressed through the excessive authority and impudence of the preachers' (Spinoza 1928, p. 206, letter 30). And when the work was published in 1670, he explained that he had been prompted by the 'fierce controversies of the philosophers in church and state' (*TTP*, preface, 1924, III, p. 9). His library contained copies of the de la Courts' *Polityke Weeg-Schaal* (the enlarged second edition of the *Consideratien*) and *Discoursen*

(Freudenthal 1899, pp. 161–2), and he described the former work as 'extremely shrewd' (*Tractatus politicus* (henceforth cited *TP*), VII.31). If Pieter de la Court was not the author of *De jure ecclesiasticorum*, then the most likely candidate is Lodowijk Meyer, a Cartesian doctor and theologian who was a close friend of Spinoza (Spinoza 1928, p. 50; Meinsma, 1896, pp. 146–50).

The anti-clerical, tolerationist, republican writings of the 1660s form the main background to Spinoza's political works; but of course his own personal history had also given him cause to consider the relation between religion, state power, and individual freedom. Baruch (Benedictus in Latin) de Spinoza was the son of a Portuguese Jew; born in Amsterdam in 1632, he was educated at a Jewish school up to the age of thirteen, and probably attended a Yeshivah (a society for the study of the Bible, the Talmud, and the Torah) for several years thereafter (Meinsma 1896, pp. 58–65; Vaz Dias and van der Tak 1932, pp. 56–61). But in 1656 he was excommunicated from the synagogue for 'the horrible heresies which he taught and practised'; the exact nature of his offence is not known, but all the evidence suggests that he had propounded a rationalist, deist theology which demoted the status of the Bible as divine revelation, questioned its historical accuracy, and probably cast doubt on the immortality of the soul (Revah 1959). According to some early sources, he wrote a thoroughly unapologetic 'Apology' after his excommunication, which contained an historical critique of the Bible and a wide-ranging attack on the Jewish religion (Préposiet 1973, pp. 345, 417). If this is so, then it is reasonable to assume that some of this material was put to use in the *Tractatus theologico-politicus*. However, the main outlines of the political theory in that book are drawn not from debates within Judaism but from the Dutch Hobbesian–republican tradition. Even the lengthy discussions of the Old Testament in that treatise may also owe something directly to Hobbes: although Spinoza did not read English, he was a friend of the man who was translating *Leviathan* into Dutch in the period 1665–7, and he may also have had time to benefit from the Latin translation of *Leviathan* (1668) before finishing the *Tractatus theologico-politicus* in 1670 (Schoneveld 1983, pp. 8, 40).

The main arguments of the treatise are succinctly summarised by Spinoza himself. He argues first that philosophy and theology are radically different in nature, 'and that the latter allows each person to philosophise freely' (*TTP*, ch. 16, 1924, III, p. 189); then 'that rights over religion belong entirely to the sovereign, and that external acts of worship must be adapted to serve the peace of the state' (ch. 19, 1924, III, p. 228); and finally that freedom of speech 'is not only compatible with civil peace, piety and the right of the sovereign, but in fact ought to be permitted in order to preserve all those things' (ch. 20, 1924, III, p. 247). The separation of philosophy and theology is carefully managed, in a way which preserves an apparent respect for the special nature of revelation while at the same time suggesting that it is ultimately unnecessary. Philosophy can teach both virtue and the knowledge of God (these two things being inseparable in Spinoza's theory); theology, on the other hand, which is based on revelation, aims only at teaching obedience to God (chs. 7, 14, 15). For this purpose the teachings of the Old Testament were 'adapted' to the understandings of ordinary people of the time: the validity of a theological doctrine lies not in its truth but in its power to instil obedience (ch. 14, 1924, III, pp. 176–7). Only gradually does Spinoza make it plain that obedience is an inferior substitute for understanding, that the principal contents of revelation – prophecy and miracles – are fictions adapted for weak minds which cannot understand that God works in nature by means of immutable laws, and that the peculiar injunctions given to the Jews in the Old Testament were essentially political devices, designed to further political obedience and social cohesion. Some of these arguments may have derived from Moses Maimonides' theory of divine law, which stressed that divine commands were adapted to historical conditions in the Old Testament, and suggested that the dietary and ceremonial laws were simply devices for instilling moral virtues – virtues which could in principle be arrived at philosophically, without the use of revelation (Maimonides 1975, pp. 71–2, 1904, pp. 312–80). But Spinoza's comments on the use of religion as an instrument of political power also reflect his careful reading of Tacitus and Machiavelli.

This is particularly apparent in his account of the Jewish state in chapter 17 of the treatise, where he implies that when the Jews made God their sovereign they were in fact being cleverly manipulated by Moses, who became their effective ruler as God's representatives on earth. Since religion is such a powerful force in human psychology (combining love, fear, and admiration – the last two of which are the products of defective understanding), this pseudo-theocracy was a very successful form of covert monarchy; but Moses' system of government was flawed, Spinoza argues, because it allowed the Levite priests to retain a form of religious jurisdiction, and in later generations they were able to assume political power and reduce the Jewish nation to civil war (ch. 18).

Spinoza's theory of the nature and purpose of political power is set out in the *Tractatus theologico-politicus* (esp. ch. 16) and in the first six chapters of his later, unfinished work, the *Tractatus politicus*. Like the de la Courts, he starts with the assumption that men are passionate creatures, guided by short-term self-interest; as they become more rational, they will be guided by longer term self-interest, but self-interest remains the key to all human actions (*TTP*, ch. 17, 1924, III, pp. 215–16). Social cooperation is necessary for leading a secure and pleasant life. The more rational a man is, the more he will desire cooperation because he understands this; but political power, wielding coercive force, is needed to keep irrational men from pursuing their own short-term interest against the interests of society at large. And since rulers as well as ruled will be subject to passions, constitutions must be designed to ensure that subjects and rulers will subordinate or assimilate their own interests to the interests of the whole state (ch. 17, 1924, III, p. 203). In the *Tractatus politicus* Spinoza intended to show how this could be achieved in each form of constitution (monarchy, aristocracy and democracy); unfortunately he died before completing his section on democracy, which he held to be the most natural and most rational of the three forms. Like the de la Courts, he argued in the *Tractatus theologico-politicus* that the subjects of a democracy would enjoy a greater sense of freedom, because in obeying the sovereign they were obeying themselves (ch. 16, 1924, III, p. 195); and he also followed the de la Courts in claiming that the process of decision-making in a large assembly would cancel out individual passions and ensure the prevalence of reason (ch. 16, 1924, III, p. 194; on his debt to the de la Courts in *TP* see Haitsma Mulier 1980, pp. 187–208).

Thus far, Spinoza's theory seems confined to the bare analysis of motivation and power structures. Much of the interest of his theory, however, lies in the way in which he assimilates the concepts of 'right' and 'contract' into his argument. He makes use of the concept of 'right', but identifies it completely with 'power'. This is not a piece of casual cynicism on his part: it flows from the heart of his philosophical theology, which attributes both infinite right and infinite power to God, and identifies the physical universe as an expression of God's nature. It follows from this that every event in the physical world is an expression both of God's power and of His right. 'Whatever man does, whether he is led to do it by reason or only be desire, he does it according to the laws and rules of nature, that is, by natural right' (*TP*, II.5, 1924, III, p. 277). Where Hobbes argued both that natural rights were all-encompassing and that there were some actions (contrary to self-preservation) which people did *not* have the right to perform, Spinoza can argue both that men have the right to do whatever they can do, and that an order of preference can be established when considering alternative courses of action: actions which help ensure the agent's self-preservation will increase his right because they increase his power, so that in some sense he will have less right to perform those actions which diminish his power.

Just as Spinoza uses the term 'right' but reduces it to 'power', so too he uses the term 'contract' but reduces it to a relationship of power. In chapter 16 of the *Tractatus theologico-politicus* he describes, in terms reminiscent of *De Cive*, how people must have transferred their natural right to the sovereign through a 'contract' ('pactum' or 'contractus'). In the later *Tractatus politicus* this account of a contract is notably absent: the notion of 'agreement' ('consensus') is used instead, and men are said to 'come together' to form a state not because they are led by reason but because they are driven by common passions (VI.1, 1924, III, p. 295). This has led some commentators to suggest that Spinoza believed, in the earlier work, in an historical contract which the founders of society had entered into out of 'rational foresight', and that he later abandoned this belief (Wernham 1958, pp. 25–6). Yet the real differences between the two accounts are not so great. A transfer of right, as the earlier work has already made clear, can only amount to a transfer of power, and this is something which can come about without 'rational foresight' playing any special role. Spinoza emphasises in the *Tractatus theologico-politicus* that 'a contract is binding only by reason of its utility' (ch. 16, 1924, III, p. 192); as soon as it becomes advantageous for someone to break his contract, he will have the right to do so. This means that men keep their contract of obedience only because the sovereign wields real power. Such a view is entirely compatible with the idea that the origins of the state go back not to a set of formal articles of agreement but to a gradual coalescence of human power relations. When Spinoza introduces the idea of a contract in chapter 16 of the *Tractatus theologico-politicus* he says, in a revealing construction, that men 'must have' contracted (1924, III, p. 191); the notion of a contract is nothing more than a device for describing a power-relationship which is informed by an understanding of mutual benefit, and to describe such an arrangement as rational does not imply that it can only have been introduced through a conscious act of reason.

Spinoza seems to have adopted, at this point in the earlier treatise, a Hobbesian terminology of 'transferring' natural rights, because he wanted to make the Hobbesian anti-clerical point that *all* rights belonged to the sovereign. (This was the first stage of his tolerationist argument, aimed at removing the jurisdictional powers of the clergy which would otherwise be deployed against freedom of opinion.) At one point he says that the subject must have 'completely yielded' his natural right (ch. 16, 1924, III, p. 195). But this is a misleading form of words for Spinoza to use, and it can only amount to saying that the subject is sufficiently motivated to act always in complete accordance with the will of the sovereign. For each person, in Spinoza's theory, retains natural right so long as he retains natural power: when asked by a friend to explain the difference between his theory and Hobbes', he replied that it 'consists in this, that I ever preserve the natural right intact, so that the Supreme Power in a State has no more right over a subject than is proportionate to the power by which it is superior to the subject' (Spinoza 1928, p. 269).

This is the essential argument which enables Spinoza to conclude that the toleration of religious and philosophical opinions is both compatible with the sovereign's power and beneficial to it. In Spinoza's state the power of the sovereign can rise or fall, according to how the subjects become more or less fully motivated to obey it. More power, and therefore more right, inheres in a policy which is popular: it is in the interests of the sovereign to avoid alienating his subjects. Laws forbidding beliefs are, as Hobbes pointed out, fatuous; but Spinoza adds that laws forbidding people to express their beliefs will render those people sullen and hostile, and thereby weaken the power of the state (*TTP*, ch. 20). Only the preaching of seditious doctrines must be proscribed; all opinions which do not disturb the peace of the state are to be allowed.

Despite, or perhaps because of, his reductive style of power analysis, Spinoza seems possibly to have arrived at a liberal, pluralistic theory of the state which matches the liberal elements of Hobbes' theory. It is possible to argue that the role of the Spinozan state is simply to provide an external framework of peace and security within which individuals can continue to pursue their own interests (den Uyl 1983, esp. pp. 111–28). Such an interpretation, however, ignores the implications of Spinoza's metaphysics and psychology. His major exposition of these subjects, the *Ethics*, was completed concurrently with the writing of the *Tractatus theologico-politicus* in the second half of the 1660s, and he referred to the *Ethics*, implying that it was part of the same systematic body of theory, in chapter 2 of the *Tractatus politicus* (1924, III, p. 276). Only from the *Ethics* do we learn just how radically different Spinoza's metaphysics were from Hobbes', and therefore how completely his theory of reason and his theory of human liberty differed from Hobbes' too.

In Spinoza's metaphysics, all reality is comprehended in God, who is the only substance, that is, the only absolutely self-subsistent being. God is knowable through an infinite number of 'attributes', of which only two are actually known to us: extension and thought. A human body is a 'mode' (i.e. a modification, a particular entity) of extension, and a human mind is a mode of thought. There is a strict parallelism between these modes of different attributes: neither can act causally on the other, but each is an expression (in a completely different dimension, so to speak) of the same component of the divine substance. Thus a human mind is the 'idea of' a human body; the development of the mind and the development of the body will consist of the same development being manifested in different forms.

Physical bodies exist in an order of causes; thought exists in an order of reasons or implications. The human mind, being the idea of the human body, contains the ideas of the experiences which the body undergoes. If the mind fails to understand these ideas 'adequately' (that is, if it fails to recognise the way in which each is implicitly part of the whole system of the divine substance) then it experiences an impairment of power, a passive emotion, or 'passion' (e.g. fear). But if the cause or reason is understood adequately by the mind, then the mind is exercising and enlarging its power of action, and the passion is transformed into an active emotion (e.g. love). All active emotions are ultimately forms of the love of God, because they derive from acts of understanding which involve relating particular things to the totality of things, which is God. The more active the mind is – the more, in other words, it 'contains' the causes of its action within itself – the more free it is. Spinoza is a classic exponent of the rationalist theory of freedom (cf. *TP* II.7), and therefore lies at the opposite pole from Hobbes' view of freedom as the absence of impediment.

In Part IV of the *Ethics* Spinoza explains that while passions are individual and particularising, reason is universal and harmonising. 'Men can be opposed to each other insofar as they are afflicted with emotions which are passions' (prop. 34, 1924, II, p. 231); 'men necessarily agree with one another insofar as they live according to the dictates of reason' (prop. 35, dem., 1924, II, p. 233). This 'agreement' is a real harmonising and converging of minds, not just an attitude of liberal non-interference: as Spinoza wrote in his early *Short Treatise*, if I teach knowledge and the love of God to my neighbours, 'it brings forth the same desire in them that there is in me, so that their will and mine become one and the same, constituting one and the same nature, always agreeing about everything' (xxvi.4, 1924, I, p. 112).

Although in his metaphysics he rejected teleology in the strict sense, Spinoza's account of reason as the defining feature of the 'human essence' gives rise to a quasi-teleological scale of values for mankind: man fulfils his nature more fully when he acts rationally. Such a theory could not be further removed from Hobbes' view, in which reason is simply the servant of the desires. Even the apparent agreement between the two writers on the primacy of self-preservation is removed by Spinoza's argument that a man's true self, his 'power of acting', is his reason (*Ethics*, part 4, prop. 52, dem., 1924, II, p. 248).

The aim of Spinoza's state is to make men rational and free. 'When I say that the best state is one in which men live harmoniously together, I mean a form of life . . . which is defined above all by reason, the true virtue and life of the mind' (*TP*, v.5, 1924, III, p. 296). Spinoza recognises that the state must be constructed to contain those who are not predominantly rational and virtuous; but the state can aim gradually to mould its citizens into a more rational kind of existence by imposing rational laws on them. In very general terms, we might say that the history of republicanism in political philosophy presents two fundamentally different defences of republican government. There is a mechanistic type of theory, which sees the construction of a republic as the solution to the problem of organising and balancing a mass of conflicting individual forces; and there is the rationalist-idealist type of theory, which believes that in a republic men are freed from the corrupting ties of dependence on or subjection to personal authority, and are enabled to participate most fully as rational beings in the rationality of the state and its laws. Spinoza manages to combine both types of theory in a single system: that is the distinction, and the ambiguity, of his achievement.

V
Natural law and utility

19
Pufendorf

ALFRED DUFOUR

The Saxon philosopher Samuel Pufendorf has, for three reasons, an unusual place in the history of modern political thought. First, unlike Hobbes or Montesquieu, he has often been consigned to oblivion. He was famous in his own time and a central figure in eighteenth-century writing, through the texts translated, compiled and popularised by Jean Barbeyrac, Jean-Jacques Burlamaqui, and Jean-Jacques Rousseau. Gradually, however, his work became discredited, becoming overshadowed by Christian Thomasius, Christian Wolff, and Kant in Germany, and by Locke and Rousseau in the English and French traditions. His reputation was never secure, and even contemporaries passed contradictory judgements. Leibniz denigrated him as 'no lawyer, and scarcely a philosopher at all' (Leibniz 1768, p. 261). Thomasius lauded him as 'the first in Germany to think of establishing a science of morality in accordance with mathematical methods' (Thomasius 1719, p. 6). Secondly, unlike Bodin, Locke, or Rousseau, Pufendorf left a disparate body of work, seemingly lacking in unity and containing no major political text. He wrote voluminously on practical philosophy and public law, and monumental historical works. Yet he does not look like a classical political thinker. Thirdly, unlike, say, Machiavelli or More, Pufendorf's political thought is characterised not by the originality of his own ideas, but by his eclecticism. He borrowed the epistemological and methodological principles of the Jena Cartesian Erhard Weigel and sought to combine the opposing anthropological and political concepts of Hobbes and Grotius. Consequently, for a long time he was seen as 'a thinker of secondary importance', at worst 'a dull and indigestible compiler' (Derathé 1970, p. 78; Belime 1856, p. 11). Pufendorf's reputation has, therefore, suffered, not so much because of the vicissitudes of the current of thought of

This chapter was translated from the French by Dr J.C. Whitehouse and abridged by Dr Mark Goldie.

which he was the most prominent representative, that of modern natural law, but from the enormous complexity of his work and the stature of his great contemporaries and successors.

Pufendorf was a pioneer of German theories of natural law and of the state, and an exponent of the doctrine of the interests of states. His main legacy, after his *Elements of Universal Jurisprudence* (1660), is his *On the Law of Nature and Nations* (1672) and *On the Duty of Man and the Citizen* (1673), his treatises on practical philosophy which became authorities throughout Europe, shaping the rise of the school of the law of nature and nations, and serving as justifications for regimes based either on enlightened despotism or on declarations of the rights of man.

Pufendorf was early attracted to political problems and quickly became an authority on public law, examining the natural foundations and historical forms of the state, as in his essay *On the Constitution of the German Empire* (1667) and his studies *On the Irregular Republic* (1677) and *On the Systems of States* (1677), which gained him a solid reputation amongst publicists. He also examined ecclesiastical law and church–state relationships, as in his treatise *On the Relation of the Christian Religion to Civil Life* (1687), which put him firmly in the Lutheran tradition of the subordination of religious communities to civil authority.

He was later appointed official historiographer to the kings of Sweden in 1677 and to the Electors of Brandenburg in 1686, and produced two impressive *Histories of Sweden* (1695 and 1696) and two *Histories of the Electors of Brandenburg* (1695 and 1734), painstakingly based on diplomatic archives, a milestone in German historiography. He also produced an *Introduction to the History of the Principal Kingdoms and States of Europe* (1682). This, by highlighting 'the interests of states', shows him to be one of the first German theoreticians of the idea of reason of state. It was a theme already adumbrated in his *Constitution of the German Empire*, and was a result of his openness to knowledge acquired both from experience and the demands of reason. It is not surprising that at the beginning of this century Meinecke, the historian of reason of state, should regard Pufendorf as freeing the theory of the state 'from the shackles of theology' and building instead upon the master conception of 'reason of state and the interests of nations' (Meinecke 1924, p. 280).

A deep coherence underlies the diversity of Pufendorf's work. Its unity lies in his central preoccupation with the nature of the state and the primacy of the political. His approach is marked by eclecticism, and he cannot be reduced to any particular school. There is something in common with the rationalistic optimism common at the time, yet his ideas remain open to the experience history provides. He is certainly within the tradition of Ockham's voluntarist nominalism, but that does not prevent Pufendorf maintaining that divine decrees are rational insofar as they respect the requirements of the order of Creation. Similarly, the part he allots to consent in the foundation of all authority does not mean he can be seen as offering an early form of liberal individualism, nor does the favourable way he seems to regard monarchy allow of an opportunistic absolutism.[1] He is fundamentally to be seen as a mediator and reconciler, a man of compromise.[2] He embodies in secular philosophy the syncretic and conciliating spirit which, a hundred years earlier, was represented in theology by Suárez. As a German Suárez, he lacks the theological and metaphysical temper of the Spanish Jesuit, but he shares his eclecticism and ability to reconcile conflicting theses. This is first evident if we examine the philosophical bases of his political thought.

i The philosophical bases of Pufendorf's thought

Pufendorf's overriding aim was to take advantage of the methodology of the physical and mathematical sciences in order to confer on the human sciences the certitude that the Aristotelian scholastic tradition denied them (Pufendorf (1660) 1931, p. 1/xxviii, (1672) 1934, I.ii.1, pp. 14–15/22).[3] In this he was profoundly influenced by Descartes, introduced to him by his Jena master, the philosopher and mathematician Weigel (Spiess 1881). Although Pufendorf was convinced of the appropriateness of applying the new scientific methodology to socio-moral reality, either in its resolutive-compositive form, to which Hobbes showed him the way, or in its demonstrative form, for which Spinoza provided the example, he nevertheless took care not to fall into the mechanistic materialism of the former or the sociological naturalism of the latter, who both reduced the socio-moral universe to that of physical reality ((1672) 1934, II.ii.3, pp. 108–11/158–62). Thus it was that he set himself the preliminary task of

---

1. For some of these theses see Welzel 1958, pp. 6–7, 38–9, 1962, pp. 130–1; and Sauter 1932, p. 136n.
2. On Pufendorf's eclecticism see his letter to Thomasius (19 June 1688) in Pufendorf 1893, pp. 30–1. For recent commentary see Krieger 1965, p. 3; Denzer 1972, pp. 9, 324.
3. References in the text and notes to Pufendorf's *On the Law of Nature* ((1672) 1934), *Elements* ((1660) 1931), and *On the Duty of Man* ((1673) 1927) give page numbers of the Latin texts and of the English translations; in the case of *On the Law of Nature* and *On the Duty of Man* page references are preceded by book and section numbers. In references supplied in the text 'Pufendorf' is omitted where it is obvious that his work is being cited.

establishing the autonomy of the socio-moral world and defining the specificity of the human sciences.

Pufendorf fulfilled this task by a theory of moral realities (*entia moralia*) which enabled him to stress the irreducibly separate origins of the socio-moral world (Welzel 1958, pp. 19–21; Krieger 1965, pp. 73–81). This was a singularly innovative theory of culture, yet a misunderstood one. The epistemological considerations underlying the *Elements of Universal Juris-prudence* and *On the Law of Nature,* under the rubric of *entia moralia,* are the key to his legal and political thought ((1660) 1931, p. 1/xxviii, Def. I–XXI, pp. 1–242/1–206; (1672) 1934, i.i, pp. 1–14/3–21). In some aspects they are close to modern thinking. They foreshadow the neo-Kantian view of the *Geisteswissenschaften* and the *Naturwissenschaften* as opposites: a distinction between the realm of culture, which is the creation of freedom, and the realm of nature, which is dominated by necessity (Welzel 1958, pp. 19–21; 1962, pp. 132–3). It renders the science of humankind separate from the natural sciences. To Pufendorf, human beings are different from all other natural beings, who are motivated solely by instinct, not only by virtue of their faculties of knowing and willing, but also in their ability to invent and apply means of directing them or providing for their needs. Those means are ideas, which serve to clarify the understanding, and moral entities, which serve as rules for acts of the will ((1672) 1934, i.i.2, pp. 2/4–5). In thus defining the cultural world, Pufendorf is able to synthesise the sciences of the mind and the moral and social sciences on the basis of this theory of moral entities.

Following the model of the creation of natural reality either by the imposition of the will of God, 'who did not wish men to live without culture or morals, like the beasts', or of human will, to fulfil the needs of communal life, moral entities are ordained for the perfection of human life insofar as it is susceptible of order and harmony ((1672) 1934, i.i.3–4, p. 3/5). Pufendorf sees these realities as *modes,* which do not subsist of themselves but are always supported by physical realities ultimately serving as substances for them, and affecting them in conformity with the will that brought them into being ((1672) 1934, i.i.3, p. 2/5). Since they owe their existence solely to the free decisions of beings endowed with reason (as a shadow owes its existence solely to light), they disappear once those decisions have been revoked, with no resultant change in the physical substance of the realities they affect ((1672) 1934, i.i.4, p. 3/6, i.i.23, p. 14/21). In maintaining that moral realities have no effect of a physical kind and hence stressing the radical heterogeneity of the socio-moral and physical worlds, Pufendorf was seeking to avoid both the terrible confusions of scholastic thought still weighing upon contemporary political theologies and the reductive materialist contaminations of the physical and mathematical sciences jeopardising the rise of modern political philosophy.

Once he had determined the status of moral realities, Pufendorf defined their different categories, conceptualising them on the model of the traditional metaphysical categories of space, time, substance, quality, and quantity. He differentiated the following four moral categories ('space' and 'time' being combined in the first of them). First, states (*status*), which, by analogy with space and time, form the framework within which moral beings function ((1672) 1934, I.i.6, p. 4/7). By 'state' Pufendorf meant any condition, in principle involving rights and duties, in which people are placed in order to carry out certain actions ((1673) 1927, II.i.1, p. 98/89). By analogy with space, he distinguishes the state of nature (*status naturae*), which arises from the imposition of divine will, and adventitious states (*status adventitii*), which are the result of human wishes (marriage, domestic and political society). By analogy with time, he distinguishes youth and age, which arise from the order imposed by God, and minority and majority, which depend on the arbitrary conventions of humankind ((1672) 1934, I.i.7–10, pp. 4–6/7–10). Secondly, moral persons (*personae morales*), having the role of substances, which, though grounded in physical realities, do not lose their moral character. By moral person Pufendorf means not only any individual, but also any group of persons, in relation to the moral state they find themselves in. He contrasts the single person (*persona simplex*) and the composite person (*persona composita*) and in each case the political or ecclesiastical public and private person ((1672) 1934, I.i.12–13, pp. 7–9/11–13). Thirdly, moral qualities, which are affective modes and cover every modification affecting persons at the moral level. Pufendorf distinguishes *formal qualities* (such as titles of honour), and *operative qualities* (such as powers, rights, and obligations, and honour, credit, and infamy).[4] Fourthly, *moral quantities*, which are estimative modes, reflecting the degree of esteem that can be granted to things and actions in accordance with human judgement, such as consideration (*existimatio*) and price (*pretium*).[5] These apparently highly academic

4. For the definition of the moral qualities see Pufendorf (1672) 1934, I.i.17–18, pp. 11–12/16–17, (1660) 1931, Def. XIIff, pp. 80ff/71ff; for the distinctions, see (1672) 1934, I.i.17–21, pp. 11–13/16–20.
5. Pufendorf (1672) 1934, I.i.17, 22, pp. 11–14/17–21, (1660) 1931, Def. X, XVIII, pp. 72–6/64–70, 220–9/181–96.

distinctions were vital parts of Pufendorf's renovation of the traditional theory of society, law, and the state.

These innovatory concepts were strikingly different from the still-dominant scholasticism, and though he did take up some of its ideas, they acquired a different meaning in his hands. This is particularly true of the 'state of nature'. By this phrase he did not mean the scholastic notion of the 'condition which nature intended should be most perfect', but that condition which humankind is in 'by the mere fact of its birth, all inventions and institutions . . . being disregarded' ((1672) 1934, II.ii.1, p. 105/154). The state of nature is derived from an analysis of humankind in its present state, and not from speculation about origins or alleged essential purposes. It was not thereby merely an abstraction or fiction, but a juridical reality characteristic of the life of people and societies bereft of all connections other than those that exist because they are similar by nature. The state of nature contrasts with every form of civilisation and civil society, it is prior to any institutions.[6] From this basis, Pufendorf determines the basic rights and duties of man qua man, – 'total independence from all but God' and 'complete equality before all men' – and also the elementary rules which govern the relations of people and states living outside any political community.[7]

In affirming the freedom and basic equality of all men in the state of nature, and in going against traditional doctrines like those of Filmer and Bossuet, Pufendorf undermined the current conception of natural authority, which derived the right to command from physical or intellectual superiority ((1672) 1934, I.vi.11, pp. 68–70/99–101). In its place he put a new theory of power in which all kinds of authority were grounded in agreement or free consent ((1672) 1934, III.ii.8, pp. 232/341–2). This doctrine of 'conventionalism' has close links with the epistemological principles embedded in his idea of moral entities. All social power is a moral quality grounded in acts of will. 'Sovereignty, as a moral entity of one man over another, does not exist without a human act and is not intelligible without obedience.' Thus, for instance, 'no obligation to obey lies upon a woman before she has with her own consent subjected herself to a man' ((1672) 1934, VI.i.12, p. 587/863). Authority is hence grounded in the *impositio* of the free will. And as in the case of most moral entities, this *impositio* takes the form of an agreement, as in marriage or the civil pact,

6. Pufendorf (1672) 1934, I.i.7, p. 4/7, II.ii.1–4, pp. 105–72/154–63; (1673) 1927, II.i.4–5, pp. 99/89–90.
7. Pufendorf (1672) 1934, II.ii.3, 5–11, pp. 108–9/158–9, 113–21/165–76, (1673) 1927, II.i.8, pp. 90–1, 100–1; 1677, pp. 463–5, 472, 482–9.

and generates the differing adventitious states, such as marriage and citizenship, as well as the 'moral persons', exemplified in households, magistrates, and corporations.[8]

Amongst all the 'moral persons' created by an act of human will, Pufendorf pays particular attention to what he calls 'composite moral persons'. These include corporations of merchants and artisans as well as the higher organs of state, as opposed to 'simple moral persons', such as officers or magistrates ((1672) 1934, I.i.12–14, pp. 7–11/11–13). This step displaces the traditional distinction between 'artificial' and 'natural' persons, and gives to composite moral persons a specific reality (Gierke 1902, p. 193). 'A composite moral person is constituted when several individual men so unite that whatever, by reason of that union, they want or do, is considered as one will, one act, and no more' ((1672) 1934, I.i.12, p. 7/11). Far from being imaginary, such persons are real; they have their own life and ends, deriving their autonomy from the will that animates them, and distinct from their creators ((1672) 1934, I.i.15, p. 10/15). It is precisely in this way that Pufendorf sees the state. 'A state is a compound moral person, whose will, intertwined and united by the pacts of a number of men, is considered the will of all' ((1672) 1934, VII.ii.13, p. 672/984).

ii The background of law: anti-realism and voluntarism

It is difficult to underestimate the degree to which epistemological considerations underpin the whole range of Pufendorf's practical philosophy. His theory of moral entities offered a new basis for a general theory of law and the state which was clearly anti-realist. A reading of the *Elements of Universal Jurisprudence* and *On the Law of Nature and Nations* reveals that Pufendorf was reacting against the errors and confusions entailed in scholastic attempts to define moral realities in terms of a naive realism. He rejected the idea of real and eternal essences, separate from definite concrete actuality. His thinking challenged the validity of ontological assumptions on which the distinction of essence and existence was based. In his view, it was erroneous to affirm that essences were eternal and not dependent on the will of God. His thought is resolutely nominalist and denies the reality of universals, or essences, regarding all things as dependent on the contingent

8. Pufendorf (1672) 1934, I.i.4, 7, 12–13, 19, pp. 3–12/5–19, also VI.i.11–12, pp. 571/839–40, 584–7/859–63, VII.iii.1, pp. 683/1000–1.

will of God. Following the path established by Ockham's voluntarist nominalism, he directly questioned the objective nature of values and the doctrine of the *perseitas moralis* of human acts. Since there was no longer any essence independent of the divine will, there was consequently no good or evil *in se*, and values simply stemmed from the unfathomable decrees of a legislating will.[9]

Nevertheless, Pufendorf did not follow Ockham into his paradoxical reflections on the imperative nature of the Decalogue. This was because to him it seemed that if God is free to create, he is nonetheless bound by his creation. Thus, if he has created man as a reasonable and social being, he is necessarily bound to accept a defined order of value. This necessity is no doubt a relative one and quite distinct from that posited by intellectualist metaphysical realism, but it does bring out the fact that Pufendorf's voluntarism is rational in nature ((1672) 1934, II.iii.4, pp. 125–6/184; Denzer 1972, pp. 52–5).

The resolutely nominalist nature of his thinking, with its denial of a realm of essences, completes a decisive break with the Thomist metaphysical tradition still apparent in Grotius. Pufendorf's position does not only challenge the existence of good and evil *in se*, but also rejects the realist notion of human nature as an eternal and immutable reality and asserts, in opposition to traditional essentialism, the pure contingency of nature and the values imposed on it.

Pufendorf's voluntarist theory of moral entities brought in its wake a change in the concept of natural law. This came to be seen not in terms of the original nature of humankind in the Garden of Eden, nor an essential nature common to all living beings, but a matter of culture, of the world characteristic to humankind in its concrete history. He turned to the empiricism of the nominalist-voluntarist tradition and based his thought on the contingent nature of humankind as it appears with all those tendencies that are the fruit of the contingent decrees of divine providence ((1672) 1934, II.iii.14, p. 141/205). Our reason can, by examining humankind's estate, demonstrate the need to live according to the norm of natural law, and make plain its precepts by solid and convincing demonstrations. Pufendorf applies the resolutive-compositive method in his search for the fundamental principle of natural law. This is achieved first by breaking down human nature into a bundle of elementary tendencies:

---

9. Pufendorf (1672) 1934, I.ii.6, pp. 18–21, 1706, pp. 235–6; Welzel 1958, pp. 36–8; Denzer 1972, pp. 51–4.

self-love, ignorance, weakness, and the undeniable malice (*pravitas*) of the soul.[10] He then goes on to reconstitute the fundamental law of nature, the *fundamentum legis naturalis*, namely the law of 'sociability' (*socialitas*), which he conceives to be not a natural disposition to live together in society, such as Grotius' *appetitus societatis*, but a prime principle of social behaviour:[11]

> Man is an animal extremely desirous of his own preservation, in himself exposed to want, unable to exist without the help of his fellow-creatures, fitted in a remarkable way to contribute to the common good, and yet at all times malicious, petulant . . . For such an animal to live and enjoy the good things . . . it is necessary that he be sociable, that is, be willing to join himself with others like him, and conduct himself towards them in such a way that, far from having any cause to do him harm, they may feel there is reason to preserve and increase his good fortune.   ((1672) 1934, II.iii.15, pp. 142/207–8)

The basis of natural law, then, is that each man should maintain towards all men a peaceable sociability, in conformity with the nature and end of the human race in its entirely. It follows that everything necessary for that sociability is prescribed by natural law, and everything contrary to it is forbidden by it ((1673) 1927, I.iii.9, pp. 21–2/19).

Yet despite his anti-metaphysical temperament, Pufendorf retained certain distinctions with regard to natural law that had been elaborated by scholastic philosophers. In the range of precepts derived from the principle of sociability, he distinguished those which were absolute and those which were hypothetical, taking up Suárez' differentiation between 'preceptive' and 'compelling' natural law.[12] This distinction, which Pufendorf admits drawing from Grotius, marks the essential difference between precepts of a transhistorical nature, which bind all people in whatever state they find themelves and independently of institutions brought about by their will, and precepts which presuppose a state or other voluntary institution. The distinction echoes that between 'state of nature' and 'adventitious states' ((1672) 1934, II.iii.24, p. 158/229; 1673 (1927), I.vi.1, p. 37). Alongside obligations arising from nothing other than the natural community, there are further ones which, although they impose themselves with all the force of natural law, nevertheless depend on free human choices. 'There are many things which man is free to do or not to do, but once they have been

---

10. Pufendorf (1660) 1931, II Obs. III, 1–2, pp. 273–5/233–4, (1672) 1934, II.iii.14, pp. 141–2/205–7; (1673) 1927, I.iii.1–7, pp. 18–21/17–19.
11. Pufendorf (1672) 1934, II.iii.15, pp. 142–3/207–8; (1673) 1927, I.iii.7–9, pp. 21–2/19; cf. Welzel 1958, pp. 43–8; Krieger 1965, pp. 93–8; Denzer 1972, pp. 93–6.
12. Pufendorf (1672) 1934, II.iii.24, p. 158/229; cf. Suárez (1612) 1971–81, II.xiv.14–16, IV, pp. 31–4.

Natural law and utility

done, they entail a certain moral necessity, an obligation arising from some precept of the natural law that governs their mode and their circumstances' ((1672) 1934, II.iii.24, p. 158/229).

In this way Pufendorf integrates history into the field of moral law. Hypothetical precepts, which are always as rigorously binding as absolute ones, are linked to the manifold variety of factual reality in historical time. The main institutions determining the nature of hypothetical precepts are word, property, and the fixing of prices, together with the power of one person over another, all of which correspond to the various adventitious states people construct by their will.[13] By making the institutions necessitated by social life, from marriage to the state, into the foundation for specific obligations under natural law, a law people cannot escape, Pufendorf comes close to seeing the positive laws of political societies as having the same compelling force as natural law, even though he is careful not to confuse them. And in recognising that it is hypothetical natural laws that give positive laws their compelling authority in human courts, he takes the first step towards the hypostatising of positive law, which, during the Enlightenment, led to seeing obedience to the positive law of the state as an obligation arising from natural law ((1672) 1934, II.iii.24, p. 158/230). Pufendorf thus not only gave the political community a dominant role in the field of hypothetical natural law, but also became the first representative of 'a state version of the natural law' (Wolf 1963, p. 324).

iii   The foundations of the state

The whole of Pufendorf's philosophy of society, law, and history is centred on the state, and consequently his political thought emerges primarily as a reflection on the foundations of political society (natural or contractual), its distinctive power (sovereignty), and its historical manifestations (forms of the state, political regimes, and the interests of states). Although the eclectic nature of his philosophical positions is apparent – Aristotelian sense for synthesis inherited through Suárez and Grotius from the scholastic school, Ockhamist voluntarism from Hobbes – there is another, more radical aim at the heart of Pufendorf's thinking, and that is to free it systematically from theology. For him, there can be no other basis for social theory than data and hypotheses produced by reason and observation. Pufendorf's

13. Pufendorf (1672) 1934, IV.i.1–4, pp. 309–15/457–65; IV.iii–iv, pp. 356–80/524–57; V.iff, pp. 457–74ff/675–98ff, II.iii.24, p. 158/230. See also (1673) 1927, I.x, pp. 62–5; I.xii–xiii, pp. 69–77/62–9; I.xivff, pp. 78–82ff/70–3ff.

work of rationalisation and secularisation, which continued what Galileo, Harvey, and Descartes had already achieved and followed Hobbes and Spinoza into the social and political fields, is nowhere more evident than in his investigation of the foundations of the state ((1672) 1934, I.ii.2–3, pp. 11–16/22–4, (1660) 1931, pp. 4–6/xxix–xxx).

In this investigation Pufendorf has recourse, once the autonomy of the moral realm has been established, primarily to the methodology of the physical and mathematical sciences, understood in its resolutive-compositive rather than in its demonstrative form. This emerges less from his treatises on natural law than from his occasional writings. It is worth making particular mention of his *Dissertation on the Natural State of Man* (1677), in the opening of which he states, in terms reminiscent of Hobbes' preface to *De Cive*, that:

Those who have devoted themselves to the study of physical bodies have not merely considered their outward appearance . . . but have attempted to penetrate them and break them down into their main component elements. Indeed they have . . . reduced everything corporeal to some prime matter, understood as being without any particular form and as something beyond which it is impossible to go. That same method has also been applied by all those wishing to examine the most important of moral bodies, the state. They have not been content with showing its external administration, the diversity of magistracies . . . Rather they have examined its inner structure . . . and they have . . . carefully distinguished the parts of which this huge body is made up. They have gone much further, seeing the final aim of their science as transcending all societies and as conceiving of the condition and state of men outside society and without all means and human institutions. (1677, pp. 458–9)

The final stage of Pufendorf's resolutive procedure is an analysis of the state of nature from a point of view which excludes theology. The concept of the state of nature is the *prima materia* of his political thought, the starting point of the compositive procedure.

Pufendorf not only points out its elementary tendencies at an anthropological level (self-love, extreme weakness, a congenital need for others, malice), but is also concerned to show its specific characteristics at the social level; here, he differs from Hobbes and initially refuses to see the state of nature as a state of *perpetual warfare* and describes it rather as a state of *relative sociability*.[14] In that state, men are ruled not only by their sense-impressions, but also by reason, which, Pufendorf believes, will, even in the natural state, readily reveal the fundamental maxims of natural law.

14. Pufendorf (1672) 1934, II.iii.14, pp. 141–2, 205–7; II.ii.5, pp. 113–14/165–6; (1673) 1927, II.i.8, pp. 100–1/90–1.

Natural law and utility

If any man would adequately define a state of nature, he should by no means exclude the proper use of reason . . . Now since man can heed not merely the craving of his passions but also the call of a reason which does not measure itself simply by its own advantage, he is dissuaded from such a war as is described by the phrase 'of all men against all others'. ((1672) 1934, II.ii.9, p. 118/172)

As well as *anthropological* and *social* considerations, there is also *historical* evidence to suggest that societies in the state of nature are not perpetually engaged in warfare, but rather have ties of amity ((1672) 1934, II.ii.8, pp. 117/171-2).

Although Pufendorf sees the natural state as one of 'relative sociability' and even finds some advantages in it, such as freedom and equality, he is fully aware of its limitations. In language reminiscent of Hobbes and heralding Locke, he indicates its defects as insecurity, the lack of any recognised judge or power of constraint.

In the natural state each man is protected by his own powers only, in the community by those of all . . . In the natural state, if a man does not willingly perform for another what he ought under an agreement, or if he has injured him, or if some controversy arises otherwise, there is no one who by authority can compel the other to perform what he ought. ((1673) 1927, II.i.9-10, p. 102/91).

Thus, though Pufendorf rejects Hobbes' perpetual warfare, he still sees the natural state as the antithesis of the political state, and shows the defects which make urgent the establishment of political society ((1672) 1934, II.ii.2, p. 108/157).

When considering the way political societies are set up, Pufendorf pays less attention to the historical than to the logical reasons for the formation of states. It is not so much human needs, our awareness of our insecurity and of the malice of others, as our natural propensity for political order which interest him. He turns to assess the degree of this propensity. He rejects Hobbes' position, which denies such a propensity, but nonetheless does not accept the Aristotelian notion of man as a political animal. In his view, the political state is radically different from the social state. Man is both sociable and disinclined to accept authority. Political society implies a radical change in the human condition, namely that man 'gives up his natural liberty and subjects himself to sovereignty, which embraces, among other things, the right over him of life and death', as well as the disposal of goods. Such a change cannot arise directly from nature. It can only be set up on the basis of an act of will following upon a rational consideration ((1672) 1934, VII.i.4, pp. 650-2/953-6, II.iii.14, p. 142/207).

This brings Pufendorf to the social contract. He adopts a viewpoint similar to that of Suárez. The Hobbesian formula of the contract of subjection absorbing the contract of association was unacceptable to him, and instead he maintained the necessity of a twofold consent of the will for the introduction of political society and the establishment of government.[15] In fact, he went further than Suárez and converted the twofold contract into a three-phase theory. He sees the movement from the natural to the political state as involving, first, a contract of association (*pactum associationis*); secondly, a contract of subjection (*pactum subjectionis*); and, between, an intervening agreement (*decretum*) for the establishment of the supreme instrument of government. Each of these three stages, the *pacta* or the *decretum*, explains one of the constituent elements of the political order ((1673) 1927, II.vi.7, p. 120/107).

The first stage of the formation of the state thus lies in the *contract of association*. It is a voluntary agreement, 'every individual with every other one . . . it is necessary for each and all to give their consent . . . whoever does not do so . . . remains outside the future state' ((1672) 1934, VII.ii.7, p. 665/974). Pufendorf goes on to say that:

> The wills of many men can be united in no other way, than if each subjects his will to the will of one man, or one council, so that henceforth, whatever such a one shall will concerning things necessary to the common security, must be accounted the will of all, collectively and singly . . . When a union of both wills and powers has been brought about, then at last a multitude of men is quickened into the strongest of bodies, a state.   ((1672) 1934, II.vi.5–6, p. 120/107)

If he makes clear that it is only on this basis that a state emerges, his purpose is also to insist that this first contract is not sufficient to establish it, having as its function the creation of a people from a multitude: it is the 'rudiments and beginnings of a state' ((1672) 1934, VII.ii.7, pp. 664–5/972–4).

The second stage is for the people to agree on the preliminary conditions of the *contract of subjection*, by passing a decree wherein the people agree a type of government, be it monarchical, aristocratic, or democratic, that is to direct the state, and to which they will commit themselves by the second contract. It is only when the form of government has been decided that the third stage is reached with the *contract of subjection*, which constitutes both the holder of power, monarch, council, or assembly, and the reciprocal commitments that a person or a body will enter into with those who have made the choice. 'The rulers bind themselves to the care of the common security and safety, and the rest to render them obedience' ((1672) 1934, VII.ii.8, p. 665/975, cf. (1673) 1927, II.vi.9, p. 121/107).

Pufendorf sees the movement from the state of nature to the political

15. Suárez (1612) 1973, III.i.3, p. 8, III.iii.6, p. 32, III.iv.6, p. 43.

state in a traditional way, and as grounded in agreement, but he nevertheless stresses that it is the second contract which establishes the *civitas* and makes it into a particular body, a *person* ((1672) 1934, VII.ii.13, p. 671/983). His innovativeness lies here: he sees the will of the people as creating a new moral reality, the composite moral person of the state, the distinctive attribute of which is *sovereignty*.

Pufendorf here expresses a new concept of the personality of the state. Its novelty lies in its realism and autonomy (Denzer 1972, pp. 185–8; Gierke 1902, pp. 192–5). It is far removed from Hobbes, who is still vaguely tied to the idea of representation. The personality of the state, for Pufendorf, is not a legal fiction, but a specific and autonomous moral reality, a compound person, grounded in his theory of *entia moralia*. Such a real person has its own life and tasks, and specific attributes. The state has its own will and characteristic power, sovereignty.[16] This realist concept of the state was not perhaps fully developed by Pufendorf, but it nevertheless played a threefold part in his general theory of the state. First, it allows him to distinguish between the patrimony of the state and that of the prince. Secondly, it ensures that the state will have an unchallenged status at the international level ((1672) 1934, VIII.vi, pp. 879ff/1292ff). Thirdly, and in particular, it is the immediate reason for the need for a unified and centralised organisation of state power. In consequence, it calls for a doctrine of sovereignty so absolute that it represents a marked contrast to the assent-based view which inspired Pufendorf's understanding of the formation of political society.

iv The doctrine of sovereignty

This is a modern and innovative aspect of Pufendorf's political thought. It completes his theory of the personality of the state, determines his view of both absolutism and the right to resist, and shapes his typology of the forms of the state and of government. Like Bodin, Pufendorf sees sovereignty as 'the soul of the state' ((1672) 1934, VII.iii.1, p. 683/1000).

The problem of the origin of sovereignty is not as simple as it seems. It has its immediate origin in a human agreement which directly founds it. Certainly it is grounded in consent, 'not upon violence but upon the free subjection and consent of the citizens'. And because of this the 'supreme

---

16. Pufendorf (1672) 1934, I.i.13, 15, pp. 8/13, 10/15; VII.ii.13, p. 671/983; (1673) 1927, II.vi.10, p. 121/108.

sovereignty comes about as a moral quality' ((1672) 1934, VII.iii.1, p. 683/1000). But this does not mean that the civil power is but a human invention arising from the random play of individual wills. In his care to avoid any charge of relativism or subjectivism that his emphasis on consent might seem to justify, Pufendorf carefully distinguishes between the order of human will and that imposed by the Creation. Taking up the scholastic distinction between *causa proxima* and *causa remota*, he stresses this point. 'He who says that sovereignty results directly from pacts does by no means detract from the sanctity of supreme civil authority, or base the authority of a prince merely on human and not on divine right.' Hence it is that 'sovereignty came from God as the author of natural law', for what 'men have contrived under the guidance of sound reason' they do 'in order that they might fulfil the obligation enjoined upon them by God' ((1672) 1934, VII.iii.1–2, pp. 683–4/1000–1). Pufendorf is here following the example of Suárez and attacking the doctrine of popular sovereignty, which reduces civil power to the status of a purely human institution, and that of divine right, which sees sovereignty as purely divine in origin, in which rulers are immediately invested with power by God. Against this, he argues that sovereignty proceeds at once *mediately* from God as the Creator and *immediately* from men as the founders of political societies (see Suárez (1612) 1971–81, III.iii.2, p. 29).

We should not be deceived in this matter by his lengthy refutation of his contemporary J.F. Horn, the German theorist of the divine right of kings.[17] Far from indicating any allegiance to the doctrine of popular sovereignty, this refutation enabled him to dissociate himself from any form of theological thought in his affirmation of the mediate divine origin of sovereignty. This emerges clearly from his observations on J.H. Boecler's commentary on Grotius: the supreme power, Boecler says, lies 'not alone in an act of men but also in the command of God and the law of nature, or in such an act of men as is made in an effort to conform to the law of nature', so that, Pufendorf adds, 'the command of God to establish states manifested itself through the dictate of reason' ((1672) 1934, VII.iii.2, pp. 684/1001–2). By virtue of this doctrine of the natural divine right of the origin of sovereignty, Pufendorf can be seen largely in agreement with the view of Suárez, in which it proceeds from God as the author of nature, by means of our natural reason, but not without the intervention of the will of men (Suárez (1612), 1971–81, III.iii.2, 5, 6, pp. 29, 31, 32).

---

17. See especially Horn 1664.

By analogy with the human soul, Pufendorf saw sovereignty, the 'soul of the state', as having as many 'potential parts' as it produced different actions in the pursuit of its own ends. Sovereignty was the 'operative' and 'active' moral quality of the composite moral person which the state constitutes and it has certain proper characteristics.[18] Of the 'parts' of sovereignty which correspond to what traditional doctrine called 'powers', Pufendorf lists over half-a-dozen. These parts relate to the power to make laws and inflict punishments, to settle differences between citizens, to make war and peace, to appoint magistrates and impose taxes, and to control education ((1672) 1934, VII.iv.2, p. 691/1011). His object in specifying these legislative, punitive, legal, confederative, and fiscal powers is by no means to suggest a separation of powers, but, on the contrary, their profound unity and the exclusion of any separation since 'each power must necessarily depend upon one and the same will' ((1672) 1934, VII.iv.11, p. 695/1017).

The characteristics of sovereignty are indivisibility, absoluteness, and sacrosanctity. The nature of the state postulates indivisibility: to tear asunder the parts of sovereignty is to destroy the state ((1672) 1934, VII.iv.11, pp. 695–6/1017). Since sovereignty is indivisible, it is, like the freedom of individuals in the natural state, absolute and unlimited. In the natural state there exists 'the highest and absolute liberty of individual men' to act 'in accordance with their own wish and judgement'; so also the state has

the same liberty, or faculty to decide by its own judgement about the means that look to the welfare of the state. And this liberty is attended with absolute sovereignty, or the right to prescribe such means for citizens, and to force them to obedience. Therefore, there exists in every state in the strict sense of the word, an absolute sovereignty, at least in habit and theory, if not always in practice.

((1672) 1934, VII.vi.7, pp. 728/1063–4)

The indivisible nature of sovereignty also implies 'Caesaropapism', full power in religious matters. It cannot be allowed that a putative religious duty interrupts the command of the sovereign.

For if a man commands citizens to do something upon penalty of natural death and another persuades them that by such a deed they will incur the penalty of eternal death, and each of them does this by his own right . . . it follows that not only can citizens, though innocent, be rightfully punished, but that the commonwealth will be dissolved into an irregular status with two heads.

((1672) 1934, VII.iv.11, p. 696/1017)

---

18. Pufendorf (1672) 1934, VII.iv.1–2, pp. 690–1/1010–11; VII.vi.1ff, pp. 722ff/1055ff.

There can be no sharing of spiritual power, and here Pufendorf follows the Lutheran doctrine of *jus circa sacra*, the denial of any external or internal limitation of state power by means of the indirect power of the church as provided by Suárez' theory of the *potestas directiva* ((1672) 1934, VII.iv.11, pp. 695–6/1077; cf. Suárez (1612) 1971–81, III.vi.3, pp. 70–2).

The outcome of the indivisibility, absoluteness and sacrosanctity of sovereignty is the obligation to obey. 'And surely no sane man will at all doubt that it is wrong to resist rulers so long as they stay within the limits of their power. For it is patent from the end and genius of sovereignty that there should necessarily be joined to it the obligation of non-resistance' ((1672) 1934, VII.viii.2, p. 755/1103). In approaching the problem of obeying unjust laws, Pufendorf sees the subordination of the state to natural laws as secondary to the primacy of the established order. His analysis of the sacrosanctity of sovereignty culminates when he states that 'there is always a presumption of justice on the part of the prince' and that 'anyone who finds the burdens intolerable can go elsewhere' (*alio migrandi potestas est*) ((1672) 1934, VII.viii.3, 6, pp. 756, 760/1104, 1110).

Such ideas of the sanctity of sovereignty seem to go totally against his theory of the state. After taking the state of nature as his starting point, and maintaining both that there are natural laws and that consent is the foundation of all power, he later shows himself to be a defender of established power, even an advocate of absolutism. But this is not an incoherence, but the result of a deliberate intention to establish state sovereignty peremptorily and incontestably by refusing to set it any external or internal limits (cf. Derathé 1970, pp. 212, 324). If sovereignty is implied to be limited by natural law, in fact it is the sovereign who is deemed 'the best judge of the common good'; his laws have the obligatory force of natural laws, by the doctrine of hypothetical natural law and by the contract of subjection. Neither may the church provide external limits nor the people internal limits to sovereignty ((1672) 1934, II.iii.24, p. 158/230, VII.viii.1, p. 755/1103).

In the same way, contrary to what might be expected of the consensual foundations of political society, Pufendorf is very far from being an apologist for the right to resist.[19] Any right of private persons to resist unjust laws and commands is absorbed in the unconditional duty of patience. The procedure he adopts here is influenced by scholastic casuistry,

19. See the typical approach to the right of resistance in Pufendorf (1672) 1934, VII.viii, pp. 755–64/1103–16. For a general statement of Pufendorf's doctrine see Krieger 1965, pp. 143–4, and Denzer 1972, pp. 194–205, whose critical appreciations are much more positive than mine.

and ranges from stressing that grievances against the government should be
kept to a minimum – whether they come from the common people
ignorant of the real needs of the state, or from the magnates, embittered by
their exclusion from power – to making much of the subject's obligation
to obey ((1672) 1934, VII.viii.3, 6, pp. 756, 760/1104–11). He insists on the
duty of the private citizen to overlook the shortcomings of rulers.

> Since such is the condition of human life that it cannot do without some
> inconveniences . . . it would be foolish as well as imprudent to wish to rise in
> revolt against a prince for merely any kind of grievance, especially as we ourselves
> are not always so exact in meeting our full duty toward him, and since the laws
> commonly overlook the lesser shortcomings of private citizens. How much more
> fair would it be, therefore, to overlook the slight shortcomings of a prince . . .
> And added weight is given this consideration by the fact that experience is witness
> to the great slaughter of citizens and mighty shock to the state with which the
> overthrow even of the worst princes has been attended . . . This also is certain: that
> even when a prince with hostile intent threatens a most frightful injury, to leave the
> country, or protect oneself by flight, or seek protection in another state is better
> than to take up arms. ((1672) 1934, VII.viii.5, pp. 758/1106–7)

Pufendorf goes on to consider the extreme case of a prince who threatens
death to a manifestly innocent citizen. In such a case, 'in assuming by this
act the role of an enemy instead of a prince, he is understood to have
released the citizen also from obligation . . . Yet in such a case there should
be resort to flight, so far as possible, and the protection sought of some third
person who lies under no obligation to that prince.' So that even such an
extreme situation does not imply a right of resistance, for 'if flight be not
possible, a man should be killed rather than kill, not so much on account of
the person of the prince, as for the sake of the whole commonwealth,
which is usually threatened with grave tumults under such circumstances'
((1672) 1934, VII.viii.5, p. 759/1108).

   Nonetheless, in a case of tyranny against a whole people, Pufendorf is
forced to concede a right of legitimate self-defence when brought to the last
extremity by 'the unjust violence of its prince'. Such defence, 'when
successful', brings liberty, for a prince, in becoming an enemy, himself frees
a subject from obligation to him. Pufendorf was later to confirm this
doctrine in the light of his *ex post* judgement that the Glorious Revolution
in England was legitimate. Yet even so, the scope of self-defence is
restricted, both by the opportunism implicit in the notion of 'defence,
when successful', and by the further apologia for absolutism he builds upon
the same original concept of contract. For, he argues, it is by no means
necessarily improper for a people to consent to slavery, 'for this civil

servitude . . . is not so foreign to nature as some fancy, so that, when a man has at one time felt it necessary to agree to it, so as to avoid a greater evil, he can later cast it off, when the opportunity arises, on the plea that nature gives him the right'. He may not repudiate a bargain just because he may 'realise later that the bargain was not to his advantage' ((1672) 1934, VII.viii.6, pp. 760/1110–11).

The parameters of Pufendorf's concept of the right to resist are, therefore, set less by his theory of the social contract and by his concept of sovereignty, than by the absolute nature of sovereignty and the opportunistic character of his understanding of reason of state (see Denzer 1972, p. 199). Furthermore, his concept of the right to resist gives an exemplary illustration of the extent to which his contractualist theory of state formation gave way to his absolutist doctrine of sovereignty. Pufendorf was here attempting to provide a new basis for the state and a better intellectual foundation for sovereignty than those based on the concept of divine right, in order to free political thought from theological domination. He comes close to offering a new, radical, and secular basis for the legitimisation of absolutism. 'Pufendorf's natural foundation of state power', as J. Sauter judiciously notes, 'is no more than an accommodation with the absolutism of his time, which sought to replace every form of trancendental justification by a "natural' one. Politically it could be as advantageous, or even more so, than a theocratic justification' (Sauter 1932, p. 136n).

v   The state in history

Nothing could be more fallacious than to see Pufendorf's political thought merely as a theory of the state produced by a natural law rationalist speculating totally outside the realms of historical reality, or to contrast in his work an abstract natural law theory of the state and an historian's pragmatic thought on the interests of states (see Meinecke 1924, p. 287). His thought only conceives of the state as anchored in history, whether his aim be to investigate its typical forms or its political regime or to formulate the principles governing its changes in time. His categories, distinctions, and theses concerning the typology of states are by no means abstract, but sharpened and tested by the observation and experience of an historian – a court historian at that – who had become familiar with the vicissitudes of the principal states of the civilised world.

Filled with a lofty idea of state power, which could neither be diminished nor divided, and anxious to describe the complexity of historical reality, of which the Holy Roman Empire of his age provided a striking example, Pufendorf, following Francisco de Vitoria and Bodin, sought to give new life to the classical theory of the forms of the state, which was Aristotelian in origin. In this regard, he made a distinction between forms of state and forms of government on the one hand, and on the other he gave up the criterion of rectitude in favour of that of the unity of sovereignty; he also rejected any idea of a mixed form. Thus he replaced the Aristotelian typology of pure forms (monarchy, aristocracy, and republic) and degenerate forms (tyranny, oligarchy, and democracy) with a new one based on regular and irregular forms of state, in terms of the way in which sovereignty is divided or left whole within each state. Where not everything in the state 'appears to proceed from one soul and will, nor is each and every person to be controlled by virtue of sovereignty', then the state is irregular ((1672) 1934, VII.V.2, 14, pp. 701, 712/1024, 1040, 1677, §6, p. 311). The criterion of regularity, grounded in unity of power, lies at the heart of his typology.

Pufendorf also differentiates between 'simple' or 'unitary' and 'composite' states, and 'unions of states'.[20] Composite states had interested him since his 1664 thesis on Philip of Macedon. Pufendorf was amongst the first to study comparative constitutional law and one of the earliest publicists to take an interest in the phenomenon of federation. He subdivided composite states into personal unions (where more than one state has the same monarch) and confederations of states (where two or more states are constituted into a single body by treaty). But his judgement of such unions is determined always by the criterion of regularity, for as soon as a confederated state is able to impose its will on another, the sovereignty of the latter is diminished and the union becomes irregular, or even turns into a unitary state.[21]

Despite his insistence on the indivisibility of sovereignty, Pufendorf retains the classical distinction of three forms of government – monarchy, aristocracy, and democracy – for sovereignty may reside in 'one simple person, or one council, composed of a few, or all the citizens' ((1672) 1934, VII.V.3, pp. 701/1024–5). He does, however, put aside the Aristotelian typology of degenerate forms, for 'although there is the greatest difference

20. See Pufendorf 1677c, §6, p. 310; see too the quite clear definitions in 1677d, §2, p. 211, and (1672) 1934, VII.V.16, p. 714/1043.
21. Pufendorf (1672) 1934, VII.V.16–21, pp. 715–20/1043–51; 1677c, §17, pp. 332–3. See also 1677b, pp. 86ff; 1677d, pp. 210ff.

between a healthy and a sickly state', nonetheless 'vices change neither the nature of power itself nor its proper object' ((1672) 1934, VII.V.11–14, pp. 708–12/1035–40). Similarly, the idea of 'mixed' forms must be dispensed with, for any apparently mixed state is best called irregular. Pufendorf appears here to follow Bodin closely. Sovereignty may lie in a body of persons as well as in an individual prince, but that is no sanction for talk of mixed regimes. Bodin drew a distinction between sovereignty and the manner of its administration, and Pufendorf follows suit. Hence, a sovereign monarch may choose to refer difficult matters to a senate or to the people, or a sovereign people permit the administration of affairs to lie in the hands of a principal magistrate. Such a regime is either, exceptionally, one in which sovereignty remains essentially undivided, or, more likely, is an irregular state ((1672) 1934, VII.V.13, pp. 711–2/1039–40).

The idea of the mixed state had, in Polybius, been the kernel of an idea of the best state. But Pufendorf rejects that too. There can be no absolute 'best regime', only that which has fewest evils, for all states are subject to inconveniences 'by reason of the slothfulness or the wickedness of the rulers' ((1672) 1934, VII.V.22, p. 721/1052). It is this relativist attitude that plays the major part in how he determines the suitability of different political regimes to the individual situation of each state, leading him to see monarchy as inadequate for a city-state and democracy as inappropriate for the government of an extensive empire or for people amongst whom there is a large number of proud and ambitious men.[22] The same attitude also induces him to prefer monarchy over democracy and aristocracy, because 'a monarch . . . is ever endowed with power sufficient to exercise acts of sovereignty': a popular or senatorial regime requires appointed times and places for assembling and deliberating ((1672) 1934, VII.V.9, p. 707/1033). Even so, there is an open-mindedness in Pufendorf that also allows him to insist that democracy is a regime of great antiquity and that it is a regular regime. He expresses this in terms which take us forward to Rousseau's distinction between the 'general will' and the 'will of all'. Majesty may 'as much belong to a moral compound person as to one man' ((1672) 1934, VII.V.4–10, pp. 701–8/1023–34).

Even a man of little wit can comprehend the difference between all the people and individuals, between a council of the people, and the members as they scatter to their homes . . . the whole is an actual moral person distinct from the individual members, to which a special will, as well as actions and rights, can be attributed, which do not fall to the individuals.   ((1672) 1934, VII.V.5, pp. 703/1027–8).

22. Pufendorf (1672) 1934, VII.V.22, pp. 721/1033–5; VII.vi.5, p. 725/1059.

The same open-mindedness extends to the incorporation of the principle of limited monarchy into his theory. In some states kings are limited 'to a certain manner of procedure'. The judgement of a single person 'may be easily misled in seeking out what is for the welfare of the state', and so 'it has appeared advisable to many peoples not to commit in so absolute a fashion such power as this to a single man . . . but to prescribe for him a definite manner of holding the sovereignty'. This is especially appropriate where 'certain institutions and a particular manner of conducting affairs are best suited to the genius of a people'. For instance, a people 'could lay down a law for the king, when they crowned him, that he would not on his own authority make any change in matters of the religion of the land' ((1672) 1934, VII.vi.7, 9, 11, pp. 727–30, 734/1063–6, 1072). In conclusion, we can see that Pufendorf's thinking in this area, though relativistic in temper, does not verge on indifference, but is grounded in an acute sense of historical peculiarities and a consequent eye for the regime best suited to each state in its own circumstances.

Pufendorf had decisively broken with the 'pathological' typology of regimes characteristic of traditional political thinking, to which the theory of the best regime was a kind of therapeutic adjunct. He transforms this classical theory into a view of changes within states centred on historical modifications of the form and destiny of states rather than abstract typologies of regime. He is also once again governed by his fundamental distinction between regular and irregular states. He instances states which combine to form a new single state, either by mutual consent or military pressure, and states which disband by virtue of their inhabitants scattering. Like a methodical entomologist, Pufendorf lists the characteristic ways in which 'the moral tie which binds' the 'community of right' may be broken. He draws many of his instances from the historians of antiquity, Livy, Tacitus, and Plutarch, and from the modern writers, George Buchanan, Grotius and Hobbes ((1672) 1934, VIII, xii, 1, 5–9, pp. 924, 926–8/1360, 1362–7). Similarly, Pufendorf examines the manifold ways in which irregular states may come about or become transformed. There are states in which, at the outset, the people 'bargained for such jurisdictions and privileges for themselves, that they cannot be regarded as true subjects'. Institutions which begin in 'usurpation, faction, or contumacy' may come to 'pass thereafter as right or privilege', though it be of irregular form ((1672) 1934, VII.v.14, pp. 712/1014–15). Not the least example of an 'irregular' state hallowed by time is the Holy Roman Empire, in which Pufendorf had a close interest, as an 'enlightened patriot' of the empire (see Wolf 1963, p. 333).

Indeed, although he devoted an entire thesis to the example of ancient Rome (*On the Form of the Roman Republic*, 1677) dealing with the metamorphoses of the monarchy and the singular republic that succeeded it, and although he dwells on Rome up to the time of the division of the empire (*divisio imperii*), it is nonetheless the Holy Roman Empire which Pufendorf finds most instructive (1677, pp. 357ff; (1672) 1934, VII.V.15, pp. 712–14/1041–3). Under the pseudonym of Severinus de Monzambano he devoted to it one of his most brilliant works, *On the Constitution of the German Empire* (1667). This study afforded him the opportunity of finally exposing the medieval ideology of the *translatio imperii*, which fraudulently formed the basis for seeing the Holy Roman Empire as the continuation of that of Ancient Rome, an interpretation which in Pufendorf's view could be of no service to anyone except the papacy. It also allowed him to attack the *Reichspublizistik* of his own age, which was attempting to incorporate the empire into one of the customary categories of the traditional theory of states. Some writers, such as Bogislav Philipp von Chemnitz, saw it as an aristocratic state, others, like Henning Arnisaeus and Dietrich Reinkingk, as a monarchical state.[23] The fact is that the empire of his time belonged to none of the forms of states proposed by traditional thought, and, furthermore, its history provides an exemplary illustration of the process of degeneration at the origin of irregular states.

There remains therefore nothing for us but to describe the German Empire, if we ·wish to classify it according to the rules of political science, as an irregular body resembling a monster which, over the centuries, as a result of the negligence of the emperors, the ambition of its princes and the plotting of its ecclesiastics, has constituted itself from a regular form of monarchy and an irregular form of state, which is no longer a limited monarchy, whatever appearance of such it may have, but nor is it a federation of several states, since it represents something between the two. (1667, VI.9, p. 157).

Pufendorf does not, however, merely adopt the impartial stance of the student or historian of comparative institutions. He offers a diagnosis, even a prognosis, of this classic case of constitutional irregularity.

That situation is the lasting cause of a mortal sickness for the empire and of all its internal troubles, for on the one hand the emperor strives to refound his monarchical power and on the other the states of the empire tend towards total liberty . . . It will not be possible to bring Germany back to its original form without the greatest upheavals and total confusion, and, indeed, that country is of

23. Chemnitz (alias Hippolithus a Lapide) 1640; on him see Hoke 1977. Arnisaeus 1610; on him see Dreitzel 1970. Reinkingk 1619; for him see Link 1977.

its own accord becoming once more like a federation of states. And if we remove the mutual resistance of emperor and the states of the empire, it is already a kind of confederation of unequal allies. (1667, VI.9, pp. 157–8).

Pufendorf goes on to make recommendations to prevent the condition of the empire from deteriorating further. Proper forms of state should be established and their specific interests defined. This is what emerges in the final chapter of his *German Empire*, with the significant Latin title of *De Statu Imperii Germanici*, where he takes the opposite positions to those recommended by von Chemnitz (1667, VIII.2, 4, pp. 186, 191–5). A chief aim of politicians must be to give more attention 'to preserving what is possessed than to achieving new conquests'. If the confederation should appoint a leader, 'the greatest precautions must be taken lest he aspire to sovereignty'. That leader must be limited by precise laws and 'also by the addition of some permanent council that represents the confederate states'. In short, the German states must understand themselves as regular states, confederated together. In this discussion, Pufendorf has gone beyond the role of a student of comparative state systems, to that of theorist of the interests of states, as befits a counsellor and court historian (1667, VIII.4, pp. 192–5).

Pufendorf's new doctrine of reason of state, which finds fullest expression in his historiographical work, flagrantly disproves any suggestion that natural law philosophy was not open to historical reality. His doctrine was the first important modification of the Italian theory of reason of state, as adapted in the France of Richelieu. In the latter, the general theory of political art came to be applied chiefly to the individual interests of states in their relationships with each other. It was this French modification of the theory, with its implied preeminence of foreign over domestic policy, that Pufendorf was so decisively to transplant to Germany. This he did less in his works on public and natural law than in his historical works, particularly in his *Introduction to the History of the Principal Kingdoms and States of Europe*.[24]

Pufendorf distinguishes several categories of interests, of which the two major ones are the 'imaginary' and the 'real' interest of states. The former is of a sort that can only be sustained by a universal injury to, and contention with, other states, such as an aspiration to 'the monarchy of Europe, or a universal monopoly; such things being the fuel with which the whole

---

24. See Pufendorf 1667, VIII.4, pp. 192–3; (1672) 1934, VIII.vi,14, pp. 882–3/1305–7, VIII.ix.5–6, pp. 908–9/1334–7.

world may be put into a flame'. The real interests of states may be further divided into 'perpetual and temporary'. 'The former depends chiefly on the situation and constitution of the country, and the natural inclinations of the people; the latter, on the condition, strength, and weakness of the neighbouring nations' (1682, pp. 3–4/3).

He goes on to apply these theoretical distinctions to particular cases, such as those of England, Holland, and the Swiss Cantons. Thus, for instance, he observes the interests of England in relation to constitutional history, national character, and the situation of the country:

> England ought to take special care, that it does not fall into civil dissensions, since it has often felt the effects of the same, and the seeds of them are remaining yet in the nation; which chiefly arises from the difference in religion, and the headstrong temper of this nation, which makes it very fond of novelties. Nevertheless a wise and courageous king may easily prevent this evil, if he does not act against the general inclination of the people, maintains a good correspondence with the Parliament; and as soon as any commotions happen, takes off immediately the ringleaders. Lastly, England and Scotland being now comprehended in one island, whose chief strength lies in a good fleet, it is evident, that this king need not make any great account of such states as either are remote from the sea, or else are not very powerful in shipping. Wherefore . . . the king of England takes no great notice of Germany . . . It is the chief interest of England, to keep up the balance betwixt France and Spain, and to take a special care, that the king of France does not become master of all the Netherlands . . . Holland seems to be the only obstacle that the English cannot be sole masters of the sea and trade.
>
> (1682, I.iv.37, pp. 314–15/146–7)

The doctrine of the interests of states is not simply representative of Pufendorf's subtle political judgement, but established norms that are assigned to the sovereign in the government of states. For the doctrine completes the theory of hypothetical natural law by giving sovereigns a privileged role in determining and putting into effect the rules of natural law. Once the pursuit of the public good is accepted as the first of these rules (*salus populi suprema lex esto*) and one which every ruler exercising sovereignty must obey, the reason of state specified in his teaching on the interests of states is that which will give content to the right reason of princes ((1672) 1934, VII.ix.3, p. 766/1118; cf. Reibstein 1956, p. 65).

Pufendorf's doctrine is more than a mere transposition of natural law to the field of relationships between states. He is categorically on the side of those who see natural law and the law of nations (*jus gentium*) as one and the same thing ((1672) 1934, II.iii.23, p. 156/226). He sees the moral persons constituted by states as partaking in the same rights as physical persons in the state of nature (((1672) 1934, VIII.xii.4, p.926/1362). Just as with individuals, the principle of sociability is compromised by the right to act in our interest, where there is no common sovereign arbitrator. For instance, he holds that in entering into treaties with other states a prince always makes this implicit exception: 'Provided considerations of his own kingdom can conveniently allow it.' For, 'since a king is bound to no one more closely than to his citizens, no promise of his to a foreigner can be valid if it is clearly to the disadvantage of the latter'. Pufendorf then cites Lord Bacon: 'For princes there is but one true and fitting basis of faith, necessity' (((1672) 1934, VIII.ix.5, pp. 908–9/1334–5). No state is irrevocably bound by international agreements if they conflict with its own interests. Pufendorf's overriding proposition at the international law level – and here he echoes Spinoza – seems not that of sociability, but that of reason of state. This latter legitimises both absolutism and the fact of international anarchy.[25]

Throughout Europe, Pufendorf's political thought soon exerted exceptional influence. There are many reasons for this: the course of his life, which combined the freedom of the republic of letters with the privileges of a courtier; the eclectic nature of his inspiration, which was nourished on the realist and organicist tradition of high scholasticism and the nominalist and individualist currents of the later stages of that movement; and the diversity of ways in which he achieved literary expression, from the polemical essay to the more academic genres of his philosophical and historical treatises.

This conjunction of features explains why his chief writings as a publicist, philosopher, and historian, *On the Constitution of the German Empire*, *On the Law of Nature and Nations*, and the *Introduction to the History of the Principal Kingdoms*, went through ten to twenty editions, and the short work *On the Duty of Man and the Citizen* over sixty editions, in the century after their publication, being translated into all the important European languages, Danish and Russian included (Denzer 1972, pp. 359–73). It also explains why a number of these editions and translations, with substantial commentaries, served as text-books for the study of natural law, politics, and public law in most of the universities of Protestant Europe, from Scotland to Switzerland; they became obligatory

---

25. See Spinoza 1670, XVI. On Spinoza's conception of international relations, especially in regard to reason of state, see Mugnier-Pollet 1976, pp. 155–62.

reading for the higher education of the young. Pufendorf was to be recommended by Diderot in his plans for a Russian university, by Locke and Rousseau for the education of young noblemen, and was echoed in the training of Frederick the Great and Joseph II.[26]

Pufendorf's many theses left their mark on the political language of the eighteenth century: concerning the state of nature, the three-phase social contract, the establishment of state power upon the basis of (irrevocable) consent, his absolutist view of sovereignty, his typology of states. He was popularised by a galaxy of commentators in the chairs of law and philosophy in the German-speaking universities (Denzer 1972, pp. 318–19; Dufour 1972, pp. 206–11). Pufendorf bestrides the rise of the German school of modern natural law, a fact encapsulated by Schiller at the close of the eighteenth century:

> Leave then the wild wolves' fiercer station,
> Accept the state's more lasting obligation.
> Thus teaches, pen in hand, his nostrum,
> Pufendorf, from his high rostrum.
>
> (Schiller 1964, II, p. 131)

His political theses were spread in the translations and commentaries of the French Huguenot Barbeyrac (1674–1744) and the compilations of the Genevan Burlamaqui (1694–1748).[27] They shaped key ideas of Rousseau and Diderot (in his *Encyclopédie* articles), as well as, in Anglo-Saxon writing, Locke's concept of the natural state and William Blackstone's remarks on the foundations of state power (Derathé 1970, pp. 78–84; Dufour 1985). In America they shaped the manifesto of John Wise (1652–1725) on the democratisation of the New England churches, the defence of the rights of colonies propounded by James Otis (1725–83), as well as the ideas of the American Founding Fathers, Samuel and John Adams, Thomas Jefferson and Alexander Hamilton.[28]

---

26. For Europe in general see Othmer 1970, pp. 135–49; Dufour 1985; for French Switzerland see Dufour 1976, pp. xiii–xv, 1–5. For France see Rousseau 1824, p. 50; Diderot 1875, p. 492. For England see Locke 1963 (*Thoughts Concerning Education*). For Pufendorf's influence on Frederick the Great see Baumgart 1979, pp. 143–54, and on Emperor Joseph II see Voltelini 1910, pp. 71–2.
27. On Barbeyrac's life and work, before and after the Berlin years, see Meylan 1937; for his philosophy of law see Dufour 1976, pp. 11–25. On Burlamaqui see Gagnebin 1944 and Harvey 1937.
28. For Pufendorf's influence on John Wise see Welzel 1952, with Wise's text of *A Vindication of the Government of the New England Churches* (1717). For Pufendorf's significance for the political thought of the American Revolution see Krieger 1965, pp. 259–60, and Reibstein 1972, pp. 291, 294, 295, 310.

His manner of grounding state power on contract served 'enlightened despots' and angered revolutionaries. When Frederick the Great acceded to the throne, a medal was struck with the inscription 'Fredericus rex natura' (Baumgart 1979, p. 143). At the end of the consultation on the general code for the Prussian states drawn up in 1787 (Baumgart 1979, p. 143) its main author, Carl Gottlieb Svarez (1746–96), remarked: 'From now on, the social contract will be more than an attractive hypothesis' (Svarez 1787; Conrad 1961). In 1793, in the midst of revolutionary upheavals, A.L. Schlözer offered disenchanted reflections: 'The people may resist, compel, depose, punish and do all these things within the idea of a contract . . . The people has these rights, the old public lawyers tell us, *but does not have the right to exercise them*' (Schlözer 1793, p. 105).

In the twentieth century Pufendorf's reputation has been ambiguous. Few doubt that his breadth of vision, the rigour and novelty of his legal and historical methods, and the radical nature of his political criticism, all make him an outstanding figure.[29] But judgements remain opposed. For some, he was above all a defender of absolutism and the established order.[30] For others, he was more a pioneer, a publicist for the urban bourgeoisie, or a theorist of modern conceptions of human rights and fundamental freedoms.[31] Yet it would be risky to take the latter view. By building upon a social contract, Pufendorf may seem to offer a prelude to our fundamental freedoms, but, as we have seen, he tends rather to set the ultimate seal on state power. The hypothesis of the state of nature serves less to remind rulers of the original rights of subjects than to induce the latter to greater submission to the former. 'I myself', Pufendorf remarked, 'believe that the complaint of the masses about the burdens and drawbacks of civil states could be met in no better way than by picturing to their eyes the drawbacks of the state of nature' ((1672) 1934, II.ii.2, p. 108/157). In the Old World his authority served to establish state power independently of any theological limitations. If, in the New World, and occasionally, in revolutionary upheavals, in the Old, his authority was to be cited in defence of peoples' natural rights, it was because in their circumstances the natural state was no longer a rhetorical figure but, uniquely, it was a reality (Vossler 1930). In such circumstances, Pufendorf's political thought came to have an impulse far different from that of its original conception.

29. See Wolf 1927, p. 75; Sauter 1932, p. 114; Dunning 1947; Gough 1957, p. 119; and more recently Tuck 1979, p. 156. See also Welzel 1962, pp. 130ff, and Röd 1970, pp. 81ff, for the juridical methodology. See Meinecke 1924, p. 280; Krieger 1965, pp. 66–8 and pp. 189–92; Krieger 1960; Hammerstein 1972, pp. 239–41; and Hammerstein 1977, pp. 193–4.
30. See Jellinek 1900, p. 187; Gough 1957, p. 125n; Sauter 1932, p. 136n; Bloch 1961, p. 65.
31. Wolf 1963, p. 333; Denzer 1979, p. 73; Welzel 1958, p. 6; Welzel 1962, p. 131.

20

The reception of Hobbes

MARK GOLDIE

i   The polemic against Hobbes: the theological
premises

The German philosopher Leibniz, the most persistent and percipient of
Hobbes' continental critics, believed that the crux of the quarrel between
them lay in Plato's Euthyphro Dilemma. Socrates wanted to know of
Euthyphro whether a thing was 'just' (or 'good' or 'true') by virtue of God
having willed it, or whether God willed it because it was of itself just.[1] If the
former, then justice is arbitrary, having no essential nature; it subsists
contingently, by divine fiat, and can be humanly known only as empirical
knowledge of the facts of God's utterances. This is called the voluntarist, or
nominalist, doctrine. But if the latter answer is correct (and Socrates
thought it was), then justice does have an essence distinct from its being
willed, and it can be intuited by rational agents. This answer is known as the
essentialist, or realist, doctrine. In the biblical terms of seventeenth-century
debate this dilemma was expressed as the choice between the awesome,
peremptory God of Abraham and Isaac, or of Job, and the philosophical,
rational God of the Johannine Logos. Because God told Abraham to kill
Isaac it seemed that killing one's son was not an immutable evil, but only
evil until God said otherwise: justice is contingent upon God's command.
Yet if, on the other hand, God is the supreme light of reason, then He will
act only in accordance with self-consistent rules embodied in the natural
order. Whilst the former view guarantees God's omnipotent will, it does so
at the cost of His reasonableness. The latter view, conversely, establishes
divine wisdom, but at the risk of turning God into a metaphor for Reason
and Nature. This is the cardinal dilemma in the theology of God's

---

1. Plato, *Euthyphro*, 9E–10E; Leibniz 1972, p. 45. Plato in fact is discussing 'holiness', but this gloss on
Euthyphro is standard.

government of the world. And because its terms are immediately translatable into the temporal jurisprudence of the sovereign's government of the state, and into the moral government of the individual over himself, it is fundamental in political and ethical theory too: for is justice constituted by the will of the sovereign (or the self) *in vacuo*, or does justice flow from, and participate in, the essential nature of things?

Plato, Aristotle, and the medieval scholastics of the school of Aquinas, were essentialists, and Leibniz agreed with them. He was emphatic about this when engaged in refuting Hobbes' overwhelming insistence upon the voluntarist answer. Hobbes' predication of justice, goodness, and truth upon will and power alone was, Leibniz thought, fraught with appalling consequences for human conduct. In the second half of the seventeenth century many English and continental philosophers challenged Hobbes on the same ground. To study the reception of Hobbes is to discover, among his enemies, a powerful continuation of scholastic Aristotelian styles of philosophy, and, among his allies, an urgent campaign to dethrone scholasticism. Archbishop John Bramhall was the most penetrating of Hobbes' English critics and his quarrel with Hobbes in the 1650s laid out all the main points in contention.[2] The controversy, vigorous and vivid through several decades, exhausted itself by the time Leibniz endorsed Bramhall's position in his *Theodicy* (1710). The arguments are best epitomised and most accessible in Leibniz's essay, *Meditation on the Common Concept of Justice* (*c.* 1702).[3] Because the civil aspects of Hobbism – his notions of sovereignty, morality, and ecclesiology – were taken to be derivations from the Euthyphro Dilemma, much of the debate was metaphysical and theological in character. This pervasiveness of philosophical theology is not properly recognised in modern histories of political thought written from a secular standpoint. But this familiarity, with its easy transitions between talk about God's nature and talk about political society, was taken for granted even in the demotic 'Dialogues' and 'Characters' designed for the coffee houses of Restoration England. Accordingly, we shall need at each step to take account of the metaphysical crux which Leibniz posed. The source material is primarily English, but the

2. The debate took place privately in the 1640s, and was published later. The appearance of Hobbes' *Of Liberty and Necessity* (1654) provoked in turn, Bramhall 1655; Hobbes, *The Questions Concerning Liberty, Necessity and Chance* (1656); and Bramhall 1658.
3. Printed in Leibniz 1972, pp. 45–64, and 1956, pp. 911–32. His other main discussions of Hobbes are in *Caesarinus Furstenerius* (1972, pp. 111–20), and in the appendix to *Theodicy* (1952, pp. 393–404). There are comments scattered throughout his works, e.g. 1956, pp. 278–83, 690–5. See also Riley 1973; Jolley 1975.

responses of such continental writers as Pufendorf, Spinoza, Bayle, and especially Leibniz will be noted.[4]

Concerning God's attributes, there was no difficulty in identifying Hobbes' unequivocal position. God was sovereign power. Leibniz complained that Hobbes (like Descartes and Spinoza) held that in respect of God, truth, goodness, and justice were fictions, conjured by His omnipotent will. The outcome was that creation was emptied of its moral economy: goodness was a superaddition of God's categories upon the amoral chaos of nature. For Hobbes, truth and worth were not instantiated in natural substances but were 'arbitrary because they depend on nominal definitions' (1956, p. 452; cf. 1972, pp. 45ff; 1956, pp. 278ff, 355). God's utterances bind only because grounded in God's power. Hobbes 'maintains that all that which God does is just, because there is none above him with power to punish and constrain him'. And he who has power of defining may redefine without rhyme or reason. Hobbes' God is sovereign, but is also a tyrant (1952, p. 394). Thomas Tenison similarly objected that for Hobbes 'there is no rule God may not most justly break, because he is almighty', since 'power irresistable justifieth all actions' (1670, p. 144). John Eachard asserted that Hobbes had 'turned all the attributes of God . . . into power, making divine goodness, divine mercy, and divine justice to be nothing but power' (1673, p. 79).

The critics' own position concerning God's attributes was, however, more equivocal. They were anti-voluntarists, but as Christians they could not allow God to be merely a metaphor for reason, or permit that goodness subsisted regardless of His volition. Hence they wished to say that uniquely in God a perfect knowledge of the good is harmoniously and inseparably united with his sovereign power. Leibniz constantly asserted that God has knowledge and understanding as well as power and will. God discovers the good in his intellectual nature, wills what He knows to be good, and by His power transforms right into fact. God's nature 'is based not only on the sovereign power but also on the sovereign wisdom which he possesses'. His omnipotence gives existence to what ought to be, and the 'ought to be' of goodness and justice 'have grounds independent of will and of force' (Riley 1973, p. 324; Leibniz 1972, pp. 46, 50). Richard Baxter, the eminent Presbyterian divine, likewise insisted that God has 'sapiential excellencies'

4. For general accounts of the reception of Hobbes see Bowle 1951; Mintz 1962; Skinner 1965, 1966a, 1966b, 1969, 1972; Redwood 1976; and Yale 1972. Mintz 1962, pp. 157–60, gives a checklist of English anti-Hobbes literature 1650–1700. The most approachable of Hobbes' English critics are Bramhall 1655 and 1658; Tenison 1670; Eachard 1672 and 1673; and Hyde 1676.

as well as 'potencies'. He rules in virtue of his creative and causal power, but also morally, as a rational agent governing a community of angelic and human rational agents. God is both *Dominus* and *Rector* (1659, pp. 17–18, 36; cf. Lawson 1657, pp. 150–1; Lamont 1979, pp. 136–41).

The critics' formula was that justice equals Will plus Understanding. The relationship between Will and Understanding is the heart of the whole Hobbes debate. Hobbes' failure lay in his suppression of the latter half of the equation. Bramhall argued that 'as the will of God is immutable, always willing what is just and right and good, so his justice likewise is immutable'. It is true that 'nothing is impossible to God's absolute power', but since his power 'is disposed by his will', of which good is the object, 'he cannot change his own decrees, nor go from his promise' (1655, p. 85, 1658, p. 154). Tenison protested that 'by the absolute sovereignty of God, you affront his other attributes', for it was a deep mistake to say that God's 'arbitrary government and . . . imperious will' allows Him to change His rules. Justice is a perfection eternally present in God's mind, so that justice is 'inseparable from the First Cause' (1670, pp. 144–5). Leibniz, echoing Bramhall, asserted that God did not in fact will that Abraham kill Isaac, for God could not will an intrinsically wrong act (1952, pp. 401–2; cf. Pufendorf 1934, p. 97).

This redressing of Hobbes' unbalanced theology was also undertaken by his ostensible followers. Pufendorf, whom Leibniz contemptuously regarded as Hobbes' poodle, devoted considerable energy, in his massive *De Jure Naturae et Gentium* (1672), to the need to give a 'favourable interpretation' to the master's overstatements, often softening the starkness of *Leviathan* by citations from the more mellow *De Cive*. God's right of command 'should in no way be derived only from His bare omnipotence' for 'it does not seem consonant with God's goodness'. In *De Cive*, Hobbes had properly said that honour to God is an opinion of power 'joined with goodness' (1934, pp. 97, 158–9, 1245–6). Another theorist who broadly followed Hobbes' jurisprudence was Richard Cumberland. In his *De Legibus Naturae* (1672), he made this crucial adjustment, saying that Hobbes was mistaken in 'resolving the divine dominion into His irresistable power', for there is no licit dominion without right annexed (1727, p. 319). A third example is Samuel Parker, in his manifesto of 'Modern' against 'Ancient' philosophy, *A Free and Impartial Censure of the Platonick Philosophy* (1666). In Part II he considered 'the nature and extent of the divine dominion'. God's dominion is in accordance with right reason, and is hence 'the lawful use of power', so that God will only do those things 'that will comply with the reputation of his other attributes'. Despite this, however, Parker praised *De Cive* and followed Hobbes in placing greatest weight on divine dominion, for he thought it a Platonic, essentialist mistake to make 'all the effects of God's power be the natural emanations of his goodness', whereas 'the notion of him in Scripture never refers to his essence, but always to his power and empire' (1666, pp. 2, 25–6). Because of this, Parker was regularly denounced as a Hobbesian.

For Hobbes' enemies, human beings are rational subjects of God's universe and not merely craven slaves of divine will. An important context of this claim was the furious debate concerning the means of salvation, the quarrel between the strict Calvinist doctrine of predestination, and the Arminian reassertion of the Thomist and Catholic notion of human cooperation in salvation. Voluntarist philosophy was instinctively associated with the view that people are saved or damned by God's arbitrary election, and Hobbes was repeatedly linked with Luther, Calvin, and with their medieval nominalist-voluntarist predecessors, particularly Ockham. This association is conspicuous in Baxter (among the moderate Presbyterians), in Thomas Pierce (among the high neo-Thomist Anglicans), and in Ralph Cudworth (among the Cambridge Platonists).[5] Leibniz echoed them, saying that 'Ockham himself was not more nominalistic than is Thomas Hobbes', and that an intellectual descent lay in 'Bradwardine, Wyclif, Hobbes and Spinoza' (1956, p. 199, 1952, pp. 159–60, 234, 395). It is odd to find Hobbes cast as a Reformation theologian by those who were abandoning Reformation orthodoxy, but what prompted them was an intense fear of the antinomian consequences of Calvinism, coupled with the conviction that Hobbes offered (as we shall see) a kind of secular antinomianism. Hobbes, like strict Calvinists, emptied the world of its natural moral economy, and left humanity at the mercy of preponderant or anarchic wills.

Hobbes' critics, albeit Protestants, were unabashed about conceding that the most satisfying modern synthesis of God's intellect and will was that of the Jesuit neo-Thomist Suárez. Baxter, noting that 'it is a great controversy whether it be the Reason or the Will . . . that informeth laws', and that the chief contenders on each side were Aquinas and Ockham, judged that Suárez was right to say 'that it is both', for God is not God, nor is a person a person, nor is a law a law, without both 'intellect and will' (1659, p. 323).

5. See (for Baxter) Lamont 1979, pp. 136–45; Pierce 1658; Cudworth 1678; Tenison 1670, p. 144. This aspect of Hobbes' philosophy is considered in Malcolm 1983.

Bramhall likewise wished that Hobbes were better versed in Suárez' works 'that he might not be so averse from the Schools' (1658, p. 69). But Suárez notwithstanding, it was difficult not to construe the debate in simpler terms, as a war between Hobbes and Aristotle. There is barely a chapter in *Leviathan*, and, it seems, hardly a coffee house virtuoso, not engaged in guerrilla operations against the neo-Thomism which still formed the backbone of Protestant academic education, and which indeed was enhanced in defence of crown and church in the wake of the Puritan Revolution. Alexander Ross' *Leviathan Drawn out with a Hook* is chiefly a paean to 'the prince of philosophers', Aristotle, whose 'brightness doth so much dazzle his [Hobbes'] weak light'. 'Why should not divines thank . . . Aquinas and other Schoolmen' for correctly holding that 'we honour God not so much for his greatness . . . as for his goodness?' (1653, pp. 16, 96–7). George Lawson, a Presbyterian friend of Baxter, complained that Hobbes 'undervalues the Philosopher [Aristotle] so much, as far below him, though he was far above him' (1657, p. 93). The schoolmasterish Bramhall lectured Hobbes on the concepts of the 'Schoolmen' and 'Doctors of the Church', defending them from 'new-fangled speculations' and from Hobbes' 'paroxysm . . . of inveighing against them' (1655, pp. 156–7, 200, 1658, p. 341; cf. Eachard 1672, pp. 32, 35). The polemic against Hobbes might be summarised as the last gasp of scholastic Aristotelianism.

ii Sovereignty and constitutionalism

We can now consider the ways in which the scholastic doctrine of the duality of God's attributes was applied to civil jurisprudence. Civil sovereignty was said to have an identical form with divine sovereignty because human government was a microcosm of, and participated in, providential government. Human intuitions about the right ordering of the state will naturally mirror the divine archetype of the order of creation. Thus legitimate temporal sovereignty was said, like God's rule, to be a fusion of will with wisdom and virtue. If the latter elements go missing, then sovereignty becomes tyranny, and rational citizenship gives way to the master–slave relationship. In Aristotle's terms, despotical relations replace political ones. The crucial difference between God's rule and human regimes is the propensity of the latter to exercise power in the absence of right reason. The temporal sovereign, unlike God, has limited resources of virtue and wisdom, which is why Christian princes need

education and counsel. This is where customs and constitutions, laws and
parliaments, come in, for they supply the defect of the single intellect. The
institutions of temporal magistracy are therefore embodiments of both will
and understanding, and they replicate in human affairs God's own nature.
Grasping this idea will resolve for us a puzzle about seventeenth-century
political theory. It tends to be supposed that in examining seventeenth-
century writers, they shall be found to be either constitutionalists or
absolutists, depending upon whether binding institutional checks or rights
of popular resistance are asserted or denied. It is clear that English
parliamentarians and Whigs took up constitutionalist theories. But there is
disagreement about the position of royalists and Tories, and it is
(paradoxically) they, not the Whigs, who wrote most of the critiques of the
absolutist Hobbes. How, then, do the critics stand in relation to Hobbes'
theory of absolute sovereignty?

Once again there was no ambiguity about Hobbes' own view. He aimed
at monarchical absolutism by a strict doctrine of sovereign power.
According to Lawson, his 'intention is to make men believe, that the Kings
of England were absolute monarchs . . . the Parliaments of England
merely nothing but shadows'. He thought *Leviathan* was addressed to a
precise contemporary issue. Hobbes' insistence (ch. 20) upon the nullity of
any grant of powers to subjects by the sovereign, such as would incapacitate
his sovereignty, was, Lawson believed, a repudiation of the proposed Isle of
Wight treaty of 1648 by which Charles I nearly came to terms with the
victorious parliament (1657, pp. 37, 73–5). The treaty was overtaken by the
army coup and the king's execution, but thereafter parliamentary
Presbyterianism and the Whiggism of 1688 were projects for the fulfilment
of 1648. Many talked of an 'Isle of Wight' regime as a 'mixed monarchy',
because it included elements of aristocracy and democracy, a concept for
which Hobbes had unmixed contempt.

There is doubt about where most royalists stood. One study of Hobbes'
critics, most of whom were royalist divines or lawyers, takes them to be
committed to common law, custom, and the representative institutions
which restrained monarchical fiat, a conservative constitutionalism which
differed from the parliamentarians only in degree (Bowle 1951). It has often
been said that when Edward Hyde (later earl of Clarendon) persuaded
Charles I to issue the *Answer to the Nineteen Propositions* in 1642 (which
Hobbes also denounced), royalism was set on the path of moderation. In
another version of this view, it has been argued that Sir Robert Filmer, the
most prominent royalist theorist and Locke's adversary in the *Two*

Treatises, was close to Hobbes in adopting a strict legal positivism, and was correspondingly distant from his royalist contemporaries, who remained wedded to the customary diffusion of powers in the Ancient Constitution (Daly 1979). There is some support for this in remarks (considered below) of Leibniz and of Locke's friend James Tyrrell, who both coupled Filmer with Hobbes. These arguments place Hobbes in sharp contradistinction to most royalists. It is true that Hobbes' bullish irreverence for common law was unusual, and true that although Hobbes and Bramhall were both royalist exiles in Paris in the 1640s, they were intellectually utterly at odds.

But it has also been argued that, on the contrary, most royalists agreed with Hobbes about the king's sole sovereignty, perhaps blenching only at his impatient boldness of formulation. This seems the correct view, although one which will need qualification. The royalists all grasp the indefeasible and illimitable nature of sovereignty and locate it firmly in crown not parliament. They rehearse the standard corollaries. There can be no appellate jurisdication above the king, for if there were then that jurisdiction, and not the king's, would be sovereign (as was said to be so in the nominal kingdoms of Poland, Venice, and ancient Sparta). Common law, they said, was not properly law, and parliaments not of right, except insofar as they are deemed laws and rights by the king's will and concession. England is a pure monarchy, without admixture of aristocracy or democracy, and the *Answer to the Nineteen Propositions* was mistaken in saying otherwise. They constantly recite the Roman law dictum that *princeps* is *legibus solutus* – the prince is the sole legislator.[6] All these points coincide with Hobbes' teaching in *Leviathan, Behemoth*, and the *Dialogue of the Common Laws*. The royalists usually acknowledge a debt to Bodin and his epigoni Henning Arnisaeus and Christian Besold, but occasionally they cite Hobbes. Filmer, who published the first sustained commentary upon *Leviathan*, wrote that 'with no small content I read Mr Hobbes' book *De Cive*, and his *Leviathan*, about the rights of sovereignty, which no man, that I know, hath so amply and judiciously handled' (1949, p. 239). More grudgingly, Tenison conceded that 'in some things you are just to the prerogative of Kings' (1670, p. 165). Moreover, Cavalier commonplaces about royal absolutism quickly came to be called Hobbesian by their enemies. In 1661 Henry Oldenburg noted 'the asserting of Hobbes' principles in Parliament', which refers to a speech by the speaker of the

---

6. This could be documented in almost all the royalist treatises from the 1640s to the 1680s, but there is not space to do so here. Restoration royalism will be considered in my forthcoming *The Tory Ideology: Politics, Religion, and Ideas in Restoration England* (Cambridge University Press).

House of Commons in praise of the king's sovereignty and in denigration of aristocracy and democracy. In 1680 the Whig lawyer William Petyt wrote of 'our new politicians the Hobbists, who place all the ...tue of the French government in its absoluteness'.[7] A thoroughgoing absolutism is to be found in Restoration England: Locke combated a pervasive and not an isolated theory of monarchical sovereignty (Goldie 1983).

Yet royalist treatises are still initially confusing. They criticise parliamentarians and Whigs for the conceptual muddles and desperate dangers of 'mixed' or 'balanced' polities, and condemn rights of resistance, but they also fulsomely defend custom and the necessity of parliament, condemn arbitrary rule, and stress the obligation of subjects in some cases to disobey kings. Roger Coke's *Justice Vindicated* is a case in point. On the one hand, 'the Common Law and Statute Law of this realm were nothing but the declared will of the King'. A monarch is 'not obliged by his own laws' and it is folly to say any law can oblige the maker of it, 'unless a man will grant that an effect may be prime and superior to the cause' (1660b, pp. 61, 45). On the other hand, laws must certainly be made in parliament, and the king must abide by 'custom and usage' and by those things 'which have been so time out of mind'. Moreover, 'Princes ought not to be obeyed, when they command in derogation of God's majesty' (1660b, pp. 50, 104, 111–12). The resolution of this paradox lies in understanding the Suárezian union of will and intellect. We shall not find, in any but an arrant voluntarist, an unqualified defence of arbitrary fiat, but neither do we find an extreme Thomist view that laws can subsist in the absence of agents to promulgate them and apply coercive sanctions. Hobbes' royalist critics were clear that a precept, when given by a subject, or by custom, or by a sovereign uttering other than *ex cathedra*, was not a law properly so-called, for there is no law without proper signification and without the sword. These are attributes annexed only to sovereignty – and to expatiate on them is to sound Hobbesian. But, correlatively, there is more to law and politics than swords and significations, for there is also virtue and right reason – and this is the Aristotelian reproof to Hobbes.

Hobbes' enemies held that sovereignty is not to be construed as mere will, for, like any adequate rational agent, and like God, sovereigns do not exercise volition *in vacuo*. The sovereign's will does not simply equate with, or occupy the same space as, justice, for, in legislating he deliberates among many possible goods and means, and gives legal force to some of them. He

---

7. Oldenburg 1965, p.410; Petyt 1954, p.463.

will do this with a greater or lesser degree of moral success, depending upon the quality of his education as a virtuous prince, and the quality of his consultation with the community's resources of moral wisdom, his council, parliament, and church. To uphold such institutions was no detriment to the juristic quality of sovereign will nor to the puissance of the sword, but to negate them transforms a landscape of common moral striving for the public good into a tyrannical, Hobbesian wilderness. There are, then, no legitimate coercive limitations upon a king, who is legislatively omnipotent, but there are moral limits. A virtuous prince will freely choose to constrain his actions within the boundaries of the good, and through channels of rational public deliberation. His sovereignty is not impaired by the plenitude of these concessions, indeed, as a person he becomes freer the more he acts for the common good, and the less in accordance with private desires. Such virtuous practices were held to be so habitual and ingrained in English constitutional procedures that when royalists descanted upon them they sounded like 'constitutionalists'. In a sense they were so: England is an absolute *and* limited regime, but it is not a 'mixed' or 'balanced' one, for it is virtue and not mechanical force which restrains kings. Royalist theologians applauded Charles II's divine sovereignty and yet deplored Hobbism; they believed that whilst no earthly power should compel a king, nonetheless they were the keepers of the king's conscience, and if the king did not listen to them he would soon be a tyrant. The same cardinal point about the compatibility of estates and counsel with absolute kingship was put with particular felicity by Pufendorf. 'Sovereignty does not cease to be absolute by the establishment of . . . a senate', for 'the nature of absolute sovereignty is not that a king may do whatever he pleases . . . but that he has the final decision on his own judgement in matters which concern the commonwealth'. Therefore 'although the advice given a king by such a senate does not obligate him of itself . . . it nevertheless furnishes the occasion for an obligation, insofar as it calls to his attention the manner in which he can fulfil his duty' (1934, p. 1075).

When, therefore, English absolutists cited, as they frequently did, the authority of 'Bracton' and Fortescue, often regarded as the canonical medieval 'constitutionalists', they were neither muddled nor disingenuous, for they were right to see that the Bractonian sense of the king's limitations lay in Aristotelian moral metaphysics, and not in the political mechanics with which Hobbes familiarised the world (see Nederman 1984). Hobbes accordingly received many lectures out of Aristotle's *Ethics*. The critics constantly moved between questions of God's attributes, of human moral action, and of the English constitution, often borrowing vocabulary from one sphere into another, since 'all created rectitude is but a participation of divine rectitude' (Bramhall 1655, p. 85). Indeed, what is called the theory of the 'Divine Right of Kings' often turns out to be a meditation upon the congruence between modes of action in all rational agents, divine, human, and magistratical. An example is William Falkner's *Christian Loyalty*, an able defence of Charles II's absolutism, yet anxious to dissociate itself from Hobbism, and keen to bruit the church's authority. He argued that 'it is neither necessary, nor most suitable to supremacy of government, that the rules by which the governor proceedeth, should be altogether at his own will and pleasure', for after all, 'it is no abatement of the high sovereignty of the glorious God over the world, that all His government and executing judgement, is ordered according to the natural and eternal rules and measures of goodness and justice, and not by any such arbitrary will, which excludeth all respect thereto' (1679, pp. 10–11). Bramhall explained more fully. 'The will which affecting some particular good, doth engage and command the understanding to consult and deliberate what means are convenient for attaining that end.' The 'will is the lady and mistress of human actions, the understanding is her trusty counsellor, which gives no advice, but when it is required by the will'. In the public realm, the king embodies will, the counsellors or parliament embody understanding. 'The greatest propugners of sovereign power think it enough for Princes to challenge [i.e. claim] an immunity from coercive power, but acknowledge that the law hath a directive power over them.' Hobbes was, he continued, correct to say that sovereignty cannot be mixed or overruled, yet it can be 'tempered or moderated'. Hobbes thinks that 'whatever they do by power, they do justly', and he thereby overthrows all deliberation, counsel, advice, praise and blame. We have duties not only to act with competency of will and signification, but also to know good ends as objects of the will: there are epistemic duties as well as practical ones. 'He who hath an erroneous conscience is doubly obliged: first to reform it, and then to follow it.' Hobbes, by contrast, enslaves the people to the king, and the king to his passions. 'The dominion of reason, or of a reasonable man, over his sensitive appetite, is not despotical, like the government of a master over his slave, but political, like that of a magistrate over the people' (1655, pp. 30–1, 82–3, 91, 1658, pp. 305, 309, 527–8). Without the appropriate ethics, Bramhall rightly concluded, Aristotle's crucial distinction between political and despotical rule becomes meaningless, and Hobbes was repeatedly accused of seeing no difference between monarchy and tyranny or slavery.

In *Justice Vindicated*, Roger Coke provided a manifesto for the Restored monarchy predicated upon a refutation of Hobbes' 'monstrous and blasphemous' denial of right reason as a necessary attribute of divine and human sovereignty. Justice, he explained, is not only effective command, but also 'upright doing', which, said Cicero, is 'a habit of mind' in the virtuous. So it is utterly wrong to say that 'Kings might make their will the rule of their actions', for 'there is nothing more to be wished in the world, than that the will of them which command, might be moderated and restrained by reason'. Princes are deserving of blame when they act not for the public good but 'either by passion, or to pleasure factious men'. As for the compatibility of parliaments with absolute monarchy, the case was simple. 'It is as clear as the sun at noonday, that a King of England, by the ancient usages of this nation, is as free and absolute in the session of Parliament, as out. And the act of a King in Parliament, is the free and voluntary act of an absolute monarch.' This was no different from individual human agency, since 'my will, being a faculty of my soul . . . takes information from my understanding or reason', as 'counsel is to law' (1660b, pp. 49–50, 67, 116, 121–2).

If this duality of will and understanding had its primary application in the concept of law, it had another use in the vexed question of the legitimacy of sovereigns who acquired their power in successful revolutions. Recent scholarship has demonstrated the part Hobbes played in the Engagement Controversy in the 1650s by encouraging the view that plenary possession of the civil sword, and thereby of the power to protect subjects, was all that counted for legitimate sovereignty (Skinner 1965, 1966a, 1972; cf. Yale 1972). For instance, Marchamont Nedham appended quotations from Hobbes to his *Case of the Commonwealth* in order to vindicate his claim 'that the power of the sword gives title to government' (1969, p. 129). Hobbes' Cavalier critics repeatedly denounced him as a publicist for the 'usurper' Cromwell, and pointed to Hobbes' failure to understand that licit governors must hold authority *de jure*, by rational rules of legitimacy, and not only *de facto*, by mere power (Hyde 1676, pp. 44–5, 60–1, 189, 317–18; Tenison 1670, sig. A3v). Ironically, however, in the aftermath of the Revolution of 1688–9, a number of Hobbes' erstwhile enemies found themselves dangerously close to his doctrine, that right is predicated on power, because they now wished to support this considerably more acceptable revolution. This is conspicuously so of Leibniz himself (who had the interests of his Hanoverian masters to think of), and of the English writer upon whom Leibniz wrote a commentary, William Sherlock, who was the leading Tory defender of William of Orange's new regime. Sherlock's painful attempts to distance himself from Hobbes were unconvincing (Riley 1973; Jolley 1975). This is not to say that scholastic theorists were wholly false to themselves in leaning towards the sword in revolutions of which they approved. For, as Baxter said, conquest may not create right but it does make the conqueror 'materiam dispositam' – capable of receiving right. Any government that lacks effective executive power cannot be sovereign, for it is 'materia indisposita et incapax formae' (1659, pp. 163, 134). As every good Aristotelian knew, reality consisted in both form and matter, and it was as dangerous to succumb to a fantasy of pure form (sentimental legitimism) as to the barbarism of mere matter in motion (the naked sword). The willingness of seventeenth-century theorists to accept the conquering sword was an outcome of their sense of the juristic necessity of will and power, in addition to reason and understanding in human affairs.

Most of Hobbes' adversaries who sought to uphold the claims of right reason against voluntarism were royalists and Tories, or conservative-minded Presbyterians. We have seen that moderate Presbyterians like Baxter and Lawson were in agreement on metaphysical fundamentals with diehard Cavaliers like Bramhall and Coke. It would, however, be mistaken to suppose that the revolutionaries of mid-century were by contrast committed to a new 'empirical' politics (cf. Gunn 1969). The radical Puritans, the Levellers, Independents, and republicans, were not harbingers of democracy or popular consent, in the modern sense of the aggregation of contingent wills, but equally were seekers after righteousness. According to the Leveller John Lilburne the point about Magna Carta and the Petition of Right was not that they were expressions of the people's will, but that there were 'divers things in them founded upon the principles of pure reason'. So that, as John Wildman put it, 'reason and equity . . . is not prostrate at the feet of the Parliament's will'.[8] The republican Algernon

---

8. Quoted in M.M. Dzelzainis, 'The Ideological Context of John Milton's History of Britain', Cambridge University PhD thesis (1984), pp. 197–8, cf. pp. 206–7. Several scholars have recently suggested that at the Putney Debates Ireton adopted a quasi-Hobbesian position against the Levellers, insisting on the primacy of contingent volition and upon the hopelessness of trying to reach common agreement on the substance of 'right reason' in human political relations. See Tuck 1979, p. 156, and Hampsher-Monk 1976, pp. 397–422. The latter emphasises the importance of the Levellers' denial of citizenship to Cavalier 'delinquents', who were not rational agents but brute beasts, servants of Charles I's tyranny, for they were self-enslaved to passion and interest and had deposed the empire of reason in their own souls.

Sidney believed deeply that tyranny in any human relationship was to be defined as dependence on the mere will of another: it is 'letting will rule for reason' (Scott 1988, pp. 35ff). All sides were committed to the Aristotelian definition of tyranny: it was any type of regime which failed to serve the public good. Despotism was not so much the absence of a constitution but the absence of virtue. Hence pure monarchy might be virtuous, and democracies might be factious and despotical.

It would be difficult to overestimate the enormous degree of consensus that commonwealths should manifest an objectively rational human order, where 'reason' meant roughly what Plato and Aristotle took it to mean. Scholastic accounts of the moral element in sovereignty tend to lack cogency nowadays, and in consequence we are apt not to notice them. There were, of course, seventeenth-century theorists who talked about constitutional balances or fulcra, or about the mechanics of power, or the calculus of 'interests' (cf. Gunn 1969; Greenleaf 1964). They reflect the philosophical revolution of which Hobbes was a part – but it was a slow revolution. To his critics, Hobbes was preeminently a philosopher of the will who overthrew right reason in human affairs. Since he conceived of reason as simply instrumental to the capricious will, he was thought, far from constructing a 'rationalist' politics, to have left 'reason . . . dejected at the feet of affection [i.e. the passions]' (Bramhall 1655, p. 182). A commonwealth is a community 'of reasonable men, not a Leviathan, which is an irrational brute' (Lawson 1657, p. 5). In spite of the modern presumption that Hobbes produced a 'rationalist' politics, this Aristotelian standpoint never wholly fell from sight, and in many respects was to be brilliantly revived by Hegel and the Idealist and Romantic political traditions.

iii   Contract and the limits of obligation

Just as Hobbesian sovereignty was seen to be the exercise of contingent will, so too was the act of consent in the Hobbesian subject. His opponents understood consent to be, not an expression of preference or taste, but the occasion upon which the recalcitrant human will was bent to embrace God's rational purposes – purposes which should be visible to any rightly educated understanding. Hobbes seemed to overthrow the notion of civil society as a natural community engaged in a collective seeking after virtue. He proposed instead a minimal state designed to protect whatever private persons took to be good for themselves. The critics were struck by those passages, particularly in *De Cive*, which seemed to limit the scope of the social contract to the subjects' sense of what was necessary for 'the common peace and safety'. Lawson pronounced that it was 'false and dangerous' to hold that 'the sole or principal cause of the constitution of a civil state is the consent of men, or that it aims at no further end than peace and plenty' (1657, pp. 1–2). Leibniz' *Common Concept of Justice* reflects on Hobbes' impoverishment of the aims of political society. Hobbes (who interestingly is coupled with Filmer) considers the state only from the standpoint of *ius strictum*, the only precept of which is to keep the peace and to avoid causing harm to others. Both Hobbes and Filmer abandon 'equity', 'piety', and 'honeste vivere' as objects of the commonwealth, rejecting Aristotle's 'beautiful' notion of the mutual striving after virtue (1972, p. 60; cf. 1956, pp. 690–5).

In this context, Hobbes' preference for monarchy was separable from, and philosophically less important than, his insistence that sovereignty, wherever it lay, was simply the aggregate of private wills. It was, therefore, not inappropriate that his critics should reprove him for encouraging the dangers of democracy. Bramhall reminded him that a law might be unjust although it had the consent of all. He berated him for failing to understand the point of Plato's account of the death of Socrates at the hands of the Athenian *demos* (1658, pp. 495–6). Lawson commented that many societies proceed by majority vote, yet 'the major part may err, because they are not infallible', for 'men's votes are inferior to reason' and it is possible that 'the major part be a faction . . . not for public good so much as for private interest' (1657, pp. 26–7).

Hobbes' doctrine at best impoverished the human community, but at worst was downright subversive of civil society. The subversive element was located in Hobbes' claim in *Leviathan* that, since the paramount desire of individuals was to preserve their lives, subjects were not obligated to a sovereign who tried to kill them. This caveat seemed the profoundest flaw in an argument otherwise intended to shore up an almost limitless authority. It opened wide the possibility of private judgement of the sovereign's care of their welfare. Pufendorf was worried by this theoretical leakiness, for it might lead to holding that nobody was bound to obey further than that point at which the ruler was perceived to be no longer securing peace, safety, or indeed welfare (1934, p. 980). Rulership was hence upheld by nothing more secure than the fact that people habitually obeyed. For English royalists, Hobbes not only thereby legitimised the usurper Cromwell, but encouraged rebellion. In Eachard's *Dialogue*

Philautus remarked that the subject had given up all his power to the sovereign; 'but', Timothy replied, 'by your principles, he can call for it again, when he thinks it for his advantage' (1673, pp. 242–3). Tenison said Hobbes' books sowed 'seeds of sedition' (1670, p. 161), Hyde that he gave subjects a 'wonderful latitude' (1676, p. 100). Filmer remarked that 'in his pleading the cause of the people, he arms them with a very large commission of array; which is, a right of nature for every man, to war against every man when he please' (1949, p. 239). For Cumberland, Hobbes allowed any individual to act upon his opinion that the commonwealth was about to inflict harm upon him, a principle which will 'excite subjects to rebellion'. The Hobbesian sovereign had feet of clay: 'Hobbes, whilst he pretends with one hand to bestow gifts upon Princes, does with the other treacherously strike a dagger to their hearts' (1727, p. 377, cf. pp. 288, 355–9, 375–1).

Because of these dangers inherent in contract theory almost all the royalists firmly rejected the notion that civil society is the product of individual wills and pacts. It is a concept 'very absurd and insecure' thought Tenison (1670, p. 131). Filmer, in the passage in which he praised Hobbes' doctrine of sovereignty, went on to say, 'I consent with him about the rights of exercising government, but I cannot agree to his means of acquiring it' (1949, p. 239; cf. Hyde 1676, p. 52; Falkner 1679, pp. 407–9). With Aristotle and Aquinas, the royalists held that civil society and political authority were natural, not conventional. Since power does not derive from the people, it cannot revert to them; people find themselves under government, they are born unfree and unequal. The royalists were also patriarchalists in holding that monarchy is God's natural ordinance; fatherhood is the paradigm of all authority, the family is the archetype of the state. They constantly cite Book 1 of Aristotle's *Politics*, and Genesis. Coke is typical: 'from the evidence of all sacred and profane history, no time was ever recorded, in which men were not in subjection to one another'. The 'highest Philosopher', Aristotle, gives testimony that 'commanding and obeying is not human artifice or invention' and that 'there was never any man born, but was born in subjection' (1660b, pp. 1, 28). Hobbes they take to be impious because he denied the Adamic origins of human authority. His natural state of free and equal people must presuppose the separate appearance of myriad people, a scandalous notion given publicity by the publication in 1656 of Isaac de la Peyrère's *Men before Adam* (Popkin 1987). The critics said Hobbes borrowed from the story of Cadmus' teeth in Ovid's *Metamorphoses*, or that his natural people were 'mushroom men' spontaneously generated, or that his source was Epicurus (Pufendorf 1934, p. 163; Tenison 1670, pp. 131–3; Hyde 1676, pp. 38–9; Eachard 1672, pp. 76–80; Filmer 1949, p. 241; Bramhall 1658, p. 531). It is, however, the case that a few untypical royalist writers did adopt Hobbes' contractarian stance. The most conspicuous are Dudley Digges' *Unlawfulness of Subjects taking up Arms* (1643) and Matthew Wren's *Monarchy Asserted* (1659). Sovereignty, as Wren put it, arises from the 'compact of every man to part with his private power' (p. 100). Yet, unlike Hobbes, both are emphatic that the right of self-preservation is wholly renounced under the social pact: any continuance into civil society of private natural rights is implicitly subversive (Tuck 1979, pp. 102–4).

If such writers, in the context of the Civil War, were anxious to foreclose leakages in the authoritarian deductions from contractarian premises, others were later no less keen to exploit the liberal implications of Hobbism, and deliberately placed boundaries on the scope of political authority. Spinoza's only explicit emendation of Hobbes was on these lines. 'The difference . . . between Hobbes and myself, consists in this, that I always preserve natural right intact, and only allot to the chief magistrates in every state a right over their subjects commensurate with the excess of their power over the power of the subjects' (1909, II, p. 369). That sovereigns have only such powers as were granted them by their subjects is a point more clearly made in his *Tractatus politicus* (*c.* 1675): 'the natural right of every man does not cease in the civil state. For man, alike in the natural and in the civil state, acts according to the laws of his own nature, and consults his own interest' (1909, I, p. 302). Similarly, Pufendorf seeks to liberalise *Leviathan* by way of familiar passages in *De Cive*, and concludes that when Hobbes seems to give sovereigns unlimited power, 'we must bear in mind the intention or thought with which men made up their minds to establish states'.[9] Tyrrell, an early student of Pufendorf, covered identical ground, cleverly insinuating Hobbes into Whiggism by way of *De Cive*. Hobbes could be said to hold that 'nobody is understood to have conferred more power by his will upon the monarch, than a reasonable man can judge necessary to that end', namely 'common peace and safety' (1681, pp. 257). The liberal minimalist state was discovered in Hobbes at an early stage.

9. 1934, p. 1077. For Pufendorf's numerous adjustments of Hobbes see, e.g., pp. 25–6, 124, 158–9, 171–2, 383, 1138. His general drift is that some knowledge of the law of nature is after all possible, and therefore some justice precedes human covenants.

iv   Ethical relativism and sceptical politics

In the Puritan Revolution 'right reason' too easily had its outcome in parliamentary or military dictatorship, as surely as 'right reason' for royalists indubitably meant Stuart absolutism. The fact that everyone agreed that civil society should embody rational principles, which all could intuit, did not prevent manifold disagreements about their substantive content. This was the starting point of Hobbes' scepticism. The light of reason shines in desperately variegated ways; so that it may as well be said that it shines not at all. There is no consensus about rational principles, and what is called 'the law of nature' generally turns out to be custom, prejudice, or preference. Some said this was because of the weakness of human intellect, but Hobbes took the radically sceptical standpoint that it was because justice had no essence, so that there could be no common intuition of it. Now it is possible to hold, voluntaristically, that although there is no innate knowledge of the good, nonetheless God has given humanity moral rules pellucidly in scripture (see Lawson 1657, pp. 159–63, 102–7). In other words, it can be held that truth and rightness are fictions to God, because he makes them, and yet they are real and absolute for humans, because given in Revelation. But for Hobbes not only was humanity not possessed of innate knowledge of the good, but it also had no incorrigible hermeneutic for knowing the meaning of scripture. God's ways are unknowable and He has left us to our own moral and epistemic devices. Consequently, God's arbitrariness is exactly mirrored in human arbitrariness. Both His and our volition operate *in vacuo*. Accordingly, the human sovereign must, without firm divine guidance, fabricate such laws of good and evil as shall seem necessary for social peace.

Hobbes did, of course, talk of laws of nature, and of things which all humanity knew to be true about human nature. But his critics were struck by what seemed the appalling extent of his Pyrrhonism. Coke and Tenison likened his doctrine to the classical sceptical relativism of Carneades (1660a, sig. b4r; 1670, p. 162; cf. Tuck 1983, 1988). They stressed Hobbes' denial of innate moral knowledge, and the subjectivist ethics which followed. Eachard's dialogues had a clever way of encapsulating Hobbism in the character of Philautus. Philautus remarks on the 'perpetual lamps, that some philosophers speak of, which have got a trick of going out always when people go to see them'; 'metaphysical term-drivers do love to talk of instrinsical and essential right and wrong'. There was no more common remark than Eachard's that Hobbes allows the sovereign 'to be the maker of good and evil' (1672, pp. 146, 110). Bramhall said that for Hobbes the names good and evil 'signify nothing but at the pleasure of the sovereign Prince' (1658, pp. 571–2). Tyrrell remarked on Hobbes' notion that there is 'no other measure of good and evil, right or wrong but the Prince's will' (1681, p. 236). The coffee-house tract *The Character of a Town Gallant* had it that 'he denies there is any essential difference between good and evil'. The Hobbesians denied the scholastics' constant contention that intuitions of the good are 'writ in the hearts of men', 'imprinted', 'innate', the 'noble light of the soul' (e.g. Bramhall 1655, p. 100, 1658, pp. 187, 201, 467).

The dangerous outcome of Hobbes' ethical scepticism was seen to be downright libertinism. In *Leviathan* he pronounced that 'where law ceaseth, sin ceaseth' (ch. 27). In the late 1660s an intensification of the attack on Hobbes was combined with moral outrage at the licentiousness of Charles II's court, which also protected the ageing Hobbes from ecclesiastical wrath. The theologian Herbert Thorndike called for a renewal of ecclesiastical excommunication, against the three great unpunished evils of the day, adultery, duelling, and Hobbes, for 'the law of the land lays no hold' on them (1854, p. 463, cf. pp. 336, 374–5). The divines pressed their point home in the recantation which Daniel Scargill, a Cambridge don expelled for Hobbism and 'great licentiousness', was forced to make in 1669. The beliefs which he professed included 'that all right of dominion is founded only in power', and 'that all moral righteousness is founded only in the law of the civil magistrate'. His notion that 'God's law is founded in power' he now confessed was 'inconsistent with the being of God, and destructive to human society' (Scargill 1669, pp. 1–2, 4; Axtell 1964, p. 103).[10] The gamut of the Hobbes controversy was encapsulated in this recantation. We can see here again a perception of the way in which politics and ethics were deduced from metaphysical and theological premises. A sense of these connections was enhanced by the considerable éclat of Hobbes' *Liberty and Necessity* (1655), part of the Bramhall debate, which arguably was more widely read than his major works. Pierce and Eachard gave it great attention (1658; 1673). Pepys read it in bed, several years

10. Many examples of discussions of libertinism could be given, but an interesting contrast is that between Chief Justice John Vaughan's Hobbesian (or, rather, Seldenian) claim in 1669 that no form of sexual or marital practice is naturally wrong, but only civilly so (Tuck 1979, pp. 113–15), and Tenison's counter-claim, in a discussion of buggery, that some practices are indeed offences under natural law (1670, pp. 137–40). Teeter 1936 discusses the use of Hobbism in Restoration drama; in Thomas Crowne's *Caligula*, for example, the emperor attempts a seduction with the words 'Yes, madam, now 'tis treason to be chaste' because 'I'm the fountain whence all honour flows' (p. 161). Compare Pufendorf's citation of Seneca: 'She is not unchaste who was summoned by the tyrant' (1934, p. 1141; cf. pp. 1137–8). See also (on Hobbes and Dryden) Bredvold 1956.

before acquiring *Leviathan* (Diary, 20 November 1661). Thomas Shadwell's play *The Libertine* (1675) includes verbatim quotations from it. Leibniz debated it in his *Theodicy*, and the freethinker Anthony Collins used it in his *Philosophical Inquiry Concerning Human Liberty* (1717). And with it Tenison could reduce Hobbes' whole teaching to a few phrases: 'God Almighty is incomprehensible' and so 'that which men make amongst themselves here by pacts and covenants' they 'call by the name of justice' (1670, pp. 27, 29).

The *Liberty and Necessity* controversy also served to publicise a profound ontological dilemma that stalks the metaphysics of all the debates we have been examining. For Bramhall and Leibniz, God in his creativity must be said to choose freely between possibilities, for such choice is an activity of his intellectual and virtuous nature. By his power he turns prior right into created fact. Thus, essence precedes existence, and this world is the best of possible worlds, for God chooses the best. But if so, the impieties seemingly entailed are that there are things which precede God's creativity, and that his creativity is not exhaustive. To avoid this impiety Hobbes and Spinoza insist that existence exhausts essence; there are no non-existing essences, and this world is the only possible one. This doctrine in turn has its own blasphemy: that God does not have the good for His object and purpose. Once again the metaphysical dilemma had a political metonym. For the Aristotelian, the temporal sovereign, in legislating, chooses between several alternative goods; he operates in a pre-existent moral landscape. But for Hobbes, the good is what the sovereign says it is: his legislative activity coincides with, and exhausts, the possibilities of social justice. Beyond it there is only an amoral chaos, and there cannot be said to be determinable essences of justice which have failed of existence (Leibniz 1956, p. 420). The anti-libertine critics of Charles II's court believed that too many essences were failing of existence: if the good was what the sovereign willed, and the sovereign bedded Nell Gwyn, then it was difficult, on voluntarist grounds, to say that adultery was wicked; it could only be deplored on Christian Aristotelian grounds.

Given the degree to which, for the neo-scholastics, ethical rules, and theological dogmas, were seen to depend upon human intuitions of the divine essence, it is not suprising that in the next generation Locke's famous attack on innatism in his *Essay Concerning Human Understanding* (1690) was seen by many to be continuous with Hobbes' subversion of Christian certitude. The salient instance is Leibniz, who at many points in his *New Essays Concerning Human Understanding* (1703–5) took Locke to task for crypto-Hobbism, and presumed Locke's epistemological project to have a similar political and theological bearing (Jolley 1975, 1984). Similarly Isaac Newton's initial response to Locke's *Essay* was to say that the denial of innate ideas 'struck at the root of morality', so that 'I took you for a Hobbist' (Locke 1976– , IV, p. 727). The Hottentot in Charles Leslie's *Finishing Stroke*, a book aimed at Whiggism, is a figure compounded of Hobbesian and Lockian anti-essentialism: the Hottentot, lacking in his state of nature the interposition of sovereign will, holds the maxim '*Quod libet, licet* . . . we may justly do, whatever we have power to do' (1711, p. 135). Again, William Oldisworth's *Dialogue* links Hobbes and Locke as exponents of the doctrine epitomised ironically as 'self-love . . . is the only innate principle' (1709, pp. 19, 23). On this view, the point about Hobbes' state of nature was not that it was characterised by physical violence – the tendency to viciousness in fallen humanity was no news – but that it is a state in which people could not know what the good is. Hobbes had dissolved the human essence and presented 'pure terse human nature' (Eachard 1672, p. 89), with 'nothing more divine . . . than matter and motion' (Tenison 1670, p. 105). The state of nature was a vale of tears because it was behind a veil of ignorance.

Hobbes neglected the acquired, habituated, and experiential moral knowledge which society historically accumulates, which becomes 'second nature', and which can stand in for the lack of innate moral knowledge. Succeeding moralists were to repair this lacuna. Early followers were Cumberland, Pufendorf, and Matthew Hale (Cumberland 1727, pp. 15ff; Tuck 1979, pp. 162ff). Some writers (later aided by Locke's *Essay*) began to explore the notion of acquired moral propensities through a psychological account of sensation and sympathy. This, the dominant style of eighteenth-century moral philosophy, was early apparent in Walter Charleton's *Natural History of the Passions* (1674). A more directly political application of Hobbes' account of natural ignorance is given in Thomas White's *Grounds of Obedience and Government* (1655), a defence of allegiance to Cromwell. There is, White contends, much noise about laws of nature, but these laws turn out to be rules by 'custom and consent', for it cannot be shown that 'there be, in nature, radicated such an order of rights and [things] naturally just or due' (pp. 37–9). By nature we are left to our own epistemic devices. Most of what we say we 'know' we take on trust; we do not suppose our physician is infallible, but we trust him. Life is too short and hazardous for us not to proceed probabilistically. We 'must rely on the credit of others', because 'rational belief [i.e. probable truth] is necessary to human action' (p. 12). By the social compact the subject has 'made away all power of judgeing and caring for the common good'. The sovereign may make mistakes about what is best, but he is more likely to be right than we, who are busy on private affairs, and there is an overwhelming probability of social disaster if we challenge him (pp. 88, 98, 101–2). If the subject 'interpose his opinion', he 'breaketh his promise and engagement to his governor'. Rebellion is defined as the setting up of 'another judge or knower', it is a failure 'to keep the subject in the nature of ignorance, in which is grounded his being a subject' (pp. 98–9, 110).[11]

Hobbes' critics constantly rebuked him for this obliteration of natural moral judgement. Hobbes 'taint[s] the very foundation of practical reason' (Eachard 1673, p. 286), he dissolves 'synteresis' (Bramhall 1658, p. 201). Given that they also wished to deny that subjects might pass judgement on sovereigns in the form of armed resistance, they were placed in an awkward position. The Whig Tyrrell pressed Filmer on this score: he wished to force royalists to concede either that they renounced all judgement, like Hobbes, or that they allowed resistance, like Locke and the Whigs. The standard royalist response was the doctrine of 'passive obedience' – in fact a doctrine of passive resistance, akin to modern ideas of civil disobedience. 'Passive obedience', Bramhall explained, 'is a mean between active obedience and rebellion. To just laws which are the ordinances of right reason, active obedience is due. To unjust laws which are the ordinances of reason erring, passive obedience is due' (1658, p. 167; cf. Leibniz 1972, p. 187). Tyrrell thought Filmer closer to Hobbes, for in *Patriarcha* Filmer had said that a servant (or subject) has 'no authority or liberty to examine and judge whether his master sin or no' (1949, p. 105). This, said Tyrrell, 'savours of Mr Hobbes' divinity' (1681, pp. 137–8, 209, 232). And so it did.

v   Erastianism, toleration, and the power of the
church

Not the least of Hobbes' deductions from voluntarist and sceptical premises was what Leibniz called the 'strange and indefensible' claim that 'doctrines

11. A remarkable treatise is Hall 1654, full of lively dicta, and extraordinarily faithful to Hobbes. The state of nature is that in which we are 'gods unto ourselves, in the knowledge of good and evil'; sovereignty is the 'submitting . . . politically to have each private will swayed by a public'; rebellion is private judgement; 'private equity is public iniquity'; people do not conduct their lives by truth but by 'the highest probability they can get', and even Christianity we take on 'the hazard of birth and education' (pp. 8, 10, 305, 219, 322). Spinoza also defines the compact as an abandonment of the natural right 'of being one's own judge' (1909, I, p. 302).

touching the divinity depend entirely upon the determination of the sovereign' (1952, p. 394). Since, for Hobbes, our knowledge of God is limited to the proposition that He is the omnipotent First Cause, it followed that no further question of dogma or forms of worship was resolvable with certainty. They were 'things indifferent' and there was never good ground in conscience to disobey the arbitrament of the sovereign. To allow that private conscience, or the church, may be judge of religious truth immediately opened a Pandora's box of religious warfare and persecution, the conflict of state, church, and disaffected sects. Above all, Hobbes sought to construct an ecclesiology which would cure England's wars of religion. Thus, as the critics noted, for Hobbes there is 'in matters of religion . . . a state of nature, without any sovereign representative to determine for them, what they shall believe or profess'. People's rival opinions are such that 'whatever a man worships, is his God, . . . though that God may to his neighbour seem a devil'.[12] The sovereign must construct such religion as shall seem conducive to the peaceful worship of God; the anarchy of private conscience is, by the contract, displaced by a 'public conscience'. Hobbes turned the secular magistrate into the 'head of the Church and judge of faith' (Coke 1660b, p. 82); to this sovereign we must trust 'our eternal salvation, we must captivate our judgement' (Lawson 1657, p. 156). Hobbes' 'public conscience', the equation of religion and sovereignty, was seen to dissolve wholly the claims of church against state. Religious truth was turned into a human fabrication, the shared significations of a civil community. The church's understanding was collapsed into the state's will. Hobbes, said Coke, aimed 'to make all faith, and religion, as well as society, a mere invention and policy of man' (1660a, p. 30). But, protested Bramhall, 'the Church is the ground and pillar of truth, not the sovereign Prince' (1658, p. 428).

It would be difficult to overestimate the persistence of a neo-scholastic (and ultimately Catholic) account of the nature of the church, within both Anglican and Presbyterian traditions. The church was a visible society, a self-governing corporation, distinctive from civil society. 'Church and state', wrote Lawson, 'are two distinct commonwealths, the one spiritual, and the other temporal, though they consist of the same persons', and it is 'as great an offence for the state to encroach upon the Church, as for the Church to encroach upon the state' (1657, pp. 138–9). Bramhall insisted

---

12. Wotton 1706, p. 5; Oldisworth 1710, p. 111. Both these remarks were addressed to Hobbes via a critique of Tindal's *Rights of the Christian Church*, for which see below.

that though the sovereign was God's representative, the church was Christ's, whereas Hobbes made 'his sovereign to be Christ's lieutenant upon earth, in obedience to whose commands true religion doth consist' (1658, p. 572). Hobbes dissolved the Keys into the Sword, priesthood into kingship, yet 'there is a plain difference between civil and ecclesiastical power, between the Sword and the Keys' (Lawson 1657, pp. 8, 138). Kings emphatically do not have sacerdotal power (Coke 1660b, p. 85; cf. Bramhall 1655, p. 304).

Leviathan and *De Cive* were the most ambitious statements of Erastianism on record. Accordingly, on each occasion when Erastianism came to be urgently debated, the doctrines of Hobbes were foremost. This was so in the 1650s, when Hobbes was seen to be a publicist for the Cromwellian regime's attempt to create a national yet pluralist church, aiming to overcome both the anarchic sects and the theocratic demands of Presbyterians and 'Prelatists'. Hobbes' views were associated with, and exploited by, such Cromwellians as Henry Stubbe, John Hall, and Louis du Moulin.[13] It was again so after the Restoration when latitudinarians like Edward Stillingfleet and John Tillotson were accused of Hobbism. Stillingfleet suffered at the hands of high churchmen for his *Irenicum* (1661), and was forced to modify his Erastian doctrine of the church as 'incorporated into the state' by restating a conventional ecclesiology of the church as a 'separate society' (Marshall 1985). When Tillotson became archbishop of Canterbury, Leslie launched a ferocious attack on his 'super-Hobbism'. Tillotson's theology was said to reduce all doctrine and scripture to uncertainty and so to make religion 'a perfect tool and engine of state' (1695, pp. 4–5, 13–16). The charge of Hobbist Erastianism was loudest against Matthew Tindal's (misleadingly entitled) *Rights of the Christian Church* (1706). The striking feature of this quarrel was the constant Tory association of Hobbes with the campaign of the low-church Whigs, who were engaged in defending the parliamentary church of the Revolution and the Toleration Act of 1689 against high-church theocracy. The Tories said that the Whig idea of parliamentary religious supremacy fulfilled Hobbes' 'mighty miracles of giving the spirit by vote, and making divines

13. This is a matter which has yet to be fully documented, but on Stubbe see Jacob 1983. Strikingly Hobbesian and Seldenian defences of Cromwell's church settlement are: Hall 1654, and Du Moulin 1656. The republican James Harrington's ecclesiology was quickly associated with Hobbes: see Harrington 1977, pp. 77ff, 369ff. The fullest Anglican attack on Hobbes for his Erastian-Independency are Thorndike's *Epilogue to the Tragedy of the Church of England* (1659) and *Just Weights and Measures* (1662) (in Thorndike 1854). For similar use of Hobbes on behalf of De Witt's anti-clerical republicanism in Holland see Tuck 1979, pp. 139–42.

and divinity by the poll' (Oldisworth 1709, p. 388). According to Jonathan Swift, behind the Whigs stood 'their Apostle Tindal', and behind them all, said George Hickes, 'their dear Fathers, Hobbes, Selden and Spinoza'.[14]

In this context, Hobbism was identified with tolerant indifference, within the boundaries of sober Christian essentials, free of fanatical 'enthusiasm', atheism, and Romish idolatry – the marks of Enlightenment liberal Protestantism. But *Leviathan* also seemed in principle considerably more outlandish. Hobbes seemed to allow that were a sovereign to demand of the subject idolatrous worship, then the subject would commit no sin in obeying. This was the lesson Hobbes drew from the prophet Elisha's licensing of Naaman, the Syrian servant, to worship Rimmon at the command of his master, an instance which appalled the divines.[15] Hobbes here seemed to sanction the dissolution of any visible profession of Christ, and showed sovereigns how they might turn 'the Alcoran into Gospel' (Tenison 1670, sig. A3v). To call Hobbism 'the Mahometan religion' became a commonplace. The exponents of 'natural religion', who did away with Christian revelation altogether, became firmly associated with Hobbes, especially after the publication in 1683 of Charles Blount's *Miracles no Violation of the Laws of Nature*, a series of passages copied from Hobbes and Spinoza. Blount, one of the originators of English deism, was denounced because he 'overthrows the foundations of both law and gospel, overthrows the credit and authority of divine revelation, and remits us . . . to a bare religion of nature'.[16] Even more outlandish was the occasional association between Hobbism and Catholicism. Under James II, one of Hobbes' most devoted disciples, Sir William Petty, expended considerable intellectual energy to reconciling a thorough doctrinal scepticism with Roman Catholicism (Petty 1927, I, pp. 113–45; Goldie 1984). It is a striking, and unnoticed, fact that the very first reference in print to *Leviathan*, in August 1651, was in a plea by a Roman Catholic for toleration. This tract quoted Hobbes (ch. 45) on the cultural variety of ways of worshipping God, and the arbitrariness of human symbols. 'Thus', concluded the Catholic, 'in my judgment doth that learned Protestant absolutely clear the Papists of idolatry.'[17] Similarly, White's *Grounds of*

---

14. Swift, *The Examiner*, No. 19 (1712); Hickes 1707, p. xviii.
15. 2 Kings 5:17–19; *Leviathan*, ch. 42. See Eachard 1673, pp. 271–3; Tenison 1670, p. 199; Bramhall 1658, pp. 491–2.
16. Browne 1683, p. 2. On the continent this association of Hobbes with deism was influentially established by Kortholt 1680.
17. Austin 1651, pp. 12–13. I am grateful to Martin Dzelzainis for this point.

Obedience, noticed earlier, was a veiled address to Cromwell for toleration for sober and unjesuited Catholics.

In all these examples Hobbes was taken to lean towards religious toleration. But his ecclesiastical reputation remained ambivalent, for Erastianism could also justify the repression of religious nonconformity. The most notorious case of this was Parker's *Discourse of Ecclesiastical Polity* (1670), the most ferocious of Restoration assaults upon the dissenters. Although the book explicitly attacked 'the consequences that some men draw from Mr Hobbes' principles in behalf of toleration', it was itself quickly charged with the 'divinity of *Leviathan*', and justly so. In a ruthlessly nominalist manner, Parker argued that all public actions, such as religious ceremonies, were 'arbitrary', and that external symbols are 'changeable according to the variety of customs and places', so that what is piety in one culture is superstition in another. All 'actions are made significant by agreement', and once the sovereign's 'public conscience' had pronounced, all 'clamour' concerning worship was groundless (pp. 135, 99, 106–7). Locke asked rhetorically 'how far is this short of Mr Hobbes' doctrine?' (MS Locke, c. 39, fo. 5).

When Bayle wrote his article on Hobbes in his *Historical and Critical Dictionary* (1696) he dwelt especially on the anti-clericalism of *De Cive*, a book 'restoring to the civil powers those rights of which they had been robbed by ecclesiastics in the ages of ignorance'. Hobbes 'taught that the authority of kings ought to be absolute, and that in particular the externals of religion, as being the most fruitful cause of civil wars, ought to depend upon their will' (1952, pp. 130–1; cf. Pufendorf 1934, pp. 1014–15). It was Hobbes' systematic fusion of Christianity with civil sovereignty that later earned praise from Rousseau in the chapter on 'Civil Religion' in the *Social Contract* (Bk IV, Ch. 8): 'of all Christian authors, the philosopher Hobbes is the only one who saw clearly both the evil and the remedy, and who dared to propose reuniting the two heads of the eagle and fully restore that political unity without which neither the state nor the government will ever be well constituted'. Hobbes himself thought he had been too pusillanimous in his task, remarking that 'he durst not write so boldly' as Spinoza had in the *Tractatus theologico-politicus*. Edmund Waller, who sent Hobbes a copy of the *Tractatus*, believed, nonetheless, that Hobbes, although 'a private person, pulled down all the churches, dispelled the mists of ignorance, and laid open their priestcraft' (Aubrey 1898, I, pp. 358).

Hobbes' friends regarded the destruction of priestcraft as both a metaphysical and a practical political task. It required the dissolution of the

Aristotelian perversion of Christianity, upon which was built the material power of priestly castes, priests whose talk of innate truths, and of authority and sovereignty in church and state, were ideological weapons for imposing their own values. Abraham Cowley, in his ode 'To Mr Hobbes' (1656) wrote that before Hobbes 'Long did the mighty Stagirite retain / The universal intellectual reign'. He depicts the 'barbarous' schoolmen as being slain by Hobbes, the 'great Columbus of the Golden lands of new Philosophies'.[18] When Hall in the 1650s, and Tindal in the 1700s, borrowed Hobbes' work to construct respectively a Cromwellian and a Whig civil religion, they portrayed the vanquishing of priestcraft as the recovery of true religion from the sway of the scholastic 'Antichrist' (Hall 1654, ch. 12; Oldisworth 1710, p. 373; cf. Pocock 1973). For Hobbes and his disciples, the secularisation of politics was an eschatological project: voluntarist theology was 'true religion' and it generated true politics. Modern secular politics of the Hobbesian sort is voluntarist metaphysics which has shed its theological premises. But those premises remained highly visible in the political theory of Hobbes' contemporaries.

18. Cowley 1949, pp. 43–4. The Stagirite is Aristotle.

21

Locke

JAMES TULLY

The political thought of John Locke is concerned with four problems that every major political theorist faced in the seventeenth century. These are: a form of government that would not lead to oppression or civil war, an arrangement of religion and politics that would end the religious wars, a set of applied arts of governing appropriate to the early modern mercantile states in a balance of power system, and the epistemic status of religious and political knowledge. This chapter is a survey of Locke's response to the first two problems: sections i to vi consider the first and section vii the second (for an introduction to the latter two, see Tully 1988). Recent scholarship has shed indispensable light on the political events and pamphlet literature in England which provided the immediate context of Locke's writings on government and religion (Franklin 1978; Ashcraft 1980, 1986; Goldie 1980a, 1980b). In addition to this context, I will suggest, the political issues Locke confronted and the concepts he used were also part of a larger, European crisis in government and sustained theoretical reflection on it (Rabb 1975).

i Government

The first problem is, what is government – its origin, extent, and end? It is classically posed in the subtitle of the *Two Treatises of Government*. Locke worked on this issue from the *Two Tracts on Government* (1660–1), to the

The following abbreviations are used in this chapter:

DJB Hugo Grotíus, *De Jure Belli ac Pacis libri tres* (Amsterdam, 1646). Repr. in Classics of International Law (Oxford: Clarendon Press, 1925).

DJR George Buchanan, *De jure regni apud Scotos*, in *Opera Omnia*, vol. 1 (Edinburgh, 1715).

LT John Locke, *A Letter Concerning Toleration*, ed J. Tully (Indianapolis: Hackett Publishing Company, 1983).

TT John Locke, *Two Treatises of Government*, ed. P. Laslett (Cambridge: Cambridge University Press, 1960).

616

Locke

Two Treatises (1681–9), moving from a solution of absolutism and unconditional obedience to one of popular sovereignty and the individual right of revolution. The question is not about the nature of the state as a form of power over and above rulers and ruled, although he was familiar with this reason of state way of conceptualising early modern politics and sought to undermine it (*TT*, I.ix.93, p. 248, II.xiv.163, p. 394). Rather, it is about 'government' in the seventeenth-century sense of the problematic and unstable relations of power and subjection between governors and governed.

According to the first three introductory sections of the Second Treatise the problem of government is taken to be a problem about political power. Government is composed of three relations of power: federative (international relations), executive, and legislative (including the judiciary) (*TT*, II.xii.143–8, pp. 382–4). The controversy is over the origin, extent, and limits of these forms of power and how they differ from other relations of governance (*TT*, II.ii.2, p. 308). The foremost problem of politics is, Locke reflects late in life, 'the original of societies and the rise and extent of political power' (Locke 1968, p. 400).

What, in turn, rendered political power problematic? For Locke, as for his contemporaries, the religious and civil wars that accompanied the consolidation and formation of early modern states as exclusive, or at least hegemonic, ensembles of domination were struggles for political power (Dunn 1979). This crisis in both the ability to govern and in the way of governing threw into question the nature and location of political power. The great conflicts in practice, in the age of 'agrarian and urban rebellions' and of 'revolutionary civil wars', were over the same problem of political power as arose in political theory (Zagorin 1982): 'the great Question which in all Ages had disturbed mankind, and brought on them the greatest part of those Mischiefs which have ruin'd cities, depopulated Countries, and disordered the Peace of the World, has been, Not whether there be Power in the World, nor whence it came, but who should have it' (*TT*, I.xi.106, pp. 236–7).

Unless both the historical and causal question of which arrangements of political power do and which do not dissolve into civil wars, and the moral-jurisprudential question of who has and who has not the 'right' to political power can be answered satisfactorily, Locke continues, Europe will remain in 'endless contention and disorder'. The *Two Treatises* is an answer to both these questions and it is the most radical answer that had yet been given: each individual does have and should have political power.

617

This European problem of continual conflicts over political power was also, of course, the overriding issue of English political thought and action from 1640 to 1690 (Franklin 1978, Weston and Greenberg 1981). During the planning for an insurrection in 1681–3 Locke wrote the *Two Treatises* as a populist resolution of the problem: for the people to reappropriate their political power through a revolution and to 'continue the Legislative in themselves or erect a new Form, or under the old form place it in new hands, as they think good' (*TT*, II.xix.243, p. 446; cf. Ashcraft 1986). In 1689 he published the *Two Treatises* to recommend that King William could 'make good his title' to power only if his conquest were grounded 'in the consent of the People', thus acknowledging their sovereignty, by means of a constitutional convention (*TT*, Preface, 1.6, p. 155; Goldie 1980a, 1980b). However, because it is written in the juridical language of European politics, the *Two Treatises* is a contribution to both the English conflict and the European crisis. Not only were English difficulties about power similar to those of other European states, the English conflict was itself part of the wider European context. A major aim of the 1681–3 agitations, as Locke saw it, was to stop England from becoming aligned with and subordinate to France. Also, William of Orange conquered England in 1688 in order to draw it into a European war against France, the Nine Years War, and the *Two Treatises*, grants him unlimited 'federative' or war-making power, unchecked by parliament (*TT*, II.xii.147, pp. 383–4). Indeed, this war is Locke's main concern in 1689 (Locke in Farr and Roberts 1985, pp. 395, 397–8). Thus, the context in which Locke explicitly places the *Two Treatises* is the practical contests and theoretical debates over political power of his generation and of the previous sixty years (Locke 1968, p. 400) – the struggles between king, parliament, and people, and theoretical discussion of them from the publication of Hugo Grotius' *The Laws of War and Peace* (1625) to the *Two Treatises* (1689).

Locke's solution to the problem of government and political power comprises five steps: the definition of political power; the origin of political power; the rule of right in accordance with which it is exercised; the conditional entrusting of political power to government by the consent of the people; and the way the three parts of political power are exercised by government and limited by law and revolution. These five features make up a classic theory of individual popular sovereignty, succinctly summarised in section 171 of chapter 15. Each one, except the first, is unique to Locke in certain specific respects. I shall survey these features in a way that brings out both what is conventional and what is distinctively Locke's own, as well as the practical and theoretical difficulties that provoked his innovations.

ii Political power

Political power is defined as a tripartite right: to make laws both to preserve and to regulate the lives, activities, and possessions of subjects (legislative power); to use the force of the community to execute these laws with penalties of death and lesser penalties (executive power); and to wage wars to preserve the community, including colonies and subjects abroad, against other states (federative power). The end of political power is the 'public good'.[1] This view of the power of government is closely tied to the actual claims and practices of the early modern mercantile states, with which Locke, as a member of the Board of Trade, was professionally familiar. It would have been seen as a commonplace by his contemporaries (see Harper 1939, pp. 9–18).

Next, to determine who should have political power, Locke, like other juridic theorists, reduces it to an 'original' or 'natural' form of power from which the present tripartite power, and the author's preferred location, extent, and limit, can be historically and logically derived and justified. The objective of this second step is to answer the question, who naturally or originally possesses political power? Locke's answer is that political power is a natural property of individuals. That is, 'the *Execution* of the Law of Nature is in that State [of nature], put into every man's hands, whereby every one has a right to punish the transgressors of that Law to such a degree, as may hinder its Violation' (*TT*, II.ii.7, p. 289, cf. II.ii.8, p. 290). It follows from this premise of political individualism that people are naturally self-governing, because they are capable of exercising political power themselves; naturally free, because they are not naturally subject to the will of another; and naturally equal, because they possess and have the duty and right to exercise political power.[2] Therefore, first, prior to and independent of the establishment of institutionalised forms of government people are able to govern themselves; and, second, the power of institutionalised forms of government is derived from the original powers

1. *TT*, II.i.3, p. 286, II.ix.131, p. 371, II.x.135, pp. 375–6, II.xv.171, pp. 399–400.
2. *TT*. II.ii.4, p. 287, II.ii.7, pp. 289–90. Compare II.ii.5–6, 8–15, pp. 288–96, II.iv.22, pp. 301–2, II.vii.87, pp. 341–2, II.vii.90–1, pp. 344–5, II.ix.123, p. 368, II.xv.171, pp. 399–400.

of the individual members of the political society (*TT*, II.vii.87–9, pp. 342–3, II.ix.127–31, pp. 370–1; II.xv.171, pp. 399–400).

Locke says, 'I doubt not but this will seem a very strange Doctrine to some Men' (*TT*, II.ii.9, p. 290, cf. II.ii.13, p. 293). His premise of political individualism *is* strange: it is one of the major conceptual innovations in early modern political thought. To see this let us contrast it with the two conventional ways of conceptualising the origin of political power available to him and with reference to which Locke situates the *Two Treatises*: the traditions of 'natural subjection' and 'natural freedom'.

The *Two Treatises* is written in response to the defence of natural subjection and refutation of natural freedom put forward by Sir Robert Filmer in his *Patriarcha* and other political writings, written between 1628 and 1652 to justify unconditional obedience to absolute monarchy. These were republished in 1680 to justify obedience to the Stuart monarchy during the unsuccessful attempt to exclude the future James II from succeeding to the throne (Daly 1979). The thesis of natural subjection is that political power resides naturally and originally in the monarch to whom lesser political bodies and all citizens are naturally subject. Since this relation of subjection is unlimited and natural no resistance to it is ever justified. In Filmer's version, the political relation is patriarchal. The political power that monarchs naturally exercise over their subjects is identical with the unlimited and arbitrary power patriarchs exercise naturally over their wives, children, slaves, and private property (Filmer 1949, pp. 57–63; TT, I.i.1, p. 159, I.ii.9, pp. 165–6).

In opposition to natural subjection is the more complex tradition of natural freedom. This includes all theories which posit that the people are naturally free in the sense of not being subject to the will of another. It follows that political subjection must be based on some kind of convention: consent, contract, or agreement.[3] In setting out to attack this whole tradition Filmer characterises it as consisting in the following propositions: mankind is naturally endowed with freedom from all subjection; mankind is at liberty to choose what form of government it pleases; the power which any man has over another was at first by human right bestowed according to the discretion of the human multitude; and, therefore, kings are made subject to the censures and deprivations of their subjects. This account of political power, he argues, is 'the main foundation of popular sedition'

3. Locke explicitly places the *Two Treatises* in the tradition of natural freedom and in opposition to natural subjection: *TT*, I.i.3–5, pp. 160–1, I.ii.6, p. 162, I.iii.15, p. 169, II.ii.4, p. 287, II.viii.95, pp. 348–9.

because it supports the practical conclusion 'that the multitude have the power to punish or deprive the prince if he transgresses the laws of the kingdom' (Filmer 1949, pp. 53–4, cf. p. 68). The whole tradition, according to Filmer, must be repudiated if the rebellions of the early modern period are to end.

Filmer is well aware that this is an old tradition with its roots in Roman law and the renaissance of juridical political theory in the twelfth century (Filmer 1949, pp. 55, 73–4). He is also aware that not only theories of limited government and the right to resist constituted authority had been built on its premises. The most prestigious theories of absolutism in the seventeenth century also came out of the natural freedom tradition: those of William Barclay, Hugo Grotius, Thomas Hobbes, and, after Filmer's death, Samuel Pufendorf, Richard Cumberland, and the unpublished *Two Tracts* of the young Locke (see ch. 12 above). Although the absolutist theories of natural freedom hold that the people completely alienate their natural freedom to the king, they always leave an exception where, in extraordinary circumstances, the people may withdraw their consent and defend themselves against a murderous tyrant (Filmer 1949, pp. 54, 66–73). This exception in even the most absolutist theories opens the way to justify resistance, as in fact Locke confirmed by using Barclay's absolutist theory in precisely this way (see below, p. 638). Many agreed with Filmer, especially after the failed radical Whig uprising and the Rye House Plot of 1681–3: the major tenets of natural freedom were condemned by Oxford University, and Locke's fellow revolutionary Algernon Sidney was executed for holding them (Sidney 1772, pp. 3–32: Scott 1991).

In writing the *Two Treatises* Locke's task is not only to refute Filmer's natural subjection theory but also to rework the tradition of natural freedom in a form that both answers Filmer's criticisms and justifies constitutional government and revolution against the predominant natural freedom theories of absolutism. The first move Locke makes is, as we have seen, to place political power in the hands of individuals. Natural freedom theorists were willing to grant that individuals naturally have a right to defend themselves and their possessions from attack, even to kill the attacker if necessary. This right of defence, however, was never described as political power. Second, political power was said to come into being when the people agreed to establish institutionalised government. It is granted to the people by God or, according to Grotius, it 'immediately arises' at the moment of constitution of government (*DJB*, I.iv.2, p. 1, 1646, p. 80, 1738, pp. 102–3). Third, political power inheres in the people as a corporate body, not individually. Fourth, the people as a whole never exercises political power. Rather, the people consents either to delegate (in limited constitutional theories) or to alienate (in absolute theories) its political power to a person or body that naturally represents them: king, parliament, or both (in theories of mixed sovereignty). Finally, in the case of legitimate resistance to tyranny, the people, either individually, or corporately acting through their natural representative body, exercise their natural rights to defend themselves or their community from attack. That is, the rebellions of the early modern period were not conceptualised as political activity but as individual or corporate acts of self-defence against attack (Tully 1986).

Therefore, the tradition of natural freedom is holistic with respect to political power until Locke. Although the people is or are naturally free, this natural freedom is non-political. Politically, the individual is naturally subject to the community and the community to its natural representative bodies, with respect to the exercise of political power. This is true even for the most radical theorists such as George Buchanan (*DJR*, pp. 3–4, 38), George Lawson (1657, pp. 45, 58), Richard Overton (1647), and Algernon Sidney (1772, pp. 456–64). For example, in George Lawson's theory of mixed monarchy, when king and parliament are in deadlock political power devolves back not to the people but to their natural representatives: the original forty courts of the forty counties, that is, to the local gentry (1689, p. 15). No one was willing to grant that the people either individually or collectively had the capacity to exercise political power themselves. In positing political individualism or individual popular sovereignty Locke thus repudiates 500 years of elite political holism and reconceptualises the origins of political power in a radically populist way. And this in turn is groundwork, as we shall see, for reconceptualising rebellion as a political activity of the people.[4]

iii   The origin of political power

Turning now to the original nature of political power. Locke argues that it is the duty and right of each individual to settle 'controversies of Right'.

---

4. There are two qualifications to this claim. In *De Iure Praedae* (1605) Grotius argues that the state's power to punish is derived from its individual members. However, he never published this manuscript and he explicitly repudiated this individualist thesis in *DJB*, returning to a traditional political holism. Second, Hobbes also derives punishing power from individuals, in *Leviathan*, ch. 28 (the reaction to it shows how unconventional it was). However, the natural power of punishment of both Grotius and Hobbes is the power of self-defence; it is not like Locke's jurisdictional power to judge controversies of right, to execute one's judgement and to seek reparations in one's own case and in the case of others.

This comprises three capabilities of governing oneself and others: to judge by means of 'trial' or 'appeal' if any person has transgressed the rule of right (natural law); to execute the judgement by means of coercive punishment of the guilty party; and to seek reparations for the injured party (*TT*, II.ii.7–12, pp. 289–93). The three powers of present governments developed historically, and can be logically derived from this original form of political power. The distinction between the 'state of nature' and 'political society' is thus that in the former each individual is judge and executioner of the (natural) law, whereas in the latter the right to judge is voluntarily and conditionally entrusted to a common legislature and judiciary, and the right to execute is entrusted to an executive (prince or monarch) (*TT*, II.vii.87, pp. 341–2; II.vii.88–93, pp. 342–6). Hence, political societies are constituted by *representative* governing institutions, and natural societies by direct, non-institutional practices of self-government (*TT*, II.vii.87, lines 24–32, p. 342).

What evidence could Locke advance for his view of the nature of political power prior to the placing of political power in monarchies or representative bodies? Seen in this light, Locke's account of the individual and self-governing origins of political power would have been seen as historically plausible by his audience, even though it was 'strange' and subversively populist. The reason is that it is a fairly accurate redescription of the *accusatory* system of justice by which Europeans governed themselves until the legal revolution of the twelfth and thirteenth centuries; until, that is, the inquisitorial system of justice and the juridical institutions of government expropriated political power. The accusatory system was supplanted by institutionalised and fiscalised forms of juridical government roughly during the reign of Henry II in England, and it was officially banned throughout Europe at the fourth Lateran Council of 1215 (Kuttner 1982; Rightmire 1932; Berman 1983, pp. 434–58).

Locke's account conforms remarkably well to what we know of this 'natural' jurisprudence. Accusations of transgressions were made by private individuals, not public officials, and not only by the injured party. The court of appeal was *ad hoc* in Locke's sense that it had no paid, permanent officials. The accuser who brought the charge swore an oath to the truth of his charge. Other members of the community, compurgators, supported the accuser's oath and others could come in on the side of the accused. Thus, if this was thought to be insufficient a trial by ordeal of some kind would take place, on the assumption that God would make the correct judgement visible through the outcome of the ordeal. The most important technique for Locke is the third one: a 'trial by battle' or combat, understood as an 'appeal to Heaven', again on the assumption that God would judge through the battle's outcome. This is of course precisely the language Locke used to describe revolution and no one could miss his point that a revolution consists in people taking back their original political power and exercising it in the 'natural' or accusatory way. Finally, the whole community had a hand in executing the punishment. This overwhelmingly took the form of reparation by means of payment of goods or services of the guilty to the injured party, and the majority of disputes in the century prior to the system's abolition were, as Locke argues, about property.[5]

Why should Locke conceptualise political power in this way? First, at the tactical level, he required a theory to justify revolt against the oppression of religious dissent (see section vii). After the failure to gain toleration through parliament the Dissenters had to initiate revolt themselves. They had no support from the Anglican local gentry so could not appeal to any constituted body, as Lawson had done. Second, he had to justify armed resistance in support of an oppressed minority by those not immediately affected (since the Dissenters made up barely 10 per cent of the population). His conception of political power serves these tactical needs well, while conventional self-defence theories do not.

At a more general level, the representation and explanation of rebellions in the seventeenth century were constrained by the vocabulary of self-defence by isolated individuals or representative bodies against direct attacks. This conceptual scheme became increasingly implausible as the great contests of the century unfolded, especially the English Revolution where people not directly attacked joined in, the people judged and executed their king, and set up a new form of government. Locke's conceptual revolution enables him to represent these struggles more accurately and, for the first time in European thought, as revolutions involving the exercise of political power by the people. His involvement in the organisation of revolution in 1681–3, and for the Monmouth Rebellion of 1685, must have helped him to see that the people in fact make political judgements and act upon them.

Locke presents two arguments on the basis of accepted practice for his premise of political individualism. In circumstances where individuals cannot appeal immediately to the law they are said to have the right to

---

5. *TT*, II.v.36–8, 50–1, pp. 310–13, 319–20, II.ix.136, pp. 376–7, and below. The centrality of property disputes in the transition period has been substantiated by Little 1978 and Coleman 1985.

Locke

defend themselves and their possessions from attack by the use of force
(*TT*, II.iii.18, pp. 297–8). This alleged natural principle of justice was
traditionally used to justify resistance to tyranny. However, for it to work
for Locke the act of self-defence would have to entail the exercise of
jurisdictional power, and this is what writers such as Pufendorf were able to
show self-defence did not involve (Pufendorf, VII.viii.7, 1688, p. 761, 1934,
pp. 1111–12). Also, governments punish aliens. Since aliens do not consent,
governments must exercise some natural power of judgement and
execution (*TT*, II.ii.9, pp. 290–1; cf. Grotius 1950, p. 92).

iv   Public good and natural law

The third step is the explication of the rule of right in accordance with
which political power is exercised, justified, and limited. For Locke this is
the law of nature, which enjoins the preservation of mankind. The law of
nature is the means of translating the end of government into natural duties
and rights of preservation. As we have seen in his definition of political
power the end of government is the 'public good'. The public good is the
preservation of society and, as far as this is compatible with the preservation
of the whole, the preservation of each member. The public good and
natural law perform a triple function in the *Two Treatises*: as the standard
by which controversies are adjudicated in the state of nature; as the guide
for legislation and executive action in political society; and as the rule by
which people judge their government.[6]

Filmer's first criticism of natural freedom is that any state of nature, even
Grotius', must be a Hobbesian state of lawlessness in practice, due to the
conflict of judgements, and thus a condition of licence, not freedom (Filmer
1949, pp. 264, 273–4, 285–6). Locke himself believed this in the *Two Tracts*
but changed his mind in the *Essays on the Law of Nature* (1661–2). By
arguing in the *Two Treatises* that the state of nature has a natural law
enforced by the accusatory system he responded to Filmer and showed that
natural freedom is not Hobbesian 'absence of restraint' (or 'negative
liberty') but the traditional juridical form of freedom as action within the
bounds of and subject to law (*TT*, II.iv.22, pp. 301–2, II.vi.57, pp. 323–4; cf.
Tully 1984).

It follows from the constitutive role of natural law that individuals who

6. *TT*, II.ii.4.7, pp. 287, 289–90, II.iv.22, pp. 301–2, II.xi.135, pp. 375–6, II.xiii.149, pp. 384–5,
II.xv.171, pp. 399–400. For Locke's theory of natural law see Von Leyden 1970; Urdang and
Oakley 1966; Tully 1980, pp. 35–43; and Colman 1983.

transgress it, in civil or natural society, by using '*Force without Right*' or manifesting a 'declared design' to do so, place themselves outside moral human society, and thereby in a 'state of war' (*TT*, II.iii.16, 19, pp. 296–7, 298–9, II.ii.8, 11, pp. 290, 291–2). If they then refuse the appeal to law and adjudication, or if there is no time for an appeal, then 'the want of such an appeal gives a man the Right of War' against the defiant lawbreaker (*TT*, II.iii.19–20, pp. 298–300, II.ii.10–11, pp. 291–2). It is important to see the careful structure of this argument because the right of war Locke lays out in chapter 3 is the foundation of the right to take up arms against a monarch or legislature who transgresses natural law, as he immediately points out (*TT*, II.iii.17, 20–1, pp. 297, 299–300). The right of war is thus a juridical decision by arms: the right to judge and proceed against a recalcitrant transgressor by force of arms in 'an appeal to heaven' (*TT*, II.iii.20–1, pp. 299–300 and reference in fn). As Locke interprets the biblical account of Jephthah leading his people to battle against the Ammonites, 'then Prosecuting [judging], and relying on his *appeal* [to Heaven], he leads out his army to battle' (*TT*, II.iii.21, p. 300). This means of enforcing the law of nature continues 'until the aggressor offers Peace, and desires reconciliaton' on just terms (*TT*, II.iii.20, p. 299).

Locke supports the right of war first by reference to the (alleged) natural right to kill an attacker or a thief (*TT*, II.iii.19, pp. 298–9, II.xvi.176, pp. 403–4). Since this is too weak to justify the exercise of the right of war in the defence of the attacked by those not directly involved, he appeals to a right of all mankind to prosecute a common murderer (*TT*, II.ii.11, pp. 291–2). Since this in turn is too weak to support activating a right of war in response to any violation of natural law (where other appeals have been exhausted) he argues that any design to violate natural freedom, to use force without right, threatens 'to take away every thing else', including preservation, and so is like a direct attack (*TT*, II.iii.17, p. 297). By these means Locke stretches the traditional justifications of defence to the generalised right of proceeding against those who break natural law. Following Buchanan he conceptualises this as warfare, and war in turn, not as an act of self-defence, but as a juridical and accusatory contest of decision by arms (*DJR*, p. 38; 1949, pp. 141–2). Since tyranny and usurpation can now be defined in terms of any violation of natural law, as the use of power beyond right and of power without right respectively (*TT*, II.xviii.199, pp. 416–17, II.xvii.197, p. 415), he broadens the base for justified revolt and redescribes it as a juridico-political activity of war, as Jean LeClerc pointed out in his review in *Bibliothèque Universelle* (XIX, p. 591).

The reworking of conventional legal arguments for resistance is complemented by an innovation in the content of natural law. As a result of the wars of religion and the sceptical attack on the claims of warring Christian churches, most seventeenth-century political thinkers agreed that the basic role of the state is to *preserve* and 'strengthen' society and its members, not to uphold the 'true' religion, unless it could be shown to be useful in bringing about preservation (Raeff 1983, pp. 11–43; Tully 1988). Accordingly, the basic concept of natural law that was said to guide and legitimate legislation was the law of self-preservation. This received its classical formulation in Grotius' formula of a natural duty and right of self-preservation and dominated the political thought of the century (Tuck 1979, pp. 58–82). Locke's innovation here is to argue that the fundamental natural law is not self-preservation but *'the preservation of mankind'* (*TT*, II.xi.135, pp. 375–6). It is this change which explains and grounds the distinctive set of natural duties and rights he is able to develop and which provides further support for a broader account of revolution (Tully 1980, pp. 53–156).

The preservation of mankind is broken into two natural duties: the traditional natural law duty to preserve oneself and, when one's preservation is not sacrificed, a new, positive and other-regarding duty to preserve the rest of mankind (*TT*, II.ii.6, pp. 288–9). Two natural rights to preserve oneself and others follow from the natural duties (*TT*, II.ii.7–8, pp. 289–90). Thus, when people accuse and adjudicate controversies involving others in the natural accusatory system they are exercising their natural rights and duties to preserve others. Hence, as we shall see, these rights and duties provide the justification for the wider population coming to the revolutionary aid of an oppressed minority; exactly the form of action Locke needed to legitimate and which, as the Levellers had discovered, could not be justified in their Grotian framework of self-preservation (Tuck 1979, p. 150). These in turn correlate with the traditional negative duty to abstain from that which belongs to another (*TT*, II.ii.6, pp. 288–9).

Further, two different kinds of power are employed in the exercise of each of these natural rights and duties: the power to preserve one's life and the life of others by punishing (natural) lawbreakers (political power) and the power to preserve oneself and others from starvation (labour power or productive power) (*TT*, II.ix.129–30, pp. 370–1). Locke discusses the natural rights and duties of labour power in chapter 5. If humans have the duty and right to preserve themselves and others from starvation, then they must have the right to 'Meat and Drink and such other things, as Nature affords for their Subsistence' (*TT*, II.v.25, pp. 303–4). Therefore, the world must belong to 'Mankind in common' in the sense that each has a natural claim to the means necessary for 'support and Comfort' (*TT*, II.v.26, p. 304). This modifies the popular seventeenth-century premise in the natural freedom tradition that the world belongs to no one but is open to the appropriation of each.[7] Filmer's criticism of this is that each act of appropriation would require the consent of all and so everyone would starve waiting for universal consent (1949, p. 273). Locke's famous reply is that consent is not required in the early stages of history (*TT*, II.v.28, pp. 306–7). The exercise of one's labour power as a *person* on what is given to mankind in common bestows on the labourer a right to the product insofar as it is used for the preservation of self and others and as long as 'enough, and as good [are] left in common for others' (*TT*, II.v.27, 31, pp. 305–6. 308; cf. Yolton 1970, pp. 181–97). Thus, labour power is the means of individuating the common into individual possessions to be used for preservation (*TT*, II.v.25, 26, 28, 29, pp. 303–7). Labour power also creates products of value, insofar as they are useful, and the whole chapter underscores the productivity and importance of labour (*TT*, II.v.40–4, pp. 314–17).

In the state of nature the exercise of labour power and possession are *regulated* by political power in accordance with the 'enough and as good' proviso and the natural law enjoining use for preservation. A person who abuses possessions acquired by his own labour, or who appropriates more than one can use without spoiling, takes 'more than his share, and [it] belongs to others' (*TT*, II.v.31, p. 308). He thereby 'offended against the common law of Nature, and was liable to be punished; he invaded his neighbour's share, for he had *no right, farther than his own use*' (*TT*, II.v.37, pp. 312–13). Natural property rights are, accordingly, use-rights within a larger framework of rights and duties to preserve the community (mankind) and regulated by everyone through the accusatory system.

Increase in population, the introduction of money, development of agricultural arts, the extensive appropriation of land, the division of labour and the emergence of commercial activity all lead to interminable disputes and quarrels over property rights (*TT*, II.v.36, 37, 40, 44, 45, 48, pp. 310–12, 314, 316–17, 319). The accusatory system is ill-suited for this

---

7. *DJB*, II.ii.1–2 (1646, pp. 101–2, 1738, pp. 142–6); Pufendorf, *De Jure Naturae*, IV.iv.2 (1688, pp. 363–4, 1934, pp. 532–5).

situation and so the resulting instabilities provide one of the major causes of the historical transition from the pre-state accusatory systems to the agreements to establish the first forms of institutionalised and territorial forms of government (monarchies) and formal legal codes to regulate property (*TT*, II.v.45, p. 37, II.v.30, 50, pp. 307–8, 319–20; cf. Palmer 1985a, 1985b, for this information). I return to this transition argument below. The important points here are, first, that Locke has argued that it is a natural function of political power to regulate both labour and possessions for the sake of preservation, or the public good (*TT*, II.i.3, p. 286, II.viii.120, p. 366, II.xi.136, pp. 376–7). This provides the justification for the extensive regulation and disciplining of the labouring population in the mercantile systems of the early modern states, when this power is delegated to government, as Locke recommends in his *Report to the Board of Trade* (1697). On the other hand, this framework of natural-law rights and duties of preservation places a limit on property legislation the transgression of which justifies revolt. Once government has determined a system of 'property' – by which he means a right to some thing such that it cannot be taken without the consent of the proprietor or the consent of his representatives (*TT*, II.xvi.193, p. 413, II.xi.140, p. 380) – a transgression of these rights constitutes a violation of natural law and hence a ground for legitimate revolt, just as in the state of nature (*TT*, II.xi.138, pp. 378–9, II.xvi.119, p. 412). A further question is whether these arguments for appropriation without consent and punishment for abuse of land were used, or were intended to be used, to justify the dispossession of Amerindians and the imposition of European forms of property (Cronon 1983, pp. 54–82, 95).

v   Mutual subjection

The fourth step in the juridical argument is the way in which political power is placed in the hands of monarchs or representative bodies. It is a historical, logical, and normative question concerning the rights and conditions under which either the great centralising monarchies or the representative institutions of early modern Europe exercised political power. In the natural-freedom tradition two general genealogies were proposed. The first and dominant explanation, which Locke adopted in the *Two Tracts*, is that the people as a corporate whole, and usually acting through their natural representative body, consent to *alienate* completely political power to the monarch and to renounce the right of self-defence.

The main argument for alienation in its pure or mitigated form is that if sovereignty is shared by monarch and parliament (or estates), or if the people do not renounce their (or its) right to judge when it is a situation of self-defence, then, given human partiality, this will lead to disagreement, dissension, tumults, and so to civil war. The idea that political power is shared by parliament and monarch was castigated as a throwback to the strife-ridden feudal past and an impediment to centralisation and modernisation under absolute monarchy (Pufendorf 1667; Filmer 1949, p. 88; Shennan 1974). The second argument, famously advanced by Rousseau, is that unless alienation is complete no sovereign is formed and people remain in a quasi state of nature (Rousseau, I.vi, 1972, p. 115). Locke used both of these arguments in the *Two Tracts*.

The second genealogy is that the people, as a whole, consent or contract to entrust conditionally political power to the monarch or to monarch and parliament (in mixed monarchy theories), or to parliament (in parliamentary sovereignty) (Franklin 1978). When the ruler abuses the trust it is broken and power devolves back to the people. Then, the people may defend themselves either through parliament or, if it is a mixed monarchy, through a natural representative body such as Lawson's forty courts of the forty counties. As we have seen, no one was willing to say that dissolution of the trust returned the exercise of political power to the people.

In the *Two Treatises* Locke adopts the 'trust' theory of the relation between government and governors and adapts it to his individual account of political power. There are three reasons why he accepted the trust hypothesis. First, according to the alienation hypothesis, the sovereign is by definition outside of political society, since he is not subject to law, and thus absolutism is not a form of political society (*TT*, II.vii.90, p. 344). Further, since the people resign their right to judge and punish him for violations of natural law, it is worse than the inconveniences of the state of nature since they have no right to protect themselves against his violence. Hence it would be irrational to consent to alienate: 'to think that men are so foolish that they take care to avoid what Mischiefs may be done them by *Pole-Cats* or *Foxes* [in the state of nature], but are content, nay think it safety, to be devoured by *Lions* [in absolute monarchy]' (*TT*, II.vii.93, p. 346). This is clearly against *any* natural-freedom theory of alienation, whether that of Grotius, Hobbes, Pufendorf, or Locke himself in the *Two Tracts*. Not only is it irrational. Since it involves transferring absolute power over one's own life to another, it presupposes that individuals have the right to dispose of their own life. Locke points out to his Christian audience that only God has such a right.[8] Even if absolutism enjoys universal consent it is a form of 'despotic power' and 'slavery' that violates the natural law to preserve life by exercising unlimited power over subjects (*TT*, II.xv.172, pp. 400–1).

Locke's second reason for rejecting the alienation theory is that governments tend over time to tyranny. As states develop, rulers gain wealth and power and tend to cultivate interests different from and contrary to the people's. In addition, they become open to ideological manipulation by religious elites, who use their influence to have their beliefs imposed by political means. The resulting tyranny causes civil war.[9] Hence the alienation theory, like any absolute theory, is part of the problem rather than a solution (*TT*, I.xi.106, pp. 236–7).

The third and major reason for the change is that Locke came to believe that the alienation theory is implausible: post-Reformation, and especially post-English Civil War individuals, as a matter of fact, do not alienate their natural political power. As he classically and presciently put it in the *Two Treatises*, popular revolution is a permanent feature of modern politics, irrespective of the official ideology:

> For when the *People* are made *miserable*, and find themselves *exposed to the ill usage of Arbitrary Power*, cry up their Governors, as much as you will for sons of *Jupiter*, let them be Sacred and Divine, descended or authoriz'd from Heaven; give them out for whom or what you please, the same will happen. *The People generally ill treated*, and contrary to right, will be ready upon any occasion to ease themselves of a burden that sits heavy upon them. (*TT*, II.xix.224, pp. 432–3)

Let us turn now to the complex practice of *trust* (see Dunn 1969, pp. 120–48, 165–87, 1984, pp. 22–60, 1985, pp. 34–55). Individuals consent to entrust the two natural powers they exercise themselves in the state of nature to make up a government. First, labour power, the power '*of doing whatsoever he thought fit for the Preservation of himself*, and the rest of mankind' each individual '*gives up* to be regulated by Laws made by the Society, so far forth as the preservation of himself, and the rest of that society shall require' (*TT*, II.ix.129, pp. 370–1). That is, property and labour are now regulated by the two policy objectives of collective and individual preservation, with the individual being sacrificed to the preservation of the collectivity when these two great rationales of government conflict (*TT*, II.xi.134, pp. 373–4). Thus, as Locke stresses throughout the *Two Treatises*, the public good (preservation), not rights, is

---

8. *TT*, II.iv.23, p. 302, II.xi.135, pp. 375–6, II.xiii.149, pp. 384–5, II.xv.171, pp. 399–400, II.xix.222, pp. 430–1.
9. *TT*, II.viii.107–12, pp. 356–62, II.vii.94, pp. 347–8, II.xiv.162–3, p. 394, II.xviii.208–10, pp. 422–3.

the fundamental principle in accordance with which political power is exercised by governors and judged by the governed. This, as Locke notes, confines the liberty each had by natural law (*TT*, ii.ix.170–1, p. 371). Second, each individual 'wholly *gives up*' political power, the power of punishing, to be used to make and enforce laws, with each individual's assistance if necessary (*TT*, ii.ix.130, p. 371).

The transfer of powers involves three parts. Individuals consent with each other to give up their powers to form a political 'society' of which each becomes a member. Only explicit consent, 'by positive Engagement, and express Promise and Compact', makes one a member and constitutes a political society, and binds each to the determination of the majority until either his citizenship is revoked or the society is dissolved (*TT*, ii.viii.95–9, pp. 348–51, ii.vii.122, p. 367). The majority then constitutes the society into a form of government by placing the legislative power in specific hands. If this legislative power, as well as executive power, remains in the majority then it is a 'perfect' democracy; if in the hands of a few, oligarchy; and so on (*TT*, ii.x.132, p. 372). The legislative power is the 'supreme power' in any commonwealth because the power to make laws derives from the members' natural power to judge controversies (*TT*, ii.vii.89, p. 343, cf. ii.xix.212, pp. 425–6). Finally, the legislative entrusts the 'natural force' of the community to the executive (and, *eo ipso*, the federative) to enforce the laws and protect society, members, and colonies by means of war and diplomacy (*TT*, ii.xii.144–8, pp. 382–4).

Locke sees two objections to his thesis that lawful government is based upon explicit consent, involving the delegation of political power, and binding each member to the majority: that there are no historical instances of it, and that people are now born into and are thus naturally subject to a government (*TT*, ii.viii.100, pp. 351–2). In response to the former objection he assembles historical and anthropological evidence to illustrate that free men have commonly set rulers over themselves (*TT*, ii.viii.101–12, pp. 352–62). In these examples Locke is concerned to falsify both the natural-subjection thesis and the equally popular *de facto* thesis that lawful government can be founded in successful conquest. This aim is spliced rather awkwardly into the first section of the Second Treatise (*TT*, ii.i.1, p. 342, lines 19–25; cf. Goldie 1980b, pp. 508–18).

The latter objection is no more plausible. History furnishes many examples of people leaving their government and founding new commonwealths by consent, which would be impossible if subjection were natural. Further, present governments themselves do not assume that subjection follows from birth, but from consent, and they in fact demand express consent (*TT*, ii.viii.113–18, pp. 362–5). Recent scholarship on the origins of institutionalised forms of political power and citizenship in Europe, whether in the communes, free cities, principalities, or English commonwealth, has stressed the widespread practice of consent and oath-giving (Oestreich 1982, pp. 135–55, 166–87; Berman 1983, pp. 259–403). Explicit oaths of allegiance to the present form of church and state were precisely the form the central issue of obedience and resistance took from 1640 to 1690. In 1689 Locke insisted on explicit oaths renouncing *jure divino* doctrine (because it did not base allegiance on the *justice* of William's invasion and would equally legitimate a successful French counter-conquest) (Farr and Roberts 1985, pp. 395–8).

The most difficult question Filmer puts to the consent thesis is one of motivation. Why should anyone ever consent to give up his natural freedom and self-government, and, as Locke rephrases it, 'subject himself to the Dominion and Controul of any other Power' (*TT*, ii.ix.123, p. 368; Filmer 1949, p. 286)? Locke answers that there are three disadvantages of the natural or accusatory system that caused, or cause, people to abjure it: the lack of established, settled, or known law; the lack of a known and indifferent judge; and a want of power to execute a judgement (*TT*, ii.ix.124–6, pp. 368–9). Natural law can be known and settled, but, because people are always partial in their own cases, they will not submit to a law that applies against them. The second difficulty also turns on the jurisprudential axiom that individuals are biased judges in their own cases through 'interest' or 'partiality'. As a result, 'Passion and Revenge is very apt to carry them too far, and with too much heat, in their own Cases; as well as negligence, and unconcernedness, to make them too remiss, in other mens.' Even the third turns on partiality: since Locke argues that people will not enforce a sentence when the guilty party resists and makes punishment 'dangerous, and frequently destructive' (*TT*, ii.ix.125–6, p. 369).

Locke argues in chapter 5 that these disadvantages do not cause serious problems until the pressure of population growth on available land, the increase of, and division into, towns and villages, the development of agriculture and technology, and the introduction of money conjoin to cause disputes over property which destabilise the natural regime. He also speculates that these developments, especially money, enhanced the sense of self and thus served to enlarge, if not create, the self-interest that undermines the accusatory system (*TT*, ii.viii.107, 108, 111, pp. 356–8,

360–1, II.V.37, pp. 312–13). Thus, confusion and disorder eventually follow from a way of life in which men are 'judges in their own cases' because 'self-love will make men partial to themselves and their friends' and 'Passion and Revenge will carry them too far in punishing others' (*TT*, II.ii.13, pp. 293–4). At precisely this conjuncture in human history the greatest transformation in the way of governing occurs: from self-government to civil government. Locke immediately remarks that it is absurd to assume (as he had in the *Two Tracts*) that people would consent to absolute monarchy at this point as a remedy to their problems. Since the problem is human partiality where each is judge, what kind of a remedy is absolute monarchy 'when one Man commanding a multitude, has the Liberty to be Judge in his own Case, and may do to all his Subjects whatever he pleases, without the least liberty to any one to question or controle those who Execute his Pleasure' (*TT*, II.ii.13, pp. 293–4)? Rather, Locke advances a more plausible history of the formation of the state.

While still self-governing, people were used to entrusting their authority to a single ruler to lead them in times of war, although they retained the right, exercised in *ad hoc* councils, to declare war and peace. Only later did they turn to this custom of delegating authority to settle internal disputes (*TT*, II.viii.108, 110, 112, pp. 357–62). Thus, civil government evolved out of the practice of external war, which explains the initial plausibility of conquest theories. However, delegation of power in wartime and later in internal disputes was based on consent and a somewhat naive trust in the application of the original form of government, 'which from their infancy they had all been accustomed to'; the patriarchal family (*TT*, II.viii.107, pp. 356–7, cf. II.viii.105, 110, pp. 354–5, 359–60). Filmer is thus right in saying that the first forms of civil government are monarchies, patterned on the patriarchal family, but wrong in construing this as natural rather than a contextually rational and conventional response to the breakdown of an earlier way of life.

The initial trust was naive because people had no experience of the abuse of power and so of the need for explicit limitations, even though they understood it to be limited, like paternal care of children (*TT*, II.viii.107, pp. 356–7). As central authority developed, the monarch, through luxury and ambition, stretched his prerogative 'to oppress the People', and developed interests separate from them (*TT*, II.viii.111, pp. 360–1, cf. II.xiv.163, pp. 394–5). They then realised that it is necessary to limit monarchy by placing the legislative power 'in collective bodies of men, call them Senate, Parliament, or what you please' (*TT*, II.vii.94, pp. 247–8).

Men examined more carefully 'the *Original* and Rights of Government', and set up legislative bodies 'to *restrain the Exorbitances* and *prevent the Abuses*' of princely power, thus ushering in the present age of dispute about privilege and contests between kings and people about government (*TT*, II.viii.111, pp. 360–1, cf. II.xiv.166, p. 396). Not only did this attempt at separating and balancing power not succeed, as proponents of mixed monarchy falsely claim, but princes have been further emboldened in the present age by argument from custom and new ideologies of divine right promulgated by religious elites to advance their own interests.[10] Locke's reconceptualisation of the trust between governed and governors is thus designed to provide a solution to the problem of civil wars caused by the failure of the first attempt through representative institutions to curb the power given to princes and by the seventeenth-century resurgence of absolutism.

vi Revolution

The fifth and most important step in juridical political thought is the twofold question: how is political power exercised by governors and what prevents the abuse of power? The answer to the first question for Locke is that political power is to be exercised in accordance with the trust. This comprises: that laws should be made and executed in accordance with the common good or natural law; that governors should themselves be subject to the laws they make; and that the laws and legal rights should not be changed without the consent of the majority through their representatives (*TT*, II.ix.135, pp. 375–6, II.vi.94, pp. 347–8, II.xi.140, p. 380; cf. Grant 1987).

Locke's solution to the problem of the abuse of power, and so to the early modern crisis of government, is that the people themselves must govern their governors. They must judge when and if their governors act contrary to the trust and, when necessary, execute their judgement by a revolution and the establishment of a new government. Locke's concept of trust captures this mutual subjection practice of government. The people entrust their political power to their governors or trustees and consent to subjection as long as it is exercised in accordance with the trust. Reciprocally, the governors are under an obligation to the people to exercise power accordingly. Hence,

10. *TT*, II.viii.112, pp. 361–2. Balancing and separation are referred to in II.viii.107, p. 356, and the use of custom to legitimate absolutism at II.vii.94, pp. 347–8.

the Legislative being only a Fiduciary Power to act for certain ends, there remains still *in the People a Supreme Power* to remove or *alter the Legislative*, when they find the *Legislative* act contrary to the trust reposed in them. For all *Power given with trust* for the attaining an *end*, being limited by that end, whenever that *end* is manifestly neglected, or opposed, the *trust* must necessarily be *forfeited*, and the Power devolve into the hands of those that give it, who may place it anew where they shall think best for their safety and security   (*TT*, II.xiii.149, pp. 384–5)

How does this work in practice? In a system where the executive is separate from the legislative, the legislative, being the superior power, governs the executive which may be 'at pleasure changed and displaced' (*TT*, II.xiii.152, pp. 386–7). If the legislative fails or abuses the trust, then, as we have seen, power devolves to the people. In England, the monarch has a share in the legislative, and so is neither subordinate nor accountable to it, and thus cannot be removed by it. This section (152) ends fifty years of insoluble debate over the location of sovereignty in mixed monarchy. The legislative cannot effectively judge and constrain the executive even though this is the reason it was established. If the legislature is given authority to judge the monarch then this destroys the mixed nature of sovereignty. If the monarch is given ultimate authority the same contradiction follows (Franklin 1978, pp. 1–52). Consequently, the people, and only the people, have the power to govern both the legislative and executive when either acts contrary to the trust (*TT*. II.xix.218, 222, pp. 428, 430–2).

There are two means by which this may be done. Subjects may appeal to the legislative, not only to judge controversies among themselves, but also controversies between them and their government (unlike absolutism) (*TT*, II.vii.93–4, pp. 346–8, II.xviii.207, pp. 421–2). However, when religious Dissenters made appeals throughout the Restoration against the transgression of their civil and political rights and the confiscation of their property, their appeals were castigated as 'sedition' and 'faction' (*TT*, II.vii.93, p. 346, II.xviii.209, pp. 422–3, II.xix.218, p. 428). When this means is blocked, the trust is broken and the people turn to the second means of redress: revolution as the means of executing the law of nature (*TT*, II.xix.221–2, pp. 430–2, II.xviii.202, 204, pp. 418–20).

In chapter 19 Locke distinguishes between the dissolution of government and the dissolution of political society, states that virtually the only way political society is dissolved is by foreign conquest, and goes on to analyse cases in which government, but not political society, is dissolved by various types of breach of trust (*TT*, II.xix.211, pp. 424–5). In this revolutionary situation the people are no longer under subjection to the government, so they 'may constitute to themselves a new legislative, as they think best, being in full liberty to resist the force' of the illegitimate government (*TT*, II.xix.212, p. 426). Nor are they constrained, he continues, to act as a corporate body in resistance to unlawful authority: 'Every one is at the disposure of his own Will' (See *TT*, II.xix.220, 242, pp. 424–6, 429, 445). In these cases, the rulers (legislature or executive) are in a state of war *vis-à-vis* the people because they have acted contrary to right or used force without right.[11] Revolution then becomes an exercise of their regained natural political power to judge and execute in accordance with natural law (see *TT*, II.iii.17, p. 297).

Who has the right to judge when the trust is broken and thereby decide that political society is dissolved? Locke's unequivocally radical answer is that each individual man has this right: '*every man is Judge for himself*'.[12] Not only may any man (or woman?) make this judgement, he may make it on the basis of a *single* violation of right, on the judgement that his ancestors had been wronged by conquest (thinking of a French invasion), or even if no transgression has been committed but the individual discerns a tyrannical tendency or design.[13]

Who has the right to execute this judgement by taking up arms to punish tne government? Again, Locke replies that each individual has this right.[14] As we have seen this follows from the premises since the revolution *is* the people governing lawbreakers as they do naturally when other forms of appeal have failed. Finally, the people themselves have full constituent authority to reestablish the old form of government, to set up a new form, or to set up direct democracy – 'to continue the legislative in themselves' (*TT*, II.xii.243, pp. 445–6, cf. II.xix.220, 226, pp. 429, 433–4). To drive home his point that revolution is the exercise of natural political power by the people he calls it exactly what the right of war is called: an 'appeal to Heaven'. Here, because there is no common judge on earth, the only recourse is a decision by arms. 'And where the Body of the people, or any single Man, is deprived of their Right, or is under the exercise of a power

---

11. *TT*, II.xix.222, 232, pp. 430–2, 437, state the general argument whereas II.xix.212–19, pp. 425–9, takes up specific abuse of the trust in 1681 and 1688.
12. *TT*, II.xix.241, p. 445. Compare II.iii.21, p. 300, II.ii.9, pp. 290–1, II.xiv.168, pp. 397–8, II.xix.240, pp. 444–5.
13. *TT*, II.xiv.168, pp. 397, II.xviii.203, p. 419, II.xvi.176, pp. 403–4, II.xviii.210, p. 423, II.xix.220, p. 429.
14. *TT*, II.xix.222, 224, 228, 231, 232, 235, 239, 242, pp. 430–3, 434–5, 436–8, 439–40, 442–5. Compare II.iii.19, pp. 298–9, II.xvi.176, pp. 403–4, II.xviii.202, 207, pp. 418–19, 421–2.

without right, and have no appeal on earth, there they have a liberty to appeal to Heaven, whenever they judge the cause of sufficient moment.'[15] The elaborate account of the state of nature is thus stage-setting for the introduction of revolution as the natural and legitimate way the people govern rulers who abuse their power.

Locke attempts to make this doctrine appear less subversive than it is by making Barclay's respectable natural-freedom theory of absolutism appear more populist than it is. Buchanan had argued that a king who becomes a tyrant dissolves the constitutive pact between king and people, forfeits his rights, and so may be proceeded against by means of a judicial act of war by the body of the people or an individual, just as in the case of a common criminal (*DJR*, p. 38). In his reply Barclay countered that as an inferior can never punish a superior, so neither an individual nor the people as a whole can punish, attack, or prosecute their king. However, as we have seen, Barclay does concede that if a king becomes an *intolerable* tyrant the people as a whole, and not an individual, may defend itself as long as it does not attack the king (Barclay 1600, III.viii, cit. TT, II.xix.232–3, pp. 437–9). Although Grotius repudiated Buchanan's theory as well, he did go on to assert against Barclay that the people, individually or collectively, could defend themselves by force of arms against an intolerable tyrant who attacked them directly.[16] In this exceptional case the people exercise their natural right to defend themselves and this is justified because the reason for which people originally established government is self-preservation. Pufendorf repeated this mitigated absolutism, explicitly making the point against Barclay that the duty not to punish a superior does not apply because resistance is an act of defence, not of jurisdiction (Pufendorf, VII.viii.7, 1688, p. 761, 1934, p. 553). This line of argument, as we have seen, was used and abused – as Filmer predicted – to justify resistance throughout the century.

In his commentary on Barclay, Locke reverses this trend. Instead of saying that resistance is a non-judicial act of defence he is able to show that even Barclay admits that when a king destroys his people or alienates his own kingdom he ceases to be a king. He thereby 'divests himself of his Crown and Dignity, and returns to the state of a private Man, and the People become free and superior'; he 'sets the people free, and leaves them at their own disposal' (Barclay 1600, III.xvi, cit. *TT*, II.xix.237–8,

---

15. *TT*, II.xiv.168, pp. 397–8. Compare II.iii.21, p. 300; II.xvi.176, pp. 403–4, II.xix.241, p. 445.
16. *DJB*, I.iv.7 (1646, pp. 86–90, 1738, pp. 111–19). He refers to Barclay in I.iv.10–11 (1646, pp. 90–1, 1738, pp. 120–1).

Locke

pp. 441–2). Although Barclay is thinking of extraordinary circumstances he concedes that a king can lose his superiority and thus, as Locke immediately concludes, the rule that an inferior cannot punish a superior does not apply and so the people may prosecute him (as Buchanan originally argued) (*TT*, II.xix.239, pp. 442–4; Buchanan 1715, p. 38, 1949, p. 142). With his very different account of the natural political power of the people and his more extensive concept of tyranny firmly in place, Locke is able to exploit this opening and make it appear that his radical doctrine is not far out of line with the most respectable absolutists (*TT*, II.xix.239, pp. 442–4).

Despite Locke's exercise in feigned respectability the *Two Treatises* is unorthodox in conceiving of rebellion as a political contest involving ordinary people seizing political power and reforming government. We can measure how unconventional it is by noting two contemporary responses to its publication in 1690. First, Locke's Whig friend James Tyrrell repudiated it in *Bibliotheca Politica*, arguing that political power does not revert to the people but to representative bodies or 'great councils' (1727, p. 643; cf. Franklin 1978, p. 110). In *The Fundamental Constitution of the English Government* (1690) William Atwood stated the major objection to Locke's account:

others [Locke?] are too loose in their notions, and suppose the dissolution of this contract [James II's vacancy] to be a mere [i.e. pure] commonwealth, or absolute anarchy, wherein everybody has an equal share in the government, not only landed men, and others with whom the balance of power has rested by the constitution, but copy-holders, servants, and the very faeces Romuli which would not only make a quiet election impractical but bring in a deplorable confusion.[17]

Locke's theory thus appears to be the most implausible solution of all. Hobbes had argued that civil war is caused by each individual claiming the right to judge the law in accordance with their subjective standard of conscience or 'private judgement' (*Leviathan* II.29, 1957, p. 211). In the *Two Tracts* Locke argued that in a system of popular sovereignty members would withdraw their consent and revolt whenever a law conflicted with their private interest, claiming that it contravened the public good (1967, pp. 120–1, 137, 226). Grotius launched a blistering attack on the theory of mutual subjection of king and people, where the people (parliament) obey if the king does not abuse his trust and the king becomes dependent on the

17. Atwood 1690, p. 100. See Franklin 1978, p. 105. Five pamphlets of the 1680s are similar to the *TT* on the point of dissolution. [Wildman] 1689a and 1689b; [Humfrey] 1689; [Stephens] 1689; Ferguson 1681. See Ashcraft 1986; Goldie 1980a, 1980b.

people if he does abuse it. It would lead to confusion and disputes because king and people would judge and act differently; 'which disorder', he concludes, 'no Nation (as I know of) ever yet thought to introduce' (*DJB*, I.iii.9, 1646, p. 59, 1738, pp. 71–2). Filmer too had made the 'anarchy' of individual judgements the centrepiece of his attack on the natural freedom tradition: 'every man is brought, by this doctrine of our authors [Hunton], to be his own judge. And I also appeal to the conscience of all mankind, whether the end of this be not utter confusion and anarchy' (Filmer 1949, pp. 296–7; Franklin 1978, pp. 39–48). This argument was repeated throughout the Restoration by defenders of absolutism and mixed monarchy and it has remained the mainstay of conservative criticism of popular sovereignty.

In his reply, Locke cannot deny that people are biased in their judgement or claim that they will impartially judge in accordance with the common good. He uses the assumption of partiality to explain both the breakdown of the accusatory system and the tendency of absolutism to tyranny (*TT*, II.ii.13, pp. 293–4, II.ix.124–6, pp. 368–9, II.vii.93, p. 346). Therefore he must answer his conservative critics on their own ground, by showing that partiality does not entail confusion and anarchy. A sign that Locke may have seen his answer as the most controversial and unconventional aspect of the *Two Treatises* is that he presents it in two separate places in the text (*TT*, II.xviii.203–10, pp. 414–23, II.xix.224–30, pp. 432–6).

Here is the question (which is clearly in response to Filmer): 'May the *Commands* then *of a Prince* be opposed? May he be resisted as often as anyone shall find himself aggrieved, and but imagine he has not Right done him? This will unhinge and overturn all Polities, and instead of Government and Order leave nothing but Anarchy and Confusion' (*TT*, II.xviii.203, p. 419; cf. Sidney 1772, I.24, pp. 185–215).

Locke presents six reasons why this will not lead to 'anarchy'. First, as we have seen, people revolt when oppressed irrespective of the type of government. A government that establishes the exercise of popular sovereignty by means of appeals to courts and parliament when people find themselves aggrieved is more likely to avoid revolution than one where juridical contestation of government is forbidden (*TT*, II.xix.224, pp. 422–3, II.xviii.207, pp. 421–2). Second, just because people are partial, they will be motivated to revolt only if the oppression touches them directly (*TT*, II.xviii.208, p. 422). Third, again due to partiality, they will not in fact revolt on slight occasions but only when oppression spreads to the majority or, when it affects a minority but appears to threaten all. This is so because they will calculate that it is not in their interest to revolt unless they expect to win, and this requires a majority (*TT*, II.xviii.209, pp. 422–3, II.xix.230, pp. 435–6, II.xiv.168, pp. 397–8). (This, as we shall see below, is the sobering lesson Locke learned when the Whigs refused to support the revolution of the minority Dissenters in 1681–3.) Fourth, people will revolt only when they are persuaded in their conscience that their cause is just because they fear divine punishment for unjust rebellion (*TT*, II.xviii.209, pp. 422–3, II.iii.21, p. 300). Fifth, people are in general habituated to the *status quo* and use and custom cause them to tolerate its minor abuses (*TT*, II.xix.223, 225, 230, pp. 432–3, 435–6, II.xviii.210, p. 423). Sixth, even when there is a revolution people usually return to the old forms of government to which they are accustomed, as English history shows (*TT*, II.xix.223, p. 432). In sum, Locke plays the conservative trump card of partiality and habit against his conservative opponents, showing that these causal factors make popular sovereignty more stable than absolutism. The radical right of revolt is restrained in practice by the conservative motive of self-interest and the force of habit.

Further, Locke argues, '*this doctrine* of a Power in the People of providing for their safety a-new by a new Legislative, when their Legislators have acted contrary to their trust, by invading their Property, is *the best fence against Rebellion* and the probablest means to hinder it' (*TT*, II.xix.226, pp. 433–4). The reason is that rebellion means opposition to law and thus rulers are the most likely to rebel because they have the temptation and the means, as well as the encouragement of interested elites, close at hand. Showing them that the people will both revolt and have justice on their side brings the rulers' interest and duty in line with the public good: 'the properest way to prevent the evil [rebellion], is to shew them the danger and injustice of it, who are under the greatest temptation to run into it' (*TT*, II.xviii.226, p. 434).

However, Locke does not believe that the mere threat of revolution and the public recognition of its rightness is sufficient to guarantee good government. He grows impatient in these late sections with persuading his conservative audience that popular sovereignty is the most orderly form of government. It is, for him, enough to show that it does not lead to anarchy and confusion. Revolution is not the worst thing in politics; oppression is (*TT*, II.xix.225, 229–30, pp. 433, 434–6, II.xi.137, pp. 377–8, II.xiii.158, pp. 391–2). The only guarantee against oppression is not a doctrine but the practice of revolution itself. He argues that no form of government guarantees freedom and rights because every form can be abused (*TT*,

II.xviii.209, pp. 422–3). Only the activity of self-governing rebellion grounds freedom (*TT*, II.XIX.226, 228–9, pp. 433–5). Those who say popular sovereignty '*lays a foundation for Rebellion*' are, after all, right, but wrong to conclude that it is 'not to be allowed' because it 'is destructive to the Peace of the World'. It disrupts only the unjust peace of state oppression, and the 'unlawful violence' of 'magistrates' who act 'contrary to the trust put in them' (*TT*, II.xix.228, pp. 434–5).

The justice of resistance to oppression: this is the theme of the *Two Treatises*. As strange as it sounds, this is also the solution to civil wars. If Locke is correct about the causal constraints on popular revolts, then they occur only when the people are in fact oppressed. Hence the cause of civil wars must be the abuse of power by governors, who, being partial, cultivate oppression when it is possible and in their interest to do so.[18] If, however, they know that the people have a right to revolt and will in fact revolt when oppressed, then either their interest in avoiding civil war will outweigh their interest in oppression or it will not. If it does, then oppression has been 'fenced', government normatively and causally 'limited', and civil war avoided. If, on the other hand, the right and threat do not deter abuse of power then there is nothing that can be done short of revolt, which is both just and necessary.

vii Toleration

The second problem faced by Locke and his contemporaries is the nature of religion and the relation between religion and politics, ecclesiastical and political power, in post-Reformation Europe. The wars that swept Europe were not only struggles for power, they were also religious conflicts. Religion had become, Locke argued in 1660, 'a perpetual foundation of war and contention[:] all those flames that have made such havoc and desolation in Europe, and have not been quenched but with the blood of so many millions, have been at first kindled with coals from the altar' (1967, pp. 160–1). Twenty-five years later, still grappling with this problem, he said 'I esteem it above all things necessary to distinguish exactly the Business of Civil Government from that of Religion, and to settle the just bounds that lie between the one and the other' (*LT*, p. 26). Without this there would be no end to the controversies.

18. *TT*, II.vii.92, p. 345, II.viii.111, pp. 360–1, II.xiii.152, 158, pp. 386–7, 391–2, II.xiv.163, pp. 394–5, II.xviii.210, p. 423, II.xix.224–30, pp. 433–6.

Locke

Like the *Two Treatises*, Locke's solution, *A Letter Concerning Toleration*, has both an English and a European context. It was written in 1685 in support of the Dissenters' struggle for religious and civil liberty in England, and translated and published by William Popple for that purpose in 1689. Locke wrote it in exile in Holland to his friend Phillip von Limborch with whom he discussed the whole Reformation experience. Also, it was written immediately after not only the failed Monmouth Rebellion for toleration in England but also the Revocation of the Edict of Nantes and the persecution of Huguenots. Published at Gouda in Latin in 1689, it became a classic in the European struggle for toleration.

As early as the *Two Tracts* Locke began to explore the religious causes of war. He argued that Christian leaders had inculcated two erroneous beliefs in both princes and the laity: that there is only one true way to heaven; and that it is a Christian duty to uphold and to spread the true way by force and compulsion and to suppress heresy. Both rulers and the people consequently believe themselves to have an overriding duty and an interest (fear of hell and hope of heaven) to use the force of arms to solve religious disputes. Given the multiplicity of Christian faiths, each of which considers itself orthodox and the other heterodox, this alignment of duty and motivation leads to persecution by government and religious revolts by the people.

The clergy of *all* sects, in turn, have propagated these two false beliefs in order to use either the rulers (prince or parliament) or the populace to gain access to political power, thus achieving what they want: power, dominion, property, and the persecution of opponents.[19] In using political power in this way religious elites thus provide those who serve their purposes by taking up arms with an additional and temporal interest in performing their (alleged) religious duty (1967, p. 160). Political power is thus used not as it should be, to preserve property, but, rather, to confiscate and transfer it.

Hence, civil wars are waged in the name of religious 'reform' and religion serves as a 'vizor' or ideology which masks the struggle of competing elites for access to, and use of, political power (1967, pp. 160, 169–70). By showing the relation of ideological legitimation between religion and political power struggles Locke brings his analysis of the religious problem in line with his claim in the *Two Treatises* that the central struggle in his day is over political power.

19. Locke 1967, pp. 158, 160–2, 169–70, 211. Compare *LT*, pp. 23–5. For the persecution of religious Dissent in England see Calamy 1802; Cragg 1957; and Watts 1978.

The two true Christian beliefs are the antithesis of the widely propagated false beliefs. The first is that God allows each man to worship him in the way he sincerely believes to be right (over and above a few plain and simple essentials: the incarantion, heaven and hell, and the core Christian ethics). The second true belief is that Christianity should be upheld and spread by love and persuasion only, not by force and compulsion (1967, p. 161). Both reflect Locke's acceptance of Grotius' minimalist response (in *De Veritate Religionis Christianae*) to the sceptical attack on the claims of different churches and to the pragmatic attack on the assumption that it is the role of government to uphold true religion by force of arms. Given post-Reformation religious diversity this assumption became both the cause and justification of war. Locke's epistemological justification of the first belief is that nothing more than the essentials can be known with certainty, and of the second that the kind of belief necessary for salvation cannot be compelled, but must be voluntary (Van Leeuwen 1963: Viano 1960).

On the basis of this analysis Locke advanced two radically different solutions. The first, in the *Two Tracts*, is a theory of absolutism and the imposition of religious uniformity. The second, in *A Letter Concerning Toleration*, is a theory of popular sovereignty and religious toleration. A brief account of the former and of its failure will show how he moved to the latter and provide a better understanding of its main features. This also throws light on the *Two Treatises*, which is, in a fundamental way, Locke's repudiation of the *Two Tracts*. Both solutions turn on removing the cause and justification of the wars of religion – that it is the duty of the state to uphold the true religion – and on replacing this with preservation, or the 'public good', as the duty of government.

The *Two Tracts* is Locke's proposal for the political and religious form of the Restoration settlement of 1660–2. He argues, against a proposal for toleration based on individual conscience by Edward Bagshaw, that as long as the two false beliefs continue to be widely held, a policy of religious toleration would be used by religious groups to build up strength and, eventually, to precipitate another civil war in the attempt to gain political power (Bagshaw 1660, 1661; cf. Abrams 1967; Viano 1960). The call for toleration thus masks the underlying will to power of a clerical elite bent on domination, as he repeats even in *A Letter Concerning Toleration* (*LT*, pp. 32–3, 43). His solution is for everyone to alienate irrevocably his natural power, even over indifferent things, to an absolute monarch, Charles II. The monarch would then impose whatever forms of worship he judged necessary for peace, order, and the public good, using solely customary and prudential considerations as his guide. The magistrate does not have the duty to impose the true religion, convert his subjects or suppress heresy. Religious activity is assessed and governed in accordance with the political criterion of the 'public good' (1967, pp. 119, 124–6, 149–50, 169–70, 229–32). Locke then suggests that if the Dissenters (Baptists, Presbyterians, Quakers and Independents) were peaceful, the monarch could permit toleration in the form of a Declaration of Indulgence (as Charles II in fact wished) (1967, p. 170). Dissenters could not be tolerated on the grounds of individual conscience, as Bagshawe proposed, because this would limit the monarch's sovereignty and reintroduce a religious criterion into politics (1967, pp. 121, 137, 154).

The greatest threat to peace according to Locke comes not from the Dissenters but from the Church of England. The monarch must be absolute in order to be free of the national church, which will otherwise use the state to impose religious uniformity and gain power: '[they] know not how to set bounds to their restless spirit if persecution not hang over their head' (1967, p. 169). Throughout his writings, Locke consistently attacks the Anglican church as the greatest threat to peace and calls for its disestablishment (Goldie 1983).

Finally, as a consequence of alienation, a subject is always obligated to obey any law and not to question it, even if it prescribes forms of worship the subject believes to be unacceptable to God. This will not compromise a person's faith because faith is a matter of inner belief – judgement or conscience – whereas obedience to the law need only be a matter of will or outer behaviour. With this crucial Protestant distinction Locke could argue, like all English uniformists, that conformity and obedience are compatible with liberty of conscience (1967, pp. 220–40).

This proposal failed because Charles II was not as absolute as Locke envisaged. He was dependent on parliament and it was dominated by an Anglican–gentry alliance whose aim was the imposition of religious uniformity, the extirpation of Dissent and the control of public life. Their justification for this policy was to identify religious Dissent with sedition and civil war, as Locke notes in the *Two Treatises* and *A Letter Concerning Toleration*. Even the moderate Anglicans or 'latitudinarians', with whom Locke is sometimes erroneously grouped, opposed toleration and worked for comprehension within the established church. Charles II fought for toleration of Dissent and of his co-religionists, English Catholics, but the Anglican–gentry alliance was powerful enough to enact the Clarendon Code, a set of repressive laws designed to stamp out Dissent. These laws were enforced and augmented during the Restoration, sending thousands of Dissenters into poverty, death, jail or transportation.

Rather than causing Dissenters to conform to Anglicanism, the Clarendon Code had the opposite effect. The Dissenters refused to comply, continued to practise their religion, disobeyed the law, and suffered imprisonment and martyrdom throughout the 1660s and 1670s. The Code created a permanent underclass, oppressed and denied access to public life and to publication, who struggled for toleration until the Act of Toleration in 1689. This Act was only a partial remedy and they were treated as second-class citizens until well into the nineteenth century. By that time the Anglican–Dissent division had become the major political cleavage in English society. From 1667 onward Locke wrote in support of this minority's struggle for toleration in the twofold sense of religious and civil liberty (see Goldie 1983; Tully 1983).

Locke first changed his views and began to defend toleration in *An Essay Concerning Toleration*, 1667 (in Locke 1961). He prepared this manuscript for Anthony Ashley Cooper (soon to be the first earl of Shaftesbury), the leader of the struggle for toleration and Locke's employer and closest friend until his death in 1683. This 1667 manuscript was used to persuade Charles II to support the concerted but unsuccessful effort of the Dissenting congregations to gain an Indulgence by royal prerogative and to block new legislation to repress Dissent, especially the use of bounty-hunting informers and of transportation to the colonies in permanent servitude as punishment.

First, Locke revised his views on belief and action in the light of the Dissenters' refusal to conform from 1662 to 1667. Now, if a person sincerely believes that an article of faith is true and a form of worship is acceptable to God, and thus necessary to salvation, he evidently will profess and act accordingly. Hence, judgement and will are not separate. Rather, as he later put it in *An Essay Concerning Human Understanding*, the 'judgement determines the will', and so religious liberty must include liberty of practice as well as belief (II.xxi.48, 1975, pp. 264–5).

Second, God judges people on the sincerity, not the truth, of their beliefs, and thus if a person sincerely believes that something is necessary and not indifferent, it is necessary for salvation. This ushers in Locke's radically subjective definition of religion, which is fully articulated later in *A Letter Concerning Toleration*: 'that homage I pay to that God I adore in a way I judge acceptable to him'. Consequently, to profess or act contrary to one's religious beliefs, even if the magistrate so orders, is now the paramount sin

646

of hypocrisy and it would lead to eternal damnation: This doctrine reverses the *Two Tracts*. Duty and interest (salvation) are now aligned with disobedience to the imposition of religious uniformity, thereby justifying the Dissenters' widespread resistance to conformity. It also expresses for the first time *the* Lockean belief about the modern, post-Reformation individual: that the civil person is constituted by a moral sovereignty over one's core beliefs and practice that cannot be alienated.

The magistrate's role continues to be to uphold the public good. However, he now does not have sovereignty over his subjects' indifferent beliefs and he knows that the imposition of uniformity will in fact be resisted. Thus, a policy of uniformity causes civil unrest – it is not a response to civil unrest, as the Anglicans argued – and toleration is the pragmatic means to civil peace. Given this analysis, Locke reiterates that *any* attempt to impose uniformity under the guise of unity or conversion is a stratagem to gain power and domination. Enforced uniformity, he argues, unites all the competing sects into one hostile opposition, whereas toleration would remove the cause of the hostility, create trust, and tend to cause the proliferation of sects, thereby dividing and weakening further any potential threat to peace and security.

In 1672 Charles II introduced a Declaration of Indulgence which suspended the penal laws against Dissent. The Anglican–gentry alliance in parliament attacked it on the grounds that it undermined the rule of law and the constitution. Shaftesbury defended it as a legitimate exercise of royal prerogative. This long struggle for toleration through absolutism, and against parliament and its constitutionalist justification of opposition to Indulgence is expressed in Locke's anti-constitutionalist treatment of prerogative in the *Two Treatises*. He says that the monarch may act in his discretion not only 'beyond the law' but 'against the law' if this is in accordance with the public good (*TT*, II.xiv.164, pp. 393, 395; Weston and Greenberg 1981, pp. 171–5; Pocock 1985, pp. 227–8).

When Charles II withdrew his Indulgence one year later, abandoned his alliance with Dissent and began to go along with the uniformists in parliament, the Anglican–gentry alliance entered government under Danby, and Shaftesbury and Locke turned against Charles II and absolutism. They began to build the 'radical' Whig movement that would struggle for toleration first through parliament (1675–81), then, when this did not work, through the failed revolt of 1681–3 and the unsuccessful Monmouth Rebellion of 1685. This transition to the combination of popular sovereignty and toleration as a right that Locke presents in *A Letter*

Concerning Toleration is first sketched in *A Letter from a Person of Quality to his Friend in the Country* (1675). Locke states that what distinguishes limited from arbitrary monarchs is that they have 'the fear of human resistance to restrain them' (Locke 1823, X, p. 222). Thus, a government has a sufficient motive to rule in accordance with the public good only if it fears armed revolt, and this is a credible threat only if there is no standing army. On the other hand, the people revolt only when the government genuinely abuses the public good because they fear that the revolt will be crushed unless they have the majority on their side.

Locke concludes that when people are oppressed, as with the Dissenters, they will resist, not only passively (as in *An Essay Concerning Toleration*), but actively, by the force of arms, and they do so 'justly and rightly' (Locke 1823, X, p. 222). Understandably, Locke left for France when this pamphlet was published and did not return until 1679. The pamphlet enunciates Shaftesbury's strategy: to work for toleration through parliament with the background threat of revolt if this was blocked. It was only after Charles II dissolved three toleration parliaments and parliamentarians 'trimmed' in 1681 that Shaftesbury and Locke turned to revolution and Locke wrote the *Two Treatises* (for the dating see Ashcraft 1980). Accordingly, Locke moved from the 1675 thesis that a credible threat of revolt is sufficient to protect liberty to his mature thesis that, as we have seen, only the actual practice of revolution is sufficient to free a people from oppression. We can also see why the right to revolt had to be lodged in the hands of individuals, and not in parliament, if the Dissenters were to liberate themselves. The rebellions of 1683–5 failed and the repression was so vicious that Dissent did not resurface as a political force for almost a century, except for a tiny group around Locke in 1689 lobbying, again unsuccessfully, for the radical, religious, and civil liberty of *A Letter Concerning Toleration*. Algernon Sidney and Lord Russell were executed after the Rye House Plot in 1683 and over 100 Dissenters were hanged following the Monmouth Rebellion.

Locke fled from England to the United Provinces in 1683 and did not return until the successful invasion of England by William in 1688. *A Letter Concerning Toleration* was written while he was living in political exile in Holland during the winter of 1685. The text opens with the claim that toleration is the fundamental Christian duty and goes on to describe it as a natural right. He presents three reasons why the government is not concerned with the care of souls: individuals *cannot* alienate sovereignty over their speculative and practical religious beliefs necessary for salvation; outward force, political power, cannot induce the kind of sincere belief required for salvation, only persuasion can; and even if coercion could induce belief, there is no epistemic certainty that the religion of any particular government is the true religion (*LT*, pp. 26–8). These are used to justify toleration, the thesis that a church is a purely voluntary organisation, and the separation of church and state. That is, they free 'men from all dominion over one another in matters of religion by separating coercion and religious belief, introducing his two true beliefs, and thereby removing the cause of religious wars (*LT*, p. 38).

Nonetheless, toleration is not an absolute right. Religious beliefs and practices must be assessed and governed in accordance with the overriding criterion of the 'public good' and those judged to be injurious to it proscribed (*LT*, pp. 39, 42, 49–51; cf. Bracken 1984, pp. 83–96). What prevents a magistrate from arguing that a policy of outward religious uniformity is necessary, not to save souls or because it is true, but because the public good requires a shared public life; that the atomism of religious diversity is deeply divisive and 'inclinable to Factions, Tumults, and Civil Wars' (*LT*, p. 54)? Locke had argued in this way in 1660 and many pragmatic defenders of uniformity or comprehension did the same (Stillingfleet 1680). Locke's first answer is to argue that, as a matter of fact, religious diversity does not cause political divisiveness nor civil unrest. Conventicles are not 'nurseries of factions and seditions' as the opponents of Dissent claim and therefore cannot be repressed on prudential grounds. European history shows that quite the opposite is true: 'It is not the diversity of Opinions (which cannot be avoided) but the refusal of toleration to those that are of different Opinion, (which might have been granted) that has produced all the Bustles and Wars, that have been in the Christian World, upon account of Religion' (*LT*, p. 55).

If we ask why the imposition of uniformity has continued in the face of its failure to bring peace, Locke gives the predictable answer that the alleged purpose, of stressing the public good, is entirely spurious. The real reason is the greed and desire for domination of the clergy and their ability to manipulate rulers and people: 'The Heads and Leaders of the Church, moved by Avarice and insatiable desire of Dominion, making use of the immoderate Ambition of Magistrates, and the credulous Superstition of the giddy Multitude, has incensed and animated them against those that dissent from themselves' (*LT*, p. 55, cf. pp. 24–5, 33, 35, 43, 50). This analysis is repeated throughout *A Letter Concerning Toleration* and Locke's account of the abuse of political power in the *Two Treatises* traces it to the same religious roots (*TT*, II.viii.112, pp. 361–2, II.xviii.209–10, pp. 422–3,

II.xix.239, pp. 442–4). The *Two Treatises* and *A Letter Concerning Toleration* are two complementary analyses of civil war, or, as Locke would have it, of religious domination of civil society through the state, whether Protestant or Catholic, and justified popular resistance to it.

Locke goes on to elucidate what specifically the clergy seek to gain by their 'Temporal Dominion', thereby illuminating another important feature of the *Two Treatises* (*LT*, p. 35). He says that 'they deprive them [Dissenters] of their estate, maim them with corporal Punishments, starve and torment them in noisom Prisons, and in the end even take away their lives' (*LT*, p. 24, cf. p. 52). Yet, on Locke's account, nothing should be transacted in religion, 'relating to the possession of Civil and Worldly Goods', or civil rights (*LT*, p. 30, cf. pp. 31, 32–3, 39, 43). Further, those who favour intolerance really mean that 'they are ready upon any occasion to seise the government, and possess the Estate and Fortunes of their Fellow-Subjects' (*LT*, p. 50, cf. p. 49). Dissenters, by the imposition of uniformity, are 'stript of the Goods, which they have got by their honest Industry' (*LT*, p. 55). The preservation of property in the sense of lives, liberties, and estates earned by industry is the reason why people enter civil government in both *A Letter Concerning Toleration* and the *Two Treatises* (*LT*, pp. 47–8, *TT*, II.ix.123, p. 368). The violation of this trust is also the form of oppression Locke is specifically concerned to condemn (*TT*, II.xix.222, pp. 430–2, II.xviii.209, pp. 422–3, *LT*, pp. 48–9). *A Letter Concerning Toleration* thereby illuminates the type of property that the *Two Treatises* is written to defend. It is not the private property of the bourgeoisie but the properties – the legal, political and religious rights – of an oppressed minority who, in the course of time, became the backbone of English working-class radicalism and adopted Locke as their philosopher (Beer 1921, esp. p. 101; Ashcraft and Goldsmith 1983). Revolution, property, and toleration are all of a piece for Locke.

If the strategy of religious uniformity is as Locke suggests, then we should not expect religious elites to pay any heed to his arguments that it is the cause of civil unrest. Rather, we should expect them to defend their use of political power, the hinge on which their domination turns. This was indeed the response. Jonas Proast, chaplain of All Souls, Oxford, defended the use of force to bring Dissenters to consider the true religion in his three assaults on *A Letter Concerning Toleration* and on Locke's two following letters (Proast 1690, 1691, 1703; cf. Long 1689). In addition, *An Essay Concerning Human Understanding* (used as a text in Dissenter academies), as well as *The Reasonableness of Christianity*, were seen, correctly, as threatening the established religious order, attacked by Anglicans, and defended by Dissenters (Yolton 1956, pp. 26–72). The Toleration Act of 1689 shows how far outside reasonable opinion was Locke's call for toleration of anyone who believed in any god and for the end of coercion in religion. The Act denied freedom of worship to unorthodox Dissenters (those who denied the Trinity) and Roman Catholics, and granted it, as a revocable exemption from earlier legislation, to Protestant Trinitarian Dissenters who took the oath of allegiance and obtained a licence to meet, but denied them access to public office.

Locke was well aware that just showing that the public good is disrupted by policies of uniformity and is best served by toleration would have no positive effect on the ruling elite. As in the *Two Treatises*, he repeats that the rulers will simply claim that those who protest and dissent from the policy will be said to be the cause of unrest, and their protestations used to justify further repression (*TT*, ii.xix. 218, p. 428, *LT*, pp. 52–5). His practical solution to the problem is to argue in the same way as in the *Two Treatises* that individuals must exercise their popular sovereignty and judge for themselves whether any law concerning religious practice is for the public good. If the magistrate enjoins anything 'that appears unlawful to the Conscience of the private individual' and it is also judged to be 'directed to the publick Good', then 'a private person is to abstain from the Action that he judges unlawful [according to his conscience]; and he is to undergo the Punishment' (*LT*, p. 48). A person has the right to disobey a just law if it conflicts with his conscience, provided he recognises his political obligation to the public good by suffering the punishment.

The case Locke is, of course, primarily concerned with is when the law appears not only unlawful to the conscience but also contrary to the public good (*LT*, p. 48). What if the magistrate continues to believe it is for the public good and the subjects believe the contrary? Locke answers with the same revolutionary doctrine as in the *Two Treatises*: 'Who shall be Judge between them? I answer, God alone. For there is no judge upon earth between the Supreme Magistrate and the People' (*LT*, p. 49). And he leaves no doubt as to what this means: 'There are two sorts of Contests among men: the one managed by Law, the other by Force: and these are of that nature, that where the one ends, the other always begins.' Therefore, as in the *Two Treatises*, people are justified in turning to revolution when they are stripped of their properties and their religion and 'to defend their natural Rights . . . with Arms as well as they can' (*LT*, p. 55). Civil wars will continue as long as the 'Principle of Persecution for Religion' continues to prevail. The attempt to impose uniformity by coercion is not only the justification of revolt but also its cause. The reason is that oppression naturally causes people to struggle to cast off this 'Yoke that galls their Neck' (*LT*, p. 52).

Revolution is thus necessary to establish and protect toleration. Churches would then be required to preach toleration as the basis of their freedom, to teach that 'Liberty of Conscience is every man's natural right', and that no body should be compelled by law or force in religion (*LT*, p. 51). This would undermine the link between religious and political power that legitimates religious domination and, hence, 'this one thing would take away all ground of Complaints and Tumults upon account of Conscience'. Unlike a national church, which causes turmoil, a plurality of equally treated congregations would be, according to Locke, the best guard and support of public peace. Knowing they can do no better than mutual toleration, the churches 'will watch one another, that nothing may be innovated or changed in the Form of the Government' (*LT*, p. 53; cf. Kessler 1985). Again, his point seems to be that the only solid foundation for civil and religious liberties is the readiness to govern those who violate them by means of popular political rebellion. Popular religious sovereignty, in concert with popular political sovereignty, is the solution to the problem of oppression and war based on religion.

Conclusion

Sharp chronological lines can seldom be confidently drawn across the page of any historical record – and never in the history of ideas. Yet a book must end somewhere, and it is desirable that the point at which it ends should be supported by some kind of rationale. In the present case, that rationale cannot well be derived from the general history of the period. The turn of the century in 1700 was not, even if we allow for some years' margin on either side, distinguished by any significant turning point in European development. Yet in intellectual history there is at least a certain sense, at that point or soon afterwards, of a stage being cleared by the demise of leading characters. Of the major thinkers discussed above perhaps only Leibniz (d. 1716) survived much beyond the earliest years of the new century.[1] And by coincidence the year 1704 was marked by the deaths of two figures whose ideas encapsulate some of the main contrasting and indeed conflicting tendencies in the political thought of early-modern Europe.

John Locke and Jacques-Bénigne Bossuet did not, it is true, meet in controversy as Filmer did, posthumously, with Locke. Yet there is, it can be said, an implicit dialectic in which the thesis advanced by Bossuet, particularly in his *Politique tireé des propres paroles de l'Ecriture sainte*,[2] is met and challenged in Locke's *Two Treatises of Government*. Where Locke sees an all but indissoluble link between power that is absolute and power that is arbitrary, and an almost inevitable degeneration from that conjuncture into the tyranny of the ruler and the slavery of his subjects, Bossuet rejects both the equation and the deduction: for him the king's absolute power, neither despotic nor tyrannical, is 'sacred, paternal, and subject to reason'.

---

1. And even so the works of Leibniz that are most relevant here were largely written a decade or more before his death.   2. Not published until 1709, but written several decades earlier.

Conclusion

In this, plainly, Bossuet was adopting a traditional and, for that very reason, a backward-looking approach to the problems of political society. Even in the defence of absolute power, more original, less time-worn concepts were by then being vigorously applied. Yet it is important to bear in mind that the doctrine or ideology of 'divine right' kingship retained at least its formal place in the politics of most of Europe throughout the eighteenth century and was not finally extinguished even by the revolutionary upheavals of 1789 and after.

It is only subject to that not insubstantial proviso that we may say (as we may indeed and doubtless must) that the future of European political thinking lay with the newer ideas that had emerged and advanced towards maturity in the period covered by this book. More especially in the last hundred years or so of that period, the sense of novelty, of a more or less radical break with the received ideas of a long past, is inescapable. We may think here of the 'modernised' theory of natural law developed by Grotius and elaborated by Pufendorf; of both the empiricism and the mathematically inspired rationalism generated by the new forms of natural science; of the materialism and mechanistic models we find in Hobbes; of the connections Harrington suggests between property and power and between both and 'political personality' (Pocock 1975, p. 386); of the radical individualism some would see coming to fulfilment in Locke after adumbrations in the Leveller tracts of the Puritan Revolution. In all these, and in other phases of seventeenth-century thought, that sense of innovation, of new departures, is insistently present.

On the other side of the same coin we see, or seem to see, a corresponding pattern of rejection. Locke's rejection of traditional royalist ideology is an obvious example. More fundamentally, in the intellectual life of the period, we have the various ways in which scholastic and Aristotelian ideas were rejected. It is entirely appropriate that the volume should, already in its penultimate part, be concerned with 'the end of Aristotelianism', and noteworthy that the sceptics and 'Tacitists' are joined there in the obsequies by thinkers of such radical originality as Grotius, Hobbes, and Spinoza. Hobbes' contempt for the schoolmen (p. 132 above) is relevant again here, and perhaps especially his attack on the folly of those who use – that is, misuse – the 'counters' of language as money, valuing words 'by the authority of an *Aristotle*, a *Cicero*, or a *Thomas*, or any other Doctor whatsoever, if but a man' (Hobbes 1651, p. 29). Yet it may be as well to recall also that if the end had indeed now come it had been long in coming. The humanist contention with scholasticism had begun before the period

Conclusion

of this book opened; and well within our first century the doctrines of such a schoolman as John Mair were earning the contempt of adversaries as diverse as Melanchthon and Rabelais.

Was it, in any case, the end even now? Were the 'obsequies' premature? Too much need not be made of the fact that, as late as 1706, substantial texts in medieval political thought were reproduced in the Ellies Dupin edition of the works of Jean Gerson. For this there were no doubt political reasons connected with the stubborn relevance of 'Gallicanism' in the French church. More important perhaps is the persistence – for example, in Leveller literature – of what has been called (p. 442 above) 'second-hand scholastic philosophy'. Again, when Locke himself, preparing his Second Treatise for publication, decided to bolster its arguments by quoting at length from Hooker's *Ecclesiastical Polity*, he was among other things helping to preserve and transmit the ideas Hooker had in his turn borrowed from Thomas Aquinas. Facts such as these, whatever their intrinsic importance, may be valuable pointers towards something more significant. In the dialectic of scholastic and anti-scholastic thinking there was perhaps a genuine moment of synthesis and not merely a confrontation of opposites. If Pufendorf can be described as 'a German Suárez' (p. 563 above); if Leibniz – himself 'a great admirer of Suárez'[3] – was concerned in part 'to rescue what was valuable in . . . scholasticism' (p. 681 below): granted these points, there must be a sense in which scholastic thinking died to rise again.

This makes it not less but more important to recognise that, insofar as synthesis took place, it was no mere amalgam of discordant elements. The 'modern theory of natural law' – for this is above all what is at issue here – was much more than that and certainly much more than the tired restatement of second-hand Thomism it has sometimes been made to appear (cf. Tuck, in Pagden 1987, esp. pp. 99–103). Grounded in a sceptical rethinking of the foundations of moral philosophy and jurisprudence, that doctrine became 'in many ways the most important language of politics and ethics in Europe' (*ibid.*, p. 119). The Europe of the Enlightenment had that language made available most extensively through the work of Jean Barbeyrac and his translators, who ensured the diffusion of the writings of Grotius and Pufendorf in French and English as well as in their original Latin. To recall the importance of that kind of political science for thinkers

3. Trentman in Kretzmann, Kenny, and Pinborg 1982, p. 826. The whole chapter, 'Scholasticism in the Seventeenth Century', provides valuable background to matters discussed here.

655

as diverse as Rousseau and Blackstone is one way of appreciating the impact on eighteenth-century thought of some of the crucial ideas analysed in these pages.

To say that is not, of course, to imply that the Enlightenment of the eighteenth century was no more than a culture of inheritance from the past. Already beneath the surface, as it were, of seventeenth-century intellectual life, still newer departures were beginning. Giambattista Vico was thirty-two when the century ended. Montesquieu was then a boy of eleven; but his *Lettres persanes* saw the light four years before Vico's *Scienza nuova*, and his mature ideas were, of course, to have far greater contemporary effect. By the time *De l'esprit des lois* was published in 1748, yet another new dimension had been added by the publication – 'dead-born' though it may have been – of David Hume's *Treatise of Human Nature*. 'New sciences' of man and society were no doubt in the making, and a new world was in many ways to emerge when an age of revolution succeeded the age of Enlightenment. What was new, however, still marched alongside what was old; and the old had lost neither its savour nor its sting. When, in 1801, *The British Critic* said of a recently published work that 'the chief principle . . . is of a dangerous tendency' and added, 'we cannot consider this as a well-timed publication', the subject was not some newly written piece of Jacobin pamphleteering: it was Robert Macfarlan's translation of George Buchanan's *De jure regni apud Scotos*.

Biographies

These notes provide outline biographies for the principal writers discussed in this book. Their chief works are mentioned either in these notes or can be found in the Bibliography, where details of editions are given. At the end of each entry there is a guide to secondary literature, together with an indication of the part of the bibliography in which the items are to be found.

ALCIATO, ANDREA
1492–1550. As a professor of law at the Universities of Avignon, Pavia, Bologna, Ferrara, and Bourges, Alciato combined the new humanist learning and methods associated with the work of his friend Erasmus with the old-fashioned ('Bartolist') science of law and defended the papal as well as the imperial political tradition. Besides his fundamental study of the Digest title 'On the Meaning of Words' (*De Verborum significatione*), Alciato published various philological and historical essays on the law, collected especially in his *Parerga Praetermissa Paradoxa* and *Dispunctiones*. His new humanist style of teaching and writing was later called the 'French method' (*mos gallicus iu is docendi*) after his disciples at the University of Bourges.
SECONDARY LITERATURE (part I): Viard 1926; Kelley 1970a.

ALLEN, WILLIAM
1532–94. A devout Catholic, Allen left Oxford for Louvain in 1561. Ordained priest at Mechlin, he opened a seminary at Douai in 1568 to train English exiles as missionary priests to reconvert England. In 1578 the seminary moved to Reims, and Allen also helped to establish a college at Rome in 1579. In 1584 he responded in print to William Cecil's assertion that English Catholics were not persecuted for their religion but for their secular disloyalty. He lived in Rome in his last years, being made a cardinal in 1587. At this time he no longer preached loyalty to Queen Elizabeth but encouraged rebellion in support of Phillip II's Armada.
SECONDARY LITERATURE (part II): Clancy 1964; Kingdon, in Allen 1965; Pritchard 1978; Holmes 1982.

ALMAIN, JACQUES
c. 1480–1515. Born in the diocese of Sens, studied and taught in arts and theology at Paris, where he was a pupil of John Mair. Soon after obtaining his doctorate in theology in 1512 he was commissioned by the faculty to reply to the anti-conciliarist views expressed by Tommaso de Vio (Cajetan) and directed against the claims of the Council of Pisa–Milan (1511–12). This produced Almain's *Libellus de auctoritate ecclesiae*. His ecclesiology and

political thought were further developed in *Expositio circa decisiones quaestionum M. Guillermi Ockham, super potestate summi pontificis*; but this, like many of Almain's other works, was published only after his premature death.
SECONDARY LITERATURE (part I): Oakley 1964–5; La Brosse 1965; Oakley 1977; Farge 1980, pp. 15–19; Burns 1983a.

ALTHUSIUS, JOHANNES

1557–1638. Born in Westphalia, studied at Cologne and Basle. He taught law at the University of Herborn, founded by Count John of Nassau, whose counsellor Althusius became. Summoned to Emden, the centre of northern Calvinism, in 1604, he had an active and influential career as syndic of the city. His major work, *Politica methodice digesta*, appeared in 1603, with later much expanded editions in 1610 and 1614. His *Dicaelogicae libri tres* (1617) attempted to establish a system of universal jurisprudence from elements of scriptural, Roman, and various customary laws.
SECONDARY LITERATURE (part II): Friedrich, in Althusius 1932; Gierke 1929, 1966; Mesnard 1952; Salmon 1959; Carney, in Althusius 1965.

AMMIRATO, SCIPIONE

1531–1600. Born in Lecce in southern Italy, Ammirato spent much of his life (from 1569 on) in Medici service, writing on history and other subjects. His best-known work is the *Discorsi sopra Cornelio Tacito* (1594).
SECONDARY LITERATURE (part IV): Berner 1970; Cochrane 1973.

ANDREAE, JOHANN VALENTIN

1586–1654. Son of a Lutheran cleric, and grandson of an important Lutheran theologian, Jakob Andreae (1528–90). Like three of his brothers Andreae became a Lutheran pastor. Education at Tübingen, he returned there, after extensive travels, to be ordained in 1614 and to take up a life of pastoral activities and writing. In the next six years he produced almost twenty works, including *Christianopolis* and a series of social satires in the Erasmian/Lucianic tradition. He was interested in the idea of a Societas Christiana dedicated to moral and social reform. His pastoral and intellectual work was severely disrupted by the Thirty Years War.
SECONDARY LITERATURE (part II): Held, in Andreae 1916; Montgomery 1973.

ANDREWES, LANCELOT

1555–1626. An ecclesiastic and scholar, Andrewes was educated at Cambridge, where his distinguished academic career culminated in his appointment as Master of Pembroke College. Under James I, he rose to high office in the church, as bishop first of Chichester, of Ely, and finally of Winchester. In theology, Andrewes inclined towards Arminianism, but his absolutist political ideas were typical of highly placed Jacobean clerics of all theological complexions. His political views are set out especially in *Tortura Torti* (1609) and *Responsio ad apologiam Cardinalis Bellarmini* (1610).
SECONDARY LITERATURE (part III): Reidy 1955.

ANTONINUS (Antonino Pierozzi), ST, OF FLORENCE

1389–1459. Born in Florence, he entered the Dominican order aged sixteen at Fiesole. After novitiate studies at Cortona, he came rapidly to the fore as prior of a succession of Dominican houses, including the Minerva in Rome. In 1436 he founded the convent of San Marco in Florence; and in 1446, having taken a major part in the Council of Florence, was nominated by Eugenius IV as archibishop there. An outstanding diocesan bishop and ecclesiastical statesman, Antoninus was also a notable scholar. His principal works were the

Biographies

Summa Theologica (or *Summa moralis*), written between 1440 and 1459; and the *Chronicon*, an account of world history for the purposes of moral edification.
SECONDARY LITERATURE (part I): Morçay 1914; Gaughan 1931; Walker 1933; *Dizionario Biográfico degli Italiani; Dictionnaire de Théologie Catholique; Dictionnaire d'Histoire et de Géographie Ecclésiastiques.*

ARNAULD, ANTOINE (the elder)

1560–1619. Educated at Paris and Bourges, Arnauld, despite his Calvinism, succeeded his father as *procureur-général* and auditor in the household of Catherine de Médicis. He converted to Catholicism, and wrote eloquently against the League and its Spanish allies on behalf of Henri IV. He gained forensic fame as an *avocat* before the *parlement* of Paris. He persuaded the *parlement* to decree the expulsion of the Jesuits in 1594, and pleaded against their return in 1603. A member of a family of the robe, he held the hereditary office of *conseiller de la ville* in Paris. His many children, including the younger Antoine Arnauld, were the founders of the Jansenist movement.
SECONDARY LITERATURE (part II): Sedgwick 1977.

ARNISAEUS, HENNING

1576/9–1636. A physician by training, he was also an erudite Aristotelian with a special interest in political theory. In 1620 he became a political adviser to King Christian IV of Denmark as well as his personal physician. A theorist of sovereignty in the Bodinian style, he advocated undivided and absolute sovereignty in the ruler and rejected the right of resistance (*De auctoritate principum in populum semper inviolabili*, 1611). Yet Arnisaeus was among the first to show that the main rights of sovereignty could be separated. His three main works on politics – *Doctrine politica* (1606), *De jure majestatis* (1610), and *De republica* (1615) – move toward a remarkably systematic and comprehensive treatise on the public law of sovereignty.
SECONDARY LITERATURE (part II): Dreitzel 1970.

ARUMAEUS, DOMINICUS

1579–1673. He spent his entire career as a teacher of law at Jena beginning in 1600. Despite occasional service to the court at Weimar as an adviser and ambassador, he was above all an academic, and even died at a faculty meeting at the ripe age of ninety-four. His main contribution was his pioneering effort to establish public law as an independent academic discipline through a programme of disputation at Jena in which a highly influential corpus of scholars was formed. And papers delivered there – together with other writings of his own, his colleagues, and his students – were put before the public in two important collections: the *Discursus academici de jure publico* (6 vols., 1615–23) and the *Discursus academici ad Auream Bullam* (1617).

ATWOOD, WILLIAM

c. 1661–*c.* 1705. Petyt's friend and disciple, this little-studied Whig barrister and pamphleteer advocated shared parliamentary sovereignty in his *Jani Anglorum Facies Nova* (1680), *Jus Anglorum ab Antiquo* (1681), and *Fundamental Constitution of the English Government* (1690). Taking issue with Locke, Atwood argued that government devolved in 1689 on the Convention Parliament but not on the community. In this he was representative of the Whig leadership in parliament. In a response subsequently to William Molyneux, Atwood asserted the English parliament's sovereignty over Ireland. In 1701 he became chief justice of New York, but, quarrelling with the royal governor, he returned to England, where his pamphleteering ended only with his death.
SECONDARY LITERATURE (part III): Pocock 1957; Franklin 1978; Ashcraft 1986.

Biographies

BACON, FRANCIS
1561–1626. Son of Sir Nicholas Bacon and nephew of Lord Burghley, Bacon was educated at Trinity College, Cambridge, and Gray's Inn. His political career under Elizabeth I was frustrated by rivalry with the Cecils and a finally abandoned but dangerous alliance with Essex. Under James I he rose to be lord chancellor only to be impeached in 1621. His writings represent a brilliant flourishing of Ramist anti-Aristotelianism in natural philosophy, and of Machiavellianism tempered by royalist pessimism and Anglican sympathy. His vision of the advancement of natural philosophy, the *Great Instauration*, exercised great influence on mid-seventeenth-century scientific, educational, and social reformers.
SECONDARY LITERATURE (part II): Rossi 1968; Vickers 1968; Webster 1975.

BANCROFT, RICHARD
1544–1610. An ecclesiastical commissioner and canon of Westminster, Bancroft defended episcopacy by divine right against the Marprelate tracts. An inveterate critic of Presbyterianism, he became chaplain to Archbishop Whitgift in 1592, and published *Dangerous Positions* and *Survey of the Pretended Holy Discipline*, condemning resistance theory, in the following year. Bishop of London in 1597, he encouraged loyalist Catholic secular priests in their controversy with the Jesuits. In 1604 James I appointed him archbishop of Canterbury. He defended the ecclesiastical courts against common law claims of jurisdiction.
SECONDARY LITERATURE (part II): Cross 1969; Collinson 1982.

BARCLAY, WILLIAM
c. 1546–1608. Educated first at Aberdeen, Barclay moved to France in 1571, and studied and taught Roman law at Bourges. He then became professor of civil law at the University of Pont-à-Mousson in Lorraine. There he was involved in a struggle for control of the university between the faculties of law and humanities, the latter being dominated by the Jesuits. Barclay was a vigorous defender of absolute monarchy. His best-known book, *De regno* (1600), was an attack upon both Catholic and Protestant theorists of resistance. He was offered posts and pensions by James I on condition he became an Anglican, but refused. He died at Angers where he had become dean of the law faculty. He also wrote against the temporal power of the papacy.
SECONDARY LITERATURE (part II): Carlyle 1936; Allen 1941; Collot 1965.

BARON, EGUINAIRE
1495–1550. Among Alciato's first students at the University of Bourges, Baron went on to teach in the law faculty there until his death. Besides a defence of the new 'method' of Alciato, which included the study of history and philology as well as philosophy, Baron published several 'bipartite' commentaries on the Digest and Institutes of Roman law, drawing extensive, often invidious, comparisons with corresponding French legal, social, and political institutions. He was a pioneer in the new field of comparative law and the study of the modern 'law of nations' (*jus gentium*), anticipating in some ways the work of Bodin and the seventeenth-century school of natural law.
SECONDARY LITERATURE (part I): Kelley 1981b.

BAXTER, RICHARD
1615–91. The most influential and most prolific of the Presbyterian theologians of the English Civil War and Restoration. His autobiography and devotional works are classics of English Puritan literature. He was a chaplain in the parliament army and later suffered for his

Biographies

nonconformity. His intellectual outlook was a traditional English Reformed mixture of Calvinism and Aristotelianism, so that, although hostile to Cavaliers and Anglicans, he shared many of their assumptions in the controversy with Hobbes. His most sustained political work is *A Holy Commonwealth* (1659); its arguments were considerably derived from his friend George Lawson.
SECONDARY LITERATURE (part V): Lamont 1979.

BAYLE, PIERRE

1647–1706. A canonical founder figure of the Enlightenment. When Louis XIV's drive against the Huguenots intensified, Bayle fled to Holland in 1681. Whilst some Huguenots continued to uphold traditional Calvinist theological and ecclesiological dogmas (following Pierre Jurieu), Bayle adopted a sceptical, anti-clerical, and tolerationist approach. His journals became a clearing house for the European Republic of Letters. His *Historical and Critical Dictionary* (1696) is his principal monument, its ideas expressed in the form of encyclopaedia articles.
SECONDARY LITERATURE (part V): Labrousse 1983.

BECAN, MARTIN

1550–1624. A Jesuit, born in Brabant; in later life taught theology in Mainz, Wurzburg, and Vienna. He was confessor to the emperor Ferdinand II. He published several works against James I and his supporters in the oath of allegiance controversy. So extreme was his view of papal authority that Paul V was obliged to censure his *Controversia Anglicana* in 1613.
SECONDARY LITERATURE (part II): McIlwain 1918.

BELLARMINE (ST), ROBERT

1542–1621. Entered the Jesuit order at eighteen, and in the 1570s taught theology at Louvain. From 1576 he taught at the college in Rome founded by Gregory XIII. Sixtus V sent him to France in 1590 with the legate Cardinal Gaetano. Clement VIII made him a cardinal in 1598, and Paul V appointed him keeper of the Vatican library in 1605. He took part in many controversies as the indefatigable champion of papal authority (*De potestate summi pontificis*, 1610). He played a major part in the controversy over James I's oath of allegiance.
SECONDARY LITERATURE (part II): Brodrick 1961.

BELLERS, JOHN

1654–1725. Son of a prosperous London merchant and prominent Quaker, Bellers became an important Quaker organiser and philanthropist. He married into the Gloucestershire gentry and combined the life of a country gentleman with religious activities, scientific interests (he became FRS in 1718) and the promotion of schemes for social improvement, religious toleration, and European peace. His best-known tract is the *Proposals for Raising a College of Industry* (1695).
SECONDARY LITERATURE (part II): Fry 1953; Bernstein 1963; Davis 1981a; Clarke, in Bellers 1987.

BELLOY, PIERRE DE

1540–1613. Belloy studied law in Toulouse and pleaded before the *parlement* there as an *avocat*. He was appointed a judge in the Toulouse *présidial*. A dedicated royalist, he defended the claim of Catherine de Médicis to the Portuguese crown in 1582. From 1585 he published several outspoken attacks upon the Catholic League. He was arrested by the League in Paris during the barricades of May 1588, and was held for a year before escaping. Henri IV

Biographies

appointed him *avocat-général* in the Toulouse *parlement* in 1593, but he could not return to the city until the League surrendered there in 1596.
SECONDARY LITERATURE (part II): Weill 1891; Allen 1941.

BERNARDINO OF SIENA, ST
1380–1444. Born at Massa Marittima in Tuscany of a distinguished Siennese family, the Albizeschi, he became a Franciscan in 1402 at Siena. Ordained priest in 1404, he began a long and influential career as a preacher throughout Italy. In 1430 he became vicar-general of the Franciscans of the Strict Observance, whose effectual second founder he became: numbers grew more than tenfold by the time of his death. Despite earlier Observant hostility to learning, Bernardino insisted on the study of theology and canon law as part of the friars' training. His own learning is demonstrated by his having addressed the Greek participants in the Council of Florence in their own language.
SECONDARY LITERATURE (part I): Ferrers Howell 1913; Oppelt 1977; *Analecta Bollandiana*, 71 (1953): 282–322.

BESOLD, CHRISTOPH
1577–1638. A jurist who taught at Tübingen and Ingolstadt. After converting to Catholicism in 1635, he was invited to Bologna by the pope and to Vienna by the emperor. His erudition was formidable in depth and range and extended not only to public law but to history, comparative government, religion, and philology. He was a lifelong friend of Johannes Kepler. In addition to important studies of the rights of sovereignty and of the mixed constitution, Besold provided a highly influential theory of federalism to account for the structure of the German Empire. Most of his work in political science is in the form of collected monographs. A convenient brief introduction to this political thought is his *Synopsis doctrinae politicae* (1623).
SECONDARY LITERATURE: *Neue Deutsche Biographie*.

BEZA, THEODORE
1519–1605. After studying law at Orleans, he went to Paris and gained a reputation as a Latin poet. A serious illness in 1548 led to his conversion to Protestantism, and he went to Geneva to join Calvin. He became a professor of Greek at Lausanne and spent several years travelling through Europe to promote the Protestant cause. In 1559 he became the first rector and professor of theology at the new academy in Geneva. He became the leader of the Genevan church after Calvin's death in 1564 and thereafter directed the spread of the Reformed church. Of his many publications, the one which deals most fully with politics is his *Du droit des magistrats*, first published in 1574.
SECONDARY LITERATURE (part II): Dennert 1968; Kingdon 1988.

BIEL, GABRIEL
c. 1410–95. Born at Speyer, studied at Heidelberg, Erfurt and, Cologne. As a member of the cathedral clergy at Mainz he wrote his *Defensorium Obedientiae Apostolicae* in 1462 on the papal side in the conflict over the archiepiscopal succession there. In the late 1470s he presided over the Brethren of the Common Life at Urach. In 1484, despite his advanced age, he became professor of theology (in the *via moderna*) at Tübingen, where he taught for seven years. He died in retirement with the Brethren of the Common Life at Einsiedel. His major works are the *Canonis Missae Expositio* and the *Collectorium in quattuor libros Sententiarum*.
SECONDARY LITERATURE (part I): Hermelink 1906; Ott 1952; Oberman 1967a; Picascia 1979; *Dictionnaire de Théologie Catholique; Dictionnaire d'Histoire et de Géographie Ecclésiastiques; Lexikon für Theologie und Kirche*.

Biographies

BILSON, THOMAS
1547–1616. A strong defender of episcopacy, an critic of resistance theory. Bilson was warden of Winchester College. He became bishop of Worcester in 1596, and was transferred to Winchester in the following year. He delivered the sermon at the coronation of James I.
SECONDARY LITERATURE (part II): Cross 1969; Collinson 1982.

BLACKWOOD, ADAM
1539–1613. A Scotsman, educated in humanities at Paris and law at Toulouse. A strong defender of monarchical absolutism, Blackwood published the first parts of *De conjunctione religionis et imperii* in 1575, maintaining a complementarity between temporal and spiritual powers. His *Pro regibus apologia* of 1581 was an attack upon Calvinist resistance theory in general, and George Buchanan in particular. His defence of Mary Queen of Scots after her execution in 1587 was widely known. He held office as a judge at Poitiers.
SECONDARY LITERATURE (part II): Weill 1891; Allen 1941.

BOCCALINI, TRAIANO
c. 1556–1613. From Loreto in the Papal States, where, after a training in law at the Universities of Perugia and Padua, he held low-ranking administrative posts. He died at Venice (but the story of his murder has been shown to be without foundation). His *Ragguagli da Parnasso* (satirical 'News from Parnassus') were published in 1612–13; his *Pietro del Paragone Politico* (a more outspoken continuation of the *Ragguagli*), posthumously, in 1615; and the *Osservationi sopra Cornelio Tacito*, only in 1678, in a volume entitled *Bilancia Politica*.
SECONDARY LITERATURE (part IV): Meinecke 1957; Varese 1958.

BODIN, JEAN
1529/30–96. Born at Angers, studied civil law at Toulouse, where he also taught. Practised as an *avocat* in Paris in the 1560s, when he also wrote his *Methodus ad facilem historiarum cognitionem* (1566) and his *Response à M. de Malestroit* (1568) on price-inflation. He joined the duke of Alençon's household in 1571 and took part in the 1576 meeting of the Estates at Blois. The same year saw the publication of his *Les Six Livres de la République*, of which a Latin version appeared ten years later. He became *procureur du roi* for Laon in 1587 and collaborated with the Catholic League. His controversial (and posthumous) *Colloquium Heptaplomeres* argued for religious toleration and indicated that his own religious belief had a Judaised character.
SECONDARY LITERATURE (part II): Mesnard 1952; McRae, in Bodin 1962; Franklin 1963, 1973; Denzer 1973; Skinner 1978; Rose 1980.

BOSSUET, JACQUES-BENIGNE
1627–1704. A Catholic controversialist and orator, Bossuet was born at Dijon, and educated at the Jesuit college there, and then at Paris. He was ordained priest and took a doctorate of divinity in 1652. In 1669 he was designated bishop of Condom, but resigned on becoming tutor to the Dauphin in 1670. In 1681 he was appointed bishop of Meaux. He was renowned for the eloquence of his funeral orations. His outlook was typical of the Gallican brand of Catholic orthodoxy, viewing monarchical absolutism as a bulwark against papalist pretensions. Bossuet's writings include the *Discours sur l'histoire universelle* (1681) – a providentialist account of history – and his main political work, the *Politique tirée des propres paroles de l'Ecriture sainte*, written in two stages and finally published posthumously in 1709.
SECONDARY LITERATURE (part III): Martimort 1953; Calvet 1968.

Biographies

BOTERO, GIOVANNI

1544–1617. From Bene in Piedmont, Botero joined the Jesuits and taught in Jesuit colleges in Italy and France, but was recalled from Paris because of his political activities during the religious wars. He became secretary to Carlo Borromeo, archbishop of Milan and adviser to his nephew Federico; his *Relazioni Universali*, a geopolitical world survey (published in 1591), originated as a collection of information on the environment of Catholic missions. From 1599 to 1610 he was in the service of the duke of Savoy. His best-known work is the *Ragione di Stato* (1589), the first of a long line of books discussing 'reason of state'. His analysis of urban growth, the *Grandezza delle città* (1588) also deserves an important place in intellectual history.

SECONDARY LITERATURE (part IV): Meinecke 1957; Chabod 1967.

BOUCHER, JEAN

1548–1644. A member of a prominent Parisian bourgeois family, Boucher taught at Reims for some years before joining the Sorbonne in 1576. He served as prior, then rector of the university, taking his doctorate in theology in 1583. Appointed curé of Saint-Benoît, he became a fervent member of the Catholic League, preaching sermons and writing satires and treatises against Henri III and his favourite, the duc d'Epernon. He was a leader of the revolutionary radical group, the Sixteen, and called for the assassination of Henri III and Henri IV (*De iusta Henrici Tertii abdicatione*, 1589). He fled to the Netherlands when Henri IV recovered Paris in 1594, and lived at Tournai until his death.

SECONDARY LITERATURE (part II): Baumgartner 1975; Salmon 1987.

BRACCIOLINI, POGGIO

1380–1459. Born at Terranuova near Montepulciano, Poggio became a member of the humanistic circle around Coluccio Salutati in Florence. Working with Niccolò Niccoli, he took part in the discovery of many little-known Latin classical texts, especially during his time at the Council of Constance (1414–18). He served in the papal curia for much of his career, and in 1453–8 was chancellor of Florence. In this period he wrote a history of Florence from the mid-fourteenth century to the Peace of Lodi. Poggio engaged in famous controversies with other humanists, notably Guarino of Verona and Lorenzo Valla. His political and social writings, notably the dialogue. *On Avarice* are more remarkable for vivid satire than for strong positions.

SECONDARY LITERATURE (part I): Walser 1914; Kohl and Witt 1978, pp. 231–9.

BRADY, ROBERT

1627–1700. Educated at Cambridge in arts and medicine, master of Gonville and Caius College from 1660 until his death, having gone into exile after the parliamentary victory in the Civil War. He served Charles II and James II as physician and took to historical scholarship late in life, entering the controversy over the history of English institutions in 1681. In his major works, *Introduction to the Old English History* (1684) and *A Complete History of England* (1685–1700), Brady emphasises the importance of the Norman conquest and argued for strong monarchical power.

SECONDARY LITERATURE (part III): Pocock 1951, 1957; Weston 1972; Weston and Greenberg 1981.

BRAMHALL, JOHN

1594–1663. The epitome of Cavalier Anglican churchmanship, he became a bishop in Ireland in 1634 and was an energetic executor of Archbishop Laud's and Charles I's policies. He was jailed in 1641, and later fled to Paris. Here he met Hobbes; their famous controversy concerning 'liberty and necessity' was published in the 1650s. In 1661 he became archbishop

Biographies

of Armagh. In the nineteenth century his works were published in the Library of Anglo-Catholic Theology.
SECONDARY LITERATURE (part V): Bowle 1951; Mintz 1962.

BRANDOLINI, AURELIO LIPPO
c. 1454–97. Born in Florence, he emigrated around 1466 with his father to Naples, where he received, although half-blind (lippus), a humanist education. Author of poems in Latin and Italian, of an oration on the dignity of the art of war and of literature, and of a commentary on the Georgics, he went to Rome in c. 1480 and to Buda in 1489, where he composed for King Matthias Corvinus De humanae vitae conditione et toleranda corporis aegritudine and the De comparatione reipublicae et regni, completed in Florence after the death of Matthias in 1490, and dedicated to Lorenzo de Medici. Around 1491 he joined the Augustinian order in Florence.
SECONDARY LITERATURE (part I): Thorndike 1929, pp. 233–60; Dizionario biografico degli Italiani, XIV, pp. 26–8.

BRUNI, LEONARDO
1370–1444. Born in Arezzo, Bruni became the preeminent protégé of Salutati and a deft student of the Byzantine scholar Manuel Chrysoloras. He translated and adapted numerous Greek works, providing versions of Aristotle's Politics and the pseudo-Aristotelian Oeconomica, among other works, using a more classical and attractive Latin than the medieval versions. His own works on moral philosophy and history (notably the History of the Florentine People) and his early Praise of Florence established him as the most eloquent of all Renaissance spokesmen for the Ciceronian view that the only life worthy of a free man was active life in the service of the republican state. He served as chancellor of Florence from 1427 until his death.
SECONDARY LITERATURE (part I): Baron 1967, 1968, 1988; Kohl and Witt 1978, pp. 121–33; Griffiths et al. 1987.

BUCER, MARTIN
1491–1551. A reformer of humanist sympathies who had become a Dominican friar in 1506, secured papal dispensation from his vows in 1521, and married in 1522, he began to preach a modified version of Luther's evangelical theology in 1523 and went on to lead the reform at Strasburg for the next quarter of a century. As the natural leader of the Reformed churches of Switzerland, the Rhineland and South Germany after Zwingli's death in 1531, he sought unsuccessfully to mediate between Protestants and Catholics. In 1549 he went to England, taught at Cambridge, and set forth his ideas for the reform of Christian society in his De regno Christi, posthumously published in 1551.
SECONDARY LITERATURE (part II): bibliography in De Kroon and Krüger 1976.

BUCHANAN, GEORGE
1506–82. Educated at St Andrews and Paris (with John Mair among his teachers), he taught in Paris, Bordeaux, and Coimbra (where he fell foul of the Inquisition). He became one of the leading humanists of his generation, noted especially as a Latin poet, publishing Latin plays on biblical themes (Jephthes, Baptistes) and a Latin paraphrase of the psalms. Returning to Scotland in 1561 and converted to Calvinism, he served as moderator of the General Assembly of the Kirk and later as keeper of the privy seal and tutor to the young king James VI. He developed his political ideas in defence of the deposition of Mary Stuart, especially in his De jure regni apud Scotos (written 1567–8, published 1579). His Rerum Scoticarum Historia was completed shortly before his death.
SECONDARY LITERATURE (part II): Trevor-Roper 1966; Skinner 1978; McFarlane 1981; Mason 1982; Salmon 1987.

Biographies

BUDÉ, GUILLAUME

1468–1540. The greatest Hellenist of his day, Budé was a champion not only of 'encyclopaedic' humanism – *Philologia*, which was the title of one of his scholarly works – but also of the French monarchy and its cultural mission. Following Italian antecedents, especially Lorenzo Valla, and Angelo Poliziano, he carred on the critical, philological, and historical study of Roman law in his *Annotations on the Pandects* of 1508, which assailed the ignorance and philistinism of legal scholasticism and contained digressions on French institutions such as the *parlement* of Paris and his own office (*maître des requêtes*). Budé's political views are also displayed in his *Institution of the Prince*, which was a more conventional and moralistic contribution to the 'Mirror of Princes' genre, closer to that of his rival Erasmus than to Machiavelli.

SECONDARY LITERATURE (part I): Kelley 1970a; McNeil 1975.

CAJETAN, TOMMASO DE VIO, CARDINAL

1468–1534. Born at Gaeta, he entered the Dominican order in 1484 and studied at Naples, Bologna, and Padua until 1493. At Padua he taught philosophy in the Thomist mode and theology from 1495 to 1499. After teaching for two years in Milan, he went to Rome, where he taught philosophy and scripture. As the master-general of the order, he took part in the fifth Lateran Council from 1512 to 1517. He became cardinal in the latter year and was deeply involved in theological controversy with Luther. In addition to his important Aristotelian commentaries, his most influential work was his edition, with commentary, of Aquinas' *Summa Theologiae*; but for specifically political ideas his controversial writings of 1511–12 – *Auctoritas Papae et Concilii sive Ecclesiae Comparata* and *Apologia de Comparatione Auctoritatis Papae et Concilii* – are of particular significance.

SECONDARY LITERATURE (part I): Hennig 1966; Wicks, in Cajetan 1978; *Dictionnaire d'Histoire et de Géographie Ecclésiastiques; Dictionnaire de Théologie Catholique.*

CALVIN, JOHN

1509–64. His career as a lawyer, based on training at Orleans, and as a classical humanist, based on study in Paris, was cut short by a sudden conversion to Protestantism. He fled to Basle and there published in 1536 the first edition of his *Institutes of the Christian Religion*, which he expanded and revised for the rest of his life. It became the most influential single summary of Protestant theology, and includes occasional reflections on politics. After brief periods as public lecturer in Geneva and as pastor to a church of French refugees in Strasburg, the city of Geneva in 1541 asked him to lead its Reformed church. He spent the rest of his life making of that city a 'Protestant Rome', a model community that profoundly influenced the life and thought of the Reformed throughout the world.

SECONDARY LITERATURE (part II): Bohatec 1937; Chenevière 1937; Parker 1975; Lloyd 1981a; Höpfl 1982.

CAMPANELLA, TOMMASO

1568–1639. A shoemaker's son of Calabria, Campanella entered the Dominican order in 1582. His defence of Telesio, Galileo, and the validity of empirical observation caused him to be examined before the Holy Office in Padua. He argued in favour of papal world supremacy but in 1599 was committed to a Neapolitan prison on charges of heresy and conspiracy. He was to remain in confinement for the next twenty-seven years. During this time he wrote many works, including the *Città del Sole* and his defence of Galileo. Released in 1626 he fled to France in 1634 and placed himself under the protection of Richelieu and Louis XIII. His last years were spent working for the conversion of the Protestants and trying to prolong his life by astrology.

SECONDARY LITERATURE (part II): Meinecke 1957; Bonansea 1969.

Biographies

CARAFA, DIOMEDE

1406/8–87. Neapolitan statesman and soldier. Having entered the service of Alfonso of Aragon, king of Naples, he became one of the chief counsellors of his son and successor Ferrante, who conferred high offices on him. He wrote a number of memoranda (*memoriali*) containing advice for princes, among them the *Memoriale sui doveri del principe* for Eleonora of Aragon, wife of Ercole d'Este, duke of Ferrara, another for her brother Alfonso, duke of Calabria, heir to the Neapolitan throne, for whom he also wrote, during the war of the Pazzi conspiracy, a treatise on the art of war. There are two Latin translations of the *Memoriale*, one of them, by Giovanni Battista Guarino, commissioned by Eleonora.
SECONDARY LITERATURE (part I): Persico 1899; *Dizionario Biografico degli Italiani*, XIX, pp. 524–30.

CARBONE, LODOVICO

1435–82. A student of Guarino da Verona, Carbone lectured at Ferrara in the 1450s and wrote many orations and dialogues. The one in memory of Guarino provided a very influential portrait of the greatest of humanist teachers.
SECONDARY LITERATURE (part I): Garin 1952, p. 381.

CASAUBON, ISAAC

1559–1614. A classical scholar, born in Geneva. His parents were Huguenot refugees. Casaubon taught at Geneva and Montpellier before moving to Paris, where in 1604 he became keeper of the royal library. In 1610 he was invited to England and he spent the remainder of his life there. In addition to producing texts of a number of classical authors, Casaubon also defended Venice against the Interdict in *De libertate ecclesiastica* (1607), and attacked papalist ideas in *Ad Frontonem Ducaeum S.J. Theologum Epistola* (1611), and in *De rebus sacris et ecclesiasticis exercitationes XVI* (1614).
SECONDARY LITERATURE (part III): Pattison 1892.

CASTELLIO, SEBASTIAN (Chateillon, Sébastien)

1515–63. Born in Savoy, he received a humanist education at Lyons. In 1541 he went to Geneva, recommended by Calvin, as rector of the college there; but his theological and scriptural views – notably his rejection of the belief that Christ descended into hell and his regarding the Song of Solomon as simply an erotic poem – alienated him from Calvin and he left Geneva in 1544 for Basle, where he spent the rest of his life. In 1554 he published, pseudonymously, his *De Haereticis*, condemning the execution of Servetus and strongly defending religious toleration. He also published, in the early 1550s, Latin and French translations of the Bible.
SECONDARY LITERATURE (part II): Buisson 1892; Ozment 1973.

CASTIGLIONE, BALDASSARE

1478–1529. Born in Mantua and educated there and in Milan, he accompanied Francesco Gonzaga in his campaign against the Spaniards in the kingdom of Naples in 1503. He then served the duke of Urbino on diplomatic missions, including one to England in 1506. Sent to Spain as papal nuncio in 1524, he died there five years later. His most celebrated work *Il libro del cortegiano*, begun in Urbino as early as 1507, was published in 1528. It achieved wide currency throughout Europe and was translated into English by Sir Thomas Hoby in 1561. Castiglione also wrote poems in both Latin and Italian and left important correspondence.
SECONDARY LITERATURE (part I): Cartwright 1908; Woodhouse 1978.

CHARRON, PIERRE

1541–1603. The son of a Paris bookseller, Charron studied philosophy and law before becoming a priest, a well-known preacher, and a canon of Condom. He adhered to the

667

Catholic League for a short time in 1589, but he became acquainted with Montaigne at this period and came to share his scepticism (in 1600 Charron had the words 'je ne scay' inscribed over the door of his house at Condom). His *Trois Vérités* appeared in 1594, under a pseudonym, and his *Sagesse* in 1601 (it was reprinted in 1604 with cuts, and in 1607 with additions).
SECONDARY LITERATURE (part IV): Battista 1966; Abel 1978, pp. 153–227; Keohane 1980, pp. 135–54.

CHASSENEUZ, BARTHELEMY DE
1480–1541. Born near Autun of bourgeois parentage, Chasseneuz studied law at several universities including Bologna, Turin, and Pavia before graduating doctor *in utroque jure* in 1502. Having already acted as *maître des requêtes* to the French governor of the Milanais, he went on diplomatic missions before returning to Autun in 1506, to practise as an *avocat* and then to serve as *bailli*. His *Commentaria in consuetudines Burgundiae*, which established his reputation, was published fragmentarily in 1517 and fully in 1528. *Conseiller* successively in the *parlements* of Dijon and Paris, he became in 1532 *président* in the *parlement* of Aix. Chasseneuz sought vigorously to reform the latter court, and he may have inspired the major Provençal judicial reform of 1535.
SECONDARY LITERATURE (part II): Pignot 1880.

CLARENDON, EARL OF: *see* HYDE, EDWARD

COKE, SIR EDWARD
1552–1634. A learned lawyer, judge of incalculable influence, and common law champion of parliamentary privilege and national liberties, Coke was educated at Trinity College, Cambridge, and the Inner Temple. Called to the bar in 1578, he became solicitor-general, speaker of the House of Commons, and attorney-general under Elizabeth; and under James I, chief justice of the common pleas (1606), and of king's bench (1613). Dismissed in 1616, he reappeared in the parliaments of the 1620s, where he was conspicuous among the promoters of the *Protestation* and the Petition of Right. After the first part of the *Institutes* appeared in 1628, Charles I, fully alert to the dangers of Cokean historiography, seized Coke's papers; and the last three parts remained in manuscript until rescued by the Long Parliament.
SECONDARY LITERATURE (part III): Thompson 1948; Kenyon 1966, 1986; Russell 1979; Weston and Greenberg 1981.

CONTARINI, GASPARO
1483–1542. Venetian patrician; held high offices in the republic before being created cardinal by Paul III in 1535. A leading figure in the movement of Catholic reform; author of works on philosophical and theological subjects and on ecclesiastical reform. He began the composition of the *De magistratibus et republica Venetorum* during his embassy to Charles V (1521–5) and completed it in Venice between 1531 and 1534. First published in Paris in 1543, in French in 1544, and in English in 1599, the work long remained the authoritative description of the Venetian constitution.
SECONDARY LITERATURE (part I): Gilbert 1969; *Dizionario Biografico degli Italiani*, XXVIII, pp. 172–92.

COQUILLE, GUY
1523–1603. Born at Decize into a family active in the judicial and municipal life of Nevers, Coquille studied arts in Paris (Collège de Navarre) followed by law at Padua and then at Orleans. In 1550 he joined the Paris bar, but soon returned to Decize and in 1568 was elected

Biographies

premier échevin of Nevers. In 1571 he became the duchy's *procureur-général* and remained there despite offers of office in the capital. A deputy at the Orleans and at the Blois Estates General (1560–1, 1576), Coquille commenced thereafter to write on law and history. His works, which included tracts on customs, an *Institution au droit des françois* and his *Histoire du pays et duché de Nivernois*, were published posthumously.

SECONDARY LITERATURE (part II): Maumigny 1910.

CORAS, JEAN DE

1513–72. Best known as the judge in the case of Martin Guerre, Coras was a distinguished professor of law at the Universities of Toulouse, Angers, and Orleans, and a convert to Protestantism. He commented extensively on the texts of Roman law and wrote various works on legal theory and practice, such as his *De Iuris arte libellus* of 1560. Arguing that jurisprudence was both 'art' and 'science', Coras carried on the ancient project of 'reducing law to an art' in the context of modern theories of 'method' and neo-Aristotelian conceptions of legal and political 'causes'.

SECONDARY LITERATURE (part I): Fell 1983–7.

COWELL, JOHN

1554–1611. Cowell was regius professor of civil law in Cambridge from 1594, and master of Trinity Hall from 1598. He was a close ally of Richard Bancroft, archbishop of Canterbury, whom he served as vicar-general from 1608, and to whom he dedicated his most famous work, the *Interpreter* (1607), a law dictionary. The political opinions expressed in this book were typical of the higher clergy under James I, but the candour with which Cowell voiced his absolutism aroused hostility in the House of Commons, and the king found it politic to suppress the work in 1610. It was reissued unaltered in 1637.

SECONDARY LITERATURE (part III): McIlwain 1918, appendix B; Sommerville 1986b, pp. 121–7.

CRAIG, SIR THOMAS

1538–1608. Educated at St Andrews from 1552, and Paris from 1555, Craig studied law under the celebrated legists Pierre Rebuffi and François Baudouin. Returning to Scotland in 1561, he was at first a barrister, and then justice-depute for the earl of Argyll. In 1566 he was the judge at the trial of underlings involved in the murder of Rizzio, secretary to Mary Queen of Scots, and in 1567 he presided at a similar trial of minor conspirators implicated in the murder of her husband, Lord Darnley. He became sheriff-depute of Edinburgh in 1573. An expert in feudal law, he published *Ius Feudale* in 1603. He also wrote on the claim of James VI and I to the English throne.

SECONDARY LITERATURE (part II): Pocock 1957.

CROMÉ, FRANÇOIS MORIN DE

fl. 1589–93. He came from a well-connected legal family in Burgundy. Like his father, he began his career as a judge in the *parlement* of Dijon and moved to Paris to become a magistrate in the *grand conseil*. After the assassination of Henri III in 1589, Cromé joined the revolutionary element in the Parisian League known as the Sixteen. He bore a grudge against Barnabé Brisson, the first president of the Leaguer *parlement* in Paris, and in 1591 Cromé and several confederates murdered Brisson as a suspected traitor to the League. Cromé escaped retribution, and while in hiding in 1593 wrote the radical tract *Dialogue d'entre le maheustre et le manant*.

SECONDARY LITERATURE (part II): Ascoli, in Cromé 1977; Barnavi 1980; Barnavi and Descimon 1985.

Biographies

CUJAS, JACQUES

1520–90. After studying civil law at the University of Toulouse, Cujas, the greatest of the 'elegant' or philological school of jurisprudence, taught at various times during the religious wars at the Universities of Cahors, Valence, and especially Bourges. Although he also wrote polemical works after the St Bartholomew's Day massacres, his scholarly life was dedicated to exegeses of the Digest and other texts of Roman law, which were collected in his massive *Observationes et Emendationes* and which were aimed at restoring the historical meaning, context, and form of classical jurisprudence. Students of Cujas, including Etienne Pasquier and the brothers Pithou, carried his philological and historical techniques over into the study of medieval law and institutions, and helped establish the fame of Cujas as the principal restorer of Roman law.

SECONDARY LITERATURE (part I): Berriat-Saint-Prix 1821.

CUMBERLAND, RICHARD

1631–1718. Became a fellow of Magdalene College Cambridge in the 1650s, and was a friend of Samuel Pepys and of the lawyer Sir Orlando Bridgeman, Lord Keeper under Charles II, to whom his great work of jurisprudence is dedicated. He was made bishop of Peterborough in 1691. His career was unremarkable, but his *De Legibus Naturae* (1672), translated as *A Treatise of the Laws of Nature* (1727), had a considerable influence on eighteenth-century ethical theory and jurisprudence. He was, broadly, a 'theological utilitarian', and despite criticising Hobbes, he shares many of his premises.

SECONDARY LITERATURE (part V): Tuck 1979; Kirk 1987.

DE DOMINIS, MARC'ANTONIO

1560–1624. The Catholic archbishop of Spalato (Split), De Dominis sided against the papacy at the time of the Venetian Interdict. Dissatisfaction with the church of Rome led him to England in 1616. There he was made Dean of Windsor and Master of the Savoy, but he became disillusioned with the English church, and in 1622 returned to Rome. Unable to persuade the authorities that he was sincere in renouncing his earlier views, De Dominis ended his life a prisoner of the Inquisition. He translated Bacon's *De sapientia veterum* into Italian, and his writings include a work on optics, but by far his most important book was *De republica ecclesiastica* (3 vols., 1617–22). The first two volumes were published by James I's printer and dedicated to the king, with whose opinions they largely agreed. The work included an attack on Suárez.

SECONDARY LITERATURE (part III): Malcolm 1984.

DE LA COURT (or Van Den Hove), PIETER and JOHAN

1618–85 (Pieter); 1622–60 (Johan). Pieter studied at Leiden; travelled abroad 1641–3 (meeting Comenius in London in 1642). He returned to Leiden University in 1643 as a theological student and became a passionate Cartesian. Next he studied medicine under Regius at Utrecht, 1645–8, and then entered the family business (cloth merchants). Supporting the republican cause in the 1650s, he published a succession of political works in the 1660s, probably incorporating material from his brother Johan's papers. He addressed a manuscript on trade to Harrington in 1674. Johan also studied at Leiden, attending Boxhorn's lectures on constitutional theory in 1643. He entered the family business, and supported the republican cause in the 1650s.

SECONDARY LITERATURE (part IV): Van Thijn 1956.

DIGGES, DUDLEY

1613–43. Born in Kent, the son of Sir Dudley, a noted lawyer and politician, he was educated at University College, Oxford, and became a fellow of All Souls in 1633. A

670

Biographies

vigorous royalist polemicist from the outset of the Civil War, he published a number of tracts. The most important was *The Unlawfulness of Subjects taking up Arms* (1643), in reply to Henry Parker's *Observations*, which went through several editions and was reprinted at the Restoration. The tract is based mainly on natural-right arguments and thus is closer to the Hobbesian than to James I's and Filmer's school of royalist thought.
SECONDARY LITERATURE (part III): Allen 1938; Judson 1949; Tuck 1979, ch. 5.

DOMAT, JEAN

1625–96. A Jansenist sympathiser and friend of Pascal, Domat published in 1689 a masterwork which was an attempt to establish a system of French law on the basis of moral principles and is one of the classics of universal, 'natural law'. A generation before Montesquieu, Domat's *Loix civiles dans leur ordre naturel* sought the 'spirit of the laws' in nature, and tried to connect the private and public spheres, although in fact his work, which constituted an important source of inspiration for the Napoleonic Code, followed for the most part the substance and conventions of Roman law.
SECONDARY LITERATURE (part I): Voeltzel 1936; Todescan 1987.

DORLÉANS, LOUIS

1542–1629. Son of a Parisian *procureur* (solicitor) Dorléans became an *avocat*. He studied with the humanist and Latin poet Jean Dorat, and himself wrote poetry. A fervent Catholic, he joined the revolutionary group of the Paris Holy League, the Sixteen. He was a prolific propagandist for the League, posing as a Catholic Englishman warning French Catholics of the danger of a Protestant ruler. In 1589 he became *avocat-général* in the Leaguer *parlement* of Paris. Growing more conservative, he dissociated himself from the Sixteen and recommended the Leaguer estates not to accept the Tridentine decrees without Gallican safeguards. He fled from Paris to Antwerp in 1594 and published a satire vilifying Henri IV. He was allowed to return in 1603. In 1622 he published reflections on Tacitus' *Annals*.
SECONDARY LITERATURE (part II): Salmon 1987.

DUDLEY, SIR EDMUND

c. 1462–1510. Equipped for public service at Oxford and the law at Gray's Inn, Dudley served Henry VII in several capacities. He gained notoriety as the agent, with Richard Empson, of a policy of legal terror conducted by the king through the exploitation of bonds and recognisances. In the reaction after Henry's death he was found guilty of constructive treason and executed. Dudley's intellectual reputation rests on *The Tree of Commonwealth* (1510) written whilst under sentence in the Tower. It is an example of the reforming genre more famously represented by More's *Utopia*, analysing the commonwealth's ills and proposing remedies. For the most part conventionally moralistic, its theme of the immutable social order reflects a growing Erastian outlook associated with the common lawyers. His concern that the nobility equip themselves by education to ward off competition for public office from their social inferiors anticipates a problem addressed by Sir Thomas Elyot's *Boke Named the Governour* (1531).
SECONDARY LITERATURE (part I): Brodie 1948; Skinner 1978.

DUGDALE, SIR WILLIAM

1605–86. This distinguished medievalist won high praise for his *Monasticon*, written with Sir Roger Dodsworth, which began to appear in 1655; his *The Antiquities of Warwickshire* (1656), and his *The Baronage of England* (1675). His political sympathies were High Tory. While in Civil War Oxford he served as secretary of the royalist commission at Uxbridge. At the Restoration he received an appointment in the College of Arms, where in 1677 he became Garter King of Arms. He worked closely with Archbishop Sancroft in mounting

Biographies

Tory propaganda on behalf of James, duke of York. He reluctantly agreed to publish his highly coloured *Short View of the Late Troubles* (1681); and at his death he was preparing a second, enlarged edition.

SECONDARY LITERATURE (part III): Pocock 1957; Weston and Greenberg 1981; Weston 1987.

DU HAILLAN, BERNARD DE GIRARD

c. 1535–1610. Born at Bordeaux, the son of a local judge, Du Haillan was the protégé of the three brothers de Noailles, two of whom he accompanied on diplomatic missions to England and elsewhere. In 1561 he became secretary to the duke of Anjou, the future Henri III. Appointed royal historiographer by Charles IX, Du Haillan retained the post under that king's successors. In addition to his *De l'Estat et succez des affaires de France* (1570), his works included translations of a good deal of Latin and Italian verse, an *Histoire de France* (1576), and a *Discours de l'extrême cherté qui est aujourd'huy en France et sur les moyens d'y remédier* (1574).

SECONDARY LITERATURE (part II): Bonnefon 1908, 1915.

DU MOULIN, CHARLES

1500–66. Born at Paris, the son of an *avocat* in the *parlement*, Du Moulin studied civil law at Orleans and canon law at Poitiers before himself practising at the Paris bar. He emerged as the most distinguished French legist of his day, notably through his lifelong work on custom. Lutheran in his religious leanings from about 1539, he then turned to Calvinism only to break with that at the outbreak of the religious wars. His position was essentially 'Gallican' – witness his *Commentaire de l'édit des petites dates* (1552) and his *Conseil sur le fait du Concile de Trente* (1564); and that position was of a piece with his firm belief in the desirability of legal uniformity under the king.

SECONDARY LITERATURE (part II): Aubépin 1855; Filhol 1953; Thireau 1980.

DU PERRON, JACQUES DAVY, CARDINAL

1556–1618. Du Perron belonged to a Huguenot family which took refuge in Switzerland. A man of great erudition, he converted to Catholicism on coming to Paris in 1576, and became a court preacher. He supported Henri IV in the wars of the League, and became bishop of Evreux in 1591. In 1600 he got the better of the celebrated Huguenot Philippe Duplessis Mornay in a debate at Fontainebleau. He became a cardinal in 1604, and then archbishop of Sens and grand almoner. When Marie de Médicis became regent in 1610, he served on the royal council as her principal adviser on religious affairs. He was a moderate Ultramontane and spoke against the third estate's proposal at the Estates General of 1614 to pass a law excluding the pope from interference in French secular affairs. He presided at the assembly of notables at Rouen in 1617.

SECONDARY LITERATURE (part II): Feret 1877; Hayden 1974.

DUPLESSIS MORNAY, PHILIPPE: see MORNAY, PHILIPPE DUPLESSIS

DU VAIR, GUILLAUME

1556–1621. Born in a Parisian *famille de robe*, he studied law and proceeded in 1572 to the Paris bar. After a period in the service of the duke of Alençon, he returned to Paris in 1582 and wrote his *Discours politiques* (1586). He played a mediating role in the conflict over the Catholic League, writing *De la Constance* during the siege of Paris in 1590 and his *Exhortation à la paix* in 1592. He was later *maître des requêtes, conseiller d'état*, and in 1616–17 *garde des sceaux*. He became bishop of Lisieux in 1618. He was one of the major representatives of the tradition of Christian Stoicism.

SECONDARY LITERATURE (part IV): Radouant 1908; *Dictionnaire de spiritualité*, III, pp. 1554–7; *Dictionnaire d'Histoire et de Géographie Ecclésiastiques*, XIV, pp. 1211–13.

Biographies

EACHARD, JOHN

c. 1636–97. Elected master of St Catharine's College Cambridge in 1675, vice-chancellor in 1679 and 1695. He is known to church historians for his *Grounds and Occasions of the Contempt of the Clergy* (1670). His two dialogues, *Mr Hobbes's State of Nature Considered* (1672) and *Some Opinions of Mr Hobbes* (1673) were immensely successful. Their clever parodies and jaunty conversational wit put Augustan prose at the service of a conventional theological attack on Hobbes. Reprinted as late as 1774, they appeared in German translation in 1680. The Tory journalist Oldisworth, who published dialogues against Hobbes, Locke, and Whiggism, drew heavily from the 'famous dialogue' of 'the incomparable Eachard' (1709, p. xiv).
SECONDARY LITERATURE (part V): Bowle 1951; Mintz 1962.

ELYOT, SIR THOMAS

c. 1490–1546. Elyot was a member of Thomas More's circle and, like More, attained high office as secretary to the king's council in the latter part of Wolsey's administration. He differed from More both on the issue of the royal divorce (conducting an embassy to Charles V in support of Henry VIII's case in 1531) and that of the royal ecclesiastical supremacy. However, he was not closely associated with the regime of the 1530s and withdrew to write. His best-known work, *The Boke Named the Governour* (1531), belongs to the genre best represented by Castiglione's *Book of the Courtier* (1528), which brought humanism to bear on the task of transforming the European nobility from chivalric warriors to civil courtiers. The book elaborates a Neoplatonic conception of the hierarchic cosmic order. Elyot shared More's enthusiasm for developing the vernacular, producing many translations from the classical corpus, the first full Latin–English dictionary (1538), as well as several moral and devotional essays.
SECONDARY LITERATURE (part I): Lehmberg 1960; Major 1964.

ERASMUS, DESIDERIUS

1466–1535. After being schooled under the Brethren of the Common Life, and abandoning a monastic vocation, Erasmus spent his career as a peripatetic scholar. Unconstrained by princely service or university teaching, he moved about Europe's centres of scholarship, advancing humanism through research, the production of critical texts, the development of a literature on stylistics and pedagogy, an admonitory propaganda. The controlling inspiration was the vision of a reformed *Respublica Christiana*, Christendom renewed spiritually, culturally, and politically. It can be summarised in the notion of the *Philosophia Christi*, the perfection of human wisdom through divine revelation. The philosophical basis is laid out in the *Antibarbari* (1488–93); the idea is popularised in the devotional classic, *Enchiridion Militis Christiani* (1516). Meanwhile, Erasmus delivered devastating critiques of late medieval mores in *Encomium moriae* (1508) and in brillinat essays in succeeding editions of the *Adagia*. Later he turned to a furious assault on Luther, beginning with *De libero arbitrio* (1524).
SECONDARY LITERATURE (part I): Huizinga 1952; Kisch 1960; Tracy 1978; Bradshaw 1982.

FAUCHET, CLAUDE

1530–1602. Fauchet was the son of a *procureur* at the Paris Châtelet, and himself became a judge there. In 1568 he received a higher office as second president of the *cour des monnais*, advancing to first president in 1581. Although he had been trained in law at Orleans, he had strong literary interests, and frequented the circle of Pierre Ronsard. He left Paris during the wars of the League, and returned there in the train of the victorious Henri IV in 1594. He was one of the greatest antiquarians of his time, and published collections of medieval literary and historical sources. He also wrote a work on the origin of French magistracies, and translated Tacitus.
SECONDARY LITERATURE (part II): Espiner-Scott 1938; Kelley 1970.

Biographies

FILMER, SIR ROBERT

1588–1653. A Kentish gentleman, one of eighteen children, Filmer was educated at Trinity College, Cambridge, and Lincoln's Inn. Knighted in 1619, he inherited his father's estate in 1629. Filmer married the daughter and co-heiress of Martin Heton, bishop of Ely, and his friends included Peter Heylin, a Laudian cleric of outspokenly absolutist views. His ideas are typical of English absolutist thinking in the decades before the Civil War, though his main work, *Patriarcha*, was not published until 1680. During the Civil War he was briefly imprisoned by the parliamentarians. He wrote on blasphemy and witchcraft, and published political works including commentaries on Aristotle, Grotius, Hobbes, and Milton.
SECONDARY LITERATURE (part III): Laslett 1948; Schochet 1975; Daly 1979; Tuck 1986.

FLETCHER ANDREW

1655–1716. Heir to a country gentleman of Saltoun in East Lothian, Fletcher travelled abroad in his youth. He became associated with the Whig cause in Scotland from 1678, and joined Monmouth's unsuccessful invasion in 1685 and William III's successful one in 1688, although thereafter he struggled to contain William's powers in Scotland. His *Discourse concerning Militias* (1697–8) was the first of his major political writings, which offered incisive if nostalgic accounts of Scotland's political, economic, and social difficulties.
SECONDARY LITERATURE (part III): Robertson 1985.

FORTESCUE, SIR JOHN

c. 1395–*c*. 1477. The son of a Devonshire knight, Fortescue entered Lincoln's Inn. He was several times a member of parliament before becoming serjeant-at-law in about 1430. Having served on innumerable judicial commissions, he was appointed chief justice of King's Bench in 1442. Displaced and attainted in 1461 owing to his Lancastrian allegiance, he accompanied the queen and Prince Edward abroad. He returned with them to England in 1471 only to be captured at the battle of Tewkesbury, but eventually obtained a reversal of his attainder. Fortescue's principal works, the *De natura legis nature*, the *De laudibus legum Anglie*, and the *De dominio regale et politico*, appear all to have been composed during his decade of exile.
SECONDARY LITERATURE (part II): Chrimes, in Fortescue 1949; Burns 1985.

GANSFORT, JOHN WESSEL

c. 1419–89. Born at Groningen, he was first a pupil and then a teacher in the school at Zwolle, where he encountered the Brethren of the Common Life. After studying in the arts faculties of Cologne, Louvain, and Paris, he taught for three years at Cologne before returning to Paris in 1459, where he remained until about 1474, also twice visiting Rome. Back in Zwolle from 1475 he incurred some suspicion of heresy, but enjoyed episcopal protection and gained a considerable reputation. The last years of his life found him once more in Groningen, where he lived in the covent of the Poor Clares. Apart from correspondence, his surviving writings are on spiritual and doctrinal subjects. The most important item for his political thinking is the *De dignitate et potestate ecclesiastica*.
SECONDARY LITERATURE (part I): Miller, in Gansfort 1917, i; Van Rhijn 1933; Oakley 1988.

GARDINER, STEPHEN

c. 1490–1555. Trained in common and civil law, he came to play an important role in the unsuccessful diplomatic effort to secure papal annulment of Henry VIII's marriage to Catherine of Aragon. Appointed bishop of Winchester in 1531, he supported the royal supremacy over the English church and in its defence wrote his *De vera obedientia* (1535). His later opposition to the introduction of Protestant views led to his deprivation and

Biographies

imprisonment during the reign of Edward VI. Subsequently restored to his see by Mary Tudor, he accepted the restoration of Catholicism and became lord chancellor.
SECONDARY LITERATURE (part II): Muller 1926; Smith 1953.

GENTILI, ALBERICO

1552–1608. A jurist educated at Perugia, where his family was suspected of Protestantism. He fled to England, arriving in Oxford in 1580, where he taught law in the old scholastic style, attacking the legal humanists. Appointed regius professor of civil law in 1587, he then began publication of *De iure belli*, which established him as one of the founders of modern international law. He defended absolute monarchy in his *Regales disputationes*. He spent his last years in London, becoming advocate to the Spanish ambassador in 1605.
SECONDARY LITERATURE (part I): Phillipson, in Gentili 1933; Van der Molen 1937; Panizza 1981.

GENTILLET, INNOCENT

c. 1532–88. An active lay leader of the Protestant movement in the province of Dauphiné, particularly in the city of Vienne, Gentillet is nevertheless better known for the polemical treatises he published during two periods of exile in Geneva, from 1572 to 1578, and again from 1585 to his death in 1588. He was by training a jurisconsult and served as a member of the bi-confessional court of his native province between his periods of exile. He is best known for his *Antimachiavel*, first published in 1576, which links the amoral political thought of Machiavelli with the policy of the French royal government under the influence of Catherine de Médicis.
SECONDARY LITERATURE (part II): Meinecke 1957; Stewart 1969; Mastellone 1972.

GIANNOTTI, DONATO

1492–1573. Studied in Florence; between 1520 and 1525 lectured at Pisa on poetry, rhetoric, and Greek. When the republican regime was restored in 1527, he was elected to the post of secretary of the Ten which Machiavelli had held until 1512. Having been banished from the city after the fall of the republic in 1530, he composed the *Della repubblica fiorentina* and completed the final version of the *Libro della repubblica de' Viniziani*. After the assassination in 1527 of Duke Alessandro de' Medici, he joined the Florentine exiles at Bologna and Venice. In 1562 he settled in Venice, later in Padua, and finally in Rome. Among his literary works are Italian comedies and the *Dialogi de' giorni che Dante consumò nel cercare l'Inferno e 'l Purgatorio* (c. 1546), in which he extols the tyrannicide of Brutus. After the Sienese revolt against the Spanish in 1552, he wrote a *Discorso sopra il riordinare la repubblica di Siena*.
SECONDARY LITERATURE (part I): Ridolfi 1942; Starn 1968; Cadoni 1978b.

GOODMAN, CHRISTOPHER

c. 1520–1603. Educated at Oxford and became professor of divinity in 1548. After Mary Tudor's accession he left England for the continent and eventually settled in Geneva where, in 1555, he was appointed pastor for the church of English refugees. His *How Superior Powers Ought to be Obeyed* was published in Geneva in 1558. His writings denouncing women created a backlash in England which prevented his return there after Elizabeth's accession, and he spent six years in Scotland and four more in Ireland. He returned to England permanently in 1570 and was accused of nonconformity the following year.
SECONDARY LITERATURE (part II): Collinson 1967.

GOTT, SAMUEL

1613–71. A gentleman scholar, Gott was strongly connected with the gentry-ironmaster families of East Sussex and London. Educated at Cambridge and the Inns of Court he

Biographies

embodied that combination of classicism, hebraism, and millenarian piety to be found in the circles of Milton, Hartlib, Dury, and William Petty. He was elected to the Long Parliament in 1645 and in 1650 argued for *de facto* recognition of the new English republic. As well as *Nova Solyma* (1648) he published *An Essay of the True Happiness of Man* (1650) and *The Divine History of the Genesis of the World* (1670).

SECONDARY LITERATURE (part II): Begley, in Gott 1902; Patrick 1977; Davis 1981a, ch. 5.

GRÉGOIRE, PIERRE

1540–1617. After studying both canon and civil law Grégoire taught at Toulouse and Cahors. In 1582 Duke Charles III of Lorraine chose him as professor of both laws at Pont-à-Mousson, where Grégoire and William Barclay resisted Jesuit influence. Besides contributing to the debate on 'method' in the study of law, he published two major treatises: *Syntagma iuris universi* (1582) and *De republica* (1596), the latter modifying the absolutist views of Bodin.

SECONDARY LITERATURE (part I): Carlyle 1903–36, VI; Collot 1965; Gambino 1975.

GROTIUS, HUGO

1583–1645. Hugo Grotius (the Latinised name of Huig de Groot) was born at Delft in the United Provinces. He was educated at Leiden University, then became adviser to the Dutch statesman Oldenbarnevelt. In 1619 he was implicated in Oldenbarnevelt's fall, tried for treason and imprisoned; but he escaped and lived in exile until his death in 1645, acting as Swedish ambassador in Paris from 1634. He wrote a number of important works on Dutch politics, 1599–1619, and the manuscript *De Iure Praedae* on natural law (1605), one chapter of which was published as *Mare Liberum* (1609). His major work was *De Jure Belli ac Pacis* (1625), but his theological writings were also important, notably *De Veritate Religionis Christianae* (1627).

SECONDARY LITERATURE (part IV): Knight 1925; Tuck 1979, ch. 3.

GUEVARA, ANTONIO DE

c. 1480–1545. Born of an Asturian family, he became a page in the household of Prince Juan, son of Ferdinand and Isabella. After the prince's death in 1497, Guevara became a Franciscan and was later a celebrated preacher. He was successively inquisitor of Toledo and bishop first of Guadix and then of Mondeñado. His writings circulated widely in manuscript, the first to be published, and perhaps the most notable, being his *Relox de principes* (1529). He has been described as 'the courtier-writer *par excellence*'.

SECONDARY LITERATURE (part I): Castro 1956, pp. 53–72; Gibbs 1960; Grey 1973.

GUICCIARDINI, FRANCESCO

1483–1540. Born in Florence into a patrician family prominent under Lorenzo de'Medici, he began, after studying law, a public career in his city, and continued it, under the Medici popes Leo X and Clement VII, in the administration of the Papal States; in 1526–7 he was lieutenant of the pope in the army of the League of Cognac. After the fall of the last Florentine republic, he was governor of Bologna (1531–4) and then counsellor of Duke Alessandro de' Medici, and in 1527 played a leading role in securing Cosimo's succession. Author of two histories of Florence, the *Storia fiorentina* (1508–9) and the (fragmentary) *Cose fiorentine* (1528–9), and of the *Storia d'Italia* (1537–40), his greatest work. Apart from the *Dialogo del reggimento di Firenze* (c. 1521–c. 1525), he wrote a number of discourses on political subjects, an (unfinished) commentary on the *Discorsi* of Machiavelli (1530), maxims collected in the *Ricordi*, and memoirs.

SECONDARY LITERATURE (part I): Ridolfi 1960; Gilbert 1965; Sasso 1984.

Biographies

HAKEWILL, WILLIAM

1574–1655. One of Lincoln's Inn's most respected chief benchers, Hakewill was a member of the Society of Antiquaries and possessed copies of the *Modus*. These interests hardly endeared him to James I, nor did his opposition to impositions, yet he was made solicitor general to the queen. A veteran member of parliament, Hakewill was a proponent of the *Protestation* and in 1628 assisted Coke in a crucial conference with the Lords. Siding with the Long Parliament he became master in chancery and sat with the commissioners of the great seal to hear causes. Both his *Libertie of the Subject* and the *Manner of Holding Parliaments* were published in 1641, and the latter was enlarged as *Modus Tenendi Parliamentum* (1659, 1671).
SECONDARY LITERATURE (part III): Thompson 1948; Russell 1979; Pronay and Taylor 1980.

HALE, SIR MATTHEW

1609–76. Educated at Magdalen Hall, Oxford, and Lincoln's Inn, this legal historian and scholar was the most eminent lawyer and judge of his age. Living through the Civil War and Interregnum, he made the necessary accommodations. He was successively justice of the common pleas, lord chief baron of exchequer, and chief justice of king's bench. As a practising lawyer, he offered his services to Strafford, Laud, and Charles I, but subsequently chaired a law reform commission under Cromwell and served him as member of a trade committee of the council of state. He was an inactive member of Cromwell's first parliament and of the convention parliament of 1660. Among his published writings are *History of the Common Law* (1713) and *The Prerogatives of the King* (1976), both published posthumously.
SECONDARY LITERATURE (part III): Pocock 1957; Introductions to Hale 1971, 1976; Yale 1972.

HARDING, THOMAS

1516–72. Like John Jewel, whose defence of the Anglican church he refuted, Harding was a Devon man. He was educated at Winchester and New College, Oxford, where he became a fellow in 1536. He was appointed professor of Hebrew at Oxford and chaplain to Henry Grey, duke of Suffolk. He was a Protestant under Edward VI, but converted to Catholicism at the end of the reign, for which he was reproached by Lady Jane Grey, Suffolk's daughter. Under Mary he was chaplain to Bishop Gardiner. In 1558 he was deprived of his offices, and fled to Louvain. His various works against Jewel were published at Antwerp and Louvain in the years 1564–8.
SECONDARY LITERATURE (part II): Holmes 1982.

HARRINGTON, JAMES

1611–77. The eldest son of Sir Sapcote Harrington of Upton, Northamptonshire, Harrington was educated at Trinity College, Oxford, and thereafter travelled extensively in Europe. He avoided taking ideas in the Civil War, but in 1647, with parliament's approval, became an attendant to Charles I. His first published work, *Oceana* (1656), was his most important. It was followed by a series of shorter works. In 1659 he proposed a republican solution to the breakdown of authority that followed Cromwell's death, and chaired meetings of the Rota Club, a constitutional debating society. After the Restoration, when he published nothing, he was suspected (improbably) of conspiring against Charles II. His close friends included Henry Nevile and Andrew Marvell.
SECONDARY LITERATURE (part III): Fink 1945; Macpherson 1962; Smith 1971; Pocock, in Harrington 1977; Goldie 1987.

HAYWARD, SIR JOHN

c. 1564–1627. After taking his MA at Pembroke College, Cambridge, Hayward devoted himself to history and law. He was a client of Robert Devereux, earl of Essex, to whom in

Biographies

1599 he dedicated his account of the deposition of Richard II. His book was used as evidence of premeditation in Essex's trial after the failed coup of 1601. Hayward was imprisoned, but was restored to favour by James I, becoming historiographer to Prince Henry. He published an answer to Robert Parsons' *Conference about the Next Succession* in 1603. He was appointed to Chelsea College in 1610 and knighted in 1619. Among his other works were histories of the first Norman kings and of the reign of Edward VI.

SECONDARY LITERATURE (part II): Levy 1987.

HERLE, CHARLES

1598–1659. Puritan divine and political theorist, he was educated at Exeter College, Oxford. A period as tutor to the earl of Derby led to his acquiring the rich rectory of Winwick in Lancashire. Herle sympathised with the Long Parliament, and Anthony Wood thought him 'esteemed by the factious party the prime man of note and power among the clergy'. This remark was due to the widely influential *Fuller Answer* (1642), but also to Herle's services in the Westminster assembly, of which he became prolocutor in 1646. His tracts include *An Answer to Dr Ferne's Reply* (1643) and *Ahab's Fall* (1644). After Charles I's death Herle withdrew to Winwick and, reacting against the Commonwealth, was suspected of complicity in royalist plotting.

SECONDARY LITERATURE (part III): Weston 1965; Weston and Greenberg 1981.

HOBBES, THOMAS

1588–1679. The son of an Anglican priest, he studied at Oxford, 1603–8. Employed as tutor and secretary by the Cavendish family, he took his pupil on a tour of France and Italy in 1614–15. He worked occasionally as secretary to Bacon, *c*. 1618–25, and was a member of the Virginia Company, 1622–4. His translation of Thucydides appeared in 1629. He visited the continent again in 1629–30 and 1634–6, and developed an interest in continental science and philosophy. His first political work, *The Elements of Law*, was written in 1640. He lived in France, 1640–51, where he wrote *De Cive* (published 1642) and *Leviathan* (published 1651). He next returned to England and the service of the Cavendish family. He published a major work on logic and physics, *De copore* (1655), and engaged in scientific controversies with Wallis and Boyle in the 1650s and 1660s. Late works include *Behemoth* (a history of the Civil War) and *A Dialogue . . . of the Common Laws of England*: written in the 1660s, they were not published until 1679 and 1681 respectively.

SECONDARY LITERATURE (part IV): Polin 1953; Warrender 1957; Brown 1965; Watkins 1965; Skinner 1966a, 1966b, 1969, 1972; Cranston and Peters 1972; Pocock 1972; Oakeshott 1975; Raphael 1977; Reik 1977; Tuck 1979, 1989; Johnston 1986.

HOLBOURNE, SIR ROBERT

d. 1649. A great lawyer and royalist administrator, Holbourne was educated at Lincoln's Inn, where he became a bencher and reader in law. As a practising lawyer he defended William Prynne's *Histriomastix* (1633) and John Hampden's refusal to pay Ship Money. Holbourne was still anti-court when elected to the Short Parliament but was converted to the king's cause in the Long Parliament. At Oxford he was knighted, created DCL, and appointed attorney general to the prince of Wales. His reading on the statute of treason was published in 1642 and again in 1681. He sat in the parliament at Oxford and was at Uxbridge in 1645 but not at Newport in 1648. His last years were spent in London, where he was barred from the inns of court.

SECONDARY LITERATURE (part III): Weston 1980, 1987; Weston and Greenberg 1981; Daly 1983.

Biographies

HOOKER, RICHARD

1554–1600. Born near Exeter, and educated at the local grammar school, Hooker became a protégé of John Jewel and Edwin Sandys, two of Elizabeth's first episcopal appointees. He proceeded to Corpus Christi College, Oxford, where he became a fellow in 1577. He taught logic in the college and Hebrew in the university, and interested himself above all in theology. After a brief incumbency in Buckinghamshire he was appointed in 1585 to the mastership of the Temple and rapidly became embroiled in controversy with the Temple's puritan reader, William Travers. In 1591 he retired to the living of Boscombe in Wiltshire in order to write his *Lawes of Ecclesiasticall Politie*, moving finally (1595) to Bishopsbourne near Canterbury.

SECONDARY LITERATURE (part II): D'Entrèves 1939; Kearney 1952; Munz 1952; McGrade 1963; Cargill Thompson 1972; Sommerville 1983.

HOTMAN, FRANÇOIS

1524–90. Born at Paris, received his doctorate in law at Orleans, then practised and later taught law in Paris. After converting to Protestantism in 1547, he taught law successively in Lyons, Lausanne, and Strasburg, finally returning to France in 1563 to teach at Valence, then at Bourges. After the St Bartholomew's Day massacre, he fled to Geneva and taught there until 1578. He then moved to Basle, where he died. He was a prolific writer of both legal treatises and polemical tracts, such as his *Epistre envoiée au tigre de la France* of 1560. His most important contribution to political theory was his *Francogallia*, first published in 1573.

SECONDARY LITERATURE (part II): Reynolds 1931; Dennert 1968; Kelley 1973; Kingdon 1988.

HUNTON, PHILIP

1604–82. A puritan divine and political theorist, Hunton was educated at Wadham College, Oxford. He was schoolmaster at Avebury, minister at Devizes, and vicar in Westbury, Wiltshire. Later he was provost of Cromwell's university college at Durham. It disappeared at the Restoration, and so did his living at Westbury, where he is said to have held conventicles. His *Treatise of Monarchie* (1643) was one of the seminal tracts of the century. Published in two editions, it was defended in Hunton's *Vindication* (1644, 1651), reprinted during the Exclusion Crisis, burned by Oxford University in 1683, and reissued at the Revolution. Hunton was answered by Henry Ferne, Sir Robert Filmer, Robert Sheringham, and Nathaniel Johnston.

SECONDARY LITERATURE (part III): Judson 1964; Weston and Greenberg 1981; Wootton 1986.

HYDE, EDWARD (Earl of Clarendon)

1609–74. An opposition member of parliament in the early stages of the Long Parliament, Hyde joined Charles I's side in 1641, and shaped the king's more moderate pronouncements at the opening of the Civil War. He was Charles II's chief adviser in France in the 1650s and lord chancellor from 1660 until impeached and exiled in 1667. He devoted his last years to revising his classic *History of the Rebellion*, and to writing his *Autobiography* and *Brief View and Survey of Leviathan* (1676).

SECONDARY LITERATURE (part V): Wormald 1951.

JAMES VI and I

1566–1625. James became king of Scotland in 1567, and of England in 1603. He reacted strongly against the ideas of his tutor Buchanan and against the Presbyterians who dominated Scotland during his minority. In 1616 James published his collected writings in a substantial folio volume. Most of these works were concerned with questions of political theory, and included *The True Law of Free Monarchies* (1598), *Basilikon Doron* (1598; a book

Biographies

of advice for his son), and three treatises against papalist theories on church–state relations. James' ideas were absolutist, but he was willing to listen to criticism of his exercise of power. He did, however, resent attacks on the power itself, and this caused friction with parliament. The king's influence ensured that absolutist ideas were expressed with increasing frequency during his reign.

SECONDARY LITERATURE (part III): McIlwain, in James I 1918; Greenleaf 1964; Mason 1982; Sommerville 1986b.

JEWEL, JOHN

1522–71. As a fellow of Corpus Christi College, Oxford, Jewel fell under the influence of Peter Martyr Vermigli, the Italian Protestant professor of divinity from 1548. After the accession of Queen Mary Jewel fled to Frankfurt, where he supported the moderate Richard Cox against John Knox. He returned to England in 1559, and was consecrated bishop of Salisbury in the following year. Through his sermons at St Paul's Cross, his *Apology for the Church of England*, and other published works, he was the principal defender of the Anglican church in the first decade of Elizabeth's reign.

SECONDARY LITERATURE (part II): Cross 1969.

KECKERMANN, BARTHOLOMAEUS

1571–1608. Trained initially in theology and philosophy, Keckermann taught briefly as professor of Hebrew at Heidelberg in 1600 before returning to his native Danzig to teach philosophy until his death in 1608. Keckermann was an enterprising and untiring devotee of that 'methodising' and systematising tendency with which academics were so often preoccupied in the late sixteenth and early seventeenth centuries, even though he was more partial to Aristotle than to Ramus. Along with his *Systema disciplinae politicae* (1606) he wrote similarly entitled 'systems' of logic, mathematics, ethics, astronomy, theology, geometry, geography, and optics. His *Opera omnia* appeared in Geneva in 1614.

SECONDARY LITERATURE: *Neue Deutsche Biographie*.

KNOX, JOHN

1505–72. Having become a Protestant preacher in 1546, he spent several years in England but was forced to leave for the continent after Mary Tudor's accession. He served as pastor to the church of English refugees in Frankfurt until forced to leave in a dispute over church order; he then went to Geneva and became pastor of the English church there. He returned to Scotland in 1559 and was active in establishing the Reformation there, drawing up the Confession of Faith, the First Book of Discipline and the Book of Common Order. He published a number of political tracts, the best known of which was his *First Blast of the Trumpet Against the Monstrous Regiment of Women*, though the most thoughtful was his *Appellation to the Nobility*. He was minister of the High Kirk in Edinburgh until his death.

SECONDARY LITERATURE (part II): Janton 1967; Ridley 1968.

LANGUET, HUBERT

1518–81. He received his doctorate in law at Pádua in 1548. He converted to Protestantism after reading Melanchthon's works and spent two years in Wittenberg. After travelling extensively through Europe for several years, he returned to Paris in 1560 as diplomatic agent for the Elector of Saxony. He left in 1567 and carried out several missions for the Elector in Germany, being sent by the Elector in 1570 to Charles IX to support the cause of the Huguenots. He remained in Paris for two years and narrowly escaped death in the St Bartholomew's Day massacres. In 1576 the Elector made him diplomatic agent at the court of the emperor. The *Vindiciae contra tyrannos*, first published in 1579, is often attributed to him as well as to his friend Philippe Duplessis Mornay.

SECONDARY LITERATURE (part II): Chevreul 1852.

Biographies

LAS CASAS, BARTOLOME DE

1476–1566. Born in Seville, he studied law and went, in 1502, to Santo Domingo. He was ordained priest in 1510 and returned to the New World – to Cuba – in 1512. Two years later he gave up his grant of serfs and espoused the cause of the Indians, to which he devoted the rest of his long life. His attempts to reform the colonial regime, even with royal support, were frustrated. Having become a Dominican, he endeavoured to secure favourable conditions for the Indians of Peru before the Spanish conquest and undertook the pacification of northern Guatemala. He became bishop of Chiapas in Mexico in 1544, but in 1547 returned finally to Spain. His chief works were the product of his controversy over the treatment of the Indians with Ginés de Sepúlveda: *Apologética Historia; Historia General de las Indias; Brevissima Relación de la Destruyción de las Indias.*

SECONDARY LITERATURE (part II): Fabié 1879; Hanke 1949, 1959, 1974; Pagden 1987, ch. 4.

LAWSON, GEORGE

c. 1598–1678. A Presbyterian divine who supported the parliamentarian cause, and was a friend of Richard Baxter. His major work, *Politica sacra et civilis* (1660), a remarkable synthesis of English radical thought as developed in the 1640s and 1650s, has been credited with anticipations of Locke's theory of the dissolution of government. Lawson's ecclesiological and political ideas revived the ideas of Marsilius of Padua. Earlier there had appeared his *Examination of the Political Part of Mr Hobbes his Leviathan* (1657). Like Baxter (who copied him) his Presbyterianism did not prevent him from adopting philosophical positions which placed him close to Hobbes Anglican critics.

SECONDARY LITERATURE (part V): Bowle 1951; Franklin 1978; Condren 1989.

LE CARON, LOUIS CHARONDAS

1534–1613. A graduate in law of Bourges, where he studied with Baron and Baudoin, Le Caron was a man of letters, 'vernacular humanist', peripheral member of the *Pléiade*, and Platonist philosopher as well as jurist and historian of the French legal tradition. For him 'true philosophy' was active, not contemplative, and indeed he identified it with the profession of jurisprudence. Among his many works were his 'nationalist' panegyrics to Charles IX and his massive *Pandectes, ou Digestes du droit françois,* which correlated, and invidiously compared, the laws and institutions of the French monarchy with those of ancient Rome, and which represented an early contribution to the unification of French laws, an effort which he regarded as essential for the 'sovereign good' of the French nation.

SECONDARY LITERATURE (part I): Kelley 1976a.

LEIBNIZ, GOTTFRIED WILHELM

1646–1716. One of the greatest of German philosophers. He stands somewhat apart from figures like Descartes, Hobbes, Spinoza, and Locke (all of whom he criticised) in his determination to rescue what was valuable in Aristotle, Plato, and scholasticism, and somehow to synthesise them with modern materialist and sceptical insights. As a critic of Hobbes he generally appears remarkably Platonic. He was official historian at the court of the Elector of Hanover. He engaged with Catholics in search of a scheme to reunite Christendom; he quarrelled with Newton over which of them discovered calculus; and he undertook with Samuel Clarke a classic philosophical correspondence. Most of his political works are in the form of short essays (see Riley, in Leibniz 1972) but of special importance is his book-length *Theodicy* (1710).

SECONDARY LITERATURE (part V): Riley, in Leibniz 1972; Riley 1973; Jolley 1975, 1984.

LESCHASSIER, JACQUES

1550–1625. an *avocat* before the *parlement* of Paris until appointed *procureur-général* of that court by Henri IV. He defended the Salic law governing the descent of the French crown,

and in 1606 published a celebrated defence of Gallican independence based on ancient precedents. In 1607 he published a defence of the republic of Venice in its conflict with Pope Paul V.
SECONDARY LITERATURE (part II): Salmon 1987.

L'HÔSPITAL, MICHEL DE
1507–73. Born in the Auvergne, the son of a physician, L'Hôpital studied law at Padua and served in the Roman curia before returning to France and gaining through marriage the office of a *conseiller* in the Paris *parlement*. Thence he rose via the household of Henri II's sister and a succession of high-level judgeships to become chancellor in 1560. Coupling moderation in religion with a belief in strong monarchical rule, L'Hôpital sought judicial and administrative reforms, most notably through the edicts of Orleans (1561) and Moulins (1566). His writings, among them six volumes of Latin verse and numerous speeches, are no longer thought to include the *Traité de la réformation de la justice* once attributed partly to him.
SECONDARY LITERATURE (part II): Buisson 1950.

LILBURNE, JOHN
1615–57. Leveller. Second son of a Durham gentleman, he was apprenticed in London, and pilloried and imprisoned by the star chamber in 1638, for attacks on the bishops and calls for the separation of church and state. On his release he served in the parliamentary army, being the only officer to resign rather than take the Covenant. In 1645 his association with Walwyn and Overton began. His radical view of the rights of Englishmen led to his being imprisoned seven times, 1645–52, by various authorities (Houses of Commons and Lords, council of state). In 1649 and again in 1653 he was acquitted on charges of treason, but he was not released after his final acquittal, and died in prison, a Quaker. He wrote some eighty political pamphlets.
SECONDARY LITERATURE (part III): Greaves and Zaller 1982–4 and works cited there.

LIPSIUS, JUSTUS
1547–1606. From the neighbourhood of Brussels, the son of a burgomaster, Lipsius was educated by the Jesuits and at the university of Louvain. He became Latin secretary to Cardinal Granvelle and visited Rome in his retinue. He became a university teacher, lecturing at Jena, Leiden, and Louvain (and conforming to Lutheranism, Calvinism, and Catholicism respectively: it is thought he was a member of the underground religious group the Family of Love). Of his many works, the most famous are his editions of Tacitus and Seneca, his dialogue *De Constantia* (1584) and his treatise *Politicorum libri sex* (1589). He played an important part in launching both Tacitism and neo-Stoicism.
SECONDARY LITERATURE (part IV): Saunders 1955; Abel 1978, pp. 67–113; Oestreich 1982.

LOCKE, JOHN
1632–1704. Born in Somerset and educated at Westminster and Christ Church, Oxford. In 1667 he became physician to the earl of Shaftesbury and so was drawn into political activity. He wrote the *Two Treatises* during the Exclusion Crisis (1679–81) and *Letter Concerning Toleration* while in exile in Holland. Both books were published anonymously after his return to England in 1689. The other great works that have made him famous were also then published: *An Essay Concerning Human Understanding* (1690), *Thoughts Concerning Education* (1693), and *The Reasonableness of Christianity* (1695). A weak constitution and continuing controversy caused him to retire to Essex where he spent his last years defending and clarifying his unconventional views and his simple and austere ethics based on the gospels.

Biographies

SECONDARY LITERATURE (part V): Fox Bourne 1876; Cranston 1958; Macpherson 1962; Dunn 1969, 1985; Laslett in Locke 1970; Franklin 1978; Parry 1978; Tully 1980; Goldie 1983; Ashcraft 1986.

LUTHER, MARTIN

1483–1546. The son of a Saxon miner, he was educated at the University of Erfurt and went on to study and teach theology at the new University of Wittenberg, where, in 1511, he received the doctorate of theology and undertook the duties of professor of scripture which he was to discharge until his death. He had entered the Augustinian Eremites in 1507, and it was his unsuccessful struggle to find spiritual rest in the rigorous fulfilment of the monastic vocation that led eventually to his historic rejection of the theological foundations of medieval Catholicism. The extent of that rejection became unmistakably clear in the four crucial works he produced in 1520: *The Freedom of the Christian, The Babylonian Captivity of the Church, Address to the Christian Nobility,* and *On the Papacy at Rome.*
SECONDARY LITERATURE (part II): Bainton 1955; Cranz 1959; Bornkamm 1979; Cargill Thompson 1984.

MACHIAVELLI, NICCOLÒ

1469–1527. Son of a Florentine lawyer, elected in 1498 second chancellor of the republic. As secretary of the Ten he was active in Florentine diplomacy, his many missions taking him to France, Rome, Cesare Borgia, Germany, and various Italian cities. He achieved the establishment of a Florentine militia in the *contado* in 1506 and became secretary of the *Nove della Milizia*. His close association, from 1502, with Piero Soderini cost him his post when the Medici returned in 1512. Arrested on suspicion of conspiracy in 1513, he was released when Giovanni de' Medici became pope, but failed in his efforts to secure employment by the Medici. Commissioned in 1520 to write the history of Florence, he dedicated it to Clement VII in 1525. In 1526 he became secretary for the city's fortifications. He died shortly after the republican restoration in 1527. His works, besides *Il Principe*, the *Discorsi*, and the *Istorie fiorentine*, include the *Arte della guerra*, the life of Castruccio Castracani, and Italian poetry and plays, notably the *Mandragola*.
SECONDARY LITERATURE (part I): Chabod 1927; Gilbert 1938; Butterfield 1940; Baron 1961; Hale 1961; Gilbert 1965; Anglo 1969; Ridolfi 1972; Sasso 1980; Skinner 1981.

MAIR (Major), JOHN

c. 1468–1550. Born in East Lothian, and educated in Haddington, Cambridge, and Paris, where his first work was published in 1499. Graduating in theology in 1506, Mair soon became one of the most influential Parisian teachers of his generation. In 1518 he returned to Scotland to teach first at Glasgow and then at St Andrews. He went back to Paris in 1526 for five years, and in 1531 returned finally to Scotland and was provost of St Salvator's College, St Andrews, until his death. Mair's voluminous works include Aristotelian commentaries (especially on the *Ethics*, 1530) and a series of commentaries on Peter Lombard's *Sentences*, between 1509 and 1530. Also of importance for his political ideas are his 1518 commentary on St Matthew's gospel and his *Historia Majoris Britanniae* (1521)
SECONDARY LITERATURE (part I): Mackay, in Mair 1892, pp. xxix–cxxx; Durkan 1950a, 1950b; Burns 1954; Oakley 1962, 1964–5; Farge 1980, pp. 304–11; Burns 1981.

MARIANA, JUAN DE

1536–1624. Born in Talavera, Castile, Mariana became a Jesuit in 1554. He studied philology, theology, and history at Alcalá before teaching in Rome, Sicily, and Paris, and preaching even farther afield. In 1574 he returned homewards to Toledo and devoted

himself to writing. His *Historiae de rebus Hispaniae* was published at Toledo in 1592, his *De rege* appearing seven years later; the latter was written at Philip II's request and dedicated to Philip III. In his *De monetae mutatione* (1609) Mariana attacked monetary debasement and virtually alleged that Spain's fiscal administrators were guilty of fraud. A restive and independent-minded member of the Jesuits, he suffered in 1610 a year's imprisonment in a Franciscan house.
SECONDARY LITERATURE (part II): Backer and Backer 1853–61; Lewy 1960.

MARTYR, PETER: *see* VERMIGLI, PETER MARTYR

MELANCHTHON, PHILIP
1497–1560. A German scholar of deeply humanistic sympathies, he went on from studies at Heidelberg and Tübingen to become in 1518 professor of Greek at Wittenberg, where he began a lifelong friendship and collaboration with Martin Luther. Having embraced Luther's evangelical theology, he produced in his *Loci communes* (1521) – a work which he was to revise and amplify throughout his life – the first systematic presentation of Lutheran doctrine. In doctrinal matters he was of mediating disposition, opposing Zwingli's eucharistic teaching at the Colloquy of Marburg (1529) and later organising the church of Saxony on a quasi-episcopal footing.
SECONDARY LITERATURE (part II): Manschreck 1958; Kisch 1967.

MILTON, JOHN
1608–74. During the Puritan Revolution Milton turned from his ambition to write a great epic poem to produce pamphlets 'of the left hand'. In the earlier 1640s his principal concern was with reform of the church and liberty of conscience, ideals which he consistently advocated thereafter. His political loyalties proved more flexible, and like his friend Nedham he supported the successive coups of the Interregnum, earning employment as Latin secretary to the Commonwealth and, both under the Rump and under Cromwell, writing pamphlets for an English and a continental audience in defence of the regicide. Unlike Nedham he would not support the Restoration, when his life was for a time in danger.
SECONDARY LITERATURE (part III): Introductions to Milton 1953–82; Hill 1977; Dzelzainis 1983; Geisst 1984.

MOLESWORTH, ROBERT
1656–1725. Of an Anglo-Irish family with ancient roots amongst the Northamptonshire gentry, Molesworth was born in Dublin. He made his name in 1694 with *An Account of Denmark*, a country he had visited two years earlier and where he had been dismayed to note the social and economic consequences of despotism. His other principal contribution to political thought is his preface to an English translation of Hotman's *Francogallia* in 1711. A privy councillor for Ireland in 1697 and 1714, he was a member of the Royal Society. He enjoyed the favour of George I and under him became Viscount Molesworth.
SECONDARY LITERATURE (part III): Robbins 1959.

MOLINA, LUIS DE
1535–1600. Apparently of noble parentage, Molina was born at Cuenca and educated briefly at Salamanca and chiefly at Alcalá. In 1553 he became a Jesuit, making his profession seventeen years later. During those years he studied and taught in Portugal and in 1571 was elevated to the prime chair of theology at Evora. His *De iustitia et iure* (1592–) began as a course of lectures there, as did his commentary on Aquinas' *Prima Secundae* to which he planned to add a new *Summa theologiae* of his own. Throughout his career he espoused

unconventional opinions, notably on slavery, and, above all, on the vexed question of divine grace and human free will, his views upon which were expressed in his highly controversial *Concordia* (1588).
SECONDARY LITERATURE (part II): Backer and Backer 1853–61; Hamilton 1963.

MONTAIGNE, MICHEL DE
1533–92. A nobleman from Périgord, Montaigne received a good humanist education at the Collège de Guyenne in Bordeaux before becoming a magistrate in the *parlement* of Bordeaux. In 1570 he withdrew to his estate (and his tower library) to escape the civil wars and meditate on life, although he visited Italy (1580–1) and served two terms as mayor of Bordeaux (1581–5), as well as helping to negotiate the end of the wars of religion. He published the first two books of his *Essais* in 1580, and the third in 1588, but continued to revise them to the end of his life. He combined Stoicism, scepticism and Catholicism in a highly personal synthesis. His essays rarely deal directly with political questions, but contain many penetrating and original observations on politics.
SECONDARY LITERATURE (part IV): Battista 1966; Clark 1970; Burke 1981.

MORE, SIR THOMAS
1478–1535. More's enigmatic personality, multi-faceted genius, and tragic martyrdom, for opposition to Henry VIII's ecclesiastical supremacy, have fascinated succeeding generations. A lucrative legal career led to public service in 1516. He became lord chancellor on Wolsey's fall in 1529. His prowess as a humanist was celebrated in Erasmus' *Moriae Encomium* (1508), and his reputation sealed by his *Utopia* (1516). His passionate, often scurrilous, polemics against the Lutherans (*Responsio ad Lutherum*, 1523; *The Confutation of Tyndale's Answer*, 1532) have struck less sympathetic modern chords. More's literary and philosophical proclivities are displayed in a plethora of humanist writings: translations from Greek to Latin; satirical and edificatory Latin verse; and a biography of Richard III, which damned tyranny in brilliant English vernacular. *Utopia* is a manifesto for the idea of achieving a truly just Christian commonwealth by recourse to rational endeavour.
SECONDARY LITERATURE (part I): Chambers 1935; Hexter 1952, 1973; Surtz 1957; Dorsch 1966–7; Fenlon 1981; Kenny 1983; Bradshaw 1985; Skinner 1987.

MORNAY, PHILIPPE DUPLESSIS
1549–1623. Educated a Protestant, he spent several years in Italy and Germany after completing his education, returning to France in 1572. He wrote numerous political tracts over the next several years. The *Vindiciae contra tyrannos*, first published in 1579, has often been attributed to him as well as to his friend Hubert Languet. In 1576 he became an adviser to Henry of Navarre and carried out several diplomatic missions to England and Flanders for him. After Henry's accession to the French throne, Mornay was appointed governor of Saumur, but his influence with Henry was weakened by the king's conversion to Catholicism and Mornay's continued attacks on the Catholic view of the eucharist. He was deprived of his governorship in 1621.
SECONDARY LITERATURE (part II): Patry 1933.

MORTON, THOMAS
1564–1659. The son of a mercer of York, Morton entered St John's College, Cambridge, in 1582. He took orders and remained at Cambridge until 1598. In 1602 he accompanied his patron, Lord Eure, on an embassy in Germany and Denmark. After his return he became chaplain to Roger Manners, earl of Rutland, and began to write polemics against Rome. He was a friend of John Donne, Isaac Casaubon, and Bishop Bilson. He wrote many works against the Jesuits. He was appointed bishop of Chester in 1616, transferring to Lichfield in

Biographies

1618, and to Durham in 1632. A Calvinist in matters of free will, he was a defender of episcopacy, who was imprisoned and deprived during the Civil War.
SECONDARY LITERATURE (part II): McIlwain 1918; Sommerville 1986.

MOYLE, WALTER
1672–1721. A Cornish gentleman and antiquary, Moyle moved in literary circles in London in the 1690s, and became member of parliament for Saltash in Cornwall in 1695. He contributed to the campaign against standing armies in 1697–9, although his most important works appeared only posthumously, his *Essay upon the Constitution of the Roman Government* in 1726 and his *Essay upon the Lacedaemonian Government* in 1727.
SECONDARY LITERATURE (part III): Robbins, in Moyle 1969.

MÜNTZER, THOMAS
c. 1490–1525. Having studied at Leipzig and Frankfurt, he went on to preach radical religious and social reform at Zwickau in 1520. Claiming the direct inspiration of the Holy Spirit, he went on from challenging the appeal to scriptural authority and attacking infant baptism, to disputing with Martin Luther at Wittenberg, calling himself the 'new Daniel', openly preaching rebellion at Mülhausen in Thuringia, and inserting himself into a position of leadership in the German Peasants' Revolt in 1524–5. In 1525, after the defeat of the peasants at the battle of Frankenhausen, he was captured and put to death.
SECONDARY LITERATURE (part II): Gritsch 1967.

NAUDÉ, GABRIEL
1600–53. Studied at Padua in 1626 with the Aristotelian Cremonini. Returned to Italy, 1631–42, as librarian to Cardinal Bagni, for whom he wrote *Considérations politiques sur les coups d'estat* (1639). He was then called to Paris by Cardinal Richelieu, whose librarian he became (and Mazarin's after him). One of the so-called *libertins érudits* (together with Guy Patin, François La Mothe le Vayer, and others), he also compiled a bibliography of politics and wrote a history of the reign of Louis XI (1620) as a supplement to Commynes, and an *Apologia* (1625) 'for all the great men who have been falsely suspected of magic'.
SECONDARY LITERATURE (part IV): Meinecke 1957; Thuau 1966, pp. 318–34; Keohane 1980, pp. 145–50.

NEDHAM, MARCHAMONT
1620–78. Political journalist from Burford, educated at Oxford. After writing on the king's behalf in the late 1640s, he earned his pardon for plotting against the Commonwealth by writing in defence of the new regime as editor of *Mercurius Politicus* and author, in particular, of *The Case of the Commonwealth of England Stated* (1650). His effective trimming continued until 1660, when he fled to Holland, but he later returned to resume a royalist position. He was a friend of Milton and of Andrew Marvell.
SECONDARY LITERATURE (part III): Zagorin 1966; Frank 1980.

NEVILE, HENRY
1620–94. Raised at Billingbear in Berkshire, and educated at Merton College, Oxford. He travelled to Italy in the 1640s and again in the 1660s, and formed friendships at the court of Ferdinand II of Tuscany. He took no part in the Civil War but entered parliament after the regicide, though his political career effectively ended when he broke with Cromwell over the dissolution of the Rump in 1653. A friend and literary collaborator of Harrington, he translated works of Machiavelli in 1675. His *Plato Redivivus*, a major contribution to the political literature of the Exclusion Crisis, appeared in 1680 and was revised in 1681.
SECONDARY LITERATURE (part III): Robbins, in Nevile 1969.

686

Biographies

OTTO, DANIEL

d. 1664. Originally trained as a philosopher at Jena, he turned to law perhaps under the influence of Arumaeus who included several of Otto's works in his *Discursus academici de jure publico*. The most influential of these was his 'De jure publico Imperii Romani' which was also published separately in 1616.

OVERTON, RICHARD

fl. 1631–64. Leveller. The details of his early life are uncertain, but he was probably in turn a Baptist, a Cambridge undergraduate, and an actor. Between 1640 and 1642 he wrote some fifty pamphlets (almost all anonymous) against Catholicism and royalism. In 1644 he printed *Mans Mortalitie*, a treatise denying the natural immortality of the soul. He wrote a series of attacks on Presbyterianism, under the pseudonym Marpriest, during 1645–6. He was the author or co-author of forty Leveller tracts during the years 1645–9, and as a consequence was imprisoned 1646–7 and 1649. He was involved in anti-Cromwell plots which forced him to go briefly into exile in 1655. In 1659 he defended the Good Old Cause and served a final imprisonment.

SECONDARY LITERATURE (part III): Greaves and Zaller 1982–4 and works cited there.

PALMIERI, MATTEO

1406–75. Florentine merchant and humanist, who held a large number of high offices in the Florentine republic. A loyal and trusted supporter of the Medici, he was a member of Medicean councils (*balìe*) and, between 1458 and 1465, one of the *accoppiatori* in charge of electing the Signoria. Having received a humanist education from Carlo Marsuppini and probably Ambrogio Traversari, he wrote his first work, the *Vita civile* (*c.* 1439), in the vernacular in order to acquaint those unable to read Latin with the moral and political wisdom of the Ancients. Author of historical works, among them a universal history (*De temporibus*), a history of the Florentine conqu~ ,t of Pisa, and contemporary annals, his long didactic poem *Città di vita*, on the different kinds of angel, was criticised for containing heretical opinions.

SECONDARY LITERATURE (part I): Messeri 1894; Belloni 1978; Finzi 1984.

PARKER, HENRY

1604–52. Born in Sussex, and educated at St Edmund Hall, Oxford, he was called to the bar at Lincoln's Inn in 1637. In the Civil War he began as a Presbyterian but became an Independent. He served as secretary to the army under the earl of Essex from 1642 and to the House of Commons from 1645. He was in Hamburg in the years 1646–9, serving the Merchant Adventurers Company. On his return he became army secretary under Cromwell in Ireland, where he died. A prolific pamphleteer, his first works concerned Ship Money (1640) and episcopacy (1641). His *Observations upon Some of His Majesty's Late Answers* (1642) is one of the most important defences of the parliamentarian cause. Going beyond constitutional and historical debate, he asserted that political power derives from contract and that tyrannical power may be resisted. Also influential was his *Political Catechism* (1643).

SECONDARY LITERATURE (part III): Allen 1938; Judson 1949; Tuck 1979.

PARKER, SAMUEL

1640–88. A notorious polemicist in Restoration England, who became bishop of Oxford in 1686. He was appointed chaplain to Archbishop Sheldon in 1667 ana defended the religious intolerance of the re-established Anglican church. He ought to have been typical of Anglican Cavalier churchmanship, but not only did he become a servant of James II's Catholic policies, he was also intellectually an oddity. His best known work, *A Discourse of*

Biographies

Ecclesiastical Polity (1670) attracted an unpublished commentary from Locke, and the pungent wit of Andrew Marvell. Parker attacked the 'Hobbesian' case for religious tolerance, but his own grounds for intolerance were themselves distinctly Hobbesian.

PARSONS (or Persons), ROBERT

1546–1610. Attended St Mary's Hall, Oxford, before becoming successively fellow, bursar, and dean of Balliol. Expelled from Balliol in 1574, he went to Rome, where he became a Jesuit. He undertook a mission to England with Edmund Campion in 1580. After making numerous conversions and operating a secret press, he escaped to Rouen when Campion was arrested in 1581. With the patronage of the Guise family in France, he was involved in plots to assassinate Queen Elizabeth, serving as an intermediary with Philip II. He was in Rome from 1585 to 1588, and then in Spain for nine years, where he established English seminaries. As rector of the English College in Rome from 1597, he quarrelled with the English secular priests. As a pamphleteer for the cause of English Catholicism, he sometimes advocated loyalty and at other times rebellion.

SECONDARY LITERATURE (part II): Clancy 1964; Pritchard 1978; Holmes 1982.

PARUTA, PAULO

1540–98. Born in Venice, he took a prominent part in the affairs of the city and represented the republic on several diplomatic missions. His works include a series of dialogues *Della perfezione della vita politica*, a notable history of Venice, and the *Discorsi politici*, published in the year after his death and in English translation, *Politick Discourses*, in 1657, followed a year later by *The History of Venice*.

SECONDARY LITERATURE (part II): Monzani, in Paruta 1852; Zanoni 1903; Bouwsma 1968.

PASQUIER, ETIENNE

1529–1615. Born into a well-connected Parisian family, Pasquier studied in France and Italy under several distinguished teachers – Ramus, Hotman, Cujas, Alciato. Returning to Paris in 1549, he practised as a barrister and gained forensic fame in 1565 through his advocacy for the university against the Jesuits. From 1585 he held the office of *avocat-général* in the *chambre des comptes*. Pasquier's friends included Ronsard and other members of the *Pléiade* as well as Montaigne and a circle of historically minded legal scholars. The first book of his *Recherches de la France* appeared in 1560. His fear of plagiarism delayed publication of some of the later books, though all but Book IX (published posthumously) had appeared by 1611.

SECONDARY LITERATURE (part II): Thickett 1979.

PATRIZI, FRANCESCO

1413–94. Sienese citizen and humanist; Poggio decribed him as *doctissimus*. After studying at the Univerity of Siena, he held high office in the republic and acted often as its ambassador. Exiled in 1457, accused of having conspired to hand over the city to Jacopo Piccinino, he returned to the city owing to the intervention of his friend Pius II, who appointed him in 1461 bishop of Gaeta and governor of Foligno. After the pope's death he retired to Gaeta, where he spent the rest of his life.

SECONDARY LITERATURE (part I): Battaglia 1936.

PAURMEISTER (or Baurmeister), TOBIAS

1555–1616. Studied law at Heidelberg and Freiburg. In 1594 he became active in public service as chancellor and privy councillor to the duke of Braunschweig–Lueneberg. He was also elevated to the nobility and given a title by Emperor Rudolf II. It was then that he changed the spelling of his name and became known as Paurmeister von Kochstedt. His *De jurisdictione Imperii Romani* (1608) became an influential work on the German constitution, and he also wrote a *Commentarium rerum politicarum et juridicarum*.

688

Biographies

PETYT, WILLIAM

1637–1707. A great antiquarian lawyer, educated at Christ's College, Cambridge, and the Inner Temple. During the Exclusion Crisis he was the chief Whig polemicist in a group that included William Atwood, Edward Cooke, James Tyrrell, and Thomas Hunt. His *Antient Right of the Commons of England Asserted* was dedicated to the earl of Essex. He worked with Sir George Treby and Francis Pollexfen in preparing the legal defence of London's charter. At the Revolution Petyt was one of the eminent authorities whom the Lords consulted concerning the nature of the 'original contract'. Among his other writings are *The Pillars of Parliament* (1681) and *Jus Parliamentarium* (1739).

SECONDARY LITERATURE (part III): Pocock 1957; Weston 1972; Weston and Greenberg 1981.

PITHOU, PIERRE

1539–96. The son of an *avocat*, and an *avocat* himself at the *parlement* of Paris, Pithou studied classics under Adrien Turnèbe in Paris and law under Jacques Cujas in Bourges and Valence. As a Protestant he took refuge in Sedan and Basle in the early religious wars. He became a Catholic after narrowly escaping death at the massacre of St Bartholemew in 1572. He helped to compose the *Satire Ménippée* against the League while residing in Leaguer Paris in 1593. In 1594 Henri IV made him *procureur-général* in the Paris *parlement*. He published a famous defence of the Gallican liberties, and collected other Gallican treatises. As an antiquary, he published a text of Visigothic law and a collection of Carolingian capitularies.

SECONDARY LITERATURE (part II): Kelley 1970; Salmon 1987.

PLATINA (Sacchi), BARTOLOMEO

1421–81. Born at Piadena (Platina) near Mantua, where he studied under Ognibene Bonisoli, a disciple of Vittorino da Feltre, and tutored the sons of the marquis. In 1457 he went to Florence to study under Johannes Argyropoulos; appointed by Pius II to the papal college of abbreviators, he lost his post in 1464 when Paul II reorganised that college. His violent protest led to his imprisonment; released in 14⸱5, he was rearrested in 1468, accused of conspiracy against the pope. Released in 1469, again after Gonzaga intervention, he was rehabilitated after the accession of Sixtus IV, who made him his librarian in 1475. Besides the *De principe* and the *De optimo cive*, he wrote a history of Mantua (1466–9) and a history of the popes until Sixtus IV and, among other humanist treatises, the *De falso et vero bono* and the *De vera nobilitate* on moral philosophy, and the *De honesta voluptate et valetudine* on food and health.

SECONDARY LITERATURE (part I): Gaida, in Platina 1913–32, pp. ix–xxxiv; Rubinstein 1986.

PONET, JOHN

c. 1514–56. He received his doctorate in theology at Cambridge in 1547, having gained a reputation as a noted preacher. He was appointed bishop of Rochester in 1550 and of Winchester the following year. Deprived of his see at Mary's accession, he went to Strasburg where he wrote and published his *Shorte Treatise of Politike Power* in 1556, and it was there that he died.

SECONDARY LITERATURE (part II): Hudson 1942.

PONTANO, GIOVANNI (GIOVIANO)

1429–1503. Neapolitan humanist and statesman. Born at Cerreto in Umbria, he entered the service of Alfonso of Aragon, king of Naples, in 1447. Under his successor Ferrante he rose to eminence as royal counsellor and diplomatist; from c. 1468 to 1475 he was tutor to Ferrante's eldest son Alfonso, duke of Calabria. From 1486 the king's secretary, or chief minister, he lost this office having recognised Charles VIII as king of Naples after the French conquest. The leading Neapolitan humanist of the second half of the fifteenth century, his

Biographies

many writings include treatises on moral philosophy, dialogues on literary subjects, a treatise and two poems on astrology, and a history of the war between Ferrante and John of Anjou. He was a prolific and highly influential Latin poet.
SECONDARY LITERATURE (part I): Percopo 1938; Altamura 1941; Tateo 1972.

PRYNNE, WILLIAM

1600–69. This militant Puritan pamphleteer was educated at Oriel College, Oxford, and Lincoln's Inn and called to the bar in 1628. A prominent dissident in the 1630s, he became Laud's arch-enemy and was foremost in his impeachment. For a time member of the Long Parliament, whose sovereignty he promoted, Prynne was secluded in Pride's Purge. The king's execution confirmed Prynne's crypto-royalism. As the first polemicist to launch a full-scale attack on Coke, he was esteemed by the Restored court and made keeper of the Tower records. The most ideologically significant of Prynne's 200 tracts are his *Soveraigne Power of Parliaments* (1643) and the four volumes of parliamentary writs (1659–64).
SECONDARY LITERATURE (part III): Allen 1938; Pocock 1957; Lamont 1963; Weston and Greenberg 1981.

PUFENDORF, SAMUEL

1632–94. Born in Saxony, the son of a Lutheran pastor. After studying theology at Leipzig he went to Jena, where he studied philosophy. Next he became tutor in the household of the Swedish ambassador in Copenhagen. Whilst imprisoned during the war between Sweden and Denmark he wrote his *Elementa Jurisprudentiae Universalis* (published 1660). The Elector Palatine appointed him professor of law of nature and nations at Heidelberg, where he wrote his *De Statu Imperii Germanici* (1667). Next the king of Sweden appointed him to the new chair of natural law at Lund. There he published his *De Jure Naturae et Gentium* (1672). In 1677 he became court historiographer at Stockholm, and began his monumental histories of Sweden and the principal states of Europe. He went to Berlin in 1688 at the request of the Elector of Brandenburg, for whom he performed the same hitorical tasks.
SECONDARY LITERATURE (part V): Wolf 1927, 1963; Krieger 1965; Denzer 1969, 1972, 1979; Dufour 1972, 1976, 1985.

QUEVEDO VILLEGAS, FRANCISCO DE

1580–1645. From a wealthy family, he studied at the universities of Alcalá and Valladolid, 1596–1606, becoming a noted wit. From 1613 to 1620 he was counsellor to the duke of Osuna, viceroy of Sicily, falling from favour with the duke. A prolific poet, moralist, and polemicist, he was placed on the Index in 1632 and confined to a monastery from 1639 to 1643. He became known throughout Europe for his satires and picaresque novels. In a life dogged by adversity – ill-health, penury, lawsuits, imprisonment, a disastrous marriage, and battles with the censors – his Christian neo-Stoicism was apt enough: he admired Lipsius and translated Seneca and Epictetus. His *Política de Dios* (1626), in the Mirror of Princes tradition, is in part an elegy for the decline of Spain; an abridged translation was published to serve the Tory cause in Queen Anne's England.
SECONDARY LITERATURE (part IV): Crosby in Quevedo 1966; Ettinghausen 1972.

QUIRINI, LAURO

c. 1420–*c.* 1479. Venetian patrician and humanist, born at Venice or Candia (Crete). Studied at Venice and Padua, where he took doctorates in the liberal arts and in law; lectured in Venice on Aristotle's *Ethics*; in 1452 he left for Candia, where he appears to have spent the rest of his life. His writings include, apart from the *De republica*, three treatises on nobility, in

which he attacks Poggio's *De nobilitate* (1440), and a *Dialogus de gymnasiis Florentinis* modelled on Lucian's dialogue. One of his letters, to Nicholas V, describes the fall of Constantinople.
SECONDARY LITERATURE (part I): Introductions to Quirini 1977a and 1977b; King 1986, pp. 118–32, 419–21.

RAINOLDS, WILLIAM: *see* REYNOLDS, WILLIAM

RASTELL, JOHN
1532–77. Educated at Winchester and New College, Oxford, Rastell was ordained a priest in 1555. He left Oxford for Louvain after the accession of Queen Elizabeth, and, after a stay in Antwerp, moved to Rome, where he entered the Jesuit order in 1568. He published attacks upon Bishop Jewel's justification of the Anglican settlement. He died at Ingolstadt, where he had become vice-rector of the university.
SECONDARY LITERATURE (part II): Holmes 1982.

REBUFFI, PIERRE DE
1487–1557. Born near Montpellier, Rebuffi studied there and at Toulouse before taking his doctorate *in utroque jure* at Cahors in 1527. He taught briefly at Poitiers and then at Bourges as a colleague of the great exponent of the *mos gallicus*, Alciato. In 1534 he settled at Paris, teaching canon law and practising as an *avocat*. Although an indifferent speaker, he nonetheless gained a sufficient reputation to qualify as a prospective judge in the Roman curia. His principal works were in canon law, particularly on the question of ecclesiastical benefices. His work as a civilian, notably the *Explicatio* (1589) and the *In titulum Dig. de verborum et rerum significatione* (1576), nevertheless ranks high. His *Commentaria* appeared in 1554–5.
SECONDARY LITERATURE (part II): Chabanne 1965.

REYNOLDS (or Rainolds), WILLIAM
c. 1544–94. Educated at Winchester and New College, Oxford, he took Anglican orders but resigned his fellowship of New College in 1572 because of his Catholic beliefs. He visited Rome and studied at Douai and Reims before becoming a priest. In 1580 he assumed the chair of divinity and Hebrew at Reims. He collaborated with Gregory Martin in the Catholic translation of the Bible known as the Douai version. For the last five years of his life he served as a priest in Antwerp. There he published his major treatises on resistance to heretical and tyrannical kings, using the pseudonym 'Gulielmus Rossaeus'. He also wrote on the nature of the mass, and composed a ferocious attack on Calvinism.
SECONDARY LITERATURE (part II): Baumgartner 1975; Salmon 1987.

RICHER, EDMOND
1559–1631. He arrived in Paris from Langres in 1577. Through his academic brilliance and foreceful personality he rose from college servant to principal at the Collège Cardinal Lemoine. When he took his doctorate of theology in 1589 he was a supporter of the Ultramontane Catholic League, but subsequently became a spokesman for Gallicanism. In 1606 he published the works of Gerson with extracts from other early anti-papal writers. He became a syndic of the Sorbonne in 1608, but many in the faculty of theology opposed him. He found support in the *parlement* for his short treatise on church–state relations, published in 1611. It was censured by a commission of bishops and he resigned as syndic in 1612. He continued to oppose Jesuit influence and had to resign from his post as principal in 1615.
SECONDARY LITERATURE (part II): Preclin 1930; Salmon 1987.

Biographies

ROSSAEUS, GULIELMUS: *see* REYNOLDS, WILLIAM

RUTHERFORD, SAMUEL
c. 1600–61. Born in Roxburghshire, and educated at Edinburgh, where he was appointed regent of humanity in 1623. A popular preacher in Galloway, he got into trouble with the bishops, being suspended in 1636. Active in the Covenanter revolution, he served in London as a Scots representative, 1643–7, and member of the Westminster assembly. He was principal of St Mary's College, St Andrews, from 1647, and rector from 1651. His writings defended Presbyterianism and attacked Arminianism. His chief political work is his *Lex Rex* (1644), which defended resistance by the *pars valentior*, being firmly in the tradition of the Calvinist theory of a right of revolution in the lesser magistrates. His harangue on the duty of kings to Charles II in 1650 was reminiscent of Buchanan preaching to the young James VI.
SECONDARY LITERATURE (part III): Allen 1938, pp. 285ff; Smart 1980.

ST GERMAN, CHRISTOPHER
c. 1460–1540. Born probably in Warwickshire, the son of a knight, St German proceeded via Oxford to the Middle Temple from where he was called to the bar. He gained fame for his legal learning and sufficient professional standing to serve as Master of Requests in 1528. The first edition of his *Doctor and Student* appeared in Latin (*De fundamentis legum Anglie*) in 1523; it was augmented in 1530 by the *Secunde dyalogue* and in the following year by the *Newe Addycyons*. His treatise *Concernynge the Division betwene the Spiritualtie and the Temporaltie* (*c.* 1532) and his *Dialogue betwixte Salem and Bizance* provoked fierce disputation with More. In his closing years he produced a further series of increasingly radical tracts.
SECONDARY LITERATURE (part II): Baumer 1936–7; Fox and Guy 1986.

SALAMONIO, MARIO
c. 1450–*c.* 1532. Descended from the important Roman family of Alberteschi, Salamonio studied at the University of Rome where he later held a chair of civil law. Distinguished as a jurist, he was a member of Pope Alexander VI's commission to reform the Roman legal system, held numerous public offices in that city, and served for six months in Florence as *Capitano del Popolo*. He acted as peace negotiator in the Roman uprising of 1511, and two years later intervened to demand reforms for the city in the aftermath of Pope Julius II's death. At about this time Salamonio wrote his *Patritii Romani de Principatu*, though it remained unpublished until 1544. His other works included a volume of *Commentaria in librum primum Digestorum* (1525).
SECONDARY LITERATURE (part II): Addio 1954.

SALMASIUS, CLAUDIUS: *see* SAUMAISE, CLAUDE DE

SALUTATI, COLUCCIO
1331–1406. Born in a provincial town north of Florence, Salutati trained as a notary in Bologna and became chancellor of Florence in 1375. A public and intellectual figure of great importance, he built up a splendid library, fostered the careers of younger scholars, and brought Manuel Chrysoloras to teach Greek in Florence. A scholar of great learning, he was not a thoroughgoing, one-sided classicist and republican like Leonardo Bruni; but he established the vital role that humanists could play in articulating an ideology and defending policies.
SECONDARY LITERATURE (part I): Ullman 1963; Witt 1983.

SANDERS (or Sander), NICHOLAS
c. 1530–81. The son of the high sheriff of Surrey, he was educated, like Harding and

692

Biographies

Reynolds, at Winchester and New College, Oxford, where he became a fellow in 1548. After the death of Queen Mary he left Oxford for Rome, where he was awarded a doctorate of divinity, and took holy orders. In 1563–4 he travelled in Prussia and Poland. He was professor of theology at Louvain in the year 1565–72. For a time he was a papal commissioner for English Catholic affairs. He wrote a treatise on the authority of the pope, and endorsed Pius V' bull excommunicating Queen Elizabeth. In 1573 he went to Madrid, and for several years urged Philip II to invade England. In 1579 he accompanied an expedition to Ireland, where he survived for two years before dying of the hardship he endured. His attack on English Protestantism was published posthumously in 1585.
SECONDARY LITERATURE (part II): Holmes 1982.

SARAVIA, HADRIAN
c. 1532–1613. Born at Hesdin in Artois, Saravia fled from the Low Countries for religious reasons. Naturalised in 1568 as an Englishman, he was headmaster of King Edward VI School, Southampton, from 1572 to 1578. During the 1580s he was for a few years professor of theology at Leiden, but he returned to England, becoming rector of Tatenhill in 1588 and later holding other livings in the English church. His De diversis gradibus ministrorum of 1590 rejected Presbyterianism in favour of the divine right of bishops. In De imperandi authoritate (1593) he attacked the political ideas of both Protestant and Catholic monarchomachs, and set out a trenchantly absolutist theory of government. He was one of the translators of King James' Authorised Version of the Bible.
SECONDARY LITERATURE (part III): Nijenhuis 1980; Sommerville 1983.

SARPI, PAOLO
1552–1623. A Venetian scholar whose interests included theology, mathematics, and Oriental languages. He was one of the leading defenders of Venice at the time of the Interdict, publishing several polemical works against papalist political ideas. After the withdrawal of the Interdict, Sarpi was summoned to Rome to account for his conduct. When he refused to obey he was excommunicated, and an attempt to assassinate him narrowly failed. His Istoria del concilio Tridentino (1619) was highly critical of the papacy. Though he defended the liberty of the Venetian republic, Sarpi was an absolutist as to internal affairs. His views, and especially his hostility to clerical pretensions, attracted the approval of such figures as Voltaire.
SECONDARY LITERATURE (part III): Bouwsma 1968; Wootton 1983.

SAUMAISE, CLAUDE DE (Salmasius, Claudius)
1588–1653. A French classical scholar, he studied at Paris and Heidelberg. He became a Huguenot and in 1651 took up a professorship at Leiden, where he remained until his death, except for a year in Sweden (1650–1). In addition to his classical writings (of which the most important was Plinianae exercitationes in Solinum, 1629) he also produced a defence of usury. Saumaise's most important political work was the Defensio regia pro Carolo I, in which he attacked the English Independents and the execution of Charles I. The book attracted a reply from John Milton. Saumaise, like many Continental Protestants, was clearly anxious to distance Protestantism from the activities of Cromwell and his supporters.

SAVONAROLA, GIROLAMO
1452–98. Born at Ferrara, he joined the Dominican order at Bologna in 1475. Appointed lecturer at the Florentine convent of S. Marco, he was elected prior in 1491 and set about its reform. The French invasion of Italy in 1494 seemed to fulfil his prophecies of impending doom and vastly increased his authority in Florence, which he used, after Piero de' Medici's flight, to bring about the creation of a Great Council on the Venetian model. While

Biographies

preaching the moral regeneration of the laity in his New Jerusalem of Florence, he also demanded the reform of the church, and this, with his support of the city's French alliance, led to open conflict with Alexander VI, who excommunicated him in 1497. The following year he was imprisoned, tortured, sentenced to death for heresy, and burned. He wrote, apart from his many sermons, works on theological, moral, and philosophical subjects, among them the *Trionfo della Croce* on Catholic doctrine, as well as the *Trattato circa el reggimento e governo della città di Firenze*. He summarized his prophecies in the *Compendium revelationum*.
SECONDARY LITERATURE (part I): Ridolfi 1952; Weinstein 1970.

SCALIGER, JOSEPH-JUSTE
1540–1609. Scaliger was the tenth of the fifteen children of Jules-César Scaliger, the humanist critic of Erasmus. He studied under Marc-Antoine Muret at Bordeaux, and went to Paris on the death of his father in 1558. There he became remarkably learned in many ancient and modern languages. In 1562 he became a Calvinist, and, after visits to Italy, England, and Scotland, fought for the Huguenots in the religious wars of 1567–70. He went to Valence to study with Jacques Cujas, and fled to Geneva after the massacre of St Bartholemew. He began to establish his great reputation as a classical scholar with commentaries on Aristotle and Cicero. In 1593 he accepted the chair vacated by Justus Lipsius at Leiden. He substantially revised classical and early Christian chronology.
SECONDARY LITERATURE (part II): Grafton 1983.

SELDEN, JOHN
1584–1654. Selden was the son of a Sussex yeoman, educated at Oxford and called to the bar. He acted as legal adviser to various noble families, and sat in parliament, 1621–9 and 1640–53. He was a supporter of the opposition to the king in the 1620s, and a moderate parliamentarian in the 1640s. Between 1610 and 1617 he published a number of works on legal history, and in 1617 his *History of Tithes* in which he attacked clerical authority. He provided a sympathetic critique of Grotius in *Mare Clausum* (1635) and a sophisticated though idiosyncratic theory of natural law in *De Iure Naturali* of 1640. His last work was a major study of Hebrew government, *De Synedriis* (1650–5). A posthumous volume of *Table Talk* captured his engaging and witty conversation.
SECONDARY LITERATURE (part IV): Tuck 1979, ch. 4, 1982; Christianson 1984; Sommerville 1984.

SENAULT, JEAN-FRANÇOIS
1599–1672. Born in Angers, he studied at Douai and in Paris, where he was attracted to Bérulle's recently founded Oratory. After five years, in 1623, he left, only to return in 1628 and to become, in time, possibly the most celebrated and influential preacher of his time. In 1662 he became the fourth superior-general of the Oratory. In addition to *Le Monarque* (1661), a treatise on the duties of the sovereign, his works include *L'Homme criminel*, *L'Homme chrétien*, and *De l'usage des passions*.
SECONDARY LITERATURE: *Dictionnaire de Théologie Catholique*.

SERVIN, LOUIS
1555–1626. Servin studied law under François Baudoin. A *politique* believer in divine right monarchy, he was appointed *avocat-général* of the royalist section of the *parlement* of Paris when Henri III ordered the court to move to Tours in 1589. He retained his post when the royalist and Leaguer sections were reunited by Henri IV in 1594, and continued in office until his death. He adopted an aggressive stance against the League and its Ultramontane policies in his vindication of the Gallican church in 1590. In 1603 he published a collection of

Biographies

his forensic pleadings, only to find their extreme Gallicànism censured by the Sorbonne. In subsequent years he defended the Gallican position of Edmond Richer. He died during a *lit de justice* when Louis XIII interrupted his criticism of royal fiscal edicts.
SECONDARY LITERATURE (part II): Salmon 1987.

SEXBY, EDWARD

c. 1616–58. Leveller. Probably a gentleman's son and a London apprentice, he was a soldier and agitator in 1647, and participated in the Putney debates. He left the army between 1647 and 1649, rejoined as an officer, but was court-martialled, on flimsy charges, in 1651. He was then sent by the council of state to encourage revolution in France. From 1653 until his death in prison in 1658 he was engaged in plots against Cromwell's life, the legitimacy of which he defended in *Killing No Murder* (1657).
SECONDARY LITERATURE (part III): Greaves and Zaller 1982–4 and works cited there.

SEYSSEL, CLAUDE DE

c. 1450–1520. The illegitimate son of a Savoyard nobleman, Seyssel studied civil law at Turin and Pavia. In 1492 he entered the service of Charles VIII of France and subsequently became counsellor to Louis d'Orléans whose merits he extolled in his *Louenges du roy Louis XII* (1508). Frequently employed by that king upon diplomatic missions, Seyssel held numerous judicial and administrative offices before retiring in 1515 to his bishopric of Marseilles. His *Monarchie de France* is a book of advice for princes, but shows more awareness than did Machiavelli of the institutional and cultural conditions of stability; it inspired new studies of French legal antiquities. Seyssel's other works included commentaries in Bartolist fashion on civil law, translations of classical histories, and religious tracts.
SECONDARY LITERATURE (part II): Poujol, in Seyssel 1961a; Hexter 1973; Kelley, in Seyssel 1981.

SHERLOCK, WILLIAM

c. 1641–1707. A popular High Tory polemical divine in the 1680s, he at first repudiated the Revolution of 1689; his conversion to it provoked controversy and led to his appointment as dean of St Paul's. His *Case of Allegiance* (1691) is a 'de facto' defence of the Revolution, parallel to similar Hobbesian tracts of the 1650s. Despite his talk of the divine right of providential revolutions, his critics detected Hobbism. Locke wrote a manuscript commentary against Sherlock, and Leibniz produced a more favourable essay in which he too came close to Hobbesian stances.
SECONDARY LITERATURE (part V): Riley 1973; Jolley 1975.

SIDNEY, ALGERNON

1623–83. A great-nephew of Sir Philip Sidney, and younger son of the second earl of Leicester. He fought for parliament in the Civil War and became a member of parliament after it. He achieved some prominence in the republican regime in 1652–3, but disowned Cromwell's Protectorate. He returned to politics in 1659 and took part in an embassy to the Baltic. The Restoration of 1660 ended his political influence. Most of his later years were spent in exile. He plotted with the Dutch and French against England in 1664–5, but returned in 1677. In 1683 he was executed for his part in the Rye House Plot against Charles II. His principal works are his 'Court Maxims' and his *Discourse concerning Government*.
SECONDARY LITERATURE (part III): Worden 1985; Scott 1988, 1991.

SLEIDAN, JOHANNES

c. 1506–56. After being educated in the humanities at Liège and Louvain, Sleidan moved to France in 1533, to take a degree in law at Orleans and enter the service of the prominent du

Biographies

Bellay family, helping them with several historiographic projects. His increasing interest in Calvinist Protestantism led him to move to Strasburg in 1541, where he spent the rest of his life, as a diplomat for the city and its princely allies and as an official historian. His *De statu religionis et reipublicae, Carolo Quinto Caesare* first published in 1555, was the most authoritative early history of the Reformation in Germany and paid special attention to the political consequences of religious change.

SECONDARY LITERATURE (part II): Dickens and Tonkin 1985, pp. 10–19.

SMITH, SIR THOMAS

1513–77. Born of farming stock at Saffron Walden, Essex, Smith entered Queens' College, Cambridge, in 1526, and was elected a fellow four years later. In 1540 he was appointed to the new regius chair of civil law, but then toured several foreign universities, taking a doctorate at Padua. Secretary of state under Protector Somerset, he lost favour when the Protector fell, only to re-emerge under Elizabeth. He became a member of parliament, a commissioner for the religious settlement, and (1562–6) ambassador to France. In 1572 he became the queen's principal secretary. Smith's *De Republica Anglorum*, written in France, was published in 1583; and he may also be the author of the anonymous *Discourse of the Commonweal* (1581).

SECONDARY LITERATURE (part II): Dewar 1964.

SOTO, DOMINGO DE

1495–1560. Born in Segovia, Soto was educated at Alcalá and Paris before entering the Dominican order in 1525. He proceeded to Salamanca where he taught theology. He attended early sessions of the Council of Trent and also assisted at Augsburg in preparing the Interim whereby Charle V made minor concessions to protestants. Soto's writings, of which the *De iustitia et iure* appeared in 1553–4, included much-reprinted commentaries on Aristotle and unpublished treatises criticising the Spanish conquest of the Indies. The question of the treatment of the Amerindians involved him in 1550–1 in adjudicating, with other theologians and jurists, upon the famous dispute between Sepúlveda and Las Casas.

SECONDARY LITERATURE (part II): Hamilton 1963; Hanke 1974.

SPELMAN, SIR HENRY

1562–1641. Educated at Lincoln's Inn, this cultivated Norfolk gentleman embarked late on a scholarly career. About 1614, in concert with Sir Robert Cotton, William Camden, Sir John Davies, and Hakewill, he attempted unsuccessfully to resurrect the Society of Antiquaries. In 1626 he published his *Glossary*, an historical dictionary of legal and constitutional terms; but such important works as the second volume of the *Glossary* (1664), and *Reliquiae Spelmannianae* (1698), were published posthumously. Spelman's highly developed linguistic skills and wide reading in English and continental legal sources enabled him to 'discover' feudalism and discern the impact of the Norman Conquest on English law and institutions.

SECONDARY LITERATURE (part III): Fox 1956; Pocock 1957.

SPINOZA, BARUCH (Benedict) DE

1632–77. Born in Amsterdam of an émigré Portuguese (originally Spanish) Jewish family; educated at a Jewish school up to the age of thirteen. He joined his father's business, but ceased after being excommunicated from the synagogue in 1656. He studied philosophy at Leiden, *c.* 1656–7; lived in Amsterdam again *c.* 1657–60, when he composed his first philosophical work, the *Short Treatise*. Next he lived at Rijnsburg (near Leiden), 1660–3, giving private lessons on Cartesian philosophy. During the 1660s he worked on his *Ethics*.

Biographies

He lived at or near The Hague from 1663, and was befriended there by the republican politician Jan de Witt. Began *Tractatus theologico-politicus, c.* 1665 (published 1670). The *Ethics* and the unfinished *Tractatus politicus* were published posthumously in 1677.
SECONDARY LITERATURE (part IV): Meinsma 1896; Wernham, in Spinoza 1958; Revah 1959; McShea 1968; Mugnier-Pollet 1976; Popkin 1979; Scruton 1986.

STARKEY, THOMAS

c. 1499–1538. Of Cheshire extraction, Starkey was educated at Magdalen College, Oxford, where he held a fellowship. His most influential formative experience was some thirteen years (1521–34) spent in Reginald Pole's household in Padua, where he added law to his earlier qualifications in theology. Starkey broke with Pole in 1534 on the issue of the royal ecclesiastical supremacy, returning to England in 1535, where he attached himself to Thomas Cromwell, in hopes of encouraging social and economic reformation of the commonwealth on humanist principles. He may have influenced Cromwell's legislative programme, though his plea that the wealth of the dissolved monasteries be redeployed for social reform fell on deaf ears. Most of Starkey's *Dialogue between Pole and Lupet* was probably written in 1529–32. His *Exhortation to the People Instructynge theym to Unitie and Obedience* (1537) belong to Cromwell's propaganda for the Reformation.
SECONDARY LITERATURE (part I): Zeeveld 1948; Elton 1973; Bradshaw 1979; Mayer 1989; Mayer, in Starkey 1989.

SUÁREZ, FRANCISCO

1548–1627. Born in Granada into a family distinguished by long service to the crown, Suárez studied canon law from 1561 at Salamanca. In due course he became a Jesuit and developed into an outstanding theologian. After teaching at several institutions, he became professor of theology at the Jesuit college at Rome. From there he returned to Alcalá and thence to Salamanca. Evidently more at ease as a writer than as a teacher, he was nonetheless nominated by Philip II in 1593 to the theology chair at Coimbra where he delivered the lectures which were published as *De legibus* (1612). With his *Defensio fidei* (1613) Suárez engaged in the famous controversy between James I of England and Cardinal Bellarmine.
SECONDARY LITERATURE (part II): Backer and Backer 1853–61; Hamilton 1963; Melía 1977; Sommerville 1982.

SUMMENHART, CONRAD

c. 1455–1502. Born at Calw, he matriculated in 1472 at Heidelberg, later migrating to Paris and completing his arts course in 1478 at the then recently founded University of Tübingen. In 1489 he became a doctor of theology there and is first mentioned as *ordinarius* in theology in 1497. His teaching was realist, inclining to Scotism. His most important work was the *Septipertitum opus de contractibus*.
SECONDARY LITERATURE (part I): Hermelink 1906, pp. 152–6; *Lexikon für Theologie und Kirche; Auctarium Chartularii Universitatis Parisiensis*, VI, p. 539 n. 5.

TENISON, THOMAS

1636–1715. As a fellow of Corpus Christi College, Cambridge, in the 1660s he helped procure the recantation and ejection of the 'licentious Hobbist' Daniel Scargill. His *Creed of Mr Hobbes Examined* appeared in 1670. In the 1680s he became a popular London preacher, in 1691 a bishop, and in 1694 archbishop of Canterbury. Although regarded as a latitudinarian and court Whig bishop, before the Revolution there was little to distinguish him from the political and ecclesiastical Toryism then prevailing.
SECONDARY LITERATURE (part V): Mintz 1962.

Biographies

TOLAND, JOHN

1670–1722. An Irishman best known for his controversial deist writings, above all his *Christianity not Mysterious* (1696), Toland also had an active political career from his arrival in London in the early 1690s. He edited the principal works of Harrington, wrote a life of Milton, and probably edited Sidney and Ludlow too. He was also active in the campaign against standing armies, in which he collaborated with Walter Moyle and John Trenchard and with radical Whig publishers.

SECONDARY LITERATURE (part III): Worden, in Ludlow 1978; Sullivan 1982.

TYNDALE, WILLIAM

c. 1494–1536. Born in Gloucestershire, he studied first at Magdalen College, Oxford, and then at Cambridge, where he became acquainted with the new religious ideas emanating from Wittenberg. Committing himself to the Reform and to the project of translating the Bible afresh into English, he left England for Hamburg in 1524 and never returned. His Bible was printed in 1525–6 and his political tract, *The Obedience of a Christen man and how Christen rulers ought to governe*, in 1528. Having moved to the Low Countries, he was arrested, imprisoned, and burnt at the stake as a heretic.

SECONDARY LITERATURE (part II): Mozley 1937.

TYRRELL, JAMES

1642–1718. A close friend of Locke. There are signs of the latter's collaboration in the writing of *Patriarcha non Monarcha* (1681), one of the three major Whig ripostes to the Tory's ideological flagship, Filmer's *Patriarcha*, the other two being Sidney's *Discourses* and Locke's *Two Treatises*. Tyrrell's book includes important remarks on Hobbes, and there are borrowings from Pufendorf too. In the 1690s he turned to writing history and to a résumé of Whig constitutional theory in his *Bibliotheca Politica*.

SECONDARY LITERATURE (part V): Gough 1976.

VERMIGLI, PETER MARTYR

1500–62. Born in Florence, entered the Augustinian order in 1516. He studied at Padua, then lectured on the Bible in several Augustinian convents in Italy. He was influenced by the biblical commentaries of Bucer and Zwingli and was summoned to appear before a general chapter of his order in 1542. He fled to Switzerland, then to Strasburg, where he became professor of theology. Invited to England by Cranmer, he became regius professor of divinity at Oxford in 1548. After Mary Tudor's accession he returned to Strasburg but encountered opposition to his eucharistic teaching from Lutheran pastors there and so accepted an invitation to teach at Zurich. His many published biblical commentaries, particularly on Judges and Romans, contain a number of comments on political topics.

SECONDARY LITERATURE (part II): Anderson 1975; Kingdon, in Vermigli 1980.

VIRET, PIERRE

1511–71. Born in the canton of Vaud, Switzerland. He studied theology in Paris, then returned to Switzerland where, influenced by Farel, he became a Protestant preacher. He helped establish the Reformation in Geneva and Lausanne, and as a preacher and professor at the Lausanne Academy, he organised the Reformed church in Vaud. He was forced to leave Lausanne in 1559 because of disagreements with the authorities over church discipline. He served as a preacher in Geneva, then went to southern France in 1563. In 1567 he became professor of theology at the academy established at Orthez by the queen of Navarre. Of his many theological works containing occasional references to political topics, the most important is his *Instruction chrestienne*, first published in 1556.

SECONDARY LITERATURE (part II): Linder 1964, 1966.

Biographies

VITORIA, FRANCISCO DE

c. 1483–1546. A Basque born at Vitoria in Alava, Vitoria entered the Dominican order at Burgos before proceeding to the Collège de St Jacques in Paris where he stayed as student and teacher for some sixteen years. Back in Spain, he taught at Valladolid before appointment in 1526 to the chair of theology at Salamanca. Famous as a lecturer, he eventually achieved an important curricular reform through partially replacing Peter Lombard's *Sentences* with Aquinas' *Summa*. His *De Indis* and *De jure belli Hispanorum in barbaros* began as public lectures. They form the basis of Vitoria's claim to be a founding father of international law, and of his reputation as a defender of the Amerindians.
SECONDARY LITERATURE (part II): Getino 1930; Hamilton 1963; Pagden 1987.

VIVES, JUAN LUIS

1492–1540. Vives was the most distinguished of the Spanish humanists, although most of his career was spent as a peripatetic scholar and teacher. After studies at Beauvais (1509–12) he moved to Bruges, and then taught at Louvain (1519–23) and Oxford (from 1523). He was attached to Queen Catherine of Aragon's circle, and his opposition to Henry VIII's divorce led to brief imprisonment in 1527 and retirement to Bruges. Vives' voluminous writings comprehend classical studies, patristics, moral philosophy, and psychology (*De anima et vita libri tres*, 1538), educational theory (*De disciplinis*, 1531; *De institutione feminae Christianae*, 1524), politics and social affairs (*De subventione pauperum*, 1526, on the alleviation of poverty by state-sponsored public works). His writings against war align him with the Erasmian circle.
SECONDARY LITERATURE (part I): Adams 1962; Norena 1970.

WALWYN, WILLIAM

1600–80. Leveller. Second son of a Worcestershire gentleman, apprenticed in London, he became a member of the Merchant Adventurers' Company. Beginning in 1641 he wrote a number of pamphlets in favour of religious and political freedom. Always radical in his political views, he early opposed arguments from the ancient constitution as too conservative. He defended religious toleration, but remained a member of his parish church. From 1646 to 1649 he came under attack for 'atheism', a charge he repeatedly denied. His association with the other Leveller leaders began in 1645, and he was briefly imprisoned with them in 1649. Later he developed an interest in medical practice.
SECONDARY LITERATURE (part III): Greaves and Zaller 1982–4 and works cited there.

WHITE, THOMAS

1593–1676. The most intellectually interesting Catholic priest in seventeenth-century England, condemned for heresy both by the English parliament and by Rome. His philosophical reputation was high; Leibniz linked him with Descartes and Gassendi among the leading lights of new philosophy. His alias was Blacklo; 'Blackloism' involved anti-papalism and an excessively rationalist style of theology. One of Hobbes' earliest works was a critique of White's *De Mundo*; in later years the two enjoyed arguments together; they were linked in Coke's 1660 critique and in parliament's 1666 condemnation. White's *Grounds of Obedience* (1655) is the best example of politics on Hobbes' sceptical foundations.
SECONDARY LITERATURE (part V): Mintz 1962.

WILDMAN, JOHN

1623–93. Leveller, plotter, pamphleteer. He served in the parliamentary army, and first appears as an agitator in 1647, when he helped draft the Agreement of the People. He was arrested in 1648, became a land speculator on his release, and re-entered military service, reaching the rank of major in 1653. He was a double agent under Cromwell. At the

Restoration he both won royal favour and engaged in republican plots. He was in exile 1661–7; later he was an associate of Shaftesbury and Sidney, participating in the Rye House Plot (1683), Monmouth's Rebellion and William's invasion. He briefly became postmaster-general in 1689, but was soon dismissed. He was knighted in 1692, though he had turned to Jacobite plotting.
SECONDARY LITERATURE (part III): Greaves and Zaller 1982–4 and works cited there.

WILLIAMS, ROGER

c. 1603–83. Born in London, son of a merchant tailor, he studied at Cambridge, and emigrated to Massachussetts in 1631, where he insisted on the need for complete separation from the church of England. He was expelled from Massachussetts in 1635, accused of antinomianism. He then established Providence, Rhode Island, and returned to England in 1643 to seek a charter. There he published *A Key into the Language of America*, the product of a mission to the Indians during which he had convinced himself of their land rights, and *The Bloudy Tenent of Persecution for Cause of Conscience* (1644), a defence of the rights of all believers. He returned to Rhode Island, but was back in England 1652–4, when he published *The Bloudy Tenent Yet More Bloudy*. He was prominent in Rhode Island politics until his death.
SECONDARY LITERATURE (part III): Greaves and Zaller 1982–4 and works cited there.

WINSTANLEY, GERRARD

1609–76. The son of a burgess of Wigan, Winstanley was apprenticed in 1630 to a London widow. He became a freeman of the Merchant Taylors Company in 1637 but by 1643 the collapse of his business led to his taking up agricultural employment in Surrey. In 1648 he began to publish a series of works on universal salvation and the coming millennium. *The New Law of Righteousness* (1649) announced the end of covetousness and the beginning of community. In April 1649 the famous digging experiments began at St George's Hill, Surrey. By early 1650 similar communities had developed in several midland and southern counties. They appear to have collapsed during that year. Winstanley went on to write his appeal to Cromwell. *The Law of Freedom* (1652). After the Restoration he served a Anglican churchwarden at Cobham, but may have died a Quaker corn dealer in London.
SECONDARY LITERATURE (part II): Hill 1972, 1986; Hill, in Winstanley 1973; Davis 1976, 1981a; Aylmer 1984.

ZAMPINI, MATTEO

fl. 1586–94. Born in Recanati in the March of Ancona, the jurisconsult Zampini joined the retinue of Catherine de Médicis in France. His first work to be published in France was an attempt to show that the Capetians were descended from Clovis. In 1586 he printed the *Elogia* of his patroness, followed by a study of the French Estates General in 1587 and two tracts on the right of the Cardinal de Bourbon to succeed Henri III, appearing in 1588. In 1591 he criticised the refusal of the royalist *parlements* to receive briefs from Pope Gregory XIV. He returned to Italy after Henri IV's recovery of Paris in 1594.
SECONDARY LITERATURE (part II): Allen 1941.

ZASIUS, ULRICH

1461–1535. The leading German jurist of his day, friend of Erasmus, and member (with Budé and Alciato) of an international 'imaginary triumvirate' of legal humanism, Zasius had a career both as a practising lawyer and as a teacher of law at Freiburg. Combining the old scholastic with the new humanistic styles of scholarship, he published a variety of legal works, most notably the collection of his legal opinions (*consilia*), his work on the status of

Jews, his lectures on feudal law (commentary on the Lombard *Libri Feudorum*), and a variety of critical and reformist studies of Roman law, especially his influential treatise *On the Origin of Civil Law*, which was a survey of Roman legal, institutional, and political history from the standpoint both of imperial ideology and a humanist 'sense of history'.
SECONDARY LITERATURE (part I): Rowan 1987.

ZWINGLI, HULDREICH
1484–1531. Born at Waldhaus in the Swiss canton of St Gall, he was educated at Berne, Vienna, and Basle. Ordained as a priest in 1506, he served as a pastor at Glarus until 1516 when he moved to Einsiedeln. Moved by the spirit of Erasmian humanism, and led by his scriptural studies to develop the doctrinal commitments that came later to characterise the Protestantism of the Reformed churches of Switzerland, he began the work of putting his reforming ideas into effect at Zürich after he had been elected preacher at the Old Minster there in 1518. The turning point in the reform at Zürich came in 1523 when the city council backed the doctrinal position he had defended in public disputation. He was killed at the battle of Kappel.
SECONDARY LITERATURE (part II): Walton 1967; Potter 1976.

Bibliography

Note: the bibliography is intended to provide detailed references for works cited in the text, notes, and biographical appendix. It also serves as a guide to further reading. It is divided into the five principal divisions of the book, and subdivided into primary and secondary sources under each heading. Primary works are taken to be those written before 1800, whether printed in early or in modern editions. For books printed before 1800 place of publication is given, and for those printed after 1800 both place of publication and name of publisher. At the beginning is a short list of key items of general reading for the whole period or a substantial part of it.

General works

Allen, J.W. (1928). *A History of Political Thought in the Sixteenth Century* (London: Methuen; new edn, 1961).

Burns, J.H., ed. (1988). *The Cambridge History of Medieval Political Thought, c. 350–c. 1450* (Cambridge: Cambridge University Press).

Carlyle, Sir R.W. and A.J. (1903–36). *A History of Medieval Political Theory in the West*, 6 vols. (Edinburgh and London: Blackwood).

Figgis, J.N. (1896). *The Divine Right of Kings* (Cambridge: Cambridge University Press; 2nd edn, 1922; reissue, New York: Harper, 1965).

    (1907). *Studies of Political Thought from Gerson to Grotius, 1717–1625* (Cambridge: Cambridge University Press). Reissued 1960 as *Political Thought from Gerson to Grotius 1414–1625: Seven Studies*, intro. G. Mattingley (New York: Harper).

Gierke, O. (1934). *Natural Law and the Theory of Society, 1500 to 1800*, intro. and trans. E. Barker, 2 vols. (Cambridge: Cambridge University Press).

Keohane, N.O. (1980). *Philosophy and the State in France: The Renaissance to the Enlightenment* (Princeton: Princeton University Press).

MacIntyre, A. (1967). *A Short History of Ethics* (London: Routledge and Kegan Paul).

Macpherson, C.B. (1962). *The Political Theory of Possessive Individualism* (Oxford: Clarendon Press).

Manuel, F.E., and Manuel, F.P. (1979). *Utopian Thought in the Western World* (Oxford: Blackwell).

Meinecke, F. (1957). *Machiavellism: The Doctrine of Raison d'Etat and its Place in Modern History*, trans. D. Scott, intro. W. Stark (London: Routledge and Kegan Paul). First publ. as *Die Idee der Staatsräson* (Munich: R. Oldenbourg, 1924).

Mesnard, P. (1936). *L'Essor de la philosophie politique au XVIe siècle* (Paris: Boivin).

Miller D., ed. (1987). *The Blackwell Encyclopaedia of Political Thought* (Oxford: Blackwell).

Oakeshott, M. (1946, 1975). 'Introduction' to Thomas Hobbes, *Leviathan* (Oxford: Blackwell). Repr. in *Hobbes on Civil Association* (Oxford: Blackwell).

Oakley, F. (1979). *The Western Church in the Later Middle Ages* (Ithaca: Cornell University Press).

Ozment, S. (1980). *The Age of Reform 1250–1550: An Intellectual and Religious History of Late Medieval and Reformation Europe* (New Haven: Yale University Press).

Plamenatz, J. (1963). *Man and Society*, vol. II: *Machiavelli to Rousseau* (London: Longman).

Pocock, J.G.A. (1975). *The Machiavellian Moment: Florentine Political Thought and the Atlantic Republican Tradition* (Princeton: Princeton University Press).

Skinner, Q. (1978). *The Foundations of Modern Political Thought*, 2 vols. (Cambridge: Cambridge University Press).

Tierney, B. (1982). *Religion, Law and the Growth of Constitutional Thought, 1150–1650* (Cambridge: Cambridge University Press).

Troeltsch, E. (1931). *The Social Teaching of the Christian Churches*, trans. O. Wyon, 2 vols. (London: Allen and Unwin). First publ. as *Die Soziallehren der christlichen Kirchen und Gruppen* (Tübingen: Mohr, 1911).

Tuck, R. (1979). *Natural Rights Theories: Their Origin and Development* (Cambridge: Cambridge University Press).

Wolin, S.H. (1960). *Politics and Vision: Continuity and Innovation in Western Political Thought* (Boston: Little, Brown and Company).

I Renaissance and Counter-Renaissance

Primary sources

Alciato, Andrea (1565). *De Verborum significatione* (Lyons).

(1617). *Opera omnia*, 4 vols. (Frankfurt).

Almain, Jacques (1512). *Libellus de auctoritate ecclesiae seu sacrorum conciliorum eam representatium* (Paris).

(1518). *Aurea . . . opuscula* (Paris).

Antoninus, St (1959). *Summa Theologica*, 4 vols. (Graz: Akademische Druck-u. Verlagsanstal: facsimile of the 1740 Verona edition).

Aquinas, St Thomas (1948). *De regimine principum*, ed. J. Mathis (Turin: Marietti).

Arnisaeus, Henning (1615). *De Republica* (Frankfurt).

Ayliffe, John (1714). *The Ancient and Present State of the University of Oxford*, vol. 1 (London).

Ayrault, Pierre (1576). *De l'ordre et instruction iudicaire* (Paris).

(1677). *Rerum ab omni antiquitate iudicarum Pandectae* (Geneva).

Baldus de Ubaldis (1535). *Super Digesto veteri* (n.p.).

Barbaro, Ermolao (1969). *De coelibatu. De officio legati*, ed. V. Branca (Florence: Olschki).

Baron, Eguinaire (1550). *Institutionum civilium ab Iustiniáno Caesare editarum libri IIII* (Poitou).

(1562) *Opera omnia*, ed. F. Baudouin, Digest 1 (Paris).

Baudouin, François (1559). *Commentarius de jurisprudentia muciana* (Paris).

Biel, Gabriel (1963–71). *Canonis Missae Expositio*, 5 vols., ed. H.A. Oberman and W.J. Courtney (Wiesbaden: Veröffentlichungen des Instituts für Europäische Geschichte, Mainz, Bd 31–5).

(1968). *Defensorium Obedientiae Apostolicae, et alia documenta*, ed. H.A. Oberman, D.E. Zerfoss, and W.J. Courtney (Cambridge, Mass.: Belknap Press of Harvard University).

(1973–84). *Collectorium in quattuor libros Sententiarum*, 4 vols. in 5, ed. H. Ruckert *et al.* (Tübingen: Mohr).

Bodin, Jean (1951). *Methodus ad facilem historiarum cognitionem*, in *Œuvres philosophiques*, ed. P. Mesnard (Paris: Presses Universitaires de France).

Brandolini, Aurelio (1890). *De comparatione reipublicae et regni*, ed. J. Abel (in Irodalomtörténeti Emlékek, 2: 77–183; Budapest: Magyar Tudomángos Akadémia).

Brucioli, Antonio (1982). *Dialogi*, ed. A. Landi (Naples: PRISMI, Chicago: Newberry Library).

Brûlefer, Etienne (1500). *Opuscula* (Paris).

Bruni, Leonardo (1928). *Humanistische-philosophische Schriften*, ed. H. Baron (Leipzig and Berlin: Teubner). Reprinted 1969 (Wiesbaden: Dr Martin Sandig).

I Renaissance and Counter-Renaissance

Budé, Guillaume (1535). *Annotationes . . . in quatuor et viginti Pandectarum libros* (Paris).

Busini, Giovanni Battista (1860). *Lettere a Benedetto Varchi sopra l'assedio di Firenze*, ed. G. Milanese (Florence: Le Monnier).

Cajetan, Tommaso de Vio, Cardinal (1582). *Opuscula Omnia*, vol. 1 of 3 (Turin).

(1978). *Cajetan Responds: A Reader in Reformation Controversy*, ed. and trans. J. Wicks (Washington: Catholic University of America Press).

Cantiuncula, Claudius (1545). *Topica legalia* (Basle).

Carafa, Diomede (1899). *I doveri del principe*, ed. T. Persico, in *Diomede Carafa: Uomo di stato e scrittore del secolo XV* (Naples: Pierro), pp. 261–96.

Celtis, Conrad (1948). *Selection from Conrad Celtis*, ed. L. Foster (Cambridge: Cambridge University Press).

Challine, Paul (1666). *Méthode générale pour l'intelligence des coutumes de France* (Paris).

Chasseneuz, Barthélemy de (1529). *Catalogus gloriae Mundi* (Paris).

(1586). *Catalogus gloriae mundi* (Frankfurt).

Choppin, René (1662). *Traité du domaine de la couronne de la France* (Paris).

Conring, Hermann (1666). *Exercitationes* (Helmstadt).

Contarini, Gasparo (1589). *De magistratibus et republica Venetorum* (Venice).

Coras, Jean (1560). *De Iuris arte libellus* (Lyons).

(1568). *De iustitia et iure* (Lyons).

(1572). *Petit discours sur les marriages contractés par les enfans sans l'avis, conseil et volunté des pères*, following *Edict du roy sur les marriages clandestins* (Paris).

Cowell, John (1651). *The Institutes of the Laws of England* (London).

Domat, Jean (1702). *Les Loix civiles dans leur ordre naturel* (Paris).

Dudley, Edmund (1948). *Tree of Commonwealth*, ed. D.M. Brodie (Cambridge: Cambridge University Press). Written in 1510.

Duker, Karl Andreas (1711). *Opuscula varia de latinitate jurisconsultorum veterum* (Leiden).

Elyot, Thomas (1946). *Of the Knowledge which Maketh a Wise Man*, ed. E.W. Howard (Ohio: Ohio University Press).

(1962). *The Boke Named the Governour*, ed. S.E. Lehmberg (Texas: University of Texas Press).

Erasmus, Desiderius (1936). *Institutio Principis Christiani*, trans. L.K. Born (New York: Columbia University Press).

(1965). *Convivium Religiosum*, trans. C.R. Thompson, in *The Colloquies of Erasmus* (Chicago: University of Chicago Press).

(1969–). *Opera Omnia Desiderii Erasmi Roterodami*, ed. J.H. Waszink et al. (Amsterdam: North Holland Publishing Company).

(1974–). *Collected Works*, various editors, 78 vols. (Toronto: University of Toronto Press).

(1978). *Antibarbari*, trans. M.M. Phillips, in Erasmus (1974–), vol. XXIII.

(1982, 1989). *Adagiorum Collectanea*, trans. M.M. Phillips and R.A.B. Mynors, in Erasmus (1974–), vols. XXXI–XXXII.

(1986). *Moriae Encomium*, trans. B. Radice, in Erasmus (1974–), vol. XXVII.

(1988). *Enchiridion Militis Christiani*, trans. C. Fontazzi, in Erasmus (1974–), vol. LXVI.

Ferrault, Jean (1542). *Tractatus . . . iura seu privilegia contínens* (Paris).

Ferrière, Claude de (1679). *Commentaire sur le coutume de la prevoté et vicomté de Paris* (n.p.).

Ficino, Marsilio (1576). *Theologia Platonica*, in *Opera omnia*, vol. I, pp. 78–424 (Basle; facsimile reprint 1962, Turin: Bottega d'Erasmo).

Filelfo, Francesco (1967). *Francesco Filelfo educatore e il 'codice Sforza' della Biblioteca Reale di Torino*, ed. L. Firpo (Turin: Unione Tipografico-Editrice Torinese).

Fortescue, Sir John (1949). *De laudibus legum Anglie*, ed. S.B. Chrimes (Cambridge: Cambridge University Press).

Bibliography

Fregius, Joannes Thomas (1581). *Partitiones iuris utriusque* (Basle).

Fulbeke, William (1618). *A Parallele or Conference of the Civil with the Canon Law and the Common Law of the Realm of England* (London).

Gammaro, Pietro (1584). *De Extensionibus*, in *Tractatus universi iuris*, vol. XVIII (Venice).

Gansfort, John Wessel (1917). *Life and Writings*, by E.W. Miller, and *Principal Works*, trans. J.W. Schudder, 2 vols. (New York and London: Papers of the American Society of Church History).

(1966). *Opera quae inveniri potuerunt omnia* (Nieuwkoop: Monumenta Humanistica Belgica, vol. I: facsimile of the 1614 Groningen edition).

Gennaro, Giuseppe Aurelio di (1733). *Respublica Jurisconsultorum* (Leipzig).

Gentili, Alberico (1582). *De Iuris interpretibus dialogi sex* (London).

(1933). *De iure belli libri tres*, intro. C. Phillipson, 2 vols. (Oxford: Clarendon Press).

George of Trebizond (1970). *Praefatio in libros Platonis 'De legibus'*, ed. F. Adorno, in *Studi in onore di Antonio Corsano*, pp. 13–17 (Manduria: Lacaita).

(1984). *Collectanea Trapezuntiana*, ed. J. Monfasani (Center for Medieval and Early Renaissance Studies, State University of New York at Binghampton).

Giannotti, Donato (1850). *Libro della repubblica de' Viniziani*, in *Opere*, ed. F.-L. Polidori, 2 vols. (Florence: le Monnier), vol. II, pp. 1–173.

(1990). *Republica fiorentina*, ed. G. Silvano (Geneva: Droz).

Grassaille, Charles de (1545). *Regalium Franciae libri duo* (Paris).

Grégoire, Pierre (1580). *De Iuris arte libellus* (Lyons).

(1591). *Syntagma iuris universi* (Frankfurt).

(1609). *De republica* (Frankfurt).

Gribaldi, Matteo (1541). *De Methode ac ratione studiendi* (Lyons).

Guarino da Verona (1915–19). *Epistolario*, ed. R. Sabbadini, 3 vols. (Venice: Miscellanea di Storia Veneta, series 3, vols. VIII, XI, XIV).

Guevara, Antonio de (1919). *The Diall of Princes by Don Anthony of Guevara translated by Sir Thomas North . . ., select passages*, ed. K.N. Colvile (London: Philip Allan and Co. The Scholar's Library, 1).

(1968). *Relox de principes*, trans. Sir Thomas North as *The Diall of Princes* (facsimile of the 1557 edition) (Amsterdam: Theatrum Orbis Terrarum; New York: Da Capo Press. *The English Experience*, vol. V).

Guicciardini, Francesco (1931). *Storia fiorentina dal 1378 al 1509*, ed. R. Palmarocchi (Bari: Laterza).

(1932). *Dialogo e discorsi del reggimento di Firenze*, ed. R. Palmarocchi (Bari: Laterza).

(1933). *Considerazioni intorno ai Discorsi del Machiavelli sopra la prima deca di Tito Livio*, in *Scritti politici e ricordi*, ed. R. Palmarocchi (Bari: Laterza), pp. 1–65.

(1951). *Ricordi*, ed. R. Spongano (Florence: Sansoni).

Hegendorf, Christoph (1537). *Iuris ipsius discendi Methodus*, in Alciato, *Iudiciarii processus compendium* (Paris).

Hobbes, Thomas (1971). *A Dialogue between a Philosopher and a student of the Common Laws of England*, ed. J. Cropsey (Chicago: University of Chicago Press).

Hotman, François (1560). *Partitiones iuris civilis elementaries* (Basle).

(1603). *Antitribonian* (Paris). Reproduced in the Paris law thesis (1972) of A.H. Saint-Charmaran.

(1972). *Francogallia*, ed. R.E. Giesey, trans. J.H.M. Salmon (Cambridge: Cambridge University Press).

Landino, Cristoforo (1980). *Disputationes Camaldulenses*, ed. P. Lohe (Florence: Sansoni).

Le Caron, Louis (1555). *La Philosophie* (Paris).

(1587). *Pandectes ou Digestes du droit françois*, vol. I (Paris).

(1637). *Memorables observations du droit françois* (Paris).

I   Renaissance and Counter-Renaissance

Le Conte, Antoine (1599). *Methodus de feudis*, in Freher, *De Feudis constition Karoli III* (Hanover).

Lehmann, K. (1896). *Das langobardische Lehnrecht (Consuetudines feudorum*, no. 3) (Göttingen: Dieterich).

Leibniz, Gottfried Wilhelm (1667). *Nova methodus discendae docendaeque jurisprudentiae* (Frankfurt).

Lipsius, Justus (1637). *Opera Omnia* (Antwerp).

Loisel, Antoine (1844). *Pasquier, ou Dialogue des avocats du Parlement de Paris*, ed. M. Dupin (Paris: Vidocq).

(1935). *Institutes coutumiers*, ed. M. Reulos (Paris: Sirey).

Luther, Martin (1957). *Why the Books of the Pope and his Disciples were Burned, 1520*, trans. L. Spitz, ed. H. Grimm, in *Works*, vol. XXXI, pp. 383–95 (Philadelphia: Muhlenberg Press).

Machiavelli, Niccolò (1950). *The Discourses of Niccolò Machiavelli*, trans. L.J. Walker, 2 vols. (London: Routledge and Kegan Paul).

(1960). *Il Principe e Discorsi sopra la prima deca di Tito Livio*, ed. S. Bertelli (Milan: Feltrinelli).

(1961a). *Lettere*, ed. F. Gaeta (Milan: Feltrinelli).

(1961b). *Arte della guerra e scritti politici minori*, ed. S. Bertelli (Milan: Feltrinelli).

(1961c). *The Prince*, trans. G. Bull (Harmondsworth: Penguin).

(1962). *Istorie fiorentine*, ed. F. Gaeta (Milan: Feltrinelli).

(1988). *The Prince*, trans. R. Price, ed. Q.R.D. Skinner (Cambridge: Cambridge University Press).

Maio, Iuniano (1956). *De maiestate*, ed. F. Gaeta (Bologna: Commisione per i testi di lingua; Scelta di curiosità letterarie inedite o rare, 250).

Mair, John (1509). *Quartus Sententiarum* (Paris).

(1510). *In secundum Sententiarum* (Paris).

(1516). *In quartum Sententiarum questiones* (Paris).

(1518). *In Mattheum ad literam expositio* (Paris).

(1519). *In quartum Sententiarum questiones* (Paris).

(1521). *Historia Majoris Britanniae tam Angliae quam Scotiae* (Paris).

(1528). *In tertium Sententiarum disputationes theologicae* (Paris).

(1530). *Ethica Aristotelis Peripateticorum principis. Cum Jo. Maioris Theologi Parisiensis commentariis* (Paris).

(1892). *A History of Greater Britain as well England as Scotland*, trans. A. Constable (Edinburgh: Publications of the Scottish History Society, 10).

Mazzolini da Prierio, Silvestro (1539). *Summa Summarum quae Silvestrina nuncupatur* (Lyons). First publ. Bologna, 1515.

More, Thomas (1965). *Utopia*, ed. E. Surtz and J.H. Hexter (New Haven: Yale: University Press; The Complete Works of St Thomas More, vol. IV).

(1974). *Utopia*, introd. J. Warrington (London: Dent; Everyman's Library).

Morison, Richard (1540). See Vives.

Morosini, Domenico (1969). *De bene instituta re publica*, ed. C. Finzi (Milan: Giuffrè).

Nerli, Filippo de' (1859). *Commentari dei fatti civili occorsi dentro la città di Firenze dall'anno 1215 al 1537*, 2 vols. (Trieste: Coen).

Palmieri, Matteo (1982). *Vita civile*, ed. G. Belloni (Florence: Sansoni).

Pasquier, Etienne (1621). *Les Recherches de la France* (Paris).

(1847). *L'Interprétation des Institutes de Justinian*, ed. M. le Duc Pasquier (Paris: Vidocq ainé and Durand).

Patrizi, Francesco (1594a). *De institutione reipublicae* (Strasburg).

(1594b). *De regno et regis institutione* (Strasburg).

Bibliography

Pico della Mirandola, Giovanni (1948). *Oration on the Dignity of Man*, trans. E.L. Forbes (Chicago: University of Chicago Press).

Platina (Sacchi), Bartolomeo (1913–32). *Liber de vita Christi ac omnium pontificum*, ed. G. Gaida, in *Rerum Italicarum Scriptores*, vol. III, 1 (Città di Castello: Lapi).

(1944). *De optimo cive*, ed. F. Battaglia, in Matteo Palmieri, *Della vita civile*, and Bartolomeo Sacchi detto il Platina, *De optimo cive* (Bologna: Zanichelli), pp. 177–236.

(1979). *De principe*, ed. G. Ferraù (Messina: Il Vespro).

Poggio, Giovanni Francesco (1504). *Ad S.D.N. Iulium Papam Il de officio Principis* (Rome). (1512?). *De potestate papae et concilii* (Rome).

Poliziano, Angelo (1958). *Della congiura dei Pazzi (Coniurationis commentarium)*, ed. A. Perosa (Padua: Antenore, 3).

(1979). *The 'Stanze' of Angelo Poliziano*, ed. and trans. D. Quint (Amherst: Massachusetts University Press).

Pontano, Giovanni (1952). *De principe*, in *Prosatori latini del Quattrocento*, ed. E. Garin (Milan and Naples: Ricciardi), pp. 1024–63.

Quirini, Lauro (1977a). *De nobilitate*, ed. K. Krautter, P.O. Kristeller, H. Roob, in *Lauro Quirini umanista*, ed. V. Branca (Florence: Olschki), pp. 74–98.

(1977b). *De republica*, ed. C. Senio and V. Ravegnani, in *Lauro Quirini umanista*, ed. V. Branca (Florence: Olschki), pp. 121–61.

Rachel, Samuel (1676). *De Jure Naturae et Gentium Dissertationes* (Kiel; repr. Washington: Carnegie Institute, 1916, with English trans.).

Reusner, Nicolas (1588). *XEIPAFOFIA, sive Cynosure iuris* (Speier).

Rijkel, Denis (the Carthusian), (1908). *Opera minora*, in *Opera Omnia*, vol. XXXVI (Tournai: Typis Cartusiae S.M. de Pratis).

Rinuccini, Alamanno (1957). *Dialogus de libertate*, ed. F. Adorno, in *Atti e Memorie dell'Accademia Toscana di Scienze e Lettere 'La Columbaria'*, 22:270–303.

Roper, William (1963). *The Life of Sir Thomas More, Knight*, ed. E.E. Reynolds (London: Dent).

Savonarola, Girolamo (1965). *Trattato circa el reggimento e governo della città di Firenze*, in *Prediche sopra Aggeo*, ed. L. Firpo (Rome: Belardetti), pp. 435–87.

Seyssel, Claude de (1508). *Commentarri in sex partes Digestorum et Codicis* (n.p.). (1566). *Speculum Feudorum* (Basle).

(1961). *La Monarchie de France*, ed. J. Poujol (Paris: Librairie d'Argence).

(1981). *The Monarchy of France*, trans. J.H. Hexter, intro. D.R. Kelley (New Haven: Yale University Press).

Simonetta, Giovanni (1932–59). *Rerum gestarum Francisci Sfortiae commentarii*, ed. G. Soranzo, in *Rerum Italicarum Scriptores*, vol. XXI, 2 (Bologna: Zanichelli).

Spelman, Henry (1733). *The English Works* (London).

Starkey, Thomas (1537, 1878). *The Exhortation to the People*, ed. S.J. Heritage (London: Early English Text Society).

(1989). *A Dialogue between Pole and Lupset*, ed. T. Mayer (London: Royal Historical Society; Camden Fourth Series, 37).

Stryk, Samuel (1709–12). *Specimen usus moderni Pandectarum*, erd edn, 5 vols. (Halle).

Summenhart, Conrad (1513). *Septipertitum opus de contractibus* (Hagenau).

Textor, Johann Wolfgang (1916). *Synopsis juris gentium*, ed. L. von Bar (Washington: Carnegie Institute; Classics of International Law).

Tolomei, Claudio (1517). *De Corruptis verbis iuris civilis dialogus* (Sienna).

Traversari, Ambrogie (1759). *Epistolae* (Florence).

Valla, Lorenzo (1962). *Elegantiae Latinae linguae*, vol. VI. Preface in *Opera omnia*, ed. E. Garin (Turin: Bottega d'Erasmó).

Vico, Giambattista (1911–41). *Opere*, 8 pts (Bari: Laterza).

I Renaissance and Counter-Renaissance

Vives, Juan Luís (1525, 1526, 1531, 1535). *Opera Omnia*, vols. IV and V (facsimile edition, London: The Gregg Press, 1964).

(1540). *An introduction to wysedome . . . Translated by R. Morysone* (London).

Watkins, R.N., ed. (1978). *Humanism and Liberty: Writings on Freedom from Fifteenth-Century Florence* (Columbia: South Carolina University Press).

Zasius, Ulrich (1550). On Digest I, 1 and 3, in *Opera Omnia*, vol. III (Lyons; reprinted 1964–6, Aalen: Scientia Verlag).

Secondary sources

Acton, J.E.E. (Lord Acton) (1910). *Lectures on the French Revolution*, ed. J.N. Figgis and R.V. Laurence (London: Macmillan).

Adams, R.P. (1962). *The Better Part of Valor: More, Erasmus, Colet, and Vives, on Humanism, War, and Peace, 1496–1535* Seattle: University of Washington Press).

Affölter, F.X. (1897). *Das römische Institutionen-System, sein Wesen und seine Geschichte* (Berlin: Puchkammer and Mühlbrecht).

Albertini, R. von (1955). *Das florentinische Staatsbewusstsein im Übergang von der Republik zum Prinzipat* (Berne: Francke).

Allen, J.W. (1928). *A History of Political Thought in the Sixteenth Century* (London: Methuen).

Altamura, A. (1941). *L'umanesimo nel Mezzogiorno d'Italia* (Florence: Biblioteca dell' 'Archivum Romanicum', series 1, 29).

Anglo, S. (1969). *Machiavelli: A Dissection* (London: Gollancz).

Arnaud, J-J. (1969). *Les Origines doctrinales du Code Civil français* (Paris: Librairie générale de droit et de jurisprudence).

Astuti, G. (1937). *Mos italicus e mos gallicus nei dialogi 'de iuris interpretibus' di Alberico Gentili* (Bologna: Zanichelli).

Aubépin, H. (1855). *De l'influence de Dumoulin sur la législation française* (Paris: Cotillon).

Baron, H. (1961). 'Machiavelli: The Republican Citizen and the Author of "The Prince"', *English Historical Review*, 76:217–53. Repr. Baron 1988, vol. II.

(1966). *The Crisis of the Early Italian Renaissance*, 2nd edn (Princeton: Princeton University Press).

(1967). 'Leonardo Bruni: "Professional Rhetorician" or "Civic Humanist"?', *Past and Present*, 36:21–37.

(1968). *From Petrarch to Leonardo Bruni* (Chicago: University of Chicago Press).

(1988). *In Search of Florentine Civic Humanism*, 2 vols. (Princeton: Princeton University Press).

Battaglia, F. (1936). *Enea Silvio Piccolomini e Francesco Patrizi: due politici senesi del Quattrocento* (Florence: Olschki).

Bausi, F. (1985). *I 'Discorsi' di Niccolò Machiavelli. Genesi e strutture* (Florence: Sansoni).

Bayley, C.C. (1961). *War and Society in Renaissance Florence: The 'De Militia' of Leonardo Bruni* (Toronto: University of Toronto Press).

Bec, C. (1967). *Les Marchands Ecrivains à Florence 1375–1434* (Paris and The Hague: Mouton).

Becker, J.-J. (1988). *Die Appellation vom Papst an ein allgeneines Konzil: historische Entwicklung und kanonistiche Diskussion im späten Mittelalter und in der früher Neuzeit* (Vienna and Cologne: Forschungen zur kirchlichen Rechtsgeschichte und zum Kirchenrecht, 17).

Bekker, E.I. (1871). *Die Aktionen in der römischen Privatrechts* (Berlin: F. Vahlen).

Belloni, G. (1978). 'Intorno alla datazione della *Vita civile* di Matteo Palmieri', *Studi e problemi di critica testuale*, 16:49–62.

Bentley, J.H. (1987). *Politics and Culture in Renaissance Naples* (Princeton: Princeton University Press).

Bibliography

Bergfeld, C. (1968). *Franciscus Connanus, 1508–1551* (Cologne: H. Bohlau).

Berlin, I. (1972). 'The Originality of Machiavelli', in *Studies on Machiavelli*, ed. M.P. Gilmore (Florence: Sansoni), pp. 145–206. Repr. in *Against the Current* (Oxford: Oxford University Press), pp. 25–79.

Berriat-Saint-Prix, J. (1821). *Histoire du droit romain, suivie de l'histoire de Cujas* (Paris: Neve).

Black, A.J. (1970). *Monarchy and Community: Political Ideas in the Later Conciliar Controversy, 1430–1450* (Cambridge: Cambridge University Press).

  (1979). *Council and Commune: The Conciliar Movement and the Council of Basle* (London: Burns and Oates; Shepherdstown: The Patmos Press).

Born, L.K. (1928). 'The Perfect Prince', *Speculum*, 3:470–504.

Bradshaw, B. (1979). 'The Tudor Commonwealth: Reform and Revision', *Historical Journal*, 22:455–76.

  (1981). 'More on *Utopia*', *Historical Journal*, 24:1–27.

  (1982). 'The Christian Humanism of Erasmus', *Journal of Theological Studies*, n.s., 33:411–47.

  (1985). 'The Controversial Sir Thomas More', *Journal of Ecclesiastical History*, 36:535–69.

Branca, V. (1973). 'Ermolao Barbaro and Venetian Humanism', in *Renaissance Venice*, ed. J.R. Hale (London: Faber).

Brie, S. (1898). *Die Lehre vom Gewohnheitsrecht* (Breslau: Marcus).

Brodie, D.M. (1948). 'Introduction' to Edmund Dudley, *The Tree of Commonwealth* (Cambridge: Cambridge University Press).

Brown, A.M. (1961). 'The Humanist Portrait of Cosimo de' Medici Pater Patriae', *Journal of the Warburg and Courtauld Institutes*, 24:186–221.

  (1979). *Bartolomeo Scala, 1430–1497, Chancellor of Florence* (Princeton: Princeton University Press).

  (1986). 'Platonism in Fifteenth-Century Florence and its Contribution to Early Modern Political Thought', *Journal of Modern History*, 58:383–413.

Brucker, G. (1977). *The Civic World of Early Renaissance Florence* (Princeton: Princeton University Press).

Burckhardt, J. (1890). *The Civilization of the Renaissance in Italy*, trans. S.G.C. Middlemore (London: Sonnenschein).

Burns, J.H. (1954). 'New Light on John Major', *Innes Review*, 5:83–100.

  (1955). 'John Ireland and *The Meroure of Wyssdome*', *Innes Review*, 6:77–98.

  (1981). '*Politia regalis et optima*: The Political Ideas of John Mair', *History of Political Thought*, 2:31–61.

  (1983a). '*Jus gladii* and *jurisdictio*: Jacques Almain and John Locke', *Historical Journal*, 26:369–74.

  (1983b). 'St German, Gerson, Aquinas, and Ulpian', *History of Political Thought*, 4:443–9.

  (1985). 'Fortescue and the Political Theory of *dominium*', *Historical Journal*, 28:777–97.

  ed. (1988). *The Cambridge History of Medieval Political Thought, c. 350–c. 1450* (Cambridge: Cambridge University Press).

Butterfield, H. (1940). *The Statecraft of Machiavelli* (London: Bell; 2nd edn, 1955).

Butters, H. (1986). 'Good Government and the Limitations of Power in the Writings of Niccolò Machiavelli', *History of Political Thought*, 7:411–17.

Cadoni, G. (1978a). 'Machiavelli teorico dei conflitti sociali', *Storia e Politica*, 14:197–220.

  (1978b). *L'utopia repubblicana di Donato Giannotti* (Milan: Giuffrè).

Calasso, F. (1954). *Medio evo del diritto*, arta seconda (Milan: Giuffrè).

Canning, J.P. (1987). *The Political Thought of Baldus de Ubaldis* (Cambridge: Cambridge University Press).

  (1988). 'Law, Sovereignty and Corporation Theory, 1300–1450', in Burns (1988), pp. 454–76.

712

I Renaissance and Counter-Renaissance

Cantimori, D. (1937). 'Rhetoric and Politics in Italian Humanism', *Journal of the Warburg and Courtauld Institutes*, 1:83–102.

Carlyle, Sir R.W. and A.J. (1903–36). *A History of Medieval Political Theory in the West*, 6 vols. (Edinburgh and London: Blackwood).

Carpintero, F. (1977). 'Mos italicus, mos gallicus y el Humanismo racionalista', *Ius commune*, 6:108–71.

Cartwright, J. (1908). *Baldesare Castiglione, the Perfect Courtier: His Life and Letters 1478–1529*, 2 vols. (London: John Murray).

Castro, A. (1956). *Semblanzas y estudios españoles* (Princeton: Princeton University Press).

Cavanna, A. (1983–7). *Storia del diretto moderno in Europa*, 2 vols. (Milan: Giuffrè).

Chabod, F. (1927). 'Sulla composizione de Il Principe di Niccolò Machiavelli', *Archivum Romanicum*, 11:330–83. Repr. in *Opere* (Turin: Einaudi, 1964), vol. 1: *Scritti su Machiavelli*, pp. 137–93. English trans. by D. Moore in F. Chabod, *Machiavelli and the Renaissance* (Cambridge, Mass.: Harvard University Press, 1958; repr. New York, 1965).

Chambers, R.W. (1935). *Thomas More* (London: Cape).

Cipriani, G. (1980). *Il mito etrusco nel rinascimento fiorentino* (Florence: Olschki).

Clough, C.H. (1967). 'Machiavelli Researches', *Annali dell'Istituto Universitario Orientale, Sezione Romana*, 9:21–129.

Coing, H., ed. (1973–7). *Handbuch der Quellen und Literatur der neueren europäisches Privatrechtsgeschichte*, vol. I: *1100–1500*, vol. II: *1500–1800* (Göttingen: C.H. Beck'sche Verlagsbuchhandlung).

    (1985–9). *Europäisches Privatrecht*, 2 vols. (Munich: Beck).

Collot, C. (1965). *L'Ecole doctrinale de droit public de Pont-à-Mousson* (Paris: Librairie générale de droit et de jurisprudence).

Cortese, E. (1962–4). *La Norma giuridica*, 2 vols. (Milan: Giuffrè).

Cox-Rearick, J. (1984). *Dynasty and Destiny in Medici Art* (Princeton: Princeton University Press).

Cozzi, G. (1970). 'Domenico Morosini e il De bene instituta re publica', *Studi Veneziani*, 12:405–58.

Dahm, G. (1972). 'On the Reception of Roman and Italian Law in Germany', in *Pre-Reformation Germany*, ed. G. Strauss (New York: Macmillan).

Dawson, J.P. (1960). *A History of Law Judges* (Cambridge, Mass.: Harvard University Press).

    (1968). *Oracles of the Law* (Ann Arbor: University of Michigan Law School).

Denzer, H., ed. (1973). *Jean Bodin: Verhandlungen der internationalen Bodin Tagung* (Munich: Beck).

Dickerhof, K. (1941). 'Leibniz' Bedeutung für die Gesetzgebung seiner Zeit' (Freiburg, doctoral dissertation).

Diesner, H.J. (1985). 'Die Virtù der Principi bei Machiavelli', *Zeitschrift für historische Forschung*, 12:385–428.

Dorsch, T.S. (1966–7). 'Sir Thomas More and Lucian: An Interpretation of Utopia', *Archiv für das Studium der Neueren Sprachen und Literaturen*, 203:345–63.

Duff, P.W. (1938). *Personality in Roman Private Law* Cambridge: Cambridge University Press).

Durkan, J. (1950a). 'John Major: After 400 years', *Innes Review*, 1:131–9.

    (1950b). 'The School of John Major: Bibliography', *Innes Review*, 1:140–57.

Durkan, J., and Ross, A. (1961). *Early Scottish Libraries* (Glasgow: John S. Burns & Sons).

Ebel, W. (1958). *Geschichte der Gesetzgebung in Deutschland* (Göttingen: O. Schwartz).

Ebrard, F. (1948). 'Über Methoden, Systeme, Dogmen in der Geschichte des Privatrechts', *Zeitschrift für Schweizerisches Recht*, 67:95–136.

Bibliography

Elton, G.R. (1973). *Reform and Renewal: Thomas Cromwell and the Commonweal* (Cambridge: Cambridge University Press).

Engelmann, W. (1939). *Die Wiedergeburt der Rechtskultur in Italien* (Leipzig: K.F. Koehler).

Eyssell, A.P.T. (1860). *Doneau* (Dijon: Decailly).

Farge, J.K. (1980). *Biographical Register of Paris Doctors of Theology, 1500–1536* (Toronto: Pontifical Institute of Medieval Studies).

Fasoli, G. (1958). 'Nascita di un mito', in *Studi storici in onore di Gioacchino Volpe* (Florence: Sansoni), vol. I, pp. 445–79.

Fassò, G. (1968). *Storia del filosofia del diritto*, vol. II Bologna: Il Mulino).

  (1971). *Vico e Grozio* (Napels: Guida).

Fell, A. (1983–7). *Origins of Legislative Sovereignty and the Legislative State* (Konigstein: Athenäum).

Fenlon, D. (1981). 'Thomas More,and Tyranny', *Journal of Ecclesiastical History*, 22:453–76.

Ferguson, W.K. (1948). *The Renaissance in Historical Thought* (Boston: Houghton Mifflin).

Ferrers Howell, A.G. (1913). *St Bernardino of Siena* (London: Methuen).

Figgis, J.N. (1916). *Studies of Political Thought from Gerson to Grotius*, 2nd edn (Cambridge: Cambridge University Press).

Filhol, R. (1937). *La Premier Président Christofle de Thou et la réformation des coutumes* (Paris: Sirey).

Finzi, C. (1984). *Matteo Palmieri: Dalle 'Vita civile' alla 'Città di Vita'* (Perugia: Giuffrè).

Fox, A., and Guy, J.A., eds. (1986). *Reassessing the Henrician Age* (Oxford: Blackwell).

Franklin, J.H. (1973). *Jean Bodin and the Rise of Absolutist Theory* (Cambridge: Cambridge University Press).

Fraser Jenkins, A.D. (1970). 'Cosimo de' Medici's Patronage of Architecture and the Theory of Magnificence', *Journal of the Warburg and Courtauld Institutes*, 33:162–70.

Fubini, R. (1984). 'Ficino e i Medici all'avvento di Lorenzo il Magnifico', *Rinascimento*, 2nd ser., 24:3–52.

Gaeta, F. (1961). 'Alcune considerazioni sul mito di Venezia', *Bibliothèque d'Humanisme et de Renaissance*, 32:38–75.

Gagner, S. (1960). *Studien zur Ideengeschichte der Gesetzgebung* (Stockholm: Almquist and Wiksell).

Gambino, L. (1975). *Il De Republica di Pierre Grégoire* (Milan: Giuffrè).

Garcia Gallo, A. (1956). *Curso de Historia del Derecho Español* (Madrid: Gráfica Adminsitrativa).

Garin, E. (1952). *Prosatori latini del Quattrocentro* (Milan and Naples: Ricciardi).

  (1965). *Italian Humanism*, trans. P. Munz (Oxford: Oxford University Press). First publ. 1947 as *Der italienische Humanismus* (Berne: Francke).

  (1969). *Science and Civic Life in the Italian Renaissance*, trans. P. Munz (New York: Anchor).

Gaudemet, J. (1977). 'Les Tendances à l'unification du droit en France dans les derniers siècles de l'ancien régime (XVIe–XVIIIe)', *La Formazione storica del diritto moderno* (Florence: Olschki).

Gaughan, W.T. (1931). *Social Theories of Saint Antoninus from his Summa Theologica* (Washington: Catholic University of America Press).

Geerken, J.H. (1987). 'Elements of Natural Law Theory in Machiavelli', in *The Medieval Tradition of Natural Law*, ed. H.J. Johnson (Kalamazoo: Western Michigan University Press).

Gelin, A. (1965). *The Poor of Yahweh* (Collegeville, Minnesota: Liturgical Press).

Gibbs, J. (1960). *Vida de Fray Antonio de Guevara 1481–1545* (Valladolid: Miñón).

Gierke, O. (1950). *Natural Law and the Theory of Society*, trans. E. Barker, 2 vols. (Cambridge: Cambridge University Press).

Gilbert, A.H. (1938). *Machiavelli's Prince and its Forerunners* (Durham, NC: Duke University Press).

Gilbert, F. (1939). 'The Humanist Concept of the Prince and *The Prince* of Machiavelli', *Journal of Modern History* 11:449–83. Repr. in Gilbert (1977), pp. 91–114.

(1953). 'The Composition and Structure of Machiavelli's *Discorsi*', *Journal of the History of Ideas*, 14:136–56. Repr. in Gilbert (1977), pp. 115–33.

(1965). *Machiavelli and Guicciardini: Politics and History in Sixteenth-Century Florence* (Princeton: Princeton University Press).

(1968). 'The Venetian Constitution in Florentine Political Thought', in *Florentine Studies: Politics and Society in Renaissance Florence*, ed. N. Rubinstein (London: Faber), pp. 463–500. Repr. in Gilbert (1977), pp. 179–214.

(1969). 'Religion and Politics in the Thought of Gasparo Contarini', in *Action and Conviction in Early Modern Europe*, ed. T.K. Rabb and J.E. Seigel (Princeton: Princeton University Press), pp. 90–116. Repr. in Gilbert (1977), pp. 247–67.

(1977). *History: Choice and Commitment* (Cambridge, Mass.: Harvard University Press).

Gilbert, N.W. (1960). *Concepts of Method in the Renaissance* (New York: Columbia University Press).

Gilmore, M.P. (1941). *Argument from Roman Law in Political Thought, 1200–1600* (Cambridge, Mass.: Harvard University Press).

Goez, W. (1958). *Translatio Imperii* (Tübingen: Mohr).

Goldbrunner, H. (1983). 'Laudatio urbis: Zu neueren Untersuchungen über das humanistische Stadtelob', *Quellen und Forschungen aus italienischen Archiven und Bibliotheken*, 63:313–28.

Goldthwaite, R. (1981). *The Building of Renaissance Florence* (Baltimore: Johns Hopkins University Press).

Gombrich, E. (1950). *The Story of Art* (London: Phaidon).

(1976). *The Heritage of Apelles* (Oxford: Phaidon).

(1985). *Norm and Form* (Oxford: Phaidon).

Goudy, H. (1910). *Trichotomy in Roman Law* (Oxford: Clarendon Press).

Grafton, A., and Jardine, L (1986). *From Humanism to the Humanities* (London: Duckworth).

Gray, H.H. (1963). 'Renaissance Humanism: The Pursuit of Eloquence', *Journal of the History of Ideas*, 24:497–514.

Grey, E. (1973). *Guevara, a Forgotten Renaissance Author* (The Hague; Nijhoff).

Griffiths, G., et al. (1987). *The Humanism of Leonardo Bruni* (Binghamton, N.Y.: Medieval and Renaissance Texts and Studies).

Gross, H. (1973). *Empire and Sovereignty* (Chicago: University of Chicago Press).

Grossi, P., ed. (1972). *La Seconda scolastica nella formzione del diretto privato moderno*, Quaderni fiorentini (Milan: Giuffrè).

Guillemain, B. (1976). 'Machiavel, lecteur d'Aristote', in *Platon et Aristote à la Renaissance* (XVIe Colloque international de Tours), pp. 163–73.

(1977). *Machiavel: L'anthropologie politique* (Geneva: Droz).

Guthrie, W.K.C. (1969, 1975). *History of Greek Philosophy*, vols. III and IV (Cambridge: Cambridge University Press).

Hale, J.R. (1961). *Machiavelli and Renaissance Italy* (London: English Universities Press).

Hamilton, B. (1963). *Political Thought in Sixteenth-Century Spain: A Study of the Political Ideas of Vitoria, De Soto, Suárez and Molina* (Oxford: Clarendon Press).

Hankins, J. (forthcoming). *A Life of Leonardo Bruni*.

Hennig, G. (1966). *Cajetan und Luther: ein historischer Beitrag zur Begegnung von Thomismus und Reformation* (Stuttgart: Arbeiten zur Theologie, II Reihe, vol. VII).

Hermelink, H. (1906). *Die theologische Facultät in Tübingen vor der Reformation, 1477–1534* (Stuttgart: Druck der Union deutsche Verlagsgesellschaft).

Bibliography

Hexter, J.H. (1952). *More's Utopia: The Biography of an Idea* (Princeton: Princeton University Press).

(1956). 'Seyssel, Machiavelli and Polybius VI; the Mystery of the Missing Translation', *Studies in the Renaissance*, 3:20–37.

(1957). '*Il Principe* and *lo stato*', *Studies in the Renaissance*, 4:113–38.

(1965). 'Introduction', in *Utopia*, ed. E. Surtz and J.H. Hexter (New Haven: Yale University Press; The Complete Works of St Thomas More, vol. IV).

(1973). *The Vision of Politics on the Eve of the Reformation: More, Machiavelli and Seyssel* (London: Allen Lane).

Hoke, R. (1976). 'Die Emanzipation der deutschen Staatswissenschaft von der Zivilistik im 17 Jahrhundert', *Der Staat*, 15:211–40.

Holmes, G. (1986). *Florence, Rome and the Origins of the Renaissance* (Oxford: Oxford University Press).

Huizinga, J. (1924). *The Waning of the Middle Ages* (London: Arnold).

(1952). *Erasmus of Rotterdam*, trans. J. Hopman (London: Phaidon).

Hunt, H.A.K. (1954). *The Humanism of Cicero* (Carlton, Victoria: Melbourne University Press).

Huovinen, L. (1951). *Das Bild vom Menschen im politischen Denken Machiavellis* (Annales Academiae Scientiarum Fennicae, ser. B, 74, 2).

Ianziti, G. (1988). *Humanistic Historiography under the Sforzas: Politics and Propaganda in Fifteenth-Century Milan* (Oxford: Oxford University Press).

James, M.E. (1978). 'English Politics and the Concept of honour 1485–1642', *Past and Present*, Supplement 3.

Kagan, R.L. (1981). *Lawsuits and Litigants in Castile, 1500–1700* (Chapel Hill: North Carolina University Press).

Kahn, V. (1985). *Rhetoric, Prudence and Skepticism in the Renaissance* (Ithaca: Cornell University Press).

Kalinowski, G. (1982). 'La Logique juridique et son histoire', *Archives de Philosophie du Droit*, 27:275–89.

Kantorowicz, E. (1957). *The King's Two Bodies: A Study in Medieval Political Theology* (Princeton: Princeton University Press).

Keen, M.H. (1966). *The Laws of War in the Late Middle Ages* (London: Routledge and Kegan Paul).

Kelley, D.R. (1964). '*De Origine Feudorum*: The Beginnings of an Historical Problem', *Speculum*, 39:207–28. Repr. in Kelley (1984).

(1970a). *Foundations of Modern Historical Scholarship: Language, Law and History in the French Renaissance* (New York: Columbia University Press).

(1970b). 'Murd'rous Machiavel in France', *Political Science Quarterly*, 85:545–59.

(1973). *François Hotman: A Revolutionary's Ordeal* (Princeton: Princeton University Press).

(1974). 'History, English Law and the Renaissance', *Past and Present*, 65:24–51. Repr. in Kelley (1984).

(1976a). 'Louis Le Caron Philosophe', in *Philosophy and Humanism: Renaissance Essays in Honor of Paul Oskar Kristeller*, ed. E. Mahoney (New York: Columbia University Press). Repr. in Kelley (1984).

(1976b). 'Vera Philosophia: The Philosophical Significance of Renaissance Jurisprudence', *Journal of the History of Philosophy*, 14:267–79. Repr. in Kelley (1984).

(1976c). 'Vico's Road: From Philology to Jurisprudence and Back', in *Giambattista Vico's Science of Humanity*, ed. G. Tagliacozzo and D. Verene (Baltimore: Johns Hopkins University Press). Repr. in Kelley (1984).

I Renaissance and Counter-Renaissance

(1979a). 'Civil Science in the Renaissance: Jurisprudence Italian Style', *Historical Journal*, 22:277–94. Repr. in Kelley (1984).

(1979b). 'Gaius Noster: Substructures of Western Social Thought', *American Historical Review*, 84:619–48. Repr. in Kelley (1984).

(1981a). *The Beginnings of Ideology*: Consciousness and Society in the French Reformation: (Cambridge: Cambridge University Press).

(1981b). 'Civil Science in the Renaissance: Jurisprudence in the French Manner', *History of European Ideas*, 2:261–76. Repr. in Kelley (1984).

(1983). 'Hermes, Clio, Themis: Historical Interpretation and Legal Hermeneutics', *Journal of Modern History*, 55:644–68. Repr. in Kelley (1984).

(1984). *History, Law and the Human Sciences: Medieval and Renaissance Perspectives* (London: Variorum Reprints).

(1987). 'Civil Science in the Renaissance: The Problem of Interpretation', in *The Languages of Political Theory in Early-Modern Europe*, ed. A. Pagden (Cambridge: Cambridge University Press).

(1988). '*Jurisconsultus perfectus*: The Lawyer as Renaissance Man', *Journal of the Warburg and Courtauld Institutes*, 51:84–102.

(1990). *The Human Measure: Social Thought in the Western Legal Tradition* (Cambridge, Mass.: Harvard University Press).

Kennedy, G. (1980). *Classical Rhetoric and its Christian and Secular Tradition from Ancient to Modern Times* (London: Croom Helm).

Kenny, A. (1983). *Thomas More* (Oxford: Oxford University Press; Past Masters).

Kent, F.W. (1977). *Household and Lineage in Renaissance Florence* (Princeton: Princeton University Press).

Kent, F.W. and Kent, D. (1982). *Neighbors and the Neighborhood in Renaissance Florence: The District of the Red Lion in the Fifteenth Century* (Locust Valley, N.Y.: J.J. Augustin).

King, M.L. (1986). *Venetian Humanism in an Age of Patricican Dominance* (Princeton: Princeton University Press).

Kisch, G. (1960). *Erasmus und die Jurisprudenz seiner Zeit* (Basle: Helbing and Lichtenhahn).

(1967). *Melanchthons Rechts- und Soziallehre* (Berlin: De Gruyter).

(1969). *Gestalten und Probleme aus Humanismus und Jurisprudenz* (Berlin: De Gruyter).

(1970). *Claudius Cantiuncula* (Basle: Helbing and Lichtenhahn).

(1972). *Studien zur humanistischen Jurisprudenz* (Berlin: De Gruyter).

Kohl, B., and Witt, R. (1978). *The Earthly Republic* (Philadelphia: Pennsylvania University Press).

Koschaker, P. (1958). *Europa und das römische Recht* (Munich and Berlin: Beck).

Kretzmann, N., Kenny, A., and Pinborg, J., eds. (1982). *The Cambridge History of Later Medieval Philosophy: From the Rediscovery of Aristotle to the Disintegration of Scholasticism, 1100–1600* (Cambridge: Cambridge University Press).

Kristeller, P.O. (1961). *Renaissance Thought*, vol. 1: *The Classic, Scholastic and Humanistic Strains* (New York: Harper).

(1972). *Renaissance Concepts of Man, and Other Essays* (New York: Harper).

(1979). *Renaissance Thought and its Sources*, ed. M. Mooney (New York: Columbia University Press).

(1982). 'The Renaissance in the History of Political Thought', in *The Renaissance: Essays in Interpretation*, ed. A. Chastel et al. (London: Methuen), pp. 127–51.

La Brosse, O. de (1965). *Le Pape et le Concile: la comparaison de leurs pouvoirs à la veille de la Réforme* (Paris: Unam Sanctam, 58).

Laspeyres, E.A. (1830). *Über die Entstehung und älteste Bearbeitung der Libri Feudorum* (Berlin: F. Dümmler).

Bibliography

Lebrun, A. (1932). *La Coutume* (Paris: Librairie générale de droit et de jurisprudence).

Leff, G. (1976). *The Dissolution of the Medieval Outlook: An Essay on Spiritual and Intellectual Change in the Fourteenth Century* (New York: Harper and Row).

Lehmberg, S.E. (1960). *Sir Thomas Elyot, Tudor Humanist* (Austin: Texas University Press).

Levack, B.P. (1973). *The Civil Lawyers in England 1603–1641* (Oxford: Clarendon Press).

Lombardi, G. (1947). *Sul Concetto di 'ius gentium'* (Rome: Istituto de Diritto Romano).

Longo, G. (1972). 'Utilitas publica', *Labeo*, 18:7–71.

Macke, P. (1966). *Das Rechts- und Staatsdenken des Johannes Oldendorp* (Cologne: inaugural dissertation).

McNeil, D.O. (1975). *Guillaume Budé and Humanism* (Geneva: Travaux d'Humanisme et Renaissance, 142).

Maffei, D. (1956). *Gli Inizi dell' umanesimo giuridico* (Milan: Giuffrè).

(1964). *La Donazione di Costantino nei giuristi medievali* (Milan: Giuffrè).

Maiorca, C. (1937). *La Cosa in senso giuridico* (Turin: Istituto giuridico della R. Università).

Major, J.M. (1964). *Sir Thomas Elyot and Renaissance Humanism* (Lincoln, NB: University of Nebraska Press).

Marchand, J.-J. (1975). *Niccolò Machiavelli: I primi scritti politici (1499–1512)* (Padua: Antenore).

Marius, R. (1984). *Thomas More: A Biography* (London: Dent).

Markus, R.A. (1970). *Saeculum: History and Society in the Theology of St Augustine* (Cambridge: Cambridge University Press; repr. 1988).

Martelli, M. (1969). 'I "Ghiribizzi" a Giovan Battista Soderini', *Rinascimento*, 2nd ser., 9:147–80.

(1970). 'Ancora sui "Ghiribizzi" di Giovan Battista Soderini', *Rinascimento*, 2nd ser., 10:3–27.

Mason, R. (1987). 'Kingship, Tyranny and the Right to Resist in Fifteenth Century Scotland', *Scottish Historical Review*, 66:125–51.

Matteucci, N. (1972). 'Niccolò Machiavelli politologo', in *Studies on Machiavelli*, ed. M.P. Gilmore (Florence: Sansoni), pp 207–48.

Mayer, T.F. (1989). *Thomas Starkey and the Commonweal: Humanist Politics and Religion in the Reign of Henry VIII* (Cambridge: Cambridge University Press).

Messeri, A. (1894). 'Matteo Palmieri cittadino di Firenze nel secolo XV', *Archivio Storico Italiano*, ser. 5, 13:256–340.

Meynial, E. (1908). 'Notes sur la formation de la théorie du domaine divise (domaine direct et domaine utile du XIe au XIVe siècle', *Mélanges Fitting* (Montpellier: Laros et Tenin), II, pp. 409–61.

Mochi Onory, S. (1951). *Fonti canonistiche dell'idea moderno dello stato* (Milan: Vita e pensiero).

Mommsen, T.E. (1959). *Medieval and Renaissance Studies*, ed. E.F. Rice (Ithaca: Cornell University Press).

Morçay, R. (1914). *Saint Antonin, foundateur du Couvent de Saint Marc, archevêque de Florence 1389–1459* (Paris: Gabalda).

Moreau-Reibel, J. (1933). *Jean Bodin et le droit public comparé* (Paris: Vrin).

Mortenson, L.B. (1986). 'Leonardo Bruni's *Dialogus*: A Ciceronian Debate on the Literary Culture of Florence', *Classica et Medievalia*, 37:259–302.

Müllejans, H. (1961). *Publicus und Privatus in römisches Recht und älteren kanonischen Recht* (Munich: M. Hueber).

Müllner, L. (1899). *Reden und Briefe italienischer Humanisten* (Vienna: A. Holder).

Noreña, C.G. (1970). *Juan Luís Vives* (The Hague: Archives of the History of Ideas, 34).

Oakley, F. (1962). 'On the Road from Constance to 1688: The Political Thought of John Major and George Buchanan', *Journal of British Studies*, 2:1–31.

I Renaissance and Counter-Renaissance

(1964–5). 'Almain and Major: Conciliar Theory on the Eve of the Reformation'. *American Historical Review*, 70:673–90.

(1977). 'Conciliarism in the Sixteenth Century: Jacques Almain Again', *Archiv für Reformationsgeschichte*, 68:111–32.

(1979). *The Western Church in the Later Middle Ages* (Ithaca: Cornell University Press).

(1988). 'Disobedience, Consent, Political Obligation', *History of Political Thought*, 9:211–21.

Oberman, H.A. (1967a). *The Harvest of Medieval Theology: Gabriel Biel and Late Medieval Nominalism*, 2nd edn (Grand Rapids, Mich.: Eerdmans).

(1967b). *Forerunners of the Reformation: The Shape of Late Medieval Thought*, trans. P.L. Nyhus (London: Letternorth Press).

(1977). *Werden und Wertung der Reformation. Vom Wegestreit zum Glaubenskampf* (Tübeingen: Mohr (Paul Siebeck).

(1981). *Masters of the Reformation: The Emergence of a New Intellectual Climate in Europe*, trans. D. Martin (Cambridge: Cambridge University Press).

Oppelt, J. (1974). 'Peace versus Liberty in the Quattrocento: Poggio, Guarino, and the Scipio–Caesar Controversy', *Journal of Medieval and Renaissance Studies*, 4:221–65.

(1977). 'Poggio, San Bernardino of Siena and the Dialogue *On Avarice*', *Renaissance Quarterly*, 30:564–87.

Orestano, R. (1978). *Azzione, diritto soggetivo, persone giuridichi* (Bologna: Il Mulino).

Ott, G. (1952). 'Recht und Gesetz bei Gabriel Biel: ein Beitrag zur spätmittelaltlichen Rechtslehre', *Zeitschrift der Savigny-Stiftung für Rechtsgeschichte*, 69 (Kan. Abt. 38), pp 251–96.

Ozment, S. (1980). *The Age of Reform 1250–1550: An Intellectual and Religious History of Late Medieval and Reformation Europe* (New Haven: Yale University Press).

Pampaloni, G. (1961). 'Fermenti di riforme democratiche nelle consulte della Repubblica Fiorentina', *Archivio Storico Italiano*, 119:241–81.

(1962). 'Nuovi tentativi di riforme alla Costituzione Fiorentina visti attraverso le consulte', *Archivio Storico Italiano*, 120:521–81.

Panizza, D. (1981). *Alberico Gentili, giurista ideologico nell'Inghilterra elizabettiana* (Padua).

Percopo. A. (1938). *Vita di Giovanni Pontano* (Naples: ITEL).

Persico, T. (1899). *Diomede Carafa: Uomo di stato e scrittore del secolo XV* (Naples: Pierro).

Phillips, M. (1987). *The Memoir of Marco Parenti: A Life in Medici Florence* (London: Heinemann; Princeton: Princeton University Press, 1989).

Piano Mortari, V. (1956). *Ricerche sulla interpretazione dell diritto nel secolo XVI* (Milan: Giuffrè).

(1962). *Diritto romano e diritto nazionale in Francia nel secolo XVI* (Milan: Giuffrè).

(1978). *Diritto, logica, metodo* (Naples: Jovene).

Picascia, M.L. (1979). *Un Occamista quattrocentesco: Gabriel Biel* (Florence: Publicazioni della Facoltà di Lettere e Filosofia dell'Università di Pavia, 23, Istituto di Storia della Filosofia).

Plamenatz, J. (1963). *Man and Society*, 2 vols. (London: Longman).

Pocock, J.G.A. (1957, 1987). *The Ancient Constitution and the Feudal Law* (Cambridge: Cambridge University Press).

(1975). *The Machiavellian Moment: Florentine Political Thought and the Atlantic Republican Tradition* (Princeton: Princeton University Press).

Post, G. (1964). *Studies in Medieval Legal Thought: Public Law and the State, 1100–1322* (Princeton: Princeton University Press).

Price, R. (1973). 'The Senses of *virtù* in Machiavelli', *European Studies Review*, 3:315–45.

(1982). '*Ambizione* in Machiavelli's Thought', *History of Political Thought*, 3:383–445.

Puchta , G.F. (1828–37). *Das Gewohneitsrecht* (Erlangen: Palm).

Bibliography

Quint, D. (1985). 'Humanism and Modernity: A Reconsideration of Bruni's *Dialogues*', *Renaissance Quarterly*, 38:423–45.

Renaudet, A. (1953). *Préréforme et humanisme à Paris pendant les premières guerres d'Italie* (1494–1517), 2nd edn (Paris: Librairie d'Argences).

Reulos, M. (1935). *Etude sur L'esprit, les sources et la méthode des Institutes coutumières d'Antoine Loisel* (Paris: Sirey).

Rice, E.F. (1958). *The Renaissance Idea of Wisdom* (Cambridge, Mass: Harvard University Press).

Ridolfi, R. (1942). 'Sommario della vita di Donato Giannotti', in *Opuscoli di storia letteraria e di erudizione* (Florence: Libreria Bibliopolis), pp. 55–164.

  (1952). *Vita di Girolamo Savonarola* (Rome: Belardetti). English trans. by C. Grayson: *The Life of Girolamo Savonarola* (London: Routledge and Kegan Paul, 1959).

  (1960). *Vita di Francesco Guicciardini* (Rome: Belardetti). English trans. by C. Grayson: *The Life of Francesco Guicciardini* (London: Routledge and Kegan Paul, 1967).

  (1972). *Vita di Niccolò Machiavelli*, 5th edn (Florence: Sansoni), English trans. by C. Grayson: *The Life of Niccolò Machiavelli* (London: Routledge and Kegan Paul, 1963).

Ridolfi, R., and Ghiglieri, P. (1970). 'I "Ghiribizzi" al Soderini', *La Bibliofilia*, 72:53–74.

Ritter, G. (1963). *Via Antiqua und Via Moderna auf den deutschen Universitäten des XV. Jahrhundert* (zweite Auflage) (Heidelberg: Sitzungsberichte der Heidelberger Akademie der Wissenschaften, Phil. Hist. Klasse 1922, Abh. 7).

Robey, D. (1973). 'Pier Paolo Vergerio the Elder: Republicanism and Civic Values in the Work of an Early Humanist', *Past and Present*, 58:3–37.

Robey, D., and Law, J. (1975). 'The Venetian Myth and the *De Republica Veneta* of Pier Paolo Vergerio', *Rinascimento*, 2nd ser., 15:3–59.

Rowan, S. (1987). *Ulrich Zasius: A Jurist in the German Renaissance 1461–1535* (Frankfurt-am-Main: Klostermann).

Rubinstein, N. (1966). *The Government of Florence under the Medici (1434 to 1494)* (Oxford: Oxford University Press).

  (1968). 'Florentine Constitutionalism and Medici Ascendancy in the Fifteenth Century', in *Florentine Studies: Politics and Society in Renaissance Florence*, ed. N. Rubinstein (London: Faber, pp. 442–62.

  (1972). 'Machiavelli and the World of Florentine Politics', in *Studies on Machiavelli*, ed. M.P. Gilmore (Florence: Sansoni), pp. 3–28.

  (1979). 'Le dottrine politiche nel Rinascimento', in *Il Rinascimento: Interpretazioni e problemi* (Rome, Bari: Laterza), pp. 181–237. English trans.: see next item.

  (1982). 'Political Theories in the Renaissance', in *The Renaissance: Essays in Interpretation*, ed. A. Chastel (London: Methuen), pp. 153–200.

  (1986). 'Il *De optimo cive* del Platina', in *Bartolomeo Sacchi il Platina*, ed. A. Campana and P. Medioli Masotti (Padua Antenore), pp. 137–44.

  (1987). 'The History of the Word *politicus* in Early-Modern Europe', in *The Languages of Political Theory in Early-Modern Europe*, ed. A. Pagden (Cambridge: Cambridge University Press), pp. 41–56.

Sabbadini, R. (1896). *La scuola e gli studi de Guarino Guarini Veronese* (Catania: Tip. F. Galati).

Sasso, G. (1957, 1958). 'Intorno al composizione dei "Discorsi" di Niccoló Machiavelli', *Giornale Storico della Letteratura Italiana*, 134:482–534; 135:215–59.

  (1967). *Studi su Machiavelli* (Naples: Morano).

  (1980). *Niccolò Machiavelli: Storia del suo pensiero politico* (revised edn., Bologna: Il Mulino).

  (1984). 'Guicciardini e Machiavelli', in *Francesco Guicciardini 1483–1983: Nel V centenario della nascita* (Florence: Olschki).

(1987–8). *Machiavelli e gli antichi e altri saggi*, 3 vols. (Milan and Naples: Ricciardi).
Scarano, E. (1980). *La ragione e le cose: tre studi su Guicciardini* (Pisa: ETS università).
Schellhase, K.C. (1976). *Tacitus in Renaissance Political Thought* (Chicago: University of Chicago Press).
Schmiedel, B. (1966). *Consuetudo im klassischen und nach-klassischen römische Recht* (Graz: H. Bohlau).
Schneider, H.P. (1967). *Justitia Universalis* (Frankfurt: Klostermann).
Schramm, P.E. (1960). *Der König von Frankreich* (Weimar: H. Böhlaus Nachfolger).
Schulz, F. (1936). *Principles of Roman Law*, trans. M. Wolff (Oxford: Clarendon Press).
(1953). *History of Roman Legal Science* (Oxford: Clarendon Press).
Scupin, H.V., Scheuner, U., and Wyduckel, D. (eds.) (1973). *Althusius-Bibliographie* (Berlin: Duncker and Humblot).
Seigel, J.E. (1968). *Rhetoric and Philosophy in Renaissance Humanism* (Princeton: Princeton University Press).
Skinner, Q. (1978). *The Foundations of Modern Political Thought*, 2 vols. (Cambridge: Cambridge University Press).
(1981). *Machiavelli* (Oxford: Oxford University Press; Past Masters).
(1986). 'Ambrogio Lorenzetti: The Artist as Political Philosopher', *Proceedings of the British Academy*, 72:1–56.
(1987). 'Sir Thomas More's *Utopia* and the Language of Renaissance Humanism', in *The Languages of Political Theory in Early-Modern Europe*, ed. A. Pagden (Cambridge: Cambridge University Press).
Sollner, A. (1975). 'Zu der Literatur-Typen der deutschen *Usus Modernus*', *Ius Commune*, 1:167–86.
Spitz, L.W. (1957). *Conrad Celtis* (Cambridge, Mass.: Harvard University Press).
Starn, R. (1968). *Donato Giannotti and his 'Epistolae'* (Geneva: Droz).
Stein, P. (1966). *Regulae iuris: From Legal Rules to Juristic Maxims* (Edinburgh: Edinburgh University Press).
Stintzing, R. (1857). *Ulrich Zasius* (Basle: Schweighauser).
Stintzing, R., and Landsberg, E. (1880–1910). *Geschichte der deutschen Rechtswissenschaft*, Abt. 1–3 (Munich, Leipzig, Berlin: R. Oldenbourg).
Strauss, G. (1986). *Law, Resistance and the State* (Princeton: Princeton University Press).
Sturm, F. (1968). *Das römische Recht in der Sicht von Gottfried Wilhelm Leibniz* (Tübingen: Mohr).
Surtz, E.L. (1957). *The Praise of Pleasure: Philosophy, Education and Communism in More's Utopia* (Cambridge, Mass.: Harvard University Press).
Tarello, G. (1971). *Le Ideologie nella codificazione nel secolo XVIII* (Genoa: Cooperativa Libraria Universitaria).
Tateo, F. (1972). *L'umanesimo etico di Giovanni Pontano* (Lecce: Milella).
Theuerkauf, G. (1968). *Lex, Speculum, Compendium iuris* (Cologne: Böhlau Verlag).
Thireau, J.-L. (1980). *Charles Dumoulin (1500–1566)* (Geneva: Droz).
Thomson, J.A.F. (1980). *Popes and Princes, 1417–1517: Politics and Polity in the Late Medieval Church* (London: Allen and Unwin).
Thorndike, L. (1929). *Science and Thought in the Fifteenth Century* (New York: Columbia University Press).
Thorne, S.E. (1976). 'English Law and the Renaissance' in *La Storia del diritto nel quadro delle scienze storiche* (Florence: Olschki).
Tierney, B. (1983). 'Tuck on Rights: Some Medieval Problems', *History of Political Thought*, 4:429–41.
Todescan, F. (1980). 'Domat et les sources du droit', *Archives de Philosophie du Droit*, 27:55–66.

(1987). *Le Radici teologiche del giusnaturalismo*, vol. II: *Il probleme della secolarizzazione nel pensiero di Jean Domat* (Milan: Giuffrè).

Tracy, J.D. (1972). *Erasmus: The Growth of a Mind* (Geneva: Droz; Travaux d'Humanisme et Renaissance, 126).

(1978). *The Politics of Erasmus* (Toronto: University of Toronto Press).

Trinkaus, C. (1970). *In Our Image and Likeness: Humanity and Divinity in Italian Humanist Thought* (Chicago: University of Chicago Press).

(1979). 'Luther's Hexameral Anthropology', in *Continuity and Discontinuity in Church History*, ed. E.F. Church and T. Grace (Leiden: Brill).

(1982). 'Themes for a Renaissance Anthropology', in *The Renaissance: Essays in Interpretation* (London: Methuen), pp. 83–125.

Troeltsch, E. (1922). *Der Historismus und seine Probleme* (Tübingen: Mohr).

Troje, H. (1969). 'Wissenschaft und System in der Jurisprudenz des 16. Jahrhunderts', in *Philosophie und Rechtswissenschaft*, ed. J. Blundorn and J. Ritter (Frankfurt: Klostermann).

(1971). *Graeca leguntur* (Cologne. H. Bohlau).

Tuck, R. (1979). *Natural Rights Theories: Their Origin and Development* (Cambridge: Cambridge University Press).

Ullman, B.L. (1963). *The Humanism of Coluccio Salutati* (Padua: Antenore).

Ullmann, W. (1975). *Law and Politics in the Middle Ages: An Introduction to the Sources of Medieval Political Thought* (London: The Sources of History; Studies in the Uses of Historical Evidence).

(1977). *Medieval Foundations of Renaissance Humanism* (Ithaca and London: Cornell University Press).

Vanderlinden, J. (1967). *Le Concept de code en Europe occidentale du XIIIe au XIXe siècle* (Brussels: Ed. de l'Institut de Sociologie de l'Université Libre de Bruxelles).

Van der Molen, G. (1937). *Alberico Gentili and the Development of International Law* (Amsterdam: H.J. Paris).

Van Kleffens, E.N. (1968). *Hispanic Law* (Edinburgh: Edinburgh University Press).

Van Rhijn, M. (1933). *Wessel Gansfort* (The Hague: Nijhoff).

Vasoli, C. (1977). 'La dialettica umanistica e la metodologia giuridica nel secolo XVI', in *La Formazione storica del diritto Moderno in Europa*, ed. B. Paradisi, 3 vols. (Florence: Olschki).

Vawter, B. (1961). *The Conscience of Israel: Pre-Exilic Prophets and Prophecy* (London: Sheed and Ward).

Viard, P.E. (1926). *André Alciat, 1492–1550* (Paris: Sirey).

Villoslada, R.G. (1938). *La Universidad de París durante los estudios de Francisco de Vitoria, O.P.* (Rome: apud aedes Universitatis Gregorianae).

Voeltzel, R. (1936). *Jean Domat, 1626–1696, essai de réconstruction de sa philosophie juridique, précédé de la biographie du jurisconsulte* (Paris: Sirey).

Vogt, W. (1971). *Franciscus Duarenus 1509–1559* (Stuttgart: W. Kohlhammer).

Wagner, H. (1978). *Studien zur allgemeinen Rechtslehre des Gaius* (Zutphen: Terra Pub. Co.).

Walbank, F.W. (1972). *Polybius* (Los Angeles and Berkeley: California University Press).

Waley, D. (1970). 'The Primitivist Element in Machiavelli's Thought', *Journal of the History of Ideas*, 31:91–8.

Walker, J.B. (1933). *The 'Chronicles' of St Antoninus: A Study in Historiography* (Washington: Catholic University of America).

Walser, E. (1914). *Beiträge zur Kulturgeschichte des Mittelalters und der Renaissance*, vol. XIV (Leipzig: Teubner).

Watkins, R.N. (1978). *Humanism and Liberty* (Columbia: South Carolina University Press).

Watson, J.S. (1986). *Cicero on Oratory and Orators* (Carbondale, IL: Southern Illinois University Press).

Weinstein, D. (1970). *Savonarola and Florence: Prophecy and Patriotism in the Renaissance* Princeton: Princeton University Press).

Weiss, R. (1947). *The Dawn of Humanism in Italy* (London: H.K. Lewis).

Whitehead, A.N. (1948). *Science and the Modern World* (New York: Macmillan).

Whitfield, J.H. (1947). *Machiavelli* (Oxford: Blackwell).

(1969). *Discourses on Machiavelli* (Cambridge: Heffer).

Wieacker, F. (1967). *Privatrechtsgeschichte der Neuzeit* (Göttingen: Vandenhoeck and Ruprecht).

Witt, R. (1982). 'Medieval *Ars Dictaminis* and the Beginnings of Humanism: A New Construction of the Problem', *Renaissance Quarterly*, 35:1–35.

(1983). *Hercules at the Crossroads* (Durham, NC: Duke University Press).

Wolf, E. (1963). *Grosse Rechtsdenker der deutschen Giestesgeschichte* (Tübingen: Mohr).

Woodhouse, J.R. (1978). *Baldessar Castiglione: A Reassessment of 'The Courtier'* (Edinburgh: Edinburgh University Press).

Woodward, W.H. (1899). *Vittorino da Feltre and Other Humanist Educators* (Cambridge: Cambridge University Press).

Wright, A.D. (1982). *The Counter Reformation: Catholic Europe and the Non-Christian World* (London: St Martin's Press).

Zattum O, (1975). *Persona giuridica e soggettività* (Padua: CEDAM).

Zeeveld, W. G. (1948). *Foundations of Tudor Policy* (Cambridge Mass.: Harvard University Press).

II Religion, civil government, and the debate on constitutions

Primary sources

Agostini, Lodovico (1957). *La Repubblica Imaginaria*, ed. L. Firpo (Turin: Istituto di Scienze Politiche, Universita di Torino).

Alciato, Andrea (1582). *Paradoxa*, in *Opera*, vol. IV (Basle).

Allen, William (1587). *The Copie of a Letter Concerning the Yeelding up of Daventrie* (Antwerp).

(1588). *An Admonition to the Nobility and People of England and Ireland* (n.p.).

(1965). *A True, Sincere, and Modest Defence of English Catholics*, ed. R.M. Kingdon (Ithaca: Cornell Univerity Press). First publ. 1584. See also Cecil (1965).

Almain, Jacques (1706). *Quaestio resumptiva . . . de dominio naturali, civili et ecclesiastico*, in Gerson (1706), vol. II, cols. 961–76.

(1706). *Tractatus de auctoritate ecclesiae et conciliorum generalium: adversus Thomam de Vio*, in Gerson (1706), vol. II, cols. 976–1011.

(1706). *Expositio circa decisiones magistri Guilielmi Occam super potestate ecclesiastica et laica*, in Gerson (1706), vol. II, cols. 1012–120.

Althusius, Johannes (1932). *Politica methodice digesta*, ed. C. J. Friedrich (Cambridge, Mass.: Harvard University Press: Harvard Political Classics).

(1965). *The Politics of Johannes Althusius: An Abridged Translation of the Third Edition of 'Politica Methodice Digesta'*, trans. and intro. F.S. Carney (London: Eyre).

Andreae, Johann Valentin (1916). *Christianopolis* (1619), ed. F.E. Held (Oxford: Oxford University Press).

Anonymous (1538). See *Treatise*.

(1550). See *Bekentnis*.

(1613–19). See *Treasurie*.

(1660). See R.H.

(1693). See *Antiquity*.

Antiquity Reviv'd (1693). (London).

Antonius, Gottfried (1614). *Disputatio apologetica de potestate imperatoris legibus soluta et hodierno Imperii statu adversus Hermannum Vulteium*, in *Politica Imperialia*, ed. M. Goldast (Frankfurt), part XIII, pp. 623–9. Written in 1608.

Arnauld, Antoine (1594). *The Arrainement of the Whole Societie of Jesuites in Fraunce* (London).

(1602). *Le Franc Discours. A Discourse Presented of Late to the French King* (London).

Arnisaeus, Henning (1606). *Doctrina politica governum methodum quae est Aristotelis reducta* (Frankfurt).

724

(1610). *De jure majestatis libri tres* (Frankfurt).

(1615). *De republica seu relectiones politicae*, 2 vols. in 1 (Frankfurt).

Arumaeus, Dominicus, ed. (1615–23). *Discursus academici de jure publico*, 6 vols. (Jena).

Bacon, Sir Francis (1627). 'New Atlantis: A Worke Unfinished', in *Sylva Sylvarum: Or A Naturall History in Ten Centuries* (London). See also R.H. (1660).

Bancroft, Richard (1593). *A Survey of the Pretended Holy Discipline* (London).

Barclay, William (1600). *De regno et regali potestate adversus Buchananum, Brutum, Boucherium et reliquos monarchomachos, libri sex* (Paris).

(1604). *Commentarius ad legem imperium D. de iurisdictione* (Angers).

(1609). *De potestate Papae an et quatenus in reges et principes seculares jus et imperium habeat* (Pont-à-Mousson).

Barnes, Joshua (1675). *Gerania: A New Discovery of a Little Sort of People, Anciently Discoursed of, called Pygmies* (London).

Barnes, Robert (1573). *The Whole Workes of W. Tyndall, John Frith, and Robt. Barnes . . . collected and compiled in one tome together* (London).

Beacon, Richard (1594). *Solon His Folie* (Oxford).

Becan, Martin (1612). *Controversia Anglicana de potestate Pontificis et Regis contra Lancellottum Andream, Sacellanum Regis Angliae, qui se episcopum Eliensem vocat, pro defensione illustrissimi cardinalis Bellarmini* (Mainz).

Begley, Walter (1902). *Nova Solyma: The Ideal City; or Jerusalem Regained*, 2 vols. (London: John Murray).

Bekentnis (1550). *Bekentnis Unterricht und vermanung der Pfarrhern und Prediger der Christlichen Kirchen zu Magdeburgk. Anno 1550. Den 13. Aprilis* (Magdeburg).

Bellarmine, Robert (1586). *De Summo Pontifice capite militantis Ecclesiae*, in *Disputationes . . . de Controversis Christianae Fidei*, 3 vols. (Ingolstadt, 1590), I, cols. 582–1081. First publ. 1586.

(1587). [Pseudonym 'Franciscus Romulus'] *Responsio ad praecipua capita Apologiae quae falso catholica inscribitur pro successione Henrici Navarreni in Francorum regnum* (n.p.).

(1606), *Riposta . . . a due libretti . . .* (Rome).

(1610). *Apologia Roberti S.R.E. cardin. Bellarmini pro responsione sua ad librum Jacobi, Magnae Britanniae regis, cujus titulus est 'Triplici nodo triplex cuneus'. Accessit eadem ipsa responsio iterum recusa, quae sub nomine Matthaei Torti anno superiore prodierat* (Cologne).

(1610). *Tractatus de potestate summi pontificis in rebus temporalibus adversus Gulielmum Barclaium* (Rome).

(1619). *De Officio Principis Christiani* (Rome).

Bellers, John (1695). *Proposals for Raising a College of Industry* (London).

(1987). *John Bellers: His Life, Times and Writings*, ed. G. Clarke (London: Routledge and Kegan Paul).

Belloy, Pierre de (1585). *Apologie catholique contre les libelles, declarations, advis, et consultationes faictes, escrites et publiées par les ligues perturbateurs du repos du royaume de France* (n.p.).

(1587). *De l'authorité du Roy et Crimes de leze majesté qui se commettent par ligues, designation de successeur et libelles escriptes contre la personne et dignité du prince* (n.p.).

Berington, Simon (1737). *The Memoirs of Sigr. Gaudentio di Lucca* (London).

Besold, Christoph (1626). *De majestate in genere ejusque juribus specialibus . . . accessit tractatus singularis de reipublicae statu mixto*, in *Opus politicum variis digressionibus philologicis et iuridicis illustratum* (Strasburg).

Bethel, Slingsby (1671). *The Present Interest of England* (London).

Beza, Theodore (1965). *De jure magistratuum* (Neukirchen-Vluyn: Neukirchener Verlag).

(1969). See Franklin.

Bibliography

(1971). *Du droit des magistrats*, ed. R.M. Kingdon (Geneva: Droz; Les Classiques de la Pensée Politique, 7).

Bilson, Thomas (1585). *The True Difference between Christian Subjection and Unchristian Rebellion* (Oxford).

(1593). *The Perpetual Government of Christes Church* (London).

Blackwood, Adam (1575). *De conjunctione religionis et imperii libri duo* (Paris).

(1581). *Adversus Georgii Buchanani dialogum de jure regni apud Scotos pro regibus apologia* (Poitiers).

Bluet, Thomas (1601). *Important considerations which ought to moue all true and sound Catholikes . . . to acknowledge that the proceedings of her Maiesty haue bene both mild and mercifull* (with an 'epistle generall' by William Watson) (n.p.).

Boccalini, Traiano (1706). *Advices from Parnassus* (London). Trans. of *Ragguagli da Parnassus*, by Henry, earl of Monmouth, first publ. London 1656.

Bodin, Jean (1583). *Les Six Livres de la République* (Paris). First publ. 1576.

(1586). *De republica libri sex* (Paris).

(1945). *Method for the Easy Comprehension of History*, ed. B. Reynolds (New York: Columbia University Press), First publ. 1566.

(1951a). *Juris universi distributio*, ed. P. Mesnard, in *Œuvres philosophiques de Jean Bodin* (Paris: Presses Universitaires de France).

(1951b). *Methodus ad facilem historiarum cognitionem*, ed. P. Mesnard, in *Œuvres philosophiques de Jean Bodin* (Paris: Presses Universitaires de France).

(1961). *Les Six Livres de la République* (Aalen: Scientia Verlag).

(1962). *The Six Bookes of a Commonweale*, trans. R. Knolles, ed. K.D. McRae (Cambridge, Mass.: Harvard University Press; Harvard Political Classics).

(1975). *Colloquium of the Seven about the Secrets of the Sublime*, ed. M.L. Daniels Kuntz (Princeton: Princeton University Press).

Botero, Giovanni (1659). *Relationi Universali* (Venice).

Boucher, Jean (1588). *Histoire tragique et mémorable de Gaverston gentilhomme gascon iadis mignon d'Edouard II roi d'Angleterre, tirée des chroniques de Th. Valsingham et tournée de latin en français, dédiée a Monseigneur le duc d'Epernon* (n.p.).

(1591). *De iusta Henrici Tertii abdicatione e francorum regno, libri quatuor* (Lyons). First publ. 1589.

(1594). *Sermons de la simulée conversion et nullité de la prétendue absolution de Henry de Bourbon, prince de Béarn, à S. Denys en France, le dimanche 25 de juillet 1593* (Paris).

(1595). *Apologie pour Jehan Chastel exécuté à la mort, et pour les pères et escholliers de la Société de Jésus, bannis du Royaume de France, contre l'arrest de Parlement donné contre eux à Paris le 29 decembre 1594* (n.p.).

Bromiley, G.W., ed. (1953). *Zwingli and Bullinger* (London: SCM Press: Library of Christian Classics, 24).

Bucer, Martin (1954–5). *De regno Christi*, ed. F. Wendel, 2 vols. (Paris: Presses Universitaires de France).

(1959). *On the Kingdom of Christ* (in Pauck (1959)).

Buchanan, George (1571), [*Detectio*]. *De Maria Scotorum Regina . . .* (n.p.).

(1579). *De jure regni apud Scotos* (Edinburgh).

(1582). *Rerum Scoticarum Historia* (Edinburgh).

(1727). *De jure regni apud Scotos* (Edinburgh).

(1949). *The Powers of the Crown in Scotland, Being a Translation, with Notes and an Introductory Essay, of George Buchanan's 'De Jure Regni Apud Scotos'*, trans. C.F. Arrowood (Austin: Texas University Press).

(1958). *The Tyrannous Reign of Mary Stewart: George Buchanan's Account*, ed. W.A. Gatherer (Edinburgh: Edinburgh University Press).

(1964). *The Art and Science of Government Among the Scots, Being George Buchanan's 'De Jure Regni apud Scotos'*, trans. D.H. MacNeill (Glasgow: MacLellan).

(1969). *De jure regni apud Scotos* (Amsterdam and New York: Da Capo Press). Facsimile reprint of the first edition, Edinburgh 1579.

Budé, Guillaume (1557). *Annotationes in Pandectas tam priores quam posteriores* (Basle).

Burnet, Gilbert (1830). *History of the Reformation of the Church of England*, ed. E. Nares, 4 vols. (London: J.F. Dove).

Burton, Robert (1932). *The Anatomy of Melancholy*, ed. H. Jackson, 3 vols. (London: Dent).

Cabot, Vincent (1752). *Variarum juris publici et privati disputationum libri duo*, in *Novus thesaurus juris civilis et canonici*, ed. G. Meerman, vol. IV (The Hague).

Calvin, Jean (1960). *Institutes of the Christian Religion*, ed. J.T. McNeill, trans, F.L. Battles, 2 vols. (Philadelphia: Westminster Press; London: SCM Press, 1961).

(1863–1900). *Ioannis Calvini Opera quae Supersunt Omnia*, ed. G. Baum, E. Cunitz, R. Reuss (Brunswick and Berlin: Schwetschke).

Campanella, Tommaso (1981). *The City of the Sun*, trans. A.M. Elliott and R. Millner, intro. A.L. Morton (London University of California Press). See also Campanella (1981): *La Città del Sole: Dialogo Poetico/The City of the Sun: A Poetic Dialogue*, trans. with intro. D.J. Donno (Los Angeles and Berkeley: California University Press).

Caraffa, Carlo Maria (1688). *Instrucción Christiana de Principes, y Reyes Sacada de le Escritura Divina*, 3rd edn (Palermo).

Carrerius, Alexander (1599). *De potestate Romani Pontificis adversus impios politicos* (Rome).

Castillo de Bobadilla, Geronimo (1597). *Política para corregidores y señores de vassallos*, 2 vols. (Madrid).

Caumont, Jean de (1585). *La Vertu de la noblesse* (Paris).

(1587). *Advertissment des advertissements* (n.p.).

Cavalcanti, Bartolomeo (1805). *Trattati . . . sopra gli ottimi reggimenti delle repubbliche antichi et moderne* (Milan: Società tipografica de' classici italiani). First publ. Venice 1570.

Cecil, William (1965). *The Execution of Justice in England*, ed. R.M. Kingdon (Ithaca: Cornell University Press). First publ. 1583. See also Allen (1965).

Chamberlen, Peter (1649). *The Poore Mans Advocate* (London).

Chasseneuz, Barthélemy de (1528). *In Consuetudines Ducatus Burgundiae* (Paris).

(1546). *Catalogus gloriae mundi* (Lyons).

(1547). *Consuetudines ducatus Burgundiae* (Paris).

Chrestien, Florent [Gilles Durant, Jacques Gillot, Pierre Le Roy, Pierre Pithous, and Nicolas Rapin] (1876). *La satyre ménippée ou la vertu du catholicon*, ed. C. Read (Paris: Editions Jouhaast). First publ. 1594.

Clary, François de (1592). *Philippiques contre les bulles et autres pratiques de la faction d'Espagne* (Tours). First publ. 1590.

Coke, Sir Edward (1658). *The Reports of Sir Edward Coke* (London).

Coquille, Guy (1703). *Les Œuvres de Maistre Guy Coquille*, 2 vols. (Bordeaux).

Coras, Jean de (1603). *De jure civili*, in *Opera*, 2 vols. (Wittenberg), vol. II.

Cowell, John (1607). *The Interpreter: or Booke containing the Signification of Words* (Cambridge).

Craig, Sir Thomas (1603). *The Right of Succession to the Kingdom of England* (London).

Cromé, François Morin de (1977). *Le Dialogue d'entre le maheustre et le manant*, ed. P.M. Ascoli (Geneva: Droz). First publ. 1594.

De Blécourt, A.S., and Japiske, N., eds. (1919). *Klein Plakkaatboek van Nederland. Verzameling van ordonnantiën en Plakkaten betreffende Regeeringsvorm, Kerk en Recht-spraak 14e eeuw tot 1749* (Groningen and The Hague: J.B. Wolters).

Dennert, J., ed. (1968). *Beza, Brutus, Hotman: calvinistische Monarchomachen*, trans. H. Klingelhofer (Cologne: Westdeutscher Verlag).

Dorléans, Louis (1586). *Advertissement des catholiques anglois aux françois catholiques* (n.p.).

(1586). *Apologie ou défence des catholiques unis les uns avec les autres, contre les impostures des catholiques associez à ceux de la prétendue religion* (n.p.).

(1588). *Responce des vrays catholiques françois à l'advertissement des catholiques anglois pour l'exclusion du Roy de Navarre de la couronne de France* (n.p.).

(1594). *Le Banquet et apresdinée du conte [sic] d'Arète, ou il se traicte de la dissimulation du Roy de Navarre, et les moeurs de ses partisans* (Paris).

(1594). *Plaidoyé des gens du Roy faict en parlement en plein audience toutes les chambres assemblées* (Arras).

Drayton, Michael (1606). *Ode to the Virginia Voyage* (London).

Du Haillan, Bernard de Girard (1609). *De l'Estat et succez des affaires de France* (Paris).

Du Moulin, Charles (1681). *Omnia quae extant opera*, 5 vols. (Paris).

Du Perron, Jacques Davy, Cardinal (1620). *Réplique à la réponse du sérénissime Roy de la Grande Bretagne* (Paris).

Eberlein von Günzburg, Johann (1521). *Wolfaria*, in *Fünfzehn Bundsgenossen* (Basle).

Elyot, Sir Thomas (1531). *The Boke Named the Governour* (London).

Erasmus, Desiderius (1965). *The Education of a Christian Prince*, trans. and ed. L.K. Born (New York: Columbia University Press. First publ. 1516.

(1969). *On Free Choice of the Will/De libero arbitrio*, in *Luther and Erasmus: Free Will and Salvation*, ed. and trans. E.G. Rupp (London: Westminster Press; Library of Christian Classics, 17).

Fauchet, Claude (1651). *Traicté des libertez de l'église gallicane*, in *Traitez des droits et libertez de l'église gallicane*, ed. Pierre Dupuy (n.p.), pp. 110–31. First publ. 1610.

Faye d'Espesses, Jacques (1583). *Advertissement sur la réception et publication du concile de Trente* (Paris).

Fénelon, François (1701). *Aventures de Télémaque Fils d'Ulysse* (The Hague).

Ferrarius, Joannes Montanus (1559). *A Work touching the Good Ordering of a Commonweal*, trans. W. Bavand (London; facsimile reprint, 1972, New York: Johnson Reprint Corporation).

Filippe, Barthomeu (1584). *Tractado de consejo y de los consejeros de los principes* (Coimbra).

Fish, Simon (1529). *The summe of the holye Scripture and ordinarye of the Christen teachyng* (translated from the Dutch of Henricus Bomelius) (Antwerp?).

Fortescue, Sir John (1949). *De laudibus legum Anglie*, ed. S.B. Chrimes (Cambridge: Cambridge University Press).

Foxe, Edward (1534). *Opus exminius de vera differentia regiae potestatis et ecclesiasticae* (London).

(1548). *The True Dyfferens between ye Regall Power and the Ecclesiasticall Power* (London).

Franklin, Benjamin (1740). *A Collection of Charters and Other Publick Acts relating to the Province of Pennsylvania* (Philadelphia).

Franklin, J.H., ed. (1969). *Constitutionalism and Resistance in the Sixteenth Century: Three Treatises by Hotman, Beza and Mornay* (New York: Pegasus).

Frantzke, George (1621). 'De statu reipublicae mixto', in *Discursus academici de jure publico*, ed. D. Arumaeus (Jena), vol. III, no. 21.

Furio Ceriol, Fadrique (1570?). *A Very Briefe and Profitable Treatise* (London).

Gardiner, Stephen (1930). *De vera obedientia/The Oration of True Obedience*, in *Obedience in Church and State: Three Political Tracts by Stephen Gardiner*, ed. P. Janelle (Cambridge: Cambridge University Press).

Gentili, Alberico (1933). *De iure belli libri tres*, intro. C. Phillipson, 2 vols. (Oxford: Clarendon Press).

Gentillet, Innocent (1968). *Antimachiavel*, ed. C.E. Rathé (Geneva: Droz; Les Classiques de la Pensée Politique, 5).

Gerson, Jean (1706). *Opera omnia*, ed. Ellies Dupin (Antwerp).

Gilbert, Claude (1700). *Histoire de Calejava ou de l'isle des Hommes raisonnables* (Dijon).

Glanville, John (1775). *Reports of Certain Cases* (London).

Goodman, Christopher (1558). *How Superior Powers Oght to be Obeyd of their Subjects* (Geneva). Facsimile reprint, 1931, intro. C.H. McIlwain (New York: Columbia University Press).

Gott, Samuel (1902). *Nova Solyma: The Ideal City*, ed. and trans. W. Begley, 2 vols. (London: Murray). First publ. 1648.

Grassaille, Charles de (1538). *Regalium Franciae iura omnia* (Lyons).

Grégoire, Pierre (1609). *De republica libri sex et viginta* (Lyons). First publ. 1596.

Guevara, Antonio de (1529). *Relox de los principes*, trans. Sir Thomas North, as *The Dial of Princes* (London, 1582).

Hale, Sir Matthew (1976). *The Prerogatives of the King*, ed. D.E.C. Yale (London: Selden Society).

Harding, Thomas (1565). *A Confutation of a Book Intituled An Apologie of the Church of England* (Antwerp).

Harrington, James (1977). *The Political Works of James Harrington*, ed. J.G.A. Pocock (Cambridge: Cambridge University Press).

Hayward, Sir John (1603). *An Answer to the First Part of a Certaine Conference* (London).

Hooker, Richard (1977–82). *Of the Lawes of Ecclesiasticall Politie*, ed. W. Speed Hill, 4 vols. (Cambridge, Mass.: Belknap Press of Harvard University; The Folger Library Edition of the Works of Richard Hooker).

Hotman, Antoine (1608). *Traicté des libertez de l'église gallicane* (Paris).

Hotman, François (1586). *The Brutish Thunderbolt, or, rather feeble fire-flash of Pope Sixtus the Fift* (London).

(1970). *Le Tigre de 1560*, ed. C. Read (Geneva: Slatkine Reprints; facsimile reprint of the 1875 edition).

(1972). *Francogallia*, ed. R.E. Giesey, trans. J.H.M. Salmon (Cambridge University Press). First publ. 1573.

See also Franklin (1969).

Hurault, Michel (1590). *Anti-Sixtus. An Oration of Sixtus the Fift: with a Confutation* (London).

James VI and I, King (1918). *The Political Works of James I*, ed. C.H. McIlwain (Cambridge, Mass.: Harvard University Press).

Jewel, John (1562). *An Apologie or Aunswer in Defence of the Church of England* (London).

John of Paris (1969). *Über königliche und päpstliche Gewalt (De regia potestate et papali)*, ed. F. Bleienstein (Stuttgart: Ernst Klett).

(1971). *On Royal and Papal Power*, ed. J.A. Watt (Toronto: Pontifical Institute of Medieval Studies).

Kamenka, E., ed. (1987). *Utopias* (Oxford: Oxford University Press).

Keckermann, Bartholomaeus (1608). *Systema disciplinae politicae* (Hanover).

Kirchner, Hermann (1614). *Respublica ad disputationis aciem methodice revocata* (Marburg). First publ. 1608.

Knox, John (1846–64). *Works*, ed. D. Laing, 6 vols. (Edinburgh: Bannatyne Club). The political works are in vol. IV.

(1949). *History of the Reformation in Scotland*, ed. W.C. Dickinson, 2 vols. (London: Thomas Nelson).

Kossmann, E.H., and Mellink, A.F., eds. (1974). *Texts Concerning the Revolt of the Netherlands* (Cambridge: Cambridge University Press).

Las Casas, Bartolomé de (1957–8). *Obras Escogidas*, 5 vols. (Madrid: Biblioteca de Autores Espanoles, 95–6, 105–6, 110).

Bibliography

Le Caron, Louis (Charondas) (1607). *Pandectes, ou Digestes du droict françois* (Paris).

Le Roy, Louis (1568). *Les Politiques d'Aristote* (Paris).

(1598). *Aristotles Politiques or Discourses of Government* (London).

Leschassier, Jacques (1607). *Consultatio Parisii cuiusdam de controversia inter sanctitatem Pauli Quinti et serenissimam rempublicam Venetam* (n.p.).

L'Hôpital, Michel de (1824–6). *Œuvres complètes*, ed. P.J.S. Dufey, 5 vols. (Paris: A. Boulland).

Locke, John (1960). *Two Treatises of Government*, ed. P. Laslett (New York: Mentor Books).

Luther, Martin (1883–1983). *Martin Luthers Werke*, 92 vols. in 105 (Weimar: H. Bohlau).

(1906–61). *Martin Luthers Werke. Die deutsche Bibel* (Weimar: H. Bohlau).

(1955–76). *Luther's Works*, ed. J. Pelikan *et al.*, 54 vols. (St Louis: Corcordia Publishing House).

Machiavelli, Niccolò (1950). *The Discourses of Machiavelli*, trans. L.J. Walker, 2 vols. (London: Routledge and Kegan Paul).

Mair, John (1519). *In quartum Sententiarum questiones* (Paris).

Mariana, Juan de (1599). *De rege et regis institutione libri tres* (Toledo).

(1605). *De rege et regis institutione libri III* (Mainz).

Marsilius of Padua (1956). *The Defensor Pacis*, ed. A. Gewirth (New York: Columbia University Press).

Martyr, Peter. *See* Vermigli, Peter Martyr.

Melanchthon. Philip (1951–75). *Melanchthons Werke in Auswahl*, ed. R. Stupperich, 7 vols. in 9 (Gütersloh: C. Bertelmanns Verlag).

(1965). *Melanchthon on Christian Doctrine: Loci communes, 1555*, ed. C.L. Manschreck (Oxford: Oxford University Press).

See also Pauck (1959).

Mendo, Andres (1662). *Principe Perfecto y Ministros Aivstados, Documentos Politicos y Morales* (Salamanca).

Molina, Luis de (1602–3). *De iustitia et iure libri sex*, 2 vols. (Mainz).

(1614). *De iustitia et jure* (Cologne). First publ. 1592.

More, Thomas (1965). *Utopia*, ed. E. Surtz and J.H. Hexter (New Haven: Yale University Press; The Complete Works of St Thomas More, vol. IV).

Morison, Richard (1539). *An Exhortation to styrre all Englyshe men to the defence of theyr countreye* (London).

Mornay, Philippe Duplessis (1585). *An Answer to the Excommunication by Sixtus V against Henry, King of Navarra, and Henry, Prince of Condé, made by the said princes* (London).

(1979). *Vindiciae contra tyrannos*, ed. H. Weber *et al.* (Geneva: Droz; Les Classiques de la pensée politique, 11).

See also Franklin (1969).

Morton, Thomas (1605). *An Exact Discovrie of Romish Doctrine in the Case of Conspiracie and Rebellion* (London).

(1606). *A Full Satisfaction concerning a Double Romish Iniquitie, Hainous Rebellion and more than Heathenish Equivocation* (London).

(1608). *A Preamble unto an Incounter with P.R. concerning the Romish Doctrine of Rebellion and Aequivocation* (London).

Müntzer, Thomas (1950). *Auslegung des zweiten Kapitels Daniels* ('*Die Furstenpredigt*', *1524*), in Thomas Müntzer, *Politische Schriften*, ed. C. Hinrichs (Halle: Niemeyer; Hallische Monographien, 17).

(1957). *Sermon before the Princes*, in G.H. Williams, ed., *Spiritual and Anabaptist Writings: Documents Illustrative of the Radical Reformation* (London: SCM Press; Library of Christian Classics, 25).

II   Religion, civil government, and the debate on constitutions

Otto, Daniel (1616). 'An princeps legibus sit solutus?', in D. Arumaeus, ed., *Discursus academici de jure publico* (Jena), vol. I, no. 14.

(1620). 'An mixtus detur reipublicae status?', in *ibid.*, vol. II, no. 22.

(1623). 'De jure publico Imperii Romani', in *ibid.*, vol. V, no. 2.

(1623). *De maiestate imperii et imperantis* (Strasburg).

Palma-Cayet, Pierre-Victoire (1823). *Chronologie novenaire*, in *Mémoires relatifs à l'histoire de France*, ed. C.B. Petitot (Paris: Foucault), 1st series, vol. XXXVIII.

Parsons, Robert (1594) [pseud. 'N. Doleman']. *A Conference about the Next Succession to the Crowne of England* (n.p.).

(1607). *A Treatise tending to Mitigation towardes Catholicke Subjectes in England* (n.p.).

(1608). *The Judgment of a Catholicke English-man concerning Triplici nodo, Triplex cuneus* (n.p.).

(1609). *A Quiet and Sober Reckoning with M.T. Morton [concerning] a Treatise of R.P.* (n.p.).

Paruta, Paolo (1657). *Politick Discourses*, trans. Henry, earl of Monmouth (London).

(1852). *Opere politiche*, ed. G. Monzani, 2 vols. (Florence: Le Monnier).

Pasquier, Etienne (1594). *The Jesuite displayed, containing the original and proceedings of the Jesuits together with the fruits of their doctrine* (London).

(1602). *The Jesuites Catechisme* (London).

(1621). *Les Recherches de la France* (Paris).

(1723). *Les Œuvres*, 2 vols. (Amsterdam).

Patrizi, Francesco (1553). *La Città felice* (Venice).

Pauck, W., ed. (1959). *Melanchthon and Bucer* (London: SCM Press; Library of Christian Classics, 19).

Paurmeister, Tobias (1608). *De jurisdictione Imperii Romani libri II* (Hanover).

Petri, Olaus (1914–17). *Samlade Skrifter af Olavus Petri*, ed. B. Hesslman, 4 vols. (Upsala: Sveriges Kristliga Studentrorelses Forlag).

Pithou, Pierre (1594). *Les libertez de l'église gallicane* (Paris).

Plockhoy, Peter Cornelius (1659?). *A Way Propounded to Make the Poor in these and other Nations Happy* (London).

Pocock, N., ed. (1870). *Records of the Reformation: The Divorce, 1527–1533*, 2 vols. (Oxford: Oxford University Press).

Pole, Reginald (1538?). *Ad Henricum Octavum Britanniae Regem, Pro ecclesiasticae unitatis defensione, libri quatuor* (Rome).

Ponet, John (1556). *A Shorte Treatise of Politike Power* (Strasburg). Facsimile in Hudson (1942): see secondary sources.

Porthaise, Jean (1594). *Cinq sermons du R.P.J. Porthaise . . . théologal de l'église de Poitiers, par lui prononcez en icelle esquels est traicté tant de la simulée conversion du Roy de Navarre que du droit l'absolution ecclésiastique* (Paris).

Psalmanazar, George (1704). *An Historical and Geographical Description of Formosa* (London).

Pufendorf, Samuel (1769). *De officio hominis et civis secundum legem naturalem libri duo*, 2 vols. (Leiden).

(1934). *On the Law of Nature and Nations* (Oxford: Oxford University Press).

R.H. (1660). *New Atlantis. Begun by the Lord Verulam, Viscount St Albans and continued by R.H., Esquire. Wherein is set forth a Platform of Mechanical Government* (London).

Rainsart, Oudart (1591). *La Représentation de la noblesse hérétique sur le théâtre de France* (n.p.).

Rastell, John (1564). *A Confutation of a Sermon Pronounced by M. Juell* (Antwerp).

Rebuffi, Pierre (1589). *Explicatio ad quatuor primos Pandectarum libros* (Lyons).

(1613). *Commentaria in constitutiones seu ordinationes regias* (Lyons).

Reinkingk, Theodor (1631). *Tractatus de regimine seculari et ecclesiastico* (Marburg).

731

Reynolds, William [or Rainolds; pseud. 'Gulielmus Rossaeus'] (1590). *De iusta reipublicae Christianae in reges impios et haereticos authoritate* (Paris).

Richer, Edmond, ed. (1606). *Ionnis Gersonii doctoris et cancelarii Parisiensis opera* (Paris).

(1611). *De ecclesiastica et politica potestate* (Paris).

Roy, William (1527). *A Brefe Dialoge bitwene a Christen Father and his stobborn Sonne* (translated from the Latin of Wolfgang Capito, (Strasburg).

Saavedra Fajardo, Diego de (1700). *The Royal Politician Represented in One Hundred Emblems*, trans. Sir J.A. Asty (London).

St German, Christopher (1535?). *An Answer to a Letter* (London).

(1974). *Doctor and Student*, ed. T.F.T. Plucknett and J.L. Barton (London: Selden Society, 91).

Salamonio, Mario (1544). *Patritii Romani de Principatu* (Rome).

Salici, Giovanni Andrea (1627). *Discorsi Politici, utili in Pace, e in Guerra al Reggimento de Principe* (Cesena).

Sampson, Richard (1534). *Oratio qua docet Anglos regiae dignitati ut obediant* (London).

Sanders, Nicholas (1571). *De visibili monarchia ecclesiae libri octo* (Louvain).

Sansovino, Francesco (1578). *Del governo et amministratione di diversi regni e republiche* (Venice).

Santa Maria, Juan de (1650). *Policy Unveiled, or Maxims of State* (London).

Saravia, Hadrian (1590). *De diversis ministrorum Evangelii gradibus* (London).

(1593). *De imperandi authoritate et Christiana obedientia* (London).

Sarpi, Paulo ['Pietro Soave'] (1620). *The Historie of the Council of Trent* (London). First publ. as *Historia del Concilio Tridentino*, ed. M.A. de Dominis, London, 1619.

Servin, Louis (1591). *Vindiciae secundum libertatem ecclesiae Gallicanae et regii status Gallo-Francorum sub Henrici IIII rege Francorum* (Tours).

(1606). *Pro libertate status et reipublicae Venetorum Gallo franci ad Philenetum epistola* (Paris).

Seyssel, Claude de (1961a). *La Monarchie de France et deux autres fragments politiques*, ed. J. Poujol (Paris: Librairie d'Argences).

(1961b). *Prohème en la translation de l'histoire d'Appian*, in Seyssel (1961a).

(1981). *The Monarchy of France*, trans. J.H. Hexter, intro. D.R. Kelley (New Haven: Yale University Press).

Sleidan, Johannes (1555). *De statu religionis et reipublicae Carolo Quinto, Caesare, Commentarii* (Strasburg).

(1689). *The General History of the Reformation*, ed. E. Bohun (London).

Smith, Sir Thomas (1982). *De Republica Anglorum*, ed. M. Dewar (Cambridge: Cambridge University Press).

Soto, Domingo de (1569). *Libri decem de iustitia et iure* (Lyons).

Starkey, Thomas (1540?). *An Exhortation to the People Instructynge them to Unitie and Obedience* (London).

(1871). *Dialogue between Cardinal Pole and Thomas Lupset*, ed. J.M. Cowper (London: Early English Text Society).

Stiblin, Gaspar [Stublinus] (1555). *De Eudaemonensium republica* (Basle).

Strachey, William (1612). *For the Colony in Virginea Britannia. Lawes Divine, Morall and Martiall* (London).

Suárez, Francisco (1612). *Tractatus de legibus ac Deo legislatore* (Coimbra). Bilingual Latin–Spanish edn by L. Perena, V. Abril, and P. Suner, 8 vols., Madrid, 1971–81.

(1613a). *Tractatus de legibus ac Deo legislatore* (Lyons).

(1613b). *Defensio fidei Catholicae et Apostolicae* (Coimbra).

(1614). *Defensio fidei Catholicae et Apostolicae* (Cologne).

(1621). *De Opere Sex Dierum* (Lyons). In *Opera Omnia*, ed. D.M. André, vol. III (Paris:

Vivès, 1856), pp. 1–447.

(1621). *De triplici virtute theologica, fide, spe et charitate* (Coimbra).

Sutcliffe, Matthew (1591). *A Treatise of Ecclesiasticall Discipline* (London).

(1600). *A Briefe Replie to a Certaine Odious Libel lately published by a Jesuit* (London).

(1604). *A Ful and Round Answer to N.D. alias R. Parsons his Warne-Word* (London).

Tanner, J.R., ed. (1951). *Tudor Historical Documents, AD 1485–1603* (Cambridge: Cambridge University Press).

Taverner, Richard (1539). *The Second Booke of the Garden of wysdome* (London).

Thou, Jacques-Auguste de (1620). *Historiarum sui temporis ab . . . 1543 . . . ad 1607 Libri* cxxxviii, 5 vols. (Geneva).

(1734). *Histoire universelle de Jacques Auguste de Thou depuis 1543 jusq'en 1607. Traduite sur l'édition Latine de Londres* ('London' [Paris]).

Torres, Juan de (1596). *Philosophia Moral de Principes para buena crianca y govierno* (Burgos).

Treasurie (1613–19). *The Treasurie of Ancient and Modern Times*, 2 vols. (London).

Treatise (1538). *A Treatise concernynge generall councilles, The Bysshopes of Rome and the Clergy* (London).

Tyndale, William (1573). *The Whole Workes of W. Tyndall, John Frith, and Robt. Barnes . . . Collected and Compiled in One Tome Together* (London).

(1848). *The Obedience of a Christen Man, and How Christen Rulers Oughte to Governe*, ed. H. Walker, in *Doctrinal Treatises and Introductions to Different Portions of the Holy Scripture, by William Tyndale* (Cambridge: Cambridge University Press; Parker Society).

Vairasse D'Allais, Denis (1702). *Histoire des Sevarambes* (Amsterdam). First publ. 1675.

Vermigli, Peter Martyr (1980). *The Political Thought of Peter Martyr Vermigli: Selected Texts and Commentary*, ed. R.M. Kingdon (Geneva: Droz).

Vitoria, Francisco de (1933–6). *De potestate civili*, in *Relecciones teologicas*, ed. L.G. Alonso Getino, 3 vols. (Madrid: Asociación Francisco de Vitoria).

Vives, Juan Luís (1782–90). *Opera omnia*, 8 vols. (Valencia).

Vulteius, Hermann (1599). *Ad titulos Codicis qui sunt de jurisdictione et foro competenti commenatarius* (Frankfurt).

Watson, William (1601). See Bluet, Thomas.

Williams, G.H., ed. (1957). *Spiritual and Anabaptist Writers: Documents Illustrative of the Radical Reformation* (London: SCM Press; Library of Christian Classics, 25).

Winstanley, Gerrard (1941). *The Works of Gerrard Winstanley*, ed. G.H. Sabine (Ithaca: Cornell University Press).

(1973). *The Law of Freedom and Other Writings*, ed. C. Hill (Harmondsworth: Penguin).

Zampini, Matteo (1578). *Degli stati di Francia et della lora potenza* (Paris).

Zwingli, Huldreich (1905–59). *Huldreich Zwinglis samtliche Werke*, ed. E. Egli and G. Finsler, 14 vols. (Berlin: Verlag Schwetschke).

(1953). *An Exposition of the Faith*, in Bromiley (1953).

Secondary sources

Addio, M.D'. (1954). *L'idea del contratto sociale dai sofisti alla Riforma e il 'De principatu' di Mario Salamonio* (Milan: Giuffrè; Pubblicazioni dell' Istituto di Diritto Pubblico e di Dottrina dello Stato dello Facoltà di Scienze Politiche dell' Università di Roma, ser. 4, no. 4).

Allen, J.W. (1941). *A History of Political Thought in the Sixteenth Century* (London: Methuen). First publ. 1928.

Anderson, M.W. (1975). *Peter Martyr, a Reformer in Exile (1542–1562)* (Nieuwkoop: De Graaf).

Aubépin, H. (1855). *De l'influence de Dumoulin sur la législation française* (Paris: Cotillon).

Aylmer, G.E. (1984). 'The Religion of Gerrard Winstanley', in *Radical Religion in the English Revolution*, ed. J.F. McGregor and B. Reay (Oxford: Oxford University Press), pp. 91–119.

Backer, A., and A. (1853–61). *Bibliothèque des écrivains de la compagnie de Jésus*, 7 vols. (Liège: L. Grandmont-Donders).

Bainton, R.H. (1955). *Here I Stand: A Life of Martin Luther* (New York: New American Library). First publ. 1950.

Barnavi, E. (1980). *Le Parti de Dieu: Etude sociale et politique des chefs de la Ligue parisienne, 1585–1594* (Brussels and Louvain: Nauwelaerts).

Barnavi, E., and Descimon, R. (1985). *La Sainte Ligue, le juge et la potence: L'Assassinat du Président Brisson* (Paris: Hachette).

Baron, H. (1966). *The Crisis of the Early Italian Renaissance*, 2nd edn (Princeton: Princeton University Press).

Bataillon, M. (1950). *Erasmo y España: estudios sobre la historia espiritual del siglo XVI* (Mexico: Fondo de Cultura Economica).

Baumer, F.L. (1936–7). 'Christopher St German: The Political Philosophy of a Tudor lawyer', *American Historical Review*, 62:631–51.

(1940). *The Early Tudor Theory of Kingship* (New Haven: Yale University Press).

Bäumer, R. (1971). *Nachwirkungen des konziliaren Gedankens in der Theologie und Kononistik des frühen 16. Jahrhunderts* (Münster: Aschendorff).

Baumgartner, F.J. (1975). *Radical Reactionaries: The Political Thought of the French Catholic League* (Geneva: Droz).

Bernstein, E. (1963). *Cromwell and Communism: Socialism and Democracy in the Great English Revolution*, trans. H.J. Stenning (London: Frank Cass).

Blockmans, W.P. (1983). 'Du contrat féodal à la souveraineté du peuple: les précedents de la déchéance de Philippe II dans les Pays-Bas (1581)', *Annali della Facoltà di Scienze Politiche* (Università di Perugia), 19:135–50.

Bohatec, J. (1937). *Calvins Lehre von Staat und Kirche* (Breslau: Marcus; repr. 1961, Aalen: Scientia Verlag).

Bonansea, B.M. (1969). *Tommaso Campanella: Renaissance Pioneer of Modern Thought* (Washington: Catholic University of America Press).

Bonnefon, P. (1908, 1915). 'L'Historien du Haillan', *Revue d'Histoire Littéraire de la France*, 15:642–96 and 21:453–93.

Bornkamm, H. (1979). *Martin Luther in der Mitte seiner Lebens* (Göttingen: Vandenhoek and Ruprecht).

Bouwsma, W.J. (1968). *Venice and the Defense of Republican Liberty* (Berkeley: California University Press).

Boyd, J.P. (1964). *Fundamental Laws and Constitutions of New Jersey 1664–1964* (Princeton: Van Nestrand; New Jersey Historical Series, 17).

Brodrick, J. (1961). *Robert Bellarmine, Saint and Scholar* (Westminster, Md: Newman Press).

Brown, E.A.R. (1972). 'Representation and Agency Law in the Later Middle Ages: The Theoretical Foundations and the Evolution of Practice in the XIIIth and XIVth Centuries', *Viator*, 3:329–64.

Buisson, A. (1950). *Michel de l'Hôpital* (Paris: Hachette).

Buisson, F. (1892). *Sebastien Castellion: sa vie et son œuvre (1515–1563)* (Paris: Hachette).

Burns, J.H. (1981). '*Politia regalis et optima:* The Political Ideas of John Mair', *History of Political Thought*, 2:31–61.

(1983). '*Jus gladii* and *jurisdictio*: Jacques Almain and John Locke', *Historical Journal*, 26:369–74.

(1985). 'Fortescue and the Political Theory of *dominium*', *Historical Journal*, 28:777–97.

Caprariis, V. de (1959). *Propaganda e pensiero politico in Francia durante le guerre di religione* (Naples: Edizioni scientifiche italiane; Biblioteca storica, nuova ser., 7).

Caravaglia, J.C. (1981). 'I Gesuiti del Paraguay: Utopia e Realtà', *La Rivista Storica Italiana*, 93:269–314.

Cargill Thompson, W.D.J. (1960). 'The Sixteenth-Century Editions of *A Supplication unto King Henry the Eighth*, by Robert Barnes, D.D.: A Footnote to the History of the Royal Supremacy', *Transactions of the Cambridge Bibliographical Society*, 3:133–42.

    (1972). 'The Philosopher of the "Politic Society": Richard Hooker as a Political Thinker', in *Studies in Richard Hooker*, ed. W. Speed Hill (Cleveland, Ohio: Case Western Reserve University Press).

    (1980). *Studies in the Reformation: Luther to Hooker*, ed. C.W. Dugmore (London: Athlone Press).

    (1984). *The Political Thought of Martin Luther* (Brighton: Harvester).

Carlyle, Sir R.W., and A.J. (1936). *A History of Medieval Political Thought in the West*, vol. VI (Edinburgh and London: Blackwood).

Cepeda Adan, J. (1956). *En torno al concepto del estado en los Reyes Católicos* (Madrid: Consejo Superior de Investigaciones Cientificas, Escuela de Historia Moderna).

Chabanne, R. (1965). 'Rebuffe', in *Dictionnaire de droit canonique*, ed. R. Naz (Paris: Letouzey et Ane), vol. VII, cols. 475–7.

Chenevière, M.E. (1937). *La Pensée politique de Calvin* (Paris: Editions 'Je Sers'; Geneva: Editions Labour; repr. 1970, Geneva: Slatkine Reprints).

Chevreul, H. (1852). *Etude sur le XVIe siècle: Hubert Languet* (Paris: L. Potier; repr. 1967, Nieuwkoop: De Graaf).

Chevrier, G. (1952). 'Remarques sur l'introduction et les vicissitudes de la distinction du "jus privatum" et du "jus publicum" dans les œuvres des anciens juristes français', *Archives de Philosophie du Droit*, n.s., 1:5–77.

Chrimes, S.B. (1936). *English Constitutional Ideas in the Fifteenth Century* (Cambridge: Cambridge University Press).

Church, W.F. (1941). *Constitutional Thought in Sixteenth-Century France* (Cambridge, Mass.: Harvard University Press; repr. 1969).

Clancy, T.H. (1964). *Papist Pamphleteers: The Allen-Persons Party and the Political Thought of the Counter-Reformation in England, 1572–1615* (Chicago: Loyola University Press).

Clebsch, W.A. (1964). *England's Earliest Protestants, 1520–1535* (New Haven: Yale University Press).

Coleman, J. (1982). 'The Continuity of Utopian Thought in the Middle Ages: A Reassessment', *Vivarium*, 20:1–23.

Collinson, P. (1967). *The Elizabethan Puritan Movement* (London: Cape).

    (1982). *The Religion of Protestants: The Church in English Society 1559–1625* (Oxford: Oxford University Press).

Collot, C. (1965). *L'Ecole doctrinale de droit public de Pont-à-Mousson* (Paris: Librairie générale de droit et de jurisprudence).

Congar, Y. M-J. (1958). '"Quod omnes tangit ab omnibus tractari et approbari debet"', *Revue Historique de Droit Français et Etranger*, ser. 4, 36:210–59.

Cranz, F.E. (1959). *An Essay on the Development of Luther's Thought on Justification, Law, and Society* (Cambridge, Mass.: Harvard University Press).

Cro, S. (1979). 'The New World in Spanish Utopianism', *Alternative Futures*, 2:39–53.

Cross, C. (1969). *The Royal Supremacy in the Elizabethan Church* (London: Allen and Unwin).

Curtin, M. (1985). 'A Question of Manners: Status and Gender in Etiquette and Courtesy', *Journal of Modern History*, 57:395–423.

Davis, J.C. (1976). 'Gerrard Winstanley and the Restoration of True Magistracy', *Past and Present*, 70:76–93.

(1981a). *Utopia and the Ideal Society: A Study of English Utopian Writing 1516–1700* (Cambridge: Cambridge University Press).

(1981b). 'Pocock's Harrington: Grace, Nature and Art in the Classical Republicanism of James Harrington', *Historical Journal*, 24:683–97.

(1984a). 'The History of Utopia: The Chronology of Nowhere', in *Utopias*, ed. P. Alexander and R. Gill (London: Duckworth).

(1984b). 'Science and Utopia: The History of a Dilemma', in *Nineteen Eighty-Four: Science between Utopia and Dystopia*, ed. E. Mendelsohn and H. Nowotny (Dordrecht and Lancaster: D. Reidel; Sociology of the Sciences Yearbook, 8).

Deane, H.A. (1963). *The Political and Social Ideas of St. Augustine* (New York: Columbia University Press).

De Kroon, M., and Krüger, F., eds. (1976). *Bucer und seine Zeit* (Wiesbaden: F. Steiner).

Dennert, J., ed. (1968). *Beza, Brutus, Hotman: calvinistiche Monarchomachen*, trans. H. Klingelhofer (Cologne: Westdeutscher Verlag).

D'Entrêves, A.P. (1939). *The Medieval Contribution to Political Thought: Thomas Aquinas, Marsilius of Padua, Richard Hooker* (Oxford: Oxford University Press).

Denzer, H., ed. (1973). *Jean Bodin: Verhandlungen der internationalen Bodin Tagung in München* (Munich: Beck).

Dewar, M. (1964). *Sir Thomas Smith: A Tudor Intellectual in Office* (London: Athlone Press).

Dickens, A.G., and Tonkin, J. (1985). *The Reformation in Historical Thought* (Cambridge, Mass.: Harvard University Press).

Dictionnaire de droit canonique (1935–65), ed. R. Naz, 7 vols. (Paris: Letouzey et Ane).

Dreitzel, H. (1970). *Protestantischer Aristotelismus und absoluter Staat. Die 'Politica' des Henning Arnisaeus (1575–1636)* (Wiesbaden: F. Steiner).

Elton, G.R. (1953). *The Tudor Revolution in Government* (Cambridge: Cambridge University Press).

(1973). *Reform and Renewal: Thomas Cromwell and the Commonweal* (Cambridge: Cambridge University Press).

(1974). *Studies in Tudor and Stuart Politics and Government*, 2 vols. (Cambridge: Cambridge University Press).

Eschmann, I.T. (1943). 'A Thomistic Glossary on the Principle of the Pre-Eminence of a Common Good', *Medieval Studies*, 5:123–65.

Espiner-Scott, J.G. (1938). *Claude Fauchet: sa vie, son œuvre* (Geneva: Droz).

Estèbe, J. (1968). *Tocsin pour un massacre, la saison des Saint-Barthélemy* (Paris: Le Centurion/Sciences Humaines).

Fabié, A.M. (1879). *Vida y escritos de fray Bartoleme de las Casas* (Madrid: Impr. de M. Ginestra).

Fell, A.L. (1983). *Origins of Legislative Sovereignty and the Legislative State*, 2 vols. (Cambridge, Mass.: Oelgeschlager, Gunn and Hain; Koenigstein: Athenäum).

Feret, P. (1877). *Le Cardinal du Perron, orateur, controversiste, écrivain* (Paris: Didier).

Ferguson, J. (1975). *Utopias of the Classical World* (London: Thames and Hudson).

Fernández-Santamaria, J.A. (1977). *The State, War and Peace: Spanish Political Thought in the Renaissance 1516–1559* (Cambridge: Cambridge University Press).

Figgis, J.N. (1965). *The Divine Right of Kings* (New York: Harper). First publ. 1896.

Filhol, R. (1953). 'Dumoulin', in *Dictionnaire de droit canonique*, ed. R. Naz (Paris: Letouzey et Ane), vol. v, cols. 41–67.

Fincham, K., and Lake, P. (1985). 'The Ecclesiastical Policy of James I', *Journal of British Studies*, 24:169–207.

Firpo, L. (1963). 'Kaspar Stiblin, Utopiste', in *Les Utopies à la Renaissance*, ed. J. Lameere (Université Libre de Bruxelles: Travaux de L'Institut pour l'Etude de la Renaissance et de l'Humanisme).
Flinn, M.W. (1957). *The Law Book of the Crowley Iron Works* (Durham: Surtees Society, 167).
Fox, A., and Guy, J.A., eds. (1986). *Reassessing the Henrician Age* (Oxford: Blackwell).
Fox, V.C. (1969). 'Deviance in English Utopias in the 16th, 17th and 18th Centuries' (PhD thesis, Boston University).
Franklin, J.H. (1963). *Jean Bodin and the Sixteenth-Century Revolution in the Methodology of Law and History* (New York: Columbia University Press).
  (1973). *Jean Bodin and the Rise of Absolutist Theory* (Cambridge: Cambridge University Press).
Fry, A.R. (1953), *John Bellers, 1654–1725, Quaker, Economist and Social Reformer: His Writings Reprinted with a Memoir* (London: Cassell).
Getino, L.G.A. (1930). *El Maestro fr. Francisco de Vitoria, su vida, su doctrina e influencia* (Madrid: Imprenta católica).
Gierke, O. (1929). *Johannes Althusius und die Entwicklung der naturrechtlichen Staatstheorien* (Breslau: Marcus). For English edn see Gierke (1966).
  (1957). *Natural Law and the Theory of Society*, ed. and trans. E. Barker (Boston: Beacon Press).
  (1966). *The Development of Political Theory*, trans. B. Freyd (New York: H. Fertig). First publ. 1939, London: Methuen; see Gierke (1929).
Giesey, R.E. (1960). 'The French Estates and the *corpus mysticum regni*', in *Album Helen Maud Cam* (Louvain: Etudes présentées a la Commission Internationale pour l'histoire des assemblées d'Etats, 23), 1:153–71.
  (1968). *If Not, Not: The Oath of the Aragonese and the Legendary Laws of Sobrarbe* (Princeton: Princeton University Press).
  (1970). 'The Monarchomach Triumvirs: Hotman, Beza and Mornay', *Bibliothèque d'Humanisme et Renaissance*, 32: 41–56.
  (1972). '"Quod omnes tangit" – a Post Scriptum', *Studia Gratiana*, 15:319–32.
Gilmore, M.P. (1941). *Argument from Roman law in Political Thought, 1200–1600* (Cambridge, Mass.: Harvard University Press).
Goldie, M. (1983). 'Obligations, Utopias and their Historical Context', *Historical Journal*, 26:727–46.
Gough, J.W. (1955). *Fundamental Law in English Constitutional History* (Oxford: Clarendon Press).
Grafton, A. (1983). *Joseph Scaliger: A Study in the History of Classical Scholarship* (Oxford: Clarendon Press).
Greenleaf, W.H. (1964). *Order, Empiricism and Politics: Two Traditions of English Political Thought 1550–1700* (Oxford: Oxford University Press).
Griffin, M.T. (1976). *Seneca: A Philosopher in Politics* (Oxford: Clarendon Press).
Griffiths, G. (1968). *Representative Government in Western Europe in the Sixteenth Century* (Oxford: Clarendon Press).
Gritsch, E.W. (1967). *Reformer without a Church: The Life and Thought of Thomas Muentzer* (Philadelphia: Fortress Press).
Gross, H. (1973). *Empire and Sovereignty* (Chicago: University of Chicago Press).
Hall, A.R. (1972). 'Science, Technology and Utopia in the Seventeenth Century', in *Science and Society 1600–1900*, ed. P. Mathias (Cambridge: Cambridge University Press).
Hamilton, B. (1963). *Political Thought in Sixteenth-Century Spain: A Study of the Political Ideas of Vitoria, De Soto, Suárez and Molina* (Oxford: Clarendon Press).

Bibliography

Hanke, L. (1949). *The Spanish Struggle for Justice in the Conquest of America* (Philadelphia: Pennsylvania University Press).

    (1959). *Aristotle and the American Indians: A Study in Race Prejudice in the Modern World* (Chicago: H. Regnerg).

    (1974). *All Mankind is One: A Study of the Disputation between Bartolomé de las Casas and Juan Ginés de Sepúlveda on the Religious and Intellectual Capacity of the American Indians* (De Kalb, Ill.: Northern Illinois University Press).

Hanley, S. (1983). *The Lit de Justice of the Kings of France: Constitutional Ideology in Legend, Ritual and Discourse* (Princeton: Princeton University Press).

Hansot, E. (1974). *Perfection and Progress: Two Modes of Utopian Thought* (Cambridge, Mass.: MIT Press).

Harder, L. and M. (1952). *Plockhoy from Zurick-Zee: A Study of a Dutch Reformer in Puritan England and Colonial America* (Newton, Kan.: Mennonite Historical Series, 2).

Hayden, J.M. (1974). *France and the Estates General of 1614* (Cambridge: Cambridge University Press).

Hexter, J.H. (1973). *The Vision of Politics on the Eve of the Reformation: More, Machiavelli and Seyssel* (London: Allen Lane).

Hill, C. (1972). *The World Turned Upside Down: Radical Ideas during the English Revolution* (London: Temple Smith).

    (1973). 'Introduction' to *Winstanley: The Law of Freedom and Other Writings* (Harmondsworth: Penguin).

    (1986). 'The Religion of Gerrard Winstanley', in *The Collected Essays of Christoper Hill: Volume Two, Religion and Politics in Seventeenth-Century England* (Brighton: Harvester).

Hofmann, H. (1974). *Repräsentation: Studien zur Wort- und Begriffsgeschichte von der Antike bis ins 19. Jahrhundert* (Berlin: Duncker and Humblot).

Hoke, R. (1968). *Die Reichsstaatsrechtslehre des Joannes Limnaeus* (Aalen: Scientia Verlag).

Holmes, P. (1982). *Resistance and Compromise: The Political Thought of the Elizabethan Catholics* (Cambridge: Cambridge University press).

Holstun, J. (1987). *A Rational Millennium: Puritan Utopias of Seventeenth-Century England and America* (Oxford: Oxford University Press).

Höpfl, H. (1982). *The Christian Polity of John Calvin* (Cambridge: Cambridge University Press).

Hudson, W.S. (1942). *John Ponet (1516?–1556), Advocate of Limited Monarchy* (Chicago: University of Chicago Press). Includes a facsimile reprint of *A Shorte Treatise of Politike Power* after p. 246.

Izbicki, T.M. (1981). *Protector of the Faith: Cardinal Johannes de Turrecremata and the Defense of the Institutional Church* (Washington: Catholic University of America Press).

Janton, P. (1967). *John Knox (c. 1513–1572): l'homme et l'œuvre* (Paris: Didier).

Jarlot, G. (1949). 'Les Idées politiques de Suárez et le pouvoir absolu', *Archives de Philosophie*, 18:64–107.

Jones, N.L. (1982). *Faith by Statute: Parliament and the Settlement of Religion, 1559* (London: Royal Historical Society).

Jones, W.R.D. (1970). *The Tudor Commonwealth, 1529–1559* (London: Athlone Press).

Kagan, R.L. (1981). *Lawsuits and Litigants in Castile, 1500–1700* (Chapel Hill: North Carolina University Press).

Kantorowicz, E.H. (1957). *The King's Two Bodies: A Study in Medieval Political Theology* (Princeton: Princeton University Press).

Kearney, H.F. (1952). 'Richard Hooker: A Reconstruction', *Cambridge Journal*, 5:300–11.

Kelley, D.R. (1970). *Foundations of Modern Historical Scholarship: Language, Law and History in the French Renaissance* (New York: Columbia University Press).

(1973). *François Hotman: A Revolutionary's Ordeal* (Princeton: Princeton University Press).

(1981). *The Beginning of Ideology: Consciousness and Society in the French Reformation* (Cambridge: Cambridge University Press).

Kingdon, R.M. (1988). *Myths about the St. Bartholomew's Day Massacres 1572–1576* (Cambridge, Mass.: Harvard University Press).

Kisch, G. (1960). *Erasmus und die Jurisprudenz seiner Zeit* (Basle: Helbing and Lichtenhahn).

(1967). *Melanchthons Rechts- und Soziallehre* (Berlin: De Gruyter).

Kossmann, E.H. (1981). 'Popular Sovereignty at the Beginning of the Dutch Ancien Regime', *Acta historiae Nederlandica*, 14:1–28.

Lachèvre, F. (1933). *La Première Utopie Française: La Royaume D'Antangil* (Paris: La Connaissance).

Lapouge, G. (1973). *Utopie et Civilisations* (Paris and Geneva: Librairie Weber).

Law, T.G. (1896). *The Archpriest Controversy* (London: Camden Society).

Lemaire, A. (1907). *Les Lois fondamentales de la monarchie française d'après les théoriciens de l'ancien régime* (Paris: A. Fontemoing).

Levin, H. (1970). *The Myth of the Golden Age in the Renaissance* (London: Faber).

Levy, F.J. (1987). 'Hayward, Daniel and the Beginnings of Politic History in England', *Huntington Library Quarterly*, 50:1–34.

Lewy, G. (1960). *Constitutionalism and Statecraft during the Golden Age of Spain: A Study of the Political Philosophy of Juan de Mariana, S.J.* (Geneva: Droz; Travaux d'Humanisme et Renaissance, 36).

Linder, R.D. (1964). *The Political Ideas of Pierre Viret* (Geneva: Droz).

(1966). 'Pierre Viret and the Sixteenth Century French Protestant Revolutionary Tradition', *Journal of Modern History*, 38:125–37.

Lloyd, H.A. (1981a). 'Calvin and the Duty of Guardians to Resist', *Journal of Ecclesiastical History*, 32:65–7.

(1981b). 'The Political Thought of Charles Loyseau (1564–1627)', *European Studies Review*, 11:53–82.

(1983). *The State, France and the Sixteenth Century* (London: Allen and Unwin).

Logan, G.M. (1983). *The Meaning of More's 'Utopia'* (Princeton: Princeton University Press).

Lubac, H. de (1944). *Eucharistie et l'église au Moyen Age* (Paris: Aubier).

Lyon, B. (1956). 'Fact and Fiction in English and Belgian Constitutional Law', *Medievalia et humanistica*, 10:82–101.

McFarlane, I.D. (1981). *Buchanan* (London: Duckworth).

McGrade, A.S. (1963). 'The Coherence of Hooker's Polity: The Books on Power', *Journal of the History of Ideas*, 24:163–82.

McIlwain, C.H. (1918). Introduction to *The Political Works of James I* (Cambridge, Mass.: Harvard University Press).

Manschreck, C.L. (1958). *Melanchthon: The Quiet Reformer* (New York: Abingdon Press).

(1965). *Melanchthon on Christian Doctrine. Loci communes 1555* (Oxford: Oxford University Press).

Manuel, F.E., and Manuel, F.P. (1979). *Utopian Thought in the Western World* (Oxford: Blackwell).

Maravall, J.A. (1972). *Estado moderno y mentalidad social (siglos XV a XVII)*, 2 vols. (Madrid: Ediciones de la Revista de Occidente).

Marin, L. (1984). *Utopics: Spatial Play*, trans. R.A. Vollrath (London: Humanities Press/Macmillan).

Martin, A.L. (1973). *Henry III and the Jesuit Politicians* (Geneva: Droz).

Martin, V. (1919). *Le Gallicanisme et la réforme catholique: essai historique sur l'introduction en France des décrets du Concile de Trente, 1563–1615* (Paris: Picard).

Mason, R. (1982). '*Rex Stoicus*: George Buchanan, James VI and the Scottish Polity', in *New Perspectives on the Politics and Culture of Early Modern Scotland*, ed. J. Dwyer, R. Mason, and A. Murdoch (Edinburgh: John Donald), pp. 9–33.

Mastellone, S. (1972). *Venalità e machiavellismo in Francia (1572–1610): All'origine della mentalità politica borghese* (Florence: Olschki).

Maugis, E. (1913–16). *Histoire du Parlement de Paris de l'avènement des rois Valois à la mort d'Henri IV* (Paris: Picard).

Maumigny, J. de (1910). *Etude sur Guy Coquille, publiciste et jurisconsulte* (Paris: Larose).

Meinecke, F. (1957). *Machiavellism: The Doctrine of Raison d'Etat and its Place in Modern History*, trans. D. Scott, intro. W. Stark (London: Routledge and Kegan Paul). First publ. as *Die Idee der Staatsräson* (Munich: R. Oldenbourg, 1924).

Melía, A.M. (1977). *Iglesia y Estado en el siglo de oro español: el pensamiento de Francisco Suárez* (Valencia: Universidad de Valencia).

Mesnard, P. (1952). *L'Essor de la philosophie politique au XVIe siècle*, 2nd edn (Paris: Vrin).

Milsom, S.F.C. (1985). *Studies in the History of the Common Law* (London: Hambledon Press).

Milward, P. (1977). *Religious Controversies of the Elizabethan Age* (Lincoln: Nebraska University Press).

(1978). *Religious Controversies of the Jacobean Age* (Lincoln: Nebraska University Press).

Moeller, B. (1965). 'Frommigkeit in Deutschland um 1500', *Archiv für Reformationsgeschichte*. 56:3–31.

(1966). *Spätmittelalter*, instalment H (pt 1) in *Die Kirche in ihrer Geschichte: Ein Handbuch*, ed. K. Schmidt and E. Wolf (Göttingen: Vandenhoeck and Ruprecht).

(1972). *Imperial Cities and the Reformation*, ed. H.C.E. Midelfort and M.V. Edwards (Philadelphia: Fortress Press).

Montgomery, J.W. (1973). *Cross and Crucible: Johann Valentin Andreae (1586–1654), Phoenix of the Theologians*, 2 vols. (The Hague: Archives Internationales d'Histoire des Idées, 55).

Morris, C. (1953). *Political Thought in England: Tyndale to Hooker* (Oxford: Oxford University Press).

Mozley, J.F. (1937). *William Tyndale* (London: Macmillan).

Muller, J.A. (1926). *Stephen Gardiner and the Tudor Reaction* (London: SCM Press).

Munz, P. (1952). *The Place of Hooker in the History of Thought* (London: Routledge and Kegan Paul).

Oakley, F. (1964–5). 'Almain and Major: Conciliar Theory on the Eve of the Reformation', *American Historical Review*, 70:673–90.

(1977). 'Conciliarism in the Sixteenth Century: Jacques Almain Again', *Archiv für Reformationsgeschichte*, 68:111–32.

(1984). *Omnipotence, Covenant and Order: An Excursion in the History of Ideas from Abelard to Leibniz* (Ithaca: Cornell Univerity Press).

(1987). 'Edward Foxe, Matthew Paris, and the Royal *potestas ordinis*', *Sixteenth Century Journal*, 18:347–53.

Oestreich, G. (1982). *Neostoicism and the Early Modern State*, ed. B. Oestrich and H.G. Koenigsberger, trans. D. McLintock (Cambridge: Cambridge University Press).

Ourliac, P., and Gilles, H. (1971). *La Période post-classique (1378–1500)* (Paris: Cujas; Histoire du droit et des institutions de l'église en Occident, 13).

Ozment, S. (1973). *Mysticism and Dissent* (New Haven: Yale University Press).

Pagden, A. (1987). 'Dispossessing the Barbarian: The Language of Spanish Thomism and the Debate over the Property Rights of the American Indians', in *The Languages of Political Theory in Early-Modern Europe*, ed. A. Pagden (Cambridge: Cambridge University Press).

Parker, T.H.L. (1975). *John Calvin: A Biography* (London: Dent).

Parry, J.H. (1940). *The Spanish Theory of Empire in the Sixteenth Century* (Cambridge: Cambridge University Press).

Patrick, J.M. (1977). '*Nova Solyma*: Samuel Gott's Puritan Utopia', *Studies in the Literary Imagination*, 10:43–55.

Patry, R. (1933). *Philippe du Plessis-Mornay, un huguenot homme-d'état (1549–1623)* (Paris: Fischbacher).

Perez, J. (1970). *La Révolution des 'Communidades' de Castille (1520–1521)* (Bordeaux: Institut d'Etudes Ibériques et Ibéro-Américaines).

(1972). 'The Science of Law in the Spain of the Catholic Kings', in *Spain in the Fifteenth Century 1369–1516*, ed. R. Highfield (London: Macmillan).

Pignot, J.H. (1880). *Un jurisconsulte au XVIe siècle: Barthélemy de Chasseneux, premier commentateur de la coutume de Bourgogne et président du parlement de Provence: sa vie et ses œuvres* (Paris: Larose).

Pissavino, P. (1985). 'Utopia e Arco Storico: linee preliminari per un'analisi differenziale', *Il Politico*, 50:41–65.

Pocock, J.G.A. (1957). *The Ancient Constitution and the Feudal Law* (Cambridge: Cambridge University Press; reissued 1987).

(1975). *The Machiavellian Moment: Florentine Political Thought and the Atlantic Republican Tradition* (Princeton: Princeton University Press).

Porter, H.C. (1958). *Reformation and Reaction in Tudor Cambridge* (Cambridge: Cambridge University Press).

Post, G. (1943). '*Plena potestas* and Consent in Medieval Assemblies', *Traditio*, 1:355–408.

(1953). 'Two Notes on Nationalism in the Middle Ages', *Traditio*, 9:281–320.

Potter, G.R. (1976). *Zwingli* (Cambridge: Cambridge University Press).

Préclin, E. (1930). 'Edmond Richer, 1559–1631: sa vie, son œuvre, le richerisme', *Revue d'Histoire Moderne*, 28:241–69; 29:321–36.

Pritchard, A. (1978). *Catholic Loyalism in Elizabethan England* (Chapel Hill: North Carolina University Press; London: Scolar Press).

Quillet, J. (1971). '*Universitas populi* et représentation au XIVe siècle', *Miscellania Mediaevalia*, 8:186–201.

Reed, C. (1960). *Lord Burghley and Queen Elizabeth* (London: Cape).

Reesor, M.E. (1951). *The Political Theory of the Old and Middle Stoa* (New York: J.J. Augustin).

Renaudet, A. (1953). *Préréforme et humanisme à Paris pendant les premières guerres d'Italie (1494–1517)*, 2nd edn (Paris: Librairie d'Argences).

Reynolds, B. (1931). *Proponents of Limited Monarchy in Sixteenth Century France: François Hotman and Jean Bodin* (New York: Columbia University Press).

Ridley, J. (1968). *John Knox* (Oxford: Clarendon Press).

Romeyer, B. (1949). 'La Théorie Suarezienne d'un état de nature pure', *Archives de Philosophie*, 18:37–63.

Rose, P.L. (1980). *Bodin and the Great God of Nature: The Moral and Religious Universe of a Judaiser* (Geneva: Droz; Travaux d'Humanisme et Renaissance, 179).

Rossi, P. (1968). *Francis Bacon: From Magic to Science*, trans. S. Rabinovitch (London: Routledge and Kegan Paul).

Rubinstein, N., ed. (1968). *Florentine Studies: Politics and Society in Renaissance Florence* (London: Faber).

Bibliography

Salmon, J.H.M. (1959). *The French Religious Wars in English Political Thought* (Oxford: Clarendon Press).

(1975). *Society in Crisis: France in the Sixteenth Century* (London: Benn).

(1987). *Renaissance and Revolt: Essays in the Intellectual and Social History of Early Modern France* (Cambridge: Cambridge University Press).

Sargent, L.T. (1979). *British and American Utopian Literature: An Annotated Bibliography* (Boston, Mass.: G.K. Hall).

Sawada, P.A. (1961). 'Two Anonymous Tudor Treatises on the General Council', *Journal of Ecclesiastical History*, 12:197–214.

Scarisbrick, J.J. (1968). *Henry VIII* (Los Angeles and Berkeley: California University Press).

Schmitt, E. (1977). '*Repraesentio in toto* und *repraesentatio singulariter*', in *Album François Dumont* (Brussels: Librairie Encyclopédique).

Sedgwick, A. (1977). *Jansenism in Seventeenth-Century France: Voices in the Wilderness* (Charlottesville: Virginia University Press).

Seguy, J. (1971). 'Une sociologie des sociétés imaginées: monachisme et utopie', *Annales, Economies, Sociétés, Civilisations*, 26:328–54.

Seibt, F. (1980). 'Liber Figurarum XII and the Classical Ideal of Utopia', in *Prophecy and Millenariansim: Essays in Honour of Marjorie Reeves*, ed. A. Williams (London: Longman), pp. 257–66.

Shklar, J. (1969). *After Utopia* (Princeton: Princeton University Press).

Skinner, Q. (1978). *The Foundations of Modern Political Thought*, 2 vols. (Cambridge: Cambridge University Press).

(1986). 'Ambrogio Lorenzetti: The Artist as Political Philosopher', *Proceedings of the British Academy*, 72:1–56.

Smith, L.B. (1953). *Tudor Prelates and Politics, 1536–1558* (Princeton: Princeton University Press).

Sommerville, J.P. (1982). 'From Suárez to Filmer: A Reappraisal', *Historical Journal*, 25:525–40.

(1983). 'Richard Hooker, Hadrian Saravia, and the Advent of the Divine Right of Kings', *History of Political Thought*, 4:229–45.

(1986). *Politics and Ideology in England 1603–1640* (London: Longman).

Stayer, J.M. (1973). *Anabaptists and the Sword* (Lawrence, Kansas: Coranado Press).

Stern, J.P. (1980–1). 'A Game of Utopia', *German Life and Letters*, 34:94–107.

Stewart, P.D. (1969). *Innocent Gentillet e la sua polemica antimachiavellica* (Florence: La Nuova Italia; Biblioteca di Cultura, 88).

Stintzing, R. von (1880–4). *Geschichte der deutschen Rechtswissenschaft*, 2 vols. (Munich and Leipzig: R. Oldenbourg).

Surtz, E.L. (1957). *The Praise of Pleasure: Philosophy, Education and Communism in More's Utopia* (Cambridge, Mass.: Harvard University Press).

Thickett, D. (1979). *Etienne Pasquier (1529–1615): The Versatile Barrister of Sixteenth-Century France* (London: Regency Press).

Thireau, J-L. (1980). *Charles Du Moulin (1500–1566)* (Geneva: Droz; Travaux d'Humanisme et Renaissance, 176).

Thomas, K. (1985). 'The Utopian Impulse in Seventeenth Century England', *Dutch Quarterly Review of Anglo-American Letters*, 15:162–88.

Thompson, I.A.A. (1982). 'Crown and Cortes in Castile, 1590–1665', *Parliaments, Estates and Representation*, 2:29–45.

Tierney, B. (1975). '"Divided Sovereignty" at Constance: A Problem of Medieval and Early Modern Political Theory', *Annuarium Historiae Conciliorum*, 7:238–56.

(1982). *Religion, Law and the Growth of Constitutional Thought, 1150–1650* (Cambridge: Cambridge University Press).

Trevor-Roper, H.R. (1966). 'George Buchanan and the Ancient Scottish Constitution', *English Historical Review*, Supplement 3.

Troeltsch, E. (1960). *The Social Teaching of the Christian Churches*, trans. O. Wyon, 2 vols. (New York: Harper).

Tuck, R. (1979). *Natural Rights Theories: Their Origin and Development* (Cambridge: Cambridge University Press).

Tuveson, E.L. (1964). *Millennium and Utopia: A Study in the Background of the Idea of Progress* (New York: Harper and Row).

Ullmann, W. (1962). 'De Bartoli sententia: *Concilium repraesentat mentem populi*' in *Bartolo da Sassoferrato: Studi e Documenti per il VI centenario*, vol. II (Milan: Università degli Studi, Perugia).

(1981). 'Calvin and the Duty of the Guardians to Resist: A Further Comment', *Journal of Ecclesiastical History*, 32:499–501.

Van Bragt, R. (1956). *De Bligde Inkomst van de Hertogen van Brabant Johanna en Wenceslas (3 Januauri 1356)* (Louvain: Nauwelaerts; Anciens Pays et Assemblées d'Etats, 13).

Van Uytven, R., and Blockmans, W. (1969). 'Constitutions and their Application in the Netherlands during the Middle Ages', *Revue Belge de Philologie et d'Histoire*, 47:399–424.

Vickers, B. (1979). 'Frances Yates and the Writing of History', *Journal of Modern History*, 51:287–316.

ed. (1968). *Essential Articles for the Study of Francis Bacon* (New York: Archon Books).

Vile, M.J.C. (1967). *Constitutionalism and the Separation of Powers* (Oxford: Clarendon Press).

Walton, R.C. (1967). *Zwingli's Theocracy* (Toronto: University of Toronto Press).

Webster, C. (1975). *The Great Instauration: Science, Medicine and Reform 1626–1660* (London: Duckworth).

Weill, G. (1891). *Les Théories sur le pouvoir royal en France pendant les guerres de religion* (Paris: Hachette; repub. New York: Burt Franklin, 1966).

Wenger, J. (1945). 'The Schleitheim Confession of Faith', *Mennonite Quarterly Review*, 19:243–53.

White, T.I. (1982). 'Pride and the Public Good: Thomas More's Use of Plato in *Utopia*', *Journal of the History of Philosophy*, 20:329–54.

Wilks, M. (1972). 'Corporation and Representation in the *Defensor Pacis*', *Studia Gratiana*, 15:251–92.

Wolgast, E. (1980). *Die Religionsfrage als Problem des Wiedenstandsrechts im 16. Jahrhundert* (Heidelberg: Sitzungsberichte der Heidelberger Akademie der Wissenschaften, Phil.-Hist. Klasse 1980, Abh. 9).

Woodhouse, J.R. (1978). *Baldessar Castiglione: A Reassessment of 'The Courtier'* (Edinburgh: Edinburgh University Press).

Zanoni, E. (1903). *Paulo Paruta nella vita e nelle opere* (Leghorn: R. Giusti).

Zeeveld, W.G. (1948). *Foundations of Tudor Policy* (Cambridge, Mass.: Harvard University Press).

III   Absolutism and revolution in the seventeenth century

Primary sources

Acherley, Roger (1759). *The Britannic Constitution: or, the Fundamental Form of Government in Britain*, 2nd edn (London).

Amyraut, Moïse (1650). *Discours de la souveraineté des Roys* (Charenton?).

Andrewes, Lancelot (1610). *A Sermon Preached before his Majestie, on Sunday the Fifth of August last* (London).

Anonymous (1640). See *Priviledges*.

  (1656). See *Copy of a Letter*.

  (1697). See *Argument*.

  (1698). See *Short History*.

Argument (1697). *An Argument Showing that a Standing Army is inconsistent with a Free Government* (London).

Atkyns, Sir Robert (1689). *The Power, Jurisdiction and Priviledge of Parliament; and the Antiquity of the House of Commons Asserted* (London).

Atwood, William (1681). *Jus Anglorum ab Antiquo* (London).

  (1690). *The Fundamental Constitution of the English Government* (London).

Austine, Robert (1644). *Allegiance not Impeached* (London).

Aylmer, G.E., ed. (1975). *The Levellers in the English Revolution* (London: Thames and Hudson).

Bacon, Sir Francis (1671). *Resuscitatio or, Bringing into Publick Light Several Pieces of the Works*, 3rd edn (London).

Bacon, Nathaniel (1647–51). *An Historical Discourse of the Uniformity of the Government of England*, 2 vols. in 1 (London).

Bagshaw, Edward (1660). *The Rights of the Crown of England, as it is Established by Law* (London).

Ball, William (1645). *Tractatus de Jure Regnandi et Regni* (London).

Balzac, Jean-Louis Guez de (1665). *Œuvres*, 2 vols. (Paris).

Baricave, Jean (1614). *La Défence de la Monarchie Françoise, et autres Monarchies* (Toulouse).

Barnes, John (1625). *Dissertatio contra Aequivocationes* (Paris).

Barret, William (1612). *Ius Regis* (London).

Baxter, Richard (1659). *A Holy Commonwealth* (London).

  (1696). *Reliquiae Baxterianae* (London).

Bethel, Slingsby (1671). *The Present Interest of England* (London).

Bignon, Jerome (1610). *De l'excellence des Roys et du Royaume de France* (Paris).

Bilson, Thomas (1603). *A Sermon Preached at Westminster before the King and Queens maiesty* (London).

Bodin, Jean (1962). *The Six Books of a Commonweale*, trans. R. Knolles, ed. K.D. McRae (Cambridge, Mass.: Harvard University Press; Harvard Political Classics).

Bolton, Robert (1635). *Two Sermons Preached at Northampton* (London).

Bossuet, Jacques-Bénigne (1966). *Politique de Bossuet: Textes Choisis et Présentés par Jacques Truchet* (Paris: Colin; Idées Politiques).

(1967). *Politique tirée des propres paroles de l'Ecriture sainte*, ed. J. Le Brun (Geneva: Droz).

Brady, Robert (1681). *A Full and Clear answer to a Book written by William Petit, Esq.* (London).

(1684). *An Introduction to the Old English History, Comprehended in Three several Tracts* (London).

(1685). *A Complete History of England*, vol. 1 (London).

Brooke, Sir Robert (1573). *La Graunde Abridgement*, ed. R. Tottell (London).

Buckeridge, John (1606). *A Sermon Preached at Hampton Court* (London).

(1614). *De potestate papae in rebus temporalibus* (London).

Burton, Thomas (1828). *The Diary of Thomas Burton*, ed. J.T. Rutt, 4 vols. (London: H. Colburn and R. Bentley).

Butler, Charles (1609). *The Feminine Monarchie (or a Treatise Concerning Bees)* (Oxford).

Casaubon, Isaac (1607). *De libertate ecclesiastica liber singularis* (Paris).

Charles I (1628). *His Maiesties Declaration to all his Loving Subjects of the Causes which Moved him to Dissolve the Last Parliament* (London).

Charron, Pierre (1604). *De la sagesse*, 2nd edn (Paris).

Coke, Sir Edward (1642). *The Second Part of the Institutes of the Laws of England* (London).

(1681). *The Fourth Part of the Institutes of the Laws of England*, 6th edn (London).

(1777). *Reports*, ed. G. Wilson, 7 vols. (London).

(1809). *The First Part of the Institutes of the Laws of England*, 16th edn (London: Hansard).

Collection (1705). *A Collection of State Tracts, Publish'd on Occasion of the Late Revolution in 1688*, vol. 1 (London). See also under *State Tracts*.

Commons Debates 1621 (1935). Ed. W. Notestein, H. Simpson, and F. Relf, 7 vols. (New Haven: Yale University Press).

Commons Debates 1628 (1977). Ed. R.C. Johnson and M. Jansson Cole, assisted by M.F. Keeler and W.B. Bidwell, 6 vols. (New Haven: Yale University Press).

Cooke, Edward (1682). *Argumentum Anti-Normannicum* (London).

Copy of a Letter (1656). *A Copy of a Letter from an Officer of the Army in Ireland.*

Coquaeus, Leonardus (1610). *Examen praefationis monitoriae* (Freiburg-im-Breisgau).

Cowell, John (1607). *The Interpreter: or Booke containing the Signification of Words* (Cambridge).

Cunaeus, Petrus (1653). *Of the Commonwealth of the Hebrews* (London).

De Dominis, Marc'Antonio (1620). *De republica ecclesiastica pars secunda* (Frankfurt). First publ. London 1617.

De la Court, Pieter (1702). *The True Interest of Holland* (London).

Digges, Dudley (1642). *An Answer to a Printed Book, intituled, Observations upon some of his Maiesties late Answers and Expresses* (Oxford).

(1643). *The Unlawfulness of Subjects taking up Arms against their Soveraigne, in what case soever* (Oxford).

Dodderidge, John (1658). *The Several Opinions of Sundry learned Antiquaries . . . Touching the Antiquity . . . of the High Court of Parliament in England* (London).

Domat, Jean (1705). *Les loix civiles dans leur ordre naturel, le droit public, et legum delectus*, (2 vols. (Paris).

Donne, John (1610). *Pseudo-martyr* (London).

Du Boys, H. (1604). *De l'origine et autorité des roys* (Paris).

745

Bibliography

Dugdale, Sir William (1666). *Origines Juridiciales* (London).

(1675). *The Baronage of England* (London).

See also Spelman (1664)

Edwards, Thomas (1977). *Gangraena* (University of Exeter: facsimile reprint of the first edn, London 1646).

Fénelon, François de S. de la M. (1920). *Fénelon: écrits et lettres politiques*, ed. C. Urbain (Paris: Bossard).

Ferne, Henry (1642). *The Resolving of Conscience* (Cambridge).

(1643). *Conscience Satisfied, that there is no Warrant for the Armes now taken up by Subjects* (Oxford).

Filmer, Sir Robert (1949). *Patriarcha and Other Political Works*, ed. P. Laslett (Oxford: Blackwell).

Fletcher, Andrew (1732). *The Political Works of Andrew Fletcher* (London).

Foxe, John (1843–9). *The Acts and Monuments*, ed. G. Townshend, 3 vols. (London: Seeley, Burnside and Seeley), vol. II.

Glanville, John (1775). *Reports of Certain Cases* (London).

Grotius, Hugo (1649). *A Treatise of the Antiquity of the Commonwealth of the Battavers, which is now the Hollanders* (London).

Hakewill, William (1641). *The Libertie of the Subject* (London).

Hale, Sir Matthew (1966). 'Reflections . . . on Mr Hobbes, His Dialogue of the Lawe', in Sir William Holdsworth, *A History of English Law*, 3rd edn, vol. v (London: Methuen), pp. 500–13.

(1971). *The History of the Common Law*, ed. C.M. Gray (Chicago: University of Chicago Press).

(1976). *The Prerogatives of the King*, ed. D.E.C. Yale (London: Selden Society).

Hall, John (1700). *The Grounds and Reasons of Monarchy Considered*, in Harrington (1700).

Haller, W., ed. (1934). *Tracts on Liberty in the Puritan Revolution, 1638–1647*, 3 vols. (New York: Columbia University Press; repr. 1965, New York: Octagon Books).

Haller, W., and G. Davies, eds. (1944). *The Leveller Tracts, 1647–1653* (New York: Columbia University Press; repr. 1964. Gloucester, Mass.: P. Smith).

Harrington, James (1700). *The Oceana and Other Works of James Harrington*, ed. John Toland (London).

(1977). *The Political Works of James Harrington*, ed. J.G.A. Pocock (Cambridge: Cambridge University Press).

Hayward, Sir John (1603). *An Answer to the First Part of a Certaine Conference* (London).

Herle, Charles (1642). *A Fuller Answer to a Treatise Written by Doctor Ferne* (London).

(1643). *An Answer to Dr Ferne's Reply* (London).

Hespérien, Pierre (1617). *Harangue faite au roi par les députés du synode national des églises réformées de France* (La Rochelle).

Heylin, Peter (1637). *A Briefe and Moderate Answer to the Seditious and Scandalous Challenges of Henry Burton* (London).

Hobbes, Thomas (1839–45). *English Works*, ed. Sir W. Molesworth, 11 vols. (London: Bohn).

Holbourne, Sir Robert (?) (1648). *The Freeholders Grand Inquest* (n.p.). Also attributed to Sir Robert Filmer.

Holles, Denzil (1693). 'Letter', in *State Tracts* (1693), pp. 458–61.

Hooker, Richard (1977–82). *Of the Lawes of Ecclesiasticall Politie*, ed. W. Speed Hill, 4 vols. (Cambridge, Mass.: Belknap Press of Harvard University; The Folger Library Edition of the Works of Richard Hooker).

Horn, Andrew (1895). *The Mirror of Justices*, ed. W.J. Whittaker, intro, F.W. Maitland (London: B. Quaritch).

Howell, James (1651). *Cottoni Posthuma* (London).

Howell, T.B. (1809–28). *A Complete Collection of State Trials*, 34 vols. (London: Hansard).

Hume, David (1762). *The History of England*, vol. 1 (London).

Hunton, Philip (1643). *A Treatise of Monarchie* (London).

Husband, Edward (1643). *An Exact Collection of all Remonstrances* (London).

Hyde, Edward, Earl of Clarendon (1676). *A Brief View and Survey of the Dangerous and Pernicious Errors to Church and State, in Mr Hobbes's Book, entitled Leviathan*, 2nd edn (Oxford).

Jacob, Giles (1729). *A New Law Dictionary* (London).

James VI and I, King (1616). *The Workes* (London).

(1918). *The Political Works of James I*, ed. C.H. McIlwain (Cambridge, Mass.: Harvard University Press).

Johnson, Samuel (1693). *An Argument Proving that the Abrogation of King James by the People of England from the Regal Throne, and the Promotion of the Prince of Orange, one of the Royal Family, to the Throne of the Kingdom in his stead, was according to the Constitution of the English Government and Prescribed by it*, 5th edn (London).

Kenyon, J.P., ed. (1966). *The Stuart Constitution 1603–1688: Documents and Commentary* (Cambridge: Cambridge University Press). Revised edn 1986.

La Bruyère, Jean de (1966). *Les Caractères* (Paris: J. Tallandier; Livre de Poche).

Lambarde, William (1568). *Archaionomia, sive De Priscis Anglorum Legibus* (London).

(1957). *Archeion or, A Discourse upon the High Courts of Justice in England*, ed. C.H. McIlwain and P.L. Ward (Cambridge, Mass.: Harvard University Press).

Le Bret, Cardin (1632). *De la souveraineté du Roy* (Paris).

Leslie, Charles (1709). *The Best Answer ever was made and to which no Answer will be made* (London).

Lever, Christopher (1608). *Heaven and Earth, Religion and Policy* (London).

Locke, John (1967). *Two Treatises of Government*, ed. P. Laslett, 2nd edn (Cambridge: Cambridge University Press).

Louis XIV (1860). *Mémoires de Louis XIV pour l'instruction du Dauphin*, ed. C. Dreyss, 2 vols. (Paris: Didier).

Ludlow, Edmund (1978). *A Voyce from the Watch Tower*, ed. B. Worden (London: Royal Historical Society; Camden Fourth Series, 21).

Mandeville, Bernard (1924). *The Fable of the Bees*, ed. F.B. Kaye, 2 vols. (Oxford: Clarendon Press).

Marca, Pierre de (1641). *De concordia sacerdotii et imperii seu de libertatibus ecclesiae Gallicanae* (Paris).

Marsilius, Johannes (1606). *Defensio Iohannis Marsilii, in favorem responsi octo propositiones continentis*, in *Controversiae memorabilis inter Paulum V. Pontificem Max. & Venetos* (Villa Sanvincentiana, 1607).

Martelière, Pierre de la (1612). *The Argument of Mr Peter de la Marteliere Advocate in the Court of Paris, made in Parliament* (London).

Maxwell, John (1644). *Sacro-Sancta Regum Majestas, or the Sacred and Royal Prerogative of Christian Kings* (Oxford).

Merlat, Elie (1685). *Traité du pouvoir absolu des souverains* (Cologne).

Milton, John (1931–40). *The Works of John Milton*, ed. F.A. Patterson et al., 20 vols. (New York: Columbia University Press).

(1953–82). *The Complete Prose Works of John Milton*, ed. D.M. Wolfe, 8 vols. (New Haven: Yale University Press).

Minsheu, John (1617). Ἡγεμὼν εἰς τας Γλωσσας, *id est, Ductor in Linguas, the guide into Tongues* (London).

Mirror of Justices. See Horn (1895).

Molesworth, Robert (1694). *An Account of Denmark* (London).

(1721). 'Preface' to English trans. of François Hotman, *Francogallia*, 2nd edn (London).

Morton, Thomas (1610). *The Encounter Against M. Parsons, by a Review of his Last Sober Reckoning*, 2 vols. (London).

Moyle, Walter (1727). *The Whole Works of Walter Moyle* (London).

(1969). *An Essay upon the Constitution of the Roman Government*, in *Two English Republican Tracts*, ed. C. Robbins (Cambridge: Cambridge University Press).

Nalson, John (1677). *The Common Interest of King and People* (London).

Nedham, Marchamont, ed. (1971). *Mercurius Politicus*, 19 vols. (London: Cornmarket Press).

Nevile, Henry, trans. (1675). Niccolò Machiavelli, *The History of Florence* (London).

(1969). *Plato Redivivus, or A Dialogue Concerning Government*, in *Two English Republican Tracts*, ed. C. Robbins (Cambridge: Cambridge University Press). First publ. 1681.

Nicholas, Sir Edward (1766). *Proceedings and Debates of the House of Commons in 1620 and 1621*, vol. II (Oxford).

Nicole, Pierre (1670). *De l'éducation d'un prince* (Paris).

Overall, John (1844). *The Convocation Book of MDCVI. Commonly called Bishop Overall's Convocation Book* (Oxford: Parker).

Overton, Richard (1968). *Mans Mortalitie*, ed. H. Fisch (Liverpool: Liverpool University Press).

Owen, David (1610). *Herod and Pilate reconciled* (Cambridge, London).

Parliamentary Debates in 1610 (1862). Ed. S.R. Gardiner (London: Camden Society).

Pateson, James (?) (1623). *The Image of Bothe Churches, Hierusalem and Babel, Unitie and Confusion, Obedience and sedition* (Tournai).

Petyt, William (1680a). *The Antient Right of the Commons of England Asserted, or, a Discourse proving by Records and the best Historians, that the Commons of England were ever an Essential Part of Parliament* (London).

(1680b). *Miscellanea Parliamentaria* (London).

(1681). *The Pillars of Parliament struck at by the Hands of a Cambridge Doctor* (London).

(1739). *Jus Parliamentarium: or, the Ancient Power, Jurisdiction, Rights and Liberties, of the Most High Court of Parliament, Revived and Asserted* (London).

Philipps, Fabian (1687). *The Established Government of England Vindicated, from all Popular and Republican Principles* (London).

Poisson de la Bodinière, Pierre (1597). *Traicté de la maiesté royalle en France* (Paris).

Priviledges (1640). *Priviledges and Practice of Parliaments* (n.p.).

Proceedings of the Short Parliament of 1640 (1977). Ed. E.S. Cope and W.H. Coates (London: Camden Society).

Pronay, N., and Taylor, J. (1980). *Parliamentary Texts of the Later Middle Ages* (Oxford: Clarendon Press).

Prynne, William (1643). *The Treachery and Disloyalty of Papists to their Soveraignes, in Doctrine and Practise. Together with The First Part of the Soveraigne Power of Parliaments and Kingdoms*, 2nd edn (London).

(1648). *The Levellers Levelled to the very Ground* (London).

(1657a). *An Exact Abridgement of the Records in the Tower of London . . . Collected by Sir Robert Cotton* (London).

(1657b). *The Third Part of a Seasonable, Legal and Historical Vindication* (London).

(1658). *A Plea for the House of Lords, and House of Peers* (London).

(1662). *Brevia Parliamentaria Rediviva* (London). (The third part of *A Brief Register*: see next item.)

(1664). *The Fourth Part of a Brief Register, Kalender and Survey of the Several Kinds, Forms of Parliamentary Writs* (London).

(1669). *Brief Animadversions on, Amendments of, and Additional Explanatory Records to, the Fourth Part of the Institutes of the Lawes of England. Compiled by the Late Famous Lawyer Sir Edward Cooke Knight* (London).

Réfuge, Eustache du (?) (1633). *Le conseiller d'estat, ou recueil des plus générales considérations servant au maniment des affaires publiques* (Paris).

Richer, Edmund (1692). *De potestate ecclesiae in rebus temporalibus, et defensio articuli quem tertius ordo comitiorum regni Franciae pro lege fundamentali ejusden regni, defigi postulavit anno Domini 1614 & 1615* (Cologne).

Rolle, Henry (1668). *Un Abridgment des plusiers Cases et Resolutions del Commun Ley*, ed. Matthew Hale (London).

Sadler, John (1649). *Rights of the Kingdom: or, Customs of our Ancestors* (London).

St Armand, George (1725). *An Historical Essay on the Legislative Power of England* (London).

Saravia, Hadrian (1611). *De imperandi authoritate*, in *Diversi tractatus theologici* (London).

Sarpi, Paulo (1606). *Apologia adversus oppositiones factas ab illustrissimo & reverendiss. Domino Card. Bellarmino*, in *Controversiae memorabilis inter Paulum V. Pontificem Max. & Venetos* (Villa Sanvincentiana, 1607).

Saumaise, Claude de (1650). *Apologie royale pour Charles I. Roy d'Angleterre* (Paris).

Savaron, Jean (1620). *De la Souveraineté du roy, et que sa Maiesté ne la peut souzmettre à qui que ce soit* (Paris).

Selden, John (1631, 1672). *Titles of Honour*, 2nd and 3rd edns (London).

Senault, Jean François (1661). *Le monarque, ou les devoirs du souverain* (Paris).

Sheringham, Robert (1660). *The Kings Supremacy Asserted* (London).

Short History (1698). *A Short History of Standing Armies* (London).

Sibthorp, Robert (1627). *Apostolike Obedience* (London).

Sidney, Algernon (1666?). 'Court Maxims'. Unpublished MS, Warwickshire Record Office.

(1772). *Discourses concerning Government*, ed. T. Hollis and J. Robertson (London).

Spelman, Sir Henry (1626). *Archaeologus. In modum Glossarii*, part I (London).

(1664). *Glossarium Archaiologicum*, ed. William Dugdale (London).

Squire, Samuel (1745). *An Enquiry into the Foundation of the English Constitution* (London).

State Tracts (1692–3). *State Tracts: Being a Collection of Several Treatises relating to the Government* (London). Repub., 2 vols. in 1, 1693. See also *Collection* (1705).

Tanner, J.R., ed. (1930). *Constitutional Documents of the Reign of James I, 1603–1625* (Cambridge: Cambridge University Press).

Toland, John (1698). *The Militia Reformed*, in *State Tracts*, 3 vols. (London, 1705–7), vol. II, pp. 594–613.

(1702). *Paradoxes of State* (London).

Twysden, Sir Roger (1696–1704). *General History of England*, 3 vols. (London).

(1849). *Certaine Considerations upon the Government of England*, ed. J.M. Kemble (London: Camden Society).

Tyrrell, James (1694). *Bibliotheca Politica: or, An Enquiry into the Antient Constitution of the English Government* (London).

(1696–1704). *General History of England*, 3 vols. (London).

Verstegan, Richard (1622). *Observations Concerning the Present Affayres of Holland*, 2nd edn (St Omer).

Weston, Edward (1613). *Iuris pontificii sanctuarium* (n.p.).

Whitelocke, Bulstrode (1766). *Notes Uppon the Kings Writt for Choosing Members of Parliament . . . being Disquisitions on the Government of England by King, Lords and Commons*, ed. C. Morton, 2 vols. (London).

Williams, Roger (1644). *The Bloudy Tenent of Persecution*, in *Works*, 7 vols. (New York: Russell and Russell, 1963) III.

Bibliography

Wolfe, D.M., ed. (1944). *Leveller Manifestoes of the Puritan Revolution* (New York: Nelson; repr. 1967, New York: Humanities Press).

Woodhouse, A.S.P., ed. (1938). *Puritanism and Liberty: Being the Army Debates (1647–9) from the Clarke Manuscripts with Supplementary Documents* (London: Dent; repr. 1950, 1965, 1986).

Wootton, D., ed. (1986). *Divine Right and Democracy* (Harmondsworth: Penguin).

Secondary sources

Allen, J.W. (1938). *English Political Thought, 1603–1644* (London: Methuen).

Amati, F., and Aspromourgos, T. (1985). 'Petty contra Hobbes', *Journal of the History of Ideas*, 46:127–32.

Ashcraft, R. (1980). 'Revolutionary Politics and Locke's *Two Treatises of Government*: Radicalism and Lockean Political Theory', *Political Theory*, 8:429–86.

  (1986). *Revolutionary Politics and Locke's Two Treatises of Government* (Princeton: Princeton University Press).

Ashton, R. (1979). *The English Civil War: Conservatism and Revolution, 1603–1649* (London: Weidenfeld and Nicolson).

Aylmer, G.E. (1970). 'Gentlemen Levellers?', *Past and Present*, 49:120–5.

  (1984). 'The Religion of Gerrard Winstanley', in *Radical Religion in the English Revolution*, ed. J.F. McGregor and B. Reay (Oxford: Oxford University Press), pp. 91–119.

Bailyn, B. (1967). *The Ideological Origins of the American Revolution* (Cambridge, Mass.: Harvard University Press).

Bercovich, S. (1967). 'Typology in Puritan New England: The Williams–Cotton Controversy Reassessed', *American Quarterly*, 29:166–91.

Bonney, R. (1978). *Political Change in France under Richelieu and Mazarin, 1624–1661* (Oxford: Oxford University Press).

Bouwsma, W.J. (1968). *Venice and the Defense of Republican Liberty* (Berkeley: California University Press).

Brailsford, H.N. (1961). *The Levellers and the English Revolution* (London: Cresset Press).

Brewer, J. (1976). *Party Ideology and Popular Politics at the Accession of George III* (Cambridge: Cambridge University Press).

Brooks, C., and Sharpe, K. (1976). 'History, English Law and the Renaissance', *Past and Present*, 72:133–42.

Burns, J.H. (1959). 'Sovereignty and Constitutional Law in Bodin', *Political Studies*, 7:174–7.

Burns, N.T. (1972). *Christian Mortalism from Tyndale to Milton* (Cambridge, Mass.: Harvard University Press).

Burrow, J.W. (1981). *A Liberal Descent: Victorian Historians and the English Past* (Cambridge: Cambridge University Press).

Butterfield, H. (1944). *The Englishman and His History* (Cambridge: Cambridge University Press).

Calvet, J. (1968). *Bossuet*, ed. J. Truchet, 2nd edn (Paris: Hatier).

Carlin, N. (1984). 'Leveller Organisation in London', *Historical Journal*, 27:955–60.

Chitty, J. (1820). *A Treatise of the Law of the Prerogatives of the Crown* (London: Butterworth; facsimile reprint, 1968, Farnborough: Gregg International).

Christianson, P. (1978). *Reformers and Babylon* (Toronto: Toronto University Press).

  (1984). 'Young John Selden and the Ancient Constitution, ca. 1610–18', *Proceedings of the American Philosophical Society*, 128:271–315.

Church, W.F. (1941). *Constitutional Thought in Sixteenth-Century France* (Cambridge, Mass.: Harvard University Press).

(1972). *Richelieu and Reason of State* (Princeton: Princeton University Press).

Clancy, T.H. (1964). *Papist Pamphleteers: The Allen-Persons Party and the Political Thought of the Counter-Reformation in England, 1572–1615* (Chicago: Loyola University Press).

Clarke, M.V. (1964). *Medieval Representation and Consent* (New York: Russell and Russell).

Colbourn, H.T. (1965). *The Lamp of Experience* (Chapel Hill: North Carolina University Press).

Daly, J. (1974). 'The Origins and Shaping of English Royalist Thought', *Historical Papers/Communications Historiques*, pp. 15–35.

(1978). 'The Idea of Absolute Monarchy in Seventeenth-century England', *Historical Journal*, 21:227–50.

(1979). *Sir Robert Filmer and English Political Thought* (Toronto: University of Toronto Press).

(1983). 'Some Problems in the Authorship of Sir Robert Filmer's Works', *English Historical Review*, 98:737–62.

Davis, J.C. (1968). 'The Levellers and Democracy', *Past and Present*, 40:174–80.

(1973). 'The Levellers and Christianity', in *Politics, Religion, and the English Civil War*, ed. B.S. Manning (London: Arnold), pp. 225–50.

Dickinson, H.T. (1977). *Liberty and Property: Political Ideology in Eighteenth-Century Britain* (London: Weidenfeld and Nicolson).

Dodge, G.H. (1947). *The Political Theory of the Huguenots of the Dispersion, with Special Reference to the Thought and Influence of Pierre Jurieu* (New York: Columbia University Press).

Dow, F.D. (1985). *Radicalism in the English Revolution, 1640–1660* (Oxford: Blackwell).

Dzelzainis, M.M. (1983). 'The Ideological Context of John Milton's *History of Britain*' (PhD thesis, Cambridge University).

Edwards, C.S. (1981). *Hugo Grotius: The Miracle of Holland* (Chicago: Nelson-Hall).

Elliott, J.H. (1969). 'Revolution and Continuity in Early Modern Europe', *Past and Present*, 42:35–56.

Elton, G.R. (1965). 'A High Road to Civil War?', in *From the Renaissance to the Counter-Reformation*, ed. C.H. Carter (New York: Random House).

Evans, E. (1938). 'Of the Antiquity of Parliaments in England', *History*, 23:206–21.

Evans, R.J.W. (1979). *The Making of the Habsburg Monarchy, 1550–1700* (Oxford: Clarendon Press).

Fink, Z.S. (1945). *The Classical Republicans* (Evanston: Northwestern University Press).

Finlayson, G.K., ed. (1908). *Catalogue of the Pamphlets, Books, Newspapers and Manuscripts Relating to the Civil War, the Commonwealth and Restoration, collected by George Thomason, 1640–1661* (London: Trustees of the British Museum).

Finlayson, M.G. (1983). *Historians, Puritanism and the English Revolution* (Toronto: Toronto University Press).

Fox, L., ed. (1956). *English Historical Scholarship in the Sixteenth and Seventeenth Centuries* (Oxford: Oxford University Press).

Foxcroft, H.C. (1898). *Life and Letters of Sir George Savile, First Marquis of Halifax*, 2 vols. (London: Longman).

Frank, J. (1980). *Cromwell's Press Agent: A Critical Biography of Marchamont Nedham 1620–1678* (Latham, Md: University Press of America).

Franklin, J.H. (1978). *John Locke and the Theory of Sovereignty* (Cambridge: Cambridge University Press).

Fussner, F.S. (1962). *The Historical Revolution: English Historical Writing and Thought 1580–1640* (London: Routledge and Kegan Paul).

Bibliography

Galland, A. (1928). 'Les Pasteurs français Amyraut, Bochart, etc., et la royauté de droit dívin de l'édit d'Alais à la Révocation (1629–1685)', *Bulletin de la Société de l'Histoire du Protestantisme Français*, 27:14–20, 105–34, 225–41, 413–23.

Gardiner, S.R. (1965). *History of England*, 10 vols. (New York: AMS Press).

Geisst, C.R. (1984). *The Political Thought of John Milton* (London: Macmillan).

Gentles, I. (1978). 'London Levellers in the English Revolution: The Chidleys and their Circle', *Journal of Ecclesiastical History*, 29:281–309.

Gilmore, M.P. (1950). 'Authority and Property in the Seventeenth Century: The First Edition of the *Traité des seigneuries* of Charles Loyseau', *Harvard Library Bulletin*, 4:258–65.

Goldie, M. (1980). 'The Revolution of 1689 and the Structure of Political Argument', *Bulletin of Research in the Humanities*, 83:473–564.

(1987). 'The Civil Religion of James Harrington', in *The Languages of Political Theory in Early-Modern Europe*, ed. A. Pagden (Cambridge: Cambridge University Press), pp. 197–224.

Gough, J.W. (1961). *Fundamental Law in English Constitutional History* (Oxford: Clarendon Press).

Gray, C. (1972). 'Bonham's Case Reviewed', *Proceedings of the American Philosophical Society*, 116, 1:35–58.

Greaves, R.L., and Zaller, R. (1982–4). *Biographical Dictionary of British Radicals in the Seventeenth Century*, 3 vols. (Brighton: Harvester).

Greenberg, J. (1989). 'The Confessor's Laws and the Radical Face of the Ancient Constitution', *English Historical Review*, 104:611–37.

Greenleaf, W.H. (1964). *Order, Empiricism and Politics: Two Traditions of English Political Thought 1550–1700* (Oxford: Oxford University Press).

Gunn, J.A.W. (1969). *Politics and the Public Interest in the Seventeenth Century* (London: Routledge and Kegan Paul).

Guy, J.A. (1982). 'The Origins of the Petition of Right Reconsidered', *Historical Journal*, 25:289–312.

Haitsma Mulier, E.O.G. (1980). *The Myth of Venice and Dutch Republican Thought in the Seventeenth Century* (Assen: Van Gorcum).

Hampsher-Monk, I. (1976). 'The Political Thought of the Levellers', *Political Studies*, 24:397–422.

Hexter, J.H. (1978). 'Power Struggle, Parliament and Liberty in Early Stuart England', *Journal of Modern History*, 50:1–50.

Hill, C. (1958). 'The Norman Yoke', in *Puritanism and Revolution: Studies in the Interpretation of the English Revolution of the Seventeenth Century* (London: Secker and Warburg), pp. 50–122.

(1971). *Antichrist in Seventeenth Century England* (Oxford: Oxford University Press).

(1972). *The World Turned Upside Down: Radical Ideas during the English Revolution* (London: Temple Smith).

(1977). *Milton and the English Revolution* (London: Faber).

(1986). 'The Word "Revolution" in Seventeenth-Century England', in *For Veronica Wedgewood These*, ed. R. Ollard and P. Tudor-Craig (London: Collins), pp. 134–51.

Holt, J.C. (1965). *Magna Carta* (Cambridge: Cambridge University Press).

(1985). 'The Origins of the Constitutional Tradition in England', in *Magna Carta and Medieval Government* (London: Hambledon Press).

Judson, M. (1949, 1964). *The Crisis of the Constitution* (New Brunswick: Rutgers University Press; republ. 1964, New York: Octagon Books).

Kelley, D.R. (1974). 'History, English Law and the Renaissance', *Past and Present*, 65:24–51.

(1976). 'A Rejoinder', *Past and Present*, 72:143–6.

Kenyon, J.P. (1966, 1986). See primary sources.

(1984). *The History Men: The Historical Profession in England since the Renaissance* (Pittsburgh: University of Pittsburgh Press).

Keohane, N.O. (1980). *Philosophy and the State in France: The Renaissance to the Enlightenment* (Princeton: Princeton University Press).

Keynes, G. (1980). *The Library of Edward Gibbon*, 2nd edn (London: St Paul's Bibliographies).

Kishlansky, M. (1981). 'Consensus Politics and the Structure of Debate at Putney', *Journal of British Studies*, 20:50–69.

Kliger, S.L. (1952). *The Goths in England* (Cambridge, Mass.: Harvard University Press).

Kossmann, E.H. (1960). 'Dutch Political Theory in the Seventeenth Century', in *Britain and the Netherlands*, ed. J.S. Bromley and E.H. Kossmann (London: Chatto and Windus), vol. I, pp. 91–110.

Kussmaul, A. (1981). *Servants in Husbandry in Early-Modern England* (Cambridge: Cambridge University Press).

Lacour-Gayet, G. (1898). *L'Education politique de Louis XIV* (Paris: Hachette).

Lamont, W.M. (1963). *Marginal Prynne, 1600–1669* (London: Routledge and Kegan Paul).

(1979). *Richard Baxter and the Millennium* (London: Croom Helm).

Laslett, P. (1948). 'Sir Robert Filmer: The Man versus the Whig Myth', *William and Mary Quarterly*, 5:523–46.

Lee, J. (1982). 'Political Antiquarianism Unmasked: The Conservative Attack on the Myth of the Ancient Constitution', *Bulletin of the Institute of Historical Research*, 55:166–79.

Lindley, K. (1986). 'London and Popular Freedom in the 1640s', in *Freedom and the English Revolution*, ed. R.C. Richardson and G.M. Ridden (Manchester: Manchester University Press), pp. 111–50.

Lossky, A. (1984). 'The Absolutism of Louis XIV', *Canadian Journal of History*, 19:1–15.

McIlwain, C.H. (1910). *The High Court of Parliament and its Supremacy* (New Haven: Yale University Press).

(1918). 'Introduction' to *The Political Works of James I* (Cambridge, Mass.: Harvard University Press).

Macpherson, C.B. (1962). *The Political Theory of Possessive Individualism* (Oxford: Clarendon Press).

(1973). *Democratic Theory* (Oxford: Oxford University Press).

Malcolm, N. (1984). *De Dominis (1560–1624): Venetian, Anglican, Ecumenist and Relapsed Heretic* (London: Strickland and Scott).

Manning, B.S. (1976). *The English People and the English Revolution* (London: Heinemann; repr. Harmondsworth: Penguin, 1978).

(1978). 'Puritanism and Democracy 1640–1642', in *Puritans and Revolutionaries*, ed. D. Pennington and K. Thomas (Oxford: Oxford University Press), pp. 139–60.

Martimort, A.-G. (1953). *Le Gallicanisme de Bossuet* (Paris: Les Editions du Cerf).

Mason, R. (1982). '*Rex Stoicus*: George Buchanan, James VI and the Scottish Polity', in *New Perspectives on the Politics and Culture of Early Modern Scotland*, ed. J. Dwyer, R. Mason, and A. Murdoch (Edinburgh: John Donald), pp. 9–33.

Mendle, J.M. (1985). *Dangerous Positions: Mixed Government, The Estates of the Realm, and the Answer to the XIX Propositions* (Alabama University Press).

Merriman, R.B. (1938). *Six Contemporaneous Revolutions* (Oxford: Clarendon Press).

Miller, P. (1953). *Roger Williams* (Indianapolis: Bobbs-Merill).

Morrill, J. (1976). *The Revolt of the Provinces* (London: Longman).

(1984). 'The Religious Context of the English Civil War', *Transactions of the Royal Historical Society*, 34:155–78.

Morton, A.L. (1970). *The World of the Ranters* (London: Lawrence and Wishart).

Mulligan, L. (1982). 'The Religious Roots of William Walwyn's Radicalism', *Journal of Religious History*, 12:162–79.

Nenner, H. (1977). *By Colour of Law* (Chicago: University of Chicago Press).

Nijenhuis, W. (1980). *Adrianus Saravia (c. 1532–1613)* (Leyden: Brill).

Norbrook, D. (1984). *Poetry and Politics in the English Renaissance* (London: Routledge and Kegan Paul).

Nuzzo, E. (1984). *La Superiorità degli Stati Liberi: I Repubblicani Inglesi (1699–1722)* (Naples: Edizioni scientifiche italiane; Publicazzioni dell'Università degli Studi di Salerno: Sezione di Studi Storici).

Pallister, A. (1971). *Magna Carta: The Heritage of Liberty* (Oxford: Clarendon Press).

Parker, D. (1980). *La Rochelle and the French Monarchy: Conflict and Order in Seventeenth-Century France* (London: Royal Historical Society).

(1981). 'Law, Society and the State in the Thought of Jean Bodin', *History of Political Thought*, 2:257–63.

(1983). *The Making of French Absolutism* (London: Arnold).

Pattison, M. (1892). *Isaac Casaubon 1559–1700*, 2nd edn (Oxford: Oxford University Press).

Pawlisch, H.S. (1985). *Sir John Davies and the Conquest of Ireland* (Cambridge: Cambridge University Press).

Pearl, V. (1961). *London and the Outbreak of the Puritan Revolution* (Oxford: Oxford University Press).

Peters, M. (1971). 'The "Monitor" on the Constitution, 1755–1765: New Light on the Ideological Origins of English Radicalism', *English Historical Review*, 86:706–27.

Pocock, J.G.A. (1951). 'Robert Brady 1627–1700: A Cambridge Historian of the Restoration', *Cambridge Historical Journal*, 10:186–204.

(1957, 1987). *The Ancient Constitution and the Feudal Law* (Cambridge: Cambridge University Press; 2nd edn, 1987).

(1971, 1972). *Politics, Language and Time* (New York: Athenaeum; London: Methuen).

(1975). *The Machiavellian Moment: Florentine Political Thought and the Atlantic Republican Tradition* (Princeton: Princeton University Press).

(1985). *Virtue, Commerce, and History* (Cambridge: Cambridge University Press).

Polizzotto, C. (1975). 'Liberty of Conscience and the Whitehall Debates of 1648–49', *Journal of Ecclesiastical History*, 26:69–82.

Pollock, Sir F., and Maitland, F.W. (1968). *The History of English Law before the Time of Edward I*, 2 vols., 2nd edn (Cambridge: Cambridge University Press).

Pronay, N., and Taylor, J. (1980). See primary sources.

Raab, F. (1964). *The English Face of Machiavelli* (London: Routledge and Kegan Paul).

Rabb, T.K., and Hirst, D. (1981). 'Revisionism Revised: Two Perspectives on Early Stuart Parliamentary History', *Past and Present*, 92:55–99.

Reeve, L.J. (1986). 'The Legal Status of the Petition of Right', *Historical Journal*, 29:257–77.

Reidy, M.F. (1955). *Bishop Lancelot Andrewes: Jacobean Court Preacher* (Chicago: Loyola University Press).

Renaudet, A. (1953). *Préréforme et humanisme à Paris pendant les premières guerres d'Italie (1494–1517)*, 2nd edn (Paris: Librairie d'Argences).

Robbins, C. (1959). *The Eighteenth-Century Commonwealthman* (Cambridge, Mass.: Harvard University Press).

Robertson, D.B. (1951). *The Religious Foundations of Leveller Democracy* (New York: King's Crown Press).

Robertson, J. (1985). *The Scottish Enlightenment and the Militia Issue* (Edinburgh: John Donald).

Rowen, H.H. (1978). *John de Witt* (Princeton: Princeton University Press).

Russell, C. (1965). 'The Theory of Treason in the Trial of Strafford', *English Historical Review*, 80:30–50.

(1979). *Parliaments and English Politics, 1621–1629* (Oxford: Clarendon Press).

Schochet, G. (1975). *Patriarchalism in Political Thought* (Oxford: Blackwell).

Schwoerer, L. (1981). *The Declaration of Rights, 1689* (Baltimore: Johns Hopkins University Press).

Scott, J. (1988). *Algernon Sidney and the English Republic 1623–1677* (Cambridge: Cambridge University Press).

(1991). *Algernon Sidney and the Restoration Crisis 1677–1683* (Cambridge: Cambridge University Press).

Seaberg, R.B. (1981). 'The Norman Conquest and the Common Law: The Levellers and the Argument from Continuity', *Historical Journal*, 24:791–806.

Shackleton, R. (1964). 'Montesquieu and Machiavelli: A Reappraisal', *Comparative Literature Studies*, 1:1–13.

Sharp, A. (1983). *Political Ideas of the English Civil Wars 1641–1649* (London: Longman).

(1988). 'John Lilburne and the Long Parliament's *Book of Declarations*: A Radical's Exploitation of the Words of Authorities', *History of Political Thought*, 9:19–44.

Sharpe, K., ed. (1978). *Faction and Parliament: Essays in Early Stuart History* (Oxford: Clarendon Press).

(1979). *Sir Robert Cotton 1586–1631* (Oxford: Oxford University Press).

Skinner, Q. (1965). 'History and Ideology in the English Revolution', *Historical Journal*, 8:155–78.

(1972). 'Conquest and Consent: Thomas Hobbes and the Engagement Controversy', in *The Interregnum: The Quest for Settlement 1649–1660*, ed. G.E. Aylmer (London: Macmillan).

Smart, I.M. (1980). 'The Political Ideas of the Scottish Covenanters, 1638–1688', *History of Political Thought*, 1:167–94.

Smith, H.F.R. (1971). *Harrington and his Oceana*, 2nd edn (New York: Octagon Books).

Smith, R.J. (1987). *The Gothic Bequest: Medieval Institutions in British Thought 1688–1863* (Cambridge: Cambridge University Press).

Snow, V.F. (1962). 'The Concept of Revolution in Seventeenth-Century England', *Historical Journal*, 5:167–74.

(1977). *Parliament in Elizabethan England: John Hooker's 'Order and Usage'* (New Haven: Yale University Press).

Solt, L. (1959). *Saints in Arms: Puritanism and Democracy in Cromwell's Army* (Stanford: Stanford University Press).

Sommerville, J.P. (1983). 'Richard Hooker, Hadrian Saravia, and the Advent of the Divine Right of Kings', *History of Political Thought*, 4:229–45.

(1986a). 'History and Theory: The Norman Conquest in Early Stuart Political Thought', *Political Studies*, 34:249–61.

(1986b). *Politics and Ideology in England 1603–1640* (London: Longman).

Stone, L. (1972). *The Causes of the English Revolution* (London: Routledge and Kegan Paul).

Straka, G.M. (1971). 'Revolutionary Ideology in Stuart England', in *Studies in Change and Revolution*, ed. P.J. Korshin (Menston: Scolar Press), pp. 3–17.

Styles, P. (1956). 'Politics and Historical Research in the Early Seventeenth Century', in *English Historical Scholarship in the Sixteenth and Seventeenth Centuries*, ed. L. Fox (Oxford: Oxford University Press).

Sullivan, R. (1982). *John Toland and the Deist Controversy* (Cambridge, Mass.: Harvard University Press).

Tanner, J.R., ed. (1930). See primary sources.

Bibliography

Thomas, K. (1972). 'The Levellers and the Franchise', in *The Interregnum: The Quest for Settlement 1646–60*, ed. G.E. Aylmer (London: Macmillan), pp. 57–78.

(1973). *Religion and the Decline of Magic* (Harmondsworth: Penguin).

Thompson, C. (1980). 'Maximilian Petty and the Putney Debate on the Franchise', *Past and Present*, 88:63–9.

Thompson, F. (1948). *Magna Carta: Its Role in the Making of the English Constitution, 1300–1629* (Minneapolis: University of Minnesota Press).

Thorne, S.E. (1938). 'Dr Bonham's Case', *Law Quarterly Review*, 54:543–52.

Thuau, E. (1966). *Raison d'état et pensée politique à l'époque de Richelieu* (Paris: Armand Colin).

Tierney, B. (1982). *Religion, Law and the Growth of Constitutional Thought, 1150–1650* (Cambridge: Cambridge University Press).

Tolmie, M. (1977). *The Triumph of the Saints* (Cambridge: Cambridge University Press).

Trevor-Roper, H.R. (1967). *Religion, the Reformation and Social Change* (London: Macmillan).

Tuck, R. (1979). *Natural Rights Theories: Their Origin and Development* (Cambridge: Cambridge University Press).

(1986). 'A New Date for Filmer's *Patriarcha*', *Historical Journal*, 29:183–6.

Wallace, D.D. (1982). *Puritans and Predestination* (Chapel Hill: North Carolina University Press).

Wallace, J.M. (1968). *Destiny his Choice: The Loyalism of Andrew Marvell* (Cambridge: Cambridge University Press).

Webster, C. (1975). *The Great Instauration: Science, Medicine and Reform 1626–1660* (London: Duckworth).

Weston, C.C. (1965). *English Constitutional Theory and the House of Lords 1556–1832* (London: Routledge and Kegan Paul).

(1972). 'Legal Sovereignty in the Brady Controversy', *Historical Journal*, 15:409–31.

(1980). 'The Authorship of the *Freeholders Grand Inquest*', *English Historical Review*, 95:74–98.

(1984). 'Co-ordination: A Radicalising Principle in Stuart Politics', in *The Origins of Anglo-American Radicalism*, ed. M. Jacob and J. Jacob (London: Allen and Unwin), pp. 85–104.

(1987). 'The Case for Sir Robert Holbourne Reasserted', *History of Political Thought*, 8:435–60.

Weston, C.C., and J.R. Greenberg (1981). *Subjects and Sovereigns: The Grand Controversy over Legal Sovereignty in Stuart England* (Cambridge: Cambridge University Press).

Wharam, A. (1972). 'The 1189 Rule: Fact, Fiction or Fraud', *Anglo-American Law Review*, 1:262–78.

Woolrych, A. (1986). 'Putney Revisited: Political Debate in the New Model Army in 1647', in *Politics and People in Revolutionary England*, ed. C. Jones, M. Newitt, and S. Roberts (Oxford: Blackwell), pp. 95–116.

Wootton, D. (1983). *Paolo Sarpi: Between Renaissance and Enlightenment* (Cambridge: Cambridge University Press).

(1986). See primary sources.

(1990). 'From Rebellion to Revolution: The Crisis of the Winter of 1642/3 and the Origins of Civil War Radicalism', *English Historical Review*, 105:654–69.

Worden, B. (1977). *The Rump Parliament 1648–1653* (Cambridge: Cambridge University Press). First publ. 1974.

(1981). 'Classical Republicanism and the Puritan Revolution', in *History and Imagination: Essays in Honour of H.R. Trevor Roper* (London: Duckworth), pp. 182–200.

(1985). 'The Commonwealth Kidney of Algernon Sidney', *Journal of British Studies*, 24:1–40.

(1986). 'Friend to Sir Philip Sidney', *London Review of Books*.

Yale, D.E.C. (1972). 'Hobbes and Hale on Law, Legislation and the Sovereign', *Cambridge Law Journal*, 31:131–56.

Yardeni, M. (1985). 'French Calvinist Political Thought. 1534–1715', in *International Calvinism 1541–1715*, ed. M. Prestwich (Oxford: Clarendon Press).

Zagorin, P. (1966). *A History of Political Thought in the English Revolution* (London: Routledge and Kegan Paul).

(1969). *The Court and the Country* (London: Routledge and Kegan Paul).

IV   The end of Aristotelianism

Primary sources

Ammirato, Scipione (1594). *Discorsi sopra Cornelio Tacito* (Florence).
Anonymous (1849). 'Illustrations of the State of the Church during the Great Rebellion', *The Theologian and Ecclesiastic*, 7:47–64, 118–29, 137–52, 276–93, 373–85.
Aubrey, John (1898). *Brief Lives*, ed. A. Clark, 2 vols. (Oxford: Clarendon Press).
Béthune, Philippe de (1633). *Le Conseiller d'Etat, ou Recueil des plus générale considérations servant au maniment des affaires publiques* (Paris).
Boccalini, Traiano (1678). *Osservationi politiche sopra i sei libri degli Annali* (Castellana [Chatelaine, near Geneva]).
   (1910–12). *Ragguagli da Parnasso*, ed. G. Rua, 2 vols. (Bari: Laterza). First publ. Venice, 1612–13. English trans. by Henry, earl of Monmouth, as *Advertisements from Parnassus* (London, 1656).
Botero, Giovanni (1589, 1956). *The Reason of State*, trans. P.J. and D.P. Waley (London: Routledge and Kegan Paul). First publ. Venice 1589, as *Ragione di Stato*.
Boxhorn, Marcus Zuerius (1649). *Commentariolus de statu confoederatarum provinciarum* (The Hague).
   (1663). *Varii tractatus politici* (Utrecht).
Buonaventura, Federigo (1623). *Della ragion di stato e della prudenza politica libri quatro* (Urbino).
Canonhiero, Pietro Andrea (1614). *Dell'Introduzzione alla politica, alla ragion di stato, et alla practica del buon governo, libri dieci* (Antwerp).
Cavendish, William (1620). *Horae subsecivae* (London).
Cavriana, Filippo (1597). *Discorsi sopra i primi cinque libri di Cornelio Tacito* (Florence).
Charron, Pierre (1601). *De la Sagesse* (Bordeaux). English trans., *Of Wisdome*, London, c. 1612; repr. New York: Da Capo Press, 1971.
Chiaramonti, Scipione (1635). *Della Ragione di stato* (Florence).
'Constans, Lucius Antistius' [pseud.] (1665). *De jure ecclesiasticorum* ('Alethopolis').
Cope, E., and Coates, W., eds. (1977). *Proceedings of the Short Parliament of 1640* (London: Royal Historical Society; Camden Fourth Series, 19).
Corvinus, Joannes Arnoldus (1622). *Petri Molinaei Novi Anatomici Nala Encheiresis* (Frankfurt).
De la Court, Johan and Pieter (1660). *Consideratien en exempelen van staat, omtrent de fundamenten van allerley regeringe* (Amsterdam).
   (1662a). *Politieke discoursen handelde . . . van steeden, landen, oorlogen, kerken, regeeringen, en zeeden* (Amsterdam).
   (1662b). *Interest van Holland ofte gronden van Hollands-welvaren* (Amsterdam).
   (1911). *'t Welvaren der stad Leiden*, ed. F. Driessen (Leiden: Nijhoff).

IV   The end of Aristotelianism

Du Vair, Guillaume (1622). *A Buckler against Adversity*, trans. A. Court (London). Originally publ. as *De la Constance* (Paris, 1594).

Felden, Johannes (1653). *Annotata in Hug. Grotium, De Iure Belli ac Pacis* (Amsterdam).

Frachetta, Girolamo (1592). 'Discorso della ragione di stato', in *Idea de'governi* (Venice).

Grotius, Hugo (1630). *De Antiquitate Reipublicae Bataviciae Liber Singularis* (Leiden). First publ. Leiden 1610.

    (1646). *De Jure Belli ac Pacis libri tres* (Amsterdam). Repr. in Classics in International Law (Oxford: Clarendon Press, 1925).

    (1647). *De imperio summarum potestatum circa sacra* (Paris).

    (1649). *A Treatise of the Antiquity of the Commenwealth of the Battavers, which is now the Hollanders* (London).

    (1679). *Opera Theologica*, 3 vols. (London).

    (1738). *The Rights of War and Peace*, ed. Jean Barbeyrac (London). First edn *De Jure Belli ac Pacis* (Paris, 1625).

    (1801). *Parallelon Rerumpublicarum Liber Tertius: De Moribus Ingenioque Populorum Atheniensium, Romanorum, Batavorum*, ed. J. Meerman (Haarlem: A. Loos).

    (1928). *Briefwisseling van Hugo Grotius*, vol. I, ed. P.C. Molhuysen (The Hague: Nijhoff).

    (1936). *Briefwisseling van Hugo Grotius*, vol. II, ed. P.C. Molhuysen (The Hague: Nijhoff).

    (1950). *De Iure Praedae Commentarius*, trans. G.L. Williams, 2 vols. (Oxford: Clarendon Press; Carnegie Endowment for International Peace). First edn, ed. H.G. Hanaker (The Hague: Nijhoff, 1868).

    (1967). *Briefwisseling van Hugo Grotius*, vol. VI, ed. B.L. Meulenbroek (The Hague: Nijhoff).

    (1969). *Briefwisseling van Hugo Grotius*, vol. VII, ed. B.L. Meulenbroek (The Hague: Nijhoff).

Historical Manuscripts Commission (1893). *Thirteenth Report, Part II: Manuscripts of His Grace the Duke of Portland*.

Hobbes, Thomas (1651). *Leviathan* (London).

    (1839–45a). *English Works*, ed. Sir W. Molesworth, 11 vols. (London: Bohn).

    (1839–45b). *Opera Latina*, ed. Sir W. Molesworth, 5 vols. (London: Bohn).

    (1889). *Behemoth or the Long Parliament*, ed. F. Toennies (London: Simpkin Marshall).

    (1909). *Hobbes's Leviathan Reprinted from the Edition of 1651 with an Essay by the Late W.G. Pogson Smith* (Oxford: Clarendon Press).

    (1928). *The Elements of Law Natural and Politic*, ed. F. Toennies (Cambridge: Cambridge University Press).

    (1968). *Leviathan*, ed. C.B. Macpherson (Harmondsworth: Penguin).

    (1971). *A Dialogue between a Philosopher and a Student of the Common Laws of England*, ed. J. Cropsey (Chicago: University of Chicago Press).

    (1973). *Critique du 'De mundo' de Thomas White*, ed. J. Jacquot and H.W. Jones (Paris: Vrin-CNRS).

    (1983). *De Cive: The English Version*, ed. J.H. Warrender (Oxford: Clarendon Press).

    (1986). *Briefe of the Art of Rhetorique*, ed. J. Harwood (Carbondale, IL: Southern Illinois UP).

Hooker, Richard (1888). *Works*, ed. J. Keble, R. Church, and F. Paget, 3 vols. (Oxford: Clarendon Press).

La Rochefoucauld, François, duc de (1946). *Réflexions morales*, in *Maxims*, ed. F.C. Green (Cambridge: Cambridge University Press). First publ. 1665.

Lipsius, Justus (1584). *De Constantia Libri Duo* (Antwerp). English trans. J. Stradling, as *Two Books of Constancy* (London, 1595).

    (1589). *Politicorum sive civilis doctrinae libri sex* (Leiden).

Maimonides, Moses (1904). *The Guide for the Perplexed*, ed. M. Friedlaender (London: Routledge and Kegan Paul).

(1975). *Ethical Writings*, ed. R.L. Weiss and C. Butterworth (New York: Dover Publications).

Mersenne, Marin (1963, 1967). *Correspondance*, vols. VIII and X, ed. C. de Waard (Paris: Editions du Centre National de la Recherche Scientifique).

Montaigne, Michel de (1580–8). *Essais* (Paris). The standard modern edition is in the Pléiade series (Paris: Gallimard, 1962).

Naudé, Gabriel (1639, 1711). *Considérations politiques sur les coups d'estat* (Paris). English trans. 'Dr King—', as *Political Considerations upon Refin'd Politicks and the Master-Strokes of the State* (London, 1711).

Palazzo, Giovanni Antonio (1606). *Discorso del Governo e della Ragion vera di Stato* (Venice).

Pasquale, Carlo, ed. (1581). *C.C. Taciti . . . Annalium libri quatuor priores* (Paris).

Patin, Gui (1846). *Lettres*, ed. J.H. Reveille-Parise, 3 vols. (Paris: J.B. Baillière).

Quevedo, Francisco de (1966). *Política de Dios*, ed. J.O. Crosby (Madrid: Editorial Castalia).

Rist, Johan (1647, 1972). *Das Friedewunschende Teutschland*, repr. in *Samtliche Werke*, vol. II, ed. E. Mannack (Berlin: De Gruyter).

Rohan, Henri, duc de (1638). *De l'interest des Princes et Estats de la Chrestienté* (Paris).

Selden, John (1726). *Opera Omnia*, ed. D. Watkins, 3 vols. (London).

Settala, Lodovico (1627). *Della Ragion di Stato libri sette* (Milan).

Spinoza, Baruch (1924). *Opera*, ed. C. Gebhardt, 4 vols. (Heidelberg: Carl Winters Universitätsbuchhandlung).

(1928). *The Correspondence of Spinoza*, ed. A. Wolf (London: Allen and Unwin).

(1958). *The Political Works. The Tractatus Theologico-Politicus in part and the Tractatus Politicus in Full*, ed. and trans. with an introduction and notes by A.G. Wernham (Oxford: Clarendon Press).

Stevin, Simon (1599). Αιμενευζετικη. *sive Portuum Investigandorum Ratio* (Leiden).

(1611). *Vita Politica. Het Burgerlyk Leven . . .* (Delft). Written in 1590.

Van Velthuysen, Lambert (1651). *Epistolica dissertatio de principiis justi et decori, continens apologiam pro tractatu clarissimi Hobbaei de Cive* (Amsterdam).

(1660a). *Het predick-ampt en 't recht der kercke, bepaelt nae de regelen van Godts woordt, en de gronden van onse reformatie* (Amsterdam).

(1660b). *Ondersoeck of de christelijcke overheydt eenigh quaedt in haer gebiedt mach toe laeten* (Middelburg).

Voetius, Gisbertus (1663). *Politica Ecclesiastica* (Amsterdam).

Walaeus, Antonius (1643). *Responsio ad Censuram Ioannis Arnoldi Corvini*, in *Opera Omnia*, vol. II (Leiden).

Wassenaar, G. (1657). *Bedekte konsten in regeringuen en heerschappien* (Utrecht). Later plagiarised by P. de la Court as *Naeuwkeurige consideratie van staet* (Amsterdam, 1662).

Zinano, Gabriele (1626). *Della Ragione degli stati libri XII* (Venice).

Zuccolo, Ludovico (1621). *Della Ragione di Stato* (Venice?). A selection is available in *Politici e Moralisti del '600*, ed. B. Croce (Bari: Laterza, 1930), pp. 23–41.

Secondary sources

Abel, H. (1978). *Stoizismus und frühe Neuzeit: zur Entstehungsgeschichte modernen Denkens im Felde von Ethik und Politik* (Berlin: De Gruyter).

Auerbach, E. (1959). 'On the Political Theory of Pascal', repr. in *Scenes from the Drama of European Literature* (New York: Meridian Books).

Battista, A.M. (1966). *Alle origini del pensiero politico libertino: Montaigne e Charron* (Milan: Giuffrè).

Beats, L. (1978). 'Politics and Government in Derbyshire 1640–1660' (PhD thesis, Sheffield University).

Berner, S. (1970). 'Florentine Political Thought in the Late Cinquecento', *Il Pensiero Politico*, 3:177–99.

Bredvold, L. (1934). *The Intellectual Milieu of John Dryden* (Ann Arbor: Michigan University Press).

Brown, K.C., ed. (1965). *Hobbes Studies* (Oxford: Blackwell).

Burke, U.P. (1969). 'Tacitism', in *Tacitus*, ed. T.A. Dorey (London: Routledge and Kegan Paul).

(1981). *Montaigne* (Oxford: Oxford University Press; Past Masters).

Chabod, F. (1967). 'Giovanni Botero', in *Scritti sul Rinascimento* (Turin: Einaudi), pp. 271–458.

Christianson, P. (1984). 'Young John Selden and the Ancient Constitution, ca. 1610–18', *Proceedings of the American Philosophical Society*, 128:271–315.

Church, W.F. (1972). *Richelieu and Reason of State* (Princeton: Princeton University Press).

Clark, C.E. (1970). 'Montaigne and the Imagery of Political Discourse in Sixteenth-century France', *French Studies*, 24:337–54.

Cochrane, E. (1973). *Florence in the Forgotten Centuries* (Chicago: University of Chicago Press).

Cranston, M., and Peters, R.S., eds. (1972). *Hobbes and Rousseau: A Collection of Critical Essays* (Garden City, N.Y.: Anchor Books).

De Michelis, F. (1967). *Le Origini Storiche e Culturali del Pensiero di Ugo Grozio* (Florence: La Nuova Italia).

Den Tex, J. (1973). *Oldenbarnevelt*, 2 Vols. (Cambridge: Cambridge University Press).

Den Uyl, D.J. (1983). *Power, State and Freedom* (Assen: Van Gorcum).

Dickinson, H.T. (1977). *Liberty and Property: Political Ideology in Eighteenth-Century Britain* (London: Weidenfeld and Nicolson).

Etter, E.-L. (1966). *Tacitus in der Geistesgeschichte des 16. und 17. Jahrhunderts* (Basle and Stuttgart: Helbing and Lichtenhahn).

Ettinghausen, H. (1972). *Francisco de Quevedo and the Neostoic Movement* (Oxford: Oxford University Press).

Fernández-Santamaria, J.A. (1980). 'Reason of State and Statecraft in Spain (1595–1640)', *Journal of the History of Ideas*, 41:355–79.

Forsyth, M. (1981). 'Thomas Hobbes and the Constituent Power of the People', *Political Studies*, 29:191–203.

Freudenthal, J. (1899). *Die Lebensgeschichte Spinoza's in Quellenschriften, Urkunden und nichtamtlichen Nachrichten* (Leipzig: Von Veit).

Freund, J. (1975). 'La Situation exceptionelle comme justification de la raison d'état chez Gabriel Naudé', in Schnur (1975).

Gert, B. (1965). 'Hobbes, Mechanism and Egoism', *Philosophical Quarterly*, 15:341–9.

(1967). 'Hobbes and Psychological Egoism', *Journal of the History of Ideas*, 28:503–20.

Geyl, P. (1947). 'Het stadhouderschap in de partij-literatuur onder de Witt', *Mededeelingen der koninklijke Nederlandsche akademie van wetenschapen*, afd. Letterkunde, n.s., 10:17–84.

Gunn, J.A.W. (1969). *Politics and the Public Interest in the Seventeenth Century* (London: Routledge and Kegan Paul).

Haitsma Mulier, E.O.G. (1980). *The Myth of Venice and Dutch Republican Thought in the Seventeenth Century* (Assen: Van Gorcum).

(1984). 'De *Naeuwkeurige consideratie van staet* van de gebroeders De la Court. Een nadere beschouwing', *Bijdragen en mededelingun betreffende de geschiedenis der Nederlanden*, 99:396–407.

Bibliography

Harrison, A.H.W. (1926). *The Beginnings of Arminianism to the Synod of Dort* (London: University of London Press).

Johnston, D. (1986). *The Rhetoric of Leviathan* (Princeton: Princeton University Press).

Keohane, N.O. (1980). *Philosophy and the State in France: The Renaissance to the Enlightenment* (Princeton: Princeton University Press).

Knight, W.S.M. (1925). *The Life and Works of Hugo Grotius* (London: Sweet and Maxwell; Grotius Society Publications, 4).

Kossmann, E.H. (1960). *Politieke theorie in het zeventiende-euwse Nederland* (Amsterdam: Noord-Hollandsche Uitg. Mij.; Verhandelingen der koninklijke Nederlandse akademie van wetenschappen, n.s. 67, no. 2).

McShea, R.J. (1968). *The Political Philosophy of Spinoza* (New York: Columbia University Press).

Malcolm, N.R. (1981). 'Hobbes, Sandys, and the Virginia Company', *Historical Journal*, 24:297–321.

   (1984). *De Dominis (1560–1624): Venetian, Anglican, Ecumenist and Relapsed Heretic* (London: Strickland and Scott).

Marx, K. (1977). *Capital*, vol. 1, trans. B. Fowkes (Harmondsworth: Penguin; London: New Left Review).

Meinecke, F. (1957). *Machiavellism* (London: Routledge and Kegan Paul). First publ. as *Die Idee der Staatsräson* (Munich: R. Oldenbourg, 1924).

Meinsma, K.O. (1896). *Spinoza en zijn kring. Historisch-kritische studien over Hollandse vrijgeesten* (The Hague: Nijhoff).

Molhuysen, P.C. (1913–24). *Bronnen tot de geschiedenis der Leidsche Universiteit*, 7 vols. (The Hague: Nijhoff).

Momigliano, A. (1977). 'The First Political Commentary on Tacitus', in *Essays in Ancient and Modern Historiography* (Oxford: Blackwell).

Mosse, G.L. (1957). *The Holy Pretence: A Study in Christianity and Reason of State from William Perkins to John Winthrop* (Oxford: Blackwell).

Mugnier-Pollet, L. (1976). *La Philosophie politique de Spinoza* (Paris: Vrin).

Oakeshott, M. (1946, 1975). 'Introduction' to Thomas Hobbes, *Leviathan* (Oxford: Blackwell). Repr. in *Hobbes on Civil Association* (Oxford: Blackwell).

Oestreich, G. (1982). *Neostoicism and the Early Modern State*, ed. B. Oestrich and H.G. Koenigsberger, trans. D. McLintock (Cambridge: Cambridge University Press).

Pocock, J.G.A. (1972). 'Time, History and Eschatology in the Thought of Thomas Hobbes', in *Politics, Language and Time* (London: Methuen).

Polin, R. (1953). *Politique et philosophie chez Thomas Hobbes* (Paris: Presses Universitaires de France).

Popkin, R. (1979). *The History of Scepticism from Erasmus to Spinoza* (Los Angeles and Berkeley: California University Press).

Post, G. (1964). '*Ratio publicae utilitatis, Ratio Status* and Reason of State 1100–1300', in *Studies in Medieval Legal Thought* (Princeton: Princeton University Press). First publ. 1961.

Préposiet, J. (1973). *Bibliographie spinoziste* (Annales littéraires de l'université de Besançon).

Radouant, R. (1908). *Guillaume du Vair, l'homme et l'orateur jusqu'à la fin des troubles de la Ligue* (Paris: Société française d'imprimerie et de librairie).

Raphael, D.D. (1977). *Hobbes: Morals and Politics* (London: Allen and Unwin).

Reik, M. (1977). *The Golden Lands of Thomas Hobbes* (Detroit: Wayne State University Press).

Revah, I.S. (1959). *Spinoza et le Dr Juan de Prado* (Paris: Mouton; Etudes juives, 1).

Rossi, M. (1942). *Alle fonti del deismo e del materialismo moderno* (Florence: La Nuova Italia).

Salmon, J.H.M. (1980). 'Cicero and Tacitus in Sixteenth-Century France', *American Historical Review*, 85:307–31.

(1989) 'Stoicism and Roman Example: Seneca and Tacitus in Jacobean England', *Journal of the History of Ideas*, 50:199–225.

Saunders, J.L. (1955). *Justus Lipsius: The Philosophy of Renaissance Stoicism* (New York: Liberal Arts Press).

Schellhase, K.C. (1976). *Tacitus in Renaissance Political Thought* (Chicago: University of Chicago Press).

Schnur, R., ed. (1975). *Staatsräson: Studien zur Geschichte eines politischen Begriffe* (Berlin: Duncker and Humblot).

Schoneveld, C.W. (1983). *Intertraffic of the Mind: Studies in Seventeenth-Century Anglo-Dutch Translation* (Leiden: Leiden University Press and Brill).

Scruton, R. (1986). *Spinoza* (Oxford: Oxford University Press; Past Masters).

Skinner, Q. (1966a). 'The Ideological Context of Hobbes' Political Thought', *Historical Journal* 9:286–317. Repr. in *Hobbes and Rousseau*, ed. M. Cranston and R.S. Peters (New York: Doubleday, 1972).

(1966b). 'Thomas Hobbes and his Disciples in France and England', *Comparative Studies in Society and History*, 8:153–67.

(1969). 'Thomas Hobbes and the Nature of the Early Royal Society', *Historical Journal*, 12:217–39.

(1972). 'Conquest and Consent: Thomas Hobbes and the Engagement Controversy', in *The Interregnum: The Quest for Settlement 1649–1660*, ed. G.E. Aylmer (London: Macmillan).

Sommerville, J.P. (1984). 'John Selden, the Law of Nature, and the Origins of Government', *Historical Journal*, 27:437–47.

Stackelberg, J. von (1960). *Tacitus in der Romania* (Tübingen: Niemeyer).

Stolpe, S. (1959). *Från stoicism till mystik: studien i drottning Kristinas maximen* (Stockholm: Almquist and Wiksell).

Syme, R. (1958). *Tacitus*, 2 vols. (Oxford: Oxford University Press).

Thuau, E. (1966). *Raison d'état et pensée politique a l'époque de Richelieu* (Paris: Colin).

Todd, W. (1973). 'An Early MS of Hobbes's *Leviathan*', *Notes and Queries*, 218:181.

Toffanin, G. (1921). *Machiavelli e il Tacitismo* (Padua: Draghi).

Tuck, R. (1979). *Natural Rights Theories: Their Origin and Development* (Cambridge: Cambridge University Press).

(1982). '"The Ancient Law of Freedom": John Selden and the Civil War', in *Reactions to the English Civil War 1642–1649*, ed. J. Morrill (London: Macmillan).

(1983). 'Grotius, Carneades and Hobbes', *Grotiana*, n.s., 4:43–62.

(1989). *Hobbes* (Oxford: Oxford University Press; Past Masters).

Van der Linde, A. (1961). *Benedictus Spinoza: Bibliografie* (Nieukoop: De Graaf).

Van Eysinga, W.J.M. (1955). 'Eene Onuitgegeven Nota van de Groot', *Mededelingen Koninklijke Akademie van Wetenschappen, afd. Letterkunde. Nieuwe Reeks*, 18:235–52.

Van Gelder, H.A.E. (1972). *Getemperde vrijheid* (Historische studies, van het Instituut voor geschiedenis der Rijksuniversiteit Utrecht, 26).

Van Thijn, T. (1956). 'Pieter de la Court. Zijn leven en zijn economische denkbeelden', *Tijdschrift voor geschiedenis*, 69:304–70.

Varese, C. (1958). *Traiano Boccalini* (Padua: Liviana).

Vaz Dias, A.M., and W.G. van der Tak (1932). *Spinoza mercator & autodidactus. Oorkonden en andere authentike documenten betreffende des wijsgeers jeugd en diens betrekking* (The Hague: Nijhoff).

Viola, F. (1979). *Behemoth o Leviathan? Diritto e obbligo nel pensiero di Hobbes* (Milan: Giuffrè).

Bibliography

Wansink, H. (1981). *Politieke wetenschappen aan de Leidse Universiteit, 1575–c. 1650* (Utrecht: HES).

Warrender, J.H. (1957). *The Political Philosophy of Hobbes: His Theory of Obligation* (Oxford: Clarendon Press).

Watkins, J.W.N. (1965). *Hobbes's System of Ideas* (London: Heinemann).

Wernham, A.G. (1958). 'General Introduction' to Spinoza, *The Political Works* (Oxford: Clarendon Press).

Zagorin, P. (1978). 'Thomas Hobbes's Departure from England in 1640: An Unpublished Letter', *Historical Journal*, 21:157–60.

V Natural law and utility

Primary sources

Arnisaeus, Henning (1610). *De Jure Majestatis Libri Tres* (Frankfurt).

Atwood, William (1690). *The Fundamental Constitution of the English Government* (London).

Aubrey, John (1898). *Brief Lives*, ed. A. Clark, 2 vols. (Oxford: Clarendon Press).

Austin, John ('William Birchley') (1651). *The Christian Moderator, or Persecution for religion condemned* (London).

Bagshaw, Edward (1660). *The Great Question Concerning Things Indifferent in Religious Worship* (London).

    (1661). *The Second Part of the Great Question* (London).

Barbeyrac, Jean (1729). 'An Historical and Critical Account of the Science of Morality', in Samuel Pufendorf, *The Laws of Nature and Nations*, trans. B. Kennett (London).

Barclay, William (1600). *De regno et regali potestate adversus Buchananum, Brutum, Boucherium et reliquos monarchomachos, libri sex* (Paris).

Baxter, Richard (1659). *A Holy Commonwealth* (London).

Bayle, Pierre (1952). *Selections from Bayle's Dictionary*, ed. E.A. Butler and M. du P. Lee (Princeton: Princeton University Press).

Blackstone, William (1781). *Commentaries on the Laws of England* (London).

Bramhall, John (1655). *A Defence of True Liberty from Antecendent and Intrinsicall Necessity. Being an Answer to a Late Book of Mr Thomas Hobbes of Malmesbury, intituled, A Treatise of Liberty and Necessity* (London).

    (1658). *Castigations of Mr Hobbes* and *The Catching of Leviathan* (London). The two items continuously paginated.

Browne, Thomas (1683). *Miracles Works Above and Contrary to Reason or, An Answer to a late Translation out of Spinoza's Tractatus Theologico-Politicus, [and] Mr Hobbes's Leviathan* (London).

Buchanan, George (1715). *De jure regni apud Scotos*, in *Opera Omnia*, vol. 1 (Edinburgh).

    (1949). *The Powers of the Crown in Scotland, being a Translation, with Notes and an Introductory Essay, of George Buchanan's 'De Jure Regni Apud Scotos'* trans. C.F. Arrowood (Austin: Texas University Press).

Calamy, Edmund (1802). *The Non-Conformists' Memorial, being an Account of the Ministers who were Ejected or Silenced after the Restoration*, 2 vols. (London: Button).

Charleton, Walter (1674). *Natural History of the Passions* (London).

Chemnitz, Bogislav Philipp von [pseud. 'Hippolitus a Lapide] (1640). *Dissertatio de Ratione Status in Imperio Romano-germanico* (Stettin).

Cicero, Marcus Tullius (1949). *De Inventione* (Cambridge, Mass.: Harvard University Press; Loeb Classical Library).

Clarendon. See Hyde.

Coke, Roger (1660a). *Justice Vindicated from the False Fucus put upon it, by Thomas White gent, Mr Thomas Hobbes and Hugo Grotius* (London).

(1660b). *Elements of Power and Subjection* (London). This is the second part, separately paginated, of 1660a.

Collins, Anthony (1717). *Philosophical Inquiry Concerning Human Liberty* (London).

Cowley, Abraham (1949). *Poetry and Prose*, ed. L.C. Martin (Oxford: Clarendon Press).

Cudworth, Ralph (1678). *True Intellectual System of the Universe* (London).

Cumberland, Richard (1727). *A Treatise of the Laws of Nature*, trans. J. Maxwell (London). First publ. as *De Legibus Naturae* (London, 1672).

Diderot, Denis (1875). *Plan d'une Université pour le Gouvernement de Russie*, in *Œuvres complètes*, ed. J. Assezat (Paris: Garnier), vol. III, pp. 429–534.

Digges, Dudley (1643). *The Unlawfulness of Subjects taking up Arms against their Soveraigne, in what case soever* (Oxford).

Du Moulin, Louis (1656). *Paraenesis ad aedificatores imperii in imperio . . . adversus Amyraldum* (London).

Eachard, John (1672). *Mr Hobbes's State of Nature considered, in a Dialogue between Philautus and Timothy* (London).

(1673). *Some Opinions of Mr Hobbes Considered, in a Second Dialogue between Philautus and Timothy* (London).

Falkner, William (1679). *Christian Loyalty* (London).

Ferguson, Robert (1681). *A Just and Modern Vindication* (London).

Filmer, Sir Robert (1949). *Patriarcha and Other Political Works*, ed. P. Laslett (Oxford: Blackwell).

Grotius, Hugo (1646). *De Jure Belli ac Pacis libri tres* (Amsterdam). Repr. in Classics of International Law (Oxford: Clarendon Press, 1925).

(1738). *The Rights of War and Peace*, ed. Jean Barbeyrac (London). First edn *De Iure Belli ac Pacis* (Paris, 1625).

(1950). *De Jure Praedae Commentarius* (Oxford: Clarendon Press; Classics of International Law).

Hall, John (1654). *Of Government and Obedience* (London).

Harrington, James (1977). *The Political Works of James Harrington*, ed. J.G.A. Pocock (Cambridge: Cambridge University Press).

Hickes, George (1707). *Two Treatises, one of the Christian Priesthood, the Other of the Dignity of the Episcopal Order* (London).

Hobbes, Thomas (1957). *Leviathan*, ed. M. Oakeshott (Oxford: Blackwell).

Horn, Johann Friedrich (1664). *Politicorum pars architectonica de Civitate* (Utrecht).

Humfrey, John (1689). *Good Advice before it be too late*, in *Somers Tracts*, x, pp. 198–202.

Hyde, Sir Edward (Earl of Clarendon) (1676). *A Brief View and Survey of the Dangerous and Pernicious Errors to Church and State in Mr Hobbes's book, entitled Leviathan* (London).

Kortholt, Christian (1680). *De Tribus Impostoribus Magnis* (Kiel).

Lawson, George (1657). *An Examination of the Political Part of Mr Hobbes his Leviathan* (London).

(1689). *Politica sacra et civilis* (London). First publ. 1660.

Leibniz, Gottfried Wilhelm (1768). *Opera omnia nunc primum edita*, ed. L. Dutens (Geneva).

(1952). *Theodicy: Essays on the Goodness of God, the Freedom of Man, and the Origin of Evil*, ed. A. Farrar, trans. E.M. Huggard (London: Routledge and Kegan Paul). First publ. 1710.

(1956). *Philosophical Papers and Letters*, ed. and trans. L.E. Loemker, 2 vols., continuously paginated (Chicago: University of Chicago Press).

V Natural law and utility

(1972). *The Political Writings of Leibniz*, ed. and trans. P. Riley (Cambridge: Cambridge University Press; reissued 1989).

Leslie, Charles (1695). *The Charge of Socinianism against Dr Tillotson considered* (Edinburgh).

(1711). *The Finishing Stroke: Being a Vindication of the Patriarchal Scheme of Government* (London).

Locke, John. The Lovelace Collection of the Papers of John Locke: Locke Room, Bodleian Library, Oxford. (For details of those manuscripts that have been published, see under secondary sources, Schankula 1973, 1974.)

(1823, 1963). *The Works of John Locke*, 10 vols. (London). Facsimile reprint (Aalen: Scientia Verlag).

(1960, 1970). *Two Treatises of Government*, ed. P. Laslett, 1st and 2nd edns (Cambridge: Cambridge University Press; reissued 1988).

(1961). *John Locke: Scritti Editi e Inediti Sulla Tolleranza*, ed. C.A. Viano (Turin: Taylor Publications).

(1963). *Some Thoughts Concerning Reading and Study for a Gentleman* (1690), in Locke (1823, 1963), vol. III, pp. 291–300.

(1963). *Some Thoughts Concerning Education* (1693), in Locke (1823, 1963), vol. IX, pp. 1–210.

(1967). *Two Tracts on Government*, ed. P. Abrams (Cambridge: Cambridge University Press).

(1968). *Some Thoughts Concerning Education*, in J. Axtell, ed., *The Educational Writings of John Locke* (Cambridge: Cambridge University Press).

(1970). *Essays on the Law of Nature*, ed. W. von Leyden (Oxford: Clarendon Press).

(1970). *Two Treatises of Government*. See (1960).

(1975). *An Essay Concerning Human Understanding*, ed. P. Nidditch (Oxford: Clarendon Press).

(1976–). *The Correspondence of John Locke*, ed. E.S. De Beer, 9 vols. (Oxford: Clarendon Press).

(1980). *Draft A of Locke's Essay Concerning Human Understanding*, ed. P. Nidditch (Sheffield: University of Sheffield).

(1983). *A Letter Concerning Toleration*, ed. J. Tully (Indianapolis: Hackett Publishing Company).

Long, Thomas (1689). *The Letter for Toleration Decipher'd and the Absurdity of an Absolute Toleration Demonstrated* (London).

Machiavelli, Niccolò (1978). *The Discourses*, ed. B. Crick (Harmondsworth: Penguin).

Marvell, Andrew (1776). *The Works of Andrew Marvell* (London).

Nedham, Marchamont (1969). *The Case of the Commonwealth of England, Stated*, ed. P.A. Knachel (Charlottesville: Virginia University Press). First publ. 1650.

Nevile, Henry (1969). *Plato Redivivus, or A Dialogue Concerning Government*, in *Two English Republican Tracts*, ed. C. Robbins (Cambridge: Cambridge University Press). First publ. 1681.

Oldenburg, Henry (1965). *The Correspondence of Henry Oldenburg*, vol. I, ed. A.R. Hall and M.B. Boas (Madison: University of Wisconsin Press).

Oldisworth, William (1709, 1710). *A Dialogue between Timothy and Philatheus*, 2 vols. (London).

Overton, Richard (1647). *Appeale from the Degenerate Representative Body . . . to the Free People* (London).

Parker, Samuel (1666). *An Account of the Nature and Extent of the Divine Dominion and Goodness* (Oxford). This is the second part of his *Free and Impartial Censure of the Platonick Philosophy*.

(1670). *A Discourse of Ecclesiastical Polity* (London).

Petty, Sir William (1927). *The Petty Papers*, ed. Marquis of Lansdowne, 2 vols. (London: Constable; facsimile repr., New York: A.M. Kelley, 1967).

Petyt, William (1954). *Britannia Languens*, in J.R. McCulloch, ed., *Early English Tracts on Commerce* (Cambridge: Cambridge University Press).

Pierce, Thomas (1658). *Autokatacrisis, or, Self-Condemnation Exemplified* (London).

Proast, Jonas (1690). *The Argument of the Letter Concerning Toleration Briefly Considered and Answered* (Oxford).

(1691). *The Third Letter Concerning Toleration* (Oxford).

(1703). *A Second Letter to the Author of the Three Letters for Toleration* (Oxford).

Pufendorf, Samuel (1660). *Elementorum Jurisprudentiae Universalis Libri Duo* (The Hague). Facsimile of the Cambridge edn of 1672, with English trans. by W.O. Oldfather, 2 vols. (Oxford: Oxford University Press; Carnegie Endowment, 1931).

[pseud. 'Severinus de Monzambano'] (1667). *De Statu Imperii Germanici ad Laelium Fratrem, Dominum Trezolani, Liber Unus* ('Geneva': in fact The Hague). English trans. London 1696.

(1672, 1934). *De Jure Naturae et Gentium Libri Octo* (Lund). Facsimile of the Amsterdam edition of 1688, with English trans. by C.H. and W.A. Oldfather, 2 vols. (Oxford: Oxford University Press; Carnegie Endowment, 1934).

(1673). *De Officio Hominis et Civis Juxta Legem Naturalem Libri Duo* (Lund). Facsimile of the Cambridge edition of 1682, with English trans. by F.G. Moore, 2 vols. (New York: Carnegie Endowment, 1927).

(1677a). *De Forma Reipublicae Romanae*, in *Dissertationes Academicae Selectiores* (Uppsala), pp. 357–404.

(1677b). *De Rebus gestis Philippi Amyntae*, in *Dissertationes Academicae Selectiores* (Uppsala), pp. 86–154.

(1677c). *De Republica Irregulari*, in *Dissertationes Academicae Selectiores* (Uppsala), pp. 301–57. First publ. Frankfurt-am-Main 1669.

(1677d). *De Systematibus Civitatum*, in *Dissertationes Academicae Selectiores* (Uppsala), pp. 210–61.

(1677e). *Dissertatio de Statu Hominum naturali*, in *Dissertationes Academicae Selectiores* (Uppsala), pp. 458–96.

(1682). *Einleitung zu der Historie der vornehmsten Reiche und Statten so itziger Zeit in Europa sich befinden* (Frankfurt-am-Main). English trans. by J. Crull (London, 1699).

(1686). *Commentariorum de Rebus Sueciis Libri XXVI ab expeditione Gustavi Adolphi in Germaniam ad abdicationem usque Christinae* (Utrecht).

(1686). *Specimen controversiarum circa Jus naturale*, in *Eris Scandica* (Frankfurt-am-Main). Edition of 1706 used here, pp. 162–276.

(1687). *De Habitu Religionis Christianae ad Vitam Civilem* (Bremen). Trans. J. Crull (London, 1698).

(1695). *Commentariorum de rebus Gestis Friderici Wilhelmi Magni Electoris Brandenburgici Libri XIX* (Berlin).

(1696). *De Rebus a Carolo Gustavo Sueciae Rege Gestis Commentariorum Libri VII* (Nuremberg).

(1734). *De Rebus Gestis Friderici III. Electoris Brandenburgici* (Berlin).

(1893). *Briefe*, ed. K. Varrentrapp, *Historische Zeitschrift*, 70:1–51 and 193–232.

(1934). See (1672).

Reinkingk, Dietrich (1619). *Tractatus de Regimine seculari et ecclesiastico* (Giessen).

Ross, Alexander (1653). *Leviathan Drawn out with a Hook* (London).

Rousseau, Jean-Jacques (1762, 1964). *Du Contrat Social*, in *Œuvres complètes*, ed. B. Gagnebin, vol. III (Paris: Gallimard), pp. 347–470.

V Natural law and utility

(1824). *Projet pour l'éducation de M. de Sainte-Marie, in Œuvres complètes*, ed. Musset-Pathay (Paris: P. Dupont), vol. x, pp. 26–51.

(1972). *Du Contrat Social*, ed. R. Grimsley (Oxford: Clarendon Press).

Scargill, Daniel (1669). *The Recantation of Daniel Scargill* (Cambridge).

Schiller, Johann Christoph Friedrich von (1964), *Werke*, ed. P. Stapf, 2 vols. (Berlin, Darmstadt: Der Tempel-Verlag).

Schlözer, August Ludwig (1793). *Allgemeines Statsrecht und StatsVerfassungsLere* (Göttingen).

Sidney, Algernon (1772). *The Works of Algernon Sidney* (London).

Smith, Adam (1976). *An Inquiry into the Nature and Causes of the Wealth of Nations*, ed. R.H. Campbell and A.S. Skinner, 2 vols. (Oxford: Clarendon Press).

Somers Tracts (1809–15). *A Collection of scarce and valuable Tracts . . .*, 2nd edn, ed. W. Scott, 13 vols. (London: Cadell and Davies).

Spinoza, Baruch (1670). *Tractatus theologico-politicus* (Amsterdam).

(1909). *The Chief Works of Benedict de Spinoza*, ed. and trans. R.H.M. Elwes, 2 vols. (London: Bell).

State Tracts (1689, 1693). *State Tracts: Being a Collection of Several Treatises relating to the Government* (London). Repub., 2 vols. in 1, 1693.

Stephens, Edward (1689). *Important Questions of State*, in *State Tracts*, I, pp. 167–75.

Stillingfleet, Edward (1680). *The Mischief of Separation* (London).

(1681). *The Unreasonableness of Separation* (London).

Suárez, Francisco (1612). *Tractatus de Legibus ac Deo Legislatore* (Coimbra). Edition used: Latin–Spanish edition, ed. L. Pereña, V. Abril, and P. Suñer, 8 vols. (Madrid: Consejo Superior de Investigaciones Científicas, 1971–81).

(1621). *De Opere Sex Dierum* (Lyons). Edition here used: *Opera omnia*, ed. D.M. André (Paris: Vivès, 1856), vol. III, pp. 1–447.

Svarez, Carl Gottlieb (1787). *Entwurf eines Allgemeinen Gesetzbuches für die Preussischen Staaten* (Berlin, Leipzig).

Tenison, Thomas (1670). *The Creed of Mr Hobbes Examined* (London).

Thomasius, Christian (1719). *Historia Juris naturalis* (Halle, Magdeburg).

Thorndike, Herbert (1854). *The Theological Works of Herbert Thorndike*, vol. v (Oxford: Parker; Library of Anglo-Catholic Theology).

Tyrrell, James (1681). *Patriarcha non Monarcha* (London).

(1727). *Bibliotheca Politica, or an Enquiry into the Ancient Constitution of the English Government*, 2nd edn (London). First publ. 1694.

White, Thomas (1655). *The Grounds of Obedience and Government* (London).

Wildman, John (1689a). *Some Remarks upon Government*, in *State Tracts*, I, pp. 149–62.

(1689b). *A Letter to a Friend Advising in this Extraordinary Juncture, How to Free the Nation from Slavery Forever*, in *Somers Tracts*, x, pp. 195–6.

Wotton, William (1706). *The Rights of the Clergy in the Christian Church* (London).

Wren, Matthew (1659). *Monarchy Asserted* (Oxford).

Secondary sources

Abrams, P. (1967). 'Introduction' in John Locke, *Two Tracts on Government*, ed. P. Abrams (Cambridge: Cambridge University Press).

Ashcraft, R. (1980). 'Revolutionary Politics and Locke's *Two Treaties of Government*: Radicalism and Lockean Political Theory', *Political Theory*, 8:429–86.

(1986). *Revolutionary Politics and Locke's Two Treatises of Government* (Princeton: Princeton University Press).

Bibliography

Ashcraft, R., and Goldsmith, M.M. (1983). 'Locke, Revolution Principles and the Formation of Whig Ideology', *Historical Journal*, 26:773–800.

Axtell, J. (1964). 'The Mechanics of Opposition: Restoration Cambridge versus Daniel Scargill', *Bulletin of the Institute of Historical Research*, 38:102–11.

(1968). *The Educational Writings of John Locke* (Cambridge: Cambridge University Press).

Baumgart, P. (1979). 'Naturrechtliche Vorstellungen in der Staatsauffassung Friedrichs des Grossen', in *Humanismus und Naturrecht in Berlin, Brandenburg, Preussen*, ed. H. Thieme (Veröffentlichungen der Historischen Kommission zu Berlin, 48), pp. 143–54.

Beer, M. (1921). *A History of British Socialism* (London: The National Labour Press).

Behrens, B. (1941). 'The Whig Theory of the Constitution in the Reign of Charles II', *Cambridge Historical Journal*, 7:42–71.

Belime, W. (1856). *Philosophie du Droit ou Cours d'Introduction à la science du Droit* (Paris: Durand).

Berman, H. (1983). *Law and Revolution: The Formation of the Western Legal Tradition* (Cambridge, Mass.: Harvard University Press).

Bloch, E. (1961). *Naturrecht und menschliche Würde* (Frankfurt-am-Main: Suhrkamp).

Bluntschli, J.C. (1881). *Geschichte der neueren staatswissenschaft* (Munich, Leipzig: R. Oldenbourg).

Bobbio, N. (1947). *Il Diritto naturale nel secolo XVIII* (Turin: G. Giappichelli).

Bowle, J. (1951). *Hobbes and his Critics: A Study in Seventeenth Century Constitutionalism* (London: Frank Cass; repr. 1969).

Bracken, H.M. (1984). *Mind and Language: Essays on Descartes and Chomsky* (Dordrecht: Foris Publications).

Bredvold, L. (1934, 1956). *The Intellectual Milieu of John Dryden* (Ann Arbor: Michigan University Press).

Burns, J.H. (1983). '*Jus gladii* and *jurisdictio*: Jacques Almain and John Locke', *Historical Journal*, 26:369–74.

Coleman, J. (1985). '*Dominium* in Thirteenth- and Fourteenth-Century Political Thought and its Seventeenth-Century Heirs: John of Paris and John Locke', *Political Studies*, 33:73–100.

Colman, J. (1983). *John Locke's Moral Philosophy* (Edinburgh: Edinburgh University Press).

Condren, C. (1989). *George Lawson's 'Politica' and the English Revolution* (Cambridge: Cambridge University Press).

Conrad, H. (1961). *Rechtsstaatliche Bestrebungen im Absolutismus Preussens und Öesterreichs am Ende des 18. Jahrhunderts* (Cologne: Opladen).

Cox, R. (1960). *Locke on War and Peace* (Oxford: Clarendon Press).

Cragg, G.R. (1957). *Puritanism in the Period of the Great Persecution 1660–1688* (Cambridge: Cambridge University Press).

Cranston, M. (1958). *John Locke, a Biography* (London: Longman; repr. 1985).

Cronon, W. (1983). *Changes in the Land: Indians, Colonists, and the Ecology of New England* (New York: Hill and Wang).

Daly, J. (1979). *Sir Robert Filmer and English Political Thought* (Toronto: University of Toronto Press).

Denzer, H. (1969). 'Pufendorf', in *Klassiker des Politischen Denkens*, ed. H. Maier, H. Rausch, H. Denzer (Munich: Beck), vol. II, pp. 27–52.

(1972). *Moralphilosophie und Naturrecht bei Samuel Pufendorf, Eine geistes- und wissenschaftsgeschichtliche Untersuchung zur Geburt des Naturrechts aus der praktischen Philosophie* (Munich: Beck).

(1979). 'Pufendorfs Naturrechtslehre und der brandenburgische Staat', in *Humanismus und Naturrecht in Berlin, Brandenburg, Preussen*, ed. H. Thieme (Veröffentlichungen der Historischen Kommission zu Berlin, 48), pp. 62–75.

Derathé, R. (1970). *Jean-Jacques Rousseau et la science politique de son temps*, 2nd edn (Paris: Vrin).

Dilthey, W. (1901). 'Das achtzehnte Jahrhundert und die geschichtliche Welt', *Deutsche Rundschau*, repub. in *Gesammelte Schriften*, 12 vols. (Stuttgart: Teubner; Göttingen: Vandenhoeck and Ruprecht, 1957–60), vol. III, pp. 209–68.

Dreitzel, H. (1970). *Protestantischer Aristotelismus und absoluter Staat: Die 'Politica' des Henning Arnisaeus (1575–1636)* (Wiesbaden: F. Steiner).

Dufour, A. (1972). *Le Mariage dans l'Ecole allemande du droit naturel moderne au XVIIIeme siècle* (Paris: Librairie générale de droit et de jurisprudence).

(1976). *Le Mariage dans l'Ecole romande du droit naturel au XVIIIeme siècle* (Geneva: Georg).

(1985). 'Pufendorfs Ausstrahlung im französischen und im anglo- amerikanischen Kulturraum', in *Samuel von Pufendorf, 1632–1982*, ed. K.A. Modeer (Stockholm: Institutet för Rättshistorisk).

Dunn, J. (1969). *The Political Thought of John Locke* (Cambridge: Cambridge University Press).

(1984). 'The Concept of "Trust" in the Politics of John Locke', in *Philosophy in History*, ed. R. Rorty, J.B. Schneewind, and Q. Skinner (Cambridge: Cambridge University Press).

(1985). *John Locke* (Oxford: Oxford University Press; Past Masters).

Dunn, R.S. (1979). *The Age of Religious Wars, 1559–1715* (New York: W.W. Norton).

Dunning, W.A. (1947). *A History of Political Theories* (New York: Macmillan).

Dzelzainis, M.M. (1984). 'The Ideological Context of John Milton's History of Britain', Cambridge University PhD thesis.

Farr, J. (1986). '"So Vile and Miserable an Estate": The Problem of Slavery in Locke's Political Thought', *Political Theory*, 14:263–89.

Farr, J., and Roberts, C. (1985). 'John Locke and the Glorious Revolution: A Rediscovered Document', *Historical Journal*, 28:385–98.

Fiore, P. (1868). *Nouveau Droit international public* (Paris: Durand et Pedone-Lavriel).

Fox Bourne, H.R. (1876). *The Life of John Locke*, 2 vols. (London: King).

Franklin, J.H. (1978). *John Locke and the Theory of Sovereignty* (Cambridge: Cambridge University Press).

Furley, O.W. (1957). 'The Whig Exclusionists: Pamphlet Literature in the Exclusion Campaign, 1679–81', *Cambridge Historical Journal*, 13:19–36.

Gagnebin, B. (1944). *Burlamaqui et le Droit naturel* (Geneva: Editions de la Frégate).

Gierke, O. (1902, 1929). *Johannes Althusius und die Entwicklung der naturrechtlichen Staatstheorien*, 2nd and 4th edns (Breslau: Marcus).

Goldie, M. (1977). 'Edmund Bohun and Jus Gentium in the Revolution Debate', *Historical Journal*, 20:569–86.

(1980a). 'The Roots of True Whiggism, 1688–1694', *History of Political Thought*, 1:195–236.

(1980b). 'The Revolution of 1689 and the Structure of Political Argument', *Bulletin of Research in the Humanities*, 83:473–564.

(1983). 'John Locke and Anglican Royalism', *Political Studies*, 31:61–85.

(1984). 'Sir Peter Pett, Sceptical Toryism and the Science of Toleration in the 1680s', in W.J. Sheils, ed., *Persecution and Toleration* (Oxford: Blackwell; Studies in Church History, 21).

Gough, J.W. (1957). *The Social Contract: A Critical Study of its Development* (Oxford: Oxford University Press).

(1976). 'James Tyrrell, Whig Historian and Friend of John Locke', *Historical Journal*, 19:581–610.

Grant, R. (1987). *John Locke's Liberalism* (Chicago: University of Chicago Press).

Greenleaf, W.H. (1964). *Order, Empiricism and Politics: Two Traditions of English Political Thought 1550–1700* (Oxford: Oxford University Press).

Gunn, J.A.W. (1969). *Politics and the Public Interest in the Seventeenth Century* (London: Routledge and Kegan Paul).

Hammerstein, N. (1972). *Jus und Historie, Ein Beitrag zur Geschichte des historischen Denkens an deutschen Universitäten im späten 17. und im 18. Jahrhundert* (Göttingen: Vandenhoeck and Ruprecht).

(1977). 'Samuel Pufendorf', in *Staatsdenker im 17. und 18. Jahrhundert*, ed. M. Stolleis (Frankfurt-am-Main: Metzner), pp. 174–97.

Hampsher-Monk, I. (1976). 'The Political Theory of the Levellers: Putney, Property and Professor Macpherson', *Political Studies*, 24:397–422.

Harper, L. (1939). *The English Navigation Laws: A Seventeenth-Century Experiment in Social Engineering* (New York: Columbia University Press).

Harvey, R.F. (1937). *Jean-Jacques Burlamaqui: A Liberal Tradition in American Constitutionalism* (Chapel Hill: North Carolina University Press).

Hoke, R. (1977). 'Hippolithus a Lapide', in *Staatsdenker im 17. und 18. Jahrhundert*, ed. M. Stolleis (Frankfurt-am-Main: Metzner), pp. 118–28.

Hundert, E.J. (1972). 'The Making of Homo-Faber: John Locke between Ideology and History', *Journal of the History of Ideas*, 33:3–22.

Hutchins, J. (1940). *Jonas Hanway, 1712–1786* (London: SPCK).

Jacob, J.R. (1983). *Henry Stubbe, Radical Protestantism and the Early Enlightenment* (Cambridge: Cambridge University Press).

Janet, P. (1887). *Histoire de la science politique dans ses rapports avec la Morale* (Paris: Alcan).

Jellinek, G. (1900). *Allgemeine Staatslehre* (Berlin: O. Haring).

Jolley, N. (1975). 'Leibniz on Hobbes, Locke's *Two Treatises* and Sherlock's *Case of Allegiance*', *Historical Journal*, 18:21–35.

(1984). *Leibniz and Locke: A Study of the New Essays on Human Understanding* (Oxford: Clarendon Press).

Jones, J.R. (1961). *The First Whigs: The Politics of the Exclusion Crisis 1678–1683* (Oxford: Oxford University Press).

Kessler, S. (1985). 'John Locke's Legacy of Religious Freedom', *Polity*, 17:482–503.

King, P. (1864). *The Life of John Locke* (London: H. Colburn and R. Bentley).

Kirk, L. (1987). *Richard Cumberland and Natural Law* (Cambridge: James Clarke).

Krieger, L. (1960). 'History and Law in the Seventeenth Century: Pufendorf', *Journal of the History of Ideas*, 21:198–210.

(1965). *The Politics of Discretion: Pufendorf and the Acceptance of Natural Law* (Chicago: University of Chicago Press).

Kuttner, S. (1982). 'The Revival of Jurisprudence', in *Renaissance and Renewal in the Twelfth Century*, ed. R.L. Benson and G. Constable (Cambridge, Mass.: Harvard University Press).

Labrousse, E. (1983). *Bayle* (Oxford: Oxford University Press; Past Masters).

Lamont, W.M. (1979). *Richard Baxter and the Millennium* (London: Croom Helm).

Laslett, P. (1969). 'John Locke, the Great Recoinage, and the Origins of the Board of Trade, 1695–1698', in *John Locke: Problems and Perspectives*, ed. J. Yolton (Cambridge: Cambridge University Press).

(1970). 'Introduction', in John Locke, *Two Treatises of Government*, 2nd edn (Cambridge: Cambridge University Press).

Laurent, P. (1982). *Pufendorf et la loi naturelle* (Paris: Vrin).

Leites, E., ed. (1988). *Conscience and Casuistry in Early Modern Europe* (Cambridge: Cambridge University Press).

V Natural law and utility

Link, C. (1977). 'Dietrich Reinkingk', in *Staatsdenker im 17. und 18. Jahrhundert*, ed. M. Stolleis (Frankfurt-am-Main: Metzner), pp. 78–99.

(1979). *Herrschaftsordnung und bürgerliche Freiheit, Grenzen der Staatsgewalt in der älteren deutschen Staatslehre* (Vienna, Cologne, Graz: Böhlau).

Little, L. (1978). *Religious Poverty and the Profit Economy in Medieval Europe* (Ithaca: Cornell University Press).

Macpherson, C.B. (1962). *The Political Theory of Possessive Individualism* (Oxford: Clarendon Press).

Malcolm, N. (1983). 'Thomas Hobbes and Voluntarist Theology', Cambridge University PhD thesis.

Manning, B. (1978). *The English People and the English Revolution* (Harmondsworth: Peregrine).

Marshall, J. (1985). 'The Ecclesiology of the Latitude-men 1660–89: Stillingfleet, Tillotson and "Hobbism"', *Journal of Ecclesiastical History*, 36:407–27.

Marx, K. (1977). *Capital*, vol. I, trans. B. Fowkes (New York: Random House).

Meinecke, F. (1924). *Die Idee der Staatsräson in der neueren Geschichte* (Munich: R. Oldenbourg).

Merea, P. (1943). 'Escolastica e jusnaturalismo: o problema da origem do poder civil em Suarez e em Pufendorf', *Boletin da Facultade de Direito, Coimbra*, 19:289–306.

Mesnard, P. (1952). *L'Essor de la philosophie politique au XVIe siècle*, 2nd edn (Paris: Vrin).

Meylan, P. (1937). *Jean Barbeyrac (1674–1744) et les débuts de l'enseignement du Droit naturel dans l'ancienne Académie de Lausanne, Contribution à l'histoire du Droit naturel* (Lausanne: F. Rouge).

Mintz, S.I. (1962). *The Hunting of Leviathan: Seventeenth-Century Reactions to the Materialism and Moral Philosophy of Thomas Hobbes* (Cambridge: Cambridge University Press).

Mugnier-Pollet, L. (1976). *La Philosophie politique de Spinoza* (Paris: Vrin).

Nederman, C.J. (1984). 'Bracton on Kingship Revisited', *History of Political Thought*, 5:61–77.

Oestreich, G. (1982). *Neostoicism and the Early Modern State*, ed. B. Oestrich and H.G. Koenigsberger, trans. D. McLintock (Cambridge: Cambridge University Press).

Othmer, S.C. (1970). *Berlin und die Verbreitung des Naturrechts in Europa, Kultur-und sozialgeschichtliche Studien zu Jean Barbeyrac Pufendorf-Übersetzungen und eine Analyse seiner Leserschaft*, (Berlin: Veröffentlichungen der Historischen Kommission zu Berlin, 30).

Palmer, R.C. (1985a). 'The Origins of Property in England', *Law and History Review*, 3:1–50.

(1985b). 'The Economic and Cultural Impact of the Origins of Property, 1180–1220., *Law and History Review*, 3:375–96.

Parry, G. (1978). *John Locke* (London: Allen and Unwin).

Pocock, J.G.A. (1957). *The Ancient Constitution and the Feudal Law* (Cambridge: Cambridge University Press; 2nd edn, 1987).

(1973). 'Time, History and Eschatology in the Thought of Thomas Hobbes', in *Politics, Language and Time* (London: Methuen).

(1985). *Virtue, Commerce, and History* (Cambridge: Cambridge University Press).

Popkin, R. (1979). *The History of Scepticism from Erasmus to Spinoza* (Los Angeles and Berkeley: California University Press).

(1987). *Isaac le Peyrere (1596–1676): His Life, Work and Influence* (Leiden: Brill).

Rabb, T.K. (1975). *The Struggle for Stability in Early Modern Europe* (Oxford: Oxford University Press).

Raeff, M. (1983). *The Well-Ordered Police State* (New Haven: Yale University Press).

Bibliography

Redwood, J. (1976). *Reason, Ridicule and Religion: The Age of Enlightenment in England 1660–1750* (London: Thames and Hudson).

Reibstein, E. (1956). 'Pufendorfs Völkerrechtslehre', *Öesterreichische Zeitschrift für öffentliches Recht*, 7:43–72.

(1972). *Volkssouveranität und Freiheitsrechte, Texte und Studien zur politischen Theorie des 14–18. Jahrhunderts* (Freiburg, Munich: K. Alber).

Rightmire, G. (1932). *The Law of England at the Norman Conquest* (Columbus, Ohio: F.J. Heer).

Riley, P. (1973). 'An Unpublished MS of Leibniz on the Allegiance Due to Sovereign Powers', *Journal of the History of Philosophy*, 11:319–36.

Röd, W. (1970). *Geometrischer Geist und Naturrecht, Methodengeschichtliche Untersuchungen zur Staatsphilosophie* (Munich: Beck, for Verlag der Bayerischen Akademie der Wissenschaften).

Rommen, H. (1947). *Die ewige Wiederkehr des Naturrechts*, 2nd edn (Munich: J. Kösel).

Sauter, J. (1932). *Die philosophischen Grundlagen des Naturrechts, Untersuchungen zur Geschichte der Rechts-und Staatslehre* (Vienna: J. Springer).

Schankula, H.A.S. (1973). 'A Summary Catalogue of the Philosophical Manuscript Papers of John Locke', *Bodleian Library Record*, 9:24–35.

(1974). 'A Summary Catalogue of the Philosophical Manuscript Papers of John Locke: Additions and Corrections', *Bodleian Library Record*, 9:80–2.

Schnur, R. (1964). *Zur Geschichte der Erklärung der Menschenrechte* (Darmstadt: Wissenschaftliche Buchgesellschaft).

Schochet, G. (1974). *Patriarchalism in Political Thought* (Oxford: Blackwell).

Schwoerer, L. (1974). *No Standing Armies!* (Baltimore: Johns Hopkins University Press).

Scott, J. (1988). *Algernon Sidney and the English Republic 1623–1677* (Cambridge: Cambridge University Press).

(1991). *Algernon Sidney and the Restoration Crisis 1677–1683* (Cambridge: Cambridge University Press).

Shapiro, B.J. (1983). *Probability and Certainty in Seventeenth-Century England* (Princeton: Princeton University Press).

Shennan, J.H. (1974). *The Origins of the Modern European State 1450–1725* (London: Hutchinson).

Skinner, Q. (1965). 'History and Ideology in the English Revolution', *Historical Journal*, 8:155–78.

(1966a). 'The Ideological Context of Hobbes' Political Thought', *Historical Journal*, 9:286–317. Repr. in *Hobbes and Rousseau*, ed. M. Cranston and R.S. Peters (New York: Doubleday, 1972).

(1966b). 'Thomas Hobbes and his Disciples in France and England', *Comparative Studies in Society and History*, 8:153–617.

(1969). 'Thomas Hobbes and the Nature of the Early Royal Society', *Historical Journal*, 12:217–39.

(1972). 'Conquest and Consent: Thomas Hobbes and the Engagement Controversy', in *The Interregnum: The Quest for Settlement 1649–1660*, ed. G.E. Aylmer (London: Macmillan).

(1978). *The Foundations of Modern Political Thought*, 2 vols. (Cambridge: Cambridge University Press).

Smith, A.E. (1947). *Colonists in Bondage: White Servitude and Convict Labor in America, 1607–1776* (Chapel Hill: North Carolina University Press).

Spiess, E. (1881). *Erhard Weigal, der Lehrer von Leibniz und Pufendorf* (Leipzig: J. Klinkhardt).

Teeter, L. (1936). 'The Dramatic Use of Hobbes's Political Ideas', *English Literary History*, 3:140–69.

Thayer, J.B. (1898). *A Preliminary Treatise at the Common Law* (Boston: Brown and Co.).

Tierney, B. (1982). *Religion, Law and the Growth of Constitutional Thought, 1150–1650* (Cambridge: Cambridge University Press).

Treitschke, H. von (1875). 'Samuel Pufendorf', *Preussische Jahrbücher*, 35:614–55; 36:61–109.

Tuck, R. (1979). *Natural Rights Theories: Their Origin and Development* (Cambridge: Cambridge University Press).

    (1983). 'Grotius, Carneades and Hobbes', *Grotiana*, n.s., 4:43–62.

    (1986). 'A New Date for Filmer's *Patriarcha*', *Historical Journal*, 29:183–6.

    (1988). 'Optics and Sceptics: The Philosophical Foundations of Hobbes's Political Thought', in Leites (1988), pp. 235–63.

Tully, J. (1980). *A Discourse on Property: John Locke and his Adversaries* (Cambridge: Cambridge University Press).

    (1983). 'Introduction', in John Locke, *A Letter Concerning Toleration*, ed. J. Tully (Indianapolis: Hackett).

    (1984). 'Locke on Liberty', in *Conceptions of Liberty in Political Philosophy*, ed. Z. Pelczynski and J. Gray (London: Athlone Press).

    (1986). 'The Origins of Political Individualism', *Proceedings of the Annual Congress of Canadian Learned Societies* (Winnipeg: University of Manitoba).

    (1988). 'Governing Conduct', in Leites (1988), pp. 12–71.

Urdang, E.W. and Oakley, F. (1966). 'Locke, Natural Law, and God', *Natural Law Forum*, 11:92–109.

Van Leeuwen, H. (1963). *The Problem of Certainty in English Thought 1630–1690* (The Hague: Nijhoff).

Viano, C.A. (1960). *John Locke, dal Razionalismo al'Illuminismo* (Turin: Einaudi).

Voltelini, H.V. (1910). 'Die naturrechtlichen Lehren und die Reformen des 18. Jahrhunderts', *Historische Zeitschrift*, 105:65–104.

Von Leyden, W. (1970). 'Introduction', in John Locke, *Essays on the Law of Nature* (Oxford: Clarendon Press).

Vossler, O. (1930). 'Studien zur Erklärung der Menschenrechte', *Historische Zeitschrift*, 142:516–45.

Walker, D.P. (1964). *The Decline of Hell* (London: Routledge and Kegan Paul).

Watts, M. (1978). *The Dissenters: From the Restoration to the French Revolution* (Oxford: Clarendon Press).

Webb, S. and B. (1927). *English Local Government, English Poor Law History. Part I: The Old Poor Law* (London: Longmans, Green and Company).

Webb, S.S. (1979). *The Governors General: The English Army and the Definition of Empire* (Chapel Hill: North Carolina University Press).

Welzel, H. (1952). 'Ein Kapitel aus der Geschichte der amerikanischen Erklärung der Menschenrechte (John Wise und Samuel Pufendorf)', in *Rechtsprobleme in Staat und Kirche: Festschrift für Rudolf Smend* (Göttingen: O. Schwartz). pp. 387–411.

    (1958). *Die Naturrechtslehre Samuel Pufendorfs* (Berlin: De Gruyter).

    (1962). *Naturrecht und materiale Gerechtigkeit*, 4th edn (Göttingen: Vandenhoeck and Ruprecht).

Weston, C.C., and Greenberg, J.R. (1981). *Subjects and Sovereigns: The Grand Controversy over Legal Sovereignty in Stuart England* (Cambridge: Cambridge University Press).

Williams, E.N. (1983). *The Ancien Régime in Europe* (Harmondsworth: Penguin).

Wilson, C.H. (1958). *Mercantilism* (London: Historical Association Pamphlets).

Wolf, E. (1927). *Grotius, Pufendorf, Thomasius: Drei Kapitel zur Gestaltgeschichte der Rechtswissenschaft* (Tübingen: Mohr).

    (1963). *Grosse Rechtsdenker der deutschen Geistesgeschichte*, 4th edn (Tübingen: Mohr).

Bibliography

Wood, N. (1983). *The Politics of Locke's Philosophy: A Social Study of An Essay Concerning Human Understanding* (Los Angeles and Berkeley: California University Press).

(1984). *John Locke and Agrarian Capitalism* (Los Angeles and Berkeley: California University Press).

Worden, B. (1985). 'The Commonwealth Kidney of Algernon Sidney', *Journal of British Studies*, 24:1–40.

Wormald, B.H.G. (1951). *Clarendon: Politics, History and Religion 1640–1660* (Cambridge: Cambridge University Press).

Yale, D.E.C. (1972). 'Hobbes and Hale on Law, Legislation and the Sovereign', *Cambridge Law Journal*, 31:131–56.

Yolton, J. (1956). *John Locke and the Way of Ideas* (Oxford: Clarendon Press).

(1970). *Locke and the Compass of Human Understanding* (Cambridge: Cambridge University Press).

Zagorin, P. (1982). *Rebels and Rulers 1500–1660*, 2 vols. (Cambridge: Cambridge University Press).

Zuber, W. (1939). 'Die Staatsperson Pufendorfs im Lichte der neueren Staatslehre', *Archiv für öffentliches Recht*, 30:33–70.

Index of names of persons

This index is intended to include the names of all persons mentioned in the text (and, where appropriate, in the footnotes) together with the Biographies (the latter distinguished by the abbreviation 'biog.'). Figures in bold type refer to chapters, sections, or other extended passages. The names of modern scholars are included only where their work is discussed, and not simply referred to, in the text.

Index of names of persons

Hall, Arthur, 394n
Hall, John, 612, 615
Haloander, Gregor, 85
Hamilton, Alexander, 587
Hammond, Henry, 364
Handel, George Frederick, 489
Harding, Thomas, 241, 677 (biog.)
Harrington, James, 339, 434, 444, 447, **450–5**,
    456, 457, 458, 459, 460, 462, 463, 464, 465,
    466, 467, 468, 469, 470, 471, 472–3, 474–5,
    612n, 654, 677 (biog.)
Hartlib, Samuel, 472
Hayward, Sir John, 249, 250, 354, 359, 365,
    677–8 (biog.)
Hedley, Thomas, 378n
Hegel, G. W. F., 602
Hegendorf, Christoph, 86
Heimburg, Gregor, 146
Henri II, king of France, 206, 231
Henri III, king of France, 212, 218, 220, 221,
    222, 223, 225, 231, 232, 481, 496
Henri IV, of Navarre, king of France, 218,
    220, 222, 228, 229, 232, 233, 236, 249, 252,
    284, 356, 361
Henry I, king of England, 380, 381, 382, 383,
    388, 394, 399, 400, 408
Henry II, king of England, 382, 391, 401, 623
Henry III, king of England, 380, 384, 400, 405
Henry VII, king of England, 452, 458
Henry VIII, king of England, 82, 177, 178,
    181, 452
Henry of Knighton, 385
Henry of Rimini, 36
Herle, Charles, 396, 397, 399, 678 (biog.)
Hespérien, Pierre, 357
Heylyn, Peter, 359
Heynlin, Johann, 138
Hickes, George, 613
Hippocrates, 483, 486
Hobbes, Thomas, 4, 89–90, 132, 363, 442, 444,
    445, 450, 462, 471, 499, 522, 527, 529,
    534–45, 547–9, 551, 555–6, 557, 561, 563,
    570, 571, 572, 582, **589–615** (reception of),
    621, 622n, 630, 639, 654, 678 (biog.); on
    authorisation and representation, 542–3; on
    church, state, and religion, 543–5; on
    conflict, war, and peace, 535–6; on contract
    and covenant, 538–40; on democracy, 541–2;
    on desire and reason, 533–4; on existence
    and essence, 532–3; on law, 540–1; on laws
    and right of nature, 535–8; on self-
    preservation and benevolence, 534–5; on
    sovereignty, 541–3; on state of nature, 536–9
Hoeck, Jacobus, 136
Hoffmann, Melchior, 188

Holbourne, Sir Robert, **398–400**, 406, 678
    (biog.)
Holinshed, Ralph, 391
Holles, Denzil, 464
Holmes, O. W., jun., 67
Hooker, John, 391
Hooker, Richard, 247–8, **279–83**, 294, 655, 679
    (biog.)
Horace, 27, 506
Horn, Andrew, 390
Horn, Johann Friedrich, 575
Hostiensis, 143n
Hotman, Antoine, 222, 233
Hotman, François, 79, 82, 83, 89, 206, **208–9**,
    221, 225, 232, 235, 270, 271, 327n, 461, 503,
    679 (biog.)
Houssaye, Amelot de la, 497
Hübmaier, Balthasar, 189
Hugh, bishop of Constance, 183
Hume, David, 410–11, 451, 475, 656
Hunton, Philip, 397, 679 (biog.)
Hurault, Michel, 232
Hut, Hans, 188
Hutchinson, John, 412
Hyde, Sir Edward, see Clarendon

Ingulphus of Croyland, 384, 408
Innocent III, pope, 105
Ireland, John, 139
Ireton, Henry, 415, 425, 440
Isaac, 589, 592
Isidore of Seville, St, 257, 267
Isocrates, 25

Jackson, Thomas, 359
James IV, king of Scotland, 139
James VI and I, king of Scotland and England,
    154, 198, 215, 216, 235, 237, 238, 239,
    247–53, 350, 352, 365, 373, 374–5, 377,
    378n, 391, 394, 395, 452, 500, 522, 679–80
    (biog.)
James VII and II, king of Scotland and
    England, 373, 386, 406, 410, 458, 613, 620
James, Richard, 493
Jefferson, Thomas, 587
Jehoiada, 226
Jephthah, 626
Jewel, John, 241, 244, 680 (biog.)
Job, 589
John the Baptist, St, 493
John, king of England, 380, 382, 384, 405, 409
John of Paris, 149, 256
John of Salisbury, 25
Jonghe, John Junius de, 271–2
Jonson, Ben, 488

Index of names of persons

West, Thomas, 340
Weston, Edward, 370
White, Thomas, 533, 609–10, 613–14
Whitehead, A. N., 4, 67
Whitelocke, Bulstrode, 385
Whitgift, John, archbishop of Canterbury, 247
Wildman, John, 425, 440, 601, 699–700 (biog.)
William I, the Conqueror, king of England, 364, 365, 369, 382, 383, 384, 400, 401, 403, 405, 406, 407, 408, 409, 427
William II, prince of Orange, 547
William III, prince of Orange, king of England and Scotland, 366, 547, 601, 618, 633, 648
Williams, Roger, 438, 439, 441, 442, 700 (biog.)
Winstanley, Gerrard, 338, 425, 426, 700 (biog.)

Wise, John, 587
Wolff, Christian, 561
Wood, Anthony, 398
Wren, Matthew, 605
Wyclif, John, 356, 593

Xenophon, 487, 490

Zabarella, Jacopo, 526
Zampini, Matteo, 221, 222, 700 (biog.)
Zasius, Ulrich, 77–8, 700–1 (biog.)
Zinano, Gabriele, 479n
Zomeron, Henry, 135
Zuccolo, Ludovico, 339, 479n, 481
Zwingli, Huldreich, 173, **182–5**, 186, 187, 189, 190, 193, 701 (biog.)

Index of subjects

Figures in bold type refer to chapters, sections, or extended passages devoted to particular subjects or themes

absolute rule/power/sovereignty, absolutism, 27, 31, 52, 54, 57, 63, 68, 69, 77–8, 81, 89, 153, 155, 220, **233–6**, 238–9, 247–9, 275, 276, 279, 297, 299, 307–9, 313, 317, 318, 319, **347–73**, 421, 447, 480, 488, 492, 519–20, 531, 563, 576, 577, 578, 579, 587, 588, 591, 592, 595–7, 599, 606, 630–1, 634, 640, 644–5, 653–4; absolute and ordained/ordinary power, 248; limits of absolutism, **367–73**; meaning of 'absolutism', **347–50**; see also sovereignty

accusatory system, 623–4, 627, 640

action, 69–70 (as legal category), 90–1

agrarian law, 453

agreement (composition, *compromis, conventio*), 283, 286, 295, 550, 566–7; see also contract(s)

Agreement of the People: first, 412, 413, 419, 425; second, 430–4; third, 434

Alcalá (university of), 240

allegiance/fealty (oaths of), 319, 325, 633; controversy over English, 249–50

Allstedt, 190

America: influence of Pufendorf in, 587; republican tradition in, 443, 475; see also Indians; New World

Amerindians, see Indians

Amsterdam, 489, 511, 551

Anabaptists, **187–91**, 210; see also Baptists

'ancient constitution': English, 373, **374–411**, 427–8, 448, 451, 459; French, 208–9, 221, 225, 285–6; see also 'Gothic' polities

'ancients' and 'moderns' (battle of), 85

Anglicanism, Anglicans, 219, 235, 240, 241, **244–7**, 253, 543–4, 611–12, 647

Anglo-Dutch War, 460

anointing (of kings), 373, 497

anti-clericalism, 159, 473, 523, 528, 550, 551, 555

antinomianism, 437, 593; see also libertinism

antiquaries, 380–1, 384–5

antiquity, antiquities, 24, 68, 71–2; see also 'ancient constitution'

'appeal to heaven', 623–4, 626, 637–8

Aragon, 292–3

Arcadia, 332, 340, 341, 343

arcana imperii, 482

archpriest controversy, 243–4, 253

Argentina, 340

aristocracy, aristocrats, 38, 260, 311, 323, 331, 348, 351, 352, 355, 395, 451, 454, 466, 490, 503, 542, 573, 580; see also constitution(s), mixed constitution, nobility

Aristotelianism, Aristotelian ideas, 19, 20–1, 37, 40–1, 72, 74, 86–7, 99, 107, 131, 171–2, 195, 197, 227, 237, 263–4, 264–5, 276, 283, 289, 321, 444, 445, 447, 448, 453, 464, 484, 499, 507, 518–19, 520, 525, 526–7, 529, 532–4, 563, 580, 590, 594, 597, 598, 599, 601, 602, 603, 604, 614–15, 654–5

Armada, 242

Arminianism, Arminians, 474, **509–14**

assemblées politiques, 209

astrology, 18–19

Athens, 13, 14, 502

Augsburg, 200, 202

Augustinianism, Augustinian ideas, 106, 114–16, 117–18, 123, 131, 161–2, 258, 265

Austria, 188

authorisation, 542–3, 548; see also authority

authority of rulers and governments, 143–4, 145, 148–50, 154–5, 159–92 passim, 169–71, 176–7, 217, 223–8, 233–6, 238–41, 247–9,

790

law(s), (*cont.*)
308–9, 324, 326, 371–2; public vs. private,
69; *see also* common law; international law;
law of nations; natural law(s); Roman law
law of nations (*jus gentium*), 69, 84–6, 92, 94,
585–6; *see also* international law
law(s) of nature, *see* natural law(s)
lawgiver, legislator, 48, 276, 342, 343, 390,
450, 465
Laws of Edward the Confessor, 379–82, 384,
386, 390, 391, 397, 400, 403, 405–6, 407, 408
League, *see* Catholic/Holy League
legal profession, 91, 93, 284
legislation, legislative power, 75, 80, 257,
266–7, 283, 286–7, 290, 294, 295, 304, 362,
389–90, 410, 423, 512, 576, 617, 619, 632,
636, 637, 641; *see also* sovereignty
légistes, legists, 68, 71, 82, 286
Leiden, 509
Leipzig, 202
letrados, 71
Levellers, 400, **412–42**, 462, 601; True, *see*
Diggers
lex regia, 250
libertinism, 607–8; *see also* antinomianism
liberty, liberties, 39, 46, 59, 62, 63, 69, 72, 83,
90, 93, 224, 225, 238, 256, 259, 264, 363–4,
374, 381, 382, 384, 387, 414, 451, 491,
508–9, 525, 541, 545, 557, 566, 619–22, 625,
630, 637, 641; *see also* Christian freedom;
conscience; nature (state of); toleration; will
London, 243, 413–14, 428–9
Long Parliament, 395, 453
Lords (House of), 381, 385, 397, 399, 400, 406,
420, 427, 428, 443, 452, 459; *see also*
parliament
loyalism, 372
Lutheranism, Lutherans, **163–82**, 200–3, 236

Magdeburg, 83, 202–3, 204, 205–6
magistrate(s), magistracy, 184–5, 186, 508, 595,
647; inferior, as agents of resistance, 196,
198–9, 201, 202, 210, 213–14; *see also*
authority
Magna Carta, 379, 381, 382, 383, 392, 393,
395, 401, 402, 406, 408, 409, 427, 523, 601
majesty, *maiestas*, 32–3, 67–8, 275, 277, 287,
290, 316; real vs. personal, 312–13, 316, 317
manhood suffrage, *see* franchise
maritime law/jurisdiction, 504, 524, 527–8
market relations, *see* mercantile society
marriage, 21; *see also* husband and wife
mathematics (and ethics), 505
medicine (and politics), 486; *see also* body
politic
Mediterranean history, 456

Melchiorites, 191
mendicant friars, 19–20
Mennonites, 188, 189
mercantile society, merchants, 16, 19–20, 21–3,
140, 414
meritocracy, 38, 61
metaphysics, *see* philosophy
Milan, 15, 25, 26, 30, 31, 42
military revolution, 492–3
militia, 42–3, 65, 339, 463; *see also*
conscription; standing armies
Militia Ordinance, 528
millenarianism, millenniallism, millenarian
ideas, 337, 342–3, 423, 424
miracles, 79
Mirror of Justices, 386, 390–1
mixed constitution/government, 36–7, 48–9,
59, 61, 64–5, 238, 270, **273–9**, 302–3,
309–28, 338–9, 395, 447, 502–3, 580–1, 597;
see also constitution(s); mixed monarchy;
sovereignty
mixed monarchy, 80, 447, 595
Modena, 31
Modus tenendi Parliamentum, 386, 390–3, 397,
401–2, 410
monarchomachs, 218, 312, 362; *see also*
resistance to rulers
monarchy, monarchies, monarchism, 1–2,
25–9, **30–41**, 80, 96, 118–19, 120, 128–9,
151–2, 153, 154–5, 220, 223, 224, **233–6**,
243, **247–50**, **273–9**, 295, 301, 311, 317, 320,
324, 331, 341, **350–8**, 367, 395, 427, 443,
446–7, 451, 452, 456, 472, 474, 492, 542,
546, 563, 573, 582, 595, 602, 603, 630, 636;
see also emperor(s); king(s); mixed
monarchy; prince(s)
monasteries (dissolution of), 452
monastic ideal, 333, 343
money (introduction of), 633–43
Monmouth Rebellion (1685), 624, 647, 648
moral philosophy, 499, 520, 522, 525, 526–7,
563–7, 606–10, 655–6; *see also* morality and
politics
morality and politics, 55–6, 62, 329–44 *passim*,
479–98 *passim*, 606–10; *see also* moral
philosophy
mos gallicus, 76, 79–80
mos italicus, 71–2
Münster, 187, 188, 190, 191
Müntzerites, 191
musical analogy, 277–8
mystical body: church as, 163; *corpus mysticum
reipublicae*, 274; of the realm, 287

Naples (kingdom of), 25, 26, 30, 31, 32–3, 41,
42

Index of subjects